Poetry
Criticism

Guide to Gale Literary Criticism Series

For criticism on	Consult these Gale series
Authors now living or who died after December 31, 1999	*CONTEMPORARY LITERARY CRITICISM (CLC)*
Authors who died between 1900 and 1999	*TWENTIETH-CENTURY LITERARY CRITICISM (TCLC)*
Authors who died between 1800 and 1899	*NINETEENTH-CENTURY LITERATURE CRITICISM (NCLC)*
Authors who died between 1400 and 1799	*LITERATURE CRITICISM FROM 1400 TO 1800 (LC)* *SHAKESPEAREAN CRITICISM (SC)*
Authors who died before 1400	*CLASSICAL AND MEDIEVAL LITERATURE CRITICISM (CMLC)*
Authors of books for children and young adults	*CHILDREN'S LITERATURE REVIEW (CLR)*
Dramatists	*DRAMA CRITICISM (DC)*
Poets	*POETRY CRITICISM (PC)*
Short story writers	*SHORT STORY CRITICISM (SSC)*
Literary topics and movements	*HARLEM RENAISSANCE: A GALE CRITICAL COMPANION (HR)* *THE BEAT GENERATION: A GALE CRITICAL COMPANION (BG)* *FEMINISM IN LITERATURE: A GALE CRITICAL COMPANION (FL)* *GOTHIC LITERATURE: A GALE CRITICAL COMPANION (GL)*
Asian American writers of the last two hundred years	*ASIAN AMERICAN LITERATURE (AAL)*
Black writers of the past two hundred years	*BLACK LITERATURE CRITICISM (BLC-1)* *BLACK LITERATURE CRITICISM SUPPLEMENT (BLCS)* *BLACK LITERATURE CRITICISM: CLASSIC AND EMERGING AUTHORS SINCE 1950 (BLC-2)*
Hispanic writers of the late nineteenth and twentieth centuries	*HISPANIC LITERATURE CRITICISM (HLC)* *HISPANIC LITERATURE CRITICISM SUPPLEMENT (HLCS)*
Native North American writers and orators of the eighteenth, nineteenth, and twentieth centuries	*NATIVE NORTH AMERICAN LITERATURE (NNAL)*
Major authors from the Renaissance to the present	*WORLD LITERATURE CRITICISM, 1500 TO THE PRESENT (WLC)* *WORLD LITERATURE CRITICISM SUPPLEMENT (WLCS)*

ISSN 1052-4851

Poetry Criticism

Excerpts from Criticism of the Works of the Most Significant and Widely Studied Poets of World Literature

Volume 127

Michelle Lee
Project Editor

GALE
CENGAGE Learning

Detroit • New York • San Francisco • New Haven, Conn • Waterville, Maine • London

GALE
CENGAGE Learning®

Poetry Criticism, Vol. 127

Project Editor: Michelle Lee

Editorial: Dana Barnes, Sara Constantakis, Kathy D. Darrow, Kristen Dorsch, Dana Ferguson, Jeffrey W. Hunter, Michelle Kazensky, Jelena O. Krstović, Marie Toft, Lawrence J. Trudeau

Content Conversion: Katrina D. Coach, Gwen Tucker

Indexing Services: Tonya Weikel

Rights and Acquisitions: Leitha Etheridge-Sims

Composition and Electronic Capture: Gary Oudersluys

Manufacturing: Rhonda Dover

Product Manager: Mary Onorato

Gale
27500 Drake Rd.
Farmington Hills, MI, 48331-3535

LIBRARY OF CONGRESS CATALOG CARD NUMBER 81-640179

ISBN-13: 978-1-4144-8454-9
ISBN-10: 1-4144-8454-2

ISSN 1052-4851

Printed in Mexico
1 2 3 4 5 6 7 16 15 14 13 12

Contents

Preface vii

Acknowledgments ix

Literary Criticism Series Advisory Board xi

Preface

*P*oetry Criticism (*PC*) presents significant criticism of the world's greatest poets and provides supplementary biographical and bibliographical material to guide the interested reader to a greater understanding of the genre and its creators. Although major poets and literary movements are covered in such Gale Literary Criticism series as *Contemporary Literary Criticism* (*CLC*), *Twentieth-Century Literary Criticism* (*TCLC*), *Nineteenth-Century Literature Criticism* (*NCLC*), *Literature Criticism from 1400 to 1800* (*LC*), and *Classical and Medieval Literature Criticism* (*CMLC*), *PC* offers more focused attention on poetry than is possible in the broader, survey-oriented entries on writers in these Gale series. Students, teachers, librarians, and researchers will find that the generous excerpts and supplementary material provided by *PC* supply them with the vital information needed to write a term paper on poetic technique, to examine a poet's most prominent themes, or to lead a poetry discussion group.

Scope of the Series

PC is designed to serve as an introduction to major poets of all eras and nationalities. Since these authors have inspired a great deal of relevant critical material, *PC* is necessarily selective, and the editors have chosen the most important published criticism to aid readers and students in their research. Each author entry presents a historical survey of the critical response to that author's work. The length of an entry is intended to reflect the amount of critical attention the author has received from critics writing in English and from foreign critics in translation. Every attempt has been made to identify and include the most significant essays on each author's work. In order to provide these important critical pieces, the editors sometimes reprint essays that have appeared elsewhere in Gale's Literary Criticism Series. Such duplication, however, never exceeds twenty percent of a *PC* volume.

Organization of the Book

Each *PC* entry consists of the following elements:

- The **Author Heading** cites the name under which the author most commonly wrote, followed by birth and death dates. Also located here are any name variations under which an author wrote, including transliterated forms for authors whose native languages use nonroman alphabets. If the author wrote consistently under a pseudonym, the pseudonym will be listed in the author heading and the author's actual name given in parenthesis on the first line of the biographical and critical introduction. Uncertain birth or death dates are indicated by question marks. Single-work entries are preceded by the title of the work and its date of publication.

- The **Introduction** contains background information that introduces the reader to the author and the critical debates surrounding his or her work.

- The list of **Principal Works** is ordered chronologically by date of first publication and lists the most important works by the author. The first section comprises poetry collections and book-length poems. The second section gives information on other major works by the author. For foreign authors, the editors have provided original foreign-language publication information and have selected what are considered the best and most complete English-language editions of their works.

- Reprinted **Criticism** is arranged chronologically in each entry to provide a useful perspective on changes in critical evaluation over time. All individual titles of poems and poetry collections by the author featured in the entry are printed in boldface type. The critic's name and the date of composition or publication of the critical work are given at the beginning of each piece of criticism. Unsigned criticism is preceded by the title of the source in which it appeared. Footnotes are reprinted at the end of each essay or excerpt. In the case of excerpted criticism, only those footnotes that pertain to the excerpted texts are included.

- Critical essays are prefaced by brief **Annotations** explicating each piece.

- A complete **Bibliographical Citation** of the original essay or book precedes each piece of criticism.

- An annotated bibliography of **Further Reading** appears at the end of each entry and suggests resources for additional study. In some cases, significant essays for which the editors could not obtain reprint rights are included here. Boxed material following the further reading list provides references to other biographical and critical sources on the author in series published by Gale.

Cumulative Indexes

A **Cumulative Author Index** lists all of the authors that appear in a wide variety of reference sources published by Gale, including *PC*. A complete list of these sources is found facing the first page of the Author Index. The index also includes birth and death dates and cross references between pseudonyms and actual names.

A **Cumulative Nationality Index** lists all authors featured in *PC* by nationality, followed by the number of the *PC* volume in which their entry appears.

A **Cumulative Title Index** lists in alphabetical order all individual poems, book-length poems, and collection titles contained in the *PC* series. Titles of poetry collections and separately published poems are printed in italics, while titles of individual poems are printed in roman type with quotation marks. Each title is followed by the author's last name and corresponding volume and page numbers where commentary on the work is located. English-language translations of original foreign-language titles are cross-referenced to the foreign titles so that all references to discussion of a work are combined in one listing.

Citing *Poetry Criticism*

When citing criticism reprinted in the Literary Criticism Series, students should provide complete bibliographic information so that the cited essay can be located in the original print or electronic source. Students who quote directly from reprinted criticism may use any accepted bibliographic format, such as University of Chicago Press style or Modern Language Association (MLA) style. Both the MLA and the University of Chicago formats are acceptable and recognized as being the current standards for citations. It is important, however, to choose one format for all citations; do not mix the two formats within a list of citations.

The examples below follow recommendations for preparing a bibliography set forth in *The Chicago Manual of Style,* 14th ed. (Chicago: The University of Chicago Press, 1993); the first example pertains to material drawn from periodicals, the second to material reprinted from books:

Linkin, Harriet Kramer. "The Language of Speakers in *Songs of Innocence and of Experience.*" *Romanticism Past and Present* 10, no. 2 (summer 1986): 5-24. Rpt. in *Poetry Criticism.* Edited by Michelle Lee. Vol. 63. Detroit: Gale, 2005. 79-88. Print.

Glen, Heather. "Blake's Criticism of Moral Thinking in *Songs of Innocence and of Experience.*" In *Interpreting Blake,* edited by Michael Phillips. Cambridge: Cambridge University Press, 1978. 32-69. Rpt. in *Poetry Criticism.* Edited by Michelle Lee. Vol. 63. Detroit: Gale, 2005. 34-51. Print.

Suggestions are Welcome

Readers who wish to suggest new features, topics, or authors to appear in future volumes, or who have other suggestions or comments are cordially invited to call, write, or fax the Associate Product Manager:

Product Manager, Literary Criticism Series
Gale
27500 Drake Road
Farmington Hills, MI 48331-3535
1-800-347-4253 (GALE)
Fax: 248-699-8054

Acknowledgments

The editors wish to thank the copyright holders of the criticism included in this volume and the permissions managers of many book and magazine publishing companies for assisting us in securing reproduction rights. Following is a list of the copyright holders who have granted us permission to reproduce material in this volume of *PC*. Every effort has been made to trace copyright, but if omissions have been made, please let us know.

COPYRIGHTED MATERIAL IN *PC*, VOLUME 127, WAS REPRODUCED FROM THE FOLLOWING PERIODICALS:

Angelaki, v. 15, August, 2010. Copyright © 2010 by Taylor & Francis Group, LLC. Reproduced by permission of Taylor & Francis, Ltd., http//:www.tandf.co.uk/journals and the author.—*Cambridge Quarterly*, v. 39, March, 2010. Copyright © 2010 by Oxford University Press. By permission of Oxford University Press.—*Contemporary Literature*, v. 32, winter, 1991. Copyright © 1991 The Board of Regents of the University of Wisconsin System. All rights reserved. Reproduced by permission.—*EAPSU Online*, v. 4, fall, 2007. Copyright © 2007 by English Association of the Pennsylvania State Universities. Reproduced by permission.—*English Studies*, v. 84, no. 4, 2003, pp. 330-46 for "Driving the Darkness: W. E. Henley's 'The Song of the Sword' as Uneasy Battle Cry" by R. van Bronswijk. Reprinted by permission of the publisher (Taylor & Francis Group, http://www.informaworld.com).—*English Studies in Canada*, v. 15, June, 1989; v. 24, June, 1998. Copyright © 1989, 1998 by The Association of Canadian College & University Teachers of English. Reproduced by permission.—*Huntington Library Quarterly*, v. 37, February, 1974. University of California Press, 1974.—*Journal of Modern Literature*, v. 28, summer, 2005. Copyright © 2005 by Indiana University Press. Reproduced by permission.— *Literature and Theology*, v. 12, June, 1998. Copyright © 1998 by Oxford University Press. Reproduced by permission.— *Malahat Review*, October, 1982 for "W. S. Graham: Constructing a White Space" by David Punter. Copyright © 1982 by David Punter. Reproduced by permission of the author.—*Modernism/modernity*, v. 8, September, 2001; v. 14, September, 2007. Copyright © 2001, 2007 by The Johns Hopkins University Press. Reproduced by permission of The Johns Hopkins University Press.—*Paideuma*, v. 33, fall and winter, 2004 for "'This Is No Rune nor Symbol': The Sensual in H. D.'s Feminized Sublime" by S. Renée Faubion; v. 33, fall and winter, 2004 for "Forgotten Memories and Unheard Rhythms: H. D.'s Poetics as a Response to Male Modernism" by Helen V. Emmitt. Copyright © 2004 by S. Renée Faubion. Reproduced by permission of the author.—*Parnassus: Poetry in Review*, v. 9, spring/summer, 1981 for "The Poetry of W. S. Graham" by Jeffrey Wainwright. Copyright © 1981 by Jeffrey Wainwright. Reproduced by permission of the publisher and the author.—*Poetry Review*, v. 76, June, 1986 for "I Would Say I Was a Happy Man': W. S. Graham Interviewed by John Haffenden" by John Haffenden. Copyright © 1986 by John Haffenden. Reproduced by permission of the author.— *South Atlantic Review*, v. 69, fall, 2004. Copyright © 2004 by Georgia State University, Department of English. Reproduced by permission.—*Theology*, v. 97, September, 1994. Copyright © Martha Greene Eads. Reproduced by permission.—*Twentieth Century Literature*, v. 44, winter, 1998; 49, winter, 2003. Copyright © 1998, 2003. Hofstra University Press. Reproduced by permission.—*Victorian Newsletter*, spring, 1993. Copyright © 1993 by *The Victorian Newsletter*. Reproduced by permission of *The Victorian Newsletter* and the author.—*Victorian Periodicals Review*, v. 28, spring, 1995. Copyright © 1995 by The Johns Hopkins University Press. Reproduced by permission of The Johns Hopkins University Press.—*Victorian Poetry*, v. 38, spring, 2000 for "H. D. and the Years of World War I" by Norman Kelvin. Copyright © 2000 by Norman Kelvin. Reproduced by permission of the author.—*Yearbook of English Studies*, v. 17, 1987. Copyright © 1987 by Carcanet Press Ltd. Reproduced by permission of Carcanet Press Limited.

COPYRIGHTED MATERIAL IN *PC*, VOLUME 127, WAS REPRODUCED FROM THE FOLLOWING BOOKS:

Buckley, Jerome Hamilton. From *William Earnest Henley: A Study in the "Counter-Decadence" of the 'Nineties*. Princeton University Press, 1945.—Christodoulides, Nephie J. From *'And Never Know the Joy': Sex and the Erotic in English Poetry*. Rodopi, 2006. Copyright © 2006 Editions Rodopi BV. Reproduced by permission.—Corbett, John. From *Edinburgh Companion to Twentieth-Century Scottish Literature*. Edinburgh University Press, 2009. Copyright © 2009 by Edinburgh University Press. Reproduced by permission. www.euppublishing.com.—Flora, Joseph M. From *William Ernest Henley*. Twayne, 1970. Copyright © 1970 by Joseph M. Flora. Reproduced by permission of the author.—Fraser, Kathleen. From *H. D. and Poets After*. University of Iowa Press, 2000. Copyright © 2000 by University of Iowa Press. Reproduced

Gale Literature Product Advisory Board

The members of the Gale Literature Product Advisory Board—reference librarians from public and academic library systems—represent a cross-section of our customer base and offer a variety of informed perspectives on both the presentation and content of our literature products. Advisory board members assess and define such quality issues as the relevance, currency, and usefulness of the author coverage, critical content, and literary topics included in our series; evaluate the layout, presentation, and general quality of our printed volumes; provide feedback on the criteria used for selecting authors and topics covered in our series; provide suggestions for potential enhancements to our series; identify any gaps in our coverage of authors or literary topics, recommending authors or topics for inclusion; analyze the appropriateness of our content and presentation for various user audiences, such as high school students, undergraduates, graduate students, librarians, and educators; and offer feedback on any proposed changes/enhancements to our series. We wish to thank the following advisors for their advice throughout the year.

W. S. Graham
1918-1986

Scottish poet.

INTRODUCTION

A poet often compared to Dylan Thomas because of his unconventional imagery and syntax, Graham produced several volumes of poetry that were virtually ignored during his lifetime. In recent years, a number of critics have come to appreciate his work, which has now been included in some important anthologies.

BIOGRAPHICAL INFORMATION

Graham was born in Greenock, Scotland, on November 19, 1918, to a working class family. His parents were Margaret Macdiarmid Graham, and Alexander Graham, an engineer. He was raised in Clydeside, on the western coast of Scotland, where he attended school until the age of fourteen. At that time he was apprenticed to an engineering firm in Glasgow. He later studied engineering at Stow College and then took up the study of literature at Newbattle Abbey College. Graham worked in a variety of jobs before the publication of his first book of poetry in 1942, after which he moved to Cornwall. In 1947, Graham traveled to America, where he conducted a reading tour and taught briefly at New York University. The following year he moved to London, but eventually returned to Cornwall where he lived in a state of near poverty near the St. Ives artist colony. His financial situation improved greatly when he was awarded a Civil List pension in 1974. Graham was married to fellow poet Agnes Kilpatrick Dunsmuir. He died in Madron, Cornwall, on January 9, 1986.

MAJOR WORKS

Graham's first book of poetry, *Cage without Grievance,* was published in 1942; it contains fifteen poems as well as drawings by Robert Frame and Benjamin Crème. It was followed two years later by *The Seven Journeys,* a collection of narrative poems, also featuring drawings by Frame. Neither of these first two collections generated much critical response. In 1945, Graham produced *2nd Poems,* which attracted a bit of attention, and three years later published *The Voyages of Alfred Wallis* in pamphlet form. It was later included in his last volume of the decade, *The White Threshold* (1949), usually considered Graham's first important book. It was the first of his works to gain serious notice by critics and reviewers. It contains thirty-one poems, many of which had been previously published in various periodicals in England and North America. *The Nightfishing* was published in 1955, and is considered by many scholars to be Graham's masterpiece. He produced no new poetry for the next fifteen years until 1970, when he published *Malcolm Mooney's Land,* which was followed seven years later by *Implements in Their Places,* containing twenty-six new poems. Graham's previously published work appeared in *Collected Poems, 1942-1977* (1979) and *Selected Poems* (1980). His last collection, *Aimed at Nobody* was published posthumously in 1993.

CRITICAL RECEPTION

Early in his career, Graham was often called the Scottish Dylan Thomas, and like Thomas, he was often associated with the neo-Romantics. At that time, his poetry was considered obscure and inaccessible. Jascha Kessler (see Further Reading) contends that it was characterized by "that nearly impenetrable syntax, those agglutinating iambics marching, so many stressed monosyllables and new Teutonic compounds." By the time *The White Threshold* was published, Graham's style was changing—the influence of Thomas was fading and his work was becoming clearer and more precise. Although critics still complained that he was too preoccupied with the theme of language, they began to acknowledge his originality and intensity, and by the time his later volumes were published Graham was finally earning some degree of recognition.

The poet's relationship with language has been explored by Jeffrey Wainwright who reports that in Graham's poem "Approaches To How They Behave," language is not controlled by the writer and "words are not complaisant and pliable . . . but unruly, susceptible, willful." Wainwright contends that the poem is "self-satirical, adopting the manner of a plain man, well-meaning and persisting through the varieties of deviousness the words produce." David Punter describes Graham's uneasy relationship with language, contending that "he has been turned into a monument to linguistic suffering." In his discussion of *Cage without Grievance,* Punter argues that not only are many of the volume's poems "syntactically strange," but they are also "crammed with too many connections, too many separate relations between words, complex, showy and pointless." John Haffendon reports that Graham himself identified one of his major themes as "the difficulty of communication," and Mark Andrew Silverberg addresses the "frustrated relationship" between Graham and his reader that characterizes so much of his work. "While his poems demand or beg a response," contends Silverberg, "they set up linguistic situations in which it is impossible for a response to be had." Ruth Grogan, however, calls the 1979 volume, *Collected Poems,* "an extraordinary exploration of human communication and dialogue" characterized by "a mercurial combination of light-heartedness, tenderness, linguistic inventiveness, and philosophical depth."

Several critics trace the evolution of Graham's work from the poetry he produced at the beginning of his career to his later work written after 1970. Damian Grant notes the differences between Graham's early work and his later, less challenging poetry beginning with *Malcolm Mooney's Land,* but maintains that there are also a number of thematic and linguistic continuities between the two phases of his career. John Redmond also addresses the changes in Graham's work over the several decades of his career, describing it as "deliriously lush at the beginning, ascetically spare at the end." However, he finds that one characteristic of Graham's work remained constant, that is, that "each poem is treated as what we might call an existential field . . . inseparable from life."

Graham's poetry is now praised by a number of scholars, although he still remains a fairly unknown poet. Wainwright notes that Graham's early style, similar to the "colored cloquence associated with Dylan Thomas," had a detrimental effect on his literary reputation. Grant, who contends that Graham's admirers consider him "one of the most rigorous and rewarding British poets," believes that the well-established difficulty of his work accounts for his obscurity, but it was exacerbated by bad timing. Grant cites as an example the appearance of the "demanding" volume *The Nightfishing* coinciding with the publication of a far more accessible collection by Philip Larkin. Since Graham's second to last volume, *Implements in Their Places,* contains his most accessible poetry, Grant advises new readers to approach his work backwards, working from the less difficult to the more difficult material written during the early years. Grogan expresses the hope that Graham's work will be

reevaluated within the context of studies on the nature of dialogue by such theorists as Martin Buber and Mikhail Bakhtin. Redmond also contends Graham's poetry was ahead of its time and that its neglect is undeserved. "Anticipating a linguistic turn in postmodern poetry, his work sees language as an obstacle and a gift," according to Redmond.

PRINCIPAL WORKS

Poetry

Cage without Grievance [drawings by Benjamin Crème and Robert Frame] 1942
The Seven Journeys [drawings by Robert Frame] 1944
2nd Poems, 1945
The Voyages of Alfred Wallis 1948
The White Threshold 1949
The Nightfishing 1955
Malcolm Mooney's Land 1970
Implements in Their Places 1977
Collected Poems, 1942-1977 1979
Selected Poems 1980
Uncollected Poems 1990
Aimed at Nobody: Poems from Notebooks 1993
W. S. Graham: Selected Poems 1996

Other Major Works

The Night Fisherman: Selected Letters of W. S. Graham (letters) 1999

CRITICISM

Damian Grant (essay date 1980)

SOURCE: Grant, Damian. "Walls of Glass: The Poetry of W. S. Graham." In *British Poetry since 1970: A Critical Survey,* edited by Peter Jones and Michael Schmidt, pp. 22-38. New York: Persea Books, 1980.

[*In the following essay, Grant discusses the continuities as well as the evolution displayed by Graham's poetry throughout his career, describing* Implements in Their Places *as his most accessible work.*]

I

W. S. Graham has published seven books of poetry in over thirty years, and is unquestioningly acknowledged by his select audience as one of the most rigorous and rewarding British poets; but he has never been popular or even widely known. This may partly be due to the fact that he has been 'somewhat unlucky in his timing', in that (as Edward Lucie-Smith once noted) his demanding volume *The Nightfishing* appeared the same year as Philip Larkin's more accessible *The Less Deceived.* But the intrinsic reason lies in the difficulty of his poems, especially his early poems; a point which has always been conceded in the little criticism that has appeared of Graham's work. On the appearance of *The White Threshold* in 1949 Edwin Morgan remarked how Graham had 'moved into the front rank of those who are striving to light up the imaginative dialogue of poet and reader without resort to well-laid fuses of moral or social response', and applauded the integrity, the 'undeviating and dangerous singlemindedness' of his determination to 'remain undistracted and unwooed'. Reviewing *Malcolm Mooney's Land* twenty years later, Robin Skelton said that 'W. S. Graham resolutely avoids the public stance; his poems are directed to individual listeners and not to crowds'. Calvin Bedient contrasts Graham with the poet who would 'wear the common language like a consecrated robe': 'Graham wants to cut his own cloth, show by his style that he is *not* the public. His cultivated eccentricity argues the right to stand alone'.

And he has stood alone; the negative evidence is there to confirm these observations. Graham's poems have never been widely anthologized, imitated, or (mercifully) set for examinations. *Collected Poems 1942-1977* have now (1979) appeared from Faber, who have never before published a selection. The only representative selection from his work appeared in volume 17 of the Penguin Modern Poets in 1970 (a volume which also featured David Gascoyne and Kathleen Raine). His poems continue to make their rare appearances in magazines; but he is almost like the ghost of a poet, whose visitations are perceived by a few initiates but pass unnoticed by the majority—even the majority of the readers of poetry. One of Graham's finest poems, **'Johann Joachim Quantz's Five Lessons'**, concludes with this sober injunction from the musician to his pupil:

> Do not be sentimental or in your Art.
> I will miss you. Do not expect applause.

It would seem then that Graham has been prepared to do without applause for most of his career. The purpose of this essay is not to set the echoes ringing with combative assertions, but to offer an interpreta-

tive introduction to Graham's work for the reader who may well (and quite excusably) have missed one of the rarest talents in English poetry. The opportunity is provided by the fact that Graham's last two volumes, *Malcolm Mooney's Land* (1970) and *Implements in their Places* (1977), were both published in the 1970s.

II

W. S. Graham's first book of poems *Cage Without Grievance* was published by David Archer's Parton Press in Glasgow in 1942 when Graham was twenty-four. There followed *The Seven Journeys* two years later; *2nd Poems* in 1945. A pamphlet poem *The Voyages of Alfred Wallis* was published in 1948 by a small press in Cornwall, where Graham (who had left his native Scotland first for London and then for New York) was shortly to make his home, and where he still lives. These early poems show Graham drunk with words and prodigal of images; dazed with Dylan Thomas (whom he had met in London, among the poets who congregated in Soho) and blown about with the windy rhetoric of the New Apocalypse:

> This flying house where somewhere houses war
> World of the winding world hands me away
> Hauls at my tugging blood for words to wear
> Like rose of rising in the mercury counting sky
>
> ('Warning Not Prayer Enough', *2nd Poems*)

And so on. The excitement is purely verbal, the 'lonely energy' of the poetry (as Graham was later to call it) runs to earth without discharging its meaning. On the technical side, one notices especially the enfeebling fondness for what one might call the poetic participle: for the much-abused -ing (and also the agent -er) forms, which set up an easy rocking rhythm without making much demand on the syntax.

But nevertheless these poems do clearly initiate some of Graham's permanent themes (the drama of identity, in the multiplying of the self; the paradoxes of communication, with particular reference to the mystery of the poem; the metaphoric voyage; time) and also introduce us to his favourite contrastive images of land and sea, tree and wave, owl and gull, voice and silence. The successful poem **'My Glass World Tells of Itself'** (*2nd Poems*) presents us with the image of a ship in a bottle, which (as we shall see) is to recur throughout Graham's work as his personal symbol of the timeless and motionless world of art: his Grecian Urn.

Graham's first important book was *The White Threshold,* published by Faber in 1949. This is still disfigured by the influence of Dylan Thomas (indeed, the influence of Thomas on both the language and the imagery of many of these poems is if anything more marked) but it was also now apparent that Graham had a voice of his own. In poems like **'Listen. Put on Morning'**, **'The White Threshold'**, and the **'Three Letters'** with which the volume concludes, one recognizes a poet of authority and rigour, the assurance of whose style and the finished beauty of whose poems could not fail to attract the reader—despite his frequent and uncompromising obscurity. One important technical advance in this volume was the development of a short, three-stressed line (Robin Skelton informs us that Graham 'studied the three-stress line over a long period by keeping a journal whose every entry was written in this form'), which certainly helped Graham to pare down his rhetorical excess and allowed for that verbal precision and rhythmical originality which have since become the hallmark of his mature style.

The Nightfishing appeared in 1955, when 'it became immediately apparent that we were in the presence of a master'; then, strangely, there was a gap of fifteen years before the publication of *Malcolm Mooney's Land* in 1970—a volume which reminded older readers of Graham's existence and as it were announced him as a new poet now in his fifties to others. *Implements in their Places* followed in 1977, confirming the fact that Graham had earned what John Berryman celebrates in his elegy for William Carlos Williams,

> the mysterious late excellence which is the crown
> of our trials & our last bride.

It is this 'late excellence' which must be the main subject of this essay; but it is essential I feel to spend a little time with *The Nightfishing* before proceeding. One is not surprised to learn that W. S. Graham doesn't like to think of himself as having 'improved' as a poet if this means that his early work should therefore be neglected, if not entirely forgotten. Many of the early poems, one must agree, do present more difficulty than many readers will be prepared to encounter without better assurance that the effort will be rewarded. But the title poem **'The Nightfishing'**, and the **'Seven Letters'** which relate to it, besides providing a basis for the understanding of Graham's later work, and clues to his subsequent development, are also important poems in themselves which will reward our attention.

'The Nightfishing' is an accomplished and beautiful poem, but even so one of formidable difficulty. Michael Schmidt has rightly remarked that Graham's poems resist prose paraphrase; but it is necessary at least to indicate the area of exploration of the poem, however inadequate an idea this may give of its final effect. At one level the poem is about a fishing trip. The central section describes how a fishing boat sets out from Greenock, trawls for herring, and returns to the port at dawn. And simply as description it works magnificently—illustrating how a debt to Hopkins has been repaid:

> Over the gunwale over into our deep lap
> The herring come in, staring from their scales,
> Fruitful as our deserts would have it out of
> The deep and shifting seams of water. . . .

But the outer sections of the poem confirm the fact that this description is densely metaphoric, and functions as part of a larger meaning. Calvin Bedient has written, rather portentously, that the poem 'is a profound experience; its nineteen pages put us amid Being'. However one chooses to express it, certainly the poem works at the deepest and dumbest levels of our selves, among our own 'deep and shifting seams'. Section I introduces the poet confronted with the mystery of being, hinging as it does on the determination of the self:

> Now within the dead
> Of night and the dead
> Of my life I hear
> My name called from far out.

He is called, uttered, born. The second section provides some vivid, surreal images of birth (still reminiscent of Thomas's obstetric imagery) and then we move into the third and longest section, where in fact the underlying metaphor frequently surfaces:

> The steep bow heaves, hung on these words, towards
> What words your lonely breath blows out to meet it.
> It is the skilled keel itself knowing its own
> Fathoms it further moves through, with us there
> Kept in its common timbers, yet each of us
> Unwound upon
>
> By a lonely behaviour of the all common ocean.

The boat is the physical vessel of the self, the body which is common to all humanity ('its common timbers') yet distinct in its own individual activity, its 'lonely behaviour'. The vessel is white-rigged with thought (like Keats's 'branched thoughts' in the 'Ode to Psyche'); the nets trailed in the sea are nerves. The sea itself is the great inclusive, inexhaustible image of all life, all time, all consciousness, on which and in which each individual must venture all he has and is. The caught herrings (possibly) are words, articulated moments rescued from the wash of time—but also killed. But to separate out the symbolism too thoroughly is also to kill or at least denature the poem. We notice that the sea itself is frequently described as a 'mingling element', mingling our own multiple selves, our separate selves (as it does in Virginia Woolf's *The Waves*), mingling all the living and all the dead (as does the falling snow in Joyce's story *The Dead*). The sea is also an agent of change; there is submerged reference to *The Tempest* ('Pearled behind my eyes') and the idea of a 'sea-change' remains strong.

The fourth section finds the poet returned to 'that loneliness' which was 'Bragged into a voyage', and which is not assuaged by the ambiguous phrase 'There we lay / Loved alone'. In the fifth the poet attempts to locate the self in a place, 'fastened with movement'. But the self is never stable; the consciousness which determines identity is itself a mingling element:

> This is myself (who but ill resembles me).
> He befriended so many
> Disguises to wander in on as many roads
> As cross on a ball of wool.

The self is in fact the first of our necessary fictions. The sixth section is crucial, presenting as it does man as poet and poem as object, both beyond change; through the image (once more) of the ship in a bottle:

> The rigged ship in its walls of glass
> Still further forms its perfect seas
> Locked in its past transparences.

Graham is a deftly allusive poet, and I would think there is a strong possibility that he means us to recall here the beautiful image of permanence invoked by Shakespeare in sonnet number 5:

> Then were not summer's distillation left
> A liquid prisoner pent in walls of glass . . .

The last section is valedictory; the restless self is committed (like Tennyson's Ulysses) to another journey, 'Out into the waving / Nerves of the open sea'; while the poem of the self comes to rest in its 'breathless still place'. The reader new to and curious about Graham would do well to go back to **'The Nightfishing'** and to the **'Seven Letters'** which accompany it. But meanwhile we must move on to consider the work which Graham has published during the present decade.

III

Despite the fifteen-year silence, there is a clear continuity between Graham's earlier and his later work. He takes up his themes and images in *Malcolm Mooney's Land* exactly where he left off:

> Language swings away
> Before me as I go
> With again the night rising
> Up to accompany me
> And that other fond
> Metaphor, the sea.

('The Dark Dialogues')

But it would be a mistake to conclude that nothing has changed, or that Graham is simply repeating himself. The whole process or pretence of communication has become more problematical, beset with more obstacles and even dangers than formerly. Instead of the fish-rich seas of the earlier work, the title poem introduces us to an Arctic world of ice and snow where words themselves have frozen, and from which he can look back almost nostalgically to 'old summers / When to speak was easy'. Now it is a glacier rather than a boat that drives its keel; now he is in a tent rather than a room, words are 'buried under the printed snow' (we note the characteristic pun) rather than swarming like herring in the sea. Language has become more resistant, more dubious as a means of communication:

> Out at the far off edge I hear
> Colliding voices . . .
> Tomorrow I'll try the rafted ice.
> Have I not been trying to use the obstacle
> Of language well? It freezes round us all.

The growing blizzard is 'filled with other voices' than Mooney's (which is itself a projection of the poet's own voice); he can no longer distinguish him, 'Becoming shapeless into / The shrill swerving snow'. And if contact with himself is threatened, the poet has also lost confidence in the connection between word and thing, which must hold as the hinge of all adequate communication. 'Sit / With me between this word / And this . . . Yet not mistake this / For the real thing'. Graham leaves us to resolve the paradox that his language is actually more than adequate to detain the 'real thing' in words:

> Tell him I came across
> An old sulphur bear
> Sawing his log of sleep
> Loud beneath the snow.
> He puffed the powdered light
> Up on to this page
> And here his reek fell
> In splinters among
> These words.

The effect is similar to that achieved in Ted Hughes's poem 'The Thought Fox', where the animal is persuaded to leave its prints on the page. Mastery of the language does not alter the fact—or the irony—that language mocks itself; like a recurring decimal, it can never be *exact*. And there is another sinister enemy. The poet is now almost morbidly conscious of the ultimate silence that overlooks and overhears all that we try to do and say.

> From wherever it is I urge these words
> To find their subtle vents, the northern dazzle
> Of silence cranes to watch.

Although the poet has tried to commune with himself and with others in the poem, writing a diary and telling stories, he ends with the inevitable admission of his loneliness:

> I have made myself alone now.
> Outside the tent endless
> Drifting hummock crests.
> Words drifting on words.
> The real unabstract snow.

It is typical of Graham's orientation towards reality— and also of the way his enclosing metaphor controls his material—that the poem actually alludes in many of its details to the voyage of the Norwegian explorer Nansen towards the North Pole in 1893-6. Nansen deliberately had his ship the Fram become locked in ice, on the theory—which proved correct—that ocean currents would carry it safely northwards. (Could this provide another appropriate meaning for Graham's 'walls of glass'?). I have suggested several parallels with other writers already in this essay, parallels which help I think to establish the scope as well as the seriousness of Graham's work. But this seems a good point to remark upon the most important and illuminating parallel, which is with Samuel Beckett. According to Michael Schmidt, Graham has acknowledged a debt to Beckett, but even without this the reader could not fail to be struck by the close correspondence between the ideas, themes, and literary technique of the poet and those of the prose writer and dramatist. The revolving obsession with identity, consciousness, and articulation; the telling of stories to create the fiction of the self, and the creation of voices and personae to evade the implosion of the self; the reliance on pun and allusion as a literary method; the deepening pessimism (which this implies) as to the possibility of communication with our kind, and the admission of loneliness as one's ultimate condition, are all themes of Beckett's Trilogy (especially of the last piece, *The Unnamable*); and it is these same themes which move Graham to his most memorable utterance. If Beckett has insisted that 'art is the apotheosis of solitude', Graham likewise once wrote that the poet

> is concerned with putting into words those sudden desolations and happiness that descend on us uninvited there where we each are within our lonely rooms never really entered by anybody else and from which we never emerge.

The obsessions of both writers converge in the relentless questioning of language itself, whose capacity to redeem us from this solitude turns out to be largely an illusion. Language is conceived now as a kind of double agent which both serves and betrays, revealing us to ourselves (and others) and at the same time disguising the fugitive self which can never be known. Robin Skelton has observed that Graham uses language 'as a metaphor for the human condition'; this is an es-

sential point to recognize if we are to respond to the passion of Graham's exhaustingly reflexive mode of expression:

> I stop and listen over
> My shoulder and listen back
> On language for that step
> That seems to fall after
> My own step in the dark

> ('The Dark Dialogues')

Beckett's Unnamable is unable to establish 'what I am, where I am, whether I am words among words or silence in the midst of silence' (392). He is 'made of words' but they are 'others' words' (390), he is 'made of silence' but the silence is continually invaded by voices and cries (417). Language diffuses his identity, he can never confidently say 'I'. Three things he says have conditioned his existence, three things which we can see are really one and the same, a kind of existential trinity: 'the inability to speak, the inability to be silent, and solitude' (400). Now the fifteen sections of Graham's poem **'Approaches to How They Behave'** (which clearly looks forward to the title poem of Graham's more recent volume) reflect very similar concerns. Speaking has the same ambiguous relation to silence:

> Having to construct the silence first
> To speak out on I realize
> The silence even itself floats
> At my ear-side with a character
> I have not met before.

> (XV)

His words are not under his exclusive control; they derive a life of their own from the silence that surrounds them, and which is also inhabited by other people:

> What does it matter if the words
> I choose, in the order I choose them in,
> Go out into a silence I know
> Nothing about, there to be let
> In and entertained and charmed
> Out of their master's orders?

> (I)

The words he sends out 'In roughly your direction' (III) may freeze, become hazardous 'floating bergs to sink a convoy' (IV). Because one is conscious all the time that 'Speaking is difficult', 'one tries / To be exact' (II); but despite our efforts, what we naively call communication can never be said to have occurred:

> The words are mine, the thoughts are all
> Yours as they occur behind
> The bat of your vast unseen eyes.

But despite the defensiveness of these assertions, the poem includes an interesting explicit metaphor which gives us a clue as to how Graham attempts to cope with an apparently insuperable problem.

> The inadequacy
> Of the living, animal language drives
> Us all to metaphor and an attempt
> To organize the spaces we think
> We have made occur between the words.
>
> (II)

The recalcitrant animal has to be exercised, the unreliable spaces organized in whatever ways we can discover. These may include direct confrontation, the method Graham prefers to metaphor in the searching poem **'The Dark Dialogues'.** Here he asks the direct question 'Who are you?', and confesses the need 'to say / Something and to hear / That someone has heard me', only to be driven back on himself by the language

> And whoever I meant
> To think I had met
> Turns away further
> Before me blinded by
> This word and this word.

Adapting Marvell's 'Dialogue of Self and Soul' (to which there may well be an implicit allusion here) Graham is blinded by a word, deaf with the drumming of a word: eye and ear enclose rather than liberate. Even the self he falls back on is indistinct, unutterable in words: 'There is no other place / Than where I am, between / This word and the next'; the voices and identities of his father and mother usurp his own, 'As I sit here becoming / Hardly who I know'. He can assert that 'always language / Is where the people are', but neither language nor people can be detained. I try (he says) 'To clench my words against / Time or the lack of time', but always 'Language swings away / Further before me'. In a minimal, reductive definition of his function, he is trying to teach his ears and eyes 'to observe / The behaviour of silence': a peculiarly Beckettian pastime.

In **'The Fifteen Devices',** similarly, the experience of psychological decomposition ('When who we think we are is suddenly / Flying apart') is paralleled by 'the prised / Open spaces between the flying / Apart words'. The self is a place, nameless and unlocatable; the poem is a space, an arena where potential meanings are released and then left to themselves. This last idea is developed in the beautiful and lucid poem **'The Constructed Space',** whose opening word 'Meanwhile' breaks in as it were on the continuous dark dialogue of one:

> Meanwhile surely there must be something to say,
> Maybe not suitable but at least happy

> In a sense here between us two whoever
> We are.

The poem he goes on to define as 'a public place / Achieved against subjective odds and then / Mainly an obstacle to what I mean'. The 'obstacle' lies in the fact that the meaning received need not be the same as that conveyed. The poem presents us with a sudden realization of this fact:

> Or maybe, surely, of course we never know
> What we have said, what lonely meanings are read
> Into the space we make.

After such a realization the meaning of the poem can only be described as an approximation:

> I say this silence or, better, construct this space
> So that somehow something may move across
> The caught habits of language to you and me.

'Habit is a great deadener' is another Beckettian axiom; Graham too recognizes the danger, and there is continuous evidence of his precautionary measures against the hardening of habitual phrases in the way he often indulges as a kind of exercise in puns and other word-games, subverting or reforging the conventional expression. Thus he describes himself with Joycean alertness as 'lying wordawake', and expresses the wish to 'be out of myself and / About the extra, ordinary world'. It is with such a punning phrase that Graham concludes this poem: 'Here in the present tense disguise is mortal'. Disguise is both human and deadly; we can avoid neither our humanity nor our sentence of death. And disguise in this sense, referring to the inevitable opacity of the self, the 'quick disguise' (another pun) which life condemns us to, is a theme to which Graham often returns.

'The Constructed Space' is a very explicit, almost literal statement of the theory that lies behind many of the poems. Elsewhere this theory is more richly caparisoned in metaphor. The beast in **'The Beast in the Space'** for example is a mythical monster that 'lives on silence' and 'laps my meaning up'; it is this beast that now possesses the arena of the poem.

> I am not here, only the space
> I sent the terrible beast across.

And the seven sections of the fine concluding poem **'Clusters Travelling Out'** develops very imaginatively the metaphor of the self as confined in a prison cell, trying to establish some kind of communication with his fellow-prisoners. He never knows if his message is being received:

> Are you receiving those clusters
> I send out travelling? Alas

I have no way of knowing or
If I am overheard here.

At the end of the poem (and the book) he is left 'waiting for / A message to come in now', much as Vladimir and Estragon wait hopelessly for Godot. We notice that here too the metaphor has more than one level. The tap on the wall is also the tap on the typewriter:

> I tap
> And tap to interrupt silence into
> Manmade durations making for this
> Moment a dialect for our purpose

—and also making the poem: 'It is our poetry such as it is'.

Another way in which Graham makes his theme more concrete is to consider the problem of communication with particular people. There are half a dozen poems in *Malcolm Mooney's Land* (and more in *Implements in their Places*) addressed to friends and to his wife which—although still oblique and difficult—are very moving. Here we have Graham's more personal expression of the need to find 'a way / Of speaking towards you' (in **'Wynter and the Grammarsow'**): 'I mean there must be some / Way to speak together straighter than this, / As I usually say': his need 'to be by another aloneness loved' (**'Hilton Abstract'**), which line speaks straight enough to anyone. The fine elegiac poem **'The Thermal Stair'**, for Peter Lanyon, is the most direct of all: 'Remember me wherever you listen from'. 'I leave this at your ear for when you wake' is the first and last line of the poem to his wife. But he is older, death is nearer (it has overtaken some already), and so there is due acknowledgement of the power of time. 'I stand in the ticking room' he says to his wife; 'The times are calling us in' he reminds Wynter, calling us towards 'the real sea' where the rest of the dead await our coming. But the consolation seized in these poems—perhaps surprisingly—is the traditional one that the poem can itself stand against time; we are back to the Shakespearean 'walls of glass'. From this perspective the artist's task may after all be simply expressed:

> His job is love
> Imagined into words or paint to make
> An object that will stand and will not move.

> ('The Thermal Stair')

IV

The first thing to remark about Graham's last collection, *Implements in their Places,* is that it is more accessible than any of his earlier work. (It is for this reason that the reader new to Graham might be well advised to begin with this last book, and read him

backwards). Never before has Graham written as simply and directly as in the dozen or so personal poems included in this volume. The strenuous syntactical effort of the earlier poems is replaced here by a restrained authority, a certainty of utterance which is characteristic of that 'mysterious late excellence' wherever it is encountered. **'Loch Thom'** is a beautiful example. The poem describes a visit made by the poet to the watery 'stretch of my childhood':

> And almost I am back again
> Wading the heather down to the edge
> To sit. The minnows go by in shoals
> Like iron-filings in the shallows.
> My mother is dead. My father is dead
> And all the trout I used to know
> Leaping from their sad rings are dead.

'It is a colder / Stretch of water than I remember': the poignancy of the experience is finely captured in the contrasted physical descriptions of past and present; there is no importunity on the part of the poet himself. In the poem addressed to his father (**'To Alexander Graham'**) the emotion is controlled by the use of the dream situation:

> Lying asleep walking
> Last night I met my father
> Who seemed pleased to see me.
> He wanted to speak. I saw
> His mouth saying something
> But the dream had no sound.

The visual images are sharp, the atmosphere of Greenock 'As real as life. I smelt / The quay's tar and the ropes'. Only in the last line of the poem is the feeling alluded to—tentatively, and in the perfect rather than the present tense: 'I think I must have loved him'. **'Lines on Roger Hilton's Watch'** ('Which I was given because / I loved him and we had / Terrible times together') and **'Dear Bryan Wynter'** ('This is only a note / To say how sorry I am / You died') are in the same direct idiom, moving elegies in Graham's most spare and essential style. 'Do not be sentimental or in your Art', said Johann Quantz to his pupil; and if Graham has avoided sentimentalism in these fine poems it must be largely due to his expert use of his characteristic three-stress line, on which we have commented earlier. The short line encourages a strict economy of word, breaks up familiar collocations of words into new groupings, and above all gives Graham the opportunity of setting up a tense rhythm, which is at the same time tightly controlled but fluent and expressive:

> Of course, here I am
> Thinking I want to say
> Something into the ghost

Of the presence you left
Me with between the granite
Of my ego house . . .

But despite the excellence of these 'private' poems, one cannot help feeling that it is still in the more exploratory, reflexive mode that Graham's true distinctiveness as a poet is discovered; in the poem of the self, and the poem of the poem itself: what Wallace Stevens called 'The poem of the mind in the act of finding / What will suffice'. One could suggest that there are two groups of poems in this broad category, plus the unclassifiable title poem. Graham has always been fascinated by the implications for literature of the other arts, and there are three poems here that reflect this continuing interest. The masterful **'Johann Joachim Quantz's Five Lessons'** takes the example of music. The celebrated musician is teaching the flute to his student Karl; the teaching is partly in words, and so we have the formula: 'It is best I sit / Here where I am to speak on the other side / Of language'. But the object of the lesson is music, the playing of the flute; and so a different kind of silence is invoked, a different kind of concave world:

> Now we must try higher, aware of the terrible
> Shapes of silence sitting outside your ear
> Anxious to define you and really love you.
> Remember silence is curious about its opposite
> Element which you shall learn to represent.

One thinks inevitably of Blake's great humanistic consolation: 'Eternity is in love with the productions of time'. Graham here more specifically dwells upon the mysterious correspondence between the convex world of musical art and the concave world of silence, which create the same curve from opposite sides and confirm each other with the exactness of an equation. The syntax in this poem has the perfect tautness of music; the movement and the sheer control of meaning is a positive pleasure for the reader:

> Karl, I can still put on a good flute-mouth
> And show you in this high cold room something
> You will be famous to have said you heard.

In the Fourth Lesson Quantz becomes more personal. Master and pupil pass beyond technique ('I think you are good enough / To not need me any more') to the philosophy of music: with the musician as demi-urge.

> What we have to do
> Today is think of you as a little creator
> After the big creator.

The last lesson is a kind of Master Class in artistic conscience.

> Do not intrude too much
> Into the message you carry and put out.

One last thing, Karl, remember when you enter
The joy of those quick high archipelagoes,
To make to keep your finger-stops as light
As feathers but definite. What can I say more?
Do not be sentimental or in your Art.
I will miss you. Do not expect applause.

This (as we have seen) is equally applicable to music or poetry, and contains lessons which Graham himself has scrupulously observed throughout his career.

There isn't space unfortunately to explore all these poems in the way they deserve: poems like **'The Found Picture'** and **'Ten Shots of Mr Simpson'**, although I must at least note the fact that this last poem includes once again Graham's personal symbol: 'a white-rigged ship bottled sailing'. If Mr Simpson is a prisoner of art he joins the liquid prisoner in its walls of glass.

The other poems confront the perennial themes—language, consciousness, identity—with Graham's home-made metaphors. The interrogative structure of the opening poem **'What is the Language Using Us For?'** brings a new urgency to what before was meditation. Malcolm Mooney returns as the perplexed questioner, 'moving away / Slowly over the white language', his regular habitat; and in his usual role:

> He is only going to be
> Myself and for you slightly you
> Wanting to be another. He fell
> He falls (Tenses are everywhere.)
> Deep down into a glass jail.

The glass jail is the image of art once more—an art which kills (as Mr Simpson was 'shot') as well as eternizes:

> The point is would you ever want
> To be down here on the freezing line
> Reading the words that stream out
> Against the ice?

The touch of the Muse, we remember, the touch of the White Goddess, is a freezing touch; a fact which was dramatically illustrated in Graham's poem **'Five Visitors to Madron'** in *Malcolm Mooney's Land*. The second part of the poem is more explicit: 'What I am making is / A place for language in my life / Which I want to be a real place / Seeing I have to put up with it / Anyhow'. This recalls Beckett's resigned answer to the question as to why he still used words: 'Parcequ'il n'y a rien d'autre'. We have to accept that it is through language that we perform as well as we are able the human function of art: 'we want to be telling / Each other alive about each other / Alive'. The third part resumes the seafaring metaphors of *The Night-fishing,* to coincide with a challenging series of rhetorical questions:

> What is the weather
> Using us for where we are ready
> With all our language lines aboard?
> The beginning wind slaps the canvas.
> Are you ready? Are you ready?

Once again, there are several other poems that require more careful analysis than there is space for here: poems like **'Untidy Dreadful Table', 'Enter a Cloud',** and **'The Secret Name'.** This last is a beautiful if chilling poem, one of several in which Madron Wood appears as an image of the absolute, and presumably death. Like Beckett's Unnamable, the persona of this poem listens for his own name in order to know and situate himself, but this 'hurries away / Before you in the trees to escape' leaving him in the terrifying solipsist enclosure:

> To tell you the truth I hear almost
> Only the sounds I have made myself.
> Up over the wood's roof I imagine
> The long sigh of Outside goes.

The self is divided again: 'I leave them there a moment knowing / I make them act you and me'; and the poem is the wood, the uneasy place where these selves take refuge. 'Under the poem's branches two people / Walk and even the words are shy'. But this is no 'rosy sanctuary', like that provided by Keats for Psyche. Madron Wood is more sinister, and there is obviously more threat than promise in the concluding section of the poem:

> The terrible, lightest wind in the world
> Blows from word to word, from ear
> To ear, from name to name, from secret
> Name to secret name. You maybe
> Did not know you had another
> Sound and sign signifying you.

Which brings us finally to the title poem, about which I must confess to feeling a certain uneasiness. **'Implements in their Places'** is not one poem but a gathering of 74 fragments of from one to nineteen lines, a curious mixture of impersonation and self-mockery along with some genuine Graham. We know where we are for example when the Muse breathes 'her rank breath of poet's bones' (4), or where Graham protests: 'Terrible the indignity of one's self flying / Away from the sleight of one's true hand' (56). Loch Thom reappears 'in place' of number 57 (was this I wonder the poet's age when he wrote it?):

> There is no fifty-seven.
> It is not here. Only
> Freshwater Loch Thom

> To paddle your feet in
> And the long cry of the curlew.

And Quantz's lesson on the impersonality of art is beautifully recapitulated in the two lines: 'It is only when the tenant is gone / The shell speaks of the sea' (48). The most interesting group, however, is the fifteen or so (24-40) which revolve round the poet's permanent struggle with words and meanings. Language is chastised as 'constrictor of my soul' and as 'you terrible surrounder / Of everything' (30, 35). Even the contemporary idiom is put to good use in this context. The poet is 'Commuting by arterial words / Between my home and Cool Cat / Reality' (28), he is 'Sad to have to infer / Such graft and treachery, in the name / Of communication' (29); in a moment of punning frustration he can exclaim: 'I want out of this underword' (42). Another four-line fragment gives us a description of Graham as he may see himself now, at the end of his last volume; a less heroic and more self-conscious version of Malcolm Mooney:

> Only now a wordy ghost
> Of once my firmer self I go
> Floating across the frozen tundra
> Of the lexicon and the dictionary.

> (27)

V

Seven years elapsed between *Malcolm Mooney's Land* and *Implements in their Places.* I don't know how long we shall have to wait for Graham's next volume. No shorter time, I imagine; I know of only one poem which has been published since the last book, although some more have been broadcast. Meanwhile, we have now the **Collected Poems** from Faber. This is a matter for satisfaction since the early volumes are now unobtainable and even *Malcolm Mooney's Land* is out of print. Graham himself may well be able to dispense with our applause, but that does not mean that we should have to dispense with Graham. The publication of his collected poems will at last enable a wider readership to get to know and begin to appreciate a profound, humane and generous poet now at the height of his powers; a poet who was not the victim (as many are) of excessive praise when he was described in the *Malahat Review* on the publication of his last volume as 'clearly one of the finest, if not *the* finest, poet now writing in English'.

Note

Chapters devoted to Graham in Calvin Bedient's *Eight Contemporary Poets* (1974) and Michael Schmidt's *50 Modern British Poets* (1979) represent the only extended criticism of his work. Edwin Morgan's review of *The White Threshold* in *Nine* (vol 2, 1950) is well worth reading, as is Robin Skelton's review of *Malcolm Mooney's Land* in the *Malahat Review* (no 15, 1970).

Jeffrey Wainwright (essay date spring/summer 1981)

SOURCE: Wainwright, Jeffrey. "The Poetry of W. S. Graham." *Parnassus: Poetry in Review* 9, no. 1 (spring/ summer 1981): 242-51.

[*In the following essay, Wainwright surveys Graham's work, focusing on the poet's relationship with language itself.*]

Our frequent fancy about language is that it is simply an instrument in our control. Words are marshalled into metaphors of power and command: so-and-so's "mastery of words," "command of language," such-and-such as a "powerful speaker." The writer, more winsomely, might be said to have "a way with words." This metaphor of obedience appears in W. S. Graham's poem **"Approaches To How They Behave"** except that here, "they," words, are not complaisant and pliable, "on their best behavior," but unruly, susceptible, willful. Rather like the traditionally exasperated schoolmaster, the poet chivvies his charges toward their proper destinations only to have them drawn away to some rival attraction, "entertained and charmed / Out of their master's orders," or see them pull a face and run off. Even the willing monitor, "the good word," has its own devices.

> The good word said I am not pressed
> For time. I have all the foxglove day
> And all my user's days to give
> You my attention. Shines the red
> Fox in the digitalis grove.
> Choose me choose me. Guess which
> Word I am here calling myself
> The best. If you can't fit me in
> To lying down here among the fox
> Glove towers of the moment, say
> I am yours the more you use me. Tomorrow
> Same place same time give me a ring.

So keen to make an impression ("the foxglove day") the good word's eloquent versatility becomes only embarrassing wordplay. The tone of **"Approaches To How They Behave"** is self-satirical, adopting the manner of a plain man, well-meaning and persisting through the varieties of deviousness the words produce.

> Speaking is difficult and one tries
> To be exact and yet not to
> Exact the prime intention to death.

Yet even so earnest an opening as this is instantly betrayed into punning complexity, with the familiar figure of speech "to death" dropping suddenly toward its anterior meaning. The task of speaking, of uttering "what I thought was worth saying," comes to appear a more and more quixotic ambition.

> Through the chinks in your lyric coat
> My ear catches a royal glimpse
> Of fuzzed flesh, unworded body.

But this is as close as he gets—the mere glimpse of the reality to which these words should refer and defer. Through its fifteen short sections, this poem runs deftly over an elaborate structure of metaphor. That is the condition of its subject-matter—"the inadequacy / Of the living, animal language drives / Us all to metaphor"—and once language itself is entertained, it will continue to discourse upon itself. The only companion more fearful is silence.

W. S. Graham's *Selected Poems* includes work published in England over thirty-five years from *Cage Without Grievance* (1942) to the *Collected Poems 1942-1977* that appeared in 1979. This selection, however, does not proceed chronologically but begins with a number of poems that concentrate intensely upon the problematics of language both in poetry and at large. The first, a sequence of three poems from *Implements In Their Places* (1977), with the challenging reiteration of its title **"What Is The Language Using Us For?,"** issues an announcement of the concerns Graham has come to, and stands almost as an admonition, a necessary question that must be confronted before we can proceed. The poem is deliberately difficult to settle into, switching the reader over between different voices and contexts, persistently interrogative in tones shifting from aggression to pathos. Here are the opening stanzas of the **"First Poem"**:

> What is the language using us for?
> Said Malcolm Mooney moving away
> Slowly over the white language.
> Where am I going said Malcolm Mooney.
> Certain experiences seem to not
> Want to go in to language maybe
> Because of shame or the reader's shame.
> Let us observe Malcolm Mooney.

The first two lines encourage us toward a firm four-stress rhythm that is immediately disrupted by the run-on into the dissonant third line. The recalcitrance of "certain experiences" is then mimed in the awkward lineation and syntax of the second stanza, the split infinitive over the line and the deliberate "in to." Also here the reader is implicated in these difficulties, though the stanza closes with the promise of a clear position and some enlightenment: "Let us observe." But Malcolm Mooney proves elusive, he is not even a "persona":

> Reader, it does
> Not matter. He is only going to be
>
> Myself and for you slightly you
> Wanting to be another.

Identities and identifications are confused, slipping away in the blank ice-world of language, "the white language," "the freezing line" of the poem. This imagery of the wastes of ice and snow recurs time and again in Graham's work. It is **"Malcolm Mooney's Land"** in that title poem to his 1970 collection where he fuses the notion of polar journeys with the poem's traverse of the white page: "Footprint on foot / Print, word on word and each on a fool's errand." Like Nansen's North Pole itself the goal is conceptual, not a journey to any *place*. But Malcolm Mooney himself, "the saviour," disappears from **"What Is The Language Using Us For?"** and the **"Second Poem"** of the group focuses the problem with a discursive clarity that at first seems to belie its subject. What "Communication's / Mistakes" are doing to us in what Graham calls sarcastically "the magic medium" does matter:

> So far as we want to be telling
>
> Each other alive about each other
> Alive

"Communication," that capitalized cliché of earnest, idealized "connection," hangs its smile over the whole matter, expanding to absorb any speech. Graham braves it with a glint of romantic rhetoric:

> I want to be able to speak
> And sing and make my soul occur
>
> In front of the best and be respected
> For that and even be understood
> By the ones I like who are dead.

Something is gained here, "telling / Each other alive about each other / Alive," but it is not a climax, not a breakthrough beyond the toils of **"Communication"** into untrammelled utterance. The question merely comes back,

> What is the language using us for?
> What shape of words shall put its arms
> Round us for more than pleasure?

and the next part of the poem moves into a sudden, evanescent recollection or imagining of his original home, Cartsburn Street in Greenock, a place that is frequently recalled in Graham's poems. Here the constitution of memory by language is in question. The appearance of his relative **"Thrown out of the Cartsburn Vaults"** who recognizes the speaker by his voice, is briefly vivid, but somehow Graham cannot renew acquaintance with his family: "Sam I'll not keep you," he says, the colloquial phrase lightly carrying the double meaning of the loss of the world of Cartsburn Street. The question returns once again, and

> From the prevailing weather or words
> Each object hides in a metaphor.

In the last stanzas of this section, out for a walk "On a kind of Vlaminck blue-rutted / Road," the empirical experience cannot be separated from the metaphorical, and the wires above drum language through him as he leans against the telegraph pole. The **"Second Poem"** concludes by repeating its first stanza,

> What is the language using us for?
> It uses us all and in its dark
> Of dark actions selections differ.

Each of the three sections of the difficult **"Third Poem"** begins with the title question. The first evokes a "King of Whales" (a homophonic confusion?), some kind of Malcolm Mooney-like denizen of the "blind ice-cap" between the writer and reader, between us. He must be propitiated, and the speaker tries to find

> Whatever it is is wanted by going
> Out of my habits which is my name
> To ask him how I can do better.

But no such secret is revealed. The second section, in another consideration of metaphor, instances seagoing terms which for sailing men "rigged their inner sailing thoughts" but which out of their context prove inappropriate. There is only one reader aboard, "Only myself, Sir, from Cartsburn Street." Always the problems of language dominate the poem: the **"Communication"** of speaking to others, of conveying ourselves "alive," of constituting experience and memory, and so, running through these, the issue of identity, of self. What the poem calls painfully in question is the autonomy and identity of self, of "myself, Sir, from Cartsburn Street." The question of the title posits language as a determining force, a structure that has accumulated through history a resonance and gravity separate from individual speakers and which now dominates them. The struggle of the poem, and I think of much of Graham's work, is to discover if there is a self independent of language and what their relation is. These are not theoretically discovered problems, nicely delineated and laid out with any supposedly forensic detachment, but are palpably learned and worked over in the practice of the poems. The poem as a "constructed space" (the phrase forms the title of the second poem in this selection), with its explicit, sometimes rebarbative, sometimes conciliatory relation between poet and reader, is the paradigm for all the problems which inhere in language. The quest for identity, for who is speaking to whom, is never comfortably settled. Exasperated, Graham turns on the totalizing ambitions of words in the last section of **"What Is The Language Using Us For?"**

> Have the words ever
> Made anything of you, near a kind
> Of truth you thought you were? Me
> Neither. The words like albatrosses
> Are only a doubtful touch towards
> My going and you lifting your hand
>
> To speak to illustrate an observed
> Catastrophe.

The recurrent question is transposed at the end of the poem,

> What is the weather
> Using us for where we are ready
> With all our language lines aboard?

Weather would seem to be a metaphor for what prevails outside language, what, should we have disposed and stowed language, we must then deal with. The next poem here, **"The Constructed Space"** begins, "Meanwhile surely there must be something to say."

I have spent what might appear to be a disproportionate amount of time on the first poem in this selection because it seems to me to announce so clearly what has become the major preoccupation of W. S. Graham's work. Also it seems important to consider this as it is worked through one poem. This *Selected Poems* draws predominantly upon work from *Malcolm Mooney's Land* (1970) and *Implements In Their Places* (1977) in which so many of the poems relate to the problems that cluster around language: speaking to each other, the formulation of memory and experience, and the reality and fictionality of identity. But the preoccupation is important too in respect of Graham's earlier work. As is usually noticed, Graham's work in the 1940's was marked by the colored eloquence associated with Dylan Thomas. Working from such a style has almost certainly cost his reputation dear in having to make his way against the suspicious modesty of an English poetic whose readiest recognition was for the most obviously representational and what was fancied to be ordinary speech. A few of the earlier poems are included here, the titles of some indicating their manner: **"Listen Put On Morning," "Men Sign The Sea," "Here Next The Chair I Was When Winter Went."** These are poems of pronounced effects, bold and extravagant diction and resonant conspicuous rhythms. This is from **"Men Sign The Sea,"**

> This that the sea
> Moves through moves over sea-tongued the whole
>   waters
> Woven over their breath. So can the floating fires
> Blow down on any.

The echoes of Thomas are evident enough in the alliteration and the close repetition of a forceful verb as in "The force that through the green fuse drives the flower / Drives my green age." This is a powerful poem, not least in the central idea—embodied in the title—of the impositions of our histories and meanings upon the expressionless sea. But it is a style that falls in love with the sweets of language. In this romantic "craft or sullen art," the poet speaks in tongues, with everything validated by the effects of his rhetoric. Here is the good word with his "foxglove day" that Graham was to mimic in **"Approaches To How They Behave."** Graham learned well in these poems how they behave, and they need to be held against his later sense of how problematic language is.

But I don't think this should be seen as a simple transition or "improvement." Rather it might be argued that the manifest artifice and heightened diction of those earlier poems involves a sense and recognition of rhetoric and of how much the gravities of language and metaphorical fictions form how we "express" ourselves and see the world. Graham was never persuaded of the chimera of "common speech" or of the mode of realism with their supposed transparency of meaning. So in the long poem **"The Nightfishing,"** the title poem of the book he published in 1955, the fishing voyage is consciously understood as a metaphor with the experience almost constructing itself into significance.

> In those words through which I move, leaving a cry
> Formed in exact degree and set dead at
> The mingling flood, I am put forward on to
> Live water, clad in oil, burnt by salt
> To life.

But nevertheless through this perpetual constructing—"And its wrought epitaph fathers itself / The sea as metaphor of the sea"—he strives for the romantic moment of significant experience through the nightfishing:

> So I have been called by my name and
> It was not sound. It is me named upon
> The space which I continually move across
> Bearing between my courage and my lack
> The constant I bleed on.

"The Nightfishing" moves continually between description and experience on the one hand, and the conscious awareness and idea about the experience and its embodiment in the poem on the other. Finally, at the center of the experience in the poem's midpoint, Graham relies upon rhetoric, perhaps inevitably, to render his epiphany,

> This instant,
> Bounded by its own grace and all Time's grace,
> Masters me into its measurement so that
> My ghostly constant is articulated.

In the two later books it becomes harder for the poet to name himself against the refractions of language and metaphor by the exercise of rhetoric. The fictions proliferate, Malcolm Mooney's blank whiteness or the painting in the beautiful poem **"The Found Picture"**:

> Observe how the two creatures turn
> Slowly toward each other each
> In the bare buff and yearning in
>
> Their wordless place.

Mister Simpson in **"Ten Shots Of Mister Simpson"** has lived a life evidently touched by the more desperate realities of modern history, yet it is all but impossible to represent him other than in a series of composed pictures. The poem ends:

> Ah Mister Simpson, Ah Reader, Ah
> Myself, our pictures are being taken.
> We stand still. Zennor Hill,
> Language and light begin to go
> To leave us looking at each other.

Whether this "looking at each other" is at last true discovery and recognition we are not sure, for the diction here is not permitted to rise to any apotheosis.

In a world of such possible fictions and "Communication's / Mistakes," Graham has concentrated more and more on personal relationships and has many poems that are directly addressed to particular individuals. There are fine poems to his wife **"I Leave This At Your Ear"** and **"To My Wife At Midnight,"** and poems to dead family and friends. These latter struggle with memory realized in words, and, in speaking to the dead, they figure in a specially poignant way all the difficulties of speaking with meaning. **"Dear Bryan Winter"** closes:

> I know I make a symbol
> Of the foxglove on the wall.
> It is because it knows you.

The finest of these poems to my mind, and one of the strongest in this selection, is the poem to his dead father **"To Alexander Graham."** This is a poem of astounding directness and simplicity. His father appears in a dream wanting to speak "But the dream had no sound." The dream remembers moments and scenes from childhood that convey the sense of a complex relationship in which the ready exchange of feeling and regard through words was difficult or unsuited. In one way this leaves unanswered questions,

> Dad, what am I doing here?
> What is it I am doing here?
> Are you proud of me?

which come out with the bald awkwardness which always made them impossible to utter. Alexander Graham almost turns, as though to speak, but cannot. Father and son it is a noble inarticulateness, knowing and fearful of being glib, but even so leaving the hole of something vital left unsaid. Graham himself speaks in a sentence whose syntax and difficulty show the stress of such an utterance,

> My father,
> I try to be the best
> In you you give me always

and the poem ends with his speaking half to himself, half to us, in a common understatement that implicitly speaks for both of them:

> I think he wanted to speak.
> But the dream had no sound.
> I think I must have loved him.

There is no *solution* to the problems Graham poses. There is no "coming through," no clear permanent triumph of mastery or transcendence of the word. There are successes when the language is in some measure comprehended, and many skirmishings. Part of the thrall of language in this work is certainly the obsessive attention paid to it which might in itself seem to be debilitating. But always these ***Selected Poems*** are sensuous, whether loving or pained at what they touch. They represent a poet's work of some forty years that is inventive and rigorous, which never settles comfortably into what it can do, but remains restless, awkward, uncomfortable, and so rightly discomforting. As Graham writes in the last poem in this volume, **"Implements In Their Places,"**

> The word unblemished by the tongue
> Of History has still to be got.

David Punter (essay date October 1982)

SOURCE: Punter, David. "W. S. Graham: Constructing a White Space." *Malahat Review,* no. 63 (October 1982): 220-44.

[*In the following essay, Punter traces Graham's evolving struggle with language throughout his career.*]

In critical discussion of W. S. Graham, a tradition is already emerging: he is seen as a poet dogged by bad luck. It was bad luck that his early work fell so heavily under the influence of Dylan Thomas; bad luck that his most considerable volume of poems was overshadowed in its year of publication by Philip Larkin; altogether bad luck that he should choose to write in a vein deeply counter to Movement norms. But there is—and here we already touch on Graham's own themes—a limit to the accidental; we cannot best get at the importance of this highly individual body of poetry by claiming to pare off its excesses, by treating the early volumes as mere training, or by—and this is where the conventional approach appears to have ended up—simply regarding Graham as better the less he writes.[1] Critically, he has been turned into a monument to linguistic suffering who, by his silent contortions, provides us with a signal reminder of the fate of the unattached consciousness. I want in this paper to suggest a different approach: for Graham's poetry describes a specific trajectory. Over the course of seven slim volumes, we can see his writing moving, sometimes hesitantly and sometimes with exultation, from the full to the empty sign; from the plenitude of connotation to the bounded spaces of denotation; from white heat over the "white threshold" to the white degree zero. From an inclusive consciousness which "seems to have no circumference, and to merge with whatever he writes about,"[2] Graham moves, and in moving moves *us,* towards the deconstruction of the subject, a measured and ironic dissection of himself and his reader; like the magician in Robert Coover's story, "The Hat Act," he enrols his reader as his professional assistant and then proceeds to dismember him, although unlike the magician he does so not in front of a large paying audience but in the pursuit of more private and, perhaps, vengeful satisfactions.[3] For Graham is not a comforting poet: over the years he has demonstrated in his poetry an increasingly anxious pallor before the unlocked might of language, and there can be little doubt that he means to allay some of this unease by passing it on.

With hindsight, then, we can see the first four volumes—*Cage Without Grievance* (1942), *The Seven Journeys* (1944), *2nd Poems* (1945) and *The White Threshold* (1949)—as an initially rather cheerful encounter with the contents of Pandora's box. Graham here revels in poetry as if in a child's playroom: adjectives and propositions are profuse, words change their syntactic function with deliberate sleight of hand, complex and repetitive forms are whirled before our eyes.

> I worship a skylift of Narnain blaeberry globed
> Priestlike sealed in a tensile sac in a nerve
> In the vein-geared bubble of vision.[4]

Meaning, for the early Graham, is liquid: sweet and dangerous, it is to be contained in poems as in a grapeskin, available to the "tongue like a stamen" which can blindly share the verbal euphoria. Thus although many of the poems in *Cage Without Grievance* are syntactically strange, they are not loose but taut, crammed with too many connections, too many separate relations between words, complex, showy and pointless like the Brussels Atonium. And, clearly, Graham is aware of this: the imagery of poems like **"Over the Apparatus of the Spring is Drawn," "As If in an Instant Parapets of Plants," "There was when Morning Fell"** is unified round a single concern, the relation between natural exuberance and architectonic structure. "Over the apparatus of the Spring is drawn / A constructed festival of pulleys from sky" (*CP* [*Collected Poems 1992-1977*], p. 15): the world of these poems is riotous with foliage, but it is curiously stagey, full of arbours from *Midsummer Night's Dream* in which at any moment part of the scenery might fall away to reveal a world of rather primitive machines. And this sense of the interpenetration of the free-flowing and the prearranged or determined is, in a shadowy way, related also to the poet's own identity, even at this early stage:

> After, when who I was
> Stands rarer and as fair as natural hawk
> My death will need no roof
> To trellis Spring's horizon from my head.
> Laid out with bloodshot pennies on my mind
> My dead discovery in evening corridors
> Shall bring this crossbeamed sycamore of steel
> To brace my crowded heart.[5]

Almost hidden within the contorted syntax, as within an over-lush forest, there lurks a fragile ego, incapable on its own of withstanding the sheer press of the outside, looking toward death, or at least the certainty sanctioned by the approach of death, as a crutch or break-water. There is irony in the insertion of the word "natural": where for Ted Hughes the associations of the hawk with freedom, blood and cycle might be assumed, for Graham the very category of the natural is dubious:

> I, no more real than evil in my roof
> Speak at the bliss I pass I can endure
> Crowding the glen my lintel marks,
> Speak in this room this traffic builds
> About my chair and table for my nature.
> I feel the glass collide with light and day.[6]

Again, some of the difficulty is wilful, and the insistence on subjective relativism callow; what is interesting, however, and again it is a keynote of many of the early poems, is the "collision." For the world of these poems is not static and unified; it is one in which the ego has to try to shoulder itself a space, try to find standing-room in a world already crowded; but to "build," to try to establish coherent identity and personal location, is simultaneously to enter into conflict of kinds that one could not foretell in advance. The poetic implications are obvious: Graham is not a believer in the pure word, language is already unspeakably profuse, the stage is already set for an as yet undreamed-of play. The poet can only try to move the scenery about, as "through all the suburbs children trundle cries";[7] neither the woods of Arden nor the cries of poverty or boredom reveal anything of the underlying reality of the world.

This set of half-completed metaphors about the secret springs of action and control is strongly present in *2nd Poems*: **"Explanation of a Map"** deals in the contrast between surface and deep structure, and **"His Companions Buried Him"** offers us two neatly encapsulated images:

> Always by beams of stars (and they disclose
> India Africa China Asia then that furry queen)
> I see Earth's operator within his glade
> Gloved in the fox of his gigantic hour.
>   . . . . .
> Always by beams of stars (and they disclose
> That furry queen who saunters on night's boards)
> I see Earth swing within its own explorer
> Who dangles each star lighting up his map.

> (*CP*, pp. 32-33)

In the first stanza, the secret knowledge is of the illusory quality of freedom: the dramas of history are staged for us by technicians, pilots, telephone operators, intelligence men crouched in the thickets. It is they who can fairly claim "gigantic" purposes, destinies, not the rest of us for whom the "furry queen" is all we need to know. The last stanza narrows the focus still further: the planet itself is reduced to a plaything, the stars to coloured lights, and we, presumably, to the unnamed dying alluded to in the poem's title.

The lushness offered by the visible world and by language is thus illusory: and in this context it is hardly surprising that Graham should next choose, in *The White Threshold,* to renounce these overpowering illusions in favour of a grittier, harsher attempt to break through to bedrock. Calvin Bedient says of the early volumes that the poet "has backed so far from common discourse that he makes us conscious less of what he sees than of his effort to escape convention,"[8] but the poems *feel* more the products of a writer in a cave; in *The White Threshold,* Graham turns his back determinedly on his absorbing but cloudy trophies from the underworld, and moves out to the mountains and the sea. And this is accompanied by another change: for the explosive fullness of massive instantaneous signification he substitutes the more continuous

pressure of time: short, effusive lyrics are replaced by lengthy, slender ballads and the terrifying choric structure exemplified in **"The White Threshold"** itself:

> Let me all ways from the deep heart
> Drowned under behind my brow so ever
> Stormed with other wandering, speak
> Up famous fathoms well over strongly
> The pacing whitehaired kingdoms of the sea.
>
> I walk towards you and you may not walk away.
>
> Always the welcome-roaring threshold
> So ever bell worth my exile to
> Speaks up to greet me into the hailing
> Seabraes seabent with swimming crowds
> All cast all mighty water dead away.
>
> I rise up loving and you may not move away.

> (*CP*, p. 77)

The ballads, **"The Children of Greenock," "The Children of Lanarkshire," "The Lost Other"** spin out like fishing-lines: in **"The Children of Lanarkshire"** in particular it looks at times as though Graham is deliberately replacing imagistic density with an absent-minded casualness, as though he wishes to postpone climax as a way of avoiding the overriding problem of bringing together the scattered and dislocated ego:

> And under waters of a monstrous language
> Its glow and game writes on the age
> Here loud with beast and flying offices.
> And April rising from the laws
>
> Finds in my nosed and fostering pocket
> Kingcup myrtle lintroot for my foot.
> And a good black thorn for my head.
> And a linty to sing at my deathbed.

> (*CP*, p. 57)

The last two lines are fragments of the past, not writable by the individual poet, and this is surely the point: Graham has now identified that hidden force which surreptitiously makes and remakes the world behind our backs (or when we leave the theatre each night) as language; he has realized that the discourse in terms of which he is trying to write has itself a "monstrous" and material presence which presses heavily upon the poet.

The movement into the open air is not altogether successful: his rhythms, certainly, are liberated by this unclogging of the arteries, but a poem like **"The Search by a Town,"** which promisingly begins "This step sails who an ocean crossed / and mountain climbed," nonetheless becomes redolent of Blake's doomed and circular "Mental Traveller":

For ever as the seeker turns
His worshipping eyes on prophetic patterns
Of shape arising from all men
He changes through, he shall remain

Continually stripped and clothed again.
The morning loses sound and man.
The glow invents the worm. His saint
Invents his food and feeds his want.[9]

The self here moves together and apart in purposeless gyration, solving problems in the external world which have in fact arisen purely through its own structure. The sea proves even more problematic: it allows Graham the minor triumphs of **"Shian Bay"** and **"Gigha,"** but it also prompts the reflections at the end of the third of the **"Three Poems of Drowning"**:

Now in these seas, my task of the foam-holy voyages
Charted in a bead of blood, I work. I answer
Across the dark sea's raging bridges of exchange
Proclaiming my own fought drowning, as loud laid
    under.
All arriving seas drift me, at each heartbreak, home.

(CP, p. 73)

From Pandora's box to Chinese boxes: the complex poise of the ending, whereby we are not certain whether the homeward drift connotes safety or failure of communication, or whether we are intended to see the two as necessarily interwoven, is precisely the poem's problem: whether the very *achievement* of that "complex poise" is not itself a betrayal, a refusal of communicative direction and a consequent submergence in the endless and pointless flow of the sea. Might it be the case, Graham is asking, that the density of language ends by stripping *us,* as subjects, of meaning?

Because *The White Threshold* marks out the beginnings of new formal directions for Graham, what tends to have been underestimated in it is its often successful deployment of the older mode of plenitude, notably in the **"Two Love Poems"** and **"The Bright Midnight,"** in which the resonances from Dylan Thomas remain but are set against a different kind of voice, derived from Hopkins and from the seventeenth century, almost as though, despairing at this time of finding his own voice amid the newly revealed labyrinths of language, Graham at least determined that he would test the Thomas fluidity against a poetry of sinew:

Since there (spun into a sudden place to discover)
We first lay down in the nightly body of the year,
Fast wakened up new midnights from our bed,
Moved off to other sweet opposites, I've bled
My look along your heart, my thorns about your
    head.[10]

The voice is not in itself original, but hearing a dialogue between Donne and Thomas is nonetheless

an adventure of language, another step out of the forest; but it is also, of course, a revelation of further depth within the sign, depth which can be interpreted as resonance or duplicity.

II

What I have been trying to do in the previous section is to take Graham's early works, less as variously successful or unsuccessful isolated attempts than as the complicated and hesitant beginnings of a narrative which can be seen running through his tests. I am therefore less concerned with the quality of individual poems than with the directions of a large poetic enterprise, and with getting our bearings in Graham's world before coming to firm decisions on the identity of the objects within it. In this and the other two sections, I propose to follow this hazy and winding narrative through his three more recent books, *The Nightfishing* (1955), *Malcolm Mooney's Land* (1970) and *Implements in Their Places* (1977).

The structure of *The Nightfishing* is complex, and important because the volume as a whole represents an attempt to bring the overflowing world of experience into relation with meditation on the draining away of the ego: the sea gives, but the sea takes away. The central long poem, **"The Nightfishing"** itself, contains a central section in which we are immersed in immediate experience, but this is framed between sections designed to cast doubt on the sufficiency of the unreflective empiricism which such description entails:

The rigged ship in its walls of glass
Still further forms its perfect seas
Locked in its past transparences.

(CP, p. 105)

When Bedient says that "few poems in the language resonate with so full and immediate a response to life" (Bedient, p. 168), this is certainly true of the central section: but that section is presented less for absorption than for criticism. Graham seems to see it as representing one, wished-for, way of achieving wholeness; yet also as a way impossible or illicit in the real world, achievable only within the framing confines of poetry. Thus the relation between the fully described experience and the half-hearted and half-glimpsed relations to nature which are permitted us in everyday life remains an ironized one, and this is pointed up by the other poems in the volume, which by no means share the easy, complicit tone of the fishing description.

In the first section of **"The Nightfishing,"** the poet is "called" by "the quay night bell," but his response is ambiguous:

I bent to the lamp. I cupped
My hand to the glass chimney.

Yet it was a stranger's breath
From out of my mouth that
Shed the light. I turned out
Into the salt dark
And turned my collar up.

(CP, pp. 91-92)

Ostensibly the narrator makes his way down to the herring-boat; but at the same time the poet embarks on his own descriptive voyage, thus assuring us that the poetic mode he is about to use is in no way to be seen as "natural," but instead as an artificially constructed work which may gain the weight to stand firm against the erosions of memory and the intrinsically fragmentary nature of perception and reflection. And indeed there is a further more troubling level at which we are brought to doubt whether either of these journeys are happening in any realm other than that of dream:

Far out faintly calls
The continual sea.

Now within the dead
Of night and the dead
Of all my life I go.
I'm one ahead of them
Turned in below.

I'm borne, in their eyes,
Through the staring world.

The present opens its arms.

Graham manages to find new uses for ancient imagery: if the sea is dream, how can we find in it any source of purchase? Yet this is the point: for only at sea are we freed from the "arrangements" that take place in unseen glades, only by plunging into flux can we escape the crushing massiveness of linguistic preformation. And so, says Graham, "we'll move off in this changing grace. / The moon keels and the harbour oil / Looks at the sky through seven colours" (*CP*, p. 93). What the last phrase establishes is that the escape which the sea represents is an escape from a particular kind of perceptual separateness: the central description is based, not on the poet looking at the sea, but on a dialectical relationship including an attempt, reminiscent of Hopkins or of Keats' "in-feel,"[11] to see and feel through the sea's blue senses: "Our bow heads home,"

Into the running blackbacks soaring us loud
High up in open arms of the towering sea.
The steep bow heaves, hung on these words, towards
What words your lonely breath blows out to meet it.
It is the skilled keel itself knowing its own
Fathoms it further moves through, with us there
Kept in its common timbers, yet each of us
Unwound upon

By a lonely behaviour of the all common ocean.
I cried headlong from my dead.

(CP, pp. 99-100)

In **The White Threshold,** Graham had approached an impasse: on the one hand he sensed the power of language to resist purposive shaping, while on the other he took on the responsibility for agency which writing entails, thus sharing language's historical guilt. Here we see him trying to shed that guilt, trying to enable the sea to write itself, humbling himself before the power of the word and allowing the waves of description to roll over him, as if hoping that he could by those means exhaust the enemy.

What is produced is change in the poet, and particularly in his sense of place:

So this is the place. This
Is the place fastened still with movement,
Movement as calligraphic and formal as
A music burned on copper.

At this place
The eye reads forward as the memory reads back.
At this last word all words change.
All words change in acknowledgement of the last.

. . . . .

Here is this place no more
Certain though the steep streets
And High Street form again and the sea
Swing shut on hinges and the doors all open wide.

(CP, p. 104)

But whether this change solves any problems remains ambiguous: in one way the poet's immersion has devalued other experience, enabled a metalanguage but at the expense of the sense of home. Immersion in the Other has produced not reconciliation but exile; the haunted stillness of the port enshrines traces of the poet as he was before, progress is subverted into a doomed attempt at recapture.

Home becomes this place,
A bitter night, ill
To labour at dead of.
Within all the dead of
All my life I hear
My name spoken out
On the break of the surf.
I, in Time's grace,
The grace of change, am
Cast into memory.
What a restless grace
To trace stillness on.

(CP, p. 106)

The attempt to use the sea as image and touchstone, to generate energy from its stored metaphoric power, has partly backfired: the sea now has added to its blind power a voice, whereas the fecundity suggested during the actual voyage dries up on the poet's tongue when he returns to land. The sea has caught the poet as the poet has caught herring; as he hauled them up to the surface in nets of words, attempted to impose precision and order, the sea fought back. "Far out faintly calls / The mingling sea" (*CP,* p. 107), mingling in defiance of order and real integration, calling out with the voice of language itself, imprinted with the thousand other voices which impede our direct vision of the world. Under these circumstances, the poet's fragile ego cannot survive: change, after all, is the sea's realm, and the human being cannot bear this much of it:

> So I spoke and died.
> So within the dead
> Of night and the dead
> Of all my life those
> Words died and awoke.

But the death of the ego is simultaneously a kind of non-human liberation, for the poet dies so that the word may have its own life. The thought is an alarming one: Graham seems to imply that language feeds, vampire-like, on death, on what is irrevocably past. Catching the herring was a present act: but no matter how immediate, to write experience remains a distortion, a savagery, and one within which the poet finally consumes his own substance, leaving phantom words hovering over the resultant double absence.

The **"Letters"** and **"Ballads"** meditate variously on this collection of themes, some less pessimistically than others. "I am / Trusted on the language," begins **"Letter II"** (*CP,* p. 110), but this hope turns into an agonized pleading with the bonds of the past:

> Take heed. Reply. Here
> I am driven burning on
> This loneliest element. Break
> Break me out of this night,
> This silence where you are not,
> Nor any within earshot.
> Break break me from this high
> Helmet of idiocy.

(CP, p. 111)

Implicit in many of the poems is an inverted model of communication: when Graham utters words, he loses them, and utterance thus demonstrates not communication but isolation. It is language itself which has power, mostly for destruction, always for obfuscation; far from freeing us to make contact with others, it effectively bounds us, reminding us whenever we choose to collaborate with it that only by its permission can we prepare a meaning.

> Cast in this gold
> Wicklight this night within

> This poem, we two go down
> Roaring between the lines
> To drown. Who hears? Who listens?[12]

The obverse side of the close involvement of the herring fishing scene is withdrawal and violence, reflected in the crudity of **"Baldy Bane"**:

> Through the word and through the word,
>   And all is sad and done,
> Who are you that these words
>   Make this fall upon?
> Fair's fair, upon my word,
>   And that you shall admit,
> Or I will blow your face in glass
>   And then I'll shatter it.
> Lie over to me from the wall or else
>   Get up and clean the grate.[13]

If words cannot be used for communication, perhaps they can at least be effective weapons; but the impotently threatening figure of Baldy Bane, drunk and powerless, undercuts even this possibility and gestures towards the frozen wastes of *Malcolm Mooney's Land.*

III

Malcolm Mooney's Land contains several significant genre successes: the elegy for Peter Lanyon, **"The Thermal Stair"**; the love poem, **"I Leave This at Your Ear"**; even the splendidly kinetic and colourful portrayal of a fruit machine in **"Press Button to Hold Desired Symbol,"** despite the dubious nature of the underlying set of puns (*CP,* pp. 154-57, 167-68). But these are suspended, as in aspic, in a world largely without outward-going vitality, a world which recognizes only immobility as a possible posture of defiance. The co-ordinates for Graham's vision here are, on the one hand, the Antarctic scenery of the title poem and, on the other, the long series of circular or regressive linguistic meditations which run from **"The Beast in the Space,"** through **"The Dark Dialogues,"** to **"Approaches to How They Behave"** and **"Clusters Travelling Out."** Those poems which escape debilitating introspection are the rareties, sparks cast off by the hammer with which Graham seeks to pound a glimmer of truth out of the distortions of the world; yet the paradoxical strength of the introspective poems is that the poet is fully aware of the debility, is able to take the tonal thinness and, largely by use of his twisting, squirming short lines, stretch it beyond expectation. The effect is of a discourse virtually shorn of predictable sources of interest—compelling imagery, character formation, narrative—which nonetheless succeeds in exciting us by its absolute determination to attend to words in a self-reflexive way, no matter what the danger.

And there is danger in **"Malcolm Mooney's Land"**; the landscape reminds us of those frozen wastes through which Frankenstein and his monster presumably still endlessly pursue each other, hoping against hope for an answer to Oedipus' little difficulty. The explorer who is the supposed author of the poem seems deeply uncertain of the line between the human and the monstrous: "Elizabeth / Was in my thoughts all morning and the boy," but later Elizabeth becomes the "furry / Pelted queen" whom we have met before in the glades of illusion (*CP,* pp. 143, 147). Out here in this uncertain land she is joined by a cast of other familiars, the invisible fox who leaves "prints / All round the tent and not a sound," the landlice, "always my good bedfellows," the "old sulphur bear / Sawing his log of sleep / Loud beneath the snow," the "benign creature with the small ear-hole, / Submerger under silence" (*CP,* pp. 143-46). They and the explorer share a world of minimal sound: the purpose of the journey may be to isolate the smallest of all possible sonic units, freeze them, and see whether by these means some sense may be distilled.

> Enough
> Voices are with me here and more
> The further I go. Yesterday
> I heard the telephone ringing deep
> Down in a blue crevasse.
> I did not answer it and could
> Hardly bear to pass.

Or could it be that sound and the illusion of meaning simply expand to fill up available space, that to cheat ourselves of normal human converse, however inadequate, is simply to allow the sounds of night and ice to take over?

> Out at the far-off edge I hear
> Colliding voices, drifted, yes
> To find me through the slowly opening leads.
> Tomorrow I'll try the rafted ice.
> Have I not been trying to use the obstacle
> Of language well? It freezes round us all.

At this point, language itself has become the tenor for a complex set of interlocked metaphors: language is the great obstacle to knowledge of reality, whether of the world or of others, yet it is also the only available site for activity, and as such it turns into a deadly trap, or rather, perhaps, it harbours within its own striations and folds a host of partially seen dangers. These dangers become brutally realized in **"The Beast in the Space,"** which is in some ways a more important key to the volume than **"Malcolm Mooney's Land"** itself, in that it pares down the poem to an attempted description of its own creative process:

> Shut up. Shut up. There's nobody here.
> If you think you hear somebody knocking

> On the other side of the words, pay
> No attention. It will be only
> The great creature that thumps its tail
> On silence on the other side.
>
> (*CP,* p. 147)

The technical manipulators and string-pullers of *2nd Poems* represented an image of language as determined by rigid, para-human rules; the "Great Beast" of *Malcolm Mooney's Land* shows us instead language at the service of the maliciously inarticulate and inexplicable.[14] The "sulphur bear" and the "beast in the space" are reminiscent of the ancient cave-bear in Conan Doyle's story about the Blue John mine, which is a story not about fear but about the absolute frustration its hero feels at being unable to produce any verification for his awful adventure.[15]

> The beast that lives on silence takes
> Its bite out of either side.
> It pads and sniffs between. Now
> It comes and laps my meaning up.
> Call it over. Call it across
> This curious necessary space.
> Get off, you terrible inhabiter
> Of silence. I'll not have it. Get
> Away to whoever it is will have you.
>
> (*CP,* p. 148)

That which lies between the writer and his implicit audience has come alive: stirred up finally by continual prodding, it has woken to guard that mysterious boundary area through which communication has to flow. It can be, temporarily, tamed, but remains unreliable, random; because it is the spirit of language, it is a human creation, but because we have lost our grip on our own construction it is out of our control. Our alienation, not only from words but from most aspects of our lives, emerges symbolically in **"The Lying Dear,"** where a poem which starts off by being about sex falls foul of the beast, and ends up catapulted back into no-man's land:

> Her breath
> Flew out like smoke. Her beauty
> Twisted into another
> Beauty and we went down
> Into the little village
> Of a new language.
>
> (*CP,* p. 149)

Words act as an inverted Aladdin's Lamp, sucking in energy and meaning.

In **"Dear Who I Mean,"** the only solution offered is silence:

> When the word or the word's name
> Flies out before us in winter
> Beware of the cunning god

Slinking across the tense
Fields ready to pretend
To carry in spittled jaws
The crashed message, this letter
Between us. With two fingers
I give one whistle along
The frozen black sticks
To bring him to heel.

(*CP,* p. 151)

The most primeval power of the gods is to name, and
to confer life by naming; in Malcolm Mooney's land,
symbolized by telegraph poles isolated in the waste,
the gods are always ready to take our names away.

the quick brown pouncing god
Magnifies towards us.
He crunches it up like a bird
And does not leave one word.

(*CP,* p. 152)

If in the early poems Graham practised an excessive
expansion of consciousness, dispersed his location and
perspective, here he has come full circle: he is a tiny
black dot in a white landscape, unable to move and all
but robbed of speech. The sparse words come through
gritted teeth; far from being "trusted on the language,"
he appears to have scant hope that any of his words
will still mean by the end of their impossibly difficult
journey through the space occupied by the beast.

In **"The Constructed Space,"** there is a certain
amount of fighting back. If the boundary between
sender and receiver is not rigid and immutable, if it
contains pockets wherein words can be swallowed,
might it not be possible to find our own space
somewhere within that masterless realm? Such a space
is suggested, not very hopefully, "a public place /
Achieved against subjective odds and then / Mainly an
obstacle to what I mean," yet the brilliantly and
intricately worked final stanza does after all allow
some possibility, sanctioned perhaps by love, or
perhaps by sheer shared effort:

I say this silence or, better, construct this space
So that somehow something may move across
The caught habits of language to you and me.
From where we are it is not us we see
And times are hastening yet, disguise is mortal.
The times continually disclose our home.
Here in the present tense disguise is mortal.
The trying times are hastening. Yet here I am
More truly now this abstract act become.

(*CP,* pp. 152-53)

The "caught" habits of language are finely ambiguous:
infected, but also trapped, language itself trapped by
the beast but we as speakers trapped within it. Thus a
complicated paradox: as in earlier poems, the ego

needs first to shape a space for itself, in which
something can be abstracted from the literal meaninglessness of the continuous present—a task which art
has habitually set itself—yet this very space can
become an inescapable enclosure. The phrase "disguise
is mortal" signifies the problem: it is a mysterious
shape emerging from the snowy mist, both ends lost in
ambiguity, simultaneously affirming hope for demysti-
fication and the endlessness of illusion.

"The Constructed Space" remains the highpoint of
hope in *Malcolm Mooney's Land,* the point at which
Graham comes closest to emerging from "white-out in
this tent of a place" (*CP,* p. 145) and building some
kind of more stable shelter against the cold winds.
**"The Dark Dialogues," "Approaches to How They
Behave," "Clusters Travelling Out"** represent a
series of attempts to reach out and touch words, but
they become increasingly tentative: the clusters end up
travelling beyond reach, the attempt to give an account of how words behave remains an anthropologi-
cal ruin. "I always meant to only / Language swings
away / Further before me."[16] What is most painful in
these meditations is the increasing weight of guilt;
Graham becomes almost childishly tearful before the
accumulating evidence of his inadequacy, and that
guilt which he has previously tried to account for in
terms of the pre-empting of language by history now
starts to fall back onto his own shoulders.

Before I know it they are out
Afloat in the head which freezes them.
Then I suppose I take the best
Away and leave the others arranged
Like floating bergs to sink a convoy.[17]

There are other brief moments of strenuous hope, and
more of wry humour, especially in epigrammatic form,
presumably because a brief sally into monster country
scars less badly than a lengthier engagement; but
perhaps the overall tone is best summarized in an
extract from **"Clusters Travelling Out"**:

I am learning to speak here in a way
Which may be useful afterwards.
Slops in hand we shuffle together,
Something to look forward to
Behind the spyhole. Here in our concrete
Soundbox we slide the jargon across
The watching air, a lipless language
Necessarily squashed from the side
To make its point against the rules.
It is our poetry such as it is.
Are you receiving those clusters
I send out travelling? Alas
I have no way of knowing or
If I am overheard here.
Is that (It is.) not what I want?
The slaughterhouse is next door.
Destroy this. They are very strict.

(*CP,* pp. 185-86)

Graham has arrived in the "prison-house of language," poetry is reduced to ephemeral communication in a concrete environment; as the shops are emptied, so language, in the service of Graham's still continuing and appallingly thorough attempt to find the one true, unpolluted, self-referential word which will destroy the beast and magically open the door it guards.[18]

IV

It seems doubtful whether Graham would attribute the difficulty of communication to a historically specific cultural condition, the sparseness of his own words to the draining of meaning effected by, for instance, commercial debasements of language, but of course we remain permitted to investigate such attributions. On the whole, rather surprisingly, critics have not done so; they have preferred to see the changes in Graham's work as indications of a purely private syndrome, and the reviews which greeted *Implements in Their Places* when it appeared suggest a kind of almost morally blame-worthy atrophy. "In what . . . looks like a carefully anxious career, Mr. Graham has slowly ground down his work until it is by now concentrated on a small handful of subjects essential to himself," wrote Douglas Dunn, and "*Implements in Their Places* is very much a book for private meditation, no matter how public the theme of communication might seem to be";[19] but both claims undermine the "careful" dialectic which Graham has built up. The grinding down is performed, not purely by the poet, but in the course of the continuous confrontation between the force of subjectivity and the weight of language; the "private meditation" may itself be a forced mode, may be the only pocket of resistance left for the poet in a time when the telephone lines are down. The very first poem in the collection is called **"What is the Language Using Us for?"**, and is a defiant restatement of the earlier pressing themes, an indication that this volume is going to provide no easy escape from an encounter which is now taking on the dimensions of an epic wrestling match:

> What is the language using us for?
> I don't know. Have the words ever
> Made anything of you, near a kind
> Of truth you thought you were? Me
> Neither. The words like albatrosses
> Are only a doubtful touch towards
> My going and you lifting your hand
>
> To speak to illustrate an observed
> Catastrophe. What is the weather
> Using us for where we are ready
> With all our language lines aboard?
> The beginning wind slaps the canvas.
> Are you ready? Are you ready?

                              (*CP*, pp. 195-96)

The resources of Graham's imagery—the sea, the wind, the wastes—are reinvoked in the service of an introductory poem which introduces only its eventually non-existent self; even beginning is replaced by reflexion on the possibility of beginning, bracketed and abstracted in an extreme phenomenological parenthesis according to which the "thing-in-itself" left for pure apprehension is the pattering of life in language's wainscot, *before* the writer or user himself starts to interfere.

Implements in Their Places is a volume which broadens the site of poetry. Graham's perception of the materiality of language forces him to bring the whole question of the social relation between poet and reader into the arena, and in many of the poems this actually becomes the content. The subject matter of **"Untidy Dreadful Table"** is the poet himself in the act of writing; the subject matter of **"Imagine a Forest,"** a poem written in the second person—singular—is the reader entrapped by the poem's coordinates and by his own prior experience of poetry—"you go in a deep / Ballad on the border of a time / You have seemed to walk in before" (*CP*, p. 196). It is not at all that Graham has found a way through the obstacles; it is more that, having observed the monsters which impede communication, he is now concerned to bring up more lights on the stage, to bring us and himself into greater proximity with the beast. But what happens is therefore a set of preparations: the meanings of the title of the volume are multiple, but one important one shows Graham arranging his tools for a further round in the struggle—whether or not that round will come.

> This morning I am ready if you are
> To speak. The early quick rains
> Of Spring are drenching the window-glass.
> Here in my words looking out
> I see your face speaking flying
> In a cloud wanting to say something.[20]

This is the dominant discourse of the volume, and it is in many ways a unique one. What Graham seems to have done is press through an almost adolescent subjectivism and come out on the other side; in order to squeeze through, he has had to—or perhaps more to the point, has determined to—jettison most of the paradigmatic resonance which poetry enables to flourish, as if that were baggage too heavy for the journey (through the Antarctic) and is left with the thinnest and most sinewy of syntagmatic chains, pared to the bone but as powerfully linked as steel hawser.

On the whole, the concentration on the poet's activity is less satisfying, perhaps because Graham has already tapped the vein, than the new attention to the implied reader. **"Language Ah Now You Have Me"** makes us begin all over again when we no longer feel we need to:

Language ah now you have me. Night-time tongue,
Please speak for me between the social beasts
Which quick assail me. Here I am hiding in
The jungle of mistakes of communication.

                                        (*CP,* p. 200)

But **"Ten Shots of Mister Simpson,"** one of the most important poems in the volume, has power and grace in sinister combination. It seems initially a direct address to the reader:

Ah Mister Simpson shy spectator
This morning in our November,
Don't run away with the idea
you are you spectating me.

On the contrary from this hide
Under my black cloth I see
You through the lens close enough
For comfort.

                                        (*CP,* p. 203)

Graham's attitude has changed: from a worthy, but increasingly self-pitying, fear and guilt before language, he has moved into a posture of greater aggression: here we are directly threatened by the awful complicity of "our" November, "close enough / For comfort." Why, the poem appears to ask, should the poet be the only one terrorized by the beast? Or, to put it another way, why should we as readers not also be made to feel the threat of unnaming and the meaningless? Graham then swings between Mister Simpson and a further reader:

Look at him standing sillily
For our sake and for the sake
Of preservation.

                                        (*CP,* p. 204)

"Preservation" sounds very like a jibe at Larkin's insistence on the possibility of a poetic conservation of real experience: the alternation between Simpson and a further Other ensures our discomfort, demonstrates that even the élitist complicity offered is itself fake, that language's duplicity does not always merely confound the poet, it can also provide the poet with the means to confound us.

The growing irony in the poet's stance moves at times over the boundaries of literary gentility into sarcasm: at the end of **"Enter a Cloud"** Graham, still the stage magician, emerges from behind the curtain to provide a fitting conclusion to his act:

Thank you. And for your applause.
It has been a pleasure. I
Have never enjoyed speaking more.
May I also thank the real ones
Who have made this possible.
First, the cloud itself. And now

Gurnard's Head and Zennor
Head. Also recognize
How I have been helped
By Jean and Madron's Albert
Strick (He is a real man.)
And good words like brambles,
Bower, spiked, fox, anvil, teeling.

                                        (*CP,* p. 212)

At a stroke Graham's abrasive wit scythes through the sterile problems of metaphysics and defines the poem as fiction within self-conscious fiction. Earlier in his career, when asked about his influences, he mentioned only modernist writers, leaving out, to the consternation of some critics, more overt influences like Thomas and Hopkins;[21] whether or not that was a fair account of the poems to that date, his later work has certainly vindicated a similarity of attention to, say, Beckett, and *Implements in Their Places* demonstrates a constant dislocation of form and role which reminds us at several points of Beckett's "prose." In **"Johann Joachim Quantz's Five Lessons,"** a different but related comparison springs to mind: the frozen postures, the stylized speech, the chill intensity of estrangement are the devices of the new German cinema of Fassbinder and Herzog:

Karl, you are late. The traverse flute is not
A study to take lightly. I am cold waiting.
Put one piece of coal in the stove. This lesson
Shall not be prolonged. Right. Stand in your place.
Ready? Blow me a little ladder of sound
From a good stance so that you feel the heavy
Press of the floor coming up through you and
Keeping your pitch and tone in character.[22]

Beckettian fragmentation and neo-Brechtian stylization are not improbable refuges for the harried consciousness.

Strangest among the poems are the three little horror stories, **"The Gobbled Child," "The Lost Miss Conn," "The Murdered Drinker,"** in which minor newspaper pieces are turned into Graham's distinctive five-lined non-rhyming ballad stanzas; but more significant is the long title sequence of seventy-four pieces, fragments or epigrams, beginning "somewhere our belonging particles / Believe in us. If we could only find them" (*CP,* p. 236). Rather than attempt the naturalization which would be involved in marshalling these pieces, Graham has preferred to leave them to stand on their shelves, racked like tools or implements, available for use but not foregrounding their participation in the act of poetry. It is as though we have come to a place where movement has ceased: since such movement might disturb the sulphur bear, release danger and destruction, Graham has become, temporarily, an armourer rather than a fighter: here, he says, are some weapons, but I am not about to dictate their use. And this, of course, confronts us with a choice: whether to believe, with Mister Simpson, that we can take up a passive stance to the problems Graham has outlined, or whether we are fatally embroiled in an active situation. Graham is ironic about our options, and also about our potential: in one poem he leaves us space to write in our own implement, adding after the empty lines:

> Do it with your pen.
> I will return in a moment
> To see what you have done.
> Try. Try. No offence meant.

(CP, p. 246)

It is as though, having tried in poems like **"The Constructed Space"** to persuade us of the possibility of activity by relatively non-directive means, he is now reverting to more old-fashioned pedagogy. His patience with his audience is fast running out, and we feel increasingly doubtful about the intention of his embraces:

> You will observe that not one
> Of those tree-trunks has our initials
> Carved on it or heart or arrow
> We could call ours. My dear, I think
> We have come in to the wrong wood.

(CP, p. 251)

Further reflections are prompted: whose fault, for instance, is the mistake? And what might proceed to happen if this wood is, after all, not the nice safe one which we habitually think of as poetry, but a wood altogether more wild and deep?

In *Malcolm Mooney's Land,* Graham's emptying of the over-determined and overladen sign was almost completed; greater perfection might only have been possible at the level of white noise. *Implements in Their Places,* courageously assuming that at least *that* minimal communication reached its audience, proceeds to supplement it with a question: what are we going to do about the increasingly rapid evaporation of meaning? It is as if the magician has turned into the animal-trainer, in several different senses: he wishes to train us in the use of his implements, but at the same time he wants to show us the limits of our own freedom, the extent to which we rely on the poet, depend on his strength to control language. Graham seems to feel that he has become a victim of psychological transference, that his strenuous negations have somehow made the reader dependent on him, and *Implements in Their Places* is a defining, and a partial shedding, of responsibility. There is no point, the book claims, in moving through the mazy thickets of language unless we become able to do it by ourselves, without a helpful guide at our elbow. Thus the emptying of the sign

turns into an emptying of the poet's role: where the romantic conception of the poet ends in apotheosis, Graham's conception ends in absence and silence. We are, of course, constructing a fiction of endings: no doubt there is more of Graham's poetry to come, and it will modify our impression of the whole corpus. But *Implements in Their Places* is, for all that, a still point, part retreat and part stockade, in itself a constructed space for reflection; and, as an entire volume, a powerful image for the refusals and strengths which are the keynotes of Graham's career.

Notes

1. See, e.g., Michael Schmidt, *A Reader's Guide to Fifty Modern British Poets* (London, 1979), pp. 297-304.

2. Thomas Blackburn, *The Price of an Eye* (London, 1961), p. 131.

3. See Robert Coover, *Pricksongs and Descants* (London, 1971), pp. 194-206.

4. "The Narrator," from Graham, *2nd Poems*; see Graham, *Collected Poems 1942-1977* (London, 1979), p. 38. I refer throughout to this edition, and have chosen not to make detailed reference to any of the work, including that originally published in *The Seven Journeys,* which does not appear in it; although the existence of that other work has from time to time coloured my comments.

5. "There was when Morning Fell," *CP,* p. 20.

6. "I, No More Real than Evil in My Roof," *CP,* p. 24. A relevant comparison would be, of course, with Hughes, "Hawk Roosting," *Lupercal* (London, 1960), p. 26.

7. "I, No More Real than Evil in My Roof," *CP,* p. 24.

8. Calvin Bedient, *Eight Contemporary Poets* (London, 1974), p. 162.

9. *CP,* pp. 51-52; see Blake, "The Mental Traveller," *The Poetry and Prose of William Blake,* ed. D. V. Erdman (Garden City, N.Y., 1965), pp. 475-77.

10. "Two Love Poems," I, *CP,* p. 65.

11. See John Jones, *John Keats's Dream of Truth* (London, 1969), e.g., pp. 225-26.

12. "Letter V," *CP,* pp. 120-21.

13. *CP,* p. 137. The relevant comparison for this mode of mythologization is, surprisingly, with the sadistic Glaswegian pornography of a book like Alexander Trocchi, *Thongs* (London, 1971).

14. The allusion is perhaps not as unlikely as it sounds; one of the messages the "Great Beast" Aleister Crowley tries to convey in *Diary of a Drug Fiend* (London, 1922) and elsewhere is that magic has to do with the mastery and manipulation of linguistic and quasi-linguistic codes.

15. "The Terror of Blue John Gap," *The Conan Doyle Stories* (London, 1929), pp. 506-25.

16. "The Dark Dialogues," *CP*, p. 158.

17. "Approaches to How They Behave," *CP*, pp. 170-71.

18. The specific reference is to Fredric Jameson, *The Prison-House of Language* (Princeton, N.J., 1974); Jameson's brilliant account of the problems of structuralism is deeply relevant to the nature of Graham's enterprise.

19. Douglas Dunn, "For the Love of Lumb: New Poetry," *Encounter*, L, 1 (January 1978), 82.

20. "A Note to the Difficult One," *CP*, p. 199.

21. See *Contemporary Poets of the English Language*, ed. Rosalie Murphy (Chicago and London, 1970), p. 436.

22. "The Third Lesson," *CP*, p. 223. The films which spring to mind most immediately are Fassbinder, *Fear Eats the Soul* (1973) and Herzog, *The Enigma of Caspar Hauser* (1974).

W. S. Graham and John Haffenden (essay date June 1986)

SOURCE: Graham, W. S., and John Haffenden. "'I Would Say I Was a Happy Man': W. S. Graham interviewed by John Haffenden." *Poetry Review* 76, no. 1/2 (June 1986): 67-74.

[*In the following interview, Graham discusses his influences, his creative process, and his thoughts on his own poetry.*]

W. S. Graham died on 12 January. Born in Greenock in 1918, he attended the local High School and then (for one year) the Workers Educational Association College outside Edinburgh, where he met his wife Nessie. After an early career in engineering, he published his first book, *Cage Without Grievance* (1942), through his friend and patron David Archer, who also rented a house for Graham and two painters to live in: although they had no furniture, the threesome shared a mattress on the floor, and cooked themselves leeks and potatoes whose smell infested the street long after every meal. After a dizzily deriva-

tive beginning in the Apocalyptic romanticism of the 1940s, Graham struck his distinctive poetic voice with *The Nightfishing* (1955), followed by *Malcolm Mooney's Land* (1970), and *Implements in Their Places* (1977).

On the occasion of the publication of his *Collected Poems 1942-1977* (Faber, 1979), I went down to Cornwall to interview Graham at his home in Madron. As I remember it, the day goes something like this:

Nessie Graham, fast-spoken, spry and gentle, meets me off the train, and we take a taxi the two miles up the road from Penzance. Prompt to meet us at the door, Sydney Graham hospitality greets the driver and starts to usher him towards the cottage . . . well before he sees me descend from the far side of the car. A splendid misapprehension, it somehow sets the tone of the evening, and before the night is over it stirs my host to compose for me this parody of our first encounter (typos included):

> Questions for Enlightenment & Despair
> AN ENCOUNTER
> John Haffenden & W. S. Graham
> (H for Haffenden G for Graham)

> Reality The taxi at last drives up and I say to
> the taxi-driver how are you You dont
> look like a heffenden.
> H How old are you now?
> G Well, now I suppose I must be gettin
> well nigh but dont let me make a
> fool of this certain form of a
> medium. WOW WOW. We either
> touch or do not touch.
> H Well anyhow what age are you now?
> 60 or is it sixty-one? Why do you
> keep saying I am asking the wrong
> questions?
> G My dear Heffenden.
> H Dont call me stupidly all the time.
> G Forgive me I was just about to
> H Stop that. The batteries are taking in
> Just what they can inside the Keltic
> din.
> G Certain things I have to ask.
> H What then are those, Sir?
> G Only disguised questions to find out
> if you know the least convenience of
> what words come out in our
> respective words. O O forget it eat
> the good chicken I had all lined up
> to dull your pssible brain.

It does not take me long to feel that my brain *has* possibly given up, for I've arrived with a bottle of Scotch. 'I'm already roaring,' Graham announces as we both fall to it. Florid-faced, with spriggy eyebrows and silky grey hair, Graham wears a blue smock over a blue striped shirt. By turns benign, bantering and bullying, he displays an altogether gorgeous and engross-ing manner, like an impassioned clown, and fixes me with twinkling-fierce eyes. He drinks his whisky from a beer glass, mixing it with Coca-Cola to take away the taste, and periodically complains of heartburn. I find myself cast in the role of the serious young soul who needs jollying up; Graham caps himself as the entertainer, feeling perhaps threatened by my tape recorder, and seems to be possessed by a state of emotional ebullition. Throughout the interview he indulges in persiflage and imprecations, snatches of unannounced song, and remarks such as 'You look like Perseus in this light, my dear John!' He pauses heavily before answering each question, and then understandably expostulates that they're not the right questions, we're not speaking the same language. He pantomimes, side-steps, enunciates deeply and clearly, growls at me, and from time to time—in an amiable but convincingly threatening manner—invites me to come outside for him to knock my block off. Im-mensely discontented with questions about his early life and activities, he wants above all to speak about the techniques of poetry. 'Ask me what you like,' he avers nonetheless. 'I will answer anything.' But he still fumes at my lame efforts.

'"Are you really interested in poetry? Do you think it's a good thing? Do you think it should really go on?" Those are the only things to ask,' he tells me. 'Keep off questions like, "Where do you get your inspiration from?" My dear John, I'm really best and more articulate when I'm speaking about technical things, the length of lines or why I persist in using capitals at the beginnings of lines. Those seem real to me. I also think that if you've come to interview me you should like my poetry so much that you should inveigle me occasionally into quoting bits, to hear what we're talking about.'

Elsewhere he had correctly characterised his major themes as 'The difficulty of communication; the dif-ficulty of speaking from a fluid identity; the lessons in physical phenomena; the mystery and adequacy of the aesthetic experience; the elation of being alive in the language'—all of which I am more eager to discuss than line-lengths and capital letters. Although my ques-tions dissatisfy him, he encourages and likes the way I read his verse. 'It helps me to hear my own poems coming from someone else's voice,' he remarks. 'Say me a page-long poem.' I recite one of my favourites, **'I leave this at your ear'**. 'You say it beautifully, my dear', he compliments me. 'I could hear a tear not very far behind your voice. Good boy!' He himself declaims in the grand manner, passionately engaged.

Nessie Graham, who had left us to it for much of the evening, comes back downstairs with the remark 'Coming in newly . . .', to which he responds delight-

edly 'You see what she says—she's influenced by my verse.' Our meal-time becomes a matter of collective bargaining; Nessie and I eventually eat chicken towards midnight, while Sydney overlooks the food and has another little drink. Their home is a spare, cold-water cottage where they have lived by grace of an admirer for 12 years. The single downstairs room leads straight into a kitchen of lean-to style; beyond a small garden lies the loo. A paraffin heater warms us for the evening. They seem to live a simple life, draw-ing small financial rewards from publishing poems and giving readings.

Later still, after supper, I essay more questions; but I am heavily diverted, both oppressed and enchanted, by the combination of the bard and the booze. Soon Syd-ney says, 'Let's switch the bugger off', and then 'You're not a particularly good interviewer, but you bring another bit out of me for strange reasons.' As we retire to our beds (where Nessie has provided me with a wonderful hot waterbottle), I can hear Sydney watch-ing the midnight movie on TV. 'Whisht', comes a loud mutter through the partition wall. 'Good boy'. In the morning he brings me a bowl of hot water, soap and sponge. Presently I find him at the sink downstairs. 'I am washing the front of my face' he says. 'Only the front!'

If I too feel dissatisfied with my questions, I find some feeble consolation in the knowledge that nobody else seems to have managed any better with this subject (see, for example, Penelope Mortimer's affectionate effort 'A Poet's Interview with Himself', *Antaeus* 34, Summer 1979). This transcription salvages the best that can be made of the tape; I reproduce it here not as any significant contribution to the critical literature on Graham (he fairly thought it a 'porridge', and preferred not to see it in print all the while he might have a say), but simply as a fond memorial tribute to a greatly gifted poet—a delightful man who loved and lived the language.

[*Haffenden*]: *What do you prefer to offer in a public reading—recent work, or a spectrum of your whole career?*

[Graham]: It would be a sprinkling, an editing. I'm a very good art-conscious man, and I take great effort to think out the shape of a reading. One is tempted—a terrible thing—to read simple poems which go down well, poems which are not necessarily beautiful but a great gift for someone to read (that's me) with a wee bit of acting feeling in them. It's great floating out your words, and being technically in command. But one wants also to read poems which are difficult in thought and articulation (I mean, the tongue getting round various bits). I don't like the English saying 'wales', when they mean 'whales'! The poet should always be an entertainer, no matter what the poem seems to say.

I will tell you, if there is one way I differ from perhaps most other poets, it is because I write in verse with a distinct rhythm. I mean, we have all read what Eliot says about *vers libre*; it is something I'm not very happy with, although I do like Pound. I need to know where I am, counting out my lines inside myself—as though a metronome were going—to allow myself to make things within the beat, which of course makes rhythmic shapes more easy to do. If you don't get the beat established silently in the centre of the words and within the words' sense, you can't make anything which goes out from the rhythmic beat. Free verse is not free verse at all: it curtails; it is like not using certain instruments in the orchestra.

Do you still have a high regard for the poems you wrote much earlier in life?

One has to watch not to take it as a natural thing that the poems should get better and better through one's career. They change. Of course I'm tempted to say I like my later poems more than earlier ones, but I couldn't add a page to my early books. They have a quality which is no longer in me: one is no longer made of the same stuff, one can't put out the same cloth. I wouldn't like it to be easily accepted that those were boyish balloons and effervescence. No, I get a certain kick out of early poems that I don't get out of later work—speaking about my father, for example. In a *kind* of way maybe I get less worse, but it's not just like that. Certain things occurred in the early poems which couldn't occur now, and make not just a random shape out of ignorance but something else.

You wouldn't at all accept the view that your early work is derivative, and gradually gained in accomplishment?

I'm against that being thought of; it shouldn't be taken for granted.

You have acknowledged that your poetry is influenced by the prose of Joyce and Beckett, and by the verse of Marianne Moore, Pound and Eliot. Would you say something about such influences?

Of course those people have influenced me. Joyce . . . and Marianne Moore, who seems his opposite. Her beautiful self-conscious language: you realise that every word has been thought of and put down there absolutely for its purity. How beautiful!

One writer you didn't mention is Dylan Thomas. Yet your verse of the 1940s was vivid and adjectivally dense in a way that must owe a lot to Thomas.

But of course I might not have started in that way but for Dylan Thomas, who was so exciting at that time, and I think I tried to write like him. But looking back now, in my **Collected Poems,** as far as I can see, they're not as like Thomas as I thought I was being at the time; I can see another thing; I hope I'm not rationalising. But certainly I was conscious that he was one of the people who gave me great pleasure and joy—the great upsurge of his words.

Were you trying to emulate his verbal exuberance?

I would say that. But at the same time, reading Edith Sitwell's translation of Rimbaud was absolutely tremendous for me: I mean, *Les Illuminations*. No matter how good or bad a translator she was, boy it was great! The lovely beginning of *The Deluge*. I found that book filled with something so scintillating and visually colourful, more than I had ever met before in English poetry. It's unusual that a translation should give you a good bang. I found it better than any other translation of Rimbaud, even one which may have had more fidelity—although the best one is by Norman Cameron, a great man. 'Those famed old trundlers of the dead, says he'—translating hexameters into pentameters.

Did you know Dylan Thomas?

Quite well. We were both very greedy . . . though I'm not claiming the same magnitude. I'd met my match. I could be quite happy with him all the time; we stayed many a night in the same house. Dylan would get up in the morning and wash his face with great noise, throwing the water over his face and bubbling. 'We Celts have to make Celtic noises', he'd say. (That's just a small thing). I knew him in America as well.

Why did you specifically name Joyce, Pound and Eliot as influences?

Well, for different reasons. Joyce for his absolutely super awareness of language, not just in puns but every word . . . *Finnegans Wake,* a great shoosh, a lovely thing to me. Eliot, because I had a phase of his lovely, fairly cold ways of speaking and handling words in the *Quartets*. In the earlier work—

> Apeneck Sweeney spreads his knees
> Letting his hands hang down to laugh

. . . he uses this lovely lyrical poem, in a way. Whether or not the *Quartets* have affected me more, those early poems were absolutely devastating in their originality and strangeness. 'The circles of the stormy moon / Slide westward toward the River Plate . . .

She yawns and draws a stocking up . . .' ['Sweeney Among the Nightingales']. 'The Love Song of J. Alfred Prufrock' is also a fantastic thing, a great poem to have written. It has a lovely beginning, not great brass instruments: it enters as though a curtain has been drawn aside and the poem has been going on before and has just let you hear. All poets of any worth are good beginners, have good first lines. Think of Housman, who I think a great man and still underestimated, writing

> Tell me not here, it needs not saying,
>   What tune the enchantress plays
> In aftermaths of soft September

—an absolutely enchanting line! He has a line in another poem, 'There, by the starlit fences', which I even used in a poem of my own, knowing it was by him; it has the whole feeling of the glint of the stars and being out at night.

I think too that de la Mare is quite a good poet; everybody does if they have any sensitivity at all.

Pound is very near me, and I have put some weight of feeling on understanding him, and I know what he represents to me—the 'King of Montage', putting one phrase against another. He followed up Browning and took more from Browning than most other poets. It made a new thing in the medium of verse.

Could you say something about what I'll crudely call your central themes or concerns: the sense of transience, the shifting state of one's identity, your meditations upon Time?

My dear, no poet could *not* write about Time, whether it's Walter de la Mare or Beckett. The awareness of time is part of the awareness of being in the world, of oneself changing. One doesn't know oneself the next morning, to some degree; it's a journey of identity. One is constantly a wee bit astonished by what one finds one has become. That sounds a bit pompous— putting it as 'one'—but it's very true. Call it moods or not, but it's more than moods.

Do you feel a great sense of insecurity?

I don't think so, any more than anybody else. It's the changing self that one is constantly perplexed by . . . when you think you're getting to know yourself, pulling yourself together a wee bit . . . Here's an example, to illustrate the terrible moods that sometimes assail one, and how one's identity seems to flow, sometimes for good and sometimes for bad, away from oneself. I'll give you some lines from a poem called **'The Fifteen Devices'**:

> When who we think we are is suddenly
> Flying apart, splintered into
> Acts we hardly recognize
> As once our kin's curious children,
> I find myself turning my head
> Round to observe and strangely
> Accept expected astonishments
> Of myself manifest and yet
> Bereft somehow as I float
> Out in an old-fashioned slow
> Motion in all directions. I hope
> A value is there lurking somewhere.

Do you find that poems start more from moods than subjects?

Sometimes a first line seems to come up, and one goes on . . . and it brings a question which one tries to answer, and then another question: one is then speaking, and finding out about oneself even, so that one has suddenly become a person saying his bit.

You mean that a form evolves itself through that process of question-and-answer?

Occasionally one thinks of the absolute physical form before an emotion; mind you, not often. Occasionally I set down a metre and suddenly see something to fill that up, and that's a great thing; it doesn't happen very often. At other times, after beginning a poem, you find that the first three lines have a pattern, and you carry out the pattern. In the long storm passage of **'The Nightfishing'**, for example, I decided to use long iambics with short lines to alleviate them. If a poem is going to go on for a long time speaking about the same thing, one has to use one's syntactical wit to make it filled with good things within the actual sense, because one is writing for both an intellect and an ear. One uses everything to make it so that when the reader puts the poem down, at times he doesn't even know why the words have stuck in his head as a great pleasure or entertainment.

Is pleasure the nub of what you like to achieve?

A poem has to be a pleasure. The remembrance of a poem, even it you don't have it word by word, is a lovely thing. All good poems are entertaining.

In one poem you speak of words as being 'an aside from the monstrous'. What do you mean by that?

As one of the many reasons to be living this life—that is, as a poet—one creates a place which happens simultaneously with writing, a place to hide from the monstrous. You don't make a paradise, but you make a place at that time where you can feel more truly *in*. Now that is one of the reasons why one writes poetry. The opposite of that could be: 'I want to describe something exactly' (which maybe Marianne Moore might have said, but I doubt it). You make a world for yourself at the time, not suggesting that you are side-stepping reality. That I really believe in, I've said it in my poetry in various ways.

Some of your poems seem to suggest that words are mercurial, chimerical, or frightening, that they can say certain things and yet jump away . . .

A chimera is something that can change shape into various forms of monster. I would claim that I use the words—at least at my best—in a way that brings out the sense *right* for the first time.

Do you think that words can have a betraying power, as I think Michael Schmidt has suggested?

No, I don't think so. (Maybe I'm better at writing about what I think where words should be, because the few times I've written didactic poetry are very clear, clearer than I am speaking to you now.)

Can you comment on what I think George Barker once said in a review, that you are too concerned with stylistic effects and not thoughtful enough about subjects?

I'd rather be called out for that . . .

You find that acceptable, not a criticism?

I think so, oh yes. If there is something lurking in the middle of a technical manipulation of language, it will not sink, it will be there. That is the great thing. In trying to write poetry, when you feel you have no idea, when you're alone saying to yourself 'What am I doing anyhow?', the thing is to get your typewriter out and put down something, even lists of words; the point being that you must be on the spot when the angel descends to give you a miraculous beginning or something. Now I know that's a wee bit romantic, but if you don't *work* and be near the language, the Muse won't deign to look at you. A bit much!

There is also a sense in which you're speaking across a void to your reader.

Of course it is an attempt to communicate from one aloneness to another; one has to try to steer language, to make something that will come across. Let me read you a bit. This is me speaking about how difficult it is to judge what the poem is going out as . . . it is difficult to judge if one is only using one's own nostalgia . . . or whether it's going to work for other people. It's called **'Approaches to How They Behave'.**

1

What does it matter if the words
I choose, in the order I choose them in,
Go out into a silence I know
Nothing about, there to be let
In and entertained and charmed
Out of their master's orders? And yet
I would like to see where they go
And how without me they behave.

2

Speaking is difficult and one tries
To be exact and yet not to
Exact the prime intention to death.
On the other hand the appearance of things
Must not be made to mean another
Thing. It is a kind of triumph
To see them and to put them down
As what they are. The inadequacy
Of the living, animal language drives
Us all to metaphor and an attempt
To organize the spaces we think
We have made occur between the words.

Does criticism upset you, or can you use it?

Do critics disturb me and put me down? Of course they do; not always, occasionally. If they're too stupid or far-out I don't mind so much, but if criticism strikes me as true, of course it matters. If you feel that nobody has said anything about a particular poem which you thought a real humdinger—and maybe very new, you thought—you've got to watch not to mistrust your own poem.

You have continued to mine your own vein; you must feel a great strength in your gift?

This is not a boast: I don't feel critics have helped or changed me much, although one is human and easily wounded; one wants acclaim and love . . . even to be famous. If you show your poetry to others, that is already under measurement.

Perhaps you could comment on one point, which is that critics have complained about a narrowness in your subject matter?

It's a bit daft, because one's subjects, if you want to lump them all up—like 'Time' or 'Oneself' or 'How Alone One Is'—those are all true things and can't be written to death. I can ring the changes on the best things: there's that poem to Nessie, and I speak about Life and Death (that's too much to put it like that), or about my cat . . . and I've even written a poem about the hairs in the corner of my nose . . .

What I think reviewers perhaps haven't sufficiently commented on is your sense of exultation, of celebrating life . . .

I would say I was a happy man.

. . . as in 'Ten Shots of Mister Simpson'.

Yes, that poem's filled with light, and the Zennor Hill and the great sky.

Why do you think readers have so often failed to remark upon the delight and jokiness in your poems?

I don't understand it myself, because Nessie and I see many of them as very funny. Very few critics have the courage to take a measurement from themselves, keeping away from the prevailing fashion.

Are there certain kinds of poems you haven't felt able to write . . . such as a dramatic monologue?

If I'm blessed with health, I feel technically—I mean, the soul is good, new things are coming up also—I feel I can almost do anything. I purposely don't attempt a play—although I want to be more dramatic . . . but then it comes out in a different way in poems. I'd love to write a play, but there are so many other kinds of poem I want to write; I feel very good about that.

What do you prefer to offer in a public reading—recent work, or a spectrum of your whole career? Can you say something about the writing of 'The Nightfishing', which is a highly crafted and evocative poem?

I was living alone for a while in Mevagissey, in a cottage for five shillings a week, and I worked each day like a fury. I was taking the benzedrine, which seemed to be quite good for me physically, and it meant that I could stay up two days running. It was a great thing to feel myself sparking, it certainly gave me energy to keep going—good energy, not agony. It was a lovely time in my life. The poem just started, and then grew, and because I was so alone and had so much energy I was able to get into the whole thing of fishing for herring. It was all terribly actual: great things came into my mind that I hadn't thought I had observed about the sea and the behaviour of the sea. I lived in that poem, it was great. I haven't read **'The Nightfishing'** for a year or two. Nessie thinks it's the best. I now know what's wrong with it—imagine me saying that! The fishing section is too long and filled with the same stuff. If it was Mozart writing that as music—and I'm not speaking of the sound of the poem—he wouldn't have gone on as long as that. It's not filled with enough invention. I find it very difficult to read aloud, although all the individual lines are great. I like better, at the beginning, 'Very gently struck / The quay night bell', and then it starts off with the sound of the clump of the rubber boots of the men going down at about four in the morning, and me cupping my hands to the glass chimney to puff out the oil lamp. It's all quite real. The third section is too rhetorical.

Why did you devise the figure of Malcolm Mooney?

All kinds of poets have made people that they speak through to give them another dimension in the poem, like Yeats's Red Hanrahan. 'Red Hanrahan Looks at Ireland': great thing.

Which of my poems do you like reading? which gives you pleasure?

'Enter a Cloud' *is one I really enjoy . . .*

It's a nice kind of original poem, don't you think?

. . . and **'Implements in Their Places'** *has a wonderfully crisp epigrammatic quality. 'It is only when the tenant has gone / The shell speaks of the sea'.*

Good boy! (When I say 'Good boy!', that comes from loving my cat who died some time ago. I found the word 'boy' entering my poems, and gradually forgetting where it came from; and I say it to everyone—even Nessie—out of sheer affection.)

Why haven't you undertaken to write criticism?

I never started it, just because I think too much of the whole thing of criticism . . . it would really make a great change of gear in me. Of course I have thought about the place of criticism. If I turned to that, it would gradually diminish another bit of me, I think. I don't want to put 'great power' into that. If I started to write criticism, it would be half philosophy about one person—Hopkins . . . or maybe Eliot (but I doubt it: he's too erudite for me to have covered the things he uses as subjects). I think the theatre of reviewing in the magazines is a terrible low, a pseudo-intellectual soup.

Poets are awful people, filled with jealousy. A painter is somehow more attractive to me; he's more physically involved in his work, which usually produces a more balanced person.

Has music meant a lot to you?

My dear, it's part of my life. Shakespeare has been set very well. I'd like to have my poems set to music, and I'd dearly love to write a song cycle. It's one of the sadnesses of my life that I didn't apply myself to knowing the language of how to set down music.

Do you have a place for religion in your life and work?

I find that my efforts to make an object of art of a particular kind help to sustain me in the world. It doesn't cut me off from the world in the least: on the contrary, it makes me try to see deeper into nature or natural occurrences. That is something else, let us not call it religion.

Can you explain why you're so often drawn to the metaphor of darkness in your poems?

Do you know, my dear John, I don't know . . . except that when I put my mind into thinking about night I find my words coming easier. I find myself wanting to write about night more than day, except that I wrote that lovely poem—Christ, isn't it terrible to find oneself saying that?—of lying on the hill. What is that fantastic ungrammatical beginning?—'Gently disintegrate me / Said nothing at all . . .'. I only mean, *that* is a poem filled with light and sun and glare, where the sun becomes blue by its very intensity at the end. I also like winter better than summer.

What would you like people to value most in your work?

I would just like people to read my book. That's the only measurement. But I also feel that I have made some poems which have gone *through* the usual ways and shapes of thinking. I think I have pushed things in my poems a wee bit forwards . . . well, it doesn't matter about forward, but I think I've made the language make something up a bit more than the fashionable poets of our time. But I have to watch: obviously I would want to claim such a thing, which is the best thing to claim. I could write poems people might want, but I decide to put out the more difficult ones because I am *interested*. I'm trying to break new ground—what a terrible phrase. I tear up many draft poems, as Nessie and I look through them . . . the fire is filled with poems which I haven't let go. I want to say things about feelings that we have inside the very centre which are more difficult to put into verse, a poem which is like no other being written just now.

Edwin Morgan (essay date 1987)

SOURCE: Morgan, Edwin. "The Sea, the Desert, the City: Environment and Language in W. S. Graham, Hamish Henderson, and Tom Leonard." *Yearbook of English Studies* 17 (1987): 31-45.

[*In the following essay, Morgan discusses the place of three specific environments in the poetry of three Scottish poets—in Graham's case, the presence of the sea in many of his better-known poems.*]

I wish to consider three Scottish poets whose work has been strongly marked by a specific environment, each environment being topographically identifiable

and describable, but at the same time being the occasion for great extensions of meaning. W. S. Graham (1918-86) was born and brought up in Greenock, on the Firth of Clyde, but then moved south and lived for the rest of his life on the coast of Cornwall. In both environments he was on the edge of the sea, and the sea dominates his poetry, as both a literal and a metaphorical presence. Hamish Henderson (b. 1919) served as an officer with the Highland Division in North Africa during the Second World War, and his poetry starts out by dealing with the actual conditions of desert warfare but also opens much more widely into thoughts and feelings about 'the desert' as such. Tom Leonard (b. 1944), born and brought up in Glasgow, has committed himself to developing a Glasgow poetry which will not only recreate a range of social experience within that city but will frequently use the language(s) of Glasgow speech; all this within a broader recognition of the meaning and importance of 'the city'.

The three environments, although two are natural and one is man-made, hold tensions and oppositions which make them attractive to poets. The sea is the most alien, the most uninhabitable except briefly (in boats) or under special conditions (on oil-rigs); yet a source and image of both life (fishing; biological evolution) and death (drowning). The desert, dangerous and precarious to live in, a challenge to resourcefulness and survival, baffling in its dune-shifting and mirages, can yet be magnetic to certain temperaments for its colours, its silences, its starry skies, its strange extremes of heat and cold, its buried or half-buried relics of ancient cultures. And the city, which for some may be as dangerous and precarious as the desert, is also a wonderfully varied and vigorous arena for every sort of human relationship and action and voice; alienating to some, and to others as natural as the sea is to fish.

W. S. Graham began publishing his poetry in the early 1940s, when the New Apocalypse movement was in the ascendant and when James Joyce had recently brought out *Finnegans Wake*. Linguistic intoxication made this early poetry almost impenetrable and, although an inchoate poetic force was always felt to be there, it was only with the appearance of *The White Threshold* (London, 1949) and more especially *The Nightfishing* (London, 1955) that his full talent could be recognized. It is significant that a powerful group of poems in *The White Threshold* took up seriously for the first time the subject and theme of the sea which were later to become so much his trademark, as if this particular concentration had effected a release of feelings previously blocked and confused behind thick verbal entanglements. He has done his exercises, he has packed his luggage, and now he is ready to set out into the unknown, to cross the white threshold, to go on a nightfishing. That the idea of such a release was important to him can be seen in his essay 'Notes on a Poetry of Release (*Poetry Scotland*, 3 (July 1946), 56-58), where the sense of unbinding or uncaging is applied to the reader rather than to the poet, except that without the potential of release with which the poet has charged the poem from his own experience, using the flux of always-changing language as a sailor uses the flux of the always-changing ocean, no release would be carried across the gap to the reader:

> The most difficult thing for me to remember is that a poem is made of words and not of the expanding heart, the overflowing soul, or the sensitive observer. A poem is made of words. It is words in a certain order, good or bad by the significance of its addition to life. . . . The poem itself is dumb but has the power to release. . . . A poem is charged to that power of release that even to one man it goes on speaking again and again beyond behind its speaking words, a space of continual messages behind the words.

This 'space of continual messages behind the words' became very characteristic of Graham's poetry. Even when he is most directly evoking memories of his early days on the Clyde and his move from training as engineer to training as poet, as for example in **'Letter II'** from *The Nightfishing* (*Collected Poems* (London, 1979), p. 110), he gives the reader the bonus of grappling with the idea of a continuous shedding of selves, an involuntary sloughing of each dead 'I' as the next living 'I' is resurrected from it, all this summed up in the startling last two lines with his claim that his long-dead Clydeside tenement days are still fecund in a way that cannot be spelled out:

> Younger in the towered
> Tenement of night he heard
> The shipyards with nightshifts
> Of lathes turning their shafts.
> His voice was a humble ear
> Hardly turned to her.
> Then in a welding flash
> He found his poetry arm
> And turned the coat of his trade.
> From where I am I hear
> Clearly his heart beat over
> Clydeside's far hammers
> And the nightshipping firth.
> What's he to me? Only
> Myself I died from into
> These present words that move.
> In that high tenement
> I got a great grave.

Where more than reminiscence is at work, as in the sudden eruption of sea themes in *The White Threshold,* with poems like **'Night's Fall Unlocks the Dirge of the Sea'**, **'At Whose Sheltering Shall the Day Sea'**, **'Three Poems of Drowning'**, **'The Voyages of Alfred Wallis',** and the title-poem, the sea itself, accompanied fairly quickly by its metaphorical possibilities, moves to the centre of the picture to interlock with problems of language, art, and communication. In the very fine **'Night's Fall . . .'** the speaker lies at night listening to the sea breaking on the shore, and although he is 'Dressed warm in a coat of land in a house' he can neither write nor sleep, thinking about the ambiguous image the ocean presents, morally innocent and aesthetically beckoning yet filled with drowned people and sunken treasures, the 'Grief sea with a purse of pearls and debt | Wading the land away with salt in its throat'. In the elegy on the Cornish naive painter Alfred Wallis (1855-1942), whose pictures celebrate seas and ships and coastal towns, the artist is presented through fantastic images, his death a keelhauling to Heaven, the land he leaves behind floating past him like a ship with gulls in the rigging of the roofs, he himself both sailor ('waved into boatfilled arms') and keel ('grounded on God's great bank'). This poem is one of several in which Graham pays tribute to painters who have lived and worked on the Cornish coast (Peter Lanyon, Roger Hilton, Bryan Wynter) and whom he sees as fellow-strugglers with the idea or the reality of the sea, whether they make of it something representational or something entirely abstract.

The title-poem, **'The White Threshold',** is a longer piece, in five sections, strong and striking in parts but less than clear in overall structure; a first run, in a sense, for the more solidly achieved **'The Nightfishing'.** The title does not mean, as George Barker once in friendly banter with Graham translated it, the well-scrubbed doorstep (though it might almost imply that too, Empsonianly) but, of course, the wave-crests and foam, the 'pacing white-haired kingdoms of the sea', that lure the watcher on the shore to enter, to cross the threshold, to cast off, to try that other kingdom, and then (deepening the metaphor) to descend and rise again, to announce the creative abyss to others, to welcome others at the threshold, to bring the messages and memories of the drowned, the dead (the real dead, or one's own dead selves), to show that Melville's harpooned whale is also the human heart, the 'caaing thresher' in its 'splendid blood'. And the speaker, the poet, is like the Ancient Mariner who has a tale to tell you: 'I walk towards you and you may not walk away.' The poem ends with a statement: the poet is at the threshold of his own ambitious and distinctive conception of poetry, the sense of his potential being stirred up as the sea stirs up the sand, the nature of the power being an interaction of present and past not unlike that of Wordsworth:

> This midnight makes, more than the sea its sand,
> My daily dead puff up an ambitious dust

Through native pain endured and through my earliest
Gesture towards the first fires of my past.

(*Collected Poems*, p. 83)

That ambition shows itself most fully and satisfactorily in **'The Nightfishing'**. Here, structure and underpinning are provided by a narrative, the story of a boatload of fishermen (who are present but scarcely mentioned: there is only one observer/speaker) sailing out at night, casting their nets, waiting, hauling the herring catch aboard, and returning to the harbour in the morning through rough seas. The oddly solipsistic effect of the invisibility of the crew has been criticized, and the only defence must be that the realism of the poem is deliberately meant to go so far and no further. There are plenty of clear and straightforward references: 'The cross-tree light, yellowing now', 'the rudder live and gripped in the keel-wash', 'a sailing pillar of gulls', 'we cut the motor quiet', the nets 'sawing the gunwale | With herring scales', the rope 'feeding its brine | Into our hacked hands'. But we are never allowed to forget that, while all this perfectly recognizable fishing activity is going on, the boat is at the same time sailing through dark seas of language for a shimmering catch of poetry (that is, the poem), and even beyond that, for a catch of near-mystic experience that may feed the speaker's poetry in the future. The moment of pause after the nets have been cast is the centre of the poem, and as the men rest back, and the bilges slap in the first faint grey light, and gulls settle on the water, there is a strange abstracted stillness which is described as 'grace arriving'. Echoes of Eliot's 'Marina' accompany the sense of an unexpected, inexplicable moment of happiness and joy:

This grace, this movement bled into this place,
Locks the boat still in the grey of the seized sea.
The illuminations of innocence embrace.
What measures gently

Cross in the air to us to fix us so still
In this still brightness by knowledge of
The quick proportions of our intricacies?
What sudden perfection is this the measurement of?

(*Collected Poems*, p. 97)

These unanswered questions, and the rather forced quality of the writing, make it hard to believe that the poem comes sufficiently sharp and clear at its most crucial point, and only the power of the surrounding narrative permits us to take on trust at least something of the 'still brightness', the 'instant written dead', the 'script of light'. Perhaps, when one thinks of the bilges slapping at the speaker's feet, the abstract language, continuing for several stanzas, has imposed a too conscious abreption from the story for the reader to be other than slightly suspicious of it; and perhaps, in that sense, the poet should have kept closer to the

concrete imagery he uses so well. But, whatever one's momentary reservations, this remains an impressive poem, not easily forgotten.

'The Nightfishing' represents the furthest or deepest point of Graham's exploitation of sea imagery. After publishing the volume of *The Nightfishing* he had no book till fifteen years later, when *Malcolm Mooney's Land* (London, 1970) appeared, and his next volume after that, *Implements in Their Places* (London, 1977), was his last. In these late collections the sea is still present from time to time, but it is no longer the commanding obsession it was in his middle period. The Old Quay in Greenock where he 'smelt the tar and the ropes' is used as a setting in a moving poem about his father, **'To Alexander Graham',** and in the title-poem, **'Malcolm Mooney's Land',** there are allusions to the heroic Arctic voyages of Nansen in his ship *Fram*; the great virtue of Nansen, as Graham records elsewhere and would doubtless apply to the creative artist too, was that 'he knew when to allow himself to be drifted and when to act'.[1] The seventy-four quasi-epigrammatic sections of the title-poem in *Implements in Their Places* have a habit of adverting or reverting to the sea, at times wryly or humorously, at times with what seems like a consciously valedictory note, at times with literary references to other 'sea' associates (Shelley, Crane, Melville, 'Maybe even Eliot'). Two moods come across strongly, and with the same economy. One is grim, though not lacking in a final touch of black humour:

From my bunk I prop myself
To look out through the salted glass
And see the school of black killers.
Grampus homes on the Graham tongue.

(*Collected Poems*, p. 250)

The other is light, playful, self-perceptively resigned:

When I was a buoy it seemed
Craft of rare tonnage
Moored to me. Now
Occasionally a skiff
Is tied to me and tugs
At the end of its tether.

(*Collected Poems*, p. 237)

The death of Graham early in 1986 gives this piece an added pathos, but its well-cut outline remains typical of the engineer who did not go to sea but wrote about it instead.

It could be argued that Graham's devotion to the sea had both positive and negative aspects, in that it instigated most of his best poetry in the post-war years to 1955 but may also have encouraged him into an isolation which cut him off from too many human sources of feeling, his late attempt to recapture these (largely through reminiscence) and also to write more 'communicatively' through clearer meaning or lighter tone, being heroic but fragmented. When we turn to Hamish Henderson a similar question poses itself. Although he has published poems intermittently in magazines over the years, Henderson's only volume of his own poetry is *Elegies for the Dead in Cyrena-ica* (1948; second edition, with some added material, Edinburgh, 1977), and that book sums up his experience of the desert, and of desert warfare, so intensely, in poems written between 1942 and 1947, that it must have been deeply problematic whether the desert, like Graham's sea, could somehow be carried forward to integrate with other and more ordinary facets of experience.

Hamish Henderson has become extremely well known as a collector, writer, and singer of songs, and his work with the School of Scottish Studies in Edinburgh, on ballads and folklore and indeed everything connected with oral tradition, has made him a revered figure in that area of culture where scholarly and popular can meet. There is some disagreement as to the continuities between his *Elegies* and his later songs. The *Elegies* use in general a 'high' literary style, with a recurring suggestion of the classical hexameter as well as hints of Pound and Eliot in line-breaks and in international vocabulary, yet there is also a fair amount of colloquial language, there are snatches of song, and the reader is certainly not being held at arm's length. For all that, the book stands out very distinctively in his work, and has been undervalued for what it is in itself.

The desert, in these poems, is shown as having such a powerful presence that it controls the reactions of soldier and poet to the war being waged. In his original 'Foreword', Henderson relates how the main theme of the sequence was suggested to him when he heard a captured German officer say: 'Africa changes everything. In reality we are allies, and the desert is our common enemy' (p. 59). It is, on the one hand, a perfectly real North African desert, and the book abounds with place-names: Sollum, Halfaya, El Adem, El Eleba, Himcimat, Munassib, Cyrene, Alexandria, Libya, Egypt. But it is also 'the dead land . . . insatiate and necrophilous', 'the brutish desert', 'the limitless | shabby lion-pelt', 'the heretic desert' with its bad trinity of 'sand rock and sky', 'this bleak moon-surface | of dents and ridges, craters and depressions', an 'imbecile wasteland', 'the unsearchable desert's | moron monotony', 'The tawny deadland' under silent 'African constellations', 'the envious desert', 'the ennui | of limestone desert', 'the benighted deadland', 'this barbarous arena', 'the lunar qattaras, the wadis like family trees'. It is a brutal, animal place, a pseudo-

Trinity of material elements. Also, in the desert warfare within that barbarous arena (the Latin derivation is perfect), the shifting sands, the violent winds, and the mirages add a disorientating effect, so that the enemy appears as a *doppelgänger,* a mirror reflection of oneself, as the battle swirls back and forward:

> And these, advancing from the direction of Sollum,
> swaddies in tropical kit, lifted in familiar vehicles
> are they mirage—ourselves out of a mirror?
> No, they too, leaving the plateau of Marmarica
> for the serpentine of the pass, they advancing towards
>   us
> along the coast road, are the others, the brothers
> in death's proletariat, they are our victims and betray-
>   ers
> advancing by the sea-shore to the same assignation.
> We send them our greetings out of the mirror.

> (p. 22)

If the 'other' is the 'brother', it is not only because the killed of both sides must join 'death's proletariat', it is equally a feature of the curious quasi-camaraderie of the desert campaign, where each side would take, use, and have retaken equipment or stores belonging to the other; where the haunting song 'Lili Marlene' was on Axis and Allied lips indiscriminately; and where Rommel was a German general whom his enemies could respect in a half-legendary way. So the desert is both alien and familiar, both savage and reconciling. The humanitarianism of the sequence, which would at first sight surely seem bizarre to anyone who had fought on the Russian front or been sent to a concentration camp, is strongly qualified at certain points. Although one of the best of the elegies, the seventh ('Seven Good Germans'), gives a sympathetic but unsentimental thumbnail sketch of the seven dead Nazis under their crosses at El Eleba, the interlude ('Opening of the Offensive') between the fifth and sixth elegies, which describes the fearsome barrage at Alamein in October 1942, is an outburst of the warlike spirit that could only fail to satisfy the most patriotic by extending its anger into politics in an ambiguous (not really ambiguous!) fashion:

> Meaning that many
> German Fascists will not be going home
> meaning that many
> will die, doomed in their false dream
> We'll mak siccar!
> Against the bashing cudgel
> against the contemptuous triumphs of the big bat-
>   talions
> mak siccar against the monkish adepts
> of total war against the oppressed oppressors
> mak siccar against the leaching lies
> against the worked out systems of sick perversion
> mak siccar
>   against the executioner

against the tyrannous myth and the real terror
mak siccar

(pp. 28-29)

The use of the Scots phrase *mak siccar* (make sure) reminds us that it is a Highland division which is at the centre of the action, but this is also a means of introducing analogies and allusions, as is done elsewhere throughout the book. One desert is in Africa, but tracts of northern and western Scotland are also a desert, where the Clearances have replaced people with sheep, or indeed with nothing at all: 'the treeless machair', 'Burning byres', 'Dark moorland bleeding | for wrong or right'. And what of the Pharaohs of earlier millenniums, did they defeat the desert with their monuments or did the desert defeat them? The very interesting eighth elegy ('Karnak') inclines to the view that the desert 'had its own way at last', almost in collusion with a kind of desert, a death-wish, a 'craved annihilation' in the minds of the Egyptians. The Hyksos, the Greeks, the Arabs, the 'barbarians' of Cavafy, and now 'Rommel before the gates of Alexandria' are all perhaps 'the necessary antithesis', 'the standard-bearers of the superb blasphemy'. If the thesis is the 'stylised timeless effrontery' of the Ancient Egyptian desert culture, and the antithesis is the barbarian at the gate, can the dialectic complete itself?

> Synthesis is implicit
> in Rilke's single column, (die *eine*)
> denying fate, the stone mask of Vollendung.
> (Deaf to tarbushed dragoman
> who deep-throatedly extols it).

(p. 40)

Rilke too visited the Egyptian desert, and its imagery appears in his *Duino Elegies*. But whereas Rilke wanted us to interiorize, and change in terms of art, the great monuments of the past, Henderson is more concerned to ask questions on the historical level, and in the dialectic of history (wars, invasions, oppressions, and minglings of culture) he remains impressed by the extraordinary power of a desert civilization to 'deny fate', not only the fate of destruction and dispersal but even the fate of having its ruins extolled by puny successors. There is a useful discussion of the relation between the elegies of Henderson and Rilke by Richard E. Ziegfeld.[2]

The tenth and last elegy ('The Frontier') makes it clear that Henderson sees how his duty as an elegist must include something more than remembrance: there must be something more active, if the dead are to be appeased, more active even than Wilfred Owen's warnings. The dead will hold us in contempt if we fail to change society, reform government, make freedom and justice efficacious.

Here gutted, or stuck through the throat like Buon-
  conte,
or charred to grey ash, they are caught in one corral.
We fly from their scorn, but they close all the passes:
their sleep's our unrest, we lie bound in their inferno—
this alliance must be vaunted and affirmed, lest they
  condemn us!
Lean seedlings of lament spring like swordsmen
  around us;
the coronach scales white arêtes. Bitter keening
of women goes up by the solitary column.
Denounce and condemn! Either build for the living
love, patience and power to absolve these tormented,
or else choke in the folds of their black-edged
  vendetta!
Run, stumble and fall in our desert of failure,
impaled, unappeased. And inhabit that desert
of canyon and dream—till we carry to the living
blood, fire and red flambeaux of death's proletariat.
Take iron in your arms!

(pp. 44-45)

In passages like that it is not difficult to see a carry-forward into Henderson's later work with ballad and folk-song, his involvement with CND and protest politics, his exegesis of Gramsci. As Raymond J. Ross has written, 'in one sense, Henderson's poetry never leaves the desert. Subsequent work is imbued with that experience as it is with "the clear imperative of action" to (re)build our human house and to defend it when necessary'.[3]

The sequence has an epilogue, a 'Heroic Song for the Runners of Cyrene', which has been rightly praised, through its extreme stoicism and heroic individualism seem at odds with much that had been foregrounded in the tenth elegy. In a final shift of perspective we are taken back to an earlier Cyrenaica, to the territorial rivalry between the Cyreneans and the Carthaginians, and to their agreed method of marking the frontier at the point where two runners sent out from each capital eventually met. The fleetfooted Philaeni brothers from Carthage raced far into previous Cyrenean territory, were held to have cheated by starting too early, and were killed by the Cyreneans. Carthage raised altars to the brothers as national heroes, but Henderson writes from the side of Cyrene, a city which his note to the poem says 'is for me a symbol of civilised humanity, of our "human house"'. The Cyrenean runners, straining to challenge 'the rough bounds of the desert', to 'reclaim the dead land' for their city-stage, run to meet not simply their opponents but 'history the doppelgaenger'. At the moment of meeting, when 'history the other | emerges at last from the heat's trembling mirror', the intersecting figures are locked in a fatal embrace which solves nothing, historically speaking, for the rival cultures. Heroism is not enough, perhaps? The poem, though with a splendid gesture, escapes from saying so:

Each runs to achieve, without pause or evasion
    his instant of nothing

    they look for an opening
grip, grapple, jerk, sway
and fall locking like lovers

down the thunderous cataract of day.

                      (p. 51)

If the desert is more peopled than the sea, the city is more peopled than the desert. The topographical isolation faced by W. S. Graham on the Cornish coast, or the isolating time-warp effect Hamish Henderson had to be prepared for in writing so intently about the North African desert at one moment of its history, would not necessarily be paralleled, though it could be, in the experience of a city-dweller. Certainly James ('B.V.') Thomson, author of *The City of Dreadful Night,* and greatly admired by the third of my poets, Tom Leonard, suffered extreme isolation in London and made his fictional nocturnal city 'dreadful' through its being the haunt of lonely, alienated, or rejected figures. But Leonard, a more robust and directly provocative and entertainingly comic writer than Thomson, is well able to give the required modicum of isolation its head without brooding over its destructive potential, and his poetic world, for all that it may be delivered through a speaker of eccentric inscape ('brackets watch him he has a stoop and funny eyes'), is peopled with a rich range of characters.[4] To put the reality of urban life on the map, and to use a specific, unfictionalized place (Glasgow), were aims of Leonard's that came out of various social and linguistic irritations and challenges as well as out of a broader conviction that the non-urban world, non-urban material, had become less and less interesting. This conviction comes across with vigour in a prose piece called 'Honest', where a troubled writer wonders in Glaswegian why he has difficulty finding the right subject:

> So a thinkty ma cell, jist invent sumdy, write a story about a fisherman or sumhm. But thi longer a think, thi mair a realise a canny be *bothird* writn aboota fisherman. Whut wid a wahnti write about a fisherman fur? N am no gonny go downti thi library, nsay, huvyi enny booksn fishermen, jiss so's a can go nread up about thim, then go n write another wan. Hoo *wahntsti* read a story about fishermen anyway, apart fray people that wid read it, so's they could go n write another wan, or fishermen that read? A suppose right enough, thi trick might be, that yi cin write a story about a fisherman, so long as thi main thing iz, that thi bloke izny a fisherman, but a man that fishes. Or maybe that izny right at all, a widny no. But a do no, that as soon as a lookt up thi map ti see what might be a good name furra fishn village, nthen maybe went a walk ti think up a good name for a fisherman's boat, nthen a sat nworked out what age thi fisherman should be, nhow tall he wuz, nwhat colour his oilskins were, nthen gotim wokn iniz oilskins, doon frae thi village tay iz boat, ad tend ti

> think, whut duzzy wahnti day that fur? Kinni no day sumhm else wayiz time? Aniffa didny think that ti masell, if a jiss letm go, ach well, it's iz job, away out ti sea, ana big storm in chapter two, ahd tend ti think, either, here, sumdyz wrote that before, or, can a no day sumhm else wi ma time? An in fact, if a came across sumdy sitn readn it eftir a did write it, if a hud, ad tend ti thinkty ma cell, huv *they* got nuthn behtr ti day wi their time?

            (*Intimate Voices*, p. 72)

So no village fishermen; but teachers, schoolgirls, linguists, priests, hardmen, footballers, broadcasters, pub philosophers, electronics freaks, psychiatrists, council officials, bus conductors, and all the people living and working, or not working, in a large city that has no shortage of problems but also has a marked character, a marked language and a marked resilience, immediately attractive to the poet who is above all 'honest' and wants to start off from that point, of his native place. And native place it may be, but 'starts off from' is the important thing, as it was with the sea and desert of Graham and Henderson. As Leonard himself has said, 'just because you speak in Glasgow dialect doesn't mean you can't be interested in Bartók'.[5] Or Sibelius, as the title of his collected poems, *Intimate Voices,* indicates, referring to that composer's string quartet *Voces Intimae* (Friendly Voices, but also Inward or Secret Voices).

It is significant that Leonard expresses these claims and interests in terms of voices and sound. He uses English, or Glaswegian, or sound-poetry, as the need changes, but his book is a book of voices, and the city comes alive through what its characters say, not through their physical description or through description of the look and atmosphere of the city itself. The city poetry of Baudelaire or Thomson or Eliot makes a strong appeal to the eye, and that is true whether the presentation is realistic or hallucinatory, but in Leonard it is the ear which is the master, and any loss of a romantic or expressionist glow is compensated for by accuracy of tone, sharp compression of meaning, and thought-provoking juxtapositions of cultural shibboleths, structures, and weapons. The concentration on sound, on language, seems perfectly natural when one thinks that the main difference between country and town is that one is quiet and the other is noisy; but more to the point is Leonard's underlying and reiterated theme of the relations between language and power. In a review of a light-hearted book on Glasgow's speech habits, Albert Mackie's *Talking Glasgow* (Belfast, 1978), Leonard objected strongly to what he saw as its patronizing tone:

> I've no doubt that Albert Mackie means well, and that he does feel affection for 'they' Glasgow people he's talking about. But if you don't treat language seriously, you don't treat people seriously. . . . Nowhere will

real linguistic aggression or anger show alongside the of-course-always-bowdlerised 'humour'; the natives here are not even allowed the luxury of getting restless. There are very serious linguistic political points to be discussed here in relation to speech registers as a barometer of economic and political power in Britain, but it would be a waste of time discussing them in relation to this book.

(*Aquarius,* 12 (1980), p. 124)

It is in cities, and I am thinking of course of the Scottish context, that the full complex web of registers, from thick dialect and patois to the various kinds of standard southern English (either imitated by Scots or heard on radio or television), and including characteristic types of 'Scottish English' which are quite different from 'imitated southern standard' and often have different class and political associations, is to be felt, and Leonard's urban poetry constantly seeks to relate his subjects, whatever they may be (education, football, housing, smoking, crime, philosophy, drinking, sex, religion, unemployment, poetry), to the realities of the language situation. Sometimes the language situation is itself the subject, as in the first of a sequence called 'Unrelated Incidents':

    its thi lang-
    wij a thi
    guhtr thaht hi
    said its thi
    langwij a
    thi guhtr

    awright fur
    funny stuff
    ur
    Stanley Bax-
    ter ur but
    luv n science
    n thaht naw

    thi langwij
    a thi
    intillect hi
    said thi lang-
    wij a thi intill-
    ects Inglish

    then whin thi
    doors slid
    oapn hi raised
    his hat geen
    mi a fare-
    well nod flung
    oot his right

    fit boldly n
    fell eight
    storeys
    doon thi
    empty
    lift-shaft.

(*Intimate Voices,* p. 86)

In that poem the urban environment supplies the eight storeys and the empty lift-shaft, and the suggestion of an incident in a knockabout comedy film would also be urban, but the grotesqueness of the situation, the black humour of the comedy which is making a perfectly serious point, and the irony of the pro-English speaker's Glaswegian voice are all very much a part of Leonard's own approach. Through urban patois, or patter, he edifies as he entertains. Another poem, 'hangup', is a fragment of conversation, possibly in a pub though no background is given, offering at the same time an extreme naturalism totally sensitive to speech habits and the sudden emergence of a philosophy of art; not only is it amusing, and not only is it convincing, but it echoes his own comment on Bartók quoted above: the speaker has in fact heard about minimalism, and does not necessarily reject it, but he sticks to his belief that you 'have to say something':

    aye bit naw

    naw bit
    aye bit

    away
    away yi go
    whut

    mini whut
    minimalism

    aw minimalism
    minimalism aye

    aye right
    aye right inuff
    aye right inuff definitely

    aye bit
    naw bit

    a stull think yi huvty say sumhm

(p. 138)

A desire to 'say something' has been the ruin of not a few poets in the past. With Leonard, however, although some of his poems are epigrammatically slight, even throwaway, there is the saving grave of an awareness of the importance of popular forms (ballad, riddle, joke, proverb, folk-rhyme, tall story, music-hall song) which can often be recycled in ways that are both funny and minatory. In this short untitled poem, the nursery rhyme is not only reslanted very pointedly at the end, but given, through its Glaswegian accent, an additional relevance to the English-Scottish power situation; while in a more general way the linguistic transmogrification of the rhyme recalls what Joyce did with/to Humpty Dumpty in *Finnegans Wake*:

humpty dumpty satna wa
humpty dumpty hudda big faw

aw thi kingz hoarsyz
inaw thi kingz men

came charjn up
n trampld im inty thi grunn

(p. 107)

The 'voces intimae' of Sibelius are in Leonard both truly friendly and ironically 'friendly' (that is, button-holingly aggressive), but they may also be inward-directed, psychologically rather than socio-politically concerned. In 'A Priest Came on at Merkland Street', one of his longer poems in English, the voice is unspoken, an interior monologue from a young man travelling opposite a priest on Glasgow's underground. The poem is printed together with a map of the underground, so that the local urban context is clear. Its subtitle tells us that it is 'A very thoughtful poem, being a canonical penance for sufferers of psychosomatic asthma'. Not everyone has asthma, but the basic situation in the poem is like the very common one (at least in cities with undergrounds) described by T. S. Eliot in 'East Coker':

> Or as, when an underground train, in the tube, stops
>   too long between stations
> And the conversation rises and slowly fades into
>   silence
> And you see behind every face the mental emptiness
>   deepen
> Leaving only the growing terror of nothing to think
>   about.

(III. 18)

The young man's guilty conscience, and feelings of inadequacy and uncertainty struggling with self-assertion and acceptance, are set into action by the 'sad but dignified' face of the priest who sits opposite him; there is no conversation, but the young man's mind is itself a conversation of interior voices, his own at different periods of his life, a priest's, God's, that of Ozymandias, and that of Mahler in his Seventh Symphony. He clings to the positives of art as in Mahler, but is haunted by fears of madness and death in which the confession-box and his coffin are merged, not without an 'I-was-here' urban localization:

> I could write to a psychiatrist
> a cry from the heart
> dear sir
> my name is Ozymandias
> king of Leithland Road
> and then there's the box
> yours sincerely

(p. 30)

Also 'intimate', but at the same time reaching out into the general issues that motivate Leonard, is a pair of poems which start from father-son relationships: one (in Glaswegian) the voice of a working-class father talking about his would-be radical student son; the other (in English) the voice of an educated working-class poetry-writing son talking about his uneducated father. The first poem is 'The Qualification':

> wurk aw yir life
> nuthnty show
> pit oanthi nyuze
> same awl drivl
>
> yoonyin bashn
> wurkir bashn
> lord this
> sir soan soa thaht
>
> shood hearma boay
> sayzwi need guns
> an armd revalooshn
> nuthn else wurks
>
> awright fur him thoa
> uppit thi yooni
> tok aw yi like therr
> thats whit its fur

(p. 50)

The other poem is called 'Fathers and Sons':

> I remember being ashamed of my father
> when he whispered the words out loud
> reading the newspaper.
>
> 'Don't you find
> the use of phonetic urban dialect
> rather constrictive?'
> asks a member of the audience.
>
> The poetry reading is over.
> I will go home to my children.

(p. 140)

The scepticism of the socialist father in the first poem is balanced and perhaps overthrown by the understanding and amends-making of the son in the second. Continuity mixes with change, and with an ambiguous but possible sense of progress, when we see that the son in the second poem is himself a father, and may pass on the authenticities and indignations which have moved him to act and write.

Notes

1. *Poetry Book Society Bulletin,* 64 (Spring 1970).

2. 'The Elegies of Rilke and Henderson: Influence and Variation', *Studies in Scottish Literature,* 16 (1981), 217-34.

3. 'Hamish Henderson: In the Midst of Things', *Chapman,* 3, no. 5 (Winter 1985), 11-18 (p. 18).

4. Tom Leonard, *Intimate Voices: Selected Work 1965-1983* (Newcastle upon Tyne, 1984), p. 33.

5. *Radio Times,* 12-18 February 1977, p. 14.

Ruth Grogan (essay date June 1989)

SOURCE: Grogan, Ruth. "W. S. Graham: A Dialogical Imagination." *English Studies in Canada* 15, no. 2 (June 1989): 196-213.

[*In the following essay, Grogan discusses the philosophical and linguistic aspects of Graham's approach to dialogue and the difficulties of dialogue in his work.*]

I

W. S. Graham's *Collected Poems: 1942-1977* (Faber, 1979) is an extraordinary exploration of human communication and dialogue. Rarely has the poetic experience of dialogue, or the failure of dialogue, been set forth with such a mercurial combination of lightheartedness, tenderness, linguistic inventiveness, and philosophical depth. Yet Graham's readership has always been relatively meagre. Perhaps the present widespread interest in such dialogical thinkers as Buber and Bakhtin and in the subtleties and paradoxes of reader responses will give just the impetus necessary to bring the recognition his work merits.

From the mid-1940s until his death in 1986, Graham lived in the remote western parts of Cornwall. He was nevertheless an internationalist and modernist in his writing. Reviewers of his earlier volumes regularly mention his affinities with Dylan Thomas, whom he knew during the war years in London and whose poetry exerted a strong influence to begin with. But his intellectual connections were much wider. During the forties he knew, and was encouraged and published by, T. S. Eliot. He was also reading and absorbing Rimbaud, Hopkins, Stevens, Pound, Yeats, and Beckett. As well as having a delightful flair himself for drawing, he was interested in modern art. His deep friendships with the distinguished avant-garde painters centred around St. Ives in Cornwall during the forties, fifties, and sixties are reflected in poems dedicated to the painters Alfred Wallis, Bryan Wynter, Roger Hilton, and Peter Lanyon.

Despite a capacity for a huge and disarming conviviality with personal friends, Graham was almost obsessively private in his relation to the world at large. His geographical isolation in a small Cornish village reflects a psychological isolation. He was reluctant to open his cottage door to strangers and skittish about giving out personal information. He gave few interviews, and apart from short "statements" here and there published no memoirs, prose essays, or criticism. It would not be an undue exaggeration to say that he was a master of camouflage and secretiveness. And this is true not only of his personal behaviour but of his poetry as well. Many of his poems are the utterance of an unidentified voice calling out to someone unidentified, unidentifiable, and perhaps non-existent. Graham's readers will eventually want to search out and add to what biographical and intellectual information we have.[1] But at this stage one could argue that the elusive call to an elusive other is precisely the unique feature of his poetry, and that as readers it best behoves us to concentrate on just that.

It was in his remarkable last two volumes, **Malcolm Mooney's Land** of 1970 and **Implements in Their Places** of 1977, that Graham left behind the reflective-symbolic mode of writing (so common in poetry that we take it for granted) and adopted what I will call the "dialogical" mode. More than three-quarters of these last poems explore the relationship between a speaker, "I," and an unanswering listener, "you." The "I" yearns to communicate. It sends out messages, listens for a response, and constructs return messages out of the silence. The "you's" to whom the messages are sent out range from identifiable intimates such as wife and friends, through invented characters, the poet's own secret self, a friend's watch, a cloud, the city of his birth, the language itself, simply unidentifiable addressees, and (most significant as I will show) the reader in various guises. One could experiment in arranging the "you's" on a continuum according to their distance from the speaker; at one end would be the poet's sleeping wife, toward the middle his friend the painter Bryan Wynter, and at the far end an unidentified "Dear Pen / Pal in the distance."

What is crucial to an understanding of the entire range of dialogue is the fact that many of these addressees, whether real, invented, or problematically unidentifiable, are beyond the reach of any message. Or more accurately, there is no way of knowing whether the message ever reaches them. The poems themselves hardly ever present an answering voice. In many cases there cannot conceivably be a reply, for there is no return channel of communication. Malcolm Mooney, marooned in arctic ice, will never receive a reply to the messages he is writing to his wife in his diary. Bryan Wynter cannot reply for he is dead; indeed, the speaker in this poem hardly knows to whom or what he is speaking:

> . . . Or am
> I greedy to make you up
> Again out of memory?
> Are you there at all?
>
>   (255)

The language of these problematic messages is that of ordinary talk with another human being. The tone has an astonishing variety; it can be affectionate, peremptory, sardonic, diffident, badgering, caressing, comic, severe. It reflects the shifting moods of the speaker, and even more remarkably, it reflects the fluctuations of mood and response in the assumed hearer, as though the "I" were constantly aware of, imagining, how his listener must be responding—if only she or he *would* respond. The poems generate an immense pathos that such a compelling and fetching human voice never seems to fetch an answer.

The poems make the reader question the addressee's failure to respond in a way that would not occur in more meditative or lyrical utterances; they also differ strikingly from the classic Browningesque dramatic monologue, a point I shall return to. It becomes evident as we reflect further about them that the distance between speaker and addressee at the one end of the continuum raises the possibility of unseen or unacknowledged distances, even (perhaps especially) when speaker and addressee are apparently within call of each other. When the speaker returning from a late-night walk addresses his sleeping wife, there seems no distance at all; why should one doubt that she will wake up and talk to him in the morning? A rock-climber whom the speaker is watching through binoculars does not answer, but of course it is only that he is temporarily too far away and too occupied with his next foothold to take part in conversation. For other poems, however, towards the opposite end of the continuum, no such reassurance exists. On some occasions the addressee is dead. On other occasions there is a peculiar question as to what dimension the addressee inhabits—real-life or fictive. And then how do we pursue our interpretative inferences when the addressee is the reader? What dimension is the reader in? Once we start wondering why addressees fail to answer, we are compelled to ask, in the case of reader-directed passages, why the reader does not reply. Who is "the reader" anyhow? Is it me? What would constitute a reply? Is the reader answerable? Am *I* answerable? Once started along the path of asking why "you" does not reply to "I," it is hard to stop when "you" seems to be me.[2]

In one of Graham's few statements about poetry, made for a *Poetry Book Society Bulletin,* he said: "I am always very aware that my poem is not a telephone call. The poet only speaks one way. He hears nothing back. His words as he utters them are not conditioned by a real ear replying from the other side" (n. pag.). Oddly enough, however, our reading of the poems *is* conditioned by a real ear, or, to acknowledge the problematics more precisely, by the fluctuational merging and discriminating of a "real ear" (mine) and the fic-

tive ear of various apparent readers. In this essay I want to move toward and concentrate on the addresses to the "reader," because in the end it is these, the trickier ones, that teach us to interpret the poems that seem more straightforwardly addressed either to a real person or to an unambiguously fictional person. It is only by paying attention to the "I-you" situation as it modulates through each poem, and by becoming conscious of our own responses to the fact that the poems address a "you," that we begin to fathom the poems' meanings.

I shall begin with two quotations. The first was originally published in the 1955 volume *The Nightfishing.* In it the speaker pleads for contact with a "you":

> . . . Break
> Break me out of this night,
> This silence where you are not,
> Nor any within earshot.
> Break break me from this high
> Helmet of idiocy.

> (111)

Etymology provides essential clues. The second syllable of Graham's given name, William, is derived from *helma* 'helmet' (Withycombe 293-94), an image which appears frequently in his work, and "helmet" is derived from the Indo-European word *kel* 'conceal.' The root of "idiocy" is the Greek *idios* 'private' or 'peculiar' (*Oxford Dictionary of English Etymology*). Graham's own name thus connotes concealment, privacy, a kind of "idiotic" impermeability or disguise, from which he pleads to be released.

My other launching quotation comes from **"Implements in Their Places,"** a long poem begun in 1970. This passage also addresses an unidentified "you":

> Do not think you have to say
> Anything back. But you do
> Say something back which I
> Hear by the way I speak to you.

> (244)

Now it could be said of any conversation that one hears by the way one speaks; anyone who observes conversations knows that each speaker "hears"—interprets—the other's contributions in terms, at least partly, of what he has himself said or thought he said. But the second sentence in the passage may have even more relevance to the poet's inevitable isolation; "you do reply," it says, "but it is a reply which I must have invented and projected out of my own dialogue-craving voice." Let us suppose further that the "you" is the reader. That works too, for a poet must infer and construct his assumed reader's response from the way he himself speaks. The complexities here are not based on etymology and imagery as in the first passage, but on the reciprocity of "I" and "you," speaker and hearer, poet and reader.

Note that the poet infers the response not from *what* he says (the substance), but from the *way* he says it (the tone). Indeed, it is just that tonal casualness (heard in the second but not the first passage) which lures the reader of Graham's later poetry into the role of participator ("but you do / Say something back") rather than observer.

In seeking useful parallel explorations of the nature of dialogue, one turns inevitably to Martin Buber and Mikhail Bakhtin. Certain aspects of Bakhtin's work seem to speak directly to Graham's poems, but in general Bakhtin is concerned with "heteroglossia," the social and ideological diversity of sublanguages and their dialogical jostling and orchestration in the novel. Buber, on the other hand, conceives of dialogue more as the call of the alone to the alone. In fact, there is an extraordinary parallel between Graham's explorations of the reciprocity of "I" and "you" and Buber's philosophy of I and Thou.

What Buber calls the "sphere of the interhuman," where I and Thou confront each other, seek self-confirmation in each other, and make the world present for each other, coincides with the "I-you" sphere of Graham's poetry. For Buber, as in Graham's later poetry, language is fundamentally *spoken,* for it is the spoken word, not the thought or written word, that reaches out immediately and urgently to the other. Language is dialogical rather than monological in nature:

> A precommunicative stage of language is unthinkable. Man did not exist before having a fellow being, before he lived over against him, toward him, and that means before he had dealings with him. Language never existed before address; it could become monologue only after dialogue broke off or broke down.
>
> (115-16)

Language is dialogical even when the respondent is absent or unanswering. The spoken word

> reaches out toward a hearer, it lays hold of him, it even makes the hearer into a speaker, if perhaps only a soundless one.
>
> (112)

. . . . .

> Even when in a solitude beyond the range of call the hearerless word pressed on his throat, this word was connected with the primal possibility, that of being heard.
>
> (116)

If language is fundamentally dialogical, then so is poetry: "For the poem is spokenness, spokenness to the Thou, wherever this partner might be" (118).

Despite these similarities, Buber's thought elucidates Graham's poetry only as a conception of the ideal elucidates the impaired. Graham has the modernist feeling for the tragic inadequacies of language. In poem after poem he does not so much depict dialogue as deconstruct it, showing the contradictions, impossibilities, ironies, and humour behind the ideal conceived and desired. Graham's poems are "dialogical events" *with one half missing,* which is not to say, however, that they are monologues or soliloquies.

II

In a survey of Graham's dialogical poems, his appeal to his old friend Bryan Wynter stands out as being so direct and casual as to seem almost banal:

> Dear Bryan Wynter
>
> . . . . .
>
> This is only a note
> To say how sorry I am
> You died. You will realize
> What a position it puts
> Me in. . . .
>
> . . . . .
>
> Anyhow how are things?
> Are you still somewhere
> With your long legs
> And twitching smile under
> Your blue hat walking
> Across a place? Or am
> I greedy to make you up
> Again out of memory?
> Are you there at all?
>
> (255)

Notes of the sort that begin "This is only a note to say" belong to a distinct mode of written discourse. They are only a passing incident in a relationship usually conducted face-to-face. The pathos of Graham's poem arises from the disparity between the assumptions normally made about this sort of message and the fact that in this case the addressee is dead. Instead of dignified, elegiac language, here we have all the markers of over-the-fence chat: simple diction; a question that usually serves to fill a momentary silence ("Anyhow how are things?"); a friendly offer to help out ("Do you want anything? / Where shall I send something?"); a request for a small favour ("Bryan, I would be obliged / If you would scout things out / For me") with its wryly candid qualifier ("Although I am not / Just ready to start out"). The speaker imagines his addressee's characteristic responses—his "twitching smile," his worries about wife and children, his probable amusement that his friend back in life is still "trying to be better."

In my larger context what is to be noted here is the "position it puts / Me in":

> Speaking to you and not
> Knowing if you are there
> Is not too difficult.
> My words are used to that.

> (255-56)

Graham's words are used to reaching out in the affectionate language of a close, continuing relationship to someone who is utterly beyond affection, language, or the reception and answering of messages.

While some of Graham's addresses are identifiable as real people, others are more elusive. The "you" of **"A Note to the Difficult One"** is the poet's self:

> This morning I am ready if you are,
> To hear you speaking in your new language.
> I think I am beginning to have nearly
> A way of writing down what it is I think
> You say. You enunciate very clearly
> Terrible words always just beyond me.

> (199)

The ordinary poet who is speaking the poem on the page addresses the more mysterious poet deep within who utters "terrible words always just beyond." In language number one, which we read on the page, the speaker expresses his readiness for the terrible words of language number two. But the last three lines suggest ambiguously that languages number one and two may be identical:

> Here in my words looking out
> I see your face speaking flying
> In a cloud wanting to say something.

> (199)

The syntax permits both "I" and "your face" to be located "here in my words," thus making the poem the utterance of both. Consider further whether the "you" might be the reader, in which case the poetic intention is not simply to express the secret self (a fairly conventional notion) but to express what it is the speaker conceives the *reader* as wanting to say (a more intriguing theory).

If spokenness and dialogue are so central to Graham's poetry, how do we deal with the apparent contradiction that many of these "I-you" relationships are solicited, not in speech, but by way of letters? As a genre the familiar letter raises questions of special relevance to Graham's work. In a discussion of the readers' roles called for by written as distinct from oral communication, Walter J. Ong singles out the familiar letter as apparently exceptional. One might

think that a friendly letter is the most direct and candid kind of written discourse, no more requiring the sender to "construct" a reader or the reader to play roles than does ordinary talk. But Ong maintains that "the writer's audience is always a fiction":

> Although by writing a letter you are somehow pretending the reader is present while you are writing, you cannot address him as you do in oral speech. You must fictionalize him, make him into a special construct. Whoever saluted a friend on the street with "Dear John"? . . . [In a letter] you have no way of adjusting to the friend's real mood as you would be able to adjust in oral conversation. You have to conjecture or confect a mood that he is likely to be in or can assume when the letter comes.

> (19)

If there is role-playing of this sort in a letter, which is writing pretending to be speech, think how complicated must be the role-playing involved in a poem pretending to be a letter.

"Private Poem to Norman Macleod" is a case in point. Why (a naïve reader might enquire) would a poet include a private letter to a real person (the American poet and editor) in his *Collected Poems* when he knows (and hopes) it will be bought by strangers? And the stranger-reader who has bought the *Collected Poems* expecting poems she has a perfect right to read—how does she feel when she finds herself engaged in an unintentional act of intrusion? Reader-oriented criticism has dealt mainly with narrative fiction or descriptive and reflective poetry, the problems of which are somewhat different from those of poems taking the form of direct interpersonal messages. **"Private Poem to Norman Macleod"** plays with these issues in typically quirky fashion. The poem establishes itself as an affectionate message to an old friend across the Atlantic. Part 5 brings out into the open, however, the inconsistencies between the title and the fact that it is to be found on a page of Graham's *Collected Poems*:

> Remember the title. A PRIVATE
> POEM TO NORMAN MACLEOD.
> But this, my boy, is the poem
> You paid me five pounds for.
> The idea of me making
> Those words fly together
> In seemingly a private
> Letter is just me choosing
> An attitude to make a poem.

> (221)

All that spontaneity and authenticity is shown, a bit sardonically, to have been commissioned and paid for, and is further tainted by the distancing demanded by the poetic craft.

The next section makes three moves. First it turns to the readers, as distinct from Macleod, and charges them with eavesdropping:

> Gentle readers, this poem
> Is private with me speaking
> To Norman Macleod, as private
> As any poem is private.
>
> (221)

But in the next breath the reader's role changes from that of intruder to that of owner or collaborator:

> The spaces in the poem are yours.
> They are the place where you
> Can enter as yourself alone
> And think anything in.
>
> (222)

Curiously, the final lines of the poem re-establish the original intimacy:

> Macleod. Macleod, say
> Hello before we both
> Go down the manhole.
>
> (222)

Having published and thus publicized his private message, Graham turns back without apology to Macleod. The end of the poem is not a rational explanation of how this can be, but simply a call—a vocative plus an imperative verb—characteristic of the primal grammar of his poems. The poem shows that though the intimate voice is a device for making a poem, for going public, the intimacy is nevertheless not abandoned. Intimate and public voices are interdependent.

In **"The Secret Name,"** the "I" is irritated by and suspicious of the "you":

> Whatever you've come here to get
> You've come to the wrong place. . . .
>
>   . . . . .
>
> I am against you looking in
> At what you think is me speaking.
>
> (232)

The speaker's prickliness then melts away, first into a regret for an earlier, more innocent time when the poet-reader relationship might have been more direct and intimate:

> If I had met you earlier walking
> With the poetry light better
> We might we could have spoken and said
> Our names to each other. . . .
>
> (232)

then into a sad admission of his own solipsism:

> To tell you the truth I hear almost
> Only the sounds I have made myself.
>
> (232)

The speaker of Part 1 cannot break from his "high helmet of idiocy." Part 2 begins to deconstruct the "I-you" relationship:

> I leave them there for a moment knowing
> I make them act you and me.
> Under the poem's branches two people
> Walk and even the words are shy.
>
> (233)

Thus Part 2 acts as a "frame" for Part 1, converting it suddenly from a message (between Graham and me) to a text (*about* a message between poet and reader). If the reader had been so naïve as to think she was actually being addressed by Graham, the second part draws it to her attention that she had been watching a performance between two invented personages. This has an oddly unsettling effect on the "I-you" relationship. If the "I" and "you" of the framed Part 1 have suddenly been *re*-perceived as actors performing on a stage, the "I" and "you" of the framing Part 2 are now felt, in turn, as personal and untextualized—that is, as Graham and me. But having been framed once and alerted to the trick, the reader almost simultaneously on her own reframes and depersonalizes Part 2.

In Part 3 what Buber calls dialogue is imaged as an eerie wind:

> The terrible, lightest wind in the world
> Blows from word to word, from ear
> To ear, from name to name, from secret
> Name to secret name. You maybe
> Did not know you had another
> Sound and sign signifying you.
>
> (233)

The uncanny atmosphere dissolves the "I" and "you" into mysterious and ghostly characters, not readily reducible to real reader, virtual reader, implied reader, or any of the terms by which reader-response criticism tries to nail down the way a literary work engages readers.

Graham likes to invent fantastic stories. In **"Clusters Travelling Out"** the setting is a high-security prison. The prisoner, wary of the guards and secretive about his own identity, taps out messages to an unknown receiver:

> Clearly I tap to you clearly
> Along the plumbing . . .
>
>   . . . . .

TAPTAP. Are you reading that taptap
I send out to you along
My element? O watch. Here they come
    . . . . .
Clearly they try to frighten me
To almost death. I am presuming
You know who I am. To answer please
Tap tap quickly along the nearest
Metal. When you hear from me
Again I will not know you. Whoever
Speaks to you will not be me.

                             (184-85)

By leaving ellipsis points in the preceding quotation, I
have tried to sort out two readerly responses, the ellipses representing places where the reader is already
required to play a different role—not that of fellow-
prisoner hearing the taps along the plumbing, but
poetry-reader interpreting what looks like allegory.
Here is roughly the same section, this time with gaps
filled in:

Clearly I tap to you clearly
Along the plumbing *of the world*
I do not know enough, not
Knowing where it ends. I tap
And tap to interrupt silence into
Manmade durations making for this
Moment a dialect for our purpose.
              . . . . .
. . . Whoever
Speaks to you will not be me.
I wonder what I will say.

          (184-85; emphasis added)

The two sets of clusters test the reader's inner ear, his
sense of balance, between responding to a prisoner
tapping or a poet typing.

The sender of these messages tries out different media.
In one place he is in the prison's visiting room, in
another he is waving his arms in semaphore, in another
it is a letter ("burn this"). The "you" so variously addressed must accordingly change her imagined
distance from the sender. More disconcerting, she must
at one point change from being a sympathetic fellow-
prisoner or visitor to being the guard or executioner.

There is some temptation to look for allegorical
equivalences: is the prison the world? or art? is the
prisoner the self? is the outsider or fellow-prisoner the
reader? The allegorical move is indeed a necessary
first step, but only the first. The text itself arouses this
critical response and simultaneously frustrates it and
pushes the reader further:

If this place I write from is real then
I must be allegorical. Or maybe
The place and myself are both the one
Side of the allegory and the other

Side is apart and still escaped
Outside. And where do you come in . . .

                         (187)

The planes of logic shift like the planes in an Escher
drawing—from real to allegorical, from poem to prison
("this place"), from poet to prisoner (the "I"). "And
where do you come in"—how, where, and in what
role does the reader contribute? The text prevents us
from finding a stable set of allegorical conversion factors, and concentrates our energies on the paradoxical
and ultimately unresolvable roles of "I" and "you" in
"this place."

What crucially distinguishes Graham's poetry from
the kind of poetry normally called "dramatic" is that
the "you" summoned into the scene shifts from one
dimension to another. In **"Clusters"** the "you" shifts
not only between fellow-prisoner and prison-guard
(both in the fictive dimension) but also between
fellow-prisoner and reader of the poem (in two different dimensions—one fictive, the other real-life). The
result here, as in **"The Secret Name,"** is to make us
radically self-conscious of the problems of reader-
response. At times the text engages *me* when it says
"you," and though I can shake off that engagement
and shift back into the dimension in which I objectively
observe "I" and "you" as actors in a drama, I am
inevitably summoned, seized again by that pronoun
"you." At the end of **"Clusters,"** with the lines "Don't
hurry away, I am waiting for / A message to come in
now," even though I can force myself as a well-taught
critic to read the lines in their fictional framework, it
is almost impossible not to feel really summoned,
made responsible for a return message.

Comparing the roles of "I" and "you" in this poem to
those in a classic dramatic monologue such as
Browning's "My Last Duchess" brings us to the same
point. In "My Last Duchess" the "I" is unambiguously
the duke, the "you" is the messenger. There is nothing
in the text to direct the reader out of the fictive situation, to make us wonder about the relationship between
the duke and the poet or between the messenger and
the reader. Browning's poem is not, as Graham's poem
is, a drama deconstructing the writer-reader symbiosis.

"The Constructed Space" reads like one side of a
dialogue about the difficulty of getting started on and
participating in dialogue:

Meanwhile surely there must be something to say,
Maybe not suitable but at least happy
In a sense here between us two whoever
We are. Anyhow here we are and never
Before have we two faced each other who face
Each other now across this abstract scene
Stretching between us. This is a public place

Achieved against subjective odds and then
Mainly an obstacle to what I mean.

(152)

It is an "abstract scene" in that it displays the dynamics of dialogical language in an abstract, almost contentless way. Beginning *in medias res,* the speaker appears to be in a negotiative impasse and uses what we recognize as a sort of formula for getting unstuck: "Meanwhile surely there must be something to say." "Anyhow here we are" is another semi-ritualized pre-sequence used when a conversation or negotiation has lost impetus. And, as in **"Clusters,"** there are locutions indicating thinking in process, uncertain, concessive, qualifying: "surely," "maybe," "at least," "and then mainly."

As a poem about poetry, it conceives of the poem, not as an object for contemplation (as do other theories of poetry), but as the sphere of the dialogical event. Its "constructed space"—"the space we make"—corresponds to what Buber calls "the between." In any conversation "[the] meaning is to be found neither in one of the two partners nor in both together, but only in their dialogue itself, in this 'between' which they live together" (75). Buber describes "the between" as actualized, fulfilled; Graham—more disillusioned—depicts it only as potential, impaired, awaiting fulfilment.

Graham can also give this "between" a rollicking comic treatment. **"The Beast in the Space"** begins with the speaker in a bad temper, fending off an overture from his partner in dialogue and denying that he ever sent a message:

Shut up. Shut up. There's nobody here.
If you think you hear somebody knocking
On the other side of the words, pay
No attention. . . .

(147)

It turns out, though, that "the between" is inhabited by a great unpredictable and disobedient creature, perhaps to be interpreted as the word or poem:

The beast that lives on silence takes
Its bite out of either side.
It pads and sniffs between us. Now
It comes and laps my meaning up.
Call it over. Call it across
This curious necessary space.
Get off, you terrible inhabiter
Of silence. I'll not have it. Get
Away to whoever it is will have you.

(148)

The third stanza opens with a sigh of relief, "He's gone"; but with peace restored, the speaker acknowledges that nothing really matters except the beast:

Watch. He bites. Listen gently
To any song he snorts or growls
And give him food. He means neither
Well or ill towards you. Above
All, shut up. Give him your love.

(148)

As well as comedy, Graham's dialogical fantasy can encompass the world of dark woods, enchanted knights, and unexplained quests. **"Imagine a Forest,"** one of his finest poems, has affinities with the romantic ballads of his Scottish heritage. However, unlike the usual ballad with its third-person narrative, the protagonists of this poem are "I" and "you." And although there are many declarative sentences as would be expected in a narrative, the governing mood is imperative, the "I" directing the "you" through the stages of a journey.

The journey begins with an apparently paradoxical command: "Imagine a forest / A real forest" (196). The paradox seems at first easy enough to solve. It is surely the injunction made implicitly by any storyteller to any audience. Milton's implicit command is not "imagine an imaginary Hell" but "imagine a real Hell"; Trollope does not ask us to "imagine an *imaginary* Barchester." So on one level at least the initial command does no more than send the reader off on the imaginative and aesthetic quest of any literary work.

A further parallel with Buber suggests, however, that there is more to it. Buber speaks of a capacity he calls "imagining the real." By this he means "that I imagine to myself what another man is at this very moment wishing, feeling, perceiving, thinking, and not as a detached content but in his very reality, that is, as a living process in this man" (70). In Graham's poem the reader is directed through a dark wood to "A glinted knight lying dying / On needles under a high tree" (197). The reader must prepare to listen to the knight speak:

Ease his visor open gently
To reveal whatever white, encased
Face will ask out at you who
It is you are or if you will
Finish him off. His eyes are open.
Imagine he does not speak. Only
His beard moving against the metal
Signs that he would like to speak.

(197)

At this point there is a gap in the narrative. The next lines enjoin us to

Imagine a room
Where you are home

Taking your boots off from the wood
In that deep ballad. . . .

(197)

Disconcerted by the sudden shift of locale, the reader can hardly avoid asking: Did the knight speak? If so, what did he say? Did the reader ("you"? I?) listen properly? Did she "imagine the real" deeply enough? Is it that human kind cannot bear very much of this deeply imagined reality? The speaker insists on the importance of that meeting even though he does not reveal what happened:

Do not imagine I put you there
For nothing. I put you through it
There in that holt of words between
The bearded liveoaks and the beeches
For you to meet a man alone
Slipping out of whatever cause
He thought he lay there dying for.

(197)

It is as if the dying knight has pleaded speechlessly, "Break break me from this high / Helmet," but the reader's response is unknown.

What the reader must infer, so my hypothesis goes, is that in this incomplete narrative told to and about herself she refused the opportunity for dialogue and thereby failed the ordeal. Having failed to relieve a fellow-knight, the reader too will die lonely, speechless, her being unconfirmed in Buber's sense by any succoring stranger-listener:

You are come home but you are about
To not fight hard enough and die
In a no less desolate dark wood
Where a stranger shall never enter.

(197)

Whether the stranger who will never enter the reader's dark wood is a fellow-knight who might have listened or a Virgil-guide who might have spoken her through the wood, the conclusion of the poem is the same as the beginning: "Imagine a forest / A real forest"—the real forest in which the reader will die alone.

The baleful prophecy of the speaker's words may not, however, be the poem's final message, for the literal meaning of the words can be seen as contradicted and superseded by the dialogical situation itself. The Virgil-guide *has* entered the reader's dark wood, has already been present as the speaking "I" from the first word of the poem. Rescue is possible if "you" the reader listens so deeply to "I" the speaker as to imagine the events in the poetic forest into a real dialogue.

III

The grammatical peculiarities of that last sentence are an eruption into the sentence's surface order of deeper disruptions in our reading habits. Graham's poems continuously and in different ways make us ask disconcerting questions about who speaks, who is being addressed, and what sort of response we are responsible for.

Let us put the "normal" case first. As readers we usually respond to a poem as though we were overhearing either a monologue or an exchange between two or more voices, perhaps with the other voice temporarily suppressed. We do not feel personally summoned or immediately responsible for an answer. Our sense of poetry as essentially a "spectator activity" is reinforced by theories of the impersonality of literature and by sheer common sense. What Robert Frost called "the speaking tone of voice" may be psychologically or aesthetically necessary to the poem in that it returns the language of poetry to the language of ordinary human intercourse, but it is not ontologically necessary. Even in dramatic verse or a dramatic monologue, "the speaking tone of voice" is only something that contributes to the illusion, the spectacle. Now let us extend this "normal" sense of reading to Graham's poems, to all those poems which seem to be one half of a dialogue, to all that talkiness which seems bent on luring an answering voice out of the emptiness into which it flings itself. The fact that the poems themselves almost never present a responding voice seems to invite an obvious interpretation; the speaker, so we might construe the situation, is a character in a Beckettian world, isolated, calling toward an unresponding or non-existent companion. We seem still, as readers, to be listening in, overhearing.

We have already seen, however, that this "normal" case cannot be sustained in Graham's poetry. In certain poems, among them **"The Secret Name," "Clusters Travelling Out,"** and **"Imagine a Forest,"** Graham's use of the first- and second-person singular pronouns has that disruptive effect on the grammar of critical discourse which I illustrated and noted earlier. Enclosing the "I" and "you" in quotation marks, as I did in the earlier sentence and as I am doing in this sentence, is only a cosmetic device. The underlying disruption derives from a strategic slippage between the "you" understood as a fictive character in the poetic spectacle and the "you" who can be interpreted only as the real-life reader, me sitting here with Graham's ***Collected Poems*** in my hands. As well-trained readers we resist this slippage and try assiduously to turn "you" into narratee, mock-reader, virtual reader, or ideal reader—anything but me personally. But the personal summons which the use of the word "you" exerts is like a magnet which I can resist only intermittently. As soon as I lose concentration on interpreting "you" as a fictive "dialoguee," I find myself drifting back into what feels like a personal relationship.

The absence of a speaking part for the dialoguee is strategically crucial in producing this slippage. If Graham were to give the "you" a turn in the conversation, one of two things would happen: either the poem would become a sort of Yeatsian dialogue of self and soul which the reader would promptly interpret as a mock-dialogue between two aspects of the poet's mind, or the poem would become a mini-drama between two characters observed on an imagined stage. In neither of these cases would the reader be pushed into identifying the "I" with Graham or the "you" with me-the-reader. In other words, the objectivity of the text, its status as spectacle, would not be violated.

But in Graham's poetry the objectivity of the text does appear to be violated. The "speaking tone of voice," the absence of a fictive dialoguee, and the devices of pronominal slippage all collaborate to persuade the reader, at least intermittently, that she is personally and directly addressed by the text. The reader oscillates between two theories of poetry, two modes of experiencing herself as a reader. One moment she is overhearing a monologue; the next moment she is listening to a personal communication—one half of an entity which requires the other half, her own answer, to achieve its dialogical wholeness. Modernist and postmodernist poetry has been endlessly sceptical of its own procedures, its own ontological status as a work of art. Graham has extended this enquiry. In his poetry it is the status of the reader which is unstabilized. As a body of work, his poetry is more persistently, wittily, movingly dialogical than that of any other modern poet in English. Its value lies in reminding us—compelling us to feel and experience—that a poem may be, not an object for contemplation, but a summons from an I to a you.

Notes

1. It is not my purpose in this article to produce a bibliography of work by and on Graham. Graham's volumes of poetry were reviewed as they appeared, but there are very few sustained critical articles. Of these, two deserve special attention: Calvin Bedient, "W. S. Graham," in his *Eight Contemporary Poets* (London: Oxford UP, 1974) 159-80; and Damian Grant, "Walls of Glass: The Poetry of W. S. Graham," in *British Poetry Since 1970: A Critical Survey,* eds. Peter Jones and Michael Schmidt (Manchester: Carcanet, 1980) 22-38. A good but not widely available source of information is the Autumn 1986 issue of the *Edinburgh Review* (75 [1986]: 6-109). This presents, under the general heading "The Life and Work of W. S. Graham," a very interesting collection of letters, notebook pages, and other items by Graham himself and of memoirs and articles by

people who knew him. The material also provides a supportive context for my interpretation, showing Graham's preoccupation with language, tone of voice (what Graham termed "timbre"), and the vicissitudes of interpersonal communication.

2. Another pronominal dilemma arises in this article, besides the one just encountered in the use of "I" and "you." What should we assume is the gender of the unidentified addressee in Graham's poems, especially when the addressee merges with "the reader" in the abstract or "the reader" as me? Furthermore, though Graham is certainly masculine, does it necessarily follow that the more impersonal "speaker" or "I" of the poem is also masculine? I have arbitrarily decided—with two gender pronouns at my disposal and two "roles" being played out in my article—to assign one to each: the speaker will be "he" and the reader will be "she."

Works Cited

Buber, Martin. *The Knowledge of Man: A Philosophy of the Interhuman.* Ed. Maurice Friedman. Trans. Maurice Friedman and Ronald Gregor Smith. New York: Harper and Row, 1965.

Graham, W. S. *Collected Poems: 1942-1977.* London: Faber and Faber, 1979.

———. Statement in *Poetry Book Society Bulletin* 64 (Spring 1970): n. pag.

Ong, Walter J., s.j. "The Writer's Audience Is Always a Fiction." *PMLA* 90 (1975): 9-21.

Oxford Dictionary of English Etymology. Ed. C. T. Onions. London: Oxford UP, 1966.

Withycombe, E. G. *The Oxford Dictionary of English Christian Names.* 3rd ed. Oxford: Clarendon Press, 1977.

Mark Andrew Silverberg (essay date June 1998)

SOURCE: Silverberg, Mark Andrew. "A Readership of None: The Later Poetry of W. S. Graham." *English Studies in Canada* 24, no. 2 (June 1998): 139-55.

[*In the following essay, Silverberg analyzes the theme— pervasive in Graham's later work—of the difficult relationship between the poet as speaker and his readers.*]

I. Maimed for the Job?

The man I pretend
To think I am walked
Listening in the dark
Talking to who he liked.

I hope I do not write
Only for those few
Others like myself
Poets maimed for the job.

("From Dark Dialogues," *Aimed At Nobody* 43)

The biographical details of W. S. Graham's life have frequently led readers to cast the poet in a role in which he often casts himself (the man he pretends to think he is)—the role of tragically neglected artist. David Punter's article on Graham begins by commenting on what Punter sees as an "emerging tradition" in Graham criticism:

[Graham] is seen as a poet dogged by bad luck. It was bad luck that his early work fell so heavily under the influence of Dylan Thomas; bad luck that his most considerable volume of poems was overshadowed in its year of publication by Philip Larkin; altogether bad luck that he should choose to write in a vein deeply counter to Movement norms.

(220)[1]

Ruth Grogan's "W. S. Graham: A Dialogical Imagination" begins in the same vein. Grogan laments Graham's "meagre readership" and suggests that, in part, his limited audience was owing to his "almost obsessively private [nature] in his relation to the world at large" (196). The biographical facts presented in Tony Lopez's study of Graham contribute further to the Romantic picture of the tragically neglected artist. Graham lived most of his life in poverty. Although trained as a journeyman engineer, he made writing poems his only livelihood. Graham thus lived on his wife's meagre salary and the generosity of friends and collectors such as Robin Skelton, who sent him a monthly allowance of £25 in exchange for Graham's completed notebooks and manuscripts (Lopez 6). Lopez further notes Graham's discomfort with anyone outside of his small, close circle of friends (7). Adding to this picture of Romantic isolation is Sylvia Skelton's account of the Graham household:

They were living in one of a terrace of abandoned Coastguard cottages which had a leaking roof, no cooking stove, no electricity, an outside toilet and no bathroom. I remember visiting them and taking food with me—but there was nothing to cook it on. On my next visit I took them a primus stove—before this they were cooking on an open fire, when there was fuel. They used an oil lamp for light and a paraffin stove for heat.

(Lopez 5-6)

There is ample evidence, then, to support the picture of Graham as a poet "maimed for the job"—whether by personal choice, external circumstance, or a combination of both. Aside from the tantalizing glamour of these facts, Graham's biography also provides an important starting point for the argument of this essay. From these details, one can begin to draw a picture not only of Graham-the-man but, more importantly, of Graham-the-persona, a constant and stable voice that speaks through the vast majority of his later poems. These poems, from *Malcolm Mooney's Land* (1970) and *Implements in Their Places* (1977), make neglect their starting point. The poems are utterances of a voice cut off from others yet desperate to communicate. In various ways Graham's verse questions the idea of an audience and the possibility of being heard at all. His poems take failed communication to its critical extreme and succeed, paradoxically, precisely to the extent that they are *not* heard. How the Graham-persona deconstructs his audience or, more accurately, constructs a readership of none will be discussed below. This feat is central to the success of Graham's most important poems.[2]

II. A READERSHIP OF MANY AND A READERSHIP OF NONE

Poet and theorist Ron Silliman has made an interesting observation on the possible effect of readership upon a poet's work. Silliman reflects on how Judy Grahn's poetry was jeopardized by her growing readership:

Once she had achieved star status, [Grahn] . . . had great difficulty negotiating a more public voice and her later works have, I think, suffered for it. . . . So I'm a skeptic as to the value of larger audiences. . . . Anyone who speaks (or tries to speak) to audiences of 500+ people at one time will quickly learn how reductive one has to make his/her speech just to be broadly understood. Imagine a Ginsberg or Bly or Rich, who must take that size audience as a given. It's sort of a curse.

(Letter to the author)

Silliman's recognition that a perceived audience can have a great impact on a poet's work seems to me an important one—though I do not agree that a large audience is necessarily a curse. In the case of Adrienne Rich, as I will show, the perception of a relatively large audience is fundamental to the success of her work. With Allen Ginsberg or Robert Bly, their large audience may be read as either blessing or curse. As these poets became closely identified with their audiences, they experienced both a popular elevation and a critical decline. As cultural icons—figureheads for hippies and yuppies—Ginsberg and Bly reveal a cardinal rule of the artistic marketplace: that commercial capital accrues in inverse proportion to cultural capital. The more money these poets made, the less seriously they were taken and hence the more closely they identified (and were identified with) their popular audience.

These questions of audience are also related to Graham, whose later poetry is crucially concerned with readership—particularly with questions of the relationship between speaker and receiver, poet and reader. In fact, to understand Graham's work it is useful to contrast poets such as Bly, Ginsberg, and Rich (who have a relatively large readership) with Graham, who not only has a much smaller readership but who also pretends, in the most extreme way, to have no audience at all. Graham's poetic persona is that of the poet doomed to incomplete communication—the poet who is terminally unsure of being heard. His writing, as the title of his uncollected poems suggests, is **"Aimed at Nobody."** This title comes from a notebook entry of 1973 entitled **"Poem"**:

> It does not matter who you are,
> It does not matter who I am.
>
> This book has not been purposely
> made for any reason.
>
> It has made itself by circumstances.
> It is aimed at nobody at all.
>
> It is now left just as an object by me
> to be encountered by somebody else.

(*Aimed* xi)

Ironically, the "nobody" of line six is also the "somebody" of line eight. In fact, the significance or meaning of the "nobody" can only be realized by "somebody" reading the text. The poem is not complete until it is "encountered by somebody else." Although the poem claims to be unconcerned with "who you are" ("you" appears frequently in Graham's poems), his speaker is well aware that the "you" is just as responsible for making the poem as the "I". A great number of his poems are approaches to finding, understanding, and speaking to this undefined (and perhaps indefinable) nobody/somebody. Graham's poems thus take as their audience a paradoxical readership of none.

In *Self and Sensibility in Contemporary Poetry* Charles Altieri suggests that the most important contemporary poetry is being written by "poets who make the conditions of speaking their central thematic concern" (18). He cites as one of his two "strongest" poets Adrienne Rich, who has both a relatively large readership and a great deal of critical currency. One of the most important "conditions of speaking" surely has to do with *who* is being spoken to. In the case of Rich, this question is a pertinent one to ask. Rich writes as if she knows to whom she is speaking. Both her prose and poetry have a clear sense of audience, a community of readers, and this sense is crucial to how her poetry works. A great part of her work attempts to recover the lost voices and experiences of her assumed readers, or her readers' shared community (whether defined by gender, nationality, or, more recently, religion—as in the poems of Jewish experience in *An Atlas of the Difficult World*). Rich's writing conveys a constant awareness of the responsibility of speaking. "The relative amount of visibility that I have," Rich says in a recent interview, "that gives you a certain kind of power, and it's really important to keep thinking about how to use that power" (Rothschild 34). Much of her poetry's power comes from the assertive belief in a readership, the presumption to speak to and for a large group of people. The last section, entitled "Dedications," of her recent long poem "An Atlas of the Difficult World" works with the full recognition of a definite readership. The poem is constructed as a series of statements that confidently "find" her readers with the refrain: "I know you are reading this poem" (25). Rich's poem is made meaningful by her ability to locate her audience—to define her readers, both for herself and for them. Reinforcing her recognition of, and her sense of responsibility to, her audience, Rich says in this interview: "To a certain extent in *Atlas* I was trying to talk about the location, the privileges, the complexity of loving my country and hating the ways *our* national interest is being defined for *us*" (34; emphasis added). The emphasis has been added to highlight Rich's successful and important presumption to speak for an "us". Her poetry is an attempt to make manifest her "dream of a common language," to speak to and for an audience of many.

W. S. Graham's poetry is aware of an audience or readership in a way that is the converse of Rich's; rather than speaking to many, it presumes to speak to none. As Grogan has noted, a great deal of Graham's later poetry takes as its subject the problematic conditions of speaking to anyone. In many poems, the Graham-persona seems to address us directly as readers, and repeatedly asks us the same questions—though in a dazzling and amusing number of ways. These questions both reify and problematize the interactions between speaker and listener; they draw us into the process of the poem by challenging our position and use as readers. Thus the voice asks questions such as: *Who are you? Do you hear me? Are you reading this? Are you ready? Where shall you find us? Have I spoken to you before? Are you there at all?* and, in a question crucially related to all of the preceding: *What is the language using us for?* Graham's dialogical form seems to invite the participation of the reader. This interactive model has become increasingly important in contemporary poetry with the claims of many "language-centered" poets (frequently gathered under the L=A=N=G=U=A=G=E, or more simply "Language," banner). An avant-garde movement that couples verse and theory, Language poetry draws attention to the ways in which readers complete meaning. While both Graham and the Language poets are preoccupied with the medium of language as poetic subject and with the various players in language acts, Graham's work differs from theirs in some significant ways.

While both Graham and the Language poets have small audiences, the later group has a small *known* audience. This coterie, predominantly made up of other poets and aficionados, provides a kind of security for Language poets that is radically missing in Graham's work, since the former group knows—at least in some measure—to whom they speak. As previously discussed, this perception of audience can have an important impact on poetic form. In the case of Language poetry, the perception of a small, specialized audience allows for a degree of experimentation that would be intolerable in most lyric poetry aimed at a larger audience. Graham, on the other hand, perceives his audience as unknown. His is a potential audience that must be constantly courted, constantly won. His poetry longs to be understood and engaged, and therefore he uses forms suitable to this end. Hence while Language poetry often presents intentionally obscure and frustrating forms, Graham's later verse is eminently readable. While much Language poetry aims only to communicate with a small circle of readers, Graham's poetry wants desperately to communicate with anyone. However, while the Language poets can, ironically, except to be understood by their small group of readers, Graham's fate is to remain terminally unsure of his audience. Each poem is a further, more desperate attempt to woo an audience who, the poetry tells us, may never actually be won:

Are you Still there?

I love I love you tucked away
In a corner of my time looking
Out at me for me to put
My arm round you to comfort you.

I love you more than that as well
You know. You know I live now
In Madron with the black, perched beasts
On the shoulder of the gable-end.

The first day of October's bright
Shadows go over the Celtic fields
Coming to see you. I have tucked
You I hope not too far away.

(*Collected Poems* 199-200)

The heart of Graham's poetry has to do with the frustrated relationship between speaker and receiver. While his poems demand or beg a response, they set up linguistic situations in which it is impossible for a response to be had. The poems both create and foil the reader's desire to talk back. In section 40 of **"Implements in Their Places,"** for example, Graham leaves a space for the reader to respond:

I leave you this space
To use as your own.
I think you will find
That using it is more
Impossible than making it.
Here is the space now.
Write an Implement in it.

(*Collected* 246)

What follows in the poem is a series of dotted lines, a designated place for you-the-reader to respond:

YOU . . .
YOU . . .
YOU . . .
YOU . . .
    Do it with your pen.
    I will return in a moment
    To see what you have done.
    Try. Try. No offence meant.

The space here offered is the familiar lacuna in many of Graham's poems—a private, personal place for the reader: "The spaces in the poem are yours. / They are the place where you / Can enter as yourself alone / And think anything in" (**"Private Poem to Norman MacLeod,"** *Collected* 222). Readers quickly find, however, that "using it is more / Impossible than making it" (**"Implements,"** *Collected* 246). The space draws readers into a chasm of unanswerable questions, a "place" in which they often find themselves in Graham's poems. Waiting for the speaker to "return," readers are left to contemplate these questions: Am I really supposed to respond? How should I respond? Would a response make a difference to the poem? To Graham? What kind of difference? Filling in the space in **"Implements,"** section 40, does not answer these questions. The problems that this space (and others like it) raise are meant to be unresolvable, just as the poem that begs an answer is meant to be unanswerable. While the Language poets can presume a small audience who will know how to make their difficult forms mean, Graham's speaker can presume "nobody" yet must speak in a way cogent enough to invite "somebody".

Graham uses other strategies to create forms that simultaneously beg and refuse an answer. Many poems use an epistolary form of familiar, personal address. Ironically, though, the addressee is constructed as someone who cannot respond. Hence, Graham writes epistolary poems to people who are dead (**"Dear Bryan Wynter"**), people who are mute (**"To Alexander Graham"**), or "people" who do not exist

("**Dear Who I Mean**"). He constructs a readership of none by manufacturing a reader who cannot respond. Even occasions of great intimacy are turned into situations of silence. In "**To My Wife At Midnight**," Graham reconstructs the intimate circumstances of talking in bed as a one-way communication:

> Are you asleep I say
> Into the back of your neck
> For you not to hear me.

(Collected 262)

"**To My Wife At Midnight**" is a remarkable love poem that illustrates Graham's project perfectly—the emotional energy of the poem draws the lover in and distances her at the same time:

> Are you to say goodnight
> And turn away under
> The blanket of your delight?
>
> Are you to let me go
> Alone to sleep beside you
> Into the drifting snow?
>
> Where we each reach,
> Sleeping alone together,
> Nobody can touch.

(Collected 261)

Graham constructs all of his listeners in this ambiguous way, whether it is his wife, close friends, or an unidentified "Pen / Pal in the distance" ("**Yours Truly**," *Collected* 149-50). The listener's role is to hear and not to hear, and for that the listener (reader/ audience) is both necessary and unnecessary:

> Are you receiving those clusters
> I send out travelling? Alas
> I have no way of knowing or
> If I am overheard here.
> Is that (It is.) not what I want?

("Clusters Travelling Out," Collected 186)

Ironically, not being heard is exactly what Graham wants. The second-person "you" who appears so frequently in Graham's poems, and in much contemporary poetry, is unique in Graham's work in that this person remains radically unknown and unknowable. While Ginsberg, Bly, or Rich "place" their readers by trying to show them where they belong, Graham leaves them unconnected, at "the edge of earshot" ("**Malcolm Mooney's Land**," *Collected* 144), with little but the powerful desire for connection. Compare Rich's certainty to Graham's equivocation about who "you" are:

> I know you are reading this poem by the light
> of the television screen where soundless images jerk
>   and slide

while you wait for the newscast from the *intifada*.
> I know you are reading this poem in a waiting-room
> of eyes met and unmeeting, of identity with strangers.
> I know you are reading this poem by fluorescent light
> in the boredom and fatigue of the young who are
>   counted out,
> count themselves out, at too early an age.

("Dedications," Atlas 25)

> And who are you and by
> What right do I waylay
> You where you go there
> Happy enough striking
> Your hobnail in the dark?
> Believe me I would ask
> Forgiveness but who
> Would I ask forgiveness from?

("The Dark Dialogues," Collected 158)

The familiar lyrical "you," which normally signifies a community between speaker and reader, takes on a new, ambiguous, and unfamiliar quality in Graham's verse. Where Rich's poetry gains from a confident certainty of its audience, Graham's gains from a confident uncertainty, an equivocal assurance of a readership of none.

III. WHAT IS GAINED?

To answer the question of what Graham's poetry gains by taking this ambiguous stance towards its readership, the consequences of such a position, both intellectual and emotional, may be considered. While Graham's poetry raises a number of intellectual conundrums, particularly of the kind now associated with post-structuralist theory and often enacted by Language poetry, it also achieves a great deal of pathos. In a feat of notable skill and charm, Graham manages both to deconstruct and court his readers at the same time. As suggested above, Graham's accessibility, as well as his skill *and* charm, is a significant departure from most Language poetry, which, for all its theoretical interest, remains densely inaccessible.

Intellectually, Graham's poetry makes gains by constructing a readership of none. These gains come from the poet's intense scrutiny of how we use language and how language uses us. If Graham's poetry destabilizes and, in some cases, actually denies the idea of a reader, to whom does it speak? "**What is the Language Using Us For?**" answers this question:

> I am not making a fool of myself
> For you. What I am making is
> A place for language in my life
>
> Which I want to be a real place
> Seeing I have to put up with it
> Anyhow. What are Communication's

Mistakes in the magic medium doing
To us? . . .
I would like to speak in front
Of myself with all my ears alive
And find out what it is I want.

(*Collected* 192-93)

Graham's poems can be seen here as a way of talking to himself and, more importantly, of talking to language. They are a dialogue in and *with* the "magic medium," a process of speaking not only in order "to say something" but also in order to "find out what it is I want." In playing with the medium, Graham tackles the problems of both speaking (How do I say what I want?) and being spoken (What does the language make of me?). In the above quotation, by "speaking in front of himself" the poet-persona finds out "what he wants" and *who he is*; for he discovers that his identity is constructed in the process of speaking.

In the last quotation, it is evident how the reader appears to be ontologically insignificant for the speaker who claims to be speaking only "in front of himself" and in front of language: "I am not making a fool of myself / For you. What I am making is / A place for language in my life." In another paradoxical twist, however, the *idea of the reader* does have great importance, as section 33 of **"Implements"** makes clear:

Do not think you have to say
Anything back. But you do
Say something back which I
Hear by the way I speak to you.

(*Collected* 244)

Here the reader is both essential and unnecessary, as the speaker's discourse is shaped by the way it imagines a reader.[3] Once again a perceived audience shapes poetic utterance. It must be remembered, however, that the reader is most often imagined in Graham's poems as *absent*. What the Graham-persona "hears" and "speaks back" is the pathos of not being heard, of silence:

I speak as well as I can
Trying to teach my ears
To learn to use their eyes
Even only maybe
In the end to observe
The behavior of silence.

("The Dark Dialogues," *Collected* 162)

Graham's preoccupation with the way language "behaves," then, invites a marvelous assortment of language tricks and questions into the poems. In **"Clusters Travelling Out,"** for example, the speaker, who

is a kind of prisoner-poet, shows the reader how language creates, destroys, and recreates both speaker and listener in each new language act:

When you hear from me
Again I will not know you. Whoever
Speaks to you will not be me.
I wonder what I will say.

(*Collected* 185)

The circumstances (that is, the language situation, or what Graham calls "the constructed space") in which the subject speaks dictate not only his identity but also the identity of his assumed listener. In each language act, each participant becomes a new person, both the creator and the progeny of language. Hence we see how language creates us at the same time that we create language. Graham presents the same paradox again in **"Implements,"** section 34, which looks like a little post-structural Zen Koan:

As I hear so I speak so I am so I think
You must be. O Please Please No.

(*Collected* 244)

The qualifying "Please Please No" seems to be the only adequate response to the puzzle of untangling the relationship between hearing, speaking, being, and knowing an other.

Graham's poems variously construct and deconstruct their speaker, reader, and even the poem itself, as in **"Enter a Cloud."** Here the speaker appears in the last section of the poem as a flashy master-of-ceremonies taking his curtain call and introducing the *dramatis personae* who made the poem possible. With typical Graham wit, the speaker dissolves the poem into its constituent parts and inevitably requests the audience to consider the slippery relationship between signifier and signified:

Thank you. And for your applause.
It has been a pleasure. I
Have never enjoyed speaking more.
May I also thank the real ones
Who have made this possible.
First, the cloud itself. And now
Gurnard's Head and Zennor
Head. Also recognise
How I have been helped
By Jean and Madron's Albert
Strick (He is a real man.)
And good words like brambles,
Bower, spiked, fox, anvil, teeling.

(*Collected* 212)

In the context of the poem, signifier and signified are collapsed since the "real man" Albert Strick and "good words like brambles" are given equal weight as "the real ones" who have made the poem "possible." What, then, one wonders, is the status of the speaking "I"? Is it another "good word" or does it have a different kind of existence? How is it related to "brambles" or "Albert Strick"? What role does the "I" have in making the poem "possible"? These questions are typical entanglements in Graham's poems.

Another interesting performance in the "constructed space" of Graham's poetry is the struggle, in various contexts, between speaker and what is spoken, the poet-persona and his words. The struggle recalls Lewis Carroll's Humpty Dumpty in *Through the Looking Glass,* whose whimsical "nice knock-down arguments" are also complex linguistic time-bombs:

> "When *I* use a word," Humpty Dumpty said, in a rather scornful tone, "it means just what I choose it to mean— neither more nor less."
>
> "The question is," said Alice, "whether you *can* make words mean so many different things."
>
> "The question is," said Humpty Dumpty, "which is to be master—that's all. . . . They've a temper, some of them—particularly verbs: they're the proudest—adjectives you can do anything with, but not verbs— however, *I* can manage the whole lot of them! Impenetrability! That's what *I* say!"
>
> (269)

Graham's poems often enact this struggle for mastery between the speaker and the spoken. In this contest the balance of power is always shifting, as illustrated by two parts of **"Implements"**:

> 29
>
> These words as I uttered them
> Spoke back at me out of spite,
> Pretended to not know me
> From Adam. Sad to have to infer
> Such graft and treachery in the name
> Of communication. . . .
>
> 30
>
> Language, constrictor of my soul,
> What are you snivelling at? Behave
> Better. Take care. It's only through me
> You live. Take care. Don't make me mad.
>
> (*Collected* 243)

While these examples illustrate the typical Carroll-like whimsy of some of Graham's work, the question of who is master, and the dangers of being controlled or written *by* language are also evident in less whimsical contexts. **"What is the Language Using Us For?"** reflects on the possible inadequacy of the language as tool to express or to signify ourselves:

> What is the language using us for?
> I don't know. Have the words ever
> Made anything of you, near a kind
> Of truth you thought you were? Me
> Neither. The words like albatrosses
> Are only a doubtful touch towards
> My going and you lifting your hand
>
> To speak to illustrate an observed
> Catastrophe.
>
> (*Collected* 195-96)

Here language is conceived as a doomed system of doubtful signifiers that hang symbolically, like the Ancient Mariner's albatross, around the neck of the poet condemned to speak ("to illustrate an observed / Catastrophe"), but always imperfectly.

All of these examples demonstrate the intellectual gains Graham achieves by constructing a readership of none. Since "no one" is listening, Graham's poetry takes as both its subject and its audience the poet-persona and language itself—the speaker and the spoken. His poetry does not deal with these conundrums, however, in the unwaveringly sombre way of some literary theory that tackles the same problems. In fact, some of the most challenging semantic puzzles occur in rather humorous and self-mocking poetic moments, as in part eight of **"Approaches to How They Behave"**:

> And what are you supposed to say
> I asked a new word but it kept mum.
> I had secretly admired always
> What I thought it was here for.
> But I was wrong when I looked it up
> Between the painted boards. It said
> Something it was never very likely
> I could fit in to a poem in my life.
>
> (*Collected* 172)

Graham's poetry succeeds not only because of the rigorous nature of the questions it poses but also, and perhaps more importantly, because of the style, humour, and, as will be discussed below, pathos of the work.

IV. PATHOS: GAINING THROUGH LOSS

Though intellectual dexterity is an important element in Graham's poetry, it is not an end in itself. The construction of a readership of none and the concomitant manipulation of language have emotional as well as intellectual ends. In the quotation cited at the beginning of this essay, the speaker hopes that he does not write only for other poets. The Graham-persona also hopes, it may be assumed, that he is not engaged only in clever word play (a charge often levelled against the Language poets). The voice of **"The Constructed Space"** speaks of an ineffable "something" beyond language (though paradoxically created in language) towards which the poem reaches:

I say this silence or, better, construct this space
So that somehow something may move across
The caught habits of language to you and me.

(Collected 153)

What "move[s] across / The caught habits of language"
is a great pathos, an emotional energy that paradoxically defies Graham's constructions. At the bottom of
his writing is a powerful desire to speak and be heard
coupled with the pathos of knowing that he will never
be fully, or perfectly, or perhaps even adequately,
heard.

Along with the epistolary form, another typical
structure in Graham's poetry is the elegy. His ***Collected Poems*** includes elegies for friends and fellow
artists Peter Lanyon, Roger Hilton, and Bryan Wynter,
among others. These elegies are some of the most successful poems in the collection, not only as moving
statements of personal loss but also as theoretical statements of a more general loss: the failure of communication. The poems are constructed not only as
remembrances but also as emblematic attempts to
speak to "no one." Often they try to do what seems
both logically impossible and emotionally imperative,
that is, to communicate directly with the dead. **"Dear
Bryan Wynter"** sustains a chatty tone of intimate
conversation that is all the more poignant given the
impossibility of such communication:

> This is only a note
> To say how sorry I am
> You died. . . .
> Anyhow how are things?
> Are you still somewhere
> With your long legs
> And twitching smile under
> Your blue hat walking
> Across a place? Or am
> I greedy to make you up
> Again out of memory?
> Are you there at all? . . .
> Do you want anything?
> Where shall I send something?
> Rice-wine, meanders, paintings
> By your contemporaries?

(Collected 255-56)

The numerous queries are, of course, questions that
cannot be answered. The poignancy of the poem
results not only from the specific loss but also from
the reader's cumulative knowledge that a loss of this
kind is the basis of most of Graham's poems, not only
the elegies. Specifically, the poem mourns the loss of
a friend. More generally, it is another instance of the
unanswerable message. **"Dear Bryan Wynter"** is a
missive from someone, like the prisoner in **"Clusters**

Travelling Out," who is desperate to hear something
beyond his own tapping but who is trapped in the
"prison house of language."[4] The speaker of **"Dear
Bryan Wynter"** is in the same solitary predicament:
"Speaking to you and not / Knowing if you are there /
Is not too difficult. / My words are used to that"
(***Collected*** 255-56). Although the speaker is used to
talking to himself, there is a subtext of powerful desire.
The desire is for a more important, substantial kind of
communication, a connection "on the other side / Of
language," as another poem puts it (**"Johann
Joachim,"** *Collected* 222).

The elegies, then, collapse the specific and the theoretical instances of loss in Graham's poetry. They speak
both of the personal loss of friends and the general
loss of communicative insufficiency. The ending of
"The Thermal Stair," for instance, merges the pathos
of Peter Lanyon's untimely death with the pathos of
trying to speak (or, as Graham calls it, of "taking the
word-road home"):

> Uneasy, lovable man, give me your painting
> Hand to steady me taking the word-road home.
> Lanyon, why is it you're earlier away?
> Remember me wherever you listen from.
> Lanyon, dingdong dingdong from carn to carn.
> It seems tonight all Closing bells are tolling
> Across the Duchy shire wherever I turn.

(Collected 157)

Here the "Closing bells" ring in both Lanyon's death
and the mournful sounds of the poet, stumbling on
"the word-road home."

The pairing of the specific and the theoretical may
also provide a key to Graham's moving poem for his
father, **"To Alexander Graham."** Here the specific
failure of communication between father and son
opens onto the general insufficiency of language. The
impossibility of communication is symbolically
represented in the poem as a dream without sound:

> Lying asleep walking
> Last night I met my father
> Who seemed pleased to see me.
> He wanted to speak. I saw
> His mouth saying something
> But the dream had no sound.

(Collected 215)

Within this soundless environment, the speaker reflects
on his father's desperate and unattainable desire "to
say something." Into the father's silence are cast the
son's unanswerable questions (unanswerable because
they fall not on deaf ears but on mute lips):

Dad, what am I doing here?
What is it I am doing now?
Are you proud of me?
Going away, I knew
You wanted to tell me something.

(*Collected* 216)

The failures in the filial context of the poem are linked to a more general defeat in the context of language as system. Hence, it seems natural to make the transition from the unanswerable questions of **"To Alexander Graham"** ("Dad, what am I doing here? / What is it I am doing now?") to the equally problematic questions of **"To My Wife At Midnight"** ("What is to happen to us / And what is to happen to each / Of us asleep in our places?" [*Collected* 261]). In both cases, the speakers are not only alone with intimates but also alone with and in language.

In **"To My Wife At Midnight"** the speaker imagines himself and his wife "sleeping alone together." The tenderness of the poem suggests that their aloneness is better seen as an isolation in language than a physical or emotional separation. The pathos of both this poem and **"To Alexander Graham"** comes from the feeling that language is unable to reach even those people who should, figuratively at least, be most accessible. This failure to touch even the closest of intimates is one of the great indictments of language in Graham's work. But an indictment of language is always paradoxical, as Graham well knows; for such an argument must be framed in the very system it hopes to expose—creating an impossible hermeneutic circle.

Nonetheless, Graham's problems with language have both intellectual and emotional consequences. The pathos of the elegies and the love poems is intimately connected with the rigour and self-consciousness of the more obviously "language-oriented" poems. The "language-oriented" qualification is needed because almost all of Graham's poems could, in fact, be subsumed under this heading. The poet's achievement is that he makes "language concerns" into "personal concerns." Finally, his poems are about the compulsion to communicate coupled with the fear of never being fully heard or understood. They are about calling out "across / The dead centre of the night" (**"Yours Truly,"** *Collected* 150) and listening, hesitantly, for a reply. The resonance of such a situation surely goes beyond its theoretical interest. Graham's predicament in language has a great deal to do with our own. Importantly, the knowledge of being trapped in language does not stop the Graham-persona from speaking. The poet must speak because—even though the speaker, in a final paradox, may never know his

listener—he must keep reaching, keep talking, since "always language / Is where the people are." These lines come from the first section of **"The Dark Dialogues"**:

And this is no other
Place than where I am,
Here turning between
This word and the next.
Yet somewhere the stones
Are wagging in the dark
And you, whoever you are,
That I am other to,
Stand still by the glint
Of the dyke's sparstone,
Because always language
Is where the people are.

(*Collected* 159)

In *Self and Sensibility in Contemporary American Poetry,* Charles Altieri describes "two central factors of the contemporary [poetry] scene" by remarking on:

how speculative criticism now attracts much of the audience and the energy the last decade devoted to poetry and how some poets do in fact continue to serve as antennae of the race as they face this general condition in their own way.

(27)

W. S. Graham is one of these later poets. His work faces the situation Altieri comments on by involving itself with some of the most essential questions of language in a way that is not only rigorous, but also humorous, humane, and aesthetically accomplished. In Altieri's phrase, Graham makes "a lyricism out of lucidity" (26). By re-imagining the speaker's relation to his readership, Graham's poems discover new ways of using and being used by language. His work reveals the tricks and fancies, the pleasures and dangers of language; it takes the reader into a most familiar—but also wildly new—country:

I know you cannot follow me but please
Try by example to travel even disguised
Across this part of the country even although
The season is not fashionable. O holidaymaker
On language and its environs, you are now
Entering country where only the words go.

("One Good Sound," *Aimed* 6)

Graham's poems are some of the most valuable "implements" available for exploring this new country.

Notes

1. Graham's *The Nightfishing* appeared the same year as Larkin's *The Less Deceived*. His association with the so-called "Apocalyptics" (Dylan

Thomas and others) ensured that his work was not favourably treated by the most important critics of the time, who preferred the poetics and philosophy of The Movement (Lopez 9-25).

2. This analysis is much indebted to the work of Professor Ruth Grogan, with whom I studied Graham's poetry at York University. Grogan's article, "W. S. Graham: A Dialogical Imagination," provides the framework on which my study builds. Grogan analyzes the "dialogical" nature of Graham's later poems, noting that a great number of them explore "the relationship between a speaker, 'I,' and an unanswering listener, 'you'" (197). Drawing on Bakhtin and Martin Buber's philosophy of I-and-Thou, Grogan explores the philosophical dimensions of Graham's poetry. Following this initiative, my paper attempts to broaden Grogan's analysis of the question of poetic audience and to explore further implications of Graham's method.

3. I am indebted to Grogan for this point. Her essay relates this phenomenon to Bakhtin's discussion of "double-voicing," a topic I will not take up here. See "Dialogical" 199.

4. This phrase was first used in reference to Graham by Punter (237). Punter notes: "The specific reference is to Fredric Jameson, *The Prison-House of Language*" (Punter 244).

Works Cited

Altieri, Charles. *Self and Sensibility in Contemporary American Poetry*. Cambridge: Cambridge UP, 1984.

Carroll, Lewis. *The Annotated Alice: Alice's Adventures in Wonderland and Through the Looking Glass*. Intro. and notes Martin Gardner. New York: Meridian, 1960.

Graham, W. S. *Aimed at Nobody*: Poems from Notebooks. Ed. Margaret Blackwood and Robin Skelton. London: Faber, 1993.

―――. *Collected Poems: 1942-1977*. London: Faber, 1979.

Grogan, Ruth. "W. S. Graham: A Dialogical Imagination." *English Studies in Canada* 15.2 (1989): 196-213.

Jameson, Fredric. *The Prison-House of Language: A Critical Account of Structuralism and Russian Formalism*. Princeton: Princeton UP, 1972.

Lopez, Tony. *The Poetry of W. S. Graham*. Edinburgh: Edinburgh UP, 1989.

Punter, David. "W. S. Graham: Constructing a White Space." *Malahat Review* 63 (1982): 220-44.

Rich, Adrienne. *An Atlas of the Difficult World: Poems 1988-1991*. New York: Norton, 1991.

Rothschild, Matthew. Interview with Adrienne Rich. *Progressive* 58 (1994): 31-35.

Silliman, Ron. Letter to the author. 29 January 1998.

John Redmond (essay date 2002)

SOURCE: Redmond, John. "W. S. Graham." In *British Writers: Supplement VII*, edited by Jay Parini, pp. 103-17. New York: Charles Scribner's Sons, 2002.

[*In the following essay, Redmond offers a comprehensive overview of Graham's entire body of work.*]

William Sydney Graham has claims to being one of the most important Scottish poets of the twentieth century. His poetry is not at all well known, even in Scotland, although he has gained over the years a small but influential band of admirers. He wrote about silence and being alone, and he has been left alone by many readers. In a century when many readers approach poets and other artists via the label of a group or movement, Graham had no label. In a period when writing was often politicized by writers and critics, he was not political. He lived his life—and to some degree chose to live it—at the margins of different, though ultimately interweaving, kinds of power: economic, social and literary. Self-conscious about his working-class roots, he wrote poems that were self-conscious about being made up.

Graham, however, very much deserves to be heard, and it is not necessary to take the work at its own modest face value. His poems approach subjects that may be discomforting, even depressing, but that are fundamental to our lives. They listen for things we cannot quite hear and describe states we cannot quite control and so emphasize our comparative helplessness. In the opening lines of **"Enter a Cloud,"** a simple situation—a man lying on a hill looking at the sky—is described with simple diction. Through the sophistication of the syntax and the line breaks, the poem creates a dizzying depth out of seemingly nothing:

> Gently disintegrate me
> Said nothing at all.
>
> Is there still time to say
> Said I myself lying
> In a bower of bramble
> Into which I have fallen.

Look through my eyes up
At blue with not anything
We could have ever arranged
Slowly taking place.

(Implements in Their Places, p. 33)

LIFE AND BACKGROUND

Graham was born in Greenock in Renfrewshire, Scotland, on 19 November 1918. Known to his friends as Sydney, he was the son of Alexander Graham, a journeyman engineer, and Margaret McDermid. The family lived on the top floor of a tenement building, which overlooked the "winches and steel giants" of the dockyards. Graham left school at the age of fourteen and became a draftman's apprentice with a Glasgow engineering firm.

The location of Greenock plays an influential role in Graham's poetry. Glasgow, during the period when it styled itself as the second city of the British Empire, owed much of its economic prosperity to the river Clyde. But deepwater ships, coming from the west, had not always been able to navigate the whole length of the river (it was widened and deepened at various points in its history) and sometimes would deliver their cargo at more accessible locations. Greenock, downriver of Glasgow to the west, is located at the point where the Clyde widens dramatically into its firth (or fjord) before flowing into the sea proper, and it is easily in reach of deepwater shipping. Hence it was a place of traditional, labor-intensive industries, of fishing and shipbuilding, as well as being decidedly secondary in relation to the major city it served, a place through which traffic was always passing, a "threshold," to use Graham's term, between Glasgow and the sea.

Graham, too, lived his life at the periphery. Like Greenock he lived downriver of the big city, whether that city was Glasgow, London, or New York. He could stay in such places for a short period of time but could never put down roots. Most of his life was lived in the relative seclusion of Cornwall, in the southwest corner of England, far removed from Scotland. His early years, like the ships and cargoes, passing through Greenock, had an itinerant, provisional quality, as he moved, always unsettled, and sometimes unsettling to others. His working-class background remained an issue, as he once said, jokingly: "Am I a poet? Or am I just a boy from Greenock?"

Graham's alcoholism, which played a considerable role in his life, also partly derives from a Clydeside background where hard drinking was common, the one easily available release for men from lower-class backgrounds. The pub, though, was more to Graham than a place where he could easily indulge himself. The culture of the pub was close to the center of his work, and a pub named Mooney's features numerous times in his later poetry, including the title of arguably his best book, ***Malcolm Mooney's Land.*** For Graham the pub was where views could be exchanged and roles tried out and tested and where free-flowing, heightened language was possible. He was fascinated by the pub scene in *The Waste Land,* with its slangy, side-of-the-mouth conversation. David Wright, his friend and fellow writer, has recorded examples of Graham's sometimes abrasive pubtalk. Once confronted by a literary bore, Graham burst out:

> In three days I will begin the novel of my life with—"Unlike my brother, the Grand Duke Ferdinand . . .". There is no reply—You have to sit and be talked to—OK OK Reply reply if you dare. Well well eh? So what? You don't know eh?—Yeheeh—Alright?, lay cards on table—I thought so. No cards eh?

(David Wright, "W. S. Graham in the Forties," in Edinburgh Review 75 [1987], p. 52.)

Perhaps one of the most puzzling aspects of Graham's character was how someone so voluble and gregarious could also write such delicate, quiet, almost self-erasing poems. It was a trait he shared with other poets of the periods, notably Dylan Thomas and Patrick Kavanagh, whose desire to become "characters" with the help of alcoholic inspiration masked fundamental sensitivity and shyness. A Celtic poet of the time could be expected, especially by an English audience, to play a bardic role, to play up to the stereotype of the mercurial, verbose, extravagant clown. Of course this role was also a trap

Most of Graham's life was lived in conditions that dipped in and out of poverty, and he was always dependent, to a greater or lesser extent, on others. From his teenage years, however, it was clear that he wished to improve himself, though in a nonmaterialistic way. To the consternation of his traditionally minded parents, he took evening classes in art appreciation and literature at Glasgow University and then, in 1938, began a year of study at Newbattle Abbey Adult Residential College. Unusually progressive for the time, Newbattle modeled itself on an Oxford College and was open to working students who were not from prosperos backgrounds. There Graham embarked on a mixed program of subjects, mainly concentrating on arts and philosophy. At this point he had already gained a reputation among his classmates for writing poetry, as well as for being something of a character or, more unkindly, a poseur. One of the students Graham met there was the woman he would eventually marry, Agnes Dunsmuir, who was known as Nessie.

Graham's mother was Irish and much of his work leans sympathetically toward the Irish culture of the singer John McCormack and the writers J. M. Synge, James Joyce, and Samuel Beckett. It was not surprising when, in 1939, seeking to avoid conscription into the armed forces, he went to Ireland, which was neutral during the Second World War, and sought work. The jobs he found were mixed—on a farm, with a fair, on the docks—and short-lived. He also drifted from place to place. Later, he returned to Scotland, where a medical examination revealed an ulcer, which made him unfit for military service. In a belated contribution to the war effort, he put his engineering skills to use in a torpedo factory.

All of these occupations tended to suck him back into the limited cultural expectations of his upbringing. More rewarding opportunities and contacts were to be gained through the artistic circles in which he was beginning to move. Graham's first book, *Cage Without Grievance,* was taken up by David Archer, who published it with his Parton Press in 1942. Archer, a literary philanthropist with many contacts, was one of a line of figures who played a generous, avuncular role in Graham's life, recognizing his talent and providing him, from time to time, with financial and moral support. Graham lived for a while in Archer's flat in Glasgow, and the circles of his artistic friends became significantly wider and more elevated. Through the cultural events Archer organized, Graham met the poets Hugh McDiarmid and Dylan Thomas and the painters Robert Colquhoun and Robert MacBryde.

These contacts also led further afield to London, where Graham moved in 1944. He became associated with the wartime literary community, especially the Fitzrovia scene, which was based around pubs in Soho in the center of London. That same year he had a daughter by Mary Harris. Pleading his unsuitability in the role, he gave up his responsibilities as a father. He had little contact with either daughter or her mother subsequently.

In late 1944, Graham moved with Nessie Dunsmuir to Cornwall. Initially they lived a spartan existence in a pair of vans. Graham is said to have worked as a casual laborer and fisherman during the early part of his residence while his wife supplemented their income with seasonal work for a local hotel.

In 1946, the couple moved into a cottage in Mevagissey, Cornwall. Soon thereafter, they separated for six years. Graham began a relationship with the American academic Vivienne Koch, which was to have a considerable influence on him. It led to his living in New York for a year, giving a series of lectures on literature at New York university, and winning an Atlantic Award in 1947. Koch obligingly wrote about his work in *Sewanee Review,* helping him to become better known. His cultural horizons broadened, and there is an evident deepening of his style in his collection *The White Threshold,* which was published in 1949.

Graham returned to England in 1948, briefly to Cornwall and then to London. His health was poor. Under pressure of an inadequate diet and, especially, the excessive drinking that was becoming a permanent feature of his life, he had agitated his ulcer. Some of Graham's contemporaries around this time remembered him as being difficult and prickly. Julian Maclaren-Ross, in his *Memoirs of the Forties* (London, 1963), draws a picture of Graham holding forth in the literary pubs and recalling how difficult it could be even to say hello to him. Except with close personal friends, Graham found communication stressful. In order to counteract his difficulty, he would fuel himself up with alcohol and treat each meeting as a performance, even a high-wire act. A reading, an interview or the most casual encounter became an adventure. However jovial his intentions, he tended to put his listeners, interlocutors, and, indeed, readers on edge—or, as he might have seen it, made them aware that the edge was where they had been all along. Edwin Morgan, in "W. S. Graham and Voice,'" records this kind of baiting in a 1978 interview with Graham by Penelope Mortimer, in *The Observer,* which is also a good example of Graham's humor:

> PM: Tell me about your parents.
>
> WSG: My dear. You must ask me something very small. Like "Why do you put capitals at the beginning of the lines of your verse?"
>
> PM: Why do you put capitals at the beginning of lines of your verse?
>
> WSG: To make people realize it's poetry.
>
> (p. 78)

Graham lived with a friend in London and then again with Vivienne Koch until their separation, in 1950. In the same year he worked briefly for an advertising agency. He was writing the long poem for which he would become best known, **"The Nightfishing."** By 1953 he had reunited with Nessie Dunsmuir, who had been living in Paris. In 1955, Graham moved back to Cornwall with Nessie as his wife (they had married the previous year). His first significant collection, *The Nightfishing,* was published in 1955.

Graham developed friendships with many of the painters based around St. Ives, in Cornwall. In a setting he Graham found agreeable, St. Ives combined a traditional (if declining) fishing community with the bohemian atmosphere created by an influx of painters. The bombing of London in the Blitz meant that many were eager to escape the city. Property was going cheap in Cornwall, and painters went there attracted by the quality of the light, the chance to buy studio space, and the congenial presence of their peers. Graham met and made friends with many who would prove important to the history of postwar British painting—like Peter Lanyon, Roger Hilton, and Bryan Wynter—writing poems about all of them.

The subject and methods of Graham's approach to writing found echoes in the attitudes of the painters. The style of the primitive painter Alfred Wallis was a major influence in St. Ives, emphasizing an existential approach where the borderline between subject and object crumbled. The painting (or the poem) could now be seen as an experience, not so much a commentary on life as an extension of it, and therefore more appropriate to the way we actually live. As the St. Ives scene also represents the beginning of a coming to terms with Abstract Expressionism in British painting, Graham's position could be compared with the American poets Frank O'Hara and John Ashbery, of the New York School, who were coming to terms with Abstract Expressionism around the same time.

There is a synesthetic aspect to Graham's work—not only could he appreciate art forms other than poetry, he saturated himself in them. Graham's readings often became a dialogue between different kinds of art. Before a performance he would decorate a room with his own paintings and hangings, light the area with candles, and play music by Bartok or Mozart. The audience was encouraged to join in and make dramatic sounds (the noise of a storm perhaps), while different poems were read by different voices. Graham's sheer exuberance was striking; he sought in any given moment the transcendence that art can afford. As he once wrote, "I happen to feel most alive when I am trying to write poetry."

Such combinations were also a part of his working methods. When composing a poem over a long period Graham used a wall, rather as a painter uses a canvas, and pinned up phrases he found particularly resonant. His notebooks are composed in different inks, with lettering of different sizes, sometimes painted over with a wash of color. His letters often read like excerpts from Joyce's *Finnegans Wake*; a long list of puns and variations on words unwound, creating a playful, intoxicating effect.

Despite its being well received, Graham did not follow up *The Nightfishing* with a new collection for fifteen years, when *Malcolm Mooney's Land* was published in 1970. He seemed to disappear from the literary scene at the moment he should have been most visible. One of Graham's significant patrons during this bleak period in his life was the poet Robin Skelton (1925-1997), who had interceded with publishers on his behalf and who was interested in collecting Graham's manuscripts. Skelton notes the extent of Graham's vanishing in his introduction to an edition of Graham's notebooks: "When in the late sixties I asked Faber & Faber why they had not seen fit to bring out a new Graham book I was astonished to be told that they had lost touch with him and did not know he was still writing" (*Aimed at Nobody,* p. viii).

Faber may have forgotten about Graham simply because he went out of fashion. Partly, this was because the style of the Movement writers, dominant in the 1950s, was far removed from Graham's new style. The typical Movement poem was ironic, English, low key, and featured a lyric self acting in recognizable contemporary situations, whereas the typical Graham poem was contemplative, Scottish, and featured a fragmented self acting in metaphorical, psychologized landscapes. Philip Larkin's *The Less Deceived,* a popular triumph of the Movement style, was published in the same year as *The Nightfishing* and probably helped to overshadow it.

Nor did Graham receive his due from his homeland. He was never fully accepted by the Scottish Renaissance movement, which was at its height between the years 1920 and 1945. The movement laid heavy stress on the use of a literary version, or versions, of the Scots dialect, an emphasis with which Graham was out of sympathy. Graham, through his literary style and his decision to move away from Glasgow to Cornwall, was perhaps not obviously Scottish enough. Admittedly, to remove himself to Cornwall was to withdraw to the other end of the island of Britain. He could hardly get much further away. However, Graham never stopped seeing himself as Scottish. His fundamental stance, in any case, was of solitude—he did not exist for formal groups or alliances, and neither did they exist for him. During periods when it was fashionable to be explicitly political, particularly in the 1960s, he was obviously not so. Although poets in the late twentieth century usually didn't live off their poetry but from activities peripheral to it, Graham made no sustained effort to promote his works through, for example, broadcasting, reviewing, or lecturing. As much as anything else, this contributed to his neglect.

By 1958 Graham had started to supplement his income by selling some of his manuscripts. He remained in a precarious financial position, however, still reliant on friends for aid. In 1962, the Grahams stayed in a house lent by a friend, the painter Nancy Wynne-Jones, with whom they traveled in 1964 to Greece, a location that would feature later in his work. In 1968 they moved into a cottage she owned and were allowed to stay without paying rent. An arrangement was worked out whereby Graham received a regular if modest income in return for sending all his drafts and manuscripts to Skelton, who had moved to Canada and was teaching at the University of Victoria. In 1973 Graham visited Canada, where he gave a series of poetry readings at universities and colleges. The 1970s saw a reawakening of interest in his work, as he published two of his most important collections with Faber, an *American Selected Poems* in 1979, and in the same year his *Collected Poems* **1942-1977.** Graham remained in demand for poetry readings through the 1980s, despite illness and the strain of traveling. He died, after a long battle with cancer, on 9 January 1986.

Cage Without Grievance

The advent of Graham's publishing career was not much appreciated by his family. David Wright records one of Graham's more rueful, and probably painful memories of *Cage Without Grievance*:

> My father gave 5 dozen copies away to the paper salvage people about 4 years ago. He just handed out the two packages which were unopened, straight from the printers. I had left them in the house when I went to Cornwall—thinking "well I'll always have those safe anyhow"—but there you are!

(David Wright, "W. S. Graham in the Forties," p. 54)

As a consequence of Graham's friendship with so many painters, his first book bore illustrations by Benjamin Crème and Robert Frame. This is significant in view of his later life, but the drawings do not help to elucidate the book. The first poem in *Cage Without Grievance* combines pastoral with industrial images:

> Over the apparatus of Spring is drawn
> A constructed festival of pulleys from sky.

(p. 7)

We must remember that Graham, like his father, trained to be an engineer in an area where engineering was a traditional activity. Although his later poetry has a somewhat pastoral appeal, it also draws much of its imagery from mechanical, technical activity. Fishing, of which Graham had firsthand experience, and which features so memorably in his long poem **"The Nightfishing,"** was also an important traditional feature of the area. The Clydeside landscape where Graham grew up was indeed industrial, but it was within easy reach of some outstanding natural beauty. So Graham was combining a picture of natural beauty with an industrial, or increasingly post-industrial, landscape in an environment that featured this very combination. This opening poem concludes:

> A derrick in flower swings evening values in
> And wildernight or garden day frames government
> For thieves in a prison of guilt. Birches erect
> The ephemeral mechanism of welcoming.
> And Spring conquests the law in a cuckoo's school.

(p. 7)

Most of the poems in the book confront us with a simple question: "What does this mean?" The sense of the passage above is difficult to catch, as the different levels of diction clash—the concrete "birches" seem to be operating on the same plane as the abstract "law," the pastoral and the industrial jostle with the administrative. We may gather that some kind of conflict is taking place along the lines of sexuality versus culture, in which presumably the former comes out on top. But it is not clear who the thieves are in the "prison of guilt" or what it is that constitutes "the cuckoo's school." Several influences are at work on Graham in this collection: Hopkins, Dylan Thomas, and W. H. Auden. These are influences to which much of Graham's generation responded. From Hopkins, Graham is taking the headlong rhythms, the compulsion to coin new words like "wildernight," and the packing of stresses in alliterative clusters ("garden day frames government"). From Auden he is taking the familiar psychologized landscape of 1930s British poetry, with its often-sinister combination of pastoral and industrial images. From Thomas, however, he takes the most. In his essay "W. S. Graham: Professor of Silence," Denis O'Driscoll draws attention to features of Dylan Thomas' style identified by John Berryman, the same features with which O'Driscoll notes Graham's poems become saturated:

> . . . unusual epithets, compound words, notions of dichotomy, marine imagery. Graham seemed to seize on all of them without allowing words the breathing space which Thomas did.

(*The Constructed Space*, p. 52)

Thomas' poems tend to place a hazily identified speaker, a kind of supercharged ego, within a network of conflicting and powerful associations: love, grief, guilt, spring, summer. In this vein, Graham's first poem mysteriously touches on "jealous agonies" and "funnels of fever." The poem makes a hymn out of this drama, as it measures the force of powerful feelings without defining them. The action of the poem has a surreal coloring; Graham rarely lingers to describe any specific, recognizable state, such as a man walking down a street or a casual conversation. The collection as a whole depends on the inclusion of powerful ingredients, and when a poem fails it is usually through the inclusion of too many, rather than too few, of these ingredients.

A framework of sexuality and regeneration occasionally renders Graham's universal dramas, in which this self is so enigmatically engaged, a little more comprehensible. Again, the evocation is relatively hazy, and there is no attempt made to complicate the matter by delineating realistic but difficult emotional situations. This element, combined with some of the formal features (particularly the songlike rhythmical qualities), gives the ordinary reader something on which to fasten and with which he can identify.

> Blood builds its platform on a love-me-not
> And calculates from exile the seed's dominion.
> Love cascades myrtle gospels from the nipple's hill.
> Who, with a nettle forefinger sparking covenants
> Will sting humanity and point the docken ground?

(Cage Without Grievance, p. 8)

Although the surface of this untitled poem is busy, one can pick out a basic thread of meaning. It is that love or desire creates the essential tension or conflict from which vital writing emerges. This was not a surprising position for Graham to hold; indeed, it is something of an adolescent commonplace. The language is unnecessarily twisted—the rather silly variation on "forget-me-not," portentous phrases like "seed's dominion," and the dubious personifications of "Blood" and "Love." The sexual imagery is straight out of the Dylan Thomas cosmology.

Although Graham's poetry changed profoundly over the course of his writing career —deliriously lush at the beginning, ascetically spare at the end—one feature remains constant. Each poem is treated as what we might call an existential field, that is to the say, the poem is not seen as removed, commenting on life. Each poem is inseparable from life. One of the ways of looking at how his poetry changed is to say that the poems themselves become ever more sharply aware of—and ever more self-conscious about—their experiential immediacy.

Graham's second book is really a pamphlet—its eight poems seldom exceed the length of a page and the book was issued as part of a Poetry Scotland series. Like his first book, it features artwork by Robert Frame. Graham advances a metaphor that will stay with him throughout his career: the journey. The seven journeys of the title are related to the reader in the breathless, Thomasesque rhetoric found in *Cage Without Grievance.* **"The First Journey,"** for example, concludes:

> My flourishing prophet on cockhorse scatters the sun
> Through dragonfly graves dark on my pith of travel.
> SHEER I break AGAINST those EVERMORE GLIT-
> TERING SEASONS.

(n.p.)

The poem conveys a sense of motion, if not exactly of journeying, through its active verbs ("spins," "scatters," "break"). The first word of the poem is "launched," and indeed we do have a sense of some tremendous energy, however indiscriminate, being released. The "I" of the poem is not so much an everyman as a superman, and the material of the poem provides an appropriate backdrop, or stage, for his declarations. The speaker's actions are invested with power, and evidently there is a certain amount of wish fulfillment in this immature fantasy of assuming godlike status. The uppercase typography adds extra emphasis.

Some of the excesses of the collection's rhetoric are contained by the occasional hint that these journeys are not exercises of godlike power but poetic journeys within domestic spaces or spiritual journeys—that the project is seeing the universe, as Blake saw it, in a grain of sand. Such moments anticipate developments in Graham's later work. In **"The Third Journey"** he says, "I build an iliad in a limpet dome." The poems exhibit a jumble of romantic protagonists: swains, clowns, saints, harlequins, acrobats, mermaids, and leopards. None stays in focus longer than it takes to register their elusive presence.

The burden of meaning seems to indicate that the poet is dependent on himself, not on institutionalized religion. "I call the ocean my faith," Graham writes in **"The Sixth Journey,"** and he asks:

> Who times my deity, defines my walking sin
> In curfew inches on a chain of printed chimes?
> What text is my breath on resurrected reefs
> Where west records my teething bliss of helms?

(n.p.)

Most of the nouns in the poems are accompanied by unexpected adjectives, even in this passage, where the sense is clearer than usual. The passage seems to suggest that there is no law, no institution, that can anticipate the experience of any moment. Each moment is a new experience, and the definition of its spirituality remains open.

2ND POEMS

2nd Poems is a relatively short book of twenty-three poems. The rather obscure title refers in part to Graham's future wife—To (2) Nessie (N) Dunsmuir (D). The poems in this book are more carefully shaped than before—there is a noticeable use of refrain and a more restrained use of adjectives. The "I" of the poems is fractionally less impersonal and less supercharged than in the earlier work, and Graham settled on a recognizable northern coastal landscape. From this point on, the "temperature" of the environment in his poetry, almost Mediterranean in his first, over-heated book, begins to lower, till it reaches the arctic conditions of *Malcolm Mooney's Land.* Graham also began to settle on the roughhewn diction associated with his later work, interspersing his verse with some harshly accented, monosyllabic lines, as in **"The Bright Building"**:

> You in a squad of dead pecked by the tides
> Speak as likely as the sea rolls its stones
>
> (*2nd Poems,* p. 18)

The objects with which the poems are furnished swing toward the recognizable. The volume also illustrates a tendency firmly established in his style: the use of compound nouns to create heavily stressed neologisms. Graham was particularly fond of coining compounds with the word "sea," such as "seanight" and "sealaw."

However, to adopt a phrase used by Seamus Heaney, Graham still had the veins bulging in his biro. The first five lines of **"The Crowd of Birds and Children"** illustrate some of the improvements in as well as the lingering vices of Graham's style:

> Beginning to be very still
> I know the country puffed green through the glens.
> I see the tree's folly appleing into angels
> Dress up the sun as my brother
> And climb slow branches and religious miracles.
>
> (*2nd Poems,* p. 27)

Here the opening line exhibits the syntactic ambiguity that also features at the start of **"The Nightfishing."** The subordinate clause of the first line might be referring to any, or even all, of the nouns in the next line. It could also be taken as a statement about itself, or even about the change that was taking place in Graham's poetry, which was beginning to be very still. The second line features the typically quirky adjective "puffed," which is just about successful, but the neologistic verb "appleing" in the third line is excessive, especially when surrounded by the portentous religious imagery. In later volumes, Graham retained the kind of dignity he achieves in the first two lines of **"The Crowd of Birds and Children,"** but he progressively dropped the overheated rhetoric of the next three.

The more recognizable landscape of these poems is partly generated by Graham's use of names that refer to the Scottish landscape, such as Calder and Lanarkshire. Equally important, he used fewer exotic proper nouns drawn from books rather than from experience. The result was greater consistency in the texture of the verse.

THE WHITE THRESHOLD

This significant transitional volume was also the first of Graham's to be published by the preeminent British poetry firm Faber and Faber. The book was accepted for publication by T. S. Eliot. Eliot and Graham often met for lunch to discuss poetic form, a development that was immensely flattering to the young Scot.

An important feature of the book was Graham's adoption of the three-stress line. The tempo suited his contemplative style. Graham was reported to have trained himself in the form by using it to record every entry in one of his journals, an indication both of his ambitious formalism and of his singlemindedness. It is not just the three-stress line, however, that indicates a growing attention to form in his work of the period. The poems in *The White Threshold* are carefully shaped in a variety of ways with regular stanza forms, including ballad forms, tercets, quatrains, Yeatsian nine-line stanzas, and stanzas with patterned alterations of their line lengths. There are a vast number of compounds in this book based on the word "sea": "seawind," "sea-lamb," "sea-tombs," "seagreat," "seachanged," "sea-martyrdom," "seabraes," and "seabent"—a list that could readily be extended. The influence of the sea can even be felt in the titles: **"Men Sign the Sea," "Night's Fall Unlocks the Dirge of the Sea," "Three Poems of Drowning,"** and **"The Voyages of Alfred Wallis"** (the latter significantly draws a parallel between voyaging and painting). Drowning is a major motif, eliciting comparisons to J. M. Synge's *Riders to the Sea* as will be discussed later. Such consistency of diction and subject matter allows the poems to speak to each other, and *The White Threshold* works well as a book. It ends with three letters to members of Graham's family—his brother, father, and mother—again demonstrating his fondness for the letter as a form.

The use of adjectives is markedly restrained, making descriptions crisper, and the diction becomes more harsh and clipped. This more measured style allows individual lines to stand out in a way they could never have in his earliest work, as in the last stanza of **"Shian Bay"**:

> Last gale washed five into the bay's stretched arms,
> Four drowned men and a boy drowned into shelter.
> The stones roll out to shelter in the sea.
>
> (*The White Threshold,* p. 39)

The dignified finality of the last line, charged by the disturbing ambiguity of the word shelter marks a new, more powerful kind of effect in Graham's work. The diction is unforced and simple, and the effects are gained by the use of somber understatement. Since the book is so wholly given over to maritime influences, it is fitting that the poem ends with the word "sea." The use of the sea as a constant point of reference had become a fully established motif by the time of *The White Threshold,* although Graham had yet to make such startling use of it as later on.

The White Threshold (the title also refers to the sea) was an attempt at self-definition, through an analysis of the poet's environment—the geographical and social factors that shaped his community and himself. As such, it was the closest Graham came to the mainstream of postwar British poetry, which he subsequently approached only to pass far beyond. The style of the Movement (as it was colorlessly known) called for restrained diction, careful observations and description and, more negatively, avoidance of grandiose poses and statements or mystification of any kind. Since Graham was writing ***The White Threshold*** in the years before the Movement became established, he could not be said to be adhering to any program. Nevertheless, the book showed a temporary convergence with the cultural aims of some of his contemporaries, aims that would sharply diverge.

THE NIGHTFISHING

The Nightfishing is dominated by two sequences, the title poem and **"Seven Letters."** The epistolary sequence (an echo of ***The Seven Journeys***) marked a significant advance in Graham's technique. The letters are addressed to his wife and are filled with his signature motifs, in particular the use of a landscape that is densely metaphorical and yet has recognizable features (the loch, the moor, the shore, a pub called Mooney's) combined with an increasingly self-reflexive focus on language:

> My love my love anywhere
> Drifted away, listen.
> From the dark rush under
> Us comes our end. Endure
> Each word as it breaks at last
> To become our home here.
> Who hears us now? Suddenly
> In a stark flash the nerves
> Of language broke. The sea
> Cried out loud under the keel.
> Listen. Now I fall.

(p. 62)

The use of the sea and the invocation to listen are prominent features of **"The Nightfishing,"** Graham's first major work. The poem opens with sound, not a voice: the striking of a bell. The sound has qualities of command and strangeness, a solemnity that announces change. That the poem opens with a sound also reminds us of Graham's knowledge of, and love for, music. As a young man he was an enthusiast for choirs and singers and traveled into Glasgow whenever he could to hear the best of them. **"The Nightfishing"** has a markedly musical form, opening with a slow, dignified movement and gradually accelerating into the sonic storm of the long third section, until calming toward its conclusion. When reading this poem,

Graham performed like a cross between an opera singer and a stage actor, as his friend Edwin Morgan has testified:

> I have his own copy of the programme he used for a reading at the Institute of Contemporary Arts in London on 26 November 1957, and the margins are spattered with handwritten commands to himself, almost in the manner of musical annotation, indicating exactly how particular lines are (or are not!) to be delivered. He writes: "as clearly enunciated as possible," "as formal and mechanical as possible," "slow easy conversational," "shock," "take it easy," "these words slow and separate," "don't ham this," "almost casual," "slay them."
>
> (Edwin Morgan, "W. S. Graham and Voice,'" in *The Constructed Space,* pp. 76-77)

The opening of **"The Nightfishing"** is a call to attention, reminding us of Graham's uneasy desire to make a connection with the listener. He treated the poem as a tour de force but began by starting slowly, recognizing the dramatic value of understatement.

> Very gently struck
> The quay night bell

The opening illustrates some of the enlivening syntactical ambiguity that operates in nearly all of Graham's poetry. It is not clear whether or not the inversion of the clause is party to an ellipsis. Is the bell striking or is it being struck? Is it the object or the subject? The opportunity to listen that the poem extends remains at the heart of his work from this collection onward. Uncertainty about who or what is acting or being acted upon permeates the work and is one of its most apparent themes. The adverbial opening, also characteristic of some of his work, asks us to pay attention not only to action but to that which qualifies it.

Although the poem is presented as a journey out to sea, the reader is less conscious of where the speaker is going than of what he is undergoing. We are not conscious of having arrived at a particular significant point; rather, we have a sense of rising and falling (particularly falling) within an ambiguous environment. **"The Nightfishing"** creates a poetics of the wave, the nature of its odyssey the oscillation. If there is progress then it is circular in nature, like Shakespeare's "waves which approach the pebbled shore, / each one changing place with that which went before."

When he was at college, Graham took part in a production of J. M. Synge's *Riders to the Sea,* a one-act tragedy that invokes the sea as a symbolic force while at the same time depicting the actual appalling conditions for fishermen on the west coast of Ireland. In his play, Synge effectively evokes the death of one of the fishermen, and anticipates the death of another, through the clothes retrieved from a drowned body. Although none of the action actually takes place on the sea, it figures as an immensely powerful offstage presence, with the islanders like prisoners encircled by its malevolence. The atmosphere is of doom and foreboding. In **"The Nightfishing,"** the outlook is not as bleak, informed as it is by Graham's energetic melancholy. Nevertheless, Graham uses clothing in a way similar to Synge; the sea is presented as an all-encompassing, all-penetrating entity, which has even worked its way into what the speaker wears:

> Here we dress up in a new grave,
> The fish-boots with their herring-scales
> Inlaid as silver of a good week,
> The jersey knitted close as nerves

> *(The Nightfishing,* p. 18)

This quote from section II of the poem follows the speaker's discussion of the material conditions in which he has grown up. Again, as in Synge, the encroaching symbolism of the sea as a force of nature is not allowed to obscure bald observations about how harsh living conditions are for the speaker. This kind of grounding is absent from Graham's first book, ***Cage Without Grievance.*** The use of clothing details is of a piece with points of technical authenticity ("tethers and springropes," "corks / And bladders") sprinkled throughout the text, from which the poem greatly benefits.

If Graham's poem is not a depiction of physical death, as in *Riders to the Sea,* it nevertheless anticipates and conveys a metaphysical death undergone by the speaker. The experience of the sea, which becomes a metaphor for all life-changing experience, focuses on the death of identity through experience—words are inadequate to convey what happens and need constantly to be renewed, as in the third section:

> This mingling element
> Gives up myself. Words travel from what they once
> Passed silence with. Here, in this intricate death,
> He goes as fixed on silence as ever he'll be.

> *(The Nightfishing,* p. 27)

Another point of connection between **"The Nightfishing"** and *Riders to the Sea* is the association of the grave with domestic space:

> I sat rested at the grave's table
> Saying his epitaph who shall
> Saying his epitaph who shall
> After me to shout farewell.

> *(The Nightfishing,* p. 31)

Other antecedents of the poem include Pound's "The Seafarer," Nansen's *Far North,* and *Moby-Dick.* It also bears comparison with the maritime imagery and religious or quasi-religious existentialism in Robert Lowell's "The Quaker Graveyard at Nantucket," T. S. Eliot's "Little Gidding," and parts of David Jones's much longer modernist sequence, "The Anathemata."

MALCOLM MOONEY'S LAND

Before embarking on a reading tour of Canada in 1973, when he was promoting ***Malcolm Mooney's Land,*** Graham wrote to a lecturer friend at the Calgary School of Art. Asking about the best approach to Canadian audiences, Graham revealed how he saw the relationship between his background and his poetry:

> About the class thing. What shall I do? I suppose I am lower working class. Shall I be superior or inferior? How shall I behave? What shall I wear? I'm coming anyhow and I'll have to make the best of it fuckthem.

Graham's anxiety and self-consciousness were reflected in the stance he took in his poetry. Calvin Bedient, in *Eight Contemporary Poets,* speaks of Graham's style as "having gained the surprised ring of one who had never expected to hear himself speak" (p. 173). One might add that part of the pathos of his later poetry in particular is the articulation of a voice that does not assume it will be heard. In their varying ways, the more public poets of the 1960s, like Robert Lowell and Allen Ginsberg, wrote to command attention; an audience was readily assumed to exist. Graham never counted on an audience. The neglect of his writing must have hurt and it is mirrored by the startling isolation of the speakers in ***Malcolm Mooney's Land.***

Graham's apprehensions about language come starkly into view in the book. They could be considered with reference to lines from W. H. Auden's elegy "In Memory of W. B. Yeats": "The words of a dead man / Are modified in the guts of the living." Graham could not be certain about his words once they had been digested by his readers, and this troubled him.

The volume opens spectacularly with the title poem, which introduces us to the frigid landscape of the whole book, a snowscape that in its emptiness, is even more uncompromisingly metaphorical than the seascapes of his earlier work. In the title poem, which is divided into five sections, we read, as if in a journal, the words of an arctic explorer who is trying to come to terms with the extreme conditions of his journey. Here, then, is the definitive Graham figure, a seeker thrown entirely on his own resources, desperate to connect with others, yet facing the obstacles of the definitive Graham landscape, the blinding, page-like whiteness of the snow. The seeker is surrounded by figures and memories that rise beguilingly out of the whiteness as if to mock him with their presence. From time to time, he hallucinates a surreal yet significant event:

Enough
Voices are with me here and more
The further I go. Yesterday
I heard the telephone ringing deep
Down in a blue crevasse.
I did not answer it and could
Hardly bear to pass.

(p. 12)

Commenting on his own book for a *Poetry Society Bulletin,* Graham wrote that he was aware that a poem was not like a telephone call, because you can never hear a voice speaking back. Thus the unanswered imaginary telephone in the ice of **"Malcolm Mooney's Land"** partly stands for a possibility that is closed to this explorer and to any poet.

Again indicating Graham's fondness for the epistolary form, the explorer in **"Malcolm Mooney's Land"** sometimes writes his journal as if it were a letter that has been found or is about to be found, like a message in a bottle. He dreamily addresses two figures in particular (not to be confused with any actual people in Graham's life) who may be his loved ones, "Elizabeth" (possibly his wife or lover) and "the boy" (possibly his son). Speaking of his expedition, the explorer urges Elizabeth to let the boy understand it in the form of a story:

Tell him I came across
An old sulphur bear
Sawing his log of sleep
Loud beneath the snow.
He puffed the powdered light
Up on to the page
And here his reek fell
In splinters among
These words.

(p. 15)

The attractive simplicity of these lines, with their almost reassuring tones, relates them to other forms we usually encounter in childhood, the fairytale, the beast fable, and the cartoon. With its imaginary creatures and its puzzling rules of behavior, the book's imaginary landscape often resembles the imaginary landscape of a child.

After the opening poem, the figure of the explorer is replaced by others who are engaged in similar existential struggles. These figures remain isolated; they are never seen as part of a cohesive group. Often, they are artists, though other figures that feature are the climber, the gambler, and the prisoner. Their lonely struggles, taken to an extreme, against conditions they may never overcome, are meant to be seen as parallel.

Given that the poems have started to consider themselves as literature, it is not surprising that other literary writings become prominent within them. One of

the foremost presences in the book is Samuel Beckett, with whom Graham admitted he was fascinated. In his novels in particular, Beckett presented a solitary voice that fails to come to terms with its own existence, although it can see no alternative to the attempt. In his essay "Walls of Glass: The Poetry of W. S. Graham," Damian Grant lists the features that Beckett's novels have in common with Graham's later poetry:

The revolving obsession with identity, consciousness, and articulating the telling of stories to create the fiction of the self; the reliance on pun and illusion as a literary method; the deepening (which this implies) as to the possibility of communication with our kind, and the admission of loneliness as one's ultimate condition . . .

(*British Poetry Since 1970,* p. 28)

Although the poems in the book are self-conscious, they are not overwhelmingly cerebral or abstract. Graham does not allow us to forget that words are spoken by creatures of flesh and blood, especially in those poems that adopt the form of a letter. Characteristically, Graham's poems have a strong emotional tug; they remain human appeals from one person to an imagined other, although he is usually able to stop just the right side of sentimentality. These qualities are particularly sharply felt in **"The Thermal Stair,"** his elegy for a painter friend, Peter Lanyon:

Uneasy, lovable man, give me your painting
Hand to steady me taking the word-road home.
Lanyon, why is it you're earlier away?
Remember me wherever you listen from.

(p. 27)

Childhood again appears in **"The Dark Dialogues,"** a long poem at the center of the book that Graham, toward the end of his life, thought was his most successful. Here the landscape of the snow shifts into a ghostly evocation of Graham's own childhood, in which he daringly imagines being, and speaks in the voice of, his parents. He describes the Greenock flat where he grew up:

Here, this is the door
With the loud grain and the name
Unreadable in brass.
Knock, but a small knock,
The children are asleep.
I sit here at the fire
And the children are there
And in this poem I am,
Wherever elsewhere I am,
Their mother through his mother.

(p. 31)

Graham's use of pronouns, as in **"The Nightfishing,"** unsettles easy identity. When we read this for the first time, we are not aware that the "I" here is not the "I" of the poem's other sections, that it is meant to be Graham's mother who is speaking. At least, the "I" is mainly Graham's mother, for the poem is too self-conscious not to admit the poet's presence himself within the mother, as in the next section he is a ghostly presence in his own father. At the same time, the poem traces a dizzying circle where Graham's mother is looking at the boy who will imagine being his mother looking at him.

Unlike his earliest work, where the poem was a kaleidoscopic field for any number of heterogeneous impressions, most of which were not arranged in any satisfactory relationship to each other, in *Malcolm Mooney's Land* the situations described and the memories revived are integrated, so that the poems behave like close relatives. The title of the collection is taken from the name of a chain of pubs, and it also has a distinctly Irish resonance. Christian names feature prominently and help to give an air of informality. The lunar associations of Mooney contribute to the evocation of a white, inhospitable landscape. In this book, consideration of language has become much more self-conscious, to an extent that some readers may feel uncomfortable. At a philosophical level, the poems have come to a point where they distrust the relationship between words and the realities to which they refer. The poems puzzle over the gaps between what is said and what was intended to be said.

IMPLEMENTS IN THEIR PLACES

To some extent *Implements in Their Places* is a book that speaks to its predecessor, despite the seven-year gap between dates of publication. The pair share a common territory and can usefully be studied side by side. *Implements in Their Places* is seen as Graham's most accessible book, which owes something to the frankness and directness of its approach to the reader; it was also to be his last. It begins with a poem in sections, **"What Is the Language Using Us For?"** In its first section, an explorer strikes out over the frozen wastes: "What is the language using us for? / Said Malcolm Mooney moving away / Slowly over the white language" (p. 11). The opening question becomes a refrain in the poem and echoes throughout the rest of the book. Reflecting Eliot's use of everyday speech in parts of *The Waste Land*, the poem includes snatches of humdrum conversation. Language is seen as limiting description, just as the "sailing terms" of sailors condition their "inner-sailing thoughts." In the final section, Graham allows himself one of his swift, sudden addresses to the reader:

> What is the language using us for?
> I don't know. Have the words ever

> Made anything of you, near a kind
> Of truth you thought you were? Me
> Neither.

> (p. 15)

The word "flying" and the figure of flight arise often and unexpectedly after periods of direct and seemingly straightforward speech, dramatically heightening the tone and suggesting a lingering unreality. **"Flying"** describes woods both in **"The Murdered Drinker"** and **"How Are the Children Robin"** and jungles in **"Language Ah Now You Have Me,"** and in each case it gives the poetry an eerie valedictory air. In the final stanza of **"A Note to the Difficult One,"** the poet finishes addressing a mysterious other (himself? a friend? the reader?) who is trying to speak:

> This morning I am ready if you are
> To speak. The early quick rains
> Of spring are drenching the window-glass.
> Here in my words looking out
> I see your face speaking flying
> In a cloud wanting to say something.

> (p. 20)

The image of flight crops up again in the book's concluding elegy, **"Dear Bryan Wynter,"** where it seems to change the scene into something phantasmagorical: "The house and the whole moor / Is flying in the mist" (p. 84). This kind of consistent use of a term or image is common in Graham's poetry, although the device is probably overused here, consistent with a slight slackening of tension compared with *Malcolm Mooney's Land.*

The emphasis on flight might be paralleled with the late work of Seamus Heaney. In *Seeing Things*, Heaney reaches a state where he is engaged with the element of air. The quality of fading into a common substance serves as a poetic equivalent to being assumed into heaven. In Graham, if not in Heaney, the movement is often downward. Journeying still takes place without any progress. As fragment No. 68 in the title poem puts it:

> The earth was flat. Always
> The mind or earth wanderer's choice
> Was up or down, a lonely vertical.

> (p. 80)

The title poem marks something of a departure in Graham's work. A sequence of small fragments (there are seventy-four of them) that have not been worked into an obvious shape, it is the closest Graham came to a poetry of process. The poem resembles one of his workboards, where a set of vaguely interrelated pieces is pinned up. Graham wished to explore the possibilities of finishing a poem without applying the polish of complete finish. The difference is not just that he is writing about language but that he is writing, intermittently, about his own technique:

> Nouns are the very devil. Once
> When the good nicely chosen verb
> Came up which was to very do,
> The king noun took the huff and changed
> To represent another object.
> I was embarrassed but I said something
> Else and kept the extravert verb.
>
> (No. 26, p. 69)

The emphasis on technique, which is more than just friendly advice for other artists, is given a fuller treatment in the well-finished **"Johann Joachim Quantz's Five Lessons,"** in which a teacher instructs his student in how to play the flute (only the first of these lessons had appeared in **Malcolm Mooney's Land**). Here the emphasis on technique has a philosophical basis. As Tony Lopez, in *The Poetry of W. S. Graham*, explains, the title poem includes:

> the use of material from early Greek philosophy, the idea of language actively participating in the fullness of creation; that is, the whole matter of the poem is most likely derived from Heidegger.
>
> (p. 106)

Graham seems to be examining how we come to know the world through the implements that we have, and the techniques that we have for employing them, a central concern in Heidegger's very influential book *Being And Time*. The fragments are what Graham makes his world out of—they are implements themselves.

Twenty of the poems Graham wrote after **Implements in Their Places** was published (plus a few not collected before) are to be found in the posthumously published **Uncollected Poems.** These are variable in quality, and some, such as **"Look at the Children"** and **"To Leonard Clark,"** seem underwritten and sentimental. Tributes to other artists proliferate, including two for writers who were old drinking companions: **"For John Heath-Stubbs"** and **"An Entertainment for David Wright on His Being Sixty."** A few stand with his best work, including **"I Will Lend You Malcolm"** and **"Look at the Cloud His Evening Playing Cards."** Overall, we have a sense of a new collection in the making, perhaps a quarter of the way to being completed.

CONCLUSION

W. S. Graham does not deserve to be neglected. From *The Nightfishing* onward, he wrote poetry of unusual dexterity and originality. His stance and his style are very much his own, and **Malcolm Mooney's Land** is probably one of the five or six best individual collections from Britain since the Second World War. He is important because he showed British poetry an alternative to the conservative poetics of the Movement. Anticipating a linguistic turn in postmodern poetry, his work sees language as an obstacle and as a gift. Experience, for Graham, cannot be detached from the problems of language, nor can it be detached from the problems of where there is no language—and only silence.

Selected Bibliography

I. POETRY. *Cage Without Grievance* (Glasgow, 1942); *The Seven Journeys* (Glasgow, 1944); *2nd Poems* (London, 1945); *The White Threshold* (London, 1949); *The Nightfishing* (London, 1955); *Malcolm Mooney's Land* (London, 1970); *Implements in Their Places (London, 1977); Collected Poems 1942-1977* (London, 1979); *Selected Poems* (New York, 1979); *Uncollected Poems* (Warwick, 1990); *Aimed at Nobody: Poems from Notebooks* (London, 1993); *The Nightfisherman: Selected Letters of W. S. Graham,* ed. by Michael Snow and Margaret Snow (Manchester, U.K., 1999).

II. BIOGRAPHICAL AND CRITICAL STUDIES. Calvin Bedient, *Eight Contemporary Poets* (London, 1974); Damian Grant, "Walls of Glass; The Poetry of W. S. Graham," in Peter Jones and Michael Schmidt, eds., *British Poetry Since 1970* (Manchester, U.K., 1980); David Wright, "W. S. Graham in the Forties—Memoirs and Conversations," in *Edinburgh Review* 75 (1987), a special issue on Graham; Tony Lopez, *The Poetry of W. S. Graham* (Edinburgh, 1989); Ronnie Duncan and Jonathan Davidson, eds., *The Constructed Space: A Celebration of W. S. Graham* (Lincoln, U.K., 1994).

Edward Larrissy (essay date 2007)

SOURCE: Larrissy, Edward. "Languages of Modernism: William Empson, Dylan Thomas, W. S. Graham." In *The Cambridge Companion to Twentieth-Century English Poetry,* edited by Neil Corcoran, pp. 131-44. Cambridge: Cambridge University Press, 2007.

[*In the following essay, Larrissy sketches a number of contrasts and continuities in the approaches of Graham, William Empson, and Dylan Thomas to poetic modernism.*]

If one wishes to understand the attitude to their craft of British poets of the mid-twentieth century, the influence of T. S. Eliot, both in his poetry and his criticism, is one of the most important facts to consider. This is true even where that influence is mediated or qualified, but in the case of William Empson it is direct and avowed. Empson's *Seven Types of Ambiguity* (1930) and *The Structure of Complex Words* (1951) are developments of Eliot's shift away from 'personality' and 'emotion' towards the discovery of feelings of which the identifiable components of the poem were the only true gauge. A more proximate influence on Empson's thinking was his Cambridge tutor, I. A. Richards, but Eliot lies behind Richards too and is a more pervasive point of reference for poets.

The revolution that Eliot wrought in the reading and criticism of poetry can best be illustrated by a compilation of assertions from the essays collected in *The Sacred Wood*. In the best-known of these, 'Tradition and the Individual Talent' (1919), he states that 'The poet's mind is . . . a receptacle for seizing and storing up numberless feelings, phrases, images, which remain there until all the particles which can unite to form a new compound are present together.'[1] The word 'compound', in evoking a scientific analogy, suggests that 'impersonality' which Eliot lauds in the essay, and this consorts well with another implication: the poem becomes an object—a variegated object, compounded of different elements, but an object nevertheless. As such, it can be understood and analysed. In the essay (1919) on *Hamlet* from the same volume, Eliot makes an assertion which extends the definition of the 'compound': 'The only way of expressing emotion in the form of art is by finding an "objective correlative"; in other words, a set of objects, a situation, a chain of events which shall be the formula of that *particular emotion*; such that when the external facts are given, the emotion is immediately evoked.'[2] The 'formula' makes, or perhaps is, the 'compound'; and when the different components are put together in the right way, the 'particular emotion' will be evoked as a direct result, and without the requirement for any statement about how one is feeling. There is an analogy with the formulations of other Modernist writers, most obviously with Joyce's concept of 'epiphany'.

Eliot was an influence on the criticism produced in the dynamic Cambridge English Faculty of the 1920s and 1930s. The following formulation from I. A. Richards's *Principles of Literary Criticism* (1924) is quite similar in import to Eliot's pronouncements, and that is no accident:

> To make the work 'embody', accord with, and represent the precise experience upon which its value depends is [the artist's] preoccupation . . . and the dissipation of attention which would be involved if he considered the communicative side as a separate issue would be fatal to most serious work.[3]

The 'compound' that embodies the precise experience or emotion may be analysed and specified by the critic. And it was to this exercise that Empson brought an unparalleled clarity of purpose and thoroughness of execution.

In *Seven Types of Ambiguity*, he refers to the popular assumption 'that what the poet has conveyed is no assembly of grammatical meanings, capable of analysis, but a 'mood', an 'atmosphere', a 'personality', an attitude to life . . .'[4] He goes on to speculate that '[t]his belief may in part explain the badness of much nineteenth-century poetry'. Empson, by contrast, assumes that 'atmosphere' is the consciousness of what is implied by the meaning. He proceeds to engage in a virtuoso analysis of Macbeth's speech, 'Come, seeling Night' (III.ii.50). In particular, he fastens on the lines 'Light thickens, and the Crow / Makes wing to th' Rookie Wood.' He refers to the associations of 'thickens' with blood which have already been established elsewhere in the play. He then makes explicit the associations which radiate from the idea of the rook: it is ill-omened; and there is a distinction between *rook* and *crow,* the former social, the latter solitary. Macbeth is in the position of the solitary crow. The way he describes his rejoining society simultaneously figures his intention to murder, his sense of distinction from the mass of his subjects, and his fear of his own solitude. Empson also tries to show how the sounds of the words contribute to the overall effect, with clicking sounds being reminiscent of footsteps in a wood at night.

The technique is analytic, and while there may indeed be 'atmosphere' in these lines, it is the sense of embodied thought and feeling that Empson prizes, rather than a belief that good poetry must always make the hair stand on end. The dissection of 'atmosphere' is congruent with an attitude to poetry which takes ideas and intellection to be a natural, even if not a necessary, part of it. In this yet again Empson is true to the influence of Eliot, who, in his essay 'The Metaphysical Poets' (1921), had spoken of a malign 'dissociation of sensibility' which had divorced thought from feeling in much poetry written since the late seventeenth century.[5] The metaphysicals, however, pre-dated this catastrophe: John Donne, Eliot implies, felt his thought immediately as 'the odour of a rose'.[6] In the same spirit, the modern poet would be able to bring together the experiences of falling in love, the sound of the typewriter, the smell of cooking and reading Spinoza. This formulation is actually yet another version of the 'compound', or the 'formula'; but one needs to weigh the full implications of the idea of reading Spinoza. Empson's poetry, in its 'conceited' character, conforms with Eliot's sense that intellection was a natural part of poetry, and in particular with his high valuation of the metaphysicals. Leaving aside the question of Eliot's influence, it is in any case on record that Empson claimed that he 'definitely was not bitten by Donne until Cambridge and it became clear I wanted to write argumentative poetry'.[7] As with Eliot's account of the metaphysicals, intellection may well comprise 'wit', and witty conceitedness is a marked characteristic of Empson's poetry. This is where the play on meanings touches on that other interest of his, ambiguity.

It seems appropriate therefore to find a way into the texture of Empson's poetry at the stylistic level. Yet as so often, there is a link between style and substance, and one of Empson's most celebrated poems, 'This Last Pain' (*CP* [*The Complete Poems*], 52-3), is apt for the illustration of style, substance and link. The poem begins with a summary of the doctrine of the 'beatific vision': that is, the teaching of the Church Fathers that the cruellest punishment of doomed souls was that, before being consigned to Hell, they would be able to see and feel for a moment the bliss experienced in Heaven by the blessed. As Empson puts it, 'This last pain for the damned the Fathers found: / "They knew the bliss with which they were not crowned."' Much of the subsequent development of this idea is comprised in the following two lines: 'Such, but on earth let me foretell, / Is all, of heaven or of hell'. This is congruent with Empson's well-known and strongly professed atheism, but it also ascribes a perverse structure to the human experience of happiness. Yes, the only happiness is to be found on earth; but it is acquired only at a distance, so to speak, and always just before being snatched away. It is really this conception of the true condition of human life which is subject to development and conclusion. The following stanza indicates the development: 'Man, as the prying housemaid of the soul, / May know her happiness by eye to hole . . .'. It also provides a conveniently rich example of the uses to which Empson puts ambiguity. As for the general idea, it is close to the conclusion of the first stanza: that we only know happiness temporarily and at a remove. But the proof of the pudding, with Empson, is in the ambiguity, which is structural. 'Man' appears to be separate from 'soul', as an inferior being, a housemaid. Is it his own soul from which he is separate, or some larger entity: the soul of the world, perhaps? There is a sense in which both are true: the implication is that, just as man is not entirely identified with the sacred in the universe, so he is not at one with the part of

himself that aspires to such identification. In any case, man knows the happiness of the soul by peering through a keyhole at her bliss. But the very fact that it is something that can be peered at in this way suggests that the soul's happiness contains elements that are not as 'pure' as most people think: at the very least, something to be savoured in privacy and isolation. But there is another ambiguity: it is not clear whether 'her' happiness is that of the housemaid or the soul, since both qualify as antecedent nouns. If it is the housemaid's happiness that man may know, it is precisely a prurient satisfaction of curiosity which is the most blessed experience to which humanity can aspire. One must, however, toy with both readings, which in any case are not entirely incommensurate with each other. The effect is of a fundamental investigation of the human condition, one which embodies the suggestion that there can be no unified explanation of it, and which forces the reader to confront the deep-rooted influence of sexuality, power and selfishness in those high matters we had thought were the province of the 'soul'.

In other words, this poem indicates that 'ambiguity' is more than a matter of double meanings: it may be essential to experience. Nor is it likely to be 'double' only. As Empson himself says about the meaning of his poem 'Bacchus', 'the notion is that life involves maintaining oneself between contradictions that can't be solved by analysis; e.g. those of philosophy, which apply to all creatures, and the religious one, about man being both animal and divine' (*CP*, 290). Note that these are given as examples: they are not the only contradictions involved in life. Furthermore, not only do both philosophy and religion comprise their own contradictions, they must be to some extent in contradiction with each other, since what applies to all creatures cannot apply to a creature half divine.

Empson's meditation on contradiction is as compact with implication as many examples of ambiguity in the poems. Faced with the situation he describes, he is inclined to suggest that 'it may be that the human mind can recognize actually incommensurable values, and that the chief human value is to stand up between them'.[8] However, as Christopher Ricks has noted, this leads to an ironic danger: that one may accord an 'absolute status' to the rejection of absolutes.[9] It is a danger of which Empson was aware. Speaking of the 'embarrassing' way in which Richards, Ogden and Wood appear to posit 'Absolute Beauty' in their *Foundations of Aesthetics,* Empson remarks that: 'It is a familiar paradox; any serious attempt at establishing a relativity turns out to establish an absolute. . . .'[10]

This was a danger signalled in the very first pages of the powerful collection with which Empson first attracted notice, *Poems* (1935). Its epigraph, reprinted in the *Collected Poems* of 1955, is Empson's 'synthesized translation' of the Buddha's Fire Sermon, which evokes the weariness occasioned by the empty fires of passion consuming the unenlightened life. Enlightenment, indeed, is true freedom from these things, for one becomes 'weary of the feeling which arises from the contact of the visible, be it pleasure, be it pain' (*CP*, 3). These constitute a major example of life's contraries, and possess an analogy with what Empson refers to as 'contradictions'. But the Buddha goes on to specify that one also grows weary of the visible, 'be it neither pleasure nor pain'. This implies that one should seek 'non-attachment' even to those states of mind where one would have thought there was no attachment in any case. John Haffenden's notes to this epigraph run to several pages (*CP*, 138-52) and make it clear that Empson did not regard the epigraph as a key to his work. Yet John Wain raised the obvious question, why he should therefore continue its apparent sway by reprinting it in the 1955 collection. Empson conceded that he 'perhaps should not have put it at the front'. He does not feel that the life-denying attitude makes people any better. Yet 'it has a quieter kind of merit'. This merit is partly to do with the stance of the Buddha, beyond both contraries and the rejection of contraries, which mirrors the uncommitted stance for which the poet strives. It also has something to do with the way in which the Buddha's depiction of the human condition reflected the fears of a writer who could not accept the consolation proffered by the Christian story of salvation.

Indeed, Empson's poems are full of intimations of mortality. One of the finest, 'To an Old Lady' (*CP*, 24), develops the conceit of comparing a still arresting old woman to an exotic but 'cooling' alien planet—or to one who inhabits such a planet. So Empson not untypically connects the facts of individual mortality to a scientifically informed view of cosmic entropy. A stark paradox, framed around the contradictions noted earlier, structures one of the central thoughts of the poem: the old lady is related to the divine by being on another planet, for other planets, unlike ours, are given the names of gods. However, 'Our earth alone given no name of god / Gives, too, no hold for such a leap to aid her' This could be because her contact with the divine is something with which the modern observer, understanding the fatuity of faith, cannot empathise. Or it could be that the poem momentarily concedes that she, like us, is really of the earth and is gloriously exiled from the harsh truth about humanity. This compound ambiguity is typical of Empson.

Another poem about the inevitable approach of death concentrates on the waste which presages and prefigures it. 'Missing Dates' (*CP*, 79) is a villanelle, the repetitiveness of whose form mimics the sense of time as unredeemed repetition. Yet again, a sense of life's contrarieties is central to its thought:

> Not to have fire is to be a skin that shrills.
> The complete fire is death. From partial fires
> The waste remains, the waste remains and kills.

The three conditions outlined here contain echoes of the Buddha's Fire Sermon, but they are more sharply differentiated in their unsatisfactoriness: not to have fire, a position not fully outlined by the Buddha, is to be empty. The complete fire is death, a claim with which the Buddha would agree, but which here takes on, by contrast with lack of fire, a sense of grand if terrifying excess. Partial fire kills by the slow but relentless accumulation of toxic waste but is presumably the condition of most of humanity. It also suggests an affinity with that position, poised between alternatives, which seems Empson's recommendation for an approach to life. The poem thus develops an alternative view of his own favoured stance: a negative contrary, exhibiting his capacity to doubt even his commitment to sagacious uncommittedness.

The verse form of 'Missing Dates' is highly pondered and memorably sonorous. It is easy to forget, adverting necessarily to Empson's intellectuality, those stylistic features of his poetry which go beyond, even as they help to support and embody, the argumentative. It is not only the conceit that Empson shares with the metaphysicals: he also deploys rhetorical figures to structure an argument and he has a good ear for the music of a line, qualities evident in the concluding stanza of 'This Last Pain':

> Imagine, then, by miracle, with me,
> (Ambiguous gifts, as what gods give must be)
>   What could not possibly be there,
>   And learn a style from a despair.

The 'then' is an example of rhetorical connectedness: this is the conclusion of the preceding argument. The sentence is cast in the imperative mood: only a strong conclusion dares to start with a command. The command itself takes on added force from the alliteration on 'm' ('Imagine', 'miracle', 'me'), as does the next line, with its hard 'g' alliteration. While the 'm' in the first line might seem to suggest the dreamlike, it is arguable whether or not it is onomatopoeic, but it does draw together imagery and miracle in such a way as to suggest that the former is miraculous. The connection with 'me' reinforces the essential subjectivity of such a state of mind: one which, in order to share, we might have to submit to some pressure from another person, in this case the speaker of the poem. The most notable thing about verbal music in Empson is the way in which it operates as an autonomous means of linking ideas and images.

Empson's poetry, then, is an intense amalgam of intellection and feeling involved in a passionate scrutiny of the contradictions of human life; and considered from a technical point of view, it offers an appropriate and absorbing intensity of artifice. In these respects it is similar to the work of a poet whom Empson profoundly admired—Dylan Thomas. Empson would have no truck with the notion that Thomas heedlessly threw his feelings onto the page, regardless of their sense. In his review of Thomas's *Collected Poems* he says of the obscurity of the early poems that 'they hit you before you know how, but that is no reason for not wanting to know how'.[11] This is similar to the argument for analysing 'atmosphere', and it certainly implies that Thomas's meaning can be analysed. On Empson's account, Thomas would have agreed, and ironically enough, in the same terms as were employed by his critics. This is clear from his 'Poetic Manifesto', which appeared in the *Texas Quarterly* in 1961. Based on replies given to a research student's questions in 1951, it is thus a late work.[12] Thomas speaks of the influences on his work, and claims that the earliest of these, 'that first made me love language', were 'nursery rhymes and folk tales, the Scottish Ballads, a few lines of hymns, the most famous Bible stories and the rhythms of the Bible, Blake's Songs of Innocence and the quite incomprehensible magical majesty and nonsense of Shakespeare heard, read, and near-murdered in the first forms of my school.'[13] The 'nonsense' is not as approved as it might appear to be, for it is a product of the inadequacy of school education. That Thomas has no abiding respect for the irrational is underlined by his response to the attempt to enlist him in the Surrealist movement. Thomas disagrees 'profoundly' with the Surrealists' method, because they juxtapose words and images with 'no rational relationship', whereas he believes that poetic images 'must go through all the rational processes of the intellect'.[14]

Yet the issue shows how, even in his own day, Thomas was often regarded as an irrationalist. His Romantic themes, combined with the incantatory reading offered by his sometimes repetitive rhetoric and rhythms, made him seem a natural ally for neo-Romantic poets such as those of the New Apocalypse, including Henry Treece and Vernon Watkins.[15] Yet Thomas did not repay their admiration. He would have prized John Goodby's estimate that 'the naïvely Romantic response to postwar conditions of the New Apocalypse poets bears little resemblance to the dense complexity and lucid control of Thomas's poems'.[16] Arguably, Thomas has been the victim of an ill-considered response, motivated partly by the vagaries of literary fashion, partly by class and national prejudice, partly by the

accident of his happening to die just as the Movement was initiating a reaction against the New Apocalypse poetry with which his work had been misleadingly identified.

It is Thomas's themes which should be associated with Romanticism, but no serious critic can conclude that this proves him an irrationalist. His poetry offers a celebration of the fecundity of the natural cycle, combined with an awareness of death's inexorable place therein, and a visionary interpretation of that cycle in terms of its birth, flourishing, renewals, fading and final end. An aspect of the tentative myth Thomas constructs consists of the presence within it of what threatens life and creativity. If that sounds Blakeian, one may feel that Thomas's own avowal of the early influence of Blake is indeed accurate.[17] At the same time, as is true also of Blake, the myth, if that is not too strong a term for the tendencies in his work, has a strongly Christian basis.

But as for his style, Empson's admiration was indeed procured for 'dense complexity and lucid control', and for the conceited and metaphysical character of the complexity. The way in which Blakeian themes are conveyed in a metaphysical style is epitomised in 'There Was a Saviour'.[18] This poem describes a tyrannical god, reminiscent of Blake's Urizen, who can only hold sway over his subjects while they are enslaved in their own minds. When one escapes from his control, one emerges into a state of innocent sexual love. The saviour has his own kind of truth, though his excessive adherence to it turns it into something else: 'crueller than truth'. This appearance of truth is related to other ambiguities: while the saviour has a 'golden note', it turns repetitiously 'in a groove', so that what might have appeared positive becomes suspect in such a way that the very word 'golden' accrues some of the more negative connotations of gold: that it glitters, that it represents superficiality.

The internalisation of this tyrant's control is memorably conveyed at the end of the first stanza: 'Prisoners of wishes locked their eyes / In the jails and studies of his keyless smiles'. To be the prisoner of a wish is not quite the same thing as being simply the prisoner of the saviour: it is to have been reduced to the state of wishing rather than acting in the first place. In that case, one becomes blind to a range of things: to the fruits of satisfied desire, but also to the nature of the imprisonment itself. Jails and studies compound physical and mental enslavement, as Blake might have depicted. But the fact that these are constituted by the saviour's 'keyless smiles' suggests a psychological domination no less damaging for its apparent subtlety. The 'keyless' smiles are certainly not liberating, but they are also unnervingly hard to decode or find the 'key' to; and this is presumably a technique for unsettling the saviour's victims. But they are also smiles that do not show the white teeth resembling a piano's keyboard, and thus they are closed, ungenerous and probably at best insincere, at worst a disguise for viciousness. Finally, although the 'saviour' has a 'golden note', it is out of 'key', and thus not attuned to the harmony of things, which is a condition one would expect in a genuine saviour.

These lines are broadly characteristic of much of Thomas's work and do not conform to the caricature sometimes drawn of him. It is easy to see why he elicited the admiration of Empson. The two poets might be further compared in their use of ambiguity. With Thomas, as for Empson, the device merges with the topic of life's contradictions: for instance, there are those who appear to be saviours but are actually murderers in virtue of their very narratives of salvation. Yet for Thomas this is a recurring kind of contradiction, fastening him more securely to a repeated structure of thought than is the case with Empson. That repeated structure, as already suggested, is a fundamentally Romantic, and often Blakeian, one. Thus, in 'Fern Hill' (*DTCP* [*Collected Poems*], 134-5), we are informed that 'Time held me green and dying / Though I sang in my chains like the sea'. Here, time is both the basis of the singing and the perpetrator of the ambiguous limitations which are necessary to any formed expression. Time is also the principle of death. Thus it is that, as with the 'saviour', we are presented with a phenomenon of dual aspect. On the one hand, Time is the impetus of the natural cycle; on the other, its terminus. Yet unlike with the 'saviour' there is a life-giving aspect to it. Contemplating the radiant pastoral imagery, and the 'lamb white days' of the child in the country, one feels, alongside that of Blake, the influence of the Wordsworth of the 'Intimations' Ode. However, one only needs to think of how one might isolate the destructive form of Time as a separate figure to see how it might indeed be related to the 'saviour' and other life-denying figures in Thomas's verse. This shows how he is not really offering different kinds of cycle, but rather playing with the attitudes appropriate to different stages and positions in the same one. Thus, in addition to the opposition of life and death, what is thought life-enhancing may in fact be destructive, and what is thought destructive may be the agent of a frightening but necessary process of liberation. Such cyclical patterns, stretching between contrary poles, and either fundamentally identical or exhibiting strong parallels with each other, repeat themselves over and over in Thomas. Since they revolve around a quasi-mythical representation of the great themes of life, death and sexuality, they may sometimes give rise to the thought expressed by Neil

Corcoran that, for all their 'glamour and charm', they are 'elaborate tautologies'.[19] They certainly court this danger, and that only underlines the difference from Empson already suggested: that where his ambiguities open onto numerous points of view, Thomas's grand Romantic themes offer a sharply defined and repeated structure. This, rather than incoherence, is the identifying feature of Thomas's neo-Romanticism.

W. S. Graham is himself often seen as a neo-Romantic, and one who in his earlier work was overly indebted to Thomas. They were friends, and Graham's first book, *Cage Without Grievance* (1942), was published by David Archer's Parton Press, which had also brought out Thomas's first collection. Graham sometimes felt that he might be overfond of what he himself saw as the 'rich clutter of language' in Thomas, and aspired to something more than that.[20] That something was the 'TECHNIQUE OF MENTAL VERSE', by which he meant that, alongside the manipulation of sound, the poet had a craft for handling ideas. He explains this in terms of the way in which metaphors, and the links between metaphors, further a rich complexity of meaning.[21] And, while it is true that Graham's early poetry can be self-indulgent, in the way that it is often claimed that Thomas's is, precision is necessary here also. Graham's earlier poetry, that of *Cage Without Grievance, The Seven Journeys* (1944) and *2nd Poems* (1945), is sometimes reminiscent of the Thomas of 'Altarwise by Owl-light'. But no more than with Thomas is this because we are confronted by free association. As with Thomas at his least successful, the poem can be the result of too much care of the wrong kind. Calvin Bedient offers a number of examples of unsuccessful writing by Graham, accurately claiming that 'This is the poetry of the whirligig, the words spinning so fast that the imperial order of the world, its arrangement of time and death, is lost in the blur.'[22] He quotes the first verse of **'Let Me Measure my Prayer with Sleep'**:

> Let me measure my prayer with sleep as an
> Infant of story in the stronghold eyelid
> Left by a hedge with a badge of campions
> Beats thunder for moles in the cheek of spring.[23]

Bedient assumes that the lines are supposed to make sense, and decodes them thus: 'So prayer will consist of a dream inspired by a glimpse of nature (the hedge) and joyfully participating in its fertility (beating thunder for moles).'[24] This seems right, though Bedient would presumably not have regarded it as an exhaustive explication. Thus, that prayer should be measured with sleep suggests the moderating influence of dreams, even as they further a prayer which is formed by the waking mind, but which may perhaps be too insistent at that level. So dream is protective, and this is why it is said to occur within the stronghold of the eyelid. What it protects is the innocent imagination of one who is like an 'Infant of story'. But the dreaming imagination is itself protected by Nature, for the hedge is also protective. This is the emblem of a creativity quietly gestating potential, and it is fitting that it should wear the apparently insignificant but eye-catching 'badge of campion', a flower whose pinkish violet petals make a startling contrast with the hedgerows where it grows. The imagination still at some level deals with the actual, for while it is in a dreaming sleep, it 'Beats thunder for moles'—moles who are under the hedgerow where the infant sleeps. And since the infant is sleeping on the ground, its cheek is on the ground. So it is cheek-to-cheek with Nature, and the thunder of the pulse in its head is heard by the moles, which is to say by a representative part of Nature, a part to be found in its very depths. The overall idea is thus of a reciprocal relationship between Nature and Imagination.

As with Thomas, then, the effect is of an intense compression of multiple meanings into a charged metaphorical space. Whatever one may think about the aesthetic effect, there is more to say about it than can be summarised in terms of metaphor. For a whole poem constructed in this way, while it certainly does not look like a representation of everyday thought, docs look like some kind of—strange, exalted—representation of thought. It is as if Graham were depicting an intense mode of imaginative apprehension poised between the connection-making power of dream and the ordering faculty of consciousness. This concern with presenting a mode of poetic consciousness is typical and forms a central strand in the continuity between the earlier Graham and the later, though the later becomes more and more sensitive to the role of language in consciousness, and thus in the poem.

This investigation of consciousness is connected to a thoroughly Modernist sense of impersonality. In particular, Graham does not see imaginative consciousness as identical with the mundane self or ego. Along with this goes an impersonal sense of the poet as craftsman with language:

> The most difficult thing for me to remember is that a poem is made of words and not of the expanding heart, the overflowing soul, or the sensitive observer. A poem is made of words. It is words in a certain order, good or bad by the significance of its addition to life and not to be judged by any other value put upon it by imagining how or why or by what kind of man it was made

> ('Notes on a Poetry of Release', *Poetry Scotland*, No. 3, July 1946).[25]

In Graham's later work, the poet as linguistic craftsman and the poet as explorer of imaginative conscious-

ness coalesce. Thus it is that two of the most arresting poems in *Implements in their Places* (1977) are **'What Is the Language Using Us For?'** (*NCP* [*New Collected Poems*], 199-204) and **'Language Ah Now You Have Me'** (*NCP*, 207-9). One common element in both titles is lack of control by the ego. Indeed, language as the medium for a fundamental exploration of a wider and deeper self may lead to places that surprise and unsettle the ego:

> Language now you have me
> Trying to be myself but changed into
> The wildebeest pursued or the leo pard . . .

> (*NCP*, 208)

Appropriately, Graham is often, as Corcoran puts it, 'improvisatory and impulsive'.[26] Indeed, the rigour with which he is these things can, as his work develops, start to resemble thinking aloud, or the attempt to make a poem out of something so similar to thinking aloud that it remains only just on the right side of the shaping faculty:

> In from the West a fine smirr
> Of rain drifts across the hedge.
> I am only out here to walk or

> Make this poem up. The hill is
> A shiny blue macadam top.

> (*NCP*, 202)

Even these lines, though, confirm that the world does exist for Graham; and in his finest poem, *The Night-fishing* (1955), he makes the sea an emblem of the way in which the world of Nature, irresistibly strong, can also be so protean in appearance as to prove a fitting emblem of the interrelationship of world and interpretation. The extraordinarily dense, detailed, precise and inventive descriptions of the sea can be appreciated simply for their virtuoso fidelity, but in the end have to be understood in a wider symbolic light.

A significant fact about composing an essay on Empson, Thomas and Graham is the ease with which one may construct a linear account, moving from one to the next, picking up the same themes, and observing how these are exemplified differently in each. This is because each enacts a Modernist emphasis on the poet as rational and impersonal craftsman with words. In their particular expression of this emphasis, in terms of metaphor and word play capable of rational interpretation, they reveal their indebtedness to the revolution in poetics wrought by Eliot. It is only once this fact has been established that one can proceed to specify Thomas's poetry as neo-Romantic in its themes, and Graham's as neo-Romantic in its exploration of the imagination at work.

Notes

1. T. S. Eliot, 'Tradition and the Individual Talent', *The Sacred Wood,* 2nd edn (London: Methuen, 1928), p. 55.

2. T. S. Eliot, 'Hamlet and his Problems', *The Sacred Wood,* p. 100.

3. I. A. Richards, *Principles of Literary Criticism,* 2nd edn (London: Kegan, Paul, Trench, Trubner, 1926), pp. 26-7.

4. William Empson, *Seven Types of Ambiguity,* 3rd edn (London: Chatto and Windus 1953), p. 17.

5. T. S. Eliot, 'The Metaphysical Poets', *Selected Essays,* 2nd edn (London: Faber, 1934), p. 288.

6. *Ibid.,* p. 287.

7. Quoted in William Empson, *The Complete Poems,* ed. John Haffenden (London: Allen Lane, 2000), p. xlii. Future references given in the main text as *CP,* followed by page number.

8. William Empson, *The Structure of Complex Words* (London: Chatto and Windus, 1951), p. 421.

9. Christopher Ricks, 'Empson's Poetry', in Roma Gill (ed.), *William Empson: The Man and His Work* (London and Boston: Routledge and Kegan Paul, 1974), p. 150.

10. William Empson, *Argufying: Essays on Literature and Culture,* ed. John Haffenden (London: Chatto and Windus, 1987), p. 212.

11. *Ibid.,* p. 392.

12. Dylan Thomas, 'Poetic Manifesto', in Walford Davies (ed.), *Dylan Thomas: Early Prose Writings* (London: J. M. Dent and Sons, 1971), pp. 154-60.

13. *Ibid.,* p. 157.

14. *Ibid.,* p. 159.

15. [J. F. Hendry, ed.], *The New Apocalypse: An Anthology of Criticism, Poems and Stories* (London: Fortune Press, 1939).

16. John Goodby, '"Very Profound and Very Box-Office": The Later Poems and *Under Milk Wood*', in John Goodby and Chris Wigginton (eds.), *Dylan Thomas* (Basingstoke: Palgrave, 2001), p. 201.

17. Edward Larrissy, *Blake and Modern Literature* (Basingstoke: Palgrave, 2006), pp. 51-5.

18. Dylan Thomas, *Collected Poems 1934-1953,* ed. Walford Davies and Ralph Maud (London: Dent, 1988), pp. 104-5. Subsequent references are given in the main text as *DTCP* followed by page number.

19. Neil Corcoran, *English Poetry Since 1940* (Harlow: Longman, 1993), p. 44.

20. Undated letter to Edwin Morgan [*c.* 1950], W. S. Graham, *The Nightfisherman: Selected Letters of W. S. Graham,* ed. Michael Snow and Margaret Snow (Manchester: Carcanet, 1999), p. 118.

21. Letter to William Montgomerie, 20 August 1944, *The Nightfisherman,* p. 20.

22. Calvin Bedient, *Eight Contemporary Poets* (New York: Oxford University Press, 1974), p. 162.

23. W. S. Graham, *New Collected Poems,* ed. Matthew Francis, foreword by Douglas Dunn (London: Faber and Faber, 2004), p. 24. Subsequent references are given in the main text as *NCP* followed by page number.

24. Bedient, *Eight Contemporary Poets,* p. 162.

25. Graham, *The Nightfisherman,* pp. 379-80.

26. Corcoran, *English Poetry Since 1940,* p. 53.

Further Reading

Bedient, Calvin, *Eight Contemporary Poets,* New York: Oxford University Press, 1974

Constable, John (ed.), *Critical Essays on William Empson,* Aldershot: Scolar Press, 1993

Corcoran, Neil, *English Poetry Since 1940,* Harlow: Longman, 1993

Davies, Walford (ed.), *Dylan Thomas: New Critical Essays,* London: Dent, 1972

Gill, Roma (ed.), *William Empson: The Man and His Work,* London and Boston: Routledge and Kegan Paul, 1974

Goodby, John and Chris Wigginton (eds.), *Dylan Thomas,* Basingstoke: Palgrave, 2001

Lopez, Tony, *The Poetry of W. S. Graham,* Edinburgh: Edinburgh University Press, 1989

John Corbett (essay date 2009)

SOURCE: Corbett, John. "Language, Hugh MacDiarmid and W. S. Graham." In *Edinburgh Companion to Twentieth-Century Scottish Literature,* edited by Ian Brown and Alan Riach, pp. 112-22. Edinburgh: Edinburgh University Press, 2009.

[*In the following essay, Corbett discusses the similarities of approach to the issue (and difficulties) of poetic language in Graham and fellow Scottish poet Hugh MacDiarmid.*]

In March 1955, the year of the publication of Hugh MacDiarmid's *In Memoriam James Joyce* and W. S. Graham's **The Nightfishing,** a literary dinner was held to present an award to John Betjeman. In a book on poetic language, published three years later, the critic John Press recalls a *Daily Telegraph* report on the dinner, which was made newsworthy by Lord Samuel robustly denouncing much recent poetry as being afflicted by 'this fashion of deliberate and perverse obscurity', citing lines by Dylan Thomas to illustrate his point.[1] MacDiarmid and Graham's poetry can generally be accused of 'deliberate and perverse obscurity', and indeed the two major poems published in 1955 directly address the vexed issue of poetic language, if in quite different ways. With particular reference to these two poems, this chapter explores each poet's linguistic concerns in the context of contemporary and later attitudes to language and literature.

Christopher Murray Grieve, or 'Hugh MacDiarmid' (1892-1978) and William Sydney Graham (1918-86) might be seen as poets whose literary careers and poetic concerns are diametrically opposed. MacDiarmid's early lyrics brought him literary fame, and his combative personality, controversial political interventions and poetic ambition sustained his public profile and won him a circle of followers and a loyal audience, even when his style and opinions chopped and changed over the decades. During his life, he combined his poetry with careers as a journalist, editor, controversialist, political activist and academic, without ever yielding to the temptation of the kind of stable employment that might bring financial security and temper his opinions. His poetry in Scots and English is public, attention-seeking and encyclopaedic in reference. In twentieth-century Scottish letters, he is an inescapable monument, and he is still a household name, even amongst those who read little or no poetry.

By contrast, W. S. Graham is still a less celebrated figure, even in literary circles. Born and raised in industrial Greenock, he served his apprenticeship as an engineer before enrolling in Newbattle Abbey, an Adult Education College, in the late 1930s. He published his first collection of poems in the early 1940s; around this time, through David Archer, his publisher, he came into contact with poets (including MacDiarmid) and artists who converged on Archer's flat and the Arts Centre that Archer had opened on Scott Street in Glasgow. Through these personal contacts, Graham moved with his partner and their daughter to Cornwall in 1944; there, amongst the colony of artists in St Ives, he spent much of the rest of his life, with occasional sojourns in North America, London and Paris. His poetry, in English peppered with the stray Scottish word, is inwardly directed,

philosophical, elusive. It suffered from general neglect: after the appearance of **The Nightfishing** in 1955 he published no collection until **Malcolm Mooney's Land** in 1970, followed seven years later by **Implements in their Places.** During this long period he contributed to the sustenance of his family by selling manuscripts of his work to friends and patrons. With the publication of his **Collected Poems** in 1979, and the public admiration of such cultural icons as Harold Pinter, Graham's standing gradually grew. Since his death, his poetry has been relaunched by the prestigious publisher Faber, his letters have been edited, and his work as a whole has received dedicated attention from an expanding coterie of enthusiasts. Monographs have been published by Lopez (1989)[2] and Francis (2004)[3] alongside a critical anthology edited by Pite and Jones (2004),[4] while **Malcolm Mooney's Land** is one of three key texts chosen by Christopher Whyte to evoke the 1970s in his survey of *Modern Scottish Poetry* (2004). It is interesting to note that MacDiarmid's *In Memoriam James Joyce* is one of Whyte's three key poems of the 1950s.

Despite the apparent gulf between the life and literature of MacDiarmid and Graham, a comparison of their work yields considerable insights into Scottish poetry in the mid-twentieth century and its relationship to broader cultural concerns. This chapter takes as its starting point Alan Riach's suggestion, in his extensive discussion of MacDiarmid's later poetry: 'It seems to me that Graham and MacDiarmid might be considered as poets whose enquiry into the nature and function of language is equally essential, but which led them to develop completely different poetics.'[5]

An explicit engagement with language is clearly crucial to the poetry of both Graham and MacDiarmid. Douglas Dunn, in his foreword to Graham's **New Collected Poems** contrasts the erudite 'synthetic English' of MacDiarmid's *In Memoriam James Joyce: A Vision of World Language* (1955) with Graham's obsession with 'communication itself, with the imperatives of listening and reading, and the improbability of being entirely heard or understood'.[6] A concern with language is by no means confined to Graham and MacDiarmid. Shari Benstock characterises Modernist poets' assumptions in terms that apply equally to MacDiarmid and Graham:

> The one sacred belief common to them all seemed to be the indestructibility of the bond between the word and its meanings, between symbol and substance, between signifier and signified. Multiple linguistic experiments—juxtaposition of like words, typographical experimentation, translations of language into the dreamworld of the night or the idiolect of the mad—only reinforced the linguistic claims on meaning. The word was the one thing in this modern world that

remained sacred: it survived wars, resisted the claims of materialist culture, masked despair and exposed cultural hypocrisy. The word held within it the possibilities of restructuring and rewriting the world. The writer would succeed where God had failed.[7]

For Benstock, the writer who showed Modernists the way was James Joyce, who with *Finnegans Wake* had mastered and re-imagined the potential of language, releasing its energy anew. MacDiarmid's *In Memoriam James Joyce* pays explicit homage to the Irish novelist, and, according to Matthew Francis, Joyce was cited by Graham as one of the major influences on his work, and 'was arguably the greatest and most durable of them all'.[8] Of course, the poetry of MacDiarmid and Graham shares at least one distinctive quality with the later fiction of Joyce: all of these writers are very difficult to read. This fact is so obvious as to be a commonplace, and yet the challenging quality of their work is worth revisiting, because, although MacDiarmid and Graham's poetry might be difficult to read for similar intellectual motivations, it is not, as Riach observes in the quotation above, difficult in the same way.

The 'difficulty' of modern poetry has troubled many readers and critics; a live issue in the 1950s, it resurfaces even today. In 1958, John Press published *The Chequer'd Shade: Reflections on Obscurity in Poetry,* which begins with an account of the literary dinner alluded to at the very beginning of this chapter. Fifty years later, a feature article on current poetry, written by John Mullan in *The Guardian,* attests to the fact that difficult poetry and adventuring in dictionaries remain fixtures in the poetic firmament. Rather than Dylan Thomas, however, the avant-garde poet in question is J. H. Prynne (to whom Lopez's monograph on Graham is dedicated):

> Prynne's poems are likely to defeat the common reader; even an admirer calls them 'dense and alarming'. Though most have a poetic shape on the page, there is no recognisable human voice speaking to you in them. They are places where vocabularies from different places (economics or science, for instance) unexpectedly intersect. They do not tell stories or describe experiences. They are usually about language itself. They will probably not make you look at nature afresh, but they might send you for an interesting trip through the Oxford English Dictionary.[9]

The construction of the 'common reader' is itself a critical response to a set of challenging poetic strategies. The 'common reader' is someone who might well query the value of engaging with a poetry that, from poets such as MacDiarmid and Graham through to Prynne, flaunts its dense, alarming near-incomprehensibility. From the perspective of the late 1950s, Press's defence of obscure poetry appeals to spiritual qualities that only a departure from the expected norms of everyday language can evoke:

> Poetry is less a means of communication than a way of communion, more intense, more profound and more personal than the casual intercourse of our social life. Those who desire to share in this communion must learn to accept the strangeness and even the obscurity of a world in which the syntax and the vocabulary of analytical reason have been transformed into the grammar of assent and the language of the heart.[10]

Press's vocabulary of 'communion' and his assertion that linguistically difficult poetry can conjure an intense, profound and personal response in those who accept its challenges echo MacDiarmid's Introduction to *In Memoriam James Joyce*. MacDiarmid's Introduction and the poem that follows it both envisage an intellectual elect. Quoting an unnamed contemporary who asks 'Why should the fences be lowered till even the donkeys can jump them?',[11] the poet forms an allegiance with John Milton and T. S. Eliot, both of whom demanded for their work 'fit audience, though few'. MacDiarmid's intellectual élitism does, however, allow for self-mockery, as when he describes his poem as 'jujitsu for the educated'.

Graham, too, writes obsessively in his poetry about the difficulty of communicating, a difficulty compounded, for the 'common reader', by the wilful opacity of his writing. His early poems followed the contemporary trend of the 'New Apocalyptics', a grouping of predominantly Scottish, Welsh and Irish poets such as Dylan Thomas, J. F. Hendry, Norman MacCaig and G. S. Fraser, who sought to bring a rapturous intensity and fervour to their poetry. It is the kind of poetry easily represented by a brief sequence of lines such as the following, from **'The Sixth Journey'**:

> With Judas my head, the thunderclapping hub
> The joywheel ring of tempest-engendered wrack
> Peels round my Crusoe sky a drunken almanac
> Lights on this Galway inish my island's negro
> And swings the wrinkling sea on a servant hinge.[12]

The reader is faced with the challenge of making sense from this string of potent and provocative cultural images ('Judas . . . Crusoe . . . negro'), Anglo-Saxonish compound modifiers ('thunderclapping . . . joywheel') and half-obscured syntax ('the ring . . . peels round . . . lights . . . and swings'). The relationship between the phrases is ambiguous: does the joywheel ring light my island negro on this Galway inish, or does the joywheel ring light on this Galway inish, which *is* my island negro? The 'common reader' might complain that whichever reading is preferred, the outcome is nonsensical. We shall return to the issue of interpretation later; for now, it is sufficient to note that while Norman MacCaig relinquished and disowned his poetry of the New Apocalyptic period, Graham continued to uphold the value of his earlier work.

Indeed, much of his more celebrated and ambitious later work develops the themes and techniques found in his early verse.

Both *In Memoriam James Joyce* and **The Nightfishing** are long poems. The former was the result of a protracted process of composition and reconfiguration lasting two decades, while Graham finished his first draft of the latter in 1949. The two poems represent, as Riach observes, a very different set of poetics, linked by a fundamental interest in language. MacDiarmid's 'vision of world language' is a voracious autodidact's common-place book versified: a long, energetically rambling collage of prose passages reworked and assembled into a piece of found art. The materiality of the poetic enterprise is accentuated in the original publication by 'decorations' by J. D. Fergusson, described in MacDiarmid's Introduction as 'that splendid octogenarian and doyen of Scottish painters, who knew James Joyce in Paris'.[13] Fergusson's 'decorations' announce the poem as an *objet d'art*; while controversial in their day, the many 'plagiarisms' in the poem situate it as an *objet trouvé* in the line of Marcel Duchamp's 'readymades', his bicycle wheel, urinal and bottle-rack, exhibited as sculptures, to public consternation, from 1915 on. The appropriation of found texts into 'original' poems was always central to MacDiarmid's versifying and can be seen in his ransacking of Jamieson's dictionary for his early lyrics. *In Memoriam James Joyce* extends and intensifies the process. Robert Crawford notes that

> The technique of building fragments of older work into a new text was a common modernist practice, used by Pound, Joyce, Eliot and others, but, as in the case of Eliot, so with MacDiarmid this collage technique could bring charges of plagiarism. Later he would take long passages of other people's prose and, often with a very fine feel for line-breaks and verse movement, realign them as verse.[14]

The 'long passages of other people's prose' in *In Memoriam James Joyce* were largely unacknowledged by the poet himself, and it has been left to sleuthing if sympathetic commentators such as Kenneth Buthlay and Alan Riach to track them down.[15] The sources include novels such as T. H. White's well-known *The Sword in the Stone* (1938) and less familiar sources such as J. S. Martin's *Orchardford* (1924) and John Buchan's *A Prince of the Captivity* (1933). If there is a continuing unease about MacDiarmid's silently reworking passages from these sources into his own work, it is mitigated by the acknowledgement that transgressive, even unethical, practices can be seen in the light of Modernist appropriation of 'ready-made' texts. That Joyce offered a direct model for the method MacDiarmid adopted is evident in Eloise Knowlton's observations on the 'difficulty' of *Finnegans Wake*:

> So, what is difficult about *Finnegans Wake*? Simply put, it has no quotation marks, no means of bordering one semantic unit from another or one period of history from another. It has no ultimate singular source by which to name and refer it, reliably. It has no narrator, no 'author.' [. . .] It is from our necessarily fixed positions as modern (not yet as 'postmodern') that we find the textuality of *Finnegans Wake* transgressive, unsettling, *out of control* [original emphasis].[16]

This passage could easily be adapted to describe *In Memoriam James Joyce*. It too has no quotation marks, acknowledging the diversity of voices that contribute to its textuality. Author and interlocutor waver, unreliably. It celebrates unity by insisting on diversity, takes us on a roller-coaster trip beyond the settled solidities of individual perspective, and denies us the comfort of expected poetic conventions. Christopher Whyte is one of a range of critics to affirm that MacDiarmid's technique of uncontrolled collage is a meaningful attempt to redefine what it means to be a poet in a post-Romantic age; he notes that:

> Concepts such as originality, subjectivity and intellectual property collapse in the maelstrom of MacDiarmid's compilation which, though it can sound both overwhelming and forbidding when described like this, is at the same time an entertaining and enormously playful text.[17]

Whyte is pleasingly sensitive to the playfulness that offsets the seeming intellectual arrogance of *In Memoriam James Joyce*; after all, in his Introduction to the poem, MacDiarmid appeals not only to an intellectual élite but to 'Miss Mae West', whom he quotes approvingly as having observed, 'Well, Shakespeare had his technique, and I have mine.'[18] MacDiarmid's poetic technique in this poem is 'to illustrate the concept [. . .] of the unity of all mankind' by explicitly and repeatedly placing the reader in the uncommon position of having fully absorbed the 'literature of all times and languages, the merely good as well as the great'.[19] Time and again the reader is exhorted to recall that he enjoys a dizzying command of knowledge. By accepting the exhortation, the reader might aspire to the spiritual condition that Press alludes to in *The Chequer'd Shade*, namely, a profound communion with other minds that results in an altered perception of the world. The poem addresses the reader directly, sometimes positioning that person as James Joyce, sometimes as W. B. Yeats, sometimes as the poet's wife, Valda Trevlyn, but always as someone who has read and understood a wealth of literature, science and myth in a dazzling range of often untransliterated languages. J. D. Fergusson's illustrations sit alongside a rash of glyphs whose meaning is both concrete and (to the 'common reader') elusive. To be the ideal reader of *In Memoriam James Joyce* is to join the interlocutor in a privileged community of hyper-intellectuals, whose sagacity encompasses all human endeavour. It is not an easy reader-position to adopt; the narrator continually urges you to recall texts and writers with whom you are likely only to have the merest, if any, acquaintance; for example:

> This rag-bag, this Loch Ness monster, this impact
> Of the whole range of *welt literatur* on one man's
>   brain,
> In short this 'friar's job' as they say in Spain
> Going back in kind
> To the Eddic, 'Converse of Thor and the All-Wise
>   Dwarf'
> (Al-viss Mal, 'Edda die lieden des Codex Regius'
>   120, I f)
> Existing in its present MS form
> Over five centuries before Shakespeare.
> You remember it?[20]

While Shakespeare remains a cultural benchmark, both in the Introduction and the body of the poem, MacDiarmid is notoriously, unapologetically, anglophobic in his sentiments throughout the text, most explicitly in the section 'England is our Enemy'. Further examination shows that it is a cast of mind that MacDiarmid associates with 'Anglo-Saxondom', a genteel philistinism sanctioned by 'English official literary criticism' that might be summed up best as a lack of national ambition, a complacent tendency to belittle rather than enlarge. MacDiarmid identifies this belittling mindset with the advocacy of 'Basic English', a reduced form of English devised in the 1930s by C. K. Ogden for use in the teaching of English to speakers of other languages[21] and championed by I. A. Richards.[22] However, MacDiarmid rebuts what he refers to as 'linguistic imperialism', anticipating by over three decades Robert Phillipson's 1992 volume which takes this phrase as its title.[23] In *In Memoriam James Joyce,* MacDiarmid engages explicitly with the Basic English movement (which in an altered guise has returned in the form of current debates on English as a lingua franca today; see, for example, Jennifer Jenkins, *World Englishes*).[24] MacDiarmid acknowledges that the adoption of Basic English as a world language would carry with it the implication that 'We are richer, more numerous / More civilised, more virtuous than the rest!' and suggests instead that a world language might be composed of a core vocabulary assembled from 'the vast international vocabulary which already exists'.[25] This suggestion triggers a typical digression on potential sources of an international vocabulary and grammar, sources that include Sanskrit *sūtras,* the grammar of Wasiri Pashto (an Afghan language), various Chinese languages, Greek and Latin, three dialects of Albanian, Japanese, Hebrew, Yiddish, Tupi (an Amazonian Indian language), Continental and Brazilian Portuguese, Castilian and Argentinian Spanish, Bantu, Amerindian languages, amongst others. MacDi-

armid, of course, in this poem and elsewhere, advocated a 'poetry of fact'; it is useful to lay the stress on the first rather than the second of those two nouns: fact is here the substance from which a poetic perspective is distilled.

MacDiarmid's technique for evoking this poetic perspective, then, is to place his readers in a position where they experience a totalising epiphany, a position where they are imaginatively conversant with all the languages and literatures of the world and so apprehend imaginatively the unity of all humankind. This technique is one source of the 'difficulty' of this poem—the reader might think they need to know all the allusions, references, citations and quotations, overt and covert, in all the languages and scripts referred to and represented. They do not. They just need to accept MacDiarmid's generous invitation to *imagine* that they know them, and, like him, to snarl at anyone who might wish to belittle their vision or offer a pallid 'Basic' alternative. Despite its notorious 'difficulty', if the reader accepts the near-omniscient role offered, *In Memoriam James Joyce* can be, as Christopher Whyte acknowledges, 'an extremely easy poem to read'.[26] The arcane knowledge, languages and scripts on ostentatious display can be relished simply as displays of humankind's endless diversity and ingenuity; quarrying for deeper meaning can be reserved for later contemplation.

In contrast, as we have already seen, W. S. Graham's poetry places more immediate obstacles in the way of the reader's comprehension. The obscurity of his poetry is more in line with that identified by John Press in *The Chequer'd Shade,* namely, a departure from the expected norms of syntax and lexical usage. Matthew Francis argues that Graham, particularly in his early poems, uses the figure of 'catachresis', that is, the deliberately unusual collocations of words, or even incongruous images, such as the following:

> My need reads in light more specially gendered and
> Ambitioned by all eyes that wide have been
> Me once.[27]

Here the collocations are incongruous and perplexing: why should 'need' 'read'? Why should 'light' be 'more specially gendered'? How has 'light' been 'ambitioned by all eyes'? The grammar does not help, the syntax playing against the line division to suggest first that 'all eyes' have been 'wide' before suggesting that 'all wide eyes' have been 'me once'. Francis follows Michael Riffaterre in arguing that catachresis is a signal that the reader should strive beyond the literal meaning of the language towards a metaphorical significance.[28] The 'common reader', picking up *The Nightfishing,* then, faces a different set of challenges from those afforded by *In Memoriam James Joyce.* Instead of being swiftly borne along in a role that implies superhuman erudition, Graham's reader must slowly puzzle out the sense of evocative, but semantically opaque, wordings. The rewards, no less than the effort demanded, are different.

Gnomic poetry is as old as any recorded literature in the English language. Anglo-Saxon poets compressed images and deferred meanings in their riddles, elegies and religious visions. Chris Jones has argued strongly for a rediscovery of Old English poetics by Modernist writers, and he notes that Graham acknowledged that Ezra Pound's translation of 'The Seafarer' was beside him when he was composing *The Nightfishing.*[29] Jones also remarks on the occasional influence of Old English versification on Graham's other poetry, most obviously 'The Voyages of Alfred Wallis', which is marked by unusual compounds and heavy alliteration. Another more immediate and pervasive influence is T. S. Eliot's *Four Quartets,* whose phraseology *The Nightfishing* persistently echoes, as Ian Sansom observes: '"N. F." is in fact stuck together from little bits from "Tommy E.", beginning with an echo from "The Dry Salvages" [. . .] and continuing with many reminders of the rest of *Four Quartets.*'[30] There are other poems that could be referred to, not least Robert Lowell's *The Quaker Graveyard in Nantucket* (1946), which, like 'The Seafarer' and 'The Dry Salvages' is one of a sub-genre of Modernist poems that treat of sea-voyages and drowning in an elegiac mode. Matthew Francis confirms this point: 'A glance at any anthology of poetry of the period [1930s and 1940s] reveals a number of laments for the drowned.'[31] *The Nightfishing,* in common with many other poems by Graham, therefore invites its readers to make sense of its linguistic conundrums against a narrative frame of seafaring that extends back to the earliest verse in English and which enjoyed a recrudescence in the Modernist period. The ubiquity of the sea in Graham's poetry is perhaps at the root of Robert Crawford's characterisation of the 'surging obscurity' of his earlier work.[32] Its presence might be explained by Graham's upbringing in the Clydeside port of Greenock; it might equally be explained by the attraction of the archetypal trope of sea-voyaging to many Modernist poets.

The Nightfishing, then, offers the reasonably erudite 'common reader' a set of familiar images—the haunting bell from 'The Dry Salvages', the cry of gulls and the lonely voyager from 'The Seafarer', the sea's harvest from *The Quaker Graveyard in Nantucket*—and so the poem can at least be quickly apprehended as a variation on a theme. However, as in Graham's earlier, more apocalyptic work, the elusiveness of the literal sense of many of the lines ensures that the reader cannot regard their meaning as unproblematic.

In his exploration of Graham's poetic language, Mathew Francis[33] invests a substantial part of his argument in suggesting that Graham's 'difficulty' represents a critique of the metaphor of language as a conduit, that is, Graham's poetry problematises the view of language as a simple container for transferring ideas from one individual to another. This metaphor is unquestioned in MacDiarmid's 'vision of world language'. The notion that language is a conduit, and that it therefore automatically evokes a particular cognitive response lies (however ironically) behind some of the litanies in *In Memoriam James Joyce*; as in, for example, the following extract:

> And [we] are learned in all manners of hypnagogic
>   images
> Verbal reflexes, visual onomatopoeia
> Word-physiognomy, colour associations, tactile values,
> The psychological experiences differentiating
> Noun-consciousness from verb-consciousness,
> And the adjective state of mind from the adverb.
> The psychomotor effects of different sound combina-
>   tions,
> The fact that poetry is largely tonal and that the sounds
>   of poems,
> Especially those of lyric poetry, yield of themselves
> A mood comparable to that of the original poem
>   [. . .][34]

The suggestion here, particularly in the last lines quoted, is that the substance of language is a guarantee of its meaning, or at least of its mood. W. S. Graham struggles with the contrary notions that there is in fact no guarantee that he will find the right words to convey his ideas or mood, and that, even if he is satisfied by his own wordings, he cannot be sure that they will have communicated his thoughts and emotions effectively. *Malcolm Mooney's Land* contains two of the most familiar of many, many lines that address the inadequacy of communication. Graham asks: 'Have I not been trying to use the obstacle / Of language well? It freezes round us all.'[35] Frozen wastes, inhospitable seas, chasms whose silence is punctuated by the surreal ringing of neglected telephones—these images do not hold sufficient meaning in themselves but invoke metaphorical interpretations from readers who are primed by their knowledge of poetry, intensified by the shock of Graham's obscure rhetoric, to read texts non-literally.

The linguistic theory best suited to guiding the 'common reader' through Graham's work is not the structuralism celebrated by MacDiarmid, but later pragmatic approaches to textual interpretation formulated by linguistic philosophers such as Paul Grice and John Searle.[36] Grice famously sought to account for the human capacity to understand non-literal utterances by devising a 'co-operative principle' underpinned by four 'maxims', namely quality (that is, tell the truth), quantity (give a sufficient amount of information), manner (avoid obscurity) and relevance (remain on the topic of conversation). As Grice recognised, much communication is characterised by the breaking or 'flouting' of these maxims, and indeed most literature flouts the maxim of quality (by being fictional), quantity (by leaving the reader to infer information), manner (by being 'perversely and deliberately obscure'), and relevance (by being about strange or elusive topics). Grice's point is not that the flouting of the maxims disables communication; rather it enriches it by signalling that the co-operative reader must resort to *implicatures* to make sense of the utterances. And so, say, the co-operative reader makes sense of Ezra Pound's 'In a Station of the Metro' by establishing an unstated connection of relevance between the apparition of the faces in the crowd, and petals on a wet, black, bough. A co-operative reader will recognise that the simple assertion of these two images in conjunction with each other is sufficient to reveal a hitherto unrecognised truth, and the reader may conclude that the manner in which the comparison is made is therefore orderly and transparent.

Of course, if the reader considers that the writer is *not* co-operating, and simply producing meaningless babble, then communication breaks down. The distinction between the co-operative and unco-operative reader, the reader who will work with the poet in the mutual construction of meaning versus the reader who simply throws a book of 'difficult' poetry across the room, perhaps correlates to the Modernist notion of the 'fit audience' versus the 'common reader', though some poems, like Graham's earlier oeuvre, seem to defeat even his more ardent admirers. Even a fit audience must still be teased with exotic reading positions, sensuous imagery, ghostly allusions to a rich tradition, or the promise of a metaphorical understanding. We see Matthew Francis adopting several of these strategies in his analysis of *The Nightfishing*:

> [T]he narrator's equivalent of home is language. The ghost crew to which he belongs is the community of all those who have used the language before him. For this reason, like the Ancient Mariner, surrounded by his ghostly shipmates, he is a lonely and alienated figure, but at the same time not alone. Language is both the ghost crew and the sea itself, 'the all common ocean' whose 'lonely behaviour' causes him to cry 'headlong from my dead'.[37]

The Nightfishing is read, here, metaphorically, as a voyage to fix and capture language, seen variously as the ghost crew (with its allusion to Coleridge), the sea, and the shoals of herring that are being fished. The critic's engagement with the poet to co-construct meaning through the medium of the poem is itself a necessary negotiation of individual perspective and scholarly authority; it is part of an echoing, overlapping, ongoing dialogue between a 'fit audience' of sympathetic critics, more sceptical 'common readers' and the poets themselves. MacDiarmid, in his typically provocative manner, does the sums and calculates 'the fraction of readers / for the best work today' as five per one hundred thousand.[38] His work and that of Graham in the mid-1950s represent different ways of using the 'obstacle of language' to challenge that minority of readers without losing their co-operative and sympathetic engagement.

Notes

1. John Press, *The Chequer'd Shade: Reflections on Obscurity in Poetry* (London: Oxford University Press, 1958), p. 1.

2. Tony Lopez, *The Poetry of W. S. Graham* (Edinburgh: Edinburgh University Press, 1989).

3. Matthew Francis, *Where the People Are: Language and Community in the Poetry of W. S. Graham* (Cambridge: Salt Publishing, 2004).

4. Ralph Pite and Hester Jones (eds), *W. S. Graham: Speaking Towards You* (Liverpool: Liverpool University Press, 2004).

5. Alan Riach, *Hugh MacDiarmid's Epic Poetry* (Edinburgh: Edinburgh University Press, 1991), p. 206n.

6. W. S. Graham, *New Collected Poems,* ed. Matthew Francis; intro. Douglas Dunn (London: Faber and Faber, 2004), p. xvi.

7. Shari Benstock, 'Beyond the Reaches of Feminist Criticism: A Letter from Paris' [1987], reprinted in Michael H. Whitworth (ed.), *Modernism* (Oxford: Blackwell, 2007), p. 226.

8. Matthew Francis, *Where the People Are,* p. 148.

9. John Mullan, 'What are our Poets Writing About?', *The Guardian,* 5 October 2005, http:// books.guardian.co.uk/forwardprize2005/story/ 0,16299,1585250,00.html, accessed 6 June 2008.

10. John Press, *The Chequer'd Shade: Reflections on Obscurity in Poetry* (London: Oxford University Press, 1958), p. 24.

11. Hugh MacDiarmid, *In Memoriam James Joyce: A Vision of World Language* (Glasgow: William Maclellan, 1955), p. 18.

12. W. S. Graham, *New Collected Poems,* p. 10.

13. Hugh MacDiarmid, *In Memoriam James Joyce,* p. 18.

14. Robert Crawford, *Scotland's Books: The Penguin History of Scottish Literature* (London: Penguin, 2007), p. 553.

15. For example: Kenneth Buthlay, 'The Ablach in the Gold Pavilion', in *Scottish Literary Journal* 15 (2) (1988), pp. 39-57; Alan Riach, *Hugh MacDiarmid's Epic Poetry* (Edinburgh: Edinburgh University Press, 1991).

16. Eloise Knowlton, *Joyce, Joyceans and the Rhetoric of Citation* (Gainesville: University of Florida Press, 1998), p. 10.

17. Christopher Whyte, *Modern Scottish Poetry* (Edinburgh: Edinburgh University Press, 2004), p. 94.

18. Hugh MacDiarmid, *In Memoriam James Joyce,* p. 13.

19. Ibid., p. 14.

20. Ibid., p. 35.

21. Charles Kay Ogden, *Basic English: A General Introduction with Rules and Grammar* (London: Kegan Paul, Trench, Trubner, 1930).

22. I. A. Richards and Christine Gibson, *Learning Basic English: A Practical Handbook for English-Speaking People* (New York: W. W. Norton and Co., 1945).

23. Robert Phillipson, *Linguistic Imperialism* (Oxford: Oxford University Press, 1992).

24. Jennifer Jenkins, *World Englishes* (London: Routledge, 2003).

25. Hugh MacDiarmid, *In Memoriam James Joyce,* pp. 61, 62.

26. Christopher Whyte, *Modern Scottish Poetry,* p. 97.

27. From *The Nightfishing,* in W. S. Graham, *New Collected Poems,* ed. Matthew Francis; intro. by Douglas Dunn (London: Faber and Faber, 2004), p. 109.

28. Matthew Francis, *Where the People Are,* p. 59.

29. Chris Jones, *Strange Likeness: The Use of Old English in Twentieth Century Poetry* (Oxford: Oxford University Press, 2006), p. 153n; see also Michael and Margaret Snow (eds), *The Nightfisherman: Selected Letters of W. S. Graham* (Manchester: Carcanet, 1999), pp. 104, 117.

30. Ian Sansom, '"Listen": W. S. Graham', in Ralph Pite and Hester Jones (eds), *W. S. Graham: Speaking Towards You* (Liverpool: Liverpool University Press, 2004), p. 16.

31. Matthew Francis, *Where the People Are,* p. 81.

32. Robert Crawford, *Scotland's Books,* p. 617.

33. Matthew Francis, *Where the People Are,* pp. 3-12.

34. Hugh MacDiarmid, *In Memoriam James Joyce,* p. 77.

35. W. S. Graham, *New Collected Poems,* p. 155.

36. See, for example: H. P Grice, 'Logic and Conversation' [1967], reprinted in P. Cole and J. L. Morgan (eds), *Syntax and Semantics 3: Speech Acts* (New York: Academic Press, 1975), pp. 41-58; Mary Louise Pratt, *Towards a Speech Act Theory of Literary Discourse* (Bloomington: Indiana University Press, 1977).

37. Matthew Francis, *Where the People Are,* p. 105.

38. Hugh MacDiarmid, *In Memoriam James Joyce,* p. 123.

Natalie Pollard (essay date March 2010)

SOURCE: Pollard, Natalie. "'The pages are bugged': The Politics of Listening in the Poetry of W. S. Graham." *Cambridge Quarterly* 39, no. 1 (March 2010): 1-22.

[*In the following essay, Pollard argues for the essential public and political nature of Graham's poetry—in contrast to perhaps the majority of Graham critics.*]

. . . this dedication is for others to read:
These are private words addressed to you in public.

'A Dedication to My Wife', T. S. Eliot

'The poetry of a people takes its life from the people's speech and in turn gives life to it', T. S. Eliot wrote in 1932.[1] Eliot's pronouncement underlines at least one respect in which twentieth-century writers insisted that we explore language—colloquial and academic, political and aesthetic—as a powerful political and cultural force. This essay takes as its focus a contemporary writer for whom that Eliotic notion significantly shapes the sense of writing as a peopled, civil act: the Scottish poet W. S. Graham. One might recall Graham as a neo-Romantic 1940s poet, whose densely verbally playful early lyrics were initially detrimentally associated with Dylan Thomas and the New Apocalypse. Graham began to rise to critical acclaim in the 1950s, with the publication of his volume ***The Nightfishing***.[2] Subsequent publication of his modernist-inflected volumes ***Malcolm Mooney's Land*** and ***Implements in Their Places*** saw a largely favourable reception.[3] Today, however, Graham remains a peripheral figure, not easily aligned with the Scottish Renaissance, the New Apocalypse, or the Movement poetics of the 1950s and 1960s. Although in Scotland his poetry has achieved something like canonical status, Graham's English and American audiences have often complained that the work seems uncomfortably out of step with the major poetic movements of its day.[4]

When reading Graham, however, one encounters a poet insistent that literary acts cannot be conducted single-handedly by an isolated figure. Graham's letters and poems envisage the writer taking shape through linguistic co-operation and interchange within the *polis*—through what Eliot termed 'the poetry of a people'. Writing, in a late poem, to his personal friend and literary colleague John Heath-Stubbs, Graham makes clear that this is not private correspondence:

> Of course I meet you here in public
> In the pages of your Aquarius.
> It is not the best place to talk in
> The pages are bugged but we must make
> Do[5]

Although the poem is addressed in the intimate second person voice, to a known recipient, it also emphasises its reception by many others. If the poem contacts its personal auditor, it must do so through publication 'Upon the pages of the world', and, specifically, in Heath-Stubbs's literary magazine *Aquarius*. When Graham adds that 'literature with courage is a thousand men', he is asserting, with a certain bravado, that the poet can 'make I Do' in that busy world of public hearings and listenings-in. Such determination ('we must') gestures at poetic triumph over uninvited auditors, but it also implies that these eavesdropping civil figures are *productively* comprising the poet by invading and scripting him, rather than the other way round: 'literature [. . .] *is* a thousand men', a meeting point of identities and voices (*NCP* [*New Collected Poems*], p. 274). Language, as Graham often insists, even as early in his career as 1945, is 'a shape arising from all men', 'wording the world awake'.[6] Similarly, in his poem **'The Nightfishing'**, where 'Each word speaks its own speaker', Graham again emphasises language's role in formulating changing identities, and alterable social worlds:

> Who asks to listen? And who
> Do these words listen to
> In some far equivalent?
> Through me they read you through.
> Present your world. Reply
> Now at the growing end
> As words rush to become
> You changing at your best.[7]

Graham's sense that language organises each speaking subject ('words rush to become I You', 'Present your world'), hints that *I* and *you* possess continually altering identities: 'You changing at your best', 'Through me they read you through'. Yet Graham's poetry is simultaneously wedded to the notion that flux provides a paradoxically consistent verbal meeting space: 'This I Is the place fastened still with movement', he also writes in **'The Nightfishing'**, 'at this last word all words change', 'my place constantly anew' (*NCP*, pp.

116-17). For Graham, the mutability of being 'Between this word and the next' is less an isolating than a shared condition. Similarly, the poet's personal language is not merely a private resource but an entrenchedly social act that binds the speaker to others—audiences, dedicatees, recipients, publishers, friends, book-buying publics, and 'the people's speech'.[8] In addition, as we will come to see, not only the poet, but 'the people' too, change, and change in, Graham's negotiable public-poetical world.

Graham's critics have often complained that his oeuvre is repetitively subjectivist, 'essentially private'.[9] Some have considered him solipsistic, obsessed with isolation, or vainly struggling for connection. Others have regarded his verse as intellectually abstracted, trapped in 'its own intoxication with language', 'excessively literary', exhibiting 'a tenuous, mistrustful dependence on the word'.[10] In contrast, I shall argue that even (or especially) at its most personal, Graham's poetry insists upon art's opening onto, and involvement in, the politics of the civil sphere. 'A way of speaking, if it is any good [. . .] creates its understanders', he wrote in a letter to Ruth Hilton in 1967.[11] The phrase, taken from Graham's personal correspondence to a close companion, insists that words are a means of mutual sense-making and social organisation. Throughout his poetical oeuvre, too, Graham uses the letter form to emphasise that personal discourse is not a refuge from the public sphere, but a means of 'creating', forging, and reworking the roles of speakers, recipients, 'understanders'.[12] Words alter and create, giving birth to selves and relations. In this, as I will argue, Graham's lyrics differentiate themselves from the mid-century realist poetics of Philip Larkin or D. J. Enright, in so far as these writers attempted faithfully to represent an amenable, agreed-upon world. Graham, in contrast, depicts a world in which words will not be obediently representative, and language neither serves as a vehicle for self-expression, nor lends itself to autobiography. Graham's sense of provisionality is repeatedly evident, from his idea in **'The Dark Dialogues'** that, 'in this poem I am I Whoever elsewhere I am' (*NCP*, p. 169), to his insistence in **'The Nightfishing'** that:

> At this last word all words change.
> All words change in acknowledgement of the last.
> Here is their mingling element.
> This is myself (who but ill resembles me).
> He befriended so many
> Disguises to wander in on as many roads
> As cross on a ball of wool.
> What a stranger he's brought to pass
> Who sits in on this place.
>
> (*NCP*, p. 117)

In such lines, any appeal to a 'true' self or experience before language is unreliable, suspect, since 'W. S.

Graham' is not a single coherent entity, nor really 'myself', but an abstract 'stranger', distanced to a shape-shifting 'he': 'He befriended so many'. If 'all words change in acknowledgement of the last', the identities of speakers and listeners are also continually on the move. The poet-figure is a shape-shifting itinerant who provisionally 'sits in on this place', just as the auditor finds himself disconcertingly listening in. Such a poet-figure is portrayed as a meeting-place of 'disguises', 'mingling elements' altering in language, a crossroads of identities and guises, where even 'myself [. . .] ill resembles me'. Semblance and dissemblance play through this writing, for each *I* cannot remain coincident with itself. Any attempt to claim a stable role as '*Me*—the present writer of | The present poem' is likely playfully to reveal itself—as does *Don Juan*'s writerly negotiation of Byron's authorial persona—as a stagey device negotiating a public readership, a self-consciously performative forgery.[13]

For Graham then, lyric language is not—nor should the poet let it appear—simply reflective, representational, or personal. Rather, one's language '*makes* a world of ideas enriching to enter'. That comment comes from Graham's complimentary, and not untactical, letter to the English poet C. H. Sisson:

> although A POSSIBLE ANGLICANISM is (as far as its paraphrasable subject goes) not near my interest it really speaks about some things which, in no language (if that is possible), are near us all. Each essay makes a world of ideas enriching to enter. [. . .] Please if you can spare a copy of anything, remember to send it.[14]

Paving the way for what is to become a series of fruitful literary exchanges between the two writers, Graham's own act of verbal 'making' in writing to Sisson establishes a shared 'world of ideas' that both can step into. Graham's way of speaking makes out of Sisson a new 'understander', a real poetic co-respondent and ally. Such agile verbal negotiation of his poetic contemporaries takes place in both Graham's poems and letters. To my mind, this indicates that his writing is not, as many of his critics have argued, an entry point into a private verbal realm, 'a bounded, protected place [. . .] [where] the author can play freely without interference from anybody else'.[15] Rather, for Graham, language is an opening onto the flexible public sphere, an assertion of one's place in the world of writers, readers, artists, critics, reviewers, publishers. In the letters, this is a world in which such well-known literary figures as Edwin Morgan, Sven Berlin, David Wright, Harold Pinter, and J. F. Hendry are addressed. In the poems, too, Graham speaks to a host of artists and writers, including the poet and critic Robin Skelton, the St Ives painters Bryan Wynter, Roger Hilton, and Peter Lanyon, and the American poet and editor Norman Macleod.

Retaining his position within these communities, however, demands a good measure of worldly savvy from the impoverished Scottish writer. 'I am well aware I write to you for my own furtherance', Graham confesses wryly in a 1969 letter to Edwin Morgan.[16] His need to beg furtherance forms a familiar refrain in the letters, which often find themselves shame-facedly requesting favours (usually financial) from colleagues and fellow writers. As if in exchange for money, goods, or poetic recommendation, Graham repeatedly proffers a conspicuous display of verbal ingenuity:

> EMBARRASSING LETTER but hold fast. It is not too bad.
>
> Dear Roger, Nessie's hotel is closed for a month and we must get over this bare bit. I would like you to lend me £5. I do mean *lend*. [. . .] I enclose a stamped, addressed envelope and hope we shall have the favour of your business in the future. It is a pleasure to deal with your firm. Yours truly, chairman of the bored, W S Graham.
>
> THE MILK OF HUMAN KINDNESS IS CONDENSED.[17]

Graham's daily realities turn out to be dependent upon clever verbal contact: language is his means of securing simple, domestic necessities: 'The £5 is necessary to pay milk and existing grocery bill and get some coal against the season's blast', 'first let me get this over with [. . .] The Electricity Bill and a bill for the glazier have come in [. . .] Now would it be best for you to post to us two cheques for those amounts'.[18] On the one hand, poetry-writing is viewed in such a lean, economic light. Writing is Graham's primary means of paying his way, not just some elitist luxury: 'This is against POETRY (Chicago), paying me in June the amount of £26 10 0. Remember this is not a funny half-blackmail-lone [*sic*]. I'll send POETRY'S cheque and you please will cash it', 'the Scottish Arts Council have awarded me £300. That is an inside WC on to our house [. . .] a wee bit recognition'.[19] But luxuries are not necessarily private matters, and singing for his supper does not prevent Graham from luxuriating in that song. If Graham's words operate as currency, the process of barter remains laced with mischief and delight, as well as prosaic frugality. It is, after all, precisely because Graham is being paid for it that he can afford a private joke, on the Scottish Arts Council's expenses: 'an inside WC [. . .] a wee bit recognition'.

For Graham, lyricism is not separate from the workaday world, from proletarian concerns, or from the economic drive for money and success. His poems and letters are public spaces, desirous to circulate and, in certain respects, to co-opt addressees. Graham is not afraid of starkly pointing up the politics of poetic patronage, even in apparently personal addresses to friends in 'private poems':

Remember the title. A PRIVATE
POEM TO NORMAN MACLEOD.
But this, my boy, is the poem
You paid me five pounds for.
The idea of me making
Those words fly together
In seemingly a private
Letter is just me choosing
An attitude to make a poem.[20]

Such writing enables Graham to poke fun at the idea of writing as an ideal realm of exclusive privacy and pure personal contact. He leads us on, of course: the title, and the style of the poem itself, are set up to lure us into thinking of the lyric as autobiographical, with readers listening in on Graham's personal correspondence. Direct address between the named author (Graham) and the really existing, named recipient (Graham's friend, the painter Norman Macleod) creates the impression of immediate dialogue, as if the poem were conversing in front of us, unmindful of its readers. The poem is written in the second person, the pronominal form commonly associated with personal contact, one-to-one conversation: 'you', 'my boy'. Notational and casual idiom—'Remember the title'—similarly conspire to create the impression of direct contact between Graham and Macleod, a correspondence that seems so caught up in speaking with its addressee that it forgets its audience. But the poem, it turns out, is highly attentive to audience reception, to being scoured more generally, by 'the vast bat of unseen eyes'. Concerned to put on a fine performance, Graham dons the guise of privation in order to entertain and intrigue his unknown readership. He writes at least as much to conjure, through address, this book-buying audience as his named interlocutor. Continually alert to its future published, public status, and to the appeal of tapping into the form of poem as letter, the poem uses the notion of lyricism as private correspondence to attract future readers. They will want most of all, Graham predicts, to listen in on words not intended for them to hear. This writing pulls the concepts of reader and writer, speaker and addressee, *I* and *you* into a complex network of relations and contacts. Such addressees are at least as much Graham's readers as his explicit, known recipients. This slippery *you* calls out for further investigation.

Graham's lyric focus on saying *you,* then, takes shape as he performs complex negotiations in the political-cultural fray. His address oscillates between resistance to and fascination with the shaping forces of social and national identity. Born in Greenock in 1918, and growing up during the second-generation Scottish Renaissance (1920-45), Graham could not fail to be aware of the significance that many of his poetic contemporaries, in particular Hugh MacDiarmid, placed upon constructing a specifically Scottish literary language. Graham was a contemporary and occasional correspondent of MacDiarmid's, but he was not a follower of the Scottish Renaissance, and he did not regard his own poetry as a platform for the assertion of national identity or cultural independence: 'I do recognise a Scots timbre in my "voice" although I can't see myself, in any way, as characteristic of Scots poetry'.[21] Graham is also strongly critical of Hugh MacDiarmid's insistence upon using, and upon making others use, poetic language as a nationalist statement. In a characteristic parody of MacDiarmid's eager reconstitution of Lowland Scottish or 'Synthetic Scots' dialects, Graham writes: 'I now consider myself as banished, more or less, from the Scottish Lit Scene, which I don't hold with and seems to get more embarrassing with its playing bards glumerin lufts keekin wi sna.'[22]

Although Graham regarded many of the aims of the Scottish literary scene as prescriptive and artificial, the poems do not reject his Greenock background. Until the end of his career Graham continued to draw frequently on memory, place, and the past, as the titles of poems such as **'A Page About My Country'** (*NCP,* p. 281), **'Loch Thom'** (*NCP,* p. 220), **'Sgurr Na Gillean Macleod'** (*NCP,* p. 223), and **'To Alexander Graham'** (*NCP,* p. 222) make clear. The lyrics also frequently incorporate early experiences of Clydeside speech and life, and **'Baldy Bane', 'The Broad Close',** and **'The Greenock Dialogues'** are interspersed with dialect words and specifically Scottish ballad rhythms.[23] Anthologists of the 1940s and 1950s, however, repeatedly turned a blind eye to Graham: his exclusion from *An Anthology of the Scottish Renaissance 1920-1945*[24] caused him anger at the time ('the smug insensitive cheek of it'), and wounded pride subsequently.[25] As late as 1970 he writes: 'I have always been a wee bit hurt (JOKE OR NOT JOKE?) that Scotland have never said anything about their exiled boy here, me.'[26]

'Exile' is an interesting choice of word, indicating banishment by others, rather than a choice willingly made, while the grammatically incorrect 'Scotland have' sets up the language of a victimising group of others ('them') against the final, isolated 'me'. That 'me'—thrust towards Graham's reader, friend, and fellow-poet, Robin Skelton—comes close to a performed address, in which Graham is able to stage a version of himself as a sufferer of years of cultural and financial estrangement (even as he invites his interlocutor to share his energetic delight in having 'just had word that the Scottish Arts Council have awarded me £300'). If Graham felt estranged from Scotland as a result of his relocation to St Ives in 1954, those feelings were, of course, partly a result of his own self-exile—not merely inflicted upon him, as the syntax of his address to Skelton rather misleadingly implies. Graham's phrasing ('their [. . .] boy') indicates both his persisting sense of belonging, and his ability loudly to insist upon it, in spite of his stated intellectual and geographical banishment. As Ralph Pite and Hester Jones comment, 'His writing arises out of a sense of non-affiliation, partly chosen and partly imposed upon him.'[27]

In the poems too, relationships with others are a mixture of choice and imposition, taking their shape as much from accident as from intention, and as much from willed exile as affinity. Alignment with others, particularly with established movements or schools of thought, is beset with difficulties: perpetual alteration and reworking make alignments precarious, changeable, unstable. Meanwhile, the desire for alignment often involves, Graham would argue, a mistaken belief that changeless stability is preferable to flux. In his essay 'Notes on A Poetry of Release' Graham writes that he *wishes* to be 'a man who searches continually [who] is a new searcher with his direction changing at every step'; a man flexible enough to continue negotiating his sense of what, and whom, he belongs to.[28] To Graham's mind, flexibility depends on resisting the urge to follow in others' footsteps. A writer who longs for a greater fixity of direction will search for more well-trodden ground, affiliating himself to institutions, disciplines, funding bodies, or vociferously forging national allegiances. Or he may court favour, attention, popular recognition. Graham, in contrast, is uneasy about setting too much store by others' veneration: 'Everybody seems to love me. But That is Not The Point.'[29]

In a letter to Moncrieff Williamson in 1950, Graham writes of his indebtedness to Eliot, who had supported him in his early work, and had shown a good deal of enthusiasm about his long poem **'The Nightfishing'**: 'A nice letter from Tommy E. saying the N.F. is a whizz for sticking together and being a long poem.'[30] Graham's phrasing is casual ('Tommy E.', 'a whizz'), and his tone lightly self-ironising. The thrill of approbation is to be played down. Even on occasions of fairly unambiguous literary success, Graham remains suspicious that recognition, flattery, and fame might anchor him, rather too rigidly, to the designs of others. Gleeful at being awarded a Civil Pension in 1974 he writes: 'Christ, what a responsibility. Dammit does this mean I will no longer be able to excuse my laziness and drunkenness by pleading money-worry?'[31] Similarly, after a trip to Canada, full of heady excitement at the success of his poetry readings, Graham is keen to deflate his ego with a reminder of the institutional character of that praise. He has some fun at the faculty's expense: 'every reading went well. I have never read better. When I came back Nessie had

had a pile of postcards from various deans, administers, fuckulty members, and plain wild students, saying how great the poetry and the readings were.'[32] If aligning himself too thoroughly with their approval would risk sliding into staid, faculty acceptability, an iconoclastic description of his admirers goes some way towards distancing him from the praise they offer. Their compliments, Graham feels, remained positioned, political, for the 'members' are keen to reward only what they already believe a poet ought to offer. In spite of their praise, 'I could feel impatience in me at their constant effort to make a Canadian culture'.[33]

Emerging clearly from Graham's work is the sense that a poet is inadequately and incompletely defined though his exclusive relation with cultural or national identity. One has to avoid confining poetry's significance to how well, or ill, it fits with literary movements, with the Movement, or modernism, or the New Apocalypse poets. But exiling oneself from trends is not the same as being excludingly private, 'inward-directed', or 'obsessed with the self'. Graham is likely to have had much sympathy with a comment made by the poet and essayist Geoffrey Hill: 'What we call the writer's "distinctive voice" is a registering of different voices.'[34] 'Distinctive' speaks of distinction, of being perceived as unique, and distinguishable. What work, then, does this 'registering of different voices' perform upon a writer's distinguished personal voicing? Hill's remark questions, first, the notion of uniqueness as individual and unrepeatable, by implying a writer's unique tone is, at least in part, derivative. Distinctive voices are not pure and original but always informed by the interlocutions of other writers and writings, manoeuvring the common circumstances of language spoken to, and with, other *you*s. Secondly, Hill disturbs the notion of authority and praise implicit in being distinguished. The gravity and poise associated with honoured poetic distinction arrives only after the messy creative event, for *I*'s 'distinctive voice' is a result of differences that have been knit together precariously: the influence of past literary masters, the tastes of the poet's present readership, the current political climate.

This voicing, then, however distinctive, is not solipsistic. 'He do the police in different voices', Eliot wrote, and used as his working title for *The Waste Land*.[35] That is a registering of the different, and authoritative, voice of Eliot that polices Hill's own comment from *The Enemy's Country*. Eliot's words are a circumstance of language that contextualises Hill's more recent noticing. Uniqueness of voice leads us back to other users, and uses, of the language. Uniqueness, in that sense, is social, negotiated with other *you*s. Those writers who receive praise for distinctiveness are likely to tell us as much about their audience, and its current preoccupations and established modes of thought, as about their radically singular departure from it. Distinctiveness, for Graham too, is inevitably measured against recognisable (read social and worldly) circumstances of language.

Viewing the poems in this public light involves reading Graham against the grain of much contemporary commentary. Tony Lopez has written of Graham's poems as 'largely isolated from an extended social world [. . .] The social presences it implies are more often drawn out of memory than from any sense of current community.'[36] Community is again sounded in the title of Matthew Francis's more recent monograph, *Where the People Are,* so that one might think Francis's book will gesture towards the existence of wider social influences at play in Graham's poems.[37] But for Francis, the community of Graham's poems is merely an *imagined* verbal gathering; and the addressees are not contact with others, but an 'extension of his [Graham's] own mind'.[38] Francis, like Lopez, speaks repeatedly of Graham's '*failure* to escape [. . .] from self-reference'. Not dissimilarly, the chapter on 'Dependence' in Peter Robinson's *Twentieth Century Poetry,* though it speaks at length of Graham's 'primary need for relationship', writes of 'this aloneness and isolation of the self [. . .] [as] an irreducible condition' that is 'only temporarily relieved' by Graham's lyric addresses to loved ones.[39]

On reading Graham it is easy to see why the idea that his work is a private, set-apart activity has been dominant. The poems repeatedly conduct intimate addresses to lovers, family members, and close friends. The *I* of a Graham poem speaks **'To My Brother'** (*NCP,* p. 98), **'To Alexander Graham'** (*NCP,* p. 222), to **'Dear Bryan Wynter'** (*NCP,* p. 258), **'To My Wife at Midnight'** (*NCP,* p. 166). Graham's addresses to *you* flag up their status as personal correspondence, as imagined dialogues between the poet and those closest to him. Graham's address to his sleeping fiancée, 'I leave this at your ear', offers a good example of what appears to be such lyric privacy at work:

> I leave this at your ear for when you wake,
> A creature in its abstract cage asleep.
> Your dreams blindfold you by the light they make.
> The owl called from the naked-woman tree
> As I came down by the Kyle farm to hear
> Your house silent by the speaking sea.

> (*NCP,* p. 166)

Such lines are not only addressed personally to Graham's loved one, they also catch her at a moment of unconsciousness, of unexpected vulnerability. It is easy for the reader to feel like a trespasser on a private scene between author and recipient. One is made to

witness an intimacy that is seemingly not intended for one's own eyes and ears; this intimate exchange between Graham and his privately hailed auditor. The poem's dedication to a *named* recipient—'(**For Nessie Dunsmuir**)'—heightens one's temptation to think of the lyric as recounting an actual occurrence from Graham's life: a real encounter with Nessie. So too, the accessibility of the writing contributes to the impression of mimesis. The poem/cage may be 'abstract', but this lyric, unlike Graham's more 'difficult' writing, presents an instantly recognisable domestic scene, in clear, familiar language: 'I leave this at your ear for when you wake'. Graham, it seems, is directly identifiable as this *I*; an *I* speaking directly, exclusively to his fiancée. Readers listen in, observers of the poet's estrangement, but distanced from him, too.

Is Francis right, then, when he points out that, in Graham's poems, 'text [. . .] substitutes for the real-time, personal, meaningful encounter between living human beings'?[40] Like Francis, we might read such lyrics as examples of Graham's tendency to draw real individuals into a constructed poetry world. Here, only imagined verbal contact can be made. Since Nessie embodies the position of both addressee *and* intended future reader, we might think we are encouraged to see 'you' as Graham's exclusive, privately hailed double-recipient. There is no room here for other auditors to participate in the dialogue, to interrupt Graham's aloneness. On this view, the poem creates a sphere of private contacts and contexts, shielding its speakers and recipients from the public realm, but also locking them in lyric solitude.

Yet these are, in several respects, illusory impressions. The lyric will not, and cannot, confine Graham and Nessie, or *I* and *you,* to passivity and textual isolation. The act of naming Nessie gives her a curiously active verbal presence. 'Nessie Dunsmuir' cannot also occupy the position of 'reader' without effecting a series of curious and illogical reversals. How could Nessie give voice to the poem's first line, for instance: 'I leave this at your ear for when you wake'? Were Nessie herself to read/speak this line, Graham's *you* would become her *I*; she would become the waiting addresser, addressing only herself. Logically, Nessie must occupy the position of sleeping listener in relation to the poem's speaker. The poem knowingly threatens mischief. If Graham's *I* becomes Nessie's own, if *you* turns into the poem's real reader and takes command of words addressed to her, the poem's sense is imperilled. The poem is not gravely, isolatedly **'For Nessie Dunsmuir'**, but a playful exploration of what it might mean for poems to encounter and address others. More accurately still, the poem is questioning the conditions required in being *for you,* and it brings that privately wielded pronoun into the resonant space of the published address, like Eliot's 'private words addressed to you in public', in the epigraph to this article. Graham, like Eliot, is teasing about the extent to which an intimate lyric of address must be spoken *by* its poet, *to* other recipients: 'A PRIVATE | POEM TO NORMAN MCLEOD. | But this, my boy, is the poem | You paid me five pounds for.' As poetic *you*, Nessie must occupy the position of sleeping listener, enabling the lyric to be 'left at her ear' for Graham's readers publicly to witness. Francis writes that Graham 'dreams of speech, and of the intimacy that can take place between people who are physically present to each other'.[41] But the poem is not merely waiting about for the waking of its addressee; it is already in the fullest moment of being when she is sleeping. In that sense, the poem enjoys its state of anticipation, a state of play that neither poet nor audience is desirous to end.

This might look as if it opens Graham to another common critical charge, of 'hiding in the safety of the text'; of a navel-gazing reluctance to make contact with his addressee. But on that reading it is difficult to account for the relationship between Graham's *I* and *you*, which is curiously mutual, oddly dialogic. Since the poem, is written '*for* when you wake', both the lyric and the woman remain 'abstract', caged, and 'asleep', corresponding counterparts, mirroring each other. The poem, in one sense, is immediate, for it is spoken almost entirely in the speaker's present tense: *I* 'leave', 'wake', 'make', 'stand', 'take'. But the poet-figure's speech and all of his present-tense actions are motivated by an event which he hopes will take place in a shared future: '*when* you wake', '*for* [. . .] you'. The phrasing implies that the lyric's own awakening will correspond with receiving *your* attention. In the meantime, the poem, like its recipient, metaphorically slumbers. Unable to prevent himself imagining that his lines require the 'ear' of Nessie to come fully into being, he imagines his poem as passive, mere potential: 'abstract [. . .] asleep'. Are 'these words', then, as Francis thinks they are, 'a poor substitute for hugs and kisses'; a lament at the loneliness of the textual condition? Graham's poem tests out this view: it implies that saying *you* is an impotent act until the address is really received by another's (Nessie's) ears. It suggests that to speak to another, in the fullest sense, one needs to be heard. Full of potential sounds, then, Graham's lines remain in a state of stilled anticipation, longing to be received by another. Yet the poem will not endorse a view of language as verbal isolation, for it turns silence itself into a form of intense provocation.

Clearly, Graham's writing to 'Nessie Dunsmuir' is neither a straightforwardly autobiographical nor an isolated address: Graham's work sets out to explore the effects of saying *you* to many others, designating a series of changeable listeners, hearers, and addressees. The impression of the poet's isolation is a carefully negotiated effect. Paradoxically, in creating the appearance of solitude the poet must pay close attention to being received in the public fray, to the presence of a readership's watchful eyes. Such a lyric neatly comes full circle, closing as it begins, in a state of unrelieved anticipation of its encounter with *you*. This *you* is both a public and a private recipient, a real readership as well as its named fiancée.

Pite and Jones have observed, correctly I think, that 'Graham's poetry often arises out of and refers to [. . .] friendships with other writers and artists'— predominantly his St Ives community of poets and painters that included Bryan Wynter, Norman MacLeod, Brian Higgins, and Roger Hilton.[42] In this, too, one should remember that Graham's apparently exclusive addresses to friends and lovers are often only in part to those named figures. His ear is closely attuned to 'speaking to you in public', and fascinated by what responses that public world will give. In repeatedly hailing private recipients that cannot, or will not, respond, Graham's poems make room for unknown voices and strangers to enter. 'I leave this at your ear' addresses Graham's wife as a sleeping interlocutor; **'Dear Bryan Wynter'** and **'Lines on Roger Hilton's Watch'** are elegies to his recently deceased friends. **'To my Mother'** and **'To Alexander Graham'** are addressed to deceased family members, while in **'Private Poem to Norman Macleod'** Graham's address attempts to span vast geographical distances after a much-lamented gap in correspondence. Such poems turn from their declared recipients, to whomever else may be listening, opening themselves to an unknown, unquantifiable *you*. These addresses are inherently double: a plural, public *you* exists behind or beyond the specifically denominated known, familiar 'you'.

One way in which Graham's poems issue this flexible invitation is by complicating the roles of speaker and addressee, often by poking fun at the notion of a stable specificity of address. Other Graham titles seek out deliberately underspecified auditors: **'A Note to the Difficult One'** (*NCP*, p. 206), **'Dear who I mean'** (*NCP*, p. 160). These poems might seem esoteric and asocial: their evasion of particular contexts and persons seems to produce abstracted addresses, unanchored pronominal play. But Graham's poems, even as they flirt with the beyondness of address, are very much inured to conversational habits from the quotidian world, and can speak as plainly, as directly, as a Larkin poem. 'I hardly see you nowadays | Being down here on the jetty | Out of town', Graham writes in

'For John Heath-Stubbs'; 'Don't fool me. Is it you', he writes in **'Implements in Their Places'.**[43] Meanwhile, a title such as **'Dear who I mean'** hardly demonstrates profound estrangement from the daily world. Rather, it indicates the text's reliance upon the everyday social sphere in which letter-writing addresses are exchanged, and from which this poem's own address takes shape. What is witty and disconcerting about Graham's lyric is that its realist details knowingly exploit the conventions of addressing speech or writing to a known other, questioning the limits of familiar correspondence:

> Dear who I mean but more
> Than because of the lonely stumble
> In the spiked bramble after
> The wrecked dragon caught
> In the five high singing wires
> Its tail twisting the wind
> Into visibility, I turn
> To where it is you lodge
> Now at the other end
> Of this letter let out
> On the end of its fine string
> Across your silent airts.

(NCP, p. 160)

Toying with the interlocutor's expectation that letter-writing will be specific, private contact, the poem uses a conventional, personal address form as the first word of the poem: 'Dear'. Yet in refusing to confirm that the words are directed at any one *you*, 'who I mean' tests out the privacy of the letter's address upon many, or any, *you*s. **'Dear who I mean'** is the poem's shrug of the shoulders at the notion of any one personal addressee (implying *'whoever'*), and it turns aside the very notions of personal address that it taps in using the letter form. The line that pulls 'who I mean' into question immediately slips out of that mode of questioning: 'who I mean but *more* . . .' More of what? More recipients? More meaning, specifically more meaning than the speaker can procure alone?

One might expect the lyric to invite 'you' to answer, but *I* dissolves the possibility of response, collapsing the question in detail: '*In* the spiked bramble', '*after* | The wrecked dragon', '*To* where it is', '*Across* your silent airts'. Perhaps Graham refuses to contact whoever might be addressed by such lines, speaking at, not with, *you*. Yet if the poem's verbal evasiveness closes down the possibility of receiving a letter back, in another sense, Graham's repeated deferrals set the stage for *your* impatient rebuke. This increasingly meandering address seems increasingly unlikely to supply the answers its speaker strains for. His audience might well be provoked to retort, or interrupt. The speaker's evasiveness works as a form of provocation to *you*, precisely to the extent that *I* appears to

vex the possibility of hearing *your* response. Graham's lines are, as so often in the late work, both 'speaking to you and not', avoiding and maintaining particular contacts.

One might also view Graham's poems as 'speaking to you and not' in a rather different sense. Graham's named *you*s slip out of their designated contexts, and beckon to an unknown audience. This readership is not companionably comprised in Graham's image, 'one like me', but figured as an amorphous crowd, or a disconcerting stranger: 'I seem to know your face from some | One else I was'.[44] This *I* speaks to *you*, but also past *you*, to unspecified, unimaginable others: 'you, whoever you are, | That I am other to', 'that step | That seems to fall after | My own step in the dark'.[45] In **'Wynter and the Grammarsow',** a 1970 poem addressed to his friend Bryan Wynter, Graham combines both the familiar and discomfiting rhythms of address:

> The titles are finished
> It was a way
> Of speaking towards you.
>
> Maybe we could have a word before I go,
> As I usually say. I mean there must be some
> Way to speak together straighter than this,
> As I usually say.

(NCP, p. 187)

This is a moment of easy companionability with a close friend: 'speaking towards you'. 'Maybe we could have a word before I go' is a way of quickly securing attention, with the unelevated and idiomatic 'have a word', just as 'a way | Of speaking' catches the colloquial 'in a manner of speaking'. Such poetry offers a great example of 'speaking straighter' than one might expect a poem to be able to. The conversation with Wynter is not conducted on a higher plane than ordinary talk, nor is it inaccessible to readers.

Yet the lines are simultaneously a comment on the complexity of such directness, and the use of the accessible and the everyday in art. Any belief in the existence of a 'way to speak [. . .] straighter than this' is undermined by the addition, 'As I usually say', which places straightness in the straitjacket of unvarying routine. The generative possibilities syntactically established at the beginning of the sentences—'we could', 'there must be'—settle down twice over into the too easy familiarity of 'As I usually say'. The inclusion of 'As I usually say' might be regarded as comfortingly commonplace, a further example of the speaker's enjoyment of the rhythms of 'straighter' speech. However, its repetition produces a slide from potentiality into inertia. The rising possibilities set up at the beginning of both sentences collapse into ungratified wistfulness, banality: something repeatedly unattained, perhaps unattainable. Although the lines declare that it 'must be' possible to attain a straighter style of speech, to iron out asymmetries, they are reluctant to do so.

After all, Graham's attempt to shape his words clearly and accessibly for Wynter's comprehension is also a way of buttonholing Wynter (and the reader). 'A word before I go' spells out the imminent departure of the speaker: *you* need to listen up, and listen carefully. The lines are in one sense speaking plainly, but they are also motivated by a desire to secure a listener's attention by creating an ingeniously crafted, familiar sound effect. Accessible phrases are part of its arsenal. They enable *I* to secure *your* assent to its interpretation of art's role, by speaking winningly, exploiting familiar diction. Such lines are as much outward-directed commentary on the difficulty of clear speech, of straight talking in art and poetry, as a private correspondence with a single interlocutor. Hailing anyone who will listen, Wynter and Graham are embarked on a shared project of mutual address, 'we', and their addressees are as much the readers and viewers of artistic works as each other.

If, however, speaking plainly is more complex than it first appears, the apparent benefits of straight speech may themselves also be called into question. It is precisely when Graham attempts to speak 'straighter than this' that his address sounds most rehearsed and comically affected: 'As I usually say'. Beckett's wittily woeful line, 'No one that ever lived ever thought so crooked as we'[46] ghosts Graham's address, here, running that isolated, exceptional 'No one' alongside much more commonplace misalignment. Graham's amusingly crooked syntactical re-modifications underline the provisional quality of the descriptive mode, hinting that language, like thought, will not stay still politely. There is a sense that any single literal, or naturalistic, description cannot be trusted; that multiple perspectives, speeches, *hearings,* are needed. For Graham, as for Eliot, Joyce, and Beckett, words and thoughts are continually on the move, and will not settle down to obey an artist's, or an addressee's, demands for straightforward representation. Words reverse the expected polarity of obedience, and start organising the poet's world for him:

> the words
> I choose, in the order I choose them in,
> Go out into a silence I know
> Nothing about, there to be let
> In and entertained and charmed
> Out of their master's orders[47]

The close repetition of '*I* choose' draws attention to the speaker's controlling impulses, his pride in deliberately selecting his language, and organising it into a well-structured sentence. But the very lines that demonstrate his single-handed precision simultaneously reveal that his meticulousness has failed to produce a regulated effect. Who is it that has charmed 'the words | I choose' from him? And to whom are the poem's current words addressed? If Graham's words have been 'charmed | Out of their [. . .] orders', are there other speakers and listeners shadowing the lines, giving orders, taking control? The poem may offer a hint in this direction when it details the 'ins' and 'outs' of its syntactical ordering. It creates a liminal spatial zone which is neither quite in nor out, but repeatedly turning between: '*in* the order I choose them *in*', 'Go *out into*', 'ab*out*', 'let | *In*', 'charmed | *Out*'.

Eliot, too, included that motif of 'turning' in his vignette-laden poem 'Gerontion'—'Who turned in the hall, one hand on the door'—between deliberate stalling and active transit.[48] The ins and outs of 'Gerontion' might be allied with the 'time to turn back' in 'The Love Song of J. Alfred Prufrock', which fluctuates between fear of *you* and desire to secure *you* as auditor; engagement with, and escape from, an interlocutor.[49] Betweenness can also be traced in 'the key' that is made to 'Turn in the door and turn once only', in *The Waste Land.*[50] Here too, turning is poised perpetually between imprisonment and release, desired solitude and a demand for correspondence. Graham's work, like Eliot's, is fascinated by language's comings and goings, contacts and avoidances. In **'Approaches'**, 'in' occurs four times, wrestles with 'out' (which occurs twice), and the tussle between them even breaks apart and exploits individual words for their capacity to carry semantic possibilities: 'ab*out*', '*in*to', '*enter*tain*e*d'.

For both poets, 'turning' flirts with a turn away from contact, as well as turning between possibilities. But Eliot's turns and returns, hesitations and delays, often speak of the frozen indecisiveness felt when poised before fearful choices: 'a thousand small deliberations | Protract the profit of their chilled delirium', 'And time yet for a hundred indecisions, | And for a hundred visions and revisions | Before the taking of a toast and tea'.[51] Such 'turning' and 'returning', 'indecisions [. . .] visions and revisions' are far from bereft of aural and semantic pleasure. The lines enjoy the repetition of rhyme on 'indecision', 'revision', getting a kick out of the very 'deliberations' they say they find chilling. Eliot's verbal ingenuity, then, holds at bay the fear of descending into the routine drudgery of 'the taking of a toast and tea', the series of mechanically repetitive actions that leave agents caught between futile alternatives: 'delaying', 'coming and going', 'one hand on the door'. Graham's verbal turns, in comparison, feel less discomfited by 'indecisions' and revisions: the playfulness of the rhythms and rhymes is less an attempt to stave off a sense of sterility or futility about making linguistic choices than a celebration of the irregularity of returns, revisions. For Graham, even repetitions are manifested differently each time, susceptible to mutation: the poems do not appeal to a fixed original act or object, from which copies can be made, assessed, or corrected. This leaves a poet's words at risk of being unregulated, wayward. But Graham finds 'entertainment' and 'charm' in this change and disruption, where another poet might identify merely a failure of verbal mastery ('out of [. . .] order'), a loss of aesthetic transcendence.

Revealing one's susceptibility to the disruption of 'what I thought was worth saying' indicates a positive adaptability for Graham, a delight in address's capacity to exhibit change, and to produce a certain degree of disorder. But Graham is less anarchically opening the work to disorganisation than exploring alternative forms of organisation. It is an exploration that is often envisaged as co-operation with its interlocutors. 'At least I keep you wound I And put my ear to you I To hear Botallack tick', Graham writes in his elegy to Roger Hilton, which imagines addressing the fiery, often raging, drunk, Hilton 'through' the deceased's watch:

> Which I was given because
> I loved him and we had
> Terrible times together.
>
> O tarnished ticking time
> Piece with your bent hand,
> You must be used to being
> Looked at suddenly[52]

Graham's address is keeping time with *you* (in both senses), and also making 'you I [. . .] tick'. But even when the speaker is able to keep his relationship with *you* going like clockwork, this consensual co-operation is simultaneously a fraught collaboration. The address, as so often in Graham, is simultaneously a plea to be co-opted by its recipient and a demand for verbal tussles: 'it is time I wound I You up again', he puns, brilliantly, extending the play on enraging *you*, on making you 'tick' as the very means of ordered poetic and temporal progression (*NCP*, p. 237). Is the poem a well-wrought object if what opens and closes the text is the foregrounding of struggle, disorder, angularity in its relations: 'I loved him and we had I Terrible times together' (*NCP*, p. 235)? Graham moves at once to create the semblance of a circular, balanced poetic order out of the disruptive and destructive 'terrible' relations between *I* and *you*, and indicates that any poetic order it achieves is still created from what is 'terrible' and unruly. The poem's end may be neatly in its beginning, but in the poem, as in the clock, what keeps such verbal tidiness in orbit is the unstable drive

for being 'wound up' by its audience, by a circular, clockwise motion that, like time's own 'tarnished ticking' 'with your bent hand' has no destination, end point or beginning.

'This living hand, now warm and capable I Of earnest grasping [. . .]—See here it is—I I hold it towards you', wrote Keats.[53] Like Keats, Graham's negotiations of his audience, and his focus on the slippery poetic relations between *I* and *you,* underline how self and other, speaker and recipient, are fluid tenets of language, continually up for change and reconstruction. This fluidity becomes clearest in poetic addresses when deictic figures of speech are used: 'I' and 'you', as well as 'here', 'there', 'this', 'that', 'now'. Antony Easthope, drawing on the work of linguists such as Emile Benveniste and Tzvetan Todorov, has used the helpful term 'marks of utterance' for these self-declaring aspects of writing (demonstratives, second person pronouns, and deictics). Easthope combines what Benveniste calls 'signs of person' with Todorov's idea of revealing 'the imprint of the process of enunciation in the utterance'. Easthope's terminology helps one to differentiate between texts that flag up their performative aspect (vocative poems, for example, that present an *I* speaking to a *you*), and texts that play down the impression of themselves as speech-acts (often realist novels written in the third person); as Benveniste puts it, commenting on Balzac, 'events seem to narrate themselves'.[54]

Yet in poems that address others as *you,* 'signs of person' are all too often mistaken for signs of the immediately personal; 'the poet himself' speaking directly to 'the reader', as though both were stable, embodied figures, occupying the same textual time and space. Graham treats *I* and *you* less as fixed and discrete entities than as changeable linguistic potentials. Terms such as 'author' and 'audience', 'writer' and 'reader' are viewed as fluid and alterable, akin to pronominal categories. Moving away from the notion that lyric address is the manoeuvre of a monologic private self estranged from others, I too have attempted to set up an alternative picture of lyric interlocutions. Address, I have argued, is a continually negotiated feature of language that establishes changeable identities, that *gives rise* to *I*s and *you*s, speakers and listeners, authors and readers. This focus on poems as audience negotiation offers new openings onto the social, the historical, and the political. Graham's work emphasises the inescapably public nature of poetic language in general, as well as its anchorage in the changeably particular public contexts of twentieth-century speech, writing, and gesture.

Notes

1. T. S. Eliot, *The Use of Poetry and the Use of Criticism* (Cambridge, Mass. 1933) p. 5.

2. London 1955.

3. *Malcolm Mooney's Land* (London 1970); *Implements in Their Places* (London 1977).

4. 'W. S. Graham remains an anomaly', writes Ian Sansom in '"Listen": W. S. Graham', in Ralph Pite and Hester Jones (eds.), *W. S. Graham: Speaking Towards You* (Liverpool 2004) pp. 11-23: 11. 'Graham has never fitted into any of the movements or canons of literary history', writes Angela Leighton in 'W. S. Graham: In the Mind's Ear', in *On Form: Poetry, Aestheticism and the Legacy of a Word* (Oxford 2007) pp. 198-219: 198. See also Christopher Whyte, 'The 1970s', in *Modern Scottish Poetry* (Edinburgh 2004) pp. 149-73.

5. 'For John Heath-Stubbs', *Aquarius*, 10 (1978), repr. in *New Collected Poems* [*NCP*] (London 2004) p. 274. All references to Graham's poetry are to this volume.

6. 'Explanation of a Map', *2nd Poems* (1945); repr. in *NCP*, p. 34.

7. 'The Nightfishing', *Botteghe Oscure*, 9 (1951); repr. in *NCP*, pp. 115, 134.

8. 'The Dark Dialogues', *Botteghe Oscure*, 23 (1959); repr. in *NCP*, p. 174.

9. See Alan Bold, *Modern Scottish Literature* (London 1983) pp. 71-5. Damien Grant writes of Graham's 'obsession with identity, consciousness and articulation' in 'Walls of Glass: The Poetry of W. S. Graham', in Peter Jones and Michael Schmidt (eds.), *British Poetry since 1970: A Critical Survey* (Manchester 1980) pp. 22-38: 28.

10. John Kinsella, 'Under the Surface', review of *New Collected Poems, Observer*, 29 Feb. 2004, p. 17; Kenneth Allott, *The Penguin Book of Contemporary Verse* (Harmondsworth 1962) p. 309; Michael Schmidt, *An Introduction to Fifty Modern British Poets* (London 1979) p. 302.

11. 21 Mar. 1967, in *The Nightfisherman: Selected Letters of W. S. Graham* (Manchester 1999) p. 210. Unless otherwise stated, all references to Graham's letters are to this source (*Selected Letters*).

12. See, in *NCP*, the poems 'Dear who I mean' (pp. 160-1), 'Seven Letters' (pp. 121-40), 'Three Letters' (pp. 98-101), '2nd Letter' (pp. 27-8), 'I leave this at your ear (for Nessie Dunsmuir)' (p. 166), 'Dear Bryan Wynter' (pp. 258-60), and 'For John Heath-Stubbs' (pp. 274-5).

13. *Don Juan*, VII. 3, in *The Poetical Works of Lord Byron* (London 1859) pp. 578-760: 677.

14. 31 Dec. 1967 (*Selected Letters*, p. 212; my emphasis).

15. Matthew Francis, *Where the People Are: Language and Community in the Poetry of W. S. Graham* (Cambridge 2004) pp. 24-5. Francis believes that poems are unavoidable forms of social engagement, but that Graham works under the illusion that they offer him 'bounded, protected places'. Graham's words thus leave his speakers and recipients feeling isolated from one another.

16. 14 Oct. 1969 (*Selected Letters*, p. 234).

17. Letter to Roger Hilton, 8 Nov. 1968 (ibid., pp. 222-3).

18. Letter to Roger Hilton, 8 Nov. 1968 (ibid, p. 223); letter to Bryan Wynter, 11 May 1968 (ibid., pp. 213-14).

19. Letter to Bryan Wynter, 11 May 1968 (ibid., p. 214); letter to Robin Skelton, 7 May 1970 (ibid., p. 241).

20. 'Private Poem to Norman Macleod', *Pembroke Magazine*, 5 (1974); repr. in *NCP*, p. 227.

21. Quoted in James Vinson and D. L. Kirkpatrick (eds.), *Contemporary Poets*, 2nd edn. (New York 1975) p. 575.

22. Letter to Moncrieff Williamson, undated, *circa* Jan. 1949 (*Selected Letters*, p. 80).

23. 'Baldy Bane', *Nimbus*, 2/3 (1954), and 'The Broad Close', *Botteghe Oscure*, 9 (1954) are reprinted in *NCP*, pp. 145-50 and 141-5. Both draw on Scottish places, dialects, and rhythms in their ballad form. 'The Greenock Dialogues' (*NCP*, pp. 319-23) incorporates dialect words, while many sections of the long poem 'Implements in Their Places' (*NCP*, pp. 240-57) vividly evoke Scotland.

24. Ed. Maurice Lindsay (London 1946).

25. Letter to William Montgomery, undated (?) Aug. 1946 (*Selected Letters*, p. 68).

26. Letter to Robin Skelton, 7 May 1970 (ibid., p. 241).

27. 'Introduction: Contacting Graham', in Pite and Jones (eds.), *W. S. Graham: Speaking Towards You*, pp. 1-9: 3.

28. *Poetry Scotland*, 3 (July 1946); repr. in *Selected Letters*, pp. 379-83.

29. Letter to Nessie Graham, 21 Nov. 1973 (*Selected Letters*, p. 269).

30. Quoted in 'The Life and Work of W. S. Graham', *Edinburgh Review*, 75, ed. Peter Kravitz (1987) pp. 6-109: 10; not included in *Selected Letters*.

31. Letter to Robin Skelton, 31 Jan. 1974 *Selected Letters*, (p. 274).

32. Letter to Bill and Gail Featherstone, 4 Dec. 1973 (ibid., p. 270).

33. Letter to Charles Monteith, 29 Mar. 1974 (ibid., p. 277).

34. Geoffrey Hill, 'Dryden's Prize Song', in *The Enemy's Country: Words, Contextures and Other Circumstances of Language* (Stanford 1991) pp. 63-82: 80.

35. This sentence, found at the top of some of the typed pages of the manuscript of *The Waste Land*, is from chapter 16 of Dickens's *Our Mutual Friend*: the boy Sloppy is described as a 'beautiful reader of a newspaper. He do the Police in different voices.'

36. Tony Lopez, *The Poetry of W. S. Graham* (Edinburgh 1989) p. 127.

37. See n. 15 above.

38. Francis, *Where the People Are*, p. 26.

39. Peter Robinson, *Twentieth Century Poetry: Selves and Situations* (Oxford 2005) pp. 74, 70.

40. Francis, *Where the People Are*, p. 24.

41. Ibid., p. 25.

42. Pite and Jones (eds.), *W. S. Graham: Speaking Towards You*, p. 6.

43. 'For John Heath-Stubbs' (*NCP*, p. 274); 'Implements' was first published, in different form, in *Malahat Review*, 17 (July 1972); repr. in *NCP*, p. 240.

44. 'Clusters Travelling Out' (*NCP*, p. 192). {?}

45. 'Dialogues' (*NCP* pp. 168, 173). {?}

46. *Endgame*, first performed 3 Apr. 1957 as *Fin de partie*, at the Royal Court, London; first pub. 1958; repr. in *Samuel Beckett: The Complete Dramatic Works* (London 1986), p. 97.

47. 'Approaches to How They Behave', in *Malcolm Mooney's Land*; repr. in *NCP*, pp. 178-82: 178.

48. In *Poems* (Richmond 1920); repr. in *T. S. Eliot: Collected Poems 1909-1962* (London 1963) p. 40.

49. In *Prufrock and Other Observations* (London 1917), repr. in *Collected Poems*, pp. 13-17.

50. *Collected Poems*, pp. 61-86: 79.

51. 'Gerontion', ibid., p. 38; 'Prufrock', ibid., p. 14. {?}

52. 'Lines on Roger Hilton's Watch', *Malahat Review*, 39 (July 1976), repr. in *NCP*, pp. 235-7.

53. 'This Living Hand', *The Complete Poems of John Keats* (Hertfordshire 2001) p. 461.

54. All quotations are from Easthope, *Poetry as Discourse* (London 1983) p. 41.

FURTHER READING

Criticism

Hendry, Diana. "W. S. Graham Writes. . . ." *PN Review* 27, no. 5 (May-June 2001): 35-6.
Recalls a 1979 poetry reading by Graham.

Kessler, Jascha. "Coming Down (W. S. Graham)." *Parnassus: Poetry in Review* 6, no. 2 (spring/summer 1978): 205-12.
Review of *Implements in Their Places,* comparing it to Graham's earlier work.

H. D.
1886-1961

(Full name Hilda Doolittle; also wrote under the pseudonym John Helforth) American poet, novelist, playwright, translator, editor, and essayist.

For more information on H. D.'s life and career, see *PC,* Volume 5.

INTRODUCTION

Known for her work as an Imagist, as a modernist, and as a feminist, Hilda Doolittle, who published under the initials H. D., repeatedly transformed herself as a writer. Influenced early in her career by Ezra Pound and later by Sigmund Freud, H. D. also responded viscerally to both World War I and World War II. These events shaped her poetry as much as the men in her life did. As an Imagist, the label bestowed upon her by her early mentor, Ezra Pound, H. D. rejected traditional verse forms and looked to the image as the primary inspiration for her poetry. Imagism as a poetic movement corresponded with the experimental mode of early modernist literature. Later, as modernism evolved to incorporate a variety of avant-garde approaches, H. D. turned toward classicism and Hellenism as a new source of inspiration. Her interest in mythology, occultism, and psychoanalysis informed her work at this time as well. H. D. additionally had a close working relationship with Sigmund Freud, who treated her as a psychoanalyst. Involved for a number of years in romantic relationships with both men and women, H. D. was labeled a bisexual by Freud. The poet's understanding of this perceived sense of duality in terms of gender and desire informs a number of her later writings. Although not overtly a political advocate for women's rights, H. D. has been dubbed a feminist by many modern critics for her depiction of strong female figures and for her open approach to her own sexuality.

BIOGRAPHICAL INFORMATION

H. D. was born in 1886 in Bethlehem, Pennsylvania, to an astronomer father with a Puritan background and a pianist mother with Moravian roots. Influenced by her father's New England intellectualism and her mother's spiritual mysticism, H. D. attended Bryn Mawr College for two years. She was welcomed into a literary community that included the poets Marianne Moore, William Carlos Williams, and Ezra Pound, to whom she was briefly engaged. H. D.'s father terminated the engagement in 1907. After leaving college in 1906, H. D. sought publication in newspapers and journals. Her success was limited, and H. D. later travelled to Europe, in 1911, initially as a vacation. The move, however, was a permanent one; she never lived in the U. S. again. H. D. settled in London, and through Pound, who had moved to England in 1908, H. D. met many of the aspiring writers in the London literary community. With Pound's help and encouragement, and largely due to his desire to initiate the Imagist movement, H. D. published a number of poems in the journal *Poetry* in 1913. The same year, H. D. married fellow Imagist poet Richard Aldington. With Aldington, H. D. had a daughter, Perdita, after H. D.'s first pregnancy ended in miscarriage. The couple separated in 1919 after Perdita's birth. H. D. then became involved romantically with Winifred Ellerman, who wrote under the pseudonym Bryher. They settled in Switzerland in 1924 after extensive travelling. In the 1930s, H. D. was periodically psychoanalyzed by Sigmund Freud. Although H. D. disagreed with Freud about some issues, the relationship was greatly influential on H. D.'s subsequent work. H. D. lived and worked in London during World War II, and her views on violence and the role of patriarchy in the modern world stem from her experiences during the war years. After the war, H. D. returned to Switzerland and with Bryher's help recovered from a breakdown suffered in 1945. There, she continued to publish poetry and fiction. H. D. suffered a stroke in 1961 and died later that year.

MAJOR WORKS OF POETRY

H. D. published *Sea Garden* in 1916. In this, and in her other early works of poetry, such as *Hymen* (1921), H. D.'s reputation as an Imagist was established. In these collections, H. D. employs concrete visual images, particularly those with sensual connotations, and uses them in tandem with innovative rhythm patterns and concise verbal expression. Three long poems were published in the aftermath of World War II. These include *The Walls Do Not Fall* (1944), *Tribute to the Angels* (1945), and *The Flowering of the Rod* (1946).

These poems were later collected in a single volume and published under the title *Trilogy* in 1973. In these poems, H. D. reflects on violence, warfare, patriarchy, and religion. She argues that war stems from failings of a patriarchal-based society, and explores beliefs about death and faith while highlighting a sense of spirituality in which a transcendental union with God is the goal. Her last major work of poetry was *Helen in Egypt,* published in 1961. The work combines poetry with prose and explores the myth of Helen and Achilles. The work is sometimes regarded as a synthesis of the themes H. D. explored on some level throughout the length of her career.

CRITICAL RECEPTION

H. D.'s success as an Imagist poet led to her critical reputation as an innovator of poetic form, although the work of the Imagists was often regarded among readers in a less favorable light. Despite her shift in focus as a poet, her reputation as a technically skilled artist remained largely intact throughout her career. Recent critics take a variety of approaches to H. D.'s work, and often focus on either her early work, such as *Sea Garden,* or on the later epic poetry in *Helen in Egypt.* Recent scholarship has also centered heavily on the way H. D.'s personal history shaped her approach to poetry and has emphasized the impact of World War II on the poems that later comprised the collection *Trilogy.* In discussing H. D.'s early collection *Sea Garden,* Norman Kelvin focuses on H. D.'s approach as an Imagist to the poetry's rock and flower imagery, maintaining that these function not simply as symbols, but are used as a means of accessing the conflict between the emotion and intellect that H. D. explores. H. D.'s flower imagery in this collection is further explored by Lesley Wheeler, who examines H. D.'s use of flower imagery in its relationship to womanhood and literary creation, and demonstrates that in *Sea Garden,* H. D. takes pains to sever the notions of womanhood and domesticity.

The poems in *Trilogy* and the way they draw their inspiration from modern warfare is the focus of critics such as Marti Greene, who examines the poems' subversive treatment of Christian themes, and Susan Acheson, who discusses H. D.'s neo-Romantic treatment of time and death in the poems. Julie Goodspeed-Chadwick (see Further Reading) finds in the poems collected in *Trilogy* a feminist reimagining of the world. The critic identifies the poetic tools through which H. D. recasts traditional female roles in poetry. H. D.'s last major poetic effort, *Helen in Egypt,* garners a great deal of critical attention from recent scholars. Many regard it as a culmination of H. D.'s work.

Susan Edmunds, for example, identifies in the work H. D.'s condemnation of war and its patriarchal sources, as well as the influence of Freud and his views on hysteria in H. D.'s characterization of Helen. Robert O'Brien Hokanson (see Further Reading) regards the work as a self-reflexive examination of the tension between experience and identity, while Jeffrey Twitchell-Waas studies the poem as a modernist reaction to Ezra Pound and his work. Like Edmunds, Brian Brodhead Glaser and Sarah Jackson trace the influence of Freud in H. D.'s work. Glaser identifies traces of Freud's analysis in H. D.'s feminist treatment of Helen in *Helen in Egypt.* Jackson sees Freud's influences specifically in H. D.'s poetic exploration of the tactile and the desire toward and prohibition against touching. In Jenn Wolford Watson's estimation, H. D. utilized her experiences as a female poet in a postwar society as a means of creating a poetic harmony between male and female in her work. Watson suggests that H. D.'s use of both male and female deities in her poetry demonstrates H. D.'s desire for regeneration.

PRINCIPAL WORKS

Poetry

Sea Garden 1916
The Tribute and Circe: Two Poems by H. D. 1917
Hymen 1921
Heliodora, and Other Poems 1924
Collected Poems of H. D. (poetry and translations) 1925
H. D. 1926
Red Roses for Bronze (poetry and translations) 1929; enlarged edition, 1931
*The Walls Do Not Fall 1944
What Do I Love? 1944
*Tribute to the Angels 1945
*The Flowering of the Rod 1946
By Avon River (poetry and prose) 1949
Selected Poems of H. D. 1957
Helen in Egypt (poetry and prose) 1961
Hermetic Definition 1972
Collected Poems, 1912-1944 1983
Selected Poems 1989

Other Major Works

Palimpsest (novel) 1926; revised edition, 1968
Hippolytus Temporizes (drama) 1927; revised edition, 1985
Hedylus (novel) 1928; revised edition, 1980

Kora and Ka (novel) 1934
Nights [as John Helforth] (novella) 1935
The Hedgehog (juvenile fiction) 1936
*Tribute to Freud, with Unpublished Letters to Freud by
   the Author* (memoir) 1956; enlarged edition, 1975
Bid Me to Live (A Madrigal) (novel) 1960
†*End to Torment: A Memoir of Ezra Pound* (memoir)
   1979
HERmione (novel) 1981
The Gift [abridged edition] (memoir) 1982

*These works were published as *Trilogy* in 1973.

†This work includes "Hilda's Book," a collection of poems by Ezra
Pound.

CRITICISM

Susan Edmunds (essay date winter 1991)

SOURCE: Edmunds, Susan. "'I Read the Writing When
He Seized My Throat": Hysteria and Revolution in
H. D.'s 'Helen in Egypt.'" *Contemporary Literature* 32,
no. 4 (winter 1991): 471-95.

[*In the following essay, Edmunds examines H. D.'s*
Helen in Egypt, *demonstrating the ways in which H. D.
drew on Sigmund Freud's analytical views on hysteria
and arguing that her dramatic poem is a reaction
against war and the patriarchal constructs that enable
it.*]

Between 1952 and 1955, H. D. wrote her montage
poem, **Helen in Egypt,** which returns to Stesichorus's
Palinode and Euripides' *Helen* to resurrect the argument that a phantom Helen presided over the Trojan
War while her real counterpart was held captive by the
gods in Egypt. Yet where Euripides' play is a marriage
comedy in which Helen proves her innocence and wins
back her husband, H. D.'s poem is a more somber
meditation on the trauma of war, in which Helen and
her three male lovers—Achilles, Paris, and Theseus—
gather in Egypt and Leuke to brood over their part in
the killing at Troy. The poem has strong autobiographical underpinnings. Modeling Helen after herself and
her mother, Helen Wolle Doolittle, H. D. takes Lord
Hugh Dowding, air chief marshal during the Battle of
Britain and a fellow spiritualist, as her model for
Achilles; her friend Erich Heydt, a young psychiatrist
at the Küsnacht sanatorium, as the model for Paris;
and Sigmund Freud as the model for Theseus. H. D.'s
trip to Egypt with her mother and Bryher in 1923,
which included a visit to Tutankhamen's newly opened
tomb, informs the poem's setting in ancient Egypt.

And, as Susan Friedman has argued, H. D.'s experiences during the London Blitz inform both the poem's
condemnation of war as an inevitable effect of
patriarchy and its attempts to recover a lost matriarchal
and pacifist tradition (253-72).

While Friedman is certainly correct in identifying
World War II as a major impetus for the writing of
Helen in Egypt, the postwar revolution in Egypt also
provides an important, but currently overlooked,
historical backdrop to the poem. The years of **Helen
in Egypt**'s composition span the forced abdication of
King Farouk in 1952, the rise of an independent
republic under President Naguib in 1953, and the final
evacuation of British troops in 1955. An entry for
September 18, 1955, in "Compassionate Friendship"
records Bryher's acute distress over these events. Noting Bryher's alarmed response upon learning of Erich
Heydt's fanciful proposal to move to Egypt with her,
H. D. writes:

> Bryher sent me a book about modern Egypt, *The Picnic
> at Sakkara* by P. H. Newby. I remember Erich's talks
> about Egypt, last winter—my Egypt of Karnak and the
> Tomb of 1923 is not this Egypt, as I tried to explain in
> the snow, on that memorable trip. "I had no illusions,"
> I had said to Bryher, when I told her all this, at Lugano,
> last summer. But she seems to have sent me this story,
> all the same, to stress her own "but this [proposal] is
> dangerous."

(139)[1]

While H. D. does not declare her own position on
recent events in Egypt here, she does indicate a
familiarity with postwar Egyptian nationalism dating
from at least the winter of 1954-55 and suggests a
nostalgic preference for the ancient dynastic Egypt
which she associated with Howard Carter's discoveries outside Karnak.

In Friedman's analysis, H. D.'s conflation of the Trojan
War and World War II allows her to move beyond an
account of specific historical conflicts to a more
general and radical account of the contrasting ethos of
matriarchal and patriarchal traditions (259-60).
However, **Helen in Egypt**'s nostalgic evocation of an
Egypt laid bare by British excavators during the final
years of the Egyptian revolution reasserts the poem's
historical embeddedness in the contemporary politics
of colonial dismantlement and complicates the terms
both of its pacifism and of its critique of patriarchy.
Given this embeddedness, we need to ask (1) what
declared political purposes, feminist or otherwise, are
served by the poem's use of an ancient Egyptian setting and mythology, and (2) what relationship obtains
between the poem's evocation of ancient Egypt and
the rapid changes in modern Egypt which stand behind
it.

Deferring a consideration of the second question until the end of my argument, I approach the first by proposing that H. D. grounds her poem's project of social reconstruction in a return to the model of familial peace offered by the ancient Egyptian myth of Isis. Here I build on Rachel Blau DuPlessis's analysis of Helen's efforts to construct a "sufficient family" which nurtures women's abilities, but I identify Freud's model of the destructive oedipal family, rather than DuPlessis's paradigm of "romantic thralldom," as the target of Helen's reforms ("Romantic Thralldom" esp. 201-2; *Writing* 76-83). Conflating the project to reconstruct society with the project to "reconstruct the legend" of Troy (**Helen in Egypt** 11), Helen recovers forgotten traces of Egyptian writing within later Greek drama in order to "transpose or translate" the Greek oedipal "legend of murder and lust" back into an earlier, and preoedipal, Egyptian legend of familial reparation and reunification (1, 88). This peculiarly literary revision of the nuclear family depends on Helen's initial act of "reading" a lily whose hallucinatory image organizes her promotion of two peripheral details in Euripides' Helen plays to central, and revelatory, positions within H. D.'s own montage narrative.

Here I argue that H. D. draws heavily on Freud's analysis of hysteria in forging the terms of Helen's visionary reading and of its power to reconstruct society. Freud identifies hysterics' practice of registering repressed memories on the body's surface and in hallucinations, their inability to compose coherent life histories, their unconscious use of fantasy to reassemble childhood memories into new wholes, and their appropriation of other people's bodily traits and symptoms as debilitating manifestations of a neurotic disorder. In H. D.'s hands, however, these same symptoms of hysteria function as effective strategies of visionary reform.[2] Allowing Helen and her male lovers to uncover the cultural "memory forgotten" of an earlier, redemptive past in Egypt within their personal memories of a traumatic Greek past, these strategies also provide a way to grant that ancient memory material expression in the present (304). Implicit in the project to render ancient Egypt present again, however, is the constitution of modern Egypt's own present as a new "memory forgotten" which holds a similar power to return at the surface of a narrative which would enforce its suppression.

In their joint *Studies on Hysteria* (1895), Josef Breuer and Freud propose that "*hysterics suffer mainly from reminiscences*" (Freud 2: 7). Repressing memories which cause mental conflict and pain, the hysteric experiences partial amnesia and produces bodily symptoms, or "stigmata," which serve as "mnemic symbols" of the memories barred from consciousness. These bodily symptoms, such as tics, spasms, impaired mobility and/or speech, and various kinds of sensory hallucinations *become* the reminiscences from which the hysteric suffers; relief comes only to those who regain conscious access to their forgotten memories through verbalization and thus dissolve the symptoms which mark their repression.

While in 1895 the population considered most susceptible to hysteria was one of housewives and adolescent girls, Freud noted in 1920 that "the terrible war which has just ended gave rise to a great number of illnesses" among the predominantly male veterans; these illnesses were classified as war neuroses, whose "symptomatic picture . . . approaches that of hysteria in the wealth of its similar motor symptoms" (18: 12). In the meantime, however, Freud had sharply revised the clinical picture of hysteria, first advancing his seduction theory, which traces hysterical suffering back to early scenes of sexual assault, often in the form of father-daughter incest, and then retracting it in favor of a theory of a universal fantasy life, which redefines the scenes of sexual assault which hysterics themselves take to be memories as "phantasies erected on the basis of memories" (5: 491) and the symptoms of hysteria as the somatic manifestations of these same unconscious fantasies.

This later move entailed its own complications, as Freud was well aware. He wrote in 1911 of "the difficulty of distinguishing unconscious phantasies from memories which have become unconscious," when the unconscious itself "equate[s] reality of thought with external actuality and wishes with their fulfillment—with the event" (12: 225).[3] In **Helen in Egypt,** characters have a similar difficulty distinguishing between "phantom and reality" (3). Unable to prevent each other's hidden wishes from distorting their joint account of the past, they are equally unable to decide whether they possess autonomous bodies in the Egyptian afterlife or merely exist as hallucinated effects of one another's fantasies. Where Freud views such indeterminacy as an obstacle to disinterested and truthful historiography, however, H. D. celebrates it as the condition of her poem's extraordinarily fluid and assertedly redemptive transactions between wish and event, between bodies, memories, and desire.

Helen in Egypt's first part, **"Pallinode,"** opens on Helen's solitary meditations in the temple of her father: "Amen (or Zeus we call him)" (2). Cast as a woman badly shaken by the long battle at Troy and the final victory—"Troy-gates broken / in memory of the Body" (7)—Helen has lost the desire to remember which continues to drive the limping war veteran Achilles; she complains: "I would rather forget, / / but a phantom pursues him; / shall a phantom threaten my peace? / what does it matter, / / who won, who lost? /

must the Battle be fought and fought / in his memory?" (35). However, Helen's wish for the peace of oblivion must compete with an earlier vow to remember made during a scene of physical and sexual struggle with Achilles on their first night together in Egypt. On that occasion (which takes place before the poem's meditative action begins), Helen reverses a plea to forget when Achilles' "attack" turns to lovemaking, praying anew to his sea mother, Thetis, *"let me remember, let me remember, / forever, this Star in the night"* (18, 17).[4] Her vow to remember this night fuels Helen's larger commitment to search her Greek past for the causes of war at Troy.

While the bulk of *Helen in Egypt*'s narrative presents questions, ambiguities, and conflicts which arise among the various accounts of the past offered by Helen and her three lovers, these conscious proceedings are punctuated at four points by repressed memories which abruptly return. By the end of the poem, these latter memories emerge as the components of a hidden logic of recovery, which both invokes and revises Freud's therapeutic program for hysteria and the related condition of war neurosis. The first repressed memory returns to Achilles when Helen reads Thetis's name in the shape of a flying bird on their first night in Egypt; this memory, which takes shape as the image of Thetis's figurehead on his warship at Aulis, prompts Achilles' attack. However, H. D. does not narrate the memory's return directly until well into **"Eidolon,"** the poem's last part (239-40). She initially registers its effects only indirectly, through Helen, whose visionary "reading" of a lily in **"Pallinode"** functions both as a distorted version of Achilles' memory and as a divine clue to its actual contents (25). A second "suppressed memory and unspoken name—Paris" returns to Helen at the opening of the poem's middle part, **"Leuke,"** while the third repressed memory—of abandoning her young daughter to follow Paris to Troy—returns to Helen early in **"Eidolon"** (109, 228). This third memory leads directly to Helen's recovery of Achilles' memory of the Thetis figurehead and the concomitant knowledge of his love for his mother.

Thus the poem's chain of returning memories eventually links the initial moment of a son's inscrutable anger at the sound of his mother's name to the final moment of revelation that he loves her. H. D. leaves the reader uncertain as to the status of this entire memory chain, however, at one point inscribing it within the fantasy of God the Father and at another reinscribing it within the fantasy of his daughter. On the verge of Achilles' attack, Helen cries out in her defense: "Zeus be my witness . . . / it was he, Amen dreamed of all this / phantasmagoria of Troy, / / it was dream and a phantasy" (17). At the other end of the

poem, H. D. suggests that the heroes of Troy inhabit Helen's fantasy instead—"Yes, Achilles spoke, Paris spoke. Greece and Troy challenged and contradicted each other in her fantasy"—but then retracts this suggestion in the sentences following (225). Sharply raising the stakes of this double inscription, H. D. invokes the central scene of the seduction theory in the middle of **"Leuke."**

When Helen flees a hostile interview with Paris to the snowy refuge of her aging "god-father," the Freud figure Theseus, he greets her with the memory of his failed attempts to take her as his child bride (156). Although Theseus notes that Helen might yet "fear my touch," he persists in pressing his claim, proposing, discreetly enough, "you must have loved me a little, / frail maiden that you still were, / when your brothers found you" (149, 148).[5] Yet if these remarks seem to identify Helen as a survivor of sexual assault, Theseus elsewhere doubts the accuracy of his own memories, going so far as to declare his famous battle with the Minotaur "an idle fancy, / a dream, . . . / hallucination of infancy" (168). In light of Helen's own silence on the subject, H. D. leaves open the possibility that the seduction attempt may be merely another idle fancy of an overly fond analyst and thus foregrounds the distorting effects of the analyst's own counter-transference, which pass unnoticed in Freud's first accounts of hysteria. Yet when placed within the poem's wider frameworks of fantasy, Theseus's memories might record not his own wishes but the contradictory wishes of either Zeus-Amen or Helen that the father seduce the daughter and/or that the father of psychoanalysis be discredited for his wish to seduce the daughter.

H. D.'s attribution of *Helen in Egypt*'s narrative to both Helen's and her father's fantasies raises the possibility of the father's and daughter's complicity as well as of their conflict, a possibility reinforced by the fact that Helen conducts her inquiries into the past on the grounds of her father's temple. In the end, H. D. declares neither for nor against Freud's desire to trace hysteria back to the daughter's fantasies rather than the father's acts of seduction; instead she multiplies Freud's own designated alternatives to place the vertiginous question of female complicity and/or resistance with respect to paternal desire and, more loosely, patriarchal designations at the literal and figurative center of *Helen in Egypt.*

Yet while the poem's involuted frameworks of fantasy position Helen ambiguously with respect to paternal desire, hysterical fantasy also provides Helen with a structure for revising the unhappy and even traumatic parts of her own past. In *The Interpretation of Dreams,* Freud analyzes the relationship between the daytime fantasies which give rise to hysterical symptoms and the childhood memories from which they derive: "If we examine [such fantasies'] structure, . . . the wishful purpose that is at work in their production has mixed up the material of which they are built, has rearranged it and has formed it into a new whole" (5: 492). H. D. appears to evoke this very structure in Helen's description of "the million personal things, / things remembered, forgotten, / remembered again, assembled / and reassembled in different order / as thoughts and emotions" (289) which constitute the greater part of the characters' own reminiscences and of the poem's narrative content. Reproducing fantasy's method of rearranging memories into a new whole, both the characters' meditative reorderings of their personal pasts and H. D.'s montage reordering of her epic and mythic source materials open avenues for expressing wishes that have gone unfulfilled in the actual past and the extant literary tradition.

Opening up new, more satisfying versions of the hysteric's own history, fantasy also allows the hysteric to appropriate aspects of other people's histories through hysterical identification. In identifying with one another, hysterics "catch" each other's symptoms to express a shared investment in the events and/or fantasies that lie behind them. Thus Freud declares that hysterical identification "enables patients to express in their symptoms not only their own experiences but those of a large number of other people; it enables them, as it were, to suffer on behalf of a whole crowd of people and to act all the parts in a play single-handed" (4: 149). As I will argue in detail shortly, Helen's appropriation of Achilles' wounded heel when she enters Theseus's cabin with wounded feet in "Leuke" can be read as just such a moment of hysterical identification, grounded in the sharing of a somatic symptom (151, 153). In the logic of H. D.'s poem, this identification underwrites Helen's ability to recover the repressed childhood memories of Thetis which return to Achilles on their first night in Egypt, even though Achilles himself never verbalizes their content. Furthermore, through a series of somatically registered identifications with other women, Helen makes use of the hysteric's ability to "act all the parts in a play single-handed" in order to transfer entire life histories from one set of characters to another via their joint association with herself: identified with Jocasta and Hecuba as well as Thetis and Isis, she stands as the bridge between the oedipal family and the divine Egyptian family, upon whose example her reconstruction of Achilles' personal past, and her wider project of social reconstruction, will depend.

H. D.'s appropriation of hysterical fantasy as a valued method of social reconstruction revises the relationship between hysteria and its cure promoted by Freud.

For Freud, hysterics' impaired memories force them to patch over lost links between events with "false connections" that only increase the disorder and incoherence of their self-reported life histories (2: 37; 7: 16). Yet beneath the fraudulent and disturbed surface of their accounts, Freud insists that a repressed history "in some fashion lies ready to hand and in correct and proper order" (2: 287); it rests with the analyst to restore this "proper order" to consciousness, so as to dissolve the bodily symptoms which symbolize the repressed parts of the hysteric's past and thus to cure her or his suffering.[6]

Where Freud opposes hysterical suffering, grounded in fantasy's debilitating reorderings, to a psychoanalytic cure grounded in the analyst's ability to reconstruct the true order of history, H. D. conflates hysteria with its cure to confer on hysterical fantasy's own reorderings the power to reveal a true, and curative, order outside history—the order of the divine family of Isis. Using hysterical fantasy both to retrieve clues to this lost Egyptian order from ancient Greek texts (and from their characters' life histories) and to remake those texts (and life histories) in this order's image, H. D. reconstitutes a mental disorder historically linked to the degradation and abuse of women as the means of society's reconstruction and women's positive "reinstatement" (*Helen* 1).

Helen in Egypt's visionary program of reform begins with Helen's "reading" of the lily as Achilles chokes her on the Egyptian beach. Intuitively identifying a flying "night-bird" as the hieroglyph of "Isis, . . . or Thetis," Helen rouses Achilles' anger and quickly tries to avert blame by blackening her face and arms with ash "like the prophetic *femme noire* of antiquity" (13-15).[7] Her strategy backfires. Cursing her as "Hecate," "a witch," "envious Isis, / . . . a vulture, a hieroglyph," Achilles accuses Helen of causing the deaths of his Greek warriors at Troy: "you stole the chosen, the flower / of all-time, of all-history, / my children, my legions; / for you the ships were burnt" (16-17). During the struggle and lovemaking that ensue, Helen has her "vision," whose terms of presentation recall H. D.'s own hallucinatory visions at Corfu in 1920.

In a preliminary headnote, H. D. distinguishes the Greek warships which Helen "visualizes" from the "death-ship of Osiris" and insists that "her vision is wholly Greek"; however, the story of Osiris's death ship clearly underwrites Helen's vision (24). In ancient Egyptian myth, the sun god, Ra, travels each night by ship through the underworld as a dead Osiris, only to emerge at dawn from a lotus flower as the newborn Horus. Horus, in turn, is the hawk-headed god whom his mother, Isis, conceives after Osiris's death and raises to avenge his father's murder. Horus fights Typhon, his father's brother and murderer, but Isis intervenes to reconcile them. In the nightly rehearsal of Osiris's death and resurrection, Horus and Typhon guard over Osiris-Ra's journey, protecting him from further harm. Horus here assumes Isis's role of reconstituting and reviving his father's dismembered body. He also takes the lotus, the flower of his mother's womb, as his hieroglyph, which ancient Egyptians endowed with the god's own powers of resurrection.[8] Helen's vision directly recalls this myth cycle when, amid a swirl of wing feathers, ship sails, and flower petals, she sees "the thousand sails" of the Greek war fleet converge as the "thousand-petalled lily" sacred to Horus (25, 29). At the same time, this composite image of Greek sails and lily petals literalizes Achilles' figure of the Greek host as "the flower / of all-time":

> no, I was not instructed, but I "read" the script,
> I read the writing when he seized my throat,
>
> this was his anger,
> they were mine, not his,
> the unnumbered host;
>
> mine, all the ships,
> mine, all the thousand petals of the rose,
> mine, all the lily petals. . . .
>
> (25)

As she stands in the Amen temple, Helen relates this vision to the actual lotus hieroglyphs lining the temple's corridors: "I have 'read' the lily, / / I can not 'read' the hare, the chick, the bee, / I would study and decipher / the indecipherable Amen-script" (21). However, there are no walls of writing in the original scene of her vision, which takes place near an open campfire "that first night / on the desolate beach": the "writing" she "'reads'" when Achilles seizes her throat is hallucinatory (38). Both the hallucinatory status of Helen's vision and the tropes of reading and pictography she invokes to define her relationship to it link Helen's vision to H. D.'s account of her own series of projected images at Corfu in 1920. In *Tribute to Freud*, H. D. describes her visions—which Freud would later declare her "only actually dangerous 'symptom'"—as "picture-writing" and asserts, "it was I . . . who was seeing the pictures, who was reading the writing or who was granted the inner vision" (41, 48, 51).

Similarly, Freud repeatedly invokes tropes of reading and pictography to describe the multiple relations among hysteric patients, their visual symptoms, and their psychoanalytic cure. He compares one hysteric's orderly progress through a series of pictorial memories to "reading a lengthy book of pictures, whose pages were being turned over before her eyes" (2: 153). But he also asserts that the hysteric who "reads" these im-

ages aloud dissolves them: "*The patient is, as it were, getting rid of it* [the memory picture] *by turning it into words*"; after all memories associated with it have been verbalized, "the picture vanishes, like a ghost that has been laid" (2: 180-81). Extending his analogies further, Freud defines even nonvisual hysterical symptoms as a kind of somatic picture writing. He writes: "We had often compared the symptomatology of hysteria with a pictographic script which has become intelligible after the discovery of a few bilingual inscriptions. In that alphabet being sick means disgust" (2: 129).

As Freud's example here suggests, his "bilingual inscriptions" record the same message not in two different languages—verbal and pictographic—but in two different orders or levels of the same language— figurative and literal; hysterical symptoms literalize absent verbal figures associated with repressed memories and/or fantasies. However, Freud goes on to declare that hysteric symptom formation may bypass verbal figures entirely:

> In taking a verbal expression literally . . . , the hysteric is not taking liberties with words, but is simply reviving once more the sensations to which the verbal expression owes its justification. . . . These [sensations] may now for the most part have become so much weakened that the expression of them in words seems to us only to be a figurative picture of them, whereas in all probability the description was once meant literally; and hysteria is right in restoring the original meaning of the words in depicting its unusually strong innervations.
>
> (2: 181)

This explanation makes for clumsy linguistics and clumsy science, and Freud, in fact, immediately provides examples which contradict it. H. D., on the other hand, puts the terms of Freud's discussion to quite skillful poetic use in a reading of Euripides' *Helen* which underwrites Helen's own hysterical "reading" of the lily.

As Menelaus prepares to overthrow the Egyptian crew on the getaway ship passed off as his own death ship, he addresses his small party of Greeks with Achilles' figure of the "flower / of all-time":

> τί μέλλετ᾽, ὦ γῆς Ἑλλάδος λωτίσματα,
> σφάζειν, φονεύειν βαρβάρους, νεώς τ᾽ ἄπο
> ῥίπτειν ἐς οἶδμα[9]

Here the Greek phrase Ἑλλάδος λωτίσματα, literally meaning "the flower of Hellas," already carries the figurative meaning of "choicest" or "best" for Euripides. Yet the roots of the Greek figure point directly back to Egypt: λώτισμα derives from λωτός, meaning "lotus," or even "Egyptian lotus" (Lindell). Both Euripides' Menelaus and H. D.'s Achilles employ the flower figure to represent the superiority of the Greek host—the former as a means of inciting his men to slaughter, the latter in an elegy for his men's own slaughtering. Thus in transposing Euripides' figure to a new context, H. D. ironizes it, revealing that strength in arms is never proof against death, but rather its agent. More importantly, however, Helen's response to Achilles' use of the figure indicates that its very figurality is of a piece with its violent associations: in a series of translations and semantic abstractions from the original Egyptian hieroglyph through the Greek to Achilles' English usage of "flower" as a synonym for "chosen," the lotus's magical powers of resurrection have been lost.

Through a reverse translation which exploits Freud's conflation of the verbal and figurative over and against the pictographic and literal, Helen literalizes Achilles' flower figure as the visionary lily with sails for petals. Gathering the lost ships of his dead "children" into the form—and sign—of the lotus hieroglyph, she uses its recovered power to reconstitute "the scattered host / (limbs torn asunder) / . . . the Osiris" as the reborn Horus, "the one name for the thousand lost" (27, 41). At the same time, H. D. dislodges the flower figure from its peripheral and ornamental status in Euripides' text and promotes it to a primary and generative place in her own narrative. This act of intertextual transposition functions simultaneously as an act of feminist revaluing of hysterics' and/or women's powers of vision. For Helen's complex "reading" of the lily marks *Studies on Hysteria* itself as a hysterical text which symptomatically manifests a linguistic "memory" it does not consciously possess: if Freud thinks to remind his reader that "hysteria" is "derived from the Greek word for 'uterus'" (2: 247), Breuer more absently reports, "The overflowing productivity of their minds has led one of my friends to assert that hysterics are the flower of mankind, as sterile, no doubt, but as beautiful as double flowers" (2: 240).

Where Breuer exalts hysterics as the flower of mankind only to condemn their indubitable sterility, Helen discovers a literally generative and curative power in her visionary "productions" that has been lost in the abstract verbal language Freud would use to remove them.[10] Turning Freud's and Breuer's own verbal figures back into visionary pictures, she revives dead men and dead metaphors alike and raises all the ghosts they would lay to rest. For Helen's visionary conflation of the Greek warships and the Egyptian womb-flower literally resurrects Achilles' "lost legions" as phantom agents of love and peace; "encircling" and "sheltering" her as she faces Achilles' murderous wrath, "the invisible host" converts his rage into ardor: "it was they, the veil / that concealed

yet revealed, / that reconciled him to me" (38, 40, 41, 44). As Helen will later reveal, their protection ushers in an actual moment of impregnation under Achilles' cloak, whose fruit will be a savior child (17, 185).

Helen's "reading" of the lily closely reproduces the major types of literalization which Margaret Homans traces in nineteenth-century women's writing: it stages a woman's translation of a male text, represents the virgin birth of the Word (of Horus), and occasions the conception of an actual child (29-32). However, where Homans uses the terms "literal" and "literalized" interchangeably, opposing both to the substitutive action of figures, the transformative power of Helen's vision depends on a necessary distinction between these terms. For the hysteric, the literalization of a figure does not shake off that figure's tenor to re-establish a prefigural, or literal, meaning but acquires the figure's tenor as its own.[11] Likewise, when Helen translates the Euripidean flower figure from English and Greek back into Egyptian, she does not simply restore to the lotus hieroglyph the "original meaning" it had before it was translated into Greek but instead reassigns to it the tenors of later flower figures. Thus the visionary lily with sails for petals embodies and manifests the life-restoring powers not only of the Egyptian Isis and Horus (to whom these powers are originally, and solely, attributed), but also of the mentally productive hysteric, Helen, and the chosen Greek legions. In fact, it is precisely because Helen's vision bestows on both herself and the Greek host the powers of life traditionally ascribed to the Egyptian mother and child that she can hope to reconstruct and redeem, rather than merely replace, the Greek legend of the destructive oedipal family.

Helen grounds her reconstruction of the oedipal family in a hysterical identification with Isis, which she registers on her skin at the time of her vision. Recalling how Achilles cursed her as an "envious Isis," she speculates, "in the dark, I must have looked / an inked-in shadow; but with his anger, / that ember, I became / what his accusation made me, / Isis, forever with that Child, / the Hawk Horus" (17, 23). As the emphasis on her darkness suggests, this transformation entails a putative change of race.[12] Having blackened her face and arms after sighting the "night-bird" of Isis and just before Achilles' attack, Helen laments, "I could not hide my eyes" (38). In an echo of Freud's unorthodox claim that Moses was an Egyptian rather than a Semite, Achilles later recalls this moment, describing Helen as "another / whose eyes slant in the old way" and asking, "is she Greek or Egyptian?" (254). However, if Helen's slanting eyes give her away not as a masquerading but as a newly literal Egyptian, Egypt itself must be understood as H. D.'s literalizing synthesis of a number of earlier, Freudian figures.

In his case histories of the Wolf Man and Leonardo da Vinci, Freud compares unconscious syncretic thinking to the ancient "Egyptian pantheon," which manifests a parallel tendency to fuse the identities of its various gods (11: 93; 17: 119). Mental derivatives of the unconscious posing as conscious thoughts remind him of "individuals of mixed race who . . . betray their coloured descent by some striking feature or other, and on that account are excluded from society" (14: 191). He calls adult female sexuality a "'dark continent' for psychology" (20: 212) and compares the surprising discovery of a preoedipal period of female sexuality (which he claims is "especially intimately related to the aetiology of hysteria") to "the discovery . . . of the Minoan-Mycenean civilization behind the civilization of Greece" (21: 227, 226).

Against this background of Freudian analogies, H. D. adjusts her long-standing poetic use of ancient geography to equate Parnassus and Athens with "reality," "Greek creative thought," and "the delight of the intellect" and to link Egypt, Crete, and Eleusis as common strongholds of "dream," "magic," and the "Mysteries" of the mother goddesses Demeter and Isis (168-69, 209, 212, 89).[13] In this strangely literal landscape of the mind, Egypt *becomes* the ground of the unconscious, of female sexuality and hysteria, and of the preoedipal phase and thus provides the enabling conditions for Helen's attempts to realize her vision "in material terms" (11). As the unconscious itself, Egypt equates "wishes with their fulfillment—with the event," while as the "dark continent" of female sexuality and the preoedipal phase, it stands as antecedent and antidote to the oedipal family, target of Helen's project of reconstruction.

In becoming Isis, Helen "transposes or translates" the Greek legend of the slaying son, Oedipus, into the earlier, Egyptian myth of the saving son, Horus, by exploiting a structural parallel between these two cultures' accounts of the nuclear family. Like Jocasta, Isis forms an alliance with her son in the aftermath of her husband's murder; but where, for Jocasta, this alliance only compounds Oedipus's crimes against Laius, for Isis, it becomes a means of reprisal and reparation: conceiving Horus after Osiris's fatal battle with their brother Typhon, she raises him to avenge his father's death and eventually gives him the words of power used to reunite and revive Osiris's dismembered body. Throughout the various cycles of the myth, Isis intervenes to prevent further killing and to consolidate a family which, like Osiris himself, seems bent on fragmentation. Situated ambiguously between Greece and Egypt, Helen views the hostility between her two lovers, the youthful Paris and the fatherly Achilles, as a version of the oedipal struggle: thus her question "How reconcile Trojan and Greek?" reappears as the question "must youth and maturity quarrel?" (157, 181). Her solution will be an act of "subtle genealogy" whereby the oedipal Paris is reconstituted as a Horus, who comes not to destroy but to restore the life of his new father, Achilles (184). In identifying with Isis, then, Helen identifies with a program of family reunification in which an alliance between mother and son, far from threatening the father's kingly place, preserves it.

Yet the terms of Helen's proposed reconstruction of the legend, embodied in her vision of the lily which conflates the sign of the child savior with the image of his mother's womb, meet with resistance from her fellow Greeks. In fact, the first to resist is Helen herself; following Achilles' soliloquy delineating the patriarchal power structure of the Achaeans ("The Command was bequest from the past, / from father to son"), she impulsively takes to "living in fantasy, the story of her sister," Clytaemnestra, whose alliance with her child does cause her to threaten the father's reign—in fact, to rule in his stead and murder him when he returns home (61, 85). Clytaemnestra's loyalty to Iphigenia also prompts the poem's only fantasy of an all-female family, like the one in which H. D. and Bryher raised Perdita: equating her daughter Hermione with Iphigenia, Helen reads her own relationship with Clytaemnestra into the Amen temple's depiction of "Isis with Nephthys, / the Child's other mother," while Helen's homoerotic fantasy of Iphigenia's wedding day, in which daughter and mother stand "together / as one, before the altar," evokes the text of Christian matrimony to describe what might otherwise pass as a moment of identification (68, 74).

But the story of her sister proves incompatible with the vision of the lily which Helen reviews from her father's temple; in a bribe Proteus delivers to her through his own daughter Thetis, Helen is offered deification if she agrees to forget her sister: "seek not to know / / too much; . . . / grieve not for Clytaemnestra" (105). She accepts. While **"Pallinode"** thus ends with the calculated suppression of the sororal bond in favor of paternal endorsement, **"Leuke"** begins with Helen's involuntary retrieval of "the so far suppressed memory and unspoken name—Paris." Banished from "Pallinode," Paris returns, symptomatically, in the memory of an even earlier banishment, inflicted at birth because Hecuba dreamed he would bring war to his father's city (109-10). Linked to Achilles' accusation that Helen caused the deaths of his "children" by a common theme of maternal violence, this memory of Paris will continue to trouble Helen's attempts to realize her vision and its promise of family reunification long after she leaves Paris himself behind. Thus, when she considers her Trojan lover for the part of Horus during her visit with Theseus, she wonders: "did he hate Hecuba? / she exposed him on Ida, / / like Oedipus, to die; / tell me, godfather, / how can I be his mother?" (156).

Like Hecuba and unlike Clytaemnestra, Jocasta values her husband's power over her child's life and agrees to destroy the son destined to overcome his father; thus the early period of maternal attachment which stands at the center of the Freudian child's oedipal complex never materializes for Oedipus himself. Yet when Helen finally goes through with her plan to convert Paris into another Horus—the "new Euphorion" "engendered under the cloak" of Achilles during her vision of the Greek host as lily—she focuses exclusively on extirpating the son's crimes against the father by converting the slaying son, Oedipus, into the savior of the slain father, Horus (217, 185). As H. D. tells it, "The slayer becomes the son of the slain," and as Helen herself tells it, Paris, who shot the arrow that killed Achilles, "is Achilles' son, he is incarnate / Helen-Achilles . . . / / alike but different, apart from the heroes slain, / / but one, one other, *the* other, / incarnate, manifest Egypt" (184-85). What Helen leaves out of her reconstruction of the family here is the anxious memory of the mother's complicity in the father's crimes against the son.

Nor is Paris the first son in **Helen in Egypt** to take after Oedipus. Achilles, too, was a son destined to be greater than his father—a destiny which prompted Zeus to hand Thetis over to her rapist, Peleus, an insignificant mortal. Moreover, Achilles drags Oedipus's "swollen foot" with him to Egypt as the somatic "token" of "his mortality" (9). Yet as Helen remembers it, Achilles' fatal wound takes on unmistakably erotic characteristics in a fantasy not of death but of female sexuality:

> though the Achilles-heel treads lightly,
> still I feel the tightening muscles,
> the taut sinews quiver,
>
> as if I, Helen, had withdrawn
> from the bruised and swollen flesh,
> the arrow from its wound.
>
> (8)

Under the lens of Helen's fantasy, Achilles' wound functions as a vagina (or more loosely, a womb) thrilling not to a touch, but to its withdrawal. As such, it becomes, quite literally, a hysterical "stigma," marking the male body with the sign both of "woman" and of her withdrawal, in accord with Freud's late work on hysteria, which traces symptoms to fantasies which perform "contradictory actions" simultaneously and have "a bisexual meaning" (9: 166). Preserving the memory of his stay on Skyros, when his mother

dressed him "in woman's robe and ornament" to hide him from the Greek war faction, his wound also recalls the time when Thetis "had forgotten to dip the heel / of the infant Achilles / / into the bitter water" (214, 253). Where Oedipus's pierced ankles mark his body with his parents' unambiguous intent to destroy him, Achilles' vulnerable heel, like the fatal wound to follow, poses a contradiction: as the place on his body where his mother held him over the immortalizing waters, it testifies both to her literal attachment to her child and to the limits of that attachment, to her forgetfulness, her "careless, unspeakable" detachment (253).

Achilles' somatic memory of maternal detachment thus acts as the antithetical condition of Helen's vision; it is both what the lotus hieroglyph, conflating womb and child, tries to deny and what Helen must eventually admit to consciousness if the lotus's promise of family reunification is to be fulfilled. In the meantime, the conflicted connection between his wound and her vision marks out a space of ambivalence toward the mother which **Helen in Egypt** will traverse in the very act of celebrating her.[14] Thus Helen feels "anxiety about the Sea-goddess" when she enters **"Leuke"** and worries, "will she champion? / will she reject me?"—a worry later related to Helen's fear that Achilles' initial attack was an attempt to sacrifice her to his mother (117, 244, 270). Moreover, in "Leuke," Helen approaches Theseus's fireside with "wounded" feet: appropriating the oedipal stigmata from Achilles, she bears somatic testimony of her hysterical identification with his grievances against Thetis (151). However, this identification also rests on Helen's desire to repress her own history as a mother.

When Paris returns in **"Eidolon"** to question Helen's visionary reform of the family, his insistent enumeration of the children betrayed by their parents' loyalty to "the old story" prompts Helen's last, painful memory of her daughter, Hermione, whom she abandoned for a new life with Paris himself (217). Staring after a mother who "never looked back," Hermione upsets her mother's nestlike "work-basket": as "the reels rolled to the floor / and she did not stoop to pick up / / the scattered spools" (228), she signals both her mother's "overturning" of her maternal role and her own abrupt relinquishment of a *fort-da* game which Freud's grandson also played with a reel in an attempt to supervise his mother's comings and goings (18: 15); Hermione's gesture embodies the hysterical knowledge that *her* mother is not coming back.[15]

While this memory's very painfulness would, in Freudian terms, register a conflict between Helen's desires and her daughter's, the rest of the poem will play out that pain as simple regret and use Helen's revised sense of her maternal duties to resolve the conflicts building up in *Helen in Egypt*'s previous books. Helen's acknowledgment of her daughter's anger and grief at losing her mother allows her to trace Achilles' opening attack to the same cause. Thus, if H. D. initially appears to follow Homer in linking Achilles' heroic anger before the gates of Troy to the "memory of the Body" of Patroclus, she eventually uncovers the more distant memories of a lost maternal body that lie behind the force of Achilles' grief for his male lover on the Scamander plains (7). When Helen's vicarious retrieval of Achilles' repressed love for his mother returns Thetis to the picture, Thetis's own mourning, "like Hecuba, for Hector dead," repeats and justifies Achilles' mourning for Patroclus and his other "children" and performs the final transformation of the destructive oedipal mother, Hecuba, into a grieving Isis (296).

Retrieving a moment between her naming of Thetis and Achilles' attack during their first night on the beach, Helen reports:

> I think he remembered everything
> in an instantaneous flash . . .
>
> but he only saw the ships
> assembled at Aulis,
> he only remembered his own ship
>
> that would lead them all,
> he only saw an image, a wooden image,
> a mermaid, Thetis upon the prow.

>   (239-40)

Underwriting this vicarious memory of Achilles' Nereid sea mother, a chorus of women in Euripides' *Iphigenia at Aulis* look out over the Greek fleet at Aulis and report:

> These are Achilles' ships.
> On the prow of each
> A goddess sheds gold:
> Sea-spirits are cut in tiers of gold.[16]

Here Helen's vision of the Greek ships as a lotus resolves down to a single ship whose figurehead embodies Achilles' memories of Thetis. Relating the Thetis figurehead to an earlier, childhood eidolon of Thetis, Helen "reads" the Thetis effigies as mnemonic symbols which both replace and represent Achilles' absent mother, in order to learn "the bitterness of his loss" and the fact that "he loved" (260). Once retrieved *from* history, this loss can be negated *as* history and replaced by an eternal attachment between mother and child, through Egypt's unconscious capacity to equate wishes with their fulfillment. Granting her son's wish for victory while shattering his false sense of immortality, Thetis has let Achilles die avenging his male lover at Troy only to resurrect him in Egypt as a heterosexual pacifist newly committed to the reconstituted nuclear family. Thus the lotus of Helen's earlier vision finally serves as the transcendental guarantee of a maternal love which both abrogates and appeases the "bitterness" of Achilles' martial and mortal experience.

Where Isis and Horus gather up the scattered fragments of the father's body, H. D. reads Euripides' plays for scattered traces of the mother's presence. "Assembled / and re-assembled in different order" in her own montage narrative, Euripides' obscurely Egyptian images of the lotus flower and golden sea goddesses together release the "memory forgotten" of the mother's powers of resurrection and reconciliation, a memory grounded in Egyptian myth and retained in trivialized and distorted form throughout the Western literary tradition (289, 304). In an act of restoration *and* revision, H. D. reconstructs the oedipal legend and reconciles its conflicts by rendering these obscured images of the appeasing mother newly visible. Yet while the celebration of motherhood need be no more antithetical to a feminist agenda than it has been to a patriarchal one, the terms of *Helen in Egypt*'s celebration of motherhood are not feminist. Thetis, a mother by rape, who caters to her adult son's wishes, executes her father's will, censors the memory of the rebel queen Clytaemnestra, and remains vaguely threatening to Helen herself presents little challenge to Victorian white middle-class norms of ideal womanhood, and we might well complain with Paris that "this is the old story / no new Euphorion" (217), were it not for a final twist which marks the poem as a work of the 1950s.

Concluding *Helen in Egypt* with the solitary Achilles' lonely thoughts of Thetis before a Homeric sea, H. D. forcibly excludes the characters most consistently linked with Egypt from the final picture of Greek mother love which it has taken Egypt to make visible and legible. Thus just before Helen herself disappears from the poem, she aggressively dissolves her bond with Paris. H. D.'s unsatisfying explanation for Helen's late show of hostility—"in this last phase or mood, it seems inevitable and perhaps wholly human for Helen to turn on her Trojan lover" (299)—begs the question of Paris's "inevitable" dismissal. What has he done—or undone—to deserve it? Paris, the son newly celebrated as "incarnate, manifest Egypt," was, we recall, originally the son who "would undo / the work of his father, Priam" (185, 112). Banished from the family and from memory for this very reason, he returns to consciousness when Helen agrees to suppress her sister's memory at the end of **"Pallinode."** Paris is also the last to invoke Clytaemnestra's name, bidding Helen to "remember Clytaemnestra's / last words to Orestes, / / *remember Iphigenia*" in **"Eidolon"** after Helen herself fails to answer Theseus's parting query in **"Leuke"**: "you sought / (do you still seek?) / Clytaemnestra in Egypt" (219, 188). And it is Clytaemnestra, "child of darkness" and "shadow of us all," whose angry violence to her king and lord the poem as a whole must struggle to remember and forget (187, 2).

Linked to each other and to Egypt throughout the poem, Paris and Clytaemnestra pose threats to the father's life and power which contradict the terms of Helen's visionary reform of the oedipal family. Yet while their crimes against the Crown evince a resistance *to* Egypt's promise of familial peace, such violence also evinces the resistance *of* Egypt, which was to secure its full independence from Britain while H. D. was writing her poem. When read against this history, H. D.'s repeated need to ban Paris and Clytaemnestra from the poem's project of redemption begins to look like a displaced attempt to "banish the memory" of modern Egypt, whose own insurrection contradicts the poem's evocation of an eternally gentle and conciliatory land (13). However, at one point in the poem, H. D.'s portrayal of this gentler Egypt itself breaks down, and Egypt emerges as "an enemy to be conquered" (181). Theseus cautions Helen: "Crete would seduce Greece, / Crete inherited the Labyrinth from Egypt, / the ancient Nile would undermine / / the fabric of Parnassus." Helen later repeats Theseus's reasoning in order to justify a sudden show of aggression against "Crete-Egypt": "Crete inherited the Labyrinth, / and Crete-Egypt must be slain, / / conquered or overthrown" (169, 182).

In an accompanying headnote, H. D. instructs us to take Helen's remark figuratively. Although the Egypt of Isis and Horus has consistently signified peace and second life, Theseus equates Egypt with the Cretan Minotaur and with "Death," an equation H. D. recalls when she identifies the "enemy to be conquered" in the guise of "Crete-Egypt" as "Death" (168-69, 181-82). However, H. D.'s elaborate figures for this abstract victory over death are highly overdetermined; drawing on a discourse of war, empire, and revolution, they evoke the very situation in modern Egypt which the rest of the poem would suppress. Indeed, if we follow Helen herself in ignoring H. D.'s instructions to read this remark figuratively, we come up with an unauthorized, literal reading which clearly identifies Egypt rather than death as the enemy who must be conquered or overthrown. As H. D.'s efforts to stave it off suggest, such a literal reading cannot be consciously admitted into the poem; however, in an unconscious or repressed register, a wish to defeat or punish modern Egypt may hereby gain representation. Thus while H. D.'s express (and proprietary) preference for a prewar

Egypt falls short of Bryher's reactionary panic in "Compassionate Friendship," a literal reading of these lines suggests an active resentment toward anticolonial resistance which H. D. may not yet have acknowledged even to herself.[17]

Suppressing this literal reading under a figurative one, H. D. further obscures its possibility by supplying a crime to justify Helen's retributive violence, much as the hysteric supplies "false connections" to replace the missing logical links in his or her life story. Thus, by Theseus's account, "Crete-Egypt" is guilty of seduction. As such, it functions as a criminal version not of modern Egypt, whose current relations with the British are decidedly noncooperative, but of its more hospitable, ancient counterpart; indeed, its crime inheres in the fact that it has become too hospitable, too inviting. But what kind of seductress proves so dangerous that she "must be slain"? The witch, burned to death in the United States's own colonial period for reputed crimes of sexual excess and communion with the devil. Freud follows Jean Martin Charcot in identifying witches as hysterics (19: 72), while Achilles, we recall, tries to strangle Helen after she blackens her face with a burnt stick, crying: "what sort of enchantment is this? / what art will you wield with a fagot? / are you Hecate? are you a witch?" (16).[18]

Helen's fantasy of slaying the seductive "Crete-Egypt" both rationalizes and disguises her sudden desire to conquer a suspiciously modern Egyptian enemy by mapping an earlier, more brutal script of the hysteric's fate onto an earlier, more inviting Egypt. Moreover, by locating this fantasy in a conversation between Helen and her "godfather," abductor, and analyst, H. D. shifts the blame for the father's possible sexual crimes against the daughter and indirectly clears Helen herself of the charges of wantonness she faces from the Greek host as well as the more deeply repressed charge that she desires to follow her dark sister, Clytaemnestra, into violent revolt. Instead, H. D. assigns to Helen the role of condemning another "wanton" to death—the wanton who is simultaneously "Crete-Egypt" and her own "blackened," Egyptian self (50).

Raising such issues as father-daughter incest, lesbian desire, and involuntary and/or rejected motherhood, *Helen in Egypt* provides considerable evidence of women's grievances within the patriarchal nuclear family. Yet such evidence has an insecure status within a narrative ultimately committed to the reconstruction of the good (white) family woman, enjoined to stand as guardian both of the family's peace and the father's power. Moreover, in H. D.'s treatment of the figure of a seductive "Crete-Egypt" who would "undermine the fabric of Parnassus," the injunction to uphold the father's power temporarily proves stronger than the need to keep the peace. This figure can be read as a condensation of contemporary conflicts between women and the patriarchal family and between Egypt and the British Empire; in calling for the slaughter and/or conquest of Egypt, Helen resolves those conflicts violently and at the rebels' expense. But Helen's attempt to distinguish herself from the poem's rebel element backfires; her fantasy of slaying a subversive seductress simultaneously returns H. D.'s celebratory representations of hysteria to their violently misogynist antecedents and thus subverts the poem's own narrative strategies for white women's "reinstatement." Given this entire dynamic, we need to be cautious about endorsing the poem's feminism. Instead, I would argue, **Helen in Egypt**'s interest for feminists lies in H. D.'s ability to render the acute tension between her strongly articulated desire to reform the patriarchal family and her resilient nostalgia for it, with complexity and force.

Notes

1. *The Picnic at Sakkara* portrays the comic adventures of a British English professor who nearly loses his life during the violent student demonstrations in Cairo instigated by the Moslem Brotherhood in the late forties. Published in 1955, the novel looks back from the recent successes of the Egyptian revolution to its immediate roots in postwar militant Egyptian nationalism. In letters to H. D. during a 1954 trip to India and Pakistan, Bryher frequently compares the "picturesque" people she sees to "the Egypt of my childhood"; in contrast, on her return through Cairo, she notes "how Egypt has changed" and complains of how "difficult" the Egyptians have become, "unlike our dear Pakistanis" (3 Feb. 1954; 26 Feb. 1954).

2. H. D.'s own war experience may inform her portrayal of Helen as a hysteric. Writing to Bryher from London in the spring of 1940, she records "symptoms" of nausea at the sound of the air-raid sirens, "waves" of "emotional-paralysis," and "a blank, black depression that comes down over ones [*sic*] head." She explains: "apparently having had the first infant while threat of air raids was on, I may go through sort of hysterical symptoms"; "One almost 'times' these seizures of mental weakness and despair like birth-pains"; "I am sure we are all 'travailling' together for this birth of a new era, and now I have faced it, I simply rush about between 'pains' and tell a few (not many) of this, my theory" (30 May 1940; 2 June 1940; 3 June 1940). H. D.'s links between war, hysteria, birth pain, and a "new era" will find direct parallels in Helen's "reading" of the lily. See Friedman 17-22 for a summary of H. D.'s knowledge of Freudian psychoanalytic theory and practice. Here I consider hysteria as a model for H. D.'s vision-

ary program of reform, not as a model for wider feminist practice. Because the ideas represented by hysterical symptoms conflict with the hysteric's own conscious standards of conduct, they are by definition cut off from the sphere of voluntary political practice. For two nuanced critiques of recent feminists' celebratory appropriations of hysteria, see Catherine Clement's untitled piece in *New French Feminisms* and Jacqueline Rose's "Dora—Fragment of an Analysis" (27-47).

3. For opposing positions on the significance of Freud's retraction of the seduction theory for feminists, see Masson and see Rose's astute critique of Masson's argument (1-23).

4. In contrast to previous chronologies of the poem's opening events, I place the events on the desolate beach before the poem's meditative action begins, and Helen's initial naming of Thetis before rather than after Achilles' attempt to strangle her. After using the present tense in her opening speeches in the temple, Helen adopts the past tense to recount the entire sequence of events which took place during "that first night / on the desolate beach" (38) and then returns to the present tense at the beginning of "Pallinode," Book 3, to narrate her subsequent interactions with Achilles (1, 6-25, 35 ff.). Two headnotes indicate that Helen is alone in the temple when she reviews the beach encounter with Achilles, and that he rejoins her in the temple only after she has finished her account (11, 35). In sections 7 and 8 in Book 1 of "Pallinode," Achilles' attack on Helen immediately follows her initial invocations of Thetis (13-17). For previous chronologies, see Friedman 60 and DuPlessis, "Romantic Thralldom" 193.

5. This reference to Helen's history of barely averted childhood sexual abuse at the hands of her analyst has generally gone unremarked by the poem's critics. Paul Smith, who briefly notes Theseus's abduction of the young Helen, is an exception (121). However, DuPlessis suggests that the scene in H. D.'s *The Gift,* in which the young Hilda abruptly escapes from the milk cart of a male stranger, might encode a moment of attempted sexual assault (*H. D.* 78-79).

6. Steven Marcus offers an illuminating account of Freud's association of sound narrative practices with mental health (56-91, esp. 71).

7. In *Le Tarot,* a book H. D. owned, Jean Chaboseau identifies the *femme noire* as the black priestess seated at the threshold of the Sanctuary on one of the tarot cards. The sacred ankh around her neck and the Book of Thoth in her lap link her to Isis, while her race is said to represent the obscurity undergone by the hermetic tradition in recent times (46-47).

8. Budge recounts Horus's ceremonial assumption of Isis's role in reuniting and reviving the body of Osiris (*Osiris* 70-86). H. D.'s copy of this book is housed at Beinecke. He also discusses the ancient Egyptians' practice of endowing signs with the spirits and powers of their referents (*Gods* 10).

9. In H. D.'s copy of his bilingual edition of *Helen,* Arthur Way translates these lines as follows: "Wherefore delay, O flower of Hellas-land, / To smite, to slay the aliens, and to hurl / Into the sea?" (600-601).

10. Helen's translation of the Euripidean flower figure back into the Egyptian lotus hieroglyph can also be read as a literal attempt to reinvest language with the "living quality" which H. D. misses in everyday verbal communication. Thus in *Tribute to Freud* she prefers the startling force of Walter Schmideberg's neologisms in his second language to standard English usage, arguing that "the impact of a language, as well as the impact of an impression may become 'correct,' become 'stylized,' lose its living quality" (15).

11. Thus in literalizing the figure "to get off on the wrong footing," the hysteric who stumbles signifies an inauspicious beginning, not faulty locomotion. For a similar example, see Freud 2: 179.

12. H. D. may follow Budge in portraying Isis as a black woman. He identifies Isis as an African, most likely from the Sudan, on the grounds that her retreat to the swamps to bear Horus resembles Sudanese birthing practices (*Osiris* 301-4).

13. Two patterns emerge in current evaluations of H. D.'s shifting symbolic use of ancient geography. One pattern traces H. D.'s links between Greece, the mother, and preoedipal union, while the other traces H. D.'s opposition of Greece and Egypt, in which Greece stands as a violent patriarchal culture and Egypt as "a symbol of the mother and therefore of fusion, incest, desire and death" (DuPlessis, *H. D.* 113-14; also see 18-30, 52-55). See also Friedman 131-32 and Gregory 86-87. The latter pattern conforms to H. D.'s habitual orientalist conflation of "the West" with virility and strength and "the East" with effeminacy and erotic abandon. In "People of Sparta" (1920), for instance, H. D. imagines a decadent feminizing of the West as Xerxes invades Greece: "shall this our earth be a creature of sensuous, high strung, feminine, changeable, fluid character, given first to the lure of the senses, . . . or shall the West prevail?" (76). See also Said 180-90, 206 for a discussion of the Western habit of associating the East with femininity. Of course, Freud's analogies evince a similar orientalism. I am proposing, then, not that H. D. here adopts Freud's analogies as an alien symbolic system, but that she absorbs them into an existing version of her symbolic geography.

14. For previous discussions of H. D.'s treatments of ambivalence toward the mother, see Friedman 140-42; DuPlessis, *H. D.* 44-55; and Kloepfer 46-51 and 117-40. However, Friedman also argues that *Helen in Egypt*'s portrayals of traditional mother goddesses are not ambivalent (271).

15. After drafting this essay, I discovered that Kloepfer makes different use of the same allusion to Freud (166).

16. This is H. D.'s own translation (*Collected Poems* 74).

17. In *Vale Ave,* begun a month after Ghana's independence in March 1957, H. D.'s possible anxiety over the breakup of the British Empire is suggested in still starker terms. There, a woman at the fall of Rome fears that "barbaric hordes"—"beasts in their wild-beast pelts"—will "swoop and tear me, helpless, hapless here" and "leer" as they decide whether to cage or burn her (23-24). When Lionel Durand died while covering the Algerian War for *Newsweek,* H. D. toyed with blaming his death on his interest in the politics of decolonization. She writes: "I could say that I have not cared for Lionel's intense political commitments. He died really as the result of his visit to Algeria. I read the article he wrote afterwards, with interest, with reserve, with resentment. What was he doing there?" (Diary entry, 1 June 1961).

18. I thank Roz Carroll for pointing out to me Freud's connections between hysteria and Europe's witch trials.

Works Cited

Bryher. Letters to H. D., Feb. 1954. H. D. Papers. Beinecke Rare Book and Manuscript Library, Yale University.

Budge, E. A. Wallis. *The Gods of the Egyptians.* Vol. 1. Chicago: Open Court; London: Methuen, 1904. 2 vols.

———. *Osiris and the Egyptian Resurrection.* Vol. 1. London: Medici Society, 1911. 2 vols.

Chaboseau, Jean. *Le Tarot: Essai d'interprétation selon les principes de l'hermétisme.* Paris: Editions Niclaus, [1946].

Clement, Catherine. Untitled essay. *New French Feminisms.* Ed. Elaine Marks and Isabelle Courtivron. Amherst: U of Mass P, 1980. 130-36.

DuPlessis, Rachel Blau. *H. D.: The Career of That Struggle.* Bloomington: Indiana UP, 1986.

———. "Romantic Thralldom in H. D." *Contemporary Literature* 20 (1979): 178-203.

————. *Writing beyond the Ending: Narrative Strategies of Twentieth-Century Women Writers.* Bloomington: Indiana UP, 1985.

Freud, Sigmund. *The Standard Edition of the Complete Psychological Works of Sigmund Freud.* Trans. and ed. James Strachey. 24 vols. London: Hogarth, 1955-1974.

Friedman, Susan. *Psyche Reborn: The Emergence of H. D.* Bloomington: Indiana UP, 1981.

Gregory, Eileen. "Scarlet Experience: H. D.'s *Hymen."* *Sagetrieb* 6.2 (1987): 77-100.

H. D. [Hilda Doolittle]. "Compassionate Friendship." Ts. H. D. Papers. Beinecke Rare Book and Manuscript Library, Yale University.

————. Diary, 1961. H. D. Papers. Beinecke Rare Book and Manuscript Library, Yale University.

————. *The Gift.* New York: New Directions, 1982.

————. *H. D.: Collected Poems, 1912-1944.* Ed. Louis Martz. New York: New Directions, 1983.

————. *Helen in Egypt.* 1961. New York: New Directions, 1974.

————. Letters to Bryher, May and June 1940. Bryher Papers. Beinecke Rare Book and Manuscript Library, Yale University.

————. "People of Sparta." "Notes on Euripides, Pausanius and Greek Lyric Poets." Ts. H. D. Papers. Beinecke Rare Book and Manuscript Library, Yale University.

————. *Tribute to Freud.* c. 1974. New York: New Directions, 1984.

————. *Vale Ave.* New Directions in Prose and Poetry 44. Ed. James Laughlin. New York: New Directions, 1982.

Homans, Margaret. *Bearing the Word: Language and the Female Experience in Nineteenth Century Women's Writing.* Chicago: U of Chicago P, 1986.

Kloepfer, Deborah Kelly. *The Unspeakable Mother: Forbidden Discourse in Jean Rhys and H. D.* Ithaca: Cornell UP, 1989.

Lindell, H. G. *Greek-English Lexicon.* 1978 ed.

Marcus, Steven. "Freud and Dora: Story, History, Case History." *In Dora's Case: Freud, Hysteria, Feminism.* Ed. Charles Bernheimer and Claire Kahane. New York: Columbia UP, 1985. 56-91.

Masson, Jeffrey Moussaieff. *The Assault on Truth: Freud's Suppression of the Seduction Theory.* 1984. New York: Penguin, 1985.

Newby, Percy Howard. *The Picnic at Sakkara.* New York: Knopf, 1955.

Rose, Jacqueline. *Sexuality in the Field of Vision.* London: Verso, 1986.

Said, Edward. *Orientalism.* New York: Pantheon, 1978.

Smith, Paul. *Pound Revised.* London: Croom Helm, 1983.

Way, Arthur, trans. and ed. *Euripides.* Vol. 1. London: Heinemann, 1916. 4 vols.

Marti Greene (essay date September 1994)

SOURCE: Greene, Marti. "H. D.'s Challenge to the Institution in 'The Flowering of the Rod.'" *Theology* 97, no. 779 (September 1994): 344-52.

[*In the following essay, Greene maintains that although H. D.'s "The Flowering of the Rod" is suffused with Christian images and themes, a thorough and detailed study of the work reveals the poet's subversive attitudes about Christianity.*]

In the final decades of the twentieth century, women have examined like never before the foundations of Western culture. As their struggle for equality has advanced, women have sought to identify their place in the spiritual realm. Many have found Christianity's patriarchal imagery and structure deeply dissatisfying and have struggled to develop other forms of spiritual expression. Some, unwilling to sever all ties to Christianity, have worked to transform the Church to include women in worship and service, and have even developed a concept of a deity with feminine as well as masculine qualities. Even though increasing numbers of women are finding ministry roles, the debate continues. Should women serve as priests? What is their place in terms of Christian tradition, and what responsibilities do women have to convey or transform that tradition? How should Christians think of God with regard to gender, and what effects do such concepts have on believers' views of themselves?

In the context of this struggle, the voice of H. D. rings forth with new relevance. In **'The Flowering of the Rod',** the third poem in her war-time work ***Trilogy,*** H. D. addresses questions of gender in theology in an almost prophetic manner. In offering an alternative to what she perceives to be a society built on principles of destruction, H. D. says much about women's role in the spiritual life of humanity. Can the Church learn from her work, or is H. D.'s vision inimical to Christianity?

H. D. operates from a position which many Christians will, at first glance, find comfortingly familiar. Born in 1886 in Bethlehem, Pennsylvania, Hilda Doolittle grew up in a Protestant home where the Bible and church traditions were central to her consciousness. In her autobiographical novel *The Gift,* H. D. describes how hymns, Scripture stories, and Christian legends wind through young Hilda's thoughts as easily as episodes from fairy tales.[1] One of the pictures in her parents' house is of 'someone in the Bible, Mary-someone in a cave with long hair'.[2] Her familiarity with Christian tradition, especially the legends surrounding that 'Mary-someone', equips H. D. to write in terms Christians understand.

In **'The Flowering of the Rod'**, H. D. creates a tapestry of stories about Christ's birth and his association with Mary Magdalene. The poet's account of meetings between Mary and Kaspar the Mage has a dream-like quality because she continually undermines the situations she poses. She appropriates the traditional conflation of Mary Magdalene, Mary of Bethany, and the sinful woman who washes Christ's feet (Sect. 12.7-8; Sects. 21-23) and establishes Kaspar's identity only to suggest that he *might* be 'Chaldean, not an Arab at all, / . . . Balthasar, Melchior, / or that other of Bethlehem; / . . . an Angel in Disguise / . . . an old lover / of Mary Magdalene . . . / some say he was Abraham, / some say he was God' (20.7, 9-10, 12, 19-20, 23-4). Underlying H. D.'s ambiguity is her awareness of the contradictory nature of accounts of these stories. The Gospels provide four different versions of a woman's anointing of Christ, never identifying her as Mary Magdalene (Matt. 26.6ff., Mark 14.3ff., Luke 7.36ff., and John 12.1ff.; 11.2). Faulting H. D. for using poetic licence hardly seems fair in the light of the information available.

Despite the fluid quality of her characterizations, H. D. works with familiar figures. What if Mary Magdalene *did* obtain oil from one of the magi? What significance does such a conceit have, other than providing readers with a fanciful story? Plenty, Rachel Blau DuPlessis asserts. She explains that H. D.'s weaving together of stories is 'an act of critical delegitimation of culturally sacred narratives, because it inserts a line of causation where no such relation had existed'.[3] By working within a Christian framework, H. D. puts Western readers at ease before launching her attack on their system.

A look at H. D.'s biography uncovers the roots of her dissatisfaction with Western society and its foundations in traditional Christianity. Her family's faith, Moravianism, developed in fifteenth-century Europe out of a similar dissatisfaction with the established Church. In her analysis of Moravianism's impact on H. D., Jane Augustine relates that the poet was intrigued by the group's receptiveness to different traditions, including mysticism and the religions of non-white races. She writes: 'For H. D. the Moravian Church propagates a universal eternal spirituality transcending human divisions—competing sects, warring nations, the personal opposition of male versus female.'[4] The overcoming of the opposition of male and female is a concern H. D. addresses throughout her work, and Moravianism offers her clues for reaching such a resolution.

Moravianism not only presents possibilities for an understanding of God as female, at least in part, but H. D.'s awareness of Moravianism's mystical elements comes to her through the maternal line. Hilda's grandmother, 'Mamalie', recounts discovering a record of a meeting between Moravian settlers and native Americans who worshipped in harmony. Upon reading the document, Mamalie acquired an uncanny knowledge of the peace-producing ceremonies her forebears and the Indians had shared a century earlier.[5] H. D. takes up the idea of a religion of peace, a faith which transcends traditional Church teachings while retaining Christian imagery, transmitted by women and incorporating feminine characteristics. In *The Gift,* Mamalie tells that the suspension of ceremonies with the Indians resulted in a curse of war upon the land.[6] **'The Flowering of the Rod'** suggests that H. D. accepts the view her grandmother offers in *The Gift*: that practising the peace-loving, feminine-encompassing religion of the Moravian-Indian fellowship will bring unity; those who condemn such beliefs will bring war and death upon humankind. Writing both *The Gift* and ***Trilogy*** in London during the Blitz, H. D. had good reason to explore the possibilities for peace her grandmother's revelation had promised.

H. D. establishes her position in the Christian tradition from the outset of **'The Flowering of the Rod'.** The poem's title is packed with religious associations, and it begins with what appears to be a tribute to Christ: 'O the beautiful garment, / the beautiful raiment—' (1. 1-2). A closer reading, however, uncovers her real meaning: think not of this man and his glory—at least not in the Church's terms. Traditional Christianity looks appealing, H. D. warns, but it has engendered a society of '. . . anger, frustration, / bitter line of destruction: / . . . the smouldering cities below' (1. 21-3).[7] H. D. continues her assault on Christianity, referring to the sharpening of steel into weapons and to skulls, suggesting that those who seek meaning in traditional religion are 'senseless[ly] wheeling' with a dangerously limited view of reality (6.10ff.).

Unwilling to join the ranks of those who condemn but fail to construct, H. D. shares her hopes for a better system. She challenges society to abandon Christianity for a religion of genuine love (1. 27-30). She offers clues about the nature of this religion in the planting imagery of the second section. Although sowing and reaping images are common in the Gospels, H. D.'s language also brings to mind fertility cults and such figures as Demeter and Astarte. The poet suggests that she is capable of restoring life to Western civilization, much as a fertility goddess would bring life to a field. She writes:

> I go to where I belong, inexorably
> as the rain that has lain long
>
> in the furrow I have given
> or would have given
>
> life to the grain;
> but it would not grow or ripen
>
> with the rain of beauty,
> the rain will return to the cloud;
>
> the harvester sharpens his steel on the stone;
> but this is not our field.
>
> We have not sown this;
> pitiless, pitiless, let us leave
>
> The-place-of-a-skull
> to those who have fashioned it.
>
> (2. 5-18)

Abandoning this worn-out soil, H. D. points the way to a new religion. Turning her back on the 'iron, steel, metal' of her society, H. D. looks toward antiquity for salvific secrets. She compares the message of the past to Atlantis or the Hesperides, submerged but still compelling to the birds who remember the paradisiac islands (5.12-26). Although her search for meaning, like that of the birds for the Hesperidean apples, seems vain, H. D. is confident that it will be worthwhile. She says boldly that she 'would rather drown, remembering' than live unquestioningly (6.1).

H. D. compares antiquity's message to an unfolding lily, 'each petal a kingdom, an aeon, / and it is the seed of a lily / that having flowered, / will flower again' (10.19-23). Her description of the unfolding, seed-bearing lily, reappearing in Kaspar's reveries, also suggests the cyclic nature of her vision. Her language about circles, spirals, and echoes (Sects. 28-32) is reminiscent of imagery at the poem's beginning (Sect. 6), and H. D. describes Kaspar's memory of his visit to the Bethlehem stable, which happened before the poem's action begins, at the poem's end (Sects. 42-43). Structurally, then, H. D.'s work circles on itself and underlines her assertion that time operates in a spiral rather than in a line.

H. D.'s 'eternal recurrence' view of time is the basis for the layering of events and characters in the poem. H. D. writes often of her notion of the 'palimpsest', an inscribed tablet from which an earlier message has been erased. According to H. D., traces of the old message will influence the reading of the new. She demonstrates palimpsesting in **'The Flowering of the Rod'** by layering her characters: multiple Maries and Simons and an assortment of magi figures. She layers events, presenting them as memories, visions, and fulfillments of prophecies.

According to DuPlessis, H. D.'s psychotherapy and study with Freud convinced her that both people and events are symbols or abstractions and that similarities in human experience point toward universal truth. 'By knowledge of eternal recurrence,' she explains, 'specific pain can be dissolved, enobled, and emboldened.'[8] Susan Stanford Friedman clarifies the issue, writing: '[Freud's] theory that individual development recapitulates the patterns of growth in human history provided her with a way to connect her personal myth to the records of early civilization in both religion and art.'[9] At the source of art and religion, H. D. asserts, lies the seed of the gospel she preaches: a memory of the Mother-Goddess. In her notes for *The Gift*, H. D. writes:

> Under every shrine to Jupiter, to Zeus-pater, or Theus-pater or God-the-father . . . there is an earlier altar. There is, beneath the carved superstructure of every temple to God-the-father, the dark cave or grotto or inner hall or *cella* to Mary, Mere, Mut, mutter, pray for us.[10]

Friedman examines the primacy of goddess religions in her work on the poet, explaining that Freud led H. D. to believe that the mother 'holds a prior, even primal position in the unconscious of the individual and the collective unconscious of the race'.[11] Adrienne Rich looks at Freudian theories which assert that the initial dependence of humans on their mothers results in a universal experience of dreaming about and mythologizing 'an archetypal powerful woman'.[12] She suggests that female physiology established woman as the source of life and rightful deity—known in pre-Christian societies by such names as Tiamat, Rhea, Isis, Ishtar, Cybele, Demeter, and Diana.[13]

H. D.'s conviction of the importance of Mother-Goddess cults grew not only out of her faith in Freudian theory but also from her familiarity with ancient cultures. She has Mary Magdalene identify herself with 'that myrrh-tree of the gentiles / . . . the Mother of Mutilations' (16.11, 15). The classical figure Myrrha, in an incestuous union with her father Cinyras, bore Adonis, whom H. D. mentions in association with Attis and Tammuz (16.16).[14,15] Attis was the consort of the goddess Cybele, whose festival involved a 'Day of Blood' commemorating Attis' castration and death.[16] Conflating Myrrha and Cybele yields a 'Mother of

Mutilations', and H. D. links this figure to Christ's mother by layering her Mary characters. Adonis is often identified with Christ, also the child of a woman and her father—albeit a heavenly one.[17] Many of H. D.'s mythological figures are associated with fertility, reinforcing her planting imagery.

H. D. reintroduces this imagery in her account of Kaspar's recognition of Mary Magdalene's links to pagan goddesses. She contrasts Kaspar's view of Mary with that of Simon, a Jew who considers any association with goddesses demonic. Kaspar, however, sees the goddesses not as devils but as *daemons,* attendant or indwelling spirits. H. D. writes:

> . . . Simon might have heard
> that this woman from the city,
>
> was devil ridden or had been;
> but Kaspar might call
>
> the devils *daemons*
> and might even name the seven
>
> under his breath, for technically
> Kaspar was a heathen;
>
> he might whisper tenderly, those names
> without fear of eternal damnation,
>
> Isis, Astarte, Cyprus
> and the other four;
>
> he might re-name them,
> Ge-meter, De-meter, earth-mother
>
> or Venus
> in a star.

(25.15-30)

In her work on Greek religion, Jane Harrison explains antiquity's association of femininity with crop fertility and alludes to the corresponding link between masculinity and destruction. She asserts that in the time when men were busy hunting and fighting, women would naturally have been responsible for agriculture and its rituals.[18] Worship by females within a female sphere of responsibility logically resulted in the development of goddess traditions. Harrison believes that the existence of goddess cults indicates that the earliest societies were matriarchal but became patriarchal as men gave up their belief in women's magical powers. Harrison describes how men altered myth to undermine matriarchy, remaking goddesses into temptresses and playthings.[19] The overturning of the 'kinder, gentler' matriarchal societies put men in power, but at great cost. H. D. points to the effects of two world wars as proof of man's inability to rule.

H. D. depicts resistance to a female liberator in the responses of Simon and Kaspar to Mary Magdalene.

They view her as unclean and dangerous. Looking at her, Kaspar reminds himself that 'no secret was safe with a woman'—the ultimate irony, considering the power of the secrets H. D. believes women safeguard (14.24). Mary's hair symbolizes the 'other-ness' of feminine power, and both men view it with mingled fascination and repulsion.

Although both Simon and Kaspar look upon Mary Magdalene's hair with trepidation, Kaspar is at least free of Simon's specifically Jewish prejudices against women. In spite of his own misogynistic attitudes, 'when he saw the light on her hair / like moonlight on a lost river, / Kaspar / remembered' (27.17-20). H. D. describes Kaspar's memory/vision as revealing glimpses from the Golden Age—of the Islands of the Blest, the Hesperides, Atlantis. As his vision plumbs collective memory, 'through spiral upon spiral of the shell / of memory that yet connects us / with the drowned cities of prehistory, / Kaspar understood and his brain translated: / *Lilith born before Eve / and one born before Lilith*' (33.17-22). This one born before Lilith must surely be the lost Mother-Goddess. H. D. suggests the presence of the Mother-Goddess in connection with another Mary in Kaspar's memory of his visit to the Bethlehem stable. In his recollection, related in the final lines of the poem, Kaspar sees a mother who is 'shy and simple and young, / . . . he did not know whether she knew / the fragrance came from the bundle of myrrh / she held in her arms' (43.2, 6-8). Instead of showing Mary with Christ on her lap, H. D. depicts her holding vegetation as a fertility goddess would.

H. D. points out that despite his resistance to receiving the vision, Kaspar finds joy in it. 'What he saw made his heart so glad', she writes, 'that it was as if he suffered, / his heart laboured so / with his ecstasy' (28.36-9). Although he delights in the vision's beauty, Kaspar finds the sense of fulfilment it conveys even more rewarding. He sees how his vision fits into the mysteries his forefathers have passed to him (much as Mamalie shared maternal secrets with Hilda in *The Gift*), but the vision also reveals how Kaspar himself has come full circle. He realizes that the jar of myrrh Mary has obtained from him is one of a set, the first of which he had presented to Jesus in Bethlehem. Kaspar had resolved to 'someday . . . bring the other', and Mary's use of the second jar for anointing Jesus fulfils his resolution (42.2). Through her depiction of Kaspar, H. D. suggests that the recovery of the Mother-Goddess will return humankind to its foundations, resulting in universal stability and fulfilment.

The religion of **'The Flowering of the Rod'** is inviting, promising a revitalized, harmonious society through recognition and worship of a Mother-Goddess (or, at least, a deity who is both male and female). Many Christians will, however, be wary of the implications of H. D.'s work. Even those who agree that the Church has limited women's spiritual productivity will find her understanding of Christ's role and her appeal to the Mother-Goddess religions troubling. Although Christ is an important character in the poem, H. D. never suggests that he is 'the way, the truth, and the life' in any unique sense. Her handling of the Moravian/Indian worship in *The Gift* indicates that she regards Christianity as one of a number of spiritual avenues. Furthermore, Christianity's foundation in Judaism grounds it in a tradition which opposes Mother-Goddess religions. In an unpublished paper entitled 'The Church and Inclusive Language for God?', Charles Talbert explains that the Hebrews avoided feminine language for God because creation by a goddess implies birthing, leading to a view of the world as an extension of God.[20] Those who hold such a position see sin as offence against the world, not against a Creator who is separate from creation.[21] Such a view is theologically untenable for Christians, even those who recognize that the Church has made grave mistakes in its treatment of women. Talbert warns:

> For one committed to the Apostolic Faith, . . . it would seem that guaranteeing equality for women and men in Christ should not be allowed to subvert the Faith we profess and on the basis of which we strive for sexual equality. We need to be able to distinguish between feminism as fairness and feminism as anti-Christian ideology and to support the former while holding the line against the latter.[22]

Examining **'The Flowering of the Rod'** from Talbert's perspective uncovers the heresy within H. D.'s theology while acknowledging the importance of her search for a faith which recognizes the equality of women and men.

H. D.'s **'Flowering of the Rod'** is deeply relevant for twentieth-century thinkers, both for its critique of Western culture's violence and for its expression of women's longings to find a place in organized religion. Her understanding of psychology, her familiarity with myth and Scripture, and her powerful style, enable H. D. to articulate some of modernity's most disturbing questions: should Western society be satisfied with its warring, patriarchal structure? Is Christianity in its traditional form the only source of spiritual truth? Christians who place their faith in a transcendent God will find the implications of H. D.'s work unacceptable, but her cry for peace and justice serves as a rebuke to those who have constructed a religion of oppression and violence from a gospel which proclaims that 'there is neither Jew nor Greek, slave nor free, male nor female, for you are all one in Christ Jesus' (Galatians 3.28).

Notes

1. H. D., *The Gift* (Virago 1984), pp. 7-9, 12-18, 27, 30, 59-60, 83.

2. H. D., *The Gift*, p. 38.

3. R. B. DuPlessis, *Writing Beyond the Ending* (Indiana 1985), p. 120.

4. J. Augustine, 'The Mystery Unveiled: The Significance of H. D.'s "Moravian" Novel' (*HD Newsletter*, Spring 1991), p. 15.

5. H. D., *The Gift*, pp. 86-8.

6. H. D., *The Gift*, p. 91.

7. H. D., 'The Flowering of the Rod' in L. Martz (ed.), *Trilogy* in *H. D.: Collected Poems, 1912-1944* (New Directions 1986), p. 577. All subsequent references to this work cited in the text.

8. DuPlessis, *Writing Beyond the Ending*, p. 50.

9. S. S. Friedman, *Psyche Reborn: The Emergence of H. D.* (Indiana 1981), p. 70.

10. D. Collecott, 'Introduction to the British Edition', *The Gift*, p. xvii.

11. Friedman, *Psyche Reborn*, p. 144.

12. A. Rich, *Of Woman Born* (Norton 1976), p. 73.

13. Rich, *Of Woman Born*, p. 73.

14. M. Cary et al. (eds.), *The Oxford Classical Dictionary* (Clarendon 1949), pp. 966, 6-7.

15. W. F. Allbright, *Yahweh and the Gods of Canaan* (Athlone 1968), p. 128.

16. Cary et al., *The Oxford Classical Dictionary*, pp. 119, 689.

17. Cary et al., *The Oxford Classical Dictionary*, p. 7.

18. J. Harrison, *Prolegomena to the Study of Greek Religion* (Cambridge 1922), p. 272.

19. Harrison, *Prolegomena*, p. 285.

20. C. Talbert, 'The Church and Inclusive Language for God?' (Wake Forest University 1990), p. 17.

21. Talbert, 'The Church and Inclusive Language for God', p. 6.

22. Talbert, 'The Church and Inclusive Language for God', p. 20.

Jeffrey Twitchell-Waas (essay date winter 1998)

SOURCE: Twitchell-Waas, Jeffrey. "Seaward: H. D.'s *Helen in Egypt* as a Response to Pound's *Cantos*." *Twentieth-Century Literature* 44, no. 4 (winter 1998): 464-83.

[*In the following essay, Twitchell-Waas identifies the ways in which H. D.'s* Helen in Egypt *may be regarded as a reaction to Pound's work, and additionally studies the epic poem as a distinctly modernist response to warfare that emphasizes the collective cultural psyche of the age.*]

Despite the firm nook in the modernist pantheon that H. D. has acquired over the past quarter century, she remains an oddly isolated figure within the larger matrix of poetic modernism. Recent scholarship has correctly shifted attention to her late long poems, but there has been little consideration of how these ambitious works relate to other long poems by her contemporaries.[1] Over the last two decades of her life, H. D. composed nine long sequences (if we consider the *Trilogy* as discrete poems), which at the very least are clearly distinctive from the comparable works by Pound, Eliot, Crane, Williams, Stevens, and others that are commonly taken to be at the center of American poetic modernism. Undoubtedly, the ethereal mode of her work, which tends to filter out the messiness and vulgarities of present history, goes against the grain of contemporary developments. Yet, despite their apparent difference in manner and perspective, H. D.'s long sequences were written within the context of these other works and the larger cultural project in which they are engaged. In this essay, I will focus on the most obvious point of contact: H. D.'s relationship with Pound, and specifically *Helen in Egypt* as a response to Pound's *Cantos.* Few readers will be surprised at the suggestion of a significant relationship between these two works, yet the question has received little attention.[2]

From the time she was composing *Helen in Egypt* (1952-55), H. D. frequently mentioned Pound and his *Cantos* in her correspondence with Norman Holmes Pearson, and evidently approved, was even flattered by, Pearson's reference to *Helen in Egypt* as her *"cantos"* (Friedman 216).[3] More important, if more difficult to pinpoint, is that for H. D. and many others Pound defined the ambitiousness of the modernist poet. In the cases of H. D. and Williams, there appears little in the work of their early decades that would indicate an inevitable evolution toward the composition of long poems, yet both, late in their careers, felt compelled to produce deliberately planned, epic-scale works. In *End to Torment,* H. D. remarks that "Thinking of Ezra's work, I recall my long *Helen* sequence. Perhaps, there was always a challenge in his creative power. Perhaps, even, [. . .] there was unconscious—really unconscious—rivalry" (41). For H. D. personally, Pound represented her simultaneous initiation into both love and poetry, which remained inextricable and mutually motivating throughout her work. But most important, in the *Cantos,* as well as in his advocacy of other modernists, Pound promoted a conception of the "serious artist" responding comprehensively to the sense of

cultural crisis during the period of world wars. For the older generation of American modernists, who for all their rebelliousness inherited a strong streak of Victorian earnestness, the social and spiritual catastrophe that manifested itself in the First World War and its aftermath obligated an attempt to identify the causes of cultural dysfunction and to offer positive answers for renewal. In this sense, *Helen in Egypt,* despite its very different mode of procedure, is of a piece with these other modernist epics.

H. D.'s ambitious late work, though, was not conceived as simply another rival modernist project alongside those of Pound and others, but as complementary work. This is evident in her unique memoirs—*Tribute to Freud* and *End to Torment,* and I would also include *Bid Me to Live*—which examine her relationships with other major modernists. While commentators have emphasized H. D.'s critiques of Freud, Pound, and Lawrence, this has sometimes obscured the memoirs' deeper intent to dialectically define her companionship with their work. This requires recognizing what distracts from the authentic impulse of their work, including prominently their masculinism, in order to reveal where H. D. joins them in a common effort. Throughout her late work, H. D. repeatedly refers to her participation in a heretical band of artists and cultural workers—"bearers of the secret wisdom" as she rather immodestly puts it in *The Walls Do Not Fall* (*CP* 517)—who whatever their superficial differences and disagreements are ultimately united in a common purpose, a conspiracy for world peace (see *By Avon,* esp. 83-85). In *Helen in Egypt,* after Helen and Achilles's fateful encounter on the beach and the latter's rebirth as the "new Mortal," each goes separately about their work: *"both occupied with the thought of reconstruction, he 'to re-claim the coast with the Pharos, the light-house,' she to establish or re-establish the ancient Mysteries"* in the Temple of Amen (63; see also 89).[4] In the mutual project of world peace, there appears to be a division of labor whereby Achilles attends to the more pragmatic and public sphere, while Helen attends to the sacred and psychological forms of salvation and reconstruction.

Although H. D. had moved away from classical Greek materials after the 1930s, her decision to work with broadly Homeric materials in *Helen in Egypt* was no doubt in part a response to those megaworks of Anglo-American modernism, Joyce's *Ulysses* and Pound's *Cantos.* The story that Helen was not at Troy but had been divinely whisked off to Egypt during the war represents a well-established, if minority, alternative to the orthodoxy of the Homeric version, and so problematizes the classic narrative drawn on by Joyce and Pound.[5] Actually, *Helen in Egypt* does not so much reject the Homeric narrative for a preferable alternative as it sets the two in dialogue and so complicates both. It is notable, however, that H. D. addresses the matter of the *Iliad* rather than that of the *Odyssey.* Well before Pound and Joyce, Odysseus had been taken as a type of the modern man. Curious for experience as an end in itself and pragmatically responding to each new circumstance, he and his story naturally have had more resonance with the modern sensibility than with the inflexible warrior ethos. For Pound, it is important that Odysseus's tale begins after the war and recounts a return home to reestablish the peacetime kingdom. For all its deviations into various hells, the *Cantos* begins with Odysseus seeking prophetic advice about how to get back home, and the poem was intended to help instigate a cultural revitalization to ensure that war was left behind for good, which is why the poem ground to a halt during World War II and its trajectory drastically altered when Pound returned to it at Pisa. In choosing to work with the *Iliad* materials, H. D. insists it is necessary to go not away from but back into the war. Since hers is a psychological, even a psychoanalytic epic rather than a historical one, it is necessary to reveal the psychic causes that for her lie beneath all social manifestations. By examining Achilles rather than Odysseus, she implies that the former is not an outdated type but remains an accurate model of the psychological economy of patriarchal power.

Helen in Egypt situates itself with respect to Pound's poem as the latter's textual unconscious, insisting on and exploring those spaces of the personal and psychological which tend to be repressed in the *Cantos.* H. D.'s epic argues that war is due to repression, the cultivation of an ethos of egocentric strength that requires the repression of the maternal. In Achilles's case, this means the sea, Thetis, the flowing, unbounded, vulnerable realm of experience that would undermine the iron discipline of the warrior. According to the mythic logic behind the figure of Achilles, he becomes the apotheosis of the warrior ideal precisely because his mother is the sea: the extreme powers of repression necessary for him to forget the maternal dialectically transform him into the model of military rigidity. This is a self-perpetuating ethos: the repression that makes possible the warrior manifests itself in violence and war, which in turn motivate the need for the warrior. What is left out is the "feminine," not simply all those designated "women," which might just as well cover all manner of "inferior" classes of peoples, but the whole sphere of the personal, of those human relations requiring a degree of surrender of the ego and the possibility of the transformation and interpenetration of selves. The Achilles' heel in all this is that he has a mother, manifest as Helen, the supposed cause of the war justifying the boys' need to busy themselves as repressed war machines. Helen is the cause of the Trojan War, since as a sort of eidolon for Thetis, she is the Achilles that Achilles must deny in order to become Achilles[6]—which is why Helen is the central issue yet always appears as deflected to the margins of the war. In *Helen in Egypt,* Achilles is "killed" when he exchanges a look with Helen up on Troy's walls, a gaze he describes as "shimmering as light on the changeable sea" (54). In other words, he sees Thetis as himself mirrored in Helen's eyes, a reflection that will be repeated for a final time when he washes up on the beach in Egypt. Achilles in fact melts or is scattered and immediately finds himself transported from the dry plains of Troy to a boat crossing the sea to Egypt, identified with the death ship of Osiris—who was similarly scattered, then reassembled by the Egyptian Thetis, Isis, and reborn as Horus, who in characteristic mythic logic then becomes both husband and son.

If we consider this reading of Achilles and the Trojan War as a psychological allegory in relation to Pound and the *Cantos,* we discern some interesting parallels. Pound's "poem including history" is predominately concerned with historical, economic, and political materials on the assumption that herein lies the sickness of Western culture that must be made transparent so that the spiritual and aesthetic values that are the proper focus of living can achieve full potential. The fact that in strictly quantitative terms, the historical materials tend to overwhelm and obscure the more spiritual concerns, which presumably are the underlying impetus of the *Cantos,* is symptomatic of Pound's perception of the dire state of modern culture and the threatened role of the artist-poet within modernity. Pound's commitment to clearing up the social superstructure in order for rather simplistically valorized natural energies to freely unfold themselves leads him to reject the unconscious. As many commentators have argued, Pound's anti-Semitic, sexist, and authoritarian views are grounded in the need to separate out clarity, the spiritual light that is such a central presence in his poem, from all manner of intermixture and contamination. Pound's manichaeism became increasingly entrenched under the pressure to commit himself and his poem to the trend of contemporary history, to throw in his lot with a pragmatic manifestation of the improved society he envisioned. This above all required the suppression of the anarchic impulses of the unconscious, and the *Cantos* of the late 1920s through the 30s would see an increased emphasis on Enlightenment figures of right reason, such as John Adams and Confucian emperors. But of course the *Cantos* are everywhere marked by repression, as it is surely one of the most mixed, oblique, and contaminated of literary works.

Perhaps emblematic of this repression is an interesting instance of revision in the early stages of the *Cantos*. When reworking the initial false start that he had published in 1917, Pound moved the journey to the underworld passage translated from book XI of the *Odyssey* to the opening of his epic, but he also did some minor trimming. Whereas now the translation breaks off with the name of Odysseus's mother, Anticlea, and then sputters out with a few more lines of paraphrase mentioning the Sirens and Circe, originally Pound had included several more lines in which Odysseus speaks with his mother and tries vainly three times to embrace her shade.[7] Thinking about the *Cantos* from the perspective of H. D.'s concerns, we might take this editing out of Odysseus's poignant attempt to embrace his mother as indicative of the direction Pound and his poem would take. The *Cantos* begins with Odysseus "Set[ting] keel to breakers, forth on the godly sea" (1/3), Canto II is taken up with watery Dionysian transformations, and much in the earliest Cantos deals with mythic and visionary materials.[8] However, it can be argued that Pound could not fully follow the implications of this launching forth and increasingly insisted on attempting to control his materials with "the beak of his ego," as Charles Olson put it (82). In this sense, there are striking parallels to the warrior Achilles, who is described by H. D. in decidedly fascistic terms (esp. 51-56). Of course Odysseus too is a conflicted figure: desiring new experience and its risks, yet maintaining control, as is most strikingly illustrated in the episodes with the Sirens and Circe, both of whom surface as seductive dangers to the poet in the *Cantos*.[9]

We can say with reasonable certainty that, whatever Pound's intentions, the *Cantos* did not end up being the poem he had in mind. The form of the *Cantos* committed Pound to risk, uncertainty, self-contradiction, impurity, and failure as the only possible success. The ideogrammic method as he deployed it meant that innumerable voices and scraps from all over enter the poem, and however severely Pound edited, even deformed, his sources, it was impossible to keep control over them. Surely no poem before the *Cantos* relies so heavily on quotation, which to some degree is a surrender of authorial control. From this perspective, there is a deep passivity about the paratactic method of the *Cantos,* a willingness to allow, even a dependency on allowing, other voices, texts, and languages to do the speaking, in however truncated a manner, rather than to absorb them into a more consistent authorial voice as Pound had in fact done in the Ur-Cantos of 1917. The agglutinative immensity itself of Pound's poem makes it difficult to see how he could have kept it under control, as he unquestionably desired. But beyond this, responding in part to the challenge posed by the realist novel, Pound attempted to anchor the *Cantos* in the objective reality of history, and as Michael André Bernstein has lucidly demonstrated, the ultimate authority of the poem relied on certain concrete historical changes in society. Short of such historical manifestations, despite the reiterated allusions to and assertions of stability, order, and clarity, the poem floats on shifting water, and it is quite impossible for us to read these assertions as other than strongly shadowed by Pound's anxieties and groping, and the poem as other than deeply conflicted.

Helen in Egypt is a poem of epic ambition without history, focusing instead on the cultural psyche, with material history conceived of as epiphenomena. To a significant degree, this is dictated by the fact that H. D. was female, so that "history" in a sense was unavailable to her. This is not only a question of the very attenuated agency attributed to women in history as we know it, but also the sphere of "knowledge" from which H. D. writes is naturally more that of personal relations and consciousness. In her famous defense of "Modern Fiction," Virginia Woolf strategically designates the realist novel as "materialist" in order to argue for the more authentic realism of the psychological novel she advocates. Without making the point explicitly, Woolf attempts to relocate the focus of the novel, where women stand at least equal to men, which indeed is superior precisely because of its universality. In "The Guest," written in the immediate aftermath of World War II, H. D. suggests that much of the poetic genius of the Elizabethan age was stunted and dissipated because of various poets' engagement with the public sphere, whereas Shakespeare's genius achieved fulfillment because he resisted the lures of immediate history (*By Avon,* esp. 81-85, 94-96). The poet is the voice of the repressed in the cultural psyche that embodies those desires that must be recognized and satisfied, or at least sublimated in some positive manner, if there is to be any hope for an improved society. Ultimately, this may amount to conceiving of the poet's task as insisting on "anachronistic" values in the face of the historical forces of global rationalization and instrumentalization: thus the emphasis on the poet's task as anamnesis. H. D. is one of the more extreme examples among modernist poets who cultivated disreputable and obsolete "knowledge": the occult, alchemy, gnosticism, spiritualism, cabala— "sciences" whose utter delegitimization by modernity indicates to H. D. areas of cultural repression.[10]

H. D. read the *Pisan Cantos* shortly after its publication in 1948, and, according to Barbara Guest's biography, she wrote to their old mutual friend Viola Baxter Jordan that she found them "heartbreaking" (290). "Heartbreaking" is from Guest's paraphrase, and it would be interesting to know if H. D. actually used this word, since the very last stanza of **Helen in Egypt** reads: *"only Achilles could break his heart / and the world for a token, / a memory forgotten"* (304). I take the phrase "break his heart" to represent the cracking of the isolate ego and the opening up to the emotions and the destabilizing psyche. The "memory forgotten" that shatters the "iron-ring" round his heart is that of Achilles's mother, Thetis, the sea goddess. In this final stanza, Helen is one last time affirming her choice of Achilles over Paris because the latter knows nothing of the sea; indeed, in the poem Paris is strictly a landlubber. **Helen in Egypt** argues for the acceptance of the sea, identified with the mother, but implying memory, dissolution of the ego, expansiveness, sensuality, risk, vulnerability, uncertainty—that is, the surrender of an ethos of control and power. This sea is also poetry, the muses, with the suggestion that its basis is in the presymbolic: *"its beat and long reverberation, / its booming and delicate echo, / / its ripple that spells a charm / on the sand"* (304)—the sea spells a charm on the blank page of the beach. The sea is inclusive, as the "Image or Eidolon of Thetis" tells Helen:

> A woman's wiles are a net;
> they would take the stars
> or a grasshopper in its mesh;
>
> they would sweep the sea
> for a bubble's iridescence
> or a flying-fish;
>
> they would plunge beneath the surface,
> without fear of the treacherous deep
> or a monstrous octopus

(93)

and so on.

As a response to the *Cantos,* **Helen in Egypt** attempts to perform a rescue operation, to recall Pound to the sea, to accept the uncertainty that his poem proposes but which he is constantly at odds with and attempts to manhandle.[11] Often in H. D.'s later sequences, perhaps most explicitly in **Vale Ave,** we find the female protagonist drawing out the lover-poet from the soldier figure. Achilles's transformation into the New Mortal begins when at the peak of his military power the glance he exchanges with Helen evokes dim memories of Thetis and sets off a process of self-questioning. In many respects, the broken Achilles who finds himself cast up on the shores of Egypt, still somewhat shell-shocked and suffering bouts of paranoia, is an apt image of Pound at Pisa. The well-known Dryad passage in Canto 83 is usually understood to be addressed to H. D.; certainly, she would have understood the prayer as calling out to her: "Δρνας [Dryad], your eyes are like the clouds over Taishan / When some of the rain

has fallen / and half remains yet to fall [. . .] / / Dryad, thy peace is like water" (83/530).[12] Surely, H. D. would have read the *Pisan Cantos* as the cracking of Pound's ego; in a moment of self-examination, Pound himself admits (quoting Villon): "Les larmes que j'ai crées m'inondent / Tard, très tard je t'ai connue, la Tristesse, / I have been hard as youth sixty years" (80/513).[13] Of course, what is most striking about the *Pisan Cantos* is their more personal voice, whose sense of lost hopes for society, and with it his poem, is most poignantly expressed in the remembrance of past friendships. Pound attempts to recover some grounds for his poem through the flooding up of memory, to a large degree memories of the London years when H. D.'s and Pound's lives, both personally and poetically, were so intertwined. Consequently, the texture of the *Pisan Cantos* is more flowing and less collaged out of his reading than most of the Cantos that precede and follow. There is also a renewed assertion of the mythopoetic, the desire to connect with the natural process and the consequent diminution of the belief in willfully remaking history.

However, during his years at St. Elizabeths, Pound was unable to pursue his poem in a manner that would incorporate such self-doubt. While working on **Helen in Egypt,** H. D. received a letter in which Pound with characteristic tact asserted, "Have felt yr / vile Freud all bunk / [. . .] You got into the wrong pig sty, ma chère. But not too late to climb out" (qtd. by Pearson in H. D., *Tribute* xii). At about the same time he was writing Canto 91, with the notorious passage that reads in part

> Democracies electing their sewage
> till there is no clear thought about holiness
> a dung flow from 1913
> and, in this, their kikery functioned, Marx, Freud
> and the american beaneries
> Filth under filth. . . .

(91/613-14)

Not only is this a unique instance in the *Cantos,* as far as I know, where Pound italicizes a passage written in his own voice, but also this appears in the middle of one of the more sustained visionary moments of the entire poem, full of water and light, a Canto that has some striking parallels with a number of passages in **Helen in Egypt.** Pound here deliberately sabotages or at least scars his own vision—symptomatic of his own weakening ability to maintain the utopian within history. The contaminating forces of modernity that he fears will erase "holiness" from human experience have taken hold of Pound's own voice, and although he would name that which prevents his vision from full, flawless realization, we cannot but see that what he would deny is what he needs to recognize: the unconscious and the underclasses, which the names of Freud and Marx designate.

In the final *Drafts and Fragments,* overwhelmed by a sense of futility, Pound once again allows his personal voice and feelings of vulnerability to sound through his verse. Several months after his release from St. Elizabeths in 1958, H. D. sent Pound the as yet unpublished *Helen in Egypt,* shortly followed by her memoir *End to Torment* (Robinson 432). Although apparently Pound's response to the poem was noncommittal, it is nonetheless notable that only in the last pages of the *Cantos* is H. D. explicitly named for the first time:

> But for the sun and serenitas
> > (19th May '59)
> H. D. once said "serenitas"
> > > (Atthis, etc.)
> > > at Dieudonné's
> > > > in pre-history.
>
> > > > > (113/787)

Again, Pound recalls the London years before the First World War ("in pre-history"), the time of youthful ambition and prior to his entanglements in history. We know from a letter Pound wrote H. D. in September 1959 that this passage refers to a specific event—an imagist dinner in 1914 at the Dieudonné restaurant in London where H. D. made this remark about a Sappho fragment addressed to Atthis—but which more generally is remembered by the elderly Pound as a time of relative tranquillity: "Not since Briget [Patmore], Richard [Aldington], the four of us, has there been any harmony around me" (qtd. in Materer 275).[14] As at Pisa, H. D. evidently recalls Pound to a time of youthful optimism and artistic companionship that he hoped would lead to a new renaissance. H. D.'s appearance here is particularly telling, since the underlying sentiment of Canto 113 is Pound's inability to rest, to stop his compulsiveness: "but the mind as Ixion, unstill, ever turning" (113/790). Undoubtedly, it would be too much to claim that here or elsewhere in the final Cantos Pound is acknowledging and responding to H. D.'s poem, yet H. D. remains a figure in his consciousness for a serenity lost.

Considering *Helen in Egypt* as a critical response to the *Cantos* may go some way toward situating H. D.'s poem within the larger field of poetic modernism, but the more consequential and perplexing question concerns the form of H. D.'s poem and its relationship with other modernist epics. Superficially, *Helen in Egypt* appears unrelated to the Poundian epic and other modernist specimens, which perhaps explains its

absence from general discussions of the genre. The challenge facing H. D. was not simply to offer critique or an alternative narrative to the patriarchal versions, but also to create a form that somehow enacts what the poem proposes, that, like the exchange between Helen and Achilles, acts on the readers in such a way that their more generous but repressed impulses are called forth.

In developing a long form out of imagist practice, Pound treated the imagist poem as essentially a realist fragment that could be collaged into complex constructions capable of containing an indefinite diversity. Pound's most fundamental innovation in the *Cantos* was to create a form capable not only of incorporating any sort of subject matter but also that could include virtually all registers of discourse, breaking down the protective wall separating the poetic from the discursive—what Bakhtin calls the novelization of the epic (6-7, 39). The poem becomes a space into which a multiplicity of discourses can be put into dialogue, and this became the general formal model for a major tradition of modernist long poems, such as Williams's *Paterson,* Zukofsky's *"A,"* Olson's *The Maximus Poems,* and Duncan's *Passages.* By breaking down the barrier between, and putting into juxtaposition, discursive and lyrical discourses, Pound wanted to make his poem capable of engaging with the practical world, and also to participate in the utopian amelioration of society by showing how the spheres of historical and aesthetic experience could be brought into accord.

When *Helen in Egypt* is put alongside Pound's "poem including history," what is immediately striking is the de-historicization and linguistic purity of H. D.'s poem. H. D.'s imagist practice focuses on the poem as visionary, in opposition to the material and historical present and rejecting the limitations of the real as is. H. D.'s poetry characteristically uses a limited and simple vocabulary (except for the numerous, often exotic proper names of divinities, flora, and places), is set in a mythologized past, and focuses on a few, frequently reiterated images. Even compared with the more aesthete of her contemporaries, say Wallace Stevens, the deliberateness with which H. D. expunges the historical present from her poetry is striking.[15] There are exceptions, but it is interesting that her most adventurous experiment in collaging different linguistic registers and historical materials, **"Good Frend"** (incorporated into *By Avon River*), was the last sequence H. D. wrote before beginning on *Helen in Egypt,* thus highlighting the deliberateness of her choice to return to mythological Greek materials.

Often accused of being escapist, H. D. accepted this characterization, since the poet's concern is to hold open the possibilities of desire against the admonitions of "the real," and the poem's tension is the inevitable asymmetry of desire and the real.[16] Consequently, the collage method as employed by Pound and Williams, although similarly intended to activate a deadened reality, was still too committed to a representational aesthetics, since it tended to treat discreet fragments as realist data. Robert Duncan has suggested that H. D.'s relative formal conservatism is a measure of her openness to the sea and was needed to limit "the riot of the imagination" ("H. D. Book, 2": 117). While H. D. adopts a more conventional narrative or lyrical voice for her poem, this voice has a propensity to shift, to include or contain other voices or consciousnesses, creating a most disorienting effect.

To be true to its own proposition, *Helen in Egypt* must ground itself on the groundlessness of the sea. The poem offers itself as the impossibility of a 300-page lyric, a quest narrative without telos, an epic of negative capability. To keep open possibilities beyond the real as given, it must avoid being confined by its own arguments. To propose an alternative narrative, a transposition of values such that the feminine or maternal replaces the masculine death cult risks simply inversely repeating the cycle of repression. The maternal sea is not proposed as the antithesis of the masculine warrior ethos but its actual basis, which is repressed, thus locking the mind into antitheses. The Great Goddess subsumes all such antitheses, is death as much as birth and love (17); in fact, in H. D.'s work "she" is as likely to appear as Zeus, Amen, God, Proteus "the Nameless-of-many-Names" (106), or Father as Thetis, Isis, Aphrodite, or Mother.[17] Achilles's repression of the goddess is an effort to deny death, to achieve immortality, which is why Thetis is responsible for his famous weak point. The effort to deny death manifests itself in the desire for dominance and violence toward others, a psychological substitute for a sense of immortality. So Helen-H. D. must not stop at offering a defense of herself; she must accept vulnerability as the grounds for an alternative ethos to that of power and dominance, and the first step is to reveal dominance itself as grounded in vulnerability. Vulnerability and its uncertainties become something like the ever-shifting ground of the human condition. *Helen in Egypt* in a sense acts therapeutically for the poet and on the readers to foster a mode of consciousness beyond argument. The texture of the poem—its constant circularity, folding back on itself, and apparent contradictoriness—is intended to release us from irritable reaching after certainties. H. D. often

acknowledges the threat and terror of the dissolution and shedding of old selves her poetry proposes, and the consequent need to pull back and establish some coherence. Her late sequences characteristically proceed in a centrifugal-centripetal manner, most famously emblematized in the image of the seashell in *The Walls Do Not Fall,* which alternately opens itself up to and closes out the sea tide (*CP* 512-14).

What is largely lacking in H. D.'s work is a sense of the sinister or of evil, such as one finds in, say, Djuna Barnes or Mary Butts. On the rare occasion when evil is mentioned—"Evil was active in the land / . . . Devill was after us" (*CP* 511)—it appears too much like medieval allegory for its terror to be convincing. No doubt, this in part explains why some readers feel a thinness in H. D.'s work, presumably reflecting the limitations imposed by the privileged life she lived. On the other hand, this lack of an irredeemably dark side reflects H. D.'s rejection, like Pound and unlike Eliot, of humankind's essential sinfulness, and her understanding of poetry's task as that of acceptance, as promoting an inclusive consciousness. I have been suggesting that for H. D. to identify an other as beyond transformation was to risk locking herself into an antithesis that simply perpetuates history's antagonisms. Pound was an obvious illustration of such entanglement, one in which he described himself as being "furious from perception"—an expression he evidently applied to Hitler (90/606, 104/741).

What distinguishes *Helen in Egypt* from other modernist epics is its acceptance and enactment of the consequences of its writtenness, which is certainly due to its author's self-consciousness of her social narratization as "female." Understandably, the usual assumption on approaching the poem is that Helen's exploration of the possibilities of self-hood will provide the narrative continuity of the poem, however obliquely. Robert O'Brien Hokanson has effectively pointed out the problems such an assumption inevitably encounters in attempting to rationalize the poem. The poem's initial starting point presumably takes up the alternative tale that Helen was never at Troy but *"had been transposed or translated from Greece into Egypt"* (1). However, soon enough Helen herself appears uncertain as to whether or not she was at Troy, and the likelihood is that she was, if only in the sense that the dominant narrative of herself would insist that she was. There are even hints of an explanatory link between these versions since, as Troy is falling, Helen escapes down a spiral stairway, apparently makes her way to the harbor, and then presumably is transported to Egypt (127-28, 143, 266-67). So, early on we have less alternative versions to choose between than two, held in dialogue with Helen learning to accept her complicity in both. This doubleness characterizes the figure of Helen throughout the classical tradition (Austin 48n, 83-89), and H. D. reiterates many of its traditional manifestations: Helen's double twin birth (Clytemnestra and the Dioscuri) and their twinned destinies, her double fatherhood (Zeus and Tyndareus), her double kidnapping (Theseus and Paris), her two husbands (Menelaus and Paris). As mentioned, Achilles too is double, and Helen acts to bring forth the lover-poet out of the warrior. The spiraling staircase down which Helen flees is obviously another version of H. D.'s favorite image of the seashell whose involutions spiral back to the groundlessness of the rhythms of the sea, an image of poetry itself. In this sense, Helen at Troy dissolves back into the sea, the shifting matrix of poetry, to be reborn as Helen in Egypt.[18]

The opening headnote's somewhat peculiar assertion that Helen was *"transposed or translated"* rather than "transported" to Egypt already hints that the poem will concern itself more with questions of writing and reading than asserting the authority of one narrative over others. To begin with at least, the poem seems to propose that the "present" of the poem has Helen in the Temple of Amen, and the body of the poem consists of her recollections and reconstructions of her past. Clearly this is a theater of reverie in which the imaginary and the "real" freely interpenetrate. If we privilege this moment with Helen in the Temple, we find that she is reading hieroglyphics on the walls, although she does not know the script. The fascination of Egyptian hieroglyphics is that they present themselves as natural language, signifying without being understood, so that Helen-H. D. is reading a language she does not understand, "the indecipherable Amen-script" (21). This is emblematic of H. D.'s poetry in which the image vibrates signification but the dictionary is missing. On the one hand, the hieroglyph-image is irreducible to a single, static meaning; while on the other, there is the possibility that the meanings are no more than subjective projections—the hieroglyph can mean anything and thus nothing. In this situation of too much or too little signifying, the reading (or writing) is endless, a constant process of revision with no guarantee of "progress." In contrast with Pound, whose image is relatively static and takes on further meaning through juxtaposition, H. D. constantly returns to an image to unfold through rereading further possibilities. Meaningfulness resides in the wandering reading itself, compounded by the participation of others in the reading, or as Duncan has remarked on H. D.'s hieroglyph: "Here, to experience is to read, to be aware involves at once the senses and the translation into language of our own" ("H. D. Book, 2": 28).

Consequently, if the poem is concerned with Helen's sense of identity, it is discovered in this interminable process of rereading, by others as well as herself, which is why Helen "herself is the writing" (22).[19] Achilles's transforming sea journey also proves to be a process of reading as he "measured the stars / with the sway of a ship's mast" (205; also 58, 59, 274)—learning to decipher the stars from a free-floating position.

Taking a closer look at the overall sequence of **Helen in Egypt,** one might suggest that a general development can be discerned, although it is more like devolution. I suspect that most readers would agree that each of the three major parts of the poem becomes increasingly difficult to keep in focus, which is more than merely a matter of accumulated complexity. In fact, it is not at all clear that the poem attempts to consecutively build on itself. The first part, **"Pallinode,"** is the easiest to follow because it is appropriately the most argumentative, including the critique of war outlined previously. **"Pallinode"** also contains another defense, that of Clytemnestra for murdering Agamemnon in retaliation for the sacrifice of their daughter to appease the gods for his own sacrilege. However, Helen's justification of her sister repeats patriarchy's own logic: patriarchy's crime against Clytemnestra has created its mirror image in her, and consequently her "justice" ultimately serves to perpetuate the logic of violence she would condemn. At this point there is the first appearance of the voice or eidolon of Thetis herself, telling or speaking through Helen:

> Clytaemnestra struck with her mind,
> with the Will-to-Power, . . .
>
> does it even the Balance
> if a wife repeats a husband's folly?
>
> never; the law is different;
> if a woman fights,
> she must fight by stealth.

(97)

While such passages make some readers uneasy, H. D.'s conviction is that the poet's response must move beyond forensics, otherwise one is condemned to mirror and be limited by that which is critiqued. At least, once having made the argument, it can then be kicked aside like Wittgenstein's ladder. As mentioned, this presumably was how H. D. felt Pound had entrapped himself.

Consequently, Thetis's instructive admonition to Helen to leave aside argument concludes the **"Pallinode"** and leads into part 2, **"Leuké."** The overall structure of **"Leuké"** is determined by Helen's revisitations of past selves with past men, first Paris and then Theseus; she recognizes the limits of those past selves as defined by those men. When the men attempt to insist on their perception of Helen, she does not so much reject as simply move on from them. This is particularly striking in the case of Theseus, the figure of Freud, who many commentators have taken as the councillor figure enabling Helen to achieve self-realization. Aside from the odd choice of Theseus for this role, who as we are told has a long history of abandoning women (148, 163), it is notable that Helen consistently ignores the profusion of advise he offers. H. D. here seems to replay her curious relationship with Freud, compounded of profound respect and subtle stubborn resistance. As Helen lies on the psychoanalytic couch, *"a lyric voice"* (178) begins to speak through her, which, like the eidolon of Thetis at the end of part 1, takes her beyond Theseus and into part 3. This voice alarms Theseus but then seems to subsume him as well, since we are told in the headnote to section VI.7—beginning, "Thus, thus, thus, / as day, night, / as wrong, right, / / as dark, light . . ." (190)—that this is spoken by Theseus, yet clearly this is not his voice, as if Helen has drawn out his buried other. In fact, this voice is surely Thetis again, but now even more clearly internalized, or perhaps we ought to say Helen's self is being externalized, in any case dissolved back into the sea and mysteriously transported to Egypt.

Although part 3, **"Eidolon,"** presumably takes place back in Egypt with Achilles, it is in fact difficult to fix not only in place and time but even in terms of a stable dyadic relationship. Achilles, especially, and Paris appear less as discrete characters than as part of Helen's own memory and consciousness. Helen's identity or voice at any given moment is superimposed against the ever-shifting background of Thetis the sea—"the topography of the text and the text as topo-graphy, wanders, will not stay in place" (Hirsh 441). In part 3, we are not only reminded that the poem is being woven out of Helen's reading of the Amen-script on the temple walls, but that poetry has precedence over the facts of history: "Was Troy lost for a kiss, / or a run of notes on a lyre?" (230). It is significant that H. D. picks up this thought from the *Iliad* itself, indicating that she is reading for the cracks that reveal the repressed within Homer's text.[20] The section goes on to ask if the story of Troy was intended "to inspire us with endless, / intricate questioning?" (231), and this entire section is a catalogue of questions, encapsulating the poem as a whole, which probably contains more question marks than any other poem of comparable length in the language. The following section answers these questions in the affirmative, *"Indeed it was 'Apollo's snare.' None other"* (232), or at least the headnote does, since the poetic text is again a

series of questions. The line-by-line reading experience of the poem is a process of constant, at times wearying, shifting and folding back on itself. The poetry itself has a sealike oscillation with gradual movements toward epiphanic moments where Helen asserts clarity, followed by dissolving plunges back into the ocean to start over again.

Helen in Egypt concludes with what purports to be a culminating insight, the "key or clue to the rest / of the mystery"; and the final lines preceding the brief coda are:

> there is no before and no after,
> there is one finite moment
> that no infinite joy can disperse
>
> or thought of past happiness
> tempt from or dissipate;
> now I know the best and the worst;
>
> the seasons revolve around
> a pause in the infinite rhythm
> of the heart and of heaven.
>
> (303-04)

This passage apparently asserts the present moment in its unequivocal finitude, always opening toward the uncertainty of the future rather than freezing the present in relation to some past moment or some abstracted future. If this is a plausible understanding of Helen-H. D.'s intent, then this cannot be allowed in turn to become frozen into an argument. So this privileging of the subjective experiential present, if we are correct in conflating the "finite moment" with "a pause" in the last stanza, is folded back into the larger contexts of the continuity of both the individual and the cosmos. However, the headnote to this section is hardly reassuring: *"One greater than Helen must answer, though perhaps we do not wholly understand the significance of the Message"* (303). Nonetheless, I have been arguing that *Helen in Egypt* proceeds on the unstable grounds of this "one finite moment," such that the paradoxes, circular logic, and contradictions on the level of abstract concepts reflect H. D.'s effort to develop a poetic thought of process and acceptance.

Hardly lacking in ambition, H. D. attempted to develop an "epic" work without the messianic impulses characteristic of the American long poem since at least Whitman. The woman's epic could not simply offer itself as critique of and parallel alternative to its male counterparts, although such critique is contained in H. D.'s poem. In terms of poetic materials and discursive range, *Helen in Egypt* is comparatively limited to what would be acceptable within a fairly conventional conception of the lyric. Yet, the poem is clearly of epic intent; H. D. works within or beneath the comparable texts of her peers, problematizing the act of reading itself. **Helen in Egypt** gives us a way to read Homer and the *Cantos* anew, preparing us for change, personally and culturally.

Notes

1. Several studies that offer themselves as comprehensive examinations of the American modernist epic or long poem, but at best give H. D. only passing mention, are Dickie, Miller, Rosenthal and Gall, and Walker. Keller's study of long poems by contemporary women poets gives some indication of the extensive impact H. D. has had on subsequent generations of poets working in long forms.

2. Friedman has discussed *Helen in Egypt* within the context of the epic tradition with very brief remarks on the *Cantos* (216); see also Langeteig.

3. In *End to Torment,* H. D. reiterates Pearson's linkage with the *Cantos* almost every time she mentions *Helen in Egypt* (32, 41, 49), and apparently even refers to her poem as "*Cantos*" in correspondence with Pound (Robinson 432).

4. The published text of *Helen in Egypt* italicizes the prose headnotes H. D. added later to each section of the poem, which is helpful in distinguishing between the prose and poetry texts when quoting from the work. An exception is the coda, entitled "Eidolon," which is italicized and the only section without a headnote, possibly suggesting it was added later as well.

5. H. D. indicates the two main literary sources for this alternative Helen narrative, Stesichorus's "Palinode" (a brief fragment preserved in Plato's *Phaedrus* 243a) and Euripides's *Helen.* Appropriately, these two sources represent the lyric and dramatic traditions in opposition to the epic. The Sophist Gorgias wrote a defense of Helen as well, although this may be more an exercise in showing off his rhetorical skills in defending a difficult case.

6. Cf. Norman Austin's intriguing remark on the *Iliad*:

   > The mysteries of the Mother, if we are authorized to read Helen as one of the icons of the Mother, have been translated into the male quest for beauty and honor, into the study of the function of beauty and its effect on the libido in human behavior.

   (133)

7. The "Ur-Cantos" version of this passage can be found in the revised edition of *Personæ* 245. Between the appearances of the two *Cantos* versions, Pound also published this translation from Andreas Divus's Latin translation of Homer in

"Translators of Greek: Early Translators of Homer" (*Literary Essays* 262-64), which includes the full Anticlea passage. In all three versions, only very minor changes were made in the translation except for the progressive elimination of lines from the end of the passage.

8. References to the *Cantos* will give the Canto number followed by page number(s) separated by a slash. Pagination in the most recent printings of the *Cantos* has been altered by the long belated interpolation of Cantos 72 and 73 into their proper place in the sequence; references in these printings can be located by simply adding 20 pages to the references I have given.

9. Hatcher argues that in the *Cantos* Circe is the mark of the active feminine principle that is the necessary complement to the masculine Odyssean principle.

10. Cf. Robert Kelly's remark:

    > The traditional sciences [the occult], which can by our social forms be made superstitious holdovers, represent at best that empirical speculativeness which constitutes our best mind—study thereof can make us perceptive of conditions, states, rhythms we are no longer *in our bodies* conscious of.

    (6)

11. Hatlen has argued persuasively that Pound uses a variety of what might be called mytho-philosophical discourses, which, while having many analogies, are not necessarily compatible with each other, ranging from a polymorphous polytheism to rigid manichaeism. At any given point in the *Cantos,* there might be a different mix and (im)balance between these discourses. Hatlen's argument complements my point that, in reading Pound, H. D. attempts to draw out his better side, which can become lost when his more manichaean mode predominates.

12. For more extensive commentary on this passage, see French, who argues that Pound wrote it on or within a day or two of H. D.'s birthday.

13. At the very end of his life in 1968, Pound was interviewed by Pier Paolo Pasolini and, responding to a question concerning the personal in the *Pisan Cantos,* remarked: "When I was young, I didn't think about myself. In one of my Pisan cantos I also wrote: tard, très tard, je t'ai connue, la tristesse. Late, very late, I came to know sadness" (Anderson 342).

14. Materer gives the entire letter, as well as commenting on both the background and poetic context of this allusion to H. D. in Canto 113. Aldington made a free translation of Sappho's poem, which Pound admired, and Pound provided a

partial paraphrase of his own in Canto 5/17-18. Pound's 1916 poem "Ιμερρω" [O Atthis] was composed around certain words and phrases from both Sappho and Aldington's version and has widely been understood as addressed to H. D.: "I long for thy narrow breasts, / Thou restless, un-gathered" (*Personæ* 116). For commentary on these various versions and Sappho's presence throughout the *Cantos,* see Kenner's chapter "The Muse in Tatters" (54-75).

15. In a 1959 letter to Pound speaking of "Winter Love," H. D. refers to her "*altmodisch* manner" (Robinson 432). Also worth recalling is Williams's "Prologue" to *Kora in Hell,* where he quotes a 1916 letter from H. D. justifying her extensive deletions of "flippancies" from a poem of his she published in *The Egoist*:

> I consider this business of writing a very sacred thing! [. . .] I feel in the hey-ding-ding touch running through your poem a derivative tendency which, to me, is not *you*—not your very self. It is as if you were *ashamed* of your Spirit, ashamed of your inspiration!

Williams responds in part:

> There is nothing sacred about literature, it is damned from one end to the other. There is nothing in literature but change and change is mockery. . . . But in any case H. D. misses the entire intent of what I am do-ing. . . . The hey-ding-ding touch *was* derivative, but it filled a gap that I did not know how better to fill at the time.

(Williams 13)

Williams effectively indicates the absence from H. D.'s work of a vast spectrum of registers and discourses, which might also remind us of Woolf's objection to Joyce's obscenity. There are obvious gender issues involved here, although other female modernists, such as Mina Loy or Djuna Barnes, had little difficulty using these lower modes for their own purposes.

16. For examples of H. D.'s characterization of the poet's work as "escapist," see *By Avon River* 74, 83-84, and Collecott 73.

17. Robert Graves's *The White Goddess,* which H. D. read while working on *Helen in Egypt,* argues ex-haustingly that the Goddess embodies the full cycle of birth-death-rebirth, and patriarchy sepa-rated out and reified the various aspects of the Goddess into different gods and goddesses in order to obscure the fact that she subsumes them all. See the notes in H. D.'s Working Notebook for *Helen in Egypt* in Gregory, esp. 105. Freud too points out the tripartite nature of the Mother God-dess in "The Theme of the Three Caskets" (73-77).

18. Graves (103) points out that spirals are primeval symbols of death and rebirth.

19. This last quoted phrase is from the prose headnote and unitalicized for emphasis. Since the headnotes were added at the suggestion of Pearson sometime after the verse version was completed, they themselves are quite literally a rereading, and it is notable that the headnotes do tend to highlight the textuality of the poem. On the addition of the headnotes, see Dembo's interview with Pearson (440).

20. In Book VI of the *Iliad,* Helen attempts to shame Paris into joining the battle and concludes with the suggestion that Zeus had designed her fate and its tragic consequences so that future generations could sing about them (lines 357-58).

Grateful acknowledgment is given to New Direc-tions Publishing Corporation for permission to quote from the following copyrighted works of H. D. and Ezra Pound: *Collected Poems 1912-1944* (Copyright © 1925 by H. D., Copyright © 1957, 1969 by Norman Holmes Pearson, Copyright © 1982 by the Estate of H. D., Copyright © 1983 by Perdita Schaffner); *End to Torment: A Memoir of Ezra Pound* (Copyright © 1979 by New Direc-tions Publishing Corporation); *Helen in Egypt* (Copyright © 1961 by Norman Holmes Pearson); *The Cantos* (Copyright © 1934, 1937, 1940, 1948, 1956, 1959, 1962, 1963, 1966, and 1968 by Ezra Pound); and *Personae* (Copyright © 1926 by Ezra Pound).

Works Cited

Anderson, David. "Breaking the Silence: The Interview of Vanni Ronsisvalle and Pier Paolo Pasolini with Ezra Pound in 1968." *Paideuma* 10.2 (1981): 331-45.

Austin, Norman. *Helen of Troy and Her Shameless Phantom.* Ithaca: Cornell UP, 1994.

Bakhtin, M. M. *The Dialogic Imagination.* Ed. Michael Holquist. Austin: U of Texas P, 1981.

Bernstein, Michael André. *The Tale of the Tribe: Ezra Pound and the Modern Verse Epic.* Princeton: Princeton UP, 1980.

Collecott, Diana. "Memory and Desire: H. D.'s 'A Note on Poetry.'" *Agenda* 25 (1987/88): 64-76

Dembo, L. S. "Norman Holmes Pearson on H. D.: An Interview." *Contemporary Literature* 10 (1969): 435-46.

Dickie, Margaret. *On the Modernist Long Poem.* Iowa City: U of Iowa P, 1986.

Duncan, Robert. "The H. D. Book, Part 2, Chapter 3." *Io* 6 (1969): 117-40.

———. "The H. D. Book: Part 2 Nights and Days, Chapter 4." *Caterpillar* 7 (1969): 27-60.

French, William. "'Saint Hilda,' Mr. Pound, and Rilke's Parisian Panther at Pisa." *Paideuma* 11.1 (1982): 79-87.

Freud, Sigmund. "The Theme of the Three Caskets." *Character and Culture*. New York: Collier, 1963. 67-79.

Friedman, Susan Stanford. "Gender and Genre Anxiety: Elizabeth Barrett Browning and H. D. as Epic Poets." *Tulsa Studies in Women's Literature* 5.2 (1986): 203-28.

Graves, Robert. *The White Goddess: A Historical Grammar of Poetic Myth* (rev.). New York: Farrar, 1966.

Gregory, Eileen. "Euripides and H. D.'s Working Notebook for *Helen in Egypt*." *Sagetrieb* 14.1, 14.2 (1995): 83-109.

Guest, Barbara. *Herself Defined: The Poet H. D. and Her World*. New York: Doubleday-Quill, 1984.

H. D. *By Avon River*. New York: Macmillan, 1949.

———. *Collected Poems 1912-1944*. Ed. Louis L. Martz. New York: New Directions, 1983.

———. *End to Torment: A Memoir of Ezra Pound*. Eds. Norman Holmes Pearson and Michael King. New York: New Directions, 1979.

———. *Helen in Egypt*. New York: New Directions, 1974.

———. *Tribute to Freud*. Fwd. by Norman Holmes Pearson. New York: New Directions, 1974.

Hatcher, Leslie. "'Circe's This Craft': The Active Female Principle in *The Cantos*." *Paideuma* 24.1 (1995): 83-94.

Hatlen, Burton. "Pound and Nature: A Reading of Canto XXIII." *Paideuma* 25.1, 25.2 (1996): 161-88.

Hirsh, Elizabeth A. "Imaginary Images: 'H. D.,' Modernism, and the Psychoanalysis of Seeing." *Signets: Reading H. D.* Ed. Susan Stanford Friedman and Rachel Blau DuPlessis. Madison: U of Wisconsin P, 1991. 430-51.

Hokanson, Robert O'Brien. "'Is It All a Story?': Questioning Revision in H. D.'s *Helen in Egypt*." *American Literature* 64.2 (1992): 331-46.

Keller, Lynn. *Forms of Expansion: Recent Long Poems by Women*. Chicago: U of Chicago P, 1997.

Kelly, Robert. *In Time*. West Newbury: Frontier, 1971.

Kenner, Hugh. *The Pound Era*. Berkeley: U of California P, 1971.

Langeteig, Kendra. "Visions in the Crystal Ball: Ezra Pound, H. D., and the Form of the Mystical." *Paideuma* 25.1, 25.2 (1996): 55-81.

Materer, Timothy. "H. D., Serenitas, and Canto CXIII." *Paideuma* 12.2, 12.3 (1983): 275-80.

Miller, James E. *The American Quest for a Supreme Fiction: Whitman's Legacy in the Personal Epic*. Chicago: U of Chicago P, 1979.

Olson, Charles. *Selected Writings*. Ed. Robert Creeley. New York: New Directions, 1966.

Pound, Ezra. *The Cantos of Ezra Pound*. New York: New Directions, 1986.

———. *Literary Essays of Ezra Pound*. Ed. T. S. Eliot. New York: New Directions, 1954.

———. *Personæ: The Shorter Poems of Ezra Pound* (rev.). Ed. Lea Baechler and A. Walton Litz. New York: New Directions, 1990.

Robinson, Janice S. *H. D.: The Life and Work of an American Poet*. Boston: Houghton, 1982.

Rosenthal, M. L., and Sally M. Gall. *The Modern Poetic Sequence: The Genius of Modern Poetry*. New York: Oxford UP, 1983.

Walker, Jeffrey. *Bardic Ethos and the American Epic Poem: Whitman, Pound, Crane, Williams, Olson*. Baton Rouge: Louisiana State UP, 1989.

Williams, William Carlos. *Imaginations*. Ed. Webster Schott. New York: New Directions, 1970.

Woolf, Virginia. "Modern Fiction." *The Gender of Modernism: A Critical Anthology*. Ed. Bonnie Kime Scott. Bloomington: Indiana UP, 1990. 628-33.

Susan Acheson (essay date June 1998)

SOURCE: Acheson, Susan. "'Conceived at the Grave's Edge': The Esoteric Eschatology of H. D.'s *Trilogy*." *Literature and Theology* 12, no. 2 (June 1998): 187-204.

[*In the following essay, Acheson analyzes H. D.'s* Trilogy *for evidence of the poet's revision of Christian eschatological beliefs and maintains that H. D. may be classed as a "New Apocalypse" poet who reframed the notions of time and death in her poetry.*]

I. INTRODUCTION

In 1942 H. D. (Hilda Doolittle, 1886-1961) embarked on three long poems which were published together after the war under the title *Trilogy*.[1] Though intensively discussed in specialist studies of the last twenty years neither the poem nor the poet are widely known. Anthologized as an imagist, H. D.'s poetry and prose was persistently experimental throughout her life. *Trilogy* opens a new phase in her published work, of neo-romanticism. At the same time, it develops a theme running through much of H. D's writing from its inception—a concern with eschatology: death, the end of time, judgement and salvation. Perhaps the approaching millenium with its attendant eschatological anxieties is an appropriate time to draw the attention of a wider readership to this aspect of her work which both reflects and interprets concern that was widespread amongst modernist writers grappling with the distress of world events and with the implications of Nietzsche's inaugural annunciation of modernity in terms of the death of God. H. D.'s imagist poems are haunted by gods in the very act of disappearing. Empty temples, missed footfalls, crushed blades of grass are signs of a presence that has dissolved into the signifiers once alleged to proclaim it. The abandonment of a dead poetic tradition is celebrated at the same time as the Greek tropes of the poetry mourn its passing. H. D.'s imagist poems search for a form rooted in language itself, a form that will replace old imagined congruencies of word and meaning, and so protect against the vertigo of the modernity they invoke.[2] In this way her early poetry exemplifies the overlap between modernism and romanticism which becomes even more evident in *Trilogy.* Responding to anxieties about 'the end' induced by the great war, the 1920s and '30s saw the further development of esoteric interests already well established before the end of the nineteenth century. Theosophy, drawing from Greek and Indian traditions, evaded the orthodox Christian notion of linear history progressing to an end and instead posits a series of temporal cycles, each of which transforms the previous one onto a higher plane. Death, for the enlightened, is endlessly deferred. Astrology, also, provided a comforting response to the fearsome vision of space described in popular books like James Jeans' *The Mysterious Universe,* which H. D. had read.[3] Jeans' modernist universe was populated by isolated stars and planets, each separated from the other by infinite light years. Since, as Jeans believed, the law of thermodynamics proved that the universe would one day run out of energy, and so die, all life moved towards a death that was implicated in its very origins.[4] Astrological beliefs emphasizing the intimate connection of all things in the cosmos and a cyclic view of time were popular with those who wished to avoid such pessimistic views. Although she refused to align herself wholeheartedly with esoteric philosophies, theosophy, spiritualism and astrology provided H. D. with a language which enabled her to revise the Christian eschatological programme.

In this article I shall be examining the ways in which *Trilogy* attempts to carry out this revision in the context of the eschatological discourses of the years immediately preceding and during the second world war. *Trilogy*'s first critic, Norman Holmes Pearson, wrote in a review of the first two poems, **'The Walls**

Do Not Fall' and **'Tribute to the Angels'** that this was poetry 'conceived at the grave's edge', concerned with 'time and the problem of words'.[5] Composed from 1942 onwards, *Trilogy* struggles to express a sense of death that is both imminent and immanent, but which also contains a promise of life. In *Trilogy,* H. D. 'writes beyond the ending', to borrow du Plessis' phrase, not so much in attempting to revise romantic plots, but to revise the *eschatological* plots of traditional Christianity.[6] These are mythic narratives about power and authority, the establishment of God's rule over against the state.[7] As envisaged in Revelation and in much orthodox Christian teaching based on it, history is a process inaugurated by God, and moving towards a definite end. It is a linear univocal process in which the drama of redemption or damnation is played out. The apocalypse reveals the hidden meaning of this history in a series of violent catastrophes which emphasise God's absolute power and which destroy the kingdoms of the earth. The 'saved' are gathered into a divine kingdom where all are united in praise of a God depicted metaphorically as a patriarch, and in perfect obedience to his law. H. D.'s poem challenges this power discourse, drawing on esoteric theories relating to astrology and to the myth of Atlantis. It is perhaps also indebted to the suppressed Franciscan eschatological theory of the 'eternal gospel' and the 'third age'—a doctrine declared heretical by the Church, but popular among nineteenth century writers like George Sand, Comte and George Eliot, and perhaps reaching H. D. through the fin de siècle mediation of Havelock Ellis.[8] All these ideas are mobilized to shape and inform *Trilogy*'s commitment to an open poetics, and its engagement with what Claire Buck calls its 'bisexual discourse'.[9] D. H. Lawrence had perhaps opened the way for H. D.'s vision in *Apocalypse,* where he quarrels with his idiosyncratic version of Christianity, that it tries to deny power, and so makes the world vulnerable to its abuse. 'Give homage and allegiance to a hero and you become yourself heroic', he wrote, adding 'It is the law of men. Perhaps the law of women is different'.[10] Intervening years had proved how disastrous this 'law of men' was. *Trilogy,* I shall conclude, is an attempt to mediate a new age that would begin after the war, an age which H. D. anticipates as the age of 'WOMAN [sic] in a new sense of woman', and which will be characterized by different values from those dominating the present age.[11]

II. TIME AND THE NEW APOCALYPSE

Eschatological themes coloured literary debates in London periodicals during World War II. Sections from **'The Walls Do Not Fall'** first appeared from April 1942 in *Life and Letters Today,* edited by H. D.'s friend Robert Herring. They appeared alongside the work of a now almost forgotten group of poets who called themselves poets of the 'New Apocalypse' for whom the journal provided a sympathetic forum. The group was founded by Henry Treece and J. F. Hendry who, inspired by Dylan Thomas and Herbert Read, among others, went into print with their first anthology in 1940.[12] They attempted to formulate a response to the war that addressed what they thought to be the underlying evils of the age that had led to it. Envisaging the war as apocalypse, they sought to express in their writing the vision that should accompany the Armageddon, a vision which contained the seeds for renewal.[13] They aimed to forge in their writing a transforming 'organic unity' between consciousness and unconsciousness, the individual and society so as to inaugurate a new anti mechanist and anti utilitarian age based on a transformation of the imagination.[14] 'The true poet' Treece announced in another essay, 'must necessarily be a prophet . . . [H]e may be despised because of his difficulty. Yet he shall have faith in his own word and those who have eyes to see and ears to hear shall learn from his Apocalyptic utterance . . . '.[15]

The neo-romantic and eschatological views of the New Apocalypse poets were shared in part by other literary commentators at the time. For Cyril Connolly in *Horizon,* which although it held aloof from the New Apocalypse, promoted the neo-romanticism in which the latter was embedded, the construction of a better world after the war required a rediscovery of aestheticism, art for art's sake, and an abandonment of the activist stances of the Auden group. Purged in the 'apocalyptic' experience of Dunkirk, English culture was ready for the artist who would help Britain find 'new values'.[16] Like D. H. Lawrence before him, Connolly could see no future for a society that ignored its writers' attempts to investigate' spiritual possibilities'—a materialist utopia would be a doomed one.[17] With John Lehmann in *Penguin New Writing,* Connolly called for the development of a 'new myth' which would enable healing of war torn psyche and culture.[18]

Although none of the New Apocalypse anthologies contained extracts from H. D.'s work, *Trilogy* sits comfortably in the environment of New Apocalypse and neo-romantic theory. The poet calls for a recovery of 'old values' (**WDF ["The Walls Do Not Fall"]** 2). She is 'twice born' at one level of the poem because she is a survivor of the apocalypse of the first war, and the values of her youth as an imagist are now being resought after the thirties flirtation with politics. Her voice joins with the literary critics against those who see poetry as 'non-utilitarian' and therefore irrelevant:

We are these people

wistful, ironical, willful
who have no part in

new world reconstruction
in the confederacy of labour

the practical issues of art

           (WDF 14)

as she wrote in 1942, not long after Connolly's article,

we are the keepers of the secret,
the carriers, the spinners

of the rare intangible thread
that binds all humanity

to ancient wisdom,
to antiquity

           (WDF 15)

Apocalyptic poetry was meant to challenge the basis of society, which is what *Trilogy* does. The poem struggles to bring together the head and the heart, to pursue an individual vision and to claim its authenticity for society in general, to express a personal religion unshackled, as Treece required, from a mass creed. In it the poet adopts the stance of a prophet, one of the 'Few' whose task, as Treece's friend Stefan Schimanski wrote in a review of their work, was to bring to the 'Many' consciousness of the values necessary for a humane culture.[19] 'Let us,' as the poet of **'The Walls Do Not Fall'** states,

however, recover the Sceptre,
the rod of power:

it is crowned with the lily-head
or the lily-bud:

it is Caduceus; among the dying
it bears healing:

or in invoking the dead
it brings life to the living.

           (WDF 3)

The New Apocalypse poets failed, however, to deliver what they promised. Emphasizing 'organic connection' between all aspects of life and consciousness, protesting against what they saw as the individualistic excesses of surrealism, they feared gaps, the unknown, they feared breakdown. Because it so self-consciously asserts its completeness, New Apocalypse poetry is both suffocating and incoherent. At one level, *Trilogy* may be interpreted as sharing this failure. The poem seems intent on keeping death at bay by obsessively enunciating itself, spinning out words and adding more and more lyrics—a characteristic which makes it difficult to quote. 'Take me' says the poet,

. . . anywhere
where the stars blaze through the clear air

where we may greet individually,
Sirius, Vega, Arcturus

. . . . .

where each, with its particular attribute,
may be invoked

with accurate charm, spell, prayer . . .

. . . . .

O stars, little jars of that indisputable

and absolute Healer, Apothecary,
wrought, faceted, jewelled

boxes, very precious, to hold further
unguent, myrrh, incense:

jasper, beryl, sapphire
that, as we draw them nearer

by prayer, spell,
litany, incantation

will reveal their personal fragrance . . .

(WDF 24)

In this stanza, one sentence is strung out over 28 lines in a veritable thesaurus of alternative words given for key ideas. Even the two-line stanzas that characterize most of the poem may give the impression of stringing themselves out across a fearful space. As long as there is language, the poem seems to suggest, there is no ending. And when it does finally draw to a close, it does so with a version of the nativity story, a new beginning.

On the other hand, *Trilogy* differs from its New Apocalypse contemporaries by combining this resistance to death and ending with an exemplary openness to the metonymically associated concepts of silence and unknowing. This emphasis suffuses the poem's structure as well as its content. Far from being planned in advance, the poems that compose *Trilogy* were composed piecemeal, growing out of the poet's ruminative imagination and in dialogue with her friend Norman Pearson. They share the New Apocalypse sense of crisis but precisely because they do not attempt to overcome this crisis they more successfully transform it.

The temporal vistas of the poem are complex and resist the idea that history must be a linear development culminating in a 'kingdom' in which meaning is monolithic and univocal. They also resist the idea of merely cyclic repetition. *Trilogy* offers a vision of time as constantly open to the past but moving forward. Remembering and drawing inspiration from a 'golden age' the poem does not seek to re-establish, or repeat it, but to inaugurate a new age that is both inscribed in the stars and the creation of a redeemed imagination. Thus *Trilogy* imagines time both as shaped and as open. At this level it seeks not to keep death at bay, but to incorporate it. The two line stanzas draw attention to their ample spacing, the transformative energies of the words themselves suggest a language which seeks out uncertainty. Openness, transformation, shifting meanings and shifting sounds permeate them. 'Venus' is transformed from 'venery' to 'venerate' (**TA** [**"Tribute to the Angels"**] 11, 12); 'Osiris' metamorphoses into 'Sirius' (**WDF** 40). 'Mary' is 'Mara' is 'Myrrh' in **'The Flowering of the Rod'**, reflecting the metamorphosis of Myrrha, mother of Adonis, into a myrtle, weeping thereafter tears of myrrh.

our bodies blunder

through doors twisted on hinges
and the lintels slant

cross-wise;
we walk continually

on thin air

. . . . .

we are voyagers, discoverers
of the not-known

the unrecorded . . .

(WDF 43)

The tau-cross of Hermes or Thoth, inventor of writing, marks the place where 'thin air' begins. It is the gateway to nothing, to the 'unrecorded'. Writing here does not keep death at bay, but opens the way to it. In **'Tribute to the Angels'** a similar sense of the centrality of the end is suggested by the fact the apocalyptic vision of the seven angels and of the heavenly city built of jasper occurs not, as it does in Revelation, at the end of the text, but in the middle. The poetry of *Trilogy* is after all *conceived* at the grave's edge. It achieves a form, in the end, without imposing it. 'Transformation' in *Trilogy* does not imply the search for an overarching form or shape that will lock death out, but the effort to find a way of opening up language to a constant negotiation with its opposite—silence, metonymy of death. The poem does not want to neutralize death by incorporating it into a monological language, denying the difference that it threatens, nor does it enact a hysterical ritualization of a dread it denies. On the contrary, it seeks to introduce a discourse that is always open to the opaque and destabilizing other, the unsettling silence, the space after the end.

H. D.'s conception of time has much in common with C. G. Jung's. During the 20's and '30s the latter's interest in esoteric sciences like astrology and alchemy was growing, whilst H. D. was involved in palm readings and casting astrological charts for her friends. Psychoanalysis and occult practices went as happily together in her mind as they did in his. Writing to Bryher while she prepared for her second trip to consult Freud she speaks of psychoanalysis and 'spirit analysis', analytic sessions and 'seances' in the same breath.[20] 'I am not as you know a sloppy theosophist or horoscope-ist,' she wrote in a letter of May 1933, 'but you know, I do believe in these things and think there is a whole other-science of them.'[21] She occupied her time in Vienna when not with Freud reading an 'astrological romance' although, as she wrote to Bryher, 'I feel Papa does not approve of my healthy, non-Jehovah tendencies of star-glyph.'[22]

After war broke out C. G. Jung, who had consistently couched his experiences of the 1914-1918 conflict in apocalyptic terms[23] wrote to a colleague in England:

> This is the fateful year for which I have waited more than 25 years . . . This year reminds me of the enormous earthquake in 26 BC that shook down the great temple of Karnak. It was the prelude to the destruction of all temples, because a new time had begun. 1940 is the year when we approach the meridian of the first star in Aquarius. It is the premonitory earthquake of the New Age.[24]

When H. D. prefaced 'The Walls Do Not Fall' 'To Bryher: for Karnak 1923 from London 1942' she may not only have been remembering their trip to Karnak but making an esoteric connection. Like Jung, H. D. thought of the onset of the Second World War as a 'premonitory earthquake of the New Age', the age of Aquarius. Writing to May Sarton in December 1944, just before embarking on 'The Flowering of the Rod,' she discusses 'this new Aquarian age we have been told is well under way.'[25] The astronomical observation that underpins this idea is that the point of the spring equinox on the ecliptic, or the circle which the sun appears to trace in the sky of fixed stars moves a little further backwards each year. So although the signs of the zodiac seem to revolve clockwise around the earth, every two thousand years or so the earth seems to move anticlockwise into an 'aeon' dominated by the zodiac sign preceding the present one. This is called the precession of the equinoxes. God, says the narrator in 'Majic Ring', an unpublished prose companion piece to *Trilogy*

> spread out the heavens like a cloth or a tapestry and he pricked on the cloth of heaven the pattern of day and night, of sun-rise and of sun-set, of the moon and the precession of the equinoxes. He made the measure of day and night . . . so that we have 12 hours to the day,

12 hours to the night, 12 months of the year, 12 great months (each roughly 2000 years) to the precession of the equinoxes

(43-4).

The double movement—forward through the signs of the zodiac in ordinary time, and backwards in the precession, is suggested in *Trilogy*. Section 30 of 'The Walls Do Not Fall' moves through the succession of zodiac signs—Scorpio, Sagittarius, Capricorn, Aquarius and Pisces (roughly coinciding with the months October-February). This movement connects the poem with the cycle of destruction and re-birth (autumn, winter, the beginning of spring) which H. D. transcribes onto a psychological plane: 'would climb high? then fall low'—the death of psychological disintegration must precede healing. Meanwhile, the poem also follows the backward movement of the precession. It begins in Aries, the aeon before Pisces and identified with the Egyptian mysteries of Osiris. It passes through the violent disruptions of Pisces, the fish that 'move two-ways, devour,' (**WDF** 30) the Christian era of 'pain-worship and death-symbol' (**WDF** 18) which has culminated in the war so vividly captured in the poem's opening section.

III. THE JUDGEMENT OF 'WOMAN IN A NEW SENSE'

Thus, throughout the poem, time circles backwards and forwards and, as in theosophy, in a redeeming rather than a repetitive spiral. This is the context for the poem's revision of the orthodox understanding of judgement. Instead of celebrating certainty and reason, the poem questions both. It roots its claims to wisdom in a revaluing of the irrational unconscious and the importance of uncertainty, of *not* knowing. This links with its interest in astrology, and with its sexual politics. The occluded wisdom of one aeon becomes the open wisdom of the next. In the Piscean era, overemphasis on reason, on the values of enlightenment, has resulted in conflict with the irrational unconscious. Thus the wisdom of the Aquarian will rely on a 'surrender', as the poet puts it, of 'sterile logic, trivial reason' (**WDF** 30). The Mage's 'knowledge' in the final verses of 'The Flowering of the Rod' is what he *thinks* he 'sees' in a half second, and in a 'fleck or a flaw in a gem' (*FR* [*The Flowering of the Rod*] 40). Neither he nor any one else 'will know exactly how this vision came about'. 'The Flowering of the Rod' emphasises what the mage *forgets,* what he does not know. Indeed, the value of words themselves, in which judgement is contained, are questioned. Not only, as has been already argued, is language unstable throughout the poem but finally it appears that silence is valued more than speech. The rituals of the Magi who approach Mary at the end of the poem move through speech to gesture and finally silence. Balthasar speaks 'the Great Word', Melchior 'made gesture with his hands / as if in dance or play' but Kaspar, who has allowed his inherited wisdom to be upset by the uncertainties heralded by Mary Magdalene's search for the jar of ointment, stands 'a little to one side', inclines his head 'only slightly', and says nothing (*FR* 42). Yet it is to him, whose part in the ritual is 'only negligible' that Mary speaks.

There are many 'not knowns' in the poem. It is suggested that there are plenty of stories about how Mary got her jar (*FR* 12) but only one of these is offered in the poem, and even that is never certainly opted for. Her negotiations with Kaspar remain a mystery (*FR* 20). The incident of the anointing is also told in terms of what is not known. Simon does not know who she is and thinks his Guest doesn't either (*FR* 22). His Guest's assumed ignorance leads Simon to question his identity too. He doesn't know that the 'devils' cast out of Mary are in fact 'daemons' whose release is essential for their integration and healing (*FR* 26). Kaspar, knowing this, is better off than Simon, but the poem ends with uncertainty for him all the same. Life and wisdom, are in the unknown—not just in what is presently unknown but someday may be known, but in 'unknowability' itself. This is brought home in the final exchange between Kaspar and Mary in **'The Flowering of the Rod'**. As Claire Buck points out, Kaspar, mage and patriarch, finally knows only that he does not know what the woman knows.[26] *Trilogy* which begins by setting up a question to which the poem is intended as an answer (what saved us? what for?) finally responds by undermining the whole concept of seeking answers and giving judgements.

> The price of wisdom is the risk of madness, movingly glossed in **'The Walls Do Not Fall'**
>
> so mind dispersed, dared occult lore,
>
> found secret doors unlocked,
> floundered, was lost in sea-depth
> . . . . .
>
> illusion, reversion of old values,
> oneness lost, madness.
>
> (WDF 30)

In *Trilogy* judgement is the prerogative not, as in Revelation, of 'one like a Son of Man' but of 'an unbalanced neurotic woman' (*FR* 12). The female poet who has risked this madness is empowered with judgement. Unlike her critics, she is able to 'pass judgement / on what words conceal' (**WDF** 8). She, and the female personae within the poem—Mary, Mary Magdalene and the nameless woman carrying the empty book in **'Tribute to the Angels'**—personify the

values of the Aquarian era which are themselves focused by its governing planet, Uranus. H. D. identified with this planet, sometimes signing her letters with its astronomical sign, . . .[27] In her astrology texts she read accounts of its late discovery (presaging association with a 'new era' and symbolizing all that is still 'hidden') and of its eccentric orbit, pulled away from the sun ('the light of reason') by the gravity of invisible Neptune. She was also of course well aware of Edward Carpenter's identification of the planet with homosexual—'uranian'—love. Carpenter's thesis was that all humanity was slowly evolving into homosexuality—uranism—as its final goal and highest state.[28] Carpenter concentrates on the uranian male: in *Trilogy*, H. D. focuses uranian values through the image of the woman.

For H. D. the Aquarian Age was specifically 'a woman's age in a new sense of WOMAN . . .' She had discovered this 'new sense of woman' ten years earlier during her analysis with Freud. Freud, as she had written excitedly to her friend Bryher,[29] believed that all women were bisexual, and openly homosexual or bisexual women are merely more honest about this than so-called 'normal' women. However while Freud thought that 'well adjusted' women should come to terms with their penis envy by sublimating it into motherhood,[30] H. D. interpreted his theory as a valorization of the bisexual feminine. *Trilogy* may be read as an attempt to provide an inaugurating myth and vision of the new age as an age of woman 'in a new sense'. It also explores the values that will characterize this 'bisexual' era—values of openness, undecidability, a celebration not of the mastery of knowledge, but of acceptance of unknowing.

Freud's child-bearing woman is replaced in **'Tribute to the Angels'** by a woman carrying the 'unwritten volume of the new' (**TA** 38). Though Freud thought women, fulfilled in child-bearing, could make no major cultural contribution, the Lady's book, open and open-ended, is the founding symbol of the new age. The image of the book may also connect the poem to the esoteric idea of the 'eternal evangel' or gospel. Briefly, this theory, originating with the thirteenth century Franciscan Joachim di Fiore, stated that time could be divided into three eras, each ruled by one of the three persons of the Christian Trinity, and each characterised by its own book. The Age of the Father and of the Old Testament had given way to the Age of the Son and of the New Testament. This second era is transitional: on the horizon is the Third Age, governed by the Spirit and a new gospel, surpassing the New Testament as that did the Old. The Age of the Spirit will be an age of constant inspiration and change. Its Book will not be written down, but directly communicated to each individual. Its message will be constantly renewed. According to Marjorie Reeves and Warwick Gould, versions of this theory can be found in the writing of Yeats, Joyce and Lawrence.[31] Given her close acquaintance with their writing, her interest in theosophically related ideas as well as her interest in Franciscan piety evidenced in her 1947 essay (researched during the war years) 'The Guest', it is not unlikely that H. D. was acquainted with the myth in some form.[32] The myth appropriately expresses the modernist ambivalence between form and experiment. In the end time that is modernity, the eternal gospel becomes a permanent crisis of transition, perpetually open, permeated by an afterw[o]rds it can't express. According to H. D.'s first 'analyst' and friend Havelock Ellis, the application of the new gospel will be largely 'in the hands of women'.[33] In **'Tribute to the Angels',** the new age is inaugurated by a woman bearing the Book, displacing Christ, the 'Son of Man' who is the subject of St. John's vision in Revelation. Her white veils displace his hair, white as wool. Anxious not to foreclose what the Lady represents (for in a sense she represents nothing) the poet resists identifying her with any traditional feminine figure in religious iconography—she is the image of the new age. 'Not-fear' and 'not-war' she is both a positive and a negative term; her 'attributes' are both 'different' and 'the same as before' (**TA** 39). Her colour, white, is 'all-colour' (**TA** 41)—in which the different colours of the Angels in the poem are united and transcended. She symbolizes, in her ambivalence, the open, indescribable 'bisexual' qualities of the age beyond the ending.

IV. LIFE AFTER DEATH: THE MYTH OF ATLANTIS

Trilogy's eschatological discourse is further elaborated by the myth of Atlantis which underpins its meditation on the possibility of new life. Atlantis is most directly referred to in **'The Flowering of the Rod'** as the lost island over which the flying geese circle, in remembrance of their home (**FR** 3). Kaspar sees 'the islands of the Blest . . . / / . . . the circles and circles of islands / about the lost centre island, Atlantis' (**FR** 31). In an excised section of the poem, H. D. explicitly connects Atlantis with Britain, 'this island immolated with war'.[34] Atlantis appears in **'Majic Ring'** and *Tribute to Freud* as the mysterious island the narrator can see out in the Atlantic where no land mass should be. Her ship is accompanied by dolphins which she associates with Pisces, guiding her toward the new Atlantis of the Aquarian age.[35] In **'Majic Ring'** the medium, Manisi, has a waking dream of Atlantean jars full of a 'secret energy' like the jars of **'The Flowering of the Rod'.**[36] Atlantis in H. D.'s writing stands for a lost unity between past and future, Europe and America, dream and history. It is associated with

Aquarius, the man carrying a jar of water, or of 'power and grace', and with the androgynous beings that some of her sources believed were the original inhabitants of the drowned continent. It thus encodes the poem's vision of new life beyond the splits and conflicts that have escalated into the second world war.

Books investigating the 'truth' of Atlantis were as popular between the wars as astrology was. One source for H. D.'s knowledge of the myth was H. S. Bellamy's *The Book of Revelation is History* an annotated copy of which remains in her library. Bellamy argued that the events recounted in Revelation were memories of geological catastrophes such as had drowned Atlantis, and that the last book of the Bible ought to be placed first, followed by Genesis which was really an account of a *re*-creation. This fanciful interpretation was the subject of enthusiastic correspondence between H. D. and the writer Molly Hughes in 1942, the latter writing a glowing review of it in *Life and Letters Today*.[37] Arguably, *Trilogy* follows Bellamy's proposed revised pattern in its choice to begin with an evocation of destructive apocalypse and to end with the 're-birth' in the ox-stall.[38]

The main source for allusions to Atlantis in *Trilogy* and **'Majic Ring',** however, is Dmitri Merezhkovsky's *The Secret of the West* (1933), translated by H. D.'s friend of the first world war years, John Cournos, in 1935. H. D.'s heavily annotated copy of the book is inscribed with her wartime Lowndes Square address and the date 1940-41, indicating that she had read it before embarking on *Trilogy*.[39] Merezhkovsky's book is a bizarre attempt to narrate the demise of western civilization in terms of a version of theosophy, Freudian metapsychology and his own esoteric brand of Christianity. The book endeavours, he says, using a phrase H. D. was to use of her work in *Tribute to Freud,* to 'build an ark' to preserve the seed of forgotten wisdom for future aeons.

Merezhkovsky makes no attempt to pursue a logical—or even a coherent—argument, but weaves together a number of myths to make his points. Like Joachim of Fiore, though drawing on Russian Orthodox rather than Franciscan sources, he thought that history is made up of a series of 'ages' each marked by the rise and fall of civilizations. Each civilization falls because it exaggerates certain values and splits off others. The 'civilization' of Sodom, for example erred by overemphasizing erotic, 'unisexual' love. Christianity errs the opposite way, exaggerating 'pity' and de-eroticising love. Merezhkovsky describes the Minoan culture at Knossos, recently excavated by Sir Arthur Evans, as the closest modern man can get to a glimpse of a perfect society—because, he thinks, Cretan civilization contained within it the memory of Atlantis.[40] He describes the stones of Knossos as still young; in the dim-opal whiteness of the alabaster blocks, with rose-azure veins, it is as if warm blood ran in them.[41]

The stones of Knossos are also the stones of Atlantis, and the description is closely echoed in **'Tribute to the Angels'** where the jewel distilled from the crucible is 'green-white, opalescent / with under-layer of changing blue / with rose-vein' (**TA** 13). Knossos is Atlantis is London, 'distilled' in the crucible of the blitz and the crucible of the poet's imagination.

Developing ideas in Evans' book in ways the archaeologist would not have recognised, Merezhkovsky argues that before their culture was destroyed by invading hordes from the north, the Minoans at Knossos practiced the cult of the androgyne. The masculine cult of the Bull and the feminine cult of the mother goddess, were, he thought, uniquely combined the doubleheaded axe and female knot symbols that appear with androgynous figures on official seals, signet rings and wall paintings. The 'secret of the west' is this secret of Atlantis, the androgyne. Western civilization can only survive if it evolves again bisexual beings perfectly balanced between their male and female halves. These, Merezhkovsky thinks, will be the product of the conflagration to which the west (in the 1920s) is inevitably tending, but only if people are willing to learn the lesson of the Atlanteans whose pride was the cause of their downfall. The connection between androgyny/bi-sexuality (Merezhkovsky uses the terms interchangeably) and 'unknowing' which as I have already argued is present in *Trilogy*'s astrological imagery, is present here too. The future age of the androgyne is an 'unknown' era which Merezhkovsky says he cannot describe, but it will be heralded by the return of an 'unknown Christ', the Christ not of established Christianity, but the true, androgynous Christ of the gospels, as he reads them. In the future age, as in Atlantis and in Crete, there will be no temples, but only small enclosures with low, semicircular walls, empty except for a small tree or an altar.[42]

> To Uriel, no shrine, no temple
> where red-death fell,
>
> . . . . .
>
> the lane is empty but the levelled wall
>
> is purple as with purple spread
> upon an altar
>
> (**TA** 7)

Trilogy's 'temple' is invisible, marked only by a flowering tree, a wall that is both 'there and not-there' (**TA** 20). Merezhkovsky writes: 'these enclosures are the scene of strange, non-secret mysteries, open to

all' in which the god is invoked by the ecstatic dancing of the priestess. In **'Majic Ring'** Delia dances herself into vision; in **'The Flowering of the Rod'** the hypnotic circling of the geese enables them, and the poet who identifies with them, to find 'The Islands of the Blest', Paradise and Atlantis (**FR** 7). Ecstasy, says Merezhkovsky, is the 'higher' reason, the new, unknown soul of the new age.[43]

'The Flowering of the Rod' begins with a Merezhkovskian allusion. The poet begs 'do not be beguiled / by the geometry of perfection', and calls on her readers to 'remember the snow / on Hermon'. Later in the poem H. D. refers to Hermon as the mountain of the Transfiguration—confusing it in fact with Tabor. However, she may be palimpsestically identifying the Transfiguration with an earlier encounter with the divine. Hermon, says Merezhkovsky, is the mountain where according to the Book of Enoch angels descended like a fall of snow, to tempt men with 'too much perfection', and where they mated with earthly women to breed a race of giants. In this initial encounter between earth and heaven, eros is corrupted, and its flame destroys the world, in Atlantis and later in Sodom. The present threat of war is in part, Merezhkovsky thinks, a result of a misguided search for 'perfection' in technology. 'When the northern barbarians invaded, Southern Europe got its 'geometric style'—the dry deadly mechanical order, hostile to the organic, living, developing Creto-Aegean order'.[44] The poet renounces 'iron, steel, metal', the tokens of the age of war which Merezhkovsky identifies with the pre-historic split between Atlanteans and Amazons, the male and the female principle. In an implicit criticism of her own early imagist practice the 'geometry on the wing' (10) of Enoch's fallen angels, of the war planes of the machine age is no longer to be imaged as 'patterned, a gentian / in an ice mirror' but as organic, a 'flower cone' which is a lotus, Osiris' crown, 'each petal, a kingdom, an aeon' whose seed will re-flower in each successive age (10).

The threat of war is also, Merezhkovsky argues, a result of a religion that substitutes pity for love. The poet comments in *Trilogy*:

> alas, it was pity rather than love we gave;
>
> now, having given all, let us leave all,
> above all, let us leave pity
>
> and mount higher
> to love—resurrection.
>
> (*FR* 1)

Leaving 'pity' and 'the place-of-a-skull' for 'Resurrection' means searching, in memory, for Atlantis. 'Flocks of migratory birds', writes Merezhkovsky in a passage closely quoted by H. D.:

fly every year to that spot where Atlantis has been. They circle round the water, and seek land, without finding it; some of them, out of sheer fatigue, fall into the water, while others make the return journey. That which we call 'instinct' is more eloquent than 'knowledge, memory' . . . men have forgotten it—the birds remember.[45]

So I would rather drown, remembering—
than bask on tropic atolls

. . . . .

I would rather beat in the wind, crying to these others:

yours is the more foolish circling,
yours is the senseless wheeling

round and round—yours has no reason—
I am seeking heaven;

yours has no vision,
I see what is beneath me, what is above me,

what men say is-not—I remember,
I remember, I remember—you have forgot . . .

(*FR* 6)

For H. D., the seed of secret wisdom is 'the least of all seeds' which has become 'the greatest among herbs'. Apparently a straightforward quote from the Gospel of Matthew, this is more accurately a quotation from Cournos' translation of Merezhkovsky's version of it. The word 'herb' has special significance for Merezhovsky as he associates it with a wall painting in the palace at Knossos in which the 'Herb of Life' is plucked 'not by either male or female, but by the whole human being—the two halves in one—the Androgyne'.[46]

It is with Merezhovsky's androgynous or bi-sexual being that we are confronted in the tableau vivant of the stable scene. Mary and Kaspar are a conjunction of opposites, a bi-sexual entity in which difference is not elided. In the patriarchal culture of Pisces they pulled in opposite ways—senex and virgo. Here they are united in the transforming symbol of myrrh. Uranus meets Venus; Aquarius stands before Virgo. The scene suggests healing for the splits of memory and forgetting, war and peace, past and present, reason and madness, all of which the poem addresses. It also 'heals' the split between male and female. 'WOMAN' in a 'new sense of woman' is Kaspar and Mary together, with Mary in ascendant, since the fragrance, Kaspar knows, comes from her flowers which are the source of his ointment. The healing happens through a renunciation of the epistemology of the Piscean era and an acceptance of the anti-epistemology which emphasises unknowing rather than knowing. Kaspar stands before Mary—but he does not bow low, does not abase himself, and Mary speaks to him as an equal.

She is 'shy and simple and young'. Power in the new age is unrecognizable. It is as Kaspar's hand 'just did-not touch her hand' that his vision of the pattern of life and of time opens out (*FR* 30). Confronted by Mary's myrrh, Kaspar must not only abandon the judgemental and dismissive mastery of 'it was unseemly that a woman / appear at all', he must also abandon sexual mastery. The poems substitute a sort of open agnosticism for the 'secret' wisdom or gnosis that has been hidden in the previous age.

V. Conclusion

In August 1945, after Hiroshima, Robert Herring wrote an editorial for *Life and Letters Today* that brought together some of these themes. The atom bomb had unleashed the power of the universe, promising a rule of terror in the postwar world, a rule that the war was precisely meant to prevent. Alluding perhaps to Freud's story of his grandson's 'fort-da' game in *Beyond the Pleasure Principle*, Herring likened human beings to babies who enjoy throwing things out of their cradles: they are only happy when they have not got what they want. Freud's preliminary conclusion was that the child enjoyed the control the game afforded him, in imagination, over his mother's absences and reappearances: a later conclusion was that the instinct towards death was as strong as the instinct for life. Herring concluded: 'We may be at the beginning of the Aquarian Age—and let the word 'uranium' be noted—but ages are apt to begin with the delayed actions from the last'. The power of uranium, he thought, could destroy us or enrich us. It will only do the latter if we can undergo 'the spiritual straightening' necessary to learn how to use it.[47] By weaving together its myths of Aquarius and Atlantis with all the other myths it contains, by its transforming linguistic sleights of hand, ***Trilogy*** responds to 'the sense of an ending' prevalent during the war years by proposing an eschatology that undermines the triumphalist certainties of the (Piscean) Christian vision. It attempts to create the healing myth that literary commentators in the mid-war years demanded, to transform the imagination and inaugurate an era in which the occult power of 'uranium' might become the time of Uranus, governed not by mastery and destruction but by open mysteries of love.

References

1. *Trilogy*, ed., N. H. Pearson (Manchester: Carcanet, 1988). References are included in the text and are to the sections of each poem. [*Trilogy* includes "The Walls Do Not Fall," "Tribute to Angels," and "The Flowering of the Rod."]

2. H. D.'s early poems are published in *Collected Poems 1912-1944,* ed., L. Martz (New York: New Directions, 1983).

3. J. Jeans, *The Mysterious Universe* (London: Cambridge UP, 1931).

4. 'Not with a bang but a whimper'—Eliot's vision of the end of the world in 'The Hollow Men' echoes Jeans, who wrote '[The universe] . . . is travelling the road from birth to death, just as we all are. For science knows no change except the change of growing older, and of no progress, except the progress to the grave.' *The Stars in Their Courses* (London: Cambridge UP, 1931) p. 152.

5. N. H. Pearson, 'Tribute to the Angels' (Review), *Life and Letters Today,* 46:95 (July 1945) p. 60.

6. R. B. du Plessis, *Writing Beyond the Ending: Narrative Structures of Twentieth Century Women Writers* (Bloomington: Indiana UP, 1985).

7. S. O'Leary, *Arguing the Apocalypse* (New York and Oxford: Oxford UP, 1994) p. 55.

8. H. Ellis, *The New Spirit* (London: George Bell, 1890) p. 1.

9. C. Buck, *H. D. and Freud: Bisexuality of a Feminine Discourse* (New York, London, Toronto Harvester & Wheatsheaf, 1991).

10. D. H. Lawrence, *Apocalypse and the Writings on Revelation,* ed., M. Klinis (Cambridge: Cambridge UP, 1980) p. 68.

11. H. D. to May Sarton Feb. 1941 (Berg Papers, New York Public Library).

12. *The New Apocalypse An Anthology of Criticism, Poems and Stories,* ed., J. F. Hendry and H. Treece, (London: Fortune Press, 1940). After this came *The White Horseman: Prose and Verse of the New Apocalypse* (London: Routledge, 1941) and *The Crown and the Sickle* (London: P. S. King & Staples, 1946) both edited by J. F. Hendry and H. Treece.

13. Read believed that the blitz was an apocalyptic judgement on capitalism and hoped a new, anarchist society would emerge from the flames. A. Piette, *Imagination at War: British Fiction and Poetry 1939-1945* (London & Basingstoke: Papermac, 1995) p. 40.

14. H. Treece, 'More Notes on the Image', *How I See Apocalypse,* ed., H. Treece (London: Lindsay Drummond, 1946) pp. 52-73 (p. 62).

15. H. Treece, 'Poetry and Mechanistic Ideology', *ibid.,* pp. 64-73 (p. 73).

16. C. Connolly, *Horizon,* 4:19 (July 1941) pp. 5-8.

17. *Horizon,* 1:4 (April 1940) pp. 230-1.

18. *Horizon,* 4:20 (August 1941) pp. 78-82.

19. S. Schimanski, 'The Duty of a Younger Writer', *Life and Letters Today,* 46:95 (July 1943) pp. 90-5 (p. 99).

20. H. D. to Bryher 31.5.32 (Beinecke: Bryher Papers).

21. *Ibid.,* 28.5.33 (Beinecke: Bryher Papers).

22. *Ibid.,* 30.4.33 (Beinecke: Bryher Papers).

23. In his autobiography, Jung claimed to have had a dream in 1913 which prophesied the great war. (*Memories Dreams and Reflections* (London: Fontana, 1993) p. 199). In his 1918 essay 'the Role of the Unconscious' (*CW* 10 para. 17) he warned 'As the Christian view of the world loses its authority, the more menacingly will the 'blond beast' be heard prowling about its underground prison, ready at any moment to burst out with devastating consequences.'

24. C. G. Jung to H. G. Baynes 12.8.40. *Selected Letters of C. G. Jung,* ed., G. Adler, Vol. 1 (London: Routledge & Kegan Paul, 1973) p. 285.

25. H. D. to May Sarton 6.12.44 (Berg Papers: New York Public Library).

26. C. Buck, *op. cit.,* p. 164,

27. 'The funny ♅ is Herschel, the planet, supposed to be forming our new age' H. D. to May Sarton, Feb. 1941 (Berg Papers: New York Public Library).

28. E. Carpenter, *The Intermediate Sex* (London: Swan Sonnenschein, 1908) p. 116.

29. W. Ellerman, H. D.'s partner from 1918-61.

30. S. Freud, 'Femininity', *New Introductory Lectures on Psychoanalysis,* vol. 2 (Penguin Freud Library) pp. 145-69 (pp. 162-3).

31. M. Reeves and W. Gould, *Joachim of Fiore and the Myth of the Eternal Evangel in the Nineteenth Century* (Oxford: Clarendon Press, 1987) p. 202.

32. 'The Guest' is published in *By Avon River* (New York: Macmillan, 1949).

33. H. Ellis, *The New Spirit,* quoted in Reeves and Gould, *op. cit.,* (p. 176).

34. The Flowering of the Rod: Notebook (Beinecke: H. D. Papers).

35. *Tribute to Freud,* p. 157.

36. 'Majic Ring', p. 268. (Beinecke: HD Papers).

37. M. Hughes, 'The Myth of Revelation is History' (Review) *Life and Letters Today,* 35:62 (Sept. 1942) p. 62.

38. H. D. possessed a number of books by Bellamy including *In the Beginning, God* (1940) and *Built Before the Flood* (1943) both of which also sought to 'prove' biblical myths were garbled stories of cosmic eruptions Another favourite writer was Lewis Spence whose *Will Europe Follow Atlantis?* argued that the war was a punishment for European decadence, as the Atlantean flood had been.

39. Dimitri Merezhkovsky, *The Secret of the West* (London: Jonathan Cape, 1936). C. H. Bedford explains Merezhkovsky's eschatological ideas in 'Dmitri Merezhkovsky, the Third Testament and the Third Humanity', *The Slavonic and East European Review* 42:98 (Dec. 1963) pp. 144-60.

40. Evans does not imagine connections between Crete and Atlantis. However his timetable for Minoan culture was very schematic and paralleled the Atlantis myth in some respects. The history of Knossos is traced through a series of ages, each age being subdivided into three periods, all marked at their end by some huge catastrophe, usually an earthquake. Evans' upbeat interpretation of these catastrophes as 'setbacks' out of which the Minoan and, eventually, Greek culture could rise phoenix like to new heights, appealed to postwar pessimism. (*The Palace of Minos at Knossos* (London: Macmillan, 1921) vol. 1, *passim*, especially pp. 1-28). According to her account in *Tribute to Freud*, H. D. and Freud discussed Evans' findings (p. 175).

41. *The Secret of the West*, p. 241.

42. *Ibid.*, p. 277.

43. *Ibid.*, p. 248.

44. *Ibid.*, p. 243.

45. *Ibid.*, p. 71.

46. *Ibid.*, p. 319.

47. R. Herring, 'Editorial', *Life and Letters Today*, 46:96 (Aug. 1945) pp. 70-1.

Bret L. Keeling (essay date summer 1998)

SOURCE: Keeling, Bret L. "H. D. and 'The Contest': Archaeology of the Sapphic Gaze." *Twentieth-Century Literature* 44, no. 2 (summer 1998): 176-203.

[*In the following essay, Keeling surveys the work of other critics who have identified Sappho as an influence and inspiration in H. D.'s work. Keeling goes on to contend that H. D. rejected the notion of a Sapphic gaze originating from a male perspective and instead insisted upon her own interpretation regarding the Sapphic gaze and its origins.*]

What need—
yet to sing love,
love must first shatter us.

—H. D., "Fragment Forty"
(*Collected Poems [CP]* 175)

Scholars have long documented the relationships between Sappho and her poetic successors.[1] More recently, a few critics have unearthed those between Sappho and H. D. Thirteen years ago, for example, Susan Gubar insisted that "Sappho's status as a female precursor empowered a number of female modernists" (44), including H. D., and enabled them to "try to solve the problem of poetic isolation and imputed inferiority" (46) that they experienced as women writers. Two years later, while acknowledging that H. D. never explicitly names Sappho in the poems of *Sea Garden* as the "crucial source of lyric power" ("Rose Cut in Rock" 529), Eileen Gregory viewed *Sea Garden* as "a consciously crafted whole" (536) in which H. D. "attempts to recover the imagination of goddess-centered Lesbos" as exemplified by Sappho, "the first love-possessed lyricist" (528-29).[2] Robert Babcock, indicating that Thomas Swann was the critic who "established a canon of [H. D.'s] Sapphic verses" (43), extended Gregory's thesis in 1990 by demonstrating that H. D.'s **"Pursuit"** from *Sea Garden* was based specifically on Sappho's fragment 105. Babcock proposed that "[t]he failure of [H. D.'s contemporary] critics to recognize the sources of her work or to treat her writing as a serious engagement with a literary tradition may have led H. D. to begin explicitly detailing sources in her later books" (44). Babcock referred to **"Pursuit"** as "H. D.'s earliest published version of Sappho" and concluded that it could "contribute to a fuller appreciation of the range and depth of the Sapphic influence on her writing" (46).

Today, seven years after Babcock's work, it is my intention to add my voice in order to reenvision the link between Sappho and H. D. However, I will argue that Sappho's influence on H. D. extends beyond what Gubar labels "the dynamic of collaboration" (58); beyond what Babcock identifies as H. D.'s "startling but simple" treatment of an image as an image (46); and beyond what Gregory calls "the aesthetic of H. D.'s early work," which conjures and reenacts "the experienced power of the image" ("Rose Cut in Rock" 545). I suggest that Sappho also teaches H. D. "the experienced power" and sexual erotics of a gaze that initiates not a fixed subject/object exchange but an oscillating sense of subjectivity. In this essay I demonstrate that H. D., rather than encountering a male-dominated tradition of "the gaze," creates a gaze influenced by what she interprets as the "viewing" employed by Sappho in the sixth century BC.

In the first section of this essay, I explain why readings that rely solely on ways in which male authors have oppressed women without including ways in which female authors are part of a women's literary tradition can be reductive—in a destructive as well as an analytic sense. I then examine the literary tradition of Sappho that would eventually influence H. D. In the second section, I attempt to reconstruct the ways in which I believe H. D. inherited and interpreted that tradition. In the third section, I examine H. D.'s early poem **"The Contest"** from *Sea Garden* as part of a Sapphic vision of poetry that is something other than an oppositional, perpetuating, or marginal discourse against a "patriarchal" tradition. And in the concluding section, I speculate on why H. D. might have refrained from both mere imitation and direct translation of Sappho.

> I dare more than the singer
> offering her lute,
>
> . . . . .
>
> I offer more than the lad
> singing at your steps,
>
> . . . . .
>
> I give you my praise and this:
> the love of my lover
> for his mistress.
>
> —H. D., "Fragment Forty-one" (*CP* 184)

I want to explain my use of the terms *archaeology* and *gaze* in this essay's title. The latter undoubtedly recalls film theorists such as Laura Mulvey and her articulations of visual pleasure and the "male gaze."[3] Considering H. D.'s venture into film making and film criticism in the years from 1927 through 1933, I do not discourage this association. But I also use the term *gaze* in a broader—less theoretical and less gendered—way. I use *gaze* to suggest not only a steadily intense way of looking at, but also a way of looking after (following with the eye), looking into (inquiring with the mind), looking up to (regarding with admiration), looking upon (considering and beholding), looking ahead (imagining and desiring), and looking back (reviewing and returning). I describe a Sapphic gaze as a specifically multiple way of seeing grounded in both historical and cultural moments of human sexual and erotic development that H. D. believed she could recuperate, attempt to make whole, and hope to eventually transcend.

Thus my use of the term *archaeology,* like that of *gaze,* may recall a specific theorist: Michel Foucault. Regarding knowledge, Foucault insists that he does not "study the beginning in the sense of first origin," but rather "relative beginnings" ("Order of Things" 57); and that he uses *archaeology* most explicitly "to designate something that would be the description of the archive and not at all . . . the bringing to light of

the bones of the past" (65). I emphasize Foucault's definition because my own—at least in this essay's context—appears to be both what he declares his is and what he declares it is not. That is, while I am not "searching for the first solemn moment," I am searching for "foundations" and am not at all "bothered by the idea of excavations" (57). In fact, the literal Egyptian excavations of Sappho's fragmentary poems in 1897 are central to the renewed Sappho scholarship at the turn of the century and to H. D.'s own 1923 visit to Egypt. Foucault, in order to distance himself from them, refers to "the regular historians" as those who see and reveal "continuities" (58). H. D. might be less dismissive of such historians. I believe that H. D. saw continuities—not necessarily easily, not without drama and sacrifice, not by means of conventional poetic tropes—and attempted to reveal them as they were revealed to her by way of a Sapphic gaze.

The Sapphic gaze, however, is not a way of looking that H. D. simply unearths and adopts; it is not Sappho's gaze. Rather, it is H. D.'s own gaze, H. D.'s way of looking (at, after, into, up to, upon, ahead, back) that she develops from Sappho's fragmented archives. The Sapphic gaze is H. D.'s construction of vision and viewing that relies not on narrative—there can be no logical progression of events and actions laid bare from a scattering of papyrus scraps and pottery shards—and not on spectacle, as in the "male gaze," but on analytic description. This description does more than image a scene or setting; it breaks down an object into its constituent elements without necessarily establishing an explicit relationship between the parts and the "whole"—neither as such a relationship may or may not have existed before the analysis, nor as it may or may not come to exist after the analysis. Moreover, this description does not establish a fixed relationship between the subject and the object. Such a way of analytically describing comes to H. D. by way of the material condition of Sappho's archives; all that H. D. has available to her are parts, elements, fragments of what once must have been whole poems. In this sense, H. D.'s Sapphic gaze is not a vision of archetypal synthesis but one of prototypal analysis.[4]

And yet, as we shall see in the discussions of "Notes on Thought and Vision" and "The Wise Sappho" below, H. D. eventually theorizes the (re)construction of a whole. That is, she does visualize by way of fragments a future moment of what Page duBois calls "the restoration of lost wholes" (35). Her Sapphic gaze, then, is not only analytically descriptive, it is also intermediary—a stage of development that is scopophilic in nature. Freud describes scopophilic desire as that which aims at "pleasure in looking" (23), one of the "intermediate relations to the sexual object . . .

which lie on the road towards copulation and are recognized as being preliminary sexual aims" (15). This differs from the voyeuristic impulse attributed to a "male" gaze in which sexual desire is satisfied not only by one's looking but by one's looking and not being seen. What makes visual impressions so exciting, says Freud, is that the "concealment of the body . . . keeps sexual curiosity awake. This curiosity seeks to complete the sexual object by revealing its hidden *parts*. It can, however, be diverted ('sublimated') in the direction of art, if its interest can be shifted away from the genitals on to the shape of the body as a *whole*" (22, emphasis mine). Similarly, the concealment of Sappho's "whole" poetry keeps H. D.'s curiosity in the fragments awake. She seeks to complete Sappho by revealing hidden parts. To paraphrase Freud, lingering over the intermediate sexual aim of looking offers H. D. a possibility of directing some proportion of her libido onto her artistic aims (23); she emulates Sappho's fragments in order to emphasize the fragmentation of a subject position she herself experiences as woman/object and poet/subject, but also in order to reconfigure that emphasis. As duBois suggests, "The self constituted against a background of disorder can be a self of pleasure and authority that recognizes its construction of itself out of fragmentation" (75). Sappho's fragments provide a literary and literal site where H. D. can visualize subject/object and female/male encounters in ways that extend beyond oppositional discourses. In this sense, H. D.'s Sapphic gaze is intersubjective because it is not directed toward an object but is held in relation to another subject.

H. D.'s project, then, is radical rather than merely a reaction to more recent poetic developments. When Nancy Vickers discusses the ways in which Petrarch seems to reduce Laura's image to "a collection of exquisitely beautiful disassociated objects" (266) in his poetry, she insists that this kind of "description . . . extends well beyond the confines of his own poetic age" to become the "authoritative" description of "feminine beauty" (265). Vickers views Petrarch as the originator of the gaze. At the conclusion of her essay, Vickers points out what is "understandabl[e]" in the "praise" Petrarch's description of beauty warrants: "Petrarch's poetry is a poetry of tension, of flux, of alternation between the scattered and the gathered. Laura's many parts would point to a unity, however elusive, named Laura" (277). But Vickers then goes on to address the ways in which Petrarch's figuring of the body

> implies at least two interdependent consequences. First, Petrarch's figuration of Laura informs a decisive stage in the development of a code of beauty, a code that causes us to view the fetishized body as a norm and

> encourages us to seek, or to seek to be, "ideal types, beautiful monsters composed of every individual perfection." . . . And second, bodies fetishized by a poetic voice logically do not have a voice of their own; the world of making words, of making texts, is not theirs.

> (277)

For Vickers, the male seeks the ideal, the female seeks to be idealized, and to be idealized is to be fragmented. Fragmentation here becomes an original and male exercise in power that symbolically reduces and controls a female through objectification and exhibition, one that ultimately denies her both agency and complexity.

Vickers's interpretation of a Petrarchan strategy of figuring the female body is similar to the strategy Rachel Blau DuPlessis identifies as entailing "a cluster of foundational materials" that are built into "the heart of the lyric" (71). In "Corpses of Poesy," DuPlessis presents a "case study in literary history" where she concludes that modernists Mina Loy and Marianne Moore "produced a distinctive intellectual, analytic writing fueled by their articulate suspicion of foundational assumptions of gender in poetic texts and traditions" (90). DuPlessis calls these assumptions a "foundational cluster" of the lyric poem comprised of "lyric-love-sex-beauty-Woman" (76):

> The foundational cluster concerns voice (and silencing), power (appropriation and transcendence), nature (as opposed to formation and culture), gaze (framing, specularity, fragmentation), and the sources of poetic matter—narratives of romance, of the sublime, scenes of inspiration, the muse as conduit (Vickers 1981). There is often a triangulated situation in the lyric: an overtly male "I," speaking as if overheard in front of an unseen but postulated, loosely male "us" about a (Beloved) "she" (Grossman 1992, 227). To change any of these pronouns ("I" speaking directly to a "you," for example; an "I" who is a "she"; readers claiming to be female) is to jostle, if only slightly, the homosocial triangle of the lyric (Sedgwick 1985).

> (71)

While DuPlessis, here, does not seem convinced that H. D. shares the "suspicion" she finds in Loy and Moore, she does seem to suggest that H. D. understands the "concerns" of the "cluster" by seeming to both embrace and rebuff its tenets, or as she states elsewhere, by being "characteristically both complicit and resistant" (*Career* 5). While "Loy opens poetry to analytic and ironic considerations that unmask a number of the gendered institutions on which poesy is built" (79) and "Moore makes a diction choice resistant to the poetical beauties that are linked to female beauties" (86), H. D., according to DuPlessis, remains "sometimes tempted" by a "Pretty Poetry world" (87). Moore and Loy enact a personal and social awakening that challenges, and attempts to change, existing gender representation. H. D., on the other hand, appears to employ a traditional sort of consciousness, one that accepts and includes—perhaps inverting but never transcending—gender norms.

The Vickers and DuPlessis arguments, however insightful in detailing the different ways in which women and men may acquire social and poetic identities through a viewer/object exchange, seem to be prohibitive in their rejection of visual pleasure. More importantly, both Vickers and DuPlessis approach the lyric from too advanced a point; attributing the origins of fetishism, objectification, and a standard of male gaze to Petrarch in the fourteenth century AD neglects at least 2,000 years of Western lyric poetry.[5] In addition, Vickers and DuPlessis—unintentionally, to be sure—ultimately universalize Petrarchan strategies and foundational clusters just as archaeologists used to generalize the sequences of cultural changes by way of technological traditions in Europe to include all of world history. Applying Vickers's and DuPlessis's concepts of the "scattered" and "silenced" female body to H. D.'s poem **"The Contest,"** we may be tempted to agree that H. D. does, indeed—by changing the gender of the pronouns and by speaking directly to the object—"jostle, if only slightly," the Petrarchan/foundational strategies. But I suggest that H. D.'s options here are more varied—as our evaluative tools should be. Rather than extending or distorting Vickers's exploration of a Petrarchan strategy of description, rather than imitating or rejecting DuPlessis's articulation of a Keatsian "foundational cluster," H. D.'s lyrics emulate Sappho and extend a Sapphic gaze. This gaze offers itself as neither subordinate to nor subordinating the stereotype because no such Petrarchan or Keatsian stereotypes exist.[6]

Let us turn to Sappho's work and explore the ways in which she develops a "gaze" that even Petrarch will engage. Here is her fragment 31, which duBois, Joan DeJean, and Anne Carson all address in their studies:[7]

> In my eyes he matches the gods, that man who
> sits there facing you—any man whatever—
> listening from closeby to the sweetness of your
>   voice as you talk, the
>
> sweetness of your laughter: yes, that—I swear it—
> sets the heart to shaking inside my breast, since
> once I look at you for a moment, I can't
>   speak any longer,
>
> but my tongue breaks down, and then all at once a
> subtle fire races inside my skin, my
> eyes can't see a thing and a whirring whistle
>   thrums at my hearing,

> cold sweat covers me and a trembling takes
> ahold of me all over: I'm greener than the
> grass is and appear to myself to be little
>   short of dying.
>
> But all must be endured, since even a poor

Here the poem ends. Whatever precedes, whatever follows, whatever narrative—if any—that may have once existed is lost to us.

We notice immediately in this particular lyric the presence of three figures: the first-person "I" speaker, the second-person "you," and a third-person "he." Only the third person is identified by gender, and only he remains outside the dialogue of the poem. At first we may assume the speaker intends to salute him, this man who "matches the gods" (1), but it soon becomes clear that he—like all men, "any man whatever" (2)—shares the speaker's infatuation for the second-person "you"—"the sweetness of your / voice as you talk, the / / sweetness of your laughter" (3-5). Here we may make another assumption: the speaker's objectification of the "you" will continue beyond mere voice and laughter. But instead, the speaker's attention turns to herself. Already we see deviations from DuPlessis's definition of the lyric voice as that of a man speaking to men about a woman.[8] Objectifying the "you" sets the speaker's "heart to shaking inside my breast" (6); looking at "you" prevents her from speaking (8-9), from seeing (11), and from hearing (12). In other words, objectifying the "you" causes the speaker linguistically to begin fragmenting herself—an active rather than passive process. All her senses are affected. She is covered in "cold sweat" as "a trembling takes / ahold of me all over" (13-14), and she is left a "little / short of dying" (15-16).

Compare Sappho's objectification of object and fragmentation of subject to Petrarch's. In Sonnet 3, Petrarch's speaker falls "a captive, Lady, to the sway / Of your swift eyes" (4-5) in much the same way that Sappho's speaker falls captive to the sweet voice. The power of Petrarch's "Lady's" eyes makes the speaker a "prisoner" (4) again in Sonnet 61. As Sappho's speaker articulates the effects of her beloved on her own heart, breast, voice, eyes, ears, and skin, so Petrarch's speaker blesses "the first sweet pain . . . / Which burnt my heart" and "the shafts which shock my breast, / And even the wounds which Love delivered there" (5-8). Page duBois points out that in Sappho's fragment the speaker "herself sees the disorder in the body in love, sees herself objectified as a body in pieces, disjointed, a broken set of organs, limbs, bodily functions" (70). Petrarch's speaker sees himself, the body in love, the same way—a body in pieces—which undermines any reading exclusively emphasizing broken objects and unified subjects. Was he influenced by Sappho? David M. Robinson acknowledges that Sappho was relatively unknown in medieval Europe (134), but Petrarch, who actively searched for Greek and Roman manuscripts and became the "first" writer of the Renaissance, refers to Sappho in both his *Triumph of Love* and *Tenth Eclogue* (Robinson 136). As we can see, the objectification that leads to bodily fragmentation of both object and subject may be exemplified and eroticized in Petrarch, but it does not originate here. According to duBois, it is in Sappho that we find "representation of a new stage in the thinking of existence" (7):

> Sappho and the poets who are her near contemporaries are among the first to inhabit fully the first person singular, to use the word "I" to anchor their poetic speech, to hollow out for their listeners and readers the cultural space for individual subjectivity. . . . We see in the work of Sappho the very beginnings of this process, the construction of selfhood, of the fiction of subjectivity at its origins.
>
> (6)

H. D. may or may not have considered subjectivity a "fiction," but she recognized it as a construct and clearly saw in Sappho its "origins."

> [W]hy were those slight words
> and the violets you gathered
> of such worth?
>
> —H. D., "Fragment Sixty-eight" (*CP* 188)

To expand this consideration of the gaze that H. D. articulates in **"The Contest"** as Sapphic rather than Petrarchan, we need to establish a women's literary tradition—the relationship between H. D. and Sappho—that, if not completely independent of Petrarchan influence, does not rely upon it. H. D.'s familiarity with the Greek poet's work is clear as early as 1921, with the publication of **Hymen**, H. D.'s second collection of poetry, which included **"Fragment 113"** (*CP* 131-32) and its epigraph from Sappho, "Neither honey nor bee for me." But H. D. tells us that her interest in Sappho began much earlier. Although **"Fragment Thirty-six"** (*CP* 165-68), based on Sappho's fragment, "I know not what to do: / my mind is divided," does not appear until the 1924 publication of **Heliodora**, H. D. writes in 1937 that the poem "definitely, [was] written at Corfe Castle, in 1916, the year conscription came in" ("A Note on Poetry" 1287). And while we may not be certain of the date of "The Wise Sappho," H. D.'s prose tribute to her predecessor published posthumously in 1982, we can safely assume that it originated as early as 1920.[9]

In addition, H. D. was familiar with and enchanted by Algernon Charles Swinburne's translations of Sappho.[10] In a 1925 review of a contemporary compilation and translation by Edwin Marion Cox, *The Poems of Sappho*, H. D. marvels that Cox can consider translations by Swinburne, Dante Gabriel Rossetti, and Wharton to be "out of date" ("Winter Roses"). She asks with not just a little irony, "Is it possible . . . [Cox] finds Swinburne, like others of the very *modern* schools, a little old fashioned?" (emphasis mine). Referring to a specific poem Cox has eliminated from his text, H. D. writes:

> I feel that in the gallery or galaxy of translations of Sappho that [this] particular translation of Swinburne is forever and ever wedded to that particular fragment. That no one, no matter how notable he may be has any right to omit Swinburne from any volume purporting to be an up to date compilation of critical notes and translations.

It is possible that H. D. shared Swinburne's enthusiasm for Sappho. Only two years before the publication of **Sea Garden** (and thus **"The Contest"**), a posthumous essay by Swinburne appeared in *The Living Age*. Here Swinburne wrote:

> Judging even from the mutilated fragments fallen within our reach from the broken altar of her sacrifice of song, I for one have always agreed with all Grecian tradition in thinking Sappho to be beyond all question and comparison *the very greatest poet that ever lived.*
>
> (qtd. in Robinson 11)

The fact that all that exists of Sappho's oeuvre are "mutilated fragments" may be a concern for H. D., but not necessarily an insurmountable obstacle. In "The Wise Sappho," she admits that she is "inclined to visualize these broken sentences and unfinished rhythms as rocks—perfect rock shelves and layers of rock between which flowers by some chance may grow but which endure when the staunch blossoms have perished" (58). But it is on these rocks—indeed, *from* these rocks—that "[t]he name of muse and goddess and of human woman merge" (64). As I pointed out in the discussion of archaeology above, H. D. views Sappho as a source of poetic, artistic, and cultural continuity. And it is probably not incidental that rocks—and the triumvirate of muse/goddess/woman—"endure" when we recall the last line of Sappho's fragment above: "But all must be endured" or "dared." H. D.'s **Sea Garden** poems are the flowers that grow from the enduring rock of Sappho's fragments, and her Sapphic gaze is that which dares to view and visualize from the intersubjective position of muse *and* goddess *and* woman.

While postmodern critiques of them may vary, fragments, for H. D., are part of a larger, recoverable whole.[11] She begins "Notes on Thought and Vision" with a divided—fragmented—self: "Three states or manifestations of life: body, mind, over-mind" (17). Later in the essay she rethinks and restates her claim, saying, "I think at last I have my terms clear. There are three states or manifestations—sub-conscious mind, conscious mind, over-conscious mind" (49). Fragments, symbolized by Sappho's lyrics, can be recovered. She has already insisted that "we cannot have spirit without body, the body of nature, or the body of individual men and women" (48). While "[i]t is necessary to work, to strive toward the understanding of the over-mind," once such understanding is achieved "[o]ur concern is with the body" (50). But, H. D. asks, "Where does the body come in? What is the body?" (51). She ultimately concludes that the body is "not a very rare or lovely thing. The body seem[s] an elementary, unbeautiful and transitory form of life," and yet the body has "its use," functioning as an oyster with a pearl; "the body, with all its emotions and fears and pain in time casts off the spirit, a concentrated essence," which is not itself the body but is created by the body "itself" (51). This supports her earlier declaration that the body, which "can be used as a means of approach to ecstasy" (46), is "like a lump of coal" that "fulfills its highest function when it is being consumed" (47). This also indicates that she views the body as somehow intermediary, a stage—albeit an important one—toward uncarthing an understanding of the over-mind and a construction of subjectivity.

H. D. writes that "[t]he best Greek sculpture used the bodies of young athletes as Lo-fu [her fictional Chinese poet] used the branch of the fruit tree"; she insists that "[t]he fruit tree and the human body are both receiving stations, capable of storing up energy," energy that "can be transmitted only to another body or another mind that is in sympathy with it" (46-47). What is concrete and whole—the body, the tree—can be fragmented—the body into arms and eyes, the tree into branches and leaves. And what is fragmented can be recovered and transcended, reassembled and transformed. H. D. writes:

> Lo-fu was a poet. To him that apple branch, outside in the orchard, existed as an approach to something else. As the body of a man's mistress might be said to exist as the means of approach to something else, that is as a means or instrument of feeling or happiness, so the branch in the orchard existed to Lo-fu as the means of attaining happiness, as a means of completing himself, as a means of approach to ecstasy.
>
> (45)

H. D.'s Lo-fu and his apple branch reveals a striking similarity to Sappho and another of her fragments. Wharton translates Sappho as follows in fragment 93: "As the sweet-apple blushes on the end of the bough, the very end of the bough, which the gatherers

overlooked, nay overlooked not but could not reach." Sappho's speaker draws our attention to an apple left unpicked not because it is unseen but because it is unattainable. Anne Carson calls this one "of the tactics of incompleteness by which Sappho sustains desire and desirability in the poem" (69). We do not know how Sappho's speaker regards the apple/object that cannot be secured, but we do know how Petrarch's speaker regards the beloved/object who cannot be secured: when the beloved departs—after all, "Love" is only a "guest" ("Sonnet 61" 6)—the speaker is left with "sighs" and "tears" (11) to bless "that thought of thoughts which is her [the beloved's] own, / Of her, her only, of herself alone" (13-14).

H. D.'s Lo-fu suffers no such despair. Remember Freud's discussion of the potential for curiosity in the body to be sublimated toward art. The apple branch allows Lo-fu to move beyond "a mind that may be conscious in the ordinary, scholarly, literal sense of the word" to an "over-conscious" mind that enables him "to enter into a *whole* life" (42, emphasis mine). H. D. tells us that observing the branch, Lo-fu's "conscious mind ceased wondering and, being an artist, his intensity and concentration were of a special order" (43). His gaze moves—looking at/after/into/up to/ upon/ahead/back—constantly from the apples, to their stems, to the branches, to "two leaves, continents to be explored in a leisurely manner lest his mind passing one carelessly from vein to vein" should miss any detail; but Lo-fu's mind has "only begun its search" (44). H. D. insists: "Lo-fu looked at that branch. He really did look at it. He really did see it" in such vividness that when he closes his eyes it is all the more clear. And it transforms: "That branch was his mistress now, his love. . . . Here, in his little room, the world had ceased to exist. It was shut off, shut out, forgotten. His love, his apple branch, his subtle mistress, was his. And having possessed her with his great and famished soul, she was his forever" (44-45). Petrarch's speakers objectify and are left stricken, anguished, and bleeding. H. D.'s also objectifies, but by way of the Sapphic gaze that H. D. has excavated, Lo-fu moves beyond the eroticism of fragmentation to the ecstasy of wholeness. DuBois warns, "We need to be conscious of an ongoing tension between our desire to register fragmentation and our desire to invent integrity" (20). Of course, just because H. D. describes Lo-fu in his moment of transcendent fusion—and, thus, "invent[s] integrity"—does not mean H. D. herself experiences it. But she clearly longs for its possibility.

> My mind is quite divided,
> my minds hesitate,
> so perfect matched,
> I know not what to do:
> each strives with each

as two white wrestlers
standing for a match,
ready to turn and clutch
yet never shake muscle nor nerve nor tendon. . . .

        —H. D., "Fragment Thirty-six" (*CP* 167)

H. D.'s speaker in **"The Contest"** is in the intermediate stage of the Sapphic gaze—the stage Lo-fu eventually transcends. The speaker here has only eyes. And the eye, as Freud insists, is "the [erotogenic] zone most remote from the sexual object, but it is the one which, in the situation of wooing an object, is liable to be the most frequently stimulated by the particular quality of excitation whose cause, when it occurs in a sexual object, we describe as beauty" (75). Because **"The Contest"** has been neglected in much of the H. D. criticism, I offer it below in its entirety:[12]

I.

Your stature is modelled
with straight tool-edge:
you are chiselled like rocks
that are eaten by the sea.

With the turn and grasp of your wrist
and the chords' stretch,
there is a glint like worn brass.

The ridge of your breast is taut,
and under each shadow is sharp,
and between the clenched muscles
of your slender hips.

From the circle of your cropped hair
there is light,
and about your male torso
and the foot-arch and the straight ankle.

II.

You stand rigid and mighty—
granite and the ore in rocks;
a great band clasps your forehead
and its heavy twists of gold.

You are white—a limb of cypress
bent under a weight of snow.

You are splendid,
your arms are fire;
you have entered the hill-straits—
a sea treads upon the hill-slopes.

III.

Myrtle is about your head,
you have bent and caught the spray:
each leaf is sharp
against the lift and furrow
of your bound hair.

The narcissus has copied the arch
of your slight breast:

your feet are citron-flowers,
your knees, cut from white-ash,
your thighs are rock-cistus.

Your chin lifts straight
from the hollow of your curved throat.
your shoulders are level—
they have melted rare silver
for their breadth.

                            (*CP* 12-14)

Before exploring the ways in which this poem exemplifies a Sapphic gaze, let me begin with a brief discussion of some of the poem's formal concerns. The symmetrical aspects of its form reflect, I think, H. D.'s interest in both Sappho and classical poetry.[13] Gilbert Highet says, "[S]ymmetry means a balanced proportion of parts corresponding to their importance in the general structure" (332), and one way symmetry is created and maintained is by the use of the "tricolon," a "unit made up of three parts," which Highet exemplifies by way of Lincoln's "of the people, by the people, for the people" (334).[14] H. D. recognizes this symmetrical device "invented by Greek teachers of rhetoric" and expands it by employing a tripartite structure in **"The Contest,"** which consists of three parts comprising 10 stanzas.[15] Part 1 contains four stanzas—an opening quatrain, followed by a tristich, and two more quatrains; parts 2 and 3 contain three stanzas each—two quatrains framing a distich in part 2, and three consecutive quintets in part 3. The first and third parts contain 15 lines each and frame the second, center part (which contains 10 lines) in much the same way as the second part itself is framed by the two quatrains around the distich. Each of the total 40 lines varies in irregular rhythms of dimeter, trimeter, tetrameter, and pentameter so that the alternating line lengths—two, three, four, and five stresses—mirror the alternating stanza sizes—two, three, four, and five lines—in order to underscore classical symmetry.

H. D. utilizes two different methods of imitating (neo)classical proportion in diction and syntax: chiasmus and anaphora.[16] Chiasmus is the symmetrical balance of word order through reversal. We see it in the poem's first two sentences. H. D. begins with a loose sentence: "Your stature is modelled / with straight tool-edge". The common subject-verb-object construction is followed by a prepositional phrase introduced by "with." This same preposition opens the poem's second sentence, which is—in a syntactic reversal of the first—periodic: "With the turn and grasp of your wrist / . . . / there is a glint like worn brass."

The anaphora in **"The Contest"** complements the chiasmus and suggests a stability that the content of the poem, as we shall see, resists. Where chiasmus creates, although in reverse, a balance of word order through symmetry, anaphora creates such a balance through repetition. We find it in the same sentence on consecutive lines—"and under" (9), "and between" (10); we find it in nonconsecutive lines but at the beginning of consecutive sentences—"You are white" (19), "You are splendid" (21); we find it in nonconsecutive lines and in different sentences in different syntactical arrangement—"of your bound hair" (30), "of your slight breast" (32). Finally, we see anaphora in the lines connecting the final two stanzas: "your feet are" (33), "your knees, cut" (34), "your thighs are" (35), "your chin lifts" (36), and "your shoulders are" (38). Here, anaphora emphasizes the speaker's fragmentation and objectification of the "you." The momentum created by the culmination of body parts at the end of the poem is both undermined by the repetitious balance effected by the anaphora and underscored, since repetition is not always merely repetitious.[17]

After exploring the symmetry created by chiasmus and anaphora, and detailing the symmetry of the stanzas, we see that **"The Contest"** appears to be written in a closed form; on the page it looks balanced, as though it strives for perfection. But if closed, the form is not fixed. It may inherit certain familiar elements of syntactic structure, but there are no identifiable line or stanza patterns that can be identified as Renaissance or Romantic—such as blank verse, heroic couplet, or terza rima. In addition, **"The Contest"** displays no Renaissance or Romantic conventions of context in attitude or theme. The poem's title directs us to read the text as a narrative; H. D.'s use of the definite article "the" in the title signals that this contest is specific and particular. Yet we are never fully aware of what this contest is, what it is about, or who the participants are—despite Swann's suggestion that the poem is "established in a classical background" by its images that "suggest Greek athletes" (4). Here "the contest" does not function deictically; that is, as a phrase it is not prepared for and is not explained elsewhere in the text. Instead, we are immediately involved in a second-person discourse, in medias res, as it were, without introduction to an implied "I" speaker or to the "you" addressed.

Unlike the speaker in Sappho's fragment 31 above, H. D.'s first-person speaker is implied only by the presence of the second-person "you." When an "I" speaker is present, as in Sappho's fragment, we have a sense, if not always a clear one, of the speaker's personal stakes in the action of the work. We attribute the poem's words to the speaker so that diction becomes a form of characterization. But the invisible "I" of H. D.'s poem creates tension. Who is addressing "you"? Do we, as readers, connect the "you" to ourselves? Could it be the speaker addressing herself? Is the

"you" even human? H. D.'s choice of point of view evokes a quality of indeterminacy. The "you" is depicted as a sculpture—either relief or statue—whose "stature is modelled / with straight tool-edge" (1-2), one who is "chiselled like rocks / that are eaten into by the sea" (3-4). The images of sculpture out of both stone and wood persist throughout the poem: in part 1, the word "torso" denotes the sculptured form used to represent the human trunk; in part 2, the "you" stands "rigid and mighty—/ granite and ore in rocks" (16-17); and in part 3 the "you" has knees "cut from white-ash" (34) and wears a laurel of sorts that is "sharp / against the lift and furrow / of your bound hair" (28-30).

Just as the absence of a visible "I" speaker creates tension, the use of the present tense works to create immediacy and intimacy. Notice that H. D. does not mirror Petrarch but Sappho in her use of verb tense. Petrarch's lyrics in the past tense imply the actuality and the completion of events and actions; they also imply reflection and evaluation on the part of the speaker: in Sonnet 3 the speaker looks back on the morning that "Love caught me naked to his shaft" (9) but left the "Lady" untouched (14); and in Sonnet 61 he blesses the Lady for bringing him "the sonnet-sources of my fame" (12). But for Sappho and H. D., use of the present tense allows them to exploit the intensity of the moment unfolding at hand.[18] Sappho's speaker declares, "I can't / speak any longer" (7-8), which Jeffrey Duban points out makes her "helplessness . . . complete. For a poet in a basically oral culture, to lose the power of articulation is to lose the essence of identity" (108). H. D.'s speaker has no identity to retain or lose. All that exists is the moment—are the moments?—of observing the "you." Is the speaker at the center of the objectification or merely its witness? The implied "I" speaker's relation to the "you" is significant in its present-tense ambiguity, in its unfixed dealings with time, and in its absence. To paraphrase Carson on Sappho, H. D.'s speaker does not record from past-tense security the history of a love affair, but records the anxious and present-tense instant of desire (4).

While the "you" of part 1 is inactive, "you" is still observed by the speaker in a position of movement; this object is neither static nor dynamic. The "glint like worn brass" (7) comes from "the turn and grasp of your wrist / and the chord's stretch" (5-6). The "you" here appears to be caught in the moment of pulling back the string of a bow in preparation for shooting. But the arrow has not been loosed: the muscles in the breast are "taut" (8), those of the hips are "clenched" (10). In part 2, the "you" is captured in an ambiguous stance that the speaker calls "splendid" (22) while clearly weary, resembling "a limb of cypress / bent under a weight of snow" (20-21). Part 3 presents a "you" in triumph: "Myrtle is about your head" (26). The crown may not be of laurel, but like the laurel, the myrtle is evergreen and connotes immortality and eternity. In these instances, it is as if we witness different stages of a contest—beginning, middle, end.

Such readings, however, prove unsatisfactory. H. D. has carefully concealed the genders of both the implied "I" speaker and the "you," and prevented a discussion of either "him" or "her" throughout any explication. True, in part 1 the speaker refers to "your male torso" (14), and the term *masculine* applies to socially constructed qualities characteristic of human men, while the term *male* always seems to refer to the male sex. But to assume H. D. participates in what "always seems" to be the case is dangerous. In addition, according to Cassandra Laity, "[T]he deliberate artifice of the statue in association with the loved male body creates a transgressive sexual politics. Artifice enacts the necessary denaturalization of the normative erotic body, traditionally defined as female and natural" (67). In H. D.'s **"The Contest,"** artifice is doubled, manifest in the imaging—the imagining, the conceiving—of the statue-like "you," as well as in the production—the composition, the fabrication—of the poem itself. Thus, the artifice of a "male torso" provides neither the evasion of subterfuge nor the enunciation of reality, but instead complicates notions of both. If the "you" is male, not identifying him as such has allowed H. D. to objectify the man the way the woman has been objectified—yet without overtly, directly challenging the stereotype. If the "you" is female, not identifying her as such has allowed H. D. to bring in the dimension of lesbianism. And of course, if we begin to consider the gender of the implied "I" speaker as male and not female—that is, if we separate the sex of the speaker from the sex of the poet the way we separate their voices—then the possibilities and the complexities increase. Clearly this is not an example of H. D. both complying with and resisting stereotypes. Gender is a matter of uncertainty in **"The Contest,"** and uncertainty does more than "jostle" a foundational cluster or invert a Petrarchan gaze. Uncertainty in H. D.'s poetry decenters both conventional definitions of gender and conventional hierarchizations of gender roles; and ultimately it shifts the paradigm for their analysis.

How can there be an object/subject exchange without a subject? How can there be a female/male binary without females and males? Perhaps H. D., by absenting a subject/I and fetishizing an object/you, analyzes and describes an alternative to oppositional paradigms; perhaps she analyzes and describes a fantasy where a subject, far from being fragmented and fragmenting, doubles itself as both subject and object into a new subject-position. A fantasy of this type is described by Jean Laplanche and Jean-Bertrand Pontalis:

> In fantasy the subject does not pursue the object or its sign; he appears caught up himself in the sequence of images. He forms no representation of the desired object, but is himself represented as participating in the scene although, in the earliest forms of fantasy, he cannot be assigned to any fixed place in it. . . . As a result, the subject, although always present in the fantasy, may be so in a dehumanized form, that is to say, in the very syntax of the sequence in question.
>
> (26)

"The Contest" becomes a fantasy of the Laplanche/ Pontalis variation: H. D. does not merely pursue Sappho in this wooing process but becomes entangled with her, caught up in a sequence of images that blur not only what is human and what is landscape, but *who* is subject and *who* is object, *what* is a subject and *what* is an object.

Whatever the ambiguous genders of the implied speaker and the "you," the look—the gaze—is objectifying. At least in the beginning. The speaker focuses exclusively on the body of the "you." In part 1, the speaker's gaze narrows from the "stature" (1) and moves outward along the limbs to one "wrist" (5), then returns to the center, noticing "[t]he ridge of your breast" (8) and the shadows "under each" (9), following the line of shadow to "the clenched muscles / of your slender hips" (10-11). Then the speaker's gaze seems to widen again to appreciate from head to toe the halo-like light outlining "the circle of your cropped hair" (12), "your male torso" (14), and even "the foot-arch and the straight ankle" (15). The movement of the speaker's eyes suggests a delicate eroticism reminiscent of Lo-fu's careful analysis of the apple branch. But in part 2, the speaker ceases to only objectify the "you." Now the speaker begins to metaphorize *and metamorphosize* the "you." The use of metaphor and simile in Sappho, according to duBois, "calls attention to the fragmentary status of the fragment, the thing being compared forever absent, available only to the imagination" (41). Here, H. D.'s imitation of a fragment creates the same kind of tension. While the speaker's gaze still focuses on the body—"a great band clasps your forehead" (18)—it is a body that seems to be one with the "granite and ore in rocks" (17); "you have entered the hill-straits" (24). Not only "[y]ou are white," but you are "a limb of cypress / bent under a weight of snow" (20-21). Whereas in part 1 the body of the "you" is depicted in concrete, or at least bodily, terms of tense musculature, here "your arms are fire" (23), an image as abstract as the word "splendid," which is used to describe more of what "[y]ou are" (22).

In part 3 the metamorphosis continues to oscillate between creating a human and creating a landscape. The head, hair, breast, feet, knees, thighs, chin, throat, and shoulders of the "you" still fill the gaze of the implied "I," but the pieces of the "you" blur with the surrounding landscape of the sea garden:

> The narcissus has copied the arch
> of your slight breast:
> your feet are citron-flowers,
> your knees, cut from white-ash,
> your thighs are rock-cistus.

(31-35)

Carson reminds us that, for the lover, "the moment of desire is one that defies proper edge, being a compound of opposites forced together at pressure" (30). For the object/beloved, though, this moment does not instigate the wild, emotional metamorphosis of a Daphne. The carefully constructed forms and rhythms of **"The Contest,"** mirroring the symmetry of a work of Greek sculpture, indicate that H. D. views the transformation as something creative and willed and controlled. And as a recuperation of what is continuous but has been unacknowledged. Recalling Freud's discussion of the eye as the erotogenic zone "most remote from the sexual object," yet the one "most frequently stimulated by the particular quality of excitation whose cause . . . we describe as beauty," we may view **"The Contest"** as an instance of H. D.'s wooing of Sappho—and of "you" more generally—as a subject woos an object. In this sense, the poem's images of metamorphoses function for H. D. as sublimation; she transforms the sexual energy of looking to the artistic energy of creating. But this redirection itself changes the subject/object relation. There is no experience of fusion here, as in the case of Lo-fu and the apple branch, because the "you" is not an object/branch but a subject/human. The implied "I" speaker/subject cannot fuse with the "you"/subject; the two subjects can only engage in the erotics of fragmentation—the "you" fragmented by the speaker, and the speaker fragmented by her very absence.

> Is it sweet
> to possess utterly?
> or is it bitter,
> bitter as ash?

—H. D., "Fragment Forty" (*CP* 174)

I have refused to label H. D.'s artistic construction of the Sapphic gaze an imitation. H. D. read and responded to translations of Sappho by men, but she herself did not translate the fragments. Gregory reminds us that for H. D. to assume the "role of translator and interpreter of ancient texts" was to assume "a place within a precinct universally imagined as male" (*H. D. and Hellenism* 38). In her relation-ships with Pound and (husband) Richard Aldington, H. D. had to consider not only how much knowledge of Greek to "display" to them, but how—and if?—to "display" it at all. "This question," Gregory insists, "of H. D.'s specialized knowledge . . . is bound to the spirit of gentlemen's competitive games, a model deeply implicated in the display of classical learning" (54). A "contest," indeed! With Aldington, H. D. shared a "literary hellenism" (139); and with him she edited and contributed to the Poets' Translation Series (1915-16 and 1918-19). Aldington's translations of Anyte comprised Number 1 and H. D.'s translations of Euripides's *Iphigenia in Aulis* comprised Number 3 (1916). Later, H. D. provided Number 2 of the 1918-19 series, a translation of Euripides's *Hippolytus,* which Aldington called "an improvement on the Iphigenia" (Letter 72, 173), but which (he said) required "a few minor corrections of punctuation, spelling & grammar, chiefly to preserve you from the fools who will see that & nothing else" (172). According to Caroline Zilboorg, H. D. "understood both the essential justice and the kind impulse behind Aldington's response to her compositions" (173), and Aldington surely did admire H. D.'s ability; after all, he named her Greek editor in his "Scheme" for the second Poets' Translation Series (Letter 70, 165).

But even if we acknowledge that H. D. "understood" Aldington's overall critique, we should embrace with some caution an assumption that such understanding implies H. D.'s agreement with or acquiescence to each particular criticism. In fact, H. D.'s commitment to translation extends beyond "corrections of punctuation, spelling & grammar." She saw translation as a means of bringing new life to ancient texts, extending rather than fixing meaning. As she says of her protagonist Julia in *Bid Me to Live,* "Anyone can translate the meaning of the word. She wanted the shape, the feel of it, the character of it, as if it had been freshly minted" (163). In her 1937 translation of Euripides's *Ion,* H. D. insists, "You cannot learn Greek, only, with a dictionary. You can learn it with your hands and your feet and especially with your lungs" (16). Later she adds, "I have endeavoured, in no way, to depart from the meaning," but nonetheless she makes no excuse for her use of "vers-libre," which "is the exact antithesis of [Euripides's] original" (32). If, indeed, H. D. felt apprehensive about her role as translator—her ability to both translate and share her translations—it was an apprehension she applied to all such interpreters: "There is *no* adequate translation for the Greeks *and there never will be*" ("Notes on Euripides" 137, emphasis mine).

Certainly, then, H. D. developed her own criteria of what constituted "translation." That she was fully capable of translating Sappho is evident. But while an

Aldington translation of Sappho, "To Atthis," was published in 1914, H. D. significantly refrained from translating the one poet she found capable of creating "a world of emotion, differing entirely from any present day imaginable world of emotion," a world beyond the "reach" and "song" of even "the greatest of her own countrymen" ("Wise Sappho" 58). H. D. did not translate—*imitate*—Sappho because Sappho, with "a craft never surpassed in literature" (63) was inimitable.[19] And while H. D. may have been eager to re-create the works of Euripides—a man—she may have been less inclined to tamper with and second-guess the fragments of Sappho—the woman. To paraphrase Sydney Janet Kaplan, H. D.'s translations of Euripides may have their "roots in suffering and anger" as she reflects upon "the diverse ways women have been oppressed"; but her "impetus" for Sappho "is passion and identification" (37-38).

And yet, how do we account for H. D.'s frequent allusion to Sappho? Is this—the relationship between H. D. and Sappho—the "real" contest? Rather than second-guessing Sappho through imitation, H. D. finds another means of recuperating "wholes" from fragments. As Gregory rightfully insists, it is "upon Sappho's endurance as the image of woman/poet/lover" that H. D.'s own somehow depends ("Rose Cut in Rock" 535). H. D. writes:

> Sappho has become for us a name, an abstraction as well as a pseudonym for poignant human feelings, she is indeed rocks set in a blue sea, she is the sea itself, breaking and tortured and torturing, but never broken. She is the island of artistic perfection where the lover of ancient beauty (shipwrecked in the modern world) may yet find foothold and take breath and gain courage for new adventures and dream of yet unexplored continents and realms of future artistic achievement. She is the wise Sappho.

(67)

H. D.—Hilda Doolittle—takes a pseudonym of her own because, like Sappho, she does not want her artistry to represent "poignant human feelings" but to embody—*to be*—such feelings. And she assumes the Sapphic gaze not to duplicate Sappho's "artistic perfection" but to "find foothold" for her own "artistic achievement." H. D.'s are not acts of imitation but of *emulation*. Emulation suggests competition, even rivalry, and an eventual contest—which ultimately becomes "the contest," the ideal competition where the struggle is between equals, between two subjects, and results in victory and glory for both. Emulation suggests that H. D., admiring Sappho above all artists, desires to equal her predecessor's poetic power by attempting to make whole for herself that which has come to her in shattered pieces. The erotic fragments in Sappho's archives allow H. D. to (re)construct

subjectivity independent of subject/object, female/male binarisms. Sappho's fragments, like the branch in Lo-fu's orchard, not only engage H. D. in a contest, but also serve for her as a means of attaining artistic happiness, as a means of completing herself as woman/poet/lover—muse/goddess/woman—and as a means of approach to ecstasy.

Notes

1. David Robinson's early *Sappho and Her Influence* is a delightful introduction to allusions and praise. Lawrence Lipking's "Sappho Descending" emphasizes the "battle over Sappho's name" (43) between both women and men poets:

   > Female poets required a model for their art and sex, conclusive evidence of a woman's perfect genius. And men [male poets] required an example of the hazards into which women plunge when they aspire to write—abandonment, shame, and even death await them.

   (42)

   Susan Brown, in "A Victorian Sappho," argues that women poets "enact a poetic agency that recalls recent feminist theoretical attempts to articulate viable alternatives to an identity politics" whenever women poets relate to "the figure of Sappho" (208).

2. Gregory has recently extended her readings of H. D. and Sappho, and insists that "[f]or H. D. a direct female transmission from Sappho is highly problematic" (*H. D. and Hellenism* 58). She adds: "Within H. D.'s intricate Sapphic intertextuality, one may distinguish between an overt and a covert interplay" (151).

3. In *Visual and Other Pleasures,* Mulvey revises some of her original assertions in "Visual Pleasure and Narrative Cinema."

4. I am indebted here to Rachel Blau DuPlessis's nuanced distinctions between archetype and prototype in "The Critique of Consciousness and Myth," where she says, "A prototype is not a binding, timeless pattern, but one critically open to the possibility, even the necessity, of its own transformation" (299).

5. Joel Fineman emphasizes not the originality of Renaissance imaging but rather its reliance upon "the regular force of visual imagery in the tradition of the literature or poetry of praise—a tradition that goes back to the praise of love in the *Symposium* or *Phaedrus*" (62).

6. In an examination of Sappho (and the seventeenth-century French novelist La Fayette), Joan DeJean argues against Luce Irigaray's "categorical denunciation of an erotic economy dominated by the [male] gaze," a denunciation that DeJean believes

to be Irigaray's explicit "attack" on René Girard's triangulation of desire—where "desire is never original," says DeJean, "but is inspired by the desire of a male rival," and where "the desiring subject is always a man or a woman . . . created by a man" (34). It is Girard's claim—recognizing attraction in rivalry—that Eve Kosofsky Sedgwick develops in *Between Men* (21-25) and that DuPlessis refers to in her discussion of the foundational cluster above; in *Eros the Bittersweet,* Anne Carson convincingly argues that there are "more ways . . . to triangulate desire" than merely "[t]he ruse of inserting a rival between lover and beloved" (18). DeJean suggests that Irigaray misses an important point in her "reformulation of the language of desire" because Irigaray fails to acknowledge that "[t]he gaze has been forbidden to women, but that does not mean that they have not used it" (34). In Sappho (and La Fayette), DeJean says, "Woman" is depicted as "openly speaking her desire through the eyes," a desire that "expresses itself voyeuristically, through a gaze that is mediated, although in ways that are not recognizable on the basis of male-oriented discussions of the triangulation of desire" (35). DeJean acknowledges that Sappho's gaze "may well predate the stereotypes" that a woman can only usurp, "for her female narrator," the gaze attributed to—and demanded by?—men (38). She concludes that if the gaze is often "considered 'foreign' to female criticism, it is because we are accustomed to deciphering only the male gaze. As soon as we begin to believe that women, writers at least, rather than merely avoiding a visual erotic economy, on occasion assume control over the gaze, we may well assemble information necessary to overturn Irigaray's axiom" (45).

7. The numbering of Sappho's fragments can be a source of great confusion for Sappho and H. D. scholars, since there were at least three conflicting numbering systems by 1925. In that year, Marion Mills Miller and David Moore Robinson published *The Songs of Sappho.* John Maxwell Edmonds had published his translations in *Lyra Graeca* in 1922, while the 1885 translations by Henry Thornton Wharton were still widely read and greatly admired. Fragment 31 is so named based on the (re)writings of Catullus some 600 years after Sappho's death, but in both the Wharton and Edmonds texts it is listed as fragment 2. From the titles of H. D.'s five "fragments"—36, 40, 41, 68, 113—and their Sapphic epigraphs, it is clear that H. D. used the Wharton editions (five editions appeared between 1885 and 1907), editions that she mentions briefly in her review of Edwin Marion Cox ("Winter Roses" 596).

I use the recent Powell translation because he attempts to "preserve Sappho's rhythms" (40) and her "Aeolic measures [that] transfer into English with remarkable felicity" (41); his attention to rhythms and measures is important to my argument about H. D.'s syntax and diction. The Wharton translation is prose, not verse. Since I do not claim that fragment 31/2 is the basis for "The Contest" but only that it exemplifies for H. D. the origins of a Sapphic way of "seeing," I feel this substitution of Powell for Wharton is warranted. However, I provide the Wharton translation that H. D. would have read:

> That man seems to me peer of gods, who sits in thy presence, and hears close to him thy sweet speech and lovely laughter; that indeed makes my heart flutter in my bosom. For when I see thee but a little, I have no utterance left, my tongue is broken down, and straightway a subtle fire has run under my skin, with my eyes I have no sight, my ears ring, sweat bathes me, and a trembling seizes all my body; I am paler than grass, and seem in my madness little better than one dead. But I must dare all, since one so poor . . .

8. I do not speculate on the gender of the speaker or that of the "you"—not because the gender of either or both is unimportant but because my speculation might make it seem so. For now, I am concerned with what is historically available to us—the gender of the poet. And it is the poet, after all, who breathes artistry and ideology into the gaze and the poem. Gender speculation returns in my discussion of "The Contest" below.

9. Gubar quotes H. D.'s "Notes on Sappho" from an unpublished 1920 manuscript (54). Compare this citation to H. D.'s "The Wise Sappho" (57-58).

10. Swinburne is a repeated source of inspiration for H. D. This is exemplified in *Bid Me to Live* (DuPlessis *Career* 65), *HERmione* (Friedman, *Psyche* 43), and *Asphodel* (Friedman, *Penelope* 203). For an in-depth examination of H. D.'s relationship to the work of Swinburne, see Cassandra Laity's insightful *H. D. and the Victorian Fin de Siècle.* In a discussion of H. D.'s *Paint It Today,* Laity argues:

> [Swinburne's poems] articulate a spectrum of desires and gender disruptions not available to H. D. in the high modernist discourse of the 1920s. Swinburne's hymns to the Sapphic femme fatale or the male androgyne offered to H. D. and other women writers the example of an open sexual narrative, while simultaneously maintaining the fiction of a rebel "author" whose unruly psychosexuality comprises the various songs of his deviant personae.
>
> (34)

11. Because I am indebted to duBois, I feel obligated to point out that she does not necessarily share the views of fragmentation and wholeness that I at-

tribute to H. D. DuBois says that Sappho's "poetry can produce anxiety because it exemplifies lack, and Sappho herself sometimes becomes a fetish object, made whole, perfect, sealed on the page by translators who are made uncomfortable by the holes in her writing" (27). I am not suggesting that H. D. escapes "anxiety" in reading Sappho, or that she experiences no discomfort in "the holes." But I do not share duBois's view that H. D. "engages with the past in order to generate some vision of historical difference" (75).

12. Both Thomas Burnett Swann and Eileen Gregory offer brief commentaries on "The Contest." Swann classifies it as one of H. D.'s poems about "mortal heroes" who are "free from the taints of human intercourse" (92). He reads it as a celebration of "unnamed athletes" who are "poised to begin a game" and "seem not so much living men as statues by Myron or Polycleitus" (97-98). Swann suggests that H. D. "subordinat[es] the human element to nature," that she depicts "men in terms of natural objects and sometimes los[es] sight of the men's humanity" in her attempt to describe "three heroes whose hard perfection excludes human frailties, who can commit no treacheries and bring no disillusionment to the women who may love them" (98). Gregory sees "The Contest" as an imaging of a single "human athlete" who "is humanly crafted. As image, the male figure is highly liminal; his aspects of grace and power, as experienced by the poet, reside between nature and human artifice" ("Rose Cut in Rock" 545). I agree that H. D. consciously seeks such connotations, but add that neither of these readings addresses the instability created by the poem's conflicting form and content.

13. Here I am not suggesting that H. D.'s "classicism" is necessarily Sapphic, lesbian, or Greek. What is "classical" about the forms of H. D.'s *Sea Garden* poems is, perhaps, "neoclassical." In their ordered design and in their very articulation of what is "classical"—symmetry, balance—the forms of the poems seem to react to the limitations, dualisms, and imperfections of the modern world in much the same way as the neoclassical poems of Pope reacted to the seemingly unbridled enthusiasm of the Renaissance. I reiterate here the *absence* of Renaissance, and therefore Petrarchan (as well as Romantic/Keatsian), ideals of artistry in H. D.'s *Sea Garden* poems.

14. What Highet calls a tricolon we may today call a palilogy, the deliberate repetition of words and grammatical presentations, a sort of parallelism in threes.

15. We have already explored the significance of three as it is implicated in the triangulation of desire.

Deborah Kelly Kloepfer discusses H. D.'s "trilogies" and "triptychs" and how they function differently as "structural strategies" (187) in the poetry, such as *Trilogy* and *Helen in Egypt,* and the prose, such as *Palimpsest.* We should also recall that at the beginning of the above discussion of "Notes on Thought and Vision" and "The Wise Sappho," I pointed out that H. D. divides the self into three "states or manifestations" and merges the three names "of muse and goddess and of human woman."

16. I am influenced here by Lee Edelman, although I do not suggest that H. D. employs chiasmus for the same reasons or to the same effects as Hart Crane. Discussing the ways in which Crane utilizes chiasmus, anacoluthon, and catachresis in "Voyages," Edelman finds that in Crane's poetics, "every [rhetorical] movement toward the stability of chiasmus carries a trace of the break that figures the violence of anacoluthon" (256), and such instability in language is mirrored in Crane's images: "emblems of balance and antithesis are ceaselessly created and destroyed, drowned and reborn" (263) in instances of "catachrestic borrowing[s]" (284), "catachrestic designation[s]" (285), and "catachrestic ploys" (287). Edelman reads Crane as ultimately attempting "to avoid betrayal by figural language" (290) by embracing "negativity" as "a means of stability" (291).

17. Of repetition, Gertrude Stein writes:

> [I]nsistence . . . in its emphasis can never be repeating, because insistence is always alive and if it is always alive it is never carrying anything in the same way because emphasis can never be the same not even when it is most the same that is when it has been taught.

> (171)

18. Moreover, as DeJean argues, Sappho uses the present tense so that "[s]he appears to be grounding her gaze in the instant of its generation as if to invite comparison with the focus of male erotic poetry," as well as to stage "the gaze as an act of memorialization" (39). For DeJean, "In Sappho's erotic vision, the gaze does not function as a unique occurrence," but is, instead, "doubly repetitive, both an action that takes place again and again and an original that is recreated in memory" (40). While I admire the articulation of the present tense, the idea that Sappho counters a monolithic male gaze with her own seems to align DeJean's argument, at least here, with Vickers and DuPlessis rather than with duBois.

19. H. D.'s translations of Euripides (versus her *interpretations* of him?) are explored insightfully by Eileen Gregory (*H. D. and Hellenism* 179-231). For a brief but insightful discussion of the dangers of both over- and undertranslation, see Diane J.

Rayor's "Translating Fragments," which refers specifically to Sappho and incidentally to H. D.

Works Cited

Aldington, Richard. "To H. D." 13 Dec. 1918. Letter 70. *Richard Aldington and H. D.: The Early Years in Letters.* Ed. Caroline Zilboorg. Bloomington: Indiana UP, 1992. 164-71.

———. "To H. D." 17 December 1918. Letter 72. *Richard Aldington and H. D.* 172-73.

Babcock, Robert. "H. D.'s 'Pursuit' and Sappho." *H. D. Newsletter* 3.2 (1990): 43-47.

Brown, Susan. "A Victorian Sappho: Agency, Identity, and the Politics of Poetics." *English Studies in Canada* 20 (1994): 205-25.

Campbell, David A. *Greek Lyric: Sappho Alcaeus.* Vol. 1. Loeb Classical Library. Cambridge: Harvard UP, 1982.

Carson, Anne. *Eros the Bittersweet.* 1986. Normal: Dalkey, 1998.

Chessman, Harriet Scott. *The Public Is Invited to Dance: Representation, the Body, and Dialogue in Gertrude Stein.* Stanford: Stanford UP, 1989.

Cox, Edwin Marion, trans. *The Poems of Sappho.* By Sappho. New York: Scribner's, 1924.

DeJean, Joan. "Looking Like a Woman: The Female Gaze in Sappho and Lafayette." *L'esprit créateur* 28.4 (1988): 34-45.

Duban, Jeffrey M., trans. *Ancient and Modern Images of Sappho: Translations and Studies in Archaic Greek Love Lyric.* By Sappho. Classical World Special Series. Lanham: UP of America, 1983.

duBois, Page. *Sappho Is Burning.* Chicago: U of Chicago P, 1995.

DuPlessis, Rachel Blau. "'Corpses of Poesy': Some Modern Poets and Some Gender Ideologies of Lyric." *Feminist Measures: Soundings in Poetry and Theory.* Ed. Lynn Keller and Cristanne Miller. Ann Arbor: U of Michigan P, 1994. 69-95.

———. "The Critique of Consciousness and Myth in Levertov, Rich, and Rukeyser." *Shakespeare's Sisters: Feminist Essays on Women Poets.* Ed. Sandra M. Gilbert and Susan Gubar. Bloomington: Indiana UP, 1979. 280-300.

———. *H. D.: The Career of That Struggle.* Key Women Writers. Bloomington: Indiana UP, 1986.

Edelman, Lee. "Voyages." *Modern Critical Views: Hart Crane.* Ed. Harold Bloom. New York: Chelsea, 1986. 255-91.

Edmonds, J. M. *Lyra Graeca.* Vol. 1. Loeb Classical Library. Cambridge: Harvard UP, 1922.

Fineman, Joel. "Shakespeare's 'Perjur'd Eye.'" *Representations* 7 (1984): 59-86.

Foucault, Michel. *Foucault Live: Collected Interviews, 1961-1984.* Ed. Sylvère Lotringer. Trans. Lysa Hochroth and John Johnston. New York: Semiotext(e), 1989.

———. *The Order of Things: An Archaeology of the Human Sciences.* Trans. of *Les mots et les choses.* New York: Vintage, 1973.

Freud, Sigmund. *Three Essays on the Theory of Sexuality.* Trans. James Strachey. New York: Basic, 1962.

Friedman, Susan Stanford. *Penelope's Web: Gender, Modernity, H. D.'s Fiction.* New York: Cambridge UP, 1990.

———. *Pysche Reborn: The Emergence of H. D.* Bloomington: Indiana UP, 1981.

Goldsmith, Margaret. *Sappho of Lesbos: A Psychological Reconstruction of Her Life.* London: Rich, 1938.

Gregory, Eileen. *H. D. and Hellenism: Classic Lines.* Cambridge Studies in American Literature and Culture 111. Cambridge: Cambridge UP, 1997.

———. "Rose Cut in Rock: Sappho and H. D.'s *Sea Garden.*" *Contemporary Literature* 27 (1986): 525-52.

Gubar, Susan. "Sapphistries." *Signs: Journal of Women in Culture and Society* 10 (1984): 43-62.

Hadas, Moses. *A History of Greek Literature.* New York: Columbia UP, 1950.

H. D. *Bid Me to Live (A Madrigal).* New York: Dial, 1960.

———. *Collected Poems 1912-1944.* Ed. Louis L. Martz. New York: New Directions, 1983.

———. *Ion: A Play after Euripides.* 1937. Redding Ridge: Black Swan, 1986.

———. "A Note on Poetry." *Oxford Anthology of American Literature.* Ed. William Rose Benét and Norman Holmes Pearson. 2 vols. New York: Oxford UP, 1939. 1287-88.

———. "Notes on Euripides." *Ion: A Play after Euripides.* 1937. Redding Ridge: Black Swan, 1986. 132-48.

———. "Notes on Thought and Vision." *"Notes on Thought and Vision" and "The Wise Sappho."* San Francisco: City Lights, 1982. 17-53.

———. *Tribute to Freud.* New York: McGraw, 1956.

———. "Winter Roses." Rev. of *The Poems of Sappho* by Edwin Marion Cox. *Saturday Review of Literature* 14 Mar. 1925: 596.

———. "The Wise Sappho." *"Notes on Thought and Vision" and "The Wise Sappho."* 57-69.

Highet, Gilbert. *The Classical Tradition: Greek and Roman Influences on Western Literature.* New York: Oxford UP, 1949.

Kaplan, Sydney Janet. "Varieties of Feminist Criticism." *Making a Difference: Feminist Literary Criticism.* Ed. Gayle Greene and Coppélia Kahn. New York: Routledge, 1985. 37-58.

Kloepfer, Deborah Kelly. "Fishing the Murex Up: Sense and Resonance in H. D.'s *Palimpsest." Signets: Reading H. D.* Ed. Susan Stanford Friedman and Rachel Blau DuPlessis. Madison: U of Wisconsin P, 1990. 185-204.

Laity, Cassandra. *H. D. and the Victorian Fin de Siècle: Gender, Modernism, Decadence.* Cambridge Studies in American Literature and Culture 104. Cambridge: Cambridge UP, 1996.

Laplanche, Jean, and Jean-Bertrand Pontalis. "Fantasy and the Origins of Sexuality." *Formations of Fantasy.* Ed. Victor Burgin, James Donald, and Cora Kaplan. London: Methuen, 1986. 5-34.

Lipking, Lawrence. "Aristotle's Sister: A Poetics of Abandonment." *Critical Inquiry* 10 (1983): 61-81.

———. "Sappho Descending: Eighteenth-Century Studies in Abandoned Women." *Studies in the Eighteenth Century* 12.2 (1988): 40-57.

Lobel, Edgar, trans. *The Fragments of the Lyrical Poems of Sappho.* By Sappho. Oxford: Clarendon, 1925.

Miller, Marion Mills, and David Moore Robinson. *The Songs of Sappho (Including the Recent Egyptian Discoveries).* By Sappho. New York: Frank-Maurice, 1925.

Mulvey, Laura. *Visual and Other Pleasures.* Bloomington: Indiana UP, 1989.

———. "Visual Pleasure and Narrative Cinema." *Feminism and Film Theory.* Ed. Constance Penley. New York: Routledge, 1988.

Page, Denys. *Sappho and Alcaeus: An Introduction to the Study of Ancient Lesbian Poetry.* By Sappho and Alcaeus. Oxford: Clarendon, 1955.

Petrarch. "Sonnet 3." Trans. Joseph Auslander. *Norton Anthology of World Masterpieces.* Ed. Maynard Mack et al. Vol. 1. 6th ed. New York: Norton, 1992. 1676.

———. "Sonnet 61." *Norton Anthology.* 1677.

Powell, James, trans. *A Garland: The Poems and Fragments of Sappho.* By Sappho. New York: Farrar, 1993.

Rayor, Diane J. "Translating Fragments." *Translation Review* 32/33 (1990): 15-19.

Robinson, David M. *Sappho and Her Influence.* Boston: Marshall Jones, 1924.

Rose, Jacqueline. *Sexuality in the Field of Vision.* London: Verso, 1986.

Sedgwick, Eve Kosofsky. *Between Men: English Literature and Male Homosocial Desire.* New York: Columbia UP, 1985.

The Songs of Sappho in English Translation by Many Poets. Mount Vernon: Peter Pauper, [c. 1942].

Stein, Gertrude. "Portraits and Repetition." *Lectures in America.* Boston: Beacon, 1985. 165-206.

Swann, Thomas Burnett. *The Classical World of H. D.* Lincoln: U of Nebraska P, 1962.

Tapscott, Stephen. "Williams, Sappho, and the Woman-as-Other." *William Carlos Williams Review* 11.2 (1985): 30-44.

Vickers, Nancy J. "Diana Described: Scattered Women and Scattered Rhyme." *Critical Inquiry* 8 (1981): 265-79.

Weigall, Arthur. *Sappho of Lesbos: Her Life and Times.* New York: Stokes, 1932.

Wharton, Henry Thornton. *Sappho: Memoir, Text, Selected Renderings, and a Literal Translation.* By Sappho. London: D. Scott, 1887. *History of Women* (1975): fiche reel 483, no. 3625.1.

Winkler, John J. *The Constraints of Desire: The Anthropology of Sex and Gender in Ancient Greece.* New York: Routledge, 1990.

Zilboorg, Caroline, ed. *Richard Aldington and H. D.: The Early Years in Letters.* Bloomington: Indiana UP, 1992.

Norman Kelvin (essay date spring 2000)

SOURCE: Kelvin, Norman. "H. D. and the Years of World War I." *Victorian Poetry* 38, no. 1 (spring 2000): 170-96.

[*In the following essay, Kelvin provides a detailed analysis of the rock and flower imagery in H. D.'s poetry, maintaining that through her efforts to confront the oppositional natures of these images and all that they signify, she revealed deeper intellectual and emotional struggles.*]

Why include H. D. among women poets of 1890-1918? Her life and career largely belong to much later years. The answer is that in those later years, she continuously circled back to the period of the First World War,[1] or more precisely the years 1912-1918, the period in which she first made her reputation as a poet. There is also a curious sense in which these years become, retrospectively, the conclusion to an imaginatively lived life as a Victorian, specifically as a Pre-Raphaelite. When young, several modernist poets were enthusiastic about the Pre-Raphaelites but rejected them on finding their own voices—W. B. Yeats and Ezra Pound are notable examples. H. D. reversed the process. Embracing the Pre-Raphaelites in her adolescence, when she was introduced to them by Ezra Pound, she never overtly broke her attachment to them.[2] It does disappear from view for a while but returns stronger than ever in her sixties, that is, in the late 1940s. In these years, too, she notes that friends of the World War I period had been acquainted with the Pre-Raphaelites and that their lives and works were constantly discussed. Most extraordinary of all is H. D.'s lifelong enthusiasm for William Morris.[3] Among poems read to her by the youthful Ezra Pound, Morris' gave her special pleasure. But that was only the beginning. A pattern of recurring references to Morris culminated in her writing "White Rose and the Red," a novel (completed in 1948 but still unpublished)[4] in which Morris is, arguably, the male protagonist. He is the protector of a reinvented Elizabeth Siddal who is, in numerous ways, H. D. herself.

At the heart of all this is her method of imagining. Starting perhaps in 1934, after her analysis by Freud, the process of circling back to the World War I years begins in earnest, and it proceeds through a dynamic of continuous free association of past and recent persons and events and through her use of images and characters that embody these associations. Her writing—poetry and fiction—resists the linear chronology of her life. A case in point is the novel we know as *Bid Me to Live: A Madrigal.* In her analysis by Freud, during two brief periods in 1933 and 1934, they focussed on her childhood and adolescence and gave less time to the all-important World War I period.[5] *Bid Me to Live* invites us to recognize that the novel is meant to be a psychoanalytic reliving of the World War I years. It is that, in a sense, though it is of course not a personal "history" but a novel with a very special orientation, with emphases that go counter to later references in her work to those years, and with the vivid power present in much of her work: the power to make both the absent and the unseen dramatically present and palpable.

Most important of all is that her method, circling back and freely associating along the way, made her life-work a palimpsest[6] whose uttermost layer are the years of the First World War. A necessary focus, her writing during the period gives her a presence among the poets of 1895-1918 that is reinforced rather than superseded by her subsequent career. No matter, by the way, that this is the time in which H. D. achieved fame as the foremost Imagist and that she later spoke of wanting to escape the confines of Imagist doctrine. The themes implicit in her poems of these years, and at times the technique employed in them, are the point of continuous return.

Sea Garden, published in 1916, and poems written between 1913 and 1917 and later collected as ***The God*** are essential parts of this *ur* matter and will be my focus. Because of space constraints I should qualify that. A few only will get my attention. But the imagery I think especially important is present in many poems in both collections.

Once again I cite what others have noticed: the persistent flower imagery in ***Sea Garden*** (as well as in her later work) along with the many references to water, wind, islands. But less attention has been paid to her rock imagery.[7] I intend to make much of it. Rock imagery is not only as persistent throughout her career as is that of flowers, sea, islands, and wind, but juxtaposed with flower imagery it presents the greatest challenge of all to H. D.'s endless need to confront opposites with each other and to explore the many possible ways of relating them—from deconstructing their apparent differences to transferring the defining characteristics of one form to the other without erasing the outline of either. And it is overcoming or mastering this apparently extreme polarity that enables her most forcefully, I believe, to represent the contradictions and conflicts at the heart of her life and work. By the end of the Imagist period, that is, by 1918, she had fully articulated these contradictions and conflicts: female and male, victim and priestess, Helen and Greek god or goddess (often unspecified), mother and father, sister and brother, and in this pre-Bryher period, Frances Greg and—against her—Ezra Pound, Richard Aldington, and D. H. Lawrence, the composite male lover. But inscribing binary opposites also sets in motion the struggles to overcome the divide that marks nearly all that follows.

H. D.'s flowers and rocks are not symbols abstracted from particulars. In true Imagist fashion, her flower and rock imagery condenses and energizes the emotive and intellectual struggle in her life and in her practice as a poet. And they persist in her later work. They are present, finally, in the pre-Raphaelite novel that follows all but one of her major works devoted to Greek themes. They are present, that is to say, in that 1948 layer to the palimpsest that undercuts the base period and leads forward, rather than backward, to the early years.

"The Shrine, (she watches over the sea)," the third poem in *Sea Garden,* celebrates rock imagery in a way that already suggests an absent contrasting presence:

> Are your rocks shelter for ships—
> have you sent galleys from your beach,
> are you graded—a safe crescent—
> where the tide lifts them back to port—
> are you full and sweet,
> tempting the quiet
> to depart in their trading ships?
>
> Nay, you are great, fierce, evil—
> you are the land-blight—
> you have tempted men
> but they perished on your cliffs.[8]

It is a female goddess who is apostrophized, probably Artemis,[9] and the very first line raises the possibility of transferring characteristics. That the goddess has her shrine built on a rocky shore of what looks like a haven for men but is not, associates rocks with a femininity that is more than that of a fin-de-siècle femme fatale—she is "great, fierce, evil"—words that connote a hidden strength and power. Her allure is the thinnest of "female" masks. Nevertheless, the question with which the poem begins implies that she, represented by rocks and danger, might be capable of sheltering men. That such a thought is even conceivable adds to the hard, sharp, dangerous attributes of rocks a feminized ability to encircle soothingly. And despite the explicit rejection in the second stanza of the idea that such softness is possible, the poem veers on its intellectual journey to just such a conclusion, albeit in a complex, ambivalent manner. The final two stanzas read:

> But hail—
> as the tide slackens,
> as the wind beats out,
> we hail this shore—
> we sing to you,
> spirit between the headlands
> and the further rocks.
>
> Though oak-beams split,
> though boats and sea-men flounder,
> and the strait grind sand with sand
> and cut boulders to sand and drift—
>
> your eyes have pardoned our faults,
> your hands have touched us—
> you have leaned forward a little
> and the waves can never thrust us back
> from the splendour of your ragged coast.

(*CP,* pp. 9-10)

Though still stern and powerful, the goddess has a touch—as well as eyes—that can pardon, and the waves—a treacherous but fluid force—cannot prevent the supplicant-sailors from reaching "the splendour of [her] ragged coast," so that "ragged," the condition created by rocks, finally is associated with safe haven, the haven provided by this particular goddess but surely also by extension feminine power seen as great and fierce. The strong woman, too, is shelter for the male voyager, not a danger, not the femme fatale— that is, not an incarnation of evil. Rocks, because they are strong, can play the role conventionally assigned to femininity regarded as soft and domestic.

"Garden," so often anthologized as an illustration of Imagism, is a direct and explicit juxtaposition of flowers and rocks, a transfer of the attributes of one to the other. Part I (initially published as a poem in its entirety) reads:

> You are clear
> O rose, cut in rock,
> hard as the descent of hail.
>
> I could scrape the colour
> from the petals
> like spilt dye from a rock.
>
> If I could break you
> I could break a tree.
> If I could stir
> I could break a tree—
> I could break you.

(*CP,* pp. 24-25)

Here the transfer of characteristics takes place within the flower as an autonomous figure, as was the rock an autonomous figure in **"The Shrine,"** where ideas possibly associated with flowers went unvisualized. There is some ambivalence as to whether the rose has grown up in a crevice of a rock, thus establishing the rock and flower as separate entities, or whether the rose perceived by the speaking voice as "cut in rock" is so described because its form is so precise that it suggests the attributes of a rock. Whichever it is, the speaking voice asserts the rock-like strength of the flower, reminiscent, for the moment, of the rocks representing the power of the goddess in **"The Shrine."** The coloring of the petals—which adds to the beauty conventionally associated with the rose as soft, and by extension feminine—is superficial, like the thin mask of allure of the goddess of the shrine.

Perhaps even more interesting is the potential contest of strength and will that the speaker of the poem brings to seeing the beauty of the rose. She has endowed the rose with a physical strength usually associated with maleness. But the contest cannot occur because of the enigmatic words "If I could stir." She can visually strip the rose of its superficial femininity—its color "like spilt dye [on] a rock," but she cannot fulfill her desire to pit her physical strength against the imagined physical strength of the rose. Somehow, the rose—this conventional symbol of the feminine—has paralyzed her will. Though it is gigantic power that would be needed—enough "to break a tree"—the "if" of "If I could stir" suggests that potentially she could have such strength. The poem is, finally, about two separate feminine entities, the rose and the speaker, that defy the idea of softness and yieldingness but that are, for reasons unclear, in a non-loving relationship. That all this depends on the Imagist spirit constructing the basic image—"You are clear / O rose, cut in rock, / hard as the descent of hail" demonstrates that H. D., in her Imagist beginning, used Imagist traits—directness of statement, concrete images, "crystalline" hardness to disclose, even as they are being realized, their opposites.[10]

Part II of the poem only indirectly relates to what interests me here. The opening line, "O wind, rend open the heat, cut apart the heat, rend it to tatters," endows both the wind and the heat with the attributes of solid matter—of a knife or knifelike instrument and a substance that can be cut or torn apart. It is another instance of H. D.'s method of transferring attributes from one entity to another, and though it does not explore the flower/rock binary opposition, neither does it undermine or contradict the impulse played out in Part I, and in other poems.

Two poems that extend the scope of the transference technique are **"The Cliff Temple"** and **"Sea Gods."** Both balance **"The Shrine"** in that they apply rock/flower imagery to male gods. But I shall focus on the second because it does so more explicitly and at greater length:

> They say there is no hope—
> sand—drift—rocks—rubble of the sea—
> the broken hulk of a ship,
> hung with shreds of rope,
> pallid under the cracked pitch.
> . . . . .
>
> They say you are twisted by the sea,
> you are cut apart
> by wave-break upon wave-break,
> that you are misshapen by the sharp rocks,
> broken by the rasp and after-rasp.
> . . . . .
>
> II
>
> But we bring violets,
> great masses—single, sweet,
> wood-violets, stream-violets,
> violets from a wet marsh.
>
> Violets in clumps from hills,
> tufts with earth at the roots,

> violets tugged from rocks,
> blue violets, moss, cliff, river-violets.
> . . . . .
>
> We bring the hyacinth-violet,
> sweet, bare, chill to the touch—
> and violets whiter than the in-rush
> of your own white surf.
>
> III
>
> For you will come,
> you will yet haunt men in ships,
> you will trail across the fringe of strait
> and circle the jagged rocks.
>
> You will trail across the rocks
> and wash them with your own salt,
> . . . . .
>
> For you will come,
> you will come,
> you will answer our taut hearts,
> you will break the lie of men's thoughts,
> and cherish and shelter us.

(*CP,* pp. 29-31)

There is a dazzling array—a broad all-encompassing movement—of transference here. They say the sea gods cannot be conjured, that they—the gods themselves—are cut and twisted by the ragged rocks that shipwreck humans and thus are, like humans, weaker than the force represented by nature. But we humans, by heaping violets upon some implied shrine of the sea-gods, violets that run the gamut of color possibilities and are pulled from every conceivable natural setting, including rocks, have the power to confer upon the sea gods not only a new power—the power to nurture—to "cherish and shelter us," but again in this image of a safe haven, to transform by overcoming, the encircling rocks; by "washing them with your salt" you, the sea gods, submit the rocks to a kind of rebirth: one that makes benign and nurturing their threatening power. The very strength that cut and twisted so powerful a being as a god is now, by that god's response to the offering of violets, transformed—like the god himself—into an encircling shelter, into an embrasure of nurturing arms.

Through the power—the feminine power—inherent in the violets, the power of the rocks to destroy humans is first made submissive to the awakened and inspired will of the sea gods to assist humans; and then becomes the very instrument through which the gods shelter, protect, and nurture humans, that is, "cherish" humans.

The eponymous poem will have to suffice to illustrate the recurrence of the theme in *The God,* poems of 1913-17. The fourth stanza, Part I begins:

I . . . spoke this blasphemy
in my thoughts:
the earth is evil,
given over to evil,
we are lost.

(*CP,* p. 45)

Part II continues:

And in a moment
you have altered this;

beneath my feet, the rocks
have no weight
against the rush of cyclamen,
fire-tipped, ivory-pointed,
white;

beneath my feet the flat rocks
have no strength
against the deep purple flower-embers
cyclamen, wine spilled.

(*CP,* pp. 45-46)

In Parts III and IV, which conclude the poem, there is an ambivalent hint of contemplated suicide. It is used to pit, finally, human strength against that of flowers, so that the human is identified with the rocks that "have no weight," and the god, all powerful, is, imagistically, one with the flowers.

In Part III, the speaker, who imagined herself powerful,

I thought the vine-leaves
would curl under,
leaf and leaf-point
at my touch,

the yellow and green grapes
would have dropped,
my very glance must shatter
the purple fruit

(*CP,* p. 46)

ambiguously concludes:

I had drawn away into the salt,
myself, a shell
emptied of life.

(*CP,* p. 46)

But the only power is that of the sea which, as noted, is thoroughly identified with flowers. Part IV reads:

I pluck the cyclamen,
red by wine-red,
and place the petals'
still ivory and bright fire
against my flesh;

now I am powerless
to draw back
for the sea is cyclamen-purple,
cyclamen-red, colour of the last grapes,
colour of the purple of the flowers,
cyclamen-coloured and dark.

(*CP,* pp. 46-47)

Most striking of all is how quickly the rocks lose their weight, the mass that produces their strength, when pitted against "the rush of cyclamen." And how subtly the transference of the presumed strength of rocks to flowers contrasts with the transference of the softness and kindness of flowers to the rocks in **"The Shrine"** and **"Sea Gods,"** in *Sea Garden.*

I have already said that H. D.'s 1933-34 psychoanalysis explored her childhood, adolescence, and a few subsequent years. But H. D. gave less attention to the World War I years (though there is discussion of Lawrence). By in part skipping over them to discuss experiences with Bryher that occurred later, she framed the period of interest to us between a pattern of childhood and adolescence, on the one hand, and a pattern of commitment to another woman, Bryher, that was to endure for the rest of her life. This had the further effect of making the period 1912-1918 an enclosure whose walls must fall if she was to go forward as a woman and artist.

If lack of time left the World War I years inadequately explored in her analysis, Freud himself functions in the same way that a landscape or biographical figure did in *Sea Garden* and *The Gods.* He not only "belongs" to the years preceding the World War I period but to those leading toward them, preparing the way for them, so that their absence makes them the ultimate focus of interest; but her interest in him as a subject for biography—for *Tribute to Freud* is very much a biography of Freud, as Ernest Jones observed"—introduces him into the cast of characters— family members, early Pound, and Frances Gregg— who also lead us toward Imagism. Freud is, in the constructed chronology of her life, a pre- or proto-Imagist experience.

From that viewpoint, some remarkable lines that run backwards to the World War I period are to be seen in *Tribute.* When H. D. first enters Freud's consulting room, she looks with intense absorption at Freud's famous collection of figurines, Greek and Egyptian gods and goddesses. I do not wish to strain and stretch my thesis by calling these figurines (some marble, some terracotta) "rocks," but at least we can say they are of a hard substance; and what is noteworthy is that Freud, who has entered the room, tells H. D. that she is the first patient entering that room to look first at the figurines and then at him (*TF* [*Tribute to Freud*] p.

98). Freud himself conveniently (for purposes of this article) establishes a binary division. At one extreme is Freud, a soft entity of flesh, clothes, posture, and facial expression, endowed by the perceiving imagination with a humane, humanistic interest in H. D., as well as with potential symbolic meaning. At the other are these carved or baked hard substances, endowed by the perceiving imagination with aesthetic qualities and with the authority of powerful symbols, explicit in their symbolic meaning (Isis, priestess, for example, whom, as a figurine, Freud displays, represents an entire side of H. D. the artist).

But Freud, within this binary opposition, becomes an active principle. When the analysis is far along, he wistfully, or complainingly, tells H. D. that in the transference process she has given him her mother's identity, not—as he makes plain he would have preferred—her father's. To simplify and give point to the narrative I have developed here, after recognizing the figurines in Freud's room as metaphors for the sometimes enigmatic gods and goddesses in her own World War I period poems, H. D. then, in this unstable picture, recognized the figure of the famous man who had the power to transform her. Over the next few months, she proceeded to transform Freud into a maternal, feminized nurturing being, one who, like the gods themselves paradoxically transformed by the rocks, "cherishes" her. In a play of imagination governed by indissolubly linked aesthetic and therapeutic impulses, she has actually "hardened" the soft-tissue, questioning, commenting Freud into a marble goddess, who, like the transformed rocks of **"The God,"** embraces her as a mother would. Whatever it may be from a clinical viewpoint, this transference to Freud of the symbolic power and partial function of the figurines is an Imagist move, a creative gesture and accomplishment by the leading Imagist poet of the World War I period.

As for flowers, they become an extraordinarily complex component in H. D.'s relationship with Freud. For his seventy-seventh birthday, she searches in vain throughout Vienna for gardenias, for which he has expressed enthusiasm, but at a later time, when she is back in London and asks a friend in Vienna to help, the friend writes that the florists say orchids are Freud's favorite flowers and that she has sent him orchids in H. D.'s name. Later, in 1938 in London, where Freud, a refugee from Nazified Austria, has now settled, she sends him gardenias, which by now have taken on a symbolic meaning. The note that accompanies the gardenias reads, "To greet the return of the gods" (*TF,* p. 11). This sending of flowers is tenuously connected, too, to what must be one of the more startling anecdotes about Freud, as well as, in its conclusion, moving evidence of how fine were H. D.'s

own feelings and how graciously she is able to convey to the reader their depths. H. D. recounts that one day Freud did indeed startle her when she heard him "beating with his hand, his fist, on the head-piece" of the analytic couch, on which she lay, stretched out, and heard him say, "The trouble is—I am an old man—*you do not think it worth your while to love me*" (*TF,* pp. 15-16). Quite rightly H. D. wonders whether this is meant to be a therapeutic device or a personal cry, but with her splendid ability to leave unanswered questions that have no good answers, she says and does nothing. But later in *Tribute to Freud,* she recounts a day in 1934 when the yearning for *anschluss* was strong and the Nazi presence in Vienna was everywhere and ominous. There were swastikas chalked on the sidewalk that seemed to lead to Freud's door. H. D. went to Freud's house for her scheduled session and learned that none of his other patients had come out that day. Freud said, "But why did you come? No one else has come here today, no one. What is it like outside? Why did you come out?" H. D. writes: "Again, I was different. I had made a unique gesture, although actually I felt my coming was the merest courtesy; this was our usual time of meeting . . . . our 'hour' together. I did not know what the Professor was thinking. He could not be thinking, 'I am an old man—*you do not think it worth your while to love me.*' Or if he remembered having said that, this surely was the answer to it" (*TF,* pp. 61-62).

Finally, the uses to which H. D. puts her "flower power" at one point, neatly and effectively invite this tying of H. D.'s 1933-34 analysis to the World War I period. In what must be the most extraordinary connecting of individuals in modernist literature, Freud, William Morris, Aldington, and D. H. Lawrence are for her a composite figure because all four were aware of flowers, loved them, knew their names, and cherished them.[12] As noted, Morris is both chronological forebear and latent presence in the World War I period. As noted, too, D. H. Lawrence is, personally and artistically, a central presence, perhaps the most important, in *Bid Me to Live: A Madrigal.*

The novel is one of the richest of H. D.'s several fictive and poetic returns to the World War I period. Begun in 1939, it went through many drafts and was not in fact completed until 1948.[13] But despite its having undergone multiple drafts, it is strung to the same degree of intensity as are the poems of 1912-1918. It is a vivid demonstration of H. D.'s radical revision of Wordsworth's assertion that poetry is "emotion recollected in tranquility." For H. D. all writing—including the poetic prose of her novels—is emotion recollected with increased intensity. This eliminates the time gap between the first event, often itself an act of writing, and the moment of recollection.

Bid Me to Live is structured around two of H. D.'s relationships of the period: that with her husband, Richard Aldington (Rafe Ashton in the novel); and with D. H. Lawrence (Rico Fredericks). All the other autobiographical "life stories" that belong to these years and might have been foregrounded are sharply subordinated or eliminated altogether. Most noticeably, the novel ends with H. D.'s final letter to D. H. Lawrence, and since the theme of the novel is H. D.'s quest for a self-definition as poet, what the structure says is that Lawrence was the most important person to her in the World War I years. That in her life Lawrence's last letter to her was written sometime after she had gone off to Cornwall with Cecil Gray, that Lawrence told her he hoped never to see her again, but that the novel ends by her reminding him that in a dream he had wept as she sang, tells us that closure of the novel does not end their relationship but leaves open the question of how Lawrence relates to her continued self-questing. If we allow ourselves to think for a moment that *Bid Me to Live* was written for the Freudian purpose of getting the "meaning" of all the major events and relationships in her life during the 1912-1918 period, then what we discover, as H. D./Julia Ashton did, is that Lawrence/Rico was more important to her in her growth than either Pound or Aldington, and, in some way connecting with this, that Lawrence was the man she had come to love most deeply.

All this by way of seeing *Bid Me to Live* as a layer of the palimpsest that has the World War I period as its ground. And one of the many things it does in that respect is explore more deeply and in more detail than any other work the structuring power of the flower/rock dichotomy: the power of this Imagist theme to represent literally, symbolically, and with the intensity that for H. D. characterizes the use of memory in art, the multiple meanings contained in the ever-shifting relationship, in her writing, of flowers and rocks.

How various are the meanings expressed by her flower/rock combinations. This in itself means that the binary opposition is unstable, aiming always at the transference of characteristics from one to the other. Early on, during one of Aldington/Rafe's returns on leave from France, he learns she has been sending her poems to Rico. What develops as Rafe questions Julia is a cerebral triangle, to which she gives meaning and closure by reading from a prose draft of what was to be a poem:

> Here is no flower, however sweet the scent, how deep blood-red, how purple-blue the tint, can bring the life that thyme can, growing drift on drift by a rock, your rock *is* burnt-sun in that upper light, the grain glows and the inner heart of rock gives heat. Stay on the upper earth and drink wine from the golden leaf as from a cup.[14]

It is Eurydice, in H. D.'s reinvention,[15] urging Orpheus not to try to rescue her from the underworld. But what she contrasts, in contrasting life and death, is warmth, heat, the actuality of a living love with their absence. The flowers of the underworld are inferior even to the mere thyme because the thyme is associated with the rock, with its capacity to store heat. The rock is not only the symbol of all that is most important—that is, sensory, sensual life—but even has its own visual beauty. And since it is associated with Orpheus, the rock is associated also with art: music as a gift of life.

But Orpheus is Rico/D. H. Lawrence, and finally what makes him the key figure in *Bid Me to Live* is his "man-woman" theory and Julia's final rejection of it. In criticizing her Orpheus poem, he had said, "Stick to the woman-consciousness, it is the intuitive woman-mood that matters" (*BML* [*Bid Me to Live*], p. 62). Julia rejects the theory outright—she is thinking of Rafe, of his saying he loves her but "desire[s] *l'autre*," Bella Carter (Brigit Patmore) (*BML*, p. 56) and that she, Julia, understands: understands, that is, the "man-consciousness." The glow of the sun-warmed rock is that consciousness, and the entire passage can be taken as a step along the way in Julia's quest for an identity. And a moment earlier she had said: "This mood, this realm of consciousness was sexless, or all sex, it was child-consciousness, it was heaven. In heaven, there is neither marriage nor giving in marriage" (*BML*, p. 62).

In many passages that follow, Julia will return to this assertion, not so much developing as clarifying it. What she is getting at—and will arrive at—is an ambivalent concept of the artist, and it will never be clear whether the artist is androgynous or sexless, only that "artist" is a pure concept: that of an autonomous being, neither man nor woman.

It is a slippery world she envisions herself to be in. In this reliving of the World War I years, she has stopped where there was, biographically, no closure but a chapter ending. The birth of her child will occur in the spring of 1919 (she is already pregnant, and Cecil Gray is the father when the "history" concludes, though no mention of her pregnancy is made in her long letter to Rico which concludes the novel).

In H. D.'s actual life, the birth of her child, the end (forever) of her relationship with D. H. Lawrence, and the entrance of Bryher into her life refuse final resolution of her emerging need to say I am an artist, not a woman or a man. She will always need love, and from now on there will be brief affairs with several men and women both, though Bryher will remain the central figure for her—indeed, her rock. But to speak of all this is to speak of what borders the war years. In those years themselves, her main trajectory, I would argue, was not from lesbian love (Frances Gregg) to heterosexual love (Richard Aldington and D. H. Lawrence) but from wounded wife, a victim who refuses to be a victim—to artist, which remains a complex goal for her, and one which was sought through poetic techniques which are readily and plausibly called Imagistic and are at the heart of these years for her.

The penultimate chapter of *Bid Me to Live,* which both recapitulates and concludes Julia's stay in Cornwall with Vane, and which sets the scene for her writing the long letter to Rico that ends the novel, is rich in the use of rock/flower images, and these in turn are made to bear a great span of meaning, from the pre-historical presence of Druids in Cornwall, that is to say, time, to the most intense, in-the-novelistic-present self-identification with the rock/flower multiple meanings since *Sea Garden* and *The God.*

Chapter IX begins:

> The wind was cold. Salt tasted. She tasted salt. Her lungs drank in mist and salt-mist. Under her feet was a new fragrance. She stooped to short ragged new leaf. She pinched a ragged tansy-like small leaf. It grew close to the ground. She lifted it to her nostrils. New fragrance.
>
> She walked along a path in a drawing-book. It was a symbolic drawing, over-emphasized. A large grey boulder was half-covered with ivy. . . . Stark grey stones stood up. There was an actual Druid circle on the hill, Frederick had written. . . . To her right . . . from the crest of the stony hill, lay the village where Rico and Elsa [Frieda Lawrence] had lived.
>
> The whole place was out of the world, a country of rock and steep cliff and sea-gulls. She sat down on a flat rock and wondered if the asymmetrical set of stones, just as the hill dipped, was the Druid sun-circle Rico wrote of. She found she was still clutching the weed-like leaf. She thought, "It's like something in a kitchen garden." She tied it in her handkerchief. "I will send this to Rico and ask him what it is."
>
> (*BML,* pp. 143-144).

It is Rico's country she is experiencing, even as she lives with Vane. It is Rico—close reader and critic of her poetry, challenger of her own concept of herself as a woman, and, in this novel at least, the man she loves most—who both infuses her experience of stones, rocks, and flowers with a host of meanings temporal and spiritual but centered on love, and liberates her from the present, material world: from the world in which he has in London inscribed her. It would be too much to say that the chapter tells us Rico has finally enabled her to define herself as an artist, but the themes of stones, rocks, and flowers suggest that

beauty endures, that the fragility of the flower's loveliness escapes tragedy because it is part, and only part, of a landscape that both endures and suggests "another world," that is, a world in which fragility and transience are meaningless.

There are really three Julias in the novel taken as a whole that need to be brought into relationship with each other and have their contradictions resolved. There is Julia the woman as sexual being, in search of fulfillment; there is Julia the woman as victim, in search of escape from the pain Rafe has inflicted on her; and there is Julia the artist, which, in her search, she defines in defiance of Rico's ideas. Rico in London had insisted on the man/woman dichotomy governing art. In his critique of Julia's poem "Eurydice" he had told her to stick to the experience of Eurydice and not try to understand Orpheus. But in Cornwall, liberated by scenes such as the one described above, she insists that as an artist, which she now confidently believes she is, she is "man-woman/woman-man." As such, she has the strength of the rocks and stones, which in this case she associates with maleness, and the beauty and persistence—its own kind of enduringness—that she associates with the humble plant she has pulled from between the rocks. Absorbed into the artist as man-woman is woman as victim.

In Chapter IX, following or as part of the scene described above, Julia walks on, and comes to a wall: "In the wall was another unfamiliar leaf, like a seed-pod, growing under water. It stuck parasitic roots into the almost earthless cracks of the stones, a leaf of another age, growing under water" (*BML,* pp. 144-145). Stalks of these too she will send to Rico to name, and I cannot help but feel that the "parasitic" roots cause the woman as victim to suggest itself again. For H. D.'s women-as-victims are more complex than merely beings who have been hurt by men. In her own ambivalent response to the concept of victim, H. D. partially blames the victim for being dependent, as if to say, without independence the vulnerability to feelings of victimization are natural, not moral or socially constructed. H. D. is not yet through with the theme of woman as victim.

As if to gloss the symbolizing descriptive passages quoted above, the following paragraph follows soon after the plucking of the stalks of the plant growing in the wall. It also, perhaps even more importantly, reminds us that London was not just the place where Julia struggled to hold the love of Rafe and to maintain an identity as poet in the face of Rico's criticism, but was also where she experienced World War I:

> She had walked out of a dream, the fog and fever, the constant threat from the air, the constant reminder of death and suffering (those soldiers in blue hospital

uniforms) into reality. This was real. She sat down on a rock. She . . . laid the stalk with the bulbous underwater leaves beside the leaves of the curled parsley-like plant. . . . She was Medea of some blessed incarnation, a witch with power. A wise-woman. she was seer, see-er. She was at home in this land of subtle psychic reverberations, as she was at home in a book.

(*BML*, p. 146)

That the two plucked plants are associated with her sense of power is clear. That her power is to do what an Imagist poet does, that is, to "see," is my reading of what we are told next. And if "book" is too general to stand for poetry, it at least in H. D.'s use of the word means art. The world created by art is equivalent to the otherworldliness of the nature experience she is having in Cornwall. Both it might be said, have positive, beneficent meaning. In contrast, the meaning of war is suffering, death, and most important, meaninglessness.

The novel ends—part of Chapter X and all of Chapter XI—as a long letter to Rico, in which Julia rehearses their relationship and in which her saying and repeating "I will never see you again, Rico," means a permanent break from his tyranny as definer of herself as female poet and from his tyranny as a male whom she thought was in love with her and whom she thought she loved. It is the very landscape of rocks and flowers which she associates with Rico that has set her free from him. In the course of her liberation, the rocks have been given the warmth of a nurturing figure; have been associated with the Druids, that is, history or pre-history as the history of spirit and magic; and flowers, growing—that is, persisting—against reason in earth-less crevices between the rocks, convey the strength within the seemingly fragile. The use of rocks and flowers in this way is a palimpsestic return to *Sea Garden* and *The God.* But what is added here is that much of the enterprise of finding multiple meanings in rocks and flowers and defiantly ascribing the presumed characteristics of one to the other, was carried out in the midst of a re-experiencing of World War I: carried out, that is, by turning them into a kind of shield of Achilles that both protects from war and actively opposes war, specifically, from Rafe's war-induced or war-encouraged affair with Bella Carter, and from the air-raids, the wounded soldiers in hospital uniforms. But the War has played another role, touched on in the concluding letter to Rico and developed in detail earlier in the novel. It was because Vane, finding Julia after an air-raid that had left her shaken and weakened, comforted and amused her (he took her to supper and to a film filled with symbolic meaning for her) that she had agreed to go to Cornwall with him. In the real life of H. D. the War precipitating her, as it were, into the arms of Cecil Gray led to her pregnancy,

desertion by Aldington, and near-death in child birth. *Bid Me to Live* excludes some of the events and stops short of others that constitute the extreme moment in H. D.'s life of H. D. as victim, and though she is indeed about to be rescued by Bryher—that is, beyond the boundary of *Bid Me to Live*—and about to begin the second phase of a successful career as artist, the victimization that is part sub-text to *Bid Me to Live,* part sequel, needed to be confronted through art once again.

Of the several works that could be read as a confrontation of the theme, I have chosen her unpublished novel, "White Rose and the Red." It offers many meanings for what I have suggested in this essay. It is set in the 1850s, and the characters are the Pre-Raphaelites, most notably Elizabeth Siddal, D. G. Rossetti, William Morris, and Godfrey Lushington. But through the figures of Elizabeth Siddal, Rossetti, and William Morris, it reexamines the period 1912-1918,[16] and simultaneously, *because* it is set in the 1850s and deals copiously with Morris' early writing, as well as that of Rossetti and Elizabeth Siddal, the novel is a virtual sub-layer to the palimpsest. A Pre-Raphaelite past leading toward, rather than back to, the years 1912-1918, is created and created late in H. D.'s career, for 1948 was the year the novel was finished. Even more literally, by 1948 H. D. had re-established a warm correspondence with Aldington,[17] who had returned to his own early enthusiasm for Morris, and was, as their exchange of letters shows, a key source of information in H. D.'s writing the novel.[18]

It is a fascinating development because the return to Aldington is a return to their relationship as two artists, responsive to each other's work; it makes the issue of H. D.'s victimization as a woman by Aldington extraordinarily complex, a knot that resists unraveling. As for Morris, he is a major theme in their renewed correspondence. It is Aldington who tells her that the protagonist of Morris' late prose romance, *The Glittering Plain,* is Hallblithe (*LY* [*The Later Years in Letters*], p. 94), causing her great excitement. By this time, H. D.'s genius for multiple and extended associations had been taken in hand, as it were, by her deep absorption in spiritualism, and so it was certain that Aldington's news was Morris speaking to her, for independently and prior to getting this information she had named a character in her other unpublished novel of the period, "The Sword Went Out to Sea"[19] (the title is based on a line in one of Morris' poems), "Hal Brith" and the names were for her close enough to strongly suggest mysterious forces at work. Caroline Zilboorg's comment on this is worth quoting at length:

Perhaps this is the most important statement Aldington makes in all his letters to her. . . . She felt the name 'Hallblithe' revealed the enduring intellectual, emotional, spiritual bond between them. Aldington's use of the word here short-circuited, as it were, all that had occurred between them since 1918, reinstating the period when they had worked together as artistic partners in the earliest days of their relationship. Throughout the rest of her life she would return to this moment as a turning point, a requickening of their relationship. . . . [S]he wrote to Norman Holmes Pearson on May 8, 1951: 'Richard, just like Richard, seemed to cancel out all psychic debts with his one word <u>Hallblithe</u>. How did that happen, and how did it become a double miracle, coming through Richard?'

(*LY,* 96 n. 3)

As they continued to discuss her novel titled "The Sword Went Out to Sea," H. D. became hungrier for information about Morris' life, and urged Aldington to write a play about Morris and Rossetti (she obligingly suggested that Laurence Olivier might be cast as Rossetti and Ralph Richardson as Morris) (*LY,* p. 103), intimating too that she might collaborate with Aldington in writing it. This project gradually became H. D.'s own. She subsequently "saw" it as a novel, and titled it "White Rose and the Red." On July 29, 1948, H. D. wrote Aldington: "I am deep in with Top [Morris] and Gabriel now—the first part of *White Rose and the Red* was given over to Liz [Elizabeth Siddal] and she was a bit sour puss now and again. . . . I am very happy with the book. I hope I do not finish it for some time, as I love it and live it so much" (*LY,* n. 126).

Indeed, she was living it. That part of the novel which is about the relationship of Elizabeth Siddal and Rossetti—all that can be called biography—is taken from Violet Hunt's *Wife of Rossetti,* published in 1932, which H. D. says she named.[20] But in "White Rose" Elizabeth Siddal is H. D.[21] and Rossetti and Morris are composites of the men who were part of H. D.'s life in the period 1912-1918. That she was intent on making "White Rose" an underplane for that period is indicated too by her soliciting from Aldington all the information he can give her about the Crimean War and general unrest in the 1850s. She would dearly have loved to have the Crimean War play as strong a role in "White Rose" as World War I had played in her relationship with Aldington, Pound, and Lawrence but was constrained by historical fact to keep it almost peripheral.[22] Of singular interest, given her self-identification with Elizabeth Siddal, is H. D.'s conception of her: "Elizabeth was, we know, poor, sickly, a milliner's assistant, living along Brixton way, I imagine, or that is the impression I get," she wrote to Aldington on September 3, 1947 (*LY,* p. 105). Later in the letter, "We know about Jane Morris [the Jane Morris-Rossetti affair]. But was there perhaps another woman, or more than one? I mean another woman that the 'older brother' (Gabriel) loved or possessed

first. Do we know anything at all about W. M.['s] feeling for Elizabeth? . . . Was Gabriel a 'father substitute'? . . . W. M.['s] feeling about Gabriel seems to me to be contradictory and inconsistent. Elizabeth was older and as the then companion of Gabriel, would perhaps have had some strong and subtle influence on the younger W. M." (*LY,* p. 105). That H. D. was older than Aldington when they met and married is not to be ignored.

But once into the novel, H. D. takes over from Aldington, Violet Hunt, and J. W. Mackail's *Life of William Morris,* her main source, on Aldington's recommendation, of information about Morris' life and career. Her Morris becomes Pound, Lawrence, Freud, Aldington. He is played off against Rossetti as Pound and Aldington. And with no historical encouragement at all, H. D. makes the relationship between Morris and Elizabeth Siddal central, even more important with respect to her art than is her tie to Rossetti. It is Morris who sends her his work, including manuscripts, as Pound did H. D., and it is with Morris that Liz discusses the story she is writing, the "Gold Cord." In some ways, her tale-in-progress becomes the hinge or the focus for all that is said about art and spiritualism throughout the novel, for it is Morris who instigates some of the connections and sees others. That H. D. had also unfinished business—her table-tapping and the figure of Lord Howell in "The Sword Went Out to Sea"[23]—is apparent. She ingeniously transforms the seance group in *The Sword* into the Order of Sir Galahad, the short-lived undergraduate Malory-inspired circle of friends Morris impulsively named at one point. Round tables and séance tables are palimpsestically overlaid, and it is time to mention that H. D. obtained at the sale of Violet Hunt's estate a three-legged table that had been Morris' and that she used for her table-tapping séances.[24]

There are many ways "White Rose and the Red" can be related to the period 1912-1918, the most obvious being H. D.'s own statement that it was so related, and her dependence on Aldington for historical and biographical information. However, H. D.'s Morris, a lithe figure who pads through the jungle softly like a young lion ("WRR," 3rd dr., p. 227)[25]—that is, Pound, Lawrence, or Aldington—is also Freud, the figure of the 1930s who directs H. D. back to the period 1912-18. (It is also worth noticing that Freud becomes as well the bottommost layer in what in "White Rose and the Red" is not a return to the beginning: the spiritualism, which in its full flower belongs to the World War II period and after. Freudian psychology, with its explorative attitude toward dreams, became for H. D., in "White Rose," license to see dreams as continuous with mystic other-worldly experiences and connections revealed through spiritualist séances.

My own purposes are best served by seeing in the novel the extraordinary effort to which H. D. goes to disengage from their bases the attributes of polarized entities and then to mix and rearrange them in a complex yearning for unity between the alleged opposites. And by seeing, finally, that it is Morris who provides her with an image for this elusive unity.

The whole discourse concerning opposites is framed in the novel by the "white" and the "red" rose, and the self-conscious desire to unite them is alluded to by the fictive Morris quoting Richmond in *Richard III,* "We will unite the white rose and the red," ("WRR," 4th dr., p. 415), which of course H. D. takes as a metaphysical challenge not a political one—or at least not political in the sense that Richmond's literal reference to York and Lancaster is.

A great deal of the novel is devoted to the many associations Morris, in his interior monologues and reveries, makes with Elizabeth Siddal's name, that is, with the name "Liz." Through revelations in spiritualist sessions, the name *lis* (lily) occurs, and is in turn multiplied in meanings. For example, in Rossetti's painting *The Blessed Damozel,* for which H. D. made Elizabeth the model, she holds in her hands, as she does in Rossetti's poem, three lilies.[26] But in Morris' tale "The Hollow Land"—a central connection between him and Elizabeth Siddal—(he sends her the proofs before it is published in the *Oxford and Cambridge Magazine* and she is much taken with it), the first-person narrator is Florian de Liliis, and a world of meaning is found in this heraldic family name. And remembering when he first "encountered" Liz, in a reverie on Blackfriars Bridge at night, in the snow, Morris thinks:

> This white rose, stained red, was not like the others. Lis was a snow-flower. In memory he was again whirled with the stinging snow-dust round a corner into a little courtyard. . . . But the creature beside him was tangible, though a mist of fine drifting snow veiled her occasionally. She was a white rose certainly. But he had found her, before he walked across Blackfriars Bridge with her in the snow. She was Margaret, Walter's sister in the *Unknown Church.* And she was Margaret again, a cousin perhaps, the lover who had waited for him in *The Hollow Land.*
>
> ("WRR," 4th dr., p. 269).

I know of no etymological connection between "Margaret" and "lily," but then there is none between flowers and rocks, though if H. D. was thinking of the Latin origin of the name Margaret, something of interest emerges. The Latin word *margarita* means pearl, and perhaps equally with its whiteness, the hardness of the pearl should be of interest here.

H. D.'s Morris explains the interconnections to Liz when he is with her at Hampton Court, a favorite outing for the historical William Morris but not with the historical Elizabeth Siddal. William Morris says:

> "I will ask you to think of me as happy with this lady I call Lis."
>
> "Lis?" she questioned.
>
> "It's from the story ["The Hollow Land"], I told you. I think that my rose was a lily. That is what I meant, her name, I mean, being Lis.
>
> She did not know what had happened to her. She felt like a stone being dropped down a deep well.
>
> ("WRR," 3rd dr., p. 310.)

Why someone whose name, that of a flower in Morris' view, should feel like a stone when her elusive name seems also to be that of another woman, the one who is indeed her rival for Morris' love, is another of the small but arresting matters that suit my reading of H. D.'s work. But suffice it to note that once again H. D. has erased differences, equating the white rose and the lily because they are white.

As for the red rose, the associations with the flower, the color, and the name are again multiple. Most embracing of all, "Rossetti" means "rose." In many ways, the red rose is apparently dominant; it has lethal power, potentially, to stain the white rose red. Godfrey Lushington, a minor figure in the historical life of William Morris whom the novel converts into a major character, is a key to much of the spiritualism that is woven into this tale of the Pre-Raphaelites. A beloved sister, Vivien, has died, thrown from her horse, and Godfrey's identification with her is so thorough that he not only feels guilt and loss; but in séances, as well as in visionary experiences, relives her life and suffers her death. Significantly, Vivien is also the "white rose," the dead sister of a friend, whom William Morris tells Lizzie he loves. The text reads: "Godfrey had found out that the white rose [in this case Vivien] was red. Was sacrifice always necessary? William Morris knew that it was. The white rose was stained with the blood of the heart" (*WRR,* 4th dr., p. 264). All this is enveloped in a faintly outlined larger tale. For Vivien had a lover, Carew, whom she was going to meet in the wood and who, subsequently, is killed in the Crimean War, which in the novel, as noted, works as best it can to return us (or move us forward) to World War I, and it is the blood of Carew's heart that also stains the white rose, Vivien.

And among the many other confrontations of red with white, Red Harald, in Morris' "The Hollow Land," the tale which is thoroughly explored in H. D.'s novel and which made a link between William Morris and Elizabeth Siddal, defeats in battle Florian de Liliis. But in the larger view, it is a dubious victory for Red Herald, for he sends Florian in death back to the Hollow Land, where he is reunited with his lover, Margaret, his original "white rose."

As for William Morris and Elizabeth Siddal, Rossetti, the embodiment of red, sets limits to their relationship. It is red, it seems to me, that dominates the scene of greatest intimacy between Morris and Elizabeth Siddal. They are, again, at Hampton Court, where, it should be noted, they arrange to meet frequently: "The air was fragrant with the un-trimmed climbing roses. [Morris] was seated on the window-ledge, his arms about her waist, his head bowed forward. He felt her heart under his burning forehead. It was the first time he had touched her" ("WRR," 3rd dr., p. 387). William Morris, who has said he is Florian de Liliis, has become suffused in red, given over to its power, in the scene that brings him and Lizzie Siddal closest.

This power of red, finally, has the characteristics of rocks, in relation to the easily stained and overcome embodiments of white. There are in fact passages that begin with roses and lilies and move by easy transition to rocks and flowers.

Florian de Liliis, remembering when he first enters the Hollow Land (he is first-person narrator of the tale), says: This "heaven . . . was no infinite vault [Lizzie had called the Hollow Land the inverted bowl of heaven]; . . . it was the bed of leaves . . . into which I let myself down carefully, by the jutting rocks and bushes and strange trailing flowers and there lay down and fell asleep" ("WRR," 4th dr., p. 269).27 We are back to the sheltering harbor-rocks of the islands in **"The Shrine"** and **"Sea Gods."** Though the flowers provide the soft and inviting bed, the jutting rocks also provide care: they are the sentinels. As barriers to whoever would be an easy traveler into the Hollow Land, they shelter Florian and his beloved Margaret. Significant of not, though there is reconciliation between Florian and Red Harald, the latter does not follow Florian in his final entry into the Hollow Land.

This is again the sharing of characteristics between rocks and flowers, and the movement to try to unite them as beneficial equals has begun. It is the final move in this novel, written in 1948, to find the unity that H. D. sought in 1912-1918 when she first disengaged the characteristics of rocks and flowers from their received images and attempted to achieve an unstable unity by conferring the attributes of each upon the other. It is Morris' medievalism, the Ruskinian root of his own Pre-Raphaelitism, that provides the concrete image for enduring, stable union, between the rock and the flower. It is relevant, too, that early in "White Rose and the Red," in an imagined conversation between D. G. Rossetti and John Ruskin (in history and in this novel Elizabeth Siddal's patron), Ruskin observes that women do not love line, with which, he, Ruskin, identifies through his own aesthetic. "They love colour"—a love that the text makes clear is Rossetti's concept of the basis of painting. But oddly at this early point, Rossetti answers, "What Liz wants—she as good as said so—is a rock" ("WRR," 4th dr. p. 170). Morris is the rock, and the exchange between Ruskin and Rossetti unknowingly establishes him as the answer to Lizzie's need, before he appears. But of course Morris is also—and equally—identified with flowers.

A significant narrative detail in "The Unknown Church," the second of the two early stories central to the relationship between William Morris and Elizabeth Siddal, is observed by her and moves us to the ultimate union: "It was Walter"—who Morris has told us is himself—who carved the marble "'all about with many flowers and histories'" ("WRR," 4th dr., pp. 222-233). And the text notes that before Morris as a boy went away to school, he had discovered Gerard's *Herbal*:

> That was his first great moment. Every leaf, every hedge-rose, every bluebell stalk took form. A cluster of blossoms detached itself from the maze of the thorn and became stylized, a theme for decoration. There were stone flowers in some of their northern Cathedrals, not yet "discovered." . . . The stone flowered of itself, if you let it alone.
>
> ("WRR," 4th dr., pp. 226-227).

The symbolic meaning here is remarkably apposite to a reading of H. D.'s work. It is not just that art, through its own particular power, converts flowers into stones; it is that stones—symbolizing the enduring— are the material of art, but an art that is not realized until informed by the imagery of flowers, with all its symbolism.

Elsewhere, too, the independent force exerted by flower imagery tells us that this is an enduring union. H. D.'s text continues, faithfully echoing the historical Morris (though later than the 1850s): "The living stone had gone from most of their Cathedrals, and what was left was being smothered, killed ("WRR," 3rd dr., p. 208). And Elizabeth Siddal rises, as it were, to the challenge set by the Morris who is her spiritual father, her mentor, her Freud, and the composite of her lovers of 1914-1918. In the story she is writing, the "Gold Cord," which is being accomplished through a process that is sometimes simply writing and other times use of scenes and details that emerge in her reveries, she envisions a castle: "The pillars had apparently been hewn out of the solid rock, or the rock had been cut away from them, for they were part of the floor. She could not judge the ceiling but they must be one with the rock-roof as well. . . . The doors . . . were rock doorways without doors" ("WRR," 3rd dr., p. 369). And in a discussion of her story with William Morris, he speaks first, saying "I am Florian in *The Hollow Land*." It is clear from what follows that her own vision, for her own story, is a response to "The Hollow Land": "It isn't hollow," she said, "that is, it is a mountain with the galleries cut out and those rough support-pillars. But perhaps it is hollow, but *in* the mountain. I called it the Holy Mountain" ("WRR," 3rd dr., p. 377). It was Elizabeth who had called William Morris's hollow land "an inverted bowl of heaven." Her own image here is richly suggestive. The mountain is "higher" than the hollow land. Does she aspire higher, toward a religious dimension not in "The Hollow Land"? But the mountain is hollow. Is this negative, suggesting a weakness, a "hollowness" of religious faith in her story? Or is the mountain a tall structure, surpassing all around it, waiting to be filled up, to become the dwelling place of lovers like Walter and Margaret, but a Walter and Margaret reinvented and reconceptualized by H. D.? Most interesting of all, Lizzie's castle recalls the cliff-shrine of **"The Cliff Temple"** in *Sea Garden*; it is again a joining of opposites, of Morris' medieval churches and castles with the shrines to Greek gods and goddesses. H. D.'s castle, here, resonates with her lifelong absorption in classical Greek culture, implicitly positing one more pair of opposites—classical temples and Gothic structures—in order to exchange their characteristics, a move, by the way, that would have set the historical Morris' teeth on edge.[28]

But there is, in "White Rose and the Red," the inevitable shadow question in the quest for an answer to what is art: what is an artist? As an artist, Elizabeth Siddal can compete with Rossetti's "Hand and Soul," which she acknowledges as her first inspiration, as indeed does Morris in speaking of his stories. Elizabeth Siddal can erect a mountain that is art and will house lovers within it. But the perfect union remains an hypothesis. She is engaged to Rossetti. Morris, the rock she needs in order to emerge as herself, as the image with three lilies in her hand (who is also Morris' white rose), is beyond reach. For Elizabeth Siddal, still standing for the H. D. of 1912-1918, it is not that

love for a man is impossible; it is that Aldington, Lawrence, Pound were in conflict with her as a woman, rather than figures who would enable her to fulfill herself. The idealized William Morris, a theme throughout her life, was the father-lover-brother who would have encouraged her to be an artist; who was approximated by Freud, but who, given Freud's age, his role of therapist, the brevity of the relationship, could, finally, only suggest—point in the direction in which she was traveling. The historical Elizabeth Siddal has to die, not a suicide here but a woman in search of a good night's sleep. *Bid Me to Live* stopped before the next phase in H. D.'s life began, before Bryher, thoroughly at first but ambivalently later, replaced all the men of the period 1912-1918. For different reasons H. D. had wanted to end before Elizabeth Siddal died but was persuaded by Norman Holmes Pearson to carry her to the end. H. D. wrote: "I had a vague feeling of un-ease and uncertainty about writing of the actual death of the wife of Rossetti. . . . I had so much identified myself with the story that I could not, for some strange reason, let her die."[29] I cannot, in the light of what we know, ignore the influence of Aldington on her original intention in shaping this novel.

Like Morris, Aldington is removed, beyond attainment by 1948, but he is also the Dante Gabriel Rossetti who was the chief cause of her suffering. It is H. D. as victim who finally dies. In this apparent contradiction, through the figure and life of Elizabeth Siddal she accomplished this. Morris, as an idea, as the final layer in the palimpsest, as well as the virtual, retrospectively constructed pre-1912-1918 plane, has shown the way to self-union in art, revealed the degree of self-realization and integration that is possible for the artist. But though Morris cannot, finally, erase the actual history of H. D., she could go on, now, and write *Helen in Egypt* (1961). But she could also fulfill her relationship with Aldington in the best way possible for her in these last years. Through Elizabeth Siddal, she converted the turmoil of 1912-1918 into peace, albeit the peace of death, though it is the death of H. D. as victim and sufferer at the hands of Aldington. Though "White Rose and the Red" does not initiate the return to an intimate relationship with Aldington, it cements the friendship that has emerged—his own new-found enthusiasm for Morris, and the help he gave H. D. in getting started on the novel, laid lines for what remained. With Aldington, in these late years, she finally establishes once and for all that she is artist/ woman and keeps the woman/artist subdued but self-accepting. Through redefinition, she has made a successful return to the unsettled business of 1912-18. She will always be the artist first in her correspondence with Aldington. But she will also, and simultaneously, be the woman, her love converted into caring and intimate friendship. The actual Aldington, as the ultimate layer in the palimpsest that is Morris, recombines the scattered parts of his Osiris-like career in her art, and becomes the intimate of her mind, and thus, in 1948, of her heart. I submit that it is this triumph and liberation that makes possible the fine conclusion of her career with **Helen in Egypt.** The life and meditation of the "real" Helen, as opposed to the phantom the Greeks and Trojans fought over, is her final major work, and one that does not return to 1912-18.

Notes

1. Albert Gelpi, for example, writes: "1919 marked a turning point in H. D.'s life. The previous years had been a period so filled with both achievement and anxiety, so critical and traumatic that she would spend the rest of her life mythologizing it: rehearsing it in verse, in prose, in direct autobiography and in historical and legendary personae, again and again seeking to unriddle her destiny as woman and poet" "Introduction," H. D., *Notes on Thought and Vision & The Wise Sappho* (San Francisco: City Light Books, 1982), p. 7. See also Susan Stanford Friedman, *Penelope's Web: Gender, Modernity, H. D.'s Fiction* (Cambridge: Cambridge Univ. Press, 1990).

2. Although her use of the material is different from mine, Cassandra Laity, in *H. D. and the Victorian Fin de Siècle: Gender, Modernism, Decadence* (Cambridge: Cambridge Univ. Press, 1996), has provided us with the most thorough consideration to date of H. D.'s reading of the Pre-Raphaelites.

3. References to Morris and his importance to her are scattered throughout H. D.'s autobiographical writings. Norman Holmes Pearson sums them up: "H. D. as a girl sometimes thought of William Morris as her spiritual father. 'This is the god-father I never had. . . . I did not know much about him until I was . . . about sixteen. I was given a book of his to read, by Miss Pitcher, at Miss Gordon's school;—a little later, Ezra Pound read the poetry to me. The book Miss Pitcher gave me was on furniture, perhaps an odd introduction. But my father made a bench for my room, some bookcases downstairs, from William Morris designs. My father had been a carpenter's apprentice as a boy. This 'William Morris' father might have sent me to art school but the Professor of Astronomy and Mathematics insisted on my preparing for college. He wanted eventually (he even said so) to make a mathematician of me, a research worker or scientist like (he even said so) Madame Curie. He did make a research worker of

me but in another dimension. It was a long time before I found William Morris and that was by accident, though we are told that 'nothing occurs accidentally.'" "Foreword," *Tribute to Freud* (New York: New Directions, 1974), p. x. Hereafter cited as *TF.* See also H. D.'s unpublished "Hirslanden Notebook" (p. 26), Beinecke Library, Yale University, from which Pearson quotes here.

4. The typescript is in the H. D. papers, Beinecke Library, Yale University; hereafter this document is cited as "WRR."

5. *In Tribute to Freud,* H. D. wrote that one purpose of her analysis was to prepare herself to help "war-shocked and war-shattered people. But my actual personal war-shock (1914-1919) did not have a chance. My sessions with the Professor were hardly under way before there were preliminary signs and symbols of the approaching ordeal" (pp. 93-94).

6. Again, "palimpsest" is a term regularly used by critics and scholars writing about H. D., as well as by H. D. herself in referring to her life and work. One novel, actually three stories thinly related, is titled *Palimpsest* (1926). For a particularly interesting use of the concept, see Erika Rohrbach, "H. D. and Sappho: A Precious Inch of Palimpsest," *Re-Reading Sappho: Reception and Transmission,* ed. Ellen Greene (Berkeley: Univ. of California Press, 1997), pp. 184-198. For a reading of H. D.'s novel, see Deborah Kelly Kloepter, "Fishing the Murex Up: Sense and Resonance in H. D.'s *Palimpsest,*" *ConL* [*Contemporary Literature*] 27, no. 4 (1986): 553-573; repr. in *Signets: Reading H. D.,* ed. Susan Stanford Friedman and Rachel Blau Duplessis (Madison: Univ. of Wisconsin Press, 1990), pp. 185-204.

7. Eileen Gregory calls attention to words in "The Wise Sappho" that, though my own interest here is not in H. D. and Sappho, have relevance to my theme. Sappho's fragments, H. D. writes, are not roses or orange blossoms even, "but reading deeper we are inclined to visualize these broken sentences and unfinished rhythms as rocks— perfect rock shelves and layers of rock between which flowers by some chance may grow but which endure when the staunch blossoms have perished." Sappho's fragments are "not roses but . . . a world of emotion, differing entirely from any present day imaginable world of emotion" (Gelpi, p. 58). See also Eileen Gregory, "Rose Cut in Rock: Sappho and H. D.'s *Sea Garden,*" *ConL* 27, no. 4 1986): 535; repr. in *Signets: Reading H. D.,* pp. 129-154. See also Burton Hatlen, "The Imagist Poetics of H. D.'s *Sea Garden,*" *Paideuma: A Journal Devoted to Ezra Pound Scholarship* 24 2.3 (1995): 119-120.

8. *H. D.: Collected Poems, 1912-1944,* ed. Louis L. Martz (New York: New Directions, 1983), p. 7. Hereafter cited as *CP.*

9. Thomas Burnett Swann makes the probable identification. See his *The Classical World of H. D.* (Lincoln: Univ. of Nebraska Press, 1962), p. 30.

10. For a reading of "Garden" different from my own, see Gregory, pp. 544-545. See also Gary Burnett, "The Identity of 'H.': Imagism and H. D.'s *Sea Garden,*" *Sagetrieb* 8, no. 3 (Winter 1989): 72-74.; and Hatlen, pp. 122-123.

11. In his review, which appeared in *The International Journal for Psycho-Analysis* 1 XXVII (1957): 126, Jones wrote: "The book, with its appropriate title, is surely the most delightful and precious appreciation of Freud's personality that is ever likely to be written. Only a fine creative artist could have written it. It is like a lovely flower. and the crude pen of a scientist hesitates to profane it by attempting to describe it. . . . It will live as the most enchanting ornament of all the Freudian biographical literature." Quoted also by Norman Holmes Pearson, "Foreword," *Tribute to Freud,* p. vi. For an engrossing exploration of H. D.'s psychoanalysis, and thus of her relationship with Freud, see Susan Stanford Friedman, *Psyche Reborn: The Emergence of H. D.* (Bloomington: Indiana Univ. Press, 1987), pp. 17-154.

12. For a slightly different reading—Freud is included only indirectly—see Laity, p. 155.

13. In "H. D. by Delia Alton" (*The Iowa Review* 16 [Fall 1986]: 174-221), H. D. wrote: "*Madrigal* this story of War I was roughed out, summer 1939, in Switzerland. I left the MS . . . with Bryer, when I returned to England, soon after the outbreak of War II. It was returned to me last winter [1948]. . . . I had been writing or trying to write this story, since 1921. I wrote in various styles, simply or elaborately, stream-of-consciousness or straight narrative. . . . But after I had corrected and typed out *Madrigal* last winter, I was able conscientiously to destroy the earlier versions. . . . On rereading the typed MS, I realized that at last, the War I story had 'written itself'" (p. 180).

14. H. D., *Bid Me To Live (A Madrigal)* (New York: Grove Press, 1960), pp. 55-56. Hereafter cited as *BML.*

15. The finished poem is probably "Eurydice," in *The God* (*CP,* pp. 51-55).

16. H. D. said as much. In "Delia Alton," she wrote: "A labour of love (though hardly a labour) was the assembling of the story of Elizabeth Siddall, Dante Gabriel Rossetti, and William Morris. I call this narrative *White Rose and the Red,* and it is an attempt to re-create the atmosphere of the London of the mid-years of the last century, and the group of writers and painters of which my own acquaintances and friends were, in a sense, the inheritors" (p. 193).

17. I for one am grateful to Caroline Zilboorg for selecting, arranging, and publishing the letters H. D. and Aldington exchanged, as well as providing through commentary and annotations a reading of the relationship between H. D. and Aldington in the post World War II years that makes clear as can be that H. D. without conflict had by then reconnected with Aldington as a friend who was more than a friend, as a fellow artist, as a source of information she needed for her writing, and, as she herself referred to him, as a "friendly critic" of her work. See Caroline Zilboorg, ed., *Richard Aldington & H. D.: The Later Years in Letters* (Manchester: Manchester Univ. Press, 1995); herafter cited as *LY.*

18. See *LY,* pp. 94-110, 128 nn. 5 and 6, and 138.

19. The typescript is in the H. D. Papers in the Beinecke Library, Yale University.

20. See "Delia Alton," p. 191.

21. All women as protagonists in H. D.'s novels are H. D., but her comment in "Delia Alton" is specifically to the point here: "Something of my early search, my first expression or urge toward expression in art, finds a parallel in the life of Rossetti and Elizabeth Siddall. So, as a very subtle emotional exercise I go over and over the ground, find relationships or parallels between my own emotional starvation and hers, between the swift flowering soon to be cut down, in her case, by death, in mine, by a complete break after War I, with the group of artists described in *Madrigal*" (p. 194).

22. In her zeal, she conflated the Crimean War of 1853-56 with the Russo-Turkish War of 1876-78, asserting that Morris' anti-war poem, "Wake London Lads," concerned the first; whereas it was in fact written at the beginning of 1878 to oppose efforts by Disraeli and the Conservative government to lead England into the latter conflict on the side of the Ottoman Empire.

23. Lord Howell, of "The Sword Went Out to Sea," is Lord Hugh Caswell Tremenheere Dowding, Air Chief Marshall in command of the RAF forces that won the Battle of Britain, and thus a person whose efforts were a fulcrum on which human history turned. During the War, Lord Dowding began to conduct and attend séances, to get in

touch with RAF pilots who had been downed. H. D. was also receiving messages from RAF pilots (see n. 24) but when she tried to share her information with Lord Dowding, he rejected her, asserting his messages were from higher spiritual sources than hers.

24. After noting that the table was so used, H. D. says that the messages she received from its tapping leg were from air-men who had been lost in the Battle of Britain. See "Delia Alton," p. 187.

25. Citations will be to both the third and fourth drafts (the two final ones) of "White Rose and the Red." Since the novel was never published, it does not seem to me that one draft is more authoritative than the other.

26. Intentionally or not, H. D. seems to have conflated two of the historical Rossetti's paintings. Alexa Wilding sat for *The Blessed Damozel,* who indeed holds three lilies in her hands. Among the paintings for which Elizabeth Siddal was the model, there is one, *Beata Beatrix,* that was begun early, put aside, and not finished until 1864, that is, until after her death. Rossetti's leaving unfinished this picture for which Elizabeth Siddal posed fits the description of the painting in "White Rose." But "Beata Beatrix" holds no lilies in her hand.

27. The words which H. D. underlined are quoted directly from "The Hollow Land." See Morris, *The Hollow Land and Other Contributions to the Oxford and Cambridge Magazine* (Bristol: Thoemmes Press, 1996), p. 206.

28. Morris, like Ruskin, regarded Greek and Roman architecture as drastically inferior to Gothic. Ruskin's "The Nature of Gothic," setting out reasons for the contrast and preference, was a bible for Morris.

29. See "Delia Alton," p. 200.

Kathleen Fraser (essay date 2000)

SOURCE: Fraser, Kathleen. "The Blank Page: H. D.'s Invitation to Trust and Mistrust Language." In *H. D. and Poets After,* edited by Donna Krolik Hollenberg, pp. 163-71. Iowa City, Iowa: University of Iowa Press, 2000.

[*In the following essay, Fraser discusses Pound's influence on H. D. and her work, and explores H. D.'s persistent resistance to attempts by males, including Pound and others, to label her work and define her as a poet.*]

> *we know no rule*
> *of procedure,*
>
> *we are voyagers, discoverers,*
> *of the notknown*
>
> *the unrecorded;*
> *we have no map*
>
>   H. D., *Trilogy*

With an authentic sense of beginning at zero, a poetically mature H. D. could write in the war years of the early 1940s: "we know no rule / of procedure." Yet her contemporary readers know that rules of procedure did exist at almost every level of her early life. Even in that nontraditional world of literature toward which she leaned, achieved forms stood in place. Nevertheless, she refused the finality of the already filled page. For while others' writings often thrilled her, they did not speak for the unsaid that burned in her.

Born from doubt and extreme privacy, her own tentative language slowly invented itself out of silence. Her gift was an ability to see the empty page waiting to be inscribed and to imagine—beyond the parchment metaphor of "palimpsest"—a contemporary model for the poem that would recover a complex overlay of erotic and spiritual valuings variously imprinted, then worn away, then finally rediscovered and engraved inside her own lines. Her vision lay in the conviction of plurality—that the blank page would never be a full text until women writers (and their reader-scholars) scrawled their own scripts across its emptiness.

Even within Pound's mentoring embrace, H. D. felt a certain cautionary guardedness around the unfolding, if uneasy, project of her own work. "Ezra would have destroyed me and the center they call 'Air and Crystal,'" she admits in 1958 in her journal entry from *End to Torment.* A month later, she writes: "To recall Ezra is to recall my father. . . . To recall my father is to recall the cold blazing intelligence of my 'last attachment' of the war years in London. This is not easy" (H. D. 1979: 35, 48).

She had survived two major wars and the tyranny of gender stereotype. But fifty years later she was still trying to sort out the impact of this strange, impassioned outsider, Ezra Pound, who identified and constellated her early poetic identity while at the same time limiting its very stretch by his defining, instructive approval.

That a strong push-pull dynamic progressively marks her writer-relation to Pound and her position "on the fringes of the modernist mainstream" seems evident from passages in her fictional works and in bits of letters and journals (Friedman and DuPlessis 1990: 24). Her artistic progress is marked by self-initiated shifts in attitude and ambition—notably, her decision to try to shed the once-useful but finally limiting description of "Imagiste" given her by Pound as her poet designator. It is instructive to mark her ambivalence toward—and discomfort with—male value judgments vis-à-vis her own work and to see how she climbed, repeatedly, out of these silencing effects to again recover her own voice and to trust its foraging instincts.

We read the following words written to Pound, anticipating his criticism, in a note H. D. sent along to him in 1959 with a copy of her complete *Helen in Egypt*: "Don't worry or hurry with the Helen—don't read it at all—don't read it yet—don't bother to write of it" (quoted in Friedman and DuPlessis 1990: 12). One hears the echo and ricochet of her wariness traveling all the way back to Pound's first decisive claim on her poetic gifts, the swift and confident slash of his editor's pencil and his literal initialing—or labeling—of her for purposes of identification and value in the poetry marketplace.

In H. D.'s life, this style of "help" manifested itself in various powerful guises, notably in encounters with big-affect literary friends such as D. H. Lawrence, whose charismatic male authority was often as much a source of anxiety as support. The delicate yet powerful mythic terrain wisely appropriated by H. D. afforded protection from a merely personal accounting of her highly volatile emotional life—the more personal lyric, so liable to deliver her into the hands of male "correction." Myth finally provided a route of independent travel, a large enough page on which to incise and thus emplace her own vision of the future, spiritually enlivened by values retrieved from female life.

When she directs our attention in *Trilogy* to "the blank pages / of the unwritten volume of the new," H. D. is issuing a literal invitation of breathtaking immensity and independence to contemporary women poets. Once perceived, the page is there and yours to remake. No more alibis. The challenge is at once freeing and awesome.

As a contemporary writer, I have been called back to this blank page again and again. Let me attempt to describe a largely intuitive gathering-up of poem materials for a serial work of mine, "Etruscan Pages" (*When New Time Folds Up*), in which the layerings of old and new inscription were built from accretions of literal archaeological remnant bound together into current pages of language, visual figure and event (present-time dreams and letters).

I believe that it was H. D.'s profound connection to the contemporary relevance of ancient cultures—as well as her Egyptian experience with hieroglyph as a kind of telegram from the atemporal—that opened me and prepared me for my journey (May 1991) to the sites of three Etruscan necropolises—Tarquinia, Vulci, and Norchia—scattered north of Rome along the Maremma coast, each site marked on the map with an almost illegible triangle of black dots. Having deferred a long-held intellectual curiosity, early prompted by reading D. H. Lawrence in the sixties and an early draft of Rachel Blau DuPlessis's ground-breaking essay "For the Etruscans" in 1979 (and thinly veneered with bookish obligation), I finally took the occasion of a friend's visit to propose a journey to these three sites, and we set off early one morning with map and guidebook.

There was nothing that could have prepared me for the impact these places had on me—their absence informed by presence. The cliff tombs of Norchia might well have been entirely nonexistent if one were dependent only upon visual clues or signs along nearby roads. By guesswork we found ourselves climbing down through rough rock passages overgrown with foliage that seemed to have been there forever. The lack of any other car or human allowed the presence of birds, local wild-flowers, and the more apparent ruins of Roman conquerors—planted just across the ravine from the Etruscan cliff tombs—to resonate powerfully. I felt as if dropped through time, less and less able to talk casually of our surrounds.

Days later, the poem slowly began to rise to the surface of my listening mind. And during that time a startling convergence of dreams and events worked to push the limits of the poem into something much more layered and much less personal than any account of my own private experience could have provided. A week after the Maremma trip, I returned to the Villa Giulia, the major Etruscan museum in Rome, to see again the dancers lavishly flung across urns and the sculpted bodies of husband and wife entwined sensuously on the limestone lid covering an elongated sarcophagus. It was then I could finally begin to piece together their celebratory moment on earth with utterly changed eyes. H. D.'s invitation had allowed me to step out of the skin of verbal overlay and late-twentieth-century gloss, rendering me available to the palpable presence of these women and men.

Here are several passages from a letter, early embedded in my "page," that narrate a dream and then an archaeological episode, both given to me during the weeks of the poem's writing, as if invented for the layered record I was attempting to rewrite:

> The night you left for Paros, I dreamt I was lying on a
> stone slab at the base of the cliff tombs at Norchia,

preparing to make my transition from "this world" to "the other." I was thinking about how to negotiate the passage, when it came to me—the reason for all the layers of fine white cloth arranged and spread around me. I said to you (because you were with me), "You just keep wrapping yourself with white cloth and eventually you are in the other place."

(Fraser 1993: 26)

This from an unexpected conversation—days later—with an archaeologist:

The other source [referring to etymological studies] is the "mummy wrapping," linen originally from Egypt (probably hauled on trading ships) covered with formulaic and repetitious Etruscan religious precepts written "retro" (right to left). Even though there are over 1,200 words covering it, the total lexicon is barely 500. The mummy text is preserved in the museum in Zagreb, thus "The Zagreb Mummy." Her body had been wrapped in this shroud made of pieces of linen, written on through centuries [with Phoenician, Greek, and, finally, Etruscan characters], used as "pages" for new writing whenever the old text had faded. Her family had wrapped her in this cloth, this writing, because it was available.

(Fraser 1993: 27)

With these interventions, the actual making of the poem became immensely absorbing. H. D.'s exhortation to heed "the blank pages of the unwritten volume of the new" was pulling me away from her "air and crystal" language. My page wanted to be inscribed as if it were a canvas, my own linguistic motion and visual notation appropriating the Etruscan lexicon and alphabet as subject and object—inventions suggested directly from contact with tomb inscriptions and the beaten gold tablets at Villa Giulia, covered with the elusive remainders of their language.

For example, a passage on the imagined origins of the letter *A* is juxtaposed with a miniature lexicon composed of words that already existed throughout the larger poem's text, a word hand-scrawled in Etruscan letters (meant to resemble those scratched into burial stones), and a bit of quoted speculation by D. H. Lawrence. I wanted to place a close-up lens over particular words as well as to foreground the hand and mind at work making language through history.

Without H. D.'s precedent, it is very unlikely that I would have trusted my own particular rendering of the historic clues and layers of the Etruscan culture or understood the urgency of articulating another reading of it in the face of all the officially recognized studies preceding me, including Lawrence's narrative. While my poem "Etruscan Pages" intentionally acknowledges Lawrence's 1932 travel memoir, *Etruscan Places,* it writes the new word PAGE over the old word PLACE

to tip the reader's attention in the direction of an alternative reading introduced through a formal shift of perception. Mine is a document meant to record an alternative vision of the predominantly male archaeological point of view already well installed.

Having given Lawrence's account a rather perfunctory skim in the sixties, I was curious to go back to it—once I had a fairly realized draft of my own—just to see what had occupied him. I was pleased but not that surprised to find that there were a number of physical details and baffling absences we'd noted in common (although sixty years apart), even to particulars of asphodel (he must have been there in May) and the "nothing" that seemed to be so present in the barren fields and shut tombs around Vulci, where a sensuousness of daily life had once been so radiantly apparent.

I decided to incorporate several fragment phrases from Lawrence's text as a way of marking our meeting in parallel time—a kind of palimpsest dialogue. But I was deeply relieved to find that he'd not been to Norchia, the site that most profoundly spoke to me. I didn't want his brilliant voice-print preceding me everywhere. Its definite authority and well-installed literary history might have in some way inhibited me from capturing my own barely visible version.

I'd like to return now to the issue of asserted literary dominion versus self-confirmation as it impinges on the working life of the woman poet. For in spite of her strategies for empowerment, we recognize in H. D.'s 1959 note to Pound a residual mistrust based on the tension between her deep desire for his approval and the necessary self-affirmation of her own unmediated—and thus uninhibited—vision and writing method. Even after fifty years, a lurking fear of not meeting his standards still seems to hover in her. It isn't a simple fear of critique, for she was obviously strong-willed and utterly conscious of her aesthetic choices by then; rather, it is more like the dread of having to tangle with the absolute ego of the beloved but intrusive father/judge, forever looming in the shadow just over her shoulder, and to risk the loss of his admiration.

Reviewing H. D.'s progress toward the trust of her own "page," a contemporary woman poet might well identify with this struggle to circumvent the tremendous pressure of prevailing male ideology that has so conveniently persisted, historically viewing women contemporaries as "receptacle-like muses rather than active agents," thus reinforcing long-dominant "notions of what was properly and naturally feminine" (Friedman and DuPlessis 1990: 16).

Recently reading through a selection of letters between Pound and the young Louis Zukofsky, exchanged between 1928 and 1930, I was generally amused until

I came across such bits of Pound-heavy advice as his urging Zukofsky to form a new literary group of serious, high-energy writers but exhorting him: "NOT too many women, and if possible no wives at assembly. If some insist on accompanying their *mariti* [husbands], make sure they are bored and don't repeat offense." Later, advising Zukofsky about the selection of work for a new magazine, he says: "AND the verse used MUST be good . . . preferably by men [*sic*] under 30" (Pound 1987).

In these tossed-off bits of pecking-order jocularity are found the not very subtle codes of selection and disenfranchisement that were practiced to various degrees in the literary world I entered as a young poet in the early sixties. A primary difference between my world and H. D.'s was that nine-tenths of the once-published writing by modernist women was out of print, leaving very few female texts as models for the nontraditional poetics one felt compelled to explore.

Fortunately, change was in the air. By the early seventies, women scholars had begun to talk to each other about this problem and to investigate it in print.

This brings us again to the shaping hand of influence and the prevailing authority of installed standards of judgment—and how the effects of gender-specific valuing, editing, and explication can make a radical difference in the continuing life of the working poet.

Thinking about particular writers who shaped my early writing sensibility, I cannot find any direct H. D. imprint upon my poetics or practice, yet I know that somewhere along the line my mature writing has been significantly touched by her traces even though in the first decade of my exposure to modernist American poetry there was the now-documented, measurable obstacle blocking access to her writing.

I would guess that I first saw the initials "H. D." at the end of an anthologized poem sometime at the end of the sixties. No doubt that poem was one of the few safe and untouchable Imagist poems that editors began recirculating around that time to represent her work. We would later discover a much more complex, fecund, and demanding literary production. But for the moment, lacking any particular professor's or admired poet's passion for this mythic and (what seemed to me) very austere and impersonal voice, and swarmed as I was by every possible kind of innovative or jazzy poetic example, I was not available to H. D.'s spiritual and generative gift. I suspect that even if *Trilogy* or *Helen in Egypt* had been waved in my face at this time, I lacked sufficient conscious appetite for her alchemical and mythical vocabularies of transformation.

Eventually, in the mideighties, I had the opportunity to read *Trilogy* aloud with a small group of women poets and could finally hear H. D.'s voice, as if there were no longer any barrier. By then my inevitable share of human loss had prepared me.

In the sixties I was in love with everything that promised a fresh start and quite ready to shed a dominating mainstream "poetics of Self" that imposed its confessional hypnotic trance upon readers and young American writers. I was chafing at the confines of the typical "I"-centered, mainstream American poem that so theatrically and narcissistically positioned the writer at the hub of all pain and glory; it seemed reminiscent of pre-Renaissance science, before Galileo announced the radical news of his telescopic discovery:

Man is no longer at the center of the universe.

(H. D., of course, understood this afresh. The hierarchies forever asserting themselves were again toppled.)

Physics, action painting, field poetics, and new music—as well as fuller readings of Woolf and new encounters with Richardson, Moore, and Stein, the New York School, the Black Mountain poets, and the Objectivists—had all been registering a different dynamic involving energy fields, shifting contexts, and a self no longer credibly unitary but divided and subdivided until uncertainty called into question any writing too satisfied with its own personal suffering or too narrowly focused on cleverness and polish.

My devotion and intellectual curiosity had been claimed instead by a dozen highly inventive, nontraditional sorts of poets. I imagined, then, that I was equally open to all poetry, but, in fact, I was a young reader and writer, prone to the excitement of what I thought of as a high-modern tone and syntax, one whose surface diction and visual field promised to carry me away from what had begun to feel like the dangerous trap of lyric habit and ever closer to my own increasingly idiosyncratic compositions. I did not want to write within a language tradition too easily understood, too clearly part of an agenda rubber-stamped by most mainstream journals, but I had not yet articulated for myself the reasons for my resistance or the power relations dictating the limits of what I felt antagonistic toward.

The contemplative, as a desired place of knowledge, was beyond me; the contemporary implications and uses of myth hadn't yet hit—I mean, the understanding that myth is ahistoric, breathing in us and not merely confined to a narrative of the ancient past.

The seventies and eighties revealed a different grid, a detour meant to flaw the convenient, intact, uniform story of influence. As it turned out, H. D.'s linking of "hermetic" assignations with "secret language" and her conscious rejection of single-version narratives would become central in helping to define my own poetic process. It was not that I wanted to write *like* her but, rather, that I began hearing her urgency and experiencing in her work a kind of female enspiriting guide that I'd been lacking.

Constructing and *re*constructing this episodic moment across the space of my own blank pages, I finally understood that H. D. had used the scaffolding of locked-up myth to regenerate lopsided human stories with a new infusion of contemporary perspective. This meant the possibility—for herself and her readers—of being more fully included in the ongoing pursuit of knowledge and thus less personally stuck in the isolation of private anguish. There was, as it turned out, a place in language—even in its zero beginnings—to put one's trust.

Works Cited

[Fraser, Kathleen.] 1993. *When New Time Folds Up.* Minneapolis: Chax Press.

Friedman, Susan Stanford, and Rachel Blau DuPlessis, eds. 1990. *Signets: Reading H. D.* Madison: University of Wisconsin Press.

[II. D.] 1973. *Trilogy.* Reprint 1998, ed. Aliki Barnstone. New York: New Directions.

———. 1979. *End to Torment: A Memoir of Ezra Pound.* Ed. Norman Holmes Pearson and Michael King. New York: New Directions.

[Pound, Ezra.] 1987. *Selected Letters of Ezra Pound and Louis Zukofsky.* Ed. Barry Ahearn. New York: New Directions.

Edward Comentale (essay date September 2001)

SOURCE: Comentale, Edward. "Thesmophoria: Suffragettes, Sympathetic Magic, and H. D.'s Ritual Poetics." *Modernism/Modernity* 8, no. 3 (September 2001): 471-92.

[*In the following essay, Comentale investigates the way feminist modernist writers such as H. D. turned to classicism as an aesthetic mode that served as an alternative to the avant-garde nature of modernist writing. Comentale focuses in particular on H. D.'s appropriation of classic ritual in her poetry as a means of unifying gendered dualities.*]

INTRODUCTION

From impressionism to futurism to surrealism and beyond, the avant-garde movements of the twentieth century seem to share a rigidly oppositional logic.

These antagonistic programs are united in their efforts to construct authority against and through the rival claims of each other. For each, the attempt to establish a certain authenticity, a new perspective, a transcendent consciousness depends upon the presence of some fallen other, some decadent or marked double. Indeed, as argued by critics from Walter Benjamin to Rita Felski, it is this oppositional logic that informs the avant-garde's tendency toward violence.[1] Avant-gardism is all too easily aligned with imperialism, with discourses of racial and cultural superiority, of progress and evolutionary advance. Similarly, it often exhibits an aggressive chauvinism, a hostile and repressive attitude toward the cultural markers of the feminine. Moreover, it is precisely this oppositional logic that links the avant-garde with totalitarian politics. The aesthetic and fascist movements of the early twentieth century are united in their celebration of violent renewal, by their faith in an aesthetic transcendence of the fallen world.[2] What needs to be realized, however, is that these movements, both aesthetic and political, tend to abandon the conventional terms of tyranny—order, control, stasis—for a dialectic between stasis and change, regulation and revolt. In other words, what defines the aesthetic politics of the period is a *romantic* metaphysic in which authority exists only by way of dissent, the center by way of margins, the self in and through the other. As the romantic artist evokes a creative struggle of work and world, the nation establishes itself through "war, the world's only hygiene."[3] Importantly, as Russell Berman and Andrew Hewitt have argued, these violent dialectics move us beyond specific aesthetic and political regimes to a much more pervasive influence. The conflation of order and progress helps to affirm a specific economy. For both art and politics, only within the bourgeois struggle for significance is any significance possible—individual, national, or historical. A romantic aesthetic, as it is diffused throughout the social order, offers ontological stability to a culture driven by market relations.[4]

The British avant-garde, however, needs to be explored as part of a larger national reaction to both bourgeois liberalism and the successive invasions of romantic modernism from the continent. Artists such as T. E. Hulme, Lewis, and Ezra Pound found themselves in the peculiar position of needing to be modern after the modern had, in some ways, already occurred. The value of their work, as they saw it, was its recognition of the collusion between romanticism and reification. Modern society, they argued, may now exhibit an unprecedented state of freedom, but it has never experienced a greater standardization. Thus, throughout *Blast,* Wyndham Lewis argues that the aesthete and the average man have grown indistinguishable; chaos and conformity work together to destroy social integrity. He laments a seemingly free world given over to mechanical progress and ceaseless faddism, a world in which "there is no revolt, it is the normal state."[5] In response to this state of affairs, the British avant-garde turned to classicism. For them, classicism represented an artistic and social integrity, one that eschews bourgeois individualism and foregrounds the material tensions that define and delimit individuals, classes, and nations. The classical aesthetic, particularly in its more tragic aspects, begins with the chaotic energy of the romantic spirit, but subject and object exist in a dynamic tension that restricts the tendency of either to spin out of control. Worldly forces restrain and refine each other, producing a balanced order that is at once fluid and formal. The classical work of art expresses as it reinforces these tensions, and thus serves to halt, clarify, and redirect the violent production (and reproduction) of the world. It reveals as it challenges the material constraints of the individual and his seemingly free activity. In Hulme's famous formulation, "The classical poet never forgets this finiteness, this limit of man. He remembers always that he is mixed up with earth. He may jump, but he always returns back; he never flies away into the circumambient gas." Similarly, the classical work of art foregrounds discursive limitations, the symbolic coordinates of the individual. Again, Hulme, in his essays on political conversion, argues, "Beliefs are not only representations, they are also forces, and it is possible for one view to compel you to accept it in spite of your preference for another."[6]

I hope to show that many feminists at this time, attuned to the material and discursive structures that shape experience, turned to classicism as a viable form of aesthetic politics. For these activists, classicism functioned as a critique and alternative to the oppositional logic of the avant-garde and modernity at large. Classical art spoke to the creative tensions between the private and the public, the fallen and the pure, worldly praxis and the work of art. Specifically, though, feminists adopted and adapted the principles of classical ritual. For them, ritual explicitly united action and symbol, the body and its representation, and thus became an important tool with which to reconfigure the terms of culturally inscribed power. It was neither static nor reactionary, but served as a continuous argument, a constant construction and reconstruction of those categories that govern the social. To borrow from Jacques Rancière, this form of protest can be defined as a "process of subjectivization," in which the individual, made *subject* to others, achieves a provisional identity. According to Rancière, subjectivization is "the formation of a one that is not a self but is the relationship of a self to an other." For militants,

this process not only established their presence within the public sphere, but revealed the extent to which women participated in those processes whereby subject positions are produced and maintained. More specifically, Rancière argues that, for the disempowered, subjectivization entails an "enactment" or "demonstration" of ideal identities and positions. Insofar as this "enactment" exposes the conditional nature of authority, it confounds and subverts the traditional relations of power.[7] For the modern militant, that performance was directed at the foundational principles of the bourgeois public sphere, both its self-serving discourse of "equality" and its exclusionary construction of "universality." In the words of Janet Lyon, militant ritual, like the manifesto form, reconceived politics as "political dramaturgy" in which "the concept of universal equality is not a property available to particular groups of people, nor a coherent ideal, but rather a *logic* to be used in arguments that test the viability of the distribution of equality."[8] Ultimately, women writers and activists defined the social as a ceaselessly creative medium, one that conditions, and is conditioned by, multiple identities and relations. The individual, through ritual performance, was able to grasp and reshape the possibilities that limited her experience. According to Jane Ellen Harrison, suffragette and classicist, "Life is doomed to make for itself moulds, break them, remake them."[9] The relationship between the individual and her society is a single, conscious continuum, one in which "the soul is like a bird caught in a cage, caught and recaught ever in new births. . . ."[10]

The sections of this essay, then, explore the politics of classicism as well as the relation between feminist thinkers and modernism in general. In suffrage protest, Harrison's anthropology, and H. D.'s poetry we find a charged matrix of worldly and aesthetic praxes. Each posits human desire as the basis of expression, and thus each finds in ritual a medium at once vital and static, affective and conscious. For these activists, ritual practice both activates and defines subjects in relation to one another. It functions as part of a generative process in which a community as a whole can create and understand its condition. The following three sections, however, differ in their position along a single continuum; the essay moves from political protest to ritual performance to the written word. The first section offers protest at its most explicitly physical, the latter at its most textual. In this manner, I hope to dramatize not simply the differences between these forms of activity, but the ways in which social praxis exists as both cause and effect of all aesthetic activity. I seek to uncover the political aspects of what are often criticized as the most rarefied and escapist forms of modern literature. According to Harrison, the stages of social praxis are "life with its motor reactions, the ritual copy of life with its faded reactions, the image of the god projected by the rite, and, last, the copy of that image, the work of art."[11] For the scholar and her feminist cohorts, it was precisely this continuum that countered the oppressive logic of modernity and its avant-garde.

LIFE

"Deeds, not words!"—a fitting motto for the militant suffrage movement. From protests, pageants, and fisticuffs to sabotage, smuggling, and arson, deeds defined the movement from beginning to end. For women who had been effectively barred from public life, action was imperative and struggle a goal. Members argued that "revolt is a great and glorious thing in itself" and drew little distinction between "the joy of battle and the exultation of victory."[12] But, despite these claims, one cannot deny the spectacular, performative aspects of the campaign. Firsthand accounts reveal that punches and kicks were often only suggested or mimed. In fact, one of the very first "deeds" was nothing more than an imitation of spitting; as Christabel Pankhurst explained, "It was not a real spit but only, shall we call it, a pout, a perfectly dry purse of the mouth."[13] Often, suffragettes would tie stones to their wrists or wrap them in paper so that, when tossed, they would not cause material damage. Axes rarely fell, bricks dropped limply, and flags would poke into open windows and doors.[14] Tellingly, militants defined themselves as a "stage army" and labored under the knowledge that she "Who takes the eye takes all!"[15] According to Lisa Tickner, these forms of demonstration were understood as "a way of living the abstract relations and demands of politics."[16] Militants were well aware of the power won through representation, and therefore focused their efforts upon the symbolic. Thus, as I hope to show here, the movement ultimately attests to a mutuality of deeds *and* words, and the ability of such to transform the public sphere. Militants sought not only to exploit this mutuality, but to posit it as the basis of an alternative, intersubjective community.

Any history of the suffrage movement, however, must begin with the fact that militants consistently defined their cause in opposition to the attitudes and values of the Liberal Party. Their campaign moved well beyond the issue of the vote; its force and appeal lay in a much wider attack on a complex matrix of individualism, free trade, progress, and machinery.[17] Countless statements and speeches made by militants denounced the flat, frictionless world of Liberalism, the standardized chaos of bourgeois individualism. Moreover, they critiqued the presumed consensus of the rational public sphere, which could only obscure and uphold specifi-

cally masculine interests. Emmeline Pethick-Lawrence, for example, criticized Liberals for conceiving freedom as an "ideal only of opposition, of vested interests, of inertia, and of prejudice."[18] Dora Montefiore argued that Herbert Asquith "is against the women because they are for peace and he is on the side of the capitalist."[19] As Lyon has argued, it was precisely this critique that aligned the militant with the British avant-garde. The militant's disgust with the "sluggish respectability of the 'plain man'" clearly echoed Lewis's attack on the "abysmal inexcusable middle-class."[20] Aptly, she defines this unity as a "shared sense of deep disappointment that the promises for radical change . . . had in fact been co-opted by the modern instrumental status quo" (*M* [*Manifestoes: Provocations of the Modern*], 94).

It was in opposition to this seemingly rational order that militants developed their strategy, particularly its materialist emphasis. For Emmeline Pankhurst and her followers, history had taught that reasoned argument would only delay change and protect the status quo, while efforts to raise public sympathy proved nothing more than regressive. Thus, throughout the campaign, militants focused upon the effective power of the physical, what they called life's "hard and cruel facts."[21] In her famous address at Hartford, for example, Pankhurst describes her work as an attempt "to bring enough pressure to bear upon the government to compel them to deal with the question of woman suffrage." She argues that "it is not by making people comfortable you get things in practical life, it is by making them uncomfortable." As a whole, the movement measured effectiveness in terms of size, strength, and duration. Protests and pageants maximized pressure and discomfort upon civic surroundings. A turn to arson and vandalism sought wider and more lasting effects. As Pankhurst told her audience, "You have to make more noise than anybody else, you have to fill all the papers more than anybody else, in fact you have to be there all the time and see that they don't snow you under, if you are really going to get your reform realized."[22]

Moreover, this materialism was aligned with decisively antiproductivist and antiprogressivist attitudes. Militant activity typically slowed and retarded social machinery. Opponents dismissed most tactics as mere nuisances—scraping golf greens, painting over house numbers, home and prison blockades.[23] But larger maneuvers—refusing the census, cutting down communication lines, and a rather peculiar week of self-denial—began to reveal a pattern. These acts of insurgency replaced the passion and violence of romantic revolution within conscious strategies of obstruction. According to Pankhurst, the most effective policies worked to create "a very paralyzing situation. . . . an impossible situation."[24] Thus, upon entering the streets, militants sought to impede civic flows. One observer acknowledged that "More and more it became difficult to belittle the movement . . . which could hold up the traffic of London with processions two or three miles long, and decked from end to end with hundreds of banners, some of them of vast size. . . ."[25] Similarly, in breaking shopwindows and cutting down communication lines, militants halted the flows of the market. Their leader explained that "in this effort to rouse business men . . . we entirely prevented stock brokers in London from telegraphing stock brokers in Glasgow, and vice versa; for one whole day telegraphic and telecommunication was entirely stopped."[26] Most radically, in hunger striking, militants interfered with the activity of the female body itself. This weapon, the "weapon of self-hurt," helped not only to generate sympathy for the cause, but to bring "great pressure" upon an otherwise smoothly functioning nation.[27] As Jane Marcus explains, "When woman, quintessential nurturer, refuses to eat, she cannot nurture the nation" (*SP* [*Suffrage and the Pankhursts*], 1-2, 339). Militants thus "withheld their consent" from what was considered their most important role in a social economy defined precisely in terms of ceaseless production and consumption.[28]

Similarly, militants consistently valorized restraint. According to the leaders of the movement, "our words have always been, 'be patient, exercise self-restraint, show our so-called superiors that the criticism of women being hysterical is not true. . . .'"[29] On the one hand, this emphasis countered misconceptions about the supposedly hysterical female body. Lyon points out that a "discourse of anti-sentimentality and pure objectivity" provided access to "universalizing discourses that had been formative in the historical exclusion of women . . ." (*M*, 116). But, as important, restraint figured as a powerful antidote to a dissipated liberal community. In *The Great Scourge and How to End It*, for example, Christabel Pankhurst presents sexual restraint as a positive quality that both clarifies and increases human potential. The militant argues that the current spread of sexual disease can be directly attributed to the loose values of liberal society; sexual free trade and rampant reproduction have worked together to destroy a once healthy nation. "Men whose will-power fails them," she laments, "are constantly infecting and reinfecting the race with vile disease, and so bringing about the downfall of the nation!" In this context of bodily and national dissipation, Pankhurst outlines a metaphysics of restraint. As in the most radical modernist work, she provides an intriguing economy of energy and restriction, strength and intellect. Reversing gendered tropes, Pankhurst argues that excessive male sexuality leads only to

physical distress and irritability.[30] Incontinence figures as "a waste of vital force which impoverishes [men's] moral nature and weakens their body." She contends that passion "ought to lie dormant until legitimate occasion arises for its use, when it will be found to exist in full natural vigour" (*GS* [*The Great Scourge and How to End It*], 60-1). This dynamic system extends well beyond the body to incorporate other practices and values. Pankhurst turns to the intellect and praises the "active man who directs his energies more to his brain and muscles than to his sensual nature" (*GS*, 59). She even offers a radical aesthetic theory, one we will find echoed in the work of Harrison and H. D. She boldly concludes that "Art is creative. Sexual excess is a waste of man's creative energy" (*GS*, 127).

This very logic—in its emphasis on materiality, control, and clarity—also informs the representational strategies of militancy. Insofar as women found their efforts hampered by stereotypes and standards, they focused their attacks upon the discursive. As Cicely Hamilton notes,

> Like nearly all girls of my generation I was bred in the idea that my duty and advantage was to conform to the masculine ideal of womanhood; this or that exercise of habit was forbidden because it clashed with the ideal, and would therefore lessen our value in masculine eyes. I do not mean that this principle was a matter of bald statement; but as a tradition—spoken or half-spoken—it was a constant influence on our thoughts and a constant director of our energies.[31]

Not surprisingly, Hamilton equates her turn toward feminism with a growing suspicion of male constructed ideals and symbols, to which the female body was meant to conform. As she explains, "I became a feminist on the day I perceived that—according to the story—[a girl's] 'honour' was not a moral but a physical quality. Once that was clear to me my youthful soul rebelled . . ." (ibid.). Similarly, Emmeline Pethick-Lawrence argues that "The world as we know it today is ruled by law, by custom, and by public opinion, and women are beginning to realize that it is a man-made world in the deepest sense of the word." For her, feminism struggled against a world in which "there is nothing that expresses the woman's point of view. There is nothing that tallies with the woman's soul . . . everything is arranged on a plan different from their own, and upon a system which has taken no account of their point of view."[32] One cannot overemphasize, however, that these experiences allowed feminists to recognize and thus focus their attack upon the material aspects of language. Militants adopted an aggressive symbolism, one committed to manipulating the effective potential of the sign. They fully welcomed the spectacular, using pageants, publications, and speeches in order to control and manipulate the process of their signification. As Tickner asserts, "The raison d'être of the suffragette movement was the campaign for the vote but one of the aims that motivated its supporters . . . was the legitimizing of new representations of women. Or, more precisely, the contesting, modifying and restructuring of representations of women already in circulation or in the process of emerging" (*SW* [*The Spectacle of Women: Imagery of the Suffrage Campaign 1907-1914*], 172).

Several scholars have already explored the narratives and symbols of suffrage discourse and the manner in which they helped to shape new female identities and communities. Barbara Green, Mary Jean Corbett, and Caroline J. Howlett have each examined how even the most unique feminist experiences would inspire imitators, thereby influencing and informing other subjectivities.[33] Most suffrage statements, Green argues, "take up the performative nature of identity, revealing how feminist identities are produced through constant reiteration or performance." She adds that even "many of the seemingly less dramatic writings and speeches of suffrage also functioned in ways that constructed an oppositional identity."[34] Significantly, militant "experience" always occurred within a conscious performative loop, one in which origins and repetitions seemed to blur, lost in the infinite process of reiteration. By performing certain values or identities in public, militants inevitably called them into being. In the words of Pethick-Lawrence, "While working for the idea of political liberty, we were individually achieving liberty of a far more real and vital nature."[35] The most radical example of this reiterative process was Lady Constance Lytton's masquerade as the fictional Jane Warton. Hoping to publicize the hypocrisy of the legal system, Lytton disguised herself as a lower-class militant and was forcibly fed in prison. Her account of the affair and its aftermath suggests that even the most personal, incommunicable aspects of her experience contained performative, mimetic qualities. As she writes, "To think that I who have endured by far the least of all the 'forcibly fed' should be making people wake up more than all of them. . . . It is the other more heroic and first ones who have really done what I *seem* to have done."[36]

With Lytton's example, it becomes clear how difficult it is to separate the militants' active and representational strategies. Throughout the campaign, the militant body functioned as the site of both work and signification. While its force was inevitably expressive, its expression released implacable forces. Deeds and words combined in an aggressive struggle against the cultural inscriptions of power. "The argument of the broken pane" was perhaps the most explicit realization of this unity. In a seemingly random series of attacks on nonpartisan shops and offices, suffragettes did their best to assert female power and make Londoners very "uncomfortable." The attacks, however, also gave expression to the interconnectedness of private and public spheres, particularly as that link was informed by economics. The protest, and others of its kind, spoke from within a dynamic matrix of power. In fact, Emmeline Pankhurst's speeches described with increasing confidence her position within this larger network. As she told one audience,

> Your business man who reads important communication through the post does not want his communication to be interfered with as a regular and permanent institution. . . . Your business man, whose customers mostly are women, does not like that in the interval of buying hats, his customers may be breaking his shop windows; and your insurance companies won't like to have the drain upon their resources and their profits cut down by having to make good these insurance policies.[37]

Conversely, verbal protest tended to heighten and expose reservoirs of oppositional power. The interruption of speech evoked previously hidden hostility from the status quo. By shouting at government meetings, dinner parties, sporting events, and theater performances, suffragettes not only asserted their right to participate in a discursive order, but also heightened, and thereby gave expression to, problems that had previously been hidden within that order. Thus, Pankhurst was able to argue that one of the most effective militant acts consisted of nothing more than a question. For asking a question, just as men would have asked it, "girls were treated with violence and flung out of the meeting; and when they held a protest meeting in the street they were arrested, and were sent to prison, one for a week as a common criminal, and the other for three days."[38]

This conflation of deeds and words, power and knowledge, was most compellingly expressed in the popular slogan "You are an argument."[39] In fact, it informed the militants' conception of suffrage. Pankhurst understood the vote as both "a symbol. . . . a symbol of freedom, a symbol of citizenship, a symbol of liberty" and "an instrument, something with which you can get a great many more things. . . ."[40] Most intriguingly, this intense dualism can be detected in Pethick-Lawrence's understanding of the law. In one of her most famous speeches, she defines the law as a contingent process, a changing matrix of force and form. She claims that "In common we have felt the compulsion of this Law that has brought us into association together and has made us part of a living pattern, woven by destiny in the loom of Time, to a rhythm and rune which is making the world's story." Echoing Christabel Pankhurst, Pethick-Lawrence defines the law as the result of multiple pressures and demands. It is simultaneously revealed and transformed by the tensions that exist between various subjective positions. In fact, she argues "it is by the very enemy and the betrayer that the law is accomplished and destiny fulfilled." One cannot ignore the speaker's romantic excesses, but she consistently subsumes her mysticism within the material world. The rhythms of force and form are the rhythms of history. Power is made known only because it is contingent and immanent: it is both experienced and understood through the "material substance of things," "our own bodies."[41]

Ultimately, militancy abandoned the modern valorization of the individual for a more closely integrated community. It critiqued the myth of the universal subject and the empty abstractions of representational politics in order to explore the social as a modality of various interests and desires. The bourgeois public sphere and its seemingly rational laws, paradoxically constructed upon principles of exclusion and noninterference, were rejected in favor of what appeared to be more fluid processes of exchange and mediation. Perhaps, then, the importance of the movement exists in its awareness that modern politics are essentially *negative* in character, founded upon the belief that the "individual" must *not* be encroached upon. In response, it proposed a community that was radically positive, based upon a constructive or creative interaction between its constituents. Of course, community of this kind does not imply ideological freedom; the continuous negotiation of power denies the possibility of a stable, transcendent position from which that power can be clearly evaluated. Nevertheless, this proposed community implies a point of access from which to grasp and perhaps reconfigure specific relations. According to Pethick-Lawrence, the individual does not exist apart from the "living pattern" and only achieves "human consciousness" within that pattern.[42] It is precisely this positive sense of the limited and the contingent that defines modern classicism and its power for feminist thinkers. Jane Ellen Harrison explored this collective mode as it existed in suffrage protest as well as the more formalized realm of ancient ritual. Her work argues that power relations can be radically transfigured by the performance of public rites.

RITUAL

Perhaps in order to avoid charges of deviancy, and as a testament to their intellect and learning, suffragettes often borrowed from the art of classical antiquity. They would frequently mimic the gestures and attitudes of the Greek heroines, their pristine strength, grace, and justice. This turn to antiquity, however, also implies an awareness that militant protest—in its imagery, organization, and publicity—recalled ancient

transformative rites.[43] Participants often dressed in the robes of ministrants or supplicants, and often formalized their practical, everyday activities. Memoirs and narratives frequently reveal "saints," "martyrs," and even "an overblown Adelphi heroine."[44] Similarly, service was interpreted as a process of suffering and redemption, death and rebirth. According to Mary Gordon, the average militant was "seized and used. She was both flame and burnt offering."[45] However, it would be left to a trained scholar of antiquity to explain the modern politics of ancient ritual. Jane Ellen Harrison, self-proclaimed feminist, suffragette, and anthropologist, offers an explicit account of the feminist turn to classical practice. Her work moves away from an ideological vision of enlightened antiquity in order to celebrate the material activity of the ancient masses. It redefines the public sphere by emphasizing the desiring body and its ability to enact law. Harrison's work offers a serious challenge to the oppositional logic of the avant-garde and modernity in general, as it more fully links deed and word within a single ritualized praxis.

Harrison's *Prolegomena to the Study of Greek Religion* looks beyond the religious myths of fifth-century Greece in order to disclose the material conditions and motivations of their creators. According to her, "Some of the loveliest stories the Greeks have left us will be seen to have taken their rise, not in poetic imagination, but in primitive, often savage, and I think, always practical ritual" (P [*Prolegomena to the Study of Greek Religion*], xvii). This assertion is grounded in the conviction that every religion is essentially "conditioned by the circumstances of its worshippers" (P, 85). Myths, gods, divine names and attributes are but reflections of the mortal world, the material conditions that govern earthly life. According to her, "the gods are as many as the moods of the worshipper, i.e. as his thoughts about his gods. If he is kind, they are Kindly Ones; when he feels vengeful, they are Vengeful Ones" (P, 214). Ultimately, these ideal subjectivities owe their existence to mere mortals; for Harrison, divine power is alienated human power. In speaking of women's rites and festivals, she argues that it was the goddess "who imitated her youths and maidens," and not the reverse (P, 30).

Harrison's work, however, entails an intriguing ideological critique. She first turns to the fifth-century and its unique deities, lonesome heroes, and popular poets. These various incarnations of the divine, she argues, affirm a social order driven by individualism and commerce. The Greek of this period—with his carefully departmentalized gods, with his rituals of "tendance" or exchange—is nothing more than an "archpatriarchal bourgeois" (P, 285). His rites, his professions, and his faculties are neatly governed by "ideas of law and order and reason" (*P,* 397). More importantly, she criticizes this period for its immaterialism. Its heroism, she argues, "is for individuals"; such people "are cut clean from earth and from the local bits of earth out of which they grew" (*AAR* [*Ancient Art and Ritual*], 161). She links this immaterialism with an excessive pragmatism of language and an attendant violent aestheticism of the natural world. "Eikonism," she explains, "takes the vague, unknown, fearful thing, and tries to picture it, picture it as known, distinct, definite . . . something as far rationalized as man himself."[46] For her, *eikonism* implies a desire to control and master that which is other; it works to "comprise and confine the god within the limitations of the worshipper," affirming his power over the material world (*P,* 258).

Harrison, of course, laments the similar conditions of her own historical moment, and asks readers to look beyond the affirmative myths of the heroic age, beyond Homeric individualism and Platonic abstraction. Her work returns to an even earlier period characterized by an intense materialism, immanent deities, and sensual rites. Earlier societies are celebrated for being in "touch with the confusions of actuality" (*P,* 215). For these people, fears and joys are never abstract, but earthly, tangible; they are haunted by the "actual ghost, not a mere abstract vengeance . . ." (*P,* 217). Harrison's return to the material world suggests a return to worldly potential. She asks us to look beyond the omnipotent godhead to an originally human force, beneath Olympian abstraction to a primal, chthonic practice. Specifically, she locates an alternative model of social order and change within ritual practice, within a performative logic that unites material force and aesthetic form, bodily desire and abstraction.

Much like Pound, Yeats, and Joyce, Harrison places desire at the center of ritual practice. She claims that most, if not all, rituals are initiated through passion, the "supreme mysteries of ecstasy and love." The Eleusinian rite of sacred marriage, for example, cultivates sensuality as the precondition for the revelation of the divine. "It is indeed," Harrison writes, "only in the orgiastic religions that these splendid moments of conviction could come . . ." (*P,* 568). In *Ancient Art and Ritual,* the scholar more specifically argues that traditional ritual practice focuses on the representation of a "thing desired" (*AAR,* 25). Here, she defines ritual as a form of sympathetic magic, a conscious "mimicking of nature's processes" (*AAR,* 129). This magic, she elaborates, begins with the subject's desire for the return of certain natural events, such as the spring or the rising of crops. In remembrance of past pleasure and in anticipation of future power, the participant copies or mimics the conditions under which these might occur. In seasonal rites, for example, the "savage utters his intense desire for food." Harrison explains that "His impulse is towards food. He must eat that he and his tribe may grow and multiply. It is this that he *utters and represents* in his rites" (*AAR,* 65).

Like Christabel Pankhurst, like H. D., Harrison reveals a bias toward the creative potential of restraint. In *Ancient Art and Ritual,* she explains that the primal unity of desire and representation is founded upon an inevitable tension or restriction. She offers a psychological model that presents human constitution not as a bundle of separate faculties, but as a continuous cycle of activities. Emotion, perception, and action exist concurrently, in a ceaseless causal loop, without hierarchy or telos (*AAR,* 39-40). Harrison, however, notes that "perception is not always instantly transformed into action; there is an interval for choice between several possible actions." She argues that "Perception is pent up and becomes, helped by emotion, conscious representation." It is only out of this "momentary halt" in the cycle, this "unsatisfied desire," that "all our mental life, our images, our ideas, our consciousness, and assuredly our religion and our art, is built up" (*AAR,* 41). Thus, through restraint, Harrison connects desire with the performance or representation of its fulfillment, linking motive force with expressive form. As she explains:

> A rite is . . . a sort of stereotyped action, not wholly practical, but yet not wholly cut loose from practice, a reminiscence of an anticipation of actual practical doing; it is fitly, though not quite correctly, called by the Greeks a dromenon, "a thing done." . . . its mainspring [is] not the wish to copy nature or even improve upon her . . . but rather an impulse shared by art with ritual, the desire, that is, to utter, to give out a strongly felt emotion or desire by representing, by making or doing or enriching the object or act desired.
>
> [*AAR,* 26]

For Harrison, ritual occurs at the interface of desire and restriction, and thus it exists between the active and the symbolic, the creative and the intelligible. The ritual participant at once utters and enacts desire, proclaims and repairs the terms of his or her existence.

In some sense, for Harrison, society is always ritualized, seamlessly shifting between worldly and aesthetic praxes. It ceaselessly combines *dromenon* (things done) and *drama* (performance). She emphasizes, however, that insofar as desire is intersubjective, its ritual performance mediates intersubjective relations. For her, public ritual extends beyond the expression of bodily need in order to expose social inequality and disadvantage. In fact, for Harrison, social status exists only in its performance, in the part-practical, part-symbolic gestures of public protest. For the primitive as well as the modern, "one's ritual 'dances' are the [expression] of one's importance" (*AAR*, 31). Ritual, however, does not simply reveal, but shapes social relations; its power is transformative as well. The ritual participant does "not simply 'embody' a previously conceived idea, he begets it. From his performance springs the personification. The abstract idea arises from the only thing it possibly can arise from, the concrete act" (*AAR*, 71). Ritual, much like suffrage spectacle, serves to conceive and thus enact new modes and relations. The performance of desires arouses the spectator's desire. Power is perceived in gestures that are then mimicked by the larger population. More specifically, she contends that ritual first obstructs the spectator's habitual patterns of behavior. The rite first halts, then models and channels desire for the community as a whole. These various stages of mimicry—because conscious—are open to choice and change. At her most idealistic, Harrison argues that the process is at once active and thoughtful, infinite and infinitely negotiable.

Harrison's discussion of the "Thesmophoria" offers the clearest example of this theory and its political significance. Participants in this rite, a self-elected group of women, would gather and then lower pigs into deep clefts outside the village walls. After some time, the women themselves would descend into the clefts, retrieve the rotten flesh and "place it on certain altars, whence it was taken and mixed with seed to serve as a fertility charm" (*P*, 123). Harrison asserts that the myth of Demeter and Persephone was only later appended to this rite and thus obscures its original, sympathetic intention, the mimicking of natural cycles. But she focuses on the full name of the first deity, Demeter Thesmophoros, which is translated as "law-carrier" or "law-giver." The name of the deity, like all such names, is bound to an earlier adjectival form. Thesmophoros derives from the activity of the earlier ministrants, the original carrying and laying down of *thesmoi* or sacred objects. The goddess who represents the law took her name from the human ministrants who were "called Thesmophoroi because they carried 'the things laid down'" (*P*, 137). For Harrison, this implies that the law was laid down by the rite; it was based on an earlier "thing done," on the ritual gestures of earlier societies. She defends her argument by pointing out that most ancient rites entailed "things said" as well as "things done." Words uttered during a sacred performance correspond to specific gestures and activities (*P*, 570); they figure as an "avowal of things performed" (*P*, 156). Harrison argues that ancient law derives from these vocal components. The ritual creed developed "on its social side into the ordinance and ultimately into the regular

law" (*P*, 142). For the ancient Greek, law, ritual, and desire are inextricably linked. Power is at once symbolic and sensual.

As I mentioned above, the dynamics of ritual seem to embody what Rancière calls the "process of subjectivization." Harrison clearly echoes Rancière when she argues that "many, perhaps most of us, breathe more freely in the *medium,* literally the *midway* space, of some collective ritual" (*AAR*, 206). The strength of this theory, however, is its avoidance of the binary logic that governs bourgeois politics. As a "universal transition space," ritual confounds those dichotomies— the irrational and the rational, the marked and the fallen, the private and the public—that enforce often gendered configurations of power. Similarly, Harrison's theory offers a valuable counter to the logic of the avant-garde. By locating material tensions and restrictions at the center of representational practice, she confounds the avant-garde opposition between aesthetic and worldly praxes. While ritual permits contemplation, it denies the possibility of an autonomous, purposeless space from which the world may be addressed. In fact, we will find that the work of art, born of desire, is but "a later and more sublimated, more detached form of ritual" that yet maintains its social power (*AAR*, 225). For Harrison, as for H. D., art is always already material, purposive, and social. Its beauty is collectively determined, conditioned by "a keen emotion felt toward things and people living today . . ." (*AAR*, 237).

Finally, Harrison's theory grants contemporary women a position from which to challenge institutional configurations of power. Her work clearly celebrates an early primitive society defined by female practice. However, insofar as she defines this practice as the ritual performance of desire, she accounts for its possible return. In "Homo Sum," she argues that this return has already taken form as the contemporary struggle for suffrage. She explains that it was through her studies of antiquity that she first became receptive to the activity of the militants. The sexes have always been defined by an "artificial division of moral industry." The current struggle figures as part of a constant inscription and reinscription of the relationship between the sexes. Harrison, therefore, celebrates the suffrage movement not as an expression of essential womanhood, but as a ritualized effort to rewrite the terms of cultural power. She confirms that militant activity is based on the same unity of knowing, feeling, and acting that marked ancient ritual. The militants, she explains, have recognized that "To feel keenly is often, if not always an amazing intellectual revelation." Their work is based on an "awakening of the *desire*," which is also "the awakening of the *intention to act,* to act more efficiently and to shape the world more completely to our will."[47]

ART

For Susan Stanford Friedman, H. D.'s early work is complicated by its association with patriarchal attitudes and conservative politics, with the "totalizing mythos of the reactionary center." Imagism, in particular, comes under attack as a "critical cage from which the female poet needs 'liberation.'"[48] Consequently, Friedman praises H. D.'s turn toward nonrationalist, nonmaterialist perspectives in the mystical hermeticism of the later poems and novels. The late work is valuable as "a case in point for the gendered history of modernism, for the situation of a woman who writes out of the position of the Other."[49] Although it would be hard to deny H. D.'s romantic tendencies, I contend that her work consistently confounds the notion of otherness. If H. D.'s poetry gives voice to certain marginal experiences, it emphasizes the social tensions that define those experiences. Her verses foreground a dynamic intersubjectivity and only thus entail a certain political, if not explicitly feminist, engagement. We now turn to a third point on our continuum of deeds and words, to the most formal mode of engagement, the work of art. H. D.'s poetry reveals the effective unity of often gendered binaries, such as subject and object, public and private, work and world. Her ritualized poetry does not avoid political responsibility; rather, it raises possibilities for a community that always already incorporates the marginal, the feminine, and the poetic. As H. D. explained, "My work is creative and reconstructive, war or no war, if I can get across the Greek spirit at its highest I am helping the world, and the future."[50]

For H. D., spirit is always an immanent, effective presence. Her work celebrates powerful, irrational forces as they both inform and clarify worldly objects. Thus, while her poetry is infused with a fluid energy, its images are vibrant and crisp. Its landscapes are at once tangible and expressive, vital and intelligible. H. D.'s sea flowers, for example, are caught amidst violent drifts and tides, but it is precisely their openness to these conditions that lend them their beauty. Subject to elemental forces, their features turn "hard," "bright," and "fresh." The "marred" rose and "slashed" reed are "doubly rich" for their torment. Conversely, these precise forms, in their graceful motions and swift mutations, suggest the presence of elemental forces. The reed that is "lifted" gives shape to the wind; "pebbles drift and flung" reveal the motion of the sea.[51] In **"Sheltered Garden,"** H. D. explicitly celebrates this charged, contingent landscape. The poet first condemns the imaginative excesses of romanticism,

which figure as suffocation, solipsism, and satiety: "Beauty without strength," she declares, "chokes out life." Repulsed, the poet demands a spare, classical beauty governed by pressure, tension, and precision. The speaker turns to violent forces that "break," "snap," "scatter," and "fling," and forms that lie "torn" and "twisted." A true classicist, she seeks the beauty of a "terrible / wind-tortured place" (*CP* [*Collected Poems*], 19-22).

These aesthetics are based on processes akin to those that inform militant protest and classical ritual. H. D.'s clear, crystalline images do not exist in isolation, but are embedded, and indeed result from tensions within a dynamic field. Their existence is neither spontaneous, isolated, or permanent, but conditional, resulting from their subjection to larger forces. H. D. observed that she

> grew tired of hearing the poems referred to, as crystalline. . . . For what is crystal or any gem but the concentrated essence of the rough matrix, or the energy, either of over-intense heat or over-intense cold that projects it? The poems as a whole . . . contain that essence or that symbol, symbol of concentration and of stubborn energy.[52]

More importantly, this "energy," insofar as it informs and shapes the phenomenal world, is decisively human. The winds and tides of H. D.'s poetry suggest the power of a specifically mortal force—inspiration—which she conceives as desire itself. From early poems such as **"Pursuit," "The Cliff Temple,"** and **"Eurydice,"** to the later **"Choros Sequence"** and **"The Dancer,"** we find a passionate intensity that cuts and marks all in its path, leaving its traces on both body and world. The subject exists in a constant liminal state, between palpable forces and a formal precision. Her body is subject to contingent energy from both within and without, and thus grows powerful as well as acutely sentient. According to Eileen Gregory, the most remarkable quality of H. D.'s lyrics are their "liminality," a constant mediation of "boundaries between inner and outer, between self and other." Its central qualities are at once "deeply subjective and radically impersonal . . . they represent deep interiority infusing in outward shape or motion, making it vibrant and golden."[53]

In the 1920s, H. D. revisited her early classicism and developed a clear theory of the desiring subject. H. D.'s "Notes on Thought and Vision," argues that the subject reaches her full potential only through "definite physical relations." Sensual activity shapes identity and cultivates physical as well as intellectual "talents."[54] This unity of experience and knowledge finds its clearest expression in the image of the "over-mind":

> I should say—to continue this jelly-fish metaphor—that long feelers reached down and through the body, that

these stood in the same relation to the nervous system as the over-mind to the brain or intellect.

There is, then, a set of super-feelings. These feelings extend out and about us; as the long, floating tentacles of the jelly-fish reach out and about him. They are not different material, extraneous, as the physical arms and legs are extraneous to the gray matter of the directing brain. The super-feelers are part of the super-mind, as the jelly-fish feelers are the jelly-fish itself, elongated in fine threads.

(*NTV* [*Notes on Thought and Vision*], 19)

Albeit bizarre, H. D.'s image of the over-mind provides a consistent intersubjective model. The over-mind, subjectivity itself, exists only in mutuality, in a kinetic coupling that is at once sensuous and conscious. Moreover, for H. D., this model suggests the possibility of the subject's empowerment. "The centre of consciousness," she explains, "is either the brain or the love-region of the body" (*NTV*, 20). This conflation suggests a faculty that is at once active as well as perceptive, creative as well as conscious. To illustrate her theory, she turns to the sacred rites of Eleusis, in which "One must understand a lower wisdom before one understands a higher" (*NTV*, 31). The rites entail a three-step process that moves from "Crude animal enjoyment" to pure "over-mind consciousness." Physical lovers figure as prototypes for "spiritual lovers," the latter having the power of "concentrating and directing pictures from the world of vision" (*NTV*, 50). Like Harrison, H. D. places desire at the center of her phenomenology. Body and vision, "seed" and "word," coexist in a single, dynamic process. Thus, subjection becomes subjectivization, and a position from which to negotiate power.

As we have seen in our discussion of **"Sheltered Garden,"** H. D. associates imaginative freedom with solipsism, sensual satiety with suffocation. For this poet, true creation depends upon the constancy of desire; precision is the result of restriction or tension. Thus, her work, much like that of Pankhurst and Harrison, consistently outlines the benefits of bodily restraint. "Notes on Thought and Vision" repeatedly warns against sexual fulfillment and consummation. She pleads for chastity, claiming that the artist can "retard" his powers by "neglect of his body" (*NTV*, 52). The "love-region," she argues, must remain in a state of constant excitation, "its energy not dissipated in physical relation" (*NTV*, 22). Helen Sword's work on the visionary tradition elucidates this logic:

Eros, or desire, in fact signifies an absence so powerful that it takes on the role of a presence, so that the romantic pairings that generally characterize human sexuality—dualities, if not always necessarily of male and female, then at least of lover and beloved, self and an erotic Other—triangulate into complex constellations that include as a third party desire itself: eros as a force both motivational and mediatory.[55]

Sword here locates the expressive power of those boundaries between self and other. Eros proceeds from the absence of fulfillment, in longing, in tension and pain. The artist must struggle with and against the other, and thereby "create the desire that creates poetry" (ibid.).

Tellingly, it was H. D.'s psychic experiences in Greece that enabled her to link desire, restraint, and vision. In *Tribute to Freud,* the poet recalls how her trip was supposed to culminate with a visit to Delphi. At Itea, however, she and Bryher were told that "it was absolutely impossible for two ladies alone, at that time, to make the then dangerous trip on the winding road to Delphi. . . ."[56] H. D. dramatically depicts her feelings of restriction and longing, but she also suggests that it was precisely these intense sensations that inspired her visionary experiences. Unable to visit the oracular seat, the poet finds her desire transmuted into oracular signs. Well-versed in psychoanalytic theory, she places her projections squarely between the wish-inspired dreams of Freud's work and the mystical, otherworldly speech of the mystics. Each one can be translated, she argues, "as a suppressed desire for forbidden 'signs and wonders'" or "an extension of the artist's mind, a *picture* or an illustrated poem, taken out of the actual dream or day-dream content and projected from within . . ." (*TF* [*Tribute to Freud*], 76). Thus, for H. D., the event is both personal and impersonal; the visionary is caught between her intense passion and abstract form. One image, she claims, is "so impersonal it might have been anyone, of almost any country. And yet there was a distinctly familiar line about that head . . . dead brother? Lost friend?" (*TF*, 66). The deity that presides over this hybrid experience is none other than the winged Nike. The goddess appears upon a ladder, between two realms, the worldly and the divine. For her, the image, like those found in her early poetry, is "doubly rich" (*TF*, 83).

H. D.'s poetry repeatedly returns to this relay of desire, restraint, and creativity. Her verses are populated by "broken" lovers and distraught visionaries, whose powers exist only in a passion deferred. **"Fragment Thirty-Six,"** for example, presents the following, frustrated lament:

> I know not what to do,
> my mind is reft:
> is song's gift best?
> is love's gift loveliest?
>
> [*CP*, 165]

The speaker cannot decide whether to seek fulfillment in the arms of a lover or attenuate and thus transmute her passion into the clear words of song. Masterfully,

H. D. presents the lips as the source of both desire and language. Kissing, of course, would "slake / the rage that burns." With this act, all tension would subside as subject and object dissolve into one. The speaker, however, wonders whether she should turn away and "press lips to lips / that answer not . . . ?" The verse aptly conveys the nervous transmutation of passion into speech. In the absence of fulfillment or response, in its willed deferral, kissing becomes song. Moreover, the lips offer a precise image of that creative doubling or enfolding that defines all experience. Difference and unity, engagement and detachment—it is this "brokenness" that produces song:

> so my mind hesitates
> above the passion
> quivering yet to break,
> so my mind hesitates
> above my mind,
> listening to song's delight.

> [*CP,* 167]

With this verse, it becomes apparent that the song is already being sung. The poem itself is an expression not of a decision made, but of an attenuated state. Both sensual and sentient, aroused and detached, the speaker writes herself within the dynamics of desire. Restraint produces language, as language heightens and prolongs passion.

Not surprisingly, a similar dynamic informs the social potential of classical art. Put bluntly, modernists understood the power of classicism as its ability to occasion pain. The classical work of art both offers and denies its beauty and thus arouses passions that remain torturously unfulfilled. In other words, aesthetic distance prohibits the potential sublimation of kinetic desire. Consequently, the energy that would be lost in the work is diverted back toward the world at large. Harrison, for example, argues that while the beautiful image can "discredit the actual practical world," it never insists on its own "actuality and objectivity" (*AAR,* 227). For her, art "invigorates life, but only does it by withdrawal from these very same elementary forms of life, by inhibiting certain sensuous reactions" (*AAR,* 236). Thus, "imagination, cut off from practical reaction as it is, becomes in turn a motor-force causing new emotions, and so pervading general life, and thus ultimately becoming 'practical'" (*AAR,* 210). For H. D., also, the sterile, ascetic aspects of the work refuse immersion and enforce a return to worldly praxis. In "Notes on Thought and Vision," the poet argues that aesthetic beauty is similar to that of the "loved one," but its inaccessibility leaves the mind "enflamed and excited." While the work of art may excite the "love-region," energy is not "dissipated in physical relation" and thus "takes on its character of

mind . . ." (*NTV,* 22). More aggressively, in a 1916 review, H. D. praises poetry that "holds, fascinates and half-paralyses us, as light flashed from a very fine steel blade, wielded playfully, ironically . . . with absolute surety and with absolute disdain." As the poet explains, this hostile beauty does not simply negate, but actively confronts a "world of shrapnel and machine-guns," wages "battle against squalor and commercialism."[57] Ultimately, like other forms of protest, her poetry halts, foregrounds, and suggests alternatives to the everyday. It both arouses and impedes desire, and thereby permits consciousness, various models of behavior, and the possibility of choice. Adalaide Morris, in a stunning article on H. D.'s ***Trilogy,*** explicitly aligns this aspect of H. D.'s work with ritual practice. She argues that H. D.'s poetry "not only *means* but *does*"; "it labors to create a formal break with everyday life, a ritual space that invites the reader to return to, reexamine, and rearrange the *ethos* of a community in crisis."[58] Similarly, Gregory contends that H. D.'s lyrics "demand from the reader a distinct dramatic form of attention and participation." By short-circuiting fulfillment, by refusing to dissolve into abstraction, they turn the poetic experience "inward, so that the reader is forced *through* the singular experience of the poem." Ultimately, the mediated space of the poem becomes a space of collective mediation. It signifies as it inspires "threshold states" in which "the tribe as a whole renews itself."[59]

H. D.'s various statements on the Eleusinian rites offer the most striking account of this painful beauty and its effective power. In "Notes on Thought and Vision," the poet argues that while the "Eleusinian mysteries had to do with sex," sensuality was countered by "a certain amount of detachment . . . a certain amount of artistic appreciation"(*NTV,* 29-31). Similarly, in "Helios and Athene," she claims that the participant neither surrendered to desire nor achieved detachment, but experienced a love that is "the merging and welding of both, the conquering in herself of each element, so that the two merge in the softness and tenderness of the mother and the creative power and passion of the male" (*CP,* 330). In the poem **"At Eleusis,"** however, H. D. does not simply describe, but enacts this rite and its divine pain:

> *What they did,*
> *they did for Dionysos,*
> *for ecstasy's sake:*
>
> now take the basket,
> think;
> think of the moment you count
> most foul in your life;
> conjure it,
> supplicate,
> pray to it;

your face is bleak, you retract,
you dare not remember it:

stop;
it is too late.
The next stands by the altar step,
a child's face yet not innocent,
it will prove adequate, but you,
I could have spelt your peril at the gate,
yet for your mind's sake,
though you could not enter,
wait.

What they did,
they did for Dionysos,
for ecstasy's sake:

Now take the basket—
(ah face in a dream,
did I not know your heart,
I would falter,
for each that fares onward
is my child;
ah can you wonder
that my hands shake,
that my knees tremble,
I a mortal, set in the goddess' place?)

[*CP,* 179-80]

The italicized refrain clearly suggests a worldly enactment of the divine. An anonymous, ecstatic "they" perform the power of the god. Through their activity, they do not merely conjure, but become that which they desire. Thus, with the poem's contrasting registers, H. D. presents a rich doubling of deed and word, power and thought. Her verses alternate between the abject and the divine, between passionate engagement and formal gesture. The poet, however, is not content with description or even suggestion, for she demands the reader's complicity and thereby enacts the intersubjective nature of this rite. The speaker engages us directly, calls forth an erotic potential thus far obscured. However, the speaker demands our understanding as well. Thus, the differing registers inspire and impede our desire, encourage and deny the possibility of fulfillment. This call for restraint is most dramatically seen in the transition between the second and third verse, when the speaker shouts "Stop." With this "sudden halt," the moment of unity is forestalled, and thus power and power relations are made conscious. The priestess bars entry, and commands us to "wait," presumably in order to achieve understanding, for "mind's sake." Ultimately, we turn away, but now enflamed by a conscious desire, by a renewed potential that still seeks outlet. Passion is heightened, but now mediated and made thoughtful. Consummation is yet possible, but informed by consciousness. The painful feeling of restriction transforms dream into knowledge. As mortals, we wield the power of the divine.

Classical modernism, particularly as it finds expression in ritual practice, complicates those categories with which we tend to organize modernist literature: commitment and reaction, abstraction and objectivity, masculine and feminine style. Not surprisingly, classical modernism also complicates the distinctions that inform the logic of modernity at large. First and foremost, it defines the individual as inseparable from the material and discursive forces that shape experience. Ritual performance consistently foregrounds the tensions that exist between the desiring subject and its objective surroundings. Related to this, classical modernism blurs the boundary between expressiveness and the physical body, between the symbolic and the kinetic. In protest as in poetry, image and desire are eternally yoked, together urging the forces of history. Finally, and perhaps most importantly, classical modernism confounds the relationship between modernism and its legacy, namely, the politics of postmodernity. Oddly, while classicism, particularly in its approach to gender, anticipates postmodern strategies and attitudes, its most vocal advocates—Lewis, Hulme, and H. D.—have either been dismissed as reactionaries or dropped out of discussion altogether. Conversely, those modernists who were most often criticized as romantic—Woolf, Stein, and Joyce—meet today with almost universal approval. This complex genealogy raises valuable questions not only about literary history, but about political and economic history as well. The debate between classicism and romanticism masked a much larger battle over the terms of postwar society. It is time to revisit that debate and its consequences.

Notes

1. Walter Benjamin, "The Work of Art in the Age of Mechanical Reproduction," ed. Hannah Arendt, trans. Harry Zohn, in *Illuminations* (New York: Schocken Books, 1968) and "Theories of German Fascism: On the Collection *War and Warrior,*" ed. Ernst Jünger, trans. Jerolf Wikoff, *New German Critique* 17 (spring 1979): 120-128; See also Rita Felski, *The Gender of Modernity* (Cambridge, Mass.: Harvard University Press, 1995), chs. 1, 6.

2. Most recently, this connection can be found in Modris Eksteins, *Rites of Spring: The Great War and The Birth of The Modern Age* (New York: Anchor Books, 1989).

3. F. T. Marinetti, *Let's Murder the Moonshine: Selected Writings,* ed. R. W. Flint, trans. R. W. Flint and Arthur A. Coppotelli (Los Angeles: Sun and Moon Classics, 1991), 50.

4. See Russell A. Berman, *Modern Culture and Critical Theory: Art, Politics, and the Legacy of the Frankfurt School* (Madison: University of Wiscon-

sin Press, 1989), 46, 48; Andrew Hewitt, "Fascist Modernism, Futurism, and Post-modernity," in *Fascism, Aesthetics, and Culture,* ed. Richard J. Golsan (Hanover: University Press of New England, 1992), 44, 54. See also, Renato Poggioli, *The Theory of the Avant-Garde,* trans. Gerald Fitzgerald (Cambridge, Mass.: Harvard University Press, 1968); Peter Bürger, *Theory of the Avant-Garde,* trans. Michael Shaw (Minneapolis: University of Minnesota Press, 1984).

5. Wyndham Lewis et al., *Blast 1* (Santa Rosa: Black Sparrow Press, 1992), 42.

6. *The Collected Writings of T. E. Hulme,* ed. Karen Csengeri (New York: Oxford University Press, 1994), 62, 136.

7. Jacques Rancière, "Politics, Identification, Subjectivization," *October* 61 (summer 1992): 60-2.

8. Janet Lyon, *Manifestoes: Provocations of the Modern* (Ithaca, N.Y.: Cornell University Press, 1999), 36; hereafter abbreviated as *M.* My understanding of modern ritual finds its historical foundation in the work of David Cannadine, "The Context, Performance and Meaning of Ritual: The British Monarchy and the 'Invention of Tradition', c. 1820-1977," in *The Invention of Tradition,* ed. Eric Hobsbawm and Terence Ranger (New York: Cambridge University Press, 1983) and Richard Sennett, *Flesh and Stone: The Body and the City in Western Civilization* (New York: W. W. Norton and Company, 1994).

9. Jane Ellen Harrison, "Alpha and Omega," in *Alpha and Omega* (London: Sedgwick and Jackson, 1915), 218.

10. Jane Ellen Harrison, *Prolegomena to the Study of Greek Religion* (Princeton, N.J.: Princeton University Press, 1990), 570-1; hereafter abbreviated as *P.*

11. Jane Ellen Harrison, *Ancient Art and Ritual* (1913; Montana: Kessinger Publishing Company, n.d.), 191-2; hereafter abbreviated as *AAR.*

12. Christabel Pankhurst, "Speech Delivered by Christabel Pankhurst. Queen's Hall, December 22, 1908," in *Speeches and Trials of the Militant Suffragettes,* ed. Cheryl R. Jorgensen-Earp (London: Associated University Press, 1999), 90-1; hereafter abbreviated as *ST*; Emmeline Pankhurst, "Why We Are Militant: A Speech Delivered in New York October 21st, 1913," in *Suffrage and the Pankhursts,* ed. Jane Marcus (London: Routledge and Kegan Paul, 1987), 162; hereafter abbreviated as *SP.*

13. Christabel Pankhurst, *Unshackled: The Story of How We Won the Vote* (London: Hutchinson and Company, 1987), 52.

14. See Commentary (*ST,* 101, 104); Brian Harrison, *Peaceable Kingdom: Stability and Change in Modern Britain* (Oxford: Clarendon Press, 1982), 51; Antonia Raeburn, *The Militant Suffragettes* (London: Michael Joseph Limited, 1973), 121, 135-6; Sandra Stanley Holton, "In Sorrowful Wrath: Suffrage Militancy and the Romantic Feminism of Emmeline Pankhurst," in *British Feminism in the Twentieth-Century,* ed. Harold L. Smith (Amherst: University of Massachusetts Press, 1990), 21.

15. Christabel Pankhurst, "The Commons Debate on Woman Suffrage" (*SP,* 31). Mary Lowndes, "Banners and Banner-Making," in Lisa Tickner, *The Spectacle of Women: Imagery of the Suffrage Campaign 1907-1914* (Chicago: University of Chicago Press, 1988), 263; hereafter abbreviated as *SW.*

16. Ibid., 287.

17. George Dangerfield persuasively argues that the Women's Social and Political Union (W.S.P.U.) helped to initiate a larger social revolt against Liberalism that eventually transformed the face of British politics. George Dangerfield, *The Strange Death of Liberal England 1910-1914* (New York: Capricorn Books, 1935), 139-213.

18. Emmeline Pethick-Lawrence, "Speech at Albert Hall, November 16, 1911" (*ST,* 142).

19. Quoted in Raeburn, *Militant Suffragettes,* 19.

20. Elaine Kidd, *Materialism and the Militants* (Hampstead: Macdonald, n.d.), 1; Lewis et al., *Blast,* 18.

21. Sylvia Pankhurst, "Minimum Wage for Women" (*SP,* 264).

22. Emmeline Pankhurst, "Address at Hartford" (*ST,* 332-3).

23. See Commentary (*ST,* 272).

24. Emmeline Pankhurst, "The Women's Insurrection" (*ST,* 290).

25. Quoted in *SW,* 58.

26. Emmeline Pankhurst, "Hartford" (*ST,* 336).

27. Constance Lytton, "A Speech by Lady Constance Lytton" (*ST,* 109).

28. As Lyon explains, hunger striking served to challenge the "'natural market' ideology of free trade economics" and to expose "the joints between economic coercion and sexual subjection" (*M,* 116). It should also be noted that the Liberal government responded in every possible way to restrict women to their former activity. The most

violent of these efforts, force-feeding, expresses clearly the extent to which this patriarchal order was dependent upon the constant activity of production and consumption.

29. Quoted in F. W. Pethick-Lawrence, "The Trial of the Suffragette Leaders" (*SP,* 77).

30. Christabel Pankhurst, *The Great Scourge and How to End It* (London: E. Pankhurst, 1913), 12, x-xi; hereafter abbreviated as *GS.*

31. Cicely Hamilton, *Life Errant* (London: J. M. Dent and Sons Limited, 1935), 282.

32. Emmeline Pethick-Lawrence, *The Meaning of the Women's Movement* (London: Woman's Press, n.d.), 4-5.

33. Barbara Green, *Spectacular Confessions: Autobiography, Performative Activism, and the Sites of Suffrage 1905-1938* (New York: St. Martin's Press, 1997); Mary Jean Corbett, *Representing Femininity: Middle-Class Subjectivity in Victorian and Edwardian Women's Autobiographies* (New York: Oxford University Press, 1992); and Caroline J. Howlett, "Writing on the Body? Representation and Resistance in British Suffrage Accounts of Forcible Feeding," in *Bodies of Writing, Bodies in Performance,* ed. Thomas Foster, Carol Siegel, and Ellen E. Berry (New York: New York University Press, 1996).

34. Green, *Spectacular Confessions,* 7, 16.

35. Emmeline Pethick-Lawrence, *My Part in a Changing World* (London: Victor Gollancz, 1938), 215.

36. Quoted in Howlett, "Writing on the Body," 41.

37. Emmeline Pankhurst, "Women's Insurrection" (*ST,* 290).

38. Emmeline Pankhurst et al., "Closing Days of the Trial" (*ST,* 238).

39. Quoted in *SW,* 102.

40. Emmeline Pankhurst, "Emmeline Pankhurst's Speech in the Portman Rooms, London. March 24, 1908" (*ST,* 31).

41. Emmeline Pethick-Lawrence, "The Rune of Birth and Renewal" (*ST,* 283, 285).

42. Ibid., 284.

43. See Commentary in Raeburn, *Militant Suffragettes,* 77.

44. Elizabeth Robins, *The Convert* (1907; Old Westbury: The Women's Press, 1980), 87; May Sinclair, *The Tree of Heaven* (New York: The Mac-Millan Company, 1917), 229.

45. *Letters of Constance Lytton,* ed. Betty Balfour (London: William Heinemann Limited, 1925), 129.

46. Harrison, "Alpha and Omega," in *Alpha,* 202.

47. Harrison, "Homo Sum," in *Alpha and Omega,* 81.

48. Susan Stanford Friedman, *Psyche Reborn: The Emergence of H. D.* (Bloomington: Indiana University Press, 1981), 17, xi.

49. Susan Stanford Friedman, *Penelope's Web: Gender, Modernity, H. D.'s Fiction* (New York: Cambridge University Press, 1990), 19.

50. Quoted in Barbara Guest, *Herself Defined: The Poet H. D. and Her World* (New York: Doubleday and Company, 1984), 218.

51. H. D., *Collected Poems 1912-1944,* ed. Louis L. Martz (New York: New Directions Publishing Corporation, 1983), 5, 14, 25-6, 21; hereafter abbreviated as *CP.*

52. H. D., "H. D. by Delia Alton," *Iowa Review* 16, no. 3 (1986): 184.

53. Eileen Gregory, "Rose Cut in Rock: Sappho and H. D.'s *Sea Garden,*" in *Signets: Reading H. D.,* ed. Susan Stanford Friedman and Rachel Blau DuPlessis (Madison: University of Wisconsin Press, 1990), 133.

54. H. D., *Notes on Thought and Vision and The Wise Sappho* (San Francisco: City Lights Books, 1982), 17; hereafter abbreviated as *NTV.*

55. Helen Sword, *Engendering Inspiration: Visionary Strategies in Rilke, Lawrence, and H. D.* (Ann Arbor: University of Michigan Press, 1995), 131, 133, 138.

56. H. D., *Tribute to Freud* (New York: Pantheon Books, 1956), 73; hereafter abbreviated as *TF.*

57. H. D., "Marianne Moore," *The Egoist* 3 (1916): 118.

58. Adalaide Morris, "Signaling: Feminism, Politics, and Mysticism in H. D.'s War *Trilogy,*" *Sagetrieb* 9, no. 3 (1990): 121-2.

59. This study is greatly indebted to Eileen Gregory's work on H. D. and Hellenism, particularly as such suggests a direct connection between H. D.'s poetry and Harrison scholarship, see especially *H. D. and Hellenism: Classic Lines* (New York: Cambridge University Press, 1997), 123-5.

Lesley Wheeler (essay date winter 2003)

SOURCE: Wheeler, Lesley. "Both Flower and Flower Gatherer: Medbh McGuckian's *The Flower Master* and

H. D.'s *Sea Garden.*" *Twentieth-Century Literature* 49, no. 4 (winter 2003): 494-519.

[*In the following essay, Wheeler compares the themes and imagery used by McGuckian with those of H. D., focusing in particular on the relationship between motherhood and poetic creation in the works of the two poets.*]

The relationship between maternity and other kinds of work remains a difficult subject for twenty-first century feminism.[1] Women writers, concerned with the particular difficulties of creating literature while bearing and raising children, have contributed significantly to this conversation. In the twentieth century, most American women writers emphasize the desperate competition between writing and motherhood for time, resources, and creative energy. For example, Tillie Olsen in *Silences*, Adrienne Rich in "When We Dead Awaken" and *Of Woman Born*, and most of the women writers interviewed in Judith Pierce Rosenberg's *A Question of Balance* characterize motherhood as a condition of interruption. Its most debilitating result for these artists is the fragmentation of the caretaker's attention. These women stress the intense love and responsibility they feel toward the interrupters, but although these feelings increase motherhood's rewards, they also make it harder to give priority to any other kind of work. The recent notoriety of Sylvia Ann Hewlett's *Creating a Life*, which decries pressures that make women choose between motherhood and "high-altitude" careers (6), shows the persistence (and, I think, the persistent validity) of this view, although Hewlett focuses on corporate rather than artistic work.

However, in the last two decades of the twentieth century, some women begin to pair these acknowledgments of motherhood's costs with theories about its "advantages" for writers (Ostriker 130).[2] In a 1983 book, Alicia Ostriker stresses maternity as a rich resource for women writers, a great subject that has been virtually unmined. Ursula K. Le Guin likewise emphasizes in 1989 that while "babies eat books" (230), active parenthood crucially reminds writers that "the supreme value of art depends on other equally supreme values." Rita Dove, like many successful contemporary women, describes trading childcare shifts with an involved partner to manage the time pressures of parenthood; however, she also notes the way children render one "a hostage to reality" (qtd. in Rosenberg 102), newly open and vulnerable to a larger world in ways that can benefit an introverted writer. In a 1998 interview, Lucille Clifton describes how traditional maternity does not prevent writing poetry so much as mandate a different kind of artistic process (81).

Like these American women writers, and perhaps to an even greater degree, contemporary Irish women poets emphasize cross-pollination rather than competition between the labors of raising children and composing poems. The literature itself provides evidence. Nuala Ní Dhomhnaill's work, for instance, strongly emphasizes women's sexual and maternal bodies, and poems such as her "First Communion" intertwine parental worry with religious critique, demonstrating the interdependence of personal and intellectual life. Essays and interviews also exemplify these attitudes. Notably, Eavan Boland structures *Object Lessons: The Life of the Woman and the Poet in Our Time* around her own quest to harmonize the roles identified in her subtitle. Admitting that a mother-poet has "no time to waste" (253), Boland provocatively asserts that material obstacles to a woman's literary production are far less significant than psychosexual ones, particularly the inherited idea that specifically female experiences don't belong in poetry (247). Boland, lyrically describing the suburban landscapes that inspired her to write through children's naps, celebrates the "subversive poetic perception" (244) that maternity can inspire, tellingly equating motherhood with womanhood throughout her book. Medbh McGuckian's many interviews touching on these subjects describe maternity less romantically than Boland does—in particular, she casts childbirth as a cataclysmic "annihilation of the self" ("Interview," ed. Sailer 114)—but still emphasize family life as a top priority and the profoundly influential context of her literary work. She observes to Kathleen McCracken that "most Irish women poets have a highly developed maternal dimension, and many write even while their babies are young" (165).[3] Portraying womanhood somewhat differently than do their American predecessors, these poets emphasize childrearing as a crucial background and inspiration for their writing.

This essay compares two poetic collections, one by a contemporary woman from the North of Ireland and one by an Anglo-American modernist, to show their contrasting approaches to womanhood and lyric poetry. Medbh McGuckian and H. D. both link poetic experiment to each author's first experience with maternity: their work metaphorically joins procreation with poetic innovation. However, for H. D., whose first pregnancy ended in stillbirth, successful poetry and motherhood require confrontation with a bracingly harsh world. For McGuckian, a conservative understanding of maternity blossoms into a radically experimental poetics. She investigates subversive possibilities within confined gardens and traditionally feminine spaces.

Significantly, these parallel volumes share a governing metaphor of flowers. As the reproductive structure of many plants as well as an emblem of poetic and feminine beauty, the flower has provided a powerful idiom for female lyricists negotiating a double role as both aesthetic objects and creators of beauty. As McGuckian phrases this doubleness in a letter, women writers may simultaneously identify with "both flower and flower-gatherer" (11 Feb. 2001), figuring their experience in the development of blossoms and their artistic labor as cultivation or arrangement. Further, these metaphors invite engagement with many issues of pressing concern to women artists, including sexuality, reproduction, and the complex relations between the natural and the artificial, wildness and domestication.[4]

No women poets, however, grant more prominence to the motif than do McGuckian and H. D. in their first full-length collections, *The Flower Master* (published in 1982, revised significantly in 1993) and *Sea Garden* (1916). Both volumes express their concerns with literary and sexual fertility primarily through flower imagery: each describes a garden whose particular beauties define the poet's aesthetic project, and each manipulates flower imagery to comment on the meanings of femininity. *Sea Garden* divorces womanhood from its conventional association with domesticity, implying that only windswept wildness can nourish women, children, and poems. *The Flower Master* inverts this gesture, stressing cultivated gardens and celebrating the productive confinements of bearing and raising children. Although McGuckian's literary garden seems to invoke and challenge H. D.'s, the Irish poet denies direct influence. She claims only limited knowledge of H. D. and Marianne Moore, another modernist poet: "Although I had heard of them I had no idea (consciously) of their work—in fact, I have not yet read *Sea Garden* and must go to the library to seek it, I have only read those women in anthologies of *Imagism* etc." (Letter 11 Feb. 2001).[5] Instead, the two books speak from opposing advantages to the same intense debate: what's the relationship of womanhood generally, and reproduction in particular, to literary work?

I begin this essay by considering the publication history of each volume. Each story intertwines with the author's first pregnancy, just as the early careers of women in other professions tend to overlap with their childbearing years. McGuckian's first volume exists in two significantly different editions; I compare them and explain my preference for the second version. H. D. did not subject *Sea Garden* to heavy revision, but I study how the original volume's physical qualities reveal the author's aesthetic priorities. Subsequently, I analyze the convergences and distinctions between H. D. and McGuckian through a focus on two pairs of poems: "Gladiolus" and **"Sea Iris,"** and "The Flower Master" and **"Sheltered Garden."** Finally, I discuss

the common sources of these collections and their larger implications as far as gender roles are concerned.

While gaps remain in H. D. studies, especially considering the huge critical industries surrounding some of her male contemporaries, H. D.'s poetry has received much more extensive treatment than McGuckian's. This essay, therefore, grants more acreage to the politics of McGuckian's garden. I also devote substantial attention to McGuckian's prose writings and interviews, some of them scattered through publications with limited circulation in the United States. In these interviews and at readings, she discusses her process and intentions with exceptional candor and provides important contexts for the poems. However, this essay also focuses on a specific maternal urgency in *Sea Garden* that the poems encode as spiritual and creative frustration. Both artistic growth and motherhood, according to H. D., require an inspiring blast of sea wind—or resuscitation of the stillborn daughter who never breathed.

FROM FLOWER TO MASTER

As is the case for many contemporary poets, pamphlets and contest recognition preceded McGuckian's first book contract, in 1982, with Oxford for *The Flower Master*.[6] *Venus and the Rain* (1984) and *On Ballycastle Beach* (1988) also appeared with Oxford, but with *Marconi's Cottage* (1991) she switched to the Gallery Press of Ireland. *The Flower Master and Other Poems*, a heavily revised new edition, appeared from Gallery in 1993.

In the *TLS* review of the 1993 edition, Steven Matthews praises the new version as "a much tighter, more concentrated book," more closely focused on floral imagery. Matthews notes that 12 poems were dropped, others repositioned, and 17 poems added, an expansion that "sharpens the book's range of tones and adds a welcome note of skepticism towards its presiding theme," rendering the book more "alert to the dangers of self-regard in any mastery of image and form." Clair Wills, too, finds the revised edition "chart[ing] even more clearly the development" from adolescence to mature womanhood ("Medbh McGuckian" 281). However, much scholarly commentary on *The Flower Master* predates the revisions, and in subsequent pieces McGuckian's critics do not sufficiently distinguish the versions or acknowledge the radical nature of the changes. McGuckian, after all, cut more than a quarter of the first volume, renamed one poem and amended its last line, shifted three short pieces into sequences, and added substantial new material. She also reorganized the lyrics, altered the dedication, and replaced the cover illustration.

Both incarnations of *The Flower Master* begin with poems of adolescence, but by deleting some poems, importing new ones, and rearranging others, McGuckian emphasizes the seasonal and floral motifs, accents the mixture of sexuality and violence that pervades the volume, and peoples the sequence more vividly with a range of female characters. For example, "Faith," "Spring," "The 'Singer,'" "Aunts," and "My Mother," all new poems appearing in the first dozen pages of the Gallery edition, present sisters, aunts, mothers, and grandmothers, joining women-centered poems already included in the first collection, such as "Slips" and "To My Grandmother." In interviews, McGuckian often describes this book's structural focus on marriage, pregnancy, and childbirth; the revisions also clarify this narrative, especially in "Lucina." This sequence begins with seeds, progresses through a "fattening moon" and "pica" (the mineral cravings of some pregnant women), and later evokes cervical dilation and birth. "The Moon Pond," which appeared in the 1982 book, assumes a new position at the end of "Lucina," making clearer sense of its "milk-fevered lady" and the bold birds ready to mate again.

Design changes mark not only the radical nature of the revisions but the poet's shifting view of her own project. The 1932 Georgia O'Keeffe painting "The White Trumpet Flower" on the cover of the 1982 edition suggests sympathies with female modernism; it also embodies McGuckian's lyrics closeup and without context, iconically feminine and verging on abstraction. For the 1993 version, the colors shift from vernal white and green to an earthy gold and brown. A bleached-out black-and-white photograph on the new cover shows a middle-aged woman kneeling to tend, or perhaps pick, flowers growing along the wall of a house. The door stands open and the woman glances up at the camera, caught at work, not posing. McGuckian here gives us not only the bloom but the gardener; further, a path beside her and a stone house in the background emphasize the gardener's connections to a larger world. The canonical familiarity of O'Keeffe's flowers stresses mastery and the ascendance of aesthetics over context; the snapshot of McGuckian's maternal grandmother[7] suggests an arrangement shaped by a particular time and place, and it accents McGuckian's artistic commitments to process and accident. Even as McGuckian seems to perfect her earlier vision, she highlights the contingent nature of her effort and the status of women both as aesthetic objects and as creators.

Two other changes affect my argument. By paring away "The Butterfly Farm" and "The Katydid," McGuckian obscures the Asian allusions in other pieces, such as "The Flower Master"—an issue I treat more fully below. Finally, the new dedication supports readings offered by Wills and Susan Porter that this volume negotiates the poet's place among female precursors. McGuckian offers *The Flower Master* (1982) to John and Liam, her husband and son. She dedicates *The Flower Master and Other Poems* (1993), however, "for my mother / without my father." The Gallery edition shows McGuckian considering womanhood as a subject with increasing deliberateness.

IN LEAF

While contemporary readers know **Sea Garden** primarily through the New Directions **Collected Poems** edited by Louis L. Martz, the volume's early presentations are revealing. Constable & Co. in London published **Sea Garden** in 1916 in a slim, well-designed volume. The American edition, published by Houghton Mifflin in 1917, imitates many of these design qualities on lower-quality stock.[8] Both editions evoke the modernist publication strategies described by Jerome McGann and Lawrence Rainey: beautiful books in limited editions suggest an elevated art self-consciously positioned against mass culture, aimed at collectors and connoisseurs. The handsomeness and rarity of such books present a metonym for the anticommercial fineness of the writing within and thereby paradoxically indicate modernist shrewdness about marketing.[9]

McGuckian has made drastic revisions to her early work and may do so again; H. D.'s revisions occurred mainly at earlier stages. Nevertheless, biographers and scholars have been surprisingly quiet about the process of H. D.'s first book-length publication. Constable & Co. was Amy Lowell's London publisher, and H. D. published **Sea Garden** at Lowell's urging (Hanscombe and Smyers 204). (H. D.'s poetry had also appeared in three anthologies published by Constable, all titled *Some Imagist Poets*; the first one appeared in 1915). H. D.'s connection with Lowell may indicate resistance to Ezra Pound's program for imagism. However, the institutions that would transmit modernism to its audience were only beginning to form. Although Pound struggled to "gather under one roof the principal authors and works of modernism" (Rainey 82), and in fact the Egoist Press eventually produced important works by Pound, Joyce, Aldington, Eliot, and others, it didn't begin publishing books until 1916, the same year **Sea Garden** appeared. The Constable & Co. of the modernist era, on the other hand, published a distinguished but not adventurous literary list, most notably including Bernard Shaw (Mumby and Norrie 279, 345-46).[10]

Although the publication history and spare presentation of H. D.'s first book have received little attention, excellent scholarship on **Sea Garden** illuminates its content and strategies, including its floral profusion. In fact, imagist poetry generally draws heavily from a botanical vocabulary. For instance, in the first imagist anthology, Pound's *Des Imagistes* (1914), of the 35 poems plus three verse satires at the end of the volume (separately subtitled "Documents"), 28 pieces contain references to flowers, plants, and gardens; 16 of the poems specifically mention flowers. Aldington's opening poem of 76 lines, "Choricos," provides a good example, invoking wreaths, leaves, flowers, gardens, hyacinths, and poppies. Related references in the same poem include a floral palette of white, green, red, and purple; allusions to Demeter's daughter, here called both Proserpine and Persephone, whose flower-gathering expedition ended in Hades; and qualities associated with flowers, including frailty, love, sweetness, beauty, and fragrance. Flowers constitute a crucial idiom for imagism partly because floral imagery represents an important resource for the classical and Asian traditions the imagists drew on (indeed, references to Greek antiquity populate the poems of *Des Imagistes* as heavily as floral allusions do, and the selections by Pound include translations from Asian sources). As Diana Collecott observes, Sappho's flowers are a key intertext for all that blooms in *Sea Garden* (211-20).

H. D. uses flower imagery throughout her whole career to a wide range of purposes: it alludes to crucial sources, encodes sexual and reproductive experience, and invokes a range of traditional meanings including beauty, poetry, love, and the fragility of human life. Her very titles testify to the persistence of the motif: her poetry collections include *Red Roses for Bronze* (1931) and *The Flowering of the Rod* (1946); the novels *Asphodel* and *White Rose and the Red* were unpublished in her lifetime. Not surprisingly, flower references also pervade her correspondence. Richard Aldington's letters persistently identify H. D. with their beauty: he wrote in 1918, for example, that "any flower makes me think of you" (60), and even more tellingly advised her against masturbation by warning a month later, "Don't talk to your flower too often—it is a strain on the nerves" (126). Such passages cast H. D. as both flower and flower gatherer, echoing the connection *Sea Garden* draws between modern poetry and sexual freedom.[11]

IRIDACEAE

McGuckian exercises her poetic freedom through a difficult style predicated on female experience and experiment. She responds to allegations of obscurity in her work by protesting to Kimberly S. Bohman, "It seems to me totally coherent" ("Surfacing" 105) and to McCracken, "They [the poems] are no more mysterious than a woman can help being to herself" (Interview 161). She generally insists, as in her interview with Sailer, that her work is "almost totally

autobiographic" (113). "Autobiographic," however, does not indicate confessional transparency for McGuckian: the personal experiences from which the poems spring emerge faintly or not at all. Peter Sirr rightly characterizes her poetry as "poetry of occasion whose occasions are meticulously withheld" (464). Such withholding encourages many readers to speculate about her allusions to published texts and affinities with literary precursors. Thomas Docherty, for instance, cites Baudelaire's *Flowers of Evil* as an influence on *The Flower Master* (193, 200). (Cassandra Laity also connects the same collection to *Sea Garden* [45, 50].) Peter Denman persuasively argues for allusions to Charlotte Perkins Gilman in a piece from *Venus in the Rain* (169). Shane Murphy and Clair Wills ("Voices from the Nursery") discuss McGuckian's collage methods of composition throughout her oeuvre, in particular her mostly uncredited arrangements of phrases from nonfiction books into new works of poetry, a strategy that partakes of a tradition rooted in modernism, although she refrains from providing the endnotes supplied by Moore or T. S. Eliot. Partly because of her difficulty and this manipulation of echoing fragments, scholars have, in fact, affiliated her not only with Moore and Eliot but also with Yeats, Joyce, James, Stevens, Stein, H. D., and Woolf.[12]

If affinities with female literary precursors seem especially important, *The Flower Master* concerns more than just writers. In fact, this volume shelters a world of women: not only aunts, sisters, mothers, and grandmothers, but sexually frustrated governesses, wet nurses, even Beatrix Potter and Mary, Queen of Scots (in "The Heiress"). Many poems evoke McGuckian's ambivalence toward those women. "The Mother," for example, depicts the title character as natural yet confined, familiar yet incomprehensible. Laura O'Connor comments that both Ní Dhomhnaill and McGuckian rely on "the enabling myth of the disabling mother" (McGuckian and Ní Dhomhnaill 609-10), seeing "hostile, rather than nurturant, mothering" as their impetus to art.[13] If this volume casts an eye backward for muses and models, it also distances itself from those women through style and tone.

Scholars have noticed similar configurations in H. D.'s poetry and prose. Deborah Kelly Kloepfer analyzes the trope of "the censored, repressed, or absent mother" (2) in H. D.'s work, finding that her poetry and prose have "both refused and solicited" (45) maternal inspiration. The modernist, on the other hand, adopts a maternal role herself much less obviously than the contemporary writer. Donna Krolik Hollenberg has convincingly argued for the importance of childbirth metaphors in H. D.'s work, though not until her productions of the Second World War; while H. D.'s works, Hollenberg asserts, "display a range of meanings and emotions associated with childbirth" (19), her imagist poetry documents how she found it "difficult to reconcile female sexual identity with creative power" (74).

In fact, the extensive common ground between *Sea Garden* and *The Flower Master* highlights their profound differences. Certainly, both collections mention flowers, plants, fruits, or seeds in every poem but one (**"The Wind Sleepers"** in H. D. and "The 'Singer'" in McGuckian). Both use flowers and their inherited associations with feminine beauty to set out aesthetic values and explore their complex status as women poets in male-dominated milieus. Both collections create erotic landscapes tenuously yoked to real places, layering sexual desire with pursuit of the divine. And both poets value image over clear statement; often McGuckian's cryptic pieces seem at least as coded as any imagist fragment.

However, for the most part the Belfast-born poet sounds drastically unlike the Pennsylvania native. The geographically loyal McGuckian enmeshes her speakers in family relationships; in contrast, the expatriate American wanders alone or with a band of initiates along an apparently Greek, but deliberately indeterminate, coastline. Both frequently apostrophize unidentified addressees, and both manipulate pronouns in intriguing ways, but McGuckian's lyrics imply mundane, domestic situations. While H. D. achieves an incantatory effect through repetition, McGuckian's tone is often discursive or wry; her verse is relatively lush, while H. D.'s lines are spare and short. Finally, McGuckian claims a value, or at least a tolerance, for inherited notions of womanliness that H. D. criticizes sharply throughout her work.

Two poems on botanically related flowers—H. D.'s iris and McGuckian's gladiolus—begin to illuminate these contrasts. H. D.'s volume, which celebrates a dangerous, liminal landscape, includes five poems with parallel titles and subjects: **"Sea Rose," "Sea Lily," "Sea Poppies," "Sea Violet,"** and **"Sea Iris."** In each, she depicts a flower rendered more precious through its exposure to a harsh environment. **"Sea Iris"** (*Collected Poems* 36-37) emphasizes the flower's struggle to endure, naming it "weed" and describing it as "brittle," "broken," and "thin." Like an object of art, the iris is "painted" and "stained"; like a maker of art, it "print[s] a shadow" and "drag[s] up colour" through its roots in the sand, transforming its sources. The single flower in the first section becomes a "band" in the second, parallel to the elite group of seekers populating many poems in this collection and reinforcing the identification between poet and flower. The word *iris* itself indicates the visual nature of H. D.'s imagist poems, indicating not only the colored

membrane of the eye but the Greek messenger goddess, whose sign is the rainbow. When H. D. compares the clump of flowers to a "fresh prow," she conjures that Hellenic reference, suggesting that the iris, too, performs a stimulating errand, transporting its discoverer in a metaphorical sense. Appropriately, in the Victorian language of flowers, the iris signified "message" or "messenger" (Seaton 180-81).

"Gladiolus," new to the 1993 edition of McGuckian's volume (31), treats a related plant, like the iris in its sword-shaped leaves and spike of brilliant flowers. The poem contains only 12 lines, most of which extend a further beat or two than those in **"Sea Iris."** While H. D. addresses the iris, McGuckian describes her gladiolus as if in a gardener's manual, meticulously remarking its "stately flowers," the shade and structure of the foliage, and its method of reproduction. Thrifty and eager to please, McGuckian's gladiolus "will not exhaust the ground" and possesses as "its only aim the art / Of making itself loved." While the flower "step[s] free of its own / Foliage," exercising a limited freedom, the words "border plant" and "collared" stress containment. Unlike H. D.'s iris, this is a domesticated, not a wild plant; McGuckian even frames this flower between two greenhouse poems, "The Sun-Trap" and "The Orchid-House." While H. D.'s tone is sympathetic and praising, McGuckian mimics objectivity, positioning herself as an expert (a master) rather than an admirer. She demonstrates her mastery, too, in playful ways: the phrase "satiny moons / Of honesty," for instance, encrypts part of that plant's Latin name (Lunaria annua).

McGuckian's attitude toward the gladiolus remains one of the most interesting ambiguities of this brief poem. Like H. D.'s flowers, it exists as a poetic object and also generates art—if one concedes, at least, that "making oneself loved" constitutes a creative endeavor. While detailed description conveys the poet's fascination with the plant—she does devote an entire poem to it, without deploying the gladiolus as an obvious conceit for some other subject—McGuckian sounds distinctly arch at several points. For instance, her flower's method of survival involves not endurance despite a hostile world but manipulation of its own appeal and a susceptibility to the "roguish draught" that lays the ovules open for pollination. These passive virtues are stereotypically feminine; indeed, this lovable candidate for sunny garden borders resembles the familiar domestic angel, ambitious only to please in her limited sphere, devoted to reproduction.

Other elements of the poem, however, complicate this reading. First, the word itself is Latin for little sword, and thus bears distinctly masculine connotations. Second, McGuckian throughout emphasizes the flower's asexual method of propagation. The poem's only end rhymes, "clone" and "own," accent this strategy, and McGuckian startles us with an image of sexual violence only to defuse it in the following line: "its grains ripped / Benignly." While McGuckian to some extent identifies her aesthetic with this plant's pleasing arts, rooting her own poetry in a narrowly observed domestic world, she also portrays this world in startling, defamiliarizing ways. Her gladiolus-woman-poet, despite these traditional attributes, possesses an ambiguous though intense sexuality and exerts her own, apparently passive, mastery of her environment. The poem remains tantalizingly ambiguous in its attitude: does McGuckian present this model with amused detachment, approval, or some other judgment?

Flowers as figures for female experience might seem to emphasize heterosexual eroticism (as Dickinson's nectar-drunken bees do) and reproduction. Hence H. D.'s wild specimens hint at her own modern marriage, in which each member exercised a sexual freedom that challenged the institution's conventions. Even McGuckian, though, finds examples in her border garden of unconventional sexuality. Talking to or about their flowers, each poet investigates a range of erotic and literary possibilities.

GARDEN VARIETIES

Unlike McGuckian's collection, H. D.'s **Sea Garden** contains no title poem. Instead, **"Sheltered Garden"** defines the antithesis of the title image (**Collected Poems** 19-21). **"Sheltered Garden"** implicitly describes the discipline of conventional femininity in withering terms, preferring the dangers of the sea's harsh weather to the safety of garden walls. She decries the "beauty without strength" fostered by constraint and declares, "it is better to taste of frost—/ the exquisite frost—/ than of wadding and of dead grass." If gardens are "deadly, sweet, and overripe paradises," as Laity puts it (45), H. D.'s paradoxical title retains only the lightest possible suggestion of the term's association with containment.[14] If H. D.'s poem desires escape from confined Victorian womanhood to modern sexual liberation, it also seeks "a new beauty / in some terrible / wind-tortured place."

H. D.'s longing for wind in **"Sheltered Garden"** and other **Sea Garden** poems suggests a search for inspiration, for an invigorated poetic voice. Chillingly, however, it also recalls the particulars of her 1915 stillbirth. Richard Aldington described the experience to Amy Lowell in a letter of 21 May: "I haven't seen the doctor, but the nurse said it was a beautiful child & they can't think why it didn't live. It was very strong, but wouldn't breathe" (16). A sheltered garden,

then, not only suggests Victorian femininity and pre-imagist aesthetics but also evokes a uterine space that promises to protect life but ultimately destroys it. This poem, in fact, describes fruit that is "smothered" by straw: "this beauty, / beauty without strength, / chokes out life" (20). While H. D. here seeks a kind of poetry repudiating old constraints, her diction also remembers a perfect yet lifeless baby whom she cannot resuscitate. Instead, she wishes to "forget, to find a new beauty": her art both memorializes the loss and hopes to supplant it with new life.

Paradoxically, then, the liberating winds of **Sea Garden** suggest the failure of maternity and a potentially fruitful future. Throughout most of the volume, as in **"Sheltered Garden,"** "fruit cannot drop / through this thick air" (25); neither poems nor children can thrive in the tame environs of Victorian culture. She therefore petitions a sea wind to create a harsher and wilder, seemingly unmaternal climate. However, H. D. can only imagine successful fruition of motherhood or poetry in such a radically changed, storm-blasted world. While her first collection does not develop a clear vision of how successful maternity and poetic creativity might coexist, her metaphors insist that they require the same conditions.

In contrast, the title poem of *The Flower Master* embraces a sheltered space, suggesting different attitudes toward poetry and womanhood. The first-person plural speaker obediently engages in her lessons: "we come to terms with shade, with the principle / of enfolding space." In fact, the immediate "master" of the poem seems to be not Baudelaire, as Docherty suggests, but a teacher of ikebana, instilling the principles of Japanese floral arrangement. (Porter also, although very briefly, notes "references to Japanese arts and custom" in this lyric [92].) Stella Coe, in her study of ikebana, uses the term "flower master" itself to refer to an expert in this discipline (22), and McGuckian's references to the Japanese festival of moon viewing and to the tea ceremony confirm the allusion. The flower master's students learn how to bend seasonally appropriate plants into designs and create the symbolic correspondences that this art often suggests. This strategy of bending rather than cutting also suggests an immediate contrast to H. D.'s rough handling, and the pliant strength of boughs manipulated for these arrangements evokes the similarly passive virtues of McGuckian's gladiolus.

The meditative function of ikebana, in fact, illuminates the entire collection. Directing would-be practitioners, Coe writes, "the way to proceed is to let your insight guide you. You want a direct, non-analytic expression of the theme in the simplest terms possible" (129). McGuckian herself and several critics have characterized her strategies in similar terms. Sirr, for instance, describes her evasions of rational discourse: "the images are not there to elucidate but to detonate and resonate in all their weird energy" (461). Elmer Andrews analyzes the "pull between logic and illogicality" (135) in her work, and Mary O'Connor sees McGuckian's "flight to the semiotic" (155) as a response to the pressures of living in Northern Ireland. In "Surfacing" McGuckian professes, "Poetry is my way of getting drunk" (105), calls the poetic process "vatic" (106), and describes her poems as patterns meant to express "my inability to speak. . . . I want to make English sound like a foreign language to itself" (105). Her works rarely present clear situations, coherent speakers, or consistent narratives; their purposes remain oblique, so that the poems serve as tokonamas enshrining their evocatively arranged sprays.

Even so, the very allusions in "The Flower Master" to ikebana intersect with literary modernism. McGuckian's speaker studies under "the school of the grass moon," a translation of Sogetsu-ryu. Although ikebana originated as a masculine discipline performed by priests, noblemen, and warriors, recent centuries democratized the pursuit and created new versions (Coe 22-23). Sogetsu, founded in the 1920s, "has a wide following both in and outside Japan, possibly because it is the most easily translated into the language of other cultures." It emphasizes individuality and originality in creating arrangements; its founder, Sofu Teshigahara, has been called "the Picasso of ikebana" (Coe 23). Thus Sogestu's movement coincides roughly with imagism, the modernist movement arising in part from H. D.'s early poems. McGuckian's interest in ikebana, moreover, echoes some modernists' preoccupation with the Orient.

Though it embraces rather than rejects bowers, "The Flower Master" does share some qualities and images with **"Sheltered Garden,"** just as the larger volumes correspond in certain points. These correspondences, further, suggest where McGuckian's view of womanhood overlaps with H. D.'s: each poet, in particular, celebrates female sexual appetite. Both "The Flower Master" and **"Sheltered Garden"** eroticize their landscapes; the students in the contemporary poem, for instance, "stroke gently the necks of daffodils / and make them throw their heads back to the sun," and collect plants with suggestive names like "sweet / sultan, dainty nipplewort." McGuckian's "sea-fans with sea-lavender" invoke H. D.'s many sea flowers, and both poems suggest an autumnal mood, H. D. through ripening fruit and McGuckian through the mid-September festival of moon viewing. These similarities, however, frame the essentially contrary stands the poems adopt. Placing her "scissors in

brocade," eschewing the wild, invigorating breakage H. D. imagines, McGuckian's speaker espouses gentleness and tradition. Even the form of "The Flower Master" resists its predecessor's. McGuckian avoids symmetry and creates a tripartite arrangement in loyalty to ikebana's aesthetics (these Japanese arrangements consist of three main lines), but she also returns to meters the imagists eschewed (Coe 43). "The Flower Master" adheres to a rough pentameter, irregularly rhymed, while **"Sea Garden"** depends for its rebellious music on jaggedly uneven lines and verses.

Whenever McGuckian herself describes poems in *The Flower Master,* she emphasizes their preoccupation with sexuality, pregnancy, and childbirth. In "My Words Are Traps" she emphasizes the book's focus on "the cruelty of birth" (117) and refers to death itself as "the flowermaster" (119), adding still another layer to that title image. In a 1996 essay, "Drawing Ballerinas," she links the private violence of such experience with the political violence of the Irish Troubles that has also shaped her life (196-97). In a letter, she drives home just how immediately she treats the particulars of parturition:

> As for flower-arranging—that poem (the title-poem) was just using the process as an image for the fear of childbirth. The images of cutting and tearing were to do with episiotomy, that horrible word. Unspellable. I just found the harnessing of fertility to be something passive that happened to me, and wanted to assert some vigorous learning-pattern against my lack of control. I wanted to be both flower and flower-gatherer. I found the whole experience of pregnancy and birth, especially the first time, very difficult and lonely, and impossible to write about. I guess in that poem I exorcised the pain of that education. There's a wash in it between tenderness and cruelty. It's related to my early church-going and the preparation of flowers for the altars and feast. Women being *allowed* to do only that, not actually serve the Mass or say it. Yet without the maternal centre, the special guest (Christ) could not be contemplated. So the poem's about this inversion of power. The ending is still very mysterious to me. How we see things from a very limited viewpoint . . . How the baby's feet kicking you are your main communication with it, you being the container or vase . . . I guess, it's about—a forceps delivery—when you would like to have smoothed the path yourself.
>
> (11 Feb. 2001)

McGuckian's generous expansion on the poem's purposes illuminate it wonderfully: the tools of ikebana suddenly translate into the instruments of modern childbirth, and ambiguities of position within the poem align with the first-time mother's own confused apprehension of an overwhelming event. Her comments in interviews and at readings, likewise, reveal the startling *literalness* of her apparently abstract, difficult poems.

"The Flower Master," then, like "Gladiolus," never lets one forget that flowers contain a plant's sexual structures, even as McGuckian celebrates their beauty and variety and invokes their traditional symbolism. Indeed, she creates a specific parallel between the flowers and the delivering woman's perineum (a genital connection that echoes Aldington's coded reference to H. D.'s "flower"). Women have only a few ways to decrease the odds of episiotomy, a minor procedure that nevertheless can cause a great deal of postpartum pain: good nutrition improves tissue elasticity; massage can help the perineum stretch ("stroke gently the necks of daffodils"); slowing the delivery can also allow the tissue to stretch gradually ("delay / The loveliness of the hibiscus dawn"). Identifying, as McGuckian writes, with "both flower and flower-gatherer," the poet both acknowledges the uncontrollable aspects of birth and searches, as pregnant women often do, for the means to master it. She poses ceremony and expertise against the terrifying violence of parturition. Likewise, the volume as a whole enacts a delicate counterpoise between powerful natural drives and equally urgent human discipline. Unlike H. D.'s early work, at least, McGuckian's poetry does put great faith in containment, ritual, and control of the world's, and her body's, utter wildness.

SCIONS

As students of overlapping traditions, H. D. and McGuckian inherit the garden trope from multiple precursors. Both certainly allude to Eden; Docherty even emphasizes references to the Fall in McGuckian's book over the pregnancy motif stressed by McGuckian herself and most of her critics. H. D.'s readers register the Hellenism in her gardens: Friedman calls *Sea Garden* "a sequence of modern pastorals," referring to Theocritus as a model (51); Gregory identifies H. D.'s "reinvention of the Orphic prayer" in this volume, drawing on romantic Hellenism (83); Collecott finds an embedded network of allusions to Sappho (159, 266-67). H. D. and McGuckian were also particularly steeped in Victorian literature, which is marked by its own horticultural obsessions, H. D. because she came of age in the early part of the twentieth century and McGuckian through her thesis research.[15] Finally, both encountered the flower trope through Dickinson's work, although at the time H. D. composed *Sea Garden,* Dickinson's work had been published only in bowdlerized versions.

However, these two poets share other important circumstances. *Sea Garden* and *The Flower Master* both constitute debut collections by ambitious women poets powerfully formed by the British literary tradition, although both felt marginal to it by reason of sex and national identity, and McGuckian felt marginal to it as well by religion. Most crucially for my argument, each first book documents pregnancy and the poet's concern with her own fertility, although neither writes plainly about the subject. The themes and vocabulary shared by these volumes reflect parallels between the poets' interests and situations. Even their metaphors, to some extent, join at the root.

McGuckian's experiments certainly build on the "papery legacies," as "The Flower Master" puts it, of previous women poets including H. D. However, the differences between these two prominently titled poems suggest how widely their attitudes toward gender diverge. While H. D. celebrates a harsh, androgynous beauty, "The Flower Master" thrives in sheltered space and admires the delicacy of its shade-loving specimens. While **"Mid-Day,"** the fourth poem in *Sea Garden,* laments "hot shrivelled seeds" (*Collected Poems* 10) scattered over pavement in a strong image of writer's block and, simultaneously, a troubled pregnancy (Friedman 49), McGuckian's collection seethes with fertility, depicting numerous crowded, feminine houses and greenhouses; collecting various nests, seeds, and children; evoking moons and milk fevers. Both compare procreation with literary composition, but H. D.'s struggling flowers imply her pessimism about a female artist's ability to nurture offspring. McGuckian expresses far more hope about the coexistence of art and motherhood. Her poetry, in fact, deeply roots itself in maternity as material, just as Ostriker prescribes.

Contrasts in the imagery, then, reflect contrasts in sexual politics, although their terms and figures share common elements. *The Flower Master,* like *Sea Garden,* depicts disruptive desires and bends readers' expectations, as hostile reviews have attested (see Ann Beer for a catalog of these). Nevertheless, when McGuckian tells Sailer, "I feel very tied by laws and very bound" ("Interview," ed. Sailer 115), she sounds as different as she possibly could from H. D. in her early poems, which, coded as they are, revel in risk, resistance, and broken mores. This contrast echoes in their comments about the relationship between womb and brain. "My womb is almost my *brain,*" McGuckian has declared, again to Sailer (121), insisting on the femaleness of her writing as deliberately as H. D. adhered to those genderless initials.[16] In her *Notes on Thought and Vision* H. D. explains creative work in comparable terms. She describes "the over-mind," her phrase for a state of insight or vision, as a closed, watery space, distinctly uterine (18-19). However, she also argues for creative activity that is not inflected by sex: "the brain and the womb are both centres of consciousness, equally important. . . . The two work separately, perceive separately, and yet make one picture" (21, 23).

McGuckian's comments to interviewers in more recent years reflect a shift in sexual politics. A few years after the Sailer interview, Brandes quotes McGuckian in a wry mood on the role of place in her poems: "keeping my place, a woman's place is in the home. Second-class citizenship" (64). Here as in "Gladiolus," McGuckian interweaves an acute, even mocking awareness of the restrictions that have been placed on female experience with an evident belief that constriction can produce positive results, in life and in art. In her published conversation with Irish poet Ní Dhomhnaill, McGuckian speaks of multiple experiences with sexual discrimination and laments the absence of women authors in her course-work, and in the Sailer interview she insists that women should receive equality of opportunity. However, she quickly qualifies her identification with feminism:

> You know, if you're *too* demanding for your freedom then you are going to destroy your home. I'm for feminism as long as it doesn't destroy in woman what is the most precious to her, which is her ability to relate and soften and make a loving environment for others as well as herself. . . . Sometimes there is something in feminism that demands you to be almost masculine and that's what frightens me a bit about it, or to sort of repudiate reproduction. . . . I find feminism attractive in theory but in practice I think it ends up influenced by lesbians and—very lonely and embittered and stressed and full of hatred.

(121)

H. D.'s rebellion against Victorian notions of pure, passionless womanhood springs partly from her bisexuality; McGuckian's version of femininity, while also libidinous, is distinctly heterosexual, even homophobic in this remark (though not in any other published comments that I have discovered). The Irish writer's program for contemporary poetry involves a partial validation of traditional femininity in contrast to how key modernist women undertook marriage and motherhood: bisexual H. D. was married and, after her 1915 stillborn delivery, bore a healthy daughter, but her marriage quickly shattered and she raised her child in an unconventional way.[17] The two individuals, certainly, seem utterly opposite as mothers: while McGuckian produced her first books at home around four small children for whom she was primarily responsible, H. D. resumed her travels shortly after childbirth, mostly delegating to others the care of Perdita, her child born of an extramarital liaison.

In *The Flower Master*, McGuckian revisits *Sea Garden*'s scenes, vocabulary, and erotic passion, but in so doing inverts H. D.'s central gesture of divorcing womanhood from domesticity. "Poets of this generation," speculates McGuckian about her own contemporaries, "are the pioneers of women who've survived

birth, survived multiple births, in order to write about it. And maintained the marriage relationship. I think the complexities of holding all these irons in the fire and keeping your inwardness intact are immeasurable" (McGuckian and Ní Dhomhnaill 606). McGuckian controversially describes biological reproduction as a precondition for poetic production and downplays potential conflicts among marriage, motherhood, and profession. Her position ignores certain gaps and problems: some twenty-first century women struggle with and redefine the institutions of marriage and maternity as vigorously as H. D. did. Nevertheless, both H. D.'s and McGuckian's gardens, pervaded by the intense and even terrifying transformations of motherhood, reconsider the traditional opposition between safe private havens and violent public arenas. H. D. forecasts a new wild world to resuscitate lost daughters, although her early poems primarily emphasize that world's necessary perils. McGuckian's poetry of vivid, physical motherhood finds a comparably empowering strangeness at home, in the scented bower.

Notes

1. Just since 2001, several new books on the subject have received substantial media attention. See for example Belkin, Crittenden, Cusk, Hewlett, and Wolf.

2. See Hollenberg's comments on the blurred distinction between creation and procreation for recent women writers (10-11) and Suleiman's discussion of psychoanalysis and women writers.

3. McGuckian gives conflicting reports on how she manages to find writing time. In "Surfacing" (1994) she tells Kimberly S. Bohman, "I can write with kids around me. I've written on this table [in the garden] with kids screaming, and sometimes those are the best poems" (95). To McCracken (1999) she asserts, "The children have to be unconscious, asleep, before I can write, and my husband and I must be at peace with each other" (170).

4. A horticultural catalog of flower-focused lyrics by women writing in English is beyond the scope of this essay; most poets, male and female, have taken a turn at this traditional metaphor. However, a short list of female poets for whom this is a persistent motif might include Emily Dickinson, whose use of the trope to register sensual and spiritual experience surely inflects most twentieth-century poetic gardens; Mina Loy, especially in "Anglo-Mongrels and the Rose"; Sylvia Plath and her brilliant, dangerous poppies and tulips; Louise Glück, the current American laureate, whose sexual flowers dramatize human vulnerability; and Rita Dove and her suburban gardens.

5. McGuckian's first book may react against H. D. more than she admits. Some of her most astute readers describe *The Flower Master*'s central search for female predecessors, including earlier women writers. Porter, commenting on this quest in McGuckian's first three book-length collections, notes how McGuckian makes "a place for herself in a female artistic tradition by acknowledging her debt to the female heritage of domestic artistry" (96) in poems including "The Seed-Picture" and locates her "in the tradition of poets like Emily Dickinson and Marianne Moore, in whose writing a bolder claim for the poet's own work is often hidden behind a more traditionally feminine, self-effacing façade" (88). In her overview for Scribner's *British Writers* series, Wills likewise characterizes *The Flower Master* as a book that "consider[s] how to create new forms of continuity and inheritance, and how tradition can be both preserved and renewed" (281). For a powerful comment on contemporary Irish women poets and their poverty in Irish precursors, see Ní Dhomhnaill's "What Foremothers?"

6. McGuckian describes her canny strategy for winning a key competition:

> I sent away for the previous year's winners and saw they liked narrative poems of about forty lines—it had to be substantial and to flitter about the place. I wrote three poems in this style and submitted them under a pseudonym, and I won. . . . They assumed that I was a male pretending to be a woman. They couldn't believe I was six months pregnant when they came over with their cameras. The big thing about it was that a well-known literary figure came second to me, and they rearranged the prize money so that I got less and he got more. I didn't care. I was pregnant, and I had won this. But the *TLS* cared. They created a huge fuss for weeks, wanting to know whether my prize money was cut from £1,000 to £500 because I was Irish, or Catholic, or a woman, or unknown. And then British publishers began writing to me—Faber wrote, and Charles Monteith was on the phone—and I ended up getting published with Oxford.

(McGuckian and Ní Dhomhnaill 592-93)

7. Identified by McGuckian, letter 27 Mar. 2001.

8. See Boughn 5-7 for a summary of these versions.

9. See also Dettmar and Watt.

10. Zilboorg's edition of letters from Richard Aldington to H. D. is the most helpful published source on H. D.'s relations with Constable & Co. Zilboorg alludes to wartime paper shortages and *Sea Garden*'s subsequent publication delay from the winter of 1916 to the following fall (22); she also mentions small, sporadic royalties from *Sea Garden*'s publication (62n) and Constable's probable rejection of H. D.'s second collection of poetry, *Hymen*, which was eventually published by the

Egoist Press in 1921 (212n). A biographical appendix identifies Edward Hutton as a reader and translator at Constable who worked closely on *Sea Garden* (219); Aldington makes several references to Hutton in his letters, alternately hopeful and disparaging. Also see Silverstein's chronology for the year 1916. For a history of Constable & Co. see Altick, Mumby and Norrie, and Sutherland. I thank Lawrence Rainey for these sources.

11. Zilboorg directed my attention to this exchange.

12. See Porter (Moore); Murphy (Eliot, H. D.); Gray (Yeats); Sailer (Joyce, Woolf); Gonzalez (Joyce); Docherty (James); Sirr (Stevens); and Cahill (Stein).

13. Many critics discuss representations of maternity in McGuckian, including Wills, *Improprieties*; Beer; Batten; and O'Connor.

14. DuPlessis also discusses *Sea Garden* as an "oxymoronic" title (12).

15. In her essay "Drawing Ballerinas," McGuckian describes her parents' "heritage of Victorian narratives and heroic tragedies they had learned in school" (189) as well as her "MA in Anglo-Irish literature, studying the nineteenth-century novelists, Griffin, Edgeworth, the Banim brothers and William Carleton" (195). She also, in "Birds and Their Masters," jokes about her "early desire to be a nineteenth-century English poet" (29). Friedman argues that "H. D.'s harsh flowers represent a repudiation of the sentimental language of flowers popularized by the Victorians," especially Kate Greenaway (59); Laity delineates H. D.'s extensive debt to decadent romanticism. On the nineteenth-century preoccupation with botany, see King, who examines the trope of the blooming girl in the Victorian novel.

16. Coincidentally, both poets chose pen names influenced by powerful male mentors. Pound famously signed "H. D., Imagiste" to Hilda Doolittle's *Poetry* submission, although H. D. has told different versions of that story and published under a variety of pseudonyms, as Friedman recounts (35-46). Medbh McGuckian, born Maeve McCaughan, chose the Irish spelling of her name after Seamus Heaney, her teacher, signed books to her that way ("Drawing Ballerinas" 195).

17. On H. D.'s unorthodox approach to motherhood, see Morris 120-48 and Schaffner (H. D.'s daughter).

I submitted an early, brief version of this essay to Linda Kinnahan's seminar on Modern and Contemporary Women Poets at the New Modernisms Conference at Pennsylvania State University in

October 1999. A slightly revised version of the seminar paper appeared in the online periodical *How2* 1.3 (2000) <http://www.departments.bucknell.ed . . . ler_center/how2>. I'm grateful to many people for their suggestions at later stages of composition: the members of Works in Progress group of the English Department at Washington and Lee; Helen Emmitt; and especially Diana Collecott and Caroline Zilboorg.

Works Cited

Aldington, Richard. *An Autobiography in Letters.* Ed. Norman Gates. University Park: Pennsylvania State UP, 1992.

Altick, Richard D. *The English Common Reader: A Social History of the Mass Reading Public, 1800-1900.* Chicago: U of Chicago P, 1957.

Andrews, Elmer. "Some Sweet Disorder—the Poetry of Subversion: Paul Muldoon, Tom Paulin, and Medbh McGuckian." *British Poetry from the 1950s to the 1990s: Politics and Art.* Ed. Gary Day and Brian Docherty. London: Macmillan, 1997. 118-42.

Batten, Guinn. "'The More with Which We Are Connected': The Muse of the Minus in the Poetry of McGuckian and Kinsella." *Gender and Sexuality in Modern Ireland.* Ed. Anthony Bradley and Maryann Gialanella Valiulis. Amherst: U of Massachusetts P, 1997. 212-44.

Beer, Ann. "Medbh McGuckian's Poetry: Maternal Thinking and a Politics of Peace." *The Canadian Journal of Irish Studies* 18.1 (1992): 192-203.

Belkin, Lisa. *Life's Work: Confessions of an Unbalanced Mom.* New York: Simon, 2002.

Boland, Eavan. *Object Lessons: The Life of the Woman and the Poet in Our Time.* New York: Norton, 1995.

Boughn, Michael. *H. D.: A Bibliography 1905-1990.* Charlottesville: UP of Virginia, 1993.

Cahill, Eileen. "'Because I Never Garden': Medbh McGuckian's Solitary Way." *Irish University Review* 24.2 (1994): 264-71.

Clifton, Lucille. "Doing What You Will Do: An Interview with Lucille Clifton by Marilyn Kallet." *Sleeping with One Eye Open: Women Writers and the Art of Survival.* Ed. Marilyn Kallet and Judith Ortiz Cofer. Athens: U of Georgia P, 1999. 80-85.

Coe, Stella. *Ikebana: A Practical and Philosophical Guide to Japanese Flower Arrangement.* Woodstock: Overlook, 1984.

Collecott, Diana. *H. D. and Sapphic Modernism 1910-1950.* Cambridge: Cambridge UP, 1999.

Crittenden, Ann. *The Price of Motherhood: Why the Most Important Job in the World Is Still the Least Valued.* New York: Holt, 2001.

Cusk, Rachel. *A Life's Work: Becoming a Mother.* New York: Picador, 2002.

Denman, Peter. "Ways of Saying: Boland, Carson, McGuckian." *Poetry in Contemporary Irish Literature.* Ed. Michael Kenneally. Gerrards Cross: Colin Smythe, 1995. 158-73.

Dettmar, Kevin J. H., and Stephen Watt, eds. *Marketing Modernisms: Self-Promotion, Canonization, Rereading.* Ann Arbor: U of Michigan P, 1996.

Docherty, Thomas. "Initiations, Tempers, Seductions: Postmodern McGuckian." *The Chosen Ground: Essays on the Contemporary Poetry of Northern Ireland.* Ed. Neil Corcoran. Chester Springs: Dufour, 1992. 191-212.

DuPlessis, Rachel Blau. *H. D.: The Career of That Struggle.* Bloomington: Indiana UP, 1986.

Friedman, Susan Stanford. *Penelope's Web: Gender, Modernity, and H. D.'s Fiction.* New York: Cambridge UP, 1990.

Gonzalez, Alexander G. "Celebrating the Richness of Medbh McGuckian's Poetry: Close Analysis of Six Poems from *The Flower Master.*" *Contemporary Irish Women Poets: Some Male Perspectives.* Westport: Greenwood, 1999. 43-63.

Gray, Cecile. "Medbh McGuckian: Imagery Wrought to Its Uttermost." *Learning the Trade: Essays on W. B. Yeats and Contemporary Poetry.* West Cornwall: Locust Hill, 1993.

Gregory, Eileen. *H. D. and Hellenism: Classic Lines.* New York: Cambridge UP, 1997.

Hanscombe, Gillian, and Virginia L. Smyers. *Writing for Their Lives: The Modernist Women 1910-1940.* Boston: Northeastern UP, 1987.

H. D. *Collected Poems: 1912-1944.* Ed. Louis L. Martz. New York: New Directions, 1983.

———. *Notes on Thought and Vision.* San Francisco: City Lights, 1982.

Hewlett, Sylvia Ann. *Creating a Life: Professional Women and the Quest for Children.* New York: Talk Miramax, 2002.

Hollenberg, Donna Krolik. *H. D.: The Poetics of Childbirth and Creativity.* Boston: Northeastern UP, 1991.

King, Amy Mae. "Bloom: The Botanical Vernacular in the English Novel: 1770-1890." *DAI* sec. A, Humanities and Social Sciences, 59.10 (Apr. 1999): 3830.

Kloepfer, Deborah Kelly. *The Unspeakable Mother: Forbidden Discourse in Jean Rhys and H. D.* Ithaca: Cornell UP, 1989.

Laity, Cassandra. *H. D. and the Victorian Fin de Siècle: Gender, Modernism, Decadence.* New York: Cambridge UP, 1996.

Le Guin, Ursula K. "The Fisherwoman's Daughter." *Dancing at the Edge of the Wold: Thoughts on Words, Women, Places.* New York: Grove, 1989. 212-37.

Matthews, Steven. "*The Flower Master and Other Poems* by Medbh McGuckian." *Times Literary Supplement* 15 April 1994: 26.

McGann, Jerome. *Black Riders: The Visible Language of Modernism.* Princeton: Princeton UP, 1993.

McGuckian, Medbh. "Birds and Their Masters." *Irish University Review* 23.1 (1993): 29-33.

———. "Drawing Ballerinas: How Being Irish Has Influenced Me as a Writer." *Wee Girls: Women Writing from an Irish Perspective.* Ed. Lizz Murphy. North Melbourne: Spinifex, 1996. 185-203.

———. *The Flower Master.* New York: Oxford UP, 1982.

———. *The Flower Master and Other Poems.* Loughcrew: Gallery, 1993.

———. Interview. Ed. Kathleen McCracken. *Writing Irish: Selected Interviews with Irish Writers from the* Irish Literary Supplement. Ed. James P. Myers Jr. Syracuse: Syracuse UP, 1999. 157-72.

———. "An Interview with Medbh McGuckian." Ed. Rand Brandes. *Chattahoochee Review* 19.3 (1996): 56-65.

———. "An Interview with Medbh McGuckian." Ed. Susan Shaw Sailer. *Michigan Quarterly Review* 32.1 (1993): 111-27.

———. Letter to the author. 11 Feb. 2001.

———. Letter to the author. 27 Mar. 2001.

———. "My Words Are Traps: An Interview with Medbh McGuckian, 1995." Ed. John Hobbs. *New Hibernia Review* 2.1 (1998): 111-20.

———. "Surfacing: An Interview with Medbh McGuckian." By Kimberly S. Bohman. *Irish Review* 16 (1994): 95-108.

McGuckian, Medbh, and Nuala Ní Dhomhnaill. "Comhrá, with a Foreword and Afterword by Laura O'Connor." *Southern Review* 31 (1995): 581-614.

Morris, Adalaide. *How to Live / What to Do: H. D.'s Cultural Poetics.* Chicago: U of Illinois P, 2003.

Mumby, F. A., and Ian Norrie. *Publishing and Bookselling.* London: Cape, 1974.

Murphy, Shane. "'You Took Away My Biography': The Poetry of Medbh McGuckian." *Irish University Review* 28.1 (1998): 110-32.

Ní Dhomhnaill, Nuala. "First Communion." *The Astrakan Cloak.* Trans. Paul Muldoon. Winston-Salem: Wake Forest UP, 1993. 33.

———. "What Foremothers?" *The Comic Tradition in Irish Women Writers.* Ed. Theresa O'Connor. Gainesville: UP of Florida, 1996. 9-20.

O'Connor, Mary. "'Rising Out': Medbh McGuckian's Destabilizing Poetics." *Éire-Ireland: A Journal of Irish Studies* 30.4 (1996): 154-72.

Olsen, Tillie. *Silences.* New York: Delacorte, 1978.

Ostriker, Alicia. *Writing Like a Woman.* Ann Arbor: U of Michigan P, 1983.

Porter, Susan. "The Imaginative Space of Medbh McGuckian." *International Women's Writing: New Landscapes of Identity.* Ed. Anne E. Brown and Marjanne E. Goozé. Westport: Greenwood, 1995. 86-101.

Pound, Ezra, ed. *Des Imagistes.* New York: Boni, 1914.

Rainey, Lawrence. *Institutions of Modernism: Literary Elites and Public Culture.* New Haven: Yale UP, 1998.

Rich, Adrienne. *Of Woman Born: Motherhood as Experience and Institution.* 10th anniversary ed. New York: Norton, 1986.

———. "When We Dead Awaken: Writing as Re-Vision." *On Lies, Secrets, and Silence: Selected Prose 1966-1978.* New York: Norton, 1979. 33-50.

Rosenberg, Judith Pierce, ed. *A Question of Balance: Artists and Writers on Motherhood.* Watsonville: Papier-Maché, 1995.

Sailer, Susan Shaw. "Women in Rooms, Women in History." *Pedagogy, Praxis, Ulysses: Using Joyce's Text to Transform the Classroom.* Ed. Robert Newman. Ann Arbor: U of Michigan P, 1996. 97-120.

Schaffner, Perdita. "A Sketch of H. D.: The Egyptian Cat." *Signets: Reading H. D.* Ed. Susan Stanford Friedman and Rachel Blau DuPlessis. Madison: U of Wisconsin P, 1990. 52-82.

Seaton, Beverly. *The Language of Flowers: A History.* Charlottesville: U of Virginia P, 1995.

Silverstein, Louis. Introduction. *Louis Silverstein's H. D. Chronology.* Ed. Heather Hernandez. Rev. 27 April 2003. <http://www.imagists.org/hd/hdchron.html>.

Sirr, Peter. "'How Things Begin to Happen': Notes on Eiléan Ní Chuilleanáin and Medbh McGuckian." *Southern Review* 31.3 (1995): 450-67.

Suleiman, Susan Rubin. "Writing and Motherhood." *The (M)other Tongue: Essays in Feminist Psychoanalytic Interpretation.* Ed. Shirley Nelson Garner, Claire Kahane, and Madelon Sprengnether. Ithaca: Cornell UP, 1985. 352-77.

Sutherland, J. A. *Victorian Novelists and Publishers.* Chicago: U of Chicago P, 1976.

Wills, Clair. *Improprieties: Politics and Sexuality in Northern Irish Poetry.* New York: Oxford UP, 1993.

———. "Medbh McGuckian." *British Writers.* Supp. 5. Ed. George Stade and Sarah Hannah Goldstein. New York: Scribner's, 1999. 277-93.

———. "Voices from the Nursery: Medbh McGuckian's Plantation." *Poetry in Contemporary Irish Literature.* Ed. Michael Kenneally. Gerrards Cross: Colin Smythe, 1995. 373-94.

Wolf, Naomi. *Misconceptions: Truth, Lies, and the Unexpected on the Journey to Motherhood.* New York: Doubleday, 2001.

Zilboorg, Caroline, ed. *Richard Aldington and H. D.: The Early Years in Letters.* Bloomington: Indiana UP, 1992.

Annette Debo (essay date fall 2004)

SOURCE: Debo, Annette. "H. D.'s American Landscape: The Power and Permanence of Place." *South Atlantic Review* 69, nos. 3 & 4 (fall 2004): 1-22.

[*In the following essay, Debo studies the ways in which H. D. layered her personal past and the American landscape beneath her explorations of Greek myth.*]

In *Paint It Today*, Hilda Doolittle, known as H. D., wrote,

> She, Midget, did not wish to be an eastern flower painter. She did not wish to be an exact and over-*précieuse* western, a scientific describer of detail of vein and leaf of flowers, dead or living, nor did she wish to press flowers and fern fronds and threads of pink and purple seaweed between the pages of her book. Yet she wanted to combine all these qualities in her writing and to add still another quality to these three. She wished to embody, as this other quality, the fragrance of the flowers.

(17)

Into this passage is inscribed Midget's hope to become a writer able to capture the essence of a place, a goal which H. D. herself achieved. Although she did not become the scientist her father had planned, H. D.

inherited his scientific modes of observation, and while he practiced the art of astronomy, she incorporates into her art her careful and intricate observations of the American land. The seascapes of Maine come to life with their scraggly pines and hardy flowers; likewise, Pennsylvania's pastures and woods are carefully ensconced in her texts—a much more permanent method of capturing landscapes than "press[ing] flowers and fern fronds and threads of pink and purple seaweed."

The ecocritical lens, through which H. D. has not yet been read, offers new ways to address H. D.'s focus on place. Orchestrating a concert of voices in *The Ecocriticism Reader,* Cheryll Glotfelty asks, in her catalog of questions posed by ecocritics, "in addition to race, class, and gender, should *place* become a new critical category?" (xix). If place is indeed a valid aspect of identity, then it becomes integral to the theorizing of the modernist self. For H. D., her American past haunted her, and throughout her life, as she repeatedly sought self knowledge through outlets as varied as psychoanalysis and the occult, she reflected back upon her childhood to formulate the relationship between her adult identity and that American childhood. In part, that preoccupation relies on a belief in the formative power of place. For example, H. D.'s narrator in *Paint It Today* stipulates that "language and tradition do not make a people, but the heat that presses on them, the cold that baffles them, the alternating lengths of night and day," underscoring the power of place—just like race, class, and gender—to construct identity (20). Furthermore, although ecocriticism became codified as a discrete critical school only in the mid-1990s, its roots stretch to H. D.'s time and beyond. H. D.'s contemporary Mary Austin made the claim that "Art, considered as the expression of any people as a whole, is the response they make in various mediums to the impact that the totality of their experience makes upon them, and there is no sort of experience that works so constantly and subtly upon man as his regional environment" (97). I contend that H. D. shared Austen's belief in the power of place and that H. D.'s connection to American places was a pivotal part of her artistic vision.[1]

My first objective then in interpreting the influence of the American land in H. D.'s work is identifying its physical presence. Because H. D. uses mythical settings in many poems, readers often do not realize that her poetic images are based on the American landscape of her youth, which I will demonstrate by tracing her images to their origins. There is also H. D.'s own testimony to consider. In 1937, when looking back on her writing to explain the sources of her poetic images to Norman Holmes Pearson, her close friend and literary executor, H. D. wrote,

> **"Leda"** was done at the same time as **"Lethe".** Lotusland, all this. It is nostalgia for a lost land. I call it Hellas. I might, psychologically just as well, have listed the Casco Bay islands off the coast of Maine but I called my islands Rhodes, Samos and Cos.
>
> They are symbols. And symbolically the first island of memory was dredged away or lost, like a miniature Atlantis. It was a thickly wooded island in the Lehigh river [in Pennsylvania] and believe it or not, was named actually, Calypso's island.
>
> (Collecott 72)[2]

In this somewhat elusive explanation, H. D. illustrates how she grafts the Grecian names of Rhodes, Samos, and Cos onto the physical bodies of the Casco Bay islands and an island in the Lehigh River, places she has lost through time (the world of childhood) and distance (the U.S.). The "first island of memory" is in the Lehigh River, which runs through Bethlehem, Pennsylvania, the town in which H. D. was born and lived until she was nine. This island, deliberately chosen because of its Greek name, becomes the physical basis of the later imagery in the poems **"Leda"** and **"Lethe."** According to Diana Collecott, Calypso's Island was also the "scene of Doolittle family holidays, before 1911," a perfect melding of American places and memories with Greek allusions. Significantly, the presence of Maine and Pennsylvania here is not an isolated incident. On the contrary, this layer is an ubiquitous component of H. D.'s palimpsest-like writing. Shards of her past are ever present, the American landscape undergirding the Greek myths and allusions she superimposed upon it. For the purposes of this article, I will use **Sea Garden,** H. D.'s earliest and justly acclaimed volume of poetry, to illustrate this point.

Once having established the presence and importance of American places for H. D. in **Sea Garden,** I will turn to how place functions in two of her novels. In H. D.'s fiction in general, place becomes an active spirit that constructs identity and shapes her as a writer. In *HERmione,* the land infiltrates the house, spreading its aura of wildness throughout, and it molds Hermione's character and influences her development as a writer. Similarly, in *Paint It Today,* when the main character, Midget, moves to Europe, she remains permanently separated even from the other artists there because both her character and her art were formed by the American environment of her youth.

I

H. D.'s use of the American landscape has received scant critical attention to date even though in 1916

John Gould Fletcher noticed the resemblance of H. D.'s coasts to the Northeastern coast of the U.S., commenting that "the scenery and the feeling are not Greek. In fact, as someone has pointed out, the whole poem might have been called 'The Coast of New Jersey'" (34). The only H. D. critic to build on his comments is Susan Stanford Friedman who has noted that "the landscape of **Sea Garden** originated in America," a conclusion she likely based on Pearson's statement that H. D. "often told me that her nature imagery . . . was never really Greek but came from her childhood reminiscences of Watch Hill and the coasts of Rhode Island and Maine, which she used to visit with her friends as a child" (Friedman 99; Dembo 437). Friedman's claim gestures toward the role the U.S. plays in H. D.'s work, but even her work provides a limited analysis of this aspect of H. D.'s writing.[3] In developing this critical thread, I maintain that the American landscape is omnipresent in H. D.'s writing because of its connection to nationality. Despite her expatriate life, H. D. always felt herself an American, even repatriating at age seventy-two, and for nationalism, the land is pivotal. Historian Robert H. Wiebe writes that *Nationalism is the desire among people who believe they share a common ancestry and a common destiny to live under their own government on land sacred to their history,"* a definition highlighting the land as "sacred" (5). As an expatriate, H. D. left behind her community and her citizenship, but in the imaginative space of her poetry, she could retain, and even revere, the sacred land of her childhood in the U.S. In **Sea Garden,** as in much of H. D.'s writing, the Greek qualities for which H. D. is better known are superimposed onto American places, which become the bedrock for all her landscape imagery. Always alert for opportunities to mingle the ancient and the contemporary as well as her American past and her European present, H. D. uses the American land, in scientific detail, in her imagery.

Certainly, H. D. infused the landscape of **Sea Garden** with her penchant for Greek allusions, and, following closely upon her 1912 visit to Capri, the volume is also inflected by H. D.'s travel to that island (Guest 53). However, while the allusions may be Greek, the landscape is American, accurately rendered by a woman who grew up in a family of scientists. From her father, a prominent astronomer, and her grandfather, an influential botanist, H. D. inherited scientific habits of method and precision which influence her poetic technique, as Adalaide Morris and Charlotte Mandel have demonstrated. Morris sees H. D. "reproduce" her grandfather's "delicate language, his transfixed, interrogating gaze, and his push for taxonomic precision" (199). Mandel writes,

Hilda Doolittle was born at the full of the Victorian-style quest for scientific knowledge by diligent personal observation, collection, notation and classification. . . . From birth, she was influenced by these devotions to exactitude at reading the universe, interpreting meaning that would be evoked by avid study of detail and its accurate rendition into drawing and written symbol. She absorbed the discipline of their concentrated search, and its mystery, for the myriad specific tiny plants and orbiting sky-presences were invisible to the naked eye.

(301)

This discipline and eye for detail give to *Sea Garden* a botanical accuracy and a proclivity "to model the ancient Greek catalogue form almost into a naming of species" as in **"Sea Gods"** with its myriad forms of violets: wood violets, stream-violets, blue violets, river-violets, yellow violets, bird-foot violets, and so on (Mandel 307). Her "catalog" replicates the many variations of a species, much as a nature illustrator might create a book of northeastern flora or a nature writer might record her explorations.

Not only do the poems read like botanical catalogs at times, but their imagery of the landscape and vegetation is as authentically drawn as the algae her grandfather painstakingly hand drew and colored for his two internationally recognized studies. The sources for H. D.'s imagery are found in her experiences in the U.S., akin to the local research in ponds and streams upon which her grandfather relied. Her cousin Francis Wolle testifies to her training in the local flora and fauna in their summer romps as children: "Chiefly under Eric's [H. D.'s brother, a scientist] guidance we got to know the birds, plants, and wild flowers" (33). H. D. began *Sea Garden* only a year after leaving Pennsylvania for Europe, and the Northeastern coast as well as the Pennsylvanian countryside clearly emerge in *Sea Garden*'s imagery.

Moreover, *Sea Garden*'s patterns of imagery locate the freedom for which the speaker longs in that landscape. Many critics have addressed how the American land and the frontier affected the development of an American identity in the Europeans who settled in the U.S. A dominant strain of thought pertaining specifically to women is that women were complicit in domesticating the land, in transforming vast forests into orderly orchards and gardens, as persuasively argued by Annette Kolodny. Similarly, Vera Norwood has shown how middle-class white women developed an interest in nature but managed to keep it within their gender role: "an enclosed flower garden filled with beautiful women at their ease remains a classic image of woman's proper role in nature" (xviii). These women found acceptable outlets in becoming landscape and garden designers, writing about the nature near to hand, creating scientific il-

lustrations, and painting and photographing the environment. On the other hand, Stacy Alaimo claims an opposing view, that "many women have, in fact, invoked nature in order to critique cultural roles, norms, and assumptions and to escape from the confines of the domestic" (15). She continues,

These women looked outward toward a natural realm precisely because this space was not already designated as "truly and unequivocally theirs" and thus was not replete with the domestic values that many women wished to escape. Nature, then, is undomesticated both in the sense that it figures as a space apart from the domestic and in the sense that it is untamed and thus serves as a model for female insurgency.

(17)

It is into *this* tradition that H. D. falls.[4]

Sea Garden is about freedom of the spirit, and "absolute freedom and wildness," to use Henry David Thoreau's phrase, is found in uncontaminated nature (161).[5] While H. D. preferred living with European people, she considered the American land more alive and vibrant, and her valuation of the landscape, like the relationship she senses with the land, echoes Transcendental beliefs.[6] The most favored landscape is the coast; its wildness is alluring and promises escape and adventure. More than half a century earlier, Thoreau looked to the West for wildness: "The West of which I speak is but another name for the Wild; and what I have been preparing to say is, that in Wildness is the preservation of the World. Every tree sends its fibres forth in search of the Wild. The cities import it at any price. Men plough and sail for it. From the forest and wilderness come the tonics and barks which brace mankind" (185). Thoreau locates the wildness for which he longs in the West because of the mythos of the frontier as a vast, unsettled wilderness, a mythology which ignores the earlier inhabitants of the Americas, considering only the land conquests of the European settlers. By 1890 this frontier had been officially closed, ending the fiction of endless, empty land. Therefore, H. D., writing in 1916, uses the sea as her imaginative space for locating wildness because it cannot be settled or domesticated by any people. Its yearly storms shift miles of sand, wreck boats, and tear down houses, and in its violent nature lies its value as an untamable space, a place of absolute freedom.

Thus, *Sea Garden*'s most prominent and revered landscape is the Atlantic coast, which H. D. visited many times and cherished. In fact, in a letter to her childhood friend Mary Herr, H. D. names Maine "a place of mine," emphasizing the significant role it continued to play for her.[7] While growing up, H. D., her best friend Margaret Snively, and another neighbor

Matilda Wells would spend several summer weeks on Bailey Island in Casco Bay, Maine with Matilda's family. H. D. also went to the Snively cottage in Watch Hill, New Jersey with Margaret (Guest 17-18). In her correspondence with H. D. in the 1950s, Margaret fondly reminisces about those summers:

> Do you remember the day when "Hilda, Matilda, and Me" went up the creek and went in bathing in the altogether and had only just got dressed again when a rowboat of boys came round the bend?

> And the other time when we were stormbound up the creek and a boy named Allen rescued us and Father made me go up to his house with him to express our thanks? I did feel an awful fool and I guess Allen did, too. That was a fine free life we led there.[8]

These trips were special, a far distance to travel at the time, as H. D.'s cousin Francis Wolle testifies that "to the rest of us who had never been further than the Jersey Coast for a vacation this seemed a tremendous trip and a great honor" (34).

This Atlantic coast is the same landscape constructed in *Sea Garden* where H. D. is not so much planting a sea garden as she is faithfully recording into her poetry the flowers which naturally adorn the seashore. For the flower poems—**"Sea Poppies," "Sea Lily," "Sea Violet," "Sea Rose,"** and **"Sea Iris"**—H. D. chooses plants that can survive on the edge between land and sea, in the danger this exposed position promises them, as many critics have noted. However, what has not yet been acknowledged is that these flowers are actually wildflowers native to New England. The sea poppy of the poem is "treasure" "caught root / among wet pebbles" with a more potent fragrance than the more cultivated poppies growing in meadows. The persona values the flower, which becomes "fruit on the sand," in the space between the pines, the boulders, and the sea (H. D., *Collected* 21). In actuality a wildflower of southern New England, the golden sea poppies grow on gravelly beaches and in waste places (Newcomb 142), places where life is perilous and where garden plants, accustomed to the luxury of cultivated beds, could not grow. Similarly, growing on the sea's edge, the sea lily is anchored to the land underwater. A sea lily is really an invertebrate marine animal whose body resembles a land lily, and the lily of the poem has the privilege of having its great head "drift upon temple-steps" but it is also "shattered / in the wind," since it has to accept the violence of the ocean in which it lives. The sand cuts the flower and "yet though the whole wind / slash at your bark, / you are lifted up"— the lily triumphs over the power of the sea (H. D., *Collected* 14). Likewise, the true sea violet, a coastal flower with a violet color and a white throat, grows in sandy soil along the southern coast of Maine

(Newcomb 34). H. D. values it beyond the scented white violet and "greater blue violets" which "flutter on the hill." The poem's sea violet is paradoxically "fragile as agate," hardy enough to withstand the wind and shells of the "sand-bank." This violet has a "frail" grasp on the sand but survives. In fact, it not only survives but becomes a star edged with fire, a powerful symbol for how the outwardly "frail" can persevere in the harshest elements (H. D., *Collected* 25-26).

Not only the flowers, but the seashore itself in *Sea Garden* is New England imagery—a beach of gravel or sand, or craggy rocks meeting the sea directly— also based on places H. D. personally knew. "The splendour of your ragged coast" in **"The Shrine"** and the "gulls and sea-birds that cry discords" in **"The Wind Sleepers"** recall Casco Bay in southern Maine, near Portland (H. D., *Collected* 10, 15). The Maine coast provides images for H. D.'s "safe crescent" beaches, her cliffs and shoals, her beautiful graves which lure the boats into a place with no shelter. The coast provides allure to boats on the open sea—"honey is not more sweet / than the salt stretch of your beach"—but the boats are beaten by the sea, finding no safe landing place on the rocky coast (H. D., *Collected* 7, 8). The steep cliffs, the craggy coasts, the rocks meeting the sea evoke the southern side of Casco Bay, Cape Elizabeth with its "endless line of rock coasts, with here and there a fine bluff . . . combinations of cove and cliff of distinguished beauty" (Nutting 52). Here, the rocks abruptly clash with the ocean, providing a panorama for H. D.'s many struggles with the sea or the borderline between elements.

II

In *HERmione,* the land becomes an active spirit which exerts power. Instead of staying peacefully outside the civilized home, the land invades the home, blurring the lines between the exhilarating woods and the stultifying domestic sphere. Hermione, in fact, invites it in to help her escape the rigidity of her gender role. Even more importantly, the land becomes an integral part of Hermione's character; its influence helps shape the woman she is becoming. Additionally, the land plays a central role in her choice to become a writer; within this novel's parameters, she must be able to represent the land accurately in her work to qualify as a writer.

As in *Sea Garden,* H. D. continues her scientific rendering of the American landscape in *HERmione,* and she models the novel's setting on the Doolittle house in Upper Darby where the family moved in 1896 when H. D.'s father became the Director of the Flower Observatory at the University of Pennsylvania

(Guest 16). The Director's residence was on seven acres, along with the Observatory buildings. H. D.'s father describes it:

> The Observatory is located in an agricultural region away from the disturbances due to the heavy traffic and electric illumination of the city; the elevation is high and altogether the location quite as favorable as can be looked for in the immediate vicinity of a large city, at the same time it is easily accessible. By the recently constructed Newtown Square electric railway it may be reached from the University buildings, West Philadelphia, in thirty minutes or less.
>
> (Doolittle 123)

This then is the landscape of *HERmione*: a house surrounded by working dairy farms, orchards, open fields, and woods—"Gawd's own god-damn country," as George Lowndes, Hermione's sometime fiancé (a character based on Ezra Pound), calls it (84)—but one that is also bordered by the West Chester Pike and is only a short trolley ride from downtown Philadelphia.

In *HERmione,* instead of the land representing the spirit as in *Sea Garden,* the land becomes an active force to which the house and its occupants belong. In fact, this house is submerged in its environment; the outdoors invades the home. In contrast to pioneer women who were domesticating the wilderness (Kolodny 12), H. D. rejects domesticity, which she can afford to do because she is not facing the actual frontier like the pioneers and because her class standing provides her with the luxury of servants who do many of the everyday household tasks. For her, "progress" means returning domestic spaces like the home and the kitchen to a wild state because the wilderness is liberating, precisely because it can only now be fantasized. This house is filled with lilies and wild azalea boughs, and intimately grounded in its land. Screen doors slam, honeysuckle overruns the porch, and the dog Jock invades the kitchen.

Like the wild invasion encroaching on the home's domesticity, Hermione is more often in the woods than in the house where her mother Eugenia and all her expectations for Hermione reside. Significantly, H. D. inflates the bucolic nature of her setting, rendering it as primeval, a space engendering "female insurgency," to use Alaimo's words, rather than an outlying city suburb. At times, the surrounding woods and river become "torrents of white water running through deep forests," using the myths of a rustic, wild America (H. D., *HERmione* 6). This land, primeval and powerful, does not remain a benign backdrop for the action but becomes an integral part of Hermione's character. Significantly, at several points Hermione is figured as a tree—an indigenous being, with long stabilizing roots in Pennsylvania—demonstrating the way the place of her birth inextricably shapes her. She thinks,

> Pennsylvania. Names are in people, people are in names. Sylvania. I was born here. People ought to think before they call a place Sylvania.
>
> Pennsylvania. I am part of Sylvania. Trees. Trees. Trees. Dogwood, liriodendron with its green-yellow tulip blossoms. Trees are in people. People are in trees. Pennsylvania.
>
> (H. D., *HERmione* 5)

The immediacy of this relationship articulates the extent to which Hermione has been shaped by the forests themselves.

However, the forest contains, as well as shapes, Hermione who is often walking in a maze-like forest of liriodendron, oak, dogwood, larch, and tulip trees (H. D., *HERmione* 3-5). The maze atmosphere and tall, blowing trees also serve to represent her confusion as she reels from failing at mathematics in college and tries to determine what she will do, since, in her opinion, she is grown too large (in age and a pun on H. D.'s 5'11" frame) for the house and has not "ever *done* anything" (109). The woods shelter, yet as in "Pursuit," they also confuse with their immensity and sameness, leaving little trace of individuality: "Trees, no matter how elusive, in the end, walled one in. Trees were suffocation" (7-8). These trees, actually open woods around cultivated farmland and no longer part of a frontier, become, in their symbolism, thick and close like the ancient American forests. They muffle sound and action, even giving Hermione the impression of being underwater, drowning as well as suffocating. Either way, the trees stifle her ability to breathe and live. For Hermione, the way out of this maze is to head for the coast. Escape, as in *Sea Garden,* lies at the seashore, which is the way she understands freedom. From her family's suffocation, Hermione envisions a solitary escape, albeit an impossible one, to their beach cottage at Point Pleasant, New Jersey: "The circles of the trees were tree-green; she wanted the inner lining of an Atlantic breaker. . . . Pennsylvania could be routed only by another: New Jersey with its flatlands and the reed grass and the salt creeks where a canoe brushed Indian paint-brush" (H. D., *HERmione* 7). The seashore pulls at Hermione with its flatlands, rather than crowding trees, and its promise of danger and adventure.

In essence, then, inland Pennsylvania and the coast seem irreconcilable and represent a fundamental opposition in Hermione, bequeathed by her father and mother. According to the novel's logic, Hermione's feelings for place are genetically directed; an attachment to place is embedded in a literal, biological way:

> In Pennsylvania, Carl Gart had found a sort of peace and a submergence of the thing that drove him, that had driven his people to New England and then West

to trek back East. In Eugenia Gart, the fibres were rooted and mossed over and not to be disrupted. If Eugenia Gart pulled up her mossgrown fibres, Pennsylvania itself would ache like a jaw from which has been extracted a somewhat cumbrous molar. . . . In Hermione Gart, the two never fused and blended, she was both moss-grown, inbedded and at the same time staring with her inner vision on forever-tumbled breakers. If she went away, her spirit would break; if she stayed, she would be suffocated.

(H. D., *HERmione* 9)

Because she inherited from both parents, Hermione contends with both desires—to stay and to leave—and both have a price, a breaking of spirit or the threat of suffocation. Eventually, Hermione plans to leave, to be directed by "her inner vision on forever-tumbled breakers," but part of her is moss-grown already, embedded into the American subsoil that she carries with her forever.

As well as controlling her character's development, the land is pivotal in shaping Hermione's sense of what it means to be a writer. Although Eugenia comments that Hermione ought to go on writing her "'dear little stories,'" mediocre magazine writing no longer satisfies Hermione; she wants to become an artist (H. D., *HERmione* 80). And in this novel, being an artist is tied to the ability to write in a way that is evocative of place. Hermione laments that she did not continue with her music and that she cannot paint; she needs artistic skills to capture the "'composition' of elements" that make up a place:

> Music might have caught the trail of the grass as she ran on across the meadow and the deep note made by a fabulous bee that sprung into vision, blotting out the edge of the stables, almost blotting out the sun itself with its magnified magnificent underbelly and the roar of its sort of booming. The boom of the bee in her ear, his presence like an eclipse across the sun brought visual image of the sort of thing she sought for . . . it had not occurred to Her to try and put the thing in writing.
>
> (13)

As the novel progresses, however, Hermione increasingly sees writing as a way to capture "the thing"— the trail of grass, the bee and his eclipse, Pennsylvania—and to redeem her failure at college: "Writing was an achievement like playing the violin or singing like Tetrazzini" (71).

As her writing develops, Hermione finds that her emphasis on Pennsylvanian materials positions her as a specifically American writer, as opposed to the European tradition which carries more caché with her worldly friend George. Unlike Hermione, George tries to reject ties to American literature and art, which, to

him, lack the sophistication and development of their European counterparts, and so she rejects his view and satirizes his youthful pomposity. While walking in Hermione's woods, George parodies the opening lines from Longfellow's poem *Evangeline*: "'*This is the forest primeval, the murmuring pines and the hemlocks,'* (George intoned dramatically; she knew why she didn't love him) *'bearded with moss and with garments green, indistinct in the twilight'*" (H. D., *HERmione* 65). Stubbornly resisting George's preference for European art, Hermione thinks, "why couldn't George ever let me alone to see things in my own way, to enjoy things even if they are provincial?" (133) George laughs at her parties and makes the museum offerings seem dowdy: "'Don't look at those things' [he says] and if this is what Europe does to people, Hermione thought, I don't want Europe" (135).

III

In *Paint It Today,* as in *Hermione,* the land wields power, shaping the central character, Midget, much the way it shaped Hermione. However, in this novel, that power operates at a much deeper level: formative environments create an essential difference between Americans and the English, thereby inextricably separating Midget from her European peers. Even though Midget has moved from the U.S. to Europe, she remains rooted in the American land of her youth. In describing how Midget's character is formed, H. D. writes, "I know that the important things in the tempering of a soul are perhaps the rough, the commonplace, that seem to youth and early maturity unimportant, stifling, even inhibiting surroundings or conditions. . . . I am trying . . . to give a picture of that being, that spider, that small, hatched bird, that flawless shell that once contained an unborn being" (H. D., *Paint* 6). The "small, hatched bird" is Midget, and her "flawless shell" is the Pennsylvania in which Midget grew up, where the novel opens. The shell, or the place, is what "tempers" the soul and creates the person.

When describing Midget at the beginning of the novel, H. D. literally describes her as her environment, again emphasizing the land's ability to shape identity: "Her portrait? Find her on the trail of the Pennsylvania foot-hills breaking her first bunches of the wax-pink mountain laurel; find her with a screwed-up knot of precious wild arbutus, or the first wandlike bough of dogwood" (5). The mountain laurel, arbutus, and dogwood, all native plants to the Pennsylvania woods, become synonymous with Midget; she becomes a native part of her surroundings, as indigenous as the plants.

However, where *HERmione* ends with the central character located in the American landscape, *Paint It*

Today transports that character to Europe and yet retains the ingrained sense of American identity. As for many expatriates, for H. D. the U.S. becomes more easily definable in contrast to Europe and more easily appropriated for the imagination after she herself left. The American landscape remains the dominant influence in Midget's perceptions, and she continually compares what she is seeing in her travels to what she had experienced in the U.S. While she grows to prefer living in Europe, the U.S. landscape remains more alive for her, and we see that Midget remains an American artist despite her decision to live in Europe: "Here in France, at Etaples, the people were a reality. In America, it was the white sand that lived, the wind, the stainless rout of stars" (H. D., *Paint* 16). All aspects of environment in Europe pale against the U.S. as when watching a sunset Midget thinks, "this was not the sun, this flameless, low-swinging, mid-European substitute" (15). Even the wind in Europe "was not yet wind, not wind that is when contrasted with that rush of swords that cut the sand stretches into snow and ice patterns and blared through the Maine pines and tore in mid-summer, tornadowise, walnut and tough oak branches from the walnut and great oak trees" (14). This rough wind is the same one cutting sand across flower petals in *Sea Garden* and ripping through the dense forests in *HERmione*.

Having established a basic difference between Europe and the U.S., and having endowed the American landscape with a certain power continental society lacks, H. D. develops that difference as one which creates a permanent, essentialized separation between peoples according to the environment of their youth. In London, Midget can fit in, appear to be English, "tall to the breaking-in-the-middle point, with fluttering hat brim and tenuous ankles, as of their own world" (H. D., *Paint* 18), and the literary people she meets are always surprised when she reveals that she is American, an alien in their country. Her American identity separates her from these English acquaintances, "in time, in space, a thousand, thousand years" apart (19). And what separates her is her sensual experience of the American land, of specifically grapevines in one case. Midget is at a party, "patter-[ing] rubbish with the best" when she hears a woman describing French vineyards second hand, as her friend in France has described them to her: "'He says he will have a house party and invite me especially next spring. It is indescribable, he says'" (17), and as the woman describes the "indescribable" event she hasn't seen, Midget reflects on the grapevines she has seen. Over her back porch in Bethlehem, H. D.'s house had a grape arbor, a favorite place for her and her cousins to play. The memory of touching, seeing, smelling those blossoms just as they open is a fragrance H. D.

inscribes into her writing and her construction of American identity. The fragrance is "*cold*," "identified with the tiny green feather bunches curling out from the very young, very small underfurred, red-tipped leaves of the grapevine. This was the fragrance of the grape flowers, if flowers these young spikes, resembling the unripe lilac blossoms, could be called" (19). The fragrance of Midget's American past is essential to her identity and delineates the line between herself and the English people she is meeting. Midget is different because of what she has experienced in her youth through her senses and her connection to the land.

Positing environment—the fragile eggshell, the sensory experience, the influence of seasons—as the crucial component constructing identity, rather than the literary and social culture one is born of and into, positions H. D. as an environmental determinist. H. D. clinches her emphasis on environment with the bald announcement, quoted in my introduction, that "language and tradition do not make a people, but the heat that presses on them, the cold that baffles them, the alternating lengths of night and day" (H. D., *Paint* 20). The physicality of place—the summer heat, the cold, the length of daylight in each season—forms people, as Midget is formed by the U.S. In some ways, this position is isolating because Midget remains an outsider in Europe, an exotic waiting to be caught. Alternatively, Midget's position gives her an outsider's insights, and her essentialized American identity can travel with her wherever she goes. Midget has earned that identity by living in the American environment, breathing the air, living through the seasons, and experiencing grape blossoms.

Reading H. D. as a writer who so emphasizes place alters our critical view of her work. Much of her current critical reputation rests on her reliance on experimental strategies, quite evident in the three texts interrogated here as well as throughout her career. But extensive exploration of that dimension of her work, and the corresponding critical assertion that her content is disconnected from the U.S., easily obscures H. D.'s equally strong reliance on physical place as a shaping factor in her work. She is too often imagined as existing in an imaginary Greek world; past critical discussions even interrogate the authenticity of the Greece she creates. In contrast, here I have shown that in H. D.'s landscapes while the Greek layer may be the top layer of H. D.'s palimpsest, it is overlaid upon a very real portrayal of the northeastern U.S. H. D.'s images, at their roots, are American, but even more significantly, these places exert the power to shape her characters' identities and ultimately H. D.'s own art, firmly aligning her texts with her own geographic roots.

Notes

1. This article is a revision of the second chapter of my dissertation.

2. This letter is also used by Eileen Gregory to support her exploration of H. D.'s involvement in hellenism. Gregory argues that the passage I have quoted here is often used as a means of collapsing H. D.'s hellenism into biographical and psychological matter—as though her early hellenic orientation were only a mask or shield for personal problems later cogently unraveled by Freud. Such a biographical interpretation misses the complexity of the hellenic fiction itself, reducible neither to biographical or Freudian allegory nor to literary conventions. (*Hellenism* 33)

My argument in this article avoids the pitfalls that Gregory critiques, but I clearly have interpreted H. D.'s letter in a far different way than her. I find Gregory's objectives in *H. D. and Hellenism* compelling, but I do believe that if critics restrict H. D. to a hellenic sphere, we have done her a disservice. Therefore, my work complements Gregory's, opening new spaces in H. D. studies.

3. Friedman was countering the claim that in *Sea Garden* "the landscape . . . is never anchored in human geography because . . . the 'country' is imaginary and symbolic" made by Barbara Guest (qtd in Friedman 98). In addition, Gregory sees in *Sea Garden* a consistent landscape, but she does not identify that landscape with a specific place ("Rose" 139).

4. The scope of this article prevents me from developing a full analysis of gender here. However, chapter three of my dissertation addresses the intersection of gender and nationality.

5. Many H. D. critics have read the symbolism of *Sea Garden*'s flowers as resistant to domestication and in favor of danger and wilderness. I am working in the same vein but claiming a broader reading of nature and spirit.

6. Friedman was the first to connect H. D. to transcendentalism. She writes that H. D.'s "use of nature as objective correlative for spirit attested to her American literary heritage—the Transcendentalism of Emerson and Thoreau" (99).

7. H. D. to Mary Herr. 1944. Hilda Doolittle Collection, Special Collections Department, Bryn Mawr College Library. I would like to thank H. D.'s Estate for permission to quote from H. D.'s unpublished letters and published texts. Copyright 1925 by Hilda Doolittle. Copyright © by The Estate of Hilda Doolittle. Copyright © 2004 by The Schaffner Family Foundation. Used by permission of New Directions Publishing Corporation.

8. Pratt to H. D. 9 July 1956. The Yale Collection of American Literature, Beinecke Rare Book and Manuscript Library, Yale University.

Works Cited

Alaimo, Stacy. *Undomesticated Ground: Recasting Nature as Feminist Space*. Ithaca: Cornell University Press, 2000.

Austin, Mary. "Regionalism in American Fiction." *English Journal* 21 (Feb 1932): 97-107.

Collecott, Diana. "Memory and Desire: H. D.'s 'A Note on Poetry.'" *Agenda* 25.3-4 (Autumn/Winter 1987-88): 65-76.

Debo, Annette. *America in H. D.'s Palimpsest: Place, Race, and Gender in her Early Poetry and Prose*. Dissertation. University of Maryland, College Park, 1998. Ann Arbor: UMI, 1998. 9836388.

Dembo, L. S. "Norman Holmes Pearson on H. D.: An Interview." *Contemporary Literature* 10.4 (Autumn 1969): 435-446.

Doolittle, C. L. "The Flower Observatory—University of Pennsylvania." *Popular Astronomy* 5 (1897-98): 122-25.

Fletcher, John Gould. "Three Imagist Poets." *The Little Review* June/July 1916: 32-41.

Friedman, Susan Stanford. "Exile in the American Grain: H. D.'s Diaspora." *Women's Writing in Exile*. Eds. Mary Lynn Broe and Angela Ingram. Chapel Hill: University of North Caroline Press, 1989. 87-112.

Glotfelty, Cheryll. Introduction. *Ecocriticism Reader: Landmarks in Literary Ecology*. Eds. Cheryll Glotfelty and Harold Fromm. Athens: University of Georgia Press, 1996. xv-xxxvii.

Gregory, Eileen. "Rose Cut in Rock: Sappho and H. D.'s Sea Garden." *Signets*. Eds. Susan Stanford Friedman and Rachel Blau DuPlessis. Madison: University of Wisconsin Press, 1990. 129-154.

———. *H. D. and Hellenism: Classic Lines*. Cambridge: Cambridge University Press, 1997.

Guest, Barbara. *Herself Defined: The Poet H. D. and her World*. London: Collins, 1984.

H. D. *Collected Poems 1912-1944*. Ed. Louis L. Martz. New York: New Directions, 1986.

―――. *H. D. papers. The Yale Collection of American Literature.* Beinecke Rare Book and Manuscript Library. Yale University. New Haven, Connecticut.

―――. *Hermione.* New York: New Directions, 1981.

―――. *Paint It Today.* New York: New York University Press, 1992.

Kolodny, Annette. *The Land Before Her.* Chapel Hill: University of North Carolina Press, 1984.

Mandel, Charlotte. "Magical Lenses: Poet's Vision Beyond the Naked Eye." *H. D. Woman and Poet.* Ed. Michael King. Orono, Maine: National Poetry Foundation, 1986. 301-318.

Morris, Adalaide. "Science and the Mythopoeic Mind: The Case of H. D." *Chaos and Order.* Ed. N. Katherine Hayles. Chicago: University of Chicago Press, 1991. 195-220.

Newcomb, Lawrence. *Newcomb's Wildflower Guide.* Boston: Little, Brown, 1977.

Norwood, Vera. *Made From This Earth: American Women and Nature.* Chapel Hill: University of North Carolina Press, 1993.

Nutting, Wallace. *Maine Beautiful.* New York: Garden City, 1924.

Thoreau, Henry David. *Excursions.* 1863. Gloucester, Massachusetts: Peter Smith, 1975.

Wiebe, Robert H. *Who We Are: A History of Popular Nationalism.* Princeton: Princeton University Press, 2002.

Wolle, Francis. *A Moravian Heritage.* Boulder: Empire, 1972.

S. Renée Faubion (essay date fall/winter 2004)

SOURCE: Faubion, S. Renée. "'This Is No Rune nor Symbol'": The Sensual in H. D.'s Feminized Sublime." *Paideuma: Studies in American and British Modernist Poetry* 33, nos. 2 & 3 (fall & winter 2004): 111-30

[*In the following essay, Faubion explores H. D.'s development of a theory of the sublime in which she treats the concept of the feminine as a construct of both identity and culture.*]

H. D.'s writing is heavily influenced by the sublime. Although she prefers the word "vision" to the term "sublime," for her the two describe a single event: the process by which we contact the infinite. H. D. does more, however, than simply rename this process. In *Notes on Thought and Vision* and *Trilogy,* H. D. offers an important example of a woman revising the sublime to open a public space within which she need not accommodate its implicitly patriarchal narrative. Through such alterations, H. D. develops a theory that valorizes the feminine both as an identity and as a cultural abstraction; indeed, the feminine becomes the most powerful, most fundamental element of her sublime.[1]

Before I turn to H. D.'s theory, however, a discussion of the aesthetic sublime and its gender implications is in order. This branch of the sublime, which presents the event as an internal, almost psychological, experience, is examined in Kant's *Critique of Judgement.* In his analysis, Kant describes the imagination as a sensory faculty, one which accumulates sensory details and impressions from the world until it is finally overwhelmed by the information it receives. He contrasts imagination with reason, which he identifies as an abstracting faculty, one which intervenes to "rescue" the imagination when the latter is overtaxed. Kant uses this scenario to justify his assertion that reason is a "supersensible" faculty superior to imagination (116). For example, Kant argues that in its efforts to comprehend the infinite power of a superhuman force, the imagination is limited by its dependence on sensory detail. Overwhelmed, it is soon paralyzed by fear and must be rescued by the reason. In such instances, Kant argues, reason allows us to envision ourselves as separate from and resistant to more powerful forces; although such resistance may ultimately be futile, it does offer us a measure of independence from the divine or natural power which initially overwhelms us. It is that independence which transforms our abject terror into a sublime experience (Kant 123-26). Thus, in *Critique of Judgement,* the imagination is always programmed to fail—or, as Kant says at one point, to "sacrifice" itself (136)—when faced with the infinite; in this way, it lays the groundwork for reason's triumph.

Although apparently innocuous, the pattern of failure and rescue central to Kant's sublime becomes problematic when the gender assumptions beneath its surface are exposed, for he links the imagination with qualities traditionally associated with the feminine and the reason with qualities traditionally assumed to be masculine. In Kant's analysis, the imagination seems frail, sensual, and easily overwhelmed—the image of women in western culture—while the reason is powerful, superior to the sensual, and capable of abstraction—that is, a likeness of men. Although implicit, Kant's gender coding is so persistent that numerous scholars, not all of them feminists, have recognized it.

Paul de Man, for example, describes Kant's interpretation of the sublime as a "story" rather than an "argument," charging that it depends on the anthropomorphization of reason and imagination (104). In his analysis, de Man emphasizes the links between the imagination and the feminine in Kant's theory: "What could it possibly mean, in analytical terms, that the imagination sacrifices itself, like Antigone or Iphigenia—for one can only imagine this shrewd and admirable imagination as the feminine heroine of a tragedy—for the sake of reason?" (104) Barbara Claire Freeman also describes imagination's role in the sublime narrative as the sacrifice of a feminine "surrogate" (69). In *The Feminine Sublime: Gender and Excess in Women's Fiction,* Freeman suggests that

> Kant's account of the ordeal of the imagination resembles eighteenth- and nineteenth-century depictions (or constructions) of sexuality, particularly those by Sade and Freud. So perfectly does Kant's description of the imagination's role conform to the notion of woman as a sexually passive vehicle who awaits a violent penetration and whose "pleasure" consists in a certain adaptation to pain, we might conclude that this model of gender relations has occasioned, if not in fact determined, the very parameters in which Kant conceives of its [imagination's] trajectory.

(73)

Freeman also likens Kant's description of imagination's role in the sublime to Freud's discussion of feminine castration; just as the woman in Freud's scenario must learn to interpret her own genitalia as an inferior version of the man's, so Kant's sublime forces the imagination to acknowledge its inferiority to reason (73). Freeman's analysis, like de Man's, suggests that for women, the Kantian sublime may lead not to a sense of the self's power but rather to a sense of its limitations.

In addition to the parallels Freeman identifies connecting the Kantian narrative to Freud's theories of feminine castration and female sexuality, many critics have also noted similarities between Kant's sublime and Freud's oedipal theory (Weiskel 93; Diehl 2-3; Arensberg 6-7).[2] According to these readings, the poet begins his contact with the sublime at odds with that experience. Just as in the oedipal narrative, where the son must learn to identify with the father rather than to oppose him, in the sublime the poet must learn to identify with the awe that strikes him in order to come to terms with it. Joanne Feit Diehl offers one of the most important feminist assessments of the consequences this patriarchal subtext presents for women writers. In *Women Poets and the American Sublime,* Diehl argues that literary tradition provides a crucial mechanism through which the male poet recovers from the psychological trauma of the sublime. He is able to regain his composure partly because he regards himself as part of a line of (male) poets who have managed to overcome the disorientation that imagination suffers in the sublime (Diehl 1-2). Moreover, the male poet's attempt to identify with the awe which temporarily paralyzes him is furthered by the fact that this awe often is coded as a patriarchal force—as an entity rather like the poet himself (Diehl 2-3). For women, however, Diehl argues, the task of coming to terms with this experience has often been far more complex, largely because it seems to exclude them. Historically, women poets have had relatively few female predecessors after which to model themselves; moreover, unlike men, they have great difficulty relating to an awe which is typed as a masculine force (Diehl 2-4). In fact, far from providing the woman poet with a sense of her own power, the infinite awe "may seem so 'ravishing' (a term long associated with the workings of the Sublime) that she is vanquished" (Diehl 3). In other words, Diehl argues that the masculine imagery which traditionally has shaped the sublime limits the woman poet's ability to interpret that experience. As a result, Diehl believes, women risk being stranded in the moment of sublime discontinuity, with no sense of how to recover from or communicate their contact with the infinite (2).

As the interpretations of critics such as de Man, Freeman, and Diehl indicate, theories of the sublime are to some extent hostile to the feminine. Nevertheless, although it has mirrored the misogyny of its culture, the sublime has also been the site of significant revision by women writers. Freeman and Diehl have both explored the potential for such revision. In her examination of novels authored by women, Freeman identifies a feminist sublime which "involves taking up a position of respect in response to an incalculable otherness" (11). Freeman describes that otherness as feminine, not because she believes it has any inherently gendered qualities but because she sees the feminine as a force that disrupts binary oppositions (9). The result is a sublime without a permanent authoritative center, one more responsive to a wide range of difference (Freeman 11-12). Thus, for her the feminine dislodges a masculine authority without actually stepping into the void which that shift creates. Diehl also defines a sublime that works against traditional patriarchal narratives. Yet the "Counter-Sublime" she identifies can be fraught with anxiety and frustration and does not always allow women writers to express themselves fully and freely. Diehl believes that even as they redesign the sublime, writers such as Emily Dickinson, Marianne Moore, and Sylvia Plath remain somehow constrained by the influence the patriarchy retains over modes of expression.

These constraints shape not only how they express themselves, but also what elements of their experience they reveal in their poetry (26-28, 50, 141).[3] H. D.'s work, particularly *Notes on Thought and Vision* and *Trilogy,* differs from the patterns identified by Freeman and Diehl in that it describes a sublime founded on a powerful sense of the feminine. In H. D.'s theory, the feminine is fully integrated into the process of vision, emerging as the central force in that experience.[4] Thus, although her theory may at times appear essentialist, it is a crucial moment in the history of the sublime.

H. D.'s revision of the sublime, particularly her tendency to emphasize the role of the sensory, can be profitably examined by comparing it with Julia Kristeva's *Revolution in Poetic Language.* Although Kristeva does not mention imagination, reason, or the sublime by name, her discussion of the semiotic and the symbolic offers important parallels to sublime theory. The semiotic, the fundamental level of the self, demonstrates strong links to the imagination as Kant understands it. Kristeva identifies the semiotic as the prelingual realm of drives; it is a primary field for information, a range of energy and response, of competing and even chaotic impulses (25, 28). These impulses constantly threaten to shatter the apparently stable identity which attempts to regulate them (Kristeva 28). Similarly, in the Kantian sublime, the imagination addresses a superabundance of detail, ultimately generating a crisis in which the self is absorbed, however temporarily, by a sense of the infinite. Thus, both Kantian imagination and the Kristevan semiotic resist resolution and stability, instead acting as channels for an excess of energy.

Parallels can also be drawn between Kantian reason and the Kristevan symbolic. According to Kristeva, the symbolic level attempts to contain and control the semiotic; it occurs at the level of language and ritual, setting up structures within which the shifting, inchoate semiotic can be channeled, however briefly, into a single meaning or identity (Kristeva 43, 70). The symbolic acts as a "social effect," governing the relationship between the self and an other; it shapes this relationship in part through language, particularly through the connection between subject and predicate (Kristeva 29, 54). Just as the grammatical subject creates a site of enunciation within a sentence, on a larger scale the symbolic level creates an apparently cohesive self whose perspective attempts to define and control the world (Kristeva 86-87). Likewise, Kantian reason articulates a relationship between the self and an other, rescuing the self from an experience of awe which otherwise threatens to engulf and obliterate it. Reason accomplishes this rescue in much the same way that the symbolic operates in Kristeva's theory, by acting

as the "positing, linking, assertive, cohesive element" which "completes the utterance and makes it finite (a sentence)" while defining "the spatio-temporal and communicational positing of the speaking subject" (Kristeva 54). That is to say, like the symbolic, reason limits the infinite, in the process establishing a position of safety and identity for the subject.

Unlike the Kantian sublime, however, which prizes control, Kristeva's theory of poetic language privileges semiotic drives for their capacity to break down and problematize oppressive symbolic narratives.[5] In her analysis, Kristeva stresses the political implications of this process, particularly the tendency of the symbolic to stifle rebellion. To combat this oppressiveness, she insists that poetic language must "disturb the logic that dominate[s] the social order and do so through that logic itself, by assuming and unraveling its position, its syntheses, and hence, the ideologies it controls" (83). It does so by "miming" reality—by reenacting the symbolic level's efforts to create meaning (79). Through this reenactment, poetic language exposes the contingency of meaning, emphasizing what the culture represses: the knowledge that the symbolic is not the whole of human experience, but merely one layer which tries to control the semiotic so that social harmony can be maintained (79-81). Poetic language thus "infinitizes" the meanings, positions, and relationships expressed in the symbolic, revealing the power of underlying semiotic impulses (56).

This process echoes the strategy H. D. engages in as she creates a feminized sublime that challenges Kant's traditional patriarchal narrative. In identifying reason as the power which permits us to come to terms with the sublime, Kant uses the symbolic to shape a semiotic, non-verbal experience and to contain the feminine elements that have been coded into that experience. In *Notes on Thought and Vision* and *Trilogy,* however, H. D. undermines Kant's symbolic narrative by strengthening the role of the feminized sensory faculty—what Kant calls the imagination—so that it becomes at least as potent an element of the sublime as is the "supersensible" faculty of reason.[6] To communicate the power of the sensory, H. D.'s sublime relies heavily on the body, both as an agent of sexual response and, more broadly, as a field for sensory information. As she draws the sensory more fully into the sublime, H. D. questions and revises the gendered meanings encoded in Kant's sublime. The result is a theory which defies the patriarchal narrative of the sublime by offering a woman-centered alternative to that narrative.

One of H. D.'s most important early statements regarding sublime vision appears in *Notes on Thought and Vision.*[7] Written in 1919, *Thought and Vision* represents an early stage in H. D.'s theory of the sublime. A series of exploratory fragments compiled as she was first becoming immersed in Freudian theory,[8] *Thought and Vision* is more overtly sexual than is H. D.'s later work, **Trilogy,** written from 1942 to 1944. Nevertheless, *Thought and Vision* is instructive for what it reveals of H. D.'s interest in the sensory and the feminine. H. D. begins *Thought and Vision* by proclaiming that there are "three states or manifestations of life: body, mind, over-mind" (17). The body and the mind are equally important to vision, a process which she divides into two categories. "Vision of the womb" is centered in the reproductive organs (H. D. calls it the "love-region" or "love-mind" [19, 23]) and is the realm of feeling and experiences, of the "majority of dream and of ordinary vision" (20-21). In contrast, the second kind of consciousness, "vision of the brain," is aligned with thought (20-21). Contrary to Kant's renderings of the sublime, however, this intellectual level of vision is not associated with the masculine. Moreover, it does not take precedence over womb vision; the two are "equally important" in H. D.'s sublime (21). In fact, as her interest in "vision of the womb" suggests, H. D.'s theory reflects her fundamental concern with the role of the feminine in this process; at one point in *Thought and Vision,* she even wonders whether it is "easier for a woman to attain this state of consciousness [the visionary union of womb and brain vision] than for a man" (20). Despite the distinction she makes between vision of the womb and vision of the brain, then, for H. D. each of these levels is centered in the feminine and in the sensual.

The significant role played by the sensory in *Thought and Vision* is evidenced in the comparison H. D. draws between womb vision and the ancient Eleusinian mysteries. After noting the importance of sexual stimulation in the Eleusinian initiation (*NTV* [*Notes on Thought and Vision*] 29-30), she suggests that those seeking enlightenment in the modern world can find "plenty of pornographic literature"—by which she means writers such as Boccaccio, Rabelais, and Sterne—to help them begin the process of vision (30). She continues by warning readers who do not respond to such writers that there is "something wrong . . . physically" with them, and that furthermore, those who "cannot read these people and enjoy them . . . are not ready for the first stage of initiation" into sublime vision (30). On the other hand, "if you do read these people and enjoy them and enjoy them really with your body, because you have a normal healthy body, then you may be ready for the second stage of initiation," the exercise of intellect (30-31). These blunt comments express a fundamental element of H. D.'s theory: the importance of the sensory in the sublime.

Well into *Thought and Vision,* H. D. shifts her focus from the body and the mind to the triad of subconscious, conscious, and over-mind. This change reflects not an abandonment of the sensual but rather her developing sense of the relationship between the sensual and all levels of consciousness. The subconscious becomes the territory of womb vision, "the world of sleeping dreams and the world great lovers enter, physical lovers, but very great ones" (*NTV* 49). In contrast, the over-mind is "the world of waking dreams," of the greatest "spiritual lovers" (49). The conscious mind—the intellect—unites these two realms (49). In this revised scheme, the body remains the catalyst for the sublime experience, for it is the body's passions which may be "transmuted to this other, this different form, concentrated, ethereal, which we refer to in common speech as spirit" (48). Conversely, to ignore the body is to "retard" the spirit (52). This is a marked departure from Kant's theory, in which the imagination's failure allows reason to resolve the sublime experience. Instead, for H. D. the sensory faculty does not fail; indeed, it is the prime mover of the sublime experience.

This link between the sensory and the process of vision shapes the expression of the sublime in H. D.'s **Trilogy.** Although **Trilogy** manages gender issues more subtly than does *Notes on Thought and Vision,* H. D.'s war epic also relies on the sensory to overturn the values implicit in the Kantian sublime and replace them with a theory of vision that is shaped by elements traditionally coded as feminine.

The connections between the sensual, the semiotic and H. D.'s theory of the sublime can be seen in the second book of **Trilogy, Tribute to the Angels,** as the speaker questions language's capacity to address vision. Through a spiritual alchemical process,[9] she has produced an "opalescent" substance which will further her advancement toward the sublime (13.2).[10] Urged by her "patron" to name the substance, she explains that she cannot, for to do so would be to separate herself from it:

> I do not want
>
> to talk about it,
> I want to minimize thought,
>
> concentrate on it
> till I shrink,
>
> dematerialize
> and am drawn into it.
>
> (14.10-16)

As this passage suggests, in the speaker's eyes naming delineates objects; it allows the symbolic to mark—perhaps even to create—a break between what something is and what it is not. This runs counter to the speaker's strategy for achieving the sublime, for she hopes to shake free of her own boundaries—to "dematerialize," as she says—and be absorbed by the infinite. Such a process differs from Kant's narrative, where the infinite is given a limit by the capacity of reason to *"completely* comprehend" it *"under* a concept" (Kant 116; emphasis in original). Kant admits that this limit is artificial—the word he uses is "aesthetical"—and distinguishes it from the actual mathematical limitlessness of the sublime (116), but this admission seems merely to emphasize the arbitrariness of his theory. While Kant attempts to devise an infinite which can be limited and absorbed by the self, H. D. confronts more directly the boundlessness of the sublime; her speaker hopes to be consumed by the infinite, rather than to define its boundaries.

The speaker in *Tribute to the Angels* achieves the sublime unity she seeks with the opalescent substance by first focusing on the sensory; her own "dematerialization" occurs through her extraordinary concentration on the materiality of the substance, which has come so fully into being that "it lives, it breaths" (*Angels* [*Tribute to the Angels*] 13.7). As the substance's phenomenal nature grows more vital, language becomes incapable of expressing its vitality:

> it gives off—fragrance?
>
> I do not know what it gives,
> a vibration that we can not name
>
> for there is no name for it. . . .
>
> > (*Angels* 13.8-11)

By using poetry to indicate the inability of words to describe the substance, H. D. forces language to participate in its own disruption; she enacts what Kristeva describes as the "permanent struggle to show the facilitation of drives within the linguistic order itself" (Kristeva 81). This struggle resurfaces in *Tribute to the Angels* as the speaker describes the opalescent substance primarily through gaps in language:

> I said lived, it gave—
> fragrance—was near enough
>
> to explain that quality
> for which there is no name. . . .
>
> > (14.3-6)

The substance exists at the semiotic level, in a world of "heart-beats" and "pulse-beats" (14.9), exceeding the symbolic but not the sensory, for it is the speaker's senses, and not her language, that best register this substance's presence. Moreover, her desire to "dematerialize" (*Angels* 14.15) reflects not a departure from

the physical but a desire to dissolve boundaries to become integrated into the materiality of the opalescent substance. In H. D.'s sublime, then, the sensory capacity which Kant had circumscribed so tightly becomes an arena for a more profound perception than language can achieve.

This semiotic, sensory element of H. D.'s vision in *Tribute to the Angels* grows more pronounced as the Lady appears. The Lady—the Virgin Mother—is a crucial figure in the speaker's advancement toward vision. Her appearance indicates the speaker's responsiveness to the sublime and offers a further illustration of H. D.'s theory, for the speaker describes this figure by once again indicating language's failure. In response to those who insist that the Lady is "a symbol of beauty" (37.1), the speaker emphasizes the sublime ineffability of this figure:

> This is no rune nor symbol,
> what I mean is—it is so simple
>
> yet no trick of the pen or brush
> could capture that impression. . . .
>
> > (*Angels* 40.1-4)

Earlier the speaker offers other evidence of language's inability to depict the Lady; she is not "hieratic," not "frozen," not "very tall," "not shut up in a cave," "not / / imprisoned in leaden bars / in a coloured window" (38.3-4, 15-18). The speaker adopts an identical strategy to describe the color that cloaks the Lady:

> when I said white,
> I did not mean sculptor's or painter's white,
>
> nor porcelain; dim-white could
> not suggest it. . . .
>
> > (*Angels* 40.9-12)

Through this process, the speaker breaks down language, yet again forcing the symbolic level to disclose its limitations.

Although not captured at the level of language, the Lady does have a physical presence:

> she was not impalpable like a ghost,
> she was not awe-inspiring like a Spirit,
>
> she was not even over-whelming
> like an Angel.
>
> > (*Angels* 40.17-20)

Her palpability is a crucial element of her being and is referred to repeatedly in *Angels.* "Visible and actual" (19.1), she "knock[s]" (25.6) and is found "actually standing there" (26.2),[11] "look[ing] so kindly at us" with a book in her arm (35.8, 10). These details give her life and force, in contrast to the numerous paintings which reduce her to a posed, lifeless figure (*Angels* 29-30). Such paintings operate at the symbolic level, relying on traditional interpretations to simplify the Lady so that she can more easily be represented as a humble queen, "her head bowed down / with the weight of a domed crown" or as "a wisp of a girl / trapped in a golden halo" (*Angels* 29.17-20). While these paintings address a frozen instant in an effort to define the Lady, the speaker in *Angels* pursues a different strategy; she suggests a semiotic space within which to perceive this vision. Such a space is defined by Kristeva as a "preverbal functional state that governs the connections between the body (in the process of constituting itself as a body proper), objects, and the protagonists of family structure" (27). Thus, the speaker concentrates not on what the Lady "means"—not on the symbolic interpretations attached to her figure—but on suggesting her as she "constitutes" a "body proper" relating to other objects. The effect of this strategy is not to define the Lady but rather to challenge traditional interpretations that depict her as something removed from this world. To put it another way, the sensory faculty releases a semiotic complexity which allows a being who escapes language nevertheless to be powerfully present.

This strategy of unraveling language and the symbolic reappears as the figure of Mary Magdalen is introduced in the final book of *Trilogy, The Flowering of the Rod.* Mary amplifies two key ideas introduced by the presentation of the Lady in *Tribute*: the role of women as seers and the importance of the sensual in the sublime. Historically, Mary Magdalen offers an emblem of the repentant sinner—the prostitute whose spiritual purity is restored through her commitment to a (male) savior (Haskins 174-76). This traditional image of Mary Magdalen also appears in *The Flowering of the Rod,* but rather than being affirmed, it is used as a foil for H. D.'s depiction of Mary as both an emblem and a prophet of the sublime. It is Kaspar who, prior to his sublime revelation, first interprets Mary as a fallen woman. Interestingly, however, his assessment of her reflects not so much a notion of her sinfulness as it does a sense of her indecorousness, of her failure to be modest and deferential as a woman in her culture is expected to be. In his eyes, Mary is a brazen, importunate figure who resists his attempts to dismiss her. Because she does not behave as a woman should, his language can scarcely contain her; he can find words only for what she is not. He describes her as being "un-maidenly" (*Flowering* 13.14; 15.16), "hardly decent" (15.17), and "unseemly" (18.5, 7). Her demeanor and determination pose a challenge to the patriarchal order which the language of that system is not quite equipped to record.[12]

Mary's indecorous behavior is intensified midway through *The Flowering of the Rod* as she is seen "deftly un-weaving / / the long, carefully-braided tresses / of her extraordinary hair" to use in anointing Christ's feet (21.16-18). The primary Biblical source for this scene is Luke 7:37-50, in which a woman who is described as a "sinner" also uses her hair to anoint Christ's feet with oil.[13] Although the woman's sin is not specifically identified by Luke, the emphasis the Biblical passage places on her hair suggests that her transgressions were sexual, according to Susan Haskins. As Haskins notes in *Mary Magdalen: Myth and Metaphor,* women were thought to be more carnal than men, and their hair was considered a particularly potent tool of seduction (153-54). More specifically, the fact that the woman in the passage from Luke wears her hair loose rather than bound indicates that she may have been a prostitute (Haskins 18). The Pharisee Simon, who is the evening's host, is particularly troubled by "who and what manner of woman this is that toucheth" Christ (Luke 7:39). Christ overrules Simon's objections, however, interpreting the woman's behavior as a sign of her love for him and of her humility and faith; that is to say, he protects her from Simon's scorn by containing the sensual force of her act. In *The Flowering of the Rod,* however, H. D. presents a more complex reading of the woman, whom she identifies as Mary Magdalen. Like Christ, H. D. sees a certain purity and even simplicity in Mary; she describes her as being "seated on the floor / / like a child at a party," unaware of the attention she draws to herself (21. 14-15). Nevertheless, in H. D.'s rendering of the scene, Mary's sensuality remains potent and, for Simon, threatening:

> he had seen something like this
> in a heathen picture
>
> or a carved stone-portal entrance
> to a forbidden sea-temple;
>
> they called the creature,
> depicted like this
>
> seated on the sea-shore
> or on a rock, a Siren. . . .
>
> (22.3-10)

Through this association, Mary becomes dangerous: "[S]ome said, this mermaid sang / / and that a Siren-song was fatal / and wrecks followed the wake of such hair" (22.12-14). Mary thus represents a deadly feminine power, the trio of women whose voices were so seductive that they could completely enfeeble men, causing them simply to waste away (Tripp 533). Simon's association of Mary with the Sirens further emphasizes her sensuality, a sensuality which is specifically coded as feminine; in connecting Mary with the sirens, Simon allows an element of her character which was muted in the Biblical account of this scene to resurface as a fundamental component of her being. Yet Simon's rendering of Mary in *The Flowering of the Rod* remains reductive. She is driven not by a desire to enervate and destroy men, as he suspects, but by a desire to restore her culture to the past as H. D. interprets it, when the feminine was valued and offered a powerful challenge to violent impulses.[14] Like the Lady in *Tribute to the Angels,* Mary escapes attempts to limit her identity. Infused with a semiotic energy, she at once inscribes and unravels both Simon's and Christ's readings of her, setting up a space within which she can be both sensual and spiritually chaste, a figure for H. D.'s feminized sublime.

One of the most important events in *The Flowering of the Rod* is Mary Magdalen's recognition of her position as a conduit for the sublime. The fact that she turns to Kaspar for myrrh—a substance whose fragrance is a metonymic indicator for contact with the infinite in the poem (*Flowering* 7.6-8)—suggests that she initially does not comprehend her own innate capacity for vision. She begins to understand this capacity only when she dissects language to uncover the significance of her name:

> I am Mary, she said, of a tower-town,
> or once it must have been towered
>
> for Magdala is a tower;
> Magdala stands on the shore;
>
> I am Mary, she said, of Magdala,
> I am Mary, a great tower. . . .

(Flowering 16.1-6)

This etymological excavation reveals to Mary her potential to act as a seer by leading her to the "Mother of Mutilations / to Attis-Adonis-Tammuz and his mother who was myrrh" (16.15-16). Here Mary alludes to Cybele, a mother-goddess figure whose story, like that of the Sirens, plays out cultural fears of the threat feminine power poses to a patriarchal order. Although she was born a hermaphrodite, Cybele's male genitalia were cut away by other gods who dreaded the power that might attend her liminal sexual status. This event was often reenacted by her priests, who castrated themselves to honor her (Tripp 179-80)—a redefinition of her mutilation as a tribute to her power rather than as a sign of her weakness. Cybele's status as a goddess of regeneration (Tripp 180) also undermines the patriarchal symbolism of her dismemberment; while regenerative powers are commonly assigned to mother-goddesses, in Cybele's case such a capacity suggests that she has the ability to undo what was done to her, to restore to herself the power of the

phallus. This threat is reflected in her crown, which depicts the turreted wall of a city. The crown thus becomes a site for text-practice, a signifying process which uncovers the symbolic level's attempts to control the semiotic and construct a unified meaning (Kristeva 100-03); it marks Cybele as a figure of authority even as it draws attention to the phallus she lacks. In this way, it highlights the continual splitting of the symbolic by the semiotic, both inscribing and undoing the "inferiority" from which women were thought to suffer.

Through her incantatory reading of her name, Mary Magdalen retrieves a piece of feminist spiritual history which reveals to her her own transformative power. She insists that "through my will and my power / Mary shall be myrrh" (*Flowering* 16.7-8) before turning away from Kaspar declaring, "I have need, not of bread nor of wine / nor of anything that you can offer me" (19.5-6).[15] Through what Kristeva calls "the expenditure of semiotic violence" (79)—that is, by shattering the symbolic interpretation of herself as a flawed and female figure in need of mediation if she is to achieve sublime vision—Mary Magdalen uncovers a more complex and more accurate sense of herself and her ability to experience the sublime. Her recognition of her own visionary power is expressed in terms which reflect the strong connection H. D. sees between the physical and the spiritual; Mary herself has become myrrh, *"the incense-flower of the incense-tree"* (19.1; emphasis in original). This transformation of Mary to myrrh reflects H. D.'s desire to include the sensual at the peak of sublime revelation. For H. D., myrrh is not just a symbol of the sublime; it is a product of the sublime. This is emphasized in the closing lines of *The Flowering of the Rod* as the infant savior is referred to as a "bundle of myrrh" and actually emits the fragrance of the resin (43.7-8). In H. D.'s theory of the sublime, such comments are to be interpreted literally. Earlier in *The Flowering of the Rod,* the speaker insists that the transformation created by vision is real and is tied to the phenomenal; she argues that it is "[n]o poetic phantasy / but a biological reality, / / a fact" (9. 1-3). Mary's transformation to myrrh is therefore to be understood as a fact, as an instance of the cosmic unity which involves the body as well as the spirit, for this physical transformation is inextricably linked to Mary's spiritual development.

In *Trilogy,* as in *Notes on Thought and Vision,* H. D. uses the sensory as a channel through which to undermine the traditionally patriarchal narrative of the sublime. By capitalizing on what Julia Kristeva will later identify as semiotic impulses, H. D. counters Kant's interpretation of the sublime, particularly his insistence on privileging the masculine over the feminine. This is not to say that H. D. does away with symbolic narrative altogether, for as Kristeva notes, the semiotic and the symbolic are interdependent (24); that interdependence is evident in H. D.'s notion of vision, which is itself an effort to create meaning, to explain the workings of the sublime. Nevertheless, while Kant struggles in *Critique of Judgement* to control the semiotic force of the imagination through the symbolic ordering of reason, H. D.'s theory allows for a greater semiotic space, one within which a complex of attributes typically identified as feminine—the sensual, the sensory, the bodily—challenges and influences the symbolic. The result is a theory of the sublime which assumes the full participation, and even the dominance, of the feminine.

Notes

1. Both Shawn Alfrey and Susan Stanford Friedman have made explicit connections between H. D.'s work and the sublime. Alfrey argues that the purpose of H. D.'s sublime is to "historicize history" (84)—that is, to make history itself an object of inquiry from which we might learn to overcome the destructive, divisive elements in our culture. Crucial to Alfrey's study is her consideration of the Modernist notion of image. According to Alfrey, H. D. resists the gendered, often fascist, heroism that her contemporaries attached to the image, and it is this strategy which allows her to view history through a more critical lens (84). Friedman's *Psyche Reborn* examines H. D.'s use of Goddess elements to create a syncretic approach to transcendence (230-32). In a brief but intriguing passage, Friedman identifies H. D.'s use of the term "corrosive sublimate" in *The Walls Do Not Fall* (2. 25) as a complex pun indicating the poet's goal for her epic. "Corrosive sublimate"—mercury chloride—is a purifying agent; similarly, Friedman notes, the goal of *Trilogy* is to purify or "sublime" the culture from the chaos of war and anti-spiritualism (245). Although she does not use the term "sublime," Adalaide Morris argues in "Signaling" that for H. D., the poet's task is to labor in ecstasy so that her vision might promote self-examination in the culture (124-25). My focus differs from these in that I explore the way H. D. reworks the mechanics of the aesthetic sublime, with its tension between reason and imagination, between the abstract and the sensory, in her theory of vision. Fritz's examination of what H. D. termed "spiritual realism"—the union of the noumenal and the phenomenal—is also relevant to this discussion. Fritz's analysis, however, focuses on H. D.'s development of the theme of the spiritual quest in *Trilogy* rather than on the epic's connections to the aesthetic sublime.

2. Hertz also offers an important extended consideration of the relationship between Freud and the sublime.

3. Diehl argues that not all women poets suffer from such repression. She identifies Elizabeth Bishop and Adrienne Rich as examples of writers who more easily overcome patriarchal literary tradition. These poets manage to create a Counter-Sublime which allows them greater freedom to depict their lives and concerns as women (110, 167-68).

4. The role of the feminine in H. D.'s work has been the subject of much study. Gubar notes that "H. D. illustrates how patriarchal culture can be subverted by the woman who dares to 're-invoke, re-create' what has been 'scattered in the shards / men tread upon'" (298). This revisioning is crucial to H. D.'s process of transcendence. DuPlessis agrees that in *Trilogy,* "H. D. is an anti-patriarchal symbolist" (89). Ultimately, DuPlessis argues, this revision of patriarchal myth operates not to exclude men but to include women (96-97)—a point echoed in Morris's *How to Live.* Morris argues that finally it is the cooperation of male and female principles via the figures of Kaspar and Mary Magdalen which enables vision in *Trilogy* (114). While I would agree with those who argue that H. D. would like to integrate the masculine and the feminine in the process of vision, her response to the Kantian division between the rational and the sensual in the sublime seems to me to privilege the feminine.

5. In "Signaling" Morris distinguishes H. D.'s work from Kristeva's project in *Revolution in Poetic Language.* According to Morris, H. D.'s goal isn't to negate or destroy but to reconstruct culture along less violent, more affirming patterns (122). While I agree that reconstruction is H. D.'s ultimate goal, I would argue that her process of rebuilding requires the kind of destruction embedded in Kristeva's theory.

6. Both Edmunds and Kloepfer have addressed the role of the body in H. D.'s work in detail. Kloepfer examines the relationship between mother and daughter in H. D.'s texts and argues that the poet uses male figures "to anchor and fortify herself as she makes her forays into the dangerous territory of lesbianism and incest" (129). This link between mother and daughter ultimately participates in the process of vision (133). Edmunds offers a reading of *Trilogy* based upon Melanie Klein's psychoanalytic theory. According to Klein, the child's relationship with the mother is rooted in its struggle to steal nourishment from the mother's

body. Through this contest between mother and daughter, Edmunds argues, a powerful female aggression is released, one which aids transcendence (55, 68). My own consideration of the sensual in *Trilogy* is rather different from these studies, moving beyond the body and desire to address the entire arena of sensory information as it is conceptualized in the aesthetic sublime.

7. References to this source will be indicated in parenthetical citations by the letters *NTV*.

8. For discussions of H. D.'s relationship with Freud and Freudian theory, see Friedman's *Psyche Reborn*; Morris's "The Concept of Projection"; H. D.'s *Tribute to Freud*; and Chisholm.

9. For a detailed discussion of the links between jewels and alchemy in *Trilogy*, see Friedman's *Psyche Reborn* 247ff. Fritz also address the links between Hermeticism and jewels in *Thought and Vision* 119ff.

10. References to *Tribute to the Angels* and *The Flowering of the Rod* will be cited by poem and line numbers.

11. Similar phrasing is used in *Angels* 25.13-14, where the Lady is described as "standing there, / actually, at the turn of the stair."

12. Interestingly, Alfrey notes that the description of Mary in poem 18 of *Flowering* echoes Samuel Monk's description of the sublime as a woman "in disarray and déshabille, slightly all over the place, not quite fit to be seen" (Monk quoted in Alfrey 107).

13. Another source for this scene appears in John 12:3, where Mary of Bethany, sister to Lazarus and Martha, neglects her household duties to tend to Christ's feet. Biblical scholars remain divided as to whether Mary of Bethany, the "sinner" of whom Luke speaks, and Mary Magdalen are one and the same (Haskins 93-96). H. D. does associate Mary Magdalen with Mary of Bethany, but only briefly (see *Flowering* 12.6-8). Consequently, the passage from Luke seems to be more relevant to this scene in *The Flowering of the Rod*.

14. Friedman addresses this aspect of H. D.'s work in conjunction with *Helen in Egypt* in "Creating a Woman's Mythology" (379-81). Interestingly, other scholars have identified a tendency in *Trilogy* to valorize feminine aggression. This interpretation is implicit in Kloepfer's work, as the incestuous drive toward the mother compels the daughter to find ways "to explore a forbidden access to" the mother (134). More overtly, Edmunds reads *Trilogy* as an effort to identify and valorize feminine aggression, in part via the Kleinian contest between mother and daughter (55).

15. In *How to Live*, Morris argues that Kaspar's decision to give Mary the myrrh "seeds the resurrection" (115), a point which contributes to her assertion that the male and female principles cooperate in the process of vision. I would argue that Mary's recognition of her own identity as myrrh seems to make Kaspar's participation unnecessary. Consequently, this passage seems to me to emphasize the preeminence of the feminine in the process of vision; even Kaspar is rather passive in his movement toward vision until Mary unleashes his memories. Alfrey offers another intriguing reading of the sublime connection between Mary and Kaspar, arguing that Mary is both the "object" or "occasion" of the sublime and a beneficiary of sublime inspiration (109).

Works Cited

Alfrey, Shawn. *The Sublime of Intense Sociability: Emily Dickinson, H. D., and Gertrude Stein.* Lewisburg, PA: Bucknell UP, 2000.

Arensberg, Mary. Introduction. *The American Sublime.* Ed. Arensberg. Albany: State U of New York P, 1986. 1-20.

Chisholm, Dianne. *H. D.'s Freudian Poetics: Psychoanalysis in Translation.* Ithaca: Cornell UP, 1992.

de Man, Paul. "Phenomenality and Materiality in Kant." *The Textual Sublime: Deconstruction and Its Differences.* Ed. Hugh J. Silverman and Gary E. Aylesworth. Albany: State U of New York P, 1990. 87-108.

Diehl, Joanne Feit. *Women Poets and the American Sublime.* Bloomington: Indiana UP, 1990.

DuPlessis, Rachel Blau. *H. D.: The Career of That Struggle.* Sussex, England: The Harvester Press Ltd., 1986.

Edmunds, Susan. *Out of Line: History, Psychoanalysis, and Montage in H. D.'s Long Poems.* Stanford: Stanford UP, 1994.

Freeman, Barbara Claire. *The Feminine Sublime: Gender and Excess in Women's Fiction.* Berkeley: U of California P, 1995.

Friedman, Susan Stanford. "Creating a Woman's Mythology: H. D.'s *Helen in Egypt*." Friedman and DuPlessis 373-405.

———. *Psyche Reborn: The Emergence of H. D.* Bloomington: Indiana UP, 1981.

Friedman, Susan Stanford, and Rachel Blau DuPlessis, eds. *Signets: Reading H. D.* Madison: U of Wisconsin P, 1990.

Fritz, Angela DiPace. *Thought and Vision: A Critical Reading of H. D.'s Poetry.* Washington, D.C.: The Catholic U of America P, 1988.

Gubar, Susan. "The Echoing Spell of H. D.'s *Trilogy.*" Friedman and DuPlessis 297-317.

Haskins, Susan. *Mary Magdalen: Myth and Metaphor.* New York: Harcourt Brace, 1993.

H. D. *Notes on Thought and Vision.* San Francisco: City Lights, 1982.

———. *Tribute to Freud.* Boston: David R. Godine, 1974.

———. *Trilogy. H. D.: Collected Poems 1912-1944.* Ed. Louis L. Martz. New York: New Directions, 1983. 505-612.

Hertz, Neil. *The End of the Line: Essays on Psychoanalysis and the Sublime.* New York: Columbia UP, 1985.

Kant, Emmanuel. *Kant's Critique of Judgement.* Trans. J. H. Bernard. 2nd ed. London: Macmillan, 1914.

Kloepfer, Deborah Kelly. *The Unspeakable Mother: Forbidden Discourse in Jean Rhys and H. D.* Ithaca: Cornell UP, 1989.

Kristeva, Julia. *Revolution in Poetic Language.* New York: Columbia UP, 1984.

Morris, Adelaide. "The Concept of Projection: H. D.'s Visionary Powers." Friedman and DuPlessis 273-96.

———. *How to Live / What to Do: H. D.'s Cultural Poetics.* Urbana: U of Illinois P, 2003.

———. "Signaling: Feminism, Politics, and Mysticism in H. D.'s War Trilogy." *Sagetrieb* 9.3 (1990): 121-33.

Tripp, Edward. *The Meridian Handbook of Classical Mythology.* New York: Meridian, 1970.

Weiskel, Thomas. *The Romantic Sublime.* Baltimore: Johns Hopkins UP, 1976.

Helen V. Emmitt (essay date fall/winter 2004)

SOURCE: Emmitt, Helen V. "Forgotten Memories and Unheard Rhythms: H. D.'s Poetics as a Response to Male Modernism." *Paideuma: Studies in American and British Modernist Poetry* 33, nos. 2 & 3 (fall & winter 2004): 131-53.

[*In the following essay, Emmitt analyzes the ways in which H. D. approached language not as duplicitous or deceptive but as ripe with possibility and multiplicity. Emmitt focuses in particular on H. D.'s treatment of language in* Trilogy *and* Helen in Egypt.]

The difficulties of placing H. D.'s poetry in a literary context are well known. Ezra Pound penned the name "H. D. Imagiste," making her the symbol of his poetic movement (indeed, her poems defined Imagism [Pondrom 86]) and at the same time creating the first literary niche H. D. tried to escape. While for many years her work was trivialized or ignored, in the wake of feminist criticism her later works have been published and read, giving a fuller sense of her *oeuvre.* Despite the renewed interest in her work, discussing H. D.'s poetics in relation to Modernist poetics more generally is complicated by the fact that she herself eschewed the slogans and definitions of her male contemporaries; thus Elizabeth A. Hirsch suggests that "'H. D.' was not a theorist—only an example of a theory, an image, her images, presented in evidence for a male-authored truth" (430).[1] By making an "example" of H. D. we have neglected both the way her ideas develop over the course of her career and the problem of the "male-authored truth" she wrote against.

Modernist poetry has been characterized by an awareness of and anxiety about what T. S. Eliot called the "dissociation of sensibility" (*Selected Essays* 247). As Frank Kermode argues, H. D.'s contemporaries, Eliot, Pound, and W. B. Yeats, all "seek a historical period possessing the qualities they postulate for the image: unity, indissociability; qualities which, though passionately desired, are, they say, uniquely hard to come by in the modern world" (145). While Pound, Eliot, and Yeats give different reasons for the dissociation and place its genesis at different historical moments, they all subscribe to the idea of a past time marked by a unified sensibility.[2] This unified sensibility is signified by the ability both to say what one means and to believe the evidence of one's sight. That is, language and sight could at one time be trusted, though as these poets themselves realize, their very awareness of their distance from the prelapserian poetic world they desire suggests the difficulty of their historical position. Pound's attempt to "gather the limbs of Osiris" finally reveals to him "the enormous tragedy of the dream" rather than a "live tradition" (*SP* [*Selected Prose*] 19-43; 74/425; 81/522). Yeats's line, "Man is in love and loves what vanishes," suggests how sight can (perhaps should) fail the viewer (*Collected Poems* 205), just as Eliot's need "to force, to dislocate if necessary, language into his meaning," since words "slip, slide, perish, / Decay with imprecision," reveals the difficulty of trying to find a language that does not belie its user (*Selected Essays* 248; *Collected Poems* 180).

Despite their belief in and nostalgic longing for a time when language, sight, and meaning coalesced, however, the poets cannot reach that moment when poets could "feel their thoughts as immediately as the odour of a rose" (Eliot, *Selected Essays* 247), except perhaps in their late poetry—and there it is a way of admitting defeat, as in Pound's late fragment:

> I have tried to write Paradise
>
> Do not move
>   Let the wind speak
>   that is paradise.
>
> (120/802)

By letting the wind speak, Pound relinquishes his role as poet, acknowledging that the wind can do more than his poetry to demonstrate the reality of his paradise. Similarly, at the end of *The Four Quartets,* Eliot defers the completion of the journey back to "the beginning" until a time when words are unnecessary,

> When the tongues of flame are in-folded
> Into the crowned knot of fire
> And the fire and the rose are one.
>
> (*Collected Poems* 208-09)

Perfect union requires not just "continual self sacrifice" but a faith "costing not less than everything"; and, like Pound's paradise, it requires of the reader a willingness to accept the assertion of a truth that the poet admits he cannot demonstrate (Eliot, *Sacred Wood* 53; *Collected Poems* 208).

In contrast to the male Modernists, H. D.'s does not take as her starting point a sense of a "broken self" resulting from an inability to connect language and sight. Indeed, H. D. rails against the power that sight confers on the beholder and that language confers on the speaker, perhaps because she seems so often to be grappling in her poetry with the strong male figures in her life to whom she feels a need to counter through her poetry, as numerous critics have noted.[3] What has received less attention is how her responses change over the course of her poetic career, from binary response poems in which she unwittingly reinstates the same power structure in which she takes umbrage to the more complex late long poems in which she explores alternatives to sight and language. That is, H. D. moves away from the idea (now a cliché of feminist criticism) of "re-vision" to a questioning of vision itself. In *Trilogy,* I argue, H. D. offers the sense of smell as the alternative to sight, and in *Helen in Egypt,* rhythm. In addition, in both poems, she explores an alchemical language in which words' inability to stay still becomes not a liability (as it is for Eliot) but a blessing. Thus H. D. does not try to overcome the duplicity of language; rather, she turns its lying duplicity into an affirming multiplicity.

Critics beginning with Susan Stanford Friedman have argued that H. D. writes from the margins, but what is remarkable in the early poetry is how often the female figure stands at the center both of the poem and of a particular gaze ("Modernism of the 'Scattered Remnant'" 116). In **"Helen,"** "All Greece" has the power of sight, which is tied to a hatred so great that Helen can only be seen or "revile[d]" in pieces ("still eyes," "white face," "white hands," "cool feet," etc.) (***Collected Poems*** 154-55). The fact that she is "God's daughter, born of love," leaves Greece "unmoved," for it "could love indeed the maid, / only if she were laid, / white ash amid funereal cypresses" (155). That is, Helen would be lovable (and paradoxically whole) only if she were dead and reduced to tiny unrecognizable fragments. This short poem offers a bizarre twist on the Petrarchan tradition of love poetry in which, as Nancy J. Vickers points out, "If the speaker's 'self' (his text, his 'corpus') is to be unified, it would seem to require the repetition of her dismembered image" (102). Here, though, Helen does not act as "the instrument by which man attains unity," but as the instrument through which an entire culture reaches unanimity, as if the woman at the center of the male's loving gaze becomes the pariah who defines the culture from which she is excluded.[4]

In **"Helen,"** the object of all the attention has no opportunity to speak, but in **"Eurydice,"** H. D. imagines Orpheus's doomed wife not as she is falling back into Hades, in the process losing sight and touch, but later, when her regret has turned bitter.[5] In the course of the poem she moves from impotence to power, but she begins with anger, describing and decrying her incarceration resulting from the malevolent, narcissistic gaze of Orpheus: "what was it you saw in my face / the light of your own face, / the fire of your own presence?" (***Collected Poems*** 52). While Virgil gives Eurydice five lines to bemoan her fate, the story in both his telling and Ovid's is essentially Orpheus's, that of the tragic poet, whose identity is constituted by the backwards glance. H. D.'s Eurydice knows, in contrast, that to realize his presence, his identity, Orpheus must look back at her.

As she becomes more accustomed to her new environment, Eurydice moves beyond outrage at losing "everything" and being left not in darkness but in "colourless light" and argues that, if she had just been able to return to the earth briefly, she could have made her life in hell bearable:

> if once I could have breathed into myself
> the very golden crocuses
> and the red,
> and the very golden hearts of the first saffron,
> the whole of the golden mass,
> the whole of the great fragrance,
> I could have dared the loss.
>
> (*Collected Poems* 53)

Though she includes color as well as odor, incipient here is an idea that becomes full-fledged in *Trilogy,* that is, scent as a substitute for sight. Eurydice counters her loss with a missed possibility, containing the scent of the beauties of the world. As the poem progresses, Eurydice moves away from the image of "the great fragrance" and asserts that her loss is not like Orpheus' loss, or like the loss he envisions her having; indeed, "such loss is no loss" (*Collected Poems* 54). Turning back to the visual realm, she avows that she has "more light" than Orpheus because of the contrast between her "fervour" and the "blackness" of her hell. And, while she has lost the flowers of the world, she has "the flowers of myself" and "my own spirit for light." Yet her "light," her "fervour," and her "flowers" (*Collected Poems* 55) exist only in opposition.[6] Like Milton's Satan, Eurydice is inextricably tied to hell, and her bravado cannot alter her actual situation.

As H. D. moves away from her early imagist poems, she tries several times to remake the situation of a woman seen and defined by the male gaze. When, in the mid-1930s she writes **"The Master,"** a poem about her association with Freud in which she (presumably) speaks in *propria persona,* she records her attempt to teach Freud and other men an alternate vision of woman's perfection.[7] In the poem, Freud makes possible H. D.'s vision of a female dancer whose "hieratic" movements form a kind of language:

> each word was separate
> yet each word led to another word,
> and the whole made a rhythm
> in the air,
> till now unguessed at,
> unknown.

> (454)

What this language offers is rhythm rather than meaning, something felt rather than understood. These separate entities which together create a combined rhythm help H. D. to explore with Freud her "two loves separate" (453), her bisexuality.

When the master, whose "tyranny was absolute" (452), responds to her need for "a neat answer" with "you are a poet," she feels that he is belittling her own revelation by treating her "like a child, a weakling" (454-55). This feeling that she is being denigrated leads to her argument with Freud, in which she "could not accept from wisdom / what love taught, / *woman is perfect*" (455). Rachel Blau DuPlessis and Susan Friedman note that H. D. here alludes to an incident in her work with Freud when he showed her a statue of Pallas Athena. In *Tribute to Freud,* she describes this incident: "one hand was extended as if holding a staff

or rod. 'She is perfect,' he said, 'only she has lost her spear'" (69). DuPlessis and Friedman believe that "in **'The Master,'** H. D. answered Freud's image of the 'perfect' castrated goddess with her own image of women's perfection, one that acknowledged and celebrated the tabooed eroticism between women ("'Woman is Perfect'" 423). Yet what disturbs her in Freud's words is both what he calls elsewhere the "fact" of women's castration and, perhaps more importantly, his implication that the idiom of 'wisdom,' which he claims to speak, is incompatible with her idiom of 'love.' In *Tribute,* she criticizes Freud's method of ascribing value, suggesting that "he was assessing [the statue's monetary] worth," not only its value as symbol "to be venerated as a projection of abstract thought" (70). H. D. counters his "assessing" with "veneration," or love, which teaches in a different way than wisdom, a way perhaps equally inaccessible to the uninitiated, as the conundrum of the next lines suggests: "She is a woman, / yet beyond woman, / yet in woman" (*Collected Poems* 455).

Joseph Riddel suggests that "[w]hat H. D. brings to Freud's room is the already doubled figure of the woman/translator/poet—hence the woman as the body of the text, neither presence nor absence, but the sign of the sign" (51). It seems to me, however, that Riddel's deconstructive reading of the *Tribute* does not account either for H. D.'s bitter attempt to reduce Freud to a Shylock ("he knew . . . his pound of flesh, . . . but this pound of flesh was a *pound of spirit* between us" [*Tribute* 70]) or for the ending of **"The Master,"** where H. D.'s ungraspable woman loses some of this quality of mutability and questioning. As her "woman" grows more powerful in the poet's imagining, she becomes more God-like, and more abstract:

> O God, what is it,
> this flower
> that in itself had power over the whole earth?
> for she needs no man,
> herself
> is that dart and pulse of the male,
> hands, feet, thighs,
> herself perfect.

> (*Collected Poems* 456)

From Freud's image of the goddess of wisdom lacking the phallic spear, H. D. moves to a vision of female dancer not castrated but embodying the male. The flower of female sexuality ("purple flower / between her marble, her birch-tree white / thighs" [456]) is mutated into a flower that has "power over the whole earth" because the female figure "needs no man / herself / is that dart and pulse of the male, / hands, feet, thighs, / herself perfect" (456). This may be a triumphant vision of female sexuality, but as Claire

Buck notes, the end result is that "the female body . . . become[s] phallicized as a result of the disavowal of castration" ("Freud and H. D." 63). Further, she has, wittingly or not, made the rhythm with which she counters Freud's logic "the dart and pulse of the male." Indeed, the language of dismemberment is reminiscent of that in **"Helen."**

Although the speaker does not see her ideal as phallicized, her belief that only she can "escape" Freud's legacy leads to an appropriation of male roles and to a substitution of prophetic wisdom or vision—Freud's mode of expression—for love, which was earlier hers (458). She envisions a time when "all men will feel / what it is to be a woman" and will see

> how long
> this thought of the man-pulse has tricked them,
> has weakened them,
> shall see woman,
> perfect.
>
> (460)

H. D. ends the poem with the future realization of her vision ("And they did") and a sort of apotheosis in which she and others "were together / we were one" (460), crying out to a flower turned sun god, "that Lord become woman" (461). By appropriating a male-centered version of the world, making woman wholly self-sufficient, all-encompassing, the vision seems to offer a positive alternative to a male-centered universe; yet the emphasis on men's sight reveals a world dependent on the gaze of the man, which in **"Eurydice"** set the woman irrevocably in hell.

Women, in **"The Master,"** attain full self-sufficiency only when men acknowledge it (and when men become the "weaklings" H. D. felt Freud's analysis made her). Indeed, she comes very close to falling into the same sort of essentialism she resents in Freud.[8] Dianne Chisholm believes that "in turning to Freud for the words to shape her writing, H. D. implicates herself in his ideas and evaluations" to the extent that she "*becomes* Freud, curing herself of the blocks and gaps that infect the telling of her life story and, at the same time, healing Freud of discursive foreclosures in scientific skepticism, Schopenhauerian pessimism, and metapsychological misogyny" (4). This not only seems rather a lot to ask, it is awkward as well, because to "become" Freud, even a Freud healed of skepticism, pessimism and misogyny, H. D. must take on just that mastery that makes her angry and suspicious to begin with. By making the female god "perfect" in the sense that she finds a "spear," she loses what *Trilogy* and *Helen in Egypt* will show to be finally more important, multiplicity and permeability. Thus, while DuPlessis and Friedman call **"The Master"** a "blueprint of H.

D.'s future development" ("Woman is Perfect" 427), I argue that while the resistance to being forced into an untenable role stays with her, the vision of the feminine utopia as a response to male dominance does not.

While the women in **"Eurydice"** and **"The Master"** react differently to the perceived threat from the male world, the "I" of the female speaker is not strong enough to combat it in either poem. The response poem is finally a limited form, whether H. D. is reinterpreting Eurydice's fate or Freud's analysis, for as Jan Montefiore argues, "interpretive story telling" risks determinism "unless the poet makes her traditional material into a new plot altogether" (55). Rather than give up the female "I" or accept a male cosmology, H. D. reexamines the options open to a woman in a setting determined by men from which she cannot remove herself. This means, in a sense, creating Montefiore's "new plot," but the exigencies of plot have their own dangers; H. D. begins to question the traditional building blocks of literary relationships between men and women: the gaze and the word. In **"Eurydice"** and **"The Master"** she suggests, perhaps without realizing it, the direction her questions will take her. Eurydice's "flowers of myself," while in that poem problematically linked to light, are also linked to scent ("the whole of the great fragrance"), an idea she will develop in *Trilogy*; the speaker of **"The Master"** suggests that words when put together form a rhythm which creates a "whole" quite unlike that suggested by the signification of each individual word, an idea H. D. will develop somewhat in *Trilogy* and most fully in *Helen in Egypt*.

In *Trilogy* (1942-44), H. D. links Mary Magdalene and the Virgin Mary through fragrance; as Mary Magdalene says, "Mary shall be myrrh; / / I am Mary—O, there are Marys a-plenty, / (though I am Mara, bitter) I shall be Mary-myrrh" (*Collected Poems* 590). Her prophecy comes true in the link between Mary and the jar of myrrh Kaspar brings to the "ox-stall" (610), not knowing whether the jar he carries contains the "yield of myrrh" from "the time of the sudden winter-rain" because "there were always two jars" and "no one can tell which is which" (609-10). Mary thanks the magus for his gift:

> Sir, it is a most beautiful fragrance,
> as of all flowering things together;
>
> but Kaspar knew the seal of the jar was unbroken.
> he did not know whether she knew
>
> the fragrance came from the bundle of myrrh
> she held in her arms.
>
> (612)

The bitter (marah) tears of one Mary are connected to the fragrant bundle held by the other, the mother. In this respect, H. D. has found the answer to Freud's wisdom. In *Tribute to Freud,* she realizes that "the Professor was not always right. He did not know—or did he?—that I looked at the things in his room before I looked at him; for I knew the things in his room were symbols of Eternity and contained him then, as Eternity contains him now" (*Tribute* 101-2). The jar of myrrh, like the statues in Freud's office, contains significance beyond the grasp of analysis. It offers not Eliot's ideal past when one could "feel [one's] thoughts as immediately as the odour of a rose," but the scent of the rose itself. Or as H. D. writes in *Paint It Today,* "You cannot paint fragrance, you cannot be a sculptor of fragrance, you cannot play fragrance on a violin. Yet you can, with a pencil, at least attempt to express something in definite terms, before which the violin, the chisel, and the brush are powerless" (17). This "something" corresponds to the ungraspable yet permeating scent of the jar of myrrh, which, like Christ ("the bundle of myrrh") himself, transcends boundaries.[9]

Susan Edmunds points to Freud's discussion of odors in *Three Essays on the Theory of Sexuality,* in which he connects the strong smell of feet and hair to fetishism, arguing that "Feet, hair, fragrance," all are associated with Mary Magdalene, and "myrrh, like the Magdalene, is strongly aligned with the sexual body, both in that it adorns and in that it expresses that body, or rather the body's forbidden sexuality, its pleasurable odors" (74). Yet as Freud and Edmunds make clear, fetishism is a result of the repression of smell; the fetishistic object is primarily visual. Maud Ellmann argues that in Joyce's *Ulysses* Leopold Bloom charts a course between the aural and visual by using the olfactory (his fart in "Sirens"). Thus, "what the ear hears, and the eye sees, give way to what the nose knows" (69). The suggestion of "an alternative modality" created by "the new womanly man" helps illuminate *Trilogy*'s use of scent as an alternative to paternal wisdom and *Helen in Egypt*'s attempt to create an androgynous character who marks the end of the old dispensation (Ellmann 66, 67).

As in H. D.'s earlier lyrics, the flowers in *Trilogy* are connected to the self, but they are also the sign of rebirth, of "the flowering of the rod"—and what is important is the scent, not the sight, for when Kaspar calls the Christ child "a bundle of myrrh," he changes the scene from the realm of the human to the visionary, in which Christ becomes the flowering, the culmination of "all flowering things together." Christ is also "the word," and thus connected to the poet.

The flowering of the rod, then, is the proliferation of words, revealed in all their power; language is the healing force, the life force, which connects and makes whole:

> I know, I feel
> the meaning that words hide;
>
> they are anagrams, cryptograms,
> little boxes conditioned
>
> to hatch butterflies . . .
>
> (540)

Words, then, are cocoons—that is, they both contain and are the thing they contain—but here that content is something greater than its container: beauty, psyche, flight. Julia, the poet of *Bid Me to Live,* wants to find the "inner words" of Greek words that "lead somewhere like that Phoenician track, trod by the old traders," so she "brood[s] over each word, as if to hatch it," believing that in this way she can go beyond translating "the meaning of the word. She wanted the shape, the feel of it, the character of it, as if it had been freshly minted" (162-63). As Julia's mixed metaphor suggests, words are both eggs and coins, seemingly irreconcilable images that come together in their potentiality, their (ex)changeability.

In Part II, **"Tribute to the Angels,"** H. D. explores this transformative power of words as alchemy, "distill[ing] / / a word most bitter, *marah,* / a word bitterer still, *mar*" into what seems to be their opposite:

> *marah-mar*
> are melted, fuse and join
>
> and change and alter,
> mer, mere, mère, mater, Maia, Mary
>
> Star of the Sea,
> Mother.
>
> (*Collected Poems* 552)

This transformation of the bitter into the sweet—or at least the maternal—is accomplished at the level of the word, by sound. Sound, like rhythm, has the power, for H. D., to create or reveal kinship between words, and their hidden content, for instance, "Venus whose name is kin / / to venerate, / venerator." (554). The kinship is partly phonic, partly etymological, but it is not arbitrary, as is the relationship between the signifier and signified in linguistics (Saussure). Importantly, sound is not the only connection—if it were, "Venus" could be "kin" to "venery" and "venereous," words to which "Venus" is also etymologically connected. By her choices, H. D. "recuperates" words (Schweik 272).[10] This sense of the slipperiness of language as healing rather than destructive is a step in a new and very different direction from that which Pound and Eliot, for example, take. Words release their hidden realities mystically. Just as in Christian tradition Aaron's rod becomes an attribute of Joseph and then a symbol of Mary's purity, so H. D. weaves together these symbolic meanings with her own images of leaking yet sealed jars and butterflies in chrysalis. In the figure of the flowering of the rod, the poet finds a way of connecting female and male imagery which is neither submission to nor appropriation of the phallus and which does not depend on the sign of a male viewer.

These ideas blossom in **Helen in Egypt** (1952-56), H. D.'s late epic revision of the Greek myth of Helen of Troy. Helen embodies the role of cocoon (which hides the butterfly) or "hieroglyph" (which is a rebus to be read) (**Helen** 15). Helen is the questor after understanding, for, as Friedman notes, reading is the action of the poem (*Psyche* 65), and "[s]he herself is the writing" (**Helen** 22).[11] Making Helen both reader and writing, both *"phantom and reality"* (**Helen** 3), H. D. does not accept the premise of the myth as she did with the story of Orpheus and Eurydice; instead, she questions where, what, and whom Helen was and is. While Stesichorus and Euripides were said to have been "restored to sight" when they retract their early vilifications of Helen (**Helen** 1), writing that she was held captive in Egypt during the Trojan war and replaced by a phantom, H. D. questions their (second) sight. She is no longer satisfied by the imposition of a positive image in place of the earlier negative one; in **Helen in Egypt** no single visual image is sufficient.

Language, specifically the power of naming, of defining in absolute terms, is also called into question. A character in H. D.'s novel *Asphodel* wonders, "Hellas, Hermione, herons, hypaticas, Heliodora . . . did names make people? Was it saying 'Hellas' and not 'Greece' that was to save her?" (168-69). The difference between "Greece" and "Hellas" is as important as the likeness between "Helen" and "Hellas." In H. D.'s peculiar linguistic alchemy, calling Greece "Hellas" not only creates a place for Helen and an identity for her ("Helen in Hellas forever" [**Helen** 190]) but also calls attention to the elusive character of "Helen of Troy," the name which relegates Helen to one place defined by its otherness to Greece. Part of the attraction of the name "Helen" for H. D. is that it allows her to create a chain of signification through the name and the place (*Hellas*), to the name of her own mother, Helen Wolle Doolittle, and finally to mothering as a central part of Helen's identity. H. D. associated her mother and her name with Greece ("Helen? Helen, Hellas, Helle, Helios, . . . you who are rival to Helios, to Helle, to Phoebus the sun" [*The Gift* 58]), to

her own role as poet ("I was physically in Greece, in Hellas (Helen)" [*Tribute* 44]) and to creativity ("the mother is the Muse, the Creator, and in my case especially, as my mother's name was Helen" [*End to Torment* 41]).

Women's relationship to the mother is mutable and fertile in **Helen,** unlike men's, and this asymmetry differentiates Helen's desire from Achilles'. As DuPlessis suggests, "H. D. shows that all desire is matrisexual" (*H. D.* 114). Yet the sight of the mother's body and the language used to place her leads Achilles to the past and Helen to the future. While Freud called H. D.'s "mother-fix" a "dangerous symptom," she suggests that mother love is more debilitating for men because they pine nostalgically for the mother-infant dyad that inspired unfulfillable desire (qtd. in DuPlessis and Friedman, "Woman is Perfect" 423; *Tribute* 51). For Achilles, mortally wounded with "love's arrow," and thus symbolically castrated, limping like Oedipus, his love for his mother is central to his sense of himself (**Helen** 9). Buck believes that the "eidolon" of the mother with which Achilles plays and the prow of his ship, which he also associates with her, "form fetish objects which allow the man to disavow his own castration through a disavowal of the mother's" ("O Careless, Unspeakable Mother" 136). Certainly, Achilles is the "new Mortal" (10), whose first words, "I thought I had lost that" (12), suggest that "making it new" is based on loss. In his devotion to the fascistic death-cult, the great warrior cuts himself off from his youthful love for his mother, transferring his love for her into love for his ship (**Helen** 248, *e.g.*). When the "careless, unspeakable mother" (253), Thetis, forgets to protect her son's heel, Achilles dies, but Helen tells us that "Love's arrow" is responsible. The transformative power of love is central to **Helen in Egypt,** but it is not clear exactly what or who Achilles as the "new Mortal" is. It seems that becoming the new Mortal is more difficult for the male than the female, for male identity is based not on identity with the mother, but on his desire for her and fear of the castration he sees (or refuses to see) in her. As Coppélia Kahn succinctly puts it, "While the boy's sense of self begins in union with the feminine, his sense of *masculinity* arises against it" (10).

In **Helen in Egypt,** we see Achilles's masculine sense of self in the fascistic war cult, while the split between his sense of self and sense of masculinity stand out also in the family unit Achilles-Helen-Paris, *"the inevitable triad"* (**Helen** 215), a version of Freud's family romance, where tribal law dictates that *"the young priest slays the old one, the son, the father"* (215). This split is even to a certain extent apparent in the family group in which Helen is united with Thetis. In this story, at the moment that "the ecstasy of desire had smitten" Achilles in his meeting with Helen on the beach, he "knew his mother" (**Helen** 260-61). When Helen says the potent name of the mother, Thetis, she does not realize that it

> would brand on his forehead
> that name, that the name
>
> and the flame and the fire
> would weld him to her
> who spoke it, who thought it.
>
> (*Helen* 277-78)

If sons kill fathers to become men, daughters become their mothers to become women.[12] Helen's ties to motherhood are complex and multiple, as the family triangles Helen-Achilles-Paris and Thetis-Helen-Achilles suggest. The latter, moreover, is transcended by Achilles and Helen and their child, Euphorion, the issue of "*the ultimate experience, La Mort, L'Amour*" (288). Euphorion, as Friedman notes, "is the androgynous One that incorporates both the archetypal polarity of mother and father and the dualities within each of them" (*Psyche* 294). The androgynous child in whom the opposites meet suggests an end to the oedipal dispensation, serving much the same function that Leo Bersani suggests Astyanax serves in Racine's *Andromaque*; the child offers "the possibility of a new order for desire" beyond "a psychology of sexual passion" (50, 5). But while Bersani believes that Astyanax provides an alternative to oedipal tragedy because he has no father, Euphorion's future is possible perhaps because he/she has so many mothers or, rather, a mother who is so multiple.

Feminist critics have wanted **Helen in Egypt** to be a more "affirmative" poem than it is and thus "have focused on other passages than the literal ending as the climax of the poem," as Robert O'Brien Hokanson shows (332, 342). He suggests that the "content and form of H. D.'s epic come together in an escape from final definition" (344). It is just this "escape," I argue, that differentiates Helen from Achilles (and Paris). Her elusiveness transcends the paradigm in which the male figures are trapped. Thus, despite the euphoric birth, the problem of Achilles' connection to a desire for his mother, symbolized by the name branded on his forehead, is not resolved with the birth of his child. Achilles is caught in a mode of knowing that forces him to ask questions requiring a single answer. His conundrum, which Helen provokes as well as enacts (for "*the symbolic 'veil' . . . now resolves itself down to the memory of a woman's scarf*" [**Helen** 55]), is "which was the dream? / was the dream, Helen upon the ramparts? / was the veil, Helen in Egypt?" There are no simple answers, and Helen can only "wonder and ask / numberless questions" in response (85). Thus

when "*Phoenix, the symbol of resurrection has vanquished indecision and doubt, the eternal* why *of the Sphinx*," Helen is "in complete harmony" with "Thetis (Isis, Aphrodite)" (93), but Achilles stands outside this newly formed group. He must continue to ask questions, to probe for something solid behind or beyond the veil. The symbol of the veil is important, not only, as Sandra Gilbert and Susan Gubar suggest, because it is "always holding out the mystery of imminent revelation, the promise or threat that one might be able to see, hear, or even feel through the veil which separates two distinct spheres" (468-69), but also because, as a sign of femininity (as it is both in **Trilogy** and **Helen**), it is, unlike the eye or the phallus, a liminal, hymenal symbol which cannot be fully grasped intellectually.

In *Gaudier-Brzeska*, Pound says, "we prefer the figure in silk on the stairs to the 'Victory' aloft on her pedestal-prow. We know that the 'Victory' will be there whenever we want her, and that the young lady in silk will pass on . . . toward the unknown and unfindable. That is the trouble with the caressable in art. The caressable is always a substitute" (97).[13] This odd Poundian pronouncement suggests quite precisely Achilles' relation to Helen, whose scarf or veil bewilders and entrances him, and to his mother, Thetis, whose doll or *eidolon* (related to the prow of his ship) he caresses. Pound also puts his finger on one of the problems of the male Modernist project—the desire for an unattainable ideal: Yeats's love that vanishes, Freud's infinitely lost object of desire. At the end of **Helen in Egypt,** H. D. furnishes Achilles with a rather precise formulation of this sense of loss: "*only Achilles could break his heart / and the world for a token, / a memory forgotten*" (**Helen** 304). A memory forgotten, like the prefallen literary state Eliot imagines before Milton, evokes a unified utopian past. Late in his life, Pound located his error in the attempt to repair that rift between the "unfindable" and the "caressable": "I tried to make a paradiso / terrestre" ("Notes for 117 et seq."/802); making "it" new reveals itself as an attempt to refind or recapture what is no longer, what never was.

In **Helen in Egypt,** on the other hand, Helen, despite her desire to understand, accepts that she has no control over the myriad palimpsestic cycles of existence:

> reconcile? reconcile?
>
> day, night, wrong, right?
> no need to untangle the riddle,
> it is very simple.
>
> (192)

Helen cannot communicate her insight (the commentary says that "*we do not know exactly what it is that she understands"* [191]) and, in fact, the moment of insight is transitory. Reconciliation is difficult, and, as the example of Oedipus suggests, untangling riddles is dangerous. This is why the dispensation of the Phoenix supercedes that of the Sphinx. Birth and rebirth transcend the need to look back and keep what one desires. As though answering Yeats's "Among School Children," H. D. shows in *Helen in Egypt* that it is not "mothers" who "worship images" that "break hearts," but rather their sons, who experience the mother only as loss (*Collected Poems* 214).

When Freud interpreted the series of visions H. D. experienced on the island of Corfu as a symptom of her "desire for union with [her] mother" (*Tribute* 44), what Freud fails to mention (or to understand?) is that the desire for the mother is complicated by the daughter's ability to be a mother, to reenact the mother's power of generation and transformation.[14] In refinding the mother-object, Helen finds herself, a self who is rediscovered through rereading. Julia Kristeva says, "Know the mother, first take her place, thoroughly investigate her jouissance and, without releasing her, go beyond her. The language that serves as a witness to this course is iridescent with a sexuality of which it does not 'speak'; it turns 'it' into rhythm—it is rhythm" (191). And indeed, Helen's version of the "memory forgotten" is "a rhythm as yet un-heard" (*Helen* 229).

In the penultimate section of *Helen in Egypt, "one greater than Helen"* speaks in a way that at least in part defies intellectual understanding (303), for the voice reconciles the great opposites of the poem, concluding

> now I know the best and the worst;
>
> the seasons revolve around
> a pause in the infinite rhythm
> of the heart and of heaven.

> (304)

The rhythm which Helen strains to hear is too great for human understanding, but is enough for her—it permits her to find herself amid all of the polarities which she embodies; there is no need to delve into the past or look to the future, for "there is no before and no after" (303). Rhythm is continuous movement—here a sort of cyclical oscillation—divisible into individual components and yet meaningless without the flow from one beat to the next. The revolving world goes beyond the ameliorative language of *Trilogy,* daring to include the bitter with the sweet.

The variability of rhythm (like the permeability of scent) stands in opposition to the monolithic *eidolon* just as its futurity contrasts with Achilles' burden of the past. Indeed, *Eidolon* is the name of the concluding section of *Helen in Egypt,* in which Achilles mourns over his forgotten memory—and the name is precise. An *eidolon* is a spectre or unsubstantial image; the root of the word is *eidos* or form which in turn derives from the Greek verb *"idein,"* to see. Sight belies Achilles. Rhythm, like the veil, cannot be caressed or "shattered," like Pound's dreams ("Notes for 117 et seq." /802), nor does it require the kind of "continual surrender," "continual self-sacrifice" that Eliot's desire for the "unification of the world" requires (*Sacred Wood* 52-53; "Religion Without Humanism" 112). H. D. does not attempt "a poem including history" because, as she puts it in *Trilogy,* "Pompeii has nothing to teach us" (Pound, *LE* [*Literary Essays*] 86; H. D., *Collected Poems* 510). Like Achilles, the male Modernists mourn the loss of a time before language belied them and fetishize a past when the center did hold. H. D.'s career reveals a movement away from a poetry of loss towards a poetry of rebirth, a movement from her early "crystalline" Imagist poems towards the "rough matrix" and "stubborn energy" that give birth to other voices, new worlds ("H. D. by Delia Alton" 184). By accepting that language belies its user, "perjures" his (or her) "eye," as Shakespeare says, H. D. makes a virtue of necessity, perhaps, but in doing so she creates a poetics that may be described as post-Freudian, and finally, post-modern.[15]

Notes

1. Hugh Kenner's *The Pound Era* makes this point clear. Not only does he suggest that "H. D. wrote 'Hermes of the Ways' as if she understood" Pound's "Doctrine of the Image" (185), but he also comments on the "impassioned sterility" of the woman and the poetry (523). In other words, H. D. could in Kenner's view create nothing. She simply wrote a good imagist poem *as if* she understood the theory which he privileges. More recently, in "Canon, Gender, and Text: The Case of H. D.," Lawrence S. Rainey chastises H. D. for her "miniscule corpus of nonfiction" (106), seeing the absence of critical writing as an effect of "the income and hospitality furnished by Bryher" which meant that H. D. felt no need to address "anyone who stood outside the coterie that surrounded her and Bryher" (106, 107) at the same time that Eliot, Pound, Moore, and Yeats were engaged in writing "critical-theoretical writings that articulated the . . . grounds for the modernist experiment" (106). Like Kenner, Rainey thus privileges theory over practice, but he is perhaps more disingenuous, since he omits the obvious parallel between H. D. and Joyce, who also relied

on patronage and wrote very little critical prose. A more balanced view is offered by Jacob Korg. See especially 25-46.

2. For Pound the dissociation comes between Cavalcanti and Petrarch, for Yeats in 1550. Eliot's is the latest, falling during the seventeenth century, between Donne and Milton. Kermode includes T. E. Hulme, whom he argues "was one of the first of the English to discover . . . some kind of disastrous psychical shift . . . about the time of the Renaissance" (124). In contrast, Wallace Stevens does not claim to have identified such an historical rupture. Instead, he declares that "Adam / In Eden was the father of Descartes" (*Collected Poems* 383). Many of Stevens's ideas resonate more fully with H. D.'s work than with that of his male contemporaries.

3. For a lengthy discussion of H. D.'s relationship with strong male figures, see Rachel Blau DuPlessis, "Romantic Thralldom in H. D." DuPlessis sees H. D. as trying various strategies to overcome her "thralldom" to a number of *"héros fatals"* (407). DuPlessis argues that H. D. moves from "resistance" to transcendence (412), finally breaking "the pattern of thralldom" in *Helen in Egypt* (415) with the notion of "the sufficient family" (425). Susan Stanford Friedman argues that H. D.'s exploration of the difficulties of artistic influence parallels Harold Bloom's approach to the problem in *The Anxiety of Influence*. But, she argues, while Bloom "described the male artist as the son who needed to declare his independence from the father, H. D. writes of the woman whose artistic autonomy depends on her ability to throw off the overwhelming male presence in literary tradition" (*Psyche* 150). More recently Friedman has shown how H. D.'s novels function as "rescriptions" of male Modernist works in "Portrait of the Artist as a Young Woman: H. D.'s Rescriptions of Joyce, Lawrence, and Pound." She develops these ideas further in *Penelope's Web: Gender, Modernity, H. D.'s Fiction.*

4. Josette Féral, "Antigone or The Irony of the Tribe," trans. Alice Jardine and Tom Gora, *Diacritics* 8 (Fall 1978): 7. Quoted in Vickers 102. The close connections between love and hate in their power to dismember are underscored by Jacques Lacan's example of *invidia* taken from St. Augustine, who sees "his brother at his mother's breast, looking at him *amare conspectus,* with a bitter look, which seems to tear him to pieces and has on himself the effect of a poison" (116).

5. Virgils's version of the story of Orpheus and Eurydice in *The Georgics* parallels the psychoanalytic theory of desire in many ways. Perhaps most obviously enacted is the paradigm of the impossibility of fulfilling desire. When Orpheus turns to see if, in fact, Eurydice, the object, is that which he desires, she falls back; that is, she is not what he desires, as she is no longer his wife, no longer alive. His glance both effects this movement from Eurydice being the object of desire to her not being, and allows him the realization that Eurydice as his wife was indeed the object of his desire. As Jacques Lacan argues, "the eye carries with it the fatal function of being in itself endowed . . . with a power to separate" (115). He further states that "the subject is strictly speaking determined by the very separation that determines the break of the *a*" (118). This can be seen as a symbolic act of castration; Orpheus can only escape hell, by leaving Eurydice, as the phallus (or *petit a*), behind. Hell is the feminine principle in which Eurydice as the image of, the phallic portion of, Orpheus is lost.

6. As Helen Sword notes, "Eurydice's determination to reign in hell if she cannot write poetry in heaven is not, perhaps, the most satisfying solution possible to the creative dilemma in which Orpheus has placed her. But it is a courageous one" (415). The problem with Eurydice's appropriation of hell (what Sword calls "the negative space of literary marginality into which the female poet has been driven" [414]) is that she has no choice, that she was, in a sense, always there. Her "Orphic turn" is a turn only in the sense that Orpheus's love is recast as greed, not that her own situation is changed (414).

7. H. D.'s suppression of the poem certainly suggests her discomfort at revealing herself without the use of a mask. This poem evinces the ambivalence of H. D.'s feelings for Freud and his ideas. She found in his ideas of the ego's dislocation a way of analyzing and theorizing her own "'jellyfish' experience of double ego"; still she was hurt by his assumptions about women that threatened her because they denied the very multiplicity she cherished in psychoanalytic theory (*Tribute* 116). See also "H. D. by Delia Alton," in which H. D. inscribes that inner schism; for example, "I would like to sign [a sequence of poems] Delia Alton but that must be left to the discretion of the publisher. For these are not fundamentally 'H. D. poems'" (199). She goes on to explain this duality as "the two streams of consciousness, running along together (the time-element and the dream or ideal element) but in separate channels. The streams . . . came together in the end, in the War II and post-War II novels that I sign Delia Alton" (221).

8. While H. D. says that Freud had a "precise Jewish instinct for the particular in the general, for the personal in the impersonal or universal, for the

material in the abstract," she believes that the importance of his work rests in finding the universal in the particular, "not the dream only of the Cumaean Sybil of Italy or the Delphic Priestess of ancient Greece, but the dream of everyone, everywhere" (*Tribute* 71). H. D. both attacks Freud for his Jewishness and praises him for his universality in terms that are often self-contradictory. The anti-Semitic comments may tend, as Joanna Spiro argues, to come at moments when Freud "refuses what we might call [H. D.'s] feminist self-understanding," while the idea of Freud's universalism moves to the center when H. D. tries to "de-Judaize Freud's work" (617, 612).

9. Rachel Blau DuPlessis's contention that "The *Logos* has become a veggie" is, as T. S. Eliot might say, "a way of putting it," but one that, however tongue in cheek, misses the way that the bundle of myrrh signals the bringing together of the genders (*H. D.* 94). Indeed, Susan Edmunds argues that myrrh is connected to "the menstruating womb" in its "proliferation of meanings, its ability to body forth several distinct and yet finally indeterminate genderings of divinity" (87). H. D. may have conceived of the Christ child here as a version of the androgynous child, Euphorion, of *Helen in Egypt*.

10. Her choices are made clearer, as Schweik shows, when H. D. writes of reading Ezra Pound's *Cantos*, "I could not see clearly but I could *hear* clearly" (*End to Torment* 30), for by concentrating on sound (and especially sounds reminiscent of her own poetry) "H. D. recuperates Pound" (Schweik 272).

11. The argument of Susan McCabe's "Borderline Modernism: Paul Robeson and the Femme Fatale" suggests to me that the film *Borderline* may have given H. D. some of the ideas that emerge in *Helen*. She argues that the pamphlet H. D. wrote about the film "represents the film's aesthetics— its deployment of discontinuous images and montage—as part of [both the director's and H. D.'s] radical strategy to question the cultural mechanics of fixing identity borders" (653).

12. In *The Reproduction of Mothering: Psychoanalysis and the Sociology of Gender* (Berkeley: U of California P, 1978), Nancy Chodorow attempts an explanation in psychoanalytic terms of the differing maternal relationships for boys and girls.

13. Stephen Dedalus makes a similar point in *A Portrait of the Artist as a Young Man*, when he suggests that Lynch's writing his name "on the backside of the Venus Praxiteles" is not artistic appreciation or desire for the statue itself (205). H. D., in contrast, writes, "The dynamic strength

of [the sculptor's] original impulse should therefore reach us less encumbered (as in the other arts) with our own impulses. In music, in painting, in poetry our own emotions are apt to intrude, to cloud over the original impulse (or as commonly called, inspiration) of the artist" (*Paint It Today* 61).

14. H. D. understood his analysis to mean, "'back to the womb' seems to be my only solution" (qtd. in Friedman, *Psyche* 132).

15. Here as throughout the essay I am indebted to Joel Fineman's subtle analysis of the ways Shakespeare's sonnets dramatize the relationship between what the eye sees and what the tongue says.

Works Cited

Bersani, Leo. *A Future for Astyanax*. Boston: Little, Brown, 1976.

Buck, Claire. "Freud and H. D.—Bisexuality and a Feminine Discourse." *m/f* 8 (1983): 53-65.

———. "'O Careless, Unspeakable Mother': Irigaray, H. D. and Maternal Origin." *Feminist Criticism: Theory and Practice*. Ed. Susan Sellers. Toronto: U of Toronto P, 1991. 129-42.

Chisholm, Dianne. *H. D.'s Freudian Poetics: Psychoanalysis in Translation*. Ithaca and London: Cornell UP, 1992.

DuPlessis, Rachel Blau. *H. D.: The Career of that Struggle*. Bloomington: Indiana UP, 1986.

———. "Romantic Thralldom in H. D." *Contemporary Literature* 20 (1979): 178-203. Rpt. in Friedman and DuPlessis, *Signets* 406-29.

DuPlessis, Rachel Blau, and Susan Stanford Friedman, "'Woman is Perfect': H. D.'s Debate with Freud." *Feminist Studies* 7 (1981): 417-30.

Edmunds, Susan. *Over the Line: History, Psychoanalysis, and Montage in H. D.'s Long Poems*. Stanford: Stanford UP, 1994.

Eliot, T. S. *Collected Poems 1909-1962*. New York: Harcourt, 1970.

———. "Religion Without Humanism." *Humanism and America*. Ed. Norman Foerster. New York: Farrar and Rinehardt, 1930.

———. *The Sacred Wood: Essays on Poetry and Criticism*. London: Methuen, 1920.

———. *Selected Essays of T. S. Eliot*. New York: Harcourt Brace, 1950.

Ellmann, Maud. "To Sing of Sign." In *James Joyce: The Centennial Symposium*. Ed. Morris Beja, et al. Urbana: U of Illinois P, 1986. 66-69.

Fineman, Joel. *Shakespeare's Perjured Eye: The Invention of Poetic Subjectivity in the Sonnets.* Berkeley: U of California P, 1986.

Friedman, Susan Stanford. "Modernism of the 'Scattered Remnant': Race and Politics in the Development of H. D.'s Modernist Fiction." *H. D.: Woman and Poet.* Ed. Michael King. Orono, ME: National Poetry Foundation, 1986. 91-116.

———. *Penelope's Web: Gender, Modernity, H. D.'s Fiction.* New York: Cambridge UP, 1990.

———. "Portrait of the Artist as a Young Woman: H. D.'s Rescriptions of Joyce, Lawrence, and Pound." *Writing the Woman Artist: Essays on Poetics, Politics, and Portraiture.* Ed. Suzanne W. Jones. Philadelphia: U of Pennsylvania P, 1991. 23-42.

———. *Psyche Reborn: The Emergence of H. D.* Bloomington: U of Indiana P, 1981.

Friedman, Susan Stanford and Rachel Blau DuPlessis, eds. *Signets: Reading H. D.* Madison: U of Wisconsin P, 1990.

Gilbert, Sandra and Susan Gubar. *The Madwoman in the Attic: The Woman Writer and the Nineteenth-Century Imagination.* New Haven: Yale UP, 1979.

H. D. *Asphodel.* Ed. Robert Spoo. Durham and London: Duke UP, 1992.

———. *Bid Me to Live (A Madrigal).* New York: Dial Press, 1960.

———. *Collected Poems 1912-1944.* Ed. Louis L. Martz. New York: New Directions, 1983.

———. *End to Torment: A Memoir of Ezra Pound.* New York: New Directions, 1979.

———. *The Gift.* New York: New Directions, 1982.

———. "H. D. by Delia Alton." *Iowa Review* 16 (1986): 174-221.

———. *Helen in Egypt.* New York: New Directions, 1961.

———. *Paint It Today.* Ed. Cassandra Laity. New York: New York UP, 1992.

———. *Tribute to Freud.* New York: New Directions, 1974.

Hirsch, Elizabeth A. "Imaginary Images: 'H. D.,' Modernism, and the Psychoanalysis of Seeing." Friedman and DuPlessis, *Signets* 430-51.

Hokanson, Robert O'Brien. "'Is it All a Story?': Questioning Revision in H. D.'s *Helen in Egypt.*" *American Literature* 65 (1992): 331-46.

Joyce, James. *A Portrait of the Artist as a Young Man.* New York: Penguin, 1964.

Kahn, Coppélia. *Man's Estate: Masculine Identity in Shakespeare.* Berkeley: U of California P, 1981.

Kenner, Hugh. *The Pound Era.* Berkeley: U of California P, 1971.

Kermode, Frank. *Romantic Image.* London: Routledge, 1957.

Korg, Jacob. *Winter Love: Ezra Pound and H. D.* Madison: U of Wisconsin P, 2004.

Kristeva, Julia. *Desire in Language: A Semiotic Approach to Literature and Art.* Ed. Leon S. Roudiez. Trans. Thomas Gora, Alice Jardine, and Leon S. Roudiez. New York: Columbia UP, 1980.

Lacan, Jacques. *The Four Fundamental Concepts of Pyscho-Analysis.* Ed. Jacques-Alain Miller. Trans. Alan Sheridan. New York: Norton, 1978.

McCabe, Susan. "Borderline Modernism: Paul Robeson and the Femme Fatale." *Callaloo* 25 (2002): 635-53.

Montefiore, Jan. *Feminism and Poetry: Language Experience, Identity in Women's Writing.* New York: Pandora, 1987.

Pondrom, Cyrena N. "H. D. and the Origins of Imagism." *Sagetrieb* 4.1 (Spring 1985): 73-100. Rpt. in Friedman and DuPlessis, *Signets* 85-109.

Pound, Ezra. *The Cantos of Ezra Pound.* New York: New Directions, 1970.

———. *Gaudier-Brzeska.* New York: New Directions, 1960.

———. *Literary Essays of Ezra Pound.* Ed. T. S. Eliot. New York: New Directions, 1968.

———. *Selected Prose 1909-1965.* Ed. William Cookson. New York: New Directions, 1973.

Rainey, Lawrence S. "Canon, Gender, and Text: The Case of H. D." *Representing Modernist Texts: Editing as Interpretation.* Ed. George Bornstein. Ann Arbor, MI: U of Michigan P, 1991.

Riddel, Joseph N. "H. D.'s Scene of Writing—Poetry as (and) Analysis." *Studies in the Literary Imagination* 12 (1979): 41-59.

Saussure, Ferdinand de. *Course in General Linguistics,* ed. Charles Bally et al. Trans. Wade Baskin. New York: McGraw-Hill, 1959.

Schweik, Susan. *A Gulf So Deeply Cut: American Women Poets and the Second World War.* Madison: U of Wisconsin P, 1991.

Shakespeare, William. *The Riverside Shakespeare.* Ed. G. Blakemore Evans et al. New York: Houghton Mifflin, 1974.

Spiro, Joanna. "Weighed in the Balance: H. D.'s Resistance to Freud in 'Writing on the Wall.'" *American Imago* 2 (2001). 597-621.

Stevens, Wallace. *The Collected Poems of Wallace Stevens.* New York: Knopf, 1954.

Sword, Helen. "Orpheus and Eurydice in the Twentieth Century: Lawrence, H. D., and the Poetics of the Turn." *Twentieth Century Literature* 35 (1989): 407-28.

Vickers, Nancy J. "Diana Described: Scattered Woman and Scattered Rhyme." *Writing and Sexual Difference.* Ed. Elizabeth Abel. Chicago: U of Chicago P, 1982. 95-109.

Yeats, William Butler. *The Collected Poems of W. B. Yeats.* New York: MacMillan, 1956.

Brian Brodhead Glaser (essay date summer 2005)

SOURCE: Glaser, Brian Brodhead. "H. D.'s *Helen in Egypt*: Aging and the Unconscious." *Journal of Modern Literature* 28, no. 4 (summer 2005): 91-109.

[*In the following essay, Glaser provides an overview of critical approaches to H. D.'s work that focus on her analytical relationship with Freud. Glaser then builds on these examinations and further explores this relationship and its impact on H. D.'s feminist perspective as it is revealed in works such as* Helen in Egypt.]

Since the 1982 publication of Susan Stanford Friedman's *Psyche Reborn: The Emergence of H. D.*, the majority of the critical works about the life and poetry of H. D. (Hilda Doolittle) have sought to tell and to re-interpret the story of how H. D. won acceptance as a female modernist and at the same time found a way to use her own aesthetic as a critique of prevailing, constricting gender roles within the modernist context. As Friedman later proposed in *Penelope's Web*, her 1990 study of H. D.'s fiction, the self H. D. fashioned "into a multiply split, gendered subject characteristic of both modernism and an oppositional discourse that positions woman within, yet against, patriarchal representations of female identity" has remained an object of admiration for a generation of critics (80). From Janice Robinson's claim in her *H. D.: The Life and Work of an American Poet* (1981) that as a woman Imagist "H. D. came to understand the poem not as an assertion of phallic desire, but as presentation, an act of birth, a means of disentanglement from the burden of inseminating thought" to Diana Collecott's recent interpretation of H. D.'s *Collected Poems* "in terms of an alternative modernist aesthetic, which is emotionally engaged and woman-identified, esteems speech and performance as much as writing and print, and cherishes the human personality as well as the poet's art," critics for nearly twenty years have celebrated an H. D. who transformed her gender-identity from a liability into a source of originality and freedom.

By the end of her life, H. D. had two notable achievements—she had become, as a woman, a central figure in a masculinist group of modernist writers, and she had extended its phenomenal experimental reach. I do not think there is more convincing evidence that H. D. had already, by the end of her life, been recognized for carrying off both of these than Robert Duncan's *The H. D. Book,* a book-length series of essays in homage to her begun in the late 1950's. In recollecting his own formative days as a poet, the few years spent most intensely absorbing influences before the publication of his own 1947 *Medieval Scenes*, Duncan says,

> For a new generation of young writers in the early 1950's, the *Pisan Cantos* and then *Paterson* had been the challenge. But for me, the **War Trilogy** [of H. D.] came earlier . . . In smoky rooms in Berkeley, in painters' studios in San Francisco, I read these works aloud; dreamed about them; took my life from them; studied them as my anatomy of what Poetry must be
>
> (114).

As he explores the idea of a late modernism that bifurcates into one pledged to the "rational imagination" and the other, more inspiring and pioneering, surrendering to "creative disorders of primitive mind," Duncan names three authors—Ezra Pound, William Carlos Williams and H. D.—as the writers who carried the living flame of modernism across the chaos and anguish of the Second World War to a moment when he could grasp it himself. "It seemed to me then that Williams, in the imagination," he said of his readings of the modernists in the late 1940's,

> had come to the same place, *under fire,* that appears in **Tribute to the Angels** where
>
> *then she set a charred tree before us,*
> *burnt and stricken to the heart*
>
> as if in London, in Pisa, in Paterson, there had been phases of a single revelation. Indeed, Williams saw that if his Paterson "rose to flutter into life awhile—it would be as itself, local, and so like every other place in the world." Was it that the war—the bombardment for H. D., the imprisonment and exposure to the elements for Ezra Pound, the divorce in the speech for Williams—touched a spring of passionate feeling in the poet that was not the war but was his age, his ripeness in life. They were almost "old"; under fire to come "to a new distinction."
>
> (111)

The "spring of passionate feeling" Duncan appreciates in his most courageous modernist predecessors comes not just from their experience of the chaos of the war but also from their sense that they had been themselves burned-out by age, and that they needed a restoration from something revealed. Against a poetics of rationality and self-consciousness, Duncan celebrates in H. D.'s work the idea that poetry emerges from rupture and uncertainty, that it comes out of and leaves unresolved a crisis of identity. "Under fire of life's either coming into a new creative phase in old age, larger and deeper, challenging a new generation of poets," he writes, "or coming to the summation of the work of a personal artist as a thing in itself, the work of Williams, like that of Pound and H. D., takes on new scope" (132). These three sought to face the challenge of writing late work by drawing from a "spring of passionate feeling" rather than perfecting the poem as "a thing in itself." They wanted to write from a place "larger and deeper" than their personal lives.

For the last thirty years of her life, dating from the sixteen weeks she spent in psychoanalysis with Sigmund Freud (early March to June of 1933), one of the ways H. D. herself thought of the transpersonal reservoir of inspiration Duncan sees her poetry seeking was in terms of the unconscious mind. Perhaps the most provocative aspect of Duncan's view of H. D.'s late modernist rebirth is the light it sheds on the relationship between her poetry and Freudian thought. "This sense that everything is meaningful if one learns to read must have drawn H. D. to Freud as a teacher," Duncan says in the same passage of his *H. D. Book* that suggests her work gives way to an identity-dissolving Mother-Tongue (ND [Nights and Days], 87). "Certainly," he continues, "her belief that the poet does not give meaning to the word but draws meaning from it, touches meaning or participates in meaning there, must have deepened in the psychoanalytic work" (87). By placing the emphasis elsewhere than on the question of gender in H. D.'s later works, Duncan emerges with a sense of the terrain opened to her through psychoanalysis. Duncan's interest in the crisis of age for H. D.'s later work and the surrender into a field of language that it provoked implies that she had taken from Freud the knowledge that subjectivity, as a realm of words, is divided or ruptured by a flux more primary than sexual difference.

In her 1945 "Writing on the Wall," a tribute written for Freud five years after his death, when H. D. was living in the place of his death, London, and completing *Trilogy,* she said of Freud's legacy for contemporary thought:

> He had dared to say that the dream [of Joseph] came from an unexplored depth in man's consciousness and that this unexplored depth ran like a great stream or ocean underground, and the vast depth of that ocean was the same vast depth that today, as in Joseph's day, overflowing in man's small consciousness, produced inspiration, madness, creative idea, or the dregs of the dreariest symptoms of mental unrest and disease. He had dared to say that it was the same ocean of universal

> consciousness, and even if not stated in so many words, he had dared to imply that this consciousness proclaimed all men one; all nations and races met in the universal world of the dream . . .

(71)

In the introduction to the recently published correspondence H. D. maintained with her close friend and patron Bryher during the course of her analysis, Friedman accurately remarks that the poet "could defy Freud while revering him, . . . analyze him while being analyzed," and that she was quite sensitive to the role of gender in shading their exchanges (xvii). There is no evidence that H. D. accepted the theory of penis envy Freud had propounded in his 1931 essay on female sexuality, and a good deal to suggest that she received with scepticism his views on women in general, as Friedman has demonstrated in *Psyche Reborn*. But when H. D. talks about her motives for her treatment with Freud, she returns to the idea of a journey into the unconscious, a realm that she consistently imagines, as above, with natural metaphors that are difficult to see as gendered. The tendency of the underground stream or ocean of the unconscious is not to multiply differences within this— paradoxically, gender-neutral—community of "man," but to be at work in each, birthing him or her into meaning in the way Duncan saw H. D. finding a meaning already inside of language. H. D. took from her experience as an analysand and "pupil" the Freudian caution that reason is not the master in its own house, that the dream is a privileged form of revelation, and so came to believe that the rational instrumentalisation of language is prone to disturbance by this "vast depth . . . overflowing man's small consciousness." Duncan's sense of her as reaching past herself out of the ripeness of age to come to a new distinction brings into sharper relief her belief in the universality of this inward, oceanic source than the gendered readings of the past thirty years, whether Friedman's notion of a gendered self-fashioning or Buck's emphasis on "H. D.'s formulation of woman's knowledge" (162).

It is ironic that H. D.'s understanding of the unconscious, from this perspective, seems much closer to Carl Jung's reservoir of archetypes and symbols than Freud's own notion of it as a repository of instinctual drives and primary process distortions, particularly since H. D. refused ever to meet Jung out of loyalty to Freud, even though she spent a good part of the last ten years of her life living in Zurich. Indeed, her study of psychoanalytic thought was quite selective—the narrative "Writing on the Wall" and her journal of the early days of her first analysis, "Advent," surprisingly, show little sign that she believed that transference played a central role in fuelling a treatment. Shocked at one early point in the analysis by Freud's "beating with his hand, with his fist, on the head-piece of the old-fashioned horsehair sofa" and his declaration that "the trouble is—I am too old—*you do not think it is worth your while to love me,*" H. D. reports that she remained "detached enough to wonder if this was some idea of *his* for speeding up the analytic content or redirecting the flow of associated images" (15-6). How was it that she, coming to Freud as both a patient and a student, remained unaware of Freud's view that engaging the analysand's libidinal energy was crucial to effective analytic action? H. D. was simply not interested in the interpersonal field of emotion that would open up to analysis as she might begin to repeat her early patterns of attachment to the withholding "Professor," or in examining how she would begin to resist talking freely about her moment-to-moment thoughts because of her fantasies about how Freud might respond. This affective ground, which by 1933 Freud thought essential to analytic progress, seems to have been unappealing to her. She wanted to explore, through a collaborative process of interpretation, the depth that she took Freud's teachings to have revealed underneath her own contingent emotions.

Freud's implication that H. D. as a patient chose to make a flight into intellectualization and away from the mortal shadows lingering around the presence of his own old age can be heard as an earlier instance of Duncan's own—much more sympathetic—view of her as turning, in her experience of the challenge of her own later-life ripeness, towards a universal, irrational, timeless language of the unconscious. That she could think of the Freudian depth as not only universal but also an escape from the linear progression of time is one of the clarities of a complex, complementary set of passages from "Writing on the Wall." The first, in the sixteenth section, begins:

> The actuality of the present, its bearing on the past, their bearing on the future. Past, present, future, these three—but there is another time-element, popularly called the fourth dimensional. The room has four sides. There are four seasons to a year. This fourth dimension, though it appears variously disguised and under different subtitles, described and more elaborately tabulated in the Professor's volumes—and still more elaborately detailed in the compilations of his followers, disciples, and pseudo-disciples and imitators—is yet very simple. It is as simple and inevitable in the building of time-sequence as the fourth wall to a room.
>
> (23)

Taking stock of the room in which she has begun a review of her past and the possibility of its new openings into her present, H. D. begins, through the notion of a fourth dimension contiguous with past, present and future, to establish an analogy between the four faces of that office and the presence of eternity in time. As this fourth "time-element" in its simplicity and inevitability points to a way out of the cyclical entrapment of time, so the fourth wall of Freud's consulting room gives way to an uncertain, equivocal but clearly underlying dimension of experience:

> If we alter our course around this very room where I have been talking with the Professor, and start with the wall to my left, against which the couch is placed, and go counter-clockwise, we may number the Professor's wall with the exit door 2, the wall with the entrance door (the case of pottery images and flat Greek bowls) 3, and the wall opposite the couch 4. This wall actually is largely unwalled, as the space there is left vacant by the wide-open double doors.
>
> The room beyond may appear very dark or there may be broken light and shadow. Or even bodily, one may walk into that room, as the Professor invited me to do one day, to look at the things on the table.
>
> (23)

In this redirection of the flow of her thought, turning it against the current of the clock and its trajectory through a present, H. D. locates an accessible space beyond the three walls of ordinary time.

H. D. lets this strand of her narrative drop at the end of the section, and it remains untouched for nearly a third of the work, as she follows instead a path of associations that lead from this office to her own father's desk and her complicity in her brother's play with a magnifying glass snatched from it. When she returns to the story of her entrance into this further room, the room's symbolic connection with time has become inflected with and intensified by a theme that this digression has uncovered through the figure of Prometheus: H. D. and Freud's shared love of the culture of Attic Greece. She writes,

> I did not always know if the Professor's excursions with me into the other room were by way of distraction, actual social occasions, or part of his plan. Did he want to find out how I would react to certain ideas embodied in these little statues, or how deeply I felt the dynamic *idea* still implicit in spite of the fact that ages or aeons of time had flown over many of them? . . . "This is my favorite," he said. He held the object toward me. I took it in my hand. It was a little bronze statue, helmeted, clothed to the foot in carved robe with the upper incised chiton or peplum. One hand was extended as if holding a staff or rod. "She is perfect," he said, *"only she has lost her spear."* I did not say anything. He knew that I loved Greece. He knew that I loved Hellas. I stood looking at Pallas Athene, she whose winged attribute was Nike, Victory, or she stood wingless, Nike A-pteros in the old days, in the little temple to your right as you climb the steps to the Propylaea on the Acropolis at Athens. He too had climbed those steps once, he had told me, for the briefest survey of the glory that was Greece. Nike A-pteros, she was called, the Wingless Victory, for Victory could never, would never fly away from Athens.
>
> (68-9)

The figures of this "other room" have survived the passage—or, staying closer to H. D.'s language, one could say the flood—of time. Freud's favorite has survived a symbolic castration as well, standing as an embodiment of the timeless preoccupation with the threat of castration his own body of teaching propounds. H. D. herself is non-committal on this implicit interpretation. Her own attention is absorbed by another figure of a woman, one in which a loss has entailed a gain. The winglessness of Nike means that she stakes an eternal claim to an ancient site. Her dismemberment at the hands of time means that she has established a dwelling outside of time. She has been wounded into the unchanging, other-worldly space of the "time-element."

What is H. D. sorting out in this telling of her encounter in the "other room"? Is she suggesting that the presence or absence of the phallus to a body is less significant than the god-forces it can embody, that a surviving Nike is less a spearless Athena than an awe-inspiring *genius loci*? This would imply that her own Hellenism is summoned against Freud's as a resource for a critique of patriarchal constructions of femininity, the motive that has so often been discerned in her work over the last 25 years of study. It would be a convincing reading of this passage. But focusing so intensely on the opposed gender-commitments of Freud and H. D. in this scene also forces one to look right past the tensions of temporality with which this exchange is charged. In the consulting room, they shuffle around the subject of Freud's age, of H. D.'s fear of loving an old man, separated by thirty years that produce a chasm in the emotional field of the treatment. Then they share an appreciation of the mythic figures in the "other room," agreeing—however divergent their own preferences among these *imagos*—on their consummate value as emblems of a realm of experience enduring outside of time. In their excursion into this myth-rich world the pressures of age, not gender, have been for a moment suspended.

The narrative span between H. D.'s noticing this "other room" and her crossing into it is taken up with two intertwining pasts, her own and Greece's. In a vision she received in a Corfu hotel room in 1920, H. D. saw the same Nike she spotted in Freud's trove, and in the order of telling in "Writing on the Wall" she recollects this encounter with the goddess before she comes back to the opening into the time-element through which she and Freud passed. The gradual conflation of her own history with the Attic past structures the narrative—as a similar conflation had in a less personally revelatory way driven her first book of poems, *The Sea Garden,* and would continue to do so throughout her writing life, from the translations for Euripides that she worked on during the First World War to her last ambitious poem, *Helen in Egypt,* finished in 1955.

Yet it is only in her later work, beginning with the *Tribute to Freud,* that the connection between the two pasts becomes more layered and more urgent. It is here that she does the work of age, defying the current of time. H. D.'s relationship to an eternal realm, populated with Greek and Egyptian gods and functioning according to the universal, unceasing dynamics of the dream, may have begun with her exchange in Freud's "other room," but it was sustained throughout the rest of her writing life through a connection with a series of mediators associated with his combination of Hellenism and analytic wisdom. Composing "Writing on the Wall" after Freud's death, H. D. summoned the first of these age-defying, myth-vivifying figures in Goethe, closing that book's recollection of the progress of her analysis with a sudden shift to her own translation of and commentary on his lyric, "Kennst du das Land, wo die Zitronen blumen." As an eminent German mind on the one hand, and, on the other, a poet, Goethe's great appeal was as a symbol of the union between analyst and analysand that H. D.'s text had been aiming to create. That his *Faust* revolves around the feat of the resurrection of Helen of Troy, creating by a stroke of neo-classical learning and dramatic imagination the same sort of newly alive Greek world H. D. found in the "time-element" of Freud's "other room," seems, with respect to this text, beyond the point.

Yet H. D. would share Faust's attempt to bring Helen back to life, after another phase of her life had passed. At the time she wrote "Writing on the Wall" she was in the middle of the most productive stretch of her late years, composing the three parts of her *Trilogy* as the bombing of London left her searching for new imaginative origins and as the steady destruction of the war turned her back towards the god figures in the tombs at Luxor in Egypt, the angels of her own Christian youth, and Kaspar, one of the three magi seeking out the Christ child. These poems were published between 1942 and 1944. This later-life search for a poetic and imaginative rebirth that Duncan found in these works and the creative outpouring of this period was also linked to an impending psychological crisis—in February of 1946, she had a nervous collapse. She was moved from London, where she had survived the war, to a sanatorium in Zurich. Her recovery progressed slowly. By the end of the year she had moved to Lausanne, where she would begin to spend winters, dividing her time between that auspicious *Kurort* and Lugano until she was moved permanently into a mental clinic in Küsnacht in 1953.

She wrote no poetry for a long time after completing the *Trilogy,* falling silent as a lyrical voice for five years after her breakdown. Then some time in 1951 she started to write the first cantos of what would become the sequence *Helen in Egypt.* One of her biographers, the poet Barbara Guest, speculates in her brief discussion of this period of H. D.'s life that Ezra Pound's *Pisan Cantos,* published in 1948, 'were the ferment on both the conscious and subconscious levels of what would become H. D.'s own book of cantos, *Helen in Egypt*' (290). The *Collected Poems* of H. D., first published in 1957 as a selection, includes only work written before the breakdown, ending its selection with the third part of *Trilogy.* H. D.'s extended autobiographical essay on the stretch of her recovery and return to poetry while living in Lausanne, Lugano and Küsnacht, "Compassionate Friendship," remains unpublished. There has been comparatively little focus on the work of H. D.'s last years, and age as a theme in H. D.'s later works has not yet been the subject of critical consideration.

In the part of *The H. D. Book* cited here, Duncan was not particularly curious about the nature of H. D.'s last works. Of the major text of the last decade he says only, "In the work of her old age, *Helen in Egypt,* she weaves, as ever, the revelation of 'these things since childhood' in terms of Homer and Euripides" (ND, 126). One could hardly formulate a more general description in the guise of critical appraisal. Still there are hints here, and in other spots in the body of H. D. criticism, as to how one might understand this text as a specifically late-life continuation of some of the projects of her art. Friedman says that "as a psychoanalytic narrative that reconstitutes Helen's past," *Helen in Egypt* "replicates the healing of repressed memories in *Tribute to Freud*" (303). Guest suggests that in addition to Pound the works of a German scholar and novelist, E. M. Butler, decisively influenced the direction of her imagination as she began her late Hellenistic text—and, as had Duncan implicitly and Friedman explicitly, Guest interprets this influence as a repetition of the pattern H. D. first established by taking Freud as a guide to her own inner life. Imagining the importance of discussions of Goethe's *Faust* for both women—Butler had published two works on the figure by the time the two women met in 1949, and would publish the third and last of the series, *The Fortunes of Faust,* in 1952—Guest suggests that H. D. came through Butler's influence to emulate the aim of Goethe's hero to resurrect Helen from a time long past: "Following Butler's lead, in reference to Goethe's Helen, H. D. developed in her own poem the ambiguities that pursued and worried the 'strange, beautiful, mythological being' in her own search for her identity" (292). The figure who opens for H. D. a

mythological, timeless world, first as Freud and then as Goethe, returns in Butler, another German scholar in H. D.'s life, one who has restored a sense of the efficacy of Goethe for vivifying the past that she had first been drawn to when she chose him as a figure of her alliance with Freud in 1944.

Helen in Egypt is an unusual text. Like *Trilogy,* it took its three-part shape only gradually, in the course of its slow composition from 1952 to 1955. It departs from a hint in the *Pallinode* of the Greek poet Steshichorus and its elaboration in the *Helen* of Euripides that Helen was never actually abducted by Paris but that she was transported to Egypt while a body-double was sent to walk the Trojan walls in her place. The poem has three segments, **'Pallinode,' 'Leuké'** and **'Eidolon,'** each divided into a number of books— seven, seven and six, respectively—which in turn are made up of eight cantos each. The cantos are in free verse tercets. At the head of each canto, a paragraph of prose summarizes, quotes, interprets and questions the language beneath it. As a narrative whole, the poem reports the story of Helen's encounters with the male figures of her past—Achilles, Paris, Theseus— and follows her from Egypt to Leuké to Sparta. Enabled by an identification with Helen—also, as many critics have noticed, her own mother's name—H. D. undertook in this poem a journey through her own history like the ones she tried in her prose of this period, the memoirs of her relationships with D. H. Lawrence, *Bid Me to Live* (finished in 1949), and with Ezra Pound, *End to Torment* (1958). Not content with the expanse for introspection allowed by prose, though, she aimed in this work to bring together both the visionary directness of her *Trilogy* and the reflective distance of these autobiographical narratives. She sought once again in this narratively connected sequence of lyrics to step out of her own story into the mythical, eternal "time-element" of a further room.

Why has this later attempt been received with less interest than the earlier effort of her *Trilogy?* Part of the answer must have to do with the tendency to compare works in an author's oeuvre. Guest stands alone in claiming that "*Helen* is an improvement over the war poetry" (293). But the text's background in virtual convalescence rather than late adulthood contributes to this aversion as well. In gauging the relative—and by contrast striking—discomfort of critics to take up this poem in its biographical context, I think it is illuminating to consider the caution of another writer who passed through Freud's Vienna in 1933, the developmental psychologist and theorist of the emotional stages of the human life cycle, Erik Erikson. Erikson devoted much of his career as a psychoanalytic theorist to establishing a model of human growth segmented into six phases, each dynamized by an opposition between a phase-appropriate ideal and a correspondingly deep danger—famously characterizing the business of adulthood as a negotiation between generativity and stagnation and that of old age as a contest between integrity and despair. Erikson consistently gave a broad definition to integrity, calling it in one of his last statements, from the 1982 *The Life Cycle Completed* "a sense of *coherence* and *wholeness*," an achieved synthesis of memory and self-knowledge for which the major asset is wisdom. He describes this quality elsewhere as "detached concern with life itself, in the face of death itself" (*LC* [*The Life Cycle Completed*], 65; *VI* [*Vital Involvement in Old Age*], 37).

Coming out of the tradition of ego psychology, a branch of the psychoanalytic movement inspired by the work of Freud's daughter Anna and dominating the psychoanalytic establishment in the United States from the 1950's to the 1970's, Erikson represents a Freudian legacy difficult to harmonize with H. D.'s own emphasis on the fathomless, eternally returning unconscious. His work is focussed on understanding the mind within and as a function of the sorts of developmental and interpersonal contingencies that H. D. considered poetry, linked to myth and dream, to be an escape from, and his normative and influential view of the emotional work of old age is phrased in ways that seem to leave little room to respect the striving for eternity that dominates her work. "Burdened by physical limitations and confronting a personal future that may seem more inescapably finite than ever before," Erikson writes in *Vital Involvement in Old Age*, a jointly-authored report on the findings of a decades-long study of hundreds of men and women born in Berkeley in 1928-9,

> those nearing the end of the life cycle find themselves struggling to accept the inalterability of the past and the unknowability of the future, to acknowledge possible mistakes and omissions, and to balance consequent despair with the sense of overall integrity that is essential to carrying on.
>
> (56)

The work of old age, in Erikson's view, is to look directly at the fact of death. It is in this context that a warning of his about the danger and allure of a particular kind of retrospection seems to cast light on the critical preference for earlier texts in H. D.'s body of work. "What is demanded here could be simply called 'integrality,' a tendency to keep things together," Erikson says in one summary of the final phase of life, before he admonishes, "And indeed, we must acknowledge in old age a retrospective mythologizing that can amount to a pseudointegration as a defense against lurking despair" (*LC*, 65). Myth is forbidden to old

age in the developmental course prescribed by the one Freudian line that has found its way to face the question. Only wisdom—not vision, imagination, dream—can be a sufficient ally against the nemesis of despair.

Viewed within the perspective of the Freudian diaspora, the enormously influential scattering of pupils and analysands who, like H. D. and Erikson, passed at one time through the consulting room at 19 Berggasse, it is ironic that the same evasion of age that Freud discerned in H. D.'s difficulties establishing a transference could be framed as a developmental failure in her later work through Erikson's terms. But this irony doesn't only suggest why H. D.'s late poem can evoke discomfort among readers sharing the assumptions and values Erikson represents. It also raises the question of how much H. D.'s work explores aspects of the Freudian legacy with respect to aging that are lost to ego psychology, a movement which tended from its inception to minimize the importance of the ineducable, unmaturing unconscious. The conflict between H. D.'s inspired mythologizing of her life at the start of her convalescence and Erikson's emphasis on a wise resignation in old age, viewed as an event within the Freudian field of influence they share, suggests that there is more to integrate than memory at this stage of life. The "other room" of the Freudian mind—the "unexplored depth in man's consciousness" and the "universal world of the dream" that H. D. felt he had led her to understand—seems to assert strongly its own claim to a vitality that does not age, giving the lie to wisdom's poised address to death. How does one integrate this inner life that has never been marked by time, that has always seemed to be at once ancient and undying, into a conscious life shaped by one's sense of inevitable finitude and the consequent interest in retrospection, understanding, and historical synthesis? This, as I see it, is the question H. D. grappled with courageously in writing **Helen in Egypt.**

Beyond Erikson's grand terms, there is not much contemporary literary criticism available for exploring the role of "old age"—the phase in which mortality gradually assumes the orienting psychological function long held by an idea of the future—in shaping literary texts. This must be partly because the experience of age, though itself of course a social construction based on biology, does not work quite the way more often discussed constructions like racial and gender identity do. One is not interpellated into old age; it is not, like having a sex or a race, a condition of recognition as an agent. It is a category into which one is drawn by some change in physical functioning. In this respect it is closer to a disability than to an identity. But, as the moralistic bent of Erikson's treatment suggests, "old age" is not understood, like many other disabilities, as primarily a physical and radically particular state. It is widely presumed of "old age," as is not of most disabilities, that one can understand what it is like without having the physical experiences that define it. And in this respect it operates less like either an identity or a discipline than like a fate—a tragic one, as Erikson frames it—a circumstance which is not an individual condition, but rather a widely intelligible message about the complexity of the human predicament.

"It is my experience that when people do speak personally about their own experience of old age or their own fears of aging and death," Kathleen Woodward writes in the introduction to her 1991 *Aging and Its Discontents,* one of the few works to explore representations of old age in modern literature, ". . . the common response of others is to reject what they say. Nervous anxiety is masked by a denial of another's subjectivity in a way that appears to be reassuring but is in reality silencing and repressive" (3). Woodward argues in the first chapter of this book that this conspiracy of silence has deep roots in the Freudian tradition, focussing on the equation of signs of aging with castration in *The Interpretation of Dreams* and the conflation of aging with death in *Beyond the Pleasure Principle* and *The Ego and the Id.* She ends her essay on Freud's own avoidance of the experience of growing old with this interpretation of the exchange between H. D. and Freud about his age:

> As [H. D.] reports it, he took her by surprise, beating his hand on the sofa, bursting out, "The trouble is—I am an old man—*you do not think it worth your while to love me.*" The posture of stoicism in old age was at this moment unforgettably breached by the desire for the attention of a much younger woman. Freud was not able entirely to renounce love, choose death, and make friends with the necessity of dying.
>
> (51)

Turning against Freud his own defensive moralism about aging, Woodward suggests that the source of the interpretive arrogance that enables Erikson's treatment of age is fear, evasion and hypocrisy. Not surprisingly, then, she finds little help for talking about aging in the tradition of ego psychology, relying instead on Lacan's notion of the mirror stage and D. W. Winnicott's idea of transitional objects to analyze the function of aging in a series of contemporary narratives.

As might already be clear, I do not agree entirely with Woodward's understanding of Freud's desire in the exchange she interprets, though I am in sympathy with her sense of the "occlusion of old age in Freud's work" (37). For judging from the formulations of analytic technique he had published in the decades before H. D.'s analysis, Freud was likely to want H. D.'s love not primarily as a gratification of his own desire for

"attention" but rather for its capacity, as a mobilization of her affectively charged memories, to bring to light more of her unconscious life. This central element of Freudian thought—the need to find the opening through which the unconscious can continue to take a place in emotional life—does not play a prominent role in Woodward's critique or correction of its treatment of old age.

And so one is left without any ready critical predecessor to bring to bear on the text in which H. D. attempts her own integration of this unconscious life into her "old age" sense of self. We return to the question posed earlier, informed by both the telling critique and the interpretive limitation of Woodward's groundbreaking study—how could H. D. write a poem that would give an undying, mythic world its place in a retrospective synthesis of the major events and relationships of her life? I think the brief description of the nature of the text above has already led a step in the direction of an answer. For read in the context of the psychological demands of "old age," the hybrid structure of the narrative—part prose argument, part lyrical outpouring—seems to create a recursive interplay of citation and iteration by which the words of the poem are at once foreknown and freshly meaningful, giving the timeless voice of Helen a place in the process of retrospective interpretation that the narrative enacts.

I want to devote the rest of this essay to establishing what I mean by this. The beginning of the work offers a sense of this aspect of structure. "Do not despair" are the first three words of the poem, an imperative powerful for its indiscriminate directness and its candid acknowledgment of the threat. These words come at us as it were directly from the heart of old age, as Erikson describes it—push back, this voice says, against the shadows of meaninglessness. Yet it is crucial to our experience of this address that it is preceded by two paragraphs of expository prose, an opening passage which begins in a different tone: *"We all know the story of Helen of Troy,"* H. D. writes there, *"but few of us have followed her to Egypt. How did she get there?"* (1). The most obvious function of the writing that follows this question is to set a bibliographical frame around the story, informing us that this narrative will be based on hints from Stesichorus and Euripides, and expressing the narrator's own unwavering belief in their version of events, her conviction that the *"Greeks and Trojans alike fought for an illusion"* (1). Throughout the text, this narrative voice continues to have such a blandly informative role. But apart from anticipating and answering the questions surrounding this version of history, the narrative voice also performs the less familiar function of interpreting the lyric voice before it speaks—though this interpretation itself often comes couched in a set of questions and is rarely conclusive.

The notoriously insufficient tools of paraphrase and summary are even less useful than usual in looking at this aspect of the text, since it is a phenomenon that only appears in the space opened up between its two levels of writing. By its nature it eludes quotation. Rather than describe a handful of the more striking moments of this interplay, then, I want to focus on one canto from the **"Pallinode,"** quoting it in full. This way the need for exposition is confined to establishing the place of the passage in the narrative arc of the work.

The canto comes in the middle of the fifth book, the section in which the work's themes begin to converge. The first book depicts the encounter between Helen and Achilles in a temple, a meeting that begins in a confused mixture of suspicion and attraction and ends with Achilles trying to strangle Helen in a rage, as Helen prays, *"let me remember, / forever, this Star in the night"* (17). The poems and prose passages of the second book convey Helen's painstaking interpretation of this attack, dwelling at length on the analogies between her relationship to Achilles and the restorative sibling romance of Isis and Osiris. In the third book Achilles, reconciled to Helen and captivated by her apparent understanding, poses a question that H. D. will return to for the rest of the book—"Helena, which was the dream, / which was the veil of Cytharaea?" Released by his acknowledgment of Helen's reality in this Egyptian setting, Achilles in the fourth book recounts his dimming memories of the Trojan War, a simultaneous summoning and relinquishing of the past that Helen then repeats in the fifth book, where she probes the question of why her life has taken a less bloody path than that of her sister Clytemnaestra. She continues drifting somewhat dreamily over this question in the middle of the sixth book, whose fifth canto reads this way:

> *The dream? The veil? Helen is still concerned with Achilles' question. 'I have not answered his question.' She has tried to answer the question by returning to an intermediate dimension or plane, living in fantasy, the story of her sister. Death? Love? The problem remains insoluble. Does it? No. The mind can not answer the 'numberless questions' but the heart 'encompasses the whole of the indecipherable script,' when it recalls the miracle, 'Achilles' anger' and 'this Star in the night.'*

> Clytaemnestra gathered the red rose,
> Helen, the white,
> but they grew on one stem,

> one branch, one root in the dark;
> I have not answered his question,
> which was the veil?

which was the dream?
was the dream, Helen upon the ramparts?
was the veil, Helen in Egypt?

I wander alone and entranced,
yet I wonder and ask
numberless questions;

the heart does not wonder?
the heart does not ask?
the heart accepts,

encompasses the whole
of the undecipherable script;
take, take as you took

Achilles' anger, as you flamed
to his Star,
this is the only answer;

there is no other sign nor picture,
no compromise with the past;
yet I conjure the Dioscuri,

those Saviours of men and ships,
guide Achilles,
grant Clytaemnestra peace.

(85-6)

H. D.'s prose "argument" or preface to this poem reads its searching shifts closely but, at first glance, merely descriptively, so that one is left wondering how both texts are necessary to the progress of the narrative. Stopping short of interpretation, offering no sense of the role of this canto in the development of the narrative, pre-empting some of its stronger lines by citing them out of context—what, other than blunt the poem's immediacy, does this introduction do?

In terms of the challenge of late-life retrospection and its confrontation with the ageless voice of the unconscious, I think this uncertain, incorporative voice is the most significant accomplishment of the poem. Subordinated in one sense to the poem that follows it, the source of the language it quotes, it also sustains a process of reflection that subsumes the more desperate certainties of the tercets. In this respect, the preface's quotations are the natural home of the phrase "encompasses the whole / of the undecipherable script" and Helen's own words are the repetition. At their first appearance, the words are already marked as a voice from another register, from a mythical dimension, and so when they appear the second time without this mark of incorporation they are both immediate and twice-framed. This is not only to say that the voice of the preface exemplifies a capacity for integration of the language of an eternal imago because that imago's most telling words are always already spoken. More important than this is its accomplishment of a narration capable of doubt, interruption and self-correction, a reflective consciousness which unfailingly sets the parameters within which the dream-narration, the language of immediacy, of possession and eternity, can be thought about rather than simply yielded to.

This reading of the poem does not square easily with the ones departing from the feminist version of H. D. that has predominated for the last generation of scholarship. Buck, for instance, argues that the function of the narrative voice of the prefaces is to own from within the Freudian notion of woman as unknowable, claiming that in "the face of the reader's expectations, the author as reader persists in denying knowledge" so that finally H. D. establishes a paradoxical reversal of the epistemic problem of woman in conventional psychoanalytic thought by "defining knowledge of woman as something you can know by knowing that you do not know it" (161, 164). Eileen Gregory frames the difficulties of interpretation that trouble the narrative voice throughout as coming from "an intimate intertextual engagement with Euripides' *Helen*" whose "epistemological questioning in the context of a recognition of divine mysteries opens for H. D. the complex querying and weaving" of a text where influence is not anxious, where she can reap the benefit of a wishful, intuitive classicism dismissed by her masculinist modernist contemporaries as nostalgic (231). Rachel Blau DuPlessis, from a more formalist and overtly psychoanalytic perspective, reads the Helen of the poem as "a site of resistance by being plural . . . and palimpsestic, as a series of eras overlayer and are read in relation" (109).

Indeed there is certainly room to follow these critics' lead and read this canto as an empowering repossession of a female role. Helen's "the heart accepts, / / encompasses the whole / of the indecipherable script" can be heard as a figuration of wisdom in the terms of the feminine role in sexual intercourse, turning what could be presented as passivity into a figure for comprehension. Similarly, Helen's conjuration of the Dioscuri, a two-star constellation made up of her brothers Castor and Pollox, traditionally the patrons of lost and shipwrecked sailors, can be thought of as a re-imagining of Helen's own legendary powers of attraction, presenting them not in terms of the sexual allure that is central to the myth of the start of the Trojan War but rather as having a hierophantic or priestly dimension. Helen becomes in this canto the "site of resistance" elucidated by Rachel Blau DuPlessis by subsuming and transposing the raw sexuality for which that character has been so long idealized and disparaged.

From this perspective, the uncertain quality of the narrative voice prepares the way for and is dissolved by the dramatic lyric assurance of Helen's voice in the poems. In order to read this way, though, we cannot place much emphasis on the way that Helen's strongest lines come to us as already spoken, that her dramatic resolution to the question—which was the dream? which was the veil?—in the decision to "take, take as you took / Achilles' anger" has already been narrated to us before it is spoken. For this effect seems to mitigate precisely the sense of authenticity and autonomy of the character Helen on which feminist critics placed so much emphasis.

The reading I have proposed is an addition to and not a refutation of the feminist H. D. "No compromise with the past" is the self-assured pledge of Helen as she stakes her own claim to understand the dream and the veil of Aphrodite, the illusions and revelations of love that had given her such inordinate power in the minds of men. But it is also spoken as she is trying to come to terms with the claims made on her by the memory of both her sister, Clytaemnestra, who lost her daughter Iphigenia as a sacrifice for winds that would allow the Greek ships to sail for Troy, and Achilles, one of the great heroes of that war, the warrior to whom Iphigenia was falsely said to be promised in marriage so that Clytaemnestra would let her go. This conflict of loyalties establishes a set of symmetries in the ramifications of Helen's lines. Is her invocation of the Dioscuri, as a turn towards her brothers, a signal of her sympathy with Clytaemnestra's valuing of family over military ends, an implicit acceptance of her sister's murderous resentment against Agamemnon for his having sacrificed their child? Or is it, as an address to the wind gods, an attempt at a symbolic repetition of Agamemnon's own propitiation of winds by sacrifice of his daughter, signalling the limits of her sympathy with her sister? Is it an attempt to include her partner in Egypt, Achilles, in her sense of family, by enlisting her brothers as an aid to him, the shipwrecked warrior on the strange coast where they stand? The final lines of Helen's verse—"Saviors of men and ships, / guide Achilles, / grant Clytaemnestra peace"—suggest all three of these impulses are somehow balanced, since she finds something to ask from her brothers for both her sister and her consort. "No compromise with the past" means, in this context, that she need not choose sides between these archetypes of bellicose hero and wronged female guardian of the hearth. She can recognize her intimate ties to both of them.

So viewed, Helen exemplifies a way that femininity can be constitutive, essential to identity, and yet not confining of the capacity to establish empowering roles in familial and love relationships. It need not matter whether her lines seem immediate or already framed by the more distant voice of the preface—in either case, the H. D. presents a character who is coping imaginatively with the challenge of establishing her independence from within her gendered position. Like a dream, her words move through and arrange a network of associations so that the conflictual question of her loyalties as a woman is resolved with a symbolic act—the invocation of her brothers—rather than a 'compromise.'

I have suggested this reading of the verses H. D. gives Helen because I think it traces some of the relatively elusive meanings of those lines, and because it is compatible with the feminist view of H. D. that has informed my understanding of her poetry. But this reading is most significant in the context of my argument because the preface—what I have called the most significant achievement of the poem—casts this reading into doubt. The prefaces, in my view, not only distance us from the immediacy of Helen's words, suggesting the necessity of analytic distance in reading them, but they also point towards a set of interpretive clues which draw us away from the most plausible reading of any canto taken on its own terms. Any given preface does not merely frame the poem as an experience that requires interpretation. It also places the poem in a context that alters the relative plausibility of readings. It is an act of integration.

Two phrases from the preface of this particular section (cited above) stand out in this respect: "miracle," a loaded word with no counterpart in the poem itself, and "this Star in the night," a phrase repeated not from the canto that will follow but from the last canto of the first book, the words of Helen's prayer as she is clutched to the attacking body of Achilles. Notice the effect these phrases have on the symmetry of loyalties towards Clytaemnestra and Achilles that structure the poem itself. The canto begins and ends with the name of Helen's sister, establishing her as a double not only to Achilles but to the speaker herself—an emphasis that gives a double meaning to the gesture of Helen's invocation of their brothers at the end. But the preface frames this gesture very differently. It begins and ends, for its part, with Achilles, his continually preoccupying question and his cold, piercing visitation in his first approach to Helen—coming as a star in the night. From the perspective of this retrospective, interpretive voice, the "miracle" of Achilles, not the equally strong claims of Achilles and Helen, are what fascinate Helen.

So understood, the frame this particular preface sets around the words of the following poem that it quotes does more than insist on the necessity of interpreting the words. It neutralizes some of their dramatic strength in part so that the weight of meaning can be more widely distributed, some back onto Helen's earlier sense of her visitation by Achilles as a heavenly presence, some onto this voice's original assessment of that visitation as a "miracle." This contextual shift, in turn, establishes a contrast between the invocation of the dark twin stars of the Dioscuri, Helen's brothers who can be summoned, and the uncontrollable singular star of Achilles. The balance that the poem seems to establish between Helen's status as consort and her status as a sister is skewed by the emphasis of the preface. Supported by both the record of Helen's verses that have preceded this one and its own understanding of the meaning of that record, this voice acknowledges the inordinate importance of Achilles for Helen—a threatening sense of fascination that she, in the moment of seeking out imaginative resolutions to her conflicted identities, seems inclined to hold off. The prose voice's implicit recognition that erotic fascination can be understood as a repetition of a pattern is the lesson that H. D.'s own resistance to loving an aging Freud may have spared her in Vienna. Myth has now become not an escape from the finitude of life but a layer of the inner life to which old age gives new meaning.

Neither of these readings is the "real" reading. The two experiences of the canto, one maintaining a firm separation between the two discourses of **Helen in Egypt** and the other weighing the clues of the prefaces for understanding the corresponding canto, work together to convey a sense of late-life integration of the forceful persistence of dream and fantasy in personal history. One's fantasy life does not run on a parallel track to one's real experiences. The two intersect, shade each other, and diverge again. So in the poem the two realms carry out a persistent exchange. H. D.'s remarkable achievement in this poem comes, in my view, from the courage of trying to integrate her persistent fantasies into her understanding of the meaning of the events of her life. This discipline leads to a voice capable of allowing the menagerie of the unconscious its own efficacy but also framing that power with what has been learned by living so long fascinated by one "Star in the night."

Note

H. D. does write in a letter of March 10, 1933 to Bryher, "My TRANSFERENCE seems to have taken place and what is it? This—Chiron, big and remote and dumb is father-symbol and papa is a sort of old Beaver [Helen Doolittle]. Isn't that odd?" (69) Though she was familiar with the concept of the transference, it seems to me that her notion of how the analysis should proceed emphasized intellectual rather than affective exchanges.

Works Cited

Buck, Claire. *H. D. and Freud: Bisexuality and a Feminine Discourse.* New York: Harvester Wheatsheaf, 1990.

Collecott, Diana. *H. D. and Sapphic Modernism: 1910-1950*. Cambridge UP, 1999.

Duncan, Robert. 'The H. D. Book. Part Two: Nights and Days. Chapter 9.' *Chicago Review* 30:3 (1979). 37-88.

DuPlessis, Rachel Blau. *H. D.: The Career of That Struggle*. Sussex, England: The Harvester Press, 1986.

Erikson, Erik H. *The Life Cycle Completed*. New York: Norton, 1982.

Erikson, Erik H., Joan M. Erikson & Helen Q. Kivnick. *Vital Involvement in Old Age*. New York: Norton, 1986.

Friedman, Susan Stanford. 'Introduction.' *Analyzing Freud: Letters of H. D., Bryher, and their Circle*. New York: New Directions, 2002. xiii-xxxviii.

———. *Penelope's Web: Gender, Modernity, H. D.'s Fiction*. Cambridge UP, 1990.

———. *Psyche Reborn: The Emergence of H. D.* Bloomington: Indiana UP, 1982.

Gregory, Eileen. *H. D. and Hellenism: Classic Lines*. Cambridge UP, 1997.

Guest, Barbara. *Herself Defined: The Poet H. D. and Her World*. Garden City, NY: Doubleday & Co., 1984.

H. D. (Hilda Doolittle). *Analyzing Freud: Letters of H. D., Bryher, and Their Circle*. Susan Stanford Friedman, ed. New York: New Directions, 2002.

———. *Helen in Egypt*. New York: New Directions, 1961.

———. 'Writing on the Wall.' *Tribute to Freud*. 1-112. New York: New Directions, 1974.

Robinson, Janice S. *H. D.: The Life and Work of an American Poet*. Boston: Houghton Mifflin Co., 1982.

Woodward, Kathleen. *Aging and Its Discontents: Freud and Other Fictions*. Bloomington: Indian UP, 1991.

Nephie J. Christodoulides (essay date 2006)

SOURCE: Christodoulides, Nephie J. "Triangulation of Desire in H. D.'s *Hymen*." In *"And Never Know the Joy": Sex and the Erotic in English Poetry*, pp. 317-36. New York: Amsterdam, 2006.

[*In the following essay, Christodoulides analyzes the motif of desire in H. D.'s poetry collection* Hymen *and traces the biographical and Freudian influences on this work.*]

In her book *Tribute to Freud*, where she reflects on her psychoanalytic sessions with Freud, H. D. notes, "There were two's and two's and two's in [her] life",

implying, as Eileen Gregory puts it, an erotic triangulation.[1] In light of this, her poems in **Hymen** (1921) can be read as the very manifestation of the triangle motif. Dedicating the volume to her daughter Perdita and her companion Winnifred Ellerman (Bryher), H. D. sings the erotic bonds that have sustained her and celebrates her "marriage" with them (hence the title). Figures such as Demeter, Thetis, Leda, Helen, Phaedra and Hippolyta are employed as poetic masks to draw into focus the mother's desire for the lost daughter, the woman's erotic animation, and the daughter's desire for homoerotic union with the mother, which are the main driving forces of the collection.

In *Powers of Horror*, Julia Kristeva develops her theory of the "abject", its relation to the concept of the mother and its significance in the constitution of the subject. The realm of the mother, the semiotic *chora*, is characterized by a lack of differentiation between child and mother, a pre-verbal dimension of language marked by sensual impressions, echolalias, bodily rhythms, sounds and incoherence. The mother must be repudiated and expelled ("abjected" is Kristeva's term) so that the child will be able to turn towards the father, to the realm of paternal symbolic order, structured by language that conforms to the linguistic rules of grammar, syntax, propriety and, of course, socialization. The expulsion ("abjection") of the mother is not only the precondition for entrance into the symbolic, but it also becomes the precondition for an idealization that is the basis of love as *agape* (paternal) always in conflict with *eros* (maternal, passionate and destructive love).[2]

Although the child constitutes the mother's authentication in the symbolic, the loving mother—different from "the clinging mother"—is willing to facilitate the intervention of the third party, the father, to allow the subject to be formed.[3] Thus, the process follows a triangular pattern from which any diversion will entail disruption in the formation of the subject. A glimpse into H. D.'s childhood years reveals an inadequately structured triangle:

> A girl-child, a doll, an aloof and silent father form the triangle, this triangle, this family romance. . . . Mother, a virgin, the Virgin . . . adoring with faith, building a dream, and the dream is symbolized by the third member of the trinity, the child, the doll in her arms.

The loosely joined sides, however, were never meant to be fixed permanently for the father was "a little un-get-able, a little too far away";[4] an inaccessible figure engrossed in planets and stars, "who seldom even at table focused upon anything nearer literally, than the moon".[5] An equally absent mother would direct her maternal semiotic force into painting, but was never the one who would draw the girl to her, imbue her with her semiotic and then release her to enter the symbolic. She would instead favour the younger brother as more advanced, "quaint and clever", and ignore "Mignon"[6] as "not very advanced",[7] but "wispy and mousy".[8]

In her effort to reconstruct the triangle, the adult H. D. first turned to the remote maternal figure and sought ways to rediscover her. She longed to share her art. She recalls that the sight of her mother's hand-painted dishes "fired [her] very entrails with adoration" and she wanted "a fusion or a transfusion of [her] mother's art": "I wanted to paint like my mother."[9]

As we have seen, according to Kristeva the speaking subject revolves round two conceptual and dialectical categories, the semiotic and the symbolic. The semiotic is pre-verbal, characterized by rhythms, musicality, pulses, unspeakable energy, and drives. This is the category which is associated with the mother and which as poetic language ruptures the symbolic, the language of logic, grammar, the paternal language. Therefore, for H. D. another way to recover the mother is in signs, in her use of the maternal semiotic flow in writing. Although she finds the self vacillating between the maternal semiotic and the paternal symbolic, being, as she puts it, "on the fringes or in the penumbra of the light of [her] father's science and [her] mother's art", she "derives her imaginative faculties through [her] musician-artist mother".[10]

Then she started psychoanalysis with Freud: "The Professor had said . . . that I had come to Vienna hoping to find my mother."[11] Freud believed that H. D. saw her mother in his face: "Why did you think you had to tell me?. . . . But you wanted to tell your mother."[12] He saw her problem as a "mother fix", a "desire for union with [her] mother":

> Mother? Mamma. But my mother was dead. I was dead, that is the child in me that had called her mamma was dead.

Even Freud's "old-fashioned porcelain stove that stood edge-wise in the corner" recalls the mother: "*The Nürnberg Stove* was a book my mother had liked."[13]

Homosexuality is another means for a new subject formation. Freud in "Female Sexuality" argues that the girl who achieves normal femininity turns away from her mother "in hate" when she discovers that they are both castrated. Instead she loves her father and sublimates her desire for a penis into the wish for his child. Some girls, however, never give up their desire for their mother and their wish for a penis. Among these are women whom Freud considered neurotic, as

well as those he identified as having a "masculinity complex".[14] These are the women who want to be men, a desire that manifested in their attempt to do what men do. For Freud they represent the "extreme achievement of the masculinity complex" and the women they love function psychically as substitutes for their mothers, upon whom they remain, in the unconscious, fixated.[15]

An early passion for Frances Josepha Greggs, a friend of a schoolmate from Bryn Mawr College that H. D. attended briefly, and her later lifelong relationship with Bryher constitute the two landmarks of her homoerotic journey. Like other contemporary lesbian writers, however, she was silenced by a society characterized by a "climate that produced secrecy, coding, and self-censorship".[16] Since society would not accept her homoeroticism, she used it as an intertextual layer mostly in her autobiographical novels (*HER, Asphodel*). Freud was convinced that H. D. did not repress her early psychological and sexual bisexuality, as most people do, but instead stuck to it because of her problematic connection with her mother. He suggested that H. D. should find a way to unite her split self, a feat H. D. never seems to have accomplished.[17]

The mother fixation, however, leads H. D. to the brother. She thinks that fusion with the brother will give access to the mother: "If I stay with my brother, become part almost of my brother, perhaps I can get nearer to *her*."[18] She starts with a new family romance:

> My triangle is mother-brother-self. That is early phallic mother, baby brother or smaller mother and self.[19]

However, as the maternal quest became an endless task that she did not seem to succeed in accomplishing, there was no point in turning to the quest for the father figure, since to merge with the father or a substitute paternal figure would entail no subject formation without the mother. She, therefore, sought to be involved in triangular patterns of a different nature to make up for it or merely to live a triangular relationship she never seemed to have experienced. She placed herself between males and females: she married Richard Aldington but the shadow of Ezra Pound was always cast on them, even moving into the same apartment block, "just across the hall".[20]

In 1914 H. D. met D. H. Lawrence and originally their relationship was "intensely cerebral" mostly exchanging manuscripts, but Frieda Lawrence set them up for an affair "so that she could have one of her own with Cecil Gray". In 1918, she met Bryher who became her lifelong companion, and in 1926 she "experience[d] an intense affair" with Kenneth Macpherson who later married Bryher. About this *ménage a trois* she wrote:

"We seem to be a composite beast with three faces."[21] A new triangle had been formed which, however, would soon dissolve because of Macpherson's affairs with men, and the next *ménage* consisted of H. D., Bryher, and Perdita (H. D.'s daughter by Cecil Gray).[22]

Since her life always informed her work, constituting its intertextual layer, triangulation is to be found everywhere in her work from **Hymen** to the *Palimpsest* trilogy, three stories about three seemingly different women in different historical eras. Commenting on the choice of "hymen" as the collection's title, Renée Curry notes that apart from the obvious denotation of the word suggesting "the connective attributes related to Hymen, god of marriage in classical mythology", **Hymen** "resonates with allusions to . . . the membranous connective qualities of the anatomical hymen".[23] But I take this association a step further and see the use of "hymen" as suggestive of the marriage of the several forms of desire, which encapsulates maternal passion, passion for the daughter, daughterly homoerotic passion for the mother and female heterosexual passion. **Hymen,** like *Asphodel,* was written during a bitter and sometimes distraught period of H. D.'s life after the dissolution of her marriage and Aldington's refusal to keep his promise about recognizing Perdita. Thus, it can be said that it constitutes her own lay analysis, her articulation of her predicaments, H. D.'s own *felix culpa,* her speaking sin, "the joy of [her] dissipation set into signs".[24]

The introductory poem or play draws into sharp relief the notion of triangulation of desire. Sixteen matrons from the temple of Hera (protector of marriage), "tall and dignified, with slow pace" bring gladioli with "erect, gladiate leaves and spikes", chanting:

> Of all the blessings—
> Youth, joy, ecstasy—
> May one gift last[25]

The unnamed gift is implicitly stated through the phallic symbol of the gladioli and encompasses the orgasmic ecstasy induced by the phallus. The next group of very young girls carries crocuses. According to ancient Greek mythology, Crocus was a friend of Hermes who killed him accidentally while playing. According to another myth, Crocus was a young man who turned into a flower because of his unfulfilled passion for the nymph Smilax. In this way, the flowers are suggestive of alternative forms of erotic desire: homoerotic and heterosexual.

The next group of slightly older girls is boyish in appearance, suggesting the blur of boundaries between male and female. They carry hyacinths, implying the homosexual love of Apollo for Hyacinthus[26] and the blurring of gender boundaries. They are attendants of Artemis, endorsing her forcibly maintained virginity, perhaps celebrating the Bride's virginity which is soon to be lost. Finally the Bride enters—she is an amalgamation of purity and desire, anticipating a woman's heterosexual erotic animation. Beneath her "bleached fillet", her myrtle-bound head, and "underneath her flowing veil", she is white, pure and fair, but

> All the heat
> (In her blanched face)
> Of desire
> Is caught in her eyes as fire
> In the dark center leaf
> Of the white Syrian iris.

Following the entrance of the Bride, "Four tall young women, enter in a group".[27] They carry "fragrant bays" and their reference to "laurel-bushes" and "laurel-roses" commemorates Apollo's unfulfilled passion for Daphne and her transformation into a laurel tree. Then "older serene young women enter in processional form"[28] carrying coverlets and linen, chanting a song about their use of different kinds of fragrant wood to alleviate the pain caused by the Bride's defloration. It is important to recall here Freud's observation concerning defloration and the pain it causes. As he puts it, this pain is to be seen as a substitute for "the narcissistic injury which proceeds from the destruction of an organ and which is even represented in a rationalized form in the knowledge that loss of virginity brings a diminution of sexual value".[29]

Thus, the several kinds of fragrant wood are meant to comfort the bride, perhaps soothing her psychical and physical pain with their fragrance. Finally a "tall youth crosses the stage as if seeking the bride door". Love enters as Eros: he has wings and his flame-like hair commemorates the myth of Psyche and Eros as narrated by Apuleius in his *Metamorphoses (The Golden Ass).* He carries a "tuft of black-purple cyclamen" and his song strongly echoes the sexual act: the cyclamen have phallic "honey-points / Of horns for petals".[30] The phallic "points" recall the clitoris as the sexual organ of the woman[31] which is perceived by little girls as a castrated penis.[32]

> There with his honey-seeking lips
> The bee clings close and warmly sips,
> And seeks with honey-thighs to sway
> And drink the very flower away.
>
> (Ah, stern the petals drawing back;
> Ah, rare, ah virginal her breath!)
>
>   . . . . .
>
> (Ah, rare her shoulders drawing back!)
> One moment, then the plunderer slips
> Between the purple flower-lips.[33]

The bee that is about to sip the nectar from these points is male, strongly suggesting the bridegroom who is going to taste the bride's virginity, whereas the flower petals "which draw back" when the bee attempts to sip suggest the behaviour of the vagina in sexual intercourse. As Helene Deutsch notes: "The breaking of the hymen and the forcible stretching and enlargement of the vagina by the penis are the prelude to woman's first complete sexual enjoyment." After the penetration of the penis, Deutsch observes, there are "localized contractions [in the vagina] that have the character of sucking in and relaxing".[34] In the poem, the "stern" (stiff and reluctant) petals draw back, but this is momentary; soon the bee enters lifting the flower-lips, penetrating through that which "suck" him in.

Once Love "passes out with a crash of cymbals", a band of boys advance. They are unmistakably male: "their figures never confuse one another, the outlines are never blurred." They carry torches and "Their figures are cut against the curtain like the simple, triangular design on the base of a vase or frieze".[35] Their posture strongly recalls the triangular pattern of desire as will be sung in **Hymen** and which begins with the song of Demeter. This is the mother's longing for the lost daughter that becomes a passion similar to the secret passion of the boy for the mother. Immobilized like a statue "sit[ting], / wide of shoulder, great of thigh, heavy in gold . . . press[ing] / gold back against solid back / of the marble seat", Demeter pleads with her daughter, Persephone, not to forget her but to "keep [her] foremost", "before [her], after [her], with [her]", and thence demolishing any boundary meant to separate the two.[36]

Demeter refers to Bromios, Dionysus, as another instance of mother-child separation, due as she puts it, to the gods' desertion and indifference. The analogy, however, can be further extended to imply not only the dissolution of the mother-daughter dyad in the way Bromios was taken away from the dead mother's body after she had been blasted by Zeus' light, but also the repetition of the mother-son passion in the mother-daughter dyad. Demeter says:

> Though I begot no man child
> all my days,
> the child of my heart and spirit,
> is the child the gods desert
> alike and the mother in death—
> the unclaimed Dionysos[37]

The force of the secret passion of the male child for the mother and his feelings of jealousy and competitiveness towards his father, whom he inevitably and intuitively perceives as a rival for the mother's affection, is replicated in Demeter and Persephone. In this case, there is observed dissolution of the mother-daughter dyad by a third party, the husband. The mother, however, is keen to call her daughter back, suggesting that although the abductor is physically stronger than she is, her own maternal passion is deeper, which implies that he could never replace her, since his passion was no match for hers:

> Ah, strong were the arms that took
> (ah, evil the heart and graceless),
> but his kiss was less passionate![38]

The connective attributes of the hymen join the passion of the bereaved mother with the passion and desire of the woman who wishes to rediscover the mother. For Julia Kristeva the mother-daughter bond, that Freud conspicuously neglected, is a seminal aspect that governs both a mother's life and her daughter's. She talks about the loss of the mother and her rediscovery in signs. Our articulation of the loss in language is but a recovery of the mother:

> "I have lost an essential object that happens to be my mother," is what the speaking being seems to be saying. "But no, I have found her again in signs, or rather since I consent to lose her I have not lost her (that is the negation), I can recover her in language."[39]

As Kelly Oliver puts it, commenting on Kristeva's notion of the necessity of matricide in *Black Sun*:

> The child must agree to lose the mother in order to be able to imagine her or name her. The negation that this process involves is not the negation of the mother. Rather, it is the negation of the loss of the mother that signals proper entry into language.[40]

In "Stabat Mater" Kristeva also talks about another means of maternal rediscovery in childbirth—the blissful union of mother and child recalling another fusion, that of the daughter and the mother:

> Recovered childhood, dreamed peace restored, in sparks, flash of cells, instants of laughter, smiles in the blackness of dreams, at night, opaque joy that roots me in her bed, my mother's, and projects him, a son, a butterfly soaking up dew from her hand, there, nearby, in the night. Alone: she, I, and he.[41]

In addition, in *About Chinese Women*, Kristeva commemorates the call of the mother that "generates voices, 'madness,' hallucinations" but if the ego is not strong enough to defeat it, it leads to suicide: "Once the moorings of the ego begin to slip, life itself can't hang on: slowly, gently, death settles in."[42] In *Black Sun*, proceeding further, Kristeva states that many women "know that in their dreams their mothers stand for lovers or husbands".[43]

The maternal quest and the homoerotic passion it entails is another instance of passion evident in **Hymen**. "The Islands", which many critics have seen merely as a classification of Greek islands reminiscent of Homer's listing of ships in *The Iliad*[44] is but the prelude to a series of poems focusing on maternal passion. Discussing a 1937 note by H. D. on her early poetry—"I call it Hellas. I might, psychologically, just as well, have listed the Casco Bay islands off the coast of Maine . . ."—Rachel Blau DuPlessis remarks: "But to call it Hellas means 'it' (this special source of writing) is going to be a version of her mother's name", that is Helen.[45]

In **"The Islands",** the persona wonders what the Greek islands stand for her. And here it is important to note prevalent images of roundness strongly suggesting the female body in gestation: "What. . . . The Cyclades' [κύκλος, circle] / white necklace?" Eileen Gregory observes a pattern of containing and contained "island within island",[46] a motif that once more recalls the semiotic pre-oedipal union with the mother or even the fusion of mother and child in gestation where there is alterity within but there does not seem to be a division of subject and object.

At the same time, however, phallic images are noted as well: "What is Samothrace, / rising like a ship", "What is Greece—/ Sparta, rising like a rock?" Further the persona commemorates Sparta "entering", penetrating Athens, and the Greeks are said to be tall.[47] Circular motifs suggest the maternal semiotic, but phallic images make the mother a phallic, a pre-Oedipal, mother with whom the child wants to be fused, and who, since she is not castrated and can grant gratification, is always phallic.

If the mother, the addressed "you", Helen, Hellas, is lost then the islands will be lost since they constitute part of her: "What are the islands to me / if you are lost?"

> What can love of land give to me
> that you have not,
> what can love of strife break in me
> that you have not?
>
> I have asked the Greeks
> from the white ships,
> and Greeks from ships whose hulks
> lay on the wet sand, scarlet
> with great beaks.
> I have asked bright Tyrians
> and tall Greeks—
> "what has love of land given you?"
> And they answered—"peace."[48]

The expected answer "peace" is likely to be the outcome of the fusion with the mother, but at the same time this "peace" will be the outcome of "strife", a struggle perhaps between mother and child: "the immemorial violence with which a body becomes

separated from another body, the mother's, in order to be"; a "violent, clumsy, breaking away, with the constant risk of falling back under the sway of a power as securing as it is stifling".[49] However, this entire struggle will be wasted away if the mother "draw[s] back / from the terror and cold splendor of song / and its bleak sacrifice".[50] If the mother refuses to endow the daughter with semiotic elements to rupture the symbolic, if she refuses to be sacrificed—lost—so that her daughter will recover her in signs, then the islands will come to nothing.

Fusion with the mother, which is associated with erotic passion, is manifested in a series of three poems concentrating on Phaedra, Theseus, Hippolytus, and Hippolyta. In **"Phaedra"** H. D. contrasts Phaedra's passion—which the persona, Phaedra, feels to be diminishing—with Hippolyta's chastity which in this case is to be equated with frigidity. Phaedra, implores the "Gods of Crete" to grant her "soul / the body that it wore" for she feels that

> The poppy that [her] heart was,
> formed to bind all mortals,
> made to strike and gather hearts
> like flame upon an altar,
> fades and shrinks, a red leaf
> drenched and torn in the cold rain.[51]

Phaedra juxtaposes her passion with that of Hippolyta who prays to be endowed with Artemis' chastity:

> I never yield but wait,
> entreating cold white river,
> mountain-pool and salt:
> let all my veins be ice,
> until they break
>
> . . . . .
>
> forever to you, Artemis, dedicate
> from out my veins,
> those small, cold hands.[52]

In **"She Rebukes Hippolyta",** Phaedra sees Hippolyta's passion wasted on martial activities and her own chastity as a form of frigidity begotten out of this drain of passion. She keeps asking, "Was she so chaste?",[53] as if trying to find what lurks behind chastity. She sees her chastity as a form of frigidity; for she is "wild" and Phaedra assumes that Hippolyta would normally displace her wild feeling on sexual passion. Since she does not do so, she feels that she is frigid. She rebukes her as she sees her own passion diminishing as well. For by fusing with Hippolytus she fuses with his mother, too and acquires her frigidity.

Helene Deutsch associates feminine depression with frigidity by noting that they both stem from the vagina's biological fate of being the receptacle of death anxiety. The death anxiety accompanies mother-hood and is mobilized in pregnancy and delivery and it is this anxiety that seems to prevent sexual responses in the vaginal part of the female organ.[54] Kristeva proceeds a step further, adding that a woman uses fantasy to enclose an inaccessible object (her mother) inside her body. The mother figure imprisoned is the bad mother whom the woman locks within her to prevent losing her, to dominate her, to put her to death, or even to kill herself inside. An imagined partner is the one who will be able to dissolve the mother imprisoned within the daughter "by giving [her] what she could and above all what she could not give [her], another life".[55] In the poem, however, the lover simply transfers frigidity to Phaedra and does not liberate her, for he does not seem to have been released by the maternal figure.

"Egypt", a poem H. D. dedicates to Edgar Allan Poe, recalls his poem "Helen" as well her own play ***Helen in Egypt*** (1952-54) in which, as DuPlessis notes, "she shows that all desire is matrisexual; that all polarities, including major oppositional conflicts (love and death, Eros, and conflict), can be sublated through the mother".[56]

The personae in **"Egypt"** feel that they have been cheated by Egypt who "took through guile and craft / [their] treasure and [their] hope".[57] Most probably the deception the personae attribute to Egypt goes back to Stesichorus' *Palinode* and Euripides' tragedy *Helen.* Euripides and Stesichorus give their own versions of the myth of Helen: it was Helen's phantom that triggered the war; the real Helen was "stowed away in Egypt under the protection of its virtuous king Proteus".[58] However, the persona exclaims that "Egypt [they] loved" for she "had given [them] knowledge" which they "took, blindly, through want of heart". Egypt had given them "passionate grave thought", "forbidden knowledge" and "Hellas [was] re-born from death".[59] Egypt, although she cheated the Greeks and Trojans by housing Helen, taught them that mother Helen was not to be lost, but just lay dormant until she was resurrected. Previous attempts to reach her through a lover proved unsuccessful as they only gave out frigidity. Now the personae seemed to have rediscovered her in signs: she offered a "spice", forbidden knowledge, which caused the flow of the semiotic poetic language.

How could this be achieved? As the poem prefigures H. D.'s ***Helen in Egypt,*** one can say that the semiotic poetic language is what is presented as Helen's acquisition of the ability to decipher hieroglyphs: she undertakes the difficult task of "translating a symbol of time into time less / time / the hieroglyph, the script".[60] Further in the play both Helen and Achilles are re-united with the mother Thetis: "Thetis commanded, / Thetis in her guise of mother, who first summoned you here."[61] As Rachel Blau DuPlessis puts it in "Romantic Thralldom in H. D.": "the poem concerns the parallel quests of Helen and Achilles which are not journeys to each other, but quests for access to the unifying mother. . . . both have found Thetis at the end."[62] For by finding and unifying with the mother one can get her semiotic power.

Years later during her psychoanalytic session with Freud, H. D. brings up Egypt:

> We talked of Egypt. . . . Then I said that Egypt was a series of living Bible illustrations and I told him of my delight in our Gustave Doré as a child. I told him of the Princess and the baby in the basket. He asked me again if I was Miriam or saw Miriam, and did I think the Princess was actually my mother?[63]

Egypt is associated with H. D.'s childhood as she recalls the illustrated Bible she loved to browse through as a child. Going back to this incident it is as though she is telling Freud that she is regressing in a final effort to locate the triangle before she resorts to other ways of reconstructing it. Freud's question unmistakably leads to the mother. Was the Princess her mother or the mother who would rescue her after the desertion by the real mother, the way Moses was rescued by the Princess?

In more than one way, **"Egypt"** commemorates the homoerotic union with the mother, which, however, will not entail sexual passion but semiotic passion as another way of fulfilment. As I have already suggested, the dedication of the poem to Edgar Allan Poe is appropriate since it recalls his "Helen". But unlike his persona who says that he "had come home to the glory that was Greece",[64] she seems to be saying that Greece—Hellas—Helen—is to be found in Egypt: in the recovery and rediscovery of the mother in hieroglyphs, in the semiotic poetic power.

Erotic passion is the focus of **"Thetis",** which one may say rests oddly between **"Simaetha"** and **"Circe"** as if to break the continuity of witchcraft. As Eileen Gregory puts it, "body is by no means a clear fact—rather, it is (or it arrives at being) a presence, experienced through manifold erotic thresholds".[65] The poem focuses on Thetis' sexed erotic body and its boundary crossing:

> On the paved parapet
> you will step carefully

from amber stones to onyx
flecked with violet,
mingled with light.[66]

The female element abounds in the poem: "the island disk", the "curved" white beach, the "crescent" of the moon,[67] as if prefiguring the impregnated female body, when as Ovid puts it, Peleus "planted Achilles" in Thetis' womb.[68] But

> Should the sun press
> too heavy a crown,
> should dawn cast
> over-much loveliness,
> should you tire as you laugh,
> running from wave to wave-crest,
> gathering the flower to your breast. . . .

Then she should step deeper and deeper "to the uttermost sea depth". This threshold crossing will lead her beyond culture and further into nature, where the "anemones and flower of the wild sea-thyme / cover the silent walls / of an old sea city at rest".[69] She will go deeper into the maternal sea, fuse with her, not only achieving "an indissoluble bond, of being one with the external world", a feeling Freud would call "oceanic",[70] but also rediscovering the mother in the conception of the child.

In **"Thetis"** the sexed erotic body is allowed *jouissance* in motherhood, whereas in **"Leda"**, Leda enjoys erotic heterosexual *jouissance*. Amid a landscape characterized by boundary crossings where "the slow river meets the tide", "the level lay of sun-beam / has caressed / the lily", "the slow lifting / of the tide, / floats into the river" Leda enjoys the fusion with the swan:

> Ah kingly kiss—
> no more regret
> nor old deep memories
> to mar the bliss; . . .[71]

In **"Evadne"**, another poem characterized by erotic passion, Evadne recalls her sexual initiation by Apollo, but her passion is characterized by orality. She talks about her hair "made of crisp violets or hyacinths", recalling Poe's "Helen" whose hair is "hyacinth". Equally Apollo's hair feels "crisp" to her mouth and she still remembers his mouth "slip[ping] over and over" between her "chin and throat".[72] Both lovers seem to be governed by devouring tendencies that lead back to the child's oral stage, which is characterized by strong dependence on the mother, with food-taking constituting the first, and "most archaic relationship" between mother and child.[73] Once again, erotic passion is associated with the homoerotic union with the mother.

In **"Simaetha",** Simaetha, the sorceress, turns her wheel and concocts her love potion to bring her lover Delphis back to her:

> Drenched with purple
> drenched with dye, my wool,
> Turn, turn, turn, my wheel!
>
> Drenched with purple,
> steeped in the red pulp
> of bursting sea-sloes—
> turn, turn, turn my wheel!
>
> Laurel blossom and the red seed
> of the red vervain weed
> burn, crackle in the fire.[74]

"Simaetha" is modelled upon Theocritus' "Idyll 2: Pharmaceutria":

> Give me the bay-leaves, Thestylis, give me the
>   charms;
> Put a circlet of fine red wood around the cup.
> Hurry! I must work a spell to bind my lover
> . . . . Turn, magic wheel, and force my lover home.[75]

However, H. D.'s Simaetha is equipped with a wheel, which is not only the "magic wheel" Theocritus' Simaetha is imploring to turn, and "force [her] lover home", but also the spinning wheel. Simaetha is not simply a sorceress but resembles Arachne in her spinning vocation. Her own *pharmakon* is not merely the love potion prepared for Delphis, but her song, the poem. The "red pulp" and the "sloe" may not merely denote the red flesh of "the small, sour blackish fruit of the blackthorn *Primus Spinosa*",[76] which is one of the ingredients of the potion, but they could be seen as metaphors for the page and the ink, and metonymically poetry itself.

At this point, it is important to consider an excerpt from *Asphodel,* which is strongly reminiscent of Simaetha and her spinning vocation. The protagonist, Hermione, is lost in a stream-of-consciousness reverie in which she identifies with Morgan le Fay: "Weave, that is your *métier* Morgan le Fay, weave subtly, weave grape-green by grape-silver and let your voice weave songs."[77] Although many legends see Morgan le Fay as an instigator of the plot against King Arthur, she is also presented as a healer and a shape-changer (in *Sir Gawain and the Green Knight,* in the *Vulgate Lancelot,* attributed to Walter Map, and in Geoffrey of Monmouth's *Vita Merlini*). Morgan's healing powers resemble Simaetha's magic gift that enable her to prepare the magic potion and heal her own erotic malady by bringing Delphis back. What joins the two figures, however, is the ability of both to use textile (through weaving) as text and produce words and not simply material. After all text is textile (ME < ML text[us], woven [participle of texēre]).[78]

While spinning, Simaetha is worried whether Delphis will find her "blooming" when he comes or "worried of flesh, / left to bleach under the sun".[79] Her worry, H. D. seems to be saying is groundless. Since she is spinning—not merely manipulating the spinning wheel but also spinning words, poems, songs—she is a poet and her journey back to the semiotic becomes certainly shamanic. The shaman, as Mircea Eliade said, is the witch doctor, the sorcerer, the traveller to the other world either to retrieve the souls of the people who are in danger of death or to bring back news and healings. His words or songs and poetry are thought to have magical powers. Thus, Simaetha becomes a shamaness, for by entering the world of the semiotic, she moves outside the norms and like a shaman (shamanism is an "archaic technique of ecstasy") she becomes the master of ecstasy (ἐκ στάσεως = stepping outside). Coming back to the symbolic, equipped with her poetic semiotic power, she is resurrected the way a shaman is resurrected after his dismemberment.[80]

At this point, it is important to recall H. D.'s fourth vision in Corfu as she describes it in *Tribute to Freud*:

> Two dots of light are placed or appear on the space above the rail of the wash-stand, and a line forms, but so very slowly. . . . There is one line clearly drawn, but before I have actually recovered from this, or have time to take breath, as it were, another two dots appear and I know that another line will form in the same way. So it does, each line is a little shorter than its predecessor, so at last, there it is, this series of foreshortened lines that make a ladder or give the impression of a ladder set up there on the wall above the wash-stand. It is a ladder of light. . . . I have the feeling of holding my breath under water for some priceless treasure. . . . in a sense, it seems I am drowning . . . to come out on the other sides of things (like Alice with her looking glass or Perseus with his mirror?) I must be born again.[81]

The trip H. D. narrates is certainly shamanic, the ladder being her ascent to the other world to acquire ecstasy. At the same time, however, the journey could be experienced as a descent to the sea bottom to enjoy fusion with the mother, "back to the womb"[82] to acquire the semiotic forbidden knowledge.

Like H. D., Simaetha as a shamaness comes back rejuvenated, eternally young to bring back news of goings on in the transcendent realm, using her poetic *pharmakon* for eternal poetic youth. In *Notes on Thought and Vision*, H. D. stresses the importance of sexuality for people, but most importantly for creative people who need it to "develop and draw forth their talents".[83] In the same way, Simaetha shows that sexuality will not fade away but can lead to the power to generate. By spinning the wheel to bring her lover back and quench her erotic thirst, she can at the same time spin the wheel as part of her creative drive, producing words and with her sexuality becoming the impetus for her creativity.

Simaetha's worry about eternal youth becomes Circe's despair about her own witchcraft's lack of effectiveness. She seeks a way to bring her lover, Odysseus, back: "how shall I call you back?" If she cannot have the man she desires, she would give up "The whole region / of [her] power and magic".[84] It is as though she is renouncing the power of magic as erotic *pharmakon,* as if implying that witchcraft can be used differently, perhaps as successful word alchemy, as Simaetha has proved before.

It was in 1920 during a trip to Corfu with Bryher that H. D. had a series of six visions, what in *Tribute to Freud* she called "Writing on the Wall". The experience of these visions that drained her physically and mentally were seen by Freud as a "dangerous symptom" in the sense that they were manifestations of "the unconscious forcing its cryptic speech into consciousness by disrupting the mind's perception of external reality".[85] Apart from the dangerous disruption of the external reality and the blurring of the boundaries between consciousness and the unconscious, however, these visions can be regarded as the "leakage" of the unconscious into consciousness perhaps revealing her preoccupations and predicaments. Her fifth vision can be particularly illuminating in terms of her obsession with triangulation.

In this vision a Victory, a Niké figure, resembling a Christmas or Easter card angel, a three dimensional figure with her back turned towards H. D. "moves swiftly" with a "sure floating" that "gives [her] mind some rest, as if [it] had now escaped the bars. . . . no longer climbing or caged but free with wings":

> On she goes. Above her head, to her left in the space left vacant on this black-board (or light-board) or screen, a series of tent-like triangles forms. I say tent-like triangles for though they are simple triangles they suggest tents to me. I feel that the Niké is about to move into and through the tents, and this she exactly does.[86]

What the unconscious seems to telling H. D. is that for any kind of victory to be achieved, the route to be followed is by way of triangulation. The triangles do not simply represent "tents or shelters to be set up in another future content", as H. D. thought they were.[87] They recall the missed triangle of H. D.'s childhood that she strove so hard to reconstruct seeking triangulation in every niche of her life. Niké's moving into and through these triangles suggests that her passing may well have imbued them with her presence making them partake in her victory-giving properties, implying that real victory is to be achieved through triangulation.

Notes

1. Eileen Gregory, *H. D. and Hellenism,* Cambridge, 1997, 35.

2. Julia Kristeva, *Tales of Love,* trans. Leon S. Roudiez, New York, 1987, 34 and 50.

3. Julia Kristeva, *Powers of Horror,* trans. Leon S. Roudiez, New York, 1982, 9-10 and 13.

4. H. D., *Tribute to Freud,* New York, 1977, 10.

5. Norman Holland, *Poems in Persons,* New York, 1989, 13.

6. H. D. was "small for [her] age, *mignonne"* (*Tribute to Freud,* 10).

7. Holland, *Poems in Persons,* 19.

8. H. D., *Tribute to Freud,* 10.

9. *Ibid.,* 150-51 and 117.

10. *Ibid.,* 145 and 121.

11. H. D., *Tribute to Freud,* 17.

12. Holland, *Poems in Persons,* 25.

13. *Analyzing Freud: Letters of H. D., Bryher, and Their Circle,* ed. Susan Stanford Friedman, New York, 2002, 120 (*The Nürnberg Stove* is by Ouida).

14. Sigmund Freud, "Femininity", in *New Introductory Lectures on Psychoanalysis,* trans. James Stratchey, London, 1991, 155 and 158-59.

15. Sigmund Freud, "Female Sexuality", in *On Sexuality,* trans. James Stratchey, London, 1991, 376; "Femininity", 164.

16. *Analyzing Freud,* 180.

17. *Ibid.,* 468.

18. Holland, *Poems in Persons,* 19.

19. *Richard Aldington and H. D.: Their Lives in Letters 1918-61,* ed. Caroline Zilboorg, Manchester, 2003, 142.

20. *Ibid.,* 11.

21. *Analyzing Freud,* 565, xxxii.

22. *Signets: Reading H. D.,* eds Susan Stanford Friedman and Rachel Blau Duplessis, Wisconsin, 1990, 36, 37, 39.

23. Renée Curry, *White Women Writing White,* Westport: CT, 2000, 35.

24. Kristeva, *Powers of Horror,* 131.

25. H. D., *Collected Poems,* New York, 1986, 101 and 102.

26. See Michael Grant and John Hazel, *Who's Who in Classical Mythology,* London, 1993, 178-79.

27. H. D., *Collected Poems,* 106.

28. *Ibid.,* 107.

29. Sigmund Freud, "The Taboo of Virginity", in *On Sexuality,* 275.

30. H. D., *Collected Poems,* 108.

31. In "Female Sexuality", Freud sees the clitoris as analogous to the male organ (*On Sexuality,* 142 and 374).

32. Julia Kristeva, *New Maladies of the Soul,* trans. Ross Guberman, New York, 1995, 197.

33. H. D., *Collected Poems,* 109.

34. Helene Deutsch, *The Psychology of Women,* New York, 1944, II, 71 and 73.

35. H. D., *Collected Poems,* 109.

36. *Ibid.,* 111.

37. *Ibid.,* 114.

38. *Ibid.,* 115.

39. Julia Kristeva, *Black Sun,* trans. Leon S. Roudiez, New York, 1989, 43.

40. Kelly Oliver, *Reading Kristeva: Unravelling the Double-bind,* Bloomington, 1993, 62.

41. Kristeva, *Tales of Love,* 247.

42. Julia Kristeva, *About Chinese Women,* trans. Anita Barrows, New York, 1986, 39.

43. Kristeva, *Black Sun,* 76-77.

44. Gregory, *H. D. and Hellenism,* 33.

45. Rachel Blau DuPlessis, *H. D.: The Career of That Struggle,* Brighton, 2000, 1 and 15.

46. Gregory, *H. D. and Hellenism,* 36.

47. H. D., *Collected Poems,* 124, 115 and 126.

48. *Ibid.,* 125-26.

49. Kristeva, *Powers of Horror,* 10 and 13.

50. H. D., *Collected Poems,* 127.

51. *Ibid.,* 135-36.

52. *Ibid.,* 136.

53. *Ibid.*, 138.

54. Deutsch, *The Psychology of Women*, 78.

55. Kristeva, *Black Sun*, 78.

56. DuPlessis, *H. D.: The Career of That Struggle*, 114.

57. H. D., *Collected Poems*, 140.

58. *Signets: Reading H. D.*, 440.

59. H. D., *Collected Poems*, 140-41.

60. H. D., *Helen in Egypt*, New York, 1974, 156.

61. *Ibid.*, 210.

62. *Signets: Reading H. D.*, 417.

63. H. D., *Tribute to Freud*, 108, 119.

64. Holland, *Poems in Persons*, 29.

65. Eileen Gregory, "Ovid and H. D.'s 'Thetis'" (www.imagists.org/hd/hder111.html, 2).

66. H. D., *Collected Poems*, 116.

67. *Ibid.*, 117.

68. Ted Hughes, *Tales from Ovid*, London, 1997, 104.

69. H. D., *Collected Poems*, 118.

70. Sigmund Freud, "Civilization and Its Discontents", in *Civilization, Society, and Religion*, trans. James Stratchey, London, 1991, 251-52.

71. H. D., *Collected Poems*, 120-21.

72. *Ibid.*, 132.

73. Kristeva, *Powers of Horror*, 75.

74. H. D., *Collected Poems*, 115-16.

75. Theocritus, *The Idylls*, trans. Robert Wells, London, 1988, 60.

76. *Webster's Unabridged Encyclopedic Dictionary*, New York, 1989, 1342.

77. H. D., *Asphodel*, London, 1992, 169.

78. *Webster's Unabridged Encyclopedic Dictionary*, 1469.

79. H. D., *Collected Poems*, 116.

80. Mircea Eliade, *Shamanism: Archaic Techniques of Ecstasy*, trans. Willard R. Trask, London, 1989, 34.

81. H. D., *Tribute to Freud*, 53-54.

82. *Analyzing Freud*, 142.

83. *Signets: Reading H. D.*, 279.

84. H. D., *Collected Poems*, 118 and 120.

85. *Analyzing Freud*, 119.

86. H. D., *Tribute to Freud*, 55.

87. *Ibid.*, 56.

Marsha Bryant and Mary Ann Eaverly (essay date September 2007)

SOURCE: Bryant, Marsha, and Mary Ann Eaverly. "Egypto-Modernism: James Henry Breasted, H. D., and the New Past." *Modernism/Modernity* 14, no. 3 (September 2007): 435-53.

[*In the following essay, Bryant and Eaverly explore the archaeological tropes and Egyptian influences in H. D.'s* Helen in Egypt.]

The paradoxical directive both to "make it new" and to retrieve a usable past has become a commonplace in accounts of American literary modernism. For Pound, Eliot, and H. D., the Classical tradition and its literary monuments provided foundations on which to reinvent poetic form. Moreover, such cultural artifacts served the purpose of articulating an American modernity; as Celena Kusch has argued, American modernists felt "considerable pressure to create an ancient well of artistic experience and ability for themselves."[1] In achieving these goals, making it new and retrieving the past were neither mutually exclusive activities, nor exclusive to creative writers. As H. D.'s generation of modern poets came of age, Egyptology emerged as an American academic discipline—a key intersection that critics have largely overlooked. James Henry Breasted, the father of American Egyptology and founder of the Oriental Institute of the University of Chicago, would formulate a "New Past" that positioned the United States as Egypt's cultural inheritor. Influenced by modernist Egyptology as well as by her travels, H. D. came to share with Breasted a belief in Egypt's cultural primacy. And like Breasted, she would seek a monumental past that did not simply re-inshrine the traditional Greco-Roman one. If Europe had a lock on Classical monuments, and the United States lacked monuments in the traditional sense, ancient Egypt offered these Egypto-modernists a new usable past that rerouted Eurocentric cultural transmission.

This essay crosses disciplines both in terms of its central figures and its methodology—a collaboration between a literary critic and a Classical archaeologist. For Breasted and H. D., archaeology proved fundamental to understanding Egypt. Indeed, archaeological tropes inflected a wide range of artistic, scholarly, and popular discourses during the modernist period, as the editors reminded us in the *Modernism/modernity* special issue "Archaeologies of the Modern." Jeffrey Schnapp, Michael Shanks, and Matthew Tiews note that archaeology has contributed to "historical, national, and international myths of origin and (dis)continuity: of group identity formation (nationalisms), race (ethnicity), technological progress, the rise and fall of civilizations."[2] Breasted's excavation projects were important means of acquiring artifacts for the Oriental Institute, furthering his academic career and enhancing his popular appeal as a lecturer and fund raiser. In his writing Breasted would link archaeology to the discourse of evolution in formulating the New Past. H. D. owned copies of his *A History of Egypt* and five-volume *Ancient Records of Egypt,* as well as *A Concise Dictionary of Egyptian Archaeology.* When H. D.'s critics have addressed archaeology, they tend to focus on Freudian psychoanalysis, which, as Julian Thomas states, offers the clearest "metaphorical use" of the discipline in modern thinking.[3] And yet as we shall see, her stratigraphy is more materialist than Freud's. H. D. insists, for example, that she had seen Karnak's Amun temple pictured on Freud's wall, while "he had not."[4] Both H. D. and Breasted were drawn especially to this ancient site, which figures prominently in their work.

Each writer in fact shared an archaeological sensibility that "mak[es] material culture the equal of text," as Gavin Lucas puts it.[5] Breasted validated his cultural work by emphasizing his proximity to ancient archaeological sites. For example, he stresses that his textbook *A History of the Ancient Egyptians* is "based directly and immediately upon the monuments" and is thus distinct from the growing number of books produced "at second and third hand."[6] H. D.'s story "Secret Name: Excavator's Egypt" contains four scenes in which the protagonist simulates excavation: "she paused, digging with her gloved finger down some inches (it seemed) into the incurve (cut clean in the stone)." In **Helen in Egypt** the protagonist effects a spiritual epigraphy by decoding hieroglyphic inscriptions in the Amun temple, seeking to "realize the transcendental in material terms."[7] Epigraphy, a subdiscipline of archaeology and a major component of Breasted's research, involves the transcription and translation of hieroglyphs. He founded the Epigraphic Survey of the Oriental Institute in Luxor in 1924 to record ancient inscriptions and reliefs that were rapidly deteriorating. Although H. D. could not read hieroglyphics, the fact that women were often employed as transcribers in such projects may have furthered her sense of physical connection. Breasted and H. D. valued the inscribed nature of ancient Egyptian monuments, and they drew on these artifacts to ground their alternative depictions of Egypt.

Comparing the archaeologically-inflected views of Breasted and H. D. with other modernist representations of Egypt complicates our understanding of how Western thinkers positioned its ancient culture. Breasted's numerous excavations helped establish him as the first professor of Egyptology in the United States, and prompted his influential New Past theory. H. D.'s engagement with Egypt's ancient sites was a crucial factor in her move to the long poem and major status. Although Egypt would ultimately prove more heterogeneous for H. D. than for Breasted, both constructed an American Nile through which they asserted cultural authority and national identity. During the chaos and destruction engendered by two global wars, Breasted and H. D. would turn to ancient Egypt as a source of spiritual stability and renewal. Their revaluation and repositioning of Egypt as central to Western civilization's development—which we term *Egypto-modernism*—provides an alternative to the Hellenistic frameworks that shaped mainstream modernist thought.

ANCIENT EGYPT'S SHIFTING TERRAINS

Breasted and H. D. were well aware that their explorations of ancient Egypt circulated within a culture that had become saturated with popular misconceptions. Even before the discovery of Tutankhamun's tomb, there was a fashion for things Egyptian in Europe, Britain, and America. In the first decade of the twentieth century, exotic renderings of Egypt shaped popular music such as the Oriental foxtrot and the 1905 song "There's Egypt in Your Dreamy Eyes."[8] Antonia Lant notes that a proliferation of mummy films appeared in the U.S. between 1912 and 1915, "at least four film companies" worked in Egypt before World War I, and five Cleopatra films were produced "between 1908 and 1918 alone."[9] Indeed, the emphasis on female licentiousness in both Biblical and Classical literary traditions shaped the *femmes fatales* of early cinema, which included Potiphar's wife (Jacob's would-be seducer), as well as Cleopatra. With the exception of Biblical films about Moses and the book of Exodus, exotic conceptions of Egypt had begun to overshadow the despotic vision of pharaoh present in the Hebrew captivity narrative. Americans' fascination with ancient Egypt preceded the emergence of academic Egyptologists like Breasted, who noted in his journal that the Egyptian *Book of the Dead* had already "become, in title at least, a household word in the Western world."[10] So when Howard Carter began excavating Tut's treasures in 1922, the effect "was a bit like adding gasoline to a fire," as Michael North puts it. Sarah Witte notes that Egyptian influenced fashions were prominent in both *Vogue* and *Ladies' Home Journal* throughout the 1920s.[11] H. D.'s story "Secret Name: Excavator's Egypt" reflects this oversaturation when protagonist Helen Fairwood perceives that "'everything seems painted . . . cardboard,'" a vocabulary similar to the one H. D. used to deride overdone sets in historical epic films. In the story, Captain Rafton's response to Fairwood points to the popular sources of her perceptual bias: "'You mean you seem to have seen all this before? But it's on everything, cigarette boxes posters in the underground; cigarette boxes [sic], magazine ads'" (*P* [*Palimpsest*], 188). Because Westerners tended to view Egypt as source of the exotic and mysterious rather than of civilization, tourists' initial impressions could be unsatisfactory—even when viewing ancient monuments.

The Tutankhamun excavations and other archaeological sites proved crucial to H. D.'s and Breasted's revaluation of Egypt's role in cultural transmission. Breasted entered Tutankhamun's tomb several times at Howard Carter's request, deciphering seals on the doorways and providing other historical information. Although he was a seasoned Egyptologist, Breasted was nonetheless jarred by Tutankhamun's treasures: "Here was the magnificence which only the wealth and splendor of the Imperial Age in Egypt in the fourteenth century before Christ could have wrought or conceived." The golden royal chariots—which Breasted saw as "not vulgar and ostentatious magnificence, but the richness of matured and refined art"—made "the splendor of Nineveh and Babylon" appear to be "but a rough foil for setting off the civilization of Egyptian Thebes" (qtd. in *PP* [*Pioneer to the Past*], 331, 337). H. D. saw one of the chariot wheels brought from the tomb. Filtering her perception through Helen Fairwood in the "Secret Name" story, she describes its startling brightness as being "brought to birth, brought back after four thousand years, to light. The very chariot wheel, gold, too gold, not even with the softness of some Mycenaean or Grecian burial to tone it down, to give it semblance of antiquity" (*P*, 191). Here "too gold" both reinforces Orientalist conceptions of a gaudy East, and troubles temporal boundaries by appearing new. The Tutankhamun discovery, which North has termed "the first truly modern media event,"[12] circulated widely in the press and popular imagination, drawing crowds to Carter's excavation. Although Tut's tomb was a significant site for Breasted and H. D., the monumental expansiveness of Karnak would allow them more room to articulate their Egypto-modernism.

Both were especially influenced by Karnak's vast temple complex dedicated to the sun god Amun, one of the chief gods of the Egyptian pantheon. Before the Tut phenomenon, continuing excavations at Karnak made it one of the most studied Egyptian sites in the early twentieth century. Every ancient Egyptian pharaoh from the Middle Kingdom (c. 2000 B.C.E.) until the Ptolemaic period (c. 330 B.C.E.) made additions to Karnak, so that it constituted for Breasted "a great historical volume";[13] most of the columns and walls are covered with hieroglyphs. Spreading across ten acres and including the colossal temple to Amun, the main complex has hundreds of lotus bud columns, statues, and obelisks. An additional eighty-five enclosed acres are filled with smaller temples and storehouses. Breasted's writings emphasize the sheer size and scale of the buildings, noting that in "the greatest colonnaded hall ever erected by man" each column capital "is large enough to contain a group of a hundred men standing crowded upon it at the same time" (*CC* [*The Conquest of Civilization*], 99). These particular columns are approximately seventy feet high. H. D. is similarly impressed with Karnak's colossal scale. Her surrogate character Helen Fairwood, who has "hard-won" expertise in Classics, notes that "the Parthenon itself" would fit into the "enormous court-yard" of Tuthmoses II's banquet chamber, with sufficient room to include "such tiny exquisite toys as the Erechtheum and the Nike," other major buildings of the Acropolis (*P*, 176, 214). The Parthenon is widely considered the greatest achievement of ancient Greek sacred architecture. And yet for H. D., Karnak's divine proportions challenge the Classical world's use of humans as the standard of measurement:

> In Greece, even in so late a building as the Italian Paestum there was that strange insistence upon human achievement. One measured oneself by the tiny Nike temple, out-jutting on the Acropolis. Even in the more massive Paestum, one measured oneself and one's status by some known and intellectual formula. Here was magnificence of another order."
>
> [*P*, 208]

H. D. would struggle to let go of her Hellenism which, as Eileen Gregory points out, gave her writing an "orientation within historical, aesthetic, and psychological mappings."[14] Fairwood reflects this dilemma because in order to reach her epiphany, she must revalue ancient Greek cultural achievement with respect to Egypt's.

"Secret Name" also compares Egyptian lotus bud columns to Classical Greek architecture: "Great fervid buds, not like the columns of the Greeks that hold in their straight fair line a sort of challenge, not an appeal so much as a command to the intellect to soar up and up. These bulbous buds, enormous, pregnant, seemed endowed after these four thousand years with some inner life; to hold that possibility of sudden bloom-burst" (*P*, 213). As with Tut's golden chariot wheel, Fairwood perceives that these columns incarnate a living spirituality so that their power results from neither intellect nor fascination. Meredith Miller argues that H. D.'s language challenges art critic T. E. Hulme's "binary distinction" between Egyptian hardness and Greek vitality.[15] Other parts of "Secret Name" also interrogate prevailing cultural refinement narratives, assigning "starkness" to the Greek rather than Egyptian side: "It was utterly Athenian starkly to define, to outline in terms of thought every human emotion, not making allowance for this intermediate state where shadows of bronze palms were soft and fern-like, where thought and emotion were delicately merged" (*P*, 193). This characterization sharply contrasts W. B. Yeats's story of Western art's emergence in "Under Ben Bulben": "Measurement began our might: / Forms a stark Egyptian thought, / Forms that gentler Phidias wrought."[16] H. D.'s Egypto-modernism begins when Karnak challenges her contemporaries' cultural investment in Greece, including her male compatriots Pound and Eliot. As Breasted noted in his groundbreaking 1916 textbook *Ancient Times,* "the habit of regarding ancient history as beginning with Greece has become so fixed that it is not easily to be changed."[17]

H. D. was not the only American poet who incorporated Egyptian artifacts into her writing, but she placed them into fuller archaeological contexts than her peers and predecessors. This quality distinguishes her work from Marianne Moore's object-centered "An Egyptian Pulled Glass Bottle in the Shape of a Fish," in which the artifact operates primarily as a figure for poetry. H. D.'s mythic references to Egypt are similarly grounded, so that her allusions to *The Book of the Dead* are not as displaced as those in Muriel Rukeyser's documentary poem of the same name (which memorializes a mining disaster). Walt Whitman anticipates some aspects of H. D.'s Egypto-modernism, although he never traveled to Egypt. In "Salut du Monde!," for example, he marvels at hieroglyphic inscriptions as a kind of stone papyrus: "I look on chisell'd histories, records of conquering kings, dynasties, cut in slabs of sand-stone, or on granite-blocks." As John Irwin notes, Whitman read widely in Egyptology during the 1840s and 1850s, and was a frequent visitor at Dr. Abbott's museum of Egyptology in New York.[18] H. D. and her partner Bryher had many books on Egyptology in their library, which included studies of hieroglyphics, mythology, history, and material culture. Besides Breasted's studies, they owned Janet R. Buttles's *The Queens of Egypt* (1908), Arthur E. P. Weigall's *A Guide to the Antiquities of Upper Egypt* (1913), A. Bothwell Gosse's *The Civilization of the Ancient Egyptians* (1915), Mary G. Houston and Florence S. Hornblower's *Ancient Egyptian, Assyrian and Persian Costumes & Decorations* (1920), Margaret Alice Murray's *Egyptian Sculpture* (1930), and A. Lucas's *An-*

cient Egyptian Materials (1926). The library also contained several books by E. A. Wallis Budge, including *The Dwellers on the Nile* (1899), *Easy Lessons in Egyptian Hieroglyphics* (1902), *Egyptian Religion* (1908), *Egyptian Literature* (1912), *The Egyptian Heaven and Hell* (1905), *Osiris and the Egyptian Resurrection* (1911), and *The Book of the Dead: An English Translation* (1938).[19] Because Budge was such a prolific publisher, it is not surprising that he is so well represented in H. D.'s collection. The few critics who address H. D.'s relationship to Egyptology focus almost exclusively on Budge, but his views were by no means the dominant perspective on ancient Egypt at this time.

DEBATES WITHIN ACADEMIC EGYPTOLOGY

Modernist Egyptology was an international discipline of competing claims on Egypt's sites and artifacts, and conflicting interpretations of their significance. As the major colonizing powers in the region, European nationals took the lead in these endeavors. The development of a sophisticated ancient culture on non-European (especially African) soil posed a major dilemma, casting doubt upon the hitherto accepted superiority of the West. Scholars partially solved this problem by dislocating Egypt from continental Africa, placing it instead within the cultural milieu of the Orient (variously termed the Ancient Near East, or the Near Orient). So widely accepted was this cartography that Nancy Cunard's influential *Negro* anthology omitted Egypt from its map of Africa. A corollary of this view was that Egyptian civilization was not indigenous and therefore required an outside impetus for its development. In the late nineteenth century, for example, British archaeologist Sir William Flinders Petrie proposed conquest by a "Dynastic Race" as the civilizing catalyst, basing his theory on skeletal remains.[20] Such formulations date back to the mid nineteenth century, when Americans used phrenology to justify slavery. Although Petrie's theory would be discredited, the debate over indigenous or nonindigenous development continued to be an important one for two of the most prominent Egyptologists of the modernist era: Budge and Breasted.

Budge believed that a savage native population was civilized by invaders from the East, while Breasted believed that Egyptian civilization was indigenous and influenced the East. Because Breasted's chain of cultural influence began with Egypt, it became the source rather than the recipient of civilization. Disagreeing with Budge was not unusual for Breasted. Key differences also appear in both men's interpretation of Egyptian religion. Breasted admired the pharaoh Akhenaten's transformation of Egypt's solar religion from polytheism, viewing this change as a precedent for Western monotheism. In contrast, Budge positioned it—and indeed dynastic civilization itself—as the result of "an Asiatic element" which "invaded the country and conquer[ed] the natives"—a people he saw as fundamentally primitive. Indeed, Budge argued in 1904 that the Egyptians could not "become metaphysicians in the modern sense of the word . . . the mere construction of the language would make such a thing impossible, to say nothing of the ideas of the great Greek philosophers, which belong to a domain of thought and culture wholly foreign to the Egyptian."[21] Thus for Budge, the primitivism he perceived in the ancient Egyptians compromised their cultural achievements.

While Budge argued that Egypt's ancient civilization came from elsewhere, Australian scholar Sir Grafton Elliot Smith took the opposite view that its influence extended practically everywhere. Advocating for an extreme version of Egyptian primacy, Smith proposed a "hyperdiffusionist" theory that affirmed Egyptian technological presence in the pre-conquest civilizations of the New World—and in areas as remote from Egypt as Oceania. Smith denied critics' charges that he attributed "the customs and beliefs of the whole world to Egypt."[22] However, in outlining his theories in a series of books beginning with *The Migration of Early Cultures* (1915), he dismissed the contemporary theory of independent invention. As far as Smith was concerned, if embalming was practiced in Peru and Egypt then Egypt had to be the source. His map of the transmission of technologies published in *The Diffusion of Culture* links Egypt directly to almost every region of the earth. Modernist Egyptology could be "wildly inventive," as Alice Gambrell notes, even within scholarly communities.[23]

Because the U.S. was a relative newcomer in academic Egyptology, Breasted often took an adversarial stance towards his international counterparts, especially Budge. He noted in his journal that Egyptology had "only a handful of *competent* followers, and even these often disagreed violently among themselves in fundamental matters of chronology, philology, archaeology and history" (qtd. in *PP,* 85). Having trained in Germany Breasted had a high regard for the Berlin school, which emphasized close and careful translation. By contrast, he had little respect for Budge. Breasted in fact considered Britain's prolific scholar to be incompetent, despite his prestigious post as Keeper of Egyptian Antiquities for the British Museum. To Breasted the inadequacies of the British Museum reflected Budge's own work:

> I showed him one of the most important monuments in the entire collection, so ridiculously labeled that it was evident those who had installed it knew nothing about

it. Budge himself now showed that he was ignorant of it. . . . He . . . pled the onerous duties of his office—the labels were old, put on before his time, etc., etc. But his own books, filled with egregious errors, belied him.

[qtd. in *PP,* 84]

Reporting on his own survey of Nubia in 1905-1906, Breasted repeatedly chronicles Budge's erroneous conclusions about the date and significance of monuments.[24] Other contemporary scholars also denigrated Budge for inaccurate and careless translations since he persisted in using an antiquated system of transcription. In addition, Budge's many excavations, while garnering numerous artifacts for the British Museum, were criticized for lack of scholarly rigor. In contrast Breasted was noted for his careful translation of hieroglyphic texts (many of which are still used today), and his sponsorship of systematic excavations. Vincent Arieh Tobin's recent characterization of Breasted's *Development of Religion and Thought in Ancient Egypt* is a case in point: "Although published originally in 1912, this work is still a classic study of Egyptian religion and myth and is well worth a careful reading."[25] H. D.'s critics have tended to elide scholarly Egyptology with Budge—a problematic position given his compromised status within the academy.

Breasted's disagreements with Budge did not extend to countering the prevailing scholarly opinion about race, which separated Egypt from Africa and by inference from Negro America. Although Breasted positioned Egypt as foundational to Western culture, he mirrored the contemporary racial climate in assigning whiteness to its ancient inhabitants. We see this ideology as late as 1941, when *National Geographic* illustrations for "Daily Life in Ancient Egypt" depict its inhabitants as "a light-colored, not even very suntanned people," as Bruce Trigger notes.[26] Breasted considered the Egyptians to be part of what he terms "The Great Northwest Quadrant," a geographical area which includes the Mediterranean and whose inhabitants "as far back as we know anything about prehistoric men, have all been members of the white race." This Quadrant is "bordered on the east by the Mongoloids and south by the Negroes." While Breasted admits that these two groups "occupy an important place in the modern world," he denies any contribution on their part to the development of *Western* civilization. He does allow that the Chinese branch of the Mongoloids created an "impressive" civilization in their own right, but equates the Negroes with the "teeming black world of Africa," who neither influenced nor were influenced by Egypt—and thus lacked civilization (*CC,* 43-45). Such racial constructions grow out of debates within mid-nineteenth-century Egyptology which, as Malini Johar Schueller argues, "generated anxieties about the capabilities of different races in the United States."[27] Breasted's separation of Egypt from Black Africa and the (American) Negro would surely have facilitated his acceptance among the general public.

Establishing Egyptology as a university discipline in the United States, Breasted developed the influential New Past theory, which promoted Egypt as foundational for western civilization. For Breasted the New Past made it possible to view "an imposing panorama of the human career in a vista of successive ages such as no earlier generation has ever been able to survey."[28] As the first link in the chain, Egypt was responsible for nothing less than "the emergence of civilization, the most important event that has yet occurred in the universe so far as it is known to us" (*CC*, 7). Thus Breasted never equated ancient Egypt with primitivism—a feature that distinguishes his work from Freud's recapitulation theory, as well as from Schnapp, Shanks, and Tiew's view that archaeology posits "evolutionary schemes" of "an earlier, more primitive stage."[29] In particular Breasted praised Egypt's invention of hieroglyphic writing as "having had a greater influence in uplifting the human race than any other intellectual achievement in the career of man" (*CC*, 61). This foregrounding of Egypt marks a major shift from the traditional emphasis on the Classical past or Biblical tradition as the sources of Western civilization—what we might term the old past.

Rather than requiring the direct contact advocated by Smith, the New Past viewed civilization as a "rising trail" extending from Egypt to modern America. Breasted distilled this theory in his design for the sculpted tympanum over the entrance to the Oriental Institute, titled "The East Teaching the West." The two central figures are, on the left, an Egyptian scribe (identifiable by the writing paraphernalia slung over his shoulder), and on the right, a WPA-styled American man. The scribe and his important gift (writing) represent the East; note the men from other ancient civilizations (Persian, Assyrian, Babylonian) shown behind him. The scribe also holds a fragment from a temple wall—symbol of the importance of monumental architecture as both an enduring surface for writing, and a major element of human achievement in its own right. The significance of Egyptian architecture is further emphasized by the choice of a lotus bud column capital (lying behind the Egyptian scribe), which is identical to those from the Amun temple complex at Karnak. While a pyramid would be a more iconic choice for representing Egypt (there is a small pyramid on the left side), Breasted chooses a column to further link Egypt and the West. Columns, important elements of the Greco-Roman architectural vocabulary, are ultimately derived from Egypt.

The sun with suspended ankh symbols and rays ending in human hands fills the central area above both figures. This image comes from the religion of the eighteenth-dynasty pharaoh Akhenaten, revered by Breasted and many Western scholars of his time as the first monotheist. Breasted's march of civilization is thus connected to the Hebrew/Western conception of God the Father. By placing his sculptural decoration in a tympanum, Breasted also alludes to Christian sacred architecture. He saw in the Amun temple's Hypostyle Hall the source of "the columned nave and side aisles" of European cathedrals: "Egypt furnished the later world with this beautiful architectural form."[30] Indeed, the use of relief sculpture in the tympanum is in itself a tribute to Egyptian cultural primacy, since the practice of decorating buildings in this way goes back from cathedrals to Classical and Near Eastern civilizations, and ultimately to Egypt.

The Egyptian scribe dwarfs the representatives of the other Near Eastern civilizations just as, according to the New Past theory, Egypt's civilization surpassed theirs. Similarly, American man's size suggests that his civilization will (or is) surpassing the Western civilizations of Greece and Rome depicted behind him on the right. While the American Man and Egyptian scribe are the same size, subtle stylistic devices indicate that American will surpass his Egyptian counterpart. Borrowing compositional techniques from ancient Egyptian sculpture used to express dominance, Breasted's design emphasizes American man by placing his left foot in front of the scribe's so that his bent knee intrudes into the center of the frame. In effect, modern America is poised to assume ancient Egypt's legacy and continue the march of civilization. As Breasted sees it, Egypt offers a site through which his own newer, American culture can enter the panorama of history, ultimately usurping Europe's position and becoming the culmination of Western civilization's development.

H. D.'s writing shows an awareness of debates within Egyptology—especially those involving nationality, geography and race. The name of her "famous Egyptologist" in "Secret Name: Excavator's Egypt" (Bodge-Grafton) combines Budge and Grafton Elliot Smith. This wordplay suggests not only that Budge "botched" his interpretations, as Sarah Witte has noted, but also signals ideological splits within the field of Egyptology more generally.[31] Ironically, this fictional Egyptologist represents "the amethyst Athenian values" from which the protagonist—his Classically-trained research assistant—must free herself. He leaves with his "disappointed party" when the Tutankhamun excavations force him to modify his "monumental and final volume" (*P*, 190). Although she does not invoke Breasted directly, H. D.'s rendering of Bodge-Grafton intersects with his Egypto-modernist departures from Classical frameworks.

H. D.'s conceptions of ancient Egypt were more fluid than Breasted's, shifting back and forth between Eastern and African, white and black. In the "Secret Name" story, Egypt straddles Eastern and African inflections. A bejeweled Orientalism infuses Helen Fairwood's account of Amenophis II's burial chamber, which H. D. figures as "a moon opal" housing the "exquisite gem, black opal" of the pharaoh's body. The protagonist likens this cultural "inheritance" to another opal fixed on her forehead, appropriating Eastern culture for herself as Miller has argued. At the same time, Fairwood's sense of being in Africa makes her feel "comforted" because she feels that its "unfamiliar" and "innumerable" stars place her closer to the sun—and thus closer to the source of divinity. Godhood as well as racial difference make Egypt seem "another planet" (*P,* 183, 211, 226). In *Tribute to Freud,* H. D.'s dream figure of an ancient Egyptian princess hovers between definite Eastern inflections (she wears an Indian sari) and racial ambiguity (she is a "dark lady"). As Friedman has argued, H. D.'s linking of dark and female others reflects a "modernism of the 'scattered remnant'" that sometimes breaks with Eurocentric racial hierarchies.[32] The protagonist of **Helen in Egypt** "blacken[s] her face like the prophetic *femme noire* of antiquity" (**HE** [**Helen in Egypt**], 15) an act which, as Susan Edmunds suggests, renders a black Egyptian Helen through "a moment of actual racial conversion."[33] In her most multiracial figuration—and H. D.'s starkest contrast from Breasted—the African-American maid character in *HER* manifests ancient Egypt, as well as Roman and Etruscan attributes; this combination departs from both popular and academic versions of ancient Egypt.[34] H. D.'s mergings of black Africa with Classical antiquity intersect somewhat with the Afrocentrism that Cheikh Anta Diop posited in his 1951 thesis, which considered Egypt to be the first black civilization. While it would be going too far to label H. D.'s Egypto-modernism Afrocentric, it does avoid some of the rigid racial distinctions that Martin Bernal has traced in Western scholarship on ancient Egypt and Classical antiquity.[35] Consequently, H. D.'s Egypt will never rest squarely on either side of the dualities with which her contemporaries defined it. H. D.'s model of cultural influence was not as linear as Breasted's because, as Gregory has noted, it involved "dissemination, dispersion, and diaspora," but neither was it as diffuse as Smith's.[36]

THE AMERICAN NILE

Although Breasted and H. D. approached Egypt from their respective vantage points of cross-Atlantic intellectual movements—modernist Egyptology and art—their American national identities played a more significant role in their perceptions than many critics acknowledge. Breasted's writings especially convey a sense that Americans are uniquely suited to perceive cultural kinship with the ancient Egyptians. This results not only from an imperialist belief in "Egypt as Western inheritance," as Miller notes, but also from each writer's transposition of America's mythic West onto the expansiveness of Karnak.[37]

For Breasted and H. D., Egypt was not "the 'Gateway to India'" and "foothold" that it constituted for Britain and Continental Europe.[38] Although neither embraced the idea of Egyptian independence, both writers give negative impressions of British soldiers and officials in their accounts of archaeological sites. In his journals, for example, Breasted wrote of "the fundamental Philistinism of the British government"; he was especially angry that a Nile dam project would ruin Ptolemaic relics (qtd. in *PP,* 143). H. D. diminishes British characters in "Secret Name: Excavator's Egypt." As noted above, Bodge-Grafton is expelled from the story when his research is disproved. Another minor character, Jerry Cope, sports "a totally overdone school-boy affectation," engaging in "monkey-like" antics that break the spell of Karnak's Amun temple (*P,* 212). More pertinent to the story, Helen Fairwood will ultimately reject as guide and companion the British Captain Rafton, Great War veteran and Public Works administrator in Cairo. In short the British characters are either ridiculed or rejected, thus clearing space for an American reappraisal of Egypt's ancient sites. Both find Egypt's cultural legacy especially significant during a period of shifting cultural hegemony to the United States.

The title of Charles Breasted's biography of his father—*Pioneer to the Past*—reflects the Egyptologist's sense of Western civilization as a "rising trail" leading westward to America. Early on the biographer characterizes his father as "a lone young American Egyptologist pitted against the rather self-superior complacency of Old World scholarship" (*PP,* 65). As Gerry Scott explains, the fact that Europe rather than America played the "major role" in discoveries, excavations, and epigraphy often prompted a discourse of "adventurous travel" rather than scientific inquiry.[39] As pioneer to Egypt's past, Breasted also faced the challenge of steering his fellow citizens into regions largely unknown to them except in the popular imagination: "In America, Egypt really did not exist at all—and here was I, proposing single-handedly to introduce it into a Middle Western community which for the most part did not even know the origin of the names Cairo, Illinois, and Memphis, Tennessee" (qtd. in *PP,* 85). His solution to this dilemma would link the rise of Egyptian civilization to American Manifest

Destiny. "Just as in America," he asserted before the American Historical Association in 1928, Egypt had forged "a great society" from the "wilderness." Clearing indigenous peoples from the American West, Breasted's address reinscribes constructions of an antithetical East to justify a "New Crusade" of "scientific effort in the ancient Orient." Breasted sought to inspire recruits ("modern pilgrims") for the Oriental Institute's archaeological surveys, so he extolled his audience to "set their faces to the East." And yet Breasted's sense of "returning to ancestral shores" also implies kinship with Egypt, so that going East opens up a new American frontier.[40] One might dismiss Breasted's nationalism as a rhetorical device to open the hearts and pockets of his American audience, but it proves a major trope in his writing as a whole. In *The Dawn of Conscience,* for example, Breasted interposes the Biblical world as an intermediate phase between ancient Egypt and "modern Man," who was best exemplified by America (*DC* [*The Dawn of Conscience*], 13). Throughout his career, he drew consistent parallels between Egypt (fertile ground for the world's first civilization) and America (the next great step in the West's development).

H. D. also perceived traveling to Egypt as a kind of homecoming, but for her the issue of Americanness is more vexed because of her extended expatriotism. She constructs an American Nile most fully when depicting the ways in which archaeological sites stimulate Helen Fairwood's awareness of her latent national identity. For much of the narrative, H. D.'s protagonist occupies a transnational identity that shifts on the ancient plane between Greece and Egypt, and on the modern plane between America and England. Just as she initially represses her newfound admiration of Egypt, Fairwood also represses her Americanness. For example, she refuses to join in Jerry Cope's attempts at American slang, and recoils when Mary Thorpe's mother speaks confidentially to her in the manner of "any American." Repelled by the party of nouveau-riche American tourists and their "ice-and-lemonade civilisation," Fairwood nonetheless concedes that New York "couldn't in the march of civilisations be brushed aside." Thus like Breasted, H. D. sees the U.S. as the West's emergent civilization. Fairwood will also come to acknowledge the American sensibility that has traveled with her: "Here in Egypt across her room in Luxor, America, herself gazed, as in the mirror a moment since at herself. It faced her, herself, her own school; names" (*P,* 195, 185, 199). Ultimately she is drawn to Mary Thorpe not only because of her gender, the reason other critics have emphasized, but also because of their shared nationality. In fact, Fairwood grounds this link by thinking of her young compatriot as "Maryland."

Mary's presence prompts Helen Fairwood to envision an American Nile on both of her visits to Karnak. She frames her first entry through the Avenue of the Sphinxes with "the gigantic stretches" of her childhood New Jersey shore: "the incurve of the sand about these sphinxes is somehow familiar." (This passage anticipates H. D.'s plea for the god Amen-Ra to take her "home" to the Nile in *Trilogy.*) Leaving the site, Fairwood feels that "eventually one must surely reach a sea, the rim of a New Jersey seacoast." Her second visit to Karnak, this time with Mary as her sole companion, triggers iconic images of the American West. Fairwood sees the two American women as characters in "some Wild West show" who had ridden "across strange fields where buffalo were grazing." Significantly, it is with Mary that Fairwood finally achieves a fully satisfying encounter with monumental Egypt. The two of them, Helen perceives, constitute a feminized version of the American Western hero: "this type, this American, beaten and weathered machine type, thin as rails, steel-bone and sinew, that mounted ponies and endured the change of tropic and zero weather . . ." (*P,* 203-4, 218, 235, 231). Like Breasted's sense of himself as a pioneer, H. D.'s characterization of Helen and Mary reflects the "distinctly American trait" of rugged individualism that Scott sees inflecting American approaches to Egyptology in the nineteenth century.[41] Paradoxically, the closing of the American frontier in 1890 expanded its mythic boundaries in the American imagination, enabling Breasted and H. D. to invoke it as a means of extending America's past to ancient Egypt.

ADVOCATING FOR A NEW PAST

Although monumental Egypt prompted H. D. and especially Breasted to articulate their American identities, these advocates for Egyptian cultural primacy often assumed that their respective audiences would disagree with them. This perception arose in part from the fundamental role the Bible played in U.S. nationalism. According to his son's biography, Breasted's textbook *Ancient Times* was denounced by Scopes Trial prosecutor William Jennings Bryan for supposedly destroying the nation's Christian faith (*PP,* 230). The New Past Theory attributes nothing less than the development of moral conscience to ancient Egypt rather than the traditional Biblical sources. In reading Egyptian literature, Breasted found that "the Egyptians had possessed a standard of morals far superior to that of the Decalogue over a thousand years before the Decalogue was written." He also relates his boyhood puzzlement at the lack of a commandment against lying, considering this a fundamental flaw in Biblical morality (*DC,* xii). H. D. effects a similar revaluation of ancient Egypt in *Trilogy,* which asserts that the Egyptian god Amun "is our Christos" and "not at all like Jehovah."[42] Working through layers of ancient Mediterranean cultures in the first section, H. D. reveals the Egyptian precedents for Classical and Christian symbols; for example, Pharaoh's "erect king-cobra crest" lies beneath both the Greek caduceus and the Christian Tau cross with Brazen Serpent (*T* [*Trilogy*], 13). H. D. "turned repeatedly to Egypt as a symbol for the sacred," as Friedman notes."[43] And like Breasted, her Biblical knowledge enhanced rather than diminished her appreciation of ancient Egyptian spirituality.

H. D. anticipates considerable resistance to her fullest articulations of Egypto-modernism: *Trilogy* and *Helen in Egypt.* Like other "impure" influences that Gregory and Cassandra Laity have discussed (Alexandrian Hellenism and Decadent Romanticism, respectively), her advocacy for Egypt would prove suspect to Eliot and Pound.[44] In *Trilogy* the speaker-as-scribe defends ancient Egypt from an adversarial "you" that views Isis as "a harlot," sacred symbols as "charms," and divine Egyptian headdress as "trival / intellectual adornment" (*T*, 5, 14). In *Helen in Egypt,* all the male characters accost the protagonist for her new Egyptian identity. Achilles rebukes Helen in the very first section: "O cursèd, O envious Isis, / you—you—a vulture, a hieroglyph" (17). Paris perceives that Helen is tainted with "Egyptian incense," while Theseus fears that Egyptian influences destroy Greek rationality:

> Crete would seduce Greece,
> Crete inherited the Labyrinth from Egypt,
> the ancient Nile would undermine
>
> the fabric of Parnassus;
>
> [*HE*, 17, 141, 169]

As home to the Minotaur, Crete's Labyrinth is domain of darkness, bestiality, and corruption—the antithesis to Helen's (and H. D.'s) sacred Amun temple. Significantly, Theseus's labyrinthine image of Egypt also intersects with a major point of contention for archaeologists in the modernist period. While some saw Crete as Europe's first autonomous civilized society, Breasted and others posited Egypt as the island's civilizing force (*CC,* 89). Although H. D.'s advocacy for Egypt is always put on the defensive, her Egypto-Modernism allowed her to write outside the confines of Classical warrior band myths. As Dianne Chisholm points out, H. D.'s revisionary writing, unlike Western literary history, is not dominated by the Greek text."[45] Thus it is her Egyptian influences, as well as her female protagonist, that make *Helen in Egypt* an alternative modern epic.

Egypt's ancient archaeological sites—especially Karnak—gave H. D. and Breasted a generative space in which to create new pasts unencumbered by the weight of traditional Eurocentric frameworks. For them Egypt became paradoxically ancient and new: "the same—different—the same attributes, / different yet the same as before," as H. D. writes (*T,* 105). The need for a regenerative past became more urgent in the face of global war, prompting Breasted and H. D. to view Egypt as a source of spiritual stability. Stricken by the carnage of World War I and cognizant of the emerging crisis in Europe during the early 1930s, Breasted wrote *The Dawn of Conscience* as an antidote to the horrors of war. In the foreword to this history of moral thought, he asserts: "The World War has now demonstrated the appalling possibilities of man's mechanical power of destruction. The only force that can successfully oppose it is the human conscience" that originated in Egypt (*DC,* ix). With Europe on the verge of ruin once more, Breasted sees an unscathed America ready to inherit an older source—and renew the West's usable past. If the Old World and its past are in effect dead, "the stone papyrus" of Karnak will "continue to prophesy," as H. D. writes in *Trilogy.* Excavating backward from Blitz-torn London through the remains of Pompeii and ultimately to Egypt, H. D. senses that Karnak's inscribed hieroglyphs still "pursue unalterable purpose." When the speaker-scribe asserts that "Pompeii has nothing to teach us," she means not only that Londoners know too much of airborne destruction, but also that the Classical past proves insufficient for facing it—and for healing what will remain (*T,* 3, 4). As a whole *Trilogy* effects a perpetual return to Egypt, beginning at Karnak and ending just before the Christian Holy Family flees from Herod to the Nile. While H. D. never discounted the legacies of Classical poetry and Hellenic beauty, Egypt allowed her war poems to "rearrange a culture in crisis," to borrow Adalaide Morris's evocative phrase.[46]

Malleable in a way that the Classical tradition can never be, Egypto-modernism allowed Breasted and H. D. to rewrite traditional narratives of Western culture by making Egypt its source and spiritual center. In their memorial tribute to Breasted, Ludlow Bull, Ephraim Speiser and Albert TenEyck Olmstead noted: "He often said that, much as he admired the marvellous contributions of Greece to art and philosophy, he was weary of the prevalent belief among educated laymen that 'everything began with the Greeks.'"[47] H. D.'s surrogate Helen Fairwood starts off with this view, but comes to accept that *"The Greeks came to Egypt to learn"* (*P,* 217). Reading H. D. through Breasted reveals that modernist Egyptology was a major influence on her career, surely as important as the psychoanalytic frameworks that have dominated H. D. studies. While Breasted was not the only professional Egyptologist who influenced H. D., his advocacy for Egypt and the New Past is similar to the Egypto-modernist perspective she would develop after *Palimpsest*. As we have seen, ancient Egypt held plural and even conflicting meanings in popular, literary, and intellectual discourse of the modernist period—despite the immense stability of its dynastic culture across millennia. Ideologically-inflected accounts of Egypt were hardly limited to its emergence from British colonial rule. By recovering H. D.'s intersections with academic Egyptology—especially its emergence in the United States—we can situate her career more fully within modernist intellectual history.

Notes

We would like to thank Dr. Magnus Widell, Head of Research Archives at the "Oriental Institute of the University of Chicago", for assisting us with Breasted's publications. We presented an earlier version of this essay at MSA7 in Chicago (2005).

1. Celena Kusch, "How the West Was One: American Modernism's Song of Itself," *American Literature* 74, no. 3 (September 2002): 517-38, 521.

2. Jeffrey Schnapp, Michael Shanks, and Matthew Tiews, "Archaeology, Modernism, Modernity," *Modernism/modernity* 11, no. 1 (January 2004): 1-16, 3.

3. Julian Thomas, "Archaeology's Place in Modernity," *Modernism/modernity* 11, no. 1 (January 2004): 17-34, 28.

4. H. D., *Tribute to Freud* (New York: New Directions, 1974), 9.

5. Gavin Lucas, "Modern Disturbances: On the Ambiguities of Archaeology." *Modernism/modernity* 11, no. 1 (January 2004): 109-20, 111.

6. James Henry Breasted, *A History of the Ancient Egyptians,* History Series for Bible Students, Vol. 5 (New York: Charles Scribner's Sons, 1908), vii.

7. H. D., *Palimpsest* (1926), rpt. (Carbondale: Southern Illinois University Press, 1968), hereafter abbreviated *P*; H. D., *Helen in Egypt* (New York: New Directions, 1961), 11, 216; hereafter abbreviated *HE*.

8. Richard A. Fazinni and Mary E. McKercher, "Egyptomania," in *The Oxford Encyclopedia of Ancient Egypt,* Vol. 1, ed. Donald B. Redford (Oxford, U.K.: Oxford University Press, 2001), 458-65, 463.

9. Antonia Lant, "The Curse of the Pharaoh, or How Cinema Contracted Egyptomania," in *Visions of the East: Orientalism in Film,* ed. Matthew Bernstein and Gaylyn Studlar (New Brunswick, NJ: Rutgers University Press, 1997), 69-98, 81-2.

10. Quoted in Charles Breasted, *Pioneer to the Past: The Story of James Henry Breasted, Archaeologist* (New York: Charles Scribner's Sons, 1943), 322; hereafter abbreviated *PP*.

11. Michael North, *Reading 1922: A Return to the Scene of the Modern* (New York: Oxford University Press, 1999), 21; Sarah E. Witte, "The Archaeological Context of H. D.'s 'Secret Name' and 'Hesperia,'" *Sagetrieb* 15.1-2 (1996): 51-68.

12. North, *Reading 1922,* 19.

13. James Henry Breasted, *The Conquest of Civilization* (1926), rev. ed. (New York: Harper and Brothers, 1938), 93; hereafter abbreviated *CC*.

14. Eileen Gregory, *H. D. and Hellenism: Classic Lines* (Cambridge, U.K.: Cambridge University Press, 1997), 1.

15. Meredith Miller, "'Enslaved to Both These Others': Gender and Inheritance in H. D.'s 'Secret Name: Excavator's Egypt,'" *Tulsa Studies in Women's Literature* 16, no. 1 (Spring 1997): 77-105, 96.

16. *Selected Poems and Two Plays of William Butler Yeats,* ed. M. L. Rosenthal (New York: Collier, 1962), 191.

17. James Henry Breasted, *Ancient Times: A History of the Early World* (Boston, Mass.: Ginn and Company, 1916), v.

18. Walt Whitman, *Leaves of Grass,* ed. Emory Holloway (New York: Doubleday, 1927), 120; John T. Irwin, *American Hieroglyphics: The Symbol of the Egyptian Hieroglyphics in the American Renaissance* (New Haven, Conn.: Yale University Press, 1980), 21.

19. See Virginia Smyers, "H. D.'s Books in the Bryher Library," *H. D. Newsletter* 1, no. 2 (Winter 1987): 18-25. We are grateful to Susan Stanford Friedman for sharing her research notes, which contain several Egyptology titles that do not appear in Smyers' bibliography.

20. See Ann Macy Roth, "Afrocentrism," in *The Oxford Encyclopedia of Ancient Egypt,* Vol. 1, ed. Donald B. Redford (New York: Oxford University Press, 2001), 29-32.

21. E. A. Wallis Budge, *The Gods of the Egyptians: Studies in Egyptian Mythology* (1904), rpt. (Mineola, N.Y.: Dover Publications, 1969), xii, 143.

22. See Jayne McIntosh, *The Practical Archaeologist: How We Know What We Know about the Past* (London: Paul Press Ltd, 1986), 32; Grafton Elliot Smith, *The Diffusion of Culture* (London: Watts and Co., 1933), 217.

23. Alice Gambrell, *Women Intellectuals, Modernism, and Difference: Transatlantic Culture, 1919-1945* (Cambridge U.K.: Cambridge University Press, 1997), 172.

24. James Henry Breasted, "The Temples of Lower Nubia—Report of the Expedition 1905-6," *The American Journal of Semitic Languages and Literatures* 23, no. 1 (October 1906): 3, 87, 102.

25. Vincent Arieh Tobin, "Myths: an Overview," in *Oxford Encyclopedia of Ancient Egypt,* Vol. 2. (Oxford: Oxford University Press, 2001): 464-8, 468.

26. Bruce Trigger, "Egyptology, Ancient Egypt, and the American Imagination," in *The American Discovery of Ancient Egypt,* ed. Nancy Thomas (Los Angeles County Museum of Art, 1995), 21-36, 32.

27. Malini Johar Schueller, *U.S. Orientalisms: Race, Nation, and Gender in Literature, 1790-1890* (Ann Arbor: University of Michigan Press, 2001), 35.

28. James Henry Breasted, *The Dawn of Conscience* (New York: Charles Scribner's Sons, 1934), 14; hereafter abbreviated *DC*.

29. Schnapp, Shanks and Tiews, "Archaeology, Modernism, Modernity," 10.

30. James Henry Breasted, *Egypt Through the Stereoscope: A Journey Through the Land of the Pharaohs* (New York: Underwood, 1905), 234.

31. Sarah E. Witte, "H. D.'s Recension of *The Egyptian Book of the Dead in Palimpsest*," *Sagetrieb* 8, nos. 1-2 (1989): 121-47, 141.

32. H. D., *Tribute to Freud,* 36; Susan Stanford Friedman, "Modernism of the 'Scattered Remnant': Race and Politics in the Development of H. D.'s Modernist Vision," in *H. D.: Woman and Poet,* ed. Michael King (Orono, Maine: National Poetry Foundation, Incorporated, 1986), 91-116, 107.

33. Susan Edmunds, *Out of Line: History, Psychoanalysis, & Montage in H. D.'s Long Poems* (Stanford, Calif.: Stanford University Press, 1994), 120.

34. H. D., *HERmione* (New York: New Directions, 1981), 89.

35. See Martin Bernal, *Black Athena: The Afro-Asiatic Roots of Classical Civilization* (Rutgers, N.J.: Rutgers University Press, 1987).

36. Gregory, *H. D. and Hellenism,* 2.

37. Miller, "'Enslaved to Both These Others,'" 88.

38. Lant, "The Curse of the Pharaoh," 79.

39. Gerry D. Scott III, "Go Down into Egypt: The Dawn of American Egyptology," in *The American Discovery of Ancient Egypt,* ed. Nancy Thomas (Los Angeles County Museum of Art, 1995), 37-47, 37.

40. See Breasted's 1928 Presidential Address to the American Historical Association <www.historians.org/info/AHA_History/jhbreasted.htm>.

41. Scott, "Go Down into Egypt," 37.

42. H. D., *Trilogy* (New York: New Directions, 1973), 27, 25; hereafter abbreviated *T*.

43. Susan Stanford Friedman, "Hilda Doolittle (H. D.)," *Dictionary of Literary Biography: American Poets, 1880-1945,* Vol. 45 (Detroit, Mich.: Gale Research Press, 1983), 115-49, 129.

44. See Gregory, *H. D. and Hellenism: 1880-1945,* and Cassandra Laity, *H. D. and the Victorian Fin de Siécle: Gender, Modernism, Decadence* (Cambridge, U.K.: Cambridge University Press, 1996).

45. Dianne Chisholm, *H. D.'s Freudian Poetics: Psychoanalysis in Translation* (Ithaca, N.Y.: Cornell University Press, 1992), 40.

46. Adalaide Morris, "Signaling: Feminism, Politics, and Mysticism in H. D.'s War Trilogy," *Sagetrieb* 9, no. 3 (1990): 121-33, 122.

47. Ludlow Bull, Ephraim A. Speiser, and Albert TenEyck Olmstead, "James Henry Breasted 1865-1935," *Journal of the American Oriental Society* (1936): 113-20, 116.

Jenn Wolford Watson (essay date fall 2007)

SOURCE: Watson, Jenn Wolford. "Embracing the Liminal Space: H. D.'s Androgynous Language in *Trilogy*." *EAPSU Online: A Journal of Critical and Creative Work* 4 (fall 2007): 119-34.

[*In the following essay, Watson asserts that H. D. employed both male and female deities in her poetry collection* Trilogy *as a means of establishing a sense of harmony and regeneration through the merging of these figures.*]

As H. D. composed sections of **Trilogy** in the midst of World War II, bombs literally dropped outside her window covering her typewriter with debris. Consequently, her desire to create a sense of harmony through her poetics proves unsurprising. Because H. D. aligns war with hegemonic masculinity, she often invokes the goddess figure as a symbol of rebirth to offset the discord which has arisen out of a patriarchal society. However, H. D. summons the male deity as a figure of regeneration as well, implying that both the female and male deity play an equal role in rebirth. As she merges the two in her poem, feelings of new life spring forth. This illustrates a breaking down of the binaries that are often centered on ideas of masculinity and femininity and pit the two against each other. In combining the male and female deities, H. D. obliterates this binary structure and consequently creates a fluid gap between the two. It is in this liminal space that a more elastic language becomes possible, and indeed H. D.'s poetic words take on an androgynous quality as they oscillate between a more masculine and feminine style of writing. As her words simultaneously embrace a single identity within their individual context and then inflate to accept a multiplicity of meanings, they reflect ideas about masculinist and feminist writing respectively. Luce Irigaray states that while a more "masculine" style of writing may revolve around the fixity of words with a single reading, a "feminine" style is one which *"is constantly in the process of weaving itself, [. . .] embracing words and yet casting them off to avoid becoming fixed, immobilized"* (1470). H. D. is concerned with both the fixed definition of a word and also how a single word may be inflated to encompass a variety of meanings. It is within this androgynous, and decidedly modern, space that words may contract and expand as they glide between a masculine and a feminine form. Thus, through the examination of H. D.'s use of phonetics and "etymological alchemy" in her amalgamation of the male and female deities, one may observe how she creates a sense of harmony through the elasticity of an androgynous language (Friedman 247).

In *Notes on Thought and Vision,* H. D. marks the poetic vision, and thus poetic language, as one that contains masculine and feminine elements. She states, "The majority of dream and of ordinary vision is vision of the womb," initially linking the poet's mind to certain feminine characteristics (21). However, along with the creativity of the womb, she notes that one must have the intense imagination of the mind, which proves to be the more important of the two. She notes, "Most of the so-called artists of today have lost the use of their brain. There is no way of arriving at the over-mind, except through the intellect" (21). Without the mind, an organ shared by both sexes, one cannot reach the level of poetic vision and language. As to the actual nature of the lyrical brain, it is significant that H. D. states, "We must be 'in love' before we can understand the mysteries of vision [. . .]. The minds of the two lovers merge, interact in sympathy of thought: The brain, inflamed and excited by this interchange of ideas takes on its character of over-

mind" (22). Here, the mind fuses together like two lovers, symbolizing the union of the masculine and feminine. As Lisa Rado observes, H. D. "represents the over-mind, or transcendental imagination, in terms of a confrontation between rarified male and female elements" (65). It is from this figurative marriage that a profusion of poetics breaks forth. As the masculine and feminine merge, the binaries between the two are liquidated. This creates the expansive liminal space in the mind where language becomes malleable. The "inflamed and excited" brain is raised to a level where the language it produces is androgynous, or to a point where each word may oscillate freely between a masculine fixity and a feminine fluidity where it maintains a plurality of readings. This is precisely the idea that H. D. plays with in *Trilogy* as she invokes the god and goddess with a poetic language whose pliable properties mirror the masculine and feminine bond.

H. D. discusses the elasticity and transformative properties of language itself in *Trilogy*'s first book, *The Walls Do Not Fall* [*WDNF*]. Rather than forcing words to remain within the confines of a specific definition, H. D. allows them to retain both a singular meaning and take on a plurality of readings which represents the all-encompassing nature of the masculine and feminine union:

> too little: I know, I feel
> the meaning that words hide;
>
> they are anagrams, cryptograms,
> little boxes, conditioned
>
> to hatch butterflies . . .
>
> (*WDNF* 53)

For the speaker, linguistic games may be played as the inherent elasticity of language lends itself to these tricks. An anagram allows any individual word to retain a precise meaning within a given context, but this word may then be deconstructed and rewritten to create a different message. Thus, it relies on both the masculine form of writing where the fixity of words is retained, and the feminine style where words spread out to maintain a variety of readings. In the case of a cryptogram, a secret contained within a word or phrase may only be revealed by yet another word. In other terms, a specific word with a certain definition may be implemented to unlock a variety of meanings harbored within other verbal cues, again reflecting Irigaray's idea of the masculine and feminine use of words. Indeed, words are mutable and playful entities which, because of their contracting and expanding nature, create both a finite and infinite number of meanings. As Helen V. Emmitt correctly states, "H. D. does not try to overcome the duplicity of language; rather, she turns its lying duplicity into an affirming multiplicity" (133). H. D. appropriately employs the image of a butterfly hatching out of its cocoon to illuminate how the flexible nature of words gives birth to a variety of readings. In her connection between words and butterflies, H. D. may even have been referencing Woolf's strikingly similar idea regarding the nature of language:

> Perhaps the one reason why we have no great poet, novelist, or critic writing today is that we refuse words their liberty. We pin them down to one meaning, their useful meaning, the meaning which makes us catch the train, the meaning which makes us pass the examination. And when words are pinned down they fold their wings and die.
>
> ("Craftsmanship" 206)

Woolf too embraces the fluidity of language, comparing words to butterflies, and asserts, like H. D., that to deny words their freedom is to deny them life. It is through this all-encompassing language which retains both singular and multiple readings that H. D. invokes both male and female deities. She even states in *Tribute to Freud* that she saw her language as one which naturally retains a tendency to "break bounds," these bounds potentially being the binaries constructed around ideas of masculinity and femininity (75). Thus, the shattering of these binaries generates the liminal space where a single word may become androgynous with its one and many meanings.

In her summoning of Osiris and Sirius, H. D. implements a more elastic language as she employs both anagrammatic and phonetic links between them. As the reader first peruses these lines, though, he or she is initially struck by the specific names H. D. summons:

> For example:
> Osiris equates O-sir-is or O-Sire-is
>
> Osiris,
> the star Sirius
>
> relates resurrection myth
> and resurrection reality
>
> though the ages
>
> (*WDNF* 54)

The reader is first and foremost drawn to the mythological tales attached to these proper nouns which essentially serve as their definitions. This highlights what Irigaray identifies as the masculine dimension of words with their fixed meanings. H. D.'s naming of Osiris is highly significant as he is the Egyptian lord of creation and fertility, thus also linking him to the perpetual birth of the word as it may, and will, take on a variety of meanings ("Osiris, Killed by Set, Is Resurrected by Isis"). However, one could not be drawn to

this possible linguistic tie, which will further be discussed, without his specific name and tale. This underscores the significance of the word with a concrete definition as it calls the image of resurrection and rebirth to the reader's mind.

H. D. also mentions Sirius which is the star aligned with the resurrection of Osiris and the flooding of the Nile ("**Sirius**"). Susan Gubar also helpfully states, "Sirius is the star representing Isis come to wake her brother [or husband] from death" (208). Isis, then, serves as a link between Osiris and Sirius and is also connected to a myth of rebirth. Indeed, she is the one who brings her husband back to life as she sews his limbs together. Again, though, it is through the name of Sirius with its specific tale that one makes the connection to Isis who also retains a fixed definition of one who brings fertility. In summoning the names of Osiris and Sirius, H. D. evokes a sense of new life which also reflects the changeability of words. Furthermore, H. D. mirrors the fluid androgynous space which enables the mutability of words through the merging of the male and female deity. H. D. even ends this particular poem with a positive image of androgyny:

> recover the secret of Isis,
> which is: there was One
>
> in the beginning, Creator,
> Fosterer, Begetter, the Same-forever
>
> (55)

Here, H. D. deconstructs the masculine and feminine binaries in the combination of the male and female deity. As a result, the original "Creator" is reborn, and with this deity comes the infinitely fertile realm where words may take on a plurality of meanings. From the simple invocation of a god or goddess' name with a fixed definition or tale comes feelings of rebirth or possibility which will feed a language's need to grow. Indeed, before H. D. may dive into her phonetic games with "Osiris" and "Sirius," she must have a fixed platform from which to jump.

After H. D. highlights the masculine fixed word through the invocation of divine names, she implements linguistic tricks to verbally demonstrate the feminine expansiveness of language. Thus, it is in this liminal androgynous space which the union of the male and female god produce that words may contract and expand. Phonetically, Osiris and Sirius are linked as they share the sounds of "sire" and "is." H. D. makes this clear as she breaks up "Osiris" into phonemes just as his brother Set divides Osiris' body. Both acts are related since Set's anger ultimately leads to Osiris' resurrection, while H. D.'s linguistic division of his name illuminates its connection to the Dog Star, a symbol of the land's fertility and Isis (**"Sirius"**). Her phonetic focus also demonstrates what Irigaray labels as the feminine ability of words to stretch and link to other seemingly dissimilar words, underscoring the fluidity of language. H. D. also pulls "Osiris" apart to create an anagrammatic connection with "Sirius" as "Osiris" may be rearranged to form a word visually similar to "Sirius." This represents the mutability of language whose wide boundaries mirror a more feminine style of poetics. H. D. also stretches the name "Osiris" and rearranges it into Sirius to demonstrate a state of androgyny. Because Sirius, as Gubar points out, is connected, if not synonymous, with Isis, the male Osiris momentarily changes into a female goddess. Thus, the gender switching god and the pliable language which illustrates this act both underscore the linguistic transformative state that lies between the feminine and masculine poles. Dianne Chisholm observes that H. D. "does not deconstruct the word into pictorial representations of the operations of nature but instead decodes its ancient mystery" (63). Indeed, the fertile androgynous space between the male and female deity lends words an elastic quality where they may retain both their original meaning and expand to embrace a variety of readings.

Similarly, in poem eight of *Tribute to the Angels* [*TA*], H. D. invokes a variety of sacred figures through her mutable language. While not all of these figures are deities per se, they each retain a large amount of power within a religious context:

> Now polish the crucible
> and in the bowl distill
>
> a word most bitter, *marah,*
> a word bitterer still, *mar,*
>
> sea, brine, breaker, seducer,
> giver of life, giver of tears;
>
> Now polish the crucible
> and set the jet of flame
>
> under, till *marah-mar*
> are melted, fuse and join
>
> and change and alter,
> mer, mere, mère, mater, Maia, Mary,
>
> Star of the Sea,
> Mother.
>
> (*TA* 71)

H. D.'s reference to the Virgin Mary recalls her invocation of "Osiris" and "Sirius," as her naming of the Virgin causes the reader to recall her Biblical tale and role of "Mother" (*TA* 71). Again, the importance

of a word or name with its fixed definition proves important as, in this case, it allows the reader to tie "Mary" with thoughts of rebirth. Although the Virgin Mary is not typically considered a goddess figure, she did essentially receive the status of one at the Council of Ephesus in 431 AD when the title "*theotokos*" was bestowed upon her (Baring and Cashford 550). Because "*theotokos*" literally means "bearer of God," Mary takes on the role of any primary cultural goddess as she gives birth to an actual deity and not just to "God made flesh." Therefore, H. D.'s conjuring of the name "Mary" forces the reader to remember her as one who will give new life, especially as Hermes Trismegistus merges his alchemical powers with her name. This specific tale which is attached to her name positions this proper noun in the realm of the masculine style of writing as its single meaning links her to the Great Mother, or to one who gives life. It is from this single definition, though, that H. D. may connect a variety of other words to her name through etymological and phonetic ties to demonstrate the feminine possibilities of language. While one could argue that Mary Magdalene is also summoned in the invocation of "Mary" since H. D. later connects Mary Magdalene to a variety of female deities, H. D. has yet to introduce Mary Magdalene in this context. Consequently, it appears that she is primarily referring to the Virgin Mother and her particular tale. H. D. does not stop at the potential Biblical goddess figure, though. Indeed, "Star of the Sea" refers to Venus as she was born of the sea, and was considered to be the brightest star in the morning and evening. Thus, through Venus' singular mythological story, the reader easily links the Roman goddess to this phrase and to her tale of love and fertility. Both Mary and Venus are called to the reader's mind with their similar definitions of ones who stand for new life. It is not until Hermes Trismegistus performs his verbal alchemy, though, that these proper nouns are linked with other significant words, allowing each word to expand its meaning with its connection to others.

Indeed, Hermes Trismegistus must be invoked before the female deities are merged into one goddess through a malleable language which also links them to a multiplicity of other words (*TA* 71). Trismegistus, a Pagan Gnostic aligned with alchemy, is also identified with the Greek god Hermes (Barnstone 177). Trismegistus' connection with this god proves quite significant since this deity was considered the "creator and orderer of the universe" (177). Even if one was unfamiliar with the figure of Hermes Trismegistus, his first name alone should be enough for one to make the immediate connection between the alchemist and the Greek god. Consequently, the reading of his name conjures a single myth of fertility, again highlighting the importance of a single definition for a name or word. Both the Greek god and Trismegistus are automatically linked by the reader to the idea of fertility and rebirth just as the goddess figures are. Furthermore, it is through this summoned Gnostic alchemist that the goddesses are unified. Friedman states, "The 'jewel' in the crucible is both the poet's mother and the sea as 'mother' of all life. Amniotic fluid cradles the beginning of individual birth, and seawater, too bitter to drink, created the biochemistry needed for all evolution" (247-48). While Friedman's point is both interesting and useful as it is the feminine word which evolves into one with a multiplicity of readings, she wrongly cuts out the role of Hermes Trismegistus, or the masculine component. It is he who must begin with the single words *"marah," "mar," "Mary,"* etc., and essentially serves as the catalyst for that transformation. Moreover, the Greek god Hermes was also thought to be the inventor of writing, and it is Trismegistus' verbal alchemy in conjunction with the names of the female deities which illustrates the pliability of H. D.'s words (Barnstone 177). Indeed, he must begin with words and their singular definitions before he can link them all together.

H. D. explores a variety of words which she connects to the goddess figures with their etymological roots and phonetic links through Hermes Trismegistus. In turn, H. D. demonstrates how an elastic language may broaden from a more masculine style which condones the fixity of words. In breaking down the binaries which appear to pit the masculine and feminine against each other, H. D. illuminates the limitless liminal space which is stretched wide between these two spheres. H. D. calls Hermes Trismegistus to heat the word *"marah,"* which is Hebrew for bitter, into the Spanish word for sea, and phonetic match, "mar" (Barnstone 187). While the speaker states that *"marah"* becomes bitterer in its transformation into *"mar,"* it is the sea which produces new life. This again highlights the significance of the single meaning of words, yet the phonetic link with the "m" and "ar" sound between the two words allows *"marah"* to transform into the more positive *"mar."* H. D. does not stop here as *"marah-mar,"* now visually bound by a hyphen, rapidly morphs into a variety of words which are both phonetically and etymologically connected. "[M]arah-*mar"* suddenly becomes "mer, mere, mère, mater, Maia, Mary" (*TA* 71). "Mar," "mer," and "mere" are all etymologically linked, and thus all pertain to the same thing: water. "Mer" is French for "sea" while "mere" is a small lake or marsh (Barnstone 187). Similarly, "mère" and "mater" are connected etymologically, and as a result they both translate to "mother." Significantly, "mer," "mere," and "mère"

are phonetically linked, while "mère" and "mater" are etymologically connected. Consequently, "mère" is the binding word in this list as it falls into both groups, pulling all of the words together. The result of this is clear. The images of water flow into the general terms for mother, and from this bond specific goddesses arise: Maia, and the Virgin Mary. It may also be of some note that "mer" is the root word for "Mary." Here, it seems quite obvious that both the individual readings of words in terms of their basic definitions prove important as one must first grasp their meanings before one can see the symbolism in their transformation. Indeed, H. D. transforms words of a potentially negative nature into those of life and regeneration. As she links these words together through an elastic language which glides between the masculine and feminine use of words, her "etymological alchemy distills the cultural accumulations of negative meaning into the word's 'root,' or pure essence" (Friedman 248). As Albert Gelpi correctly asserts, "feelings of separateness g[i]ve way to a sense of organic wholeness" (11). One should make clear that while H. D. melts and transforms these words into the single "Mother," her demonstration of how words are linked and may expand and contract in their connections reflects the liminal space between the masculine and feminine bond.

While the disruption of masculine and feminine binaries provides a fluid space for H. D.'s androgynous language, it also serves a practical purpose for her. Indeed, H. D.'s poetry evokes a feeling of harmony which both the poet and her contemporaries sought in the midst of World War II. It seems that in her writing of *Trilogy* and exploration of an elastic language, H. D. attempts to provide a view of possible peace for her readers. In *Notes on Thought and Vision,* she states, "There is already enough beauty in the world of art [. . .] to remake the world" (26). Through these words she implies that art may have a significant impact on the world in terms of healing some of its struggles and repairing its fragmentation. In ***The Walls Do Not Fall,*** H. D. illuminates the importance of the poet in this light:

> we are the keepers of the secret,
> the carriers, the spinners
>
> of the rare intangible thread
> that binds all humanity
>
> 　　　　　　　　　　　　　　　(24)

The secret that the poet, or specifically H. D., carries is the importance of harmony in the world. Indeed, as H. D. breaks down the masculine and feminine binaries to create a unified space between the two, she reflects the need for peace and balance in a war-torn world. The poet spins this truth out using the thread of an elastic language which one expands and contracts to connect "all humanity" in a state of tranquility.

H. D. even directly states that the word may conquer the sword and the violence it inflicts:

> forever; remember, O Sword,
> you are the younger brother, the latter-born
>
> your Triumph, however exultant,
> must one day be over,
>
> *in the beginning*
> *was the Word.*

(*WDNF* 17)

Not only does H. D. prophesize that the word will ultimately defeat the sword, she also states that the sword itself will always prove inferior as it is the word's younger sibling. Furthermore, because words are "healers, helpers" to H. D., their specific nature runs counter to that of the sword which exists only to inflict injury (34). Thus, H. D.'s fluid poetics gives life as it demonstrates the unity she seeks in its androgynous characteristics. Friedman agrees that H. D.'s verbal alchemy "serves as metaphor for cultural purification as well as for linguistic restoration" (Friedman 249). It alternately spreads out to embrace all things and contracts to lend a sense of closeness and intimacy.

Through her malleable androgynous language, H. D. evokes feelings of harmony as she combines the male and female deities in her poetry. The movement of her words from the masculine realm to the feminine one naturally reflects the amalgamation of Osiris and Isis as well as Mary and Hermes Trismegistus. Furthermore, as H. D. breaks down the binaries based on gender, it is clear that she desires to dismantle the boundaries between countries that are at war. Just as she finds the common denominator of fertility and rebirth between the male and female god, H. D. is implicitly calling nations at war to do the same. She desires these countries to drop their antagonistic feelings which serve as the rigid borders that prevent peace. Just as her language easily flows from a masculine state to a more feminine one, H. D. calls those involved in World War II to follow suit; to let go of their restricting nationalistic ideas and thus allow their borders to become more fluid, more elastic. Indeed, it is a lesson one would do well to remember.

Works Cited

Barnstone, Aliki. "Readers' Notes." *Trilogy*. New York: New Directions, 1998.

Baring, Anne and Jules Cashford. *The Myth of the Goddess*. London: Viking Press, 1991.

Chisholm, Dianne. *H. D.'s Freudian Poetics*. Ithaca: Cornell UP, 1992.

Emmitt, Helen V. "Forgotten Memories and Unheard Rhythms." *Paideuma* 33 (2004): 131-53.

Friedman, Susan Stanford. *Psyche Reborn*. Bloomington: Indiana UP, 1981.

Gilpi, Albert. "Introduction." *Notes on Thought and Vision*. San Francisco: City Lights, 1982.

Gubar, Susan. "The Echoing Spell of H. D.'s *Trilogy*." *Shakespeare's Sisters*. Ed. Sandra M. Gilbert and Susan Gubar. Bloomington: Indiana UP, 1999.

H. D. *Notes on Thought and Vision*. San Francisco: City Lights, 1982.

———. *Tribute to Freud*. New York: New Directions, 1984.

———. *Trilogy*. New York: New Directions, 1998.

Irigaray, Luce. "The Sex Which Is Not One." *The Critical Tradition*. Ed. David Richter. Boston: Bedford Books, 1998. 1466-71.

"Mary." *The Oxford English Dictionary*. <http://dictionary.oed.com.ezproxy.wfu.edu:3000/cgi/entry/00302708?query_type=word&queryword=Mary&first first=1&max_to_show=10&sort_type=alpha&result_place=1&search_id=IWoW-tHsj2m-17318&hilite=00302708>.

"Osiris, Killed by Set, Is Resurrected by Isis." *A Dictionary of African Mythology*. Ed. Harold Scheub. Oxford UP, 2000. *Oxford Reference Online*. Oxford UP. Wake Forest University. 28 November 2006. <http://www.oxfordreference.com/views/ENTRY.html?subview=Main&entry=t68.e289>.

Rado, Lisa. *The Modern Androgyne Imagination*. Charlottesville: Virginia UP, 2000.

"Sirius." *A Dictionary of Phrase and Fable*. Ed. Elizabeth Knowles. Oxford UP, 2006. *Oxford Reference Online*. Oxford University Press. Wake Forest 2006 <http://www.oxfordreference.com/views/ENTRY.html?subview=Main&entry=t214.e6528>.

Woolf, Virginia. "Craftsmanship." *The Death of the Moth*. San Diego: Harvest Books, 1970. 198-207.

Sarah Jackson (essay date 2010)

SOURCE: Jackson, Sarah. "Touching Freud's Dog." *Angelaki* 15, no. 2: 187-201.

[*In the following essay, Jackson studies the emphasis on tactility in H. D.'s poetry and comments on how H. D.'s relationship with Freud contributed to her poetic exploration of the conflict between the prohibition and the desire to touch.*]

Do not touch . . .[1]

It is not the first thing, but it is the second: "Do not touch," Sigmund Freud says to H. D. upon her entering analysis.[2] He is referring to his pet chow, Yofi, warning H. D. that "she snaps—she is very difficult with strangers" (98). H. D., however, challenges Freud's word of caution, and "not only continue[s] [her] gesture toward the little chow, but crouch[es] on the floor so that she can snap better if she wants to" (98). Freud's prohibition of touch and H. D.'s challenge to it—a challenge that I propose is extended in and through her writing—perform a tactile poetics, a literature of touch.

In this paper I explore Freud's warning in light of work by Jacques Derrida (*On Touching*) and Jean-Luc Nancy (*Noli Me Tangere*). Touch is always already permeated by its own interruption, requiring a handful of tact. Despite this, H. D.'s writing demonstrates a heightened sense of tactility—an attempt to make contact in new and often subversive ways. Here, I examine the ways in which H. D. performs a "remote touch" in her poetry. Indeed, it is the conflict between the prohibition and the desire to touch that forms the heart of this essay, in which I try to touch touch, to reach towards the untouchable, and to tender a tactile poetics.

I

"Do not touch," Freud says. We've heard it before: "'Keep still!—Don't say anything!—Don't touch me!'" Frau Emmy von N. warned Freud in 1889[3]—a statement that Freud appropriates in his first encounter with H. D., according to her *Tribute to Freud*:

> A little lion-like creature came padding toward me—a lioness, as it happened. She had emerged from the inner sanctum or manifested from under or behind the couch; anyhow, she continued her course across the carpet. Embarrassed, shy, overwhelmed, I bend down to greet this creature. But the Professor says, "Do not touch her—she snaps—she is very difficult with strangers."
>
> (98)

H. D., however, does touch, and so, moreover, does Freud. During his early practice, he would press his finger on a client's forehead and massage the neck and head to facilitate release.[4] His treatment of Frau Emmy, for instance, involved "warm baths, massage twice a day and hypnotic suggestion"—acts that are accompanied by "strok[ing] her several times over the eyes" (*SE* [*Studies on Hysteria*] II: 51, 53). He repeats this stroking to relieve her gastric pains a day later, despite her ongoing injunctions, "Keep Still!—Don't say anything!—Don't touch me!" (54).[5] Perhaps Freud

eventually responded to Frau Emmy's pleas, however, because he moved away from this early technique towards the psychoanalytic method—and the rule of abstinence. As Ernest Jones remarks, "The patient should be kept in a state of abstinence of unrequited love. The more affection you allow him, the more readily you reach his complexes, but the less definite the result."[6] For Didier Anzieu, French psychoanalyst and author of *The Skin Ego,* the perceived risk of eroticisation, especially during his work with hysterical women and girls, led Freud to develop his technique towards the psychoanalytic method, where he "suspended all tactile contact with the patient in favour of purely linguistic exchange."[7] "The tactile," writes Anzieu, "is fundamental only on condition that, at the necessary moment, it is prohibited" (140)—a double prohibition, in fact, that stresses the dangers of violence and of eroticisation implicit in contact.

Touch, it seems, is inhabited by the prohibition at its heart, and this *"law of tact,"* as Derrida calls it,[8] pervades our everyday professional, social and familial exchanges, extending to the psychoanalytic setting where touching is particularly taboo. This non-touching culture is everywhere and yet visible nowhere—touching tempered as if by a law of sensible handshakes. "Do not touch," we are warned in museums; "Breakages will be paid for"; "Beware—wet paint"; and "Keep off the grass." Do not touch your father-mother-sister-brother, we are told; do not even touch yourself. Touch is taboo. Addressing the taboos attached to the treatment of enemies, of chiefs or kings and of the dead, Freud explicitly links taboo and touch in *Totem and Taboo,* arguing that "We cannot be surprised at the fact that, in the restrictions of taboo, touching plays a part similar to the one which it plays in 'touching phobias', though the secret meaning of the prohibition cannot be of such a specialized nature in taboo as it is in the neurosis" (*SE* XIII: 33). Describing the clinical history of such a case of "touching phobia" or *"délire du toucher,"* Freud states that in very early childhood,

> the patient shows a strong *desire* to touch, the aim of which is of a far more specialized kind than one would have been inclined to expect. This desire is promptly met by an *external* prohibition against carrying out that particular kind of touching.
>
> (29)

"Both the desire and the prohibition" of this particular kind of touch, Freud remarks in a footnote, "relate to the child's touching of his own genitals" (29 n. 1). He continues by explaining that the prohibition is accepted because "it finds support from powerful *internal* forces" and because it is "stronger than the instinct which is seeking to express itself in the touching"

(29). Rather than *"abolishing* the instinct," however, "its only result is to *repress* the instinct (the desire to touch) and banish it into the unconscious" (29). Hence, "a situation is created which remains undealt with—a psychical fixation—and everything else follows from the continuing conflict between the prohibition and the instinct" (29). All our future "contact"—with ourselves and with other people—is determined by the tension between the desire and fear of touch.

The taboo is reiterated in Christ's prohibition: *"Noli me tangere,"* or "Touch me not," Jesus says to Mary Magdalene after his resurrection.[9] For Jean-Luc Nancy, *"Noli me tangere*—'Do not touch me'—calls to mind a prohibition of contact, a question of sensuality or violence, a recoil, a frightened or modest flight."[10] Nancy goes on to suggest:

> "Don't touch me" is a phrase that touches and that cannot touch, even when isolated in every context. It says something about touching in general, or it touches on the sensitive point of touching: on this sensitive point that touching constitutes par excellence (it is, in sum, "the" point of the sensitive) and on what forms the sensitive point within it. But this point is precisely the point where touching does not touch and where it must not touch in order to carry out its touch (its art, its tact, its grace): the point or the space without dimension that separates what touching gathers together, the line that separates the touching from the touched and thus the touch from itself.
>
> (13)

The phrase "Don't touch me" touches the heart of tactility—its implicit *untouchability. Noli me tangere* uncovers untouchability, its most "sensitive point" (13). The prohibition is further problematised by its difficult translation from the original Greek version, *"Mē mou haptou,"* which carries the implied alternative, "Do not hold me back"; "'Do not hold me back'" (15), Nancy argues, "amounts to saying 'Touch me with a real touch, one that is restrained, nonappropriating and nonidentifying.' Caress me, don't touch me" (49-50). Thus, to say "Do not touch me" appears to carry "discord at the very site of the embrace" (54); it is a prohibition on touch that touches on the *jouissance*—the pain and the pleasure, the prohibition and the desire, the invitation and the withdrawal—of contact.

The taboo on touch, then, is Janus-faced. The word "taboo," Freud tells us, "diverges in two contrary directions"; "it means, on the one hand, 'sacred', 'consecrated', and on the other 'uncanny', 'dangerous', 'forbidden', 'unclean'" (*SE* XIII: 18). Touch, in a similar fashion, has an antithetical resonance; at the same time as it is prohibited and feared it is revered for its healing potential—the laying on of hands, the

"Midas touch," the "Royal touch." Certainly, the healing powers inherent in Christ's touch are clear: "And he stretched out his hand and touched him, saying . . . 'I wish it; be clean.' And immediately his leprosy was cleansed."[11] Derrida notes that Jesus "the savior is 'touching,' he is the One who touches, and most often with his hand, and most often in order to purify, heal, or resuscitate—save, in a word" (*On Touching* 100). Touch is both reparative and threatening.

We might continue touching on touch, caressing it, perhaps even tampering with it, but I wish to turn or return, now, to the re-enactment of Christ's utterance by Freud in H. D.'s tribute. *Noli me tangere,* I suggest, is simultaneously performed and displaced by Freud, who uses the dog as a substitute for his own body in his analytic relationship with H. D. "Do not touch her," Freud says, and, in terms of transference, he means do not touch me (or do not hold me back, even do not hold me back from healing you). Reframing the resurrection scene, H. D. recognises Freud's position and represents it to Kenneth Macpherson in a letter dated 15 March 1933:

> Freud is just simply Jesus-Christ after the resurrection, he has that wistful ghost look of someone who has been right past the door of the tomb, and such tenderness with such humor, he just IS all that. I am sure he IS the absolute inheritor of all that eastern mystery and majic, just IS, in spite of his monumental work and all that, he is the real, the final healer.[12]

Freud the untouchable, Freud the real, the final healer, Freud the analyst saying, "Do not touch." And yet, H. D. does touch—not him, but his substitute, his chow, his dear Yofi:

> But, though no accredited dog-lover, I like dogs and they oddly and sometimes unexpectedly "take" to me. If this is an exception, I am ready to take the risk. Unintimidated but distressed by the Professor's somewhat forbidding manner, I not only continue my gesture toward the little chow, but crouch on the floor so that she can snap better if she wants to. Yofi—her name is Yofi—snuggles her nose into my hand and nuzzles her head, in delicate sympathy, against my shoulder.[13]

H. D. touches and Yofi returns H. D.'s touch; the "snuggle," the soothing nuzzle, indicating a "delicate sympathy," offers us, perhaps, the other side of the coin: the healing touch. So, Freud uses Yofi as a vehicle to simultaneously prohibit touch, and offer a certain tactile healing—do not hold me back. Freud's words to H. D. are both an invitation and a warning. This dynamic is not only played out in the relationship between H. D., Freud and his dog but is endlessly repeated in the letters H. D. sends to Bryher while she is in Vienna for analysis. In a letter dated 23 March 1933, H. D. writes:

Nearly through the hour, papa began to cough, and Yofi came and licked his hand, a most touching spectacle, papa apologized and said did I mind? The licking took a long time, almost five minutes, solid and solemn. F. says she always does that and it is sometimes very awkward.

(Letters 141)

A "touching spectacle," quite literally, Yofi's "licking" performs the healing touch on the untouching healer. This "dogged" touching between Freud, H. D. and Yofi is repeated and amplified when the analysis moves to Hohe Warte in the summer months, where Anna Freud's dog, Wolf, "barked the place down" and the "hounds" infiltrate all aspects of the analysis, "running in and out and jumping on the analysis couch to lick one all over" (9 May 1933, *Letters* 259). This licking all over forms part of the "corpus of tact" presented by Nancy:

A corpus of tact: skimming, grazing, squeezing, thrusting, pressing, smoothing, scraping, rubbing, caressing, palpating, fingering, kneading, massaging, entwining, hugging, striking, pinching, biting, sucking, moistening, taking, releasing, licking, jerking off, looking, listening, smelling, tasting, ducking, fucking, rocking, balancing, carrying, weighing . . .[14]

To lick: it is a most particular form of touch—an intimate, a nurturing, moreover, a loving touch; for anthropologist Ashley Montagu, "'licking,' in its actual and in its figurative sense, and love are closely connected."[15] In licking both Freud and H. D., Yofi shows her love to them, and performs their love for each other.

The extent of the role of dogs in the relationship is indicated by an incident in late May 1933. H. D. describes a fight between two of the dogs and the effect it had on Freud, who, despite deteriorating health, "flung" himself into the thick of it:

Had a terrible time yesterday. Yo-fi is back and doesn't like Lun, and flew at her in the room. We had been to the kitchen to see the pups. Freud ran like lightening and flung himself on the floor and pulled them apart, all his money fell out and Anna and the maid rushed in, Anna screaming in German of course, "pappachen beloved you shouldn't have done that," and the maid taking off Yo-fi in her arms like Jesus with a lamb.

(18 May, *Letters* 292)

Her letters following this incident are nervy and distracted, concerned with Freud's illness and the situation with the dogs. Writing to Bryher on 27 May, H. D. explains: "I think the dogs got his trouble and tried to get in to us, feeling he was sick. It was horrible. Almost too much when ones own skin is peeled off" (*Letters* 329). The dogs, then, not only break into the analytic space, but also into them, into their bodies,

flaying them, getting under their skins; Freud's dog transgresses the boundaries or skins that divide them from the dogs, as well as each other.

"Do not touch," Freud tells H. D., and he means more than he says. But H. D. does indeed touch, and so, moreover, does Freud. His touch is only present in fragments, and yet it *is* present, however displaced. For instance, he substitutes a third party—*another* dog—to affect his touching of H. D.; he touches Bryher, H. D.'s lover and life-long friend, whose pet name was "Dog," in order to make contact with H. D. In a letter to Macpherson on 14 April, Bryher writes:

I had my final interview for this visit with Dr F. to-day and he patted small dog {Bryher} and said now he had trotted into fold he must not be allowed to run out again and that every possible influence would be used to get small dog a collar.

(Letters 175)[16]

"Patting small dog," Freud both conforms to and breaks his own taboo on touching his patients: he does not touch his analysand, H. D., but at the same time he does—he touches her through Bryher, in the similar way that the analytic pair exchange forbidden "gifts" through Bryher and their daughter, Perdita.[17] Like touch, gifts are prohibited in Freudian analysis, but this prohibition is overcome and exchange is granted through the mediatory figures of Bryher and Perdita.[18] The main economy of exchange is, of course, the dogs. Certainly, many of H. D. and Bryher's letters are concerned with Freud's offer of one of Yofi's puppies:

Dawg and Dogggg.

Dandog.

The worst has happened.

Will you please put your two heads together. I feel like the Virgin Mary at the entrance of the dove. Pa-pa has offered us one of Yo-fi's pups. What will we do about it?????????????????????

(26 April, *Letters* 200)

In offering them the puppy, Freud is, in effect, offering them a means of permanent contact with Yofi, as well as with himself; the contract will be bound by the patting, snuggling and licking of dogs and their offspring. H. D. is not unaware of the significance of this gift, interpreting it as her impregnation by Freud: "I feel pregnant," she writes to Bryher on 27 April, just like Yofi (*Letters* 203). H. D., however, is adamant about this "touching" gift: "Evidently I was afraid of becoming pregnant by papa Freud, funny?????????? But no Freud-cat, or esoteric Yo-fi, I can assure you, will be stranded on your front door step like the last one, vintage 1919" (25 April, *Letters* 197).[19] This assurance follows a startling revelation concerning H. D.'s own fears. It seems that H. D. (whose pet name is "Cat" or "Kat") is afraid of the nature of Freud's touch; not only is she horrified to discover that Freud doesn't like cats[20] but she also displays anxiety about the vicious tendency of dogs towards cats. She writes to Robert Herring, who also owns chows, about the predisposition of this breed of dogs to attack cats: "You asked me, do they kill cats," he replies, "and I say, I don't think its in them, more than other dogs . . . Yo-fi I should think attacked the cat because it knows a cat goes for the eyes, and felt it had to protect the pups it was carrying—perhaps?" (n.d., *Letters* 235 n. 15). Although she repeatedly describes Freud as "tender" (*Letters* 87, 100, 165), she also appears wary of his touch by displaying anxiety about Yofi's behaviour with a "cat." Ironically, in eventually rejecting Freud's gift, H. D. is most concerned in not hurting Freud's "feelings": "we will have to use tact" (1 May, *Letters* 230); it "must be done most tactfully . . . above all, most tactfully" (24 May, *Letters* 319).

"*Tact itself: a phantom touching,*" writes Cixous in "Love of the Wolf," alluding to the haunting that always interrupts touch.[21] Steven Connor explains that "the values of tact, 'touch', subtlety, refinement and so on, all depend upon and ramify from the thought of the sensation of its particular kind of lightness of touch."[22] Tact, for him, is a touch that "retracts itself, but not fully"; it gestures towards an "infinitesimal meniscus between touching and not-touching" (262). In effect, tact, as Derrida writes, warns against the excess of touch, it is a "moderation of touch," or "some kind of reserve [that] holds it on the brink of exaggeration" (*On Touching* 47). For Derrida, "a certain tact," moreover,

> a "thou shalt not touch too much," "thou shalt not let yourself be touched too much," or even "thou shalt not touch yourself too much," would thus be inscribed a priori, like a first commandment, the law of originary prohibition, in the destiny of tactile experience.
>
> (47)

Derrida leads us by the hand back to the "law of tact"—a law that demands "one must touch without touching":

> In touching, touching is forbidden: do not touch or tamper with the thing itself, do not touch on what there is to touch. Do not touch what remains to be touched, and first of all law itself—which is the untouchable, *before* all the ritual prohibitions that this or that religion or culture may impose on touching, as suggested earlier.
>
> (66)

In insisting "it must be done most tactfully . . . above all, most tactfully" (*Letters* 319), H. D. learns "how to touch *without* touching, without touching *too much*,

where touching is already too much" (*On Touching* 67). The analysis demands that H. D. must "touch him without moving him"; as Derrida says, she must touch "almost imperceptibly, intangibly" (135). In this tactful relationship, touch and untouchable collide.

So, in a sense, tact involves a not-touching. As such, it exposes the space, the absence, the non-contact that haunts the fact of touching. Challenging both the privilege and the unity of touch, Derrida insists that there exists a "law of *parting and sharing* at the heart of touching and con-tact" (199); touch is always already inhabited by its own *différance*. I cannot touch the heart of the matter; touching you, I only ever touch the very outside of you with the very outside of me; contact is only ever at the absolute limits. Drawing attention to the heart as "absolute intimacy of the limitless secret" (267), and the fact that the heart is an "interior surface of the body" that "no 'self-touching' can ever reach" (267), Derrida shows that touch always becomes its own point of non-contact, with "interruption, interposition, detour of the between *in the middle* of contact" (229). The most we can ever do, he says, is "touch on a surface, which is to say the skin or thin peel of a limit" (6). The limits of touch, Christopher Stokes explains, mean that the "spacing, interruption or non-contact at the heart of touching" is the very condition of touch.[23] Or, as Ian Maclachlan describes it: "there can be no touching without loss of contact."[24] This is because "something always intervenes to disrupt the apparent immediacy of touch, whether it be a case of touching oneself or touching the other; touching presupposes interruption, lest touch simply vanish into consubstantiality" (58). While Maclachlan does not "deny the contacts of touch," he argues that touching always presupposes interruption, and "the resistance of skin as I feel myself touch you is testimony to this interruption" (58). Touch is always already inhabited by its own "*différance* of the *between*" (*On Touching* 229). And it is "this elementary *différance* of inter-position or intervals between two surfaces [that] is at the same time the condition of contact" (229). Touch, then, touches on the untouchable.

A "thinking of touch, this thought of what 'touching' means, must touch on the untouchable" (18), argues Derrida. This problem—"how to touch upon the untouchable" (6)—is played out in H. D.'s letters. Writing to Bryher about their terrifying housekeeper, Dorothy Hull, H. D. describes herself as "untouchable" (7 March 1933, *Letters* 60). And yet she tampers with her own status as untouchable even as she tenders it: "Deliver some chaste message to the Q {Dorothy Hull} from the 'untouchable.' I am so touched that P is gold-digging like mad" (*Letters* 42). Thus, even as she offers herself as untouchable to "the Q," she admits that she is "touched" by the behaviour of P—her daughter, Perdita. Her letters are certainly full of the "contradictory injunctions . . . at the heart of touch" (*On Touching* 76); she is both touchable and untouchable, simultaneously obeying and breaking a law of tact.

H. D.'s touching untouchability extends to the possibility of touching on H. D.'s writing corpus; physically tangible, it also bears the trace of its own untouchable quality. How is it ever possible to touch through a text? "Two bodies can't occupy the same place simultaneously," writes Nancy: "Therefore you and I are not simultaneously in the place where I write, where you read, where I speak, where you listen. No contact without displacement."[25] For Maclachlan, if "interruption inhabits the contact of touch," then the "possibility of touch may also inhabit the interruption of distance, for example the distance of writing."[26] Referring to the "infinitesimal dust of contact" that occurs during the endlessly deferred process of reading and writing, Nancy argues:

> Bodies, for good or ill, are touching each other upon this page, or more precisely, the page itself is a touching (of my hand while it writes, and your hands while they hold the book). This touch is infinitely indirect, deferred—machines, vehicles, photocopies, eyes, still other hands are all interposed—but it continues as a slight, resistant, fine texture, the infinitesimal dust of contact, everywhere interrupted and pursued.[27]

Reading H. D., an infinitesimal dust of contact drifts between us. Zsuzsa Baross suggests, however, that a sur-text, a writing *on* the text of another writer, may be an unwelcome touch:

> As offering, writing ineluctably risks giving offense, an intrusive *touch* (whose violence the biblical usage of offense as "striking against the foot" [*OED*] so well preserves), sending off as it does in the direction of the other an unsolicited missive, a perhaps unwanted gift, and so far as writing, a "false" present that would never give itself completely, without reserving something for itself.[28]

Thus, "the ever-present danger of misappropriation by the way of the hand—unlawfully grabbing, taking hold of, (another's) writing, as though 'property'" (150), renders H. D.'s writing untouchable, even as I touch upon it. Any writing, as Baross suggests of her own writing on Derrida, will have to be an "*offering*": "writing that approaches Derrida from a distance, writes *toward* him, perhaps without ever reaching him (as news or missive), perhaps without even *touching* him" (150). And thus, writing on H. D., I write towards her, ensuring the possibility of touching becomes ever more remote.

Neither immediate nor close, touch is filled with distance. Simultaneously performing her own desire "to touch and be touched," Cixous draws particular at-tention to the idea of a touch without touch, an untouchable touch, a telephonic touch: "An employee of Air France tells me on the telephone: I like your books because they touch me. We all like to touch—to be touched."[29] Touching at a distance, the telephone performs remote contact; it demonstrates that we can make contact even from afar. *"One cannot imagine closer to farther,"* she writes in *Rootprints*: the telephone is "the far in the near"; it is "the outside in the inside"; the "mother-daughter" relationship.[30] Thanks to the telephone, we touch without touching; "from very far, we launch the most restrained, the most murmured call"—the call that gives us the voices "that touch us most strongly" (49). They touch us from afar, up close. This telephonic touch, touching us from afar, up close, is re-enacted in H. D.'s letters through the idea of the "telegraphic" touch. In her letters she frequently refers to "wires" or telegraph messages received and sent. Regarding the puppies, H. D. writes on 26 April 1933, *"Please write, don't* (N.B. do *not!!!*) wire Freud, *'yes'* as I am not sure it would be feasible. Its all you, you, you, Fido. Now Fido . . . O, please I feel so very about-to-deliver" (*Letters* 200-01). The *delivery* of this telegraphic touch, like the delivery of her dog-baby, is, however, forever postponed in the text. Indeed, the wires referred to in Friedman's collection are often missing—they remain undelivered. On arrival in Vienna, H. D. writes to Bryher on 1 March:

> I sent a wire off about 4 yesterday on arrival, as I feared I would not be able to call you up, and a wire would have been as quick. This morning a notice came that it had not been received, so I was horrified, and at once sent off another, to Macpherson, Closeup, Vevey.
>
> (*Letters* 25)

Bryher and Macpherson's "telegraphic address—Closeup Vevey," Bryher writes to H. D. (*Letters* 20), is, it turns out, not so very "closeup."[31] Haunted by the space and interruption inherent in touch—even telegraphic touch—Closeup is, rather, out of reach. Bryher writes a pressing note to H. D. on 21 March:

> Urgent.
>
> Post office has changed our telegraphic address in error to *Kenwin Vevey* instead of Closeup accounting for terror on your arrival. Please note in future Kenwin Vevey.
>
> Stop Press.
>
> (*Letters* 131)

Even those "wires" received are absent from Friedman's collection, the wires bypassing or surpassing Friedman's hand-picked letters, remaining untouched. And yet the wires indicate a sense of urgency—they are quite "frantic" (*Letters* 64); displaying a certain nakedness, they undress the text. And it is returning to this naked voice that we find ourselves, once again, back in the realm of touch—a word, a letter, a wire, a gift—that touches. This demonstrates that while the hand cannot make complete contact, perhaps the written word can make a different gesture towards the untouchability of touch, moving towards an alternative, textual touch—a remote touch that functions through distance. H. D.'s poetics, I propose, are haunted by this remote touch. Rethinking contact through the written word, the second part of this paper moves on to examine the ways in which H. D.'s poetry inspires a new tact.

II

Derived from the French *touche* or *toucher,* the word "touch" not only refers to physical contact with the surface of our body but is also inextricably bound up with the notion of "feeling" and the emotionally affective (or "touchy feely") implications that this word implies. And yet touch refuses to be fixed in semantics; it is hard to put our finger on touch, hard to get a hold of it. Indeed, as Montagu notes:

> Interestingly enough, when one consults a dictionary for the various meanings of the word one finds that the entry under "touch" is likely to represent the most extensive in the volume. It is by far the longest entry— fourteen full columns—in the magnificent *Oxford English Dictionary*. This in itself constitutes some sort of testimony to the influence which the tactile experience of hand and fingers has had upon our imagery and our speech.[32]

Attempting to define touch, we move in multiple directions, not only towards physical sensation but also towards emotion and through language too. A lexicon of touch has entered our everyday language through the expression of an emotional or aesthetic experience; a "deeply felt experience is 'touching'" (6), for instance. The reciprocal relationship between sensation and feeling is also illustrated in H. D.'s letters to Bryher. In a single letter, dated 15 March 1933, H. D. writes, "About your coming on here . . . I am really terribly touched" (*Letters* 95). She goes on: "Now it is really touchingly sweet of you, darling Fido, to say you will come through. I will 'hold the right thought' and if it happens, it will be marvellous" (95), not only repeating the touching metaphor but also extending it through the act of "holding." And again, in the same letter, recounting a story of "Papa" (Freud) and Yofi, she describes it as "all very funny and touching" (96). In other ways, too, her writing exhibits a lexicon of touch: H. D. refers to getting "in touch with 'events,' if you like" (231); she is "not afraid (touch wood) of war" (283); she feels "very tender toward" England (284); and when offered a chow puppy from Freud, as I have already noted, suggests that "the only thing is to hold it over tentatively" (235) . . . and, of course, "above all, most tactfully" (319).

If touch and feeling can be brought together through language, it is especially interesting to think about the ways in which language can touch us, can make us feel. In conversation with Gilbert Tarrab and reiterating the prohibition of touch in psychoanalysis, Anzieu argues: "Experience shows me that it is sufficient to resort to symbolic touching: one can touch with the voice."[33] Words, then, have the power to touch us; they can function as symbolic touch experiences—a remote experience of touch that inspires "feeling" without bodily contact. In suggesting this, Anzieu draws on Montagu's description of infant development, whereby the original sensation of being held by the caregiver is gradually replaced through language: "The rhythm of this kind of tactual stimulation that the mother conveys to the child in her arms is almost universally reproduced in the lullabies sung or hummed to lull children to sleep" (119). Substituting the physical act of holding with a web of words, the voice becomes a surrogate for touch; words seem "up close and personal" without actually being "closeup," as in H. D.'s missing wires to Vevey. Both Montagu and Anzieu, however, in discussing the tactile properties of language or the symbolic experience of touch through the voice, are referring to the *spoken* word. I propose instead that we can take the notion of "symbolic touching" beyond the verbal by considering the remote tactility of the written word, primarily the tactile poetics of literature. I refer here to the way in which the written word can function as a symbolic touch experience; the ways in which literature can "touch" us too.

The tactile capacity of the written word is especially emphatic in the writings of Cixous. In "Writing Blind," Cixous makes the power of literature to touch explicit: "I like your books because they touch me" (188). Indeed, Cixous—well aware of the power of writing to "move me, touch me, strike me with blows of the axe"[34]—claims in "Writing Blind" to write in order to actually touch the limits: "I do not write to keep. I write to feel. I write to touch the body of the instant with the tips of the words" (195). Touching the tips of words, Cixous puts into play what Anzieu merely describes: not only does the spoken word have the power to touch, but writing can touch us too.

H. D., I propose, was profoundly aware of the power of writing to touch. In her early poem, **"The Pool,"** she alludes to the sense of touch and its relation to creativity:

> Are you alive?
> I touch you.
> You quiver like a sea-fish.
> I cover you with my net.
> What are you—banded one?[35]

Following Donna Hollenberg, who suggests that **"The Pool"** conveys "the primordial, undifferentiated quality of creativity,"[36] this poem, like many others, deals with a struggle with authorship and identity and exposes the writer's desire to "touch" the reader, even to get in touch with a reader through language rather than physical contact. Referring to both sexuality and her identity as a writer, H. D.'s poem addresses not only a pool of water but also a pool or well-spring of creativity. Thus, in writing **"The Pool,"** she conjures the (im)possibility of the written word to touch, perhaps even to penetrate the depths of this pool of literary creativity, causing it to "quiver like a sea-fish." The pool, however, is both reflective and bottomless, both real and imaginary. As Hollenberg remarks: "In very few lines **'The Pool'** deftly calls on our sense of touch to convey the elemental quality of water (and the unconscious) together with its impenetrable mystery" (75). The depths of this pool are always already untouchable, and her touch, therefore, can only touch its most "sensitive point"—its outside limit, its edge, its skin.

H. D. takes this idea of touching the untouchable in a different direction in **"Amaranth"** (*CP* 310-15). This poem is reputedly, with **"Eros"** and **"Envy,"** one of a triad of poems narrating the breakdown of her relationship with Richard Aldington. The three poems seem to mark a shift towards a more "tactile" writing in H. D.'s oeuvre, so that she is not only *describing* "touch" as in **"The Pool"** but she is, moreover, *performing* it. **"Amaranth"** voices the move away from an "indifferent" Greek dramatic mask towards a more personal and feeling writing voice.[37] Reportedly referring to H. D.'s reluctance to touch or be touched by her husband following the stillbirth of her first child and the doctor's severe warnings regarding a repeated wartime pregnancy, the narrator's cry to her lover in **"Amaranth"** is that she was not frigid to his touch: "I tell you this: / I was not asleep" (*CP* 311). She insists,

> I was not dull and dead when I fell
> back on our couch at night.
> I was not indifferent though I turned
> and lay quiet.
> I was not dead in my sleep.
>
> (312)

She is, rather, utterly feeling—sensing "flesh . . . scorched and rent, / shattered, cut apart, / and slashed open' (311). These words capture a physicality of experience; although she lies quiet, she finds

> my heels press my own wet life
> black, dark to purple
> on the smooth rose-streaked
> threshold of her pavement.
>
> (311)

This writing begins to demonstrate what I refer to as tactile poetics. Her words seem to have a material

power—they have a physicality of their own, they make us "feel"—from a distance. By this, I do not only mean that her writing is emotionally affective, nor do I solely refer to the fact that this writing "touches" on the body and draws the female bodily experience to the forefront of the poem. Rather, I argue that H. D.'s writing has the capacity to generate a tactile experience in the reader through the rhythm and the resonance of the poem. I "feel" the words on the inside of my body, under my skin. This follows Nancy's insistence:

> (I won't bother arguing that I'm not praising some dubious "touching literature." I know the difference between writing and flowery prose, but I *know of no writing that doesn't touch.* Because then it wouldn't be writing, just reporting or summarizing. Writing in its essence touches upon the body.)[38]

For Nancy, "touching upon the body, touching the body, *touching*—happens in writing all the time" (11). H. D.'s writing, it seems to me, draws this tactility to the surface; her works are invested, inhabited, even haunted by a feeling that touches the limits of felt experience. H. D.'s **"Amaranth"** is an example. Within this poem I feel the "quiet / where the fir-trees / press" (*CP* 15) and the light swaying of the poem's own rhythmic architecture. The combination of text and space, of word and breath, of press and sway, fill me like music. It is this musical quality that touches me, that makes me feel.

In *Rootprints,* Cixous argues that "the texts that touch me the most strongly, to the point of making me shiver or laugh, are those that have not repressed their musical structure" (64). She clarifies:

> I am not talking here simply of phonic signification, nor of alliterations, but indeed of the architecture, of the contraction and the relaxation, the variations of breath; or else of what overwhelms me with emotion in the text of Beethoven, that is to say the stops, the very forceful stops in the course of a symphony.
>
> (64)

In drawing attention to the breath of writing—its contraction, relaxation and emotion, Cixous alludes to what Julia Kristeva refers to as the "semiotic" in writing. Language, for Kristeva, operates in two ways within the signifying process: one, as an ordered expression of meaning (the symbolic), as in scientific discourse; and two, as a discharge of the subject's preverbal energy and drives (the semiotic).[39] The semiotic, which Kristeva later describes as introducing "wandering or fuzziness into language,"[40] is the heterogeneous modality that engages extra-verbal bodily energy and affect, allowing feelings and unconscious energy a place in the signifying process.

It is present in the babble, rhythm and echolalias of infants, and also through the rhythms and glossolalias evident in psychotic discourse. At the limit or skin of language, the semiotic "produces not only 'musical' but also nonsense effects," thus challenging "accepted beliefs and significations" (133). By paying attention to the semiotic in writing—by getting "in touch" with the body's pre-verbal drives, pulsions and natural rhythms—the writer is more able to make contact with the limits of felt experience and thus touch (without touching) the reader. The semiotic, consequently, is a vehicle for tactile poetics.

It is evident that in her transition from "H. D. Imagiste," as Ezra Pound named her in 1912,[41] to the H. D. writing late poems such as **"Sagesse"** in 1957, H. D. increasingly opened up her own writing process to the semiotic modality.[42] Interestingly, in this late poem, H. D. returns to the image of the pool, making it a significant point of comparison. Whereas the "crystalline" form of her earlier imagist writing did not fulfil her principles—"I have never been completely satisfied with any of my books, published or unpublished," she recalls of her pre-Freud work[43]—her later approach enabled her "a deeper, more probing daemonic drive."[44] Thus, we move away from the tight and precise structure of the first "pool," and in **"Sagesse,"** we find another—one that asks questions of itself, one that touches on its own existence, one that "quivers" once again with its own semiotic resonance as it threatens to flood its boundaries:

> Or is it a great tide that covers the rock-pool
> so that it and the rock are indistinguishable
>
> from the sea-shelf and are part of the sea-floor
> though the sea-anemone may quiver
> apprehensively
>
> and the dried weed uncurl painfully
> and the salt-sediment rebel, "I was salt,
>
> a substance, concentrated, self-contained,
> am I to be dissolved and lost?"
>
> ("Sagesse" 67)

Quite literally allowing the intertextual skin of her first "pool" to get under the skin of this pool, she refers to the "quiver" resulting from her first touch: "I touch you" (*CP* 56), but this time, her palimpsestic touch is permeated with its own *différance*. It is by inviting extra-verbal bodily energy and affect into her later writing that she allows the semiotic to enter her own signifying process, generating a poetic that, as Cixous might say, touches "the body of the instant with the tips of the words."[45] This time, H. D. does not say "I touch you"; rather, her writing performs this untouchable touch for her.

"Sagesse," from "Sageness, profound wisdom" (*OED*), was written just a few years before H. D.'s death, and subtly demonstrates a Kristevan dialectic between the semiotic and the symbolic in order to offer a new, tactile poetic. The voice in the poem alternates between that of an adult and that of a child in wartime, playing, as Pearson describes, "back and forth between the scenes of the child and her family in London, and the scenes in the sanitarium [*sic*] at Küsnacht" (viii), where H. D. spent the last years of her life. For Hollenberg, this adult-child dialectic

> dramatizes the restorative effect of the preoedipal mother upon the imagination of the poet-daughter by showing how the inner colloquy of the poet reproduces the empathy between mother and child that is broken by an awareness of the father and the male order of language.
>
> (216-17)

In other words, the poem dramatises a dialogue between the semiotic (what Hollenberg calls the "preoedipal mother") and the symbolic ("awareness of the father and the male order of language"). Consisting of twenty-six parts, the poem begins as the first narrator opens a copy of *The Listener* on 9 June and sees "'a white-faced Scops owl from Sierra Leone, / West Africa'" (**"Sagesse"** 58). This image takes the narrator both forward in time to her "imprisonment," like the owl, in the sanatorium following a broken hip, and backwards, to wartime London during her childhood. Allowing these childhood associations to rise up through her poetry, the narrator now sees the owl as "'comical, his baggy trousers / and spindly legs— you've still got half a bun'" (60). The child's father, insisting that the owl "'won't eat buns . . . but mice and such,'" compares him to "Guy" (Fawkes):

> the child remembers something, draws away,
> she thinks, "I never saw a farthing,
>
> it's half a ha'pence, but she said, teacher or
> somebody,
> or Mr. Spence, that there were two, not owls,
>
> some other birds, sold for a farthing—and
> what else?"
>
> (60)

In giving voice to the child's perspective, these associations unsettle the idea of a single, fixed meaning of the owl in captivity—and, furthermore, a "God" that would allow such imprisonment. Thus, in describing a vulnerable child who "may shudder" at the image of the caged owl, H. D. uses the revolutionary potential of the poetic to unsettle our idea of how language works to produce meaning.

The child's voice, it appears initially, enables H. D. to engage with the semiotic and invests her writing with a pre-verbal bodily energy that enlivens the poem.

Indeed, as the poem progresses, the semiotic—with its rhythms and associations—increasingly resonates through the child's narrative:

> "yes, they're pretty, mum,
> the deers"—does it mean animals? does
> He run, too,
>
> on little hooves like that one, does He jump
> and stand (now) like the biggest one with
> horns,
>
> straight up against the wire?
>
> (62)

In response to the unsettling idea of the owl for the child, and the power of a God to allow its captivity, the "adult" narrator appeals to a multitude of angels. "Tara," *"Dieu fontaine de sagesse,"* and "Ptébiou" are, as Hollenberg explains, "guardians and protectors who exist outside of the conventional Judeo-Christian script for men and women" (217). Thus, in appealing to figures from the occult, H. D. begins also to disturb the symbolic order of the adult voice in the poem—an accepted world of Christian mythology, where *Noli me tangere* still prevails. Allowing the symbolic to touch on or rub up against the semiotic, H. D. hands over the touching dialectic to the reader.

The revolutionary semiotic present within the adult voice strengthens as the poem develops:

> and Sister Annie brings my coffee,
> and I say, "how are you?" and she says, "gut—
> gut";
>
> Goot and Goed, Scotch and Belgium, my book
> says,
> Goot, gut and good and surely God, and so we
> play
>
> this game of affirmations and of angels' names,
> this Sunday, one week after Whitsun.
>
> (63)

This wordplay continues—"'gut—gut,' I'll say and Goot will surely answer; / God who receives sinners? What are we? / and Goed is 'gut,' actually some say 'goed' here" (63)—until we find ourselves with "Goth, Gott, *Germain*" (64). Germain—modelled on the young German psychiatrist Dr Erich Heydt, who often visited H. D. at the clinic—enters the poem through free-associative wordplay. Ironically, therefore, the male doctor—a figure of authority and order—is made present through H. D.'s use of the maternal semiotic. This wordplay leads to an almost manic repetition of the guttural "g" sound—"God" (59), "glare" (68), "ghostly" (59), "gladness" (59), "go" (60), "Guy" (60), "great" (67), *"Grande Mer"* (73) "Gawd" (77), to

name a few. We might consider the "g" as a glottal sound—"an expulsion of air animated by the sphincters at the rear of the throat . . . echoing a coughing movement of expectoration," as Leslie Hill explains in relation to Samuel Beckett's use of the letter "g."[46] G—God, Grandmother (which H. D. then was)—also leads us to gram, to glyph, graphic, gone. The glottal sound, furthermore, makes reading the poem a very physical experience, with the most untouchable word—"God"—in our throats as we utter the name. The letter G, moreover, is contrasted with the sibalance of the "s" in **"Sagesse"**: "Sotis, Sothis, Sith" (70). Indeed, the first eight lines of Part 19 are, in particular, littered with the "s" sound: "strand"; "72"; "seventh"; "Senciner"; "Seket"; "started"; "compassed"; "closed"; "circle" (76). On one level, the soft "s" and the guttural "g" sounds truly make this a tactile poem to read. On another level, as Hollenberg notes, the "chain of word origins and word-sound associations afford[s] H. D. a liberating departure from the male symbolic order" (219). Troubling the symbolic order, **"Sagesse"** demonstrates a *jouissance* associated with the semiotic modality. H. D.'s poetry is, in a Kristevan sense, revolutionary—and her use of the letters "s" and "g" make it a particularly "tactile" piece of writing. The poem unsettles the symbolic order, demonstrating the revolutionary power of poetry—its power not only to "touch" us but to "move" us in new directions too. Ending with a most touching laughter—a laughter as remains[47]—"laugh the world away, / laugh, laugh" (84)—**"Sagesse,"** as Hollenberg suggests, recovers "what Kristeva calls 'the riant well-springs of the imaginary' or 'riant spaciousness,' a joy without words that she will reinvest in the production of the new" (222-23). This laughter invites us to return to the semiotic origins in order to reinvest in the production of the new, to open ourselves to the future, to the "something to come [*il y a de l'avenir*]."[48]

It is by opening up to "something to come" that I attempt to end this paper on touch—by touching touch. Trying to touch touch, we come face to face—or hand to hand—with its unique reflexivity:

> Touch is the only one of the five external senses which possesses a reflexive structure: the child who touches the parts of its body with its finger is testing out the two complementary sensations, of being a piece of skin that touches at the same time as being a piece of skin that is touched.[49]

Thinking through the unique reflexivity of the sense of touch—our ability to touch and be touched simultaneously, Derrida seizes the way in which the verb to touch in the French language is itself reflexive—*se toucher,* to be touched, to touch itself, to self-touch—even, to self-touch you. Describing it as a "strange tautology," Derrida notes the "grammatical reflexivity" of "self-touching" in the figure of the kiss, which he allows "to oscillate from one to the other (touching *oneself* or touching *each other*?)" (*On Touching* 274, 270). Indeed, *se toucher,* the self-touch, for Derrida, is the very condition of sense, and "*to be* means *to touch* and *to touch touch*" (275). Thus, if words are symbolic touch experiences, how do I "touch on" this? How do I *touch touch*? Is it, finally, ever possible to make contact?

Rather than closing down my discussion of touch, the untouchable in touch, instead, opens up to something new, something to come. As Stokes explains in his review of Derrida's text, "a philosophy which acknowledges its own lack of mastery, its own inability to touch, opens itself up to the *other*" (372). This is precisely what this essay attempts to do. Opening itself up to the other, this paper invites you to touch its skin. It asks its readers to make contact, to seize the tactile poetics in literature, and to write "closeup," from afar.

Notes

My thanks to reviewer Sarah Wood for her helpful comments on this article.

1. H. D., *Tribute* 98

2. According to H. D., the first thing Freud says to her is "You are the only person who has ever come into this room and looked at the things in the room before looking at me" (ibid.).

3. Freud, *Studies on Hysteria* II: 49; hereafter parenthesised as *SE*.

4. For a history of Freud's use of touch, see Smith; and Beckenridge. For touch in psychotherapy more generally, see Older.

5. During later hypnosis, Freud discovered that her strange demands "related to the fact that the animal shapes which appeared to her when she was in a bad state started moving and began to attack her if anyone made a movement in her presence" (*SE* II: 56). The "final injunction 'Don't touch me!'," Freud explained, derived from an experience when her brother, unwell from too much morphine, would "seize hold of her" (56).

6. Jones 448.

7. Anzieu, *The Skin Ego* 139.

8. Derrida, *On Touching* 66.

9. John 20.17.

10. Nancy, *Noli Me Tangere* 12. Reflecting on the many ways that *"Noli me tangere"* has been interpreted in the arts and medicine, Nancy insists, "Few phrases from the Gospels have been so

widely disseminated" (109). For further readings of Christ's prohibition on touch, see Baross; Derrida, *On Touching*; and Manning.

11. Matt. 8.3 cited in Derrida, *On Touching* 100.

12. Friedman, *Analyzing Freud: Letters of H. D.* 100; hereafter parenthesised as *Letters*. Following Friedman, I present these letters without correction to spelling or grammar.

13. H. D., *Tribute* 98.

14. Nancy, *Corpus* 93.

15. Montagu 28-29.

16. The dog collar refers to Bryher's desire for acceptance into the psychoanalytic fold.

17. Perdita Macpherson Schaffner (born Frances Perdita Aldington), H. D.'s daughter to Cecil Gray, was adopted by Bryher and Macpherson.

18. See *Letters* 192-93.

19. Referring to Perdita's adoption.

20. See *Letters* 52.

21. Cixous, "Love of the Wolf" 124.

22. Connor 259.

23. Stokes 370.

24. Maclachlan 58.

25. Nancy, *Corpus* 57.

26. Maclachlan 58.

27. Nancy, *Corpus* 51.

28. Baross 150.

29. Cixous, "Writing Blind" 188.

30. Cixous with Calle-Gruber 49.

31. "Closeup" refers to cinema's first art journal, edited by Macpherson (and greatly aided by H. D.).

32. Montagu 102.

33. Anzieu, *A Skin for Thought* 78-79.

34. Cixous, *Three Steps* 36.

35. H. D., "The Pool" in *Collected Poems* 56; hereafter parenthesised as *CP*.

36. Hollenberg 75.

37. See Martz's account of H. D.'s shift away from Imagist principles and Greek mythology (xix).

38. Nancy, *Corpus* II.

39. See Kristeva's *Revolution in Poetic Language* 34.

40. Kristeva, *Desire in Language* 136.
41. See Pound.
42. H. D., "Sagesse" in *Hermetic Definition.*
43. H. D., *Tribute* 148.
44. Pearson v.
45. Cixous, "Writing Blind" 195.
46. Hill cited in Katz 31.
47. "It remains perhaps to think of laughter, as, precisely, a remains. What does laughter want to say? What does laughter want? [*Qu'est-ce que ça veut dire, le rire? Qu'est-ce que ça veut reire?*]" (Derrida, "Ulysses Gramophone" cited in Royle 64).
48. Derrida and Ferraris 13.
49. Anzieu, *The Skin Ego* 61-62.

Bibliography

Anzieu, Didier. *The Skin Ego.* Trans. Chris Turner. New Haven and London: Yale UP, 1989.

Anzieu, Didier. *A Skin for Thought—Interviews with Gilbert Tarrab on Psychology and Psychoanalysis.* Trans. Daphne Nash Briggs. London and New York: Karnac, 1990.

Baross, Zsuzsa. "Noli Me Tangere: For Jacques Derrida." *Angelaki* 6.2 (2001): 149-64.

Beckenridge, Kati. "Physical Touch in Psychoanalysis: A Closet Phenomenon?" *Psychoanalytic Inquiry* 20.1 (2000): 2-20.

Cixous, Hélène. "Love of the Wolf." Trans. Keith Cohen. *Stigmata: Escaping Texts.* London and New York: Routledge, 2005. 110-30.

Cixous, Hélène. *Three Steps on the Ladder of Writing.* Trans. Sarah Cornell and Susan Sellers. New York: Columbia UP, 1993.

Cixous, Hélène. "Writing Blind: Conversation with the Donkey." Trans. Eric Prenowitz. *Stigmata: Escaping Texts.* London and New York: Routledge, 2005. 184-203.

Cixous, Hélène with Mireille Calle-Gruber. *Hélène Cixous—Rootprints: Memory and Life Writing.* Trans. Eric Prenowitz. London: Routledge, 1997.

Connor, Steven. *The Book of Skin.* London: Reaktion, 2004.

Derrida, Jacques. *On Touching—Jean-Luc Nancy.* Trans. Christine Irizarry. Stanford: Stanford UP, 2005.

Derrida, Jacques. "Ulysses Gramophone: Hear Say Yes in Joyce." Trans. Tina Kendall and Shari Benstock. *Acts of Literature.* Ed. Derek Attridge. London and New York: Routledge, 1992. 256-309.

Derrida, Jacques and Maurizio Ferraris. *A Taste for the Secret.* Trans. Giacomo Donis. Malden, MA: Polity, 2001.

Freud, Sigmund. *Totem and Taboo and Other Works.* 1913. *The Standard Edition of the Complete Psychological Works of Sigmund Freud.* Vol. XIII. Ed. James Strachey. Trans. James Strachey with Anna Freud, Alix Strachey and Alan Tyson. London: Vintage, 2001.

Freud, Sigmund and Josef Breuer. "Case Histories." 1895. *Studies on Hysteria. The Standard Edition of the Complete Psychological Works of Sigmund Freud.* Vol. II. Ed. James Strachey. Trans. James Strachey with Anna Freud, Alix Strachey and Alan Tyson. London: Vintage, 2001. 19-181.

Friedman, Susan Stanford (ed.). *Analyzing Freud: Letters of H. D., Bryher, and their Circle.* New York: New Directions, 2002.

H. D. *Collected Poems 1912-1944.* Ed. Louis L. Martz. New York: New Directions, 1983.

H. D. *Hermetic Definition.* Oxford: Carcanet, 1972.

H. D. *Tribute to Freud: Writing on the Wall & Advent.* Manchester: Carcanet, 1985.

Hill, Leslie. *Beckett's Fiction: In Different Words.* Cambridge: Cambridge UP, 1990.

Hollenberg, Donna Krolik. *H. D.: The Poetics of Childbirth and Creativity.* Boston: Northeastern UP, 1991.

Jones, Ernest. *The Life and Work of Sigmund Freud. Volume 2. Years of Maturity, 1901-1919.* London: Hogarth, 1955.

Katz, Daniel. *Saying I No More: Subjectivity and Consciousness in the Prose of Samuel Beckett.* Evanston, IL: Northwestern UP, 1999.

Kristeva, Julia. *Desire in Language: A Semiotic Approach to Literature and Art.* Ed. Leon S. Roudiez. Trans. Thomas Gora, Alice Jardine and Leon S. Roudiez. Oxford: Blackwell, 1980.

Kristeva, Julia. *Revolution in Poetic Language: The Portable Kristeva.* Ed. Kelly Oliver. New York: Columbia UP, 2002.

Maclachlan, Ian. "Long Distance Love: On Remote Sensing in Shakespeare's Sonnet 109." *Sensual Reading: New Approaches to Reading in its Relations to the Senses.* Ed. Michael Syrontinski and Ian Maclachlan. Lewisburg: Bucknell UP, 2001. 57-66.

Manning, Erin. *Politics of Touch: Sense, Movement, Sovereignty.* Minneapolis and London: U of Minnesota P, 2007.

Martz, Louis L. "Introduction." *Collected Poems 1912-1944* by H. D. New York: New Directions, 1983. xi-xxxvi.

Montagu, Ashley. *Touching: The Human Significance of the Skin.* 2nd ed. New York: Harper, 1978.

Nancy, Jean-Luc. *Corpus.* Trans. Richard A. Rand. New York: Fordham UP, 2008.

Nancy, Jean-Luc. *Noli Me Tangere: On the Raising of the Body.* Trans. Sarah Clift, Pascale-Anne Brault and Michael Naas. New York: Fordham UP, 2008.

Older, Jules. *Touching is Healing.* New York: Stein, 1982.

Pearson, Norman Holmes. "Foreword." *Hermetic Definition by H. D.* Oxford: Carcanet, 1972. v-viii.

Pound, Ezra. "A Retrospect." *Literary Essays of Ezra Pound.* London: Faber, 1954. 3-14.

Royle, Nicholas. *After Derrida.* Manchester: Manchester UP, 1995.

Smith, Edward W. L. "Traditions of Touch in Psychotherapy." *Touch in Psychotherapy: Theory, Research and Practice.* Ed. Edward W. L. Smith, Pauline Rose Clance and Suzanne Imes. New York and London: Guilford, 1998. 3-15.

Stokes, Christopher. "Review of Jacques Derrida's *On Touching—Jean-Luc Nancy.*" *Textual Practice* 20.2 (2006): 370-73.

FURTHER READING

Criticism

Anderson, Elizabeth. "Dancing Modernism: Ritual, Ecstasy and the Female Body." *Literature and Theology* 22, no. 3 (September 2008): 354-67.

Examines the way H. D. used the motif of dance to explore issues of gender and embodiment in her modernist poetry.

Bruzelius, Margaret. "H. D. and Eurydice." *Twentieth-Century Literature* 44, no 4 (winter 1998): 447-63.

Studies H. D.'s examination of female identity and patriarchal culture in the poem "Eurydice."

Goodspeed-Chadwick, Julie. "Mary-ing Isis and Mary Magdalene in 'The Flowering of the Rod': Revisioning and Healing Through Female-Centered Spirituality." *Florida Atlantic Cooperative Studies* 10 (2007-2008): 29-54.

Demonstrates that H. D. employed a number of poetic strategies, including metonymy, synecdoche, and metaphors concerned with the body in order to validate a feminist perspective and to promote a sense of spiritual healing.

Graham, Sarah H. S. "'We Have a Secret. We Are Alive': H. D.'s 'Trilogy' as a Response to War." *Texas Studies in Literature and Language* 44, no. 2 (summer 2002): 161-210.

Investigates H. D.'s depiction of war, society, and culture in the poems collected in H. D.'s *Trilogy,* focusing in particular on the Christian elements in the poem and on H. D.'s notions of morality and mortality.

Hokanson, Robert O'Brien. "'Is It All a Story?': Questioning Revision in H. D.'s *Helen in Egypt.*" *American Literature* 64, no. 2 (June 1992): 331-46.

Focuses on the self-reflexive nature of H. D.'s *Helen in Egypt* and explores Helen's struggle in the poem to contextualize her experience and to re-establish her identity.

William Ernest Henley
1849-1903

English poet, critic, essayist, editor, and playwright.

INTRODUCTION

A well-known poet and editor during his lifetime, Henley's contributions to the contemporary discourse on literature and aesthetics influenced a number of other writers struggling to break free of the conventions of the Victorian Age. His most famous poem, "Invictus" (1875), is perhaps the only one of his works remembered today. Much of his writing has been criticized for its nationalist fervor and his support of British imperialism.

BIOGRAPHICAL INFORMATION

The eldest of six children, Henley was born August 23, 1849, in Gloucester, England. His father was a bookseller whose death in 1868 left his widow, Emma Morgan Henley, in a very distressed financial state with six young children to support. Henley attended the Crypt Grammar School for six years beginning in 1861, where he was influenced and encouraged by the headmaster, poet T. E. Brown. As a child, Henley suffered a tubercular disease of the bone, causing him to lose his left leg just below the knee. He recuperated in St. Bartholomew's Hospital in London for ten months, after which he tried his hand at freelance writing. However, his health problems continued and, faced with the possible amputation of the other leg, Henley sought treatment from surgeon Joseph Lister, whose methods were painful but effective. It was Henley's recovery from August of 1873 until April 1875 in the Royal Infirmary in Edinburgh that inspired *In Hospital* (1908). His lengthy convalescence had other lasting effects on Henley's life as well; it was in the infirmary that he met Anna Boyle, the sister of his roommate, whom he married in 1878. It was also during this time that he met Robert Louis Stevenson, with whom he would later collaborate on several dramas, none of them very successful. (Stevenson confessed that he used Henley as the model for the Long-John-Silver character in *Treasure Island*.) Among Henley's other well-known friends were J. M. Barrie, H. G. Wells, and the painter James McNeill Whistler.

Henley worked as a writer and editor for the next several years, but was barely able to survive on his earnings. In 1888, the Henleys had a daughter, Margaret, who died of cerebral meningitis at the age of six, the same year Henley lost his good friend Stevenson. After spending several months in Paris, the grief-stricken Henley returned to London. Over the course of his career, he edited six journals, including *The Scots Observer* (renamed *The National Observer*) and *The New Review*. Henley was in poor health and constant pain all his life, causing him to value courage, endurance, and the determination to overcome adversity—values that were central to his poetry. A fall in his final years exacerbated his already precarious condition. He died in Woking, England, on June 11, 1903; his memorial service was attended by a number of important literary figures, including Thomas Hardy, H. G. Wells, and George Saintsbury.

MAJOR WORKS

Henley's first book of poetry was the 1888 volume, *A Book of Verses,* divided into three sections: "In Hospital: Rhymes and Rhythms," "Life and Death (Echoes)," and "Bric-a-Brac (ballades, rondels, sonnets and quatorzains, rondeaus)." The first section is comprised of the poetry he wrote during his stay in the Royal Infirmary, while the middle section contains Henley's best-known individual poem "Invictus," whose theme involves overcoming adversity, inspired no doubt by his own struggle with the physical limitations he suffered as well as the intensely painful treatments he endured.

In 1892, Henley published *The Song of the Sword and Other Verses,* and many of the volume's poems made evident his enthusiastic support of British imperialism; the title poem was dedicated to Rudyard Kipling. The collection also includes "To James McNeill Whistler," a poem that was more successful with readers than "The Song of the Sword." A year later, Henley published *London Voluntaries and Other Verses,* which includes a revised version of *The Song of the Sword and Other Verses.* Henley again treated urban themes in 1898 with the appearance of *London Types* with drawings by William Nicholson. That same year, he published *Poems,* comprised of previously published pieces. In 1899, *Hawthorn and Lavender* was published in pamphlet form and was reissued in 1901 as *Hawthorn and Lavender, with Other Verses*. More patriotic enthusiasm characterizes the poems of the 1900 volume, *For England's Sake: Verses and Songs in Time of War*. Henley's last book of poetry was *A Song of Speed*, consisting of one long poem inspired by a ride in an automobile; it was published in 1903.

Henley's essays are contained in *Views and Reviews: Essays in Appreciation*, Volumes 1 and 2, published in 1890 and 1902 respectively. He also wrote four plays with Robert Louis Stevenson: *Deacon Brodie* (1882); *Beau Austin* (1890); *Admiral Guinea* (1897); and *Macaire* (1900). The plays were no more successful than his individual attempt at playwriting, *Mephisto* (1887).

CRITICAL RECEPTION

Although Henley was highly regarded by his peers, his work is rarely studied today. Kennedy Williamson (see Further Reading) contends that only a few of his poems are likely to endure, particularly "Invictus" and "Margaritae Sororis." William D. Schaefer (see Further Reading), however, reports that while "Invictus" is closely identified with Henley today, contemporary scholars would have considered *London Voluntaries* his most important work. Schaefer believes that Francis Thompson's 1890 poem, "The Hound of Heaven," provided the primary inspiration—conscious or otherwise—for *London Voluntaries*, and the critic cites numerous parallels between the two works. Edward H. Cohen discusses the contemporary response to the poems of *In Hospital*, reporting that in its gritty realism, the volume "challenges Victorian canons of taste." Cohen contends that the work is "an exemplary instance of realism, of imagination answerable to reality, of the connection of life and art." One of the primary reasons for Henley's critical neglect in recent years has been his attitude towards women and his support for imperialist aggression. R. van Bronswijk notes that for Henley "women serve as a vehicle for easing men's sexual passions and blood thirst" and their role is to "aid men in both their sexual and their physical struggle for survival." Meanwhile, the "loudly proclaimed jingoism and unapologetic primal screams" of "The Song of the Sword" have also seriously damaged Henley's literary reputation.

The limitations of Henley's physical condition and his constant struggle to overcome those limitations had a profound effect on his poetry. Williamson explains that "sometimes the battle-spirit in his blood caused him to shout too shrilly and with an extravagant defiance." Hamilton Buckley discusses the autobiographical

nature of the poems of Henley's *In Hospital*, noting that those verses were "polished and repolished over a period of thirteen years" and "reveal, ceaselessly at work, a dialectic of denial and assent." According to Buckley "the most complete lyrical statement of his self-assertive philosophy" is contained in "Echoes of Life and Death," the final poem of *In Hospital*. Critics typically mention Henley's preoccupation with courage and determination against all odds as the result of his battle to survive. However, another result was his zest for life and his appreciation of the natural world. Joseph M. Flora considers Henley's greatest achievement as a poet his ability "to recall, to recreate, the childhood capacity for wonder." He gave his readers "the pleasure of naïve wonder, of looking, of amazement," contends Flora.

PRINCIPAL WORKS

Poetry

A Book of Verses 1888

The Song of the Sword and Other Verses 1892

Arabian Nights' Entertainments 1893

London Voluntaries and Other Verses 1893

London Types 1898

Poems 1898

Hawthorn and Lavender 1899

For England's Sake: Verses and Songs in Time of War 1900

A Song of Speed 1903

In Hospital 1908

The Works of W. E. Henley. 7 vols. (poetry, essays, dramas, and criticism) 1908

Other Major Works

Deacon Brodie: The Double Life [with Robert Louis Stevenson] (play) 1882

Mephisto (play) 1887

Beau Austin [with Robert Louis Stevenson] (play) 1890

Views and Reviews: Essays in Appreciation. Vol. 1 (criticism) 1890

Admiral Guinea [with Robert Louis Stevenson] (play) 1897

Macaire [with Robert Louis Stevenson] (play) 1900

Views and Reviews: Essays in Appreciation. Vol. 2 (criticism) 1902

CRITICISM

Jerome Hamilton Buckley (essay date 1945)

SOURCE: Buckley, Jerome Hamilton. "Derivations." In *William Earnest Henley: A Study in the "Counter-Decadence" of the 'Nineties,* pp. 29-67. Princeton, N. J.: Princeton University Press, 1945.

[*In the following excerpt, taken from his book length study of Henley, Buckley offers some biographical details and examines the poetry of* In Hospital *and "In-victus," Henley's best-known poem.*]

> The sower must take his seedsheet and go afield into ground prepared for his ministrations; or there can be no harvest. The Poet springs from a compost of ideals and experiences and achievements, whose essences he absorbs and assimilates, and in whose absence he could not be the Poet.
>
> —Henley

CASE HISTORY. GLOUCESTER: 1849-1873

For the bookshop of William Henley in Gloucester, 1849 was an epic year. As on a seismograph, the fluctuations in local taste recorded themselves upon his ledgers. In February a fourth edition of *Modern Painters* sold well, despite its anonymity. And several weeks later it was joined by *The Seven Lamps of Architecture,* which disclosed the authorship of John Ruskin. By March Mrs. Trollope's sensational new novel, *The Lottery of Marriage,* had joined the best-seller lists. Then the *pièce de résistance* of the spring season—and probably indeed of the whole generation—the first number of *David Copperfield,* was announced for May Day. Safely launched, the Dickens serial rolled triumphantly down the months, growing in bulk and power and public estimation, until at its maturity it moved beyond time to the place of things perennial. Yet, whatever its taste for fiction, Gloucester was not deaf to the moral muse; Martin Tupper's *Proverbial Philosophy,* now almost a classic, had lost nothing of its appeal by July when a handsome reprint of the author's *Crock of Gold* arrived from London. Still, momentous or profitable as these works might prove to the bookseller, they were as nothing in comparison with the August arrival. For on the twenty-third of that month, Mrs. Henley was delivered of a first-born son. And William Ernest—as the child was christened—promptly became the bookshop's proudest acquisition. After his advent, the appearance in October of Currer Bell's *Shirley,* elsewhere so widely acclaimed, could not here but seem anticlimactic.

William Henley claimed no kinship with the Earls Henley of Northington nor with the fluent orator of Pope's second *Dunciad.* That he came of "ancient yeoman stock" was pedigree enough[1]; his sense of humor was too lively to attach much importance to the involutions of genealogy. Yet he could condone the vanity of his wife, Emma Morgan, who was inordinately proud of her descent from Joseph Warton, and who was sufficiently literate to appreciate the glory to which she by that descent was heir. Of her five sons, she saw fit to bless one with the poet-critic's name. If Anthony Warton, who made of himself a landscape painter, never achieved the eminence for which he was predestined, the salient fact yet remains that he had within him the creative impulse; and years later when "Bob" Stevenson met him in Paris, he was happily sharing in the struggles of artists more successful than himself[2]; his career was not a complete failure. The other children entered upon life without Anthony's singular advantage. One of them, surely the least gifted of the five, disappeared, nameless, into the turmoil of a busy age. Another, Nigel by name, conjoining a deep understanding of design and a patience with detail, rose to "the top of his chosen profession" as keeper of prints in the British Museum.[3] The youngest and most romantic of the boys was Edward John, born in 1861. Like Christian Buddenbrook, "Teddy" displayed from childhood an unholy faculty for mimicking his betters. Eventually he strutted his talents across a far-flung stage; he lived to see his name in bright letters on posters and marquees in London and New York, in Montreal and San Francisco.[4] Emma thus had five strong sons, each in his own way remarkable, yet each able to live in amity with his brothers. Surely her pride of lineage was not without foundation.

Throughout the 'fifties and 'sixties, William Henley pursued a precarious livelihood. The Victorians had lost nothing of their strenuous reading habits; they had gone so far as to relax their concept of Sabbatarianism in order to accommodate the Sunday perusal of lighter literature. But they were now finding new ways to circumvent book purchase. Mudie's Select Library had already begun to encroach upon the provincial bookseller's territory. Such competition intensified the difficulty of sustaining a growing family and left the elder Henley preoccupied with the problems of domestic finance. In the mid 'seventies he died penniless; and of his death, his poet-son had nothing to say. But the mother's passing in the late 'eighties was another matter. William Ernest arose from his watch by the death-bed to write the most impassioned of his elegies:

> Dearest, live on
> In such an immortality
> As we thy sons,
> Born of thy body and nursed
> At those wild, faithful breasts,
> Can give—of generous thoughts,

And honourable words, and deeds
That make men half in love with fate! . . .

Between the river and the stars,
O royal and radiant soul,
Thou dost return, thine influences return
Upon thy children as in life, and death
Turns stingless! What is Death
But Life in act? How should the Unteeming Grave
Be victor over thee,
Mother, a mother of men?

That such eloquence was something more than poetic intoxication, Edward John, three thousand miles from home, bore witness; by the news of his mother's death, the actor was "affected . . . almost to delirium."[5] In her artist-children, "half in love with fate," Emma Henley had engendered a lasting devotion; to the end she remained a symbol and an inspiration.[6]

Whatever may have been his father's shifting fortunes, William Ernest Henley read his boyhood quietly away in a Gloucester bookshop. Years later as self-appointed dictator of taste, he would revert again and again to the books that had been his first friends. It may be that his physical affliction, long before its true nature became apparent, had removed him from the society of boys his own age. In any case, the child turned at the outset from life to literature; and the romance that he imbibed from books, he brought to bear upon his actual experience. Once when he had attended a reading by Dickens in a crowded assembly hall, he had so fastened his eyes upon the lecturer's hand that he carried with him forever the image of a long white finger and a large flashing jewel.[7] Dickens the man became to him one with Dickens's own creations, one with Pickwick and Mrs. Gamp, one with Chuzzlewit and Sidney Carton; he remained "always an incarnation of generous and abounding gaiety, a type of beneficent earnestness, a great expression of intellectual vigour and emotional vivacity."[8] Woe it was to him who might prefer the viciously genteel Thackeray or that "Apotheosis of Pupil-Teachery" known as George Eliot.[9]

"I can," Henley wrote in his best-known essay, "certainly read my mother-tongue."[10] And, let who would dispute his taste, none could question his literacy. But from the beginning, he esteemed not less than native writers the great foreign romancers whom he first encountered in English translation. He valued beyond words "the friendship of the good Alonso Quijada" and the company of "old d'Artagnan."[11] If he missed the heroics of Homer, he found delight protean in the adventure of a thousand and one *Arabian Nights*. This, his Golden Book, he first knew in the rendition of Antoine Galland; a work of art, it seemed to him, beside which the later versions of Payne and Burton were as mere ethnological curiosities. Its double

columns of microscopic print strengthened rather than alienated his affection; they were an earnest of the more joy in store for him. The narrative of Zobeide, "alone in the accursed city whose monstrous silence is broken by the voice of the one man spared by the wrath of God as he repeats his solitary prayer," this ranked "with Crusoe's discovery of the footprint, in the thrilling moments of [his] life."[12] Galland's book was his passport to the enchanted kingdoms of "the magian East"; it was

> what is gallantest and best
> In all the full-shelved Libraries of Romance,—
> The Book of rocs,
> Sandalwood, ivory, turbans, ambergris,
> Cream-tarts, and lettered apes, and calendars,
> And ghouls, and genies—O, so huge
> They might have overed the tall Minster Tower
> Hands down, as schoolboys take a post!
> In truth, the Book of Camaralzaman,
> Schemselnihar and Sinbad, Scheherezade
> The peerless, Bedreddin, Badroulbadour,
> Cairo and Serendib and Candahar,
> And Caspian, and the dim terrific bulk—
> Ice-ribbed, fiend-visited, isled in spells and storms—
> Of Kaf! . . . That centre of miracles,
> The sole, unparalleled Arabian Nights!

This matter of Baghdad gave an extraordinary stimulus to his childish imagination. It brought wonderment and mystery to the sleepy grey city of his birth. It transformed Gloucester's prosaic cobbler, mending shoes at his shopdoor, into the wizened Leprechaun, cogitating the imponderables of scarlet destinies. One day the nine-year old strayed into the deserted showroom of a traveling Madame Tussaud's, where, "behind a fence of faded crimson cords," he chanced upon

> A Woman with her litter of Babes—all slain,
> All in their nightgowns all with Painted Eyes
> Staring—still staring.

From these wax images he fled in terror; but down the dark streets their insufferable Painted Eyes followed him. For weeks they leered at him 'round the minster archways. They pursued him even unto Candahar; they branded him pariah in "the Palace of the King." Some thirty-five years later he could evoke the episode with a psychological validity comparable to the opening chapter of *Great Expectations*. Even as England's most vigorous "realist," he had retained much of his capacity for romance. Yet the time came when actualities far more terrible than Painted Eyes were to reshape his whole philosophy.

Never particularly robust of physique, Henley succumbed in his twelfth year to a disease which might have been diagnosed as tubercular arthritis, but about which the surgeons of Gloucester had no real understanding. His body had grown out of all proportion to his withered limbs. An insidious enemy gnawed mercilessly at his hands and feet. The normal Victorian remedy for this complaint was amputation; and the usual result of amputation was gangrene and consequent death. But the Victorian child was expected to meet such eventualities with courage. In *The Crofton Boys,* which appeared in 1856,[13] Harriet Martineau had depicted the ideal reaction to a surgical operation, one of the few in which the victim was spared gangrenous infection. It is unlikely that the young Henley heeded the deaf sybil, whose precepts his father almost certainly must have purveyed. Yet it is not unprofitable to examine her narrative as a commentary, not wholly conscious,[14] on the barbarism of Victorian medical practice. Hugh Proctor, the hero of her fiction, has fractured his foot during a boarding-school squabble. His uncle comes with due solemnity to his bedside; and the model dialogue ensues:

> "Oh, dear! oh, dear! Uncle, do you think it a bad accident?"
>
> "Yes, my boy, a very bad accident."
>
> "Do you think I shall die? I never thought of that," said Hugh.
>
> "No; I do not think you will die."
>
> "Will they think so at home? Was that the reason they were sent to?"
>
> "No; I have no doubt your mother will come to nurse you, and to comfort you; but—"
>
> "To comfort me? Why, Mr. Tooke said the pain would soon be over, he thought, and I should be asleep tonight."
>
> "Yes; but though the pain may be over it may leave you lame. That will be a misfortune; and you will be glad of your mother to comfort you."
>
> "Lame!" said the boy. Then, as he looked wistfully in his uncle's face, he saw the truth.
>
> "Oh, uncle! they are going to cut off my leg."
>
> "Not your leg, I hope, Hugh. You will not be quite so lame as that; but I am afraid you must lose your foot."
>
> "Was that what Mr. Tooke meant by the surgeon's relieving me of my pain?"
>
> "Yes, it was."
>
> "Then it will be before night. Is it quite certain, uncle?"
>
> "Mr. Annanby thinks so. Your foot is too much hurt ever to be cured. Do you think you can bear it, Hugh?"
>
> "Why, yes, I suppose so. So many people have. It is less than some of the savages bear. What horrid things they do to their captives,—and even to some of their own boys! And they bear it."
>
> "Yes; but you are not a savage."

> "But one may be as brave, without being a savage. Think of the martyrs that were burnt! And they bore it!"

Mr. Shaw perceived that Hugh was either in much less pain now, or that he forgot everything in a subject which always interested him extremely. He told his uncle what he had read of the tortures inflicted by savages, till his uncle, already a good deal agitated, was quite sick; but he let him go on, hoping that the boy might think lightly in comparison of what he himself had to undergo. This could not last long, however. The ringing pain soon came back; and as Hugh cried, he said he bore it so very badly, he did not know what his mother would say if she saw him. She had trusted him not to fail; but really he could not bear this much longer. . . .

> "Don't let mother come," said Hugh.
>
> "No, my boy, I will stay with you," said his uncle.

The surgeons took off his foot. As he sat in a chair, and his uncle stood behind him, and held his hands, and pressed his head against him, Hugh felt how his uncle's breast was heaving,—and was sure he was crying. In the very middle of it all, Hugh looked up in his uncle's face, and said,

> "Never mind, uncle! I can bear it."

He did bear it finely. It was far more terrible than he had fancied; and he felt that he could not have gone on a minute longer. When it was over, he muttered something, and Mr. Tooke bent down to hear what it was. It was—

> "I can't think how the Red Indians bear things so."

If for a time Henley escaped this ordeal, he was forever reminded of its imminence. The enemy gnawing at his bone would leave him no peace.

As far as a suffering child's attention could be diverted from his torment, Henley was engrossed in his studies at the Crypt Grammar School of Gloucester. This ancient institution, established by Burgess John Cooke in the year 1509 for the education of "certain poor boys,"[15] provided an inefficient counterpart to the Cathedral School, where the students, for the most part sons of prosperous tradesmen, hung blue tassels from their mortarboards, lest they be confused with their indigent rivals. The Crypt had long since fallen upon evil days when the Chancery Commissioners in 1860 began inquiry into its abuses. The most effective among their reforms was the appointment of a new headmaster, Thomas Edward Brown.

"T. E. B." came to Gloucester trailing clouds of glory. He had graduated from Oxford with an enviable "double first" in Classics and Modern History.[16] He had held a fellowship at Oriel. He had been ordained deacon by Bishop Wilberforce. For five years he had served as Vice-Principal of King William's College in his native Isle of Man. At thirty he brought to the Crypt an unusual breadth of experience, a genuine enthusiasm, "a gift of exciting and a gift of teaching." But he also brought the temerity and the temper that were to be his own undoing. He was intolerant of opposition; and wherever he turned he found himself opposed. The Commissioners, like Mr. Gladstone a few years later, demanded that retrenchment accompany reform. The headmaster declared retrenchment quite impossible; he refused to accept inferior equipment; he declined to teach from outmoded, unreadable texts. Moreover, he was sufficiently ill-advised to battle with his overseers "in the local prints"; for he could, as Henley pointed out, "in nowise realise the kind of illiteracy—vain, fat-witted, beery, excessively conservative—into whose midst he had descended."[17] Inevitably, despite his talents, because of his talents, he failed. With evident relief he quitted the Crypt in September, 1863, to fill the post of Second Master at Clifton. There he remained in complete happiness for nearly thirty years, until "the Gloucester episode" had become a memory he did not choose to awaken.

From Henley's point of view, however, Brown's tenure of office had been an unqualified success,

> since it made him known to me, and opened to me ways of thought and speech that—well! since it came upon me like a call from the world outside—the great, quick, living world—and discovered me the beginnings, the true materials, of myself. . . . What he did for me, practically, was to suggest such possibilities in life and character as I had never dreamed. He was singularly kind to me at a moment when I needed kindness even more than I needed encouragement.[18]

It was a memorable day when "T. E. B." announced examination grades, and again and again Henley's name led all the rest. It was the day of the first private colloquy between master and pupil, which marked the beginning of their mutual understanding; it was a day as meaningful in the boy's life as the first wonderful meeting with John Keble was significant in the life of Cardinal Newman. From his own library shelves Brown scooped down precious volumes available in no county bookshop. The youth went home laden with the best that men had thought and said, full of his master's courage and confidence. New horizons of literature stretched out before him; the mere act of living became to him something worthwhile, something worth even the price of endurance.

Henley's interest in books did not flag with the resignation of the man who had most stimulated him. In 1867, at the age of eighteen, he passed the local Oxford examination as a senior candidate with a far more than adequate knowledge of English letters. But his poverty and ill-health made the examination of little consequence. By the following spring he had grimly accepted the verdict of incompetent surgeons. In the small hospital at Smithfield they amputated his foot. Concerning these butchers and his reaction to them, he kept a stoic's silence. His only published reference to the operation occurs in a birthday letter of May, 1900, to his friend, Austin Dobson. His one consolation in the Smithfield tragedy, it appears, had been his discovery during convalescence of Anthony Trollope's *St. Paul's Magazine,* in which were first printed Dobson's "Marquise" and the "Story of Rosina."[19]

After the operation he went back to Gloucester where he continued to live at home. Disillusioned with life, he held faith in his books. Already he was reaching for standards to guide his critical judgment. When Rossetti in 1870 poured a Pre-Raphaelite vintage, "cooled a long age in the deep delvèd earth," Henley turned instinctively to the sobriety of Pope.[20] But he was also beginning to express his own emotion in verse; and the earliest of his poems linked him to the Victorian romantics rather than the Augustan classicists:

> Life is bitter. All the faces of the years,
> Young and old, are gray with travail and with tears,
>   Must we only wake to toil, to tire, to weep?
> In the sun, among the leaves, upon the flowers,
> Slumber stills to dreamy death the heavy hours . . .
>   Let me sleep.

Obviously derivative in form and content, these lines have nonetheless considerable biographical relevance. They give some indication of Henley's state of mind during the five years following the first operation. In that time the disease had crept into his other foot; the old pains had renewed their assault. His will to live weighed lightly in the balance against his longing for release. And yet there was left in him enough of the spirit of Headmaster Brown to resist a petition for complete surrender. When the surgeons told him early in 1873 that he must submit to a second amputation, he scorned their harsh decree. Wearily, grimly, he began the trek to Edinburgh.

IN HOSPITAL EDINBURGH: 1873-1875

Sir James Simpson may have wondered in the last year of his life whether his long labors had been in vain. He could not doubt his accomplishment; the "perchloride of formyle" that he had introduced to a generation skeptical as to its religious propriety had now become the standard prelude to every surgical operation. He remembered his triumphs: how the first grateful mother to use the drug in childbirth had named her resultant daughter Anaesthesia, how the Queen herself had placed the royal approval upon his discovery during her confinement with Prince Arthur, how the late Consort had talked to him enthusiastically "of *Punch,* Scotland, and chloroform."[21] His battle lay behind him; he had made a distinct and valid contribution to the arts of healing. Yet his victory was incomplete as long as surgeons refused to see the relation of dirt to disease. A painless incision could not avert a painful infection. If the number of operations for minor ailments had multiplied tenfold, pyaemia and gangrene had increased proportionately.

In 1869 Sir James issued a sweeping indictment of Victorian medical practice. His ten-year survey of London, Glasgow, and Edinburgh hospitals revealed that two out of every five simple amputations and two out of every three amputations through the thigh proved fatal.[22] And there were no statistics to tell "of the unspeakable agony patients suffered as the gangrene gnawed at the living flesh, of the sharp cries of pain and the tragic prayers breathed to the Divine mercy for the speedy gift of death."[23] Yet the statistics themselves were sufficiently alarming to the investigator. "Do not these terrible figures," he asked, "plead eloquently and clamantly for a revision and reform of our existing hospital system?"[24] Unfortunately, however, his mind was no longer open to new ideas; he was unprepared to accept the only reform worth the name. He might have seen in Joseph Lister, who arrived in Edinburgh shortly after the publication of the report, an immediate solution to the problems he had raised. Instead he saw only a commendable enthusiasm misguided by an irrational faith in carbolic acid.

Early in 1865 Lister encountered a French periodical article concerning putrefaction, wherein the author, Louis Pasteur, contended that sepsis usually arose not from within the wound itself but from the action on the wound of minute organisms omnipresent in the atmosphere. According to this "germ theory," sepsis might be ended by the destruction of microbes already feeding on the tissue and the exclusion of others from the tissue. Lister accepted the theory as valid and at once began his search for a suitable antiseptic chemical. When he heard of the salutory effects of carbolic in removing the sewage odor at Carlisle, he obtained a quantity of the acid for experiment in his Glasgow ward. So crude of form was the dark, tarry liquid that it seemed insoluble in water. Yet, applied to the wound, it produced effects little short of miraculous; it irritated the tissue, induced bleeding, and then formed a crust with the blood. This was the first "antiseptic scab," a hermetic seal against contamination from the air. Lister's enthusiasm led him at first to exaggerate the virtues of carbolic. With more refined phenol he evolved successively a carbolic spray, a carbolic gauze, a carbolized putty.[25] He cleansed his instruments in watery carbolic acid and demanded that all assisting surgeons wash their hands in the same fluid. His methods of disinfection should not, of course, be reduced to a single formula. But the notion of a universal panacea struck the popular imagination; and we find a would-be Scottish Byron rhyming in *ottava rima*:

> To work out this solution, tooth and nail,
>   With skill and labour at it Lister went,
> Fully determined that he should not fail;
>   And many an hour, and day, and week he spent,
> Racking his very brains till he grew pale,
>   And making many an experiment,
> Until at last he found—it made him placid—
> The true *solution* in Carbolic Acid.[26]

Whatever the misinterpretation of his work,[27] Lister himself had a broad faith in the power and purpose of the antiseptic treatment. From that faith he drew courage to operate on a close relative, affected with carcinoma of the breast, at a time when other surgeons would have shrunk from the operation through fear of almost certain septic poisoning. Through that faith he was ultimately to revolutionize the concept of "hospitalism."

Lister cast his inaugural address at the Royal Edinburgh Infirmary in the form of a challenge. Pitting the Old Medicine against the New, he told both young internes and seasoned practitioners that, thanks to the researches of Pasteur, "surgery becomes something totally different from what it used to be."[28] Professor Hughes Bennett, the "master of the microscope," sat impatiently through the lecture and then rose to refute the whole absurd germ theory. His colleagues agreed that the new head surgeon was being most impractical. Thus, from the beginning, Lister found the weight of authority against him. But opposition gave impetus rather than rebuff to his unbending will. Like the husband in Trollope's novel, though with better reason, he knew he was right; his smile was "sweet with certainties." Within four years he had transformed a backward infirmary into the foremost of British hospitals. The wind from the Pentland Hills, blowing freshly through the long corridors, commingling with the pungent odor of carbolic, testified as to the extent of his achievement. Yet he could scarcely have done so much alone. While Simpson and Bennett scoffed at his campaign, the students upon whom depended the future of his cause rallied beneath the banner of reform. "I have always," he said years later, "I have always had youth on my side."[29] From August, 1873, he had also on his side, for what it was worth, the confidence of the young Henley.

Lister found his theories of antiseptic surgery nowhere more valid than in the treatment of the large abscesses that originate in the tuberculous caries of the joints.

Henley's case was, therefore, one to which he brought a lively interest and a tried experience. In it lay his opportunity of proving the new methods to a patient already mangled by the old. He would, he was sure, be able to scrape the infection from the bone without the danger of concomitant gangrene; there would be no second amputation. But the patient must not expect immediate recovery; such treatment was inevitably a long and painful process, at times testing human endurance to its limits.

Henley passed twenty months under Lister's care in the Edinburgh Infirmary; and towards the end of that time he recorded, as dispassionately as possible, his reactions, physical and psychological, to his environment.[30] His verses, *In Hospital,* polished and repolished over a period of thirteen years, present a microcosm of his whole biography. They reveal, ceaselessly at work, a dialectic of denial and assent; and they point towards the final synthesis, which, generally speaking, was to determine his whole subsequent attitude to reality. In the sense of the title-page caption,[31] they belong among the most personal poems in the language.

But, apart from any subjective connotation, the greatness of the Hospital sequence lies in the detachment from which it derives an independent dramatic unity.[32] For the appeal is calculated to be aesthetic; the author is in no way solicitous of the reader's sympathy. With amazing dispassion he follows the protagonist of his tragicomedy from his arrival in the morning mists at the bleak hospital until his departure for the high noon of life in the open air. He re-visions through the eyes of the character he has created the "gruesome world" of "Scissors and lint and apothecary's jars," and he feels once more his initial revulsion:

> The gaunt brown walls
> Look infinite in their decent meanness.
> There is nothing of home in the noisy kettle,
>   The fulsome fire.
>
> The atmosphere
> Suggests the trail of a ghostly druggist.
> Dressings and lint on the long, lean table—
>   Whom are they for?
>
> The patients yawn,
> Or lie as in training for shroud and coffin.
> A nurse in the corridor scolds and wrangles.
>   It's grim and strange.[33]

As if from a "third-personal" vantage point, he beholds the youth waiting,

>   waiting for the knife.
> A little while, and at a leap I storm
> The thick, sweet mystery of chloroform.

Follows the operation itself, described without a trace of hysteria or self-pity:

> You are carried in a basket,
>   Like a carcase from the shambles,
>   To the theatre, a cockpit
> Where they stretch you on a table.
>
> Then they bid you close your eyelids,
>   And they mask you with a napkin,
>   And the anaesthetic reaches
> Hot and subtle through your being.
>
> And you gasp and reel and shudder
>   In a rushing, swaying rapture,
>   While the voices at your elbow
> Fade—receding—fainter—farther. . . .

The aftertaste of anaesthetic, "foully sweet," lingers on as he recovers consciousness; and a "dull, new pain . . . grinds [his] leg and foot." All this is but a prelude to the lonely vigil, the dark weeks of uncertainty, when

> Lived on one's back,
> In the long hours of repose,
> Life is a practical nightmare—
> Hideous asleep or awake.
>
> Shoulders and loins
> Ache——!
> Ache, and the mattress,
> Run into boulders and hummocks,
> Glows like a kiln. . . .
>
> All the old time
> Surges malignant before me;
> Old voices, old kisses, old songs
> Blossom derisive about me;
> While the new days
> Pass me in endless procession:
> A pageant of shadows
> Silently, leeringly wending
> On . . . and still on . . . still on!

Recovery comes slowly, and with it, the ability to transcend the suffering, to find mental release in the Balzacs brought by friends,

> Big, yellow books, quite impudently French.

Better still, there is romance in the hospital itself. The sailor tells of blockade-running in the American war, of mud and chains, and Negroes on the wharf at Charleston, "Poor old Dixie's bottom dollar." The ploughman in his "crackling, hackling" voice sings

>   of bonnie lasses
> Keeping sheep among the heather.

Even in the Lady-probationer, her of the "dark eyes and shy, . . . ignorant of sin," there must be hidden wells of life:

Her plain print gown, prim cap, and bright steel chain
Look out of place on her, and I remain
Absorbed in her, as in a pleasant mystery.
Quick, skilful, quiet, soft in speech and touch . . .
"Do you like nursing?" "Yes, Sir, very much."
Somehow, I rather think she has a history.

And there is high inspiration in the heroism of Lister himself, "the Chief" who

seems in all his patients to compel
Such love and faith as failure cannot quell.
We hold him for another Herakles,
Battling with custom, prejudice, disease,
As once the son of Zeus with Death and Hell.

But the distant piping of the barrel organ engenders an irresistible nostalgia for "the blessèd airs of London"; and April, reaching through the "grimy, little window," brings a passing tingle to the blood and an abiding sense of frustration. Into his ultimate escape, the invalid pours a lifetime of thwarted joy:

Carry me out
Into the wind and the sunshine,
Into the beautiful world.

O, the wonder, the spell of the streets!
The stature and strength of the horses,
The rustle and echo of footfalls,
The flat roar and rattle of wheels!
A swift tram floats huge on us . . .
It's a dream?
The smell of the mud in my nostrils
Blows brave—like a breath of the sea!

As of old,
Ambulant, undulant drapery,
Vaguely and strangely provocative,
Flutters and beckons. O, yonder—
Is it?—the gleam of a stocking!
Sudden, a spire
Wedged in the mist! O, the houses,
The long lines of lofty, gray houses,
Cross-hatched with shadow and light!
These are the streets . . .
Each is an avenue leading
Whither I will!

Free . . . !
Dizzy, hysterical, faint,
I sit, and the carriage rolls on with me
Into the wonderful world.

So in childlike ecstasy, the patient is recalled to a life beyond the gray hospital corridors.

Considered as an artistic unit, the sequence represents an achievement in objective writing; for the author, even though drawing upon his own experience, is constantly above his subject; he remains always in complete control of his materials. But, in a broader sense, there can be no objective art; the dispassionate

technique is in itself a reflection of the artist's point of departure. This is pre-eminently true of the verses *In Hospital,* where the poet's vision throughout is conditioned by his fierce will to live. With the renascent feeling that the victory is worth the struggle, Henley looks at his world with a new intensity. If he is to understand existence at all, he must reduce it to its lowest common denominator. Accordingly, for the nebulous imagery of his earliest verse, he substitutes a concretion of detail, a sharpness of outline. As if continually obsessed with the dread that life may be slipping from him, he clings with an overzeal to the basic physical sensations. On his release, it is the sudden superabundance of acute impression—"the flat roar and rattle of wheels," "the smell of the mud," "the gleam of a stocking"—that swells his being with a joy unutterable. He focuses a hard, white light on the surfaces of things, till he has laid bare their very essences. At its best, his work satisfies the standards of steel engraving; each shadow is deliberately placed; each line takes telling effect. Within the Infirmary, there is little or no distracting color[34]; all is black and white and indeterminate gray. The flame is blanketed in smoke; the night lamp is half-guarded. A single splash of brightness is garish against the drab background; from his bedclothes, **"Case Number One"** stretches a sick foot,

Swaddled in wet, white lint
Brilliantly hideous with red.

Only the visitor is brown-eyed, "rich-tinted," "radiant with vivacity"; but then he is something of an "Apparition," come by some romantic whim from a far fairy-land. The real Edinburgh beyond the hospital windows is colorless as the gray ward; beneath an April sun, the poet sees only etched design in the "lofty, gray houses, Cross-hatched with shadow and light."

In the same intense visualization lies the power of the unique verse-portraits, by virtue of which Mr. Alfred Noyes has ranked Henley as a major poet.[35] The exigencies of the sonnet-form demand unusual economy of expression; only the significant detail remains to suggest the total character. But Henley moves easily within the medium. He forces himself to reduce a complex individuality to its elements. He contrives to find a guiding principle behind each of the persons he depicts. Lister lives by "his unyielding will," his dedication to an heroic ideal. The staff-nurse, old-style Mrs. Porter,[36] exercises at all times the benevolent despotism to which thirty years' experience entitles her. Miss Mitchelson, her new-style counterpart, is conscious of an innate superiority; even her "plainest cap is somehow touched with caste." The house-surgeon is neither more nor less than a genial

Philistine. Nevertheless, despite a fundamental simplicity of conception, all of these emerge as complete, life-size human beings. Among the most vivid portraits in the hospital gallery is that of Miss Abercromby, the sister of charity. More than the others, perhaps, it indicates the amused detachment from which the poet makes his appraisals:

Her little face is like a walnut shell
With wrinkling lines; her soft, white hair adorns
Her withered brows in quaint, straight curls, like
    horns;
And all about her clings an old, sweet smell.
Prim is her gown and quakerlike her shawl.
Well might her bonnets have been born on her.
Can you conceive a Fairy Godmother
The subject of a strong religious call?
In snow or shine, from bed to bed she runs,
All twinkling smiles and texts and pious tales,
Her mittened hands, that ever give or pray,
Bearing a sheaf of tracts, a bag of buns:
A wee old maid that sweeps the Bridegroom's way,
Strong in a cheerful trust that never fails.

In the matter of technique the comparison is once again with the graphic arts. This is a genre study done entirely without color, a simple design in black and white. But the portrait implies infinitely more than a sense of arrangement. Its strength rests on an objective sympathy, a "negative capability," an aesthetic aloofness guided by an understanding of fundamental character values.

Henley's concern with the hospital drama was not less disinterested than Miss Abercromby's charity. His psychological recovery demanded a sacrifice of the desire for personal escape to the claims of an interdependent society. He turned from his own miseries to the problems of his fellow inmates. He lent a willing ear to the reminiscences of Kate the Scrubber; and he marveled at the courage that had sustained her through trial and tribulation. He learned case histories more sordid than his own. And he succeeded in diverting the whole gaunt ward with anecdote and song and the favorite tunes he played upon a tin whistle. He could never forget the hospital New Year when he had piped "The Wind That Shakes the Barley," while Kate, a little the worse for liquor, had tripped a sprightly measure, herself the whole ballet. Again and again he rallied two small boys, Roden Shields and Willie Morrison, with games of war and "droll ditties" sung "to a rollicking air and in a strong Irish accent":

Ah, hurrah, brave boys! we're all fur marching;
Some fur Spain and some fur Belgim.
Drums are bating, colirs are flying,
Which among us thinks of dying?
    Love, farewell! darlint, farewell!
    We're all fur marching. Love, farewell!

His mere range of moods fascinated the children, who peered at him from the next cot, critical, admiring, half-afraid. Years later when Roden had become a Glasgow tailor, he remembered Henley's mirth and his gloom, his singing and the long hours of silence when

I used to watch him looking hard at the roof, thinking, smiling, and frowning as if he saw nice things and talked to people. I never dared question him in these moods, but I resolved when I was a man I would get pillows at my back and a desk fitted to my bed, and read and smile and frown like Henley.

Roden and Willie often wondered why he passed so much of his time in writing; and they were not quite satisfied by his reply that he had many letters to send to his grandmother.[37] Yet they could scarcely have known the labor involved in the verses which were recording his experience.

The decision to accept Henley's "Hospital Outlines" for publication in the *Cornhill* was one of the "boldest ventures" in the editorial career of Leslie Stephen. Such crude realism would certainly offend feminine delicacy; and "Thou shalt not shock a young lady" was, he said, "the first commandment that he had to enforce."[38] Though the acceptance itself must have meant a good deal to the convalescent poet, Stephen carried his kindness still further. While on a lecture tour to Edinburgh, he sought out Henley at the Infirmary. In a letter home he told Mrs. Stephen of "an interesting visit to [his] poor contributor" and of a plan to help him. "I went," he explained, "to see Stevenson this morning, Colvin's friend, . . . and am going to take him there this afternoon. He will be able to lend him books, and perhaps to read his Mss. and be otherwise useful. So I hope that my coming to Edinburgh will have done good to one living creature."[39] His hope was not misplaced, for that afternoon Colvin's friend came with him to the hospital. Both of them were moved by the sight of "the poor fellow" who "sat up in his bed with his hair and beard all tangled, and talked as cheerfully as if he had been in a King's palace or in the great King's palace of the blue air."[40] Saturday, the thirteenth of February, 1875[41]—it was in many respects the most significant single day in Henley's life.

Stevenson came to the Infirmary not once but many times. A remarkable figure, he seemed to Henley, something of an anachronism, a Victorian Villon, "Buffoon and poet, lover and sensualist." Passionate, impudent, energetic, he was able to make himself "useful" in ways that Stephen could not have imagined. He encouraged the patient's effort to learn Spanish and Italian; and he brought to the hospital Mrs. Fleeming Jenkin who consented to give free lessons in German. Each week he came laden with paper-bound

French novels at which Miss Mitchelson looked askance. Not all his usefulness, however, was of so academic a character; for his interest in Henley went beyond their mutual love of foreign literature. He was concerned with the individual; "Henley," he said, "has an immortal soul of his own."[42] Consequently, he sought out kindred spirits in whose presence Henley might realize his own true self. The friends whom he introduced into the ward, Charles Baxter, James Walter Ferrier, Sir Walter Grindley Simpson—these men opened vistas of life outside the invalid's narrowed experience. But above all others, "Lewis"[43] himself engendered an eagerness to accept the world for what it was, to seek from the drab reality the latent romance of living.

In April, just two months after Leslie Stephen's first visit, Henley was removed from the Infirmary to Portobello on the Firth of Forth. There Louis called every afternoon with the family carriage to drive him through the green countryside. Henley would ride in silence, his eyes fixed on "the cherry-blossoms bitten out upon the black firs, and the black firs bitten out of the blue sky." "The look of his face," said Louis, "was a wine to me."[44] On the Bridges they always lingered a moment to let Henley "enjoy the great *cry* of green that goes up to Heaven out of the river beds"; and sometimes he would ask, "'What noise is that?'—'The water.'—'O!' almost incredulously; and then quite a long time after: 'Do you know the noise of the water astonished me very much?'" Louis was "much struck by his putting the question *twice*."[45] But Henley would continue to put such questions until the end; he would never outgrow his child-like wonder. His release from the hospital had meant only that he would inflict his assertion, his positive faith, on a generation of half-believers. His voice would cut stridently across a late Victorian defeatism:

> Free . . . !
> Dizzy, hysterical, faint,
> I sit, and the carriage rolls on with me
> Into the wonderful world.

"Invictus." The Grammar of Assent

Stevenson knew nothing of the Henley who had lain, in the first Edinburgh months, helpless upon a hospital cot, doubtful as to the value of life itself. He could remember only a maimed Prometheus, scorning the decrees of angry gods. His description of the penny whistle and its effect on the ward attains an almost Henleyan grandiloquence:

> Small the pipe; but O! do thou,
> Peak-faced and suffering piper, blow therein
> The dirge of heroes dead; and to these sick,
> These dying, sound the triumph over death.

> Behold! each greatly breathes; each tastes a joy
> Unknown before, in dying; for each knows
> A hero dies with him—though unfulfilled,
> Yet conquering truly—and not dies in vain.

> So is pain cheered, death comforted; the house
> Of sorrow smiles to listen. Once again—
> O thou, Orpheus and Heracles, the bard
> And the deliverer, touch the stops again![46]

This poem is highly pertinent to any account of the Henley-Stevenson relationship. It depicts the piper as Louis wished to see him and as he himself desired to appear. And thereby it suggests the attitude towards pain of two youths who had each suffered greatly and whose common friendship was grounded in a personal experience, and a mutual defiance, of physical handicap. Critically, their tastes, their prejudices, their philosophies of living can only be measured against an incessant battle with tubercular disease. For neither was long free from some sort of bodily torment. Their war was never won; but while a shred of life remained, neither would admit it lost. In the South Seas, a month before the end, Stevenson, looking back upon his struggle, wrote to George Meredith:

> For fourteen years I have not had a day's real health; I have wakened sick and gone to bed weary; and I have done my work unflinchingly. . . . I was made for a contest, and the Powers have so willed that my battle-field should be this dingy, inglorious one of the bed and the physic bottle. At least I have not failed, but I would have preferred a place of trumpetings, and the open air over my head.[47]

Had he also been at heart "the Anxious Egotist,"[48] Henley might have written a like statement. Certainly his attitude to the contest and the ruling Powers, as expressed in his verse, was identical. And he could appreciate the sincerity behind Stevenson's histrionics. No sooner had he, freed from the hospital, recovered his own health, than he was called upon to serve as nurse to Louis, "in secret, hard by the old Bristo port."[49]

The tubercular germ that blighted both their lives may conceivably have had some effect on their powers of imagination. The thesis that "the toxins of the disease act in some way as a stimulus to the brain" might seriously be defended.[50] A recent writer on the subject, Dr. L. J. Moorman, believes that the victim of tuberculosis feels himself isolated, "no longer wholly subject to the world's conventional authority, and consequently . . . is in a position to exercise a free critical spirit." And another investigator contends that the patient, craving "a full and active life, . . . lives in an atmosphere of feverish eagerness to seize the fleeting moments before they pass."[51] Such theorists would explain only too easily the creative restlessness of Stevenson or the daring iconoclasm of Henley. They would cast new light upon the *carpe diem* motif of lines as cavalier as

O, gather me the rose, the rose,
  While yet in flower we find it,
For summer smiles, but summer goes,
  And winter waits behind it!

For with the dream foregone, foregone,
  The deed forborne for ever,
The worm, regret, will canker on,
  And Time will turn him never.

And undoubtedly these elucidations would carry weight in particular cases. But when Dr. Moorman suggests a general correlation between the decline of power in contemporary literature and the decrease in the prevalency of tuberculosis,[52] we begin to suspect the validity of even his special pleadings. A "Magic Mountain," we might argue, would tend to preclude rather than guarantee a literary renaissance. If disease gave Henley and Stevenson a heightened perceptivity, it as demonstrably weakened their efforts at self-expression. The best work of the English poet is forever to a degree overdeliberate; his richest music is marred by false tonalities. Likewise, the most graceful prose of the Scots storyteller is somehow strained in its mere precision.

As commentator on the invalid's modes of thought, the psychologist is both more convincing and more provocative than the physician. Where Dr. Moorman seeks evaluation, Dr. Adler contents himself with analysis. He assumes as obvious the interdependence of body and mind and proceeds at once to infer the self-involvement of physical debility and mental health. The invalid, constantly aware of his inferiority, becomes neurotic, subject to an endless emotional conflict; despising his own weakness, he covets a strength beyond his attainment. He, therefore, tends to measure all things by their weak and strong propensities. As he always "apperceives after the analogy of a contrast" and usually "only recognizes and gives value to relations of contrast," he dichotomizes the whole world "according to the Scheme 'Triumph-Defeat,'" and ultimately according to "the only real 'antithesis' of 'man-woman.'" His values thus conveniently simplified, he raises a defensive "masculine protest" against uncertainty, insecurity, indecision, in short, against every token of "effeminacy."[53]

The concept of the "masculine protest" would appear to have considerable relevance to the cases of Henley and Stevenson. While Dr. Adler's theory of causation is somewhat problematical, the effects that he outlines are patent in the style and thought of both writers. Antithesis is integral to the very structure of Stevenson's essays.[54] And Henley's verse is obsessed with dichotomies, while his prose revels in the odious comparison. In both, though with significant divergences, the dominant attitude is that of vigorous

masculinity. Stevenson's stories inculcate the principles of strenuous living. And Henley's imperial propaganda carries virilism to almost pathological extremes.

The dedication to *Virginibus Puerisque* makes manifest the author's outlook on reality; addressing "My Dear William Ernest Henley," Stevenson writes:

> Times change, opinions vary to their opposite, and still this world appears a brave gymnasium, full of sea-bathing, and horse exercise, and bracing, manly virtues; and what can be more encouraging than to find the friend who was welcome at one age, still welcome at another? Our affections and beliefs are wiser than we; the best that is in us is better than we can understand; for it is grounded beyond experience and guides us, blindfold but safe, from one age to another.

The world is thus a good place, "a brave gymnasium," where the manly individual can trust his basic instincts as stronger and wiser than his faculties of intellection. Such a philosophy leads inevitably to a repudiation of convention; a morality of taboos has ceased to be moral; the "masculine protest" demands a positive ethic for active living. In "A Christmas Sermon" Stevenson places gentleness and cheerfulness, "the perfect duties," before all morality. For it was "the moral man, the Pharisee, whom Christ could not away with," the uncharitable censor of other men's well-intentioned mistakes. The true Christian accepts cheerfully the inescapable fact that human beings are from the outset doomed to mortality; and without illusion he wages, undaunted to the end, a losing battle. Then, if he has struggled manfully, he will content himself with the epitaph: *"Here lies one who meant well, tried a little, failed much."* Death will have no bitterness to the happy warrior of whom it can be said: "There, out of the glorious sun-coloured earth, out of the day and the dust and the ecstasy—there goes another Faithful Failure!"

To Stevenson, then, the challenge of life lies not in the possible victory but rather in the inevitable defeat. Satisfaction of desire means the death of the spirit. Growth, struggle, assertion—these are their own rewards. Pain is but a goad to the restless soul, driving it away from the bypaths of indolence, prodding it ever on towards complete, but unattainable, realization. Happiness ceases to be the object in living. Life becomes the end in itself; other end is unimaginable in a world whose law is change and death, a world where all souls must learn the "high doctrinality of suffering."[55] The bad man is the slothful, only too willing to stagnate in the weeds of comfortable respectability. The good man is, by implication, the gallant warrior who enters the lists with steady hand and indomitable will. The bad man is the pessimist who questions the purpose of the battle. The good man is the optimist who accepts the struggle, who delights in it as did the forebears of the good Fleeming Jenkin—"They had all the gift of enjoying life's texture as it comes; they were all born optimists."[56] Renunciation is the cardinal sin; the ascetic is the chiefest of transgressors. Where Arnold found the Grande Chartreuse a refuge for the "last of the people who believe," Stevenson sees in monastic orders a contemptible escape from reality. Our Lady of the Snows serves only to inspire a longing for the active life:

> O to be up and doing, O
> Unfearing and unshamed to go
> In all the uproar and the press
> About my human business! . . .
>
> For still the Lord is Lord of might;
> In deeds, in deeds, he takes delight; . . .
> Those he approves that ply the trade,
> That rock the child, that wed the maid,
> That with weak virtues, weaker hands,
> Sow gladness on the peopled lands,
> And still with laughter, song and shout
> Spin the great wheel of earth about.[57]

In comparison with Arnold's "Stanzas," these didactic couplets are little more than doggerel. But they are nonetheless representative of Stevenson's ethical philosophy. They provide a crude illustration of the "masculine protest" that colors most of his work and thought.[58]

Henley did not write Christmas sermons. He admired Stevenson the stylist; but he had no sympathy with the "artist in morals," the "Shorter Catechist of Vailima."[59] He came to see the intellectual impotence of mere "vocalisings about duty." And yet, in spite of himself, he subscribed emotionally to Stevenson's credo. If he wrote in less explicit terms concerning the principles of strenuous living, he not the less frequently embodied those principles in his own creative and critical works.

Anticipated by the triumphant finale to the verses *In Hospital,* Henley's **"Echoes of Life and Death"** furnish forth the most complete lyrical statement of his self-assertive philosophy. Whereas the Hospital poems are relatively impersonal units in a dramatic sequence, the **"Echoes"** make no pretense at objectivity. In them the poet sings endless variations on his central theme, the incomparable romance of living:

> At whatever source we drink it,
>   Art or love or faith or wine,
> In whatever terms we think it,
>   It is common and divine. . . .
>
> The Past was goodly once, and yet, when all is said,
> The best of it we know is that it's done and dead. . . .
> Duty and work and joy—these things it cannot give;
> And the Present is life, and life is good to live. . . .

> The nightingale has a lyre of gold,
>   The lark's is a clarion call,
> And the blackbird plays but a boxwood flute,
>   But I love him best of all.
>
> For his song is all of the joy of life,
>   And we in the mad, spring weather,
> We two have listened till he sang
>   Our hearts and lips together.

Life is good and the poet clings to it with grim tenacity. But his very ardor reminds him that the goodness is passing:

> Fill a glass with golden wine,
>   And while your lips are wet
> Set their perfume unto mine,
>   And forget,
> Every kiss we take and give
> Leaves us less of life to live.

Yet man cannot afford to doubt; to question life is to squander its brief divinity:

> We must live while live we can;
>   We should love while love we may.
> Dread in women, doubt in man . . .
>   So the Infinite runs away.

These are the echoes of life calling unto man to fulfill himself in the brave gymnasium of time. But to every call from life, there comes the answering echo of death. For death is the one reality from which there is no escape. It is the grim denouement to the comedy of tears:

> Madam Life's a piece in bloom
>   Death goes dogging everywhere:
> She's the tenant of the room,
>   He's the ruffian on the stair.
>
> You shall see her as a friend,
>   You shall bilk him once or twice;
> But he'll trap you in the end,
>   And he'll stick you for her price.
>
> With his kneebones at your chest,
>   And his knuckles in your throat,
> You would reason—plead—protest!
>   Clutching at her petticoat.

The echoes of death are not always so suggestive of Holbein's macabre *Totenbilder*. But they are always acceptant. There is in them no rebellion against the inevitable. And occasionally the resignation rises to the level of transcendent mysticism, where life and death coalesce into a larger design:

> I am the Reaper.
> All things with heedful hook
> Silent I gather.
> Pale roses touched with the spring,
> Tall corn in summer,

Fruits rich with autumn, and frail winter blossoms—
Reaping, still reaping—
All things with heedful hook
Timely I gather.

I am the Sower.
All the unbodied life
Runs through my seed-sheet.
Atom with atom wed,
Each quickening the other,
Fall through my hands, ever changing, still change-
  less,
Ceaselessly sowing,
Life, incorruptible life,
Flows from my seed-sheet.

Maker and breaker,
I am the ebb and the flood,
Here and Hereafter.
Sped through the tangle and coil
Of infinite nature,
Viewless and soundless I fashion all being.
Taker and giver,
I am the womb and the grave,
The Now and the Ever.

Thus the ultimate antithesis resolves itself. Life and
death cease to be the eternal antinomies. The one
becomes unintelligible without the other; both play essential parts in the pattern of existence.

As poetry, **"I Am the Reaper"** attains the calm acceptance characteristic of Henley's last and mellowest
verses. But it is scarcely representative of the poet's
outlook on life in the spring of 1875. It conveys nothing of the fierce assertiveness that carried a jubilant
youth out from an Edinburgh hospital into the wonderful world. In the expression of a "masculine protest"
against passivity, it hardly compares with the strident
"Invictus," which dates from the same year:

Out of the night that covers me,
  Black as the Pit from pole to pole,
I thank whatever gods may be
  For my unconquerable soul.

In the fell clutch of circumstance
  I have not winced nor cried aloud.
Under the bludgeonings of chance
  My head is bloody, but unbowed.

Beyond this place of wrath and tears
  Looms but the Horror of the shade,
And yet the menace of the years
  Finds, and shall find, me unafraid.

It matters not how strait the gate,
  How charged with punishments the scroll,
I am the master of my fate;
  I am the captain of my soul.

In its context as epilogue to the hospital drama, **"Invictus"** thus acquires a significance far beyond its
value as an isolated unit. It marks the invalid's triumph

over physical handicap. It grounds an activist philosophy on a personal Darwinism, a necessary faith in the
survival of the biologically fit.

In a lecture of 1893 entitled "Ethics and Evolution,"
Thomas Henry Huxley warned his auditors that
cultural collapse must surely attend a continued belief
in "the gladiatorial theory of existence." If society was
to endure, he said, man must learn to distinguish
between records of zoological research and guide
books to moral conduct. Of educated people he
demanded spiritual wakefulness; and in support of his
demand, he cited the high resolve, the indomitable
will of Tennyson's Ulysses. By the 'nineties Henley
and Stevenson had also begun to suspect the inadequacy of a purely physical basis for the activist ethic.
The worship of life implied ultimately the deification
of the universal Life. Accordingly, Stevenson wrote
prayers at Vailima; and Henley recanted the violence
of **"Invictus"**:

Think on the shame of dreams for deeds,
The scandal of unnatural strife,
The slur upon immortal needs,
    The treason done to life:

Arise! no more a living lie,
And with me quicken to control
Some memory that will magnify
    The universal Soul.

If this later theism encouraged reflection, it also placed
upon the individual a new responsibility for active living, a regret for the dreams that might have been
deeds. Stevenson's lay morals did not lessen his love
of vigor; they gave him rather a new insight into
character. In his last and greatest novel, he drew the
heroic Gilbert Elliott, defiant, to the death, of the rob-
ber band threatening his life and property. And by the
last lines of that novel, the last lines that Stevenson
ever wrote, he conjured up a scene of tempestuous
passion, "unprovoked, a wilful convulsion of brute
nature. . . ." Similarly, that Henley had modified **"Invictus"** did not mean that he had repudiated his assent. Agnostic or theist, he remained as eager for the
full life as he had been in the first month of his release
from hospital; he could still chant:

Life—life—let there be life!
Better a thousand times the roaring hours
When wave and wind,
From the Arch-Murderer in flight
From the Avenger at his heel,
Storm through the desert fastnesses
And wild waste places of the world.

As literary critic, as political editor, he appeared to the
end the unshriven Giaour, impatient of the languorous
repose. But his inner emotional development was less

consistent, less assured, than his outwardly fierce demeanor might have suggested. The "masculine protest" indicated a realization of the ambivalence of values, of weakness commingling with strength. And the long, self-conscious search for style betrayed his feeling of uncertainty and his consequent desire for unequivocal expression. The will to live was strong, often because the fear of death was stronger.

Notes

1. See Cornford, *Henley,* p. 22.

2. For a photograph of A. W. Henley among his Parisian friends, see Will H. Low, *A Chronicle of Friendships* (New York, 1908), p. 208.

3. See Elizabeth Robins Pennell, *The Life and Letters of Joseph Pennell,* 2 vols. (Boston, 1929), I, 269.

4. See the report of an interviewer's conversation with E. J. Henley, *New York Dramatic Mirror,* xxxv (1896), 2.

5. *New York Dramatic Mirror,* xxxv (1896), 2.

6. See also the tribute of Robert Louis Stevenson, written in Honolulu, "*In Memoriam,* E. H.," *Scots Observer,* I (1889), 693.

7. See Cornford, p. 10.

8. Henley, *Works,* IV, 8.

9. *Works,* IV, 120.

10. *Works,* II, 158.

11. *Works,* IV, 84.

12. *Works,* IV, 192-93.

13. First separately published in 1856, but previously included in *The Playfellow,* 4 vols. (London, 1841), Vol. IV.

14. Miss Martineau shows no desire to attack the prevalent surgical methods; she is concerned rather with the ideal "manly" reaction thereto.

15. Henley, "T. E. B.," *Works,* II, 377.

16. See *Works,* II, 378; also Selwyn G. Simpson, *Thomas Edward Brown* (London, 1906), p. 22.

17. *Works,* II, 379.

18. *Works,* II, 380.

19. See Alban Dobson, *Austin Dobson, Some Notes* (London, 1928), p. 166.

20. See Cornford, p. 7.

21. See Eve Blantyre Simpson, *Sir James Y. Simpson* (Edinburgh, 1896), pp. 60, 63, 139.

22. See G. T. Wrench, *Lord Lister* (New York, n.d.), pp. 130, 163. In figures: of 2,089 simple amputations, 855 resulted in death; in Edinburgh, of 371 amputations, 161 resulted in death.

23. Wrench, p. 130.

24. Quoted by Wrench, p. 132.

25. See Sir Hector Clare Cameron, *Reminiscences of Lister* (Glasgow, 1927), pp. 16, 23; also Sir William Watson Cheyne, *Lister and His Achievement* (London, 1925), p. 37.

26. Quoted by Wrench, p. 272.

27. Lister claimed to use much less carbolic acid than those who imitated him; he insisted not on one antisceptic, but rather on a belief in the germ theory. See Cameron, p. 33.

28. Quoted by Wrench, p. 208.

29. Quoted by Cameron, p. 38. *Cf.* Wrench, p. 205.

30. Henley dates the hospital period, "August, 1873-April, 1875," "Hospital Sketches," *Voluntaries for an East London Hospital,* collected by H. B. Donkin (London, 1887), p. 148.

31. Henley heads *In Hospital* with a quotation from Balzac, "*On ne saurait dire à quel point un homme, seul dans son lit et malade, devient personnel.*"—*Works,* I, 2.

32. *In Hospital* has the dramatic "curve" of complication and denouement. The action is confined to distinct scenes or settings, the first of which is entitled "Enter Patient."

33. As it appears in the *Works, In Hospital* has been fully revised. This poem is roughly equivalent to Sonnet III, "The Ward," *Cornhill Magazine,* xxxII (1875), 121.

34. There are very few color words: "gray" occurs nine times in the twenty-nine poems; "brown," twice; "green," twice, but as a noun, meaning "grass" in the world *outside*; "red," twice, of blood.

35. See Noyes, "The Poetry of W. E. Henley," *Contemporary Review,* cxxi (1922), 205.

36. Identified in an unpublished letter, attached to a copy of *In Hospital* in the University of Toronto Library, written by Dr. G. A. Gibson, who was in charge of Henley's ward, and dated from Edinburgh, 1913.

37. See Roden Shields, "A Blurred Memory of Childhood," *Cornhill Magazine,* NS xix (1905), 227, 228.

38. Quoted by Frederic William Maitland, *The Life and Letters of Leslie Stephen* (London, 1906), p. 266.

39. Quoted by Maitland, p. 250. The letter is undated.

40. *Works of Robert Louis Stevenson,* 27 vols. (New York, 1911), XXIII, 98.

41. For this dating, see Rosaline Masson, *The Life of Robert Louis Stevenson* (Edinburgh, 1923), p. 250.

42. Stevenson, *Works,* XXVII, 317.

43. "Lewis": R. L. S. was baptized Robert Lewis Balfour Stevenson. Henley refused to recognize the name "Louis," which he considered sheer affectation; he, therefore, always wrote of "Lewis." In reality, the change in spelling had a quite different origin. Thomas Stevenson, it appears, ordered the new spelling when the local Radical, Lewis—odious to the Conservative Thomas—was elected town councillor. See Eve Blantyre Simpson, *Robert Louis Stevenson's Edinburgh Days* (London, 1898), pp. 16-17.

44. Stevenson, *Works,* XXIII, 107.

45. XXVII, 316-17.

46. Stevenson, *Works,* XVI, 122-23.

47. *Works,* XXIV, 362-63.

48. See Henley, "R. L. S.," *Pall Mall Magazine,* XXV (1901), 510.

49. *PMM,* XXV, 506.

50. See *Journal American Medical Association,* XCIX (1932), 2297.

51. See Lewis J. Moorman, *Tuberculosis and Genius* (Chicago, 1940), "Introduction," pp. xii, xiii.

52. In support of this theory, Moorman quotes a colleague, Dr. Jacobson, p. xv.

53. See Alfred Adler, *The Neurotic Constitution* (New York, 1917), pp. 24-25, 86, 99-101.

54. See Alice D. Snyder's stimulating article, "Paradox and Antithesis in Stevenson's Essays," *Journal of English and Germanic Philology,* XIX (1920), 540-59.

55. See Stevenson's letter to Henley, dated Dec. 11, 1879, *Works,* XXVII, 128-29.

56. *Works,* XVIII, 37.

57. "Our Lady of the Snows," *Works,* XVI, 132-33.

58. Apparently Stevenson, like the Keats of the revised *Hyperion,* thought the life of action preferable to the life of art. Will H. Low thought it "most distressing that Stevenson should continually have . . . viewed his undeniable endowment as an artist to be inferior to the other avocations of man."—See "An Epilogue to an Epilogue," *Modern Essays,* Christopher Morley, ed. (New York, 1925), p. 416.

59. Henley, *PMM,* XXV, 508.

Bibliography

Insofar as most of Henley's unsigned hack-work lies buried in the files of defunct periodicals, the following bibliography must be regarded as suggestive rather than exhaustive. Part I is designed to include the first and important later editions of Henley's published books, the titles and dates of his editorial projects, a representative group of his uncollected periodical articles, and a more or less complete check-list of critical and biographical studies casting direct light upon his life and work. Part II consists of a selection from the writings by and about Henley's contemporaries, in which we obtain the clearest picture of the Viking chief and his distinguished Regatta. Part III gathers together a few of the secondary works which have illuminated the literary, social, and historical backgrounds of Henley's career.

Unless otherwise indicated, the place of publication for all books is London.

PART I

THE WRITINGS OF WILLIAM ERNEST HENLEY

WORKS

The Works of W. E. Henley, 7 vols. 1908.

The Works of William Ernest Henley, 5 vols., including *Lyra Heroica.* 1921.

POEMS

"Hospital Sketches," *Cornhill Magazine,* XXXII (1875), 120-28.

"Hospital Sketches," H. B. Donkin, ed., *Voluntaries for an East London Hospital.* 1887.

Gleeson White, ed., *Ballades and Rondeaus, passim.* 1887.

A Book of Verses. 1888.

The Song of the Sword and Other Verses. 1892. Reissued as *London Voluntaries and Other Verses.* 1893.

London Types, quatorzains, illustrated by William Nicholson. New York, 1898.

Poems, with preface. 1898.

For England's Sake. 1900.

"Hawthorn and Lavender: Songs and Madrigals," *North American Review,* CLXIX (1899), 593-603, CLXXII (1901), 895-905, CLXXIII (1901), 418-21.

Hawthorn and Lavender. 1901.

A Song of Speed. 1903.

BIOGRAPHICAL AND CRITICAL STUDIES OF
HENLEY

Cornford, Leslie Cope, *William Ernest Henley.* 1913.

PART II

FRIENDS, CONTEMPORARIES, DISCIPLES

Thomas Edward BROWN (1830-1897):

Selwyn G. Simpson, *Thomas Edward Brown.* 1906.

Henry Austin DOBSON (1840-1921):

Alban Dobson, *Austin Dobson, Some Notes.* 1928.

Joseph, Baron LISTER (1827-1912):

Hector Clare Cameron, *Reminiscences of Lister.* Glasgow, 1927.

William Watson Cheyne, *Lister and His Achievement.* 1925.

G. T. Wrench, *Lord Lister.* New York, [1913].

Elizabeth Robins PENNELL (1855-1936):

—*The Life and Letters of Joseph Pennell* (1857-1926), 2 vols. Boston, 1929.

Leslie STEPHEN (1832-1904):

Frederic William Maitland, *The Life and Letters.* 1906.

Robert Louis STEVENSON (1850-1894):

—*The Works,* 27 vols. New York, 1911-1912.

Rosaline Masson, *The Life.* Edinburgh, 1923.

Alice D. Snyder, "Paradox and Antithesis in Stevenson's Essays," *JEGP* [*Journal of English and Germanic Philology*], XIX (1920), 540-59.

PART III

LITERARY, SOCIAL, AND HISTORICAL
BACKGROUNDS

Moorman, Lewis J., *Tuberculosis and Genius.* Chicago, 1940.

Joseph M. Flora (essay date 1970)

SOURCE: Flora, Joseph M. "W. E. Henley, Poet." In *William Ernest Henley,* pp. 119-41. New York: Twayne, 1970.

[*In the following essay, Flora examines each of Henley's volumes of poetry in turn and argues that the main achievement in most of his work is to "recall the childhood capacity for wonder."*]

The previously mentioned bronze replica of Rodin's bust of Henley, which was unveiled in the crypt of Saint Paul's Cathedral on the fourth anniversary of Henley's death, bears the words: "W. E. Henley, Poet, 1849-1903." The simple designation does not include all the facets of Henley's career, nor perhaps the chief aspect that his contemporaries most often saw. But the designation would have pleased Henley more than any other. On October 9, 1883, Henley—then editor of *The Magazine of Art*—wrote to Austin Dobson upon the receipt of Dobson's *Old-World Idylls:* "I sigh a little, as I turn the pages, and feel the good thought, the well-united verse, the happy and graceful rhymes. I should have liked to be a poet, too. And you know what I am."[1]

The critic and the journalist were of a lesser order on Henley's scale; and, at the time he wrote to Dobson, he regarded the drama as his only possible alternative to those activities. He had earlier written Dobson that his hospital verses "have been rejected by every editor in the civilized world."[2] For Henley, the publication of *A Book of Verses* in 1888 was a major occasion. Mr. Alfred Nutt had read the hospital poems and asked Henley to look for more. Hence, as Henley prepared that first collection, many old hopes were revived. "I found that, after all, the lyrical instinct had slept—not died"—so Henley explained in 1897.[3] To the Henley of this fondest role we again turn our attention, appropriately last because Henley the poet best summarizes the whole man.

I "BRIC-À-BRAC" (1877-1888)

Many late nineteenth-century poets, taking their lead from Algernon Swinburne, turned to highly artificial old French forms—the villanelle, the rondeau, the rondel, the ballade; and burly Henley could move in these forms with the best of them. Under the heading "Bric-à-brac," he later grouped poems in these restricting forms plus some sonnets. Bric-à-brac, which has mainly ornamental value, brings pleasure for its own delicate sake; and Henley noted in his villanelle defining that form: "A DAINTY thing's the Villanelle / Sly, musical, a jewel in rhyme, / It serves its purpose passing well. Dainty, jewel-like—all these French forms exist to please for their delicacy. Not every subject will suit them, but the poet of hospital Realism could delight in their manipulation.

In his several ballades, for example, he moves from **"Ballade of a Toyokuni Colour-Print"** (in itself a decorative, arty subject), to ballades with double refrains, to double ballades. Playing as it does with refrain and three or four rhymes in regular meter, the ballade is little concerned with a logical argument or with personal intimate reflection. Instead, it is suited to the creation of pictorial detail as in **"Ballade of a Toyokuni Colour-Print"** or, more commonly, to cataloguing or to seriatim effects. In **"Ballade Made in Hot Weather"** the poet lists pleasant images to contemplate—images largely from nature, though he is also pleased by "cherries and snow at will / From china bowls that fill / The senses with a sweet / Incuriousness of heat," not to mention "Dark aisles, new packs of cards, / Mermaidens' tails." The freedom of "cooling" ideas finds delightful counterpart in the strict demands of the ballade form. The poet may catalogue emotions as well as images, as in **"Ballade of Dead Actors"**:

> Where are the passions they essayed,
> And where the tears they made to flow?
> Where the wild humours they portrayed
> For laughing world to see and know?
> Othello's wrath and Juliet's woe?
> Sir Peter's whims and Timon's gall?
> And Millamant and Romeo?
> Into the night go one and all.

High-spirited, lively, Henley's ballades suit admirably his affirmative approach to life, nowhere more delightfully than in **"Double Ballade of Life and Fate"**:

> Every Jack must have his Jill
> (Even Johnson had his Thrale!):
> Forward, couples with a will!
> This, the world, is not a jail.
> Hear the music, sprat and whale!
> Hands across, retire, advance!
> Though the doomsman's on your trail,
> Fate's a fiddler, Life's a dance.

Thus, the vibrancy and high spirit of the ballade form belie the sobriety of the refrain of **"Double Ballade of the Nothingness of Things"**: "'O Vanity of Vanities!'" The form comes closer to persuading the reader to view life as a dance than to accept the spirit of the preacher of Ecclesiastes.

The rondeau—a shorter form and more susceptible to sonnet-like development—permitted Henley more personal reflection. But, again, form can be the crucial test of meaning. Hence, undergraduates can be quickly deceived by a rondeau like "The gods are dead?"; for, reading for meaning (victimized by stock responses) and not *hearing* the poem, far too many miss the underlying jocularity. Nevertheless, Henley did find the rondeau suitable for personal, intimate expression. **"When you are old, and I am passed away"** must have pleased Anna Henley often, and she must have cherished the rondeau **"What is to come we know not"** as a comforting statement of her Will's guiding faith. The simplicity of diction (not always characteristic of a Henley poem) and the few elemental images combine with the insistent rhymes (all monosyllables)

and careful caesuras to make the poem a dignified expression of achievement and resolution:

> What is to come we know not. But we know
> That what has been was good—was good to show,
> Better to hide, and best of all to bear.
> We are the masters of the days that were:
> We have lived, we have loved, we have suffered . . .
> > even so.
> Shall we not take the ebb who had the flow?
> Life was our friend. Now, if it be our foe—
> Dear, though it spoil and break us!—need we care
> > What is to come?
> Let the great winds their worst and wildest blow,
> Or the gold weather round us mellow slow:
> We have fulfilled ourselves, and we can dare
> And we can conquer, though we may not share
> In the rich quiet of the afterglow
> > What is to come.

The rondel permitted Henley no such memorable personal utterance. The requirement of the repetition of lines one and two as lines seven and eight and the repetition of line one in the concluding line (thirteen), leaves the poet with too little room for development; it permits no sonnet-like progression; and the tinkling form triumphs over matter. Hence in **"The ways of Death are soothing and serene"** there is little conviction—nor could the poet of *In Hospital* believe that such are always the ways of Death (in our century, they are hardly ever so!). But Henley liked to consider the ways of death serene as the proper reward at the end of a full life. The idea was a part of his nineteenth-century evolutionary faith. The rondel, however, was not conducive to such a theme. The poet's exercise works for a moment only, and only then if we are numb to its thought. Of all Henley's Bric-à-brac, the rondels seem most exclusively exercises.

The sonnet was an important part of the young Henley's repertoire and training in poetry. We have already seen the important use he found for the form in his hospital verses. "Bric-à-brac" quite naturally includes non-hospital examples of Henley's achievement in the form. The most ornamental of them is the sea sonnet **"At Queensferry,"** with its pervading sounds c, s, and z. Henley's verse reveals a continuous fascination with the sea. Here it is at one with the spirit of romance, for Queensferry becomes a place "Where Lancelot rides clanking thro' the haze." Two sonnets, **"From a Window in Princes Street"** and **"Back-View,"** use tetrameter lines to enforce other Romantic effects. But the Realist is more in evidence than the Romantic. **"In Fisherrow"** is a portrait of an old fisher woman; **"Croquis,"** an old fiddler on a crowded beach. **"In the Dials"** pictures in the octave two young girls jigging "As in the tumult of a witches' round"; in the sestet we find "two loitering hags / Look on dispassionate—critical—something 'mused." We are not far, therefore, from the detached observer of the realities of *In Hospital.*

In most of his Bric-à-brac poems, Henley is a pleasant poet to meet. There is facility that charms, but ultimately there is more than facility. Henley's personality emerges winningly. The buoyancy that delighted Stevenson is obvious; the singer is clearly "upsides" with life. We note, for example, the comradeship of the rondeau **"Inter Sodales"**:[4]

> Over a pipe the Angel of Conversation
>   Loosens with glee the tassels of his purse,
>   And, in a fine spiritual exaltation,
>   Hastens, a very spendthrift, to disburse
>   The coins new minted of imagination.
>
> An amiable, a delicate animation
>   Informs our thought, and earnest we rehearse
>   The sweet old farce of mutual admiration
>   Over a pipe.
>
> Heard in this hour's delicious divigation,
>   How soft the song! The epigram how terse!
>   With what a genius for administration
>   We rearrange the rambling universe,
>   And map the course of man's regeneration,
>   Over a pipe.

It is difficult to find in "Bric-à-brac" or any Henley poems the mean-minded person Henley is sometimes taken to be by some defenders of Stevenson and of Oscar Wilde.

II "ECHOES" (1872-1889)

The poems gathered as "Echoes" reveal the poet at different moods in his life extending from the Margate year, 1872, the earliest year from which Henley preserved his poems, through 1888, that transition year in Henley's career when the Stevenson friendship ended, Margaret was born, and his mother died. These events—as well as his young love for Anna and the struggle over his leg—are all echoed in this grouping. And in it Henley placed the famous **"Invictus."** The first poem in the group is the lyrical love-sea poem **"Chiming a dream by the way,"** which Henley entitled definitively **"To My Mother."** The title is misleading, for Henley's poem has nothing directly to do with his mother. Henley was given to dedicating poems, somewhat to the distraction of later readers. The lovely "The nightingale has a lyre of gold" (**Echo XVIII**), for example, was dedicated to Austin Dobson, who had singled it out as his favorite. "*To* A. D.," however, was a dedication—not a title. It seems likely that Henley titled his poem **"To My Mother"** as a dedication of larger emphasis for his first satisfying lyric at the beginning of his career as poet.

In the penultimate poem of "Echoes," one based on the death of his mother, he specifically views his work in relation to his mother's life:

> Dearest, live on
> In such immortality
> As we thy sons,
> Born of thy body and nursed
> At those wild, faithful breasts,
> Can give—of generous thoughts,
> And honourable words, and deeds
> That make men half in love with fate!
> Live on, O brave and true,
> In us thy children, in ours whose life is thine—
> Our best and theirs!

The final poem **"Crosses and troubles a-many have proved me"** (a twelve-line "sonnet") is a summary poem at the juncture in his life that "Echoes" underscores.

Although **"Matri Dilectissimae"** is in free verse, almost all of the other echoes are short lyrics in very regular stanzas—ranging from the charm of **"The nightingale has a lyre of gold"** to the indifferent **Poem XI**:

> Thick is the darkness—
>   Sunward, O, sunward!
> Rough is the highway—
>   Onward, still onward!
>
> Dawn harbours surely
>   East of the shadows.
> Facing us somewhere
>   Spread the sweet meadows.
>
> Upward and forward!
>   Time will restore us
> Light is above us,
>   Rest is before us.

As the rondeau **"What is to come"** contains a more moving affirmation of this idea, so in "Echoes" Henley treats more vitally the theme of the rondel **"The ways of Death are soothing and serene."** The rhythm of the rondeau, its movement of a perfect cycle, its simple diction, all correspond with the perfect pattern Henley praised in **"What is to come."** There form *was* his main metaphor. The rondel form, however, worked against the theme Henley wanted to express. Allegorized Death cannot be so summarily, so liltingly dismissed.

In **Poem XXIX,** however, dedicated to R. L. Stevenson, Death has a complete enough allegorization and loses the sting that persists in the rondel. Henley likens Man to a child who "Curious and innocent, / Slips from his Nurse, and rejoicing / Loses himself in the Fair." For a time he revels in his wandering, "Till, of a sudden / Tired and afraid, he beholds / The sordid assemblage / Just as it is, and runs "To the friendly and comforting breast / Of the old nurse, Death." One of the great themes of poetry is death and how one can or should meet it; and this theme is certainly a common one with Henley. In another "echo," **Poem IX ("Madam Life's a Piece in Bloom")** the ways of Death are not soothing and serene, but Henley's metaphor is amusingly concrete; and he playfully pulls the reader into recognition of a kind of justice in Death's ways. He portrays Death not as a friendly nurse, but as the ruffian pimp of Madam Life—and the ruffian eventually demands of us her price.

The most moving statement of Henley's approach to Death is the free verse **"A late lark twitters."** The poem should be compared with the one Tennyson ordered placed as the final poem in all editions of his work, his **"Crossing the Bar,"** which, incidentally, it predates. For the mid-Victorian there was the hope, but no certainty, that he would see his Pilot "face to face." For the late-Victorian—the activist who insisted that the only test of life was its creative living—there is not any longing for the Christian heaven. In the poem Henley slowly creates a picture of a late lark singing against the quiet of a sunset over "an old, gray city." With night comes the great gift of sleep. As many another nineteenth-century poet personalizes after creating a picture in nature, so Henley personalizes. But he is not moralizing; he voices an assured request, which is for him rather than for some reader in need of a moral:

> So be my passing!
> My task accomplished and the long day done,
> My wages taken, and in my heart
> Some late lark singing,
> Let me be gathered to the quiet west,
> The sunset splendid and serene,
> Death.

Like many other Victorians, Henley is aware of duty, tasks, and wages. And, also like many of the Victorians, Henley found in responsibility the hope of a death that would be soothing and serene. His poem, however, leaves us with an image and rhythm which means shared experience, shared "prayer."

At century's end, Thomas Hardy heard another late bird singing. So ecstatic was the bird's song, Hardy concludes in his famous "The Darkling Thrush": "I could think there trembled through / His happy good-night air / Some blessed Hope, whereof he knew / And I was unaware." The Apostle Paul, whom Hardy echoes, was certain that the Christian could believe with confidence "Looking for that blessed hope, and the glorious appearing of the great God and our Saviour Jesus Christ" (Titus 2:13). But Hardy can only momentarily consider hope for the new century.

His Jude Fawley describes upon the occasion of Father Time's suicide the fin de siècle pessimism more characteristic of Hardy: "the doctor says there are such boys springing up amongst us—boys of a sort unknown in the last generation—the outcome of new views of life. They seem to see all its terrors before they are old enough to have staying power to resist them. He says it is the beginning of the coming universal wish not to live."[5]

I bring Hardy into this chapter because he stands in such marked contrast to the affirmation of Henley's late-century assertions. Interestingly, both Henley and Hardy frequently allegorize Time, Chance, and Death. Hardy characteristically feels victimized by Time and Chance; Henley affirms the individual's power to mold and create, to make his Hope. Thus, the affirmation of **"Matri Dilectissimae,"** where Death comes to his mother as "the great Deliverer." Great Deliverer suggests Christ; as in **"The Ways of Death,"** Death was presented as "the Comforter," a noun with distinct Christian overtones—though used otherwise by Henley. Henley concluded **"Matri Dilectissimae"** by asking, "What is Death / But Life in act? How should the Unteeming Grave / Be victor over thee, / Mother, a mother of men?" And Henley was building his own life so that he could conclude the final poem in "Echoes": "For the end I know is the best of all." Jude Fawley would agree with the last line, but what a different meaning he and Henley would give it! Though Henley is not Christian in his views, his approach to death is nevertheless religious.

III "RHYMES AND RHYTHMS" (1889-1892)

The poems gathered as "Rhymes and Rhythms" are those of Henley's great days with the *Observer*. The grouping is a slim one for reasons already indicated: much of Henley's poetry had seemed strange and was unmarketable, and journalism was not something Henley took lightly. Both **"Prologue"** and **"Epilogue,"** however, date after 1894, for their subject is the death of Margaret, especially the great void left for Henley and Anna. "Something is dead" begins the **"Prologue."** The images of the poem—images which suggest the cosmological: moon, stars, sun, sea—are not only common Henley images, but ones that fit the dominant topics and themes of the group. The **"Epilogue"** allegorizes Time, Chance, and Change, as well as Life and Death. Even if Margaret had not died, those concepts might have appeared allegorized in any **"Epilogue"** Henley might have added. They are certainly predominant in the section—and are usually allegorized. The effect of the **"Prologue"** and the **"Epilogue"** is to sandwich in broad, universal affirmations, with a personal statement of the pain that Life-Death forces have caused. The irony is considerable.

An integral part of Henley's emphasis on universals in this section of poems is the emergence into his poetry of his allegiance to empire. The new pitch is not always a happy one, but it is consistent with Henley's growing emphasis on an ordered universe. His poems of empire are part of a sometimes evangelical evolutionary faith. The evangelicalism annoys because it is assertion above all that "We are the Choice of the Will: God, when He gave the word / That called us into line, set in our hand a sword." The result of "our" use of the sword is to equate England with Jesus: "Till now the name of names, England, the name of might, / Flames from the austral fires to the bounds of the boreal night." The case for empire could hardly be more audaciously stated.

The poet of "Bric-à-brac" with his acknowledged delight in form descends a long way in his "Some starlit garden gray with dew" which becomes offensively didactic. Here is Henley's activism in its most unpoetic:

> Think on the shame of dreams for deeds,
> The scandal of unnatural strife,
> The slur upon immortal needs,
>   The treason done to life:
>
> Arise! no more a living lie,
> And with me quicken and control
> Some memory that shall magnify
>   The universal Soul.

A part of Henley's militancy was caused no doubt by irritation at the esthetes, who took a decidedly different approach to empire and patriotism. In **Poem IX, "As like the Woman as you can,"** Henley satirizes the effeteness of the esthetic movement. Satire, however much Henley admired it in his reading, was not his way in poetry; he scarcely ever attempts it elsewhere, though **Poem XVII, "Carmen Patibulare,"** is also satirical as the poet amusedly views the idealists' plea that the hangman's occupation be abolished. **"As like the Woman as you can"** is, however, concrete as anecdote and without the stridency of some of the other poems. It is interesting as an attack on the blurring of the sexes Henley felt as a key indication of the wrongheadedness of many of "the decadents" as well as an indictment of the official Victorian repugnance to sex. Henley later asserted in *Hawthorn and Lavender*: "Love, which is lust, is the Lamp in the Tomb. / Love which is lust, is the Call from the Gloom." To deny this law of the universal rhythm was folly.

The most interesting poems of the section, however—with a few exceptions—are the "rhythms" rather than the "rhymes." If an increased concern with empire and didacticism mark the section, so does increased experi-

ment with "free verse." All of these "free-verse" poems are highly descriptive; that is, they attempt to create a visual picture. The pictures are of recognizable objects—usually—but they are also heavy; ultimately, they appear as Impressionistic, rather than Realistic, pictures. The Impressionistic effect is a reflection of the essentially allegorical nature of the poems.

One of the most successful is **Poem III, "A desolate shore."** The poem can be easily associated with the poem of empire which precedes it, but it has nothing of jingoism in it. We could view the poem simply as an impression of a sea-shore scene, but the personifications obviously invite us to go beyond picture. There is a certain flare about Henley's personifications and diction that makes the poem unique, not obviously Victorian. In a brief first stanza Henley shuns complete grammar for immediacy and sheer announcement of atmosphere and the "program" for the poem's action: "A desolate shore, / The sinister seduction of the Moon, / The menace of the irreclaimable Sea."

The Moon and the Sea turn out to be a corrupt old pair who "went out upon the pad / In the first twilight of self-conscious Time." Their purpose is to destroy ships, "Companions of the Advance." The second verse paragraph describes the ships at sea's bottom, fouled and desecrated; but, in the final stanza new ships come on, and there is a bright beacon:

> Stationed out yonder in the isle,
> The tall Policeman,
> Flashing his bull's-eye, as he peers
> About him in the ancient vacancy,
> Tells them this way is safety—this way home.

Next to this poem let us place the better known **"Space and dread and the dark,"** which moves slowly and surely in the one sentence (twelve line) opening paragraph to evoke a heavy primeval atmosphere. Against this despondency, the poet places two urgent questions which reflect a change in the visual atmosphere. In the third stanza he literally shouts an answer: "Life—life—let there be life!" And in a final paragraph he suddenly makes the poem personal: "Life—give me life until the end." The poem, the allegory, has not prepared us for this personal frenzy and final prayer. Since the "I" has not been rendered an Everyman in the allegorical presentation we have witnessed, we are not sure from whence he comes.

"Midsummer Midnight Skies" treats this same material in quieter spirit—and the quietness of the nocturne spirit renders the final transition to the poet and his lover somewhat more natural; but it is difficult to share the avowed experience, the sense of miracle. The allegory is less specific than in **"A desolate shore"**;

Henley's ghosts of the midsummer night skies do not emerge. There is nothing there but a poem of rather tired lines. The dashes, ellipses, the question marks, and exclamations are rather forced emotion.

Much more memorable is Henley's nocturne **"Trees and the menace of night."** Henley is again interested in ghosts, spirits; but their existence is more carefully asserted because the Impressionistic picture has some precise outlines. Sound, movement, from the first verse paragraph to the second, has some dramatic justification. After the picture of the first verse paragraph, the poet whispers "Hist!" And he keeps his questions about the possibly departed spirits tentative, ultimately giving a single spirit reality as "a great white moth." The poet does not mention himself, but we can imagine his reveries. We note the *Then* of line two and the *and then* of line four as the picture quietly, gradually takes form.

One final free verse should be mentioned here, for it suggests the method Henley attempted in the others. **"To James McNeill Whistler"** was not—like so many of Henley's—dedicated to someone after the event, as was **Poem XIX,** written in 1891, but not given the dedication "I. M. R. L. S." until after Stevenson's death in 1894. **Poem XIII** was written for Whistler, a painter Henley greatly admired and helped to promote. Whistler was opposed to the Victorian tradition of story painting. Paintings were not to tell stories or teach lessons; they were to be arrangements in paint. Whistler purposely named his paintings after music to separate them from literary associations. He called his portrait of his mother **"Arrangement in Black and White"**; that is not, of course, how the world knows it.

Henley's poem is tribute to Whistler's work. Henley's picture is of a favorite Whistler subject, a river and a bridge. The lines—like the river—wander wearily on, lingering to bubble:

> So melancholy a soliloquy
> It sounds as it might tell
> The secret of the unending grief-in-grain,
> The terror of Time and Change and Death,
> That wastes this floating, transitory world.

The first half of the poem proceeds in a satisfactory Impressionistic mood, but the mood starts to disintegrate when the soliloquy should start. Henley falls again into questions, and his syntax gets unnecessarily cumbersome. The questions come too vaguely:

> What of the incantation
> That forced the huddled shapes on yonder shore
> To take and wear the night
> Like a material majesty?

We are tempted to answer, "Well, what of it?" The answer apparently comes in the final four-line paragraph—after, alas, a tired exclamation: "O Death! O Change! O Time!" Henley may be praising art that built an "enchanted pleasure-house" as defense against "fatuous, ineffectual yesterdays"; but he may also be praising Death and Change and Time. It is difficult to be certain. Henley's experiment in Impressionism escaped him in the second half of the poem. The melancholy soliloquy that was to tell the terror of Time and Change and Death did not!

IV *HAWTHORN AND LAVENDER*

Henley first published **Hawthorn and Lavender** serially in the *North American Review* (1899-1901). The collection appeared as a book, with few changes in the poems, in 1901. The theme of the volume is caught in the lines from Shakespeare's Sonnet LXV which Henley had picked as an epigraph for Volume II of the definitive edition of his work: "O, how shall summer's honey breath hold out / Against the wrackful siege of battering days?" The white and pink blossoms and brightly colored fruit of hawthorn symbolize "summer's honey breath"; and the pale purple flower, the lavender, symbolizes "the wrackful siege of battering days."

Although Henley's own pain and desire for easeful death come through clearly enough in the poems, the poems of hawthorn are more numerous and give the volume its most dominant colors. As in the earlier Henley poems, the theme here is not hawthorn and lavender as two separate things; rather hawthorn-and-lavender is ever Henley's theme. Death is still but Life in act, as Henley had described it in **"Matri Dilectissimae."**

To accept the ordained cycles of the universe is to accept one's own death—or so Henley along with many poets before him sings. He announces his theme of Nature in a **"Praeludium,"** a "free-verse" poem to be read *"largo expressivo."* The poem's controlling metaphor is from music. Fall is portrayed as a "visual orchestra" which performs:

> In sumptuous chords, and strange,
> Through rich yet poignant harmonies:
> Subtle and strong browns, reds
> Magnificent with death and the pride of death,
> Thin, clamant greens
> And delicate yellows that exhaust
> The exquisite chromatics of decay. . . .

Although the volume starts with "sumptuous chords and strange," the vast majority are played on very simple instruments. Rather than a "sumptuous orchestra," we hear mainly a lyre or pipe. The poems are songs and madrigals. Even the poems in freer rhythms are rhymed, though not in simple or obvious patterns. In fact, since the poet is often singing of love, moon, June, spring, roses—common themes and common images—the reader will not, most probably, be greatly impressed by many of the poems. In fact, Henley himself had some doubts about them. When the first group appeared in the *North American Review,* he wrote to Charles Whibley: "I can't make up my mind about the new crop of lyrics. I can't argue that they're my best; but they're not so bad—there ain't too many flies on 'em, anyhow."[6]

Henley's celebration of love is more in an Elizabethan vein than in that readily identified as his own, as the ending of **"Praeludium"** is clearly Henley's—Winter is called "the obscene, / Old, crapulous Regent, who in his loins—/ O, who but feels he carries in his loins / The wild, sweet-blooded, wonderful harlot, Spring?" With reason does Henley invoke, in **Poem XIII,** the jolly ghost of the Elizabethan dramatist Thomas Heywood, whom he considered a distant ancestor, for lessons in wooing:

> Then to a pleasant shade
>   I did invite her:
> All things a concert made,
>   For to delight her:
> Under, the grass was gay;
>   Yet sang my Lady:—
> "Nay, Sweet, now nay, now!
>   I am not ready."

In **Poem XV,** the poet's lady lies sleeping. Thrice the admonishment is to "cover her with flowers." The variation on that line "makes" the pleasant lyric in the final stanza:

> Like to sky-born shadows
>   Mirrored on a stream,
> Let their odours meet and mix
>   And waver through her dream!
> Last, the crowded sweetness
>   Slumber overpowers,
> And she feels the lips she loves
>   *Craving through the flowers!*

How unlike the verse of most fin de siècle poets! Especially when we consider a bolder Henley statement like **"Love, which is lust, is the Lamp in the Tomb,"** it seems that Henley has in many of these poems recalled the Elizabethans as antidote to more common fin de siècle fare; he thumps his message: "And they that go with the Word [Love] unsaid, / Though they seem of the living, are damned and dead."

But **"Love which is lust"** is an exception to the volume's spirit. Poems that are not in a gayer Elizabethan note are often more directly intended for Anna and reflect Henley's creed of activism, as in **Poem XXXI,** which in the final stanza makes its metaphor come alive and is saved from triteness:

> These glad, these great, these goodly days
> Bewildering hope, outrunning praise,
>   The Earth, renewed by the great Sun's longing,
> Utters her joy in a million ways!
>
> What is there left, sweet Soul and true—
> What, for us and our dream to do?
>   What but to take this mighty Summer
> As it were made for me and you?
>
> Take it and live it beam by beam,
> Motes of light on a gleaming stream,
>   Glare by glare and glory on glory
> Through to the ash of this flaming dream!

There is starkness, too, in these poems and surprise in metaphor in the starker poems. In **Poem XLIX,** God (there is no talk in these poems of "whatever gods may be") is "working His will":

> But I wait in a horror of strangeness—
>   A tool on His workshop floor,
> Worn to the butt, and banished
>   His hand for evermore.

More effective is **Poem XLVI ("In Shoreham River")**—because it is even more dependent upon metaphor, and more dramatic in its dependence upon metaphor. At sunset the poet views "an old black rotter of a boat" stranded in midstream. Above the moon is "a Clown's face flour'd for work." Night comes on; the boat remains:

> Stuck helpless in mid-ebb. And I knew why—
> Why, as I looked, my heart felt crying.
> For, as I looked, the good green earth seemed dying—
> And, as I looked on the old boat, I said:—
> *"Dear God, it's I!"*

Though many of the individual poems might seem merely competent, Henley is sometimes more than that; and, as a whole, *Hawthorn and Lavender* renders the feeling of Henley's love for Anna and his abiding confidence as death nears. In his more personal poems Henley escaped the confused syntax and the bizarre diction and reliance on a spasmodic punctuation that weaken many of his late "free-verse" poems. The poems that are directly personal convince us of a personality who has suffered but has also been deepened by life's battles. Reviewing his life in **Poem XLII,** the poet ponders a pre-existence on another "old, spent star." He feels there was something else, for his love awakens old echoes in his heart, echoes on this "fortunate yet thrice-blasted shore" that he could not forget if he would.

Although Henley never accepted any creed, his poetry is certainly a record of a man who has become more fundamentally religious, a man of a religious conviction that saw no need of creed or ritual. His deepening religious sense finds its most vital expression in *Hawthorn and Lavender.* Yeats, who recognized the strain, tells a story of Henley's interest in the supernatural. Henley had seen a vision of his dead daughter and wanted to get to her.[7] Yeats was touched by Henley's appeal and need. Although Henley apparently never pursued the magic that Yeats's friends had too lightly mocked, there is a calm throughout these late poems. The late lark "With Time, finds heart to sing, / As he were hastening / The swallow o'er the seas."

V London

If Henley's poems reveal an abiding love of nature, her abundance, her renewals, her baubles as well as her insistent rhythms—the hawthorn and lavender and the sea—it is also true that he lived mostly in the city and that he never felt alienated from nature. His love for family and friends was in no way distinct from "nature." Man—no less than trees—has his magic; indeed, for Henley they shared a magic. His devotion to empire he could likewise hold without a sense of compartmentalization. The city and its people were, thus, also a part of Henley's song.

The sonnet portrait painter of *In Hospital* was called upon by William Nicholson to write accompanying verses for London types he had painted. With a sure hand, Henley wrote thirteen "quatorzains," as he called them, to accompany Nicholson's drawings. Though by 1898, the year of *London Types,* the poet had indeed been proven by "crosses and troubles" and often lauded the end which would be "best of all," there is only evidence in the London poems of the zest in the facts of the daily loves of the sundry London personalities. Henley's eye is steady and amused.

Shortly before *London Types,* Henley had completed a revised and expanded *London Voluntaries,* a work he had started some years earlier. In 1890 Henley had written to Charles Whibley, to whom this work was dedicated, that he had discerned in his approach "some possibilities of London as material for verse that may have some chance of living."[8] The city was not to be subject matter exclusively for the esthetes. The manly counterpart to estheticism joyously sang a city of no kinship to T. S. Eliot's coming "unreal city" of *The Waste Land.* Henley celebrated the English capital as vital participant in nature's cycle. The *Voluntaries* ends, in fact, with London joyously at one with the god Pan:

> The enormous heart of London joys to beat
> To the measures of his rough majestic song;
> The lewd, perennial, overmastering spell

> That keeps the rolling universe ensphered,
> And life, and all for which life lives to long,
> Wanton and wondrous and for ever well.

In *London Voluntaries* Henley utilized more grandly the music metaphor that he had struck in the opening poem to *Hawthorn and Lavender.* In five poems—voluntaries—the poet plays in five different tempos; but, as in **"Praeludium"** of *Hawthorn and Lavender,* the song is visual. Thus the opening even-song, **"St. Margaret's bells,"** in *grave* tempo, creates both a Henley nocturne portrait and the cry and call of those "brazen choristers." Ultimately, the most significant feature of the sunset scene is not the bells but the sweethearts who loiter as they did hundreds of years ago. Though the pace is quickened in the final voluntary, the lovers are still the most significant thing against the sky.

In **Poem II,** the lovers take horse for a night ride in order to feel the night pulse of the city, a pulse that is magical and romantic because so natural: the trees and the river are no less important to our view than the streets and houses. Once the journey is begun, picture after picture strikes the travelers. Eagerly they listen and observe. The poem is highly exclamatory and filled with such expressions as "And lo!" or "But see" or "And did you hear?" At the end of the joyous night ride, the poet and his lady are again in a more universal context. As they return home, it is as if they were "wandering some dispeopled star, / Some world of memories and unbroken graves." They must think, too, of death as "an exquisite night's more exquisite close."

Poem III, in *scherzando,* catches the magic of a golden October afternoon. Trafalgar Square shines like "an angel market," and London becomes El Dorado. Thus, the city echoes bright aspirations and dreams. Nightmare, of course, can also be found in London, but never the nightmare of Eliot's bats and violet griefs. In Henley the nightmare is but the **"Wind-Fiend"** of **Poem IV** (*largo e mesto*) who throttles London town. Though in the fury of storm the city seems a "nightmare labyrinthine," it is only a seeming one; the storm is but another of Nature's faces. Grim Death has its claims on the imagination as well as golden sunsets of dreams. And in the final poem we delight in the cycles of regeneration after storm. The spring rites are but the better for the Hangman wind; then Nature touches "to an ecstasy the act of seeing."

If in these descriptive voluntaries Henley runs the risk of too great excitement and too extensive cataloguing, his experiments in picture and music have their appeal. Henley's Romantic faith is expressed only as it celebrates the several moods of the London scenes.

Henley's voluntaries do not, of course, engage us in the way that Eliot's picture of urban life does. Henley's poems are far too diffuse. We need only to surrender to their Romantic vision—whereas Eliot requires great concentration; his scenes are dramatic rather than descriptive, and we earn our synthesis. But Henley's easier poem stands in a symbolic way to its age as Eliot's *The Waste Land* does to his. That such a vision was still possible in a late nineteenth-century poem is in itself remarkable. Amidst all the late nineteenth-century posing and celebration of the artistic over the natural, Henley made a spirited attempt to exult in the two as one.

VI OTHER POEMS

London Voluntaries was Henley's last major poetic effort. Few of his poems were of that length; indeed, longer poems were hardly a late nineteenth-century ideal when objets d'art in verse were more likely to please. But Henley occasionally went into longer discussions, for his enthusiasm sometimes could not be contained. In *Arabian Nights' Entertainments* (1893), it is at times almost overwhelming. In that verse essay, Henley recalls the magic of those Arabian tales for his boyhood. The poem affords interesting contrast with a similar effort by Tennyson, "Recollections of the Arabian Nights" (1830). Near the start of what we normally call the Victorian period, Tennyson in polished measure, slowly lulls (fourteen stanzas of eleven lines) his readers into the presence of Haroun Alraschid. The poem has almost no action, for Tennyson wants an atmosphere—and it is one of surrender to a distant world. In the poem, we sense the pull of "art for art's sake" in Tennyson.

Although Tennyson's poem is called "Recollections," the recollector is hardly present. In Henley's poem the case is decidedly otherwise: we cannot miss the late-Victorian activist. Henley's poem begins "Once on a time / There was a boy." He catches our eye as he appears "Antic in girlish broideries / And skirts and silly shoes with straps / And a broad-ribanded leghorn," and Henley shows us—with gusto a-plenty—that boy on his adventures. The poem excites more than Tennyson's because of the core of Realism that overlays the adventure, overlays the delight in exotic names and the other catalogues of the appeal of the magic East. There is no palace of art in Henley's Bagdad.

Henley's enthusiasm for the work of Rudyard Kipling had inspired him to another fairly long poem of high exuberance. That poem—*The Song of the Sword*—Henley dedicated to Kipling; it is now likely to be read not for its own sake but as a manifestation of jingoism. The sword's song is a blatantly militant exposition and exhortation. The sword declares its birth "a proof" of God's will, not *the* proof, but nevertheless an important one as it sifts nations:

> The slag from the metal,
> The waste and the weak
> From the fit and the strong;
> Fighting the brute,
> The abysmal Fecundity.

The sword is "Prince and evangelist" and invites its listeners to "Follow, O, follow me." Expressions like "Ho! then" and numerous commands add to the sense of religious militancy. When Henley sent the poem to Frank Harris at the *Fortnightly Review,* an assistant wrote Henley regrets and thanks for a song which had sent Harris' thoughts "back to Beowulf."[9] Henley doubtless deserved more courteous treatment, but it is difficult to consider the effort more than a tour de force.

Shortly before his death in 1903, Henley wrote an even longer song, *A Song of Speed.* He wrote Whibley "they that know say [it] is far and away better than the *Sword.*"[10] The poem is dedicated to Alfred Harmsworth, who had given Henley a ride in his new Mercédes. Henley found the motoring experience exhilarating, and he made the automobile the major symbol of the poem; the Mercédes is "one of God's messages," a message of progress, of advancement, indeed of miracle. It is doubtful that the poem is better than *The Song of the Sword*; the poem depends more on cataloguing, on seriatim. And for a contemporary reader, some of the notions have horrors that Henley sped by, as in these opening lines after the "prologue":

> Speed as a chattel:
> Speed in your daily
> Account and economy;
> One with your wines,
> And your books, and your bath—
> Speed!
> Speed as a rapture:
> An integral element
> In the new scheme of Life. . . .

As verse, the appeal of these lines is also slight. Henley himself must have felt the limits of such work, for in a letter to Whibley he later called the work "an effusion." *A Song of Speed* is mainly of biographical interest. Sick as he was, near death as he was, Henley's last verse was affirmative. But Henley's pain, agony, and doubts are in his letters. In the above-mentioned letter to Whibley, Henley observed: "Life is more or less unsatisfactory always—isn't it? But an 'effusion' helps."[11] Wracked by constant pain in these last years, Henley knew that his best work in verse—as in all things—was behind him.

He had roused himself, of course, for *A Song of Speed* and for the poems "for England's sake" which he wrote as propaganda for England's cause in the Boer

War. And though **"Pro Rege Nostro"** ("What have I done for you") is a patriotic song of dignity and is worth any number of "effusions" like *A Song of Speed,* most of the poems in *For England's Sake* are juvenile pumpings, moving only to a Henry Fleming of *The Red Badge of Courage.* Henley himself seems to have been able to see war primarily as the finest test of courage and character. Although he started his poetic career as poet of a new Realism, he sometimes fell victim to a callow Romanticism. He had experienced a hospital and could make convincing verse of that experience, but he was too much the "musketeer" to imagine the actuality of war for the common man, such as Stephen Crane did in *The Red Badge of Courage* or Thomas Hardy in a poem like "Drummer Hodge" (1899). Henley's value as a poet, fortunately, was not dependent on these late declarations.

VII THE POET AND THE MAN

Where, then, does this survey of Henley's poetry leave the reader who has found Henley's verse unexciting—that reader, let us say, mentioned in the introduction to this study who pitied James M. Barrie's admirable Bill Crichton who had as the only book on his desert island Henley's poems? What could there be in a poem like **"Or ever the knightly years were gone"** for a sensible Britisher like Crichton? For Barrie's play, of course, the poem anticipates the rest of the action and also comments on Crichton's character. But it is first of all a poem—an easy poem, but not necessarily a bad one. The diction is simple, the syntax simple; the meter simple; the rhymes easy. There are no real images—only a story, almost a simple one. Almost, but Henley never lets it become quite that. We know only that the poem's love story is painful, and we can offer some plausible outlines. The speaker cast his lover aside; now he longs for her, though she is dead; and yet he would undo nothing of the past if he could. Why? Henley gives us only hints—hints broad enough for the story to be as applicable to Crichton as to any Babylon king. There were, of course, no Christian slaves in Babylon. The story we concoct must be Romantic; there must be ideals and suffering because of ideals. There must be mystery above all. We are almost reading Henley's *Arabian Nights' Entertainments.*

Perhaps the chief value of Henley's verse—aside from *In Hospital*—is to recall, to re-create, the childhood capacity for wonder. Most of Henley's contemporaries were writing poems that took little account of this elemental function of verse. Nevertheless, in most of the matter-of-fact Crichtons there is the need for sheer romance, and every age needs poets who feel this need. And even in more Realistic settings like the London of *Voluntaries,* Henley recalls to his readers the pleasure of naïve wonder, of looking, of amazement. Trees, rivers, hawthorn, lavender—these are things which we may merely but delightedly look at. Poetry is one way of becoming as little children again. Even Henley's Impressionistic poems are geared toward an assertion of mystery and wonder. And, though Henley's hospital sequence is rightly admired for its Realism, the sequence also builds on the protagonist's primary belief in the privilege of wonder, of taking the world in. Indeed, he portrays this quality as the essence of health.

It is bracing to find Henley's assertions as the counterpart to a more fin de siècle pessimism. "Life is more or less unsatisfactory always—isn't it?" So Henley wrote to Whibley shortly before his death—at a time when he might easily have served as the protagonist for a play by Samuel Beckett: a one-legged man, painfully ill, suffering from extremes of constipation and diarrhea. We suspect, however, that Henley would have roundly condemned Beckett's heroes (and Beckett) as possessed by an inordinate amount of self-pity and self-love. Effusions help, Henley discovered. And though, in moments, Henley's life must have seemed only absurd, his whole work is a protest against absurdity. His poetry records a spirit aware of the pain of life, but a spirit that would not allow pain to be the whole of it. Like *In Hospital,* the whole of Henley's poetry summarizes a spirit that would not—even in an age given to inner broodings—surrender to despair.

Notes

1. Alban Dobson, *Austin Dobson* (London, 1928), pp. 117-18.

2. *Ibid.,* p. 112.

3. W. E. Henley, *Poems* (New York, 1922), p. viii.

4. Some of the Bric-à-brac Henley did not select for his complete works. This poem is one. It and other Bric-à-brac are printed in the "Appendix" to Volume II of the *Works.*

5. Thomas Hardy, *Jude the Obscure* (New York, 1923), p. 411.

6. Robertson, p. 343.

7. Yeats, pp. 198-99.

8. Robertson, p. 203.

9. *Ibid.,* p. 240.

10. *Ibid.,* p. 376.

11. *Ibid.,* p. 376.

Works Cited

PRIMARY SOURCES

A. STANDARD EDITIONS

Works. 7 vols. London: Nutt, 1908.

Works. 5 vols. London: Macmillan, 1921.

B. SINGLE VOLUMES

A Book of Verses. London: Nutt, 1888.

A Book of Verses. New York: Scribner & Welford, 1889.

The Song of the Sword, and Other Verses. New York: Scribner, 1892.

For England's Sake, Verses and Songs in Time of War. London: Nutt, 1900.

Hawthorn and Lavender. London: Nutt, 1901.

Hawthorn and Lavender. London & New York: Harper, 1901.

A Song of Speed. London: Nutt, 1903.

In Hospital. Portland, Me.: T. B. Mosher, 1908.

Echoes of Life and Death. Portland, Me.: T. B. Mosher, 1908.

Rhymes and Rhythms and Arabian Nights' Entertainments. Portland, Me.: T. B. Mosher, 1909.

Edward H. Cohen (essay date February 1974)

SOURCE: Cohen, Edward H. "Two Anticipations of Henley's 'Invictus.'" *Huntington Library Quarterly* 37, no. 2 (February 1974): 191-96.

[*In the following essay, Cohen documents a number of correspondences in both theme and language between Henley's* Invictus *and two of his earlier poems.*]

William Ernest Henley is known to most people by virtue of a single poem, **"Invictus"**:

> Out of the night that covers me,
>   Black as the pit from pole to pole,
> I thank whatever gods may be
>   For my unconquerable soul.
>
> In the fell clutch of circumstance
>   I have not winced nor cried aloud.
> Under the bludgeonings of chance
>   My head is bloody, but unbowed.
>
> Beyond this place of wrath and tears
>   Looms but the Horror of the shade,
> And yet the menace of the years

> Finds, and shall find me, unafraid.
> It matters not how strait the gate,
>   How charged with punishments the scroll,
> I am the master of my fate:
>   I am the captain of my soul.

Despite the efforts of our keenest scholars to deride the poet as a "declaimer on a cosmic soap box" or to condemn the poem for its "senseless swagger" and "its self-consciously heroic attitudinizing," the lyric still is widely anthologized and learned by rote and quoted.[1] Henley himself would perhaps be taken aback by the popular response to his work, for as its creative history reveals, **"Invictus"** was the fruit of a most significant personal experience—his protracted hospitalization.

In the summer of 1872, just a few days before his twenty-third birthday, Henley was forced to abandon his "bohemian" existence in London as a free-lance journalist and to take leave of his good friend Harry Nichols, a coffeehouse keeper. In his early youth he had been a victim of tubercular arthritis, and in his adolescence he had suffered the amputation of a leg; now, as the infection crept into his other foot, his only apparent hope for recovery was to take up residence in Margate, Kent, and to submit himself there to treatment at the Royal Sea-Bathing Infirmary. Of this reversal of fortune he wrote: "It was a boyish fault of mine to be strong and self-willed: I liked to have my own way. But I remember receiving my passport with complete indifference. There were probes and other instruments of surgery in the distance . . . but I think I was too tired to exercise myself with anticipation."[2] This same stoicism, once he was settled at the seaside, found expression in the letters he sent north to Harry:

> My foot!—The worst I can at present say of it is that it Will Not get better. It seems to stick in statu quo, neither improving nor getting worse.
>
> Indeed, my boy, my foot is powerful bad. [A physician] tells me that if it suppurates, I shall have a devil of a turn with it, for that indubitably the mischief will affect the bones. And you know what that means!
>
> There can no longer be a doubt that I have—literally—put my foot in it: and deeply, too. I am afeard my marching days are over.[3]

Throughout the autumn and winter his condition steadily deteriorated; but lest these citations be taken as the complete characterization, it seems wise to add that Henley also confessed to his friend several romantic involvements—with a "sweet Unknown," a "Molly Crump," a "Georgina," and any number of nurses—during this period. In October the "sweet Unknown" ("long since flown elsewhither") became the subject of a completed **"Cycle of Songs,"**[4] the individual lyrics of which are dully regular in rhyme and meter but refreshingly distinct in tone. It is only natural that the beloved should appear somewhat protean—now "a maiden wise, modest and fresh and fair"; now an aging virgin "with lips that are cold, & thoughts that are grey"—for the speaker himself is ever changeful in his attitudes. The two dominant strains of moral resolution and romantic hyperbole—as if echoes of the letters to Harry—are irregularly alternated throughout; and only in the final song does Henley fuse them:

A Love by the Sea. XX

—1—

Out of the starless night that covers me,
　(O tribulation of the wind that rolls!)
　Black as the cloud of some tremendous spell,
The susurration of the sighing sea
　Sounds like the sobbing whisper of two souls
　That tremble in a passion of farewell.

—2—

To the desires that trebled life in me,
　(O melancholy of the wind that rolls!)
　The dreams that seemed the future to foretell,
The hopes that mounted herward like the sea,
　To all the sweet things sent on happy souls,
　I cannot choose but bid a mute farewell.

—3—

And to the girl who was so much to me,
　(O lamentation of the wind that rolls!)
　Since I may not the life of her compel,
Out of the night, beside the sounding sea,
　Full of the love that might have blent our souls,
　A sad, a last, a long, supreme farewell.[5]

The parallels here to **"Invictus"** are self-evident: the dramatic first line, the heavy rhyming vowels, the sense of despair which modulates to forbearance. Equally apparent are the deficiencies of this work as an early draft; but Henley, when he first composed it, thought highly of his lyric: "My last—**The Song of the Sea**—is a long way higher than I have ever flown."[6]

It was the opinion of the doctors at Margate that there was no remedy for necrosis of the bone except amputation; but as the usual result of amputation was gangrene and consequent death, Henley, characteristically, scorned their advice. Somehow he had learned of the work of the as yet unheralded Joseph Lister, and so in August 1873 he made his way to Edinburgh and was admitted there as a patient in the Royal Infirmary.

For twenty months Henley was treated in Lister's wards, a test case for the antiseptic theory. His letters to Harry Nichols continued, and they reflected again his initial cautious optimism, his rebellion against the pain, the ennui, the despair, and his flirtation with a nurse—an "adorable wagtail"—and with a fellow patient's sister, who was to become his wife. Though isolated from the outside world, he focused his attention not inward, morbidly, but upon the realm of the hospital; and into poetry went the whole of his experience—observations of the daily routine, accounts of his two operations, representations of the staff and patients—in the sequence of "sketches and portraits" which are the best he ever wrote. As his foot slowly began to heal, however, it was perhaps inevitable that he should become more introspective; reflecting upon the ordeal he had survived, he selected an epigraph from Balzac and affixed it to the manuscript of his "hospital" poems: *"On ne saurait dire à quel point un homme, seul dans son lit et malade, devient personnel."* And at the very end of his convalescence, a week before his discharge, he composed **"A Thanksgiving"**:

From brief delights that rise to me
　Out of unfathomable dole,
I thank whatever gods there be
　For mine unconquerable soul.

In the strong clutch of Circumstance
　It has not winced, nor groaned aloud.
Before the blows of eyeless Chance
　My head is bloody, but unbowed.

I front unfeared the threat of Space
　And dwindle into dark again.
My work is done, I take my place
　Among the years that wait for men.

My life, my broken life, must be
　One long unsuccourable dole.
I thank the gods—They gave to me
　A dauntless & defiant soul.[7]

Eighteen of the "hospital" works were published in the *Cornhill Magazine* in July 1875;[8] thirteen others appeared in 1887 in a subscription volume,[9] but no version of **"Invictus"** was included in either sequence. Probably Henley was wise to omit it; for when these *In Hospital* poems at last were collected, he arranged them in a dramatic cycle—from **"Enter Patient"** to **"Discharged"**—in which traditional forms and patterns were generally rejected and the action was confined to the milieu, with the poet's sentiment admitted but implicitly.

It is widely known that Henley first published **"Out of the night that covers me"** in *A Book of Verses*;[10] but there remains some doubt as to when the earlier states were revised. His biographers maintain that his verses "were polished again and again,"[11] "polished and repolished over a period of thirteen years."[12] But Henley's own statement, in an "Advertisement" for his 1898 *Poems,* would suggest otherwise:

> The work of revision has reminded me that, small as is this book of mine, it is all in the matter of verse that I have to show for the years between 1872 and 1897. A principal reason is that, after spending the better part of my life in the pursuit of poetry, I found myself (about 1877) so utterly unmarketable that I had to own myself beaten in art, and to addict myself to journalism for the next ten years. Came the production by my old friend, Mr. H. B. Donkin, in his little book of "Voluntaries" . . . of those unrhyming rhythms in which I had tried to quintessentialize, as (I believe) one scarce can do in rhyme, my memories of the Old Edinburgh Infirmary. They had long since been rejected by every editor of standing in London—I had wellnigh said in the world; but as soon as Mr. Nutt had read them, he entreated me to look for more. I did as I was told; old dusty sheaves were dragged to light; the work of selection and correction was begun; I burned much; I found that, after all, the lyrical instinct had slept—not died; I ventured (in brief) **"A Book of Verses."**[13]

He seems to have taken his task "of selection and correction" quite seriously; for on February 21, 1888, he reported to Austin Dobson: "I sent off **'Life and Death'** yesterday; but when I'm to have proofs the Lord alone knows. Soon I hope; for I'm beginning to weary of the work."[14] When *A Book of Verses* was released later that year, it was among the rhymed lyrics of the **"Life and Death (Echoes)"** that **"Out of the Night"** was included.

It may be conjectured, then, that two of those "old dusty sheaves . . . dragged to light" early in 1888 were the texts of **"A Love by the Sea"** and **"A Thanksgiving."** As it appeared in the sequence of "Echoes," **"Out of the Night"** was dated 1875; there has never been any reason to doubt that it was first drafted in that year, but until the discovery of the dated holograph of **"A Thanksgiving,"** neither has there been proof that it was composed then nor that it was written in hospital.[15] It is likely that Henley himself in the process of revision realized that **"A Thanksgiving"** was "a premature and feeble version"[16] and that, in seeking to make the work more dramatic, he seized upon the opening line and key phrases and sonances of **"A Love by the Sea."** The idea is not implausible, for two of the three poems which precede **"Out of the Night"** in its sequence were also variants of lyrics originally composed at Margate in 1872, as part of the song cycle for the "sweet Unknown." The evidence of the conflation of these two anticipations into the poem now known as **"Invictus"** adds a new dimension of poignancy to its personal utterance; for its defiant statement may be regarded not simply as an "overdramatic speech about pessimism,"[17] but more logically as the culmination of a long and torturous struggle for life and truly as an epilogue to all the poems Henley wrote "in hospital."

Notes

1. This paper was prepared in San Marino, California, while I was studying under a 1972 award from the Henry E. Huntington Library and Art Gallery, for which I am appreciative. (The several manuscripts cited throughout—and designated "HM"—are reproduced by permission of The Huntington Library.) I am also indebted to the American Philosophical Society for a 1971 grant from its Penrose Fund, under which the research for the article was begun.

   The critical expletives quoted above are those, respectively, of John Ciardi, *How Does A Poem Mean?* (Boston, 1959), p. 850; Vivian de Sola Pinto, *Crisis in English Poetry 1880-1940* (London, 1951), p. 29; and Douglas Bush, *English Poetry: The Main Currents from Chaucer to the Present* (London, 1952), p. 178.

2. Quoted by John Connell—in *W. E. Henley* (London, 1949), p. 41—from a "Margate" essay written ca. 1880, but never published and now apparently lost.

3. Letters of William Ernest Henley to Harry Nichols: HM 30913-30914. These passages occur in two letters addressed from "3 Victoria Terrace, Marine Terrace, Margate" and dated October and November 21, 1872.

4. The "Margate Song-Cycle" was never published as a sequence. There are nearly two dozen drafts and variants of the individual lyrics in the National Library of Scotland, Blackwood Papers, MSS 4804, and in an uncataloged notebook of Henley's poems in the Beinecke Rare Book and Manuscript Library, Yale University. Five fair copies of Henley poems, each of them apparently unique, are preserved in the Huntington Library (HM 30904-30908).

5. The Huntington Library, HM 30907. The holograph [1 p., 4to] is undated; but the striking evidence of its relation to the songs which precede it, variously dated in Aug.-Sept. 1872, and of Henley's assertion to Harry Nichols—in a letter dated "10/'72"—that he had "finished her Cycle of Songs," would place its composition sometime during that early autumn.

6. Letter to Harry Nichols, dated Nov. 21, 1872 (HM 30914). Henley apparently was no mean judge of his own accomplishment. Prior to his departure for Margate, his close associate as a fellow journalist and as another of Harry Nichols' regular customers at the coffeehouse had been James Runciman; on Dec. 8, 1874, Henley was to write to Harry: "Jim has had a letter from Swinburne speaking highly of my *Love by the Sea*—the old Margate Song-Cycle,—& affirming me "de la famille" (HM 30923).

7. A fair copy reprinted by kind permission of The Pierpont Morgan Library: Henley Archive (MA 1617). The poem, unsigned, is dated: "9-10/4/75."

8. XXXII, 120-128. Henley notified Stevenson of their acceptance on Apr. 15 (Beinecke Collection, MS. 4695). A month later—on May 18—he wrote to Harry: "In July there will appear, in the *Cornhill Magazine,* a remarkable paper: Hospital Outlines, Sketches & Portraits, by a friend of ours, which his name, I will not deceive you is, not Harris, but Henley. I hope you will invest a shilling. It will be worth reading" (HM 30928).

9. *Voluntaries for an East London Hospital,* ed. H. B. Donkin (London, 1887), pp. 130-148. Henley wrote most of these poems at Portobello after his discharge from the infirmary but prior to the end of 1875; of them, he lamented to Harry ["1/11/75"]: "There is a second lot of Hospital stuff to come, but I doubt it will never see light till the author is one with the dark. I have called it *Lazarus*" (HM 30929).

10. London, 1888; pp. 56-57. The poem was printed here without a title. In the 1898 *Poems* Henley dedicated it to R. T. Hamilton Bruce; but the familiar title, "Invictus," was not affixed until long after the poet's death.

11. Connell, p. 53.

12. Jerome Hamilton Buckley, *William Ernest Henley: A Study in the "Counter-Decadence" of the 'Nineties* (Princeton, 1945), p. 45.

13. London, 1898, pp. [vii]-viii; both collections were published by David Nutt.

14. Quoted in Connell, p. 108.

15. In a letter to Harry Nichols dated May 18, 1875, Henley wrote: "Yes, I'm out of Hospital. Left five weeks ago next Saturday" (HM 30928). It follows, accordingly, that he was discharged on Apr. 17; again—see n. 7—"A Thanksgiving" was dated "9-10/4/75."

16. The quoted phrase is the adequate opinion of Frederick B. Adams, Jr., who commented upon the acquisition of "The Henley Archive" in the *Sixth Report to the Fellows of the Pierpont Morgan Library* (New York, 1955), p. 60. Opposite this page there is a reproduction of "A Thanksgiving."

17. Ciardi, p. 848.

Joseph S. Salemi (essay date spring 1993)

SOURCE: Salemi, Joseph S. "The Personification of Death in the Poems of William Ernest Henley." *Victorian Newsletter,* no. 83 (spring 1993): 31-5.

[*In the following essay, Salemi analyzes the depictions of the figure of Death in Henley's work and speculates on its possible biographical influences.*]

When William Ernest Henley published his second volume of verse, **London Voluntaries,** in 1893, two of the three great calamities of his life were already behind him. He had lost his left leg to tubercular arthritis in 1865, and a quarrel with Robert Louis Stevenson in 1888 had ended their close friendship. A third blow awaited Henley: the death of his five-year-old daughter Margaret from cerebral meningitis in 1894. Chronically ill, plagued by financial insecurity, and a victim of his own splenetic temperament, Henley might well have succumbed to the despair and pessimism that have disfigured lives less blighted than his own. He never did so, but instead after each fresh disappointment and grief pledged himself all the more fiercely to the twin Victorian deities of Duty and Work. The essentially celebratory character of Henley's poems, as well as his prodigious output of literary comment and first-rate journalism, attest to the triumph of his energy and tenacity over misfortune and disability.

It is no surprise, in the light of his manifold afflictions, that the theme of mortality is a frequent one in Henley's verse. However defiantly faced down, death was an enduring presence for Henley—one that added a somber note even to his most joyous moments. In a number of his lyrics the figure of death appears in vivid and memorable personifications, several of which are sustained for the entire length of the poem. In some instances these personifications serve to soften and humanize death; in others, they add to its horror *via* the amplification of imagery. In any case, Henley's imagined *personae* make of death a ghastly companion or familiar, reminiscent of *ces testes entassees en ces charniers* of his beloved Villon, or of the grinning skeletons in Holbein's *Totentanz.*

As early as his **In Hospital** verses, Henley had described the Royal Infirmary at Edinburgh (where he spent nearly two years in convalescence) as a place "Where Life and Death like friendly chafferers meet."[1]

The picture of death and life bargaining in a hospital must have suggested itself naturally to the bedridden Henley, surrounded by the suffering of his fellow patients and barely enduring his own. But even the *In Hospital* verses betray that strong sense of the complementarity of death and life which was to permeate many of Henley's later poems. In **"Ave, Caesar!"** (fourteenth in the series) the two are seen as linked in unending cyclical recurrence:

> From the winter's grey despair,
> From the summer's golden languor,
> Death, the lover of Life,
> Frees us for ever.
>
> Inevitable, silent, unseen,
> Everywhere always,
> Shadow by night and as light in the day,
> Signs she at last to her chosen;
> And, as she waves them forth,
> Sorrow and Joy
> Lay by their looks and their voices,
> Set down their hopes, and are made
> One in the dim Forever.
>
> Into the winter's grey delight,
> Into the summer's golden dream,
> Holy and high and impartial,
> Death, the mother of Life,
> Mingles all men for ever.

> (23)

The title ("Hail, Caesar!") obliquely alludes to the gladiatorial salute given to Roman emperors before combat in the arena: *Nos morituri te salutamus* ("We who are about to die salute you"). This reference conjures up the real fear that grips any patient facing the surgeon's knife, along with the typically Henleyan bravado that dismisses such fear as unmanly. The poem's real achievement, however, is its evocation of a calm detachment that looks upon life and death with equanimity. The achievement is largely due to the double personification of death as mother and lover, a pairing that takes many shapes in other poems by Henley: reaper and sower, womb and grave, the **"Secular Accomplices,"** the **"Twin-ministers."**

That Henley was partial to personification as a device is evident from a number of his other poems not specifically concerned with death. For example, in his extended lyric **"The Song of the Sword"** (originally the title piece in what later became *London Voluntaries*), the bulk of the poem is spoken by the sword, conceived as a symbol of imperial conquest, warfare, and virile excellence. Again, in the forty-first poem in the collection *Echoes,* the spirit of wine is given a voice to sing its own praises. More interesting than either of these two pieces, however, is the untitled third poem in *Rhymes and Rhythms,* which contains

unforgettable personifications of the moon, the sea, and sunken ships, imagined by Henley as two accomplice murderers and their hapless prey. The poem is worth quoting at length, both for its haunting imagery and as an example of Henley's skill with *vers libre*:

> A desolate shore,
> The sinister seduction of the Moon,
> The menace of the irreclaimable Sea.
>
> Flaunting, tawdry and grim,
> From cloud to cloud along her beat,
> Leering her battered and inveterate leer,
> She signals where he prowls in the dark alone,
> Her horrible old man,
> Mumbling old oaths and warming
> His villainous old bones with villainous talk—
> The secrets of their grisly housekeeping
> Since they went out upon the pad
> In the first twilight of self-conscious Time:
> Growling, hideous and coarse,
> Tales of unnumbered Ships,
> Goodly and strong, Companions of the Advance,
> In some vile alley of the night
> Waylaid and bludgeoned—
> Dead.
>
> Deep cellared in primeval ooze,
> Ruined, dishonoured, spoiled,
> They lie where the lean water-worm
> Crawls free of their secrets, and their broken sides
> Bulge with the slime of life. Thus they abide,
> Thus fouled and desecrate,
> The summons of the Trumpet, and the while
> These Twain, their murderers,
> Unravined, imperturbable, unsubdued,
> Hang at the heels of their children—She aloft
> As in the shining streets,
> He as in ambush at some accomplice door.

> (214-15)

The power of such free verse lies not merely in its precise diction, its command of English idiom, or its acute sensitivity to rhythm. More important are the unspoken yet palpable personifications at the poem's heart: the Moon and the Sea are a strolling prostitute and her male confederate, luring men (the Ships) to their deaths in dark alleys. The comparisons are nowhere explicit but still inescapable—pure products of the descriptive force of well-wrought language. One cannot help asking, in despair more than hope: in the ruck of "free verse" being published today is there anything that can match this century-old poem in the sheer polished literacy it embodies?

The prostitute-and-accomplice image must have pleased Henley as much as it discomfited his contemporaries, for he used it again in the untitled ninth poem in *Echoes,* where life and death are similarly personified, this time in trochaic quatrains. It is one of Hen-

ley's most effective poems—racy, colloquial, and
graphically imagined:

> Madam Life's a piece in bloom
>   Death goes dogging everywhere:
> She's the tenant of the room,
>   He's the ruffian on the stair.
>
> You shall see her as a friend,
>   You shall bilk him once and twice;
> But he'll trap you in the end,
>   And he'll stick you for her price.
>
> With his kneebones at your chest,
>   And his knuckles in your throat,
> You would reason—plead—protest!
>   Clutching at her petticoat;
>
> But she's heard it all before,
>   Well she knows you've had your fun,
> Gingerly she gains the door,
>   And your little job is done.
>
>   (126)

The images of death as a ruffian pimp, waylaying his
woman's clients outside her room, and of life as a duplicitous harlot, momentarily enjoyed and then ruin-
ously paid for, are daring even by relaxed late
Victorian standards. It was very likely poems of this
tenor in Henley's *National Observer* that prompted the
devoutly Catholic Coventry Patmore to cancel his
subscription, lamenting the editor's "uneconomical allusions to sex" (qtd. in Buckley 156). Nevertheless,
the erotic references in this poem and the preceding
one pale before the more dominant note of impending
threat. In both poems death is a menacing figure, a
"horrible old man" and a "ruffian" who evokes our
dread in the manner of the traditional Grim Reaper.
Two other poems in *Rhymes and Rhythms* (the seventh
and the sixteenth, both untitled) also depict death as a
coarse and brutal male. The former poem says

> Death, as he goes
> His ragman's round, espies you, where you stray,
> With half-an-eye, and kicks you out of his way
>
>   (219)

while the latter poem speaks of death as the sea's
"grey henchman" (234). In both cases Henley has
imagined a disreputable, lower-class character,
potentially violent and contemptuous of the finer feelings.

A gentler—and feminine—personification of death appears in the twenty-ninth poem of *Echoes*. Here death
is a kindly nursemaid, to whom a tired child turns for
solace:

> A child,
> Curious and innocent,

> Slips from his Nurse, and rejoicing
> Loses himself in the Fair.
>
> Thro' the jostle and din
> Wandering, he revels,
> Dreaming, desiring, possessing;
> Till, of a sudden
> Tired and afraid, he beholds
> The sordid assemblage
> Just as it is; and he runs
> With a sob to his Nurse
>
> (Lighting at last on him),
> And in her motherly bosom
> Cries him to sleep.
>
> Thus thro' the World
> Seeing and feeling and knowing,
> Goes Man: till at last,
> Tired of experience, he turns
> To the friendly and comforting breast
> Of the old nurse, Death.
>
>   (152-53)

The moralized allegory at its end gives this poem the
air of a seventeenth-century emblem—all that is
needed at the top of the text is a small woodcut of a
child running from his nurse, with the Latin motto
Mors ultima mater. In the previously quoted piece
from *In Hospital* Henley had called death "the mother
of Life." Here that notion is recalled, but with even
more vivid images of nurturing: death has a "friendly
and comforting breast," and a "motherly bosom." The
poem turns death into an icon of peaceful repose, as
quiescent and unintimidating as the ruffian pimp is
menacing. It would be idle to ask which image was
closer to Henley's heart—both are consciously crafted
conceits that, in their respective contexts, are equally
successful.

This gentle, womanly death appears again in the poem
"I[n] M[emoriam] R. G. C. B." in the collection *Bric
à Brac.* This lovely rondeau is much vaguer in it depiction—death is merely a comforting female presence—
but a memorable instance of Henley's experimentation
with fixed French forms:

> The ways of Death are soothing and serene,
> And all the words of Death are grave and sweet.
> From camp and church, the fireside and the street,
> She beckons forth—and strife and song have been
>
> A summer night descending cool and green
> And dark on daytime's dust and stress and heat,
> The ways of Death are soothing and serene,
> And all the words of Death are grave and sweet.
>
> O glad and sorrowful, with triumphant mien
> And radiant faces look upon, and greet
> This last of all your lovers, and to meet
> Her kiss, the Comforter's, your spirit lean.
> The ways of Death are soothing and serene.
>
>   (110)

The masterly use of sibilants in this poem has the double effect of uniting disparate images of "strife," "song," and death's "kiss," while at the same time charming—and lulling—the reader with an auditory smoothness that disguises the poem's harsh sense. This rondeau demonstrates what W. B. Nichols long ago called Henley's two salient characteristics, "a delicacy that is almost robust and a robustness that is almost delicate" (153).

Why this Janus-faced death, at one time kind and at another cruel? Marietta Neff once remarked about Henley's diction that "For some reason psychically significant, no doubt, he returns caressingly to 'sleep' and 'death' and 'peace' and 'dream'" (560). The reason is not far to seek, and is not peculiar to Henley. Death, which is technically beyond human experience while everpresent to reflective consciousness, always evokes equivocal responses. As La Rochefoucauld points out, "We cannot look squarely at either death or the sun." It is too terrible and indomitable a reality to be unthreatening, but it is also, for that very reason, conducive to what psychologists call reaction formation. Our hatred and fear of death compel us to imagine it sometimes in a positive light. Henley's soothing and serene death is merely the Grim Reaper in disguise, rendered less terrifying *via* feminization and sleep imagery.

The collection ***London Voluntaries*** has a sustained instance of Henley's favorite trope in its untitled fourth poem, a dazzling evocation of the discomfort caused by hot weather and fog in London. The poem begins with an image of the evil east wind that brings about such conditions:

> Out of the poisonous East,
> Over a continent of blight,
> Like a maleficent Influence released
> From the most squalid cellarage of hell,
> The Wind-Fiend, the abominable—
> The Hangman Wind that tortures temper and light—
> Comes slouching, sullen and obscene,
> Hard on the skirts of the embittered night;
> And a cloud unclean
> Of excremental humours, roused to strife
> By the operation of some ruinous change,
> Wherever his evil mandate run and range,
> Into a dire intensity of life,
> A craftsman at his bench, he settles down
> To the grim job of throttling London Town.

(196)

This is one long periodic sentence, every element perfectly subordinated, with a cumulative momentum that is truly incantatory. The triple personification, however, is its backbone. The use of three separate metaphors for the wind ("Wind-Fiend," "Hangman-Wind," and "craftsman") reveal Henley's penchant for

turning the impersonal into the personal in order to characterize it punitively. The power of the quoted description resides in the intensely negative judgment of his subject that Henley's word-portrait makes—we are not in the presence of a mere wind, but an active malevolence worthy of our hatred. The poem continues with a vivid account of London in the grip of this vile east wind and its concomitant fog, and then ends with an arresting image of death as an attending physician:

> And Death the while—
> Death with his well-worn, lean, professional smile,
> Death in his threadbare working trim—
> Comes to your bedside, unannounced and bland,
> And with expert, inevitable hand
> Feels at your windpipe, fingers you in the lung,
> Or flicks the clot well into the labouring heart:
> Thus signifying unto old and young,
> However hard of mouth or wild of whim,
> 'Tis time—'tis time by his ancient watch—to part
> From books and women and talk and drink and art.
> And you go humbly after him
> To a mean suburban lodging: on the way
> To what or where
> Not Death, who is old and very wise, can say:
> And you—how should you care
> So long as, unreclaimed of hell,
> The Wind-Fiend, the insufferable,
> Thus vicious and thus patient, sits him down
> To the black job of burking London Town?

(198-99)

The rhyme pattern here, vaguely reminiscent of some complex fixed form, provides only a fitful linkage *via* fugitive couplets and quatrains. The irregular rhythms render the seemingly fortuitous rhymes all the more striking—an effect also noticeable in the poetry of T. S. Eliot. Used together, they make for a poem that is colloquial and rhetorically polished at the same time. The implied personification of death in these lines is that of a kindly doctor at a patient's bedside, a doctor whose "well-worn, lean, professional smile" and "expert, inevitable hand" on one's windpipe and lungs are disquieting rather than calming. Henley's long stay in the Royal Infirmary may provide the personal context for this particular image, which encapsulates the simultaneous trust and dread of the medical profession felt by a chronic invalid.

Henley's seventeenth piece in *Rhymes and Rhythms,* the **"Carmen Patibulare"** (gibbet poem) provides another example of his skill with this rhetorical device. In this poem he sings the praises and the permanence of the gallows (*patibulum*), while at the same time deriding the crackpot idealism of those who would abolish it:

> But Tree, Old Tree of the Triple Bough
>   And the ghastly Dreams that tend you,
> Your growth began with the life of Man,

And only his death can end you.
They may tug in line at your hempen twine,
    They may flourish with axe and saw;
But your taproot drinks of the Sacred Springs
    In the living rock of Law.

(237)

The **"Carmen Patibulare"** is not an instance of personification in the strict sense, but rather an apostrophe to the gibbet. Nevertheless, the poem's figurative language does recall the imagery of the previously quoted texts, for when Henley speaks directly to the *patibulum,* as if it were a living being, there is an implicit personification of the thing addressed. In any case, the gallows in **"Carmen Patibulare"** is clearly another metaphoric rendering of death—not as a human being, but as a dread instrument of execution.

In the light of the foregoing discussion, one might infer that Henley's muse always hovered in funereal regions. It was not so. His poetry reveals a wide range of interests and emotional commitments, and it is a shame that he is so little read today. A perusal of his collected verse discovers well-crafted poems on love, friendship, art, nature, dreams, conflict—all of them marked by meticulous diction and a peculiar power of description that was Henley's *forte.* Though frequently alluded to, mortality is not an obsession in Henley's verse, as it is for example in John Webster or Edgar Allan Poe. On the contrary, what fuels Henley's poetic fire concerning this subject is an offhand and almost cavalier disdain for mortality, as if he were a member of the Spanish military unit that styles itself *novios de la muerte*—the sweethearts of death. The multiple personifications of death in his poetry suggest not a fascination with mortality, but rather a dismissal of it as irrelevant to the tasks of life, and as powerless before the force of imagination.

Consider the resonance of the following lines, where a full-voiced Henley calls for life, even if it must be accompanied by the "Arch-Murderer" and the "Avenger":

Life—life—let there be life!
Better a thousand times the roaring hours
When wave and wind,
Like the Arch-Murderer in flight
From the Avenger at his heel,
Storm through the desolate fastnesses
And wild waste places of the world!

Life—give me life until the end,
That at the very top of being,
The battle-spirit shouting in my blood,
Out of the reddest hell of the fight
I may be snatched and flung
Into the everlasting lull,
The immortal, incommunicable dream.

(235)

These are uncertain personifications; the syntax suggests that the murderer and the avenger represent "wave and wind," but their position in the text makes them foils to the reiterated "life." It is clear that Henley saw life as a gauntlet flung in the face of death, and that for him it was precisely the courage to stare death down that gave existence its meaning and texture.

When Henley greets death as a friend or familiar, he is neither morbid nor suicidal. He simply follows the venerable Western tradition, as old as the Homeric texts, that defines manhood in terms of what it can endure without flinching. With Hector he can say "Death is no longer far away; he is staring me in the face and there is no escaping him" (22: 300-301). The defiant Henley of the overquoted **"Invictus"** owed his bravado not to Victorian arrogance or self-conceit, but to a kind of serene clairvoyance into the utter contingency of human hopes and happiness in the face of the All-Annihilating. What Yeats called Henley's "intensity that seemed to hold life at the point of drama" (qtd. in Symons 477) is, I suggest, this unfeigned acknowledgement of death's power, and a concomitant hunger for life's feast.

Note

1. *Poems* 3. All subsequent quotations are from this comprehensive collection of his own verse that Henley put together for his publisher Alfred Nutt in 1897. The collection came out in 1898, and was reprinted frequently thereafter.

Works Cited

Buckley, Jerome H. *William Ernest Henley: A Study in the 'Counter-Decadence' of the 'Nineties.* Princeton: Princeton UP, 1945.

Henley, William Ernest. *Poems.* New York: Charles Scribner's Sons, 1909.

Homer, *Iliad.* Trans. E. V. Rieu. New York: Penguin, 1985.

Neff, Marietta. "The Place of Henley." *North American Review* 211 (1920): 555-63.

Nichols, W. B. "The Influence of Henley." *Poetry Review* 12 (1921): 153-59.

Symons, Arthur. "Some Makers of Modern Verse." *Forum* 66 (1921): 476-88.

Edward H. Cohen (essay date spring 1995)

SOURCE: Cohen, Edward H. "Henley's *In Hospital,* Literary Realism, and the Late-Victorian Periodical Press." *Victorian Periodicals Review* 28, no. 1 (spring 1995): 1-10.

[*In the following essay, Cohen examines the contemporary critical response to Henley's* In Hospital.]

"The nineteenth century dislike of Realism," wrote Oscar Wilde, "is the rage of Caliban seeing his own face in a glass."[1] For the Victorians the distinction between reality and the representation of reality was a powerful concern, and *realism* in art evolved as a term to define both a method of describing life accurately and a commitment to conceiving life comprehensively. But by the end of the century a moderate tradition in literary realism—"denying excess" and "valuing the ordinary as the touchstone of human experience"[2]— had become established as the principal convention of English fiction. Still, the conflict between life and art persisted. Critics disputed both the limits and the motives of realism in literature, and one of the most dramatic examples of their debate is the reception in 1888 of W. E. Henley's *In Hospital.*[3]

Henley in his youth had contracted tuberculosis of the bones in his hands and feet, and his early life was a sad chronicle of medical mistreatment and literary misadventure. He spent ten months at St. Bartholomew's Hospital in London, where he suffered the amputation of his left leg; three years in East End lodgings and taverns, where he dashed off imitations of Swinburne's *Poems and Ballads*; and a year at the Royal Sea Bathing Infirmary at Margate, where the physicians were unable to arrest his infection. In 1873 he was admitted to the Royal Infirmary of Edinburgh, to be treated by Joseph Lister as a test case for antiseptic surgery, and survived two tedious but successful operations on his right foot. It was during his convalescence in the dreary wards, where he lay for twenty months, that Henley began to transform his hospital episode into poetry.

In Hospital is a sequence of twenty-eight poems, from **"Enter Patient"** to **"Discharged,"** in which Henley threads accounts of personal experiences, sketches of infirmary life, and portraits of physicians, nurses, and fellow patients. Some of the poems are cast in conventional forms, others in free verse. Some are composed as dramatic occasions, others as lyric expressions. Henley situates himself as the poet in the poems, and presents himself as both poet and patient, but limits his horizon to the patient's perspective. The result is a tension between subjectivity and objectivity that is characteristic of Victorian poetry.[4] In other respects, however, *In Hospital* challenges Victorian canons of taste. Henley selects grim details—"corridors and stairs of stone and iron," "dressings and lint on the long, lean table," "this dull, new pain that grinds my leg and foot"—to signify the reality of hospital life. He describes sad cases and their symptoms—a ploughman whose face is "wan and sunken," a suicide whose throat is "strangely bandaged," a casualty whose hair drips "red and glistening"—to illustrate what Foucault has called the "truth" of debility and

disease.[5] But Henley offers neither moral nor meaning in his poems. Indeed, he once wrote that his aim in the completed sequence was simply to "quintessentialize" his memories of the Old Edinburgh Infirmary.[6] In this century *In Hospital* has been commended as "the first resolute attempt in English to use ugliness, meanness, and pain" as literary subjects, and Henley has been recognized as a "pioneer of the new realism in English poetry."[7]

In Henley's own time, however, readers' responses to his hospital verses were mixed. Before the poems were published, even before Henley was discharged from the infirmary, Robert Louis Stevenson read them in manuscript and expressed a reluctant enthusiasm. "Good man!" he penciled on one leaf, "that's what I *do* call realism, and yet like."[8] Leslie Stephen accepted a first version of the hospital sketches and portraits for the *Cornhill Magazine,* and his decision to print them has been acclaimed as one of his "boldest ventures."[9] But the editing entailed significant compromises, and the corrected texts reveal numerous revisions— consistent with contemporary standards of decorum— that Stephen demanded.[10] Henley composed a second series of hospital poems, more personal than the first, but the manuscript was rejected "by every editor of standing . . . in the world."[11]

Henley cannot have been surprised, therefore, by the range of responses to *In Hospital* in the periodical press. Almost every reviewer presented the sequence as an expression of literary realism, but they described the work as "crude" or "credible," "coarse" or "subtle," "false" or "vigilant." They associated Henley's art with photography and pathology, with naturalism and impressionism. They linked him with Crabbe and Meredith, with Heine and Verlaine and Zola. One reader felt a "shudder of revolt"; another heard a "ring of genuine humanity." One admired the portrayal of the hospital experience as a "human document"; another insisted on elevating the sequence to an allegory of the "patient's progress." Some praised the work as an experiment in poetry, while others scorned the attempt to treat a realistic theme in verse. They found the poems "ugly," "grotesque," "horrible," "original," "fascinating," "beautiful."

In the *Athenaeum* Theodore Watts-Dunton asked: "How much of that dramatic realism of which prose seems to be the natural medium can a poet—without neglecting the demands of poetic art—import into his verses?" He acknowledged that realism is a legitimate and essential "quest of the poet" but insisted that there must be "a limit to the extent to which the poet may invade the domain of the prose writer." "Perhaps when we affirm that Mr. Henley's little volume consists of poems written, or supposed to be written, in a hospital—poems describing, with a realism that is something more than Pre-Raphaelite, scenes which he witnessed as a hospital patient—the reader will be inclined to say that the limit has at length been reached."[12]

In some responses to *In Hospital,* realism was equated with the crude, the coarse, the grotesque. The *Critic* depicted Henley as "wandering at large through themes of pungent realism" and creating "a sense of recoil" in his readers.[13] The *Nation* described the sequence as a work, "unique in literature," in which "the uttermost realities of drug and knife are brought before us."[14] In the *Glasgow Herald* William Sharp wrote that "the 'Hospital Rhymes' will appear to some readers vigorous and truly poetic. To others, they will prove occasionally repulsive and, in the main, disagreeable; for Mr. Henley has adopted a morbid and false view of art. He has condescended to that pseudo-realism which is now the ready resource of those who have not much insight, imagination, or power of touching those chords and springs which the poet may legitimately handle."[15]

Of course, there were many reviewers who defended Henley's experiment in realism. In *Merry England* Alice Meynell expressed surprise at "the appearance of a group of poems that told the truth with a direct intention" and declared that Henley—"in a great sweeping manner"—had achieved "a simplicity allowing the experience in the verse to be felt immediately by any sensitive reader."[16] The *New Princeton Review* owned that the theme of Henley's hospital experience "is not a tempting one," but insisted that "it is not so strange, after all, that the poetic fire should be kindled and fed in such an atmosphere. The pathos and pain of life seem to lend themselves more readily to the poet's uses than life's joy and brightness."[17] Similarly, *St. James's Gazette* described *In Hospital* as "the literary picture of a section of human suffering which has not before found its artist. . . . That the hospital and the world as it looks to one stretched on a sick-bed in a ward are attractive subjects we do not assert. Still they are no small part of human life and are full of pathos and the possibilities of tragedy." The reviewer recognized Henley's restraint in touching on "the purely physical horrors" and affirmed that "to leave them unnamed, unindicated, would have been cowardly."[18]

Others, admiring Henley's impudence, cited his willingness to overstep the literary boundaries of "commonplace" experience and "indifferent" realism. In *Woman's World* Oscar Wilde praised the "power" of the hospital poems and characterized Henley as "an artist who is seeking to find new methods of expression, and who has not merely a delicate sense of beauty, but a real passion also for what is horrible,

ugly, or grotesque. No doubt everything that is worthy of existence is worthy also of art—at least, one would like to think so—but while echo or mirror can repeat for us a beautiful thing, to artistically render a thing that is ugly requires the most exquisite alchemy of form, the most subtle magic of transformation."[19] Reviewing the sequence for the *Pall Mall Gazette,* Bernard Shaw wrote that Henley "sings as if the world were a rack, and he stretched taut on it, with every power absorbed by the effort to endure," and he concluded that *In Hospital* "is a horrible, fascinating, and wrong, yet rightly done little book—a book which no one should be advised to read, and which no one would be content to have missed."[20]

A significant problem for reviewers was the difficulty of classifying the style of the hospital poems. Some tried to identify Henley's sources, citing most often Heine, Swinburne, and Whitman. In the *Saturday Review* George Saintsbury read the sequence as a "curious and interesting little chapter of realism" in the tradition of Crabbe, but—owing to Henley's "gift of abnormally acute and discriminating physical perception"—more "deliberately and crudely realistic."[21] Others attempted to describe his prosody. The *Scottish Leader* noted that the poems in irregular blank verse were "curiously and memorably vivid, full of deft phrasing, and perfectly free from prosaism."[22] The *Scotsman* concurred that the "freedom of expression" in these unrhymed pieces gave them "a freshness never seen in the work of writers who take an exclusive view of what should constitute a poetic vocabulary."[23]

Perhaps because the tradition of realism in English poetry had been neglected by critics,[24] several reviewers described Henley's literary technique in *In Hospital*—as they might explain the method in a realistic novel—by analogies with the visual arts. In the *Academy* Cosmo Monkhouse admired Henley's "artistic treatment" of the hospital theme,[25] and in the *Spectator* Richard Holt Hutton praised Henley's "clear eye for outline and colour."[26] *St. James's Gazette* regarded the portraits of hospital characters as "a gallery of credible human beings,"[27] and the *Critic* suggested that "a French painter of anatomy and vivisection might find a letter-text for illustration" in the vignettes of infirmary life.[28] The pictorial elements in *In Hospital,* particularly the vitality of detail in the poems, encouraged reviewers to analyze Henley's style in the painterly metaphors ubiquitous in late-Victorian criticism of fiction. But some resisted the stock expressions. Wilde remarked that the sequence contains a mixture of styles which treat aspects of the hospital experience with varying degrees of involvement, detachment, and sympathy: "Some of them are like bright, vivid pastels; others like charcoal drawings, with dull blacks and murky whites; others like etchings with deeply-bitten lines, and abrupt contrasts and clever colour-suggestions." Although he felt that some of the pieces were "inspired jottings in a note-book," rather than perfected works, Wilde nevertheless praised the hospital poems: "From the point of view of literature, they are a series of vivid concentrated impressions with a keen grip of fact, a terrible actuality, and an almost masterly power of picturesque presentation."[29]

The most perceptive interpretations of Henley's poetic practice in *In Hospital* were those, like Wilde's, that discerned his affinities with impressionist poets and painters. Meynell described Henley's studies of hospital characters as "impressionary portraits in which what appears is noted curiously, with no cheap conjecture and laborious analysis."[30] In the *Fortnightly Review* Arthur Symons noted "something of the exquisitely disarticulated style of Verlaine" in the hospital poems and hailed them as "a triumph of remembered and recorded sensation": "Here is poetry made out of personal sensations, poetry which is half physiological, poetry which is pathology—and yet essentially poetry."[31] Symons also wrote in *Harper's New Monthly Magazine* that "Verlaine's definition of his own theory of poetical writing—'sincerity, and the impression of the moment followed to the letter'—might well be adopted as a definition of Mr. Henley's theory or practice": "The poetry of Impressionism can go no further than that series of rhymes and rhythms named *In Hospital*. The ache and throb of the body in its long nights on a tumbled bed, and as it lies on the operating table awaiting 'the thick, sweet mystery of chloroform,' are brought home to us as nothing else that I know in poetry has ever brought the physical sensations."[32] For Wilde and Meynell and Symons, Henley's accomplishment in the hospital poems was his ability to capture particular moments, to transform their sensations into feelings, and to convey hospital life—with all its grim associations—as inextricable from his own experience.

Within the limits of the critical vocabulary available to them, nineteenth-century readers were confident that Henley had spoken personally and truthfully in *In Hospital*. "The verses describe a hard personal experience and the reflections that came to a suffering patient during a tedious recovery from a scrious and painful operation," wrote the *New Princeton Review*. "A man, evidently the poet, is taken to the hospital, is chloroformed, undergoes an operation, awakes to a 'dull, new pain,' and then awaits a slow return to the liberty of his fellow men."[33] Henley closed the sequence with a subscription, "The Old Infirmary, Edinburgh, 1873-75," and the device had the effect of particularizing the work, locating its situation in time and place, and conveying the sense of a landscape recreated—un-

transformed by language—by the poet's own memory and imagination. Hutton asserted that Henley's poems were "drawn in hospital" and that almost all contained "some strokes that mark true vision for that which is characteristic in place and person."[34] Monkhouse read the sequence as inherently autobiographical, as "a series of self-vivisections," and realized that Henley's subject is "primarily himself." From the subscription, he determined, "it would seem that the poet's sojourn in this sad hostelry lasted for more than a year—a little life within a life, with its own special stages between entrance and exit—a theme *prima facie* not ill adapted for artistic treatment."[35] Although they made no distinction between the "realism of correspondence" and the "realism of coherence" in their readings of *In Hospital*, the reviewers perceived the narrative as shaped by experience rather than dictated by art. The autobiographical connection authenticated the hospital experience and lent a legitimacy to its truth. "Out of the almost sordid material of a personal experience," said the *Scottish Leader*, Henley "has conjured up a set of poems which singularly combine the realism of actual and detailed description. . . . The success consists in the poet's simple and straightforward recital of the phenomena as he saw them."[36]

The evolution of literary realism reflects a growing awareness in the nineteenth century of the variety of human experience. But in English literature the spectrum of observation was often limited to circumstances that could be construed within a moral framework. George Levine, attempting to explain away "the confident moralism of which the great Victorian writers are frequently accused," asserts that "nineteenth-century realism, far from apologizing for what is, deliberately subverts judgments based on dogma, convention, or limited perception and imagination."[37] Indeed, Symons admired *In Hospital* simply "as a human document and as an artistic experiment."[38] And Monkhouse avowed that Henley "cannot be said to teach in song what he has learnt in suffering, because his muse is not didactic."[39] But one of the most persistent themes in the reviews is an effort to identify an uplifting moral in the sequence. Harry Quilter in the *Universal Review* argued that "the real excellence consists in the kindly philosophy, strong yet tender withal, which breathes from these pages—the words of a man who has seen both the gaiety and the suffering of life, who has had his share in each, and who now looks tolerantly or bravely at happiness or pain."[40] "Speaking generally," wrote Saintsbury, "we are no partisans of the realistic method in literature or of its products; but . . . there is a manly vigour, and even dignity, about these hospital poems which win us to accept the crudity."[41] Even Watts-Dunton, who condemned the treatment of "repulsive" subjects in verse, concluded nonetheless that "if the temper of the poet be sufficiently heroic to conquer the conditions of the surroundings, the surgeon's work may become beautiful and poetic; and . . . the wards of a Scotch hospital may become poetic ground if the temper of the sufferer be manly and heroic."[42]

Some months after **In Hospital** appeared, Alfred Nutt, the publisher, wrote to Henley to bolster the poet's spirits against an offensive refrain that had crept into the reviews. Sensing influences in the sequence of contemporary French art and literature, several critics had detected murmurs of naturalism. One compared the poems with the "Salon pictures."[43] Another warned that some of the scenes "would be grossly out of place even in the most 'realistic' novel by Zola."[44] "I wish you had reviewed me," Henley replied to Nutt. "Naturalism is but a word. I prefer reality. All human art has its basis in life and experience, and the closer the connection the greater the result."[45] Henley believed that he had captured the "truth" of his hospital experience and, in adopting literary realism as his mode of expression, had successfully translated that truth into art. The review that nettled him was Sharp's in the *Glasgow Herald,* where he stood accused of adopting a "false view of art."[46] "Art," Henley responded, "is treatment *et praeteria nil.* What I tried to do in **In Hospital** was to treat a certain subject—which seems to me to have a genuine human interest and importance—with discretion, good feeling, and a certain dignity. If I failed, I failed as an artist."[47]

In our time it has become customary to denounce nineteenth-century realism "as part of that great system of constraint by which the West compelled the everyday to bring itself into discourse."[48] But the Foucauldian doctrine ignores the strength that realism in Victorian literature derived from topicalities and particularities, by which readers were invited to perceive and judge the veracity of the text. "I was twenty months or so in the Infirmary," Henley once explained to John Blackwood, "and I wished in writing these verses to treat the matter as subjectively as I could. And this I have done. I pray you to believe that I have not written for effect. There is no word set down in my copy that is not true."[49] However personal its subject, **In Hospital** is an exemplary instance of realism, of imagination answerable to reality, of the connection of life and art. "To be shut up in hospital, drawn out of the rapid current of life into a sordid and exasperating inaction—to wait, for a time, in the ante-room of death: it is such things as these that make for poetry," Arthur Symons reflected. "The poet to whom such an experience has come, the man, perhaps, whom such an experience has made a poet, must be accounted singularly fortunate."[50]

Notes

1. Oscar Wilde, *The Picture of Dorian Gray,* ed. Donald L. Lawler (New York: Norton, 1988) 3.

2. George Levine, *The Realistic Imagination: English Fiction from Frankenstein to Lady Chatterley* (Chicago: U of Chicago P, 1981) 21-22.

3. William Ernest Henley, *A Book of Verses* (London: David Nutt, 1888) 1-48.

4. See Carol Christ, *Victorian and Modern Poetics* (Chicago: U of Chicago P, 1984) 17.

5. Michel Foucault, *The Birth of the Clinic: An Archaeology of Medical Perception,* trans. A. M. Sheridan Smith (1973; New York: Vintage, 1975) 95. Foucault insists that it was a new mode of discourse—the articulation of medical language—that made clinical experience possible: "From then on, the whole relationship of signifier to signified, at every level of medical experience, is redistributed: between the symptoms that signify and the disease that is signified, between the description and what is described, between the event and what it prognisticates" (xix). In Henley's poems one may discern not simply a discourse about disease but the intersection in the nineteenth century of medical and aesthetic models of representation.

6. William Ernest Henley, *Poems by William Ernest Henley* (London: David Nutt, 1898) vii-viii.

7. Vivian de Sola Pinto, *Crisis in English Poetry 1880-1940* (1951; New York: Harper, 1966) 27-28.

8. Henley Archive, Pierpont Morgan Library.

9. Frederic William Maitland, *The Life and Letters of Leslie Stephen* (London: Duckworth, 1906) 266.

10. See Edward H. Cohen, "The Evolution of Henley's *In Hospital,*" *Victorian Authors and Their Works: Revision Motivations and Modes,* ed. Judith Kennedy (Athens: Ohio UP, 1991) 57-71.

11. William Ernest Henley, *Poems by William Ernest Henley* (London: David Nutt, 1898) vii-viii.

12. *Athenaeum* 25 August 1888: 245. Watts-Dunton's authorship of this review was established by Susan Holland, who consulted the "marked file" of the *Athenaeum* in the library of the City University, London.

13. *Critic* 7 July 1888: 5.

14. *Nation* 26 December 1888: 522.

15. *Glasgow Herald* 21 June 1888: 4. The review was not signed, but Sharp's authorship may be deduced by his description of the poems as "occasionally

crude." In a letter to Sharp, dated 5 July 1888, Henley wrote that he "objected to but one expression—'occasionally crude'—in all the article"; see Elizabeth A. Sharp, *William Sharp (Fiona Macleod): A Memoir* (New York: Duffield, 1910) 139.

16. *Merry England* June 1888: 93.

17. *New Princeton Review* November 1888: 387.

18. *St. James's Gazette* 12 September 1888: 7.

19. *Woman's World* 1889: 108. Concerning his remarks Wilde wrote: "I have just finished a review of Henley's poems for my own Magazine: when it appears he will roar like the Bull of Bashan, though I think it is very complimentary"; see Stuart Mason, *Bibliography of Oscar Wilde* (London: Laurie, 1914) 223.

20. *Pall Mall Gazette* 11 June 1888: 3. In a letter to one of Henley's biographers, Shaw wrote: "I reviewed his first book of poems—the hospital ones—in the *Pall Mall Gazette*. Archer thought I underrated him; but I maintained that except when he had an experience like the hospital experience to go upon, his case was one of manner without matter"; see Kennedy Williamson, *W. E. Henley: A Memoir* (London: Shaylor, 1930) 199-200.

21. *Saturday Review* 23 June 1888: 770-71. Authorship of this review was confirmed by Dorothy Richardson Jones, who consulted the "account book" in which Saintsbury's anonymous writings are identified.

22. *Scottish Leader* 21 June 1888: 7.

23. *Scotsman* 28 May 1888: 3.

24. See V. de Sola Pinto, "Realism in English Poetry," *Essays and Studies* 25 (1939): 81-100. He contends that "the poetry of realism is . . . an essential and characteristic part of the English heritage which has been commonly ignored or at least inadequately treated by literary historians" (82).

25. *Academy* 23 June 1888: 425.

26. *Spectator* 26 May 1888: 724.

27. *St. James's Gazette* 12 September 1888: 7.

28. *Critic* 7 July 1888: 5.

29. *Woman's World* 1889: 108-09.

30. *Merry England* June 1888: 94.

31. *Fortnightly Review* 1 August 1892: 185-86.

32. "The Decadent Movement in Poetry," *Harper's New Monthly Magazine* November 1893: 867.

33. *New Princeton Review* November 1888: 387.

34. *Spectator* 26 May 1888: 724.

35. *Academy* 23 June 1888: 425.

36. *Scottish Leader* 21 June 1888: 7.

37. Levine 20.

38. *Fortnightly Review* 1 August 1892: 185.

39. *Academy* 23 June 1888: 425.

40. *Universal Review* May-August 1888: 307.

41. *Saturday Review* 23 June 1888: 770-71.

42. *Athenaeum* 25 August 1888: 246.

43. *Nation* 26 December 1889: 522.

44. *Glasgow Herald* 21 June 1888: 4.

45. William Ernest Henley. *Some Letters of William Ernest Henley,* intro. James de V. Payen-Payne (London: Hutchings and Crowsley, 1933) 18.

46. *Glasgow Herald* 21 June 1888: 4.

47. Quoted in Elizabeth A. Sharp, *William Sharp (Fiona Macleod): A Memoir* (New York: Duffield, 1910) 139-40.

48. Michel Foucault, "The Life of Infamous Men," *Power, Truth, Strategy,* ed. Meaghan Morris and Paul Patton (Sydney: Feral, 1979) 91.

49. William Ernest Henley to John Blackwood, 9 February 1877, National Library of Scotland, Blackwood Papers, MS 4360, fol. 207.

50. *Fortnightly Review* 1 August 1892: 185.

R. van Bronswijk (essay date 2003)

SOURCE: van Bronswijk, R. "Driving the Darkness: W. E. Henley's 'The Song of the Sword' as Uneasy Battle Cry." *English Studies* 84, no. 4 (2003): 330-46.

[*In the following essay, van Bronswijk gives a detailed analysis of Henley's "The Song of the Sword," focusing on the poem's ambiguous modernity.*]

LADY BROCKLEHURST.

By the way, Crichton, were there any books on the island?

CHRICHTON.

I had one, my lady—Henley's poems.

LORD BROCKLEHURST.

Never heard of him.[1]

Those occasional writers who have, since his death in 1903, tried largely in vain to drag W. E. Henley from the murky land of the neglected into the merry land of the reclaimed all complain about his undeserved dismissal from the canons and annals of literature. This is of course the prerogative of the reclaimists, although Henley himself would have had little sympathy with the usual reformulations of the canon to include women and (post)-colonial writers, two groups of society that Henley was not unappreciative of but that he would hardly have credited with profound literary and intellectual ability. In fact, looking back to more recent discussions concerning the canon, or canons, may go some way towards explaining Henley's absence in our own day. There is no sense of a gaping Long-John-Silver-shaped hole in our perception of literature or literary history because there is no obviously identifiable group of society that feels Henley's presence would add political, social or psychological validity to their identity—the terrorist Timothy McVeigh, if anything, may have cast even a deeper shadow over Henley's reputation. Some of the unease that Henley invoked and still invokes can be distilled from the reactions to his poem **'The Song of the Sword'**; the content and what lies behind the **'Sword'** reveals many of the contradictions that Henley incorporated and some of the reasons for his inability to find himself a sympathetic audience.

Henley finds himself forever mentioned as a character lurking on the peripheries of another literary or historic figure's life and times. His role was pivotal, yet alien, among a group of—often Celtic—authors much better known than himself: R. L. Stevenson, W. B. Yeats, J. M. Barrie, H. G. Wells, Joseph Conrad and Rudyard Kipling are some of the names that spring most readily to mind. At the same time, he was the face of the 'cult of manliness' which, as Murray G. H. Pittock has phrased it, was the main opposition against the 'bourgeois-bating artists'.[2] Henley's fist-shaking helped to define its object of derision, just as it defined Henley; as Frank Kermode has argued, 'A movement is strong when a man like Henley throws himself into an antithetical, activist movement, to oppose it.'[3] Yet, his absence as a literary and historic figure in his own right is as apt as it is comfortable. The relative obscurity of much of his poetry is not so much a judgement on the quality of the work itself, as it is a fair and telling reflection of the tastes and tendencies of the fin-de-siècle literary elite. The important biographies and accounts (most of them at least half a century old) and the recent volume of selected letters edited by Damian Atkinson paint the picture well enough: here was a religious man, a hot-tempered patriot with a strong admiration for traditional manliness, yet a consumptive cripple; here was someone who—true to the age—found inspiration in the Victorian city, the art of others and his own physical and emotional suffering, yet his no-nonsense Toryism watered down any sympathy for the femininity of Decadence and Aestheticism or the masculinity of the New Woman. Here was an invalid who—or so Connell tells us—spent his happiest days in a Scottish environment among Celtic friends, such as R. L. Stevenson, J. M. Barrie, Walter Blaikie and W. B. Yeats, yet for whom Parnell's efforts and the overt sentimental Romanticism of the Celtic revival were objects of scorn.[4] Here was a ruddy man of action, ever in need of money, who upheld the values of the gentry and of an earlier generation but whose use of strong sexual overtones in his poetry induced Coventry Patmore, writer of 'The Angel in the House' and friend of the Tennyson whom Henley so admired, to accuse him of immorality and end his subscription to the *Observer* on this count.[5] Henley was neither comfortably Victorian nor comfortably modern, or indeed, comfortably anything. Yet, it is not so much that he himself was uncomfortable, although this may certainly have been the case, but it is also that we as well as his contemporaries are made to feel uncomfortable by this conflicting late-Victorian figure who undeniably demands our attention but cannot fulfil the part of literary hero to our satisfaction. This is also why his slippery identity is of literary interest: it is from this uncomfortable, peripheral, yet domineering position that his art springs. Rather than reclaiming him as a reviewer and poet of central importance, or villainising him as a literary upstart who managed to alienate Wilde, Stevenson, followers of the Decadent movement and Burns devotees, who were not very pleased with his edition of the complete works,[6] it may be helpful simply to accept his alienation, partly inflicted upon him and partly self-imposed, and receive his work for what it is: something undeniably of the age.

What should be remembered is that, uncomfortably placed as he is in his late-Victorian context, Henley was not merely a background rumble. Although the actual remark is attributed to a friend, Cornford's account of Henley notes that he could 'no more be ignored than an active vulcano can be disregarded when its thunder fills your ears and the hot ashes singe your garments'.[7] Cornford's coloured account may ooze the unapologetic enthusiasm of an avid admirer, but these words do carry more than a hint of the almost violent activity that pervades at least some of Henley's poetry. In reviewing *The Song of the Sword and Other Verses* in 1892 (to be retitled *London Voluntaries, the Song of the Sword and Other Verses* the following year), Arthur Symons, perhaps unexpectedly sympathetic towards his poetry, emphasises that quality of Henley's verse, which must have stood out to a reviewer otherwise confronted with the effeminate receptive sensitivity of Aesthetic and Decadent poetry:[8]

> What Mr Henley has brought into the language of poetry is a certain freshness, a daring straight-forwardness and pungency of epithet, very refreshing in contrast with the traditional limpness and timidity of the respectable verse of the day. One feels indeed at times that the touch is a little rough, the voice a trifle loud, the new word just a little unnecessary. But with these unaccustomed words and tones Mr Henley does certainly succeed in flashing the picture, the impression upon us, in realising the intangible, in saying new things in a fascinating manner

(191).

Henley is indeed far from being 'timid' or 'limp'; his assertiveness translates into bellowed poems and ballads that resound in ringing echoes, which may euphemistically be described as 'a trifle loud'. The poem that gave its name to the first editions of the work Symons is reviewing is a case in point: the **'Song of the Sword'** is sung at the top of his voice.

It is also in the **'Sword'** that we find Henley's problematic position reflected in all its flagrant colours as well as its decibels. The very fact that the name of the volume was changed to *London Voluntaries, The Song of the Sword, and Other Verses* after the first edition could suggest it was thought proper that the poem would not draw too much attention to itself at the expense of the then added and often-praised **'London Voluntaries'**, which preceded it in the new title and the volume itself. This, in spite of the fact that the **'Sword'** seemed important enough to merit an edition in 1892 comprised otherwise of poems that had already appeared in print in *A Book of Verses* in 1888. Even though Henley's patriotic **'In Praise of England'** had been published in the *National Observer* of July 18 1891, the **'Sword'**—with its peculiar blend of not only jingoism, but also religion, highly-charged sexuality, Darwinism and blood-thirsty battling spirit— proved unpublishable in any of the leading literary periodicals of the time, in spite of these growing ever more numerous in the final decades of the nineteenth century. Then there is the poem's dedication to Rudyard Kipling, whose views it recalls but not his laughter, and who did not seem to appreciate the poem with as much wholehearted enthusiasm as Henley had shown towards the *Barrack-Room Ballads,* which had found their way into the *Scots Observer* edited by Henley himself. Finally, there is Henley's ill health and amputated leg, which rendered him an invalid and incapable of even travelling to the British Empire, let alone performing any physical battle there on behalf of her Majesty the Queen. The pain and personal struggle with his body arguably resulted in a fantastic

battle-cry which grew out of all proportion to encompass a world beyond the individual as grand as the British Empire. It is Henley's imagined battlefield prowess and masculinity that have condemned the poem ever since, and biographers writing with several wars between Henley and themselves (and, as is true of both Connell and Buckley, writing immediately after such a horrendous event), although able to forgive, cannot see beyond that concession to express their appreciation.

Buckley chooses to treat the subject of Henley's jingoism, which he sees epitomised in the **'Sword'**, with a mixture of disbelief and contempt, calling it 'incomprehensible not only intellectually but also in the light of normal emotional experience' and noting that 'Obviously the sanction behind this mystical belligerency is a naïve and misapplied Darwinism.'[9] Buckley, although dismissive of all of Henley's war poetry, is yet almost relieved to announce that the poet's proud imperialist attitude of the **'Sword'** changed into 'a fearful hysteria', lamenting the fallen, as the Boer War aimlessly progressed.[10] Yet, leaning on the language of madness, he cannot quite satisfy himself that here is a valid excuse for the invalid's blood-thirst of some years before:

> Pathological in character, this war-and-dead philosophy was but another expression of the masculine protest against preordained weakness. But even in Henley's case, the delight in blood and battle was programmatic and doctrinaire in its development, tried by a merely vicarious experience.[11]

(138)

This passage suggests that Henley's violent bellowing song was wholly the product of the dual contexts of the period and his own unfortunate life. True as this may be, the song itself confronts us with uncomfortable questions about the relationship between beauty, cruelty, the fury of enjoyment and beneficence. In this, it is an epic, primal and passionately physical, whose unapologetic assertiveness sweeps up the reader and throws his baser instincts back at him by painfully confronting him with man's (possibly the reader's own) response to the Sword's battle cry:[12]

> Bleak and lean, grey and cruel,
> Short-hilted, long shafted,
> I froze into steel;
> And the blood of my elder,
> His hand on the hafts of me,
> Sprang like a wave
> In the wind, as the sense
> Of his strength grew to ecstasy;

(33-40)

The awful beauty of battle—its alliance with waves, winds and all things terrible, sexual and elemental— invokes pagan deities as well as a Christian God of righteousness. The poem's pantheism confirms the Sword's symbolic function as man's fighting instincts made tangible; rationally, religiously and racially in opposition, a multitude of voices join in the same chant to the rhythmic clanging of Swords, strangely musical, justifying the battle by the righteousness of their cause symbolised by their God-granted victory, their faith in which is unconditional. As Tom Gibbons has observed: 'The notion that the universe was pervaded by this all-powerful and purposive evolutionary force gave a new and powerful impetus to a variety of religious philosophies based upon the doctrine that God is immanent in or permeates the whole of creation, and such venerable pantheistic religious philosophies as Brahmanism and Neo-Platonism now received the apparent support of the most up-to-date scientific thought.'[13] Whatever the moral stance of its author, the poem itself is a work that aspires to agelessness and for that very reason the product of the age which produced it. In the first place, its echoes of a heroic past emphasise the Victorian awareness of history and inherited oral and literary traditions. But the **'Sword'** also looks forward in a way that may be disconcerting, yet is hardly unexpected. André Guillaume remarked in 1972:

> L'audace novatrice de sa forme a une assez faible portée puis—qu'elle s'est heurtée à l'indifférence presque générale; mais sa signification historique demeure entière, elle est même prophétique, car l'idéologie qu'il esquisse s'écarte des grands courants du XIXème, et annonce surtout le XXème siècle. Ces vers souvent délirants contiennent une véritable religion de la force brutale, de la guerre pour la guerre, de la violence arbitraire gouvernée par les fantasmes d'angoisse; ils dressent la haine irrationnelle contre les idées libérales de Droit, de suprématie de la Loi issues de la Révolution française, contre la rationalisme à la fois scientifique et moral de l'ère victorienne; ils détournent vers leurs propres fins anti-intellectuelles, en les transformant, des idées tirées du darwinisme, et posent les principes d'un culte de la race, de la nation, avec un 'jingoism' paranoïde.[14]

The rational and irrational grounds for battle are dancing around each other in the poem, seemingly opposed, but eventually all leading down a sloping path towards those baser feelings of hatred and animosity that are innate and instinctive and satisfied with the flimsiest of excuses for drawing the sword. The stark blood rage of the **'Sword'** is padded with these irrational beliefs from all ages and with the newer rational Darwinism in a manner that calls to mind the war propaganda of the decades succeeding its publication. Even for Guillaume, writing some time after the Second World War, Henley necessarily *se range ainsi parmi les précurseurs du fascisme et de l'hitlerisme'*.[15] However, the journey of the **'Sword'** through every epic battlefield and its piling up of excuses for waging

war along the way add to the swelling sound of the song and universalise the chant to such a degree that it comes to stand for every battle fought, personal as well as national. The concept of survival—after illness or adversity—becomes the poem's justification for its universal simplicity; it translates the emotion necessary for active self-preservation and is neither moral nor immoral without any specific context. In retrospect, it is easy to spot the signs that indicate the **'Sword'** is caught up in a wave of contemporary thought charging towards a World-War scenario. Yet, we must also recognise in it all battles between clans, families, tribes, races and nations—the ones that predate the poem and from which it emanates as well as the episodes of ethnic cleansing we see around us in the world today.

In this lies much of the duality of the poem for the informed reader: when Henley's own unfortunate circumstances are superimposed onto its fighting spirit, some of the controversy is lost and the work becomes more politically correct. Connell, writing only a few years after Buckley, recognises the poem's baseness but sees in this an excusable simplicity on Henley's side, who is naively unaware of the bloody reality of the battlefield:

> It is by no means difficult to be smart about lines like these. But the invalid who wrote them was not just a vociferous braggart; nor was he just whistling to keep his courage up. All this joy of battle was not artificial or insincere. Henley, in his own life, had fought demons—plenty of them—and he had twelve more years of arduous, and far from triumphant, conflict ahead of him. But the battles which he fought were comprehensible and personal ones; and he thought, ardently enough, in their terms. They were, however, simple terms.[16]

It is questionable if Henley's poem can be dismissed so easily. Acute as his illness-related discomforts were, they were probably less 'comprehensible' to him than the suffering caused by the use of military forces fighting to maintain a healthy empire. Naivety about suffering is not the kind of simplicity that Henley could be accused of and serves as no excuse. In spite of this, it may indeed be Henley's own suffering that allowed him to express the strong emotions underlying the struggle for survival. Although he does not dwell on Henley's physical discomforts, it is this (together with his 'HATRED OF HUMBUG,' neatly printed in smallcaps) that Williamson, who does not mention the **'Sword'** specifically, identifies as a possible cause for Henley's extreme stances in general and his jingoism in particular.[17] According to Williamson, Henley's sole aim in life seemed to be to dispel cults and crazes of his day and of course 'a man who wishes to restore a balance, and to adjust the effects of a craze, may need to go as far over the mark in adverse criticism as the "fans" have gone in eulogy.'[18] This may be a very attractive and sympathetic way of reading Henley, but it presupposes a kind of calculated reasoning that is far removed from the violence of his verse and the lack of any argument in a poem like the **'Sword'**.

The brutality of the poem lies partly in its uncensored frenzied bloodlust, but also in the confrontational exposing nature that makes the reader uncomfortable not only because his own instincts are exposed, but also because he realises that the author is shamelessly prostrating his naked, baser self in all its splendid imperfection. Even in Henley's time, this was felt. In the review mentioned above, Symons, who saw the **'Sword'** as 'a hymn to the ecstasy of conflict',[19] praised the poem because it did what the Decadent poets were trying to do—it described a darker side of man. Yet, it did so in a language that was confrontational rather than evasive or suggestive, and this frankness, this Henleyan simplicity, shameless and amoral, forges an emotional response that is potentially painful. Symons recognises the strength of this strategy when he writes: 'He is ashamed of none of the natural human instincts, and writes of women like a man, without effeminacy and without offence, content to be at one with the beneficent seasons, the will of nature.'[20] Yet, this is also one explanation for the reluctance of the editors of periodicals, such as the *Nineteenth Century,* the *Fortnightly* and the *Contemporary Review* to publish the **'Sword'**, in spite of Henley's poetic reputation gained with the success of the hospital poems. As the correspondence quoted by Connell reveals, the poem was thought too long for Henley's own *National Observer.*[21] Of course, Henley may have felt that such an act of self-publication would be a battleless victory that would have compromised his credibility both as a poet and as a professional reviewer and critic by blurring the borders between these. Decadent periodicals such as the *Yellow Book* and the *Savoy* were known for the written contributions from their editors, and the blurring of distinctions between art and criticism was associated with Aesthetes and Decadents, as may be seen in Wilde's essay 'The Critic as Artist'. For them, all writing was individual, subjective and artistic and more often than not inspired by other artistic creations. Henley always violently disassociated himself from this group, as he did in a letter to Lewis Hind, referring to the decadent poet Francis Thompson, whom Henley disliked, but whose work he came to appreciate to some extent: 'I have never babbled the *Art for Art's Sake* babble. If I have, I'll eat the passage publicly.'[22]

After its publication in April 1892, in ***The Song of the Sword and Other Verses,*** it did certainly not go unnoticed. On June 4 and June 18, Henley's poetry was thought familiar enough and topical enough to be parodied in *Punch* in a series entitled 'Studies in the New Poetry' of which June 4 was the first installment.[23] Williamson tells us that the term 'New Poetry' was introduced by William Archer; it specifically referred to Henley's work and that of his associates.[24] Later 'Studies' in *Punch* were to include parodies of Rudyard Kipling, who was, rightly, closely associated with Henley. In his pioneering work of 1913, Holbrook Jackson already pointed out the significance of the adjective 'new' in the final decade of the nineteenth century, which was a label too frequently applied in those days; among his examples of the use of the word 'new', Jackson notes specifically that Henley, after the untimely demise of his *National Observer* exchanged it for the *New Review* in 1894.[25] The attempt at describing the 'New Poetry' in *Punch* not only pokes fun at free verse, but also at the attitude of the poet:

> Indeed, cases have been known of rhymes that have been left on a sort of desert island of verse, and have never been fetched away. And sometimes, when the lines have got chopped very short, the rhymes have tumbled overboard altogether. That is really what is meant by 'impressionism' in poetry carried to its highest excellence. There are, of course, other forms of the New Poetry. There is the 'blustering, hob-nailed' variety which clatters up and down with immense noise, elbows you here, and kicks you there, and if it finds a pardonable weakness strolling about the middle of the street, immediately knocks it down and tramples on it. Then too there is the 'coarse, but manly' kind which swears by the great god, Jingo, and keeps a large stock of spread eagles always ready to swoop and tear without the least provocation.

> (June 4, 1892)

In a letter dated June 4, quoted by Connell, Henley mentions the parody in *Punch,* which he must have just read, and suggests it could be subject to improvement.[26] As if the illustrious *Punch* had been looking over his shoulder when he wrote this, the next issue carried a parody which more directly ridiculed the **'Sword'**. It was called 'The Song of the Poker' and was accompanied by a drawing of an elderly gentleman in nightly attire brandishing a smoking hot iron and looking down triumphantly on what must presumably be a recently knocked-down burglar. The first lines immediately evoke the **'Sword'**:

> The Poker,
> Clanging.
> I am the Poker the straight and the strong,
> Prone in the fire-grate,
> Black at the nether end,
> Knobby and nebulous.

> (1-7; 16 July, 1892)

Punch's parody captures not only the voice of the poet, but also the blatant sexuality of the poem. Even in these pre-Freudian days, the significance of the sword was well understood and Henley's poem is not shy to dwell on the shape of the weapon, as well as the primal relation between the sex drive and the drive to kill, both essential to the success of man and the survival of races. For Henley, the Sword is both giver and taker of life, it is the 'arch-anarch, chief builder' (line 165). The drawing accompanying the *Punch* parody and the parody itself poke fun at Henley's blatant sexuality as well as his actual impotence. Even though the man in the drawing is not an invalid, his age and appearance suggest someone unlikely to be capable of fighting in wars against other men. The poker becomes a necessary aid in a situation where a young and healthy man would have been able to rely on physical strength alone. The poker in the *Punch* drawing is obviously as proud and sexual as the Sword of Henley's song, but as a traditional instrument of torture and of the home, it suggests hidden stories of domestic violence as well as the plain struggle with felons and burglars. Thus, the home becomes the battlefield and, in a brilliant twist to the story, the Poker is implicated in the ensuing legal battle, the kind of sensational court case which the newspapers frequently fed to their eager readers. Like the Sword, the Poker is an instrument in the hands of the righteous as well as the hands of the wicked; in a civilised society it does not justify itself, but needs to be tried by jury and judge.

The parodying text introduces a drunk wife-beating husband who serves as a manifestation of an attitude towards women that would have been considered stale and old-fashioned by the late nineteenth century. It was also the attitude associated with the London low-life characters that Kipling frequently gave voice to with some sympathy and that became a theme associated with the 'New Poetry'. Henley was by no means low-life or a wife beater, but he himself was eager to cultivate the image of his boisterous and non-melodramatic attitude to life that had inspired Stevenson to create his Long John Silver in *Treasure Island*. An unsentimental superiority over the weaker elements of society—be it the enemy in battle or the wife in marriage—were very much part of this attitude that is also suggested by the original, in which women serve as a vehicle for easing men's sexual passions and blood thirst:

> As he knew me and named me
> The War-Thing, the Comrade,
> Father of honour
> And giver of kingship,
> The fame-smith, the song-master,
> Bringer of women
> On fire at his hands
> For the pride of fulfilment,
> *Priest* (saith the Lord)
> *Of his marriage with victory.*

> Ho! then, the Trumpet,
> Handmaid of heroes,
> Calling the peers
> To the place of espousals!
> Ho! then, the splendour
> And glare of my ministry,
> Clothing the earth
> With a livery of lightnings!

(43-60)

The battling spirit and victory wins men their women and it is the role of women to be the 'Handmaid of heroes' and aid men in both their sexual and their physical struggle for survival. Henley's traditional view of marriage and of the role of women has been dealt with by Buckley, Flora and Connell, and although we are assured that Anne Boyle (the later Mrs Henley, or 'the *Châtelaine*') was happily suited to the role he had in mind for her, her passivity, voicelessness and relative unimportance in the biographies themselves make painful (as well as suspicious) reading.[27]

Yet, ancient though the epic voice of the Sword may sound, the poem was by no means old-fashioned; it was 'New Poetry', after all. To some extent, the survival tactics of the **'Sword'**—its loudly proclaimed jingoism, unapologetic primal screams and fiery sexuality—are useless in a mute world of print dominated by degeneracy and Decadence devoid of traditionally female trumpets willing to spur on the poem, but they are equally out of place in respectable and civilised queen-and-country-loving dinner-table conversations. The poem's subject, like its form, blends the old with the new and, as I have argued, its modernity lies in its overall historic awareness as much as in its unrhyming lines and candour. It may have been this curious blend that elicited Williamson's comment that in spite of his fiercely proclaimed Toryism, his writing would often seem 'a deep-dyed red' (116). Flora points out more clearly the underlying problematic situation of Henley the reviewer and editor:

> Perhaps no example is more informative about the *Observer* spirit than that of Rudyard Kipling, for the journal was nothing if not Tory and imperialistic. In this fact also lies a further explanation for the magazine's failure to reach a wider public; for, although there was a great wave of imperialistic fervour at the close of the century, most of those who clamoured loudly in its service were not up to the sophistication of Henley's magazine; those who were, more likely than not, worshipped at the temple of 'art for art' rather than the temple of empire.

(57)

What is true of the *Observer* is also true of the **'Sword'**; it is tempting to dismiss the poem as unsophisticated because it is loud, primal, apparently amoral and racist, bloody, overtly sexual or anything else that may make us uncomfortable, but the **'Sword'** is lovingly crafted by a poet of skill whose awareness of sound and language is able to bring to consciousness the subconscious voice. Although this is often acknowledged, the conventional view of Henley's poetry remains grounded in that uneasy sentiment, expressed by Connell in his prologue, when he writes that 'the content of much of his poetry is not equal to the technical competence and originality of its execution.'[28] The word 'execution' is poignant in this context, because it seems as if it is indeed the content of the **'Sword'** that signs the poem's death warrant as an appreciated and publishable work of art. However, Williamson contributed a similar view of Henley's lack of substance to Bernard Shaw and himself noted that 'Few writers of his eminence have paid such scant heed to science and philosophy, theology and metaphysics.'[29] It is only the ever-faithful Cornford who springs to Henley's defence by attributing to Henley a thorough dislike of philosophy of any kind and proclaiming with insight as well as admiration that 'Henley's work is so various, and embraces so wide a sphere of thought and emotion, that to suggest its character in a formula is merely impossible.'[30] This may well be a helpful key to reading Henley the poet: as not in the first place interested in capturing political or philosophical ideas or affectations and suggestions, but rather as trying to express in his language real and universal emotional states. In relation to the **'Sword'**, I would argue, that reading beyond the political motivations of Henley himself and beyond our own uneasiness, the work expresses more than mere jingoist propaganda.

Behind the voice of the poem, there is the notion that something natural, sensual and elemental echoes through the Sword's battle song, which necessarily lends it an irresistible Syrensque beauty because it appeals to basic human emotions. Mythical images of earth, clay, sand, wind, waves, fire and blood are continuously invoked and keep the poem tied to man's universal origins.[31] The Sword itself is 'Black and lean, grey and cruel' (33) and informs us: 'I froze into steel' (35). The metal of the sword lifts man out of his most primitive state and gives him the strength he needs to progress and procreate. Man remains 'the vacant, naked shell' (11) until the Sword stirs the libido and battle spirit man needs for enduring survival and identity. This is borne out perfectly by lines 36-40, already quoted. The sword is as natural (or, arguably, supernatural) as man himself and is created not by man, but by a divinity—it has mythical status itself. Its music is accompanied and inspired by the 'silver-throated' (120) sound of the 'iron' (21) Trumpet, that other image of supreme judgement, which is no less elemental and natural than the Sword: 'As He [God]

heard in the Thunder / That laughed over Eden / The voice of the Trumpet' (18-20). The Sword becomes the Trumpet's natural counterpart 'Clothing the earth / With a livery of lightnings!' (60-1). A phrase like this invites the reader to linger, because it comes amidst the rhythmically fired powerful monosyllabics that dominate the poem as a whole. The exclamation mark, but more so the breaking up of the rhythm suggests a raising of the voice before a pause, as if this is a climaxing of the energy built up in previous phrases, a final breath before inhaling anew that has something left over.

The phrase also calls forth the Gods, pagan and otherwise, in both subject and tone. The imagery of the **'Sword'** is as much steeped in pagan and primitive religious traditions as it is in Christianity and this eclectic identity underlies the universality of the Sword's battle song. The Biblical notion of the sword as both necessarily cruel and just has its echo in most religions and is found even in sacred Buddhist texts like the *Bhagavad Gita* and the *Upanishads* which elicited strong interest at the time. The exegesis of Biblical swords also comprises the compound concept of the sword and the tongue. In the book of Revelations, for instance we can read: 'And he had in his right hand seven stars: and out of his mouth went a sharp two-edged sword: and his countenance was as the sun shineth in his strength.' (Rev. 1.16). As in the poem, the singing Sword speaks to the people; it is indeed two-edged in that it does not necessarily speak one universal language, but may well convey its message 'speaking in tongues'. Even though the poem suggests the initial creator of the Sword is the Biblical God of Eden and creator of man, in the third stanza the Sword is given a variety of names reminiscent of Anglo-Saxon kennings: 'War-Thing'; 'Father of honour'; 'fame-smith'; 'Bringer of women', etc. (45-9). The poem evokes epic tales like *Beowulf* and the Deor poem, involving the Teutonic smith-god Weland, creator of invincible swords. The smith-creator is a well-known image (connected with the poet as word-smith and creator of art) and it is with the sword that man himself shapes the world.

More than any mythological tradition, perhaps, it evokes the poetic renditions of Celtic sagas, with their forceful rhythms and sing-song tones, found in old manuscripts as well as newer revivalist poetry. This may seem contradictory considering Henley's attitude towards the Irish question, and the topicality of the issue at the time Henley wrote the **'Sword'.** Yet, Henley may not have felt that his politics was at odds with a genuine admiration for the heroism of Celtic fairy tales. It has already been noted that many of Henley's friends were Celts. W. B. Yeats, for instance, who had been engaged by Henley to write for the *Observer,* was publishing his own Irish fairy-tale collections at the time.[32] Douglas Hyde's tales, published in 1890, were favourably reviewed in Henley's *Observer,* although this may have had something to do with the fact that they were published and annotated by Alfred Nutt, who also published Henley's poetry. Nutt, although an Englishman, had a special interest in Celtic fairy tales both as a publisher and a scholar. It may be that Henley was inspired by Nutt's claims for a strong influence of Celtic fairy tales on British literature and on mythologies and romances in the whole of Britain and Western Europe and by his views of universal ownership of the tales. In spite of this, Yug Mohit Chaudhry is still baffled by Yeats' attitude towards Henley:

> While writing his *Autobiographies,* why should Yeats pick up on remarks that Henley may have made to him in private but which were totally belied by his public conduct? Yeats's account of Henley tries to convey the impression that Henley was sympathetic to Ireland, that he was not as anti-Irish and as unreconstructed an imperialist as people think, that they shared an interest in folklore and Irish literature. However, the impression that it does convey is that Yeats is trying to justify his association with Henley because he is uncomfortable with the thought that people might wonder why he associated with Henley and why he was writing for as virulently anti-Irish a weekly as the *Observer.*[33]

Maybe this is true, but Henley's poetry at least betrays an interest in the Celtic that suggests Yeats may not be so misguided after all. In any case, Celtic stories were becoming increasingly popular, and not just with the Scottish and Irish revivalists. (It is possible that Henley's decision to employ W. B. Yeats may have been a business decision, taking this into account.) As more and more stories became available in print and in English translations, a new world of reference became available for the poet that was fresh, popular, attractive and accessible. In addition, it had local validity as it was (or so Nutt argued) already intertwined with the British literary tradition.

The heroes of Celtic cycles are shown with their weaknesses as well as their virtues. Like some of the mythological figures from Greek epics, they are not infallible and may die. They sometimes take on the role of villain and their awesome powers and passions are often more important to the story than their moral virtue. It is this passion that is also the subject of the **'Sword'** and, curiously, seems the only justification for the battle. With 'Life but a coin / To be staked in the pastime' (152-3), the victory that is to determine the future could be on either side. The **'Sword'** may appear jingoist propaganda, coming from a British-empire-worshipping tongue such as Henley's, but the song itself is found on the lips of all who carry their swords to battle. In the poem, it is emphatically not

Henley's voice we hear, nor is it that of an unidentified 'enemy'; it is the voice of the Sword itself, stripped of all specific racial, political or religious identity. In a sense, the **'Sword'** is the universal battle cry of seeking courage and self-justification before a confrontation. Blind trust in the superiority of the own side and own race, and the divine approval that will ensure the victory is a universal and necessary precursor to a war. Even at its most Darwinist, the argument of the Sword is that used by all sides, no matter how irrational and mutually exclusive:

> Sifting the nations,
> The slag from the metal,
> The waste from the weak
> From the fit and the strong;
> Fighting the brute,
> The abysmal Fecundity;
> Checking the gross,
> Multitudinous blunders,
> The groping, the purblind
> Excesses in service
> Of the Womb universal,

(127-37)

These may have been the lines that were so surprising and shocking to Buckley. Henley the invalid and consumptive was not in a position to comfortably count himself among 'the fit and the strong'; yet, like all warriors going to battle, he would have had an interest in doing so. Whether or not Henley, with all his jingoism, was conscious of this, in the **'Sword'** he succeeded in giving voice to the emotions underlying the will to be victorious that is essential to man's survival. This is consistent with Kennedy Williamson's view; he saw Henley as a poet for whom writing becomes the substitute for the physical exercise he was unable to engage in.[34] As a consequence, his verse is energetic, powerful and full of frustration, and it wants in the first place to assert itself; it wants to shout, scream, cry or shake its fist rather than speak about or mourn over something specific. It may be that positioning himself in his own unique place away from the sympathies of conventional views and movements helped Henley to rail against the world and assert himself.

It is of course all very well to shun the obvious and popular, but even a voice as loud as Henley's will go unheard without a sympathiser or audience. Considering the poem's dedication to Rudyard Kipling and the shared views of Kipling and Henley, it seems obvious that here, at last, may be found someone who appreciated the poem in all its dimensions. As has been elaborately described by Henley's biographers and by Kipling's biographers, the dedication proved very awkward for the latter, who was at that time making the important dual decision to get married and leave

Britain for America. Henley's patriotism did not fit in with the thoughts of a Kipling who was recovering from a nervous breakdown and thoroughly tired of things English. For Kipling, this was a transition period, as Ricketts explains in detail (169-201)—it was hectic on the personal front and his attitude towards both Britain and America was changing, away from Henley's.[35] Henley had asked him to write an accompanying piece to the **'Sword'**, but Kipling, sent him 'Tomlinson', a poem written some seven months earlier.[36] 'Tomlinson' is a narrative poem in which an effete decadent artist who has died is to justify himself before his maker; he has only 'been' things and never 'done' things and baffles St Peter at the gate with his past inactivity. On the basis of his deeds on earth, he can neither be allowed into Heaven, nor condemned to eternal suffering in Hell. The poem also attacked the Aesthetic attitude, but its refined and elaborate satire is far removed from Henley's primal battle cry. Lycett sees some significance in the poem being sent to Henley and argues it is Kipling's goodbye to Britain.[37] If this is true, it may also be regarded as a goodbye to his former patron and advisor, from whose ideas and views he was now steering away. The change in their relationship in those vital years can clearly be read in Kipling's correspondence. In a letter to Henley dated by Pinney August 10, 1891, he was still celebrating their joint views of poetry and effeminacy:

> Touching the influences of men upon each other we two especially are bound up in the queerest chain of give and take and one that I feel sure will last long. At the worst, my very dear man, you can only call me a 'bugger' for developing along strange lines, and I shall but love you all the more for it.[38]

On January 18, he wrote to Henley about the proposed accompanying piece and the dedication of the **'Sword'**. It was a delayed reply to an earlier letter from Henley and Kipling, after apologising, goes on to distance himself from the poem, albeit not without giving his former mentor some suggestions—suggestions, some of which Henley follows, as can be seen from the **'Sword'**:

> I shan't touch the **Sword**. And I don't see what the deuce my initials have to do with it. All the same, can't you work in 'mistress of mysteries, sweet-spoken, maker of honours, adored'? Something about the clean steel that carves writing on God's blank signet-ring which is the world and so forth? See if it welds in.[39]

Another eight months later, Kipling had received and read ***The Song of the Sword and Other Verses*** and his comments are playful but also critical:

> My poem please you will write over again with rhymed endings. Swords sing, O Henley Sahib! And yet the way in which your blade comes out of its scabbard inch by inch till it drives back again with a clang on the last line is Good Enough. It is a 'high irresistable song' [sic]—Most of the Book—but there are certain things, (groping round for some damned word fr'instance) for which I should in the quiet of the Savile like to heave brick-bats at you—exactly as you would like to peruse me with javelins for some of my verses most like. Glory be, that we are not all of one mind!—[40]

The last line is in stark contrast to Kipling's earlier admissions of having found a kindred spirit. What all of this meant to Henley may be distilled from his letters and the biographies. Henley was, after Stevenson, losing another of his friends to a woman and to America and was utterly disappointed.[41] In the late eighties and early nineties, Stevenson and Kipling were the success stories they were, partly because of Henley, and conceivably, with their help or public appraisal, Henley might have won greater recognition for his own work as a poet. It must have been at least frustrating for the invalid to be constantly overtaken by people as well as events.

Kipling's personal development away from Britain may have been the result of a set of opinions similar to those that made Henley shake his fist at some of the weaknesses he found in British culture. Henley's instinct was to seek direct confrontation. It was the survival mechanism that had seen him through his personal hardships and it made sense to him personally. He was strengthened in this notion by the oral traditions of all the great races as well as by some aspects of Darwinism. Henley's instinct was an animal instinct and, as the *Punch* parody shows, some elements of civilised society may have felt they had moved beyond its primitive simplicity, but to Henley, it was still the basis for survival and progress as it had always been. It was as necessary as it was irrational and there was no sound ethics that could justify it. The **'Sword'** is not in the first place, if at all, about the rights and wrongs of the British Empire; it is a poetical rendition of a terrible primal instinct that is part of man, whether he likes it or not—the Hyde inside every Jekyll. In verse, the powerful chant of this instinct, with the feelings of satisfaction that go with it, is too confrontational and embarrassingly recognisable. It seems to justify and even advocate the necessity of behaviour that abhors and frightens in the light of war-time facts and experiences. Its animalism not only goes against Victorian civilised values, but also against the 'unnatural' urges of the Decadents. It becomes a taboo for all societies that have experience of the darker side of war. But the poem itself is not political and is far removed from political rhetoric. In fact, much of its strength lies in the agelessness and the universality to which it aspires. Ironically, this agelessness also condemns the poem and the poet for our times.

Notes

1. J. M. Barrie, *The Admirable Crichton* (1902). In a reworked version of the play, the reference to Henley disappears altogether.

2. Murray G. H. Pittock, *Spectrum of Decadence: The Literature of the 1890s* (London and New York, 1993), p. 124.

3. Frank Kermode, *Romantic Image* (1957; London, 1961), p. 22.

4. John Connell, *W. E. Henley* (London, 1949), p. 10.

5. Joseph M. Flora, *William Ernest Henley* (New York, 1970), p. 60.

6. *Ibid.*, pp. ii-iii.

7. L. Cope Cornford, *William Ernest Henley* (London, 1913), p. 20.

8. Arthur Symons, 'Mr Henley's Poetry.' *Fortnightly Review* os 58, ns 52 (1892), 182-93. This Arthur Symons review has been dealt with in Linda Dowling, *Language and Decadence in the Victorian Fin de Siècle* (Princeton, NJ, 1986), pp. 219-21. Tom Gibbons has also looked at it in some detail and describes the review as 'a far more important document in the history of modern poetry than his [Symons'] better known essay, "The Decadent Movement in Literature", of 1893' [See Tom Gibbons, *Rooms in the Darwin Hotel: Studies in English Literary Criticism and Ideas 1880-1920* (Nedlands, W. A., 1973), pp. 73-4]. It is an interesting detail, pointed out by R. K. R. Thornton, that Symons initially included Henley in his 'The Decadent Movement in Literature', but left him out when he reprinted the essay in 1925 as part of his *Dramatis Personae* [See R. K. R. Thornton, '"Decadence" in Later Nineteenth-Century England', in: Ian Fletcher (ed.), *Decadence and the 1890s* (London, 1979), 15-30, p. 24 and R. K. R. Thornton, *The Decadent Dilemma* (London, 1983), p. 51].

9. Jerome Hamilton Buckley, *William Ernest Henley: A Study in the Counter-Decadence of the 'Nineties* (Princeton, NJ, 1945), p. 137.

10. *Ibid.*, p. 139.

11. *Ibid.*, p. 138.

12. This and all subsequent quotations of the poem are taken from W. E. Henley, *Poems* (London: 1898).

13. Gibbons, p. 5.

14. André Guillaume, *William Ernest Henley 1849-1903 et son Groupe* (Paris, 1972), p. 625. Guillaume, incidentally, consistently dates the poem

back to 1890 in his thesis. This is understandable, considering the confusing lay-out of the 1898 edition that he refers to; in this edition, there is a separate page for the title of the poem, its dedication to Rudyard Kipling and the date 1890. All the evidence Connell brings up in his discussion suggests that the 'Sword' was not finished until early 1892 [See Connell, pp. 234-49]. The letters between Kipling and Henley that have appeared in print first mention the poem in August 1891, but suggest that the idea, at least had already been discussed between them [See Thomas Pinney, ed., *The Letters of Rudyard Kipling,* 2 vols., (Houndsmills, Basingstoke, 1990), II: 39]. It is not impossible that the poem was begun as early as 1890, but more likely, the year appears near the dedication either because it is the year Kipling and Henley first met or because it is the year Henley began publishing Kipling's work—the 'Barrack Room Ballads'—in the *Scots Observer,* which influenced Henley's writing, or both.

15. *Ibid.*, p. 625.

16. Connell, p. 19.

17. Kennedy Williamson, *W. E. Henley: A Memoir* (London, 1930), p. 127.

18. *Ibid.*, p. 128.

19. Symons, 189.

20. *Ibid.*, 189.

21. Connell, p. 234.

22. Quoted in Williamson, p. 231.

23. It may be helpful to point out that these parodies appeared in *Punch* several years before Sir Owen Seaman, who was also renowned for parodying Henley, was asked to contribute to the magazine in 1897.

24. See Williamson, p. 173. I have not been able to locate this review. It is possible that Williamson is in fact referring to an article in *Lippincott's Magazine* of 1893 by G. Parker, which carries the title that Williamson suggests, 'The New Poetry and Mr W. E. Henley'; if so, it is interesting to note that the *Punch* verdict of Henley as 'New Poetry' predates that of Parker.

25. Holbrook Jackson, *The Eighteen Nineties* (1913; Harmondsworth, 1950), p. 20.

26. See Connell, p. 249.

27. Buckley treats Mrs Henley with more sympathy than Connell, for whom she was 'practical'; 'composed'; 'serene' and 'unintelligent', not forgetting to mention that 'she said little, and

never, apparently, wrote anything at all', [See Buckley, pp. 62-3]. Buckley, being kinder but not necessarily more politically correct, acknowledges the influence of her 'feminine reserve' and notes: 'Unobtrusively she deepened and widened Henley's whole philosophy.' without any further explanation of this statement [See Buckley, pp. 74-5].

28. Connell, p. 3.

29. Williamson, pp. 58-9 and Williamson, p. 169.

30. Cornford, pp. 98-9.

31. In the later years of the nineteenth century, comparative mythologists, the most important of which was Friedrich Max Müller, had isolated these recurring themes in world mythologies. Henley himself was not unique in his interest in myths and legends; Williamson informs us that he came across Burton's *Arabian Night's Entertainments* when very young and was greatly influenced by it [See Williamson, pp. 3-5]. His own poem 'New Arabian Nights' Entertainments', written in the same year as 'the Sword', referred in part to this but also to Tennyson and to Stevenson's collection of stories *New Arabian Nights* (1882). Henley knew Andrew Lang, who was the leading figure opposing Max Müller's views on the subject at the time and one of whose main followers was Alfred Nutt, Celtic folklorist and Henley's own publisher. The interests of W. B. Yeats in the subject have also been well documented.

32. W. B. Yeats' relation to Henley is a matter of some controversy, partly on account of Henley's anti-Irish feelings. In his *Yeats, the Irish Literary Revival and the Politics of Print,* Yug Mohit Chaudhry has recently devoted much attention to this issue [See Yug Mohit Chaudhry, *Yeats, the Irish Literary Revival and the Politics of Print* (Cork, 2001)]. For Chaudhry, there is an additional conflict between Henley's abhorrence of the weak and feminine and Yeats' interest in fairy tales. This, however, ignores Henley's poetic use of fairy tales and the late-Victorian distinction between the lower imperfect form told to children and the higher literary and epic culture from which these tales were thought to derive.

33. Chaudhry, p. 169.

34. See Williamson, p. 160-3.

35. See Harry Ricketts, *The Unforgiving Minute: A Life of Rudyard Kipling* (London, 1999), pp. 164-201.

36. Andrew Lycett, *Rudyard Kipling* (London, 1999), p. 242.

37. *Ibid.,* p. 242.

38. Pinney, ed., *The Letters of Rudyard Kipling,* 10 August 1891, ii: 40.

39. *Ibid.,* 18 January 1892, ii: 46.

40. *Ibid.,* early September 1892, ii: 58.

41. See Connell, p. 237.

FURTHER READING

Criticism

Cohen, Edward H. "Henley Among the Nightingales." *Nineteenth Century Studies* 8 (1994): 23-43.
> Discusses the history of nursing using Henley's *In Hospital* as a case study.

Newton, Joy. "Whistler and W. E. Henley." *Victorian Poetry* 33, no. 2 (summer 1995): 299-303.
> Discusses the close friendship between Henley and the painter James McNeill Whistler, touching on the poem *Nocturn,* which Henley dedicated to Whistler.

Schaefer, William D. "Henley and 'The Hound of Heaven.'" *Victorian Poetry* 5, no. 3 (autumn 1967): 171-81.
> Argues that Henley's "London Voluntaries" was heavily influenced by his reading of Francis Thompson's "The Hound of Heaven."

Williamson, Kennedy. "Chapter XI." In *W. E. Henley: A Memoir,* pp. 159-84. London: Harold Shaylor, 1930.
> Provides a general overview of Henley's poetic output, concluding that only a few of his poems will be of enduring importance.

Additional coverage of Henley's life and career is contained in the following sources published by Gale: *Contemporary Authors,* **Vol. 234;** *Contemporary Authors—Brief Entry,* **Vol. 105;** *Dictionary of Literary Biography,* **Vol. 19;** *Literature Resource Center; Reference Guide to English Literature,* **Ed. 2; and** *Twentieth-Century Literary Criticism,* **Vol. 8.**

How to Use This Index

The main references

> **Calvino, Italo**
>   1923-1985 .... CLC **5, 8, 11, 22, 33, 39,**
>   **73**; SSC **3, 48**

list all author entries in the following Gale Literary Criticism series:

AAL = *Asian American Literature*
BG = *The Beat Generation: A Gale Critical Companion*
BLC = *Black Literature Criticism*
BLCS = *Black Literature Criticism Supplement*
CLC = *Contemporary Literary Criticism*
CLR = *Children's Literature Review*
CMLC = *Classical and Medieval Literature Criticism*
DC = *Drama Criticism*
FL = *Feminism in Literature: A Gale Critical Companion*
GL = *Gothic Literature: A Gale Critical Companion*
HLC = *Hispanic Literature Criticism*
HLCS = *Hispanic Literature Criticism Supplement*
HR = *Harlem Renaissance: A Gale Critical Companion*
LC = *Literature Criticism from 1400 to 1800*
NCLC = *Nineteenth-Century Literature Criticism*
NNAL = *Native North American Literature*
PC = *Poetry Criticism*
SSC = *Short Story Criticism*
TCLC = *Twentieth-Century Literary Criticism*
WLC = *World Literature Criticism, 1500 to the Present*
WLCS = *World Literature Criticism Supplement*

The cross-references

> See also CA 85-88, 116; CANR 23, 61;
> DAM NOV; DLB 196; EW 13; MTCW 1, 2;
> RGSF 2; RGWL 2; SFW 4; SSFS 12

list all author entries in the following Gale biographical and literary sources:

AAYA = *Authors & Artists for Young Adults*
AFAW = *African American Writers*
AFW = *African Writers*
AITN = *Authors in the News*
AMW = *American Writers*
AMWR = *American Writers Retrospective Supplement*
AMWS = *American Writers Supplement*
ANW = *American Nature Writers*
AW = *Ancient Writers*
BEST = *Bestsellers*
BPFB = *Beacham's Encyclopedia of Popular Fiction: Biography and Resources*
BRW = *British Writers*
BRWS = *British Writers Supplement*
BW = *Black Writers*
BYA = *Beacham's Guide to Literature for Young Adults*
CA = *Contemporary Authors*
CAAS = *Contemporary Authors Autobiography Series*
CABS = *Contemporary Authors Bibliographical Series*
CAD = *Contemporary American Dramatists*
CANR = *Contemporary Authors New Revision Series*
CAP = *Contemporary Authors Permanent Series*
CBD = *Contemporary British Dramatists*
CCA = *Contemporary Canadian Authors*
CD = *Contemporary Dramatists*
CDALB = *Concise Dictionary of American Literary Biography*

CDALBS = *Concise Dictionary of American Literary Biography Supplement*
CDBLB = *Concise Dictionary of British Literary Biography*
CMW = *St. James Guide to Crime & Mystery Writers*
CN = *Contemporary Novelists*
CP = *Contemporary Poets*
CPW = *Contemporary Popular Writers*
CSW = *Contemporary Southern Writers*
CWD = *Contemporary Women Dramatists*
CWP = *Contemporary Women Poets*
CWRI = *St. James Guide to Children's Writers*
CWW = *Contemporary World Writers*
DA = *DISCovering Authors*
DA3 = *DISCovering Authors 3.0*
DAB = *DISCovering Authors: British Edition*
DAC = *DISCovering Authors: Canadian Edition*
DAM = *DISCovering Authors: Modules*
   DRAM: *Dramatists Module;* **MST:** *Most-studied Authors Module;*
   MULT: *Multicultural Authors Module;* **NOV:** *Novelists Module;*
   POET: *Poets Module;* **POP:** *Popular Fiction and Genre Authors Module*
DFS = *Drama for Students*
DLB = *Dictionary of Literary Biography*
DLBD = *Dictionary of Literary Biography Documentary Series*
DLBY = *Dictionary of Literary Biography Yearbook*
DNFS = *Literature of Developing Nations for Students*
EFS = *Epics for Students*
EW = *European Writers*
EWL = *Encyclopedia of World Literature in the 20th Century*
EXPN = *Exploring Novels*
EXPP = *Exploring Poetry*
EXPS = *Exploring Short Stories*
FANT = *St. James Guide to Fantasy Writers*
FW = *Feminist Writers*
GFL = *Guide to French Literature,* Beginnings to 1789, 1798 to the Present
GLL = *Gay and Lesbian Literature*
HGG = *St. James Guide to Horror, Ghost & Gothic Writers*
HW = *Hispanic Writers*
IDFW = *International Dictionary of Films and Filmmakers: Writers and Production Artists*
IDTP = *International Dictionary of Theatre: Playwrights*
LAIT = *Literature and Its Times*
LAW = *Latin American Writers*
JRDA = *Junior DISCovering Authors*
MAICYA = *Major Authors and Illustrators for Children and Young Adults*
MAICYAS = *Major Authors and Illustrators for Children and Young Adults Supplement*
MAWW = *Modern American Women Writers*
MJW = *Modern Japanese Writers*
MTCW = *Major 20th-Century Writers*
NCFS = *Nonfiction Classics for Students*
NFS = *Novels for Students*
PAB = *Poets: American and British*
PFS = *Poetry for Students*
RGAL = *Reference Guide to American Literature*
RGEL = *Reference Guide to English Literature*
RGSF = *Reference Guide to Short Fiction*
RGWL = *Reference Guide to World Literature*
RHW = *Twentieth-Century Romance and Historical Writers*
SAAS = *Something about the Author Autobiography Series*
SATA = *Something about the Author*
SFW = *St. James Guide to Science Fiction Writers*
SSFS = *Short Stories for Students*
TCWW = *Twentieth-Century Western Writers*
WLIT = *World Literature and Its Times*
WP = *World Poets*
YABC = *Yesterday's Authors of Books for Children*
YAW = *St. James Guide to Young Adult Writers*

Literary Criticism Series
Cumulative Author Index

Aldiss, Brian Wilson
    See Aldiss, Brian W.
Aldrich, Ann
    See Meaker, Marijane
Aldrich, Bess Streeter
        1881-1954 .... **TCLC 125**
        See also CLR 70; TCWW 2
Alegria, Claribel
    See Alegria, Claribel
Alegria, Claribel 1924- .... **CLC 75; HLCS 1;
    PC 26**
        See also CA 131; CAAS 15; CANR 66, 94,
        134; CWW 2; DAM MULT; DLB 145,
        283; EWL 3; HW 1; MTCW 2; MTFW
        2005; PFS 21
Alegria, Claribel Joy
    See Alegria, Claribel
Alegria, Fernando 1918-2005 .... **CLC 57**
        See also CA 9-12R; CANR 5, 32, 72; EWL
        3; HW 1, 2
Aleixandre, Vicente 1898-1984 .... **HLCS 1;
    TCLC 113**
        See also CANR 81; DLB 108, 329; EWL 3;
        HW 2; MTCW 1, 2; RGWL 2, 3
Alekseev, Konstantin Sergeivich
    See Stanislavsky, Constantin
Alekseyer, Konstantin Sergeyevich
    See Stanislavsky, Constantin
Aleman, Mateo 1547-1615(?) .... **LC 81**
Alencar, Jose de 1829-1877 .... **NCLC 157**
        See also DLB 307; LAW; WLIT 1
Alencon, Marguerite d'
    See de Navarre, Marguerite
Alepoudelis, Odysseus
    See Elytis, Odysseus
Aleshkovsky, Joseph 1929- .... **CLC 44**
        See also CA 121; 128; DLB 317
Aleshkovsky, Yuz
    See Aleshkovsky, Joseph
Alexander, Barbara
    See Ehrenreich, Barbara
Alexander, Lloyd 1924-2007 .... **CLC 35**
        See also AAYA 1, 27; BPFB 1; BYA 5, 6,
        7, 9, 10, 11; CA 1-4R; 260; CANR 1, 24,
        38, 55, 113; CLR 1, 5, 48; CWRI 5; DLB
        52; FANT; JRDA; MAICYA 1, 2; MAIC-
        YAS 1; MTCW 1; SAAS 19; SATA 3, 49,
        81, 129, 135; SATA-Obit 182; SUFW;
        TUS; WYA; YAW
Alexander, Lloyd Chudley
    See Alexander, Lloyd
Alexander, Meena 1951- .... **CLC 121**
        See also CA 115; CANR 38, 70, 146; CP 5,
        6, 7; CWP; DLB 323; FW
Alexander, Rae Pace
    See Alexander, Raymond Pace
Alexander, Raymond Pace
        1898-1974 .... **SSC 62**
        See also CA 97-100; SATA 22; SSFS 4
Alexander, Samuel 1859-1938 .... **TCLC 77**
Alexander of Hales c.
        1185-1245 .... **CMLC 128**
Alexeiev, Konstantin
    See Stanislavsky, Constantin
Alexeyev, Constantin Sergeivich
    See Stanislavsky, Constantin
Alexeyev, Konstantin Sergeyevich
    See Stanislavsky, Constantin
Alexie, Sherman 1966- ..... **CLC 96, 154, 312;
    NNAL; PC 53; SSC 107**
        See also AAYA 28, 85; BYA 15; CA 138;
        CANR 65, 95, 133, 174; CN 7; DA3;
        DAM MULT; DLB 175, 206, 278; LATS
        1:2; MTCW 2; MTFW 2005; NFS 17, 31,
        38; PFS 39; SSFS 18
Alexie, Sherman Joseph, Jr.
    See Alexie, Sherman

al-Farabi 870(?)-950 .... **CMLC 58**
        See also DLB 115
Alfau, Felipe 1902-1999 .... **CLC 66**
        See also CA 137
Alfieri, Vittorio 1749-1803 .... **NCLC 101**
        See also EW 4; RGWL 2, 3; WLIT 7
Alfonso X 1221-1284 .... **CMLC 78**
Alfred, Jean Gaston
    See Ponge, Francis
Alger, Horatio, Jr. 1832-1899 .... **NCLC 8, 83**
        See also CLR 87, 170; DLB 42; LAIT 2;
        RGAL 4; SATA 16; TUS
Al-Ghazali, Muhammad ibn Muhammad
        1058-1111 .... **CMLC 50**
        See also DLB 115
Algren, Nelson 1909-1981 ..... **CLC 4, 10, 33;
    SSC 33**
        See also AMWS 9; BPFB 1; CA 13-16R;
        103; CANR 20, 61; CDALB 1941-1968;
        CN 1, 2; DLB 9; DLBY 1981, 1982,
        2000; EWL 3; MAL 5; MTCW 1, 2;
        MTFW 2005; RGAL 4; RGSF 2
al-Hamadhani 967-1007 .... **CMLC 93**
        See also WLIT 6
**al-Hariri, al-Qasim ibn 'Ali Abu
    Muhammad al-Basri**
        1054-1122 .... **CMLC 63**
        See also RGWL 3
Ali, Ahmed 1908-1998 .... **CLC 69**
        See also CA 25-28R; CANR 15, 34; CN 1,
        2, 3, 4, 5; DLB 323; EWL 3
Ali, Monica 1967- .... **CLC 304**
        See also AAYA 67; BRWS 13; CA 219;
        CANR 158, 205; DLB 323
Ali, Tariq 1943- .... **CLC 173**
        See also CA 25-28R; CANR 10, 99, 161,
        196
Alighieri, Dante
    See Dante
al-Kindi, Abu Yusuf Ya'qub ibn Ishaq c.
        801-c. 873 .... **CMLC 80**
Allan, John B.
    See Westlake, Donald E.
Allan, Sidney
    See Hartmann, Sadakichi
Allan, Sydney
    See Hartmann, Sadakichi
Allard, Janet .... **CLC 59**
Allen, Betsy
    See Harrison, Elizabeth (Allen) Cavanna
Allen, Edward 1948- .... **CLC 59**
Allen, Fred 1894-1956 .... **TCLC 87**
Allen, Paula Gunn 1939-2008 . **CLC 84, 202,
    280; NNAL**
        See also AMWS 4; CA 112; 143; 272;
        CANR 63, 130; CWP; DA3; DAM
        MULT; DLB 175; FW; MTCW 2; MTFW
        2005; RGAL 4; TCWW 2
Allen, Roland
    See Ayckbourn, Alan
Allen, Sarah A.
    See Hopkins, Pauline Elizabeth
Allen, Sidney H.
    See Hartmann, Sadakichi
Allen, Woody 1935- ..... **CLC 16, 52, 195, 288**
        See also AAYA 10, 51; AMWS 15; CA 33-
        36R; CANR 27, 38, 63, 128, 172; DAM
        POP; DLB 44; MTCW 1; SSFS 21
Allende, Isabel 1942- ... **CLC 39, 57, 97, 170,
    264; HLC 1; SSC 65; WLCS**
        See also AAYA 18, 70; CA 125; 130; CANR
        51, 74, 129, 165, 208; CDWLB 3; CLR
        99, 171; CWW 2; DA3; DAM MULT,
        NOV; DLB 145; DNFS 1; EWL 3; FL 1:5;
        FW; HW 1, 2; INT CA-130; LAIT 5;
        LAWS 1; LMFS 2; MTCW 1, 2; MTFW
        2005; NCFS 1; NFS 6, 18, 29; RGSF 2;
        RGWL 3; SATA 163; SSFS 11, 16; WLIT
        1

Alleyn, Ellen
    See Rossetti, Christina
Alleyne, Carla D. .... **CLC 65**
Allingham, Margery (Louise)
        1904-1966 .... **CLC 19**
        See also CA 5-8R; 25-28R; CANR 4, 58;
        CMW 4; DLB 77; MSW; MTCW 1, 2
Allingham, William 1824-1889 ...... **NCLC 25**
        See also DLB 35; RGEL 2
Allison, Dorothy E. 1949- . **CLC 78, 153, 290**
        See also AAYA 53; CA 140; CANR 66, 107;
        CN 7; CSW; DA3; DLB 350; FW; MTCW
        2; MTFW 2005; NFS 11; RGAL 4
Alloula, Malek .... **CLC 65**
Allston, Washington 1779-1843 .... **NCLC 2**
        See also DLB 1, 235
Almedingen, E. M.
    See Almedingen, Martha Edith von
Almedingen, Martha Edith von
        1898-1971 .... **CLC 12**
        See also CA 1-4R; CANR 1; SATA 3
Almodovar, Pedro 1949(?)- .... **CLC 114, 229;
    HLCS 1**
        See also CA 133; CANR 72, 151; HW 2
Almqvist, Carl Jonas Love
        1793-1866 .... **NCLC 42**
**al-Mutanabbi, Ahmad ibn al-Husayn Abu
    al-Tayyib al-Jufi al-Kindi**
        915-965 .... **CMLC 66**
        See also RGWL 3; WLIT 6
Alonso, Damaso 1898-1990 . **CLC 14; TCLC
    245**
        See also CA 110; 131; 130; CANR 72; DLB
        108; EWL 3; HW 1, 2
Alov
    See Gogol, Nikolai
al'Sadaawi, Nawal
    See El Saadawi, Nawal
al-Shaykh, Hanan
    See Shaykh, Hanan al-
Al Siddik
    See Rolfe, Frederick (William Serafino
    Austin Lewis Mary)
Alta 1942- .... **CLC 19**
        See also CA 57-60
Alter, Robert B. 1935- .... **CLC 34**
        See also CA 49-52; CANR 1, 47, 100, 160,
        201
Alter, Robert Bernard
    See Alter, Robert B.
Alther, Lisa 1944- .... **CLC 7, 41**
        See also BPFB 1; CA 65-68; CAAS 30;
        CANR 12, 30, 51, 180; CN 4, 5, 6, 7;
        CSW; GLL 2; MTCW 1
Althusser, L.
    See Althusser, Louis
Althusser, Louis 1918-1990 .... **CLC 106**
        See also CA 131; 132; CANR 102; DLB
        242
Altman, Robert 1925-2006 .... **CLC 16, 116,
    242**
        See also CA 73-76; 254; CANR 43
Alurista
    See Urista, Alberto
Alvarez, A. 1929- .... **CLC 5, 13**
        See also CA 1-4R; CANR 3, 33, 63, 101,
        134; CN 3, 4, 5, 6; CP 1, 2, 3, 4, 5, 6, 7;
        DLB 14, 40; MTFW 2005
Alvarez, Alejandro Rodriguez
        1903-1965 . **CLC 49; DC 32; TCLC 199**
        See also CA 131; 93-96; EWL 3; HW 1
Alvarez, Julia 1950- .. **CLC 93, 274; HLCS 1**
        See also AAYA 25, 85; AMWS 7; CA 147;
        CANR 69, 101, 133, 166; DA3; DLB 282;
        LATS 1:2; LLW; MTCW 2; MTFW 2005;
        NFS 5, 9; PFS 39; SATA 129; SSFS 27,
        31; WLIT 1
Alvaro, Corrado 1896-1956 .... **TCLC 60**
        See also CA 163; DLB 264; EWL 3

Amado, Jorge 1912-2001 ... **CLC 13, 40, 106, 232; HLC 1**
See also CA 77-80; 201; CANR 35, 74, 135; CWW 2; DAM MULT, NOV; DLB 113, 307; EWL 3; HW 2; LAW; LAWS 1; MTCW 1, 2; MTFW 2005; RGWL 2, 3; TWA; WLIT 1

Ambler, Eric 1909-1998 .... **CLC 4, 6, 9**
See also BRWS 4; CA 9-12R; 171; CANR 7, 38, 74; CMW 4; CN 1, 2, 3, 4, 5, 6; DLB 77; MSW; MTCW 1, 2; TEA

Ambrose c. 339-c. 397 .... **CMLC 103**

Ambrose, Stephen E. 1936-2002 .... **CLC 145**
See also AAYA 44; CA 1-4R; 209; CANR 3, 43, 57, 83, 105; MTFW 2005; NCFS 2; SATA 40, 138

Amichai, Yehuda 1924-2000 .. **CLC 9, 22, 57, 116; PC 38**
See also CA 85-88; 189; CANR 46, 60, 99, 132; CWW 2; EWL 3; MTCW 1, 2; MTFW 2005; PFS 24, 39; RGHL; WLIT 6

Amichai, Yehudah
See Amichai, Yehuda

Amiel, Henri Frederic 1821-1881 .... **NCLC 4**
See also DLB 217

Amis, Kingsley 1922-1995 . **CLC 1, 2, 3, 5, 8, 13, 40, 44, 129**
See also AAYA 77; AITN 2; BPFB 1; BRWS 2; CA 9-12R; 150; CANR 8, 28, 54; CDBLB 1945-1960; CN 1, 2, 3, 4, 5, 6; CP 1, 2, 3, 4; DA; DA3; DAB; DAC; DAM MST, NOV; DLB 15, 27, 100, 139, 326, 352; DLBY 1996; EWL 3; HGG; INT CANR-8; MTCW 1, 2; MTFW 2005; RGEL 2; RGSF 2; SFW 4

Amis, Martin 1949- ... **CLC 4, 9, 38, 62, 101, 213; SSC 112**
See also BEST 90:3; BRWS 4; CA 65-68; CANR 8, 27, 54, 73, 95, 132, 166, 208; CN 5, 6, 7; DA3; DLB 14, 194; EWL 3; INT CANR-27; MTCW 2; MTFW 2005

Amis, Martin Louis
See Amis, Martin

Ammianus Marcellinus c. 330-c. 395 .... **CMLC 60**
See also AW 2; DLB 211

Ammons, A.R. 1926-2001 .. **CLC 2, 3, 5, 8, 9, 25, 57, 108; PC 16**
See also AITN 1; AMWS 7; CA 9-12R; 193; CANR 6, 36, 51, 73, 107, 156; CP 1, 2, 3, 4, 5, 6, 7; CSW; DAM POET; DLB 5, 165, 342; EWL 3; MAL 5; MTCW 1, 2; PFS 19; RGAL 4; TCLE 1:1

Ammons, Archie Randolph
See Ammons, A.R.

Amo, Tauraatua i
See Adams, Henry

Amory, Thomas 1691(?)-1788 .... **LC 48**
See also DLB 39

Anand, Mulk Raj 1905-2004 ..... **CLC 23, 93, 237**
See also CA 65-68; 231; CANR 32, 64; CN 1, 2, 3, 4, 5, 6, 7; DAM NOV; DLB 323; EWL 3; MTCW 1, 2; MTFW 2005; RGSF 2

Anatol
See Schnitzler, Arthur

Anaximander c. 611B.C.-c. 546B.C. .... **CMLC 22**

Anaya, Rudolfo 1937- ...... **CLC 23, 148, 255; HLC 1**
See also AAYA 20; BYA 13; CA 45-48; CAAS 4; CANR 1, 32, 51, 124, 169; CLR 129; CN 4, 5, 6, 7; DAM MULT, NOV; DLB 82, 206, 278; HW 1; LAIT 4; LLW; MAL 5; MTCW 1, 2; MTFW 2005; NFS 12; RGAL 4; RGSF 2; TCWW 2; WLIT 1

Anaya, Rudolfo A.
See Anaya, Rudolfo

Anaya, Rudolpho Alfonso
See Anaya, Rudolfo

Andersen, Hans Christian 1805-1875 ...... **NCLC 7, 79, 214; SSC 6, 56; WLC 1**
See also AAYA 57; CLR 6, 113; DA; DA3; DAB; DAC; DAM MST, POP; EW 6; MAICYA 1, 2; RGSF 2; RGWL 2, 3; SATA 100; TWA; WCH; YABC 1

Anderson, C. Farley
See Mencken, H. L.; Nathan, George Jean

Anderson, Jessica (Margaret) Queale 1916- .... **CLC 37**
See also CA 9-12R; CANR 4, 62; CN 4, 5, 6, 7; DLB 325

Anderson, Jon (Victor) 1940- .... **CLC 9**
See also CA 25-28R; CANR 20; CP 1, 3, 4, 5; DAM POET

Anderson, Lindsay (Gordon) 1923-1994 .... **CLC 20**
See also CA 125; 128; 146; CANR 77

Anderson, Maxwell 1888-1959 .... **DC 43; TCLC 2, 144**
See also CA 105; 152; DAM DRAM; DFS 16, 20; DLB 7, 228; MAL 5; MTCW 2; MTFW 2005; RGAL 4

Anderson, Poul 1926-2001 .... **CLC 15**
See also AAYA 5, 34; BPFB 1; BYA 6, 8, 9; CA 1-4R, 181; 199; CAAE 181; CAAS 2; CANR 2, 15, 34, 64, 110; CLR 58; DLB 8; FANT; INT CANR-15; MTCW 1, 2; MTFW 2005; SATA 90; SATA-Brief 39; SATA-Essay 106; SCFW 1, 2; SFW 4; SUFW 1, 2

Anderson, R. W.
See Anderson, Robert

Anderson, Robert 1917-2009 .... **CLC 23**
See also AITN 1; CA 21-24R; 283; CANR 32; CD 6; DAM DRAM; DLB 7; LAIT 5

Anderson, Robert W.
See Anderson, Robert

Anderson, Robert Woodruff
See Anderson, Robert

Anderson, Roberta Joan
See Mitchell, Joni

Anderson, Sherwood 1876-1941 ... **SSC 1, 46, 91, 142; TCLC 1, 10, 24, 123; WLC 1**
See also AAYA 30; AMW; AMWC 2; BPFB 1; CA 104; 121; CANR 61; CDALB 1917-1929; DA; DA3; DAB; DAC; DAM MST, NOV; DLB 4, 9, 86; DLBD 1; EWL 3; EXPS; GLL 2; MAL 5; MTCW 1, 2; MTFW 2005; NFS 4; RGAL 4; RGSF 2; SSFS 4, 10, 11; TUS

Anderson, Wes 1969- .... **CLC 227**
See also CA 214

Andier, Pierre
See Desnos, Robert

Andouard
See Giraudoux, Jean

Andrade, Carlos Drummond de
See Drummond de Andrade, Carlos

Andrade, Mario de
See de Andrade, Mario

Andreae, Johann V(alentin) 1586-1654 .... **LC 32**
See also DLB 164

Andreas Capellanus fl. c. 1185- ... **CMLC 45, 135**
See also DLB 208

Andreas-Salome, Lou 1861-1937 ... **TCLC 56**
See also CA 178; DLB 66

Andreev, Leonid
See Andreyev, Leonid

Andress, Lesley
See Sanders, Lawrence

Andrew, Joseph Maree
See Occomy, Marita (Odette) Bonner

Andrewes, Lancelot 1555-1626 .... **LC 5**
See also DLB 151, 172

Andrews, Cicily Fairfield
See West, Rebecca

Andrews, Elton V.
See Pohl, Frederik

Andrews, Peter
See Soderbergh, Steven

Andrews, Raymond 1934-1991 .... **BLC 2:1**
See also BW 2; CA 81-84; 136; CANR 15, 42

Andreyev, Leonid 1871-1919 ... **TCLC 3, 221**
See also CA 104; 185; DLB 295; EWL 3

Andreyev, Leonid Nikolaevich
See Andreyev, Leonid

Andrezel, Pierre
See Blixen, Karen

Andric, Ivo 1892-1975 .... **CLC 8; SSC 36; TCLC 135**
See also CA 81-84; 57-60; CANR 43, 60; CDWLB 4; DLB 147, 329; EW 11; EWL 3; MTCW 1; RGSF 2; RGWL 2, 3

Androvar
See Prado (Calvo), Pedro

Angela of Foligno 1248(?)-1309 .... **CMLC 76**

Angelique, Pierre
See Bataille, Georges

Angell, Judie
See Angell, Judie

Angell, Judie 1937- .... **CLC 30**
See also AAYA 11, 71; BYA 6; CA 77-80; CANR 49; CLR 33; JRDA; SATA 22, 78; WYA; YAW

Angell, Roger 1920- .... **CLC 26**
See also CA 57-60; CANR 13, 44, 70, 144; DLB 171, 185

Angelou, Maya 1928- ...... **BLC 1:1; CLC 12, 35, 64, 77, 155; PC 32; WLCS**
See also AAYA 7, 20; AMWS 4; BPFB 1; BW 2, 3; BYA 2; CA 65-68; CANR 19, 42, 65, 111, 133, 204; CDALBS; CLR 53; CP 4, 5, 6, 7; CPW; CSW; CWP; DA; DA3; DAB; DAC; DAM MST, MULT, POET, POP; DLB 38; EWL 3; EXPN; EXPP; FL 1:5; LAIT 4; MAICYA 2; MAICYAS 1; MAL 5; MBL; MTCW 1, 2; MTFW 2005; NCFS 2; NFS 2; PFS 2, 3, 33, 38; RGAL 4; SATA 49, 136; TCLE 1:1; WYA; YAW

Angouleme, Marguerite d'
See de Navarre, Marguerite

Anna Comnena 1083-1153 .... **CMLC 25**

Annensky, Innokentii Fedorovich
See Annensky, Innokenty (Fyodorovich)

Annensky, Innokenty (Fyodorovich) 1856-1909 .... **TCLC 14**
See also CA 110; 155; DLB 295; EWL 3

Annunzio, Gabriele d'
See D'Annunzio, Gabriele

Anodos
See Coleridge, Mary E(lizabeth)

Anon, Charles Robert
See Pessoa, Fernando

Anouilh, Jean 1910-1987 ..... **CLC 1, 3, 8, 13, 40, 50; DC 8, 21; TCLC 195**
See also AAYA 67; CA 17-20R; 123; CANR 32; DAM DRAM; DFS 9, 10, 19; DLB 321; EW 13; EWL 3; GFL 1789 to the Present; MTCW 1, 2; MTFW 2005; RGWL 2, 3; TWA

Anouilh, Jean Marie Lucien Pierre
See Anouilh, Jean

Ansa, Tina McElroy 1949- .... **BLC 2:1**
See also BW 2; CA 142; CANR 143; CSW

Anselm of Canterbury 1033(?)-1109 .... **CMLC 67**
See also DLB 115

Anthony, Florence
See Ai
Anthony, John
See Ciardi, John (Anthony)
Anthony, Peter
See Shaffer, Anthony; Shaffer, Peter
Anthony, Piers 1934- .... **CLC 35**
See also AAYA 11, 48; BYA 7; CA 200;
CAAE 200; CANR 28, 56, 73, 102, 133,
202; CLR 118; CPW; DAM POP; DLB 8;
FANT; MAICYA 2; MAICYAS 1; MTCW
1, 2; MTFW 2005; SAAS 22; SATA 84,
129; SATA-Essay 129; SFW 4; SUFW 1,
2; YAW
Anthony, Susan B(rownell)
1820-1906 .... **TCLC 84**
See also CA 211; FW
Antin, David 1932- .... **PC 124**
See also CA 73-76; CP 1, 3, 4, 5, 6, 7; DLB
169
Antin, Mary 1881-1949 .... **TCLC 247**
See also AMWS 20; CA 118; 181; DLB
221; DLBY 1984
Antiphon c. 480B.C.-c. 411B.C. .... **CMLC 55**
Antoine, Marc
See Proust, Marcel
Antoninus, Brother
See Everson, William
Antonioni, Michelangelo
1912-2007 .... **CLC 20, 144, 259**
See also CA 73-76; 262; CANR 45, 77
Antschel, Paul
See Celan, Paul
Anwar, Chairil 1922-1949 .... **TCLC 22**
See also CA 121; 219; EWL 3; RGWL 3
Anyidoho, Kofi 1947- .... **BLC 2:1**
See also BW 3; CA 178; CP 5, 6, 7; DLB
157; EWL 3
Anzaldua, Gloria (Evanjelina)
1942-2004 .... **CLC 200; HLCS 1**
See also CA 175; 227; CSW; CWP; DLB
122; FW; LLW; RGAL 4; SATA-Obit 154
Apess, William 1798-1839(?) .... **NCLC 73;**
NNAL
See also DAM MULT; DLB 175, 243
Apollinaire, Guillaume 1880-1918 .... **PC 7;**
TCLC 3, 8, 51
See also CA 104; 152; DAM POET; DLB
258, 321; EW 9; EWL 3; GFL 1789 to
the Present; MTCW 2; PFS 24; RGWL 2,
3; TWA; WP
Apollonius of Rhodes
See Apollonius Rhodius
Apollonius Rhodius c. 300B.C.-c.
220B.C. .... **CMLC 28**
See also AW 1; DLB 176; RGWL 2, 3
Appelfeld, Aharon 1932- ... **CLC 23, 47, 317;**
SSC 42
See also CA 112; 133; CANR 86, 160, 207;
CWW 2; DLB 299; EWL 3; RGHL;
RGSF 2; WLIT 6
Appelfeld, Aron
See Appelfeld, Aharon
Apple, Max 1941- .... **CLC 9, 33; SSC 50**
See also AMWS 17; CA 81-84; CANR 19,
54, 214; DLB 130
Apple, Max Isaac
See Apple, Max
Appleman, Philip (Dean) 1926- .... **CLC 51**
See also CA 13-16R; CAAS 18; CANR 6,
29, 56
Appleton, Lawrence
See Lovecraft, H. P.
Apteryx
See Eliot, T. S.
Apuleius, (Lucius Madaurensis) c. 125-c.
164 .... **CMLC 1, 84**
See also AW 2; CDWLB 1; DLB 211;
RGWL 2, 3; SUFW; WLIT 8

Aquin, Hubert 1929-1977 .... **CLC 15**
See also CA 105; DLB 53; EWL 3
Aquinas, Thomas 1224(?)-1274 .... **CMLC 33,**
137
See also DLB 115; EW 1; TWA
Aragon, Louis 1897-1982 .... **CLC 3, 22;**
TCLC 123
See also CA 69-72; 108; CANR 28, 71;
DAM NOV, POET; DLB 72, 258; EW 11;
EWL 3; GFL 1789 to the Present; GLL 2;
LMFS 2; MTCW 1, 2; RGWL 2, 3
Arany, Janos 1817-1882 .... **NCLC 34**
Aranyos, Kakay 1847-1910
See Mikszath, Kalman
Aratus of Soli c. 315B.C.-c.
240B.C. .... **CMLC 64, 114**
See also DLB 176
Arbuthnot, John 1667-1735 .... **LC 1**
See also BRWS 16; DLB 101
Archer, Herbert Winslow
See Mencken, H. L.
Archer, Jeffrey 1940- .... **CLC 28**
See also AAYA 16; BEST 89:3; BPFB 1;
CA 77-80; CANR 22, 52, 95, 136, 209;
CPW; DA3; DAM POP; INT CANR-22;
MTFW 2005
Archer, Jeffrey Howard
See Archer, Jeffrey
Archer, Jules 1915- .... **CLC 12**
See also CA 9-12R; CANR 6, 69; SAAS 5;
SATA 4, 85
Archer, Lee
See Ellison, Harlan
Archilochus c. 7th cent. B.C.- .... **CMLC 44**
See also DLB 176
Ard, William
See Jakes, John
Arden, John 1930- .... **CLC 6, 13, 15**
See also BRWS 2; CA 13-16R; CAAS 4;
CANR 31, 65, 67, 124; CBD; CD 5, 6;
DAM DRAM; DFS 9; DLB 13, 245;
EWL 3; MTCW 1
Arenas, Reinaldo 1943-1990 .. **CLC 41; HLC**
1; TCLC 191
See also CA 124; 128; 133; CANR 73, 106;
DAM MULT; DLB 145; EWL 3; GLL 2;
HW 1; LAW; LAWS 1; MTCW 2; MTFW
2005; RGSF 2; RGWL 3; WLIT 1
Arendt, Hannah 1906-1975 .... **CLC 66, 98;**
TCLC 193
See also CA 17-20R; 61-64; CANR 26, 60,
172; DLB 242; MTCW 1, 2
Aretino, Pietro 1492-1556 .... **LC 12, 165**
See also RGWL 2, 3
Arghezi, Tudor
See Theodorescu, Ion N.
Arguedas, Jose Maria 1911-1969 .... **CLC 10,**
18; HLCS 1; TCLC 147
See also CA 89-92; CANR 73; DLB 113;
EWL 3; HW 1; LAW; RGWL 2, 3; WLIT
1
Argueta, Manlio 1936- .... **CLC 31**
See also CA 131; CANR 73; CWW 2; DLB
145; EWL 3; HW 1; RGWL 3
Arias, Ron 1941- .... **HLC 1**
See also CA 131; CANR 81, 136; DAM
MULT; DLB 82; HW 1, 2; MTCW 2;
MTFW 2005
Ariosto, Lodovico
See Ariosto, Ludovico
Ariosto, Ludovico 1474-1533 ... **LC 6, 87; PC**
42
See also EW 2; RGWL 2, 3; WLIT 7
Aristides
See Epstein, Joseph

Aristides Quintilianus fl. c. 100-fl. c.
400 .... **CMLC 122**
Aristophanes 450B.C.-385B.C. . **CMLC 4, 51,**
138; DC 2; WLCS
See also AW 1; CDWLB 1; DA; DA3;
DAB; DAC; DAM DRAM; MST; DFS
10; DLB 176; LMFS 1; RGWL 2, 3;
TWA; WLIT 8
Aristotle 384B.C.-322B.C. .... **CMLC 31, 123;**
WLCS
See also AW 1; CDWLB 1; DA; DA3;
DAB; DAC; DAM MST; DLB 176;
RGWL 2, 3; TWA; WLIT 8
Arlt, Roberto 1900-1942 . **HLC 1; TCLC 29,**
255
See also CA 123; 131; CANR 67; DAM
MULT; DLB 305; EWL 3; HW 1, 2;
IDTP; LAW
Arlt, Roberto Godofredo Christophersen
See Arlt, Roberto
Armah, Ayi Kwei 1939- . **BLC 1:1, 2:1; CLC**
5, 33, 136
See also AFW; BRWS 10; BW 1; CA 61-
64; CANR 21, 64; CDWLB 3; CN 1, 2,
3, 4, 5, 6, 7; DAM MULT, POET; DLB
117; EWL 3; MTCW 1; WLIT 2
Armatrading, Joan 1950- .... **CLC 17**
See also CA 114; 186
Armin, Robert 1568(?)-1615(?) .... **LC 120**
Armitage, Frank
See Carpenter, John
Armstrong, Jeannette (C.) 1948- .... **NNAL**
See also CA 149; CCA 1; CN 6, 7; DAC;
DLB 334; SATA 102
Armytage, R.
See Watson, Rosamund Marriott
Arnauld, Antoine 1612-1694 .... **LC 169**
See also DLB 268
Arnette, Robert
See Silverberg, Robert
Arnim, Achim von (Ludwig Joachim von
Arnim) 1781-1831 .. **NCLC 5, 159; SSC**
29
See also DLB 90
Arnim, Bettina von 1785-1859 ...... **NCLC 38,**
123
See also DLB 90; RGWL 2, 3
Arnold, Matthew 1822-1888 ..... **NCLC 6, 29,**
89, 126, 218; PC 5, 94; WLC 1
See also BRW 5; CDBLB 1832-1890; DA;
DAB; DAC; DAM MST, POET; DLB 32,
57; EXPP; PAB; PFS 2; TEA; WP
Arnold, Thomas 1795-1842 .... **NCLC 18**
See also DLB 55
Arnow, Harriette (Louisa) Simpson
1908-1986 ...... **CLC 2, 7, 18; TCLC 196**
See also BPFB 1; CA 9-12R; 118; CANR
14; CN 2, 3, 4; DLB 6; FW; MTCW 1, 2;
RHW; SATA 42; SATA-Obit 47
Arouet, Francois-Marie
See Voltaire
Arp, Hans
See Arp, Jean
Arp, Jean 1887-1966 .... **CLC 5; TCLC 115**
See also CA 81-84; 25-28R; CANR 42, 77;
EW 10
Arrabal
See Arrabal, Fernando
Arrabal, Fernando 1932- .. **CLC 2, 9, 18, 58;**
DC 35
See also CA 9-12R; CANR 15; CWW 2;
DLB 321; EWL 3; LMFS 2
Arrabal Teran, Fernando
See Arrabal, Fernando
Arreola, Juan Jose 1918-2001 .... **CLC 147;**
HLC 1; SSC 38
See also CA 113; 131; 200; CANR 81;
CWW 2; DAM MULT; DLB 113; DNFS
2; EWL 3; HW 1, 2; LAW; RGSF 2

Arrian c. 89(?)-c. 155(?) .... **CMLC 43**
   See also DLB 176
Arrick, Fran
   See Angell, Judie
Arrley, Richmond
   See Delany, Samuel R., Jr.
Artaud, Antonin 1896-1948 ... **DC 14; TCLC 3, 36**
   See also CA 104; 149; DA3; DAM DRAM; DFS 22; DLB 258, 321; EW 11; EWL 3; GFL 1789 to the Present; MTCW 2; MTFW 2005; RGWL 2, 3
Artaud, Antonin Marie Joseph
   See Artaud, Antonin
Artemidorus fl. 2nd cent. - .... **CMLC 129**
Arthur, Ruth M(abel) 1905-1979 ..... **CLC 12**
   See also CA 9-12R; 85-88; CANR 4; CWRI 5; SATA 7, 26
Artsybashev, Mikhail (Petrovich) 1878-1927 .... **TCLC 31**
   See also CA 170; DLB 295
Arundel, Honor (Morfydd) 1919-1973 .... **CLC 17**
   See also CA 21-22; 41-44R; CAP 2; CLR 35; CWRI 5; SATA 4; SATA-Obit 24
Arzner, Dorothy 1900-1979 .... **CLC 98**
Asch, Sholem 1880-1957 .... **TCLC 3, 251**
   See also CA 105; DLB 333; EWL 3; GLL 2; RGHL
Ascham, Roger 1516(?)-1568 .... **LC 101**
   See also DLB 236
Ash, Shalom
   See Asch, Sholem
Ashbery, John 1927- ... **CLC 2, 3, 4, 6, 9, 13, 15, 25, 41, 77, 125, 221; PC 26**
   See also AMWS 3; CA 5-8R; CANR 9, 37, 66, 102, 132, 170; CP 1, 2, 3, 4, 5, 6, 7; DA3; DAM POET; DLB 5, 165; DLBY 1981; EWL 3; GLL 1; INT CANR-9; MAL 5; MTCW 1, 2; MTFW 2005; PAB; PFS 11, 28; RGAL 4; TCLE 1:1; WP
Ashbery, John Lawrence
   See Ashbery, John
Ashbridge, Elizabeth 1713-1755 .... **LC 147**
   See also DLB 200
Ashdown, Clifford
   See Freeman, R(ichard) Austin
Ashe, Gordon
   See Creasey, John
Ashton-Warner, Sylvia (Constance) 1908-1984 .... **CLC 19**
   See also CA 69-72; 112; CANR 29; CN 1, 2, 3; MTCW 1, 2
Asimov, Isaac 1920-1992 ..... **CLC 1, 3, 9, 19, 26, 76, 92; SSC 148**
   See also AAYA 13; BEST 90:2; BPFB 1; BYA 4, 6, 7, 9; CA 1-4R; 137; CANR 2, 19, 36, 60, 125; CLR 12, 79; CMW 4; CN 1, 2, 3, 4, 5; CPW; DA3; DAM POP; DLB 8; DLBY 1992; INT CANR-19; JRDA; LAIT 5; LMFS 2; MAICYA 1, 2; MAL 5; MTCW 1, 2; MTFW 2005; NFS 29; RGAL 4; SATA 1, 26, 74; SCFW 1, 2; SFW 4; SSFS 17, 33; TUS; YAW
Askew, Anne 1521(?)-1546 .... **LC 81**
   See also DLB 136
Asser -c. 909 .... **CMLC 117**
Assis, Joaquim Maria Machado de
   See Machado de Assis, Joaquim Maria
Astell, Mary 1666-1731 .... **LC 68, 183**
   See also DLB 252, 336; FW
Astley, Thea (Beatrice May) 1925-2004 .... **CLC 41**
   See also CA 65-68; 229; CANR 11, 43, 78; CN 1, 2, 3, 4, 5, 6, 7; DLB 289; EWL 3
Astley, William 1855-1911 .... **TCLC 45**
   See also DLB 230; RGEL 2
Aston, James
   See White, T(erence) H(anbury)

Asturias, Miguel Angel 1899-1974 .... **CLC 3, 8, 13; HLC 1; TCLC 184**
   See also CA 25-28; 49-52; CANR 32; CAP 2; CDWLB 3; DA3; DAM MULT, NOV; DLB 113, 290, 329; EWL 3; HW 1; LAW; LMFS 2; MTCW 1, 2; RGWL 2, 3; WLIT 1
Atares, Carlos Saura
   See Saura (Atares), Carlos
Athanasius c. 295-c. 373 .... **CMLC 48**
Atheling, William
   See Pound, Ezra
Atheling, William, Jr.
   See Blish, James
Atherton, Gertrude (Franklin Horn) 1857-1948 .... **TCLC 2**
   See also CA 104; 155; DLB 9, 78, 186; HGG; RGAL 4; SUFW 1; TCWW 1, 2
Atherton, Lucius
   See Masters, Edgar Lee
Atkins, Jack
   See Harris, Mark
Atkinson, Kate 1951- .... **CLC 99**
   See also CA 166; CANR 101, 153, 198; DLB 267
Attaway, William (Alexander) 1911-1986 .... **BLC 1:1; CLC 92**
   See also BW 2, 3; CA 143; CANR 82; DAM MULT; DLB 76; MAL 5
Atticus
   See Fleming, Ian; Wilson, (Thomas) Woodrow
Atwood, Margaret 1939- . **CLC 2, 3, 4, 8, 13, 15, 25, 44, 84, 135, 232, 239, 246; PC 8, 123; SSC 2, 46, 142; WLC 1**
   See also AAYA 12, 47; AMWS 13; BEST 89:2; BPFB 1; CA 49-52; CANR 3, 24, 33, 59, 95, 133; CN 2, 3, 4, 5, 6, 7; CP 1, 2, 3, 4, 5, 6, 7; CPW; CWP; DA; DA3; DAB; DAC; DAM MST, NOV, POET; DLB 53, 251, 326; EWL 3; EXPN; FL 1:5; FW; GL 2; INT CANR-24; LAIT 5; MTCW 1, 2; MTFW 2005; NFS 4, 12, 13, 14, 19, 39; PFS 7, 37; RGSF 2; SATA 50, 170; SSFS 3, 13; TCLE 1:1; TWA; WWE 1; YAW
Atwood, Margaret Eleanor
   See Atwood, Margaret
Aubigny, Pierre d'
   See Mencken, H. L.
Aubin, Penelope 1685-1731(?) .... **LC 9**
   See also DLB 39
Auchincloss, Louis 1917-2010 ... **CLC 4, 6, 9, 18, 45, 318; SSC 22**
   See also AMWS 4; CA 1-4R; CANR 6, 29, 55, 87, 130, 168, 202; CN 1, 2, 3, 4, 5, 6, 7; DAM NOV; DLB 2, 244; DLBY 1980; EWL 3; INT CANR-29; MAL 5; MTCW 1; RGAL 4
Auchincloss, Louis Stanton
   See Auchincloss, Louis
Auden, W. H. 1907-1973 ... **CLC 1, 2, 3, 4, 6, 9, 11, 14, 43, 123; PC 1, 92; TCLC 223; WLC 1**
   See also AAYA 18; AMWS 2; BRW 7; BRWR 1; CA 9-12R; 45-48; CANR 5, 61, 105; CDBLB 1914-1945; CP 1, 2; DA; DA3; DAB; DAC; DAM DRAM, MST, POET; DLB 10, 20; EWL 3; EXPP; MAL 5; MTCW 1, 2; MTFW 2005; PAB; PFS 1, 3, 4, 10, 27; TUS; WP
Auden, Wystan Hugh
   See Auden, W. H.
Audiberti, Jacques 1899-1965 .... **CLC 38**
   See also CA 252; 25-28R; DAM DRAM; DLB 321; EWL 3
Audubon, John James 1785-1851 . **NCLC 47**
   See also AAYA 76; AMWS 16; ANW; DLB 248

Auel, Jean 1936- .... **CLC 31, 107**
   See also AAYA 7, 51; BEST 90:4; BPFB 1; CA 103; CANR 21, 64, 115; CPW; DA3; DAM POP; INT CANR-21; NFS 11; RHW; SATA 91
Auel, Jean M.
   See Auel, Jean
Auel, Jean Marie
   See Auel, Jean
Auerbach, Berthold 1812-1882 .... **NCLC 171**
   See also DLB 133
Auerbach, Erich 1892-1957 .... **TCLC 43**
   See also CA 118; 155; EWL 3
Augier, Emile 1820-1889 .... **NCLC 31**
   See also DLB 192; GFL 1789 to the Present
August, John
   See De Voto, Bernard (Augustine)
Augustine, St. 354-430 .... **CMLC 6, 95; WLCS**
   See also DA; DA3; DAB; DAC; DAM MST; DLB 115; EW 1; RGWL 2, 3; WLIT 8
Aunt Belinda
   See Braddon, Mary Elizabeth
Aunt Weedy
   See Alcott, Louisa May
Aurelius
   See Bourne, Randolph S(illiman)
Aurelius, Marcus 121-180 .... **CMLC 45**
   See also AW 2; RGWL 2, 3
Aurobindo, Sri
   See Ghose, Aurabinda
Aurobindo Ghose
   See Ghose, Aurabinda
Ausonius, Decimus Magnus c. 310-c. 394 .... **CMLC 88**
   See also RGWL 2, 3
Austen, Jane 1775-1817 ...... **NCLC 1, 13, 19, 33, 51, 81, 95, 119, 150, 207, 210, 222, 242; WLC 1**
   See also AAYA 19; BRW 4; BRWC 1; BRWR 2; BYA 3; CDBLB 1789-1832; DA; DA3; DAB; DAC; DAM MST, NOV; DLB 116, 363; EXPN; FL 1:2; GL 2; LAIT 2; LATS 1:1; LMFS 1; NFS 1, 14, 18, 20, 21, 28, 29, 33; TEA; WLIT 3; WYAS 1
Auster, Paul 1947- .... **CLC 47, 131, 227**
   See also AMWS 12; CA 69-72; CANR 23, 52, 75, 129, 165; CMW 4; CN 5, 6, 7; DA3; DLB 227; MAL 5; MTCW 2; MTFW 2005; SUFW 2; TCLE 1:1
Austin, Frank
   See Faust, Frederick
Austin, Mary Hunter 1868-1934 .... **SSC 104; TCLC 25, 249**
   See also ANW; CA 109; 178; DLB 9, 78, 206, 221, 275; FW; TCWW 1, 2
Averroes 1126-1198 .... **CMLC 7, 104**
   See also DLB 115
Avicenna 980-1037 .... **CMLC 16, 110**
   See also DLB 115
Avison, Margaret 1918-2007 .... **CLC 2, 4, 97**
   See also CA 17-20R; CANR 134; CP 1, 2, 3, 4, 5, 6, 7; DAC; DAM POET; DLB 53; MTCW 1
Avison, Margaret Kirkland
   See Avison, Margaret
Axton, David
   See Koontz, Dean
Ayala, Francisco 1906-2009 .... **SSC 119**
   See also CA 208; CWW 2; DLB 322; EWL 3; RGSF 2
Ayala, Francisco de Paula y Garcia Duarte
   See Ayala, Francisco

Ayckbourn, Alan 1939- ...... **CLC 5, 8, 18, 33, 74; DC 13**
See also BRWS 5; CA 21-24R; CANR 31, 59, 118; CBD; CD 5, 6; DAB; DAM DRAM; DFS 7; DLB 13, 245; EWL 3; MTCW 1, 2; MTFW 2005
Aydy, Catherine
See Tennant, Emma
Ayme, Marcel (Andre) 1902-1967 ... **CLC 11; SSC 41**
See also CA 89-92; CANR 67, 137; CLR 25; DLB 72; EW 12; EWL 3; GFL 1789 to the Present; RGSF 2; RGWL 2, 3; SATA 91
Ayrton, Michael 1921-1975 .... **CLC 7**
See also CA 5-8R; 61-64; CANR 9, 21
Aytmatov, Chingiz
See Aitmatov, Chingiz
Azorin
See Martinez Ruiz, Jose
Azuela, Mariano 1873-1952 .. **HLC 1; TCLC 3, 145, 217**
See also CA 104; 131; CANR 81; DAM MULT; EWL 3; HW 1, 2; LAW; MTCW 1, 2; MTFW 2005
Ba, Mariama 1929-1981 ...... **BLC 2:1; BLCS**
See also AFW; BW 2; CA 141; CANR 87; DLB 360; DNFS 2; WLIT 2
Baastad, Babbis Friis
See Friis-Baastad, Babbis Ellinor
Bab
See Gilbert, W(illiam) S(chwenck)
Babbis, Eleanor
See Friis-Baastad, Babbis Ellinor
Babel, Isaac
See Babel, Isaak (Emmanuilovich)
Babel, Isaak (Emmanuilovich) 1894-1941(?) .... **SSC 16, 78, 161; TCLC 2, 13, 171**
See also CA 104; 155; CANR 113; DLB 272; EW 11; EWL 3; MTCW 2; MTFW 2005; RGSF 2; RGWL 2, 3; SSFS 10; TWA
Babits, Mihaly 1883-1941 .... **TCLC 14**
See also CA 114; CDWLB 4; DLB 215; EWL 3
Babur 1483-1530 .... **LC 18**
Babylas
See Ghelderode, Michel de
Baca, Jimmy Santiago 1952- . **HLC 1; PC 41**
See also CA 131; CANR 81, 90, 146, 220; CP 6, 7; DAM MULT; DLB 122; HW 1, 2; LLW; MAL 5; PFS 40
Baca, Jose Santiago
See Baca, Jimmy Santiago
Bacchelli, Riccardo 1891-1985 .... **CLC 19**
See also CA 29-32R; 117; DLB 264; EWL 3
Bacchylides c. 520B.C.-c. 452B.C. .... **CMLC 119**
Bach, Richard 1936- .... **CLC 14**
See also AITN 1; BEST 89:2; BPFB 1; BYA 5; CA 9-12R; CANR 18, 93, 151; CPW; DAM NOV, POP; FANT; MTCW 1; SATA 13
Bach, Richard David
See Bach, Richard
Bache, Benjamin Franklin 1769-1798 .... **LC 74**
See also DLB 43
Bachelard, Gaston 1884-1962 ...... **TCLC 128**
See also CA 97-100; 89-92; DLB 296; GFL 1789 to the Present
Bachman, Richard
See King, Stephen
Bachmann, Ingeborg 1926-1973 ..... **CLC 69; TCLC 192**
See also CA 93-96; 45-48; CANR 69; DLB 85; EWL 3; RGHL; RGWL 2, 3

Bacigalupi, Paolo 1973- .... **CLC 309**
See also AAYA 86; CA 317; SATA 230
Bacon, Francis 1561-1626 ..... **LC 18, 32, 131**
See also BRW 1; CDBLB Before 1660; DLB 151, 236, 252; RGEL 2; TEA
Bacon, Roger 1214(?)-1294 ... **CMLC 14, 108**
See also DLB 115
Bacovia, G.
See Bacovia, George
Bacovia, George 1881-1957 .... **TCLC 24**
See Bacovia, George
See also CA 123; 189; CDWLB 4; DLB 220; EWL 3
Badanes, Jerome 1937-1995 .... **CLC 59**
See also CA 234
Bage, Robert 1728-1801 .... **NCLC 182**
See also DLB 39; RGEL 2
Bagehot, Walter 1826-1877 .... **NCLC 10**
See also DLB 55
Bagnold, Enid 1889-1981 .... **CLC 25**
See also AAYA 75; BYA 2; CA 5-8R; 103; CANR 5, 40; CBD; CN 2; CWD; CWRI 5; DAM DRAM; DLB 13, 160, 191, 245; FW; MAICYA 1, 2; RGEL 2; SATA 1, 25
Bagritsky, Eduard
See Dzyubin, Eduard Georgievich
Bagritsky, Edvard
See Dzyubin, Eduard Georgievich
Bagrjana, Elisaveta
See Belcheva, Elisaveta Lyubomirova
Bagryana, Elisaveta
See Belcheva, Elisaveta Lyubomirova
Bailey, Paul 1937- .... **CLC 45**
See also CA 21-24R; CANR 16, 62, 124; CN 1, 2, 3, 4, 5, 6, 7; DLB 14, 271; GLL 2
Baillie, Joanna 1762 1851 ...... **NCLC 71, 151**
See also DLB 93, 344; GL 2; RGEL 2
Bainbridge, Beryl 1934-2010 ..... **CLC 4, 5, 8, 10, 14, 18, 22, 62, 130, 292**
See also BRWS 6; CA 21-24R; CANR 24, 55, 75, 88, 128; CN 2, 3, 4, 5, 6, 7; DAM NOV; DLB 14, 231; EWL 3; MTCW 1, 2; MTFW 2005
Baker, Carlos (Heard) 1909-1987 .... **TCLC 119**
See also CA 5-8R; 122; CANR 3, 63; DLB 103
Baker, Elliott 1922-2007 .... **CLC 8**
See also CA 45-48; 257; CANR 2, 63; CN 1, 2, 3, 4, 5, 6, 7
Baker, Elliott Joseph
See Baker, Elliott
Baker, Jean H.
See Russell, George William
Baker, Nicholson 1957- .... **CLC 61, 165**
See also AMWS 13; CA 135; CANR 63, 120, 138, 190; CN 6; CPW; DA3; DAM POP; DLB 227; MTFW 2005
Baker, Ray Stannard 1870-1946 .... **TCLC 47**
See also CA 118; DLB 345
Baker, Russell 1925- .... **CLC 31**
See also BEST 89:4; CA 57-60; CANR 11, 41, 59, 137; MTCW 1, 2; MTFW 2005
Baker, Russell Wayne
See Baker, Russell
Bakhtin, M.
See Bakhtin, Mikhail Mikhailovich
Bakhtin, M. M.
See Bakhtin, Mikhail Mikhailovich
Bakhtin, Mikhail
See Bakhtin, Mikhail Mikhailovich
Bakhtin, Mikhail Mikhailovich 1895-1975 .... **CLC 83; TCLC 160**
See Bakhtin, Mikhail Mikhailovich
See also CA 128; 113; DLB 242; EWL 3
Bakshi, Ralph 1938(?)- .... **CLC 26**
See also CA 112; 138; IDFW 3

Bakunin, Mikhail (Alexandrovich) 1814-1876 .... **NCLC 25, 58**
See also DLB 277
Bal, Mieke 1946- .... **CLC 252**
See also CA 156; CANR 99
Bal, Mieke Maria Gertrudis
See Bal, Mieke
Baldwin, James 1924-1987 ...... **BLC 1:1, 2:1; CLC 1, 2, 3, 4, 5, 8, 13, 15, 17, 42, 50, 67, 90, 127; DC 1; SSC 10, 33, 98, 134; TCLC 229; WLC 1**
See also AAYA 4, 34; AFAW 1, 2; AMWR 2; AMWS 1; BPFB 1; BW 1; CA 1-4R; 124; CABS 1; CAD; CANR 3, 24; CDALB 1941-1968; CN 1, 2, 3, 4; CPW; DA; DA3; DAB; DAC; DAM MST, MULT, NOV, POP; DFS 11, 15; DLB 2, 7, 33, 249, 278; DLBY 1987; EWL 3; EXPS; LAIT 5; MAL 5; MTCW 1, 2; MTFW 2005; NCFS 4; NFS 4; RGAL 4; RGSF 2; SATA 9; SATA-Obit 54; SSFS 2, 18; TUS
Baldwin, William c. 1515-1563 .... **LC 113**
See also DLB 132
Bale, John 1495-1563 .... **LC 62**
See also DLB 132; RGEL 2; TEA
Ball, Hugo 1886-1927 .... **TCLC 104**
Ballard, James G.
See Ballard, J.G.
Ballard, James Graham
See Ballard, J.G.
Ballard, J.G. 1930-2009 ..... **CLC 3, 6, 14, 36, 137, 299; SSC 1, 53, 146**
See also AAYA 3, 52; BRWS 5; CA 5-8R; 285; CANR 15, 39, 65, 107, 133, 198; CN 1, 2, 3, 4, 5, 6, 7; DA3; DAM NOV, POP; DLB 14, 207, 261, 319; EWL 3; HGG; MTCW 1, 2; MTFW 2005; NFS 8; RGEL 2; RGSF 2; SATA 93; SATA-Obit 203; SCFW 1, 2; SFW 4
Ballard, Jim G.
See Ballard, J.G.
Balmont, Konstantin (Dmitriyevich) 1867-1943 .... **TCLC 11**
See also CA 109; 155; DLB 295; EWL 3
Baltausis, Vincas 1847-1910
See Mikszath, Kalman
Balzac, Guez de (?)-
See Balzac, Jean-Louis Guez de
Balzac, Honore de 1799-1850 ... **NCLC 5, 35, 53, 153; SSC 5, 59, 102, 153; WLC 1**
See also DA; DA3; DAB; DAC; DAM MST, NOV; DLB 119; EW 5; GFL 1789 to the Present; LMFS 1; NFS 33; RGSF 2; RGWL 2, 3; SSFS 10; SUFW; TWA
Balzac, Jean-Louis Guez de 1597-1654 .... **LC 162**
See also DLB 268; GFL Beginnings to 1789
Bambara, Toni Cade 1939-1995 ..... **BLC 1:1, 2:1; CLC 19, 88; SSC 35, 107; TCLC 116; WLCS**
See also AAYA 5, 49; AFAW 2; AMWS 11; BW 2, 3; BYA 12, 14; CA 29-32R; 150; CANR 24, 49, 81; CDALBS; DA; DA3; DAC; DAM MST, MULT; DLB 38, 218; EXPS; MAL 5; MTCW 1, 2; MTFW 2005; RGAL 4; RGSF 2; SATA 112; SSFS 4, 7, 12, 21
Bamdad, A.
See Shamlu, Ahmad
Bamdad, Alef
See Shamlu, Ahmad
Banat, D. R.
See Bradbury, Ray
Bancroft, Laura
See Baum, L. Frank
Bandello, Matteo 1485-1561 .... **SSC 143**
Banim, John 1798-1842 .... **NCLC 13**
See also DLB 116, 158, 159; RGEL 2

Barthes, Roland (Gerard)
1915-1980 .... **CLC 24, 83; TCLC 135**
See also CA 130; 97-100; CANR 66; DLB
296; EW 13; EWL 3; GFL 1789 to the
Present; MTCW 1, 2; TWA

Bartram, William 1739-1823 .... **NCLC 145**
See also ANW; DLB 37

Barzun, Jacques 1907- .... **CLC 51, 145**
See also CA 61-64; CANR 22, 95

Barzun, Jacques Martin
See Barzun, Jacques

Bashevis, Isaac
See Singer, Isaac Bashevis

Bashevis, Yitskhok
See Singer, Isaac Bashevis

Bashkirtseff, Marie 1859-1884 .... **NCLC 27**

Basho, Matsuo
See Matsuo Basho

Basil of Caesaria c. 330-379 .... **CMLC 35**

Basket, Raney
See Edgerton, Clyde

Bass, Kingsley B., Jr.
See Bullins, Ed

Bass, Rick 1958- . **CLC 79, 143, 286; SSC 60**
See also AMWS 16; ANW; CA 126; CANR
53, 93, 145, 183; CSW; DLB 212, 275

Bassani, Giorgio 1916-2000 .... **CLC 9**
See also CA 65-68; 190; CANR 33; CWW
2; DLB 128, 177, 299; EWL 3; MTCW 1;
RGHL; RGWL 2, 3

Bassine, Helen
See Yglesias, Helen

Bastian, Ann .... **CLC 70**

Bastos, Augusto Roa
See Roa Bastos, Augusto

Bataille, Georges 1897-1962 .... **CLC 29;**
TCLC 155
See also CA 101; 89-92; EWL 3

Bates, H(erbert) E(rnest)
1905-1974 .... **CLC 46; SSC 10**
See also CA 93-96; 45-48; CANR 34; CN
1; DA3; DAB; DAM POP; DLB 162, 191;
EWL 3; EXPS; MTCW 1, 2; RGSF 2;
SSFS 7

Batiushkov, Konstantin Nikolaevich
1787-1855 .... **NCLC 254**
See also DLB 205

Bauchart
See Camus, Albert

Baudelaire, Charles 1821-1867 . **NCLC 6, 29,**
55, 155; PC 1, 106; SSC 18; WLC 1
See also DA; DA3; DAB; DAC; DAM
MST, POET; DLB 217; EW 7; GFL 1789
to the Present; LMFS 2; PFS 21, 38;
RGWL 2, 3; TWA

Baudouin, Marcel
See Peguy, Charles (Pierre)

Baudouin, Pierre
See Peguy, Charles (Pierre)

Baudrillard, Jean 1929-2007 .... **CLC 60**
See also CA 252; 258; DLB 296

Baum, L. Frank 1856-1919 ...... **TCLC 7, 132**
See also AAYA 46; BYA 16; CA 108; 133;
CLR 15, 107; CWRI 5; DLB 22; FANT;
JRDA; MAICYA 1, 2; MTCW 1, 2; NFS
13; RGAL 4; SATA 18, 100; WCH

Baum, Louis F.
See Baum, L. Frank

Baum, Lyman Frank
See Baum, L. Frank

Bauman, Zygmunt 1925- .... **CLC 314**
See also CA 127; CANR 205

Baumbach, Jonathan 1933- .... **CLC 6, 23**
See also CA 13-16R; 284; CAAE 284;
CAAS 5; CANR 12, 66, 140; CN 3, 4, 5,
6, 7; DLBY 1980; INT CANR-12; MTCW
1

Baumgarten, Alexander Gottlieb
1714-1762 .... **LC 199**

Bausch, Richard 1945- .... **CLC 51**
See also AMWS 7; CA 101; CAAS 14;
CANR 43, 61, 87, 164, 200; CN 7; CSW;
DLB 130; MAL 5

Bausch, Richard Carl
See Bausch, Richard

Baxter, Charles 1947- .... **CLC 45, 78**
See also AMWS 17; CA 57-60; CANR 40,
64, 104, 133, 188; CPW; DAM POP; DLB
130; MAL 5; MTCW 2; MTFW 2005;
TCLE 1:1

Baxter, Charles Morley
See Baxter, Charles

Baxter, George Owen
See Faust, Frederick

Baxter, James K(eir) 1926-1972 ...... **CLC 14;**
TCLC 249
See also CA 77-80; CP 1; EWL 3

Baxter, John
See Hunt, E. Howard

Bayer, Sylvia
See Glassco, John

Bayle, Pierre 1647-1706 .... **LC 126**
See also DLB 268, 313; GFL Beginnings to
1789

Baynton, Barbara 1857-1929 . **TCLC 57, 211**
See also DLB 230; RGSF 2

Beagle, Peter S. 1939- .... **CLC 7, 104**
See also AAYA 47; BPFB 1; BYA 9, 10,
16; CA 9-12R; CANR 4, 51, 73, 110, 213;
DA3; DLBY 1980; FANT; INT CANR-4;
MTCW 2; MTFW 2005; SATA 60, 130;
SUFW 1, 2; YAW

Beagle, Peter Soyer
See Beagle, Peter S.

Bean, Normal
See Burroughs, Edgar Rice

Beard, Charles A(ustin)
1874-1948 .... **TCLC 15**
See also CA 115; 189; DLB 17; SATA 18

Beardsley, Aubrey 1872-1898 .... **NCLC 6**

Beatrice of Nazareth 1200-1268 . **CMLC 124**

Beattie, Ann 1947- ..... **CLC 8, 13, 18, 40, 63,**
146, 293; SSC 11, 130
See also AMWS 5; BEST 90:2; BPFB 1;
CA 81-84; CANR 53, 73, 128, 225; CN
4, 5, 6, 7; CPW; DA3; DAM NOV, POP;
DLB 218, 278; DLBY 1982; EWL 3;
MAL 5; MTCW 1, 2; MTFW 2005;
RGAL 4; RGSF 2; SSFS 9; TUS

Beattie, James 1735-1803 .... **NCLC 25**
See also DLB 109

Beauchamp, Katherine Mansfield
See Mansfield, Katherine

Beaumarchais, Pierre-Augustin Caron de
1732-1799 .... **DC 4; LC 61, 192**
See also DAM DRAM; DFS 14, 16; DLB
313; EW 4; GFL Beginnings to 1789;
RGWL 2, 3

Beaumont, Francis 1584(?)-1616 .. **DC 6; LC**
33
See also BRW 2; CDBLB Before 1660;
DLB 58; TEA

Beauvoir, Simone de 1908-1986 .... **CLC 1, 2,**
4, 8, 14, 31, 44, 50, 71, 124; SSC 35;
TCLC 221; WLC 1
See also BPFB 1; CA 9-12R; 118; CANR
28, 61; DA; DA3; DAB; DAC; DAM
MST, NOV; DLB 72; DLBY 1986; EW
12; EWL 3; FL 1:5; FW; GFL 1789 to the
Present; LMFS 2; MTCW 1, 2; MTFW
2005; RGSF 2; RGWL 2, 3; TWA

Beauvoir, Simone Lucie Ernestine Marie
Bertrand de
See Beauvoir, Simone de

Becker, Carl (Lotus) 1873-1945 ..... **TCLC 63**
See also CA 157; DLB 17

Becker, Jurek 1937-1997 .... **CLC 7, 19**
See also CA 85-88; 157; CANR 60, 117;
CWW 2; DLB 75, 299; EWL 3; RGHL

Becker, Walter 1950- .... **CLC 26**

Becket, Thomas a 1118(?)-1170 .... **CMLC 83**

Beckett, Samuel 1906-1989 ... **CLC 1, 2, 3, 4,**
6, 9, 10, 11, 14, 18, 29, 57, 59, 83; DC
22; SSC 16, 74, 161; TCLC 145; WLC
1
See also BRWC 2; BRWR 1; BRWS 1; CA
5-8R; 130; CANR 33, 61; CBD; CDBLB
1945-1960; CN 1, 2, 3, 4; CP 1, 2, 3, 4;
DA; DA3; DAB; DAC; DAM DRAM,
MST, NOV; DFS 2, 7, 18; DLB 13, 15,
233, 319, 321, 329; DLBY 1990; EWL 3;
GFL 1789 to the Present; LATS 1:2;
LMFS 2; MTCW 1, 2; MTFW 2005;
RGSF 2; RGWL 2, 3; SSFS 15; TEA;
WLIT 4

Beckett, Samuel Barclay
See Beckett, Samuel

Beckford, William 1760-1844 .... **NCLC 16,**
214
See also BRW 3; DLB 39, 213; GL 2; HGG;
LMFS 1; SUFW

Beckham, Barry 1944- .... **BLC 1:1**
See also BW 1; CA 29-32R; CANR 26, 62;
CN 1, 2, 3, 4, 5, 6; DAM MULT; DLB 33

Beckman, Gunnel 1910- .... **CLC 26**
See also CA 33-36R; CANR 15, 114; CLR
25; MAICYA 1, 2; SAAS 9; SATA 6

Becque, Henri 1837-1899 .... **DC 21; NCLC 3**
See also DLB 192; GFL 1789 to the Present

Becquer, Gustavo Adolfo
1836-1870 ...... **HLCS 1; NCLC 106; PC**
113
See also DAM MULT

Beddoes, Thomas Lovell 1803-1849 .. **DC 15;**
NCLC 3, 154
See also BRWS 11; DLB 96

Bede c. 673-735 .... **CMLC 20, 130**
See also DLB 146; TEA

Bedford, Denton R. 1907-(?) .... **NNAL**

Bedford, Donald F.
See Fearing, Kenneth

Beecher, Catharine Esther
1800-1878 .... **NCLC 30**
See also DLB 1, 243

Beecher, John 1904-1980 .... **CLC 6**
See also AITN 1; CA 5-8R; 105; CANR 8;
CP 1, 2, 3

Beer, Johann 1655-1700 .... **LC 5**
See also DLB 168

Beer, Patricia 1924- .... **CLC 58**
See also BRWS 14; CA 61-64; 183; CANR
13, 46; CP 1, 2, 3, 4, 5, 6; CWP; DLB
40; FW

Beerbohm, Max
See Beerbohm, (Henry) Max(imilian)

Beerbohm, (Henry) Max(imilian)
1872-1956 .... **TCLC 1, 24**
See also BRWS 2; CA 104; 154; CANR 79;
DLB 34, 100; FANT; MTCW 2

Beer-Hofmann, Richard
1866-1945 .... **TCLC 60**
See also CA 160; DLB 81

Beethoven, Ludwig van
1770(?)-1827 .... **NCLC 227**

Beg, Shemus
See Stephens, James

Begiebing, Robert J(ohn) 1946- .... **CLC 70**
See also CA 122; CANR 40, 88

Begley, Louis 1933- .... **CLC 197**
See also CA 140; CANR 98, 176, 210; DLB
299; RGHL; TCLE 1:1

Behan, Brendan 1923-1964 ...... **CLC 1, 8, 11, 15, 79**
See also BRWS 2; CA 73-76; CANR 33, 121; CBD; CDBLB 1945-1960; DAM DRAM; DFS 7; DLB 13, 233; EWL 3; MTCW 1, 2

Behan, Brendan Francis
See Behan, Brendan

Behn, Aphra 1640(?)-1689 .. **DC 4; LC 1, 30, 42, 135; PC 13, 88; WLC 1**
See also BRWR 3; BRWS 3; DA; DA3; DAB; DAC; DAM DRAM, MST, NOV, POET; DFS 16, 24; DLB 39, 80, 131; FW; NFS 35; TEA; WLIT 3

Behrman, S(amuel) N(athaniel)
1893-1973 .... **CLC 40**
See also CA 13-16; 45-48; CAD; CAP 1; DLB 7, 44; IDFW 3; MAL 5; RGAL 4

Bekederemo, J. P. Clark
See Clark-Bekederemo, J. P.

Belasco, David 1853-1931 .... **TCLC 3**
See also CA 104; 168; DLB 7; MAL 5; RGAL 4

Belben, Rosalind 1941- .... **CLC 280**
See also CA 291

Belben, Rosalind Loveday
See Belben, Rosalind

Belcheva, Elisaveta Lyubomirova
1893-1991 .... **CLC 10**
See also CA 178; CDWLB 4; DLB 147; EWL 3

Beldone, Phil "Cheech"
See Ellison, Harlan

Beleno
See Azuela, Mariano

Belinski, Vissarion Grigoryevich
1811-1848 .... **NCLC 5**
See also DLB 198

Belitt, Ben 1911- .... **CLC 22**
See also CA 13-16R; CAAS 4; CANR 7, 77; CP 1, 2, 3, 4, 5, 6; DLB 5

Belknap, Jeremy 1744-1798 .... **LC 115**
See also DLB 30, 37

Bell, Gertrude (Margaret Lowthian)
1868-1926 .... **TCLC 67**
See also CA 167; CANR 110; DLB 174

Bell, J. Freeman
See Zangwill, Israel

Bell, James Madison 1826-1902 ..... **BLC 1:1; TCLC 43**
See also BW 1; CA 122; 124; DAM MULT; DLB 50

Bell, Madison Smartt 1957- ..... **CLC 41, 102, 223**
See also AMWS 10; BPFB 1; CA 111, 183; CAAE 183; CANR 28, 54, 73, 134, 176, 223; CN 5, 6, 7; CSW; DLB 218, 278; MTCW 2; MTFW 2005

Bell, Marvin 1937- .... **CLC 8, 31; PC 79**
See also CA 21-24R; CAAS 14; CANR 59, 102, 206; CP 1, 2, 3, 4, 5, 6, 7; DAM POET; DLB 5; MAL 5; MTCW 1; PFS 25

Bell, Marvin Hartley
See Bell, Marvin

Bell, W. L. D.
See Mencken, H. L.

Bellamy, Atwood C.
See Mencken, H. L.

Bellamy, Edward 1850-1898 ..... **NCLC 4, 86, 147**
See also DLB 12; NFS 15; RGAL 4; SFW 4

Belli, Gioconda 1949- .... **HLCS 1**
See also CA 152; CANR 143, 209; CWW 2; DLB 290; EWL 3; RGWL 3

Bellin, Edward J.
See Kuttner, Henry

Bello, Andres 1781-1865 .... **NCLC 131**
See also LAW

Belloc, Hilaire 1870-1953 ... **PC 24; TCLC 7, 18**
See also CA 106; 152; CLR 102; CWRI 5; DAM POET; DLB 19, 100, 141, 174; EWL 3; MTCW 2; MTFW 2005; SATA 112; WCH; YABC 1

Belloc, Joseph Hilaire Pierre Sebastien Rene Swanton
See Belloc, Hilaire

Belloc, Joseph Peter Rene Hilaire
See Belloc, Hilaire

Belloc, Joseph Pierre Hilaire
See Belloc, Hilaire

Belloc, M. A.
See Lowndes, Marie Adelaide (Belloc)

Belloc-Lowndes, Mrs.
See Lowndes, Marie Adelaide (Belloc)

Bellow, Saul 1915-2005 ...... **CLC 1, 2, 3, 6, 8, 10, 13, 15, 25, 33, 34, 63, 79, 190, 200; SSC 14, 101; WLC 1**
See also AITN 2; AMW; AMWC 2; AMWR 2; BEST 89:3; BPFB 1; CA 5-8R; 238; CABS 1; CANR 29, 53, 95, 132; CDALB 1941-1968; CN 1, 2, 3, 4, 5, 6, 7; DA; DA3; DAB; DAC; DAM MST, NOV, POP; DLB 2, 28, 299, 329; DLBD 3; DLBY 1982; EWL 3; MAL 5; MTCW 1, 2; MTFW 2005; NFS 4, 14, 26, 33; RGAL 4; RGHL; RGSF 2; SSFS 12, 22; TUS

Belser, Reimond Karel Maria de
1929- .... **CLC 14**
See also CA 152

Bely, Andrey
See Bugayev, Boris Nikolayevich

Belyi, Andrei
See Bugayev, Boris Nikolayevich

Bembo, Pietro 1470-1547 .... **LC 79**
See also RGWL 2, 3

Benary, Margot
See Benary-Isbert, Margot

Benary-Isbert, Margot 1889-1979 .... **CLC 12**
See also CA 5-8R; 89-92; CANR 4, 72; CLR 12; MAICYA 1, 2; SATA 2; SATA-Obit 21

Benavente, Jacinto 1866-1954 .... **DC 26; HLCS 1; TCLC 3**
See also CA 106; 131; CANR 81; DAM DRAM, MULT; DLB 329; EWL 3; GLL 2; HW 1, 2; MTCW 1, 2

Benavente y Martinez, Jacinto
See Benavente, Jacinto

Benchley, Peter 1940-2006 .... **CLC 4, 8**
See also AAYA 14; AITN 2; BPFB 1; CA 17-20R; 248; CANR 12, 35, 66, 115; CPW; DAM NOV, POP; HGG; MTCW 1, 2; MTFW 2005; SATA 3, 89, 164

Benchley, Peter Bradford
See Benchley, Peter

Benchley, Robert (Charles)
1889-1945 .... **TCLC 1, 55**
See also CA 105; 153; DLB 11; MAL 5; RGAL 4

Benda, Julien 1867-1956 .... **TCLC 60**
See also CA 120; 154; GFL 1789 to the Present

Benedetti, Mario 1920-2009 .. **CLC 299; SSC 135**
See also CA 152; 286; DAM MULT; DLB 113; EWL 3; HW 1, 2; LAW

Benedetti, Mario Orlando Hardy Hamlet Brenno
See Benedetti, Mario

Benedetti Farrugia, Mario
See Benedetti, Mario

Benedetti Farrugia, Mario Orlando Hardy Hamlet Brenno
See Benedetti, Mario

Benedict, Ruth 1887-1948 .... **TCLC 60**
See also CA 158; CANR 146; DLB 246

Benedict, Ruth Fulton
See Benedict, Ruth

Benedikt, Michael 1935- .... **CLC 4, 14**
See also CA 13-16R; CANR 7; CP 1, 2, 3, 4, 5, 6, 7; DLB 5

Benet, Juan 1927-1993 .... **CLC 28**
See also CA 143; EWL 3

Benet, Stephen Vincent 1898-1943 ..... **PC 64; SSC 10, 86; TCLC 7**
See also AMWS 11; CA 104; 152; DA3; DAM POET; DLB 4, 48, 102, 249, 284; DLBY 1997; EWL 3; HGG; MAL 5; MTCW 2; MTFW 2005; RGAL 4; RGSF 2; SSFS 22, 31; SUFW; WP; YABC 1

Benet, William Rose 1886-1950 ..... **TCLC 28**
See also CA 118; 152; DAM POET; DLB 45; RGAL 4

Benford, Gregory 1941- .... **CLC 52**
See also BPFB 1; CA 69-72, 175, 268; CAAE 175, 268; CAAS 27; CANR 12, 24, 49, 95, 134; CN 7; CSW; DLBY 1982; MTFW 2005; SCFW 2; SFW 4

Benford, Gregory Albert
See Benford, Gregory

Bengtsson, Frans (Gunnar)
1894-1954 .... **TCLC 48**
See also CA 170; EWL 3

Benjamin, David
See Slavitt, David R.

Benjamin, Lois
See Gould, Lois

Benjamin, Walter 1892-1940 .... **TCLC 39**
See also CA 164; CANR 181; DLB 242; EW 11; EWL 3

Ben Jelloun, Tahar 1944- .... **CLC 180, 311**
See also CA 135, 162; CANR 100, 166, 217; CWW 2; EWL 3; RGWL 3; WLIT 2

Benn, Gottfried 1886-1956 . **PC 35; TCLC 3, 256**
See also CA 106; 153; DLB 56; EWL 3; RGWL 2, 3

Bennett, Alan 1934- .... **CLC 45, 77, 292**
See also BRWS 8; CA 103; CANR 35, 55, 106, 157, 197, 227; CBD; CD 5, 6; DAB; DAM MST; DLB 310; MTCW 1, 2; MTFW 2005

Bennett, (Enoch) Arnold
1867-1931 .... **TCLC 5, 20, 197**
See also BRW 6; CA 106; 155; CDBLB 1890-1914; DLB 10, 34, 98, 135; EWL 3; MTCW 2

Bennett, Elizabeth
See Mitchell, Margaret

Bennett, George Harold 1930- .... **CLC 5**
See also BW 1; CA 97-100; CAAS 13; CANR 87; DLB 33

Bennett, Gwendolyn B. 1902-1981 .... **HR 1:2**
See also BW 1; CA 125; DLB 51; WP

Bennett, Hal
See Bennett, George Harold

Bennett, Jay 1912- .... **CLC 35**
See also AAYA 10, 73; CA 69-72; CANR 11, 42, 79; JRDA; SAAS 4; SATA 41, 87; SATA-Brief 27; WYA; YAW

Bennett, Louise 1919-2006 .... **BLC 1:1; CLC 28**
See also BW 2, 3; CA 151; 252; CDWLB 3; CP 1, 2, 3, 4, 5, 6, 7; DAM MULT; DLB 117; EWL 3

Bennett, Louise Simone
See Bennett, Louise

Bennett-Coverley, Louise
See Bennett, Louise

Benoit de Sainte-Maure fl. 12th cent.
- .... **CMLC 90**

Benson, A. C. 1862-1925 .... **TCLC 123**
See also DLB 98

Benson, E(dward) F(rederic)
1867-1940 .... **TCLC 27**
See also CA 114; 157; DLB 135, 153;
HGG; SUFW 1

Benson, Jackson J. 1930- .... **CLC 34**
See also CA 25-28R; CANR 214; DLB 111

Benson, Sally 1900-1972 .... **CLC 17**
See also CA 19-20; 37-40R; CAP 1; SATA
1, 35; SATA-Obit 27

Benson, Stella 1892-1933 .... **TCLC 17**
See also CA 117; 154, 155; DLB 36, 162;
FANT; TEA

Bentham, Jeremy 1748-1832 . **NCLC 38, 237**
See also DLB 107, 158, 252

Bentley, E(dmund) C(lerihew)
1875-1956 .... **TCLC 12**
See also CA 108; 232; DLB 70; MSW

Bentley, Eric 1916- .... **CLC 24**
See also CA 5-8R; CAD; CANR 6, 67;
CBD; CD 5, 6; INT CANR-6

Bentley, Eric Russell
See Bentley, Eric

ben Uzair, Salem
See Horne, Richard Henry Hengist

Beolco, Angelo 1496-1542 .... **LC 139**

Beranger, Pierre Jean de
1780-1857 .... **NCLC 34; PC 112**

Berdyaev, Nicolas
See Berdyaev, Nikolai (Aleksandrovich)

Berdyaev, Nikolai (Aleksandrovich)
1874-1948 .... **TCLC 67**
See also CA 120; 157

Berdyayev, Nikolai (Aleksandrovich)
See Berdyaev, Nikolai (Aleksandrovich)

Berendt, John 1939- .... **CLC 86**
See also CA 146; CANR 75, 83, 151

Berendt, John Lawrence
See Berendt, John

Berengar of Tours c. 1000-1088 .. **CMLC 124**

Beresford, J(ohn) D(avys)
1873-1947 .... **TCLC 81**
See also CA 112; 155; DLB 162, 178, 197;
SFW 4; SUFW 1

Bergelson, David (Rafailovich)
1884-1952 .... **TCLC 81**
See also CA 220; DLB 333; EWL 3

Bergelson, Dovid
See Bergelson, David (Rafailovich)

Berger, Colonel
See Malraux, Andre

Berger, John 1926- .... **CLC 2, 19**
See also BRWS 4; CA 81-84; CANR 51,
78, 117, 163, 200; CN 1, 2, 3, 4, 5, 6, 7;
DLB 14, 207, 319, 326

Berger, John Peter
See Berger, John

Berger, Melvin H. 1927- .... **CLC 12**
See also CA 5-8R; CANR 4, 142; CLR 32;
SAAS 2; SATA 5, 88, 158; SATA-Essay
124

Berger, Thomas 1924- .... **CLC 3, 5, 8, 11, 18,
38, 259**
See also BPFB 1; CA 1-4R; CANR 5, 28,
51, 128; CN 1, 2, 3, 4, 5, 6, 7; DAM
NOV; DLB 2; DLBY 1980; EWL 3;
FANT; INT CANR-28; MAL 5; MTCW
1, 2; MTFW 2005; RHW; TCLE 1:1;
TCWW 1, 2

Bergman, Ernst Ingmar
See Bergman, Ingmar

Bergman, Ingmar 1918-2007 ..... **CLC 16, 72,
210**
See also AAYA 61; CA 81-84; 262; CANR
33, 70; CWW 2; DLB 257; MTCW 2;
MTFW 2005

Bergson, Henri(-Louis) 1859-1941 . **TCLC 32**
See also CA 164; DLB 329; EW 8; EWL 3;
GFL 1789 to the Present

Bergstein, Eleanor 1938- .... **CLC 4**
See also CA 53-56; CANR 5

Berkeley, George 1685-1753 .... **LC 65**
See also DLB 31, 101, 252

Berkoff, Steven 1937- .... **CLC 56**
See also CA 104; CANR 72; CBD; CD 5, 6

Berlin, Isaiah 1909-1997 .... **TCLC 105**
See also CA 85-88; 162

Bermant, Chaim (Icyk) 1929-1998 ... **CLC 40**
See also CA 57-60; CANR 6, 31, 57, 105;
CN 2, 3, 4, 5, 6

Bern, Victoria
See Fisher, M(ary) F(rances) K(ennedy)

Bernanos, (Paul Louis) Georges
1888-1948 .... **TCLC 3**
See also CA 104; 130; CANR 94; DLB 72;
EWL 3; GFL 1789 to the Present; RGWL
2, 3

Bernard, April 1956- .... **CLC 59**
See also CA 131; CANR 144

Bernard, Mary Ann
See Soderbergh, Steven

Bernard of Clairvaux 1090-1153 .. **CMLC 71**
See also DLB 208

Bernard Silvestris fl. c. 1130-fl. c.
1160 .... **CMLC 87**
See also DLB 208

Bernart de Ventadorn c. 1130-c.
1190 .... **CMLC 98**

Berne, Victoria
See Fisher, M(ary) F(rances) K(ennedy)

Bernhard, Thomas 1931-1989 ..... **CLC 3, 32,
61; DC 14; TCLC 165**
See also CA 85-88; 127; CANR 32, 57; CD-
WLB 2; DLB 85, 124; EWL 3; MTCW 1;
RGHL; RGWL 2, 3

Bernhardt, Sarah (Henriette Rosine)
1844-1923 .... **TCLC 75**
See also CA 157

Bernstein, Charles 1950- .... **CLC 142,**
See also CA 129; CAAS 24; CANR 90; CP
4, 5, 6, 7; DLB 169

Bernstein, Ingrid
See Kirsch, Sarah

Beroul fl. c. 12th cent. - .... **CMLC 75**

Berriault, Gina 1926-1999 .... **CLC 54, 109;
SSC 30**
See also CA 116; 129; 185; CANR 66; DLB
130; SSFS 7,11

Berrigan, Daniel 1921- .... **CLC 4**
See also CA 33-36R, 187; CAAE 187;
CAAS 1; CANR 11, 43, 78, 219; CP 1, 2,
3, 4, 5, 6, 7; DLB 5

Berrigan, Edmund Joseph Michael, Jr.
1934-1983 .... **CLC 37; PC 103**
See also CA 61-64; 110; CANR 14, 102;
CP 1, 2, 3; DLB 5, 169; WP

Berrigan, Ted
See Berrigan, Edmund Joseph Michael, Jr.

Berry, Charles Edward Anderson
1931- .... **CLC 17**
See also CA 115

Berry, Chuck
See Berry, Charles Edward Anderson

Berry, Jonas
See Ashbery, John

Berry, Wendell 1934- ..... **CLC 4, 6, 8, 27, 46,
279; PC 28**
See also AITN 1; AMWS 10; ANW; CA
73-76; CANR 50, 73, 101, 132, 174, 228;
CP 1, 2, 3, 4, 5, 6, 7; CSW; DAM POET;
DLB 5, 6, 234, 275, 342; MTCW 2;
MTFW 2005; PFS 30; TCLE 1:1

Berry, Wendell Erdman
See Berry, Wendell

Berryman, John 1914-1972 ... **CLC 1, 2, 3, 4,
6, 8, 10, 13, 25, 62; PC 64**
See also AMW; CA 13-16; 33-36R; CABS
2; CANR 35; CAP 1; CDALB 1941-1968;
CP 1; DAM POET; DLB 48; EWL 3;
MAL 5; MTCW 1, 2; MTFW 2005; PAB;
PFS 27; RGAL 4; WP

Berssenbrugge, Mei-mei 1947- .... **PC 115**
See also CA 104; DLB 312

Bertolucci, Bernardo 1940- ...... **CLC 16, 157**
See also CA 106; CANR 125

Berton, Pierre (Francis de Marigny)
1920-2004 .... **CLC 104**
See also CA 1-4R; 233; CANR 2, 56, 144;
CPW; DLB 68; SATA 99; SATA-Obit 158

Bertrand, Aloysius 1807-1841 .... **NCLC 31**
See also DLB 217

Bertrand, Louis oAloysiusc
See Bertrand, Aloysius

Bertran de Born c. 1140-1215 .... **CMLC 5**

Besant, Annie (Wood) 1847-1933 ..... **TCLC 9**
See also CA 105; 185

Bessie, Alvah 1904-1985 .... **CLC 23**
See also CA 5-8R; 116; CANR 2, 80; DLB
26

Bestuzhev, Aleksandr Aleksandrovich
1797-1837 .... **NCLC 131**
See also DLB 198

Bethlen, T.D.
See Silverberg, Robert

Beti, Mongo 1932-2001 .... **BLC 1:1; CLC 27**
See also AFW; BW 1, 3; CA 114; 124;
CANR 81; DA3; DAM MULT; DLB 360;
EWL 3; MTCW 1, 2

Betjeman, John 1906-1984 ...... **CLC 2, 6, 10,
34, 43; PC 75**
See also BRW 7; CA 9-12R; 112; CANR
33, 56; CDBLB 1945-1960; CP 1, 2, 3;
DA3; DAB; DAM MST, POET; DLB 20;
DLBY 1984; EWL 3; MTCW 1, 2

Bettelheim, Bruno 1903-1990 .... **CLC 79;
TCLC 143**
See also CA 81-84; 131; CANR 23, 61;
DA3; MTCW 1, 2; RGHL

Betti, Ugo 1892-1953 .... **TCLC 5**
See also CA 104; 155; EWL 3; RGWL 2, 3

Betts, Doris (Waugh) 1932- ..... **CLC 3, 6, 28,
275; SSC 45**
See also CA 13-16R; CANR 9, 66, 77; CN
6, 7; CSW; DLB 218; DLBY 1982; INT
CANR-9; RGAL 4

Bevan, Alistair
See Roberts, Keith (John Kingston)

Bey, Pilaff
See Douglas, (George) Norman

Beyala, Calixthe 1961- .... **BLC 2:1**
See also EWL 3

Beynon, John
See Harris, John (Wyndham Parkes Lucas)
Beynon

Bhabha, Homi K. 1949- .... **CLC 285**

Bialik, Chaim Nachman
1873-1934 .... **TCLC 25, 201**
See also CA 170; EWL 3; WLIT 6

Bialik, Hayyim Nahman
See Bialik, Chaim Nachman

Bickerstaff, Isaac
See Swift, Jonathan

Bidart, Frank 1939- .... **CLC 33**
See also AMWS 15; CA 140; CANR 106,
215; CP 5, 6, 7; PFS 26

Bienek, Horst 1930- .... **CLC 7, 11**
See also CA 73-76; DLB 75

Bierce, Ambrose 1842-1914(?) ...... **SSC 9, 72,
124; TCLC 1, 7, 44; WLC 1**
See also AAYA 55; AMW; BYA 11; CA
104; 139; CANR 78; CDALB 1865-1917;
DA; DA3; DAC; DAM MST; DLB 11,
12, 23, 71, 74, 186; EWL 3; EXPS; HGG;
LAIT 2; MAL 5; RGAL 4; RGSF 2; SSFS
9, 27; SUFW 1

Blume, Judy 1938- .... **CLC 12, 30**
See also AAYA 3, 26; BYA 1, 8, 12; CA 29-32R; CANR 13, 37, 66, 124, 186; CLR 2, 15, 69; CPW; DA3; DAM NOV, POP; DLB 52; JRDA; MAICYA 1, 2; MAIC-YAS 1; MTCW 1, 2; MTFW 2005; NFS 24; SATA 2, 31, 79, 142, 195; WYA; YAW

Blume, Judy Sussman
See Blume, Judy

Blunden, Edmund (Charles)
1896-1974 .... **CLC 2, 56; PC 66**
See also BRW 6; BRWS 11; CA 17-18; 45-48; CANR 54; CAP 2; CP 1, 2; DLB 20, 100, 155; MTCW 1; PAB

Bly, Robert 1926- ..... **CLC 1, 2, 5, 10, 15, 38, 128; PC 39**
See also AMWS 4; CA 5-8R; CANR 41, 73, 125; CP 1, 2, 3, 4, 5, 6, 7; DA3; DAM POET; DLB 5, 342; EWL 3; MAL 5; MTCW 1, 2; MTFW 2005; PFS 6, 17; RGAL 4

Bly, Robert Elwood
See Bly, Robert

Boas, Franz 1858-1942 .... **TCLC 56**
See also CA 115; 181

Bobette
See Simenon, Georges

Boccaccio, Giovanni 1313-1375 ... **CMLC 13, 57; SSC 10, 87**
See also EW 2; RGSF 2; RGWL 2, 3; SSFS 28; TWA; WLIT 7

Bochco, Steven 1943- .... **CLC 35**
See also AAYA 11, 71; CA 124; 138

Bock, Charles 1970- .... **CLC 299**
See also CA 274

Bode, Sigmund
See O'Doherty, Brian

Bodel, Jean 1167(?)-1210 .... **CMLC 28**

Bodenheim, Maxwell 1892-1954 .... **TCLC 44**
See also CA 110; 187; DLB 9, 45; MAL 5; RGAL 4

Bodenheimer, Maxwell
See Bodenheim, Maxwell

Bodker, Cecil
See Bodker, Cecil

Bodker, Cecil 1927- .... **CLC 21**
See also CA 73-76, CANR 13, 44, 111; CLR 23; MAICYA 1, 2; SATA 14, 133

Boell, Heinrich 1917-1985 ..... **CLC 2, 3, 6, 9, 11, 15, 27, 32, 72; SSC 23; TCLC 185; WLC 1**
See also BPFB 1; CA 21-24R; 116; CANR 24; CDWLB 2; DA; DA3; DAB; DAC; DAM MST, NOV; DLB 69, 329; DLBY 1985; EW 13; EWL 3; MTCW 1, 2; MTFW 2005; RGHL; RGSF 2; RGWL 2, 3; SSFS 20; TWA

Boell, Heinrich Theodor
See Boell, Heinrich

Boerne, Alfred
See Doeblin, Alfred

Boethius c. 480-c. 524 .... **CMLC 15, 136**
See also DLB 115; RGWL 2, 3; WLIT 8

Boff, Leonardo (Genezio Darci)
1938- .... **CLC 70; HLC 1**
See also CA 150; DAM MULT; HW 2

Bogan, Louise 1897-1970 .... **CLC 4, 39, 46, 93; PC 12**
See also AMWS 3; CA 73-76; 25-28R; CANR 33, 82; CP 1; DAM POET; DLB 45, 169; EWL 3; MAL 5; MBL; MTCW 1, 2; PFS 21, 39; RGAL 4

Bogarde, Dirk
See Van Den Bogarde, Derek Jules Gaspard Ulric Niven

Bogat, Shatan
See Kacew, Romain

Bogomolny, Robert L. 1938- .... **SSC 41; TCLC 11**
See also CA 121, 164; DLB 182; EWL 3; MJW; RGSF 2; RGWL 2, 3; TWA

Bogomolny, Robert Lee
See Bogomolny, Robert L.

Bogosian, Eric 1953- .... **CLC 45, 141**
See also CA 138; CAD; CANR 102, 148, 217; CD 5, 6; DLB 341

Bograd, Larry 1953- .... **CLC 35**
See also CA 93-96; CANR 57; SAAS 21; SATA 33, 89; WYA

Bohme, Jakob 1575-1624 .... **LC 178**
See also DLB 164

Boiardo, Matteo Maria 1441-1494 .... **LC 6, 168**

Boileau-Despreaux, Nicolas
1636-1711 .... **LC 3, 164**
See also DLB 268; EW 3; GFL Beginnings to 1789; RGWL 2, 3

Boissard, Maurice
See Leautaud, Paul

Bojer, Johan 1872-1959 .... **TCLC 64**
See also CA 189; EWL 3

Bok, Edward W(illiam)
1863-1930 .... **TCLC 101**
See also CA 217; DLB 91; DLBD 16

Boker, George Henry 1823-1890 . **NCLC 125**
See also RGAL 4

Boland, Eavan 1944- ... **CLC 40, 67, 113; PC 58**
See also BRWS 5; CA 143, 207; CAAE 207; CANR 61, 180; CP 1, 6, 7; CWP; DAM POET; DLB 40; FW; MTCW 2; MTFW 2005; PFS 12, 22, 31, 39

Boland, Eavan Aisling
See Boland, Eavan

Bolano, Roberto 1953-2003 .... **CLC 294**
See also CA 229; CANR 175

Bolingbroke, Viscount
See St. John, Henry

Boll, Heinrich
See Boell, Heinrich

Bolt, Lee
See Faust, Frederick

Bolt, Robert (Oxton) 1924-1995 ...... **CLC 14; TCLC 175**
See also CA 17-20R; 147; CANR 35, 67; CBD; DAM DRAM; DFS 2; DLB 13, 233; EWL 3; LAIT 1; MTCW 1

Bombal, Maria Luisa 1910-1980 .... **HLCS 1; SSC 37**
See also CA 127; CANR 72; EWL 3; HW 1; LAW; RGSF 2

Bombet, Louis-Alexandre-Cesar
See Stendhal

Bomkauf
See Kaufman, Bob (Garnell)

Bonaventura .... **NCLC 35, 252**
See also DLB 90

Bonaventure 1217(?)-1274 .... **CMLC 79**
See also DLB 115; LMFS 1

Bond, Edward 1934- .... **CLC 4, 6, 13, 23**
See also AAYA 50; BRWS 1; CA 25-28R; CANR 38, 67, 106; CBD; CD 5, 6; DAM DRAM; DFS 3, 8; DLB 13, 310; EWL 3; MTCW 1

Bonham, Frank 1914-1989 .... **CLC 12**
See also AAYA 1, 70; BYA 1, 3; CA 9-12R; CANR 4, 36; JRDA; MAICYA 1, 2; SAAS 3; SATA 1, 49; SATA-Obit 62; TCWW 1, 2; YAW

Bonnefoy, Yves 1923- . **CLC 9, 15, 58; PC 58**
See also CA 85-88; CANR 33, 75, 97, 136; CWW 2; DAM MST, POET; DLB 258; EWL 3; GFL 1789 to the Present; MTCW 1, 2; MTFW 2005

Bonner, Marita
See Occomy, Marita (Odette) Bonner

Bonnin, Gertrude 1876-1938 .... **NNAL**
See also CA 150; DAM MULT; DLB 175

Bontemps, Arna 1902-1973 ... **BLC 1:1; CLC 1, 18; HR 1:2**
See also BW 1; CA 1-4R; 41-44R; CANR 4, 35; CLR 6; CP 1; CWRI 5; DA3; DAM MULT, NOV, POET; DLB 48, 51; JRDA; MAICYA 1, 2; MAL 5; MTCW 1, 2; PFS 32; SATA 2, 44; SATA-Obit 24; WCH; WP

Bontemps, Arnaud Wendell
See Bontemps, Arna

Boot, William
See Stoppard, Tom

Booth, Irwin
See Hoch, Edward D.

Booth, Martin 1944-2004 .... **CLC 13**
See also CA 93-96, 188; 223; CAAE 188; CAAS 2; CANR 92; CP 1, 2, 3, 4

Booth, Philip 1925-2007 .... **CLC 23**
See also CA 5-8R; 262; CANR 5, 88; CP 1, 2, 3, 4, 5, 6, 7; DLBY 1982

Booth, Philip Edmund
See Booth, Philip

Booth, Wayne C. 1921-2005 .... **CLC 24**
See also CA 1-4R; 244; CAAS 5; CANR 3, 43, 117; DLB 67

Booth, Wayne Clayson
See Booth, Wayne C.

Borchert, Wolfgang 1921-1947 .... **DC 42; TCLC 5**
See also CA 104; 188; DLB 69, 124; EWL 3

Borel, Petrus 1809-1859 .... **NCLC 41**
See also DLB 119; GFL 1789 to the Present

Borges, Jorge Luis 1899-1986 ... **CLC 1, 2, 3, 4, 6, 8, 9, 10, 13, 19, 44, 48, 83; HLC 1; PC 22, 32; SSC 4, 41, 100, 159; TCLC 109; WLC 1**
See also AAYA 26; BPFB 1; CA 21-24R; CANR 19, 33, 75, 105, 133; CDWLB 3; DA; DA3; DAB; DAC; DAM MST, MULT; DLB 113, 283; DLBY 1986; DNFS 1, 2; EWL 3; HW 1, 2; LAW; LMFS 2; MSW; MTCW 1, 2; MTFW 2005; PFS 27; RGHL; RGSF 2; RGWL 2, 3; SFW 4; SSFS 17; TWA; WLIT 1

Borne, Ludwig 1786-1837 .... **NCLC 193**
See also DLB 90

Borowski, Tadeusz 1922-1951 .... **SSC 48; TCLC 9**
See also CA 106; 154; CDWLB 4; DLB 215; EWL 3; RGHL; RGSF 2; RGWL 3; SSFS 13

Borrow, George (Henry)
1803-1881 .... **NCLC 9**
See also BRWS 12; DLB 21, 55, 166

Bosch (Gavino), Juan 1909-2001 ..... **HLCS 1**
See also CA 151; 204; DAM MST, MULT; DLB 145; HW 1, 2

Bosman, Herman Charles
1905-1951 .... **TCLC 49**
See also CA 160; DLB 225; RGSF 2

Bosschere, Jean de 1878(?)-1953 ... **TCLC 19**
See also CA 115; 186

Boswell, James 1740-1795 ...... **LC 4, 50, 182; WLC 1**
See also BRW 3; CDBLB 1660-1789; DA; DAB; DAC; DAM MST; DLB 104, 142; TEA; WLIT 3

Boto, Eza
See Beti, Mongo

Bottomley, Gordon 1874-1948 ..... **TCLC 107**
See also CA 120; 192; DLB 10

Bottoms, David 1949- .... **CLC 53**
See also CA 105; CANR 22; CSW; DLB 120; DLBY 1983

Boucicault, Dion 1820-1890 .... **NCLC 41**
See also DLB 344

Branley, Franklyn M(ansfield)
1915-2002 .... **CLC 21**
See also CA 33-36R; 207; CANR 14, 39;
CLR 13; MAICYA 1, 2; SAAS 16; SATA
4, 68, 136

Brant, Beth (E.) 1941- .... **NNAL**
See also CA 144; FW

Brant, Sebastian 1457-1521 .... **LC 112**
See also DLB 179; RGWL 2, 3

Brathwaite, Edward Kamau
1930- ... **BLC 2:1; BLCS; CLC 11, 305;**
PC 56
See also BRWS 12; BW 2, 3; CA 25-28R;
CANR 11, 26, 47, 107; CDWLB 3; CP 1,
2, 3, 4, 5, 6, 7; DAM POET; DLB 125;
EWL 3

Brathwaite, Kamau
See Brathwaite, Edward Kamau

Brautigan, Richard 1935-1984 .. **CLC 1, 3, 5,**
9, 12, 34, 42; PC 94; TCLC 133
See also BPFB 1; CA 53-56; 113; CANR
34; CN 1, 2, 3; CP 1, 2, 3, 4; DA3; DAM
NOV; DLB 2, 5, 206; DLBY 1980, 1984;
FANT; MAL 5; MTCW 1; RGAL 4;
SATA 56

Brautigan, Richard Gary
See Brautigan, Richard

Brave Bird, Mary
See Crow Dog, Mary

Braverman, Kate 1950- .... **CLC 67**
See also CA 89-92; CANR 141; DLB 335

Brecht, Bertolt 1898-1956 .... **DC 3; TCLC 1,**
6, 13, 35, 169; WLC 1
See also CA 104; 133; CANR 62; CDWLB
2; DA; DA3; DAB; DAC; DAM DRAM,
MST; DFS 4, 5, 9; DLB 56, 124; EW 11;
EWL 3; IDTP; MTCW 1, 2; MTFW 2005;
RGHL; RGWL 2, 3; TWA

Brecht, Eugen Berthold Friedrich
See Brecht, Bertolt

Brecht, Eugen Bertolt Friedrich
See Brecht, Bertolt

Bremer, Fredrika 1801-1865 .... **NCLC 11**
See also DLB 254

Brennan, Christopher John
1870-1932 .... **TCLC 17**
See also CA 117; 188; DLB 230; EWL 3

Brennan, Maeve 1917-1993 ... **CLC 5; TCLC**
124
See also CA 81-84; CANR 72, 100

Brenner, Jozef 1887-1919 .... **TCLC 13**
See also CA 111; 240

Brent, Linda
See Jacobs, Harriet A.

Brentano, Clemens (Maria)
1778-1842 .... **NCLC 1, 191; SSC 115**
See also DLB 90; RGWL 2, 3

Brent of Bin Bin
See Franklin, (Stella Maria Sarah) Miles
(Lampe)

Brenton, Howard 1942- .... **CLC 31**
See also CA 69-72; CANR 33, 67; CBD;
CD 5, 6; DLB 13; MTCW 1

Breslin, James
See Breslin, Jimmy

Breslin, Jimmy 1930- .... **CLC 4, 43**
See also CA 73-76; CANR 31, 75, 139, 187;
DAM NOV; DLB 185; MTCW 2; MTFW
2005

Bresson, Robert 1901(?)-1999 .... **CLC 16**
See also CA 110; 187; CANR 49

Breton, Andre 1896-1966 .. **CLC 2, 9, 15, 54;**
PC 15; TCLC 247
See also CA 19-20; 25-28R; CANR 40, 60;
CAP 2; DLB 65, 258; EW 11; EWL 3;
GFL 1789 to the Present; LMFS 2;
MTCW 1, 2; MTFW 2005; RGWL 2, 3;
TWA; WP

Breton, Nicholas c. 1554-c. 1626 .... **LC 133**
See also DLB 136

Breytenbach, Breyten 1939(?)- .. **CLC 23, 37,**
126
See also CA 113; 129; CANR 61, 122, 202;
CWW 2; DAM POET; DLB 225; EWL 3

Bridgers, Sue Ellen 1942- .... **CLC 26**
See also AAYA 8, 49; BYA 7, 8; CA 65-68;
CANR 11, 36; CLR 18; DLB 52; JRDA;
MAICYA 1, 2; SAAS 1; SATA 22, 90;
SATA-Essay 109; WYA; YAW

Bridges, Robert (Seymour)
1844-1930 .... **PC 28; TCLC 1**
See also BRW 6; CA 104; 152; CDBLB
1890-1914; DAM POET; DLB 19, 98

Bridie, James
See Mavor, Osborne Henry

Brin, David 1950- .... **CLC 34**
See also AAYA 21; CA 102; CANR 24, 70,
125, 127; INT CANR-24; SATA 65;
SCFW 2; SFW 4

Brink, Andre 1935- .... **CLC 18, 36, 106**
See also AFW; BRWS 6; CA 104; CANR
39, 62, 109, 133, 182; CN 4, 5, 6, 7; DLB
225; EWL 3; INT CA-103; LATS 1:2;
MTCW 1, 2; MTFW 2005; WLIT 2

Brink, Andre Philippus
See Brink, Andre

Brinsmead, H. F(ay)
See Brinsmead, H(esba) F(ay)

Brinsmead, H. F.
See Brinsmead, H(esba) F(ay)

Brinsmead, H(esba) F(ay) 1922- ...... **CLC 21**
See also CA 21-24R; CANR 10; CLR 47;
CWRI 5; MAICYA 1, 2; SAAS 5; SATA
18, 78

Brittain, Vera (Mary)
1893(?)-1970 .... **CLC 23; TCLC 228**
See also BRWS 10; CA 13-16; 25-28R;
CANR 58; CAP 1; DLB 191; FW; MTCW
1, 2

Broch, Hermann 1886-1951 ... **TCLC 20, 204**
See also CA 117; 211; CDWLB 2; DLB 85,
124; EW 10; EWL 3; RGWL 2, 3

Brock, Rose
See Hansen, Joseph

Brod, Max 1884-1968 .... **TCLC 115**
See also CA 5-8R; 25-28R; CANR 7; DLB
81; EWL 3

Brodkey, Harold (Roy) 1930-1996 .. **CLC 56;**
TCLC 123
See also CA 111; 151; CANR 71; CN 4, 5,
6; DLB 130

Brodskii, Iosif
See Brodsky, Joseph

Brodskii, Iosif Alexandrovich
See Brodsky, Joseph

Brodsky, Iosif Alexandrovich
See Brodsky, Joseph

Brodsky, Joseph 1940-1996 ..... **CLC 4, 6, 13,**
36, 100; PC 9; TCLC 219
See also AAYA 71; AITN 1; AMWS 8; CA
41-44R; 151; CANR 37, 106; CWW 2;
DA3; DAM POET; DLB 285, 329; EWL
3; MTCW 1, 2; MTFW 2005; PFS 35;
RGWL 2, 3

Brodsky, Michael 1948- .... **CLC 19**
See also CA 102; CANR 18, 41, 58, 147;
DLB 244

Brodsky, Michael Mark
See Brodsky, Michael

Brodzki, Bella .... **CLC 65**

Brome, Richard 1590(?)-1652 .... **LC 61**
See also BRWS 10; DLB 58

Bromell, Henry 1947- .... **CLC 5**
See also CA 53-56; CANR 9, 115, 116

Bromfield, Louis (Brucker)
1896-1956 .... **TCLC 11**
See also CA 107; 155; DLB 4, 9, 86; RGAL
4; RHW

Broner, E. M. 1930-2011 .... **CLC 19**
See also CA 17-20R; CANR 8, 25, 72, 216;
CN 4, 5, 6; DLB 28

Broner, Esther Masserman
See Broner, E. M.

Bronk, William 1918-1999 .... **CLC 10**
See also AMWS 21; CA 89-92; 177; CANR
23; CP 3, 4, 5, 6, 7; DLB 165

Bronstein, Lev Davidovich
See Trotsky, Leon

Bronte, Anne 1820-1849 .... **NCLC 4, 71, 102,**
235
See also BRW 5; BRWR 1; DA3; DLB 21,
199, 340; NFS 26; TEA

Bronte, (Patrick) Branwell
1817-1848 .... **NCLC 109**
See also DLB 340

Bronte, Charlotte 1816-1855 ...... **NCLC 3, 8,**
33, 58, 105, 155, 217, 229; WLC 1
See also AAYA 17; BRW 5; BRWC 2;
BRWR 1; BYA 2; CDBLB 1832-1890;
DA; DA3; DAB; DAC; DAM MST, NOV;
DLB 21, 159, 199, 340; EXPN; FL 1:2;
GL 2; LAIT 2; NFS 4, 36; TEA; WLIT 4

Bronte, Emily 1818-1848 .... **NCLC 16, 35,**
165, 244; PC 8; WLC 1
See also AAYA 17; BPFB 1; BRW 5;
BRWC 1; BRWR 1; BYA 3; CDBLB
1832-1890; DA; DA3; DAB; DAC; DAM
MST, NOV, POET; DLB 21, 32, 199, 340;
EXPN; FL 1:2; GL 2; LAIT 1; NFS 2;
PFS 33; TEA; WLIT 3

Bronte, Emily Jane
See Bronte, Emily

Brontes
See Bronte, Anne; Bronte, (Patrick) Branwell; Bronte, Charlotte; Bronte, Emily

Brooke, Frances 1724-1789 .... **LC 6, 48**
See also DLB 39, 99

Brooke, Henry 1703(?)-1783 .... **LC 1**
See also DLB 39

Brooke, Rupert 1887-1915 . **PC 24; TCLC 2,**
7; WLC 1
See also BRWS 3; CA 104; 132; CANR 61;
CDBLB 1914-1945; DA; DAB; DAC;
DAM MST, POET; DLB 19, 216; EXPP;
GLL 2; MTCW 1, 2; MTFW 2005; PFS
7; TEA

Brooke, Rupert Chawner
See Brooke, Rupert

Brooke-Haven, P.
See Wodehouse, P. G.

Brooke-Rose, Christine 1923(?)- ..... **CLC 40,**
184
See also BRWS 4; CA 13-16R; CANR 58,
118, 183; CN 1, 2, 3, 4, 5, 6, 7; DLB 14,
231; EWL 3; SFW 4

Brookner, Anita 1928- . **CLC 32, 34, 51, 136,**
237
See also BRWS 4; CA 114; 120; CANR 37,
56, 87, 130, 212; CN 4, 5, 6, 7; CPW;
DA3; DAB; DAM POP; DLB 194, 326;
DLBY 1987; EWL 3; MTCW 1, 2; MTFW
2005; NFS 23; TEA

Brooks, Cleanth 1906-1994 . **CLC 24, 86, 110**
See also AMWS 14; CA 17-20R; 145;
CANR 33, 35; CSW; DLB 63; DLBY
1994; EWL 3; INT CANR-35; MAL 5;
MTCW 1, 2; MTFW 2005

Brooks, George
See Baum, L. Frank

Brooks, Gwendolyn 1917-2000 .... **BLC 1:1,**
2:1; CLC 1, 2, 4, 5, 15, 49, 125; PC 7;
WLC 1
See also AAYA 20; AFAW 1, 2; AITN 1;
AMWS 3; BW 2, 3; CA 1-4R; 190; CANR
1, 27, 52, 75, 132; CDALB 1941-1968;

CLR 27; CP 1, 2, 3, 4, 5, 6, 7; CWP; DA;
DA3; DAC; DAM MST, MULT, POET;
DLB 5, 76, 165; EWL 3; EXPP; FL 1:5;
MAL 5; MBL; MTCW 1, 2; MTFW 2005;
PFS 1, 2, 4, 6, 32, 40; RGAL 4; SATA 6;
SATA-Obit 123; SSFS 35; TUS; WP

Brooks, Gwendolyn Elizabeth
See Brooks, Gwendolyn

Brooks, Mel 1926- .... **CLC 12, 217**
See also AAYA 13, 48; CA 65-68; CANR
16; DFS 21; DLB 26

Brooks, Peter 1938- .... **CLC 34**
See also CA 45-48; CANR 1, 107, 182

Brooks, Peter Preston
See Brooks, Peter

Brooks, Van Wyck 1886-1963 .... **CLC 29**
See also AMW; CA 1-4R; CANR 6; DLB
45, 63, 103; MAL 5; TUS

Brophy, Brigid 1929-1995 ...... **CLC 6, 11, 29,
105**
See also CA 5-8R; 149; CAAS 4; CANR
25, 53; CBD; CN 1, 2, 3, 4, 5, 6; CWD;
DA3; DLB 14, 271; EWL 3; MTCW 1, 2

Brophy, Brigid Antonia
See Brophy, Brigid

Brosman, Catharine Savage 1934- ..... **CLC 9**
See also CA 61-64; CANR 21, 46, 149, 222

Brossard, Nicole 1943- .... **CLC 115, 169; PC
80**
See also CA 122; CAAS 16; CANR 140;
CCA 1; CWP; CWW 2; DLB 53; EWL 3;
FW; GLL 2; RGWL 3

Brother Antoninus
See Everson, William

Brothers Grimm
See Grimm, Jacob Ludwig Karl; Grimm,
Wilhelm Karl

The Brothers Quay
See Quay, Stephen; Quay, Timothy

Broughton, T(homas) Alan 1936- ..... **CLC 19**
See also CA 45-48; CANR 2, 23, 48, 111

Broumas, Olga 1949- .... **CLC 10, 73**
See also CA 85-88; CANR 20, 69, 110; CP
5, 6, 7; CWP; GLL 2

Broun, Heywood 1888-1939 .... **TCLC 104**
See also DLB 29, 171

Brown, Alan 1950- .... **CLC 99**
See also CA 156

Brown, Charles Brockden
1771-1810 .... **NCLC 22, 74, 122, 246**
See also AMWS 1; CDALB 1640-1865;
DLB 37, 59, 73; FW; GL 2; HGG; LMFS
1; RGAL 4; TUS

Brown, Christy 1932-1981 .... **CLC 63**
See also BYA 13; CA 105; 104; CANR 72;
DLB 14

Brown, Claude 1937-2002 ..... **BLC 1:1; CLC
30**
See also AAYA 7; BW 1, 3; CA 73-76; 205;
CANR 81; DAM MULT

Brown, Dan 1964- .... **CLC 209**
See also AAYA 55; CA 217; CANR 223;
LNFS 1; MTFW 2005

Brown, Dee 1908-2002 .... **CLC 18, 47**
See also AAYA 30; CA 13-16R; 212; CAAS
6; CANR 11, 45, 60, 150; CPW; CSW;
DA3; DAM POP; DLBY 1980; LAIT 2;
MTCW 1, 2; MTFW 2005; NCFS 5;
SATA 5, 110; SATA-Obit 141; TCWW 1,
2

Brown, Dee Alexander
See Brown, Dee

Brown, George
See Wertmueller, Lina

Brown, George Douglas
1869-1902 .... **TCLC 28**
See also CA 162; RGEL 2

Brown, George Mackay 1921-1996 ... **CLC 5,
48, 100**
See also BRWS 6; CA 21-24R; 151; CAAS
6; CANR 37, 67; CN 1, 2, 3, 4, 5, 6;
CP 1, 2, 3, 4, 5, 6; DLB 14, 27, 139, 271;
MTCW 1; RGSF 2; SATA 35

Brown, James Wllie
See Komunyakaa, Yusef

Brown, James Wllie, Jr.
See Komunyakaa, Yusef

Brown, Larry 1951-2004 .... **CLC 73, 289**
See also AMWS 21; CA 130; 134; 233;
CANR 117, 145; CSW; DLB 234; INT
CA-134

Brown, Moses
See Barrett, William (Christopher)

Brown, Rita Mae 1944- .... **CLC 18, 43, 79,
259**
See also BPFB 1; CA 45-48; CANR 2, 11,
35, 62, 95, 138, 183; CN 5, 6, 7; CPW;
CSW; DA3; DAM NOV, POP; FW; INT
CANR-11; MAL 5; MTCW 1, 2; MTFW
2005; NFS 9; RGAL 4; TUS

Brown, Roderick (Langmere) Haig-
See Haig-Brown, Roderick (Langmere)

Brown, Rosellen 1939- .... **CLC 32, 170**
See also CA 77-80; CAAS 10; CANR 14,
44, 98; CN 6, 7; PFS 41

Brown, Sterling Allen 1901-1989 ...... **BLC 1;
CLC 1, 23, 59; HR 1:2; PC 55**
See also AFAW 1, 2; BW 1, 3; CA 85-88;
127; CANR 26; CP 3, 4; DA3; DAM
MULT, POET; DLB 48, 51, 63; MAL 5;
MTCW 1, 2; MTFW 2005; RGAL 4; WP

Brown, Will
See Ainsworth, William Harrison

Brown, William Hill 1765-1793 .... **LC 93**
See also DLB 37

Brown, William Larry
See Brown, Larry

Brown, William Wells
1814(?)-1884 .... **BLC 1:1; DC 1; NCLC
2, 89, 247**
See also DAM MULT; DLB 3, 50, 183,
248; RGAL 4

Browne, Clyde Jackson
See Browne, Jackson

Browne, Jackson 1948(?)- .... **CLC 21**
See also CA 120

Browne, Sir Thomas 1605-1682 .... **LC 111**
See also BRW 2; DLB 151

Browne of Tavistock, William
1590-1645 .... **LC 192**
See also DLB 121

Browning, Robert 1812-1889 . **NCLC 19, 79;
PC 2, 61, 97; WLCS**
See also BRW 4; BRWC 2; BRWR 3; CD-
BLB 1832-1890; CLR 97; DA; DA3;
DAB; DAC; DAM MST, POET; DLB 32,
163; EXPP; LATS 1:1; PAB; PFS 1, 15,
41; RGEL 2; TEA; WLIT 4; WP; YABC
1

Browning, Tod 1882-1962 .... **CLC 16**
See also CA 141; 117

Brownmiller, Susan 1935- .... **CLC 159**
See also CA 103; CANR 35, 75, 137; DAM
NOV; FW; MTCW 1, 2; MTFW 2005

Brownson, Orestes Augustus
1803-1876 .... **NCLC 50**
See also DLB 1, 59, 73, 243

Bruccoli, Matthew J. 1931-2008 .... **CLC 34**
See also CA 9-12R; 274; CANR 7, 87; DLB
103

Bruccoli, Matthew Joseph
See Bruccoli, Matthew J.

Bruce, Lenny
See Schneider, Leonard Alfred

Bruchac, Joseph 1942- .... **NNAL**
See also AAYA 19; CA 33-36R, 256; CAAE
256; CANR 13, 47, 75, 94, 137, 161, 204;
CLR 46; CWRI 5; DAM MULT; DLB
342; JRDA; MAICYA 2; MAICYAS 1;
MTCW 2; MTFW 2005; PFS 36; SATA
42, 89, 131, 176, 228; SATA-Essay 176

Bruin, John
See Brutus, Dennis

Brulard, Henri
See Stendhal

Brulls, Christian
See Simenon, Georges

Brunetto Latini c. 1220-1294 .... **CMLC 73**

Brunner, John (Kilian Houston)
1934-1995 .... **CLC 8, 10**
See also CA 1-4R; 149; CAAS 8; CANR 2,
37; CPW; DAM POP; DLB 261; MTCW
1, 2; SCFW 1, 2; SFW 4

Bruno, Giordano 1548-1600 .... **LC 27, 167**
See also RGWL 2, 3

Brutus, Dennis 1924-2009 ..... **BLC 1:1; CLC
43; PC 24**
See also AFW; BW 2, 3; CA 49-52; CAAS
14; CANR 2, 27, 42, 81; CDWLB 3; CP
1, 2, 3, 4, 5, 6, 7; DAM MULT, POET;
DLB 117, 225; EWL 3

Bryan, C.D.B. 1936-2009 .... **CLC 29**
See also CA 73-76; CANR 13, 68; DLB
185; INT CANR-13

Bryan, Courtlandt Dixon Barnes
See Bryan, C.D.B.

Bryan, Michael
See Moore, Brian

Bryan, William Jennings
1860-1925 .... **TCLC 99**
See also DLB 303

Bryant, William Cullen 1794-1878 . **NCLC 6,
46; PC 20**
See also AMWS 1; CDALB 1640-1865;
DA; DAB; DAC; DAM MST, POET;
DLB 3, 43, 59, 189, 250; EXPP; PAB;
PFS 30; RGAL 4; TUS

Bryusov, Valery Yakovlevich
1873-1924 .... **TCLC 10**
See also CA 107; 155; EWL 3; SFW 4

Buchan, John 1875-1940 .... **TCLC 41**
See also CA 108; 145; CMW 4; DAB;
DAM POP; DLB 34, 70, 156; HGG;
MSW; MTCW 2; RGEL 2; RHW; YABC
2

Buchanan, George 1506-1582 .... **LC 4, 179**
See also DLB 132

Buchanan, Robert 1841-1901 .... **TCLC 107**
See also CA 179; DLB 18, 35

Buchheim, Lothar-Guenther
1918-2007 .... **CLC 6**
See also CA 85-88; 257

Buchner, (Karl) Georg 1813-1837 ..... **DC 35;
NCLC 26, 146; SSC 131**
See also CDWLB 2; DLB 133; EW 6;
RGSF 2; RGWL 2, 3; TWA

Buchwald, Art 1925-2007 .... **CLC 33**
See also AITN 1; CA 5-8R; 256; CANR 21,
67, 107; MTCW 1, 2; SATA 10

Buchwald, Arthur
See Buchwald, Art

Buck, Pearl S. 1892-1973 .... **CLC 7, 11, 18,
127**
See also AAYA 42; AITN 1; AMWS 2;
BPFB 1; CA 1-4R; 41-44R; CANR 1, 34;
CDALBS; CN 1; DA; DA3; DAB; DAC;
DAM MST, NOV; DLB 9, 102, 329; EWL
3; LAIT 3; MAL 5; MTCW 1, 2; MTFW
2005; NFS 25; RGAL 4; RHW; SATA 1,
25; SSFS 33; TUS

Buck, Pearl Sydenstricker
See Buck, Pearl S.

Butler, Robert Olen 1945- .... **CLC 81, 162; SSC 117**
See also AMWS 12; BPFB 1; CA 112; CANR 66, 138, 194; CN 7; CSW; DAM POP; DLB 173, 335; INT CA-112; MAL 5; MTCW 2; MTFW 2005; SSFS 11, 22

Butler, Samuel 1612-1680 .... **LC 16, 43, 173; PC 94**
See also DLB 101, 126; RGEL 2

Butler, Samuel 1835-1902 .... **TCLC 1, 33; WLC 1**
See also BRWS 2; CA 143; CDBLB 1890-1914; DA; DA3; DAB; DAC; DAM MST, NOV; DLB 18, 57, 174; RGEL 2; SFW 4; TEA

Butler, Walter C.
See Faust, Frederick

Butor, Michel (Marie Francois) 1926- .... **CLC 1, 3, 8, 11, 15, 161**
See also CA 9-12R; CANR 33, 66; CWW 2; DLB 83; EW 13; EWL 3; GFL 1789 to the Present; MTCW 1, 2; MTFW 2005

Butts, Mary 1890(?)-1937 ... **SSC 124; TCLC 77**
See also CA 148; DLB 240

Buxton, Ralph
See Silverstein, Alvin; Silverstein, Virginia B.

Buzo, Alex
See Buzo, Alex

Buzo, Alex 1944- .... **CLC 61**
See also CA 97-100; CANR 17, 39, 69; CD 5, 6; DLB 289

Buzo, Alexander John
See Buzo, Alex

Buzzati, Dino 1906-1972 .... **CLC 36**
See also CA 160; 33-36R; DLB 177; RGWL 2, 3; SFW 4

Byars, Betsy 1928- .... **CLC 35**
See also AAYA 19; BYA 3; CA 33-36R, 183; CAAE 183; CANR 18, 36, 57, 102, 148; CLR 1, 16, 72; DLB 52; INT CANR-18; JRDA; MAICYA 1, 2; MAICYAS 1; MTCW 1; SAAS 1; SATA 4, 46, 80, 163, 223; SATA-Essay 108; WYA; YAW

Byars, Betsy Cromer
See Byars, Betsy

Byatt, A. S. 1936- .... **CLC 19, 65, 136, 223, 312; SSC 91**
See also BPFB 1; BRWC 2; BRWS 4; CA 13-16R; CANR 13, 33, 50, 75, 96, 133, 205; CN 1, 2, 3, 4, 5, 6; DA3; DAM NOV, POP; DLB 14, 194, 319, 326; EWL 3; MTCW 1, 2; MTFW 2005; RGSF 2; RHW; SSFS 26; TEA

Byatt, Antonia Susan Drabble
See Byatt, A. S.

Byrd, William II 1674-1744 .... **LC 112**
See also DLB 24, 140; RGAL 4

Byrne, David 1952- .... **CLC 26**
See also CA 127; CANR 215

Byrne, John Joseph
See Leonard, Hugh

Byrne, John Keyes
See Leonard, Hugh

Byron, George Gordon
See Lord Byron

Byron, George Gordon Noel
See Lord Byron

Byron, Robert 1905-1941 .... **TCLC 67**
See also CA 160; DLB 195

C. 3. 3.
See Wilde, Oscar

Caballero, Fernan 1796-1877 .... **NCLC 10**

Cabell, Branch
See Cabell, James Branch

Cabell, James Branch 1879-1958 .... **TCLC 6**
See also CA 105; 152; DLB 9, 78; FANT; MAL 5; MTCW 2; RGAL 4; SUFW 1

Cabeza de Vaca, Alvar Nunez 1490-1557(?) .... **LC 61**

Cable, George Washington 1844-1925 .... **SSC 4, 155; TCLC 4**
See also CA 104; 155; DLB 12, 74; DLBD 13; RGAL 4; TUS

Cabral de Melo Neto, Joao 1920-1999 .... **CLC 76**
See also CA 151; CWW 2; DAM MULT; DLB 307; EWL 3; LAW; LAWS 1

Cabrera, Lydia 1900-1991 .... **TCLC 223**
See also CA 178; DLB 145; EWL 3; HW 1; LAWS 1

Cabrera Infante, G. 1929-2005 ... **CLC 5, 25, 45, 120, 291; HLC 1; SSC 39**
See also CA 85-88; 236; CANR 29, 65, 110; CDWLB 3; CWW 2; DA3; DAM MULT; DLB 113; EWL 3; HW 1, 2; LAW; LAWS 1; MTCW 1, 2; MTFW 2005; RGSF 2; WLIT 1

Cabrera Infante, Guillermo
See Cabrera Infante, G.

Cade, Toni
See Bambara, Toni Cade

Cadmus and Harmonia
See Buchan, John

Caedmon fl. 658-680 .... **CMLC 7, 133**
See also DLB 146

Caeiro, Alberto
See Pessoa, Fernando

Caesar, Julius
See Julius Caesar

Cage, John (Milton), (Jr.) 1912-1992 .... **CLC 41; PC 58**
See also CA 13-16R; 169; CANR 9, 78; DLB 193; INT CANR-9; TCLE 1:1

Cahan, Abraham 1860-1951 .... **TCLC 71**
See also CA 108; 154; DLB 9, 25, 28; MAL 5; RGAL 4

Cain, Christopher
See Fleming, Thomas

Cain, G.
See Cabrera Infante, G.

Cain, Guillermo
See Cabrera Infante, G.

Cain, James M(allahan) 1892-1977 .. **CLC 3, 11, 28**
See also AITN 1; BPFB 1; CA 17-20R; 73-76; CANR 8, 34, 61; CMW 4; CN 1, 2; DLB 226; EWL 3; MAL 5; MSW; MTCW 1; RGAL 4

Caine, Hall 1853-1931 .... **TCLC 97**
See also RHW

Caine, Mark
See Raphael, Frederic

Calasso, Roberto 1941- .... **CLC 81**
See also CA 143; CANR 89, 223

Calderon de la Barca, Pedro 1600-1681 . **DC 3; HLCS 1; LC 23, 136**
See also DFS 23; EW 2; RGWL 2, 3; TWA

Caldwell, Erskine 1903-1987 ... **CLC 1, 8, 14, 50, 60; SSC 19, 147; TCLC 117**
See also AITN 1; AMW; BPFB 1; CA 1-4R; 121; CAAS 1; CANR 2, 33; CN 1, 2, 3, 4; DA3; DAM NOV; DLB 9, 86; EWL 3; MAL 5; MTCW 1, 2; MTFW 2005; RGAL 4; RGSF 2; TUS

Caldwell, Gail 1951- .... **CLC 309**
See also CA 313

Caldwell, (Janet Miriam) Taylor (Holland) 1900-1985 .... **CLC 2, 28, 39**
See also BPFB 1; CA 5-8R; 116; CANR 5; DA3; DAM NOV, POP; DLBD 17; MTCW 2; RHW

Calhoun, John Caldwell 1782-1850 .... **NCLC 15**
See also DLB 3, 248

Calisher, Hortense 1911-2009 .... **CLC 2, 4, 8, 38, 134; SSC 15**
See also CA 1-4R; 282; CANR 1, 22, 117; CN 1, 2, 3, 4, 5, 6, 7; DA3; DAM NOV; DLB 2, 218; INT CANR-22; MAL 5; MTCW 1, 2; MTFW 2005; RGAL 4; RGSF 2

Callaghan, Morley 1903-1990 ..... **CLC 3, 14, 41, 65; TCLC 145**
See also CA 9-12R; 132; CANR 33, 73; CN 1, 2, 3, 4; DAC; DAM MST; DLB 68; EWL 3; MTCW 1, 2; MTFW 2005; RGEL 2; RGSF 2; SSFS 19

Callaghan, Morley Edward
See Callaghan, Morley

Callimachus c. 305B.C.-c. 240B.C. .... **CMLC 18**
See also AW 1; DLB 176; RGWL 2, 3

Calvin, Jean
See Calvin, John

Calvin, John 1509-1564 .... **LC 37**
See also DLB 327; GFL Beginnings to 1789

Calvino, Italo 1923-1985 .... **CLC 5, 8, 11, 22, 33, 39, 73; SSC 3, 48; TCLC 183**
See also AAYA 58; CA 85-88; 116; CANR 23, 61, 132; DAM NOV; DLB 196; EW 13; EWL 3; MTCW 1, 2; MTFW 2005; RGHL; RGSF 2; RGWL 2, 3; SFW 4; SSFS 12, 31; WLIT 7

Camara Laye
See Laye, Camara

Cambridge, A Gentleman of the University of
See Crowley, Edward Alexander

Camden, William 1551-1623 .... **LC 77**
See also DLB 172

Cameron, Carey 1952- .... **CLC 59**
See also CA 135

Cameron, Peter 1959- .... **CLC 44**
See also AMWS 12; CA 125; CANR 50, 117, 188; DLB 234; GLL 2

Camoens, Luis Vaz de 1524(?)-1580
See Camoes, Luis de

Camoes, Luis de 1524(?)-1580 . **HLCS 1; LC 62, 191; PC 31**
See also DLB 287; EW 2; RGWL 2, 3

Camp, Madeleine L'Engle
See L'Engle, Madeleine

Campana, Dino 1885-1932 .... **TCLC 20**
See also CA 117; 246; DLB 114; EWL 3

Campanella, Tommaso 1568-1639 .... **LC 32**
See also RGWL 2, 3

Campbell, Bebe Moore 1950-2006 . **BLC 2:1; CLC 246**
See also AAYA 26; BW 2, 3; CA 139; 254; CANR 81, 134; DLB 227; MTCW 2; MTFW 2005

Campbell, John Ramsey
See Campbell, Ramsey

Campbell, John W. 1910-1971 .... **CLC 32**
See also CA 21-22; 29-32R; CANR 34; CAP 2; DLB 8; MTCW 1; SCFW 1, 2; SFW 4

Campbell, John Wood, Jr.
See Campbell, John W.

Campbell, Joseph 1904-1987 .... **CLC 69; TCLC 140**
See also AAYA 3, 66; BEST 89:2; CA 1-4R; 124; CANR 3, 28, 61, 107; DA3; MTCW 1, 2

Campbell, Maria 1940- .... **CLC 85; NNAL**
See also CA 102; CANR 54; CCA 1; DAC

Campbell, Ramsey 1946- ... **CLC 42; SSC 19**
See also AAYA 51; CA 57-60; 228; CAAE 228; CANR 7, 102, 171; DLB 261; HGG; INT CANR-7; SUFW 1, 2

Campbell, (Ignatius) Roy (Dunnachie)
1901-1957 .... **TCLC 5**
See also AFW; CA 104; 155; DLB 20, 225;
EWL 3; MTCW 2; RGEL 2

Campbell, Thomas 1777-1844 .... **NCLC 19**
See also DLB 93, 144; RGEL 2

Campbell, Wilfred
See Campbell, William

Campbell, William 1858(?)-1918 ..... **TCLC 9**
See also CA 106; DLB 92

Campbell, William Edward March
See March, William

Campion, Jane 1954- .... **CLC 95, 229**
See also AAYA 33; CA 138; CANR 87

Campion, Thomas 1567-1620 . **LC 78; PC 87**
See also BRWS 16; CDBLB Before 1660;
DAM POET; DLB 58, 172; RGEL 2

Camus, Albert 1913-1960 ...... **CLC 1, 2, 4, 9,**
11, 14, 32, 63, 69, 124; DC 2; SSC 9,
76, 129, 146; WLC 1
See also AAYA 36; AFW; BPFB 1; CA 89-
92; CANR 131; DA; DA3; DAB; DAC;
DAM DRAM, MST, NOV; DLB 72, 321,
329; EW 13; EWL 3; EXPN; EXPS; GFL
1789 to the Present; LATS 1:2; LMFS 2;
MTCW 1, 2; MTFW 2005; NFS 6, 16;
RGHL; RGSF 2; RGWL 2, 3; SSFS 4;
TWA

Canby, Vincent 1924-2000 .... **CLC 13**
See also CA 81-84; 191

Cancale
See Desnos, Robert

Canetti, Elias 1905-1994 .. **CLC 3, 14, 25, 75,**
86; TCLC 157
See also CA 21-24R; 146; CANR 23, 61,
79; CDWLB 2; CWW 2; DA3; DLB 85,
124, 329; EW 12; EWL 3; MTCW 1, 2;
MTFW 2005; RGWL 2, 3; TWA

Canfield, Dorothea F.
See Fisher, Dorothy (Frances) Canfield

Canfield, Dorothea Frances
See Fisher, Dorothy (Frances) Canfield

Canfield, Dorothy
See Fisher, Dorothy (Frances) Canfield

Canin, Ethan 1960- .... **CLC 55; SSC 70**
See also CA 131; 135; CANR 193; DLB
335, 350; MAL 5

Cankar, Ivan 1876-1918 .... **TCLC 105**
See also CDWLB 4; DLB 147; EWL 3

Cannon, Curt
See Hunter, Evan

Cao, Lan 1961- .... **CLC 109**
See also CA 165

Cape, Judith
See Page, P.K.

Capek, Karel 1890-1938 .... **DC 1; SSC 36;**
TCLC 6, 37, 192; WLC 1
See also CA 104; 140; CDWLB 4; DA;
DA3; DAB; DAC; DAM DRAM, MST,
NOV; DFS 7, 11; DLB 215; EW 10; EWL
3; MTCW 2; MTFW 2005; RGSF 2;
RGWL 2, 3; SCFW 1, 2; SFW 4

Capella, Martianus fl. 4th cent. - .. **CMLC 84**

Capote, Truman 1924-1984 . **CLC 1, 3, 8, 13,**
19, 34, 38, 58; SSC 2, 47, 93; TCLC
164; WLC 1
See also AAYA 61; AMWS 3; BPFB 1; CA
5-8R; 113; CANR 18, 62, 201; CDALB
1941-1968; CN 1, 2, 3; CPW; DA; DA3;
DAB; DAC; DAM MST, NOV, POP;
DLB 2, 185, 227; DLBY 1980, 1984;
EWL 3; EXPS; GLL 1; LAIT 3; MAL 5;
MTCW 1, 2; MTFW 2005; NCFS 2;
RGAL 4; RGSF 2; SATA 91; SSFS 2;
TUS

Capra, Frank 1897-1991 .... **CLC 16**
See also AAYA 52; CA 61-64; 135

Caputo, Philip 1941- .... **CLC 32**
See also AAYA 60; CA 73-76; CANR 40,
135; YAW

Caragiale, Ion Luca 1852-1912 ...... **TCLC 76**
See also CA 157

Card, Orson Scott 1951- ...... **CLC 44, 47, 50,**
279
See also AAYA 11, 42; BPFB 1; BYA 5, 8;
CA 102; CANR 27, 47, 73, 102, 106, 133,
184; CLR 116; CPW; DA3; DAM POP;
FANT; INT CANR-27; MTCW 1, 2;
MTFW 2005; NFS 5; SATA 83, 127;
SCFW 2; SFW 4; SUFW 2; YAW

Cardenal, Ernesto 1925- .... **CLC 31, 161;**
HLC 1; PC 22
See also CA 49-52; CANR 2, 32, 66, 138,
217; CWW 2; DAM MULT, POET; DLB
290; EWL 3; HW 1, 2; LAWS 1; MTCW
1, 2; MTFW 2005; RGWL 2, 3

Cardinal, Marie 1929-2001 .... **CLC 189**
See also CA 177; CWW 2; DLB 83; FW

Cardozo, Benjamin N(athan)
1870-1938 .... **TCLC 65**
See also CA 117; 164

Carducci, Giosue (Alessandro Giuseppe)
1835-1907 .... **PC 46; TCLC 32**
See also CA 163; DLB 329; EW 7; RGWL
2, 3

Carew, Thomas 1595(?)-1640 ..... **LC 13, 159;**
PC 29
See also BRW 2; DLB 126; PAB; RGEL 2

Carey, Ernestine Gilbreth
1908-2006 .... **CLC 17**
See also CA 5-8R; 254; CANR 71; SATA
2; SATA-Obit 177

Carey, Peter 1943- .... **CLC 40, 55, 96, 183,**
294; SSC 133
See also BRWS 12, CA 123, 127, CANR
53, 76, 117, 157, 185, 213; CN 4, 5, 6, 7;
DLB 289, 326; EWL 3; INT CA-127;
LNFS 1; MTCW 1, 2; MTFW 2005;
RGSF 2; SATA 94

Carey, Peter Philip
See Carey, Peter

Carleton, William 1794-1869 ... **NCLC 3, 199**
See also DLB 159; RGEL 2; RGSF 2

Carlisle, Henry 1926-2011 .... **CLC 33**
See also CA 13-16R; CANR 15, 85

Carlisle, Henry Coffin
See Carlisle, Henry

Carlsen, Chris
See Holdstock, Robert

Carlson, Ron 1947- .... **CLC 54**
See also CA 105, 189; CAAE 189; CANR
27, 155, 197; DLB 244

Carlson, Ronald F.
See Carlson, Ron

Carlyle, Jane Welsh 1801-1866 ... **NCLC 181**
See also DLB 55

Carlyle, Thomas 1795-1881 .... **NCLC 22, 70,**
248
See also BRW 4; CDBLB 1789-1832; DA;
DAB; DAC; DAM MST; DLB 55, 144,
254, 338; RGEL 2; TEA

Carman, (William) Bliss 1861-1929 ... **PC 34;**
TCLC 7
See also CA 104; 152; DAC; DLB 92;
RGEL 2

Carnegie, Dale 1888-1955 .... **TCLC 53**
See also CA 218

Caro Mallén de Soto, Ana c. 1590-c.
1650 .... **LC 175**

Carossa, Hans 1878-1956 .... **TCLC 48**
See also CA 170; DLB 66; EWL 3

Carpenter, Don(ald Richard)
1931-1995 .... **CLC 41**
See also CA 45-48; 149; CANR 1, 71

Carpenter, Edward 1844-1929 .... **TCLC 88**
See also BRWS 13; CA 163; GLL 1

Carpenter, John 1948- .... **CLC 161**
See also AAYA 2, 73; CA 134; SATA 58

Carpenter, John Howard
See Carpenter, John

Carpenter, Johnny
See Carpenter, John

Carpentier, Alejo 1904-1980 .. **CLC 8, 11, 38,**
110; HLC 1; SSC 35; TCLC 201
See also CA 65-68; 97-100; CANR 11, 70;
CDWLB 3; DAM MULT; DLB 113; EWL
3; HW 1, 2; LAW; LMFS 2; RGSF 2;
RGWL 2, 3; WLIT 1

Carpentier y Valmont, Alejo
See Carpentier, Alejo

Carr, Caleb 1955- .... **CLC 86**
See also CA 147; CANR 73, 134; DA3;
DLB 350

Carr, Emily 1871-1945 .... **TCLC 32, 260**
See also CA 159; DLB 68; FW; GLL 2

Carr, H. D.
See Crowley, Edward Alexander

Carr, John Dickson 1906-1977 .... **CLC 3**
See also CA 49-52; 69-72; CANR 3, 33,
60; CMW 4; DLB 306; MSW; MTCW 1,
2

Carr, Philippa
See Hibbert, Eleanor Alice Burford

Carr, Virginia Spencer 1929- .... **CLC 34**
See also CA 61-64; CANR 175; DLB 111

Carrere, Emmanuel 1957- .... **CLC 89**
See also CA 200

Carrier, Roch 1937- .... **CLC 13, 78**
See also CA 130; CANR 61, 152; CCA 1;
DAC; DAM MST; DLB 53; SATA 105,
166

Carroll, James Dennis
See Carroll, Jim

Carroll, James P. 1943(?)- .... **CLC 38**
See also CA 81-84; CANR 73, 139, 209;
MTCW 2; MTFW 2005

Carroll, Jim 1949-2009 .... **CLC 35, 143**
See also AAYA 17; CA 45-48; 290; CANR
42, 115; NCFS 5

Carroll, Lewis 1832-1898 . **NCLC 2, 53, 139;**
PC 18, 74; WLC 1
See also AAYA 39; BRW 5; BYA 5, 13; CD-
BLB 1832-1890; CLR 18, 108; DA; DA3;
DAB; DAC; DAM MST, NOV, POET;
DLB 18, 163, 178; DLBY 1998; EXPN;
EXPP; FANT; JRDA; LAIT 1; MAICYA
1, 2; NFS 27; PFS 11, 30; RGEL 2; SATA
100; SUFW 1; TEA; WCH; YABC 2

Carroll, Paul Vincent 1900-1968 ...... **CLC 10**
See also CA 9-12R; 25-28R; DLB 10; EWL
3; RGEL 2

Carruth, Hayden 1921-2008 .... **CLC 4, 7, 10,**
18, 84, 287; PC 10
See also AMWS 16; CA 9-12R; 277; CANR
4, 38, 59, 110, 174; CP 1, 2, 3, 4, 5, 6, 7;
DLB 5, 165; INT CANR-4; MTCW 1, 2;
MTFW 2005; PFS 26; SATA 47; SATA-
Obit 197

Carson, Anne 1950- .... **CLC 185; PC 64**
See also AMWS 12; CA 203; CANR 209;
CP 7; DLB 193; PFS 18; TCLE 1:1

Carson, Ciaran 1948- .... **CLC 201**
See also BRWS 13; CA 112; 153; CANR
113, 189; CP 6, 7; PFS 26

Carson, Rachel 1907-1964 .... **CLC 71**
See also AAYA 49; AMWS 9; ANW; CA
77-80; CANR 35; DA3; DAM POP; DLB
275; FW; LAIT 4; MAL 5; MTCW 1, 2;
MTFW 2005; NCFS 1; SATA 23

Carson, Rachel Louise
See Carson, Rachel

Cartagena, Teresa de 1425(?)- .... **LC 155**
See also DLB 286

Cernuda y Bidon, Luis
See Cernuda, Luis
Cervantes, Lorna Dee 1954- ..... **HLCS 1; PC 35**
See also CA 131; CANR 80; CP 7; CWP; DLB 82; EXPP; HW 1; LLW; PFS 30
Cervantes, Miguel de 1547-1616 . **HLCS; LC 6, 23, 93; SSC 12, 108; WLC 1**
See also AAYA 56; BYA 1, 14; DA; DAB; DAC; DAM MST, NOV; EW 2; LAIT 1; LATS 1:1; LMFS 1; NFS 8; RGSF 2; RGWL 2, 3; TWA
Cervantes Saavedra, Miguel de
See Cervantes, Miguel de
Cesaire, Aime
See Cesaire, Aime
Cesaire, Aime 1913-2008 .... **BLC 1:1; CLC 19, 32, 112, 280; DC 22; PC 25**
See also BW 2, 3; CA 65-68; 271; CANR 24, 43, 81; CWW 2; DA3; DAM MULT, POET; DLB 321; EWL 3; GFL 1789 to the Present; MTCW 1, 2; MTFW 2005; WP
Cesaire, Aime Fernand
See Cesaire, Aime
Cesaire, Aime Fernand
See Cesaire, Aime
Chaadaev, Petr Iakovlevich 1794-1856 .... **NCLC 197**
See also DLB 198
Chabon, Michael 1963- ... **CLC 55, 149, 265; SSC 59**
See also AAYA 45; AMWS 11; CA 139; CANR 57, 96, 127, 138, 196; DLB 278; MAL 5; MTFW 2005; NFS 25; SATA 145
Chabrol, Claude 1930-2010 .... **CLC 16**
See also CA 110
Chairil Anwar
See Anwar, Chairil
Challans, Mary
See Renault, Mary
Challis, George
See Faust, Frederick
Chambers, Aidan 1934- .... **CLC 35**
See also AAYA 27, 86; CA 25-28R; CANR 12, 31, 58, 116; CLR 151; JRDA; MAI-CYA 1, 2; SAAS 12; SATA 1, 69, 108, 171; WYA; YAW
Chambers, James .... **CLC 21**
See also CA 124; 199
Chambers, Jessie
See Lawrence, D. H.
Chambers, Robert W(illiam) 1865-1933 .... **SSC 92; TCLC 41**
See also CA 165; DLB 202; HGG; SATA 107; SUFW 1
Chambers, (David) Whittaker 1901-1961 .... **TCLC 129**
See also CA 89-92; DLB 303
Chamisso, Adelbert von 1781-1838 .... **NCLC 82; SSC 140**
See also DLB 90; RGWL 2, 3; SUFW 1
Chamoiseau, Patrick 1953- ..... **CLC 268, 276**
See also CA 162; CANR 88; EWL 3; RGWL 3
Chance, James T.
See Carpenter, John
Chance, John T.
See Carpenter, John
Chand, Munshi Prem
See Srivastava, Dhanpat Rai
Chand, Prem
See Srivastava, Dhanpat Rai
Chandler, Raymond 1888-1959 .... **SSC 23; TCLC 1, 7, 179**
See also AAYA 25; AMWC 2; AMWS 4; BPFB 1; CA 104; 129; CANR 60, 107; CDALB 1929-1941; CMW 4; DA3; DLB 226, 253; DLBD 6; EWL 3; MAL 5; MSW; MTCW 1, 2; MTFW 2005; NFS 17; RGAL 4; TUS

Chandler, Raymond Thornton
See Chandler, Raymond
Chandra, Vikram 1961- .... **CLC 302**
See also CA 149; CANR 97, 214; SSFS 16
Chang, Diana 1934-2009 .... **AAL**
See also CA 228; CWP; DLB 312; EXPP; PFS 37
Chang, Eileen 1920-1995 .... **AAL; SSC 28; TCLC 184**
See also CA 166; CANR 168; CWW 2; DLB 328; EWL 3; RGSF 2
Chang, Jung 1952- .... **CLC 71**
See also CA 142
Chang Ai-Ling
See Chang, Eileen
Channing, William Ellery 1780-1842 .... **NCLC 17**
See also DLB 1, 59, 235; RGAL 4
Chao, Patricia 1955- .... **CLC 119**
See also CA 163; CANR 155
Chaplin, Charles Spencer 1889-1977 .... **CLC 16**
See also AAYA 61; CA 81-84; 73-76; DLB 44
Chaplin, Charlie
See Chaplin, Charles Spencer
Chapman, George 1559(?)-1634 . **DC 19; LC 22, 116; PC 96**
See also BRW 1; DAM DRAM; DLB 62, 121; LMFS 1; RGEL 2
Chapman, Graham 1941-1989 .... **CLC 21**
See also AAYA 7; CA 116; 129; CANR 35, 95
Chapman, John Jay 1862-1933 .... **TCLC 7**
See also AMWS 14; CA 104; 191
Chapman, Lee
See Bradley, Marion Zimmer
Chapman, Maile .... **CLC 318**
Chapman, Walker
See Silverberg, Robert
Chappell, Fred 1936- . **CLC 40, 78, 162, 293; PC 105**
See also CA 5-8R, 198; CAAE 198; CAAS 4; CANR 8, 33, 67, 110, 215; CN 6; CP 6, 7; CSW; DLB 6, 105; HGG
Chappell, Fred Davis
See Chappell, Fred
Char, Rene 1907-1988 ..... **CLC 9, 11, 14, 55; PC 56**
See also CA 13-16R; 124; CANR 32; DAM POET; DLB 258; EWL 3; GFL 1789 to the Present; MTCW 1, 2; RGWL 2, 3
Char, Rene-Emile
See Char, Rene
Charby, Jay
See Ellison, Harlan
Chardin, Pierre Teilhard de
See Teilhard de Chardin, (Marie Joseph) Pierre
Chariton fl. 1st cent. (?)- .... **CMLC 49**
Charlemagne 742-814 .... **CMLC 37**
Charles I 1600-1649 .... **LC 13, 194**
Charriere, Isabelle de 1740-1805 .. **NCLC 66**
See also DLB 313
Charron, Pierre 1541-1603 .... **LC 174**
See also GFL Beginnings to 1789
Chartier, Alain c. 1392-1430 .... **LC 94**
See also DLB 208
Chartier, Emile-Auguste
See Alain
Charyn, Jerome 1937- .... **CLC 5, 8, 18**
See also CA 5-8R; CAAS 1; CANR 7, 61, 101, 158, 199; CMW 4; CN 1, 2, 3, 4, 5, 6, 7; DLBY 1983; MTCW 1
Chase, Adam
See Marlowe, Stephen

Chase, Mary (Coyle) 1907-1981 .... **DC 1**
See also CA 77-80; 105; CAD; CWD; DFS 11; DLB 228; SATA 17; SATA-Obit 29
Chase, Mary Ellen 1887-1973 .... **CLC 2; TCLC 124**
See also CA 13-16; 41-44R; CAP 1; SATA 10
Chase, Nicholas
See Hyde, Anthony
Chase-Riboud, Barbara (Dewayne Tosi) 1939- .... **BLC 2:1**
See also BW 2; CA 113; CANR 76; DAM MULT; DLB 33; MTCW 2
Chateaubriand, Francois Rene de 1768-1848 .... **NCLC 3, 134**
See also DLB 119; EW 5; GFL 1789 to the Present; RGWL 2, 3; TWA
Chatelet, Gabrielle-Emilie Du
See du Chatelet, Emilie
Chatterje, Saratchandra -(?)
See Chatterji, Sarat Chandra
Chatterji, Bankim Chandra 1838-1894 .... **NCLC 19**
Chatterji, Sarat Chandra 1876-1936 .... **TCLC 13**
See also CA 109; 186; EWL 3
Chatterton, Thomas 1752-1770 ..... **LC 3, 54; PC 104**
See also DAM POET; DLB 109; RGEL 2
Chatwin, Bruce 1940-1989 ... **CLC 28, 57, 59**
See also AAYA 4; BEST 90:1; BRWS 4; CA 85-88; 127; CANR 228; CPW; DAM POP; DLB 194, 204; EWL 3; MTFW 2005
Chatwin, Charles Bruce
See Chatwin, Bruce
Chaucer, Daniel
See Ford, Ford Madox
Chaucer, Geoffrey 1340(?)-1400 ... **LC 17, 56, 173; PC 19, 58; WLCS**
See also BRW 1; BRWC 1; BRWR 2; CD-BLB Before 1660; DA; DA3; DAB; DAC; DAM MST, POET; DLB 146; LAIT 1; PAB; PFS 14; RGEL 2; TEA; WLIT 3; WP
Chaudhuri, Nirad C(handra) 1897-1999 .... **TCLC 224**
See also CA 128; 183; DLB 323
Chavez, Denise 1948- .... **HLC 1**
See also CA 131; CANR 56, 81, 137; DAM MULT; DLB 122; FW; HW 1, 2; LLW; MAL 5; MTCW 2; MTFW 2005
Chaviaras, Strates 1935- .... **CLC 33**
See also CA 105
Chayefsky, Paddy 1923-1981 .... **CLC 23**
See also CA 9-12R; 104; CAD; CANR 18; DAM DRAM; DFS 26; DLB 23; DLBY 7, 44; RGAL 4
Chayefsky, Sidney
See Chayefsky, Paddy
Chedid, Andree 1920-2011 .... **CLC 47**
See also CA 145; CANR 95; EWL 3
Cheever, John 1912-1982 ..... **CLC 3, 7, 8, 11, 15, 25, 64; SSC 1, 38, 57, 120; WLC 2**
See also AAYA 65; AMWS 1; BPFB 1; CA 5-8R; 106; CABS 1; CANR 5, 27, 76; CDALB 1941-1968; CN 1, 2, 3; CPW; DA; DA3; DAB; DAC; DAM MST, NOV, POP; DLB 2, 102, 227; DLBY 1980, 1982; EWL 3; EXPS; INT CANR-5; MAL 5; MTCW 1, 2; MTFW 2005; RGAL 4; RGSF 2; SSFS 2, 14; TUS
Cheever, Susan 1943- .... **CLC 18, 48**
See also CA 103; CANR 27, 51, 92, 157, 198; DLBY 1982; INT CANR-27
Chekhonte, Antosha
See Chekhov, Anton

Chekhov, Anton 1860-1904 ...... **DC 9; SSC 2,**
28, 41, 51, 85, 102, 155; TCLC 3, 10,
31, 55, 96, 163; WLC 2
See also AAYA 68; BYA 14; CA 104; 124;
DA; DA3; DAB; DAC; DAM DRAM,
MST; DFS 1, 5, 10, 12, 26; DLB 277;
EW 7; EWL 3; EXPS; LAIT 3; LATS 1:1;
RGSF 2; RGWL 2, 3; SATA 90; SSFS 5,
13, 14, 26, 29, 33; TWA
Chekhov, Anton Pavlovich
See Chekhov, Anton
Cheney, Lynne V. 1941- .... **CLC 70**
See also CA 89-92; CANR 58, 117, 193;
SATA 152
Cheney, Lynne Vincent
See Cheney, Lynne V.
Chenier, Andre-Marie de 1762-1794 . **LC 174**
See also EW 4; GFL Beginnings to 1789;
TWA
Chernyshevsky, Nikolai Gavrilovich
See Chernyshevsky, Nikolay Gavrilovich
Chernyshevsky, Nikolay Gavrilovich
1828-1889 .... **NCLC 1**
See also DLB 238
Cherry, Carolyn Janice
See Cherryh, C.J.
Cherryh, C.J. 1942- .... **CLC 35**
See also AAYA 24; BPFB 1; CA 65-68;
CANR 10, 147, 179; DLBY 1980; FANT;
SATA 93, 172; SCFW 2; YAW
Chesler, Phyllis 1940- .... **CLC 247**
See also CA 49-52; CANR 4, 59, 140, 189;
FW
Chesnut, Mary 1823-1886 .... **NCLC 250**
See also DLB 239
Chesnut, Mary Boykin
See Chesnut, Mary
Chesnutt, Charles W(addell)
1858-1932 .... **BLC 1; SSC 7, 54, 139;**
TCLC 5, 39
See also AFAW 1, 2; AMWS 14; BW 1, 3;
CA 106; 125; CANR 76; DAM MULT;
DLB 12, 50, 78; EWL 3; MAL 5; MTCW
1, 2; MTFW 2005; RGAL 4; RGSF 2;
SSFS 11, 26
Chester, Alfred 1929(?)-1971 .... **CLC 49**
See also CA 196; 33-36R; DLB 130; MAL
5
Chesterton, G. K. 1874-1936 . **PC 28; SSC 1,**
46, 148; TCLC 1, 6, 64
See also AAYA 57; BRW 6; CA 104; 132;
CANR 73, 131; CDBLB 1914-1945;
CMW 4; DAM NOV, POET; DLB 10, 19,
34, 70, 98, 149, 178; EWL 3; FANT;
MSW; MTCW 1, 2; MTFW 2005; RGEL
2; RGSF 2; SATA 27; SUFW 1
Chesterton, Gilbert Keith
See Chesterton, G. K.
Chettle, Henry 1560-1607(?) .... **LC 112**
See also DLB 136; RGEL 2
Chiang, Pin-chin 1904-1986 .... **CLC 68**
See also CA 118; DLB 328; EWL 3; RGWL
3
Chiang Ping-chih
See Chiang, Pin-chin
Chief Joseph 1840-1904 .... **NNAL**
See also CA 152; DA3; DAM MULT
Chief Seattle 1786(?)-1866 .... **NNAL**
See also DA3; DAM MULT
Ch'ien, Chung-shu
See Qian, Zhongshu
Chikamatsu Monzaemon 1653-1724 ... **LC 66**
See also RGWL 2, 3
Child, Francis James 1825-1896 . **NCLC 173**
See also DLB 1, 64, 235
Child, L. Maria
See Child, Lydia Maria

Child, Lydia Maria 1802-1880 .. **NCLC 6, 73**
See also DLB 1, 74, 243; RGAL 4; SATA
67
Child, Mrs.
See Child, Lydia Maria
Child, Philip 1898-1978 .... **CLC 19, 68**
See also CA 13-14; CAP 1; CP 1; DLB 68;
RHW; SATA 47
Childers, Erskine 1870-1922 .... **TCLC 65**
See also BRWS 17; CA 113; 153; DLB 70
Childress, Alice 1920-1994 .... **BLC 1:1; CLC**
12, 15, 86, 96; DC 4; TCLC 116
See also AAYA 8; BW 2, 3; BYA 2; CA 45-
48; 146; CAD; CANR 3, 27, 50, 74; CLR
14; CWD; DA3; DAM DRAM, MULT,
NOV; DFS 2, 8, 14, 26; DLB 7, 38, 249;
JRDA; LAIT 5; MAICYA 1, 2; MAIC-
YAS 1; MAL 5; MTCW 1, 2; MTFW
2005; RGAL 4; SATA 7, 48, 81; TUS;
WYA; YAW
Chin, Frank 1940- ..... **AAL; CLC 135; DC 7**
See also CA 33-36R; CAD; CANR 71; CD
5, 6; DAM MULT; DLB 206, 312; LAIT
5; RGAL 4
Chin, Frank Chew, Jr.
See Chin, Frank
Chin, Marilyn 1955- .... **PC 40**
See also CA 129; CANR 70, 113, 218;
CWP; DLB 312; PFS 28, 41
Chin, Marilyn Mei Ling
See Chin, Marilyn
Chislett, (Margaret) Anne 1943- ...... **CLC 34**
See also CA 151
Chitty, Thomas Willes
See Hinde, Thomas
Chivers, Thomas Holley
1809-1858 .... **NCLC 49**
See also DLB 3, 248; RGAL 4
Chlamyda, Jehudil
See Gorky, Maxim
Ch'o, Chou
See Shu-Jen, Chou
Choi, Susan 1969- .... **CLC 119**
See also CA 223; CANR 188
Chomette, Rene Lucien 1898-1981 .. **CLC 20**
See also CA 103
Chomsky, Avram Noam
See Chomsky, Noam
Chomsky, Noam 1928- .... **CLC 132**
See also CA 17-20R; CANR 28, 62, 110,
132, 179; DA3; DLB 246; MTCW 1, 2;
MTFW 2005
Chona, Maria 1845(?)-1936 .... **NNAL**
See also CA 144
Chopin, Kate 1851-1904 .... **SSC 8, 68, 110;**
TCLC 127; WLCS
See also AAYA 33; AMWR 2; BYA 11, 15;
CA 104; 122; CDALB 1865-1917; DA3;
DAB; DAC; DAM MST, NOV; DLB 12,
78; EXPN; EXPS; FL 1:3; FW; LAIT 3;
MAL 5; MBL; NFS 3; RGAL 4; RGSF 2;
SSFS 2, 13, 17, 26, 35; TUS
Chopin, Katherine
See Chopin, Kate
Chretien de Troyes c. 12th cent.
- .... **CMLC 10, 135**
See also DLB 208; EW 1; RGWL 2, 3;
TWA
Christie
See Ichikawa, Kon
Christie, Agatha 1890-1976 . **CLC 1, 6, 8, 12,**
39, 48, 110; DC 39
See also AAYA 9; AITN 1, 2; BPFB 1;
BRWS 2; CA 17-20R; 61-64; CANR 10,
37, 108; CBD; CDBLB 1914-1945; CMW
4; CN 1, 2; CPW; CWD; DA3; DAB;
DAC; DAM NOV; DFS 2; DLB 13, 77,

245; MSW; MTCW 1, 2; MTFW 2005;
NFS 8, 30, 33; RGEL 2; RHW; SATA 36;
SSFS 31, 34; TEA; YAW
Christie, Agatha Mary Clarissa
See Christie, Agatha
Christie, Ann Philippa
See Pearce, Philippa
Christie, Philippa
See Pearce, Philippa
Christine de Pisan
See Christine de Pizan
Christine de Pizan 1365(?)-1431(?) ...... **LC 9,**
130; PC 68
See also DLB 208; FL 1:1; FW; RGWL 2,
3
Chuang-Tzu c. 369B.C.-c.
286B.C. .... **CMLC 57**
Chubb, Elmer
See Masters, Edgar Lee
Chulkov, Mikhail Dmitrievich
1743-1792 .... **LC 2**
See also DLB 150
Chung, Sonya .... **CLC 318**
See also CA 307
Churchill, Caryl 1938- .... **CLC 31, 55, 157;**
DC 5
See also BRWS 4; CA 102; CANR 22, 46,
108; CBD; CD 5, 6; CWD; DFS 25; DLB
13, 310; EWL 3; FW; MTCW 1; RGEL 2
Churchill, Charles 1731-1764 .... **LC 3**
See also DLB 109; RGEL 2
Churchill, Chick
See Churchill, Caryl
Churchill, Sir Winston
1874-1965 .... **TCLC 113**
See also BRW 6; CA 97-100; CDBLB
1890-1914; DA3; DLB 100, 329; DLBD
16; LAIT 4; MTCW 1, 2
Churchill, Sir Winston Leonard Spencer
See Churchill, Sir Winston
Churchyard, Thomas 1520(?)-1604 .. **LC 187**
See also DLB 132; RGEL 2
Chute, Carolyn 1947- .... **CLC 39**
See also CA 123; CANR 135, 213; CN 7;
DLB 350
Ciardi, John (Anthony) 1916-1986 . **CLC 10,**
40, 44, 129; PC 69
See also CA 5-8R; 118; CAAS 2; CANR 5,
33; CLR 19; CP 1, 2, 3, 4; CWRI 5; DAM
POET; DLB 5; DLBY 1986; INT
CANR-5; MAICYA 1, 2; MAL 5; MTCW
1, 2; MTFW 2005; RGAL 4; SAAS 26;
SATA 1, 65; SATA-Obit 46
Cibber, Colley 1671-1757 .... **LC 66**
See also DLB 84; RGEL 2
Cicero, Marcus Tullius
106B.C.-43B.C. .... **CMLC 121**
See also AW 1; CDWLB 1; DLB 211;
RGWL 2, 3; WLIT 8
Cimino, Michael 1943- .... **CLC 16**
See also CA 105
Cioran, E(mil) M. 1911-1995 .... **CLC 64**
See also CA 25-28R; 149; CANR 91; DLB
220; EWL 3
Circus, Anthony
See Hoch, Edward D.
Cisneros, Sandra 1954- .... **CLC 69, 118, 193,**
305; HLC 1; PC 52; SSC 32, 72, 143
See also AAYA 9, 53; AMWS 7; CA 131;
CANR 64, 118; CLR 123; CN 7; CWP;
DA3; DAM MULT; DLB 122, 152; EWL
3; EXPN; FL 1:5; FW; HW 1, 2; LAIT 5;
LATS 1:2; LLW; MAICYA 2; MAL 5;
MTCW 2; MTFW 2005; NFS 2; PFS 19;
RGAL 4; RGSF 2; SSFS 3, 13, 27, 32;
WLIT 1; YAW

Cixous, Helene 1937- .... **CLC 92, 253**
See also CA 126; CANR 55, 123; CWW 2;
DLB 83, 242; EWL 3; FL 1:5; FW; GLL
2; MTCW 1, 2; MTFW 2005; TWA

Clair, Rene
See Chomette, Rene Lucien

Clampitt, Amy 1920-1994 .... **CLC 32; PC 19**
See also AMWS 9; CA 110; 146; CANR
29, 79; CP 4, 5; DLB 105; MAL 5; PFS
27, 39

Clancy, Thomas L., Jr.
See Clancy, Tom

Clancy, Tom 1947- .... **CLC 45, 112**
See also AAYA 9, 51; BEST 89:1, 90:1;
BPFB 1; BYA 10, 11; CA 125; 131;
CANR 62, 105, 132; CMW 4; CPW;
DA3; DAM NOV, POP; DLB 227; INT
CA-131; MTCW 1, 2; MTFW 2005

Clare, John 1793-1864 .. **NCLC 9, 86; PC 23**
See also BRWS 11; DAB; DAM POET;
DLB 55, 96; RGEL 2

Clarin
See Alas (y Urena), Leopoldo (Enrique
Garcia)

Clark, Al C.
See Goines, Donald

Clark, Brian (Robert)
See Clark, (Robert) Brian

Clark, (Robert) Brian 1932- .... **CLC 29**
See also CA 41-44R; CANR 67; CBD; CD
5, 6

Clark, Curt
See Westlake, Donald E.

Clark, Eleanor 1913-1996 .... **CLC 5, 19**
See also CA 9-12R; 151; CANR 41; CN 1,
2, 3, 4, 5, 6; DLB 6

Clark, J. P.
See Clark-Bekederemo, J. P.

Clark, John Pepper
See Clark-Bekederemo, J. P.

Clark, Kenneth (Mackenzie)
1903-1983 .... **TCLC 147**
See also CA 93-96; 109; CANR 36; MTCW
1, 2; MTFW 2005

Clark, M. R.
See Clark, Mavis Thorpe

Clark, Mavis Thorpe 1909-1999 ...... **CLC 12**
See also CA 57-60; CANR 8, 37, 107; CLR
30; CWRI 5; MAICYA 1, 2; SAAS 5;
SATA 8, 74

Clark, Walter Van Tilburg
1909-1971 .... **CLC 28**
See also CA 9-12R; 33-36R; CANR 63,
113; CN 1; DLB 9, 206; LAIT 2; MAL 5;
NFS 40; RGAL 4; SATA 8; TCWW 1, 2

Clark-Bekederemo, J. P. 1935- ...... **BLC 1:1;
CLC 38; DC 5**
See also AAYA 79; AFW; BW 1; CA 65-
68; CANR 16, 72; CD 5, 6; CDWLB 3;
CP 1, 2, 3, 4, 5, 6, 7; DAM DRAM,
MULT; DFS 13; DLB 117; EWL 3;
MTCW 2; MTFW 2005; RGEL 2

Clark-Bekederemo, John Pepper
See Clark-Bekederemo, J. P.

Clark Bekederemo, Johnson Pepper
See Clark-Bekederemo, J. P.

Clarke, Arthur
See Clarke, Arthur C.

Clarke, Arthur C. 1917-2008 .. **CLC 1, 4, 13,
18, 35, 136; SSC 3**
See also AAYA 4, 33; BPFB 1; BYA 13;
CA 1-4R; 270; CANR 2, 28, 55, 74, 130,
196; CLR 119; CN 1, 2, 3, 4, 5, 6, 7;
CPW; DA3; DAM POP; DLB 261; JRDA;
LAIT 5; MAICYA 1, 2; MTCW 1, 2;
MTFW 2005; SATA 13, 70, 115; SATA-
Obit 191; SCFW 1, 2; SFW 4; SSFS 4,
18, 29; TCLE 1:1; YAW

Clarke, Arthur Charles
See Clarke, Arthur C.

Clarke, Austin 1896-1974 .... **CLC 6, 9; PC
112**
See also BRWS 15; CA 29-32; 49-52; CAP
2; CP 1, 2; DAM POET; DLB 10, 20;
EWL 3; RGEL 2

Clarke, Austin 1934- ... **BLC 1:1; CLC 8, 53;
SSC 45, 116**
See also BW 1; CA 25-28R; CAAS 16;
CANR 14, 32, 68, 140, 220; CN 1, 2, 3,
4, 5, 6, 7; DAC; DAM MULT; DLB 53,
125; DNFS 2; MTCW 2; MTFW 2005;
RGSF 2

Clarke, Gillian 1937- .... **CLC 61**
See also CA 106; CP 3, 4, 5, 6, 7; CWP;
DLB 40

Clarke, Marcus (Andrew Hislop)
1846-1881 .... **NCLC 19; SSC 94**
See also DLB 230; RGEL 2; RGSF 2

Clarke, Shirley 1925-1997 .... **CLC 16**
See also CA 189

Clash, The
See Headon, (Nicky) Topper; Jones, Mick;
Simonon, Paul; Strummer, Joe

Claudel, Paul (Louis Charles Marie)
1868-1955 .... **TCLC 2, 10**
See also CA 104; 165; DLB 192, 258, 321;
EW 8; EWL 3; GFL 1789 to the Present;
RGWL 2, 3; TWA

Claudian 370(?)-404(?) .... **CMLC 46**
See also RGWL 2, 3

Claudius, Matthias 1740-1815 .... **NCLC 75**
See also DLB 97

Clavell, James 1925-1994 .... **CLC 6, 25, 87**
See also BPFB 1; CA 25-28R; 146; CANR
26, 48; CN 5; CPW; DA3; DAM NOV,
POP; MTCW 1, 2; MTFW 2005; NFS 10;
RHW

Clayman, Gregory .... **CLC 65**

Cleage, Pearl 1948- .... **DC 32**
See also BW 2; CA 41-44R; CANR 27, 148,
177, 226; DFS 14, 16; DLB 228; NFS 17

Cleage, Pearl Michelle
See Cleage, Pearl

Cleaver, (Leroy) Eldridge
1935-1998 .... **BLC 1:1; CLC 30, 119**
See also BW 1, 3; CA 21-24R; 167; CANR
16, 75; DA3; DAM MULT; MTCW 2;
YAW

Cleese, John (Marwood) 1939- .... **CLC 21**
See also CA 112; 116; CANR 35; MTCW 1

Cleishbotham, Jebediah
See Scott, Sir Walter

Cleland, John 1710-1789 .... **LC 2, 48**
See also DLB 39; RGEL 2

Clemens, Samuel
See Twain, Mark

Clemens, Samuel Langhorne
See Twain, Mark

Clement of Alexandria
150(?)-215(?) .... **CMLC 41**

Cleophil
See Congreve, William

Clerihew, E.
See Bentley, E(dmund) C(lerihew)

Clerk, N. W.
See Lewis, C. S.

Cleveland, John 1613-1658 .... **LC 106**
See also DLB 126; RGEL 2

Cliff, Jimmy
See Chambers, James

Cliff, Michelle 1946- .... **BLCS; CLC 120**
See also BW 2; CA 116; CANR 39, 72; CD-
WLB 3; DLB 157; FW; GLL 2

Clifford, Lady Anne 1590-1676 .... **LC 76**
See also DLB 151

Clifton, Lucille 1936-2010 .... **BLC 1:1, 2:1;
CLC 19, 66, 162, 283; PC 17**
See also AFAW 2; BW 2, 3; CA 49-52;
CANR 2, 24, 42, 76, 97, 138; CLR 5; CP
2, 3, 4, 5, 6, 7; CSW; CWP; CWRI 5;
DA3; DAM MULT, POET; DLB 5, 41;
EXPP; MAICYA 1, 2; MTCW 1, 2;
MTFW 2005; PFS 1, 14, 29, 41; SATA
20, 69, 128; SSFS 34; WP

Clifton, Thelma Lucille
See Clifton, Lucille

Clinton, Dirk
See Silverberg, Robert

Clough, Arthur Hugh 1819-1861 .. **NCLC 27,
163; PC 103**
See also BRW 5; DLB 32; RGEL 2

Clutha, Janet
See Frame, Janet

Clutha, Janet Paterson Frame
See Frame, Janet

Clyne, Terence
See Blatty, William Peter

Cobalt, Martin
See Mayne, William

Cobb, Irvin S(hrewsbury)
1876-1944 .... **TCLC 77**
See also CA 175; DLB 11, 25, 86

Cobbett, William 1763-1835 .... **NCLC 49**
See also DLB 43, 107, 158; RGEL 2

Coben, Harlan 1962- .... **CLC 269**
See also AAYA 83; CA 164; CANR 162,
199

Coburn, D(onald) L(ee) 1938- .... **CLC 10**
See also CA 89-92; DFS 23

Cockburn, Catharine Trotter
See Trotter, Catharine

Cocteau, Jean 1889-1963 ... **CLC 1, 8, 15, 16,
43; DC 17; TCLC 119; WLC 2**
See also AAYA 74; CA 25-28; CANR 40;
CAP 2; DA; DA3; DAB; DAC; DAM
DRAM, MST, NOV; DFS 24; DLB 65,
258, 321; EW 10; EWL 3; GFL 1789 to
the Present; MTCW 1, 2; RGWL 2, 3;
TWA

Cocteau, Jean Maurice Eugene Clement
See Cocteau, Jean

Codrescu, Andrei 1946- .... **CLC 46, 121**
See also CA 33-36R; CAAS 19; CANR 13,
34, 53, 76, 125, 223; CN 7; DA3; DAM
POET; MAL 5; MTCW 2; MTFW 2005

Coe, Max
See Bourne, Randolph S(illiman)

Coe, Tucker
See Westlake, Donald E.

Coelho, Paulo 1947- .... **CLC 258**
See also CA 152; CANR 80, 93, 155, 194;
NFS 29

Coen, Ethan 1957- .... **CLC 108, 267**
See also AAYA 54; CA 126; CANR 85

Coen, Joel 1954- .... **CLC 108, 267**
See also AAYA 54; CA 126; CANR 119

The Coen Brothers
See Coen, Ethan; Coen, Joel

Coetzee, J. M. 1940- ..... **CLC 23, 33, 66, 117,
161, 162, 305**
See also AAYA 37; AFW; BRWS 6; CA 77-
80; CANR 41, 54, 74, 114, 133, 180; CN
4, 5, 6, 7; DA3; DAM NOV; DLB 225,
326, 329; EWL 3; LMFS 2; MTCW 1, 2;
MTFW 2005; NFS 21; WLIT 2; WWE 1

Coetzee, John Maxwell
See Coetzee, J. M.

Coffey, Brian
See Koontz, Dean

Coffin, Robert P. Tristram
1892-1955 .... **TCLC 95**
See also CA 123; 169; DLB 45

Coffin, Robert Peter Tristram
See Coffin, Robert P. Tristram

Cumberland, Richard
     1732-1811 .... **NCLC 167**
     See also DLB 89; RGEL 2
Cummings, Bruce F. 1889-1919 ..... **TCLC 24**
     See also CA 123
Cummings, Bruce Frederick
     See Cummings, Bruce F.
Cummings, E. E. 1894-1962 ...... **CLC 1, 3, 8,
     12, 15, 68; PC 5; TCLC 137; WLC 2**
     See also AAYA 41; AMW; CA 73-76;
     CANR 31; CDALB 1929-1941; DA;
     DA3; DAB; DAC; DAM MST, POET;
     DLB 4, 48; EWL 3; EXPP; MAL 5;
     MTCW 1, 2; MTFW 2005; PAB; PFS 1,
     3, 12, 13, 19, 30, 34, 40; RGAL 4; TUS;
     WP
Cummings, Edward Estlin
     See Cummings, E. E.
Cummins, Maria Susanna
     1827-1866 .... **NCLC 139**
     See also DLB 42; YABC 1
Cunha, Euclides (Rodrigues Pimenta) da
     1866-1909 .... **TCLC 24**
     See also CA 123; 219; DLB 307; LAW;
     WLIT 1
Cunningham, E. V.
     See Fast, Howard
Cunningham, J. Morgan
     See Westlake, Donald E.
Cunningham, J(ames) V(incent)
     1911-1985 .... **CLC 3, 31; PC 92**
     See also CA 1-4R; 115; CANR 1, 72; CP 1,
     2, 3, 4; DLB 5
Cunningham, Julia (Woolfolk)
     1916- .... **CLC 12**
     See also CA 9-12R; CANR 4, 19, 36; CWRI
     5; JRDA; MAICYA 1, 2; SAAS 2; SATA
     1, 26, 132
Cunningham, Michael 1952- .... **CLC 34, 243**
     See also AMWS 15; CA 136; CANR 96,
     160, 227; CN 7; DLB 292; GLL 2; MTFW
     2005; NFS 23
Cunninghame Graham, R. B.
     See Cunninghame Graham, Robert Bontine
Cunninghame Graham, Robert Bontine
     1852-1936 .... **TCLC 19**
     See also CA 119; 184; DLB 98, 135, 174;
     RGEL 2; RGSF 2
**Cunninghame Graham, Robert Gallnigad
     Bontine**
     See Cunninghame Graham, Robert Bontine
Curnow, (Thomas) Allen (Monro)
     1911-2001 .... **PC 48**
     See also CA 69-72; 202; CANR 48, 99; CP
     1, 2, 3, 4, 5, 6, 7; EWL 3; RGEL 2
Currie, Ellen 19(?)- .... **CLC 44**
Curtin, Philip
     See Lowndes, Marie Adelaide (Belloc)
Curtin, Phillip
     See Lowndes, Marie Adelaide (Belloc)
Curtis, Price
     See Ellison, Harlan
Cusanus, Nicolaus 1401-1464
     See Nicholas of Cusa
Cutrate, Joe
     See Spiegelman, Art
Cynewulf fl. 9th cent. - .... **CMLC 23, 117**
     See also DLB 146; RGEL 2
Cyprian, St. c. 200-258 .... **CMLC 127**
Cyrano de Bergerac, Savinien de
     1619-1655 .... **LC 65**
     See also DLB 268; GFL Beginnings to
     1789; RGWL 2, 3
Cyril of Alexandria c. 375-c. 430 . **CMLC 59**
Czaczkes, Shmuel Yosef Halevi
     See Agnon, S. Y.

Dabrowska, Maria (Szumska)
     1889-1965 .... **CLC 15**
     See also CA 106; CDWLB 4; DLB 215;
     EWL 3
Dabydeen, David 1955- .... **CLC 34**
     See also BW 1; CA 125; CANR 56, 92; CN
     6, 7; CP 5, 6, 7; DLB 347
Dacey, Philip 1939- .... **CLC 51**
     See also CA 37-40R, 231; CAAE 231;
     CAAS 17; CANR 14, 32, 64; CP 4, 5, 6,
     7; DLB 105
Dacre, Charlotte c. 1772-1825(?) . **NCLC 151**
Dafydd ap Gwilym c. 1320-c. 1380 ..... **PC 56**
Dagerman, Stig (Halvard)
     1923-1954 .... **TCLC 17**
     See also CA 117; 155; DLB 259; EWL 3
D'Aguiar, Fred 1960- ..... **BLC 2:1; CLC 145**
     See also CA 148; CANR 83, 101; CN 7;
     CP 5, 6, 7; DLB 157; EWL 3
Dahl, Roald 1916-1990 ...... **CLC 1, 6, 18, 79;
     TCLC 173**
     See also AAYA 15; BPFB 1; BRWS 4; BYA
     5; CA 1-4R; 133; CANR 6, 32, 37, 62;
     CLR 1, 7, 41, 111; CN 1, 2, 3, 4; CPW;
     DA3; DAB; DAC; DAM MST, NOV,
     POP; DLB 139, 255; HGG; JRDA; MAI-
     CYA 1, 2; MTCW 1, 2; MTFW 2005;
     RGSF 2; SATA 1, 26, 73; SATA-Obit 65;
     SSFS 4, 30; TEA; YAW
Dahlberg, Edward 1900-1977 . **CLC 1, 7, 14;
     TCLC 208**
     See also CA 9-12R; 69-72; CANR 31, 62;
     CN 1, 2; DLB 48; MAL 5; MTCW 1;
     RGAL 4
Dahlie, Michael 1970(?)- .... **CLC 299**
     See also CA 283
Daitch, Susan 1954- .... **CLC 103**
     See also CA 161
Dale, Colin
     See Lawrence, T. E.
Dale, George E.
     See Asimov, Isaac
d'Alembert, Jean Le Rond
     1717-1783 .... **LC 126**
Dalton, Roque 1935-1975(?) ..... **HLCS 1; PC
     36**
     See also CA 176; DLB 283; HW 2
Daly, Elizabeth 1878-1967 .... **CLC 52**
     See also CA 23-24; 25-28R; CANR 60;
     CAP 2; CMW 4
Daly, Mary 1928-2010 .... **CLC 173**
     See also CA 25-28R; CANR 30, 62, 166;
     FW; GLL 1; MTCW 1
Daly, Maureen 1921-2006 .... **CLC 17**
     See also AAYA 5, 58; BYA 6; CA 253;
     CANR 37, 83, 108; CLR 96; JRDA; MAI-
     CYA 1, 2; SAAS 1; SATA 2, 129; SATA-
     Obit 176; WYA; YAW
Damas, Leon-Gontran 1912-1978 ... **CLC 84;
     TCLC 204**
     See also BW 1; CA 125; 73-76; EWL 3
Damocles
     See Benedetti, Mario
Dana, Richard Henry Sr.
     1787-1879 .... **NCLC 53**
Dangarembga, Tsitsi 1959- .... **BLC 2:1**
     See also BW 3; CA 163; DLB 360; NFS
     28; WLIT 2
Daniel, Samuel 1562(?)-1619 .... **LC 24, 171**
     See also DLB 62; RGEL 2
Daniels, Brett
     See Adler, Renata
Dannay, Frederic 1905-1982 .... **CLC 3, 11**
     See also BPFB 3; CA 1-4R; 107; CANR 1,
     39; CMW 4; DAM POP; DLB 137; MSW;
     MTCW 1; RGAL 4

D'Annunzio, Gabriele 1863-1938 ... **TCLC 6,
     40, 215**
     See also CA 104; 155; EW 8; EWL 3;
     RGWL 2, 3; TWA; WLIT 7
Danois, N. le
     See Gourmont, Remy(-Marie-Charles) de
Dante 1265-1321 .... **CMLC 3, 18, 39, 70; PC
     21, 108; WLCS**
     See also DA; DA3; DAB; DAC; DAM
     MST, POET; EFS 1:1, 2:1; EW 1; LAIT
     1; RGWL 2, 3; TWA; WLIT 7; WP
d'Antibes, Germain
     See Simenon, Georges
Danticat, Edwidge 1969- . **BLC 2:1; CLC 94,
     139, 228; SSC 100**
     See also AAYA 29, 85; CA 152, 192; CAAE
     192; CANR 73, 129, 179; CN 7; DLB
     350; DNFS 1; EXPS; LATS 1:2; LNFS 3;
     MTCW 2; MTFW 2005; NFS 28, 37;
     SSFS 1, 25; YAW
Danvers, Dennis 1947- .... **CLC 70**
Danziger, Paula 1944-2004 .... **CLC 21**
     See also AAYA 4, 36; BYA 6, 7, 14; CA
     112; 115; 229; CANR 37, 132; CLR 20;
     JRDA; MAICYA 1, 2; MTFW 2005;
     SATA 36, 63, 102, 149; SATA-Brief 30;
     SATA-Obit 155; WYA; YAW
Da Ponte, Lorenzo 1749-1838 .... **NCLC 50**
d'Aragona, Tullia 1510(?)-1556 .... **LC 121**
Dario, Ruben 1867-1916 .... **HLC 1; PC 15;
     TCLC 4**
     See also CA 131; CANR 81; DAM MULT;
     DLB 290; EWL 3; HW 1, 2; LAW;
     MTCW 1, 2; MTFW 2005; RGWL 2, 3
Darko, Amma 1956- .... **BLC 2:1**
Darley, George 1795-1846 . **NCLC 2; PC 125**
     See also DLB 96; RGEL 2
Darrow, Clarence (Seward)
     1857-1938 .... **TCLC 81**
     See also CA 164; DLB 303
Darwin, Charles 1809-1882 .... **NCLC 57**
     See also BRWS 7; DLB 57, 166; LATS 1:1;
     RGEL 2; TEA; WLIT 4
Darwin, Erasmus 1731-1802 .... **NCLC 106**
     See also BRWS 16; DLB 93; RGEL 2
Darwish, Mahmoud 1941-2008 .... **PC 86**
     See also CA 164; CANR 133; CWW 2;
     EWL 3; MTCW 2; MTFW 2005
Darwish, Mahmud -2008
     See Darwish, Mahmoud
Daryush, Elizabeth 1887-1977 ...... **CLC 6, 19**
     See also CA 49-52; CANR 3, 81; DLB 20
Das, Kamala 1934-2009 ..... **CLC 191; PC 43**
     See also CA 101; 287; CANR 27, 59; CP 1,
     2, 3, 4, 5, 6, 7; CWP; DLB 323; FW
Dasgupta, Surendranath
     1887-1952 .... **TCLC 81**
     See also CA 157
**Dashwood, Edmee Elizabeth Monica de la
     Pasture** 1890-1943 .... **TCLC 61**
     See also CA 119; 154; DLB 34; RHW
da Silva, Antonio Jose
     1705-1739 .... **NCLC 114**
Daudet, (Louis Marie) Alphonse
     1840-1897 .... **NCLC 1**
     See also DLB 123; GFL 1789 to the Present;
     RGSF 2
Daudet, Alphonse Marie Leon
     1867-1942 .... **SSC 94**
     See also CA 217
d'Aulnoy, Marie-Catherine c.
     1650-1705 .... **LC 100**
Daumal, Rene 1908-1944 .... **TCLC 14**
     See also CA 114; 247; EWL 3
Davenant, William 1606-1668 .... **LC 13, 166;
     PC 99**
     See also DLB 58, 126; RGEL 2

Delany, Samuel Ray
See Delany, Samuel R., Jr.

de la Parra, Ana Teresa Sonojo
See de la Parra, Teresa

de la Parra, Teresa 1890(?)-1936 .... **HLCS 2; TCLC 185**
See also CA 178; HW 2; LAW

Delaporte, Theophile
See Green, Julien

De La Ramee, Marie Louise
1839-1908 .... **TCLC 43**
See also CA 204; DLB 18, 156; RGEL 2; SATA 20

de la Roche, Mazo 1879-1961 .... **CLC 14**
See also CA 85-88; CANR 30; DLB 68; RGEL 2; RHW; SATA 64

De La Salle, Innocent
See Hartmann, Sadakichi

de Laureamont, Comte
See Lautreamont

Delbanco, Nicholas 1942- ..... **CLC 6, 13, 167**
See also CA 17-20R, 189; CAAE 189; CAAS 2; CANR 29, 55, 116, 150, 204; CN 7; DLB 6, 234

Delbanco, Nicholas Franklin
See Delbanco, Nicholas

del Castillo, Michel 1933- .... **CLC 38**
See also CA 109; CANR 77

Deledda, Grazia (Cosima)
1875(?)-1936 .... **TCLC 23**
See also CA 123; 205; DLB 264, 329; EWL 3; RGWL 2, 3; WLIT 7

Deleuze, Gilles 1925-1995 .... **TCLC 116**
See also DLB 296

Delgado, Abelardo (Lalo) B(arrientos)
1930-2004 .... **HLC 1**
See also CA 131; 230; CAAS 15; CANR 90; DAM MST, MULT; DLB 82; HW 1, 2

Delibes, Miguel
See Delibes Setien, Miguel

Delibes Setien, Miguel 1920-2010 ...... **CLC 8, 18**
See also CA 45-48; CANR 1, 32; CWW 2; DLB 322; EWL 3; HW 1; MTCW 1

DeLillo, Don 1936- ..... **CLC 8, 10, 13, 27, 39, 54, 76, 143, 210, 213**
See also AMWC 2; AMWS 6; BEST 89:1; BPFB 1; CA 81-84; CANR 21, 76, 92, 133, 173; CN 3, 4, 5, 6, 7; CPW; DA3; DAM NOV, POP; DLB 6, 173; EWL 3; MAL 5; MTCW 1, 2; MTFW 2005; NFS 28; RGAL 4; TUS

de Lisser, H. G.
See De Lisser, H(erbert) G(eorge)

De Lisser, H(erbert) G(eorge)
1878-1944 .... **TCLC 12**
See also BW 2; CA 109; 152; DLB 117

Deloire, Pierre
See Peguy, Charles (Pierre)

Deloney, Thomas 1543(?)-1600 .... **LC 41; PC 79**
See also DLB 167; RGEL 2

Deloria, Ella (Cara) 1889-1971(?) ..... **NNAL**
See also CA 152; DAM MULT; DLB 175

Deloria, Vine, Jr. 1933-2005 .... **CLC 21, 122; NNAL**
See also CA 53-56; 245; CANR 5, 20, 48, 98; DAM MULT; DLB 175; MTCW 1; SATA 21; SATA-Obit 171

Deloria, Vine Victor, Jr.
See Deloria, Vine, Jr.

del Valle-Inclan, Ramon
See Valle-Inclan, Ramon del

Del Vecchio, John M(ichael) 1947- .. **CLC 29**
See also CA 110; DLBD 9

de Man, Paul (Adolph Michel)
1919-1983 .... **CLC 55**
See also CA 128; 111; CANR 61; DLB 67; MTCW 1, 2

de Mandiargues, Andre Pieyre
See Pieyre de Mandiargues, Andre

DeMarinis, Rick 1934- .... **CLC 54**
See also CA 57-60, 184; CAAE 184; CAAS 24; CANR 9, 25, 50, 160; DLB 218; TCWW 2

de Maupassant, Guy
See Maupassant, Guy de

Dembry, R. Emmet
See Murfree, Mary Noailles

Demby, William 1922- ...... **BLC 1:1; CLC 53**
See also BW 1, 3; CA 81-84; CANR 81; DAM MULT; DLB 33

de Menton, Francisco
See Chin, Frank

Demetrius of Phalerum c.
307B.C.- .... **CMLC 34**

Demijohn, Thom
See Disch, Thomas M.

De Mille, James 1833-1880 .... **NCLC 123**
See also DLB 99, 251

Democritus c. 460B.C.-c.
370B.C. .... **CMLC 47, 136**

de Montaigne, Michel
See Montaigne, Michel de

de Montherlant, Henry
See Montherlant, Henry de

Demosthenes 384B.C.-322B.C. ...... **CMLC 13**
See also AW 1; DLB 176; RGWL 2, 3; WLIT 8

de Musset, (Louis Charles) Alfred
See Musset, Alfred de

de Natale, Francine
See Malzberg, Barry N(athaniel)

de Navarre, Marguerite 1492-1549 .... **LC 61, 167; SSC 85**
See also DLB 327; GFL Beginnings to 1789; RGWL 2, 3

Denby, Edwin (Orr) 1903-1983 .... **CLC 48**
See also CA 138; 110; CP 1

de Nerval, Gerard
See Nerval, Gerard de

Denham, John 1615-1669 .... **LC 73**
See also DLB 58, 126; RGEL 2

Denis, Claire 1948- .... **CLC 286**
See also CA 249

Denis, Julio
See Cortazar, Julio

Denmark, Harrison
See Zelazny, Roger

Dennie, Joseph 1768-1812 .... **NCLC 249**
See also DLB 37, 43, 59, 73

Dennis, John 1658-1734 .... **LC 11, 154**
See also DLB 101; RGEL 2

Dennis, Nigel (Forbes) 1912-1989 ...... **CLC 8**
See also CA 25-28R; 129; CN 1, 2, 3, 4; DLB 13, 15, 233; EWL 3; MTCW 1

Dent, Lester 1904-1959 .... **TCLC 72**
See also CA 112; 161; CMW 4; DLB 306; SFW 4

Dentinger, Stephen
See Hoch, Edward D.

De Palma, Brian 1940- .... **CLC 20, 247**
See also CA 109

De Palma, Brian Russell
See De Palma, Brian

de Pizan, Christine
See Christine de Pizan

De Quincey, Thomas 1785-1859 ..... **NCLC 4, 87, 198**
See also BRW 4; CDBLB 1789-1832; DLB 110, 144; RGEL 2

De Ray, Jill
See Moore, Alan

Deren, Eleanora 1908(?)-1961 .. **CLC 16, 102**
See also CA 192; 111

Deren, Maya
See Deren, Eleanora

Derleth, August (William)
1909-1971 .... **CLC 31**
See also BPFB 1; BYA 9, 10; CA 1-4R; 29-32R; CANR 4; CMW 4; CN 1; DLB 9; DLBD 17; HGG; SATA 5; SUFW 1

Der Nister 1884-1950 .... **TCLC 56**
See also DLB 333; EWL 3

de Routisie, Albert
See Aragon, Louis

Derrida, Jacques 1930-2004 ...... **CLC 24, 87, 225**
See also CA 124; 127; 232; CANR 76, 98, 133; DLB 242; EWL 3; LMFS 2; MTCW 2; TWA

Derry Down Derry
See Lear, Edward

Dershowitz, Alan M. 1938- .... **CLC 298**
See also CA 25-28R; CANR 11, 44, 79, 159, 227

Dershowitz, Alan Morton
See Dershowitz, Alan M.

Dersonnes, Jacques
See Simenon, Georges

Der Stricker c. 1190-c. 1250 .... **CMLC 75**
See also DLB 138

Derzhavin, Gavriil Romanovich
1743-1816 .... **NCLC 215**
See also DLB 150

Desai, Anita 1937- . **CLC 19, 37, 97, 175, 271**
See also AAYA 85; BRWS 5; CA 81-84; CANR 33, 53, 95, 133; CN 1, 2, 3, 4, 5, 6, 7; CWRI 5; DA3; DAB; DAM NOV; DLB 271, 323; DNFS 2; EWL 3; FW; MTCW 1, 2; MTFW 2005; SATA 63, 126; SSFS 28, 31

Desai, Kiran 1971- .... **CLC 119**
See also BRWS 15; BYA 16; CA 171; CANR 127; NFS 28

de Saint-Luc, Jean
See Glassco, John

de Saint Roman, Arnaud
See Aragon, Louis

Desbordes-Valmore, Marceline
1786-1859 .... **NCLC 97**
See also DLB 217

Descartes, Rene 1596-1650 ... **LC 20, 35, 150, 202**
See also DLB 268; EW 3; GFL Beginnings to 1789

Deschamps, Eustache 1340(?)-1404 .. **LC 103**
See also DLB 208

De Sica, Vittorio 1901(?)-1974 .... **CLC 20**
See also CA 117

Desnos, Robert 1900-1945 ...... **TCLC 22, 241**
See also CA 121; 151; CANR 107; DLB 258; EWL 3; LMFS 2

Destouches, Louis-Ferdinand
See Celine, Louis-Ferdinand

De Teran, Lisa St. Aubin
See St. Aubin de Teran, Lisa

de Teran, Lisa St. Aubin
See St. Aubin de Teran, Lisa

de Tolignac, Gaston
See Griffith, D.W.

Deutsch, Babette 1895-1982 .... **CLC 18**
See also BYA 3; CA 1-4R; 108; CANR 4, 79; CP 1, 2, 3; DLB 45; SATA 1; SATA-Obit 33

de Vere, Edward 1550-1604 .... **LC 193**
See also DLB 172

Devi, Mahasweta 1926- .... **CLC 290**

Deville, Rene
See Kacew, Romain

Domecq, Honorio Bustos
See Bioy Casares, Adolfo; Borges, Jorge Luis

Domini, Rey
See Lorde, Audre

Dominic, R. B.
See Hennissart, Martha

Dominique
See Proust, Marcel

Don, A
See Stephen, Sir Leslie

Donaldson, Stephen R. 1947- ... **CLC 46, 138**
See also AAYA 36; BPFB 1; CA 89-92; CANR 13, 55, 99; CPW; DAM POP; FANT; INT CANR-13; SATA 121; SFW 4; SUFW 1, 2

Donleavy, J(ames) P(atrick) 1926- .... **CLC 1, 4, 6, 10, 45**
See also AITN 2; BPFB 1; CA 9-12R; CANR 24, 49, 62, 80, 124; CBD; CD 5, 6; CN 1, 2, 3, 4, 5, 6, 7; DLB 6, 173; INT CANR-24; MAL 5; MTCW 1, 2; MTFW 2005; RGAL 4

Donnadieu, Marguerite
See Duras, Marguerite

Donne, John 1572-1631 ... **LC 10, 24, 91; PC 1, 43; WLC 2**
See also AAYA 67; BRW 1; BRWC 1; BRWR 2; CDBLB Before 1660; DA; DAB; DAC; DAM MST, POET; DLB 121, 151; EXPP; PAB; PFS 2, 11, 35, 41; RGEL 3; TEA; WLIT 3; WP

Donnell, David 1939(?)- .... **CLC 34**
See also CA 197

Donoghue, Denis 1928- .... **CLC 209**
See also CA 17-20R; CANR 16, 102, 206

Donoghue, Emma 1969- .... **CLC 239**
See also CA 155; CANR 103, 152, 196; DLB 267; GLL 2; SATA 101

Donoghue, P.S.
See Hunt, E. Howard

Donoso, Jose 1924-1996 ..... **CLC 4, 8, 11, 32, 99; HLC 1; SSC 34; TCLC 133**
See also CA 81-84; 155; CANR 32, 73; CD-WLB 3; CWW 2; DAM MULT; DLB 113; EWL 3; HW 1, 2; LAW; LAWS 1; MTCW 1, 2; MTFW 2005; RGSF 2; WLIT 1

Donoso Yanez, Jose
See Donoso, Jose

Donovan, John 1928-1992 .... **CLC 35**
See also AAYA 20; CA 97-100; 137; CLR 3; MAICYA 1, 2; SATA 72; SATA-Brief 29; YAW

Don Roberto
See Cunninghame Graham, Robert Bontine

Doolittle, Hilda 1886-1961 . **CLC 3, 8, 14, 31, 34, 73; PC 5, 127; WLC 3**
See also AAYA 66; AMWS 1; CA 97-100; CANR 35, 131; DA; DAC; DAM MST, POET; DLB 4, 45; EWL 3; FL 1:5; FW; GLL 1; LMFS 2; MAL 5; MBL; MTCW 1, 2; MTFW 2005; PFS 6, 28; RGAL 4

Doppo
See Kunikida Doppo

Doppo, Kunikida
See Kunikida Doppo

Dorfman, Ariel 1942- .... **CLC 48, 77, 189; HLC 1**
See also CA 124; 130; CANR 67, 70, 135; CWW 2; DAM MULT; DFS 4; EWL 3; HW 1, 2; INT CA-130; WLIT 1

Dorn, Edward 1929-1999 .... **CLC 10, 18; PC 115**
See also CA 93-96; 187; CANR 42, 79; CP 1, 2, 3, 4, 5, 6, 7; DLB 5; INT CA-93-96; WP

Dorn, Edward Merton
See Dorn, Edward

Dor-Ner, Zvi .... **CLC 70**
Dorris, Michael 1945-1997 .... **CLC 109; NNAL**
See also AAYA 20; BEST 90:1; BYA 12; CA 102; 157; CANR 19, 46, 75; CLR 58; DA3; DAM MULT, NOV; DLB 175; LAIT 5; MTCW 2; MTFW 2005; NFS 3; RGAL 4; SATA 75; SATA-Obit 94; TCWW 2; YAW

Dorris, Michael A.
See Dorris, Michael

Dorris, Michael Anthony
See Dorris, Michael

Dorsan, Luc
See Simenon, Georges

Dorsange, Jean
See Simenon, Georges

Dorset
See Sackville, Thomas

Dos Passos, John 1896-1970 ...... **CLC 1, 4, 8, 11, 15, 25, 34, 82; WLC 2**
See also AMW; BPFB 1; CA 1-4R; 29-32R; CANR 3; CDALB 1929-1941; DA; DA3; DAB; DAC; DAM MST, NOV; DLB 4, 9, 274, 316; DLBD 1, 15; DLBY 1996; EWL 3; MAL 5; MTCW 1, 2; MTFW 2005; NFS 14; RGAL 4; TUS

Dos Passos, John Roderigo
See Dos Passos, John

Dossage, Jean
See Simenon, Georges

Dostoevsky, Fedor
See Dostoevsky, Fyodor

Dostoevsky, Fedor Mikhailovich
See Dostoevsky, Fyodor

Dostoevsky, Fyodor 1821-1881 ... **NCLC 2, 7, 21, 33, 43, 119, 167, 202, 238; SSC 2, 33, 44, 134; WLC 2**
See also AAYA 40; DA; DA3; DAB; DAC; DAM MST, NOV; DLB 238; EW 7; EXPN; LATS 1:1; LMFS 1, 2; NFS 28; RGSF 2; RGWL 2, 3; SSFS 8, 30; TWA

Doty, Mark 1953(?)- .... **CLC 176; PC 53**
See also AMWS 11; CA 161, 183; CAAE 183; CANR 110, 173; CP 7; PFS 28, 40

Doty, Mark A.
See Doty, Mark

Doty, Mark Alan
See Doty, Mark

Doty, M.R.
See Doty, Mark

Doughty, Charles M(ontagu) 1843-1926 .... **TCLC 27**
See also CA 115; 178; DLB 19, 57, 174

Douglas, Ellen 1921- .... **CLC 73**
See also CA 115; CANR 41, 83; CN 5, 6, 7; CSW; DLB 292

Douglas, Gavin 1475(?)-1522 .... **LC 20**
See also DLB 132; RGEL 2

Douglas, George
See Brown, George Douglas

Douglas, Keith (Castellain) 1920-1944 .... **PC 106; TCLC 40**
See also BRW 7; CA 160; DLB 27; EWL 3; PAB; RGEL 2

Douglas, Leonard
See Bradbury, Ray

Douglas, Michael
See Crichton, Michael

Douglas, (George) Norman 1868-1952 .... **TCLC 68**
See also BRW 6; CA 119; 157; DLB 34, 195; RGEL 2

Douglas, William
See Brown, George Douglas

Douglass, Frederick 1817(?)-1895 .. **BLC 1:1; NCLC 7, 55, 141, 235; WLC 2**
See also AAYA 48; AFAW 1, 2; AMWC 1; AMWS 3; CDALB 1640-1865; DA; DA3; DAC; DAM MST, MULT; DLB 1, 43, 50, 79, 243; FW; LAIT 2; NCFS 2; RGAL 4; SATA 29

Dourado, (Waldomiro Freitas) Autran 1926- .... **CLC 23, 60**
See also CA 25-28R; 179; CANR 34, 81; DLB 145, 307; HW 2

Dourado, Waldomiro Freitas Autran
See Dourado, (Waldomiro Freitas) Autran

Dove, Rita 1952- . **BLC 2:1; BLCS; CLC 50, 81; PC 6**
See also AAYA 46; AMWS 4; BW 2; CA 109; CAAS 19; CANR 27, 42, 68, 76, 97, 132, 217; CDALBS; CP 5, 6, 7; CSW; CWP; DA3; DAM MULT, POET; DLB 120; EWL 3; EXPP; MAL 5; MTCW 2; MTFW 2005; PFS 1, 15, 37; RGAL 4

Dove, Rita Frances
See Dove, Rita

Doveglion
See Villa, Jose Garcia

Dowell, Coleman 1925-1985 .... **CLC 60**
See also CA 25-28R; 117; CANR 10; DLB 130; GLL 2

Downing, Major Jack
See Smith, Seba

Dowson, Ernest (Christopher) 1867-1900 .... **TCLC 4**
See also CA 105; 150; DLB 19, 135; RGEL 2

Doyle, A. Conan
See Doyle, Sir Arthur Conan

Doyle, Sir Arthur Conan 1859-1930 ..... **SSC 12, 83, 95; TCLC 7; WLC 2**
See also AAYA 14; BPFB 1; BRWS 2; BYA 4, 5, 11; CA 104; 122; CANR 131; CD-BLB 1890-1914; CLR 106; CMW 4; DA; DA3; DAB; DAC; DAM MST, NOV; DLB 18, 70, 156, 178; EXPS; HGG; LAIT 2; MSW; MTCW 1, 2; MTFW 2005; NFS 28; RGEL 2; RGSF 2; RHW; SATA 24; SCFW 1, 2; SFW 4; SSFS 2; TEA; WCH; WLIT 4; WYA; YAW

Doyle, Conan
See Doyle, Sir Arthur Conan

Doyle, John
See Graves, Robert

Doyle, Roddy 1958- .... **CLC 81, 178**
See also AAYA 14; BRWS 5; CA 143; CANR 73, 128, 168, 200; CN 6, 7; DA3; DLB 194, 326; MTCW 2; MTFW 2005

Doyle, Sir A. Conan
See Doyle, Sir Arthur Conan

Dr. A
See Asimov, Isaac; Silverstein, Alvin; Silverstein, Virginia B.

Drabble, Margaret 1939- ...... **CLC 2, 3, 5, 8, 10, 22, 53, 129**
See also BRWS 4; CA 13-16R; CANR 18, 35, 63, 112, 131, 174, 218; CDBLB 1960 to Present; CN 1, 2, 3, 4, 5, 6, 7; CPW; DA3; DAB; DAC; DAM MST, NOV, POP; DLB 14, 155, 231; EWL 3; FW; MTCW 1, 2; MTFW 2005; RGEL 2; SATA 48; TEA

Drakulic, Slavenka
See Drakulic, Slavenka

Drakulic, Slavenka 1949- .... **CLC 173**
See also CA 144; CANR 92, 198; DLB 353

Drakulic-Ilic, Slavenka
See Drakulic, Slavenka

Drakulic-Ilic, Slavenka
See Drakulic, Slavenka

Drapier, M. B.
See Swift, Jonathan

Drayham, James
See Mencken, H. L.

Drayton, Michael 1563-1631 . LC 8, 161; PC 98
See also DAM POET; DLB 121; RGEL 2

Dreadstone, Carl
See Campbell, Ramsey

Dreiser, Theodore 1871-1945 .... SSC 30, 114; TCLC 10, 18, 35, 83; WLC 2
See also AMW; AMWC 2; AMWR 2; BYA 15, 16; CA 106; 132; CDALB 1865-1917; DA; DA3; DAC; DAM MST, NOV; DLB 9, 12, 102, 137, 361; DLBD 1; EWL 3; LAIT 2; LMFS 2; MAL 5; MTCW 1, 2; MTFW 2005; NFS 8, 17; RGAL 4; TUS

Dreiser, Theodore Herman Albert
See Dreiser, Theodore

Drexler, Rosalyn 1926- .... CLC 2, 6
See also CA 81-84; CAD; CANR 68, 124; CD 5, 6; CWD; MAL 5

Dreyer, Carl Theodor 1889-1968 ...... CLC 16
See also CA 116

Drieu la Rochelle, Pierre 1893-1945 .... TCLC 21
See also CA 117; 250; DLB 72; EWL 3; GFL 1789 to the Present

Drieu la Rochelle, Pierre-Eugene 1893-1945
See Drieu la Rochelle, Pierre

Drinkwater, John 1882-1937 .... TCLC 57
See also CA 109; 149; DLB 10, 19, 149; RGEL 2

Drop Shot
See Cable, George Washington

Droste-Hulshoff, Annette Freiin von 1797-1848 .... NCLC 3, 133
See also CDWLB 2; DLB 133; RGSF 2; RGWL 2, 3

Drummond, Walter
See Silverberg, Robert

Drummond, William Henry 1854-1907 .... TCLC 25
See also CA 160; DLB 92

Drummond de Andrade, Carlos 1902-1987 .... CLC 18; TCLC 139
See also CA 132; 123; DLB 307; EWL 3; LAW; RGWL 2, 3

Drummond of Hawthornden, William 1585-1649 .... LC 83
See also DLB 121, 213; RGEL 2

Drury, Allen (Stuart) 1918-1998 .... CLC 37
See also CA 57-60; 170; CANR 18, 52; CN 1, 2, 3, 4, 5, 6; INT CANR-18

Druse, Eleanor
See King, Stephen

Dryden, John 1631-1700 ..... DC 3; LC 3, 21, 115, 188; PC 25; WLC 2
See also BRW 2; BRWR 3; CDBLB 1660-1789; DA; DAB; DAC; DAM DRAM, MST, POET; DLB 80, 101, 131; EXPP; IDTP; LMFS 1; RGEL 2; TEA; WLIT 3

du Aime, Albert
See Wharton, William

du Aime, Albert William
See Wharton, William

du Bellay, Joachim 1524-1560 .... LC 92
See also DLB 327; GFL Beginnings to 1789; RGWL 2, 3

Duberman, Martin 1930- .... CLC 8
See also CA 1-4R; CAD; CANR 2, 63, 137, 174; CD 5, 6

Dubie, Norman (Evans) 1945- .... CLC 36
See also CA 69-72; CANR 12, 115; CP 3, 4, 5, 6, 7; DLB 120; PFS 12

Du Bois, W. E. B. 1868-1963 .... BLC 1:1; CLC 1, 2, 13, 64, 96; HR 1:2; TCLC 169; WLC 2
See also AAYA 40; AFAW 1, 2; AMWC 1; AMWS 2; BW 1, 3; CA 85-88; CANR 34, 82, 132; CDALB 1865-1917; DA; DA3; DAC; DAM MST, MULT, NOV; DLB 47, 50, 91, 246, 284; EWL 3; EXPP; LAIT 2; LMFS 2; MAL 5; MTCW 1, 2; MTFW 2005; NCFS 1; PFS 13; RGAL 4; SATA 42

Du Bois, William Edward Burghardt
See Du Bois, W. E. B.

Dubos, Jean-Baptiste 1670-1742 .... LC 197

Dubus, Andre 1936-1999 ..... CLC 13, 36, 97; SSC 15, 118
See also AMWS 7; CA 21-24R; 177; CANR 17; CN 5, 6; CSW; DLB 130; INT CANR-17; RGAL 4; SSFS 10; TCLE 1:1

Duca Minimo
See D'Annunzio, Gabriele

Ducharme, Rejean 1941- .... CLC 74
See also CA 165; DLB 60

du Chatelet, Emilie 1706-1749 .... LC 96
See also DLB 313

Duchen, Claire .... CLC 65

Duck, Stephen 1705(?)-1756 .... PC 89
See also DLB 95; RGEL 2

Duclos, Charles Pinot- 1704-1772 .... LC 1
See also GFL Beginnings to 1789

Ducornet, Erica 1943- .... CLC 232
See also CA 37-40R; CANR 14, 34, 54, 82; SATA 7

Ducornet, Rikki
See Ducornet, Erica

Dudek, Louis 1918-2001 .... CLC 11, 19
See also CA 45-48; 215; CAAS 14; CANR 1; CP 1, 2, 3, 4, 5, 6, 7; DLB 88

Duerrematt, Friedrich
See Durrenmatt, Friedrich

Duffy, Bruce 1953(?)- .... CLC 50
See also CA 172

Duffy, Maureen 1933- .... CLC 37
See also CA 25-28R; CANR 33, 68; CBD; CN 1, 2, 3, 4, 5, 6; CP 5, 6, 7; CWD; CWP; DFS 15; DLB 14, 310; FW; MTCW 1

Duffy, Maureen Patricia
See Duffy, Maureen

Du Fu
See Tu Fu

Dugan, Alan 1923-2003 .... CLC 2, 6
See also CA 81-84; 220; CANR 119; CP 1, 2, 3, 4, 5, 6, 7; DLB 5; MAL 5; PFS 10

du Gard, Roger Martin
See Martin du Gard, Roger

du Guillet, Pernette 1520(?)-1545 ..... LC 190
See also DLB 327

Duhamel, Georges 1884-1966 .... CLC 8
See also CA 81-84; 25-28R; CANR 35; DLB 65; EWL 3; GFL 1789 to the Present; MTCW 1

du Hault, Jean
See Grindel, Eugene

Dujardin, Edouard (Emile Louis) 1861-1949 .... TCLC 13
See also CA 109; DLB 123

Duke, Raoul
See Thompson, Hunter S.

Dulles, John Foster 1888-1959 .... TCLC 72
See also CA 115; 149

Dumas, Alexandre (pere) 1802-1870 .... NCLC 11, 71; WLC 2
See also AAYA 22; BYA 3; CLR 134; DA; DA3; DAB; DAC; DAM MST, NOV; DLB 119, 192; EW 6; GFL 1789 to the Present; LAIT 1, 2; NFS 14, 19; RGWL 2, 3; SATA 18; TWA; WCH

Dumas, Alexandre (fils) 1824-1895 ...... DC 1; NCLC 9
See also DLB 192; GFL 1789 to the Present; RGWL 2, 3

Dumas, Claudine
See Malzberg, Barry N(athaniel)

Dumas, Henry L. 1934-1968 . BLC 2:1; CLC 6, 62; SSC 107
See also BW 1; CA 85-88; DLB 41; RGAL 4

du Maurier, Daphne 1907-1989 .. CLC 6, 11, 59; SSC 18, 129; TCLC 209
See also AAYA 37; BPFB 1; BRWS 3; CA 5-8R; 128; CANR 6, 55; CMW 4; CN 1, 2, 3, 4; CPW; DA3; DAB; DAC; DAM MST, POP; DLB 191; GL 2; HGG; LAIT 3; MSW; MTCW 1, 2; NFS 12; RGEL 2; RGSF 2; RHW; SATA 27; SATA-Obit 60; SSFS 14, 16; TEA

Du Maurier, George 1834-1896 ..... NCLC 86
See also DLB 153, 178; RGEL 2

Dunbar, Alice
See Nelson, Alice Ruth Moore Dunbar

Dunbar, Alice Moore
See Nelson, Alice Ruth Moore Dunbar

Dunbar, Paul Laurence 1872-1906 .... BLC 1:1; PC 5; SSC 8; TCLC 2, 12; WLC 2
See also AAYA 75; AFAW 1, 2; AMWS 2; BW 1, 3; CA 104; 124; CANR 79; CDALB 1865-1917; DA; DA3; DAC; DAM MST, MULT, POET; DLB 50, 54, 78; EXPP; MAL 5; PFS 33, 40; RGAL 4; SATA 34

Dunbar, William 1460(?)-1520(?) .... LC 20; PC 67
See also BRWS 8; DLB 132, 146; RGEL 2

Dunbar-Nelson, Alice
See Nelson, Alice Ruth Moore Dunbar

Dunbar-Nelson, Alice Moore
See Nelson, Alice Ruth Moore Dunbar

Duncan, Dora Angela
See Duncan, Isadora

Duncan, Isadora 1877(?)-1927 .... TCLC 68
See also CA 118; 149

Duncan, Lois 1934- .... CLC 26
See also AAYA 4, 34; BYA 6, 8; CA 1-4R; CANR 2, 23, 36, 111; CLR 29, 129; JRDA; MAICYA 1, 2; MAICYAS 1; MTFW 2005; SAAS 2; SATA 1, 36, 75, 133, 141, 219; SATA-Essay 141; WYA; YAW

Duncan, Robert 1919-1988 ... CLC 1, 2, 4, 7, 15, 41, 55; PC 2, 75
See also BG 1:2; CA 9-12R; 124; CANR 28, 62; CP 1, 2, 3, 4; DAM POET; DLB 5, 16, 193; EWL 3; MAL 5; MTCW 1, 2; MTFW 2005; PFS 13; RGAL 4; WP

Duncan, Sara Jeannette 1861-1922 .... TCLC 60
See also CA 157; DLB 92

Dunlap, William 1766-1839 ..... NCLC 2, 244
See also DLB 30, 37, 59; RGAL 4

Dunn, Douglas (Eaglesham) 1942- .... CLC 6, 40
See also BRWS 10; CA 45-48; CANR 2, 33, 126; CP 1, 2, 3, 4, 5, 6, 7; DLB 40; MTCW 1

Dunn, Katherine 1945- .... CLC 71
See also CA 33-36R; CANR 72; HGG; MTCW 2; MTFW 2005

Dunn, Stephen 1939- .... CLC 36, 206
See also AMWS 11; CA 33-36R; CANR 12, 48, 53, 105; CP 3, 4, 5, 6, 7; DLB 105; PFS 21

Dunn, Stephen Elliott
See Dunn, Stephen

Everett, Percival L.
See Everett, Percival

Everson, R(onald) G(ilmour)
1903-1992 .... **CLC 27**
See also CA 17-20R; CP 1, 2, 3, 4; DLB 88

Everson, William 1912-1994 .... **CLC 1, 5, 14**
See also BG 1:2; CA 9-12R; 145; CANR 20; CP 1; DLB 5, 16, 212; MTCW 1

Everson, William Oliver
See Everson, William

Evtushenko, Evgenii Aleksandrovich
See Yevtushenko, Yevgenyn

Ewart, Gavin (Buchanan)
1916-1995 .... **CLC 13, 46**
See also BRWS 7; CA 89-92; 150; CANR 17, 46; CP 1, 2, 3, 4, 5, 6; DLB 40; MTCW 1

Ewers, Hanns Heinz 1871-1943 ..... **TCLC 12**
See also CA 109; 149

Ewing, Frederick R.
See Sturgeon, Theodore (Hamilton)

Exley, Frederick (Earl) 1929-1992 .... **CLC 6, 11**
See also AITN 2; BPFB 1; CA 81-84; 138; CANR 117; DLB 143; DLBY 1981

Eynhardt, Guillermo
See Quiroga, Horacio (Sylvestre)

Ezekiel, Nissim (Moses) 1924-2004 .. **CLC 61**
See also CA 61-64; 223; CP 1, 2, 3, 4, 5, 6, 7; DLB 323; EWL 3

Ezekiel, Tish O'Dowd 1943- .... **CLC 34**
See also CA 129

Fadeev, Aleksandr Aleksandrovich
See Bulgya, Alexander Alexandrovich

Fadeev, Alexandr Alexandrovich
See Bulgya, Alexander Alexandrovich

Fadeyev, A.
See Bulgya, Alexander Alexandrovich

Fadeyev, Alexander
See Bulgya, Alexander Alexandrovich

Fagen, Donald 1948- .... **CLC 26**

Fainzil'berg, Il'ia Arnol'dovich
See Fainzilberg, Ilya Arnoldovich

Fainzilberg, Ilya Arnoldovich
1897-1937 .... **TCLC 21**
See also CA 120; 165; DLB 272; EWL 3

Fair, Ronald L. 1932- .... **CLC 18**
See also BW 1; CA 69-72; CANR 25; DLB 33

Fairbairn, Roger
See Carr, John Dickson

Fairbairns, Zoe (Ann) 1948- .... **CLC 32**
See also CA 103; CANR 21, 85; CN 4, 5, 6, 7

Fairfield, Flora
See Alcott, Louisa May

Falco, Gian
See Papini, Giovanni

Falconer, James
See Kirkup, James

Falconer, Kenneth
See Kornbluth, C(yril) M.

Falkland, Samuel
See Heijermans, Herman

Fallaci, Oriana 1930-2006 .... **CLC 11, 110**
See also CA 77-80; 253; CANR 15, 58, 134; FW; MTCW 1

Faludi, Susan 1959- .... **CLC 140**
See also CA 138; CANR 126, 194; FW; MTCW 2; MTFW 2005; NCFS 3

Faludy, George 1913- .... **CLC 42**
See also CA 21-24R

Faludy, Gyoergy
See Faludy, George

Fanon, Frantz 1925-1961 ...... **BLC 1:2; CLC 74; TCLC 188**
See also BW 1; CA 116; 89-92; DAM MULT; DLB 296; LMFS 2; WLIT 2

Fanshawe, Ann 1625-1680 .... **LC 11**

Fante, John (Thomas) 1911-1983 .... **CLC 60; SSC 65**
See also AMWS 11; CA 69-72; 109; CANR 23, 104; DLB 130; DLBY 1983

Farah, Nuruddin 1945- .. **BLC 1:2, 2:2; CLC 53, 137**
See also AFW; BW 2, 3; CA 106; CANR 81, 148; CDWLB 3; CN 4, 5, 6, 7; DAM MULT; DLB 125; EWL 3; WLIT 2

Fardusi
See Ferdowsi, Abu'l Qasem

Fargue, Leon-Paul 1876(?)-1947 .... **TCLC 11**
See also CA 109; CANR 107; DLB 258; EWL 3

Farigoule, Louis
See Romains, Jules

Farina, Richard 1936(?)-1966 .... **CLC 9**
See also CA 81-84; 25-28R

Farley, Walter (Lorimer)
1915-1989 .... **CLC 17**
See also AAYA 58; BYA 14; CA 17-20R; CANR 8, 29, 84; DLB 22; JRDA; MAI-CYA 1, 2; SATA 2, 43, 132; YAW

Farmer, Philip Jose
See Farmer, Philip Jose

Farmer, Philip Jose 1918-2009 .... **CLC 1, 19, 299**
See also AAYA 28; BPFB 1; CA 1-4R; 283; CANR 4, 35, 111, 220; DLB 8; MTCW 1; SATA 93; SATA-Obit 201; SCFW 1, 2; SFW 4

Farmer, Philipe Jos
See Farmer, Philip Jose

Farquhar, George 1677-1707 . **DC 38; LC 21**
See also BRW 2; DAM DRAM; DLB 84; RGEL 2

Farrell, James Gordon
See Farrell, J.G.

Farrell, James T(homas) 1904-1979 . **CLC 1, 4, 8, 11, 66; SSC 28; TCLC 228**
See also AMW; BPFB 1; CA 5-8R; 89-92; CANR 9, 61; CN 1, 2; DLB 4, 9, 86; DLBD 2; EWL 3; MAL 5; MTCW 1, 2; MTFW 2005; RGAL 4

Farrell, J.G. 1935-1979 .... **CLC 6**
See also CA 73-76; 89-92; CANR 36; CN 1, 2; DLB 14, 271, 326; MTCW 1; RGEL 2; RHW; WLIT 4

Farrell, M. J.
See Keane, Mary Nesta

Farrell, Warren (Thomas) 1943- ...... **CLC 70**
See also CA 146; CANR 120

Farren, Richard J.
See Betjeman, John

Farren, Richard M.
See Betjeman, John

Farrugia, Mario Benedetti
See Bentley, Eric

Farrugia, Mario Orlando Hardy Hamlet Brenno Benedetti
See Benedetti, Mario

Fasshinder, Rainer Werner
1946-1982 .... **CLC 20**
See also CA 93-96; 106; CANR 31

Fast, Howard 1914-2003 .... **CLC 23, 131**
See also AAYA 16; BPFB 1; CA 1-4R, 181; 214; CAAE 181; CAAS 18; CANR 1, 33, 54, 75, 98, 140; CMW 4; CN 1, 2, 3, 4, 5, 6, 7; CPW; DAM NOV; DLB 9; INT CANR-33; LATS 1:1; MAL 5; MTCW 2; MTFW 2005; NFS 35; RHW; SATA 7; SATA-Essay 107; TCWW 1, 2; YAW

Faulcon, Robert
See Holdstock, Robert

Faulkner, William 1897-1962 .... **CLC 1, 3, 6, 8, 9, 11, 14, 18, 28, 52, 68; SSC 1, 35, 42, 92, 97; TCLC 141; WLC 2**
See also AAYA 7; AMW; AMWR 1; BPFB 1; BYA 5, 15; CA 81-84; CANR 33; CDALB 1929-1941; DA; DA3; DAB; DAC; DAM MST, NOV; DLB 9, 11, 44, 102, 316, 330; DLBD 2; DLBY 1986, 1997; EWL 3; EXPN; EXPS; GL 2; LAIT 2; LATS 1:1; LMFS 2; MAL 5; MTCW 1, 2; MTFW 2005; NFS 4, 8, 13, 24, 33, 38; RGAL 4; RGSF 2; SSFS 2, 5, 6, 12, 27; TUS

Faulkner, William Cuthbert
See Faulkner, William

Fauset, Jessie Redmon
1882(?)-1961 ...... **BLC 1:2; CLC 19, 54; HR 1:2**
See also AFAW 2; BW 1; CA 109; CANR 83; DAM MULT; DLB 51; FW; LMFS 2; MAL 5; MBL

Faust, Frederick 1892-1944 .... **TCLC 49**
See also BPFB 1; CA 108; 152; CANR 143; DAM POP; DLB 256; TCWW 1, 2; TUS

Faust, Frederick Schiller
See Faust, Frederick

Faust, Irvin 1924- .... **CLC 8**
See also CA 33-36R; CANR 28, 67; CN 1, 2, 3, 4, 5, 6, 7; DLB 2, 28, 218, 278; DLBY 1980

Fawkes, Guy
See Benchley, Robert (Charles)

Fearing, Kenneth 1902-1961 .... **CLC 51**
See also CA 93-96; CANR 59; CMW 4; DLB 9; MAL 5; RGAL 4

Fearing, Kenneth Flexner
See Fearing, Kenneth

Fecamps, Elise
See Creasey, John

Federman, Raymond 1928-2009 .. **CLC 6, 47**
See also CA 17-20R, 208; 292; CAAE 208; CAAS 8; CANR 10, 43, 83, 108; CN 3, 4, 5, 6; DLBY 1980

Federspiel, J.F. 1931-2007 .... **CLC 42**
See also CA 146; 257

Federspiel, Juerg F.
See Federspiel, J.F.

Federspiel, Jurg F.
See Federspiel, J.F.

Feiffer, Jules 1929- .... **CLC 2, 8, 64**
See also AAYA 3, 62; CA 17-20R; CAD; CANR 30, 59, 129, 161, 192; CD 5, 6; DAM DRAM; DLB 7, 44; INT CANR-30; MTCW 1; SATA 8, 61, 111, 157, 201

Feiffer, Jules Ralph
See Feiffer, Jules

Feige, Hermann Albert Otto Maximilian
See Traven, B.

Fei-Kan, Li
See Jin, Ba

Feinberg, David B. 1956-1994 .... **CLC 59**
See also CA 135; 147

Feinstein, Elaine 1930- .... **CLC 36**
See also CA 69-72; CAAS 1; CANR 31, 68, 121, 162; CN 3, 4, 5, 6, 7; CP 2, 3, 4, 5, 6, 7; CWP; DLB 14, 40; MTCW 1

Feke, Gilbert David .... **CLC 65**

Feldman, Irving (Mordecai) 1928- ..... **CLC 7**
See also CA 1-4R; CANR 1; CP 1, 2, 3, 4, 5, 6, 7; DLB 169; TCLE 1:1

Felix-Tchicaya, Gerald
See Tchicaya, Gerald Felix

Fellini, Federico 1920-1993 .... **CLC 16, 85**
See also CA 65-68; 143; CANR 33

Felltham, Owen 1602(?)-1668 .... **LC 92**
See also DLB 126, 151

Felsen, Henry Gregor 1916-1995 ..... **CLC 17**
See also CA 1-4R; 180; CANR 1; SAAS 2; SATA 1

Friedman, Bruce Jay 1930- ...... **CLC 3, 5, 56**
    See also CA 9-12R; CAD; CANR 25, 52,
    101, 212; CD 5, 6; CN 1, 2, 3, 4, 5, 6, 7;
    DLB 2, 28, 244; INT CANR-25; MAL 5;
    SSFS 18

Friel, Brian 1929- .. **CLC 5, 42, 59, 115, 253;**
    DC 8; SSC 76
    See also BRWS 5; CA 21-24R; CANR 33,
    69, 131; CBD; CD 5, 6; DFS 11; DLB
    13, 319; EWL 3; MTCW 1; RGEL 2; TEA

Friis-Baastad, Babbis Ellinor
    1921-1970 .... **CLC 12**
    See also CA 17-20R; 134; SATA 7

Frisch, Max 1911-1991 ...... **CLC 3, 9, 14, 18,**
    32, 44; TCLC 121
    See also CA 85-88; 134; CANR 32, 74; CD-
    WLB 2; DAM DRAM, NOV; DFS 25;
    DLB 69, 124; EW 13; EWL 3; MTCW 1,
    2; MTFW 2005; RGHL; RGWL 2, 3

Froehlich, Peter
    See Gay, Peter

Fromentin, Eugene (Samuel Auguste)
    1820-1876 .... **NCLC 10, 125**
    See also DLB 123; GFL 1789 to the Present

Frost, Frederick
    See Faust, Frederick

Frost, Robert 1874-1963 . **CLC 1, 3, 4, 9, 10,**
    13, 15, 26, 34, 44; PC 1, 39, 71; TCLC
    236; WLC 2
    See also AAYA 21; AMW; AMWR 1; CA
    89-92; CANR 33; CDALB 1917-1929;
    CLR 67; DA; DA3; DAB; DAC; DAM
    MST, POET; DLB 54, 284, 342; DLBD
    7; EWL 3; EXPP; MAL 5; MTCW 1, 2;
    MTFW 2005; PAB; PFS 1, 2, 3, 4, 5, 6,
    7, 10, 13, 32, 35, 41; RGAL 4; SATA 14;
    TUS; WP; WYA

Frost, Robert Lee
    See Frost, Robert

Froude, James Anthony
    1818-1894 .... **NCLC 43**
    See also DLB 18, 57, 144

Froy, Herald
    See Waterhouse, Keith

Fry, Christopher 1907-2005 .. **CLC 2, 10, 14;**
    DC 36
    See also BRWS 3; CA 17-20R; 240; CAAS
    23; CANR 9, 30, 74, 132; CBD; CD 5, 6;
    CP 1, 2, 3, 4, 5, 6, 7; DAM DRAM; DLB
    13; EWL 3; MTCW 1, 2; MTFW 2005;
    RGEL 2; SATA 66; TEA

Frye, (Herman) Northrop
    1912-1991 .... **CLC 24, 70; TCLC 165**
    See also CA 5-8R; 133; CANR 8, 37; DLB
    67, 68, 246; EWL 3; MTCW 1, 2; MTFW
    2005; RGAL 4; TWA

Fuchs, Daniel 1909-1993 .... **CLC 8, 22**
    See also CA 81-84; 142; CAAS 5; CANR
    40; CN 1, 2, 3, 4, 5; DLB 9, 26, 28;
    DLBY 1993; MAL 5

Fuchs, Daniel 1934- .... **CLC 34**
    See also CA 37-40R; CANR 14, 48

Fuentes, Carlos 1928- .. **CLC 3, 8, 10, 13, 22,**
    41, 60, 113, 288; HLC 1; SSC 24, 125;
    WLC 2
    See also AAYA 4, 45; AITN 2; BPFB 1;
    CA 69-72; CANR 10, 32, 68, 104, 138,
    197; CDWLB 3; CWW 2; DA; DA3;
    DAB; DAC; DAM MST, MULT, NOV;
    DLB 113; DNFS 2; EWL 3; HW 1, 2;
    LAIT 3; LATS 1:2; LAW; LAWS 1;
    LMFS 2; MTCW 1, 2; MTFW 2005; NFS
    8; RGSF 2; RGWL 2, 3; TWA; WLIT 1

Fuentes, Gregorio Lopez y
    See Lopez y Fuentes, Gregorio

Fuentes Macias, Carlos Manuel
    See Fuentes, Carlos

Fuertes, Gloria 1918-1998 .... **PC 27**
    See also CA 178, 180; DLB 108; HW 2;
    SATA 115

Fugard, Athol 1932- .... **CLC 5, 9, 14, 25, 40,**
    80, 211; DC 3
    See also AAYA 17; AFW; BRWS 15; CA
    85-88; CANR 32, 54, 118; CD 5, 6; DAM
    DRAM; DFS 3, 6, 10, 24; DLB 225;
    DNFS 1, 2; EWL 3; LATS 1:2; MTCW 1;
    MTFW 2005; RGEL 2; WLIT 2

Fugard, Harold Athol
    See Fugard, Athol

Fugard, Sheila 1932- .... **CLC 48**
    See also CA 125

Fuguet, Alberto 1964- .... **CLC 308**
    See also CA 170; CANR 144

Fujiwara no Teika 1162-1241 .... **CMLC 73**
    See also DLB 203

Fukuyama, Francis 1952- .... **CLC 131**
    See also CA 140; CANR 72, 125, 170

Fuller, Charles (H.), (Jr.) 1939- ..... **BLC 1:2;**
    CLC 25; DC 1
    See also BW 2; CA 108; 112; CAD; CANR
    87; CD 5, 6; DAM DRAM, MULT; DFS
    8; DLB 38, 266; EWL 3; INT CA-112;
    MAL 5; MTCW 1

Fuller, Henry Blake 1857-1929 .... **TCLC 103**
    See also CA 108; 177; DLB 12; RGAL 4

Fuller, John (Leopold) 1937- .... **CLC 62**
    See also CA 21-24R; CANR 9, 44; CP 1, 2,
    3, 4, 5, 6, 7; DLB 40

Fuller, Margaret 1810-1850 ...... **NCLC 5, 50,**
    211
    See also AMWS 2; CDALB 1640-1865;
    DLB 1, 59, 73, 183, 223, 239; FW; LMFS
    1; SATA 25

Fuller, Roy (Broadbent) 1912-1991 ... **CLC 4,**
    28
    See also BRWS 7; CA 5-8R; 135; CAAS
    10; CANR 53, 83; CN 1, 2, 3, 4, 5; CP 1,
    2, 3, 4, 5; CWRI 5; DLB 15, 20; EWL 3;
    RGEL 2; SATA 87

Fuller, Sarah Margaret
    See Fuller, Margaret

Fuller, Thomas 1608-1661 .... **LC 111**
    See also DLB 151

Fulton, Alice 1952- .... **CLC 52**
    See also CA 116; CANR 57, 88, 200; CP 5,
    6, 7; CWP; DLB 193; PFS 25

Fundi
    See Baraka, Amiri

Furey, Michael
    See Ward, Arthur Henry Sarsfield

Furphy, Joseph 1843-1912 .... **TCLC 25**
    See also CA 163; DLB 230; EWL 3; RGEL
    2

Furst, Alan 1941- .... **CLC 255**
    See also CA 69-72; CANR 12, 34, 59, 102,
    159, 193; DLB 350; DLBY 01

Fuson, Robert H(enderson) 1927- .... **CLC 70**
    See also CA 89-92; CANR 103

Fussell, Paul 1924- .... **CLC 74**
    See also BEST 90:1; CA 17-20R; CANR 8,
    21, 35, 69, 135; INT CANR-21; MTCW
    1, 2; MTFW 2005

Futabatei, Shimei 1864-1909 .... **TCLC 44**
    See also CA 162; DLB 180; EWL 3; MJW

Futabatei Shimei
    See Futabatei, Shimei

Futrelle, Jacques 1875-1912 .... **TCLC 19**
    See also CA 113; 155; CMW 4

GAB
    See Russell, George William

Gaberman, Judie Angell
    See Angell, Judie

Gaboriau, Emile 1835-1873 .... **NCLC 14**
    See also CMW 4; MSW

Gadda, Carlo Emilio 1893-1973 ...... **CLC 11;**
    TCLC 144
    See also CA 89-92; DLB 177; EWL 3;
    WLIT 7

Gaddis, William 1922-1998 ... **CLC 1, 3, 6, 8,**
    10, 19, 43, 86
    See also AMWS 4; BPFB 1; CA 17-20R;
    172; CANR 21, 48, 148; CN 1, 2, 3, 4, 5,
    6; DLB 2, 278; EWL 3; MAL 5; MTCW
    1, 2; MTFW 2005; RGAL 4

Gage, Walter
    See Inge, William (Motter)

Gaiman, Neil 1960- .... **CLC 195, 319**
    See also AAYA 19, 42, 82; CA 133; CANR
    81, 129, 188; CLR 109; DLB 261; HGG;
    MTFW 2005; SATA 85, 146, 197, 228;
    SFW 4; SUFW 2

Gaiman, Neil Richard
    See Gaiman, Neil

Gaines, Ernest J. 1933- ..... **BLC 1:2; CLC 3,**
    11, 18, 86, 181, 300; SSC 68, 137
    See also AAYA 18; AFAW 1, 2; AITN 1;
    BPFB 2; BW 2, 3; BYA 6; CA 9-12R;
    CANR 6, 24, 42, 75, 126; CDALB 1968-
    1988; CLR 62; CN 1, 2, 3, 4, 5, 6, 7;
    CSW; DA3; DAM MULT; DLB 2, 33,
    152; DLBY 1980; EWL 3; EXPN; LAIT
    5; LATS 1:2; MAL 5; MTCW 1, 2;
    MTFW 2005; NFS 5, 7, 16; RGAL 4;
    RGSF 2; RHW; SATA 86; SSFS 5; YAW

Gaines, Ernest James
    See Gaines, Ernest J.

Gaitskill, Mary 1954- .... **CLC 69, 300**
    See also CA 128; CANR 61, 152, 208; DLB
    244; TCLE 1:1

Gaitskill, Mary Lawrence
    See Gaitskill, Mary

Gaius Suetonius Tranquillus
    See Suetonius

Galdos, Benito Perez
    See Perez Galdos, Benito

Gale, Zona 1874-1938 .... **DC 30; SSC 159;**
    TCLC 7
    See also CA 105; 153; CANR 84; DAM
    DRAM; DFS 17; DLB 9, 78, 228; RGAL
    4

Galeano, Eduardo 1940- ... **CLC 72; HLCS 1**
    See also CA 29-32R; CANR 13, 32, 100,
    163, 211; HW 1

Galeano, Eduardo Hughes
    See Galeano, Eduardo

Galiano, Juan Valera y Alcala
    See Valera y Alcala-Galiano, Juan

Galilei, Galileo 1564-1642 .... **LC 45, 188**

Gallagher, Tess 1943- .... **CLC 18, 63; PC 9**
    See also CA 106; CP 3, 4, 5, 6, 7; CWP;
    DAM POET; DLB 120, 212, 244; PFS 16

Gallant, Mavis 1922- ..... **CLC 7, 18, 38, 172,**
    288; SSC 5, 78
    See also CA 69-72; CANR 29, 69, 117;
    CCA 1; CN 1, 2, 3, 4, 5, 6, 7; DAC; DAM
    MST; DLB 53; EWL 3; MTCW 1, 2;
    MTFW 2005; RGEL 2; RGSF 2

Gallant, Roy A(rthur) 1924- .... **CLC 17**
    See also CA 5-8R; CANR 4, 29, 54, 117;
    CLR 30; MAICYA 1, 2; SATA 4, 68, 110

Gallico, Paul 1897-1976 .... **CLC 2**
    See also AITN 1; CA 5-8R; 69-72; CANR
    23; CN 1, 2; DLB 9, 171; FANT; MAI-
    CYA 1, 2; SATA 13

Gallico, Paul William
    See Gallico, Paul

Gallo, Max Louis 1932- .... **CLC 95**
    See also CA 85-88

Gallois, Lucien
    See Desnos, Robert

Gallup, Ralph
    See Whitemore, Hugh (John)

Galsworthy, John 1867-1933 .... **SSC 22;**
    TCLC 1, 45; WLC 2
    See also BRW 6; CA 104; 141; CANR 75;
    CDBLB 1890-1914; DA; DA3; DAB;
    DAC; DAM DRAM, MST, NOV; DLB
    10, 34, 98, 162, 330; DLBD 16; EWL 3;
    MTCW 2; RGEL 2; SSFS 3; TEA

Galt, John 1779-1839 .... **NCLC 1, 110**
See also DLB 99, 116, 159; RGEL 2; RGSF
2

Galvin, James 1951- .... **CLC 38**
See also CA 108; CANR 26

Gamboa, Federico 1864-1939 .... **TCLC 36**
See also CA 167; HW 2; LAW

Gandhi, M. K.
See Gandhi, Mohandas Karamchand

Gandhi, Mahatma
See Gandhi, Mohandas Karamchand

Gandhi, Mohandas Karamchand
1869-1948 .... **TCLC 59**
See also CA 121; 132; DA3; DAM MULT;
DLB 323; MTCW 1, 2

Gann, Ernest Kellogg 1910-1991 ..... **CLC 23**
See also AITN 1; BPFB 2; CA 1-4R; 136;
CANR 1, 83; RHW

Gao Xingjian
See Xingjian, Gao

Garber, Eric
See Holleran, Andrew

Garber, Esther
See Lee, Tanith

Garcia, Cristina 1958- .... **CLC 76**
See also AMWS 11; CA 141; CANR 73,
130, 172; CN 7; DLB 292; DNFS 1; EWL
3; HW 2; LLW; MTFW 2005; NFS 38;
SATA 208

Garcia Lorca, Federico 1898-1936 ...... **DC 2;**
HLC 2; PC 3; TCLC 1, 7, 49, 181,
197; WLC 2
See also AAYA 46; CA 104; 131; CANR
81; DA; DA3; DAB; DAC; DAM DRAM,
MST, MULT, POET; DFS 4; DLB 108;
EW 11; EWL 3; HW 1, 2; LATS 1:2;
MTCW 1, 2; MTFW 2005; PFS 20, 31,
38; RGWL 2, 3; TWA; WP

Garcia Marquez, Gabriel 1928- .... **CLC 2, 3,**
8, 10, 15, 27, 47, 55, 68, 170, 254; HLC
1; SSC 8, 83, 162; WLC 3
See also AAYA 3, 33; BEST 89:1, 90:4;
BPFB 2; BYA 12, 16; CA 33-36R; CANR
10, 28, 50, 75, 82, 128, 204; CDWLB 3;
CPW; CWW 2; DA; DA3; DAB; DAC;
DAM MST, MULT, NOV, POP; DLB 113,
330; DNFS 1, 2; EWL 3; EXPN; EXPS;
HW 1, 2; LAIT 2; LATS 1:2; LAW;
LAWS 1; LMFS 2; MTCW 1, 2; MTFW
2005; NCFS 3; NFS 1, 5, 10; RGSF 2;
RGWL 2, 3; SSFS 1, 6, 16, 21; TWA;
WLIT 1

Garcia Marquez, Gabriel Jose
See Garcia Marquez, Gabriel

Garcia Marquez, Gabriel Jose
See Garcia Marquez, Gabriel

Garcilaso de la Vega, El Inca
1539-1616 .... **HLCS 1; LC 127**
See also DLB 318; LAW

Gard, Janice
See Latham, Jean Lee

Gard, Roger Martin du
See Martin du Gard, Roger

Gardam, Jane 1928- .... **CLC 43**
See also CA 49-52; CANR 2, 18, 33, 54,
106, 167, 206; CLR 12; DLB 14, 161,
231; MAICYA 1, 2; MTCW 1; SAAS 9;
SATA 39, 76, 130; SATA-Brief 28; YAW

Gardam, Jane Mary
See Gardam, Jane

Gardens, S. S.
See Snodgrass, W. D.

Gardner, Herb(ert George)
1934-2003 .... **CLC 44**
See also CA 149; 220; CAD; CANR 119;
CD 5, 6; DFS 18, 20

Gardner, John, Jr. 1933-1982 ... **CLC 2, 3, 5,**
7, 8, 10, 18, 28, 34; SSC 7; TCLC 195
See also AAYA 45; AITN 1; AMWS 6;
BPFB 2; CA 65-68; 107; CANR 33, 73;
CDALBS; CN 2, 3; CPW; DA3; DAM
NOV, POP; DLB 2; DLBY 1982; EWL 3;
FANT; LATS 1:2; MAL 5; MTCW 1, 2;
MTFW 2005; NFS 3; RGAL 4; RGSF 2;
SATA 40; SATA-Obit 31; SSFS 8

Gardner, John 1926-2007 .... **CLC 30**
See also CA 103; 263; CANR 15, 69, 127,
183; CMW 4; CPW; DAM POP; MTCW
2

Gardner, John Champlin, Jr.
See Gardner, John, Jr.

Gardner, John Edmund
See Gardner, John

Gardner, Miriam
See Bradley, Marion Zimmer

Gardner, Noel
See Kuttner, Henry

Gardons, S.S.
See Snodgrass, W. D.

Garfield, Leon 1921-1996 .... **CLC 12**
See also AAYA 8, 69; BYA 1, 3; CA 17-
20R; 152; CANR 38, 41, 78; CLR 21,
166; DLB 161; JRDA; MAICYA 1, 2;
MAICYAS 1; SATA 1, 32, 76; SATA-Obit
90; TEA; WYA; YAW

Garland, (Hannibal) Hamlin
1860-1940 ... **SSC 18, 117; TCLC 3, 256**
See also CA 104; DLB 12, 71, 78, 186;
MAL 5; RGAL 4; RGSF 2; TCWW 1, 2

Garneau, (Hector de) Saint-Denys
1912-1943 .... **TCLC 13**
See also CA 111; DLB 88

Garner, Alan 1934- .... **CLC 17**
See also AAYA 18; BYA 3, 5; CA 73-76,
178; CAAE 178; CANR 15, 64, 134; CLR
20, 130; CPW; DAB; DAM POP; DLB
161, 261; FANT; MAICYA 1, 2; MTCW
1, 2; MTFW 2005; SATA 18, 69; SATA-
Essay 108; SUFW 1, 2; YAW

Garner, Helen 1942- .... **SSC 135**
See also CA 124; 127; CANR 71, 206; CN
4, 5, 6, 7; DLB 325; GLL 2; RGSF 2

Garner, Hugh 1913-1979 .... **CLC 13**
See also CA 69-72; CANR 31; CCA 1; CN
1, 2; DLB 68

Garnett, David 1892-1981 .... **CLC 3**
See also CA 5-8R; 103; CANR 17, 79; CN
1, 2; DLB 34; FANT; MTCW 2; RGEL 2;
SFW 4; SUFW 1

Garnier, Robert c. 1545-1590 .... **LC 119**
See also DLB 327; GFL Beginnings to 1789

Garrett, George 1929-2008 ... **CLC 3, 11, 51;**
SSC 30
See also AMWS 7; BPFB 2; CA 1-4R, 202;
272; CAAE 202; CAAS 5; CANR 1, 42,
67, 109, 199; CN 1, 2, 3, 4, 5, 6, 7; CP 1,
2, 3, 4, 5, 6, 7; CSW; DLB 2, 5, 130, 152;
DLBY 1983

Garrett, George P.
See Garrett, George

Garrett, George Palmer
See Garrett, George

Garrett, George Palmer, Jr.
See Garrett, George

Garrick, David 1717-1779 .... **LC 15, 156**
See also DAM DRAM; DLB 84, 213;
RGEL 2

Garrigue, Jean 1914-1972 .... **CLC 2, 8**
See also CA 5-8R; 37-40R; CANR 20; CP
1; MAL 5

Garrison, Frederick
See Sinclair, Upton

Garrison, William Lloyd
1805-1879 .... **NCLC 149**
See also CDALB 1640-1865; DLB 1, 43,
235

Garro, Elena 1920(?)-1998 .. **HLCS 1; TCLC**
153
See also CA 131; 169; CWW 2; DLB 145;
EWL 3; HW 1; LAWS 1; WLIT 1

Garth, Will
See Hamilton, Edmond; Kuttner, Henry

Garvey, Marcus (Moziah, Jr.)
1887-1940 ..... **BLC 1:2; HR 1:2; TCLC**
41
See also BW 1; CA 120; 124; CANR 79;
DAM MULT; DLB 345

Gary, Romain
See Kacew, Romain

Gascar, Pierre
See Fournier, Pierre

Gascoigne, George 1539-1577 .... **LC 108**
See also DLB 136; RGEL 2

Gascoyne, David (Emery)
1916-2001 .... **CLC 45**
See also CA 65-68; 200; CANR 10, 28, 54;
CP 1, 2, 3, 4, 5, 6, 7; DLB 20; MTCW 1;
RGEL 2

Gaskell, Elizabeth 1810-1865 ... **NCLC 5, 70,**
97, 137, 214; SSC 25, 97
See also AAYA 80; BRW 5; BRWR 3; CD-
BLB 1832-1890; DAB; DAM MST; DLB
21, 144, 159; RGEL 2; RGSF 2; TEA

Gass, William H. 1924- . **CLC 1, 2, 8, 11, 15,**
39, 132; SSC 12
See also AMWS 6; CA 17-20R; CANR 30,
71, 100; CN 1, 2, 3, 4, 5, 6, 7; DLB 2,
227; EWL 3; MAL 5; MTCW 1, 2;
MTFW 2005; RGAL 4

Gassendi, Pierre 1592-1655 .... **LC 54**
See also GFL Beginnings to 1789

Gasset, Jose Ortega y
See Ortega y Gasset, Jose

Gates, Henry Louis, Jr. 1950- ... **BLCS; CLC**
65
See also AMWS 20; BW 2, 3; CA 109;
CANR 25, 53, 75, 125, 203; CSW; DA3;
DAM MULT; DLB 67; EWL 3; MAL 5;
MTCW 2; MTFW 2005; RGAL 4

Gatos, Stephanie
See Katz, Steve

Gautier, Theophile 1811-1872 ... **NCLC 1, 59,**
243; PC 18; SSC 20
See also DAM POET; DLB 119; EW 6;
GFL 1789 to the Present; RGWL 2, 3;
SUFW; TWA

Gautreaux, Tim 1947- .... **CLC 270; SSC 125**
See also CA 187; CANR 207; CSW; DLB
292

Gautreaux, Tim Martin
See Gautreaux, Tim

Gay, John 1685-1732 ...... **DC 39; LC 49, 176**
See also BRW 3; DAM DRAM; DLB 84,
95; RGEL 2; WLIT 3

Gay, Oliver
See Gogarty, Oliver St. John

Gay, Peter 1923- .... **CLC 158**
See also CA 13-16R; CANR 18, 41, 77,
147, 196; INT CANR-18; RGHL

Gay, Peter Jack
See Gay, Peter

Gaye, Marvin (Pentz, Jr.)
1939-1984 .... **CLC 26**
See also CA 195; 112

Gebler, Carlo 1954- .... **CLC 39**
See also CA 119; 133; CANR 96, 186; DLB
271

Gebler, Carlo Ernest
See Gebler, Carlo

Gee, Maggie 1948- .... CLC 57
    See also CA 130; CANR 125; CN 4, 5, 6,
    7; DLB 207; MTFW 2005
Gee, Maurice 1931- .... CLC 29
    See also AAYA 42; CA 97-100; CANR 67,
    123, 204; CLR 56; CN 2, 3, 4, 5, 6, 7;
    CWRI 5; EWL 3; MAICYA 2; RGSF 2;
    SATA 46, 101, 227
Gee, Maurice Gough
    See Gee, Maurice
Geiogamah, Hanay 1945- .... NNAL
    See also CA 153; DAM MULT; DLB 175
Gelbart, Larry 1928-2009 .... CLC 21, 61
    See also CA 73-76; 290; CAD; CANR 45,
    94; CD 5, 6
Gelbart, Larry Simon
    See Gelbart, Larry
Gelber, Jack 1932-2003 ...... CLC 1, 6, 14, 79
    See also CA 1-4R; 216; CAD; CANR 2;
    DLB 7, 228; MAL 5
Gellhorn, Martha 1908-1998 ...... CLC 14, 60
    See Gellhorn, Martha Ellis
    See also CA 77-80; 164; CANR 44; CN 1,
    2, 3, 4, 5, 6 7; DLB 364; DLBY 1982,
    1998
Gellhorn, Martha Ellis
    See Gellhorn, Martha
Genet, Jean 1910-1986 .. CLC 1, 2, 5, 10, 14,
    44, 46; DC 25; TCLC 128
    See also CA 13-16R; CANR 18; DA3;
    DAM DRAM; DFS 10; DLB 72, 321;
    DLBY 1986; EW 13; EWL 3; GFL 1789
    to the Present; GLL 1; LMFS 2; MTCW
    1, 2; MTFW 2005; RGWL 2, 3; TWA
Genlis, Stephanie-Felicite Ducrest
    1746-1830 .... NCLC 166
    See also DLB 313
Gent, Peter 1942-2011 .... CLC 29
    See also AITN 1; CA 89-92; DLBY 1982
Gentile, Giovanni 1875-1944 .... TCLC 96
    See also CA 119
Geoffrey of Monmouth c.
    1100-1155 .... CMLC 44
    See also DLB 146; TEA
Geoffrey of Vinsauf fl. c. 12th cent.
    - .... CMLC 129
George, Jean
    See George, Jean Craighead
George, Jean C.
    See George, Jean Craighead
George, Jean Craighead 1919- .... CLC 35
    See also AAYA 8, 69; BYA 2, 4; CA 5-8R;
    CANR 25, 198; CLR 1, 80, 136; DLB 52;
    JRDA; MAICYA 1, 2; SATA 2, 68, 124,
    170, 226; WYA; YAW
George, Stefan (Anton) 1868-1933 . TCLC 2,
    14
    See also CA 104; 193; EW 8; EWL 3
Georges, Georges Martin
    See Simenon, Georges
Gerald of Wales c. 1146-c. 1223 ... CMLC 60
Gerhardi, William Alexander
    See Gerhardie, William Alexander
Gerhardie, William Alexander
    1895-1977 .... CLC 5
    See also CA 25-28R; 73-76; CANR 18; CN
    1, 2; DLB 36; RGEL 2
Germain, Sylvie 1954- .... CLC 283
    See also CA 191
Gerome
    See France, Anatole
Gerson, Jean 1363-1429 .... LC 77
    See also DLB 208
Gersonides 1288-1344 .... CMLC 49
    See also DLB 115
Gerstler, Amy 1956- .... CLC 70
    See also CA 146; CANR 99
Gertler, T. .... CLC 34
    See also CA 116; 121

Gertrude of Helfta c. 1256-c.
    1301 .... CMLC 105
Gertsen, Aleksandr Ivanovich
    See Herzen, Aleksandr Ivanovich
Gervase of Melkley c. 1185-c.
    1216 .... CMLC 121
Ghalib
    See Ghalib, Asadullah Khan
Ghalib, Asadullah Khan
    1797-1869 .... NCLC 39, 78
    See also DAM POET; RGWL 2, 3
Ghelderode, Michel de 1898-1962 ..... CLC 6,
    11; DC 15; TCLC 187
    See also CA 85-88; CANR 40, 77; DAM
    DRAM; DLB 321; EW 11; EWL 3; TWA
Ghiselin, Brewster 1903-2001 .... CLC 23
    See also CA 13-16R; CAAS 10; CANR 13;
    CP 1, 2, 3, 4, 5, 6, 7
Ghose, Aurabinda 1872-1950 .... TCLC 63
    See also CA 163; EWL 3
Ghose, Aurobindo
    See Ghose, Aurabinda
Ghose, Zulfikar 1935- .... CLC 42, 200
    See also CA 65-68; CANR 67; CN 1, 2, 3,
    4, 5, 6, 7; CP 1, 2, 3, 4, 5, 6, 7; DLB 323;
    EWL 3
Ghosh, Amitav 1956- .... CLC 44, 153, 300
    See also CA 147; CANR 80, 158, 205; CN
    6, 7; DLB 323; WWE 1
Giacosa, Giuseppe 1847-1906 .... TCLC 7
    See also CA 104
Gibb, Lee
    See Waterhouse, Keith
Gibbon, Edward 1737-1794 .... LC 97
    See also BRW 3; DLB 104, 336; RGEL 2
Gibbon, Lewis Grassic
    See Mitchell, James Leslie
Gibbons, Kaye 1960- .... CLC 50, 88, 145
    See also AAYA 34; AMWS 10; CA 151;
    CANR 75, 127; CN 7; CSW; DA3; DAM
    POP; DLB 292; MTCW 2; MTFW 2005;
    NFS 3; RGAL 4; SATA 117
Gibran, Kahlil 1883-1931 ..... PC 9; TCLC 1,
    9, 205
    See also AMWS 20; CA 104; 150; DA3;
    DAM POET, POP; DLB 346; EWL 3;
    MTCW 2; WLIT 6
Gibran, Khalil
    See Gibran, Kahlil
Gibson, Mel 1956- .... CLC 215
    See also AAYA 80
Gibson, William 1914-2008 .... CLC 23
    See also CA 9-12R; 279; CAD; CANR 9,
    42, 75, 125; CD 5, 6; DA; DAB; DAC;
    DAM DRAM, MST; DFS 2, 28; DLB 7;
    LAIT 2; MAL 5; MTCW 2; MTFW 2005;
    SATA 66; SATA-Obit 199; YAW
Gibson, William 1948- .... CLC 39, 63, 186,
    192; SSC 52
    See also AAYA 12, 59; AMWS 16; BPFB
    2; CA 126; 133; CANR 52, 90, 106, 172;
    CN 6, 7; CPW; DA3; DAM POP; DLB
    251; MTCW 2; MTFW 2005; NFS 38;
    SCFW 2; SFW 4; SSFS 26
Gibson, William Ford
    See Gibson, William
Gide, Andre 1869-1951 ..... SSC 13; TCLC 5,
    12, 36, 177; WLC 3
    See also CA 104; 124; DA; DA3; DAB;
    DAC; DAM MST, NOV; DLB 65, 321,
    330; EW 8; EWL 3; GFL 1789 to the
    Present; MTCW 1, 2; MTFW 2005; NFS
    21; RGSF 2; RGWL 2, 3; TWA
Gide, Andre Paul Guillaume
    See Gide, Andre
Gifford, Barry 1946- .... CLC 34
    See also CA 65-68; CANR 9, 30, 40, 90,
    180

Gifford, Barry Colby
    See Gifford, Barry
Gilbert, Frank
    See De Voto, Bernard (Augustine)
Gilbert, W(illiam) S(chwenck)
    1836-1911 .... TCLC 3
    See also CA 104; 173; DAM DRAM, POET;
    DLB 344; RGEL 2; SATA 36
Gilbert of Poitiers c. 1085-1154 .... CMLC 85
Gilbreth, Frank B., Jr. 1911-2001 .... CLC 17
    See also CA 9-12R; SATA 2
Gilbreth, Frank Bunker
    See Gilbreth, Frank B., Jr.
Gilchrist, Ellen 1935- .... CLC 34, 48, 143,
    264; SSC 14, 63
    See also BPFB 2; CA 113; 116; CANR 41,
    61, 104, 191; CN 4, 5, 6, 7; CPW; CSW;
    DAM POP; DLB 130; EWL 3; EXPS;
    MTCW 1, 2; MTFW 2005; RGAL 4;
    RGSF 2; SSFS 9
Gilchrist, Ellen Louise
    See Gilchrist, Ellen
Gildas fl. 6th cent. - .... CMLC 99
Giles, Molly 1942- .... CLC 39
    See also CA 126; CANR 98
Gill, Arthur Eric Rowton Peter Joseph
    See Gill, Eric
Gill, Eric 1882-1940 .... TCLC 85
    See Gill, Arthur Eric Rowton Peter Joseph
    See also CA 120; DLB 98
Gill, Patrick
    See Creasey, John
Gillette, Douglas .... CLC 70
Gilliam, Terry 1940- .... CLC 21, 141
    See also AAYA 19, 59; CA 108; 113; CANR
    35; INT CA-113
Gilliam, Terry Vance
    See Gilliam, Terry
Gillian, Jerry
    See Gilliam, Terry
Gilliatt, Penelope (Ann Douglass)
    1932-1993 .... CLC 2, 10, 13, 53
    See also AITN 2; CA 13-16R; 141; CANR
    49; CN 1, 2, 3, 4, 5; DLB 14
Gilligan, Carol 1936- .... CLC 208
    See also CA 142; CANR 121, 187; FW
Gilman, Charlotte Anna Perkins Stetson
    See Gilman, Charlotte Perkins
Gilman, Charlotte Perkins
    1860-1935 ...... SSC 13, 62; TCLC 9, 37,
    117, 201
    See also AAYA 75; AMWS 11; BYA 11;
    CA 106; 150; DLB 221; EXPS; FL 1:5;
    FW; HGG; LAIT 2; MBL; MTCW 2;
    MTFW 2005; NFS 36; RGAL 4; RGSF 2;
    SFW 4; SSFS 1, 18
Gilmore, Mary (Jean Cameron)
    1865-1962 .... PC 87
    See also CA 114; DLB 260; RGEL 2; SATA
    49
Gilmour, David 1946- .... CLC 35
Gilpin, William 1724-1804 .... NCLC 30
Gilray, J. D.
    See Mencken, H. L.
Gilroy, Frank D(aniel) 1925- .... CLC 2
    See also CA 81-84; CAD; CANR 32, 64,
    86; CD 5, 6; DFS 17; DLB 7
Gilstrap, John 1957(?)- .... CLC 99
    See also AAYA 67; CA 160; CANR 101
Ginsberg, Allen 1926-1997 .... CLC 1, 2, 3, 4,
    6, 13, 36, 69, 109; PC 4, 47; TCLC
    120; WLC 3
    See also AAYA 33; AITN 1; AMWC 1;
    AMWS 2; BG 1:2; CA 1-4R; 157; CANR
    2, 41, 63, 95; CDALB 1941-1968; CP 1,
    2, 3, 4, 5, 6; DA; DA3; DAB; DAC; DAM

MST, POET; DLB 5, 16, 169, 237; EWL
3; GLL 1; LMFS 2; MAL 5; MTCW 1, 2;
MTFW 2005; PAB; PFS 29; RGAL 4;
TUS; WP

Ginzburg, Eugenia
See Ginzburg, Evgeniia

Ginzburg, Evgeniia 1904-1977 .... **CLC 59**
See also DLB 302

Ginzburg, Natalia 1916-1991 .... **CLC 5, 11,
54, 70; SSC 65; TCLC 156**
See also CA 85-88; 135; CANR 33; DFS
14; DLB 177; EW 13; EWL 3; MTCW 1,
2; MTFW 2005; RGHL; RGWL 2, 3

Gioia, (Michael) Dana 1950- .... **CLC 251**
See also AMWS 15; CA 130; CANR 70,
88; CP 6, 7; DLB 120, 282; PFS 24

Giono, Jean 1895-1970 .... **CLC 4, 11; TCLC
124**
See also CA 45-48; 29-32R; CANR 2, 35;
DLB 72, 321; EWL 3; GFL 1789 to the
Present; MTCW 1; RGWL 2, 3

Giovanni, Nikki 1943- ... **BLC 1:2; CLC 2, 4,
19, 64, 117; PC 19; WLCS**
See also AAYA 22, 85; AITN 1; BW 2, 3;
CA 29-32R; CAAS 6; CANR 18, 41, 60,
91, 130, 175; CDALBS; CLR 6, 73; CP
2, 3, 4, 5, 6, 7; CSW; CWP; CWRI 5; DA;
DA3; DAB; DAC; DAM MST, MULT,
POET; DLB 5, 41; EWL 3; EXPP; INT
CANR-18; MAICYA 1, 2; MAL 5;
MTCW 1, 2; MTFW 2005; PFS 17, 28,
35; RGAL 4; SATA 24, 107, 208; TUS;
YAW

Giovanni, Yolanda Cornelia
See Giovanni, Nikki

Giovanni, Yolande Cornelia
See Giovanni, Nikki

Giovanni, Yolande Cornelia, Jr.
See Giovanni, Nikki

Giovene, Andrea 1904-1998 .... **CLC 7**
See also CA 85-88

Gippius, Zinaida 1869-1945 .... **TCLC 9**
See also CA 106; 212; DLB 295; EWL 3

Gippius, Zinaida Nikolaevna
See Gippius, Zinaida

Giraudoux, Jean 1882-1944 ... **DC 36; TCLC
2, 7**
See also CA 104; 196; DAM DRAM; DFS
28; DLB 65, 321; EW 9; EWL 3; GFL
1789 to the Present; RGWL 2, 3; TWA

Giraudoux, Jean-Hippolyte
See Giraudoux, Jean

Gironella, Jose Maria (Pous)
1917-2003 .... **CLC 11**
See also CA 101; 212; EWL 3; RGWL 2, 3

Gissing, George (Robert)
1857-1903 .... **SSC 37, 113; TCLC 3, 24,
47**
See also BRW 5; CA 105; 167; DLB 18,
135, 184; RGEL 2; TEA

Gitlin, Todd 1943- .... **CLC 201**
See also CA 29-32R; CANR 25, 50, 88,
179, 227

Giurlani, Aldo
See Palazzeschi, Aldo

Gladkov, Fedor Vasil'evich
See Gladkov, Fyodor (Vasilyevich)

Gladkov, Fyodor (Vasilyevich)
1883-1958 .... **TCLC 27**
See also CA 170; DLB 272; EWL 3

Gladstone, William Ewart
1809-1898 .... **NCLC 213**
See also DLB 57, 184

Glancy, Diane 1941- .... **CLC 210; NNAL**
See also CA 136; 225; CAAE 225; CAAS
24; CANR 87, 162, 217; DLB 175

Glanville, Brian (Lester) 1931- .... **CLC 6**
See also CA 5-8R; CAAS 9; CANR 3, 70;
CN 1, 2, 3, 4, 5, 6, 7; DLB 15, 139; SATA
42

Glasgow, Ellen 1873-1945 .... **SSC 34, 130;
TCLC 2, 7, 239**
See also AMW; CA 104; 164; DLB 9, 12;
MAL 5; MBL; MTCW 2; MTFW 2005;
RGAL 4; RHW; SSFS 9; TUS

Glasgow, Ellen Anderson Gholson
See Glasgow, Ellen

Glaspell, Susan 1882(?)-1948 ..... **DC 10; SSC
41, 132; TCLC 55, 175**
See also AMWS 3; CA 110; 154; DFS 8,
18, 24; DLB 7, 9, 78, 228; MBL; RGAL
4; SSFS 3; TCWW 2; TUS; YABC 2

Glassco, John 1909-1981 .... **CLC 9**
See also CA 13-16R; 102; CANR 15; CN
1, 2; CP 1, 2, 3; DLB 68

Glasscock, Amnesia
See Steinbeck, John

Glasser, Ronald J. 1940(?)- .... **CLC 37**
See also CA 209

Glassman, Joyce
See Johnson, Joyce

Gleick, James 1954- .... **CLC 147**
See also CA 131; 137; CANR 97; INT CA-
137

Gleick, James W.
See Gleick, James

Glendinning, Victoria 1937- .... **CLC 50**
See also CA 120; 127; CANR 59, 89, 166;
DLB 155

Glissant, Edouard 1928-2011 ..... **CLC 10, 68**
See also CA 153; CANR 111; CWW 2;
DAM MULT; EWL 3; RGWL 3

Glissant, Edouard Mathieu
See Glissant, Edouard

Gloag, Julian 1930- .... **CLC 40**
See also AITN 1; CA 65-68; CANR 10, 70;
CN 1, 2, 3, 4, 5, 6

Glowacki, Aleksander
See Prus, Boleslaw

Gluck, Louise 1943- . **CLC 7, 22, 44, 81, 160,
280; PC 16**
See also AMWS 5; CA 33-36R; CANR 40,
69, 108, 133, 182; CP 1, 2, 3, 4, 5, 6, 7;
CWP; DA3; DAM POET; DLB 5; MAL
5; MTCW 2; MTFW 2005; PFS 5, 15;
RGAL 4; TCLE 1:1

Gluck, Louise Elisabeth
See Gluck, Louise

Glyn, Elinor 1864-1943 .... **TCLC 72**
See also DLB 153; RHW

Gobineau, Joseph-Arthur
1816-1882 .... **NCLC 17**
See also DLB 123; GFL 1789 to the Present

Godard, Jean-Luc 1930- .... **CLC 20**
See also CA 93-96

Godden, (Margaret) Rumer
1907-1998 .... **CLC 53**
See also AAYA 6; BPFB 2; BYA 2, 5; CA
5-8R; 172; CANR 4, 27, 36, 55, 80; CLR
20; CN 1, 2, 3, 4, 5, 6; CWRI 5; DLB
161; MAICYA 1, 2; RHW; SAAS 12;
SATA 3, 36; SATA-Obit 109; TEA

Godoy Alcayaga, Lucila
See Mistral, Gabriela

Godwin, Gail 1937- ...... **CLC 5, 8, 22, 31, 69,
125**
See also BPFB 2; CA 29-32R; CANR 15,
43, 69, 132, 218; CN 3, 4, 5, 6, 7; CPW;
CSW; DA3; DAM POP; DLB 6, 234, 350;
INT CANR-15; MAL 5; MTCW 1, 2;
MTFW 2005

Godwin, Gail Kathleen
See Godwin, Gail

Godwin, William 1756-1836 .. **NCLC 14, 130**
See also BRWS 15; CDBLB 1789-1832;
CMW 4; DLB 39, 104, 142, 158, 163,
262, 336; GL 2; HGG; RGEL 2

Goebbels, Josef
See Goebbels, (Paul) Joseph

Goebbels, (Paul) Joseph
1897-1945 .... **TCLC 68**
See also CA 115; 148

Goebbels, Joseph Paul
See Goebbels, (Paul) Joseph

Goethe, Johann Wolfgang von
1749-1832 . **DC 20; NCLC 4, 22, 34, 90,
154, 247; PC 5; SSC 38, 141; WLC 3**
See also CDWLB 2; DA; DA3; DAB;
DAC; DAM DRAM, MST, POET; DLB
94; EW 5; GL 2; LATS 1; LMFS 1:1;
RGWL 2, 3; TWA

Gogarty, Oliver St. John
1878-1957 .... **PC 121; TCLC 15**
See also CA 109; 150; DLB 15, 19; RGEL
2

Gogol, Nikolai 1809-1852 .... **DC 1; NCLC 5,
15, 31, 162; SSC 4, 29, 52, 145; WLC 3**
See also DA; DAB; DAC; DAM DRAM,
MST, POET; DLB 198; EW 6; EXPS;
RGSF 2; RGWL 2, 3; SSFS 7, 32; TWA

Gogol, Nikolai Vasilyevich
See Gogol, Nikolai

Goines, Donald 1937(?)-1974 .... **BLC 1:2;
CLC 80**
See also AITN 1; BW 1, 3; CA 124; 114;
CANR 82; CMW 4; DA3; DAM MULT,
POP; DLB 33

Gold, Herbert 1924- ... **CLC 4, 7, 14, 42, 152**
See also CA 9-12R; CANR 17, 45, 125,
194; CN 1, 2, 3, 4, 5, 6, 7; DLB 2; DLBY
1981, MAL 5

Goldbarth, Albert 1948- .... **CLC 5, 38**
See also AMWS 12; CA 53-56; CANR 6,
40, 206; CP 3, 4, 5, 6, 7; DLB 120

Goldberg, Anatol 1910-1982 .... **CLC 34**
See also CA 131; 117

Goldemberg, Isaac 1945- .... **CLC 52**
See also CA 69-72; CAAS 12; CANR 11,
32; EWL 3; HW 1; WLIT 1

Golding, Arthur 1536-1606 .... **LC 101**
See also DLB 136

Golding, William 1911-1993 . **CLC 1, 2, 3, 8,
10, 17, 27, 58, 81; WLC 3**
See also AAYA 5, 44; BPFB 2; BRWR 1;
BRWS 1; BYA 2; CA 5-8R; 141; CANR
13, 33, 54; CD 5; CDBLB 1945-1960;
CLR 94, 130; CN 1, 2, 3, 4; DA; DA3;
DAB; DAC; DAM MST, NOV; DLB 15,
100, 255, 326, 330; EWL 3; EXPN; HGG;
LAIT 4; MTCW 1, 2; MTFW 2005; NFS
2, 36; RGEL 2; RHW; SFW 4; TEA;
WLIT 4; YAW

Golding, William Gerald
See Golding, William

Goldman, Emma 1869-1940 .... **TCLC 13**
See also CA 110; 150; DLB 221; FW;
RGAL 4; TUS

Goldman, Francisco 1954- .... **CLC 76, 298**
See also CA 162; CANR 185

Goldman, William 1931- .... **CLC 1, 48**
See also BPFB 2; CA 9-12R; CANR 29,
69, 106; CN 1, 2, 3, 4, 5, 6, 7; DLB 44;
FANT; IDFW 3, 4; NFS 31

Goldman, William W.
See Goldman, William

Goldmann, Lucien 1913-1970 .... **CLC 24**
See also CA 25-28; CAP 2

Goldoni, Carlo 1707-1793 .... **LC 4, 152**
See also DAM DRAM; DFS 27; EW 4;
RGWL 2, 3; WLIT 7

Goldsberry, Steven 1949- .... **CLC 34**
See also CA 131

Granger, Darius John
　See Marlowe, Stephen
Granin, Daniil 1918- .... **CLC 59**
　See also DLB 302
Granovsky, Timofei Nikolaevich
　1813-1855 .... **NCLC 75**
　See also DLB 198
Grant, Skeeter
　See Spiegelman, Art
Granville-Barker, Harley
　1877-1946 .... **TCLC 2**
　See also CA 104; 204; DAM DRAM; DLB
　10; RGEL 2
Granzotto, Gianni
　See Granzotto, Giovanni Battista
Granzotto, Giovanni Battista
　1914-1985 .... **CLC 70**
　See also CA 166
Grasemann, Ruth Barbara
　See Rendell, Ruth
Grass, Guenter
　See Grass, Gunter
Grass, Gunter 1927- .. **CLC 1, 2, 4, 6, 11, 15,
　22, 32, 49, 88, 207; WLC 3**
　See also BPFB 2; CA 13-16R; CANR 20,
　75, 93, 133, 174; CDWLB 2; CWW 2;
　DA; DA3; DAB; DAC; DAM MST, NOV;
　DLB 330; EW 13; EWL 3; MTCW 1, 2;
　MTFW 2005; RGHL; RGWL 2, 3; TWA
Grass, Gunter Wilhelm
　See Grass, Gunter
Gratton, Thomas
　See Hulme, T(homas) E(rnest)
Grau, Shirley Ann 1929- .... **CLC 4, 9, 146;
　SSC 15**
　See also CA 89-92; CANR 22, 69; CN 1, 2,
　3, 4, 5, 6, 7; CSW; DLB 2, 218; INT CA-
　89-92; CANR-22; MTCW 1
Gravel, Fern
　See Hall, James Norman
Graver, Elizabeth 1964- .... **CLC 70**
　See also CA 135; CANR 71, 129
Graves, Richard Perceval
　1895-1985 .... **CLC 44**
　See also CA 65-68; CANR 9, 26, 51
Graves, Robert 1895-1985 ... **CLC 1, 2, 6, 11,
　39, 44, 45; PC 6**
　See also BPFB 2; BRW 7; BYA 4; CA 5-8R;
　117; CANR 5, 36; CDBLB 1914-1945;
　CN 1, 2, 3; CP 1, 2, 3, 4; DA3; DAB;
　DAC; DAM MST, POET; DLB 20, 100,
　191; DLBD 18; DLBY 1985; EWL 3;
　LATS 1:1; MTCW 1, 2; MTFW 2005;
　NCFS 2; NFS 21; RGEL 2; RHW; SATA
　45; TEA
Graves, Robert von Ranke
　See Graves, Robert
Graves, Valerie
　See Bradley, Marion Zimmer
Gray, Alasdair 1934- .... **CLC 41, 275**
　See also BRWS 9; CA 126; CANR 47, 69,
　106, 140; CN 4, 5, 6, 7; DLB 194, 261,
　319; HGG; INT CA-126; MTCW 1, 2;
　MTFW 2005; RGSF 2; SUFW 2
Gray, Amlin 1946- .... **CLC 29**
　See also CA 138
Gray, Francine du Plessix 1930- ..... **CLC 22,
　153**
　See also BEST 90:3; CA 61-64; CAAS 2;
　CANR 11, 33, 75, 81, 197; DAM NOV;
　INT CANR-11; MTCW 1, 2; MTFW 2005
Gray, John (Henry) 1866-1934 ...... **TCLC 19**
　See also CA 119; 162; RGEL 2
Gray, John Lee
　See Jakes, John

Gray, Simon 1936-2008 .... **CLC 9, 14, 36**
　See also AITN 1; CA 21-24R; 275; CAAS
　3; CANR 32, 69, 208; CBD; CD 5, 6; CN
　1, 2, 3; DLB 13; EWL 3; MTCW 1;
　RGEL 2
Gray, Simon James Holliday
　See Gray, Simon
Gray, Spalding 1941-2004 .... **CLC 49, 112;
　DC 7**
　See also AAYA 62; CA 128; 225; CAD;
　CANR 74, 138; CD 5, 6; CPW; DAM
　POP; MTCW 2; MTFW 2005
Gray, Thomas 1716-1771 . **LC 4, 40, 178; PC
　2, 80; WLC 3**
　See also BRW 3; CDBLB 1660-1789; DA;
　DA3; DAB; DAC; DAM MST; DLB 109;
　EXPP; PAB; PFS 9; RGEL 2; TEA; WP
Grayson, David
　See Baker, Ray Stannard
Grayson, Richard (A.) 1951- .... **CLC 38**
　See also CA 85-88; 210; CAAE 210; CANR
　14, 31, 57; DLB 234
Greeley, Andrew M. 1928- .... **CLC 28**
　See also BPFB 2; CA 5-8R; CAAS 7;
　CANR 7, 43, 69, 104, 136, 184; CMW 4;
　CPW; DA3; DAM POP; MTCW 1, 2;
　MTFW 2005
Green, Anna Katharine
　1846-1935 .... **TCLC 63**
　See also CA 112; 159; CMW 4; DLB 202,
　221; MSW
Green, Brian
　See Card, Orson Scott
Green, Hannah
　See Greenberg, Joanne (Goldenberg)
Green, Hannah 1927(?)-1996 .... **CLC 3**
　See also CA 73-76; CANR 59, 93; NFS 10
Green, Henry
　See Yorke, Henry Vincent
Green, Julian
　See Green, Julien
Green, Julien 1900-1998 .... **CLC 3, 11, 77**
　See also CA 21-24R; 169; CANR 33, 87;
　CWW 2; DLB 4, 72; EWL 3; GFL 1789
　to the Present; MTCW 2; MTFW 2005
Green, Julien Hartridge
　See Green, Julien
Green, Paul (Eliot) 1894-1981 .. **CLC 25; DC
　37**
　See also AITN 1; CA 5-8R; 103; CAD;
　CANR 3; DAM DRAM; DLB 7, 9, 249;
　DLBY 1981; MAL 5; RGAL 4
Greenaway, Peter 1942- .... **CLC 159**
　See also CA 127
Greenberg, Ivan 1908-1973 .... **CLC 24**
　See also CA 85-88; DLB 137; MAL 5
Greenberg, Joanne (Goldenberg)
　1932- .... **CLC 7, 30**
　See also AAYA 12, 67; CA 5-8R; CANR
　14, 32, 69; CN 6, 7; DLB 335; NFS 23;
　SATA 25; YAW
Greenberg, Richard 1959(?)- .... **CLC 57**
　See also CA 138; CAD; CD 5, 6; DFS 24
Greenblatt, Stephen J(ay) 1943- ...... **CLC 70**
　See also CA 49-52; CANR 115; LNFS 1
Greene, Bette 1934- .... **CLC 30**
　See also AAYA 7, 69; BYA 3; CA 53-56;
　CANR 4, 146; CLR 2, 140; CWRI 5;
　JRDA; LAIT 4; MAICYA 1, 2; NFS 10;
　SAAS 16; SATA 8, 102, 161; WYA; YAW
Greene, Gael .... **CLC 8**
　See also CA 13-16R; CANR 10, 166
Greene, Graham 1904-1991 .. **CLC 1, 3, 6, 9,
　14, 18, 27, 37, 70, 72, 125; DC 41; SSC
　29, 121; WLC 3**
　See also AAYA 61; AITN 2; BPFB 2;
　BRWR 2; BRWS 1; BYA 3; CA 13-16R;
　133; CANR 35, 61, 131; CBD; CDBLB
　1945-1960; CMW 4; CN 1, 2, 3, 4; DA;

　DA3; DAB; DAC; DAM MST, NOV;
　DLB 13, 15, 77, 100, 162, 201, 204;
　DLBY 1991; EWL 3; MSW; MTCW 1, 2;
　MTFW 2005; NFS 16, 31, 36; RGEL 2;
　SATA 20; SSFS 14, 35; TEA; WLIT 4
Greene, Graham Henry
　See Greene, Graham
Greene, Robert 1558-1592 .... **LC 41, 185**
　See also BRWS 8; DLB 62, 167; IDTP;
　RGEL 2; TEA
Greer, Germaine 1939- .... **CLC 131**
　See also AITN 1; CA 81-84; CANR 33, 70,
　115, 133, 190; FW; MTCW 1, 2; MTFW
　2005
Greer, Richard
　See Silverberg, Robert
Gregor, Arthur 1923- .... **CLC 9**
　See also CA 25-28R; CAAS 10; CANR 11;
　CP 1, 2, 3, 4, 5, 6, 7; SATA 36
Gregor, Lee
　See Pohl, Frederik
Gregory, Lady Isabella Augusta (Persse)
　1852-1932 .... **TCLC 1, 176**
　See also BRW 6; CA 104; 184; DLB 10;
　IDTP; RGEL 2
Gregory, J. Dennis
　See Williams, John A(lfred)
Gregory of Nazianzus, St.
　329-389 .... **CMLC 82**
Gregory of Nyssa c. 335-c. 394 ... **CMLC 126**
Gregory of Rimini 1300(?)-1358 . **CMLC 109**
　See also DLB 115
Gregory the Great c. 540-604 ..... **CMLC 124**
Grekova, I.
　See Ventsel, Elena Sergeevna
Grekova, Irina
　See Ventsel, Elena Sergeevna
Grendon, Stephen
　See Derleth, August (William)
Grenville, Kate 1950- .... **CLC 61**
　See also CA 118; CANR 53, 93, 156, 220;
　CN 7; DLB 325
Grenville, Pelham
　See Wodehouse, P. G.
Greve, Felix Paul (Berthold Friedrich)
　1879-1948 .... **TCLC 4, 248**
　See also CA 104; 141, 175; CANR 79;
　DAC; DAM MST; DLB 92; RGEL 2;
　TCWW 1, 2
Greville, Fulke 1554-1628 .... **LC 79**
　See also BRWS 11; DLB 62, 172; RGEL 2
Grey, Lady Jane 1537-1554 .... **LC 93**
　See also DLB 132
Grey, Zane 1872-1939 .... **TCLC 6**
　See also BPFB 2; CA 104; 132; CANR 210;
　DA3; DAM POP; DLB 9, 212; MTCW 1,
　2; MTFW 2005; RGAL 4; TCWW 1, 2;
　TUS
Griboedov, Aleksandr Sergeevich
　1795(?)-1829 .... **NCLC 129**
　See also DLB 205; RGWL 2, 3
Grieg, (Johan) Nordahl (Brun)
　1902-1943 .... **TCLC 10**
　See also CA 107; 189; EWL 3
Grieve, C. M. 1892-1978 ... **CLC 2, 4, 11, 19,
　63; PC 9, 122**
　See also BRWS 12; CA 5-8R; 85-88; CANR
　33, 107; CDBLB 1945-1960; CP 1, 2;
　DAM POET; DLB 20; EWL 3; MTCW 1;
　RGEL 2
Grieve, Christopher Murray
　See Grieve, C. M.
Griffin, Gerald 1803-1840 .... **NCLC 7**
　See also DLB 159; RGEL 2
Griffin, John Howard 1920-1980 ..... **CLC 68**
　See also AITN 1; CA 1-4R; 101; CANR 2
Griffin, Peter 1942- .... **CLC 39**
　See also CA 136

Gustafson, Ralph (Barker)
1909-1995 .... **CLC 36**
See also CA 21-24R; CANR 8, 45, 84; CP
1, 2, 3, 4, 5, 6; DLB 88; RGEL 2

Gut, Gom
See Simenon, Georges

Guterson, David 1956- .... **CLC 91**
See also CA 132; CANR 73, 126, 194; CN
7; DLB 292; MTCW 2; MTFW 2005;
NFS 13

Guthrie, A(lfred) B(ertram), Jr.
1901-1991 .... **CLC 23**
See also CA 57-60; 134; CANR 24; CN 1,
2, 3; DLB 6, 212; MAL 5; SATA 62;
SATA-Obit 67; TCWW 1, 2

Guthrie, Isobel
See Grieve, C. M.

Gutierrez Najera, Manuel
1859-1895 .... **HLCS 2; NCLC 133**
See also DLB 290; LAW

Guy, Rosa 1925- .... **CLC 26**
See also AAYA 4, 37; BW 2; CA 17-20R;
CANR 14, 34, 83; CLR 13, 137; DLB 33;
DNFS 1; JRDA; MAICYA 1, 2; SATA 14,
62, 122; YAW

Guy, Rosa Cuthbert
See Guy, Rosa

Gwendolyn
See Bennett, (Enoch) Arnold

H. D.
See Doolittle, Hilda

H. de V.
See Buchan, John

Haavikko, Paavo Juhani 1931- .. **CLC 18, 34**
See also CA 106; CWW 2; EWL 3

Habbema, Koos
See Heijermans, Herman

Habermas, Juergen 1929- .... **CLC 104**
See also CA 109; CANR 85, 162; DLB 242

Habermas, Jurgen
See Habermas, Juergen

Hacker, Marilyn 1942- ...... **CLC 5, 9, 23, 72,**
91; PC 47
See also CA 77-80; CANR 68, 129; CP 3,
4, 5, 6, 7; CWP; DAM POET; DLB 120,
282; FW; GLL 2; MAL 5; PFS 19

Hadewijch of Antwerp fl. 1250- ... **CMLC 61**
See also RGWL 3

Hadrian 76-138 .... **CMLC 52**

Haeckel, Ernst Heinrich (Philipp August)
1834-1919 .... **TCLC 83**
See also CA 157

Hafiz c. 1326-1389(?) .... **CMLC 34; PC 116**
See also RGWL 2, 3; WLIT 6

Hagedorn, Jessica T(arahata)
1949- .... **CLC 185**
See also CA 139; CANR 69; CWP; DLB
312; RGAL 4

Haggard, H(enry) Rider
1856-1925 .... **TCLC 11**
See also AAYA 81; BRWS 3; BYA 4, 5;
CA 108; 148; CANR 112; DLB 70, 156,
174, 178; FANT; LMFS 1; MTCW 2; NFS
40; RGEL 2; RHW; SATA 16; SCFW 1,
2; SFW 4; SUFW 1; WLIT 4

Hagiosy, L.
See Larbaud, Valery (Nicolas)

Hagiwara, Sakutaro 1886-1942 .... **PC 18;**
TCLC 60
See also CA 154; EWL 3; RGWL 3

Hagiwara Sakutaro
See Hagiwara, Sakutaro

Haig, Fenil
See Ford, Ford Madox

Haig-Brown, Roderick (Langmere)
1908-1976 .... **CLC 21**
See also CA 5-8R; 69-72; CANR 4, 38, 83;
CLR 31; CWRI 5; DLB 88; MAICYA 1,
2; SATA 12; TCWW 2

Haight, Rip
See Carpenter, John

Haij, Vera
See Jansson, Tove (Marika)

Hailey, Arthur 1920-2004 .... **CLC 5**
See also AITN 2; BEST 90:3; BPFB 2; CA
1-4R; 233; CANR 2, 36, 75; CCA 1; CN
1, 2, 3, 4, 5, 6, 7; CPW; DAM NOV, POP;
DLB 88; DLBY 1982; MTCW 1, 2;
MTFW 2005

Hailey, Elizabeth Forsythe 1938- ..... **CLC 40**
See also CA 93-96, 188; CAAE 188; CAAS
1; CANR 15, 48; INT CANR-15

Haines, John 1924-2011 .... **CLC 58**
See also AMWS 12; CA 17-20R; CANR
13, 34; CP 1, 2, 3, 4, 5; CSW; DLB 5,
212; TCLE 1:1

Haines, John Meade
See Haines, John

Hakluyt, Richard 1552-1616 .... **LC 31**
See also DLB 136; RGEL 2

Haldeman, Joe 1943- .... **CLC 61**
See also AAYA 38; CA 53-56, 179; CAAE
179; CAAS 25; CANR 6, 70, 72, 130,
171, 224; DLB 8; INT CANR-6; SCFW
2; SFW 4

Haldeman, Joe William
See Haldeman, Joe

Hale, Janet Campbell 1947- .... **NNAL**
See also CA 49-52; CANR 45, 75; DAM
MULT; DLB 175; MTCW 2; MTFW 2005

Hale, Sarah Josepha (Buell)
1788-1879 .... **NCLC 75**
See also DLB 1, 42, 73, 243

Halevy, Elie 1870-1937 .... **TCLC 104**

Haley, Alex 1921-1992 . **BLC 1:2; CLC 8, 12,**
76; TCLC 147
See also AAYA 26; BPFB 2; BW 2, 3; CA
77-80; 136; CANR 61; CDALBS; CPW;
CSW; DA; DA3; DAB; DAC; DAM MST,
MULT, POP; DLB 38; LAIT 5; MTCW
1, 2; NFS 9

Haley, Alexander Murray Palmer
See Haley, Alex

Haliburton, Thomas Chandler
1796-1865 .... **NCLC 15, 149**
See also DLB 11, 99; RGEL 2; RGSF 2

Hall, Donald 1928- ... **CLC 1, 13, 37, 59, 151,**
240; PC 70
See also AAYA 63; CA 5-8R; CAAS 7;
CANR 2, 44, 64, 106, 133, 196; CP 1, 2,
3, 4, 5, 6, 7; DAM POET; DLB 5, 342;
MAL 5; MTCW 2; MTFW 2005; RGAL
4; SATA 23, 97

Hall, Donald Andrew, Jr.
See Hall, Donald

Hall, Frederic Sauser
See Sauser-Hall, Frederic

Hall, James
See Kuttner, Henry

Hall, James Norman 1887-1951 ..... **TCLC 23**
See also CA 123; 173; LAIT 1; RHW 1;
SATA 21

Hall, Joseph 1574-1656 .... **LC 91**
See also DLB 121, 151; RGEL 2

Hall, Marguerite Radclyffe
See Hall, Radclyffe

Hall, Radclyffe 1880-1943 ...... **TCLC 12, 215**
See also BRWS 6; CA 110; 150; CANR 83;
DLB 191; MTCW 2; MTFW 2005; RGEL
2; RHW

Hall, Rodney 1935- .... **CLC 51**
See also CA 109; CANR 69; CN 6, 7; CP
1, 2, 3, 4, 5, 6, 7; DLB 289

Hallam, Arthur Henry
1811-1833 .... **NCLC 110**
See also DLB 32

Halldor Laxness
See Gudjonsson, Halldor Kiljan

Halleck, Fitz-Greene 1790-1867 .... **NCLC 47**
See also DLB 3, 250; RGAL 4

Halliday, Michael
See Creasey, John

Halpern, Daniel 1945- .... **CLC 14**
See also CA 33-36R; CANR 93, 174; CP 3,
4, 5, 6, 7

Hamann, Johann Georg 1730-1788 .. **LC 198**
See also DLB 97

Hamburger, Michael 1924-2007 ... **CLC 5, 14**
See also CA 5-8R, 196; 261; CAAE 196;
CAAS 4; CANR 2, 47; CP 1, 2, 3, 4, 5, 6,
7; DLB 27

Hamburger, Michael Peter Leopold
See Hamburger, Michael

Hamill, Pete 1935- .... **CLC 10, 261**
See also CA 25-28R; CANR 18, 71, 127,
180

Hamill, William Peter
See Hamill, Pete

Hamilton, Alexander 1712-1756 .... **LC 150**
See also DLB 31

Hamilton, Alexander
1755(?)-1804 .... **NCLC 49**
See also DLB 37

Hamilton, Clive
See Lewis, C. S.

Hamilton, Edmond 1904-1977 .... **CLC 1**
See also CA 1-4R; CANR 3, 84; DLB 8;
SATA 118; SFW 4

Hamilton, Elizabeth 1758-1816 ... **NCLC 153**
See also DLB 116, 158

Hamilton, Eugene (Jacob) Lee
See Lee-Hamilton, Eugene (Jacob)

Hamilton, Franklin
See Silverberg, Robert

Hamilton, Gail
See Corcoran, Barbara (Asenath)

Hamilton, (Robert) Ian 1938-2001 . **CLC 191**
See also CA 106; 203; CANR 41, 67; CP 1,
2, 3, 4, 5, 6, 7; DLB 40, 155

Hamilton, Jane 1957- .... **CLC 179**
See also CA 147; CANR 85, 128, 214; CN
7; DLB 350; MTFW 2005

Hamilton, Mollie
See Kaye, M.M.

Hamilton, Patrick 1904-1962 .... **CLC 51**
See also BRWS 16; CA 176; 113; DLB 10,
191

Hamilton, Virginia 1936-2002 .... **CLC 26**
See also AAYA 2, 21; BW 2, 3; BYA 1, 2,
8; CA 25-28R; 206; CANR 20, 37, 73,
126; CLR 1, 11, 40, 127; DAM MULT;
DLB 33, 52; DLBY 2001; INT CANR-
20; JRDA; LAIT 5; MAICYA 1, 2; MAI-
CYAS 1; MTCW 1, 2; MTFW 2005;
SATA 4, 56, 79, 123; SATA-Obit 132;
WYA; YAW

Hamilton, Virginia Esther
See Hamilton, Virginia

Hammett, Dashiell 1894-1961 . **CLC 3, 5, 10,**
19, 47; SSC 17; TCLC 187
See also AAYA 59; AITN 1; AMWS 4;
BPFB 2; CA 81-84; CANR 42; CDALB
1929-1941; CMW 4; DA3; DLB 226, 280;
DLBD 6; DLBY 1996; EWL 3; LAIT 3;
MAL 5; MSW; MTCW 1, 2; MTFW
2005; NFS 21; RGAL 4; RGSF 2; TUS

Hammett, Samuel Dashiell
See Hammett, Dashiell

Hammon, Jupiter 1720(?)-1800(?) . **BLC 1:2;**
NCLC 5; PC 16
See also DAM MULT, POET; DLB 31, 50

Hammond, Keith
See Kuttner, Henry

Hamner, Earl (Henry), Jr. 1923- ...... **CLC 12**
See also AITN 2; CA 73-76; DLB 6

Hampton, Christopher 1946- .... **CLC 4**
 See also CA 25-28R; CD 5, 6; DLB 13;
 MTCW 1

Hampton, Christopher James
 See Hampton, Christopher

Hamsun, Knut
 See Pedersen, Knut

Hamsund, Knut Pedersen
 See Pedersen, Knut

Handke, Peter 1942- .... **CLC 5, 8, 10, 15, 38,
 134; DC 17**
 See also CA 77-80; CANR 33, 75, 104, 133,
 180; CWW 2; DAM DRAM, NOV; DLB
 85, 124; EWL 3; MTCW 1, 2; MTFW
 2005; TWA

Handler, Chelsea 1976(?)- .... **CLC 269**
 See also CA 243

Handy, W(illiam) C(hristopher)
 1873-1958 .... **TCLC 97**
 See also BW 3; CA 121; 167

Haneke, Michael 1942- .... **CLC 283**

Hanif, Mohammed 1965- .... **CLC 299**
 See also CA 283

Hanley, James 1901-1985 ..... **CLC 3, 5, 8, 13**
 See also CA 73-76; 117; CANR 36; CBD;
 CN 1, 2, 3; DLB 191; EWL 3; MTCW 1;
 RGEL 2

Hannah, Barry 1942-2010 ... **CLC 23, 38, 90,
 270, 318; SSC 94**
 See also BPFB 2; CA 108; 110; CANR 43,
 68, 113; CN 4, 5, 6, 7; CSW; DLB 6, 234;
 INT CA-110; MTCW 1; RGSF 2

Hannon, Ezra
 See Hunter, Evan

Hanrahan, Barbara 1939-1991 .... **TCLC 219**
 See also CA 121; 127; CN 4, 5; DLB 289

Hansberry, Lorraine 1930-1965 ..... **BLC 1:2,
 2:2; CLC 17, 62; DC 2; TCLC 192**
 See also AAYA 25; AFAW 1, 2; AMWS 4;
 BW 1, 3; CA 109; 25-28R; CABS 3;
 CAD; CANR 58; CDALB 1941-1968;
 CWD; DA; DA3; DAB; DAC; DAM
 DRAM, MST, MULT; DFS 2, 29; DLB 7,
 38; EWL 3; FL 1:6; FW; LAIT 4; MAL
 5; MTCW 1, 2; MTFW 2005; RGAL 4;
 TUS

Hansberry, Lorraine Vivian
 See Hansberry, Lorraine

Hansen, Joseph 1923-2004 .... **CLC 38**
 See also BPFB 2; CA 29-32R; 233; CAAS
 17; CANR 16, 44, 66, 125; CMW 4; DLB
 226; GLL 1; INT CANR-16

Hansen, Karen V. 1955- .... **CLC 65**
 See also CA 149; CANR 102

Hansen, Martin A(lfred)
 1909-1955 .... **TCLC 32**
 See also CA 167; DLB 214; EWL 3

Hanson, Kenneth O. 1922- .... **CLC 13**
 See also CA 53-56; CANR 7; CP 1, 2, 3, 4,
 5

Hanson, Kenneth Ostlin
 See Hanson, Kenneth O.

Han Yu 768-824 .... **CMLC 122**

Hardwick, Elizabeth 1916-2007 .... **CLC 13**
 See also AMWS 3; CA 5-8R; 267; CANR
 3, 32, 70, 100, 139; CN 4, 5, 6; CSW;
 DA3; DAM NOV; DLB 6; MBL; MTCW
 1, 2; MTFW 2005; TCLE 1:1

Hardwick, Elizabeth Bruce
 See Hardwick, Elizabeth

Hardy, Thomas 1840-1928 . **PC 8, 92; SSC 2,
 60, 113; TCLC 4, 10, 18, 32, 48, 53, 72,
 143, 153, 229; WLC 3**
 See also AAYA 69; BRW 6; BRWC 1, 2;
 BRWR 1; CA 104; 123; CDBLB 1890-
 1914; DA; DA3; DAB; DAC; DAM MST,
 NOV, POET; DLB 18, 19, 135, 284; EWL

3; EXPN; EXPP; LAIT 2; MTCW 1, 2;
 MTFW 2005; NFS 3, 11, 15, 19, 30; PFS
 3, 4, 18; RGEL 2; RGSF 2; TEA; WLIT
 4

Hare, David 1947- . **CLC 29, 58, 136; DC 26**
 See also BRWS 4; CA 97-100; CANR 39,
 91; CBD; CD 5, 6; DFS 4, 7, 16; DLB
 13, 310; MTCW 1; TEA

Harewood, John
 See Van Druten, John (William)

Harford, Henry
 See Hudson, W(illiam) H(enry)

Hargrave, Leonie
 See Disch, Thomas M.

**Hariri, Al- al-Qasim ibn 'Ali Abu
 Muhammad al-Basri**
 See al-Hariri, al-Qasim ibn 'Ali Abu Mu-
 hammad al-Basri

Harjo, Joy 1951- ..... **CLC 83; NNAL; PC 27**
 See also AMWS 12; CA 114; CANR 35,
 67, 91, 129; CP 6, 7; CWP; DAM MULT;
 DLB 120, 175, 342; EWL 3; MTCW 2;
 MTFW 2005; PFS 15, 32; RGAL 4

Harlan, Louis R. 1922-2010 .... **CLC 34**
 See also CA 21-24R; CANR 25, 55, 80

Harlan, Louis Rudolph
 See Harlan, Louis R.

Harlan, Louis Rudolph
 See Harlan, Louis R.

Harling, Robert 1951(?)- .... **CLC 53**
 See also CA 147

Harmon, William (Ruth) 1938- .... **CLC 38**
 See also CA 33-36R; CANR 14, 32, 35;
 SATA 65

Harper, Edith Alice Mary
 See Wickham, Anna

Harper, F. E. W.
 See Harper, Frances Ellen Watkins

Harper, Frances E. W.
 See Harper, Frances Ellen Watkins

Harper, Frances E. Watkins
 See Harper, Frances Ellen Watkins

Harper, Frances Ellen
 See Harper, Frances Ellen Watkins

Harper, Frances Ellen Watkins
 1825-1911 . **BLC 1:2; PC 21; TCLC 14,
 217**
 See also AFAW 1, 2; BW 1, 3; CA 111; 125;
 CANR 79; DAM MULT, POET; DLB 50,
 221; MBL; RGAL 4

Harper, Michael S. 1938- .. **BLC 2:2; CLC 7,
 22**
 See also AFAW 2; BW 1; CA 33-36R; 224;
 CAAE 224; CANR 24, 108, 212; CP 2, 3,
 4, 5, 6, 7; DLB 41; RGAL 4; TCLE 1:1

Harper, Michael Steven
 See Harper, Michael S.

Harper, Mrs. F. E. W.
 See Harper, Frances Ellen Watkins

Harpur, Charles 1813-1868 .... **NCLC 114**
 See also DLB 230; RGEL 2

Harris, Christie
 See Harris, Christie (Lucy) Irwin

Harris, Christie (Lucy) Irwin
 1907-2002 .... **CLC 12**
 See also CA 5-8R; CANR 6, 83; CLR 47;
 DLB 88; JRDA; MAICYA 1, 2; SAAS 10;
 SATA 6, 74; SATA-Essay 116

Harris, E. Lynn 1955-2009 .... **CLC 299**
 See also CA 164; 288; CANR 111, 163,
 206; MTFW 2005

Harris, Everett Lynn
 See Harris, E. Lynn

Harris, Everette Lynn
 See Harris, E. Lynn

Harris, Frank 1856-1931 .... **TCLC 24**
 See also CA 109; 150; CANR 80; DLB 156,
 197; RGEL 2

Harris, George Washington
 1814-1869 .... **NCLC 23, 165**
 See also DLB 3, 11, 248; RGAL 4

Harris, Joel Chandler 1848-1908 ..... **SSC 19,
 103; TCLC 2**
 See also CA 104; 137; CANR 80; CLR 49,
 128; DLB 11, 23, 42, 78, 91; LAIT 2;
 MAICYA 1, 2; RGSF 2; SATA 100; WCH;
 YABC 1

**Harris, John (Wyndham Parkes Lucas)
 Beynon** 1903-1969 .... **CLC 19**
 See also BRWS 13; CA 102; 89-92; CANR
 84; DLB 255; SATA 118; SCFW 1, 2;
 SFW 4

Harris, MacDonald
 See Heiney, Donald (William)

Harris, Mark 1922-2007 .... **CLC 19**
 See also CA 5-8R; 260; CAAS 3; CANR 2,
 55, 83; CN 1, 2, 3, 4, 5, 6, 7; DLB 2;
 DLBY 1980

Harris, Norman .... **CLC 65**

Harris, (Theodore) Wilson 1921- ... **BLC 2:2;
 CLC 25, 159, 297**
 See also BRWS 5; BW 2, 3; CA 65-68;
 CAAS 16; CANR 11, 27, 69, 114; CD-
 WLB 3; CN 1, 2, 3, 4, 5, 6, 7; CP 1, 2, 3,
 4, 5, 6, 7; DLB 117; EWL 3; MTCW 1;
 RGEL 2

Harrison, Barbara Grizzuti
 1934-2002 .... **CLC 144**
 See also CA 77-80; 205; CANR 15, 48; INT
 CANR-15

Harrison, Elizabeth (Allen) Cavanna
 1909-2001 .... **CLC 12**
 See also CA 9-12R; 200; CANR 6, 27, 85,
 104, 121; JRDA; MAICYA 1; SAAS 4;
 SATA 1, 30; YAW

Harrison, Harry 1925- .... **CLC 42**
 See also CA 1-4R; CANR 5, 21, 84, 225;
 DLB 8; SATA 4; SCFW 2; SFW 4

Harrison, Harry Max
 See Harrison, Harry

Harrison, James
 See Harrison, Jim

Harrison, James Thomas
 See Harrison, Jim

Harrison, Jim 1937- .... **CLC 6, 14, 33, 66,
 143; SSC 19**
 See also AMWS 8; CA 13-16R; CANR 8,
 51, 79, 142, 198; CN 5, 6; CP 1, 2, 3, 4,
 5, 6; DLBY 1982; INT CANR-8; RGAL
 4; TCWW 2; TUS

Harrison, Kathryn 1961- .... **CLC 70, 151**
 See also CA 144; CANR 68, 122, 194

Harrison, Tony 1937- .... **CLC 43, 129**
 See also BRWS 5; CA 65-68; CANR 44,
 98; CBD; CD 5, 6; CP 2, 3, 4, 5, 6, 7;
 DLB 40, 245; MTCW 1; RGEL 2

Harriss, Will(ard Irvin) 1922- .... **CLC 34**
 See also CA 111

Hart, Ellis
 See Ellison, Harlan

Hart, Josephine 1942-2011 .... **CLC 70**
 See also CA 138; CANR 70, 149, 220;
 CPW; DAM POP

Hart, Moss 1904-1961 .... **CLC 66**
 See also CA 109; 89-92; CANR 84; DAM
 DRAM; DFS 1; DLB 7, 266; RGAL 4

Harte, Bret 1836(?)-1902 .. **SSC 8, 59; TCLC
 1, 25; WLC 3**
 See also AMWS 2; CA 104; 140; CANR
 80; CDALB 1865-1917; DA; DA3; DAC;
 DAM MST; DLB 12, 64, 74, 79, 186;
 EXPS; LAIT 2; RGAL 4; RGSF 2; SATA
 26; SSFS 3; TUS

Harte, Francis Brett
 See Harte, Bret

Hitler, Adolf 1889-1945 .... **TCLC 53**
See also CA 117; 147

Hoagland, Edward (Morley) 1932- .. **CLC 28**
See also ANW; CA 1-4R; CANR 2, 31, 57,
107; CN 1, 2, 3, 4, 5, 6, 7; DLB 6; SATA
51; TCWW 2

Hoban, Russell 1925- .... **CLC 7, 25**
See also BPFB 2; CA 5-8R; CANR 23, 37,
66, 114, 138, 218; CLR 3, 69, 139; CN 4,
5, 6, 7; CWRI 5; DAM NOV; DLB 52;
FANT; MAICYA 1, 2; MTCW 1, 2;
MTFW 2005; SATA 1, 40, 78, 136; SFW
4; SUFW 2; TCLE 1:1

Hoban, Russell Conwell
See Hoban, Russell

Hobbes, Thomas 1588-1679 .... **LC 36, 142, 199**
See also DLB 151, 252, 281; RGEL 2

Hobbs, Perry
See Blackmur, R(ichard) P(almer)

Hobson, Laura Z(ametkin)
1900-1986 .... **CLC 7, 25**
See also BPFB 2; CA 17-20R; 118; CANR
55; CN 1, 2, 3, 4; DLB 28; SATA 52

Hoccleve, Thomas c. 1368-c. 1437 ...... **LC 75**
See also DLB 146; RGEL 2

Hoch, Edward D. 1930-2008 .... **SSC 119**
See also CA 29-32R; CANR 11, 27, 51, 97;
CMW 4; DLB 306; SFW 4

Hoch, Edward Dentinger
See Hoch, Edward D.

Hochhuth, Rolf 1931- .... **CLC 4, 11, 18**
See also CA 5-8R; CANR 33, 75, 136;
CWW 2; DAM DRAM; DLB 124; EWL
3; MTCW 1, 2; MTFW 2005; RGHL

Hochman, Sandra 1936- .... **CLC 3, 8**
See also CA 5-8R; CP 1, 2, 3, 4, 5; DLB 5

Hochwaelder, Fritz 1911-1986 .... **CLC 36**
See also CA 29-32R; 120; CANR 42; DAM
DRAM; EWL 3; MTCW 1; RGWL 2, 3

Hochwalder, Fritz
See Hochwaelder, Fritz

Hocking, Mary 1921- .... **CLC 13**
See also CA 101; CANR 18, 40

Hocking, Mary Eunice
See Hocking, Mary

Hodge, Merle 1944- .... **BLC 2:2**
See also EWL 3

Hodgins, Jack 1938- .... **CLC 23; SSC 132**
See also CA 93-96; CN 4, 5, 6, 7; DLB 60

Hodgson, William Hope
1877(?)-1918 .... **TCLC 13**
See also CA 111; 164; CMW 4; DLB 70,
153, 156, 178; HGG; MTCW 2; SFW 4;
SUFW 1

Hoeg, Peter
See Hoeg, Peter

Hoeg, Peter 1957- .... **CLC 95, 156**
See also CA 151; CANR 75, 202; CMW 4;
DA3; DLB 214; EWL 3; MTCW 2;
MTFW 2005; NFS 17; RGWL 3; SSFS
18

Hoffman, Alice 1952- .... **CLC 51**
See also AAYA 37; AMWS 10; CA 77-80;
CANR 34, 66, 100, 138, 170; CN 4, 5, 6,
7; CPW; DAM NOV; DLB 292; MAL 5;
MTCW 1, 2; MTFW 2005; TCLE 1:1

Hoffman, Daniel (Gerard) 1923- . **CLC 6, 13, 23**
See also CA 1-4R; CANR 4, 142; CP 1, 2,
3, 4, 5, 6, 7; DLB 5; TCLE 1:1

Hoffman, Eva 1945- .... **CLC 182**
See also AMWS 16; CA 132; CANR 146, 209

Hoffman, Stanley 1944- .... **CLC 5**
See also CA 77-80

Hoffman, William 1925-2009 .... **CLC 141**
See also AMWS 18; CA 21-24R; CANR 9,
103; CSW; DLB 234; TCLE 1:1

Hoffman, William M.
See Hoffman, William M(oses)

Hoffman, William M(oses) 1939- ..... **CLC 40**
See also CA 57-60; CAD; CANR 11, 71;
CD 5, 6

Hoffmann, E(rnst) T(heodor) A(madeus)
1776-1822 ..... **NCLC 2, 183; SSC 13, 92**
See also CDWLB 2; CLR 133; DLB 90;
EW 5; GL 2; RGSF 2; RGWL 2, 3; SATA
27; SUFW 1; WCH

Hofmann, Gert 1931-1993 .... **CLC 54**
See also CA 128; CANR 145; EWL 3;
RGHL

Hofmannsthal, Hugo von 1874-1929 ... **DC 4; TCLC 11**
See also CA 106; 153; CDWLB 2; DAM
DRAM; DFS 17; DLB 81, 118; EW 9;
EWL 3; RGWL 2, 3

Hogan, Linda 1947- .... **CLC 73, 290; NNAL; PC 35**
See also AMWS 4; ANW; BYA 12; CA 120,
226; CAAE 226; CANR 45, 73, 129, 196;
CWP; DAM MULT; DLB 175; SATA
132; TCWW 2

Hogarth, Charles
See Creasey, John

Hogarth, Emmett
See Polonsky, Abraham (Lincoln)

Hogarth, William 1697-1764 .... **LC 112**
See also AAYA 56

Hogg, James 1770-1835 .. **NCLC 4, 109; SSC 130**
See also BRWS 10; DLB 93, 116, 159; GL
2; HGG; RGEL 2; SUFW 1

Holbach, Paul-Henri Thiry
1723-1789 .... **LC 14**
See also DLB 313

Holberg, Ludvig 1684-1754 .... **LC 6**
See also DLB 300; RGWL 2, 3

Holbrook, John
See Vance, Jack

Holcroft, Thomas 1745-1809 .... **NCLC 85**
See also DLB 39, 89, 158; RGEL 2

Holden, Ursula 1921- .... **CLC 18**
See also CA 101; CAAS 8; CANR 22

Holderlin, (Johann Christian) Friedrich
1770-1843 .... **NCLC 16, 187; PC 4**
See also CDWLB 2; DLB 90; EW 5; RGWL
2, 3

Holdstock, Robert 1948-2009 .... **CLC 39**
See also CA 131; CANR 81, 207; DLB 261;
FANT; HGG; SFW 4; SUFW 2

Holdstock, Robert P.
See Holdstock, Robert

Holinshed, Raphael fl. 1580- .... **LC 69**
See also DLB 167; RGEL 2

Holland, Isabelle (Christian)
1920-2002 .... **CLC 21**
See also AAYA 11, 64; CA 21-24R; 205;
CAAE 181; CANR 10, 25, 47; CLR 57;
CWRI 5; JRDA; LAIT 4; MAICYA 1, 2;
SATA 8, 70; SATA-Essay 103; SATA-Obit
132; WYA

Holland, Marcus
See Caldwell, (Janet Miriam) Taylor
(Holland)

Hollander, John 1929- .. **CLC 2, 5, 8, 14; PC 117**
See also CA 1-4R; CANR 1, 52, 136; CP 1,
2, 3, 4, 5, 6, 7; DLB 5; MAL 5; SATA 13

Hollander, Paul
See Silverberg, Robert

Holleran, Andrew 1943(?)- .... **CLC 38**
See also CA 144; CANR 89, 162; GLL 1

Holley, Marietta 1836(?)-1926 .... **TCLC 99**
See also CA 118; DLB 11; FL 1:3

Hollinghurst, Alan 1954- .... **CLC 55, 91**
See also BRWS 10; CA 114; CN 5, 6, 7;
DLB 207, 326; GLL 1

Hollis, Jim
See Summers, Hollis (Spurgeon, Jr.)

Holly, Buddy 1936-1959 .... **TCLC 65**
See also CA 213

Holmes, Gordon
See Shiel, M. P.

Holmes, John
See Souster, (Holmes) Raymond

Holmes, John Clellon 1926-1988 ...... **CLC 56**
See also BG 1:2; CA 9-12R; 125; CANR 4;
CN 1, 2, 3, 4; DLB 16, 237

Holmes, Oliver Wendell, Jr.
1841-1935 .... **TCLC 77**
See also CA 114; 186

Holmes, Oliver Wendell
1809-1894 .... **NCLC 14, 81; PC 71**
See also AMWS 1; CDALB 1640-1865;
DLB 1, 189, 235; EXPP; PFS 24; RGAL
4; SATA 34

Holmes, Raymond
See Souster, (Holmes) Raymond

Holt, Samuel
See Westlake, Donald E.

Holt, Victoria
See Hibbert, Eleanor Alice Burford

Holub, Miroslav 1923-1998 .... **CLC 4**
See also CA 21-24R; 169; CANR 10; CD-
WLB 4; CWW 2; DLB 232; EWL 3;
RGWL 3

Holz, Detlev
See Benjamin, Walter

Homer c. 8th cent. B.C.- ..... **CMLC 1, 16, 61, 121; PC 23; WLCS**
See also AW 1; CDWLB 1; DA; DA3;
DAB; DAC; DAM MST, POET; DLB
176; EFS 1:1, 2:1,2; LAIT 1; LMFS 1;
RGWL 2, 3; TWA; WLIT 8; WP

Hong, Maxine Ting Ting
See Kingston, Maxine Hong

Hongo, Garrett Kaoru 1951- .... **PC 23**
See also CA 133; CAAS 22; CP 5, 6, 7;
DLB 120, 312; EWL 3; EXPP; PFS 25,
33; RGAL 4

Honig, Edwin 1919-2011 .... **CLC 33**
See also CA 5-8R; CAAS 8; CANR 4, 45,
144; CP 1, 2, 3, 4, 5, 6, 7; DLB 5

Hood, Hugh (John Blagdon) 1928- . **CLC 15, 28, 273; SSC 42**
See also CA 49-52; CAAS 17; CANR 1,
33, 87; CN 1, 2, 3, 4, 5, 6, 7; DLB 53;
RGSF 2

Hood, Thomas 1799-1845 ..... **NCLC 16, 242; PC 93**
See also BRW 4; DLB 96; RGEL 2

Hooker, (Peter) Jeremy 1941- .... **CLC 43**
See also CA 77-80; CANR 22; CP 2, 3, 4,
5, 6, 7; DLB 40

Hooker, Richard 1554-1600 .... **LC 95**
See also BRW 1; DLB 132; RGEL 2

Hooker, Thomas 1586-1647 .... **LC 137**
See also DLB 24

hooks, bell 1952(?)- .... **BLCS; CLC 94**
See also BW 2; CA 143; CANR 87, 126,
211; DLB 246; MTCW 2; MTFW 2005;
SATA 115, 170

Hooper, Johnson Jones
1815-1862 .... **NCLC 177**
See also DLB 3, 11, 248; RGAL 4

Hope, A(lec) D(erwent) 1907-2000 .... **CLC 3, 51; PC 56**
See also BRWS 7; CA 21-24R; 188; CANR
33, 74; CP 1, 2, 3, 4, 5; DLB 289; EWL
3; MTCW 1, 2; MTFW 2005; PFS 8;
RGEL 2

Hope, Anthony 1863-1933 .... **TCLC 83**
See also CA 157; DLB 153, 156; RGEL 2;
RHW

Hope, Brian
See Creasey, John

Hope, Christopher 1944- .... **CLC 52**
 See also AFW; CA 106; CANR 47, 101,
 177; CN 4, 5, 6, 7; DLB 225; SATA 62
Hope, Christopher David Tully
 See Hope, Christopher
Hopkins, Gerard Manley
 1844-1889 .... **NCLC 17, 189; PC 15;**
 WLC 3
 See also BRW 5; BRWR 2; CDBLB 1890-
 1914; DA; DA3; DAB; DAC; DAM MST,
 POET; DLB 35, 57; EXPP; PAB; PFS 26,
 40; RGEL 2; TEA; WP
Hopkins, John (Richard) 1931-1998 .. **CLC 4**
 See also CA 85-88; 169; CBD; CD 5, 6
Hopkins, Pauline Elizabeth
 1859-1930 .... **BLC 1:2; TCLC 28, 251**
 See also AFAW 2; BW 2, 3; CA 141; CANR
 82; DAM MULT; DLB 50
Hopkinson, Francis 1737-1791 .... **LC 25**
 See also DLB 31; RGAL 4
Hopkinson, Nalo 1960- .... **CLC 316**
 See also AAYA 40; CA 196, 219; CAAE
 219; CANR 173; DLB 251
Hopley, George
 See Hopley-Woolrich, Cornell George
Hopley-Woolrich, Cornell George
 1903-1968 .... **CLC 77**
 See also CA 13-14; CANR 58, 156; CAP 1;
 CMW 4; DLB 226; MSW; MTCW 2
Horace 65B.C.-8B.C. . **CMLC 39, 125; PC 46**
 See also AW 2; CDWLB 1; DLB 211;
 RGWL 2, 3; WLIT 8
Horatio
 See Proust, Marcel
Horgan, Paul (George Vincent
 O'Shaughnessy) 1903-1995 .. **CLC 9, 53**
 See also BPFB 2; CA 13-16R; 147; CANR
 9, 35, CN 1, 2, 3, 4, 5; DAM NOV; DLB
 102, 212; DLBY 1985; INT CANR-9;
 MTCW 1, 2; MTFW 2005; SATA 13;
 SATA-Obit 84; TCWW 1, 2
Horkheimer, Max 1895-1973 .... **TCLC 132**
 See also CA 216; 41-44R; DLB 296
Horn, Peter
 See Kuttner, Henry
Hornby, Nicholas Peter John
 See Hornby, Nick
Hornby, Nick 1957(?)- .... **CLC 243**
 See also AAYA 74; BRWS 15; CA 151;
 CANR 104, 151, 191; CN 7; DLB 207,
 352
Horne, Frank 1899-1974 .... **HR 1:2**
 See also BW 1; CA 125; 53-56; DLB 51;
 WP
Horne, Richard Henry Hengist
 1802(?)-1884 .... **NCLC 127**
 See also DLB 32; SATA 29
Hornem, Horace Esq.
 See Lord Byron
Horne Tooke, John 1736-1812 ..... **NCLC 195**
Horney, Karen (Clementine Theodore
 Danielsen) 1885-1952 .... **TCLC 71**
 See also CA 114; 165; DLB 246; FW
Hornung, E(rnest) W(illiam)
 1866-1921 .... **TCLC 59**
 See also CA 108; 160; CMW 4; DLB 70
Horovitz, Israel 1939- .... **CLC 56**
 See also CA 33-36R; CAD; CANR 46, 59;
 CD 5, 6; DAM DRAM; DLB 7, 341;
 MAL 5
Horton, George Moses
 1797(?)-1883(?) .... **NCLC 87**
 See also DLB 50
Horvath, odon von 1901-1938
 See von Horvath, Odon
 See also EWL 3
Horvath, Oedoen von -1938
 See von Horvath, Odon

Horwitz, Julius 1920-1986 .... **CLC 14**
 See also CA 9-12R; 119; CANR 12
Horwitz, Ronald
 See Harwood, Ronald
Hospital, Janette Turner 1942- .... **CLC 42,**
 145
 See also CA 108; CANR 48, 166, 200; CN
 5, 6, 7; DLB 325; DLBY 2002; RGSF 2
Hosseini, Khaled 1965- .... **CLC 254**
 See also CA 225; LNFS 1, 3; SATA 156
Hostos, E. M. de
 See Hostos (y Bonilla), Eugenio Maria de
Hostos, Eugenio M. de
 See Hostos (y Bonilla), Eugenio Maria de
Hostos, Eugenio Maria
 See Hostos (y Bonilla), Eugenio Maria de
Hostos (y Bonilla), Eugenio Maria de
 1839-1903 .... **TCLC 24**
 See also CA 123; 131; HW 1
Houdini
 See Lovecraft, H. P.
Houellebecq, Michel 1958- ...... **CLC 179, 311**
 See also CA 185; CANR 140; MTFW 2005
Hougan, Carolyn 1943-2007 .... **CLC 34**
 See also CA 139; 257
Household, Geoffrey 1900-1988 .... **CLC 11**
 See also BRWS 17; CA 77-80; 126; CANR
 58; CMW 4; CN 1, 2, 3, 4; DLB 87;
 SATA 14; SATA-Obit 59
Housman, A. E. 1859-1936 . **PC 2, 43; TCLC**
 1, 10; WLCS
 See also AAYA 66; BRW 6; CA 104; 125;
 DA; DA3; DAB; DAC; DAM MST,
 POET; DLB 19, 284; EWL 3; EXPP;
 MTCW 1, 2; MTFW 2005; PAB; PFS 4,
 7, 40; RGEL 2; TEA; WP
Housman, Alfred Edward
 See Housman, A. E.
Housman, Laurence 1865-1959 .... **TCLC 7**
 See also CA 106; 155; DLB 10; FANT;
 RGEL 2; SATA 25
Houston, Jeanne Wakatsuki 1934- .... **AAL**
 See also AAYA 49; CA 103, 232; CAAE
 232; CAAS 16; CANR 29, 123, 167;
 LAIT 4; SATA 78, 168; SATA-Essay 168
Hove, Chenjerai 1956- .... **BLC 2:2**
 See also CP 7; DLB 360
Howard, E. J.
 See Howard, Elizabeth Jane
Howard, Elizabeth Jane 1923- ..... **CLC 7, 29**
 See also BRWS 11; CA 5-8R; CANR 8, 62,
 146, 210; CN 1, 2, 3, 4, 5, 6, 7
Howard, Maureen 1930- .... **CLC 5, 14, 46,**
 151
 See also CA 53-56; CANR 31, 75, 140, 221;
 CN 4, 5, 6, 7; DLBY 1983; INT CANR-
 31; MTCW 1, 2; MTFW 2005
Howard, Richard 1929- .... **CLC 7, 10, 47**
 See also AITN 1; CA 85-88; CANR 25, 80,
 154, 217; CP 1, 2, 3, 4, 5, 6, 7; DLB 5;
 INT CANR-25; MAL 5
Howard, Robert E 1906-1936 .... **TCLC 8**
 See also AAYA 80; BPFB 2; BYA 5; CA
 105; 157; CANR 155; FANT; SUFW 1;
 TCWW 1, 2
Howard, Robert Ervin
 See Howard, Robert E
Howard, Sidney (Coe) 1891-1939 .... **DC 42**
 See also CA 198; DFS 29; DLB 7, 26, 249;
 IDFW 3, 4; MAL 5; RGAL 4
Howard, Warren F.
 See Pohl, Frederik
Howe, Fanny 1940- .... **CLC 47**
 See also CA 117, 187; CAAE 187; CAAS
 27; CANR 70, 116, 184; CP 6, 7; CWP;
 SATA-Brief 52
Howe, Fanny Quincy
 See Howe, Fanny

Howe, Irving 1920-1993 .... **CLC 85**
 See also AMWS 6; CA 9-12R; 141; CANR
 21, 50; DLB 67; EWL 3; MAL 5; MTCW
 1, 2; MTFW 2005
Howe, Julia Ward 1819-1910 . **PC 81; TCLC**
 21
 See also CA 117; 191; DLB 1, 189, 235;
 FW
Howe, Susan 1937- .... **CLC 72, 152; PC 54**
 See also AMWS 4; CA 160; CANR 209;
 CP 5, 6, 7; CWP; DLB 120; FW; RGAL
 4
Howe, Tina 1937- .... **CLC 48; DC 43**
 See also CA 109; CAD; CANR 125; CD 5,
 6; CWD; DLB 341
Howell, James 1594(?)-1666 .... **LC 13**
 See also DLB 151
Howells, W. D.
 See Howells, William Dean
Howells, William D.
 See Howells, William Dean
Howells, William Dean 1837-1920 ... **SSC 36;**
 TCLC 7, 17, 41
 See also AMW; CA 104; 134; CDALB
 1865-1917; DLB 12, 64, 74, 79, 189;
 LMFS 1; MAL 5; MTCW 2; RGAL 4;
 TUS
Howes, Barbara 1914-1996 .... **CLC 15**
 See also CA 9-12R; 151; CAAS 3; CANR
 53; CP 1, 2, 3, 4, 5, 6; SATA 5; TCLE 1:1
Hrabal, Bohumil 1914-1997 ...... **CLC 13, 67;**
 TCLC 155
 See also CA 106; 156; CAAS 12; CANR
 57; CWW 2; DLB 232; EWL 3; RGSF 2
Hrabanus Maurus 776(?)-856 .... **CMLC 78**
 See also DLB 148
Hroswitha of Gandersheim
 See Hrotsvit of Gandersheim
Hrotsvit of Gandersheim c. 935-c.
 1000 .... **CMLC 29, 123**
 See also DLB 148
Hsi, Chu 1130-1200 .... **CMLC 42**
Hsun, Lu
 See Shu-Jen, Chou
Hubbard, L. Ron 1911-1986 .... **CLC 43**
 See also AAYA 64; CA 77-80; 118; CANR
 52; CPW; DA3; DAM POP; FANT;
 MTCW 2; MTFW 2005; SFW 4
Hubbard, Lafayette Ronald
 See Hubbard, L. Ron
Huch, Ricarda (Octavia)
 1864-1947 .... **TCLC 13**
 See also CA 111; 189; DLB 66; EWL 3
Huddle, David 1942- .... **CLC 49**
 See also CA 57-60, 261; CAAS 20; CANR
 89; DLB 130
Hudson, Jeffery
 See Crichton, Michael
Hudson, Jeffrey
 See Crichton, Michael
Hudson, W(illiam) H(enry)
 1841-1922 .... **TCLC 29**
 See also CA 115; 190; DLB 98, 153, 174;
 RGEL 2; SATA 35
Hueffer, Ford Madox
 See Ford, Ford Madox
Hughart, Barry 1934- .... **CLC 39**
 See also CA 137; FANT; SFW 4; SUFW 2
Hughes, Colin
 See Creasey, John
Hughes, David (John) 1930-2005 ..... **CLC 48**
 See also CA 116; 129; 238; CN 4, 5, 6, 7;
 DLB 14
Hughes, Edward James
 See Hughes, Ted
Hughes, James Langston
 See Hughes, Langston

Kastel, Warren
  See Silverberg, Robert
Kataev, Evgeny Petrovich
  1903-1942 .... **TCLC 21**
  See also CA 120; DLB 272
Kataphusin
  See Ruskin, John
Katz, Steve 1935- .... **CLC 47**
  See also CA 25-28R; CAAS 14, 64; CANR
  12; CN 4, 5, 6, 7; DLBY 1983
Kauffman, Janet 1945- .... **CLC 42**
  See also CA 117; CANR 43, 84; DLB 218;
  DLBY 1986
Kaufman, Bob (Garnell)
  1925-1986 .... **CLC 49; PC 74**
  See also BG 1:3; BW 1; CA 41-44R; 118;
  CANR 22; CP 1; DLB 16, 41
Kaufman, George S. 1889-1961 ...... **CLC 38;**
  DC 17
  See also CA 108; 93-96; DAM DRAM;
  DFS 1, 10; DLB 7; INT CA-108; MTCW
  2; MTFW 2005; RGAL 4; TUS
Kaufman, Moises 1963- .... **DC 26**
  See also AAYA 85; CA 211; DFS 22;
  MTFW 2005
Kaufman, Sue
  See Barondess, Sue K.
Kavafis, Konstantinos Petrov
  See Cavafy, Constantine
Kavan, Anna 1901-1968 .... **CLC 5, 13, 82**
  See also BRWS 7; CA 5-8R; CANR 6, 57;
  DLB 255; MTCW 1; RGEL 2; SFW 4
Kavanagh, Dan
  See Barnes, Julian
Kavanagh, Julie 1952- .... **CLC 119**
  See also CA 163; CANR 186
Kavanagh, Patrick (Joseph)
  1904-1967 .... **CLC 22; PC 33, 105**
  See also BRWS 7; CA 123; 25-28R; DLB
  15, 20; EWL 3; MTCW 1; RGEL 2
Kawabata, Yasunari 1899-1972 ..... **CLC 2, 5,**
  9, 18, 107; SSC 17
  See also CA 93-96; 33-36R; CANR 88;
  DAM MULT; DLB 180, 330; EWL 3;
  MJW; MTCW 2; MTFW 2005; RGSF 2;
  RGWL 2, 3; SSFS 29
Kawabata Yasunari
  See Kawabata, Yasunari
Kaye, Mary Margaret
  See Kaye, M.M.
Kaye, M.M. 1908-2004 .... **CLC 28**
  See also CA 89-92; 223; CANR 24, 60, 102,
  142; MTCW 1, 2; MTFW 2005; RHW;
  SATA 62; SATA-Obit 152
Kaye, Mollie
  See Kaye, M.M.
Kaye-Smith, Sheila 1887-1956 .... **TCLC 20**
  See also CA 118; 203; DLB 36
Kaymor, Patrice Maguilene
  See Senghor, Leopold Sedar
Kazakov, Iurii Pavlovich
  See Kazakov, Yuri Pavlovich
Kazakov, Yuri Pavlovich 1927-1982 . **SSC 43**
  See also CA 5-8R; CANR 36; DLB 302;
  EWL 3; MTCW 1; RGSF 2
Kazakov, Yury
  See Kazakov, Yuri Pavlovich
Kazan, Elia 1909-2003 .... **CLC 6, 16, 63**
  See also AAYA 83; CA 21-24R; 220; CANR
  32, 78
Kazanjoglou, Elia
  See Kazan, Elia
Kazantzakis, Nikos 1883(?)-1957 ..... **PC 126;**
  TCLC 2, 5, 33, 181
  See also AAYA 83; BPFB 2; CA 105; 132;
  DA3; EW 9; EWL 3; MTCW 1, 2; MTFW
  2005; RGWL 2, 3

Kazin, Alfred 1915-1998 ..... **CLC 34, 38, 119**
  See also AMWS 8; CA 1-4R; CAAS 7;
  CANR 1, 45, 79; DLB 67; EWL 3
Keane, Mary Nesta 1904-1996 .... **CLC 31**
  See also CA 108; 114; 151; CN 5, 6; INT
  CA-114; RHW; TCLE 1:1
Keane, Mary Nesta Skrine
  See Keane, Mary Nesta
Keane, Molly
  See Keane, Mary Nesta
Keates, Jonathan 1946(?)- .... **CLC 34**
  See also CA 163; CANR 126
Keaton, Buster 1895-1966 .... **CLC 20**
  See also AAYA 79; CA 194
Keats, John 1795-1821 ...... **NCLC 8, 73, 121,**
  225; PC 1, 96; WLC 3
  See also AAYA 58; BRW 4; BRWR 1; CD-
  BLB 1789-1832; DA; DA3; DAB; DAC;
  DAM MST, POET; DLB 96, 110; EXPP;
  LMFS 1; PAB; PFS 1, 2, 3, 9, 17, 32, 36;
  RGEL 2; TEA; WLIT 3; WP
Keble, John 1792-1866 .... **NCLC 87**
  See also DLB 32, 55; RGEL 2
Keene, Donald 1922- .... **CLC 34**
  See also CA 1-4R; CANR 5, 119, 190
Keillor, Garrison 1942- ..... **CLC 40, 115, 222**
  See also AAYA 2, 62; AMWS 16; BEST
  89:3; BPFB 2; CA 111; 117; CANR 36,
  59, 124, 180; CPW; DA3; DAM POP;
  DLBY 1987; EWL 3; MTCW 1, 2; MTFW
  2005; SATA 58; TUS
Keillor, Gary Edward
  See Keillor, Garrison
Keith, Carlos
  See Lewton, Val
Keith, Michael
  See Hubbard, L. Ron
Kell, Joseph
  See Burgess, Anthony
Keller, Gottfried 1819-1890 .... **NCLC 2; SSC**
  26, 107
  See also CDWLB 2; DLB 129; EW; RGSF
  2; RGWL 2, 3
Keller, Nora Okja 1965- .... **CLC 109, 281**
  See also CA 187
Kellerman, Jonathan 1949- .... **CLC 44**
  See also AAYA 35; BEST 90:1; CA 106;
  CANR 29, 51, 150, 183; CMW 4; CPW;
  DA3; DAM POP; INT CANR-29
Kelley, William Melvin 1937- .... **BLC 2:2;**
  CLC 22
  See also BW 1; CA 77-80; CANR 27, 83;
  CN 1, 2, 3, 4, 5, 6, 7; DLB 33; EWL 3
Kellock, Archibald P.
  See Mavor, Osborne Henry
Kellogg, Marjorie 1922-2005 .... **CLC 2**
  See also CA 81-84; 246
Kellow, Kathleen
  See Hibbert, Eleanor Alice Burford
Kelly, Lauren
  See Oates, Joyce Carol
Kelly, M(ilton) T(errence) 1947- ...... **CLC 55**
  See also CA 97-100; CAAS 22; CANR 19,
  43, 84; CN 6
Kelly, Robert 1935- .... **SSC 50**
  See also CA 17-20R; CAAS 19; CANR 47;
  CP 1, 2, 3, 4, 5, 6, 7; DLB 5, 130, 165
Kelman, James 1946- .... **CLC 58, 86, 292**
  See also BRWS 5; CA 148; CANR 85, 130,
  199; CN 5, 6, 7; DLB 194, 319, 326;
  RGSF 2; WLIT 4
Kelton, Elmer 1926-2009 .... **CLC 299**
  See also AAYA 78; AITN 1; BYA 9; CA
  21-24R; 289; CANR 12, 36, 85, 149, 173,
  209; DLB 256; TCWW 1, 2
Kelton, Elmer Stephen
  See Kelton, Elmer
Kemal, Yasar
  See Kemal, Yashar

Kemal, Yashar 1923(?)- .... **CLC 14, 29**
  See also CA 89-92; CANR 44; CWW 2;
  EWL 3; WLIT 6
Kemble, Fanny 1809-1893 .... **NCLC 18**
  See also DLB 32
Kemelman, Harry 1908-1996 .... **CLC 2**
  See also AITN 1; BPFB 2; CA 9-12R; 155;
  CANR 6, 71; CMW 4; DLB 28
Kempe, Margery 1373(?)-1440(?) ... **LC 6, 56**
  See also BRWS 12; DLB 146; FL 1:1;
  RGEL 2
Kempis, Thomas a 1380-1471 .... **LC 11**
Kenan, Randall (G.) 1963- .... **BLC 2:2**
  See also BW 2, 3; CA 142; CANR 86; CN
  7; CSW; DLB 292; GLL 1
Kendall, Henry 1839-1882 .... **NCLC 12**
  See also DLB 230
Keneally, Thomas 1935- .... **CLC 5, 8, 10, 14,**
  19, 27, 43, 117, 279
  See also BRWS 4; CA 85-88; CANR 10,
  50, 74, 130, 165, 198; CN 1, 2, 3, 4, 5, 6,
  7; CPW; DA3; DAM NOV; DLB 289,
  299, 326; EWL 3; MTCW 1, 2; MTFW
  2005; NFS 17, 38; RGEL 2; RGHL; RHW
Keneally, Thomas Michael
  See Keneally, Thomas
Keneally, Tom
  See Keneally, Thomas
Kennedy, A. L. 1965- .... **CLC 188**
  See also CA 168, 213; CAAE 213; CANR
  108, 193; CD 5, 6; CN 6, 7; DLB 271;
  RGSF 2
Kennedy, Adrienne (Lita) 1931- .... **BLC 1:2;**
  CLC 66, 308; DC 5
  See also AFAW 2; BW 2, 3; CA 103; CAAS
  20; CABS 3; CAD; CANR 26, 53, 82;
  CD 5, 6; DAM MULT; DFS 9, 28; DLB
  38, 341, FW; MAL 5
Kennedy, Alison Louise
  See Kennedy, A. L.
Kennedy, John Pendleton
  1795-1870 .... **NCLC 2**
  See also DLB 3, 248, 254; RGAL 4
Kennedy, Joseph Charles
  See Kennedy, X. J.
Kennedy, William 1928- .. **CLC 6, 28, 34, 53,**
  239
  See also AAYA 1, 73; AMWS 7; BPFB 2;
  CA 85-88; CANR 14, 31, 76, 134; CN 4,
  5, 6, 7; DA3; DAM NOV; DLB 143;
  DLBY 1985; EWL 3; INT CANR-31;
  MAL 5; MTCW 1, 2; MTFW 2005; SATA
  57
Kennedy, William Joseph
  See Kennedy, William
Kennedy, X. J. 1929- .... **CLC 8, 42; PC 93**
  See also AMWS 15; CA 1-4R, 201; CAAE
  201; CAAS 9; CANR 4, 30, 40, 214; CLR
  27; CP 1, 2, 3, 4, 5, 6, 7; CWRI 5; DLB
  5; MAICYA 2; MAICYAS 1; SAAS 22;
  SATA 14, 86, 130; SATA-Essay 130
Kenny, Maurice (Francis) 1929- ..... **CLC 87;**
  NNAL
  See also CA 144; CAAS 22; CANR 143;
  DAM MULT; DLB 175
Kent, Kathleen .... **CLC 280**
  See also CA 288
Kent, Kelvin
  See Kuttner, Henry
Kent, Klark
  See Copeland, Stewart
Kenton, Maxwell
  See Southern, Terry
Kenyon, Jane 1947-1995 .... **PC 57**
  See also AAYA 63; AMWS 7; CA 118; 148;
  CANR 44, 69, 172; CP 6, 7; CWP; DLB
  120; PFS 9, 17, 39; RGAL 4
Kenyon, Robert O.
  See Kuttner, Henry

EWL 3; EXPS; FANT; LAIT 3; LMFS 1;
MAICYA 1, 2; MTCW 1, 2; MTFW 2005;
NFS 21; PFS 22; RGEL 2; RGSF 2; SATA
100; SFW 4; SSFS 8, 21, 22, 32; SUFW
1; TEA; WCH; WLIT 4; YABC 2

Kircher, Athanasius 1602-1680 .... **LC 121**
See also DLB 164

Kirk, Richard
See Holdstock, Robert

Kirk, Russell (Amos) 1918-1994 .. **TCLC 119**
See also AITN 1; CA 1-4R; 145; CAAS 9;
CANR 1, 20, 60; HGG; INT CANR-20;
MTCW 1, 2

Kirkham, Dinah
See Card, Orson Scott

Kirkland, Caroline M. 1801-1864 . **NCLC 85**
See also DLB 3, 73, 74, 250, 254; DLBD
13

Kirkup, James 1918-2009 .... **CLC 1**
See also CA 1-4R; CAAS 4; CANR 2; CP
1, 2, 3, 4, 5, 6, 7; DLB 27; SATA 12

Kirkwood, James 1930(?)-1989 .... **CLC 9**
See also AITN 2; CA 1-4R; 128; CANR 6,
40; GLL 2

Kirsch, Sarah 1935- .... **CLC 176**
See also CA 178; CWW 2; DLB 75; EWL
3

Kirshner, Sidney
See Kingsley, Sidney

Kis, Danilo 1935-1989 .... **CLC 57**
See also CA 109; 118; 129; CANR 61; CD-
WLB 4; DLB 181; EWL 3; MTCW 1;
RGSF 2; RGWL 2, 3

Kissinger, Henry A. 1923- .... **CLC 137**
See also CA 1-4R; CANR 2, 33, 66, 109;
MTCW 1

Kissinger, Henry Alfred
See Kissinger, Henry A.

Kittel, Frederick August
See Wilson, August

Kivi, Aleksis 1834-1872 .... **NCLC 30**

Kizer, Carolyn 1925- ..... **CLC 15, 39, 80; PC
66**
See also CA 65-68; CAAS 5; CANR 24,
70, 134; CP 1, 2, 3, 4, 5, 6, 7; CWP; DAM
POET; DLB 5, 169; EWL 3; MAL 5;
MTCW 2; MTFW 2005; PFS 18; TCLE
1:1

Klabund 1890-1928 .... **TCLC 44**
See also CA 162; DLB 66

Klappert, Peter 1942- .... **CLC 57**
See also CA 33-36R; CSW; DLB 5

Klausner, Amos
See Oz, Amos

Klein, A. M. 1909-1972 .... **CLC 19**
See also CA 101; 37-40R; CP 1; DAB;
DAC; DAM MST; DLB 68; EWL 3;
RGEL 2; RGHL

Klein, Abraham Moses
See Klein, A. M.

Klein, Joe
See Klein, Joseph

Klein, Joseph 1946- .... **CLC 154**
See also CA 85-88; CANR 55, 164

Klein, Norma 1938-1989 .... **CLC 30**
See also AAYA 2, 35; BPFB 2; BYA 6, 7,
8; CA 41-44R; 128; CANR 15, 37; CLR
2, 19, 162; INT CANR-15; JRDA; MAI-
CYA 1, 2; SAAS 1; SATA 7, 57; WYA;
YAW

Klein, T.E.D. 1947- .... **CLC 34**
See also CA 119; CANR 44, 75, 167; HGG

Klein, Theodore Eibon Donald
See Klein, T.E.D.

Kleist, Heinrich von 1777-1811 .... **DC 29;
NCLC 2, 37, 222; SSC 22**
See also CDWLB 2; DAM DRAM; DLB
90; EW 5; RGSF 2; RGWL 2, 3

Klima, Ivan 1931- .... **CLC 56, 172**
See also CA 25-28R; CANR 17, 50, 91;
CDWLB 4; CWW 2; DAM NOV; DLB
232; EWL 3; RGWL 3

Klimentev, Andrei Platonovich
See Klimentov, Andrei Platonovich

Klimentov, Andrei Platonovich
1899-1951 .... **SSC 42; TCLC 14**
See also CA 108; 232; DLB 272; EWL 3

Klinger, Friedrich Maximilian von
1752-1831 .... **NCLC 1**
See also DLB 94

Klingsor the Magician
See Hartmann, Sadakichi

Klopstock, Friedrich Gottlieb
1724-1803 .... **NCLC 11, 225**
See also DLB 97; EW 4; RGWL 2, 3

Kluge, Alexander 1932- .... **SSC 61**
See also CA 81-84; CANR 163; DLB 75

Knapp, Caroline 1959-2002 ...... **CLC 99, 309**
See also CA 154; 207

Knebel, Fletcher 1911-1993 .... **CLC 14**
See also AITN 1; CA 1-4R; 140; CAAS 3;
CANR 1, 36; CN 1, 2, 3, 4, 5; SATA 36;
SATA-Obit 75

Knickerbocker, Diedrich
See Irving, Washington

Knight, Etheridge 1931-1991 .... **BLC 1:2;
CLC 40; PC 14**
See also BW 1, 3; CA 21-24R; 133; CANR
23, 82; CP 1, 2, 3, 4, 5; DAM POET; DLB
41; MTCW 2; MTFW 2005; PFS 36;
RGAL 4; TCLE 1:1

Knight, Sarah Kemble 1666-1727 .... **LC 7**
See also DLB 24, 200

Knister, Raymond 1899-1932 .... **TCLC 56**
See also CA 186; DLB 68; RGEL 2

Knowles, John 1926-2001 ... **CLC 1, 4, 10, 26**
See also AAYA 10, 72; AMWS 12; BPFB
2; BYA 3; CA 17-20R; 203; CANR 40,
74, 76, 132; CDALB 1968-1988; CLR 98;
CN 1, 2, 3, 4, 5, 6, 7; DA; DAC; DAM
MST, NOV; DLB 6; EXPN; MTCW 1, 2;
MTFW 2005; NFS 2; RGAL 4; SATA 8,
89; SATA-Obit 134; YAW

Knox, Calvin M.
See Silverberg, Robert

Knox, John c. 1505-1572 .... **LC 37**
See also DLB 132

Knye, Cassandra
See Disch, Thomas M.

Koch, C(hristopher) J(ohn) 1932- .... **CLC 42**
See also CA 127; CANR 84; CN 3, 4, 5, 6,
7; DLB 289

Koch, Christopher
See Koch, C(hristopher) J(ohn)

Koch, Kenneth 1925-2002 .... **CLC 5, 8, 44;
PC 80**
See also AMWS 15; CA 1-4R; 207; CAD;
CANR 6, 36, 57, 97, 131; CD 5, 6; CP 1,
2, 3, 4, 5, 6, 7; DAM POET; DLB 5; INT
CANR-36; MAL 5; MTCW 2; MTFW
2005; PFS 20; SATA 65; WP

Kochanowski, Jan 1530-1584 .... **LC 10**
See also RGWL 2, 3

Kock, Charles Paul de 1794-1871 . **NCLC 16**

Koda Rohan
See Koda Shigeyuki

Koda Rohan
See Koda Shigeyuki

Koda Shigeyuki 1867-1947 .... **TCLC 22**
See also CA 121; 183; DLB 180

Koestler, Arthur 1905-1983 ... **CLC 1, 3, 6, 8,
15, 33**
See also BRWS 1; CA 1-4R; 109; CANR 1,
33; CDBLB 1945-1960; CN 1, 2, 3;
DLBY 1983; EWL 3; MTCW 1, 2; MTFW
2005; NFS 19; RGEL 2

Kogawa, Joy 1935- .... **CLC 78, 129, 262, 268**
See also AAYA 47; CA 101; CANR 19, 62,
126; CN 6, 7; CP 1; CWP; DAC; DAM
MST, MULT; DLB 334; FW; MTCW 2;
MTFW 2005; NFS 3; SATA 99

Kogawa, Joy Nozomi
See Kogawa, Joy

Kohout, Pavel 1928- .... **CLC 13**
See also CA 45-48; CANR 3

Koizumi, Yakumo
See Hearn, Lafcadio

Kolmar, Gertrud 1894-1943 .... **TCLC 40**
See also CA 167; EWL 3; RGHL

Komunyakaa, Yusef 1947- . **BLC 2:2; BLCS;
CLC 86, 94, 207, 299; PC 51**
See also AFAW 2; AMWS 13; CA 147;
CANR 83, 164, 211; CP 6, 7; CSW; DLB
120; EWL 3; PFS 5, 20, 30, 37; RGAL 4

Konigsberg, Alan Stewart
See Allen, Woody

Konrad, George
See Konrad, Gyorgy

Konrad, George
See Konrad, Gyorgy

Konrad, Gyorgy 1933- .... **CLC 4, 10, 73**
See also CA 85-88; CANR 97, 171; CD-
WLB 4; CWW 2; DLB 232; EWL 3

Konwicki, Tadeusz 1926- .... **CLC 8, 28, 54,
117**
See also CA 101; CAAS 9; CANR 39, 59;
CWW 2; DLB 232; EWL 3; IDFW 3;
MTCW 1

Koontz, Dean 1945- .... **CLC 78, 206**
See Koontz, Dean R.
See also AAYA 9, 31; BEST 89:3, 90:2; CA
108; CANR 19, 36, 52, 95, 138, 176;
CMW 4; CPW; DA3; DAM NOV, POP;
DLB 292; HGG; MTCW 1; MTFW 2005;
SATA 92, 165; SFW 4; SUFW 2; YAW

Koontz, Dean R.
See Koontz, Dean
See also SATA 225

Koontz, Dean Ray
See Koontz, Dean

Kopernik, Mikolaj
See Copernicus, Nicolaus

Kopit, Arthur 1937- ... **CLC 1, 18, 33; DC 37**
See also AITN 1; CA 81-84; CABS 3;
CAD; CD 5, 6; DAM DRAM; DFS 7, 14,
24; DLB 7; MAL 5; MTCW 1; RGAL 4

Kopit, Arthur Lee
See Kopit, Arthur

Kopitar, Jernej (Bartholomaus)
1780-1844 .... **NCLC 117**

Kops, Bernard 1926- .... **CLC 4**
See also CA 5-8R; CANR 84, 159; CBD;
CN 1, 2, 3, 4, 5, 6, 7; CP 1, 2, 3, 4, 5, 6,
7; DLB 13; RGHL

Kornbluth, C(yril) M. 1923-1958 .... **TCLC 8**
See also CA 105; 160; DLB 8; SCFW 1, 2;
SFW 4

Korolenko, V.G.
See Korolenko, Vladimir G.

Korolenko, Vladimir
See Korolenko, Vladimir G.

Korolenko, Vladimir G.
1853-1921 .... **TCLC 22**
See also CA 121; DLB 277

Korolenko, Vladimir Galaktionovich
See Korolenko, Vladimir G.

Korzybski, Alfred (Habdank Skarbek)
1879-1950 .... **TCLC 61**
See also CA 123; 160

Kosinski, Jerzy 1933-1991 ..... **CLC 1, 2, 3, 6,
10, 15, 53, 70**
See also AMWS 7; BPFB 2; CA 17-20R;
134; CANR 9, 46; CN 1, 2, 3, 4; DA3;
DAM NOV; DLB 2, 299; DLBY 1982;
EWL 3; HGG; MAL 5; MTCW 1, 2;
MTFW 2005; NFS 12; RGAL 4; RGHL;
TUS

Levenson, Jay .... CLC 70

Lever, Charles (James)
1806-1872 .... NCLC 23
See also DLB 21; RGEL 2

Leverson, Ada Esther
1862(?)-1933(?) .... TCLC 18
See also CA 117; 202; DLB 153; RGEL 2

Levertov, Denise 1923-1997 .. CLC 1, 2, 3, 5,
8, 15, 28, 66; PC 11
See also AMWS 3; CA 1-4R, 178; 163;
CAAE 178; CAAS 19; CANR 3, 29, 50,
108; CDALBS; CP 1, 2, 3, 4, 5, 6; CWP;
DAM POET; DLB 5, 165, 342; EWL 3;
EXPP; FW; INT CANR-29; MAL 5;
MTCW 1, 2; PAB; PFS 7, 17, 31; RGAL
4; RGHL; TUS; WP

Levi, Carlo 1902-1975 .... TCLC 125
See also CA 65-68; 53-56; CANR 10; EWL
3; RGWL 2, 3

Levi, Jonathan .... CLC 76
See also CA 197

Levi, Peter (Chad Tigar)
1931-2000 .... CLC 41
See also CA 5-8R; 187; CANR 34, 80; CP
1, 2, 3, 4, 5, 6, 7; DLB 40

Levi, Primo 1919-1987 ...... CLC 37, 50; SSC
12, 122; TCLC 109
See also CA 13-16R; 122; CANR 12, 33,
61, 70, 132, 171; DLB 177, 299; EWL 3;
MTCW 1, 2; MTFW 2005; RGHL;
RGWL 2, 3; WLIT 7

Levin, Ira 1929-2007 .... CLC 3, 6
See also CA 21-24R; 266; CANR 17, 44,
74, 139; CMW 4; CN 1, 2, 3, 4, 5, 6, 7;
CPW; DA3; DAM POP; HGG; MTCW 1,
2; MTFW 2005; SATA 66; SATA-Obit
187; SFW 4

Levin, Ira Marvin
See Levin, Ira

Levin, Meyer 1905-1981 .... CLC 7
See also AITN 1; CA 9-12R; 104; CANR
15; CN 1, 2, 3; DAM POP; DLB 9, 28;
DLBY 1981; MAL 5; RGHL; SATA 21;
SATA-Obit 27

Levine, Albert Norman
See Levine, Norman

Levine, Norman 1923-2005 .... CLC 54
See also CA 73-76; 240; CAAS 23; CANR
14, 70; CN 1, 2, 3, 4, 5, 6, 7; CP 1; DLB
88

Levine, Norman Albert
See Levine, Norman

Levine, Philip 1928- .. CLC 2, 4, 5, 9, 14, 33,
118; PC 22
See also AMWS 5; CA 9-12R; CANR 9,
37, 52, 116, 156; CP 1, 2, 3, 4, 5, 6, 7;
DAM POET; DLB 5; EWL 3; MAL 5;
PFS 8

Levinson, Deirdre 1931- .... CLC 49
See also CA 73-76; CANR 70

Levi-Strauss, Claude 1908-2008 ...... CLC 38,
302
See also CA 1-4R; CANR 6, 32, 57; DLB
242; EWL 3; GFL 1789 to the Present;
MTCW 1, 2; TWA

Levitin, Sonia 1934- .... CLC 17
See also AAYA 13, 48; CA 29-32R; CANR
14, 32, 79, 182; JRDA; MAI-
CYA 1, 2; SAAS 2; SATA 4, 68, 119, 131,
192; SATA-Essay 131; YAW

Levon, O. U.
See Kesey, Ken

Levy, Amy 1861-1889 ..... NCLC 59, 203; PC
126
See also DLB 156, 240

Lewees, John
See Stockton, Francis Richard

Lewes, George Henry 1817-1878 .. NCLC 25,
215
See also DLB 55, 144

Lewis, Alun 1915-1944 .... SSC 40; TCLC 3
See also BRW 7; CA 104; 188; DLB 20,
162; PAB; RGEL 2

Lewis, C. Day
See Day Lewis, C.

Lewis, C. S. 1898-1963 .. CLC 1, 3, 6, 14, 27,
124; WLC 4
See also AAYA 3, 39; BPFB 2; BRWS 3;
BYA 15, 16; CA 81-84; CANR 33, 71,
132; CDBLB 1945-1960; CLR 3, 27, 109;
CWRI 5; DA; DA3; DAB; DAC; DAM
MST, NOV, POP; DLB 15, 100, 160, 255;
EWL 3; FANT; JRDA; LMFS 2; MAI-
CYA 1, 2; MTCW 1, 2; MTFW 2005;
NFS 24; RGEL 2; SATA 13, 100; SCFW
1, 2; SFW 4; SUFW 1; TEA; WCH;
WYA; YAW

Lewis, Cecil Day
See Day Lewis, C.

Lewis, Clive Staples
See Lewis, C. S.

Lewis, Harry Sinclair
See Lewis, Sinclair

Lewis, Janet 1899-1998 .... CLC 41
See also CA 9-12R; 172; CANR 29, 63;
CAP 1; CN 1, 2, 3, 4, 5, 6; DLBY 1987;
RHW; TCWW 2

Lewis, Matthew Gregory
1775-1818 .... NCLC 11, 62
See also DLB 39, 158, 178; GL 3; HGG;
LMFS 1; RGEL 2; SUFW

Lewis, Sinclair 1885-1951 ... TCLC 4, 13, 23,
39, 215; WLC 4
See also AMW; AMWC 1; BPFB 2; CA
104; 133; CANR 132; CDALB 1917-
1929; DA; DA3; DAB; DAC; DAM MST,
NOV; DLB 9, 102, 284, 331; DLBD 1;
EWL 3; LAIT 3; MAL 5; MTCW 1, 2;
MTFW 2005; NFS 15, 19, 22, 34; RGAL
4; TUS

Lewis, (Percy) Wyndham
1884(?)-1957 . SSC 34; TCLC 2, 9, 104,
216
See also AAYA 77; BRW 7; CA 104; 157;
DLB 15; EWL 3; FANT; MTCW 2;
MTFW 2005; RGEL 2

Lewisohn, Ludwig 1883-1955 .... TCLC 19
See also CA 107; 203; DLB 4, 9, 28, 102;
MAL 5

Lewton, Val 1904-1951 .... TCLC 76
See also CA 199; IDFW 3, 4

Leyner, Mark 1956- .... CLC 92
See also CA 110; CANR 28, 53; DA3; DLB
292; MTCW 2; MTFW 2005

Leyton, E.K.
See Campbell, Ramsey

Lezama Lima, Jose 1910-1976 .... CLC 4, 10,
101; HLCS 2
See also CA 77-80; CANR 71; DAM
MULT; DLB 113, 283; EWL 3; HW 1, 2;
LAW; RGWL 2, 3

L'Heureux, John (Clarke) 1934- ...... CLC 52
See also CA 13-16R; CANR 23, 45, 88; CP
1, 2, 3, 4; DLB 244

Li, Fei-kan
See Jin, Ba

Li Ch'ing-chao 1081(?)-1141(?) .... CMLC 71

Lichtenberg, Georg Christoph
1742-1799 .... LC 162
See also DLB 94

Liddell, C. H.
See Kuttner, Henry

Lie, Jonas (Lauritz Idemil)
1833-1908(?) .... TCLC 5
See also CA 115

Lieber, Joel 1937-1971 .... CLC 6
See also CA 73-76; 29-32R

Lieber, Stanley Martin
See Lee, Stan

Lieberman, Laurence (James)
1935- .... CLC 4, 36
See also CA 17-20R; CANR 8, 36, 89; CP
1, 2, 3, 4, 5, 6, 7

Lieh Tzu fl. 7th cent. B.C.-5th cent.
B.C. .... CMLC 27

Lieksman, Anders
See Haavikko, Paavo Juhani

Lifton, Robert Jay 1926- .... CLC 67
See also CA 17-20R; CANR 27, 78, 161;
INT CANR-27; SATA 66

Lightfoot, Gordon 1938- .... CLC 26
See also CA 109; 242

Lightfoot, Gordon Meredith
See Lightfoot, Gordon

Lightman, Alan P. 1948- .... CLC 81
See also CA 141; CANR 63, 105, 138, 178;
MTFW 2005; NFS 29

Lightman, Alan Paige
See Lightman, Alan P.

Ligotti, Thomas 1953- .... CLC 44; SSC 16
See also CA 123; CANR 49, 135; HGG;
SUFW 2

Ligotti, Thomas Robert
See Ligotti, Thomas

Li Ho 791-817 .... PC 13

Li Ju-chen c. 1763-c. 1830 .... NCLC 137

Liking, Werewere 1950- .... BLC 2:2
See also CA 293; DLB 360; EWL 3

Lilar, Francoise
See Mallet-Joris, Francoise

Liliencron, Detlev
See Liliencron, Detlev von

Liliencron, Detlev von 1844-1909 .. TCLC 18
See also CA 117

Liliencron, Friedrich Adolf Axel Detlev von
See Liliencron, Detlev von

Liliencron, Friedrich Detlev von
See Liliencron, Detlev von

Lille, Alain de
See Alain de Lille

Lillo, George 1691-1739 .... LC 131
See also DLB 84; RGEL 2

Lilly, William 1602-1681 .... LC 27

Lima, Jose Lezama
See Lezama Lima, Jose

Lima Barreto, Afonso Henrique de
1881-1922 .... TCLC 23
See also CA 117; 181; DLB 307; LAW

Lima Barreto, Afonso Henriques de
See Lima Barreto, Afonso Henrique de

Limonov, Eduard
See Limonov, Edward

Limonov, Edward 1944- .... CLC 67
See also CA 137; DLB 317

Lin, Frank
See Atherton, Gertrude (Franklin Horn)

Lin, Yutang 1895-1976 .... TCLC 149
See also CA 45-48; 65-68; CANR 2; RGAL
4

Lincoln, Abraham 1809-1865 .... NCLC 18,
201
See also LAIT 2

Lincoln, Geoffrey
See Mortimer, John

Lind, Jakov 1927-2007 ... CLC 1, 2, 4, 27, 82
See also CA 9-12R; 257; CAAS 4; CANR
7; DLB 299; EWL 3; RGHL

Lindbergh, Anne Morrow
1906-2001 .... CLC 82
See also BPFB 2; CA 17-20R; 193; CANR
16, 73; DAM NOV; MTCW 1, 2; MTFW
2005; SATA 33; SATA-Obit 125; TUS

Lindbergh, Anne Spencer Morrow
　　See Lindbergh, Anne Morrow
Lindholm, Anna Margaret
　　See Haycraft, Anna
Lindsay, David 1878(?)-1945 .... **TCLC 15**
　　See also CA 113; 187; DLB 255; FANT;
　　SFW 4; SUFW 1
Lindsay, Nicholas Vachel
　　See Lindsay, Vachel
Lindsay, Vachel 1879-1931 ..... **PC 23; TCLC
　　17; WLC 4**
　　See also AMWS 1; CA 114; 135; CANR
　　79; CDALB 1865-1917; DA; DA3; DAC;
　　DAM MST, POET; DLB 54; EWL 3;
　　EXPP; MAL 5; RGAL 4; SATA 40; WP
Linke-Poot
　　See Doeblin, Alfred
Linney, Romulus 1930-2011 .... **CLC 51**
　　See also CA 1-4R; CAD; CANR 40, 44,
　　79; CD 5, 6; CSW; RGAL 4
Linton, Eliza Lynn 1822-1898 .... **NCLC 41**
　　See also DLB 18
Li Po 701-763 .... **CMLC 2, 86; PC 29**
　　See also PFS 20, 40; WP
Lippard, George 1822-1854 .... **NCLC 198**
　　See also DLB 202
Lipsius, Justus 1547-1606 .... **LC 16**
Lipsyte, Robert 1938- .... **CLC 21**
　　See also AAYA 7, 45; CA 17-20R; CANR
　　8, 57, 146, 189; CLR 23, 76; DA; DAC;
　　DAM MST, NOV; JRDA; LAIT 5; MAI-
　　CYA 1, 2; NFS 35; SATA 5, 68, 113, 161,
　　198; WYA; YAW
Lipsyte, Robert Michael
　　See Lipsyte, Robert
Lish, Gordon 1934- .... **CLC 45; SSC 18**
　　See also CA 113; 117; CANR 79, 151; DLB
　　130; INT CA-117
Lish, Gordon Jay
　　See Lish, Gordon
Lispector, Clarice 1925(?)-1977 .... **CLC 43;
　　HLCS 2; SSC 34, 96**
　　See also CA 139; 116; CANR 71; CDWLB
　　3; DLB 113, 307; DNFS 1; EWL 3; FW;
　　HW 2; LAW; RGSF 2; RGWL 2, 3; WLIT
　　1
Liszt, Franz 1811-1886 .... **NCLC 199**
Littell, Robert 1935(?)- .... **CLC 42**
　　See also CA 109; 112; CANR 64, 115, 162,
　　217; CMW 4
Little, Malcolm
　　See Malcolm X
Littlewit, Humphrey Gent.
　　See Lovecraft, H. P.
Litwos
　　See Sienkiewicz, Henryk (Adam Alexander
　　Pius)
Liu, E. 1857-1909 .... **TCLC 15**
　　See also CA 115; 190; DLB 328
Lively, Penelope 1933- .... **CLC 32, 50, 306**
　　See also BPFB 2; CA 41-44R; CANR 29,
　　67, 79, 131, 172, 222; CLR 7, 159; CN 5,
　　6, 7; CWRI 5; DAM NOV; DLB 14, 161,
　　207, 326; FANT; JRDA; MAICYA 1, 2;
　　MTCW 1, 2; MTFW 2005; SATA 7, 60,
　　101, 164; TEA
Lively, Penelope Margaret
　　See Lively, Penelope
Livesay, Dorothy (Kathleen)
　　1909-1996 .... **CLC 4, 15, 79**
　　See also AITN 2; CA 25-28R; CAAS 8;
　　CANR 36, 67; CP 1, 2, 3, 4, 5; DAC;
　　DAM MST, POET; DLB 68; FW; MTCW
　　1; RGEL 2; TWA
Livius Andronicus c. 284B.C.-c.
　　204B.C. .... **CMLC 102**
Livy c. 59B.C.-c. 12 .... **CMLC 11**
　　See also AW 2; CDWLB 1; DLB 211;
　　RGWL 2, 3; WLIT 8

Li Yaotang
　　See Jin, Ba
Li-Young, Lee
　　See Lee, Li-Young
Lizardi, Jose Joaquin Fernandez de
　　1776-1827 .... **NCLC 30**
　　See also LAW
Llewellyn, Richard
　　See Llewellyn Lloyd, Richard Dafydd Viv-
　　ian
Llewellyn Lloyd, Richard Dafydd Vivian
　　1906-1983 .... **CLC 7, 80**
　　See also CA 53-56; 111; CANR 7, 71; DLB
　　15; NFS 30; SATA 11; SATA-Obit 37
Llosa, Jorge Mario Pedro Vargas
　　See Vargas Llosa, Mario
Llosa, Mario Vargas
　　See Vargas Llosa, Mario
Lloyd, Manda
　　See Mander, (Mary) Jane
Lloyd Webber, Andrew 1948- .... **CLC 21**
　　See also AAYA 1, 38; CA 116; 149; DAM
　　DRAM; DFS 7; SATA 56
Llull, Ramon c. 1235-c. 1316 .... **CMLC 12,
　　114**
Lobb, Ebenezer
　　See Upward, Allen
Lochhead, Liz 1947- .... **CLC 286**
　　See also BRWS 17; CA 81-84; CANR 79;
　　CBD; CD 5, 6; CP 2, 3, 4, 5, 6, 7; CWD;
　　CWP; DLB 310
Locke, Alain Leroy 1885-1954 .... **BLCS; HR
　　1:3; TCLC 43**
　　See also AMWS 14; BW 1, 3; CA 106; 124;
　　CANR 79; DLB 51; LMFS 2; MAL 5;
　　RGAL 4
Locke, John 1632-1704 .... **LC 7, 35, 135**
　　See also DLB 31, 101, 213, 252; RGEL 2;
　　WLIT 3
Locke-Elliott, Sumner
　　See Elliott, Sumner Locke
Lockhart, John Gibson 1794-1854 .. **NCLC 6**
　　See also DLB 110, 116, 144
Lockridge, Ross (Franklin), Jr.
　　1914-1948 .... **TCLC 111**
　　See also CA 108; 145; CANR 79; DLB 143;
　　DLBY 1980; MAL 5; RGAL 4; RHW
Lockwood, Robert
　　See Johnson, Robert
Lodge, David 1935- .... **CLC 36, 141, 293**
　　See also BEST 90:1; BRWS 4; CA 17-20R;
　　CANR 19, 53, 92, 139, 197; CN 1, 2, 3,
　　4, 5, 6, 7; CPW; DAM POP; DLB 14,
　　194; EWL 3; INT CANR-19; MTCW 1,
　　2; MTFW 2005
Lodge, David John
　　See Lodge, David
Lodge, Thomas 1558-1625 .... **LC 41**
　　See also DLB 172; RGEL 2
Loewinsohn, Ron(ald William)
　　1937- .... **CLC 52**
　　See also CA 25-28R; CANR 71; CP 1, 2, 3,
　　4
Logan, Jake
　　See Smith, Martin Cruz
Logan, John (Burton) 1923-1987 .... **CLC 5**
　　See also CA 77-80; 124; CANR 45; CP 1,
　　2, 3, 4; DLB 5
Lo-Johansson, (Karl) Ivar
　　1901-1990 .... **TCLC 216**
　　See also CA 102; 131; CANR 20, 79, 137;
　　DLB 259; EWL 3; RGWL 2, 3
Lo Kuan-chung 1330(?)-1400(?) .... **LC 12**
Lomax, Pearl
　　See Cleage, Pearl
Lomax, Pearl Cleage
　　See Cleage, Pearl
Lombard, Nap
　　See Johnson, Pamela Hansford

Lombard, Peter 1100(?)-1160(?) ... **CMLC 72**
Lombino, Salvatore
　　See Hunter, Evan
London, Jack 1876-1916 .... **SSC 4, 49, 133;
　　TCLC 9, 15, 39; WLC 4**
　　See also AAYA 13, 75; AITN 2; AMW;
　　BPFB 2; BYA 4, 13; CA 110; 119; CANR
　　73; CDALB 1865-1917; CLR 108; DA;
　　DA3; DAB; DAC; DAM MST, NOV;
　　DLB 8, 12, 78, 212; EWL 3; EXPS;
　　JRDA; LAIT 3; MAICYA 1, 2,; MAL 5;
　　MTCW 1, 2; MTFW 2005; NFS 8, 19,
　　35; RGAL 4; RGSF 2; SATA 18; SFW 4;
　　SSFS 7, 35; TCWW 1, 2; TUS; WYA;
　　YAW
London, John Griffith
　　See London, Jack
Long, Emmett
　　See Leonard, Elmore
Longbaugh, Harry
　　See Goldman, William
Longfellow, Henry Wadsworth
　　1807-1882 .. **NCLC 2, 45, 101, 103, 235;
　　PC 30; WLCS**
　　See also AMW; AMWR 2; CDALB 1640-
　　1865; CLR 99; DA; DA3; DAB; DAC;
　　DAM MST, POET; DLB 1, 59, 235;
　　EXPP; PAB; PFS 2, 7, 17, 31, 39; RGAL
　　4; SATA 19; TUS; WP
Longinus c. 1st cent. - .... **CMLC 27**
　　See also AW 2; DLB 176
Longley, Michael 1939- ...... **CLC 29; PC 118**
　　See also BRWS 8; CA 102; CP 1, 2, 3, 4, 5,
　　6, 7; DLB 40
Longstreet, Augustus Baldwin
　　1790-1870 .... **NCLC 159**
　　See also DLB 3, 11, 74, 248; RGAL 4
Longus fl. c. 2nd cent. - .... **CMLC 7**
Longway, A. Hugh
　　See Lang, Andrew
Lonnbohm, Armas Eino Leopold
　　See Lonnbohm, Armas Eino Leopold
Lonnbohm, Armas Eino Leopold
　　1878-1926 .... **TCLC 24**
　　See also CA 123; EWL 3
Lonnrot, Elias 1802-1884 .... **NCLC 53**
　　See also EFS 1:1, 2:1
Lonsdale, Roger .... **CLC 65**
Lopate, Phillip 1943- .... **CLC 29**
　　See also CA 97-100; CANR 88, 157, 196;
　　DLBY 1980; INT CA-97-100
Lopez, Barry 1945- .... **CLC 70**
　　See also AAYA 9, 63; ANW; CA 65-68;
　　CANR 7, 23, 47, 68, 92; DLB 256, 275,
　　335; INT CANR-7, CANR-23; MTCW 1;
　　RGAL 4; SATA 67
Lopez, Barry Holstun
　　See Lopez, Barry
Lopez de Mendoza, Inigo
　　See Santillana, Inigo Lopez de Mendoza,
　　Marques de
Lopez Portillo (y Pacheco), Jose
　　1920-2004 .... **CLC 46**
　　See also CA 129; 224; HW 1
Lopez y Fuentes, Gregorio
　　1897(?)-1966 .... **CLC 32**
　　See also CA 131; EWL 3; HW 1
Lorca, Federico Garcia
　　See Garcia Lorca, Federico
Lord, Audre
　　See Lorde, Audre
Lord, Bette Bao 1938- .... **AAL; CLC 23**
　　See also BEST 90:3; BPFB 2; CA 107;
　　CANR 41, 79; CLR 151; INT CA-107;
　　SATA 58
Lord Auch
　　See Bataille, Georges
Lord Brooke
　　See Greville, Fulke

Maas, Peter 1929-2001 .... **CLC 29**
  See also CA 93-96; 201; INT CA-93-96;
  MTCW 2; MTFW 2005

Mac A'Ghobhainn, Iain
  See Smith, Iain Crichton

Macaulay, Catharine 1731-1791 .... **LC 64**
  See also BRWS 17; DLB 104, 336

Macaulay, (Emilie) Rose
  1881(?)-1958 .... **TCLC 7, 44**
  See also CA 104; DLB 36; EWL 3; RGEL
  2; RHW

Macaulay, Thomas Babington
  1800-1859 .... **NCLC 42, 231**
  See also BRW 4; CDBLB 1832-1890; DLB
  32, 55; RGEL 2

MacBeth, George (Mann)
  1932-1992 .... **CLC 2, 5, 9**
  See also CA 25-28R; 136; CANR 61, 66;
  CP 1, 2, 3, 4, 5; DLB 40; MTCW 1; PFS
  8; SATA 4; SATA-Obit 70

MacCaig, Norman (Alexander)
  1910-1996 .... **CLC 36**
  See also BRWS 6; CA 9-12R; CANR 3, 34;
  CP 1, 2, 3, 4, 5, 6; DAB; DAM POET;
  DLB 27; EWL 3; RGEL 2

MacCarthy, Sir (Charles Otto) Desmond
  1877-1952 .... **TCLC 36**
  See also CA 167

MacDiarmid, Hugh
  See Grieve, C. M.

MacDonald, Anson
  See Heinlein, Robert A.

Macdonald, Cynthia 1928- .... **CLC 13, 19**
  See also CA 49-52; CANR 4, 44, 146; DLB
  105

MacDonald, George 1824-1905 .... **TCLC 9,
  113, 207**
  See also AAYA 57; BYA 5; CA 106; 137;
  CANR 80; CLR 67; DLB 18, 163, 178;
  FANT; MAICYA 1, 2; RGEL 2; SATA 33,
  100; SFW 4; SUFW; WCH

Macdonald, John
  See Millar, Kenneth

MacDonald, John D. 1916-1986 .. **CLC 3, 27,
  44**
  See also BPFB 2; CA 1-4R; 121; CANR 1,
  19, 60; CMW 4; CPW; DAM NOV, POP;
  DLB 8, 306; DLBY 1986; MSW; MTCW
  1, 2; MTFW 2005; SFW 4

Macdonald, John Ross
  See Millar, Kenneth

Macdonald, Ross
  See Millar, Kenneth

MacDonald Fraser, George
  See Fraser, George MacDonald

MacDougal, John
  See Blish, James

MacDowell, John
  See Parks, Tim

MacEwen, Gwendolyn (Margaret)
  1941-1987 .... **CLC 13, 55**
  See also CA 9-12R; 124; CANR 7, 22; CP
  1, 2, 3, 4; DLB 53, 251; SATA 50; SATA-
  Obit 55

MacGreevy, Thomas 1893-1967 .... **PC 82**
  See also CA 262

Macha, Karel Hynek 1810-1846 .... **NCLC 46**

Machado (y Ruiz), Antonio
  1875-1939 .... **TCLC 3**
  See also CA 104; 174; DLB 108; EW 9;
  EWL 3; HW 2; PFS 23; RGWL 2, 3

Machado de Assis, Joaquim Maria
  1839-1908 . **BLC 1:2; HLCS 2; SSC 24,
  118; TCLC 10**
  See also CA 107; 153; CANR 91; DLB 307;
  LAW; RGSF 2; RGWL 2, 3; TWA; WLIT
  1

Machaut, Guillaume de c.
  1300-1377 .... **CMLC 64**
  See also DLB 208

Machen, Arthur
  See Jones, Arthur Llewellyn

Machen, Arthur Llewelyn Jones
  See Jones, Arthur Llewellyn

Machiavelli, Niccolo 1469-1527 ... **DC 16; LC
  8, 36, 140; WLCS**
  See also AAYA 58; DA; DAB; DAC; DAM
  MST; EW 2; LAIT 1; LMFS 1; NFS 9;
  RGWL 2, 3; TWA; WLIT 7

MacInnes, Colin 1914-1976 .... **CLC 4, 23**
  See also CA 69-72; 65-68; CANR 21; CN
  1, 2; DLB 14; MTCW 1, 2; RGEL 2;
  RHW

MacInnes, Helen (Clark)
  1907-1985 .... **CLC 27, 39**
  See also BPFB 2; CA 1-4R; 117; CANR 1,
  28, 58; CMW 4; CN 1, 2; CPW; DAM
  POP; DLB 87; MSW; MTCW 1, 2;
  MTFW 2005; SATA 22; SATA-Obit 44

Mackay, Mary 1855-1924 .... **TCLC 51**
  See also CA 118; 177; DLB 34, 156; FANT;
  RGEL 2; RHW; SUFW 1

Mackay, Shena 1944- .... **CLC 195**
  See also CA 104; CANR 88, 139, 207; DLB
  231, 319; MTFW 2005

Mackenzie, Compton (Edward Montague)
  1883-1972 .... **CLC 18; TCLC 116**
  See also CA 21-22; 37-40R; CAP 2; CN 1;
  DLB 34, 100; RGEL 2

Mackenzie, Henry 1745-1831 .... **NCLC 41**
  See also DLB 39; RGEL 2

Mackey, Nathaniel 1947- .... **BLC 2:3; PC 49**
  See also CA 153; CANR 114; CP 6, 7; DLB
  169

Mackey, Nathaniel Ernest
  See Mackey, Nathaniel

MacKinnon, Catharine
  See MacKinnon, Catharine A.

MacKinnon, Catharine A. 1946- .... **CLC 181**
  See also CA 128; 132; CANR 73, 140, 189;
  FW; MTCW 2; MTFW 2005

Mackintosh, Elizabeth
  1896(?)-1952 .... **TCLC 14**
  See also CA 110; CMW 4; DLB 10, 77;
  MSW

Macklin, Charles 1699-1797 .... **LC 132**
  See also DLB 89; RGEL 2

MacLaren, James
  See Grieve, C. M.

MacLaverty, Bernard 1942- ..... **CLC 31, 243**
  See also CA 116; 118; CANR 43, 88, 168;
  CN 5, 6, 7; DLB 267; INT CA-118; RGSF
  2

MacLean, Alistair 1922(?)-1987 .. **CLC 3, 13,
  50, 63**
  See also CA 57-60; 121; CANR 28, 61;
  CMW 4; CP 2, 3, 4, 5, 6, 7; CPW; DAM
  POP; DLB 276; MTCW 1; SATA 23;
  SATA-Obit 50; TCWW 2

MacLean, Alistair Stuart
  See MacLean, Alistair

Maclean, Norman (Fitzroy)
  1902-1990 .... **CLC 78; SSC 13, 136**
  See also AMWS 14; CA 102; 132; CANR
  49; CPW; DAM POP; DLB 206; TCWW
  2

MacLeish, Archibald 1892-1982 ... **CLC 3, 8,
  14, 68; DC 43; PC 47**
  See also AMW; CA 9-12R; 106; CAD;
  CANR 33, 63; CDALBS; CP 1, 2; DAM
  POET; DFS 15; DLB 4, 7, 45; DLBY
  1982; EWL 3; EXPP; MAL 5; MTCW 1,
  2; MTFW 2005; PAB; PFS 5; RGAL 4;
  TUS

MacLennan, (John) Hugh
  1907-1990 .... **CLC 2, 14, 92**
  See also CA 5-8R; 142; CANR 33; CN 1,
  2, 3, 4; DAC; DAM MST; DLB 68; EWL
  3; MTCW 1, 2; MTFW 2005; RGEL 2;
  TWA

MacLeod, Alistair 1936- .. **CLC 56, 165; SSC
  90**
  See also CA 123; CCA 1; DAC; DAM
  MST; DLB 60; MTCW 2; MTFW 2005;
  RGSF 2; TCLE 1:2

Macleod, Fiona
  See Sharp, William

MacNeice, (Frederick) Louis
  1907-1963 .... **CLC 1, 4, 10, 53; PC 61**
  See also BRW 7; CA 85-88; CANR 61;
  DAB; DAM POET; DLB 10, 20; EWL 3;
  MTCW 1, 2; MTFW 2005; RGEL 2

MacNeill, Dand
  See Fraser, George MacDonald

Macpherson, James 1736-1796 .... **CMLC 28;
  LC 29, 196; PC 97**
  See also BRWS 8; DLB 109, 336; RGEL 2

Macpherson, (Jean) Jay 1931- .... **CLC 14**
  See also CA 5-8R; CANR 90; CP 1, 2, 3, 4,
  6, 7; CWP; DLB 53

Macrobius fl. 430- .... **CMLC 48**

MacShane, Frank 1927-1999 .... **CLC 39**
  See also CA 9-12R; 186; CANR 3, 33; DLB
  111

Macumber, Mari
  See Sandoz, Mari(e Susette)

Madach, Imre 1823-1864 .... **NCLC 19**

Madden, (Jerry) David 1933- .... **CLC 5, 15**
  See also CA 1-4R; CAAS 3; CANR 4, 45;
  CN 3, 4, 5, 6, 7; CSW; DLB 6; MTCW 1

Maddern, Al(an)
  See Ellison, Harlan

Madhubuti, Haki R. 1942- .... **BLC 1:2; CLC
  2; PC 5**
  See also BW 2, 3; CA 73-76; CANR 24,
  51, 73, 139; CP 2, 3, 4, 5, 6, 7; CSW;
  DAM MULT, POET; DLB 5, 41; DLBD
  8; EWL 3; MAL 5; MTCW 2; MTFW
  2005; RGAL 4

Madison, James 1751-1836 .... **NCLC 126**
  See also DLB 37

Maepenn, Hugh
  See Kuttner, Henry

Maepenn, K. H.
  See Kuttner, Henry

Maeterlinck, Maurice 1862-1949 .... **DC 32;
  TCLC 3, 251**
  See also CA 104; 136; CANR 80; DAM
  DRAM; DLB 192, 331; EW 8; EWL 3;
  GFL 1789 to the Present; LMFS 2; RGWL
  2, 3; SATA 66; TWA

Maginn, William 1794-1842 .... **NCLC 8**
  See also DLB 110, 159

Mahapatra, Jayanta 1928- .... **CLC 33**
  See also CA 73-76; CAAS 9; CANR 15,
  33, 66, 87; CP 4, 5, 6, 7; DAM MULT;
  DLB 323

Mahfouz, Nagib
  See Mahfouz, Naguib

Mahfouz, Naguib 1911(?)-2006 . **CLC 52, 55,
  153; SSC 66**
  See also AAYA 49; AFW; BEST 89:2; CA
  128; 253; CANR 55, 101; DA3; DAM
  NOV; DLB 346; DLBY 1988; MTCW 1,
  2; MTFW 2005; RGSF 2; RGWL 2, 3;
  SSFS 9, 33; WLIT 2

Mahfouz, Naguib Abdel Aziz Al-Sabilgi
  See Mahfouz, Naguib

Mahfouz, Najib
  See Mahfouz, Naguib

Mahfuz, Najib
  See Mahfouz, Naguib

Mantel, Hilary 1952- .... **CLC 144, 309**
See also CA 125; CANR 54, 101, 161, 207;
CN 5, 6, 7; DLB 271; RHW

Mantel, Hilary Mary
See Mantel, Hilary

Manton, Peter
See Creasey, John

Man Without a Spleen, A
See Chekhov, Anton

Manzano, Juan Franciso
1797(?)-1854 .... **NCLC 155**

Manzoni, Alessandro 1785-1873 ... **NCLC 29, 98**
See also EW 5; RGWL 2, 3; TWA; WLIT 7

Map, Walter 1140-1209 .... **CMLC 32**

Mapu, Abraham (ben Jekutiel)
1808-1867 .... **NCLC 18**

Mara, Sally
See Queneau, Raymond

Maracle, Lee 1950- .... **NNAL**
See also CA 149

Marat, Jean Paul 1743-1793 .... **LC 10**

Marcel, Gabriel Honore 1889-1973 . **CLC 15**
See also CA 102; 45-48; EWL 3; MTCW 1, 2

March, William 1893-1954 .... **TCLC 96**
See also CA 108; 216; DLB 9, 86, 316;
MAL 5

Marchbanks, Samuel
See Davies, Robertson

Marchi, Giacomo
See Bassani, Giorgio

Marcus Aurelius
See Aurelius, Marcus

Marcuse, Herbert 1898-1979 .... **TCLC 207**
See also CA 188; 89-92; DLB 242

Marguerite
See de Navarre, Marguerite

Marguerite d'Angouleme
See de Navarre, Marguerite

Marguerite de Navarre
See de Navarre, Marguerite

Margulies, Donald 1954- .... **CLC 76**
See also AAYA 57; CA 200; CD 6; DFS 13;
DLB 228

Marias, Javier 1951- .... **CLC 239**
See also CA 167; CANR 109, 139; DLB
322; HW 2; MTFW 2005

Marie de France c. 12th cent. - ...... **CMLC 8, 111; PC 22**
See also DLB 208; FW; RGWL 2, 3

Marie de l'Incarnation 1599-1672 ..... **LC 10, 168**

Marier, Captain Victor
See Griffith, D.W.

Mariner, Scott
See Pohl, Frederik

Marinetti, Filippo Tommaso
1876-1944 .... **TCLC 10**
See also CA 107; DLB 114, 264; EW 9;
EWL 3; WLIT 7

Marino, Giambattista 1569-1625 ...... **LC 181**
See also DLB 339; WLIT 7

Marivaux, Pierre Carlet de Chamblain de
1688-1763 .... **DC 7; LC 4, 123**
See also DLB 314; GFL Beginnings to
1789; RGWL 2, 3; TWA

Markandaya, Kamala 1924-2004 ...... **CLC 8, 38, 290**
See also BYA 13; CA 77-80; 227; CN 1, 2,
3, 4, 5, 6, 7; DLB 323; EWL 3; MTFW
2005; NFS 13

Markfield, Wallace (Arthur)
1926-2002 .... **CLC 8**
See also CA 69-72; 208; CAAS 3; CN 1, 2,
3, 4, 5, 6, 7; DLB 2, 28; DLBY 2002

Markham, Edwin 1852-1940 .... **TCLC 47**
See also CA 160; DLB 54, 186; MAL 5;
RGAL 4

Markham, Robert
See Amis, Kingsley

Marks, J.
See Highwater, Jamake (Mamake)

Marks-Highwater, J.
See Highwater, Jamake (Mamake)

Markson, David M. 1927-2010 .... **CLC 67**
See also AMWS 17; CA 49-52; CANR 1,
91, 158; CN 5, 6

Markson, David Merrill
See Markson, David M.

Marlatt, Daphne (Buckle) 1942- .... **CLC 168**
See also CA 25-28R; CANR 17, 39; CN 6,
7; CP 4, 5, 6, 7; CWP; DLB 60; FW

Marley, Bob
See Marley, Robert Nesta

Marley, Robert Nesta 1945-1981 ...... **CLC 17**
See also CA 107; 103

Marlowe, Christopher 1564-1593 . **DC 1; LC 22, 47, 117, 201; PC 57; WLC 4**
See also BRW 1; BRWR 1; CDBLB Before
1660; DA; DA3; DAB; DAC; DAM
DRAM, MST; DFS 1, 5, 13, 21; DLB 62;
EXPP; LMFS 1; PFS 22; RGEL 2; TEA;
WLIT 3

Marlowe, Stephen 1928-2008 .... **CLC 70**
See also CA 13-16R; 269; CANR 6, 55;
CMW 4; SFW 4

Marmion, Shakerley 1603-1639 .... **LC 89**
See also DLB 58; RGEL 2

Marmontel, Jean-Francois 1723-1799 .. **LC 2**
See also DLB 314

Maron, Monika 1941- .... **CLC 165**
See also CA 201

Marot, Clement c. 1496-1544 .... **LC 133**
See also DLB 327; GFL Beginnings to 1789

Marquand, John P(hillips)
1893-1960 .... **CLC 2, 10**
See also AMW; BPFB 2; CA 85-88; CANR
73; CMW 4; DLB 9, 102; EWL 3; MAL
5; MTCW 2; RGAL 4

Marques, Rene 1919-1979 .. **CLC 96; HLC 2**
See also CA 97-100; 85-88; CANR 78;
DAM MULT; DLB 305; EWL 3; HW 1,
2; LAW; RGSF 2

Marquez, Gabriel Garcia
See Garcia Marquez, Gabriel

Marquez, Gabriel Garcia
See Garcia Marquez, Gabriel

Marquis, Don(ald Robert Perry)
1878-1937 .... **TCLC 7**
See also CA 104; 166; DLB 11, 25; MAL
5; RGAL 4

Marquis de Sade
See Sade, Donatien Alphonse Francois

Marric, J. J.
See Creasey, John

Marryat, Frederick 1792-1848 .... **NCLC 3**
See also DLB 21, 163; RGEL 2; WCH

Marsden, James
See Creasey, John

Marse, Juan 1933- .... **CLC 302**
See also CA 254; DLB 322

Marsh, Edith Ngaio
See Marsh, Ngaio

Marsh, Edward 1872-1953 .... **TCLC 99**

Marsh, Ngaio 1895-1982 .... **CLC 7, 53**
See also CA 9-12R; CANR 6, 58; CMW 4;
CN 1, 2, 3; CPW; DAM POP; DLB 77;
MSW; MTCW 1, 2; RGEL 2; TEA

Marshall, Alan
See Westlake, Donald E.

Marshall, Allen
See Westlake, Donald E.

Marshall, Garry 1934- .... **CLC 17**
See also AAYA 3; CA 111; SATA 60

Marshall, Paule 1929- .... **BLC 1:3, 2:3; CLC 27, 72, 253; SSC 3**
See also AFAW 1, 2; AMWS 11; BPFB 2;
BW 2, 3; CA 77-80; CANR 25, 73, 129,
209; CN 1, 2, 3, 4, 5, 6, 7; DA3; DAM
MULT; DLB 33, 157, 227; EWL 3; LATS
1:2; MAL 5; MTCW 1, 2; MTFW 2005;
NFS 36; RGAL 4; SSFS 15

Marshallik
See Zangwill, Israel

Marsilius of Inghen c.
1340-1396 .... **CMLC 106**

Marsten, Richard
See Hunter, Evan

Marston, John 1576-1634 ...... **DC 37; LC 33, 172**
See also BRW 2; DAM DRAM; DLB 58,
172; RGEL 2

Martel, Yann 1963- .... **CLC 192, 315**
See also AAYA 67; CA 146; CANR 114,
226; DLB 326, 334; LNFS 2; MTFW
2005; NFS 27

Martens, Adolphe-Adhemar
See Ghelderode, Michel de

Martha, Henry
See Harris, Mark

Marti, Jose 1853-1895 ..... **HLC 2; NCLC 63; PC 76**
See also DAM MULT; DLB 290; HW 2;
LAW; RGWL 2, 3; WLIT 1

Martial c. 40-c. 104 .... **CMLC 35; PC 10**
See also AW 2; CDWLB 1; DLB 211;
RGWL 2, 3

Martin, Ken
See Hubbard, L. Ron

Martin, Richard
See Creasey, John

Martin, Steve 1945- .... **CLC 30, 217**
See also AAYA 53; CA 97-100; CANR 30,
100, 140, 195, 227; DFS 19; MTCW 1;
MTFW 2005

Martin, Valerie 1948- .... **CLC 89**
See also BEST 90:2; CA 85-88; CANR 49,
89, 165, 200

Martin, Violet Florence 1862-1915 .. **SSC 56; TCLC 51**

Martin, Webber
See Silverberg, Robert

Martindale, Patrick Victor
See White, Patrick

Martin du Gard, Roger
1881-1958 .... **TCLC 24**
See also CA 118; CANR 94, DLB 65, 331;
EWL 3; GFL 1789 to the Present; RGWL
2, 3

Martineau, Harriet 1802-1876 ...... **NCLC 26, 137**
See also BRWS 15; DLB 21, 55, 159, 163,
166, 190; FW; RGEL 2; YABC 2

Martines, Julia
See O'Faolain, Julia

Martinez, Enrique Gonzalez
See Gonzalez Martinez, Enrique

Martinez, Jacinto Benavente y
See Benavente, Jacinto

Martinez de la Rosa, Francisco de Paula
1787-1862 .... **NCLC 102**
See also TWA

Martinez Ruiz, Jose 1873-1967 .... **CLC 11**
See also CA 93-96; DLB 322; EW 3; EWL
3; HW 1

Martinez Sierra, Gregorio
See Martinez Sierra, Maria

Martinez Sierra, Gregorio
1881-1947 .... **TCLC 6**
See also CA 115; EWL 3

Mayne, William 1928-2010 .... **CLC 12**
See also AAYA 20; CA 9-12R; CANR 37, 80, 100; CLR 25, 123; FANT; JRDA; MAICYA 1, 2; MAICYAS 1; SAAS 11; SATA 6, 68, 122; SUFW 2; YAW

Mayne, William James Carter
See Mayne, William

Mayo, Jim
See L'Amour, Louis

Maysles, Albert 1926- .... **CLC 16**
See also CA 29-32R

Maysles, David 1932-1987 .... **CLC 16**
See also CA 191

Mazer, Norma Fox 1931-2009 .... **CLC 26**
See also AAYA 5, 36; BYA 1, 8; CA 69-72; 292; CANR 12, 32, 66, 129, 189; CLR 23; JRDA; MAICYA 1, 2; SAAS 1; SATA 24, 67, 105, 168, 198; WYA; YAW

Mazzini, Guiseppe 1805-1872 .... **NCLC 34**

McAlmon, Robert (Menzies)
1895-1956 .... **TCLC 97**
See also CA 107; 168; DLB 4, 45; DLBD 15; GLL 1

McAuley, James Phillip 1917-1976 .. **CLC 45**
See also CA 97-100; CP 1, 2; DLB 260; RGEL 2

McBain, Ed
See Hunter, Evan

McBrien, William 1930- .... **CLC 44**
See also CA 107; CANR 90

McBrien, William Augustine
See McBrien, William

McCabe, Pat
See McCabe, Patrick

McCabe, Patrick 1955- .... **CLC 133**
See also BRWS 9; CA 130; CANR 50, 90, 168, 202; CN 6, 7; DLB 194

McCaffrey, Anne 1926- .... **CLC 17**
See also AAYA 6, 34; AITN 2; BEST 89:2; BPFB 2; BYA 5; CA 25-28R, 227; CAAE 227; CANR 15, 35, 55, 96, 169; CLR 49, 130; CPW; DA3; DAM NOV, POP; DLB 8; JRDA; MAICYA 1, 2; MTCW 1, 2; MTFW 2005; SAAS 11; SATA 8, 70, 116, 152; SATA-Essay 152; SFW 4; SUFW 2; WYA; YAW

McCaffrey, Anne Inez
See McCaffrey, Anne

McCall, Nathan 1955(?)- .... **CLC 86**
See also AAYA 59; BW 3; CA 146; CANR 88, 186

McCall Smith, Alexander
See Smith, Alexander McCall

McCann, Arthur
See Campbell, John W.

McCann, Colum 1965- .... **CLC 299**
See also CA 152; CANR 99, 149; DLB 267

McCann, Edson
See Pohl, Frederik

McCarthy, Charles
See McCarthy, Cormac

McCarthy, Charles, Jr.
See McCarthy, Cormac

McCarthy, Cormac 1933- .... **CLC 4, 57, 101, 204, 295, 310**
See also AAYA 41; AMWS 8; BPFB 2; CA 13-16R; CANR 10, 42, 69, 101, 161, 171; CN 6, 7; CPW; CSW; DA3; DAM POP; DLB 6, 143, 256; EWL 3; LATS 1:2; LNFS 3; MAL 5; MTCW 2; MTFW 2005; NFS 36, 40; TCLE 1:2; TCWW 2

McCarthy, Mary 1912-1989 ...... **CLC 1, 3, 5, 14, 24, 39, 59; SSC 24**
See also AMW; BPFB 2; CA 5-8R; 129; CANR 16, 50, 64; CN 1, 2, 3, 4; DA3; DLB 2; DLBY 1981; EWL 3; FW; INT CANR-16; MAL 5; MBL; MTCW 1, 2; MTFW 2005; RGAL 4; TUS

McCarthy, Mary Therese
See McCarthy, Mary

McCartney, James Paul
See McCartney, Paul

McCartney, Paul 1942- .... **CLC 12, 35**
See also CA 146; CANR 111

McCauley, Stephen 1955- .... **CLC 50**
See also CA 141

McClaren, Peter .... **CLC 70**

McClure, Michael (Thomas) 1932- ... **CLC 6, 10**
See also BG 1:3; CA 21-24R; CAD; CANR 17, 46, 77, 131; CD 5, 6; CP 1, 2, 3, 4, 5, 6, 7; DLB 16; WP

McCorkle, Jill 1958- .... **CLC 51**
See also CA 121; CANR 113, 218; CSW; DLB 234; DLBY 1987; SSFS 24

McCorkle, Jill Collins
See McCorkle, Jill

McCourt, Francis
See McCourt, Frank

McCourt, Frank 1930-2009 .... **CLC 109, 299**
See also AAYA 61; AMWS 12; CA 157; 288; CANR 97, 138; MTFW 2005; NCFS 1

McCourt, James 1941- .... **CLC 5**
See also CA 57-60; CANR 98, 152, 186

McCourt, Malachy 1931- .... **CLC 119**
See also SATA 126

McCoy, Edmund
See Gardner, John

McCoy, Horace (Stanley)
1897-1955 .... **TCLC 28**
See also AMWS 13; CA 108; 155; CMW 4; DLB 9

McCrae, John 1872-1918 .... **TCLC 12**
See also CA 109; DLB 92; PFS 5

McCreigh, James
See Pohl, Frederik

McCullers, Carson 1917-1967 . **CLC 1, 4, 10, 12, 48, 100; DC 35; SSC 9, 24, 99; TCLC 155; WLC 4**
See also AAYA 21; AMW; AMWC 2; BPFB 2; CA 5-8R; 25-28R; CABS 1, 3; CANR 18, 132; CDALB 1941-1968; DA; DA3; DAB; DAC; DAM MST, NOV; DFS 5, 18; DLB 2, 7, 173, 228; FWL 3; EXPS; FW; GLL 1; LAIT 3, 4; MAL 5; MBL; MTCW 1, 2; MTFW 2005; NFS 6, 13; RGAL 4; RGSF 2; SATA 27; SSFS 5, 32; TUS; YAW

McCullers, Lula Carson Smith
See McCullers, Carson

McCulloch, John Tyler
See Burroughs, Edgar Rice

McCullough, Colleen 1937- ...... **CLC 27, 107**
See also AAYA 36; BPFB 2; CA 81-84; CANR 17, 46, 67, 98, 139, 203; CPW; DA3; DAM NOV, POP; MTCW 1, 2; MTFW 2005; RHW

McCunn, Ruthanne Lum 1946- .... **AAL**
See also CA 119; CANR 43, 96; DLB 312; LAIT 2; SATA 63

McDermott, Alice 1953- .... **CLC 90**
See also AMWS 18; CA 109; CANR 40, 90, 126, 181; CN 7; DLB 292; MTFW 2005; NFS 23

McDonagh, Martin 1970(?)- .... **CLC 304**
See also AAYA 71; BRWS 12; CA 171; CANR 141; CD 6

McElroy, Joseph 1930- .... **CLC 5, 47**
See also CA 17-20R; CANR 149; CN 3, 4, 5, 6, 7

McElroy, Joseph Prince
See McElroy, Joseph

McElroy, Lee
See Kelton, Elmer

McEwan, Ian 1948- ... **CLC 13, 66, 169, 269; SSC 106**
See also AAYA 84; BEST 90:4; BRWS 4; CA 61-64; CANR 14, 41, 69, 87, 132, 179; CN 3, 4, 5, 6, 7; DAM NOV; DLB 14, 194, 319, 326; HGG; MTCW 1, 2; MTFW 2005; NFS 32; RGSF 2; SUFW 2; TEA

McEwan, Ian Russell
See McEwan, Ian

McFadden, David 1940- .... **CLC 48**
See also CA 104; CP 1, 2, 3, 4, 5, 6, 7; DLB 60; INT CA-104

McFarland, Dennis 1950- .... **CLC 65**
See also CA 165; CANR 110, 179

McGahern, John 1934-2006 .... **CLC 5, 9, 48, 156; SSC 17**
See also CA 17-20R; 249; CANR 29, 68, 113, 204; CN 1, 2, 3, 4, 5, 6, 7; DLB 14, 231, 319; MTCW 1

McGinley, Patrick (Anthony) 1937- . **CLC 41**
See also CA 120; 127; CANR 56; INT CA-127

McGinley, Phyllis 1905-1978 .... **CLC 14**
See also CA 9-12R; 77-80; CANR 19; CP 1, 2; CWRI 5; DLB 11, 48; MAL 5; PFS 9, 13; SATA 2, 44; SATA-Obit 24

McGinniss, Joe 1942- .... **CLC 32**
See also AITN 2; BEST 89:2; CA 25-28R; CANR 26, 70, 152; CPW; DLB 185; INT CANR-26

McGivern, Maureen Daly
See Daly, Maureen

McGivern, Maureen Patricia Daly
See Daly, Maureen

McGrath, Patrick 1950- .... **CLC 55**
See also CA 136; CANR 65, 148, 190; CN 5, 6, 7; DLB 231; HGG; SUFW 2

McGrath, Thomas (Matthew)
1916-1990 .... **CLC 28, 59**
See also AMWS 10; CA 9-12R; 132; CANR 6, 33, 95; CP 1, 2, 3, 4, 5; DAM POET; MAL 5; MTCW 1; SATA 41; SATA-Obit 66

McGuane, Thomas 1939- .. **CLC 3, 7, 18, 45, 127**
See also AITN 2; BPFB 2; CA 49-52; CANR 5, 24, 49, 94, 164; CN 2, 3, 4, 5, 6, 7; DLB 2, 212; DLBY 1980; EWL 3; INT CANR-24; MAL 5; MTCW 1; MTFW 2005; TCWW 1, 2

McGuane, Thomas Francis III
See McGuane, Thomas

McGuckian, Medbh 1950- .... **CLC 48, 174; PC 27**
See also BRWS 5; CA 143; CANR 206; CP 4, 5, 6, 7; CWP; DAM POET; DLB 40

McHale, Tom 1942(?)-1982 .... **CLC 3, 5**
See also AITN 1; CA 77-80; 106; CN 1, 2, 3

McHugh, Heather 1948- .... **PC 61**
See also CA 69-72; CANR 11, 28, 55, 92; CP 4, 5, 6, 7; CWP; PFS 24

McIlvanney, William 1936- .... **CLC 42**
See also CA 25-28R; CANR 61; CMW 4; DLB 14, 207

McIlwraith, Maureen Mollie Hunter
See Hunter, Mollie

McInerney, Jay 1955- .... **CLC 34, 112**
See also AAYA 18; BPFB 2; CA 116; 123; CANR 45, 68, 116, 176, 219; CN 5, 6, 7; CPW; DA3; DAM POP; DLB 292; INT CA-123; MAL 5; MTCW 2; MTFW 2005

McIntyre, Vonda N. 1948- .... **CLC 18**
See also CA 81-84; CANR 17, 34, 69; MTCW 1; SFW 4; YAW

McIntyre, Vonda Neel
See McIntyre, Vonda N.

Merleau-Ponty, Maurice
1908-1961 .... **TCLC 156**
See also CA 114; 89-92; DLB 296; GFL
1789 to the Present

Merlin, Arthur
See Blish, James

Mernissi, Fatima 1940- .... **CLC 171**
See also CA 152; DLB 346; FW

Merrill, James 1926-1995 ...... **CLC 2, 3, 6, 8,**
13, 18, 34, 91; PC 28; TCLC 173
See also AMWS 3; CA 13-16R; 147; CANR
10, 49, 63, 108; CP 1, 2, 3, 4; DA3; DAM
POET; DLB 5, 165; DLBY 1985; EWL 3;
INT CANR-10; MAL 5; MTCW 1, 2;
MTFW 2005; PAB; PFS 23; RGAL 4

Merrill, James Ingram
See Merrill, James

Merriman, Alex
See Silverberg, Robert

Merriman, Brian 1747-1805 .... **NCLC 70**

Merritt, E. B.
See Waddington, Miriam

Merton, Thomas 1915-1968 ..... **CLC 1, 3, 11,**
34, 83; PC 10
See also AAYA 61; AMWS 8; CA 5-8R;
25-28R; CANR 22, 53, 111, 131; DA3;
DLB 48; DLBY 1981; MAL 5; MTCW 1,
2; MTFW 2005

Merton, Thomas James
See Merton, Thomas

Merwin, W. S. 1927- ... **CLC 1, 2, 3, 5, 8, 13,**
18, 45, 88; PC 45
See also AMWS 3; CA 13-16R; CANR 15,
51, 112, 140, 209; CP 1, 2, 3, 4, 5, 6, 7;
DA3; DAM POET; DLB 5, 169, 342;
EWL 3; INT CANR-15; MAL 5; MTCW
1, 2; MTFW 2005; PAB; PFS 5, 15;
RGAL 4

Merwin, William Stanley
See Merwin, W. S.

Metastasio, Pietro 1698-1782 .... **LC 115**
See also RGWL 2, 3

Metcalf, John 1938- .... **CLC 37; SSC 43**
See also CA 113; CN 4, 5, 6, 7; DLB 60;
RGSF 2; TWA

Metcalf, Suzanne
See Baum, L. Frank

Mew, Charlotte (Mary) 1870-1928 .. **PC 107;**
TCLC 8
See also CA 105; 189; DLB 19, 135; RGEL
2

Mewshaw, Michael 1943- .... **CLC 9**
See also CA 53-56; CANR 7, 47, 147, 213;
DLBY 1980

Meyer, Conrad Ferdinand
1825-1898 .... **NCLC 81, 249; SSC 30**
See also DLB 129; EW; RGWL 2, 3

Meyer, Gustav 1868-1932 .... **TCLC 21**
See also CA 117; 190; DLB 81; EWL 3

Meyer, June
See Jordan, June

Meyer, Lynn
See Slavitt, David R.

Meyer, Stephenie 1973- .... **CLC 280**
See also AAYA 77; CA 253; CANR 192;
CLR 142; SATA 193

Meyer-Meyrink, Gustav
See Meyer, Gustav

Meyers, Jeffrey 1939- .... **CLC 39**
See also CA 73-76, 186; CAAE 186; CANR
54, 102, 159; DLB 111

**Meynell, Alice (Christina Gertrude
Thompson)** 1847-1922 .. **PC 112; TCLC**
6
See also CA 104; 177; DLB 19, 98; RGEL
2

Meyrink, Gustav
See Meyer, Gustav

Mhlophe, Gcina 1960- .... **BLC 2:3**

Michaels, Leonard 1933-2003 ..... **CLC 6, 25;**
SSC 16
See also AMWS 16; CA 61-64; 216; CANR
21, 62, 119, 179; CN 3, 45, 6, 7; DLB
130; MTCW 1; TCLE 1:2

Michaux, Henri 1899-1984 .... **CLC 8, 19**
See also CA 85-88; 114; DLB 258; EWL 3;
GFL 1789 to the Present; RGWL 2, 3

Micheaux, Oscar (Devereaux)
1884-1951 .... **TCLC 76**
See also BW 3; CA 174; DLB 50; TCWW
2

Michelangelo 1475-1564 .... **LC 12**
See also AAYA 43

Michelet, Jules 1798-1874 ...... **NCLC 31, 218**
See also EW 5; GFL 1789 to the Present

Michels, Robert 1876-1936 .... **TCLC 88**
See also CA 212

Michener, James A. 1907(?)-1997 . **CLC 1, 5,**
11, 29, 60, 109
See also AAYA 27; AITN 1; BEST 90:1;
BPFB 2; CA 5-8R; 161; CANR 21, 45,
68; CN 1, 2, 3, 4, 5, 6; CPW; DA3; DAM
NOV, POP; DLB 6; MAL 5; MTCW 1, 2;
MTFW 2005; RHW; TCWW 1, 2

Michener, James Albert
See Michener, James A.

Mickiewicz, Adam 1798-1855 . **NCLC 3, 101;**
PC 38
See also EW 5; RGWL 2, 3

Middleton, (John) Christopher
1926- .... **CLC 13**
See also CA 13-16R; CANR 29, 54, 117;
CP 1, 2, 3, 4, 5, 6, 7; DLB 40

Middleton, Richard (Barham)
1882-1911 .... **TCLC 56**
See also CA 187; DLB 156; HGG

Middleton, Stanley 1919-2009 ...... **CLC 7, 38**
See also CA 25-28R; 288; CAAS 23; CANR
21, 46, 81, 157; CN 1, 2, 3, 4, 5, 6, 7;
DLB 14, 326

Middleton, Thomas 1580-1627 ...... **DC 5, 40;**
LC 33, 123
See also BRW 2; DAM DRAM, MST; DFS
18, 22; DLB 58; RGEL 2

Mieville, China 1972(?)- .... **CLC 235**
See also AAYA 52; CA 196; CANR 138,
214; MTFW 2005

Migueis, Jose Rodrigues 1901-1980 . **CLC 10**
See also DLB 287

Mihura, Miguel 1905-1977 .... **DC 34**
See also CA 214

Mikszath, Kalman 1847-1910 .... **TCLC 31**
See also CA 170

Miles, Jack .... **CLC 100**
See also CA 200

Miles, John Russiano
See Miles, Jack

Miles, Josephine (Louise)
1911-1985 .... **CLC 1, 2, 14, 34, 39**
See also CA 1-4R; 116; CANR 2, 55; CP 1,
2, 3, 4; DAM POET; DLB 48; MAL 5;
TCLE 1:2

Militant
See Sandburg, Carl

Mill, Harriet (Hardy) Taylor
1807-1858 .... **NCLC 102**
See also FW

Mill, John Stuart 1806-1873 ... **NCLC 11, 58,**
179, 223
See also CDBLB 1832-1890; DLB 55, 190,
262; FW 1; RGEL 2; TEA

Millar, Kenneth 1915-1983 .. **CLC 1, 2, 3, 14,**
34, 41
See also AAYA 81; AMWS 4; BPFB 2; CA
9-12R; 110; CANR 16, 63, 107; CMW 4;
CN 1, 2, 3; CPW; DA3; DAM POP; DLB
2, 226; DLBD 6; DLBY 1983; MAL 5;
MSW; MTCW 1, 2; MTFW 2005; RGAL
4

Millay, E. Vincent
See Millay, Edna St. Vincent

Millay, Edna St. Vincent 1892-1950 ..... **PC 6,**
61; TCLC 4, 49, 169; WLCS
See also AMW; CA 104; 130; CDALB
1917-1929; DA; DA3; DAB; DAC; DAM
MST, POET; DFS 27; DLB 45, 249; EWL
3; EXPP; FL 1:6; GLL 1; MAL 5; MBL;
MTCW 1, 2; MTFW 2005; PAB; PFS 3,
17, 31, 34, 41; RGAL 4; TUS; WP

Miller, Arthur 1915-2005 ..... **CLC 1, 2, 6, 10,**
15, 26, 47, 78, 179; DC 1, 31; WLC 4
See also AAYA 15; AITN 1; AMW; AMWC
1; CA 1-4R; 236; CABS 3; CAD; CANR
2, 30, 54, 76, 132; CD 5, 6; CDALB
1941-1968; DA; DA3; DAB; DAC; DAM
DRAM, MST; DFS 1, 3, 8, 27; DLB 7,
266; EWL 3; LAIT 1, 4; LATS 1:2; MAL
5; MTCW 1, 2; MTFW 2005; RGAL 4;
RGHL; TUS; WYAS 1

Miller, Frank 1957- .... **CLC 278**
See also AAYA 45; CA 224

Miller, Henry (Valentine)
1891-1980 .... **CLC 1, 2, 4, 9, 14, 43, 84;**
TCLC 213; WLC 4
See also AMW; BPFB 2; CA 9-12R; 97-
100; CANR 33, 64; CDALB 1929-1941;
CN 1, 2; DA; DA3; DAB; DAC; DAM
MST, NOV; DLB 4, 9; DLBY 1980; EWL
3; MAL 5; MTCW 1, 2; MTFW 2005;
RGAL 4; TUS

Miller, Hugh 1802-1856 .... **NCLC 143**
See also DLB 190

Miller, Jason 1939(?)-2001 .... **CLC 2**
See also AITN 1; CA 73-76; 197; CAD;
CANR 130; DFS 12; DLB 7

Miller, Sue 1943- .... **CLC 44**
See also AMWS 12; BEST 90:3; CA 139;
CANR 59, 91, 128, 194; DA3; DAM
POP; DLB 143

Miller, Walter M(ichael, Jr.)
1923-1996 .... **CLC 4, 30**
See also BPFB 2; CA 85-88; CANR 108;
DLB 8; SCFW 1, 2; SFW 4

Millett, Kate 1934- .... **CLC 67**
See also AITN 1; CA 73-76; CANR 32, 53,
76, 110; DA3; DLB 246; FW; GLL 1;
MTCW 1, 2; MTFW 2005

Millhauser, Steven 1943- ... **CLC 21, 54, 109,**
300; SSC 57
See also AAYA 76; CA 110; 111; CANR
63, 114, 133, 189; CN 6, 7; DA3; DLB 2,
350; FANT; INT CA-111; MAL 5; MTCW
2; MTFW 2005

Millhauser, Steven Lewis
See Millhauser, Steven

Millin, Sarah Gertrude 1889-1968 ... **CLC 49**
See also CA 102; 93-96; DLB 225; EWL 3

Milne, A. A. 1882-1956 .... **TCLC 6, 88**
See also BRWS 5; CA 104; 133; CLR 1,
26, 108; CMW 4; CWRI 5; DA3; DAB;
DAC; DAM MST; DLB 10, 77, 100, 160,
352; FANT; MAICYA 1, 2; MTCW 1, 2;
MTFW 2005; RGEL 2; SATA 100; WCH;
YABC 1

Milne, Alan Alexander
See Milne, A. A.

Milner, Ron(ald) 1938-2004 .. **BLC 1:3; CLC**
56
See also AITN 1; BW 1; CA 73-76; 230;
CAD; CANR 24, 81; CD 5, 6; DAM
MULT; DLB 38; MAL 5; MTCW 1

Milnes, Richard Monckton
1809-1885 .... **NCLC 61**
See also DLB 32, 184

Milosz, Czeslaw 1911-2004 .... **CLC 5, 11, 22,**
31, 56, 82, 253; PC 8; WLCS
See also AAYA 62; CA 81-84; 230; CANR
23, 51, 91, 126; CDWLB 4; CWW 2;
DA3; DAM MST, POET; DLB 215, 331;

North, Captain George
  See Stevenson, Robert Louis
North, Captain George
  See Stevenson, Robert Louis
North, Milou
  See Erdrich, Louise
Northrup, B. A.
  See Hubbard, L. Ron
North Staffs
  See Hulme, T(homas) E(rnest)
Northup, Solomon 1808-1863 ...... **NCLC 105**
Norton, Alice Mary
  See Norton, Andre
Norton, Andre 1912-2005 .... **CLC 12**
  See also AAYA 83; BPFB 2; BYA 4, 10,
  12; CA 1-4R; 237; CANR 2, 31, 68, 108,
  149; CLR 50; DLB 8, 52; JRDA; MAI-
  CYA 1, 2; MTCW 1; SATA 1, 43, 91;
  SUFW 1, 2; YAW
Norton, Caroline 1808-1877 .. **NCLC 47, 205**
  See also DLB 21, 159, 199
Norway, Nevil Shute
  See Shute, Nevil
Norwid, Cyprian Kamil
  1821-1883 .... **NCLC 17**
  See also RGWL 3
Nosille, Nabrah
  See Ellison, Harlan
Nossack, Hans Erich 1901-1977 .... **CLC 6**
  See also CA 93-96; 85-88; CANR 156;
  DLB 69; EWL 3
Nostradamus 1503-1566 .... **LC 27**
Nosu, Chuji
  See Ozu, Yasujiro
Notenburg, Eleanora (Genrikhovna) von
  See Guro, Elena (Genrikhovna)
Nova, Craig 1945- .... **CLC 7, 31**
  See also CA 45-48; CANR 2, 53, 127, 223
Novak, Joseph
  See Kosinski, Jerzy
Novalis 1772-1801 .... **NCLC 13, 178; PC 120**
  See also CDWLB 2; DLB 90; EW 5; RGWL
  2, 3
Novick, Peter 1934- .... **CLC 164**
  See also CA 188
Novis, Emile
  See Weil, Simone
Nowlan, Alden (Albert) 1933-1983 ... **CLC 15**
  See also CA 9-12R; CANR 5; CP 1, 2, 3;
  DAC; DAM MST; DLB 53; PFS 12
Noyes, Alfred 1880-1958 ...... **PC 27; TCLC 7**
  See also CA 104; 188; DLB 20; EXPP;
  FANT; PFS 4; RGEL 2
Nugent, Richard Bruce
  1906(?)-1987 .... **HR 1:3**
  See also BW 1; CA 125; CANR 198; DLB
  51; GLL 2
Nunez, Elizabeth 1944- .... **BLC 2:3**
  See also CA 223; CANR 220
Nunn, Kem .... **CLC 34**
  See also CA 159; CANR 204
Nussbaum, Martha Craven 1947- .. **CLC 203**
  See also CA 134; CANR 102, 176, 213
Nwapa, Flora (Nwanzuruaha)
  1931-1993 .... **BLCS; CLC 133**
  See also BW 2; CA 143; CANR 83; CD-
  WLB 3; CLR 162; CWRI 5; DLB 125;
  EWL 3; WLIT 2
Nye, Robert 1939- .... **CLC 13, 42**
  See also BRWS 10; CA 33-36R; CANR 29,
  67, 107; CN 1, 2, 3, 4, 5, 6, 7; CP 1, 2, 3,
  4, 5, 6, 7; CWRI 5; DAM NOV; DLB 14,
  271; FANT; HGG; MTCW 1; RHW;
  SATA 6
Nyro, Laura 1947-1997 .... **CLC 17**
  See also CA 194
O. Henry
  See Henry, O.

Oates, Joyce Carol 1938- .. **CLC 1, 2, 3, 6, 9,**
  11, 15, 19, 33, 52, 108, 134, 228; SSC 6,
  70, 121; WLC 4
  See also AAYA 15, 52; AITN 1; AMWS 2;
  BEST 89:2; BPFB 2; BYA 11; CA 5-8R;
  CANR 25, 45, 74, 113, 129, 165; CDALB
  1968-1988; CN 1, 2, 3, 4, 5, 6, 7; CP 5,
  6, 7; CPW; CWP; DA; DA3; DAB; DAC;
  DAM MST, NOV, POP; DLB 2, 5, 130;
  DLBY 1981; EWL 3; EXPS; FL 1:6; FW;
  GL 3; HGG; INT CANR-25; LAIT 4;
  MAL 5; MBL; MTCW 1, 2; MTFW 2005;
  NFS 8, 24; RGAL 4; RGSF 2; SATA 159;
  SSFS 1, 8, 17, 32; SUFW 2; TUS
Obradovic, Dositej 1740(?)-1811 . **NCLC 254**
  See also DLB 147
O'Brian, E.G.
  See Clarke, Arthur C.
O'Brian, Patrick 1914-2000 .... **CLC 152**
  See also AAYA 55; BRWS 12; CA 144; 187;
  CANR 74, 201; CPW; MTCW 2; MTFW
  2005; RHW
O'Brien, Darcy 1939-1998 .... **CLC 11**
  See also CA 21-24R; 167; CANR 8, 59
O'Brien, Edna 1932- ..... **CLC 3, 5, 8, 13, 36,**
  65, 116, 237; SSC 10, 77
  See also BRWS 5; CA 1-4R; CANR 6, 41,
  65, 102, 169, 213; CDBLB 1960 to
  Present; CN 1, 2, 3, 4, 5, 6, 7; DA3; DAM
  NOV; DLB 14, 231, 319; EWL 3; FW;
  MTCW 1, 2; MTFW 2005; RGSF 2;
  WLIT 4
O'Brien, E.G.
  See Clarke, Arthur C.
O'Brien, Fitz-James 1828-1862 ..... **NCLC 21**
  See also DLB 74; RGAL 4; SUFW
O'Brien, Flann
  See O Nuallain, Brian
O'Brien, Richard 1942- .... **CLC 17**
  See also CA 124
O'Brien, Tim 1946- .... **CLC 7, 19, 40, 103,**
  211, 305; SSC 74, 123
  See also AAYA 16; AMWS 5; CA 85-88;
  CANR 40, 58, 133; CDALBS; CN 5, 6,
  7; CPW; DA3; DAM POP; DLB 152;
  DLBD 9; DLBY 1980; LATS 1:2; MAL
  5; MTCW 2; MTFW 2005; NFS 37;
  RGAL 4; SSFS 5, 15, 29, 32; TCLE 1:2
O'Brien, William Timothy
  See O'Brien, Tim
Obstfelder, Sigbjorn 1866-1900 ..... **TCLC 23**
  See also CA 123; DLB 354
O'Casey, Brenda
  See Haycraft, Anna
O'Casey, Sean 1880-1964 .... **CLC 1, 5, 9, 11,**
  15, 88; DC 12; WLCS
  See also BRW 7; CA 89-92; CANR 62;
  CBD; CDBLB 1914-1945; DA3; DAB;
  DAC; DAM DRAM, MST; DFS 19; DLB
  10; EWL 3; MTCW 1, 2; MTFW 2005;
  RGEL 2; TEA; WLIT 4
O'Cathasaigh, Sean
  See O'Casey, Sean
Occom, Samson 1723-1792 .... **LC 60; NNAL**
  See also DLB 175
Occomy, Marita (Odette) Bonner
  1899(?)-1971 ..... **HR 1:2; PC 72; TCLC**
  179
  See also BW 2; CA 142; DFS 13; DLB 51,
  228
Ochs, Phil(ip David) 1940-1976 .... **CLC 17**
  See also CA 185; 65-68
O'Connor, Edwin (Greene)
  1918-1968 .... **CLC 14**
  See also CA 93-96; 25-28R; MAL 5
O'Connor, Flannery 1925-1964 ..... **CLC 1, 2,**
  3, 6, 10, 13, 15, 21, 66, 104; SSC 1, 23,
  61, 82, 111; TCLC 132; WLC 4
  See also AAYA 7; AMW; AMWR 2; BPFB
  3; BYA 16; CA 1-4R; CANR 3, 41;
  CDALB 1941-1968; DA; DA3; DAB;

DAC; DAM MST, NOV; DLB 2, 152;
DLBD 12; DLBY 1980; EWL 3; EXPS;
LAIT 5; MAL 5; MBL; MTCW 1, 2;
MTFW 2005; NFS 3, 21; RGAL 4; RGSF
2; SSFS 2, 7, 10, 19, 34; TUS
O'Connor, Frank 1903-1966
  See O'Donovan, Michael Francis
O'Connor, Mary Flannery
  See O'Connor, Flannery
O'Dell, Scott 1898-1989 .... **CLC 30**
  See also AAYA 3, 44; BPFB 3; BYA 1, 2,
  3, 5; CA 61-64; 129; CANR 12, 30, 112;
  CLR 1, 16, 126; DLB 52; JRDA; MAI-
  CYA 1, 2; SATA 12, 60, 134; WYA; YAW
Odets, Clifford 1906-1963 ..... **CLC 2, 28, 98;**
  DC 6; TCLC 244
  See also AMWS 2; CA 85-88; CAD; CANR
  62; DAM DRAM; DFS 3, 17, 20; DLB 7,
  26, 341; EWL 3; MAL 5; MTCW 1, 2;
  MTFW 2005; RGAL 4; TUS
O'Doherty, Brian 1928- .... **CLC 76**
  See also CA 105; CANR 108
O'Donnell, K. M.
  See Malzberg, Barry N(athaniel)
O'Donnell, Lawrence
  See Kuttner, Henry
O'Donovan, Michael Francis
  1903-1966 .... **CLC 14, 23; SSC 5, 109**
  See also BRWS 14; CA 93-96; CANR 84;
  DLB 162; EWL 3; RGSF 2; SSFS 5, 34
Oe, Kenzaburo 1935- ... **CLC 10, 36, 86, 187,**
  303; SSC 20
  See also CA 97-100; CANR 36, 50, 74, 126;
  CWW 2; DA3; DAM NOV; DLB 182,
  331; DLBY 1994; EWL 3; LATS 1:2;
  MJW; MTCW 1, 2; MTFW 2005; RGSF
  2; RGWL 2, 3
Oe Kenzaburo
  See Oe, Kenzaburo
O'Faolain, Julia 1932- .... **CLC 6, 19, 47, 108**
  See also CA 81-84; CAAS 2; CANR 12,
  61; CN 2, 3, 4, 5, 6, 7; DLB 14, 231, 319;
  FW; MTCW 1; RHW
O'Faolain, Sean 1900-1991 ...... **CLC 1, 7, 14,**
  32, 70; SSC 13; TCLC 143
  See also CA 61-64; 134; CANR 12, 66; CN
  1, 2, 3, 4; DLB 15, 162; MTCW 1, 2;
  MTFW 2005; RGEL 2; RGSF 2
O'Flaherty, Liam 1896-1984 .... **CLC 5, 34;**
  SSC 6, 116
  See also CA 101; 113; CANR 35; CN 1, 2,
  3; DLB 36, 162; DLBY 1984; MTCW 1,
  2; MTFW 2005; RGEL 2; RGSF 2; SSFS
  5, 20
Ogai
  See Mori Ogai
Ogilvy, Gavin
  See Barrie, J. M.
O'Grady, Standish (James)
  1846-1928 .... **TCLC 5**
  See also CA 104; 157
O'Grady, Timothy 1951- .... **CLC 59**
  See also CA 138
O'Hara, Frank 1926-1966 .... **CLC 2, 5, 13,**
  78; PC 45
  See also CA 9-12R; 25-28R; CANR 33;
  DA3; DAM POET; DLB 5, 16, 193; EWL
  3; MAL 5; MTCW 1, 2; MTFW 2005;
  PFS 8, 12, 34, 38; RGAL 4; WP
O'Hara, John 1905-1970 . **CLC 1, 2, 3, 6, 11,**
  42; SSC 15
  See also AMW; BPFB 3; CA 5-8R; 25-28R;
  CANR 31, 60; CDALB 1929-1941; DAM
  NOV; DLB 9, 86, 324; DLBD 2; EWL 3;
  MAL 5; MTCW 1, 2; MTFW 2005; NFS
  11; RGAL 4; RGSF 2
O'Hara, John Henry
  See O'Hara, John

Pearson, T.R. 1956- .... **CLC 39**
See also CA 120; 130; CANR 97, 147, 185;
CSW; INT CA-130

Peck, Dale 1967- .... **CLC 81**
See also CA 146; CANR 72, 127, 180; GLL
2

Peck, John (Frederick) 1941- .... **CLC 3**
See also CA 49-52; CANR 3, 100; CP 4, 5,
6, 7

Peck, Richard 1934- .... **CLC 21**
See also AAYA 1, 24; BYA 1, 6, 8, 11; CA
85-88; CANR 19, 38, 129, 178; CLR 15,
142; INT CANR-19; JRDA; MAICYA 1,
2; SAAS 2; SATA 18, 55, 97, 110, 158,
190, 228; SATA-Essay 110; WYA; YAW

Peck, Richard Wayne
See Peck, Richard

Peck, Robert Newton 1928- .... **CLC 17**
See also AAYA 3, 43; BYA 1, 6; CA 81-84,
182; CAAE 182; CANR 31, 63, 127; CLR
45, 163; DA; DAC; DAM MST; JRDA;
LAIT 3; MAICYA 1, 2; NFS 29; SAAS
1; SATA 21, 62, 111, 156; SATA-Essay
108; WYA; YAW

Peckinpah, David Samuel
See Peckinpah, Sam

Peckinpah, Sam 1925-1984 .... **CLC 20**
See also CA 109; 114; CANR 82

Pedersen, Knut 1859-1952 .. **TCLC 2, 14, 49,
151, 203**
See also AAYA 79; CA 104; 119; CANR
63; DLB 297, 330; EW 8; EWL 8; MTCW
1, 2; RGWL 2, 3

Peele, George 1556-1596 .... **DC 27; LC 115**
See also BRW 1; DLB 62, 167; RGEL 2

Peeslake, Gaffer
See Durrell, Lawrence

Peguy, Charles (Pierre)
1873-1914 .... **TCLC 10**
See also CA 107; 193; DLB 258; EWL 3;
GFL 1789 to the Present

Peirce, Charles Sanders
1839-1914 .... **TCLC 81**
See also CA 194; DLB 270

Pelagius c. 350-c. 418 .... **CMLC 118**

Pelecanos, George P. 1957- .... **CLC 236**
See also CA 138; CANR 122, 165, 194;
DLB 306

Pelevin, Victor 1962- .... **CLC 238**
See also CA 154; CANR 88, 159, 197; DLB
285

Pelevin, Viktor Olegovich
See Pelevin, Victor

Pellicer, Carlos 1897(?)-1977 .... **HLCS 2**
See also CA 153; 69-72; DLB 290; EWL 3;
HW 1

Pena, Ramon del Valle y
See Valle-Inclan, Ramon del

Pendennis, Arthur Esquir
See Thackeray, William Makepeace

Penn, Arthur
See Matthews, (James) Brander

Penn, William 1644-1718 .... **LC 25**
See also DLB 24

Penny, Carolyn
See Chute, Carolyn

PEPECE
See Prado (Calvo), Pedro

Pepys, Samuel 1633-1703 ... **LC 11, 58; WLC
4**
See also BRW 2; CDBLB 1660-1789; DA;
DA3; DAB; DAC; DAM MST; DLB 101,
213; NCFS 4; RGEL 2; TEA; WLIT 3

Percy, Thomas 1729-1811 .... **NCLC 95**
See also DLB 104

Percy, Walker 1916-1990 .... **CLC 2, 3, 6, 8,
14, 18, 47, 65**
See also AMWS 3; BPFB 3; CA 1-4R; 131;
CANR 1, 23, 64; CN 1, 2, 3, 4; CPW;
CSW; DA3; DAM NOV, POP; DLB 2;
DLBY 1980, 1990; EWL 3; MAL 5;
MTCW 1, 2; MTFW 2005; RGAL 4; TUS

Percy, William Alexander
1885-1942 .... **TCLC 84**
See also CA 163; MTCW 2

Perdurabo, Frater
See Crowley, Edward Alexander

Perec, Georges 1936-1982 .... **CLC 56, 116**
See also CA 141; DLB 83, 299; EWL 3;
GFL 1789 to the Present; RGHL; RGWL
3

**Pereda (y Sanchez de Porrua), Jose Maria
de** 1833-1906 .... **TCLC 16**
See also CA 117

Pereda y Porrua, Jose Maria de
See Pereda (y Sanchez de Porrua), Jose
Maria de

Peregoy, George Weems
See Mencken, H. L.

Perelman, S(idney) J(oseph)
1904-1979 .. **CLC 3, 5, 9, 15, 23, 44, 49;
SSC 32**
See also AAYA 79; AITN 1, 2; BPFB 3;
CA 73-76; 89-92; CANR 18; DAM
DRAM; DLB 11, 44; MTCW 1, 2; MTFW
2005; RGAL 4

Peret, Benjamin 1899-1959 .... **PC 33; TCLC
20**
See also CA 117; 186; GFL 1789 to the
Present

Perets, Yitskhok Leybush
See Peretz, Isaac Loeb

Peretz, Isaac Leib (?)
See Peretz, Isaac Loeb

Peretz, Isaac Loeb 1851-1915 .... **SSC 26;
TCLC 16**
See Peretz, Isaac Leib
See also CA 109; 201; DLB 333

Peretz, Yitzkhok Leibush
See Peretz, Isaac Loeb

Perez Galdos, Benito 1843-1920 ..... **HLCS 2;
TCLC 27**
See also CA 125; 153; EW 7; EWL 3; HW
1; RGWL 2, 3

Peri Rossi, Cristina 1941- .. **CLC 156; HLCS
2**
See also CA 131; CANR 59, 81; CWW 2;
DLB 145, 290; EWL 3; HW 1, 2

Perlata
See Peret, Benjamin

Perloff, Marjorie G(abrielle)
1931- .... **CLC 137**
See also CA 57-60; CANR 7, 22, 49, 104

Perrault, Charles 1628-1703 .. **LC 2, 56; SSC
144**
See also BYA 4; CLR 79, 134; DLB 268;
GFL Beginnings to 1789; MAICYA 1, 2;
RGWL 2, 3; SATA 25; WCH

Perrotta, Tom 1961- .... **CLC 266**
See also CA 162; CANR 99, 155, 197

Perry, Anne 1938- .... **CLC 126**
See also CA 101; CANR 22, 50, 84, 150,
177; CMW 4; CN 6, 7; CPW; DLB 276

Perry, Brighton
See Sherwood, Robert E(mmet)

Perse, St.-John
See Leger, Alexis Saint-Leger

Perse, Saint-John
See Leger, Alexis Saint-Leger

Persius 34-62 .... **CMLC 74**
See also AW 2; DLB 211; RGWL 2, 3

Perutz, Leo(pold) 1882-1957 .... **TCLC 60**
See also CA 147; DLB 81

Peseenz, Tulio F.
See Lopez y Fuentes, Gregorio

Pesetsky, Bette 1932- .... **CLC 28**
See also CA 133; DLB 130

Peshkov, Alexei Maximovich
See Gorky, Maxim

Pessoa, Fernando 1888-1935 .... **HLC 2; PC
20; TCLC 27, 257**
See also CA 125; 183; CANR 182; DAM
MULT; DLB 287; EW 10; EWL 3; RGWL
2, 3; WP

Pessoa, Fernando Antonio Nogueira
See Pessoa, Fernando

Peterkin, Julia Mood 1880-1961 ...... **CLC 31**
See also CA 102; DLB 9

Peter of Blois c. 1135-c. 1212 ...... **CMLC 127**

Peters, Joan K(aren) 1945- .... **CLC 39**
See also CA 158; CANR 109

Peters, Robert L(ouis) 1924- .... **CLC 7**
See also CA 13-16R; CAAS 8; CP 1, 5, 6,
7; DLB 105

Peters, S. H.
See Henry, O.

Petofi, Sandor 1823-1849 .... **NCLC 21**
See also RGWL 2, 3

Petrakis, Harry Mark 1923- .... **CLC 3**
See also CA 9-12R; CANR 4, 30, 85, 155;
CN 1, 2, 3, 4, 5, 6, 7

Petrarch 1304-1374 .... **CMLC 20; PC 8**
See also DA3; DAM POET; EW 2; LMFS
1; RGWL 2, 3; WLIT 7

Petrarch, Francesco
See Petrarch

Petronius c. 20-66 .... **CMLC 34**
See also AW 2; CDWLB 1; DLB 211;
RGWL 2, 3; WLIT 8

Petrov, Eugene
See Kataev, Evgeny Petrovich

Petrov, Evgenii
See Kataev, Evgeny Petrovich

Petrov, Evgeny
See Kataev, Evgeny Petrovich

Petrovsky, Boris
See Mansfield, Katherine

Petry, Ann 1908-1997 ...... **CLC 1, 7, 18; SSC
161; TCLC 112**
See also AFAW 1, 2; BPFB 3; BW 1, 3;
BYA 2; CA 5-8R; 157; CAAS 6; CANR
4, 46; CLR 12; CN 1, 2, 3, 4, 5, 6; DLB
76; EWL 3; JRDA; LAIT 1; MAICYA 1,
2; MAICYAS 1; MTCW 1; NFS 33;
RGAL 4; SATA 5; SATA-Obit 94; TUS

Petry, Ann Lane
See Petry, Ann

Petursson, Halligrimur 1614-1674 .... **LC 8**

Peychinovich
See Vazov, Ivan (Minchov)

Phaedrus c. 15B.C.-c. 50 .... **CMLC 25**
See also DLB 211

Phelge, Nanker
See Richards, Keith

Phelps (Ward), Elizabeth Stuart
See Phelps, Elizabeth Stuart

Phelps, Elizabeth Stuart
1844-1911 .... **TCLC 113**
See also CA 242; DLB 74; FW

Pheradausi
See Ferdowsi, Abu'l Qasem

Philip, M(arlene) Nourbese 1947- .. **CLC 307**
See also BW 3; CA 163; CWP; DLB 157,
334

Philippe de Remi c. 1247-1296 ... **CMLC 102**

Philips, Katherine 1632-1664 ..... **LC 30, 145;
PC 40**
See also DLB 131; RGEL 2

Philipson, Ilene J. 1950- .... **CLC 65**
See also CA 219

Plutarch c. 46-c. 120 .... **CMLC 60**
See also AW 2; CDWLB 1; DLB 176;
RGWL 2, 3; TWA; WLIT 8

Po Chu-i 772-846 .... **CMLC 24**

Podhoretz, Norman 1930- .... **CLC 189**
See also AMWS 8; CA 9-12R; CANR 7,
78, 135, 179

Poe, Edgar Allan 1809-1849 ..... **NCLC 1, 16,
55, 78, 94, 97, 117, 211; PC 1, 54; SSC
1, 22, 34, 35, 54, 88, 111, 156; WLC 4**
See also AAYA 14; AMW; AMWC 1;
AMWR 2; BPFB 3; BYA 5, 11; CDALB
1640-1865; CMW 4; DA; DA3; DAB;
DAC; DAM MST, POET; DLB 3, 59, 73,
74, 248, 254; EXPP; EXPS; GL 3; HGG;
LAIT 2; LATS 1:1; LMFS 1; MSW; PAB;
PFS 1, 3, 9; RGAL 4; RGSF 2; SATA 23;
SCFW 1, 2; SFW 4; SSFS 2, 4, 7, 8, 16,
26, 29, 34; SUFW; TUS; WP; WYA

Poet of Titchfield Street, The
See Pound, Ezra

Poggio Bracciolini, Gian Francesco
1380-1459 .... **LC 125**

Pohl, Frederik 1919- .... **CLC 18; SSC 25**
See also AAYA 24; CA 61-64, 188; CAAE
188; CAAS 1; CANR 11, 37, 81, 140; CN
1, 2, 3, 4, 5, 6; DLB 8; INT CANR-11;
MTCW 1, 2; MTFW 2005; SATA 24;
SCFW 1, 2; SFW 4

Poirier, Louis
See Gracq, Julien

Poitier, Sidney 1927- .... **CLC 26**
See also AAYA 60; BW 1; CA 117; CANR
94

Pokagon, Simon 1830-1899 .... **NNAL**
See also DAM MULT

Polanski, Roman 1933- .... **CLC 16, 178**
See also CA 77-80

Poliakoff, Stephen 1952- .... **CLC 38**
See also CA 106; CANR 116; CBD; CD 5,
6; DLB 13

Police, The
See Copeland, Stewart; Sting; Summers,
Andy

Polidori, John William
1795-1821 .... **NCLC 51; SSC 97**
See also DLB 116; HGG

Poliziano, Angelo 1454-1494 .... **LC 120**
See also WLIT 7

Pollitt, Katha 1949- .... **CLC 28, 122**
See also CA 120; 122; CANR 66, 108, 164,
200; MTCW 1, 2; MTFW 2005

Pollock, (Mary) Sharon 1936- .... **CLC 50**
See also CA 141; CANR 132; CD 5; CWD;
DAC; DAM DRAM, MST; DFS 3; DLB
60; FW

Pollock, Sharon 1936- .... **DC 20**
See also CD 6

Polo, Marco 1254-1324 .... **CMLC 15**
See also WLIT 7

Polonsky, Abraham (Lincoln)
1910-1999 .... **CLC 92**
See also CA 104; 187; DLB 26; INT CA-
104

Polybius c. 200B.C.-c. 118B.C. ...... **CMLC 17**
See also AW 1; DLB 176; RGWL 2, 3

Pomerance, Bernard 1940- .... **CLC 13**
See also CA 101; CAD; CANR 49, 134;
CD 5, 6; DAM DRAM; DFS 9; LAIT 2

Ponge, Francis 1899-1988 ..... **CLC 6, 18; PC
107**
See also CA 85-88; 126; CANR 40, 86;
DAM POET; DLBY 2002; EWL 3; GFL
1789 to the Present; RGWL 2, 3

Poniatowska, Elena 1932- . **CLC 140; HLC 2**
See also CA 101; CANR 32, 66, 107, 156;
CDWLB 3; CWW 2; DAM MULT; DLB
113; EWL 3; HW 1, 2; LAWS 1; WLIT 1

Pontoppidan, Henrik 1857-1943 .... **TCLC 29**
See also CA 170; DLB 300, 331

Ponty, Maurice Merleau
See Merleau-Ponty, Maurice

Poole, (Jane Penelope) Josephine
See Helyar, Jane Penelope Josephine

Poole, Josephine
See Helyar, Jane Penelope Josephine

Popa, Vasko 1922-1991 . **CLC 19; TCLC 167**
See also CA 112; 148; CDWLB 4; DLB
181; EWL 3; RGWL 2, 3

Pope, Alexander 1688-1744 ...... **LC 3, 58, 60,
64, 164; PC 26; WLC 5**
See also BRW 3; BRWC 1; BRWR 1; CD-
BLB 1660-1789; DA; DA3; DAB; DAC;
DAM MST, POET; DLB 95, 101, 213;
EXPP; PAB; PFS 12; RGEL 2; WLIT 3;
WP

Popov, Evgenii Anatol'evich
See Popov, Yevgeny

Popov, Yevgeny .... **CLC 59**
See also DLB 285

Poquelin, Jean-Baptiste
See Moliere

Porete, Marguerite (?)-1310 .... **CMLC 73**
See also DLB 208

Porphyry c. 233-c. 305 .... **CMLC 71**

Porter, Connie (Rose) 1959(?)- .... **CLC 70**
See also AAYA 65; BW 2, 3; CA 142;
CANR 90, 109; SATA 81, 129

Porter, Gene Stratton
See Stratton-Porter, Gene

Porter, Geneva Grace
See Stratton-Porter, Gene

Porter, Katherine Anne 1890 1980 ... **CLC 1,
3, 7, 10, 13, 15, 27, 101; SSC 4, 31, 43,
108; TCLC 233**
See also AAYA 42; AITN 2; AMW; BPFB
3; CA 1-4R; 101; CANR 1, 65; CDALBS;
CN 1, 2; DA; DA3; DAB; DAC; DAM
MST, NOV; DLB 4, 9, 102; DLBD 12;
DLBY 1980; EWL 3; EXPS; LAIT 3;
MAL 5; MBL; MTCW 1, 2; MTFW 2005;
NFS 14; RGAL 4; RGSF 2; SATA 39;
SATA-Obit 23; SSFS 1, 8, 11, 16, 23;
TCWW 2; TUS

Porter, Peter 1929-2010 .... **CLC 5, 13, 33**
See also CA 85-88; CP 1, 2, 3, 4, 5, 6, 7;
DLB 40, 289; WWE 1

Porter, Peter Neville Frederick
See Porter, Peter

Porter, R. E.
See Hoch, Edward D.

Porter, William Sydney
See Henry, O.

Portillo (y Pacheco), Jose Lopez
See Lopez Portillo (y Pacheco), Jose

Portillo Trambley, Estela
1927-1998 .... **HLC 2; TCLC 163**
See also CA 77-80; CANR 32; DAM
MULT; DLB 209; HW 1; RGAL 4

Posey, Alexander (Lawrence)
1873-1908 .... **NNAL**
See also CA 144; CANR 80; DAM MULT;
DLB 175

Posse, Abel .... **CLC 70, 273**
See also CA 252

Post, Melville Davisson
1869-1930 .... **TCLC 39**
See also CA 110; 202; CMW 4

Postl, Carl
See Sealsfield, Charles

Postman, Neil 1931(?)-2003 .... **CLC 244**
See also CA 102; 221

Potocki, Jan 1761-1815 .... **NCLC 229**

Potok, Chaim 1929-2002 ... **CLC 2, 7, 14, 26,
112**
See also AAYA 15, 50; AITN 1, 2; BPFB 3;
BYA 1; CA 17-20R; 208; CANR 19, 35,
64, 98; CLR 92; CN 4, 5, 6; DA3; DAM
NOV; DLB 28, 152; EXPN; INT CANR-
19; LAIT 4; MTCW 1, 2; MTFW 2005;
NFS 4, 34, 38; RGHL; SATA 33, 106;
SATA-Obit 134; TUS; YAW

Potok, Herbert Harold
See Potok, Chaim

Potok, Herman Harold
See Potok, Chaim

Potter, Dennis (Christopher George)
1935-1994 .... **CLC 58, 86, 123**
See also BRWS 10; CA 107; 145; CANR
33, 61; CBD; DLB 233; MTCW 1

Pound, Ezra 1885-1972 . **CLC 1, 2, 3, 4, 5, 7,
10, 13, 18, 34, 48, 50, 112; PC 4, 95;
WLC 5**
See also AAYA 47; AMW; AMWR 1; CA
5-8R; 37-40R; CANR 40; CDALB 1917-
1929; CP 1; DA; DA3; DAB; DAC; DAM
MST, POET; DLB 4, 45, 63; DLBD 15;
EFS 1:2, 2:1; EWL 3; EXPP; LMFS 2;
MAL 5; MTCW 1, 2; MTFW 2005; PAB;
PFS 2, 8, 16; RGAL 4; TUS; WP

Pound, Ezra Weston Loomis
See Pound, Ezra

Povod, Reinaldo 1959-1994 .... **CLC 44**
See also CA 136; 146; CANR 83

Powell, Adam Clayton, Jr.
1908-1972 .... **BLC 1:3; CLC 89**
See also BW 1, 3; CA 102; 33-36R; CANR
86; DAM MULT; DLB 345

Powell, Anthony 1905-2000 ... **CLC 1, 3, 7, 9,
10, 31**
See also BRW 7; CA 1-4R; 189; CANR 1,
32, 62, 107; CDBLB 1945-1960; CN 1, 2,
3, 4, 5, 6; DLB 15; EWL 3; MTCW 1, 2;
MTFW 2005; RGEL 2; TEA

Powell, Dawn 1896(?)-1965 .... **CLC 66**
See also CA 5-8R; CANR 121; DLBY 1997

Powell, Padgett 1952- .... **CLC 34**
See also CA 126; CANR 63, 101, 215;
CSW; DLB 234; DLBY 01; SSFS 25

Power, Susan 1961- .... **CLC 91**
See also BYA 14; CA 160; CANR 135; NFS
11

Powers, J(ames) F(arl) 1917-1999 ..... **CLC 1,
4, 8, 57; SSC 4**
See also CA 1-4R; 181; CANR 2, 61; CN
1, 2, 3, 4, 5, 6; DLB 130; MTCW 1;
RGAL 4; RGSF 2

Powers, John
See Powers, John R.

Powers, John R. 1945- .... **CLC 66**
See also CA 69-72

Powers, Richard 1957- .... **CLC 93, 292**
See also AMWS 9; BPFB 3; CA 148;
CANR 80, 180, 221; CN 6, 7; DLB 350;
MTFW 2005; TCLE 1:2

Powers, Richard S.
See Powers, Richard

Pownall, David 1938- .... **CLC 10**
See also CA 89-92, 180; CAAS 18; CANR
49, 101; CBD; CD 5, 6; CN 4, 5, 6, 7;
DLB 14

Powys, John Cowper 1872-1963 ... **CLC 7, 9,
15, 46, 125**
See also CA 85-88; CANR 106; DLB 15,
255; EWL 3; FANT; MTCW 1, 2; MTFW
2005; RGEL 2; SUFW

Powys, T(heodore) F(rancis)
1875-1953 .... **TCLC 9**
See also BRWS 8; CA 106; 189; DLB 36,
162; EWL 3; FANT; RGEL 2; SUFW

Pyle, Howard 1853-1911 .... **TCLC 81**
   See also AAYA 57; BYA 2, 4; CA 109; 137;
   CLR 22, 117; DLB 42, 188; DLBD 13;
   LAIT 1; MAICYA 1, 2; SATA 16, 100;
   WCH; YAW

Pym, Barbara (Mary Crampton)
   1913-1980 .... **CLC 13, 19, 37, 111**
   See also BPFB 3; BRWS 2; CA 13-14; 97-
   100; CANR 13, 34; CAP 1; DLB 14, 207;
   DLBY 1987; EWL 3; MTCW 1, 2; MTFW
   2005; RGEL 2; TEA

Pynchon, Thomas 1937- .. **CLC 2, 3, 6, 9, 11,**
   18, 33, 62, 72, 123, 192, 213; SSC 14,
   84; WLC 5
   See also AMWS 2; BEST 90:2; BPFB 3;
   CA 17-20R; CANR 22, 46, 73, 142, 198;
   CN 1, 2, 3, 4, 5, 6, 7; CPW 1; DA; DA3;
   DAB; DAC; DAM MST, NOV, POP;
   DLB 2, 173; EWL 3; MAL 5; MTCW 1,
   2; MTFW 2005; NFS 23, 36; RGAL 4;
   SFW 4; TCLE 1:2; TUS

Pynchon, Thomas Ruggels, Jr.
   See Pynchon, Thomas

Pynchon, Thomas Ruggles
   See Pynchon, Thomas

Pythagoras c. 582B.C.-c. 507B.C. . **CMLC 22**
   See also DLB 176

Q
   See Quiller-Couch, Sir Arthur (Thomas)

Qian, Chongzhu
   See Qian, Zhongshu

Qian, Sima 145B.C.-c. 89B.C. .... **CMLC 72**
   See also DLB 358

Qian, Zhongshu 1910-1998 .... **CLC 22**
   See also CA 130; CANR 73, 216; CWW 2;
   DLB 328; MTCW 1, 2

Qroll
   See Dagerman, Stig (Halvard)

Quarles, Francis 1592-1644 .... **LC 117**
   See also DLB 126; RGEL 2

Quarrington, Paul 1953-2010 .... **CLC 65**
   See also CA 129; CANR 62, 95, 228

Quarrington, Paul Lewis
   See Quarrington, Paul

Quasimodo, Salvatore 1901-1968 .... **CLC 10;**
   PC 47
   See also CA 13-16; 25-28R; CAP 1; DLB
   114, 332; EW 12; EWL 3; MTCW 1;
   RGWL 2, 3

Quatermass, Martin
   See Carpenter, John

Quay, Stephen 1947- .... **CLC 95**
   See also CA 189

Quay, Timothy 1947- .... **CLC 95**
   See also CA 189

Queen, Ellery
   See Dannay, Frederic; Hoch, Edward D.;
   Lee, Manfred B.; Marlowe, Stephen;
   Sturgeon, Theodore (Hamilton); Vance,
   Jack

Queneau, Raymond 1903-1976 ..... **CLC 2, 5,**
   10, 42; TCLC 233
   See also CA 77-80; 69-72; CANR 32; DLB
   72, 258; EW 12; EWL 3; GFL 1789 to
   the Present; MTCW 1, 2; RGWL 2, 3

Quevedo, Francisco de 1580-1645 ...... **LC 23,**
   160

Quiller-Couch, Sir Arthur (Thomas)
   1863-1944 .... **TCLC 53**
   See also CA 118; 166; DLB 135, 153, 190;
   HGG; RGEL 2; SUFW 1

Quin, Ann 1936-1973 .... **CLC 6**
   See also CA 9-12R; 45-48; CANR 148; CN
   1; DLB 14, 231

Quin, Ann Marie
   See Quin, Ann

Quincey, Thomas de
   See De Quincey, Thomas

Quindlen, Anna 1953- .... **CLC 191**
   See also AAYA 35; AMWS 17; CA 138;
   CANR 73, 126; DA3; DLB 292; MTCW
   2; MTFW 2005

Quinn, Martin
   See Smith, Martin Cruz

Quinn, Peter 1947- .... **CLC 91**
   See also CA 197; CANR 147

Quinn, Peter A.
   See Quinn, Peter

Quinn, Simon
   See Smith, Martin Cruz

Quintana, Leroy V. 1944- ...... **HLC 2; PC 36**
   See also CA 131; CANR 65, 139; DAM
   MULT; DLB 82; HW 1, 2

Quintilian c. 40-c. 100 .... **CMLC 77**
   See also AW 2; DLB 211; RGWL 2, 3

Quiroga, Horacio (Sylvestre)
   1878-1937 ... **HLC 2; SSC 89; TCLC 20**
   See also CA 117; 131; DAM MULT; EWL
   3; HW 1; LAW; MTCW 1; RGSF 2;
   WLIT 1

Quoirez, Francoise
   See Sagan, Francoise

Raabe, Wilhelm (Karl) 1831-1910 . **TCLC 45**
   See also CA 167; DLB 129

Rabe, David 1940- .... **CLC 4, 8, 33, 200; DC**
   16
   See also CA 85-88; CABS 3; CAD; CANR
   59, 129, 218; CD 5, 6; DAM DRAM;
   DFS 3, 8, 13; DLB 7, 228; EWL 3; MAL
   5

Rabe, David William
   See Rabe, David

Rabelais, Francois 1494-1553 .... **LC 5, 60,**
   186; WLC 5
   See also DA; DAB; DAC; DAM MST;
   DLB 327; EW 2; GFL Beginnings to
   1789; LMFS 1; RGWL 2, 3; TWA

Rabi'a al-'Adawiyya c. 717-c.
   801 .... **CMLC 83**
   See also DLB 311

Rabinovitch, Sholem 1859-1916 .... **SSC 33,**
   125; TCLC 1, 35
   See also CA 104; DLB 333; TWA

Rabinovitsh, Sholem Yankev
   See Rabinovitch, Sholem

Rabinowitz, Sholem Yakov
   See Rabinovitch, Sholem

Rabinowitz, Solomon
   See Rabinovitch, Sholem

Rabinyan, Dorit 1972- .... **CLC 119**
   See also CA 170; CANR 147

Rachilde
   See Vallette, Marguerite Eymery; Vallette,
   Marguerite Eymery

Racine, Jean 1639-1699 .. **DC 32; LC 28, 113**
   See also DA3; DAB; DAM MST; DFS 28;
   DLB 268; EW 3; GFL Beginnings to
   1789; LMFS 1; RGWL 2, 3; TWA

Radcliffe, Ann 1764-1823 .. **NCLC 6, 55, 106,**
   223
   See also BRWR 3; DLB 39, 178; GL 3;
   HGG; LMFS 1; RGEL 2; SUFW; WLIT
   3

Radclyffe-Hall, Marguerite
   See Hall, Radclyffe

Radiguet, Raymond 1903-1923 ...... **TCLC 29**
   See also CA 162; DLB 65; EWL 3; GFL
   1789 to the Present; RGWL 2, 3

Radishchev, Aleksandr Nikolaevich
   1749-1802 .... **NCLC 190**
   See also DLB 150

Radishchev, Alexander
   See Radishchev, Aleksandr Nikolaevich

Radnoti, Miklos 1909-1944 .... **TCLC 16**
   See also CA 118; 212; CDWLB 4; DLB
   215; EWL 3; RGHL; RGWL 2, 3

Rado, James 1939- .... **CLC 17**
   See also CA 105

Radvanyi, Netty 1900-1983 .... **CLC 7**
   See also CA 85-88; 110; CANR 82; CD-
   WLB 2; DLB 69; EWL 3

Rae, Ben
   See Griffiths, Trevor

Raeburn, John (Hay) 1941- .... **CLC 34**
   See also CA 57-60

Ragni, Gerome 1942-1991 .... **CLC 17**
   See also CA 105; 134

Rahv, Philip
   See Greenberg, Ivan

Rai, Navab
   See Srivastava, Dhanpat Rai

Raimund, Ferdinand Jakob
   1790-1836 .... **NCLC 69**
   See also DLB 90

Raine, Craig 1944- .... **CLC 32, 103**
   See also BRWS 13; CA 108; CANR 29, 51,
   103, 171; CP 3, 4, 5, 6, 7; DLB 40; PFS 7

Raine, Craig Anthony
   See Raine, Craig

Raine, Kathleen (Jessie) 1908-2003 .. **CLC 7,**
   45
   See also CA 85-88; 218; CANR 46, 109;
   CP 1, 2, 3, 4, 5, 6, 7; DLB 20; EWL 3;
   MTCW 1; RGEL 2

Rainis, Janis 1865-1929 .... **TCLC 29**
   See also CA 170; CDWLB 4; DLB 220;
   EWL 3

Rakosi, Carl
   See Rawley, Callman

Ralegh, Sir Walter
   See Raleigh, Sir Walter

Raleigh, Richard
   See Lovecraft, H. P.

Raleigh, Sir Walter 1554(?)-1618 .... **LC 31,**
   39; PC 31
   See also BRW 1; CDBLB Before 1660;
   DLB 172; EXPP; PFS 14; RGEL 2; TEA;
   WP

Rallentando, H. P.
   See Sayers, Dorothy L(eigh)

Ramal, Walter
   See de la Mare, Walter (John)

Ramana Maharshi 1879-1950 .... **TCLC 84**

Ramoacn y Cajal, Santiago
   1852-1934 .... **TCLC 93**

Ramon, Juan
   See Jimenez, Juan Ramon

Ramos, Graciliano 1892-1953 .... **TCLC 32**
   See also CA 167; DLB 307; EWL 3; HW 2;
   LAW; WLIT 1

Rampersad, Arnold 1941- .... **CLC 44**
   See also BW 2, 3; CA 127; 133; CANR 81;
   DLB 111; INT CA-133

Rampling, Anne
   See Rice, Anne

Ramsay, Allan 1686(?)-1758 .... **LC 29**
   See also DLB 95; RGEL 2

Ramsay, Jay
   See Campbell, Ramsey

Ramus, Peter
   See La Ramee, Pierre de

Ramus, Petrus
   See La Ramee, Pierre de

Ramuz, Charles-Ferdinand
   1878-1947 .... **TCLC 33**
   See also CA 165; EWL 3

Rand, Ayn 1905-1982 ...... **CLC 3, 30, 44, 79;**
   SSC 116; TCLC 261; WLC 5
   See also AAYA 10; AMWS 4; BPFB 3;
   BYA 12; CA 13-16R; 105; CANR 27, 73;
   CDALBS; CN 1, 2, 3; CPW; DA; DA3;
   DAC; DAM MST, NOV, POP; DLB 227,
   279; MTCW 1, 2; MTFW 2005; NFS 10,
   16, 29; RGAL 4; SFW 4; TUS; YAW

Reyes, Alfonso 1889-1959 .... **HLCS 2; TCLC 33**
See also CA 131; EWL 3; HW 1; LAW

Reyes y Basoalto, Ricardo Eliecer Neftali
See Neruda, Pablo

Reymont, Wladyslaw (Stanislaw) 1868(?)-1925 .... **TCLC 5**
See also CA 104; DLB 332; EWL 3

Reynolds, John Hamilton 1794-1852 .... **NCLC 146**
See also DLB 96

Reynolds, Jonathan 1942- .... **CLC 6, 38**
See also CA 65-68; CANR 28, 176

Reynolds, Joshua 1723-1792 .... **LC 15**
See also DLB 104

Reynolds, Michael S(hane) 1937-2000 .... **CLC 44**
See also CA 65-68; 189; CANR 9, 89, 97

Reza, Yasmina 1959- .... **CLC 299; DC 34**
See also AAYA 69; CA 171; CANR 145; DFS 19; DLB 321

Reznikoff, Charles 1894-1976 ..... **CLC 9; PC 124**
See also AMWS 14; CA 33-36; 61-64; CAP 2; CP 1, 2; DLB 28, 45; RGHL; WP

Rezzori, Gregor von
See Rezzori d'Arezzo, Gregor von

Rezzori d'Arezzo, Gregor von 1914-1998 .... **CLC 25**
See also CA 122; 136; 167

Rhine, Richard
See Silverstein, Alvin; Silverstein, Virginia B.

Rhodes, Eugene Manlove 1869-1934 .... **TCLC 53**
See also CA 198; DLB 256; TCWW 1, 2

R'hoone, Lord
See Balzac, Honore de

Rhys, Jean 1890-1979 .... **CLC 2, 4, 6, 14, 19, 51, 124; SSC 21, 76**
See also BRWS 2; CA 25-28R; 85-88; CANR 35, 62; CDBLB 1945-1960; CD-WLB 2; CN 1, 2; DA3; DAM NOV; DLB 36, 117, 162; DNFS 2; EWL 3; LATS 1:1; MTCW 1, 2; MTFW 2005; NFS 19; RGEL 2; RGSF 2; RHW; TEA; WWE 1

Ribeiro, Darcy 1922-1997 .... **CLC 34**
See also CA 33-36R; 156; EWL 3

Ribeiro, Joao Ubaldo (Osorio Pimentel) 1941- .... **CLC 10, 67**
See also CA 81-84; CWW 2; EWL 3

Ribman, Ronald (Burt) 1932- .... **CLC 7**
See also CA 21-24R; CAD; CANR 46, 80; CD 5, 6

Ricci, Nino 1959- .... **CLC 70**
See also CA 137; CANR 130; CCA 1

Ricci, Nino Pio
See Ricci, Nino

Rice, Anne 1941- .... **CLC 41, 128**
See also AAYA 9, 53; AMWS 7; BEST 89:2; BPFB 3; CA 65-68; CANR 12, 36, 53, 74, 100, 133, 190; CN 6, 7; CPW; CSW; DA3; DAM POP; DLB 292; GL 3; GLL 2; HGG; MTCW 2; MTFW 2005; SUFW 2; YAW

Rice, Elmer (Leopold) 1892-1967 ...... **CLC 7, 49; DC 44; TCLC 221**
See also CA 21-22; 25-28R; CAP 2; DAM DRAM; DFS 12; DLB 4, 7; EWL 3; IDTP; MAL 5; MTCW 1, 2; RGAL 4

Rice, Tim 1944- .... **CLC 21**
See also CA 103; CANR 46; DFS 7

Rice, Timothy Miles Bindon
See Rice, Tim

Rich, Adrienne 1929- ..... **CLC 3, 6, 7, 11, 18, 36, 73, 76, 125; PC 5**
See also AAYA 69; AMWR 2; AMWS 1; CA 9-12R; CANR 20, 53, 74, 128, 199; CDALBS; CP 1, 2, 3, 4, 5, 6, 7; CSW;

CWP; DA3; DAM POET; DLB 5, 67; EWL 3; EXPP; FL 1:6; FW; MAL 5; MBL; MTCW 1, 2; MTFW 2005; PAB; PFS 15, 29, 39; RGAL 4; RGHL; WP

Rich, Adrienne Cecile
See Rich, Adrienne

Rich, Barbara
See Graves, Robert

Rich, Robert
See Trumbo, Dalton

Richard, Keith
See Richards, Keith

Richards, David Adams 1950- .... **CLC 59**
See also CA 93-96; CANR 60, 110, 156; CN 7; DAC; DLB 53; TCLE 1:2

Richards, I(vor) A(rmstrong) 1893-1979 .... **CLC 14, 24**
See also BRWS 2; CA 41-44R; 89-92; CANR 34, 74; CP 1, 2; DLB 27; EWL 3; MTCW 2; RGEL 2

Richards, Keith 1943- .... **CLC 17**
See also CA 107; CANR 77

Richardson, Anne
See Roiphe, Anne

Richardson, Dorothy Miller 1873-1957 .... **TCLC 3, 203**
See also BRWS 13; CA 104; 192; DLB 36; EWL 3; FW; RGEL 2

Richardson, Ethel Florence Lindesay 1870-1946 .... **TCLC 4**
See also CA 105; 190; DLB 197, 230; EWL 3; RGEL 2; RGSF 2; RHW

Richardson, Henrietta
See Richardson, Ethel Florence Lindesay

Richardson, Henry Handel
See Richardson, Ethel Florence Lindesay

Richardson, John 1796-1852 .... **NCLC 55**
See also CCA 1; DAC; DLB 99

Richardson, Samuel 1689-1761 ...... **LC 1, 44, 138; WLC 5**
See also BRW 3; CDBLB 1660-1789; DA; DAB; DAC; DAM MST, NOV; DLB 154; RGEL 2; TEA; WLIT 3

Richardson, Willis 1889-1977 .... **HR 1:3**
See also BW 1; CA 124; DLB 51; SATA 60

Richardson Robertson, Ethel Florence Lindesay
See Richardson, Ethel Florence Lindesay

Richler, Mordecai 1931-2001 .... **CLC 3, 5, 9, 13, 18, 46, 70, 185, 271**
See also AITN 1; CA 65-68; 201; CANR 31, 62, 111; CCA 1; CLR 17; CN 1, 2, 3, 4, 5, 7; CWRI 5; DAC; DAM MST, NOV; DLB 53; EWL 3; MAICYA 1, 2; MTCW 1, 2; MTFW 2005; RGEL 2; RGHL; SATA 44, 98; SATA-Brief 27; TWA

Richter, Conrad (Michael) 1890-1968 .... **CLC 30**
See also AAYA 21; AMWS 18; BYA 2; CA 5-8R; 25-28R; CANR 23; DLB 9, 212; LAIT 1; MAL 5; MTCW 1, 2; MTFW 2005; RGAL 4; SATA 3; TCWW 1, 2; TUS; YAW

Ricostranza, Tom
See Ellis, Trey

Riddell, Charlotte 1832-1906 .... **TCLC 40**
See also CA 165; DLB 156; HGG; SUFW

Riddell, Mrs. J. H.
See Riddell, Charlotte

Ridge, John Rollin 1827-1867 ...... **NCLC 82; NNAL**
See also CA 144; DAM MULT; DLB 175

Ridgeway, Jason
See Marlowe, Stephen

Ridgway, Keith 1965- .... **CLC 119**
See also CA 172; CANR 144

Riding, Laura
See Jackson, Laura

Riefenstahl, Berta Helene Amalia 1902-2003 .... **CLC 16, 190**
See also CA 108; 220

Riefenstahl, Leni
See Riefenstahl, Berta Helene Amalia

Riffe, Ernest
See Bergman, Ingmar

Riffe, Ernest Ingmar
See Bergman, Ingmar

Riggs, (Rolla) Lynn 1899-1954 .... **NNAL; TCLC 56**
See also CA 144; DAM MULT; DLB 175

Riis, Jacob A(ugust) 1849-1914 ..... **TCLC 80**
See also CA 113; 168; DLB 23

Rikki
See Ducornet, Erica

Riley, James Whitcomb 1849-1916 .... **PC 48; TCLC 51**
See also CA 118; 137; DAM POET; MAI-CYA 1, 2; RGAL 4; SATA 17

Riley, Tex
See Creasey, John

Rilke, Rainer Maria 1875-1926 .... **PC 2; TCLC 1, 6, 19, 195**
See also CA 104; 132; CANR 62, 99; CD-WLB 2; DA3; DAM POET; DLB 81; EW 9; EWL 3; MTCW 1, 2; MTFW 2005; PFS 19, 27; RGWL 2, 3; TWA; WP

Rimbaud, Arthur 1854-1891 ..... **NCLC 4, 35, 82, 227; PC 3, 57; WLC 5**
See also DA; DA3; DAB; DAC; DAM MST, POET; DLB 217; EW 7; GFL 1789 to the Present; LMFS 2; PFS 28; RGWL 2, 3; TWA; WP

Rimbaud, Jean Nicholas Arthur
See Rimbaud, Arthur

Rinehart, Mary Roberts 1876-1958 .... **TCLC 52**
See also BPFB 3; CA 108; 166; RGAL 4; RHW

Ringmaster, The
See Mencken, H. L.

Ringwood, Gwen(dolyn Margaret) Pharis 1910-1984 .... **CLC 48**
See also CA 148; 112; DLB 88

Rio, Michel 1945(?)- .... **CLC 43**
See also CA 201

Rios, Alberto 1952- .... **PC 57**
See also AAYA 66; AMWS 4; CA 113; CANR 34, 79, 137; CP 6, 7; DLB 122; HW 2; MTFW 2005; PFS 11

Rios, Alberto Alvaro
See Rios, Alberto

Ritsos, Giannes
See Ritsos, Yannis

Ritsos, Yannis 1909-1990 .... **CLC 6, 13, 31**
See also CA 77-80; 133; CANR 39, 61; EW 12; EWL 3; MTCW 1; RGWL 2, 3

Ritter, Erika 1948- .... **CLC 52**
See also CA 318; CD 5, 6; CWD; DLB 362

Rivera, Jose Eustasio 1889-1928 ... **TCLC 35**
See also CA 162; EWL 3; HW 1, 2; LAW

Rivera, Tomas 1935-1984 .... **HLCS 2; SSC 160**
See also CA 49-52; CANR 32; DLB 82; HW 1; LLW; RGAL 4; SSFS 15; TCWW 2; WLIT 1

Rivers, Conrad Kent 1933-1968 .... **CLC 1**
See also BW 1; CA 85-88; DLB 41

Rivers, Elfrida
See Bradley, Marion Zimmer

Riverside, John
See Heinlein, Robert A.

Rizal, Jose 1861-1896 .... **NCLC 27**
See also DLB 348

Roa Bastos, Augusto 1917-2005 ...... **CLC 45, 316; HLC 2**
See also CA 131; 238; CWW 2; DAM MULT; DLB 113; EWL 3; HW 1; LAW; RGSF 2; WLIT 1

Roa Bastos, Augusto Jose Antonio
See Roa Bastos, Augusto

Robbe-Grillet, Alain 1922-2008 ..... **CLC 1, 2, 4, 6, 8, 10, 14, 43, 128, 287**
See also BPFB 3; CA 9-12R; 269; CANR 33, 65, 115; CWW 2; DLB 83; EW 13; EWL 3; GFL 1789 to the Present; IDFW 3, 4; MTCW 1, 2; MTFW 2005; RGWL 2, 3; SSFS 15

Robbins, Harold 1916-1997 .... **CLC 5**
See also BPFB 3; CA 73-76; 162; CANR 26, 54, 112, 156; DA3; DAM NOV; MTCW 1, 2

Robbins, Thomas Eugene 1936- . **CLC 9, 32, 64**
See also AAYA 32; AMWS 10; BEST 90:3; BPFB 3; CA 81-84; CANR 29, 59, 95, 139; CN 3, 4, 5, 6, 7; CPW; CSW; DA3; DAM NOV, POP; DLBY 1980; MTCW 1, 2; MTFW 2005

Robbins, Tom
See Robbins, Thomas Eugene

Robbins, Trina 1938- .... **CLC 21**
See also AAYA 61; CA 128; CANR 152

Robert de Boron fl. 12th cent. - .... **CMLC 94**

Roberts, Charles G(eorge) D(ouglas) 1860-1943 .... **SSC 91; TCLC 8**
See also CA 105; 188; CLR 33; CWRI 5; DLB 92; RGEL 2; RGSF 2; SATA 88; SATA-Brief 29

Roberts, Elizabeth Madox 1886-1941 .... **TCLC 68**
See also CA 111; 166; CLR 100; CWRI 5; DLB 9, 54, 102; RGAL 4; RHW; SATA 33; SATA-Brief 27; TCWW 2; WCH

Roberts, Kate 1891-1985 .... **CLC 15**
See also CA 107; 116; DLB 319

Roberts, Keith (John Kingston) 1935-2000 .... **CLC 14**
See also BRWS 10; CA 25-28R; CANR 46; DLB 261; SFW 4

Roberts, Kenneth (Lewis) 1885-1957 .... **TCLC 23**
See also CA 109; 199; DLB 9; MAL 5; RGAL 4; RHW

Roberts, Michele 1949- .... **CLC 48, 178**
See also BRWS 15; CA 115; CANR 58, 120, 164, 200; CN 6, 7; DLB 231; FW

Roberts, Michele Brigitte
See Roberts, Michele

Robertson, Ellis
See Ellison, Harlan; Silverberg, Robert

Robertson, Thomas William 1829-1871 .... **NCLC 35**
See also DAM DRAM; DLB 344; RGEL 2

Robertson, Tom
See Robertson, Thomas William

Robeson, Kenneth
See Dent, Lester

Robinson, Eden 1968- .... **CLC 301**
See also CA 171

Robinson, Edwin Arlington 1869-1935 .... **PC 1, 35; TCLC 5, 101**
See also AAYA 72; AMW; CA 104; 133; CDALB 1865-1917; DA; DAC; DAM MST, POET; DLB 54; EWL 3; EXPP; MAL 5; MTCW 1, 2; MTFW 2005; PAB; PFS 4, 35; RGAL 4; WP

Robinson, Henry Crabb 1775-1867 .... **NCLC 15, 239**
See also DLB 107

Robinson, Jill 1936- .... **CLC 10**
See also CA 102; CANR 120; INT CA-102

Robinson, Kim Stanley 1952- ... **CLC 34, 248**
See also AAYA 26; CA 126; CANR 113, 139, 173; CN 6, 7; MTFW 2005; SATA 109; SCFW 2; SFW 4

Robinson, Lloyd
See Silverberg, Robert

Robinson, Marilynne 1943- ..... **CLC 25, 180, 276**
See also AAYA 69; AMWS 21; CA 116; CANR 80, 140, 192; CN 4, 5, 6, 7; DLB 206, 350; MTFW 2005; NFS 24, 39

Robinson, Mary 1758-1800 .... **NCLC 142**
See also BRWS 13; DLB 158; FW

Robinson, Smokey
See Robinson, William, Jr.

Robinson, William, Jr. 1940- .... **CLC 21**
See also CA 116

Robison, Christopher
See Burroughs, Augusten

Robison, Mary 1949- .... **CLC 42, 98**
See also CA 113; 116; CANR 87, 206; CN 4, 5, 6, 7; DLB 130; INT CA-116; RGSF 2; SSFS 33

Roches, Catherine des 1542-1587 ...... **LC 117**
See also DLB 327

Rochester
See Wilmot, John

Rod, Edouard 1857-1910 .... **TCLC 52**

Roddenberry, Eugene Wesley 1921-1991 .... **CLC 17**
See also AAYA 5; CA 110; 135; CANR 37; SATA 45; SATA-Obit 69

Roddenberry, Gene
See Roddenberry, Eugene Wesley

Rodgers, Mary 1931- .... **CLC 12**
See also BYA 5; CA 49-52; CANR 8, 55, 90; CLR 20; CWRI 5; DFS 28; INT CANR-8; JRDA; MAICYA 1, 2; SATA 8, 130

Rodgers, W(illiam) R(obert) 1909-1969 .... **CLC 7**
See also CA 85-88; DLB 20; RGEL 2

Rodman, Eric
See Silverberg, Robert

Rodman, Howard 1920(?)-1985 .... **CLC 65**
See also CA 118

Rodman, Maia
See Wojciechowska, Maia (Teresa)

Rodo, Jose Enrique 1871(?)-1917 .... **HLCS 2**
See also CA 178; EWL 3; HW 2; LAW

Rodolph, Utto
See Ouologuem, Yambo

Rodriguez, Claudio 1934-1999 .... **CLC 10**
See also CA 188; DLB 134

Rodriguez, Richard 1944- .... **CLC 155; HLC 2**
See also AMWS 14; CA 110; CANR 66, 116; DAM MULT; DLB 82, 256; HW 1, 2; LAIT 5; LLW; MTFW 2005; NCFS 3; WLIT 1

Roethke, Theodore 1908-1963 ... **CLC 1, 3, 8, 11, 19, 46, 101; PC 15**
See also AMW; CA 81-84; CABS 2; CDALB 1941-1968; DA3; DAM POET; DLB 5, 206; EWL 3; EXPP; MAL 5; MTCW 1, 2; PAB; PFS 3, 34, 40; RGAL 4; WP

Roethke, Theodore Huebner
See Roethke, Theodore

Rogers, Carl R(ansom) 1902-1987 .... **TCLC 125**
See also CA 1-4R; 121; CANR 1, 18; MTCW 1

Rogers, Samuel 1763-1855 .... **NCLC 69**
See also DLB 93; RGEL 2

Rogers, Thomas 1927-2007 .... **CLC 57**
See also CA 89-92; 259; CANR 163; INT CA-89-92

Rogers, Thomas Hunton
See Rogers, Thomas

Rogers, Will(iam Penn Adair) 1879-1935 .... **NNAL; TCLC 8, 71**
See also CA 105; 144; DA3; DAM MULT; DLB 11; MTCW 2

Rogin, Gilbert 1929- .... **CLC 18**
See also CA 65-68; CANR 15

Rohan, Koda
See Koda Shigeyuki

Rohlfs, Anna Katharine Green
See Green, Anna Katharine

Rohmer, Eric 1920-2010 .... **CLC 16**
See also CA 110

Rohmer, Sax
See Ward, Arthur Henry Sarsfield

Roiphe, Anne 1935- .... **CLC 3, 9**
See also CA 89-92; CANR 45, 73, 138, 170; DLBY 1980; INT CA-89-92

Roiphe, Anne Richardson
See Roiphe, Anne

Rojas, Fernando de 1475-1541 ... **HLCS 1, 2; LC 23, 169**
See also DLB 286; RGWL 2, 3

Rojas, Gonzalo 1917-2011 .... **HLCS 2**
See also CA 178; HW 2; LAWS 1

Rolaag, Ole Edvart
See Rolvaag, O.E.

Roland (de la Platiere), Marie-Jeanne 1754-1793 .... **LC 98**
See also DLB 314

Rolfe, Frederick (William Serafino Austin Lewis Mary) 1860-1913 .... **TCLC 12**
See also CA 107; 210; DLB 34, 156; GLL 1; RGEL 2

Rolland, Romain 1866-1944 .... **TCLC 23**
See also CA 118; 197; DLB 65, 284, 332; EWL 3; GFL 1789 to the Present; RGWL 2, 3

Rolle, Richard c. 1300-c. 1349 ...... **CMLC 21**
See also DLB 146; LMFS 1; RGEL 2

Rolvaag, O.E.
See Rolvaag, O.E.

Rolvaag, O.E.
See Rolvaag, O.E.

Rolvaag, O.E. 1876-1931 .... **TCLC 17, 207**
See also AAYA 75; CA 117; 171; DLB 9, 212; MAL 5; NFS 5; RGAL 4; TCWW 1, 2

Romain Arnaud, Saint
See Aragon, Louis

Romains, Jules 1885-1972 .... **CLC 7**
See also CA 85-88; CANR 34; DLB 65, 321; EWL 3; GFL 1789 to the Present; MTCW 1

Romero, Jose Ruben 1890-1952 .... **TCLC 14**
See also CA 114; 131; EWL 3; HW 1; LAW

Ronsard, Pierre de 1524-1585 . **LC 6, 54; PC 11, 105**
See also DLB 327; EW 2; GFL Beginnings to 1789; RGWL 2, 3; TWA

Rooke, Leon 1934- .... **CLC 25, 34**
See also CA 25-28R; CANR 23, 53; CCA 1; CPW; DAM POP

Roosevelt, Franklin Delano 1882-1945 .... **TCLC 93**
See also CA 116; 173; LAIT 3

Roosevelt, Theodore 1858-1919 ..... **TCLC 69**
See also CA 115; 170; DLB 47, 186, 275

Roper, Margaret c. 1505-1544 .... **LC 147**

Roper, William 1498-1578 .... **LC 10**

Roquelaure, A. N.
See Rice, Anne

Rosa, Joao Guimaraes
See Guimaraes Rosa, Joao

Rose, Wendy 1948- . **CLC 85; NNAL; PC 13**
See also CA 53-56; CANR 5, 51; CWP; DAM MULT; DLB 175; PFS 13; RGAL 4; SATA 12
Rosen, R.D. 1949- .... **CLC 39**
See also CA 77-80; CANR 62, 120, 175; CMW 4; INT CANR-30
Rosen, Richard
See Rosen, R.D.
Rosen, Richard Dean
See Rosen, R.D.
Rosenberg, Isaac 1890-1918 .... **TCLC 12**
See also BRW 6; CA 107; 188; DLB 20, 216; EWL 3; PAB; RGEL 2
Rosenblatt, Joe
See Rosenblatt, Joseph
Rosenblatt, Joseph 1933- .... **CLC 15**
See also CA 89-92; CP 3, 4, 5, 6, 7; INT CA-89-92
Rosenfeld, Samuel
See Tzara, Tristan
Rosenstock, Sami
See Tzara, Tristan
Rosenstock, Samuel
See Tzara, Tristan
Rosenthal, M(acha) L(ouis)
1917-1996 .... **CLC 28**
See also CA 1-4R; 152; CAAS 6; CANR 4, 51; CP 1, 2, 3, 4, 5, 6; DLB 5; SATA 59
Ross, Barnaby
See Dannay, Frederic; Lee, Manfred B.
Ross, Bernard L.
See Follett, Ken
Ross, J. H.
See Lawrence, T. E.
Ross, John Hume
See Lawrence, T. E.
Ross, Martin 1862-1915
See Martin, Violet Florence
See also DLB 135; GLL 2; RGEL 2; RGSF 2
Ross, (James) Sinclair 1908-1996 ... **CLC 13; SSC 24**
See also CA 73-76; CANR 81; CN 1, 2, 3, 4, 5, 6; DAC; DAM MST; DLB 88; RGEL 2; RGSF 2; TCWW 1, 2
Rossetti, Christina 1830-1894 ... **NCLC 2, 50, 66, 186; PC 7, 119; WLC 5**
See also AAYA 51; BRW 5; BRWR 3; BYA 4; CLR 115; DA; DA3; DAB; DAC; DAM MST, POET; DLB 35, 163, 240; EXPP; FL 1:3; LATS 1:1; MAICYA 1, 2; PFS 10, 14, 27, 34; RGEL 2; SATA 20; TEA; WCH
Rossetti, Christina Georgina
See Rossetti, Christina
Rossetti, Dante Gabriel 1828-1882 . **NCLC 4, 77; PC 44; WLC 5**
See also AAYA 51; BRW 5; CDBLB 1832-1890; DA; DAB; DAC; DAM MST, POET; DLB 35; EXPP; RGEL 2; TEA
Rossi, Cristina Peri
See Peri Rossi, Cristina
Rossi, Jean-Baptiste 1931-2003 .... **CLC 90**
See also CA 201; 215; CMW 4; NFS 18
Rossner, Judith 1935-2005 .... **CLC 6, 9, 29**
See also AITN 2; BEST 90:3; BPFB 3; CA 17-20R; 242; CANR 18, 51, 73; CN 4, 5, 6, 7; DLB 6; INT CANR-18; MAL 5; MTCW 1, 2; MTFW 2005
Rossner, Judith Perelman
See Rossner, Judith
Rostand, Edmond 1868-1918 . **DC 10; TCLC 6, 37**
See also CA 104; 126; DA; DA3; DAB; DAC; DAM DRAM, MST; DFS 1; DLB 192; LAIT 1; MTCW 1; RGWL 2, 3; TWA

Rostand, Edmond Eugene Alexis
See Rostand, Edmond
Roth, Henry 1906-1995 ... **CLC 2, 6, 11, 104; SSC 134**
See also AMWS 9; CA 11-12; 149; CANR 38, 63; CAP 1; CN 1, 2, 3, 4, 5, 6; DA3; DLB 28; EWL 3; MAL 5; MTCW 1, 2; MTFW 2005; RGAL 4
Roth, (Moses) Joseph 1894-1939 ... **TCLC 33**
See also CA 160; DLB 85; EWL 3; RGWL 2, 3
Roth, Philip 1933- ... **CLC 1, 2, 3, 4, 6, 9, 15, 22, 31, 47, 66, 86, 119, 201; SSC 26, 102; WLC 5**
See also AAYA 67; AMWR 2; AMWS 3; BEST 90:3; BPFB 3; CA 1-4R; CANR 1, 22, 36, 55, 89, 132, 170; CDALB 1968-1988; CN 3, 4, 5, 6, 7; CPW 1; DA; DA3; DAB; DAC; DAM MST, NOV, POP; DLB 2, 28, 173; DLBY 1982; EWL 3; MAL 5; MTCW 1, 2; MTFW 2005; NFS 25; RGAL 4; RGHL; RGSF 2; SSFS 12, 18; TUS
Roth, Philip Milton
See Roth, Philip
Rothenberg, Jerome 1931- .... **CLC 6, 57**
See also CA 45-48; CANR 1, 106; CP 1, 2, 3, 4, 5, 6, 7; DLB 5, 193
Rotter, Pat .... **CLC 65**
Roumain, Jacques 1907-1944 .... **BLC 1:3; TCLC 19**
See also BW 1; CA 117; 125; DAM MULT; EWL 3
Roumain, Jacques Jean Baptiste
See Roumain, Jacques
Rourke, Constance Mayfield
1885-1941 .... **TCLC 12**
See also CA 107; 200; MAL 5; YABC 1
Rousseau, Jean-Baptiste 1671-1741 ...... **LC 9**
Rousseau, Jean-Jacques 1712-1778 .... **LC 14, 36, 122, 198; WLC 5**
See also DA; DA3; DAB; DAC; DAM MST; DLB 314; EW 4; GFL Beginnings to 1789; LMFS 1; RGWL 2, 3; TWA
Roussel, Raymond 1877-1933 .... **TCLC 20**
See also CA 117; 201; EWL 3; GFL 1789 to the Present
Rovit, Earl (Herbert) 1927- .... **CLC 7**
See also CA 5-8R; CANR 12
Rowe, Elizabeth Singer 1674-1737 ..... **LC 44**
See also DLB 39, 95
Rowe, Nicholas 1674-1718 .... **LC 8**
See also DLB 84; RGEL 2
Rowlandson, Mary 1637(?)-1678 .... **LC 66**
See also DLB 24, 200; RGAL 4
Rowley, Ames Dorrance
See Lovecraft, H. P.
Rowley, William 1585(?)-1626 ..... **DC 43; LC 100, 123**
See also DFS 22; DLB 58; RGEL 2
Rowling, J.K. 1965- .... **CLC 137, 217**
See also AAYA 34, 82; BRWS 16; BYA 11, 13, 14; CA 173; CANR 128, 157; CLR 66, 80, 112; LNFS 1, 2, 3; MAICYA 2; MTFW 2005; SATA 109, 174; SUFW 2
Rowling, Joanne Kathleen
See Rowling, J.K.
Rowson, Susanna Haswell
1762(?)-1824 .... **NCLC 5, 69, 182**
See also AMWS 15; DLB 37, 200; RGAL 4
Roy, Arundhati 1961- .... **CLC 109, 210**
See also CA 163; CANR 90, 126, 217; CN 7; DLB 323, 326; DLBY 1997; EWL 3; LATS 1:2; MTFW 2005; NFS 22; WWE 1

Roy, Gabrielle 1909-1983 .... **CLC 10, 14; TCLC 256**
See also CA 53-56; 110; CANR 5, 61; CCA 1; DAB; DAC; DAM MST; DLB 68; EWL 3; MTCW 1; RGWL 2, 3; SATA 104; TCLE 1:2
Roy, Suzanna Arundhati
See Roy, Arundhati
Royko, Mike 1932-1997 .... **CLC 109**
See also CA 89-92; 157; CANR 26, 111; CPW
Rozanov, Vasilii Vasil'evich
See Rozanov, Vassili
Rozanov, Vasily Vasilyevich
See Rozanov, Vassili
Rozanov, Vassili 1856-1919 .... **TCLC 104**
See also DLB 295; EWL 3
Rozewicz, Tadeusz 1921- ...... **CLC 9, 23, 139**
See also CA 108; CANR 36, 66; CWW 2; DA3; DAM POET; DLB 232; EWL 3; MTCW 1, 2; MTFW 2005; RGHL; RGWL 3
Ruark, Gibbons 1941- .... **CLC 3**
See also CA 33-36R; CAAS 23; CANR 14, 31, 57; DLB 120
Rubens, Bernice (Ruth) 1923-2004 . **CLC 19, 31**
See also CA 25-28R; 232; CANR 33, 65, 128; CN 1, 2, 3, 4, 5, 6, 7; DLB 14, 207, 326; MTCW 1
Rubin, Harold
See Robbins, Harold
Rudkin, (James) David 1936- .... **CLC 14**
See also CA 89-92; CBD; CD 5, 6; DLB 13
Rudnik, Raphael 1933- .... **CLC 7**
See also CA 29-32R
Ruffian, M.
See Hasek, Jaroslav
Rufinus c. 345-410 .... **CMLC 111**
Ruiz, Jose Martinez
See Martinez Ruiz, Jose
Ruiz, Juan c. 1283-c. 1350 .... **CMLC 66**
Rukeyser, Muriel 1913-1980 . **CLC 6, 10, 15, 27; PC 12**
See also AMWS 6; CA 5-8R; 93-96; CANR 26, 60; CP 1, 2, 3; DA3; DAM POET; DLB 48; EWL 3; FW; GLL 2; MAL 5; MTCW 1, 2; PFS 10, 29; RGAL 4; SATA-Obit 22
Rule, Jane 1931-2007 .... **CLC 27, 265**
See also CA 25-28R; 266; CAAS 18; CANR 12, 87; CN 4, 5, 6, 7; DLB 60; FW
Rule, Jane Vance
See Rule, Jane
Rulfo, Juan 1918-1986 .. **CLC 8, 80; HLC 2; SSC 25**
See also CA 85-88; 118; CANR 26; CD-WLB 3; DAM MULT; DLB 113; EWL 3; HW 1, 2; LAW; MTCW 1, 2; RGSF 2; RGWL 2, 3; WLIT 1
Rumi
See Rumi, Jalal al-Din
Rumi, Jalal al-Din 1207-1273 ...... **CMLC 20; PC 45, 123**
See also AAYA 64; RGWL 2, 3; WLIT 6; WP
Runeberg, Johan 1804-1877 .... **NCLC 41**
Runyon, (Alfred) Damon
1884(?)-1946 .... **TCLC 10**
See also CA 107; 165; DLB 11, 86, 171; MAL 5; MTCW 2; RGAL 4
Rush, Benjamin 1746-1813 .... **NCLC 251**
See also DLB 37
Rush, Norman 1933- .... **CLC 44, 306**
See also CA 121; 126; CANR 130; INT CA-126
Rushdie, Ahmed Salman
See Rushdie, Salman

Salinas (y Serrano), Pedro
1891(?)-1951 .... **TCLC 17, 212**
See also CA 117; DLB 134; EWL 3

Salinger, J.D. 1919-2010 ...... **CLC 1, 3, 8, 12,**
55, 56, 138, 243, 318; SSC 2, 28, 65,
146; WLC 5
See also AAYA 2, 36; AMW; AMWC 1;
BPFB 3; CA 5-8R; CANR 39, 129;
CDALB 1941-1968; CLR 18; CN 1, 2, 3,
4, 5, 6, 7; CPW 1; DA; DA3; DAB; DAC;
DAM MST, NOV, POP; DLB 2, 102, 173;
EWL 3; EXPN; LAIT 4; MAICYA 1, 2;
MAL 5; MTCW 1, 2; MTFW 2005; NFS
1, 30; RGAL 4; RGSF 2; SATA 67; SSFS
17; TUS; WYA; YAW

Salinger, Jerome David
See Salinger, J.D.

Salisbury, John
See Caute, (John) David

Sallust c. 86B.C.-35B.C. .... **CMLC 68**
See also AW 2; CDWLB 1; DLB 211;
RGWL 2, 3

Salter, James 1925- .... **CLC 7, 52, 59, 275;**
SSC 58
See also AMWS 9; CA 73-76; CANR 107,
160; DLB 130; SSFS 25

Saltus, Edgar (Everton) 1855-1921 . **TCLC 8**
See also CA 105; DLB 202; RGAL 4

Saltykov, Mikhail Evgrafovich
1826-1889 .... **NCLC 16**
See also DLB 238:

Saltykov-Shchedrin, N.
See Saltykov, Mikhail Evgrafovich

Samarakis, Andonis
See Samarakis, Antonis

Samarakis, Antonis 1919-2003 .... **CLC 5**
See also CA 25-28R; 224; CAAS 16; CANR
36; EWL 3

Samigli, E.
See Schmitz, Aron Hector

Sanchez, Florencio 1875-1910 .... **TCLC 37**
See also CA 153; DLB 305; EWL 3; HW 1;
LAW

Sanchez, Luis Rafael 1936- .... **CLC 23**
See also CA 128; DLB 305; EWL 3; HW 1;
WLIT 1

Sanchez, Sonia 1934- . **BLC 1:3, 2:3; CLC 5,**
116, 215; PC 9
See also BW 2, 3; CA 33-36R; CANR 24,
49, 74, 115; CLR 18; CP 2, 3, 4, 5, 6, 7;
CSW; CWP; DA3; DAM MULT; DLB 41;
DLBD 8; EWL 3; MAICYA 1, 2; MAL 5;
MTCW 1, 2; MTFW 2005; PFS 26; SATA
22, 136; WP

Sancho, Ignatius 1729-1780 .... **LC 84**

Sand, George 1804-1876 .... **DC 29; NCLC 2,**
42, 57, 174, 234; WLC 5
See also DA; DA3; DAB; DAC; DAM
MST, NOV; DLB 119, 192; EW 6; FL 1:3;
FW; GFL 1789 to the Present; RGWL 2,
3; TWA

Sandburg, Carl 1878-1967 ...... **CLC 1, 4, 10,**
15, 35; PC 2, 41; WLC 5
See also AAYA 24; AMW; BYA 1, 3; CA
5-8R; 25-28R; CANR 35; CDALB 1865-
1917; CLR 67; DA; DA3; DAB; DAC;
DAM MST, POET; DLB 17, 54, 284;
EWL 3; EXPP; LAIT 2; MAICYA 1, 2;
MAL 5; MTCW 1, 2; MTFW 2005; PAB;
PFS 3, 6, 12, 33, 36; RGAL 4; SATA 8;
TUS; WCH; WP; WYA

Sandburg, Carl August
See Sandburg, Carl

Sandburg, Charles
See Sandburg, Carl

Sandburg, Charles A.
See Sandburg, Carl

Sanders, Ed 1939- .... **CLC 53**
See also BG 1:3; CA 13-16R; CAAS 21;
CANR 13, 44, 78; CP 1, 2, 3, 4, 5, 6, 7;
DAM POET; DLB 16, 244

Sanders, Edward
See Sanders, Ed

Sanders, James Edward
See Sanders, Ed

Sanders, Lawrence 1920-1998 .... **CLC 41**
See also BEST 89:4; BPFB 3; CA 81-84;
165; CANR 33, 62; CMW 4; CPW; DA3;
DAM POP; MTCW 1

Sanders, Noah
See Blount, Roy, Jr.

Sanders, Winston P.
See Anderson, Poul

Sandoz, Mari(e Susette) 1900-1966 .. **CLC 28**
See also CA 1-4R; 25-28R; CANR 17, 64;
DLB 9, 212; LAIT 2; MTCW 1, 2; SATA
5; TCWW 1, 2

Sandys, George 1578-1644 .... **LC 80**
See also DLB 24, 121

Saner, Reg(inald Anthony) 1931- .... **CLC 9**
See also CA 65-68; CP 3, 4, 5, 6, 7

Sankara 788-820 .... **CMLC 32**

Sannazaro, Jacopo 1456(?)-1530 .... **LC 8**
See also RGWL 2, 3; WLIT 7

Sansom, William 1912-1976 . **CLC 2, 6; SSC**
21
See also CA 5-8R; 65-68; CANR 42; CN 1,
2; DAM NOV; DLB 139; EWL 3; MTCW
1; RGEL 2; RGSF 2

Santayana, George 1863-1952 .... **TCLC 40**
See also AMW; CA 115; 194; DLB 54, 71,
246, 270; DLBD 13; EWL 3; MAL 5;
RGAL 4; TUS

Santiago, Danny
See James, Daniel (Lewis)

Santillana, Inigo Lopez de Mendoza,
Marques de 1398-1458 .... **LC 111**
See also DLB 286

Santmyer, Helen Hooven
1895-1986 .... **CLC 33; TCLC 133**
See also CA 1-4R; 118; CANR 15, 33;
DLBY 1984; MTCW 1; RHW

Santoka, Taneda 1882-1940 .... **TCLC 72**

Santos, Bienvenido N(uqui)
1911-1996 ... **AAL; CLC 22; TCLC 156**
See also CA 101; 151; CANR 19, 46; CP 1;
DAM MULT; DLB 312, 348; EWL;
RGAL 4; SSFS 19

Santos, Miguel
See Mihura, Miguel

Sapir, Edward 1884-1939 .... **TCLC 108**
See also CA 211; DLB 92

Sapper
See McNeile, Herman Cyril

Sapphire 1950- .... **CLC 99**
See also CA 262

Sapphire, Brenda
See Sapphire

Sappho fl. 6th cent. B.C.- ... **CMLC 3, 67; PC**
5, 117
See also CDWLB 1; DA3; DAM POET;
DLB 176; FL 1:1; PFS 20, 31, 38; RGWL
2, 3; WLIT 8; WP

Saramago, Jose 1922-2010 ..... **CLC 119, 275;**
HLCS 1
See also CA 153; CANR 96, 164, 210;
CWW 2; DLB 287, 332; EWL 3; LATS
1:2; NFS 27; SSFS 23

Sarduy, Severo 1937-1993 .... **CLC 6, 97;**
HLCS 2; TCLC 167
See also CA 89-92; 142; CANR 58, 81;
CWW 2; DLB 113; EWL 3; HW 1, 2;
LAW

Sargeson, Frank 1903-1982 ..... **CLC 31; SSC**
99
See also CA 25-28R; 106; CANR 38, 79;
CN 1, 2, 3; EWL 3; GLL 2; RGEL 2;
RGSF 2; SSFS 20

Sarmiento, Domingo Faustino
1811-1888 .... **HLCS 2; NCLC 123**
See also LAW; WLIT 1

Sarmiento, Felix Ruben Garcia
See Dario, Ruben

Saro-Wiwa, Ken(ule Beeson)
1941-1995 .... **CLC 114; TCLC 200**
See also BW 2; CA 142; 150; CANR 60;
DLB 157, 360

Saroyan, William 1908-1981 ... **CLC 1, 8, 10,**
29, 34, 56; DC 28; SSC 21; TCLC 137;
WLC 5
See also AAYA 66; CA 5-8R; 103; CAD;
CANR 30; CDALBS; CN 1, 2; DA; DA3;
DAB; DAC; DAM DRAM, MST, NOV;
DFS 17; DLB 7, 9, 86; DLBY 1981; EWL
3; LAIT 4; MAL 5; MTCW 1, 2; MTFW
2005; NFS 39; RGAL 4; RGSF 2; SATA
23; SATA-Obit 24; SSFS 14; TUS

Sarraute, Nathalie 1900-1999 .... **CLC 1, 2, 4,**
8, 10, 31, 80; TCLC 145
See also BPFB 3; CA 9-12R; 187; CANR
23, 66, 134; CWW 2; DLB 83, 321; EW
12; EWL 3; GFL 1789 to the Present;
MTCW 1, 2; MTFW 2005; RGWL 2, 3

Sarton, May 1912-1995 ... **CLC 4, 14, 49, 91;**
PC 39; TCLC 120
See also AMWS 8; CA 1-4R; 149; CANR
1, 34, 55, 116; CN 1, 2, 3, 4, 5, 6; CP 1,
2, 3, 4, 5, 6; DAM POET; DLB 48; DLBY
1981; EWL 3; FW; INT CANR-34; MAL
5; MTCW 1, 2; MTFW 2005; RGAL 4;
SATA 36; SATA-Obit 86; TUS

Sartre, Jean-Paul 1905-1980 . **CLC 1, 4, 7, 9,**
13, 18, 24, 44, 50, 52; DC 3; SSC 32;
WLC 5
See also AAYA 62; CA 9-12R; 97-100;
CANR 21; DA; DA3; DAB; DAC; DAM
DRAM, MST, NOV; DFS 5, 26; DLB 72,
296, 321, 332; EW 12; EWL 3; GFL 1789
to the Present; LMFS 2; MTCW 1, 2;
MTFW 2005; NFS 21; RGHL; RGSF 2;
RGWL 2, 3; SSFS 9; TWA

Sassoon, Siegfried 1886-1967 .. **CLC 36, 130;**
PC 12
See also BRW 6; CA 104; 25-28R; CANR
36; DAB; DAM MST, NOV, POET; DLB
20, 191; DLBD 18; EWL 3; MTCW 1, 2;
MTFW 2005; PAB; PFS 28; RGEL 2;
TEA

Sassoon, Siegfried Lorraine
See Sassoon, Siegfried

Satterfield, Charles
See Pohl, Frederik

Satyremont
See Peret, Benjamin

Saul, John 1942- .... **CLC 46**
See also AAYA 10, 62; BEST 90:4; CA 81-
84; CANR 16, 40, 81, 176, 221; CPW;
DAM NOV, POP; HGG; SATA 98

Saul, John W.
See Saul, John

Saul, John Woodruff III
See Saul, John

Saunders, Caleb
See Heinlein, Robert A.

Saura (Atares), Carlos 1932-1998 .... **CLC 20**
See also CA 114; 131; CANR 79; HW 1

Sauser, Frederic Louis
See Sauser-Hall, Frederic

Sauser-Hall, Frederic 1887-1961 ..... **CLC 18,**
106
See also CA 102; 93-96; CANR 36, 62;
DLB 258; EWL 3; GFL 1789 to the
Present; MTCW 1; WP

Shiel, Matthew Phipps
See Shiel, M. P.

Shields, Carol 1935-2003 . **CLC 91, 113, 193, 298; SSC 126**
See also AMWS 7; CA 81-84; 218; CANR 51, 74, 98, 133; CCA 1; CN 6, 7; CPW; DA3; DAC; DLB 334, 350; MTCW 2; MTFW 2005; NFS 23

Shields, David 1956- .... **CLC 97**
See also CA 124; CANR 48, 99, 112, 157

Shields, David Jonathan
See Shields, David

Shiga, Naoya 1883-1971 .... **CLC 33; SSC 23; TCLC 172**
See also CA 101; 33-36R; DLB 180; EWL 3; MJW; RGWL 3

Shiga Naoya
See Shiga, Naoya

Shilts, Randy 1951-1994 .... **CLC 85**
See also AAYA 19; CA 115; 127; 144; CANR 45; DA3; GLL 1; INT CA-127; MTCW 2; MTFW 2005

Shimazaki, Haruki 1872-1943 .... **TCLC 5**
See also CA 105; 134; CANR 84; DLB 180; EWL 3; MJW; RGWL 3

Shimazaki Toson
See Shimazaki, Haruki

Shirley, James 1596-1666 .... **DC 25; LC 96**
See also DLB 58; RGEL 2

Sholem Aleykhem
See Rabinovitch, Sholem

Sholokhov, Mikhail 1905-1984 ..... **CLC 7, 15**
See also CA 101; 112; DLB 272, 332; EWL 3; MTCW 1, 2; MTFW 2005; RGWL 2, 3; SATA-Obit 36

Sholokhov, Mikhail Aleksandrovich
See Sholokhov, Mikhail

Sholom Aleichem 1859-1916
See Rabinovitch, Sholem

Shone, Patric
See Hanley, James

Showalter, Elaine 1941- .... **CLC 169**
See also CA 57-60; CANR 58, 106, 208; DLB 67; FW; GLL 2

Shreve, Susan
See Shreve, Susan Richards

Shreve, Susan Richards 1939- .... **CLC 23**
See also CA 49-52; CAAS 5; CANR 5, 38, 69, 100, 159, 199; MAICYA 1, 2; SATA 46, 95, 152; SATA-Brief 41

Shteyngart, Gary 1972- .... **CLC 319**
See also AAYA 68; CA 217; CANR 175

Shteyngart, Igor
See Shteyngart, Gary

Shue, Larry 1946-1985 .... **CLC 52**
See also CA 145; 117; DAM DRAM; DFS 7

Shu-Jen, Chou 1881-1936 . **SSC 20; TCLC 3**
See also CA 104; EWL 3

Shulman, Alix Kates 1932- .... **CLC 2, 10**
See also CA 29-32R; CANR 43, 199; FW; SATA 7

Shuster, Joe 1914-1992 .... **CLC 21**
See also AAYA 50

Shute, Nevil 1899-1960 .... **CLC 30**
See also BPFB 3; CA 102; 93-96; CANR 85; DLB 255; MTCW 2; NFS 9, 38; RHW 4; SFW 4

Shuttle, Penelope (Diane) 1947- .... **CLC 7**
See also CA 93-96; CANR 39, 84, 92, 108; CP 3, 4, 5, 6, 7; CWP; DLB 14, 40

Shvarts, Elena 1948-2010 .... **PC 50**
See also CA 147

Sidhwa, Bapsi 1939-
See Sidhwa, Bapsy (N.)

Sidhwa, Bapsy (N.) 1938- .... **CLC 168**
See also CA 108; CANR 25, 57; CN 6, 7; DLB 323; FW

Sidney, Mary 1561-1621 .... **LC 19, 39, 182**
See also DLB 167

Sidney, Sir Philip 1554-1586 .... **LC 19, 39, 131, 197; PC 32**
See also BRW 1; BRWR 2; CDBLB Before 1660; DA; DA3; DAB; DAC; DAM MST, POET; DLB 167; EXPP; PAB; PFS 30; RGEL 2; TEA; WP

Sidney Herbert, Mary
See Sidney, Mary

Siegel, Jerome 1914-1996 .... **CLC 21**
See also AAYA 50; CA 116; 169; 151

Siegel, Jerry
See Siegel, Jerome

Sienkiewicz, Henryk (Adam Alexander Pius) 1846-1916 .... **TCLC 3**
See also CA 104; 134; CANR 84; DLB 332; EWL 3; RGSF 2; RGWL 2, 3

Sierra, Gregorio Martinez
See Martinez Sierra, Gregorio

Sierra, Maria de la O'LeJarraga Martinez
See Martinez Sierra, Maria

Sigal, Clancy 1926- .... **CLC 7**
See also CA 1-4R; CANR 85, 184; CN 1, 2, 3, 4, 5, 6, 7

Siger of Brabant 1240(?)-1284(?) . **CMLC 69**
See also DLB 115

Sigourney, Lydia H.
See Sigourney, Lydia Howard

Sigourney, Lydia Howard 1791-1865 .... **NCLC 21, 87**
See also DLB 1, 42, 73, 183, 239, 243

Sigourney, Lydia Howard Huntley
See Sigourney, Lydia Howard

Sigourney, Lydia Huntley
See Sigourney, Lydia Howard

Siguenza y Gongora, Carlos de 1645-1700 .... **HLCS 2; LC 8**
See also LAW

Sigurjonsson, Johann
See Sigurjonsson, Johann

Sigurjonsson, Johann 1880-1919 ... **TCLC 27**
See also CA 170; DLB 293; EWL 3

Sikelianos, Angelos 1884-1951 .... **PC 29; TCLC 39**
See also EWL 3; RGWL 2, 3

Silkin, Jon 1930-1997 .... **CLC 2, 6, 43**
See also CA 5-8R; CAAS 5; CANR 89; CP 1, 2, 3, 4, 5, 6; DLB 27

Silko, Leslie 1948- .... **CLC 23, 74, 114, 211, 302; NNAL; SSC 37, 66, 151; WLCS**
See also AAYA 14; AMWS 4; ANW; BYA 12; CA 115; 122; CANR 45, 65, 118, 226; CN 4, 5, 6, 7; CP 4, 5, 6, 7; CPW 1; CWP; DA; DA3; DAC; DAM MST, MULT, POP; DLB 143, 175, 256, 275; EWL 3; EXPP; EXPS; LAIT 4; MAL 5; MTCW 2; MTFW 2005; NFS 4; PFS 9, 16; RGAL 4; RGSF 2; SSFS 4, 8, 10, 11; TCWW 1, 2

Silko, Leslie Marmon
See Silko, Leslie

Sillanpaa, Frans Eemil 1888-1964 ... **CLC 19**
See also CA 129; 93-96; DLB 332; EWL 3; MTCW 1

Sillitoe, Alan 1928-2010 . **CLC 1, 3, 6, 10, 19, 57, 148, 318**
See also AITN 1; BRWS 5; CA 9-12R, 191; CAAE 191; CAAS 2; CANR 8, 26, 55, 139, 213; CDBLB 1960 to Present; CN 1, 2, 3, 4, 5, 6; CP 1, 2, 3, 4, 5; DLB 14, 139; EWL 3; MTCW 1, 2; MTFW 2005; RGEL 2; RGSF 2; SATA 61

Silone, Ignazio 1900-1978 .... **CLC 4**
See also CA 25-28; 81-84; CANR 34; CAP 2; DLB 264; EW 12; EWL 3; MTCW 1; RGSF 2; RGWL 2, 3

Silone, Ignazione
See Silone, Ignazio

Siluriensis, Leolinus
See Jones, Arthur Llewellyn

Silver, Joan Micklin 1935- .... **CLC 20**
See also CA 114; 121; INT CA-121

Silver, Nicholas
See Faust, Frederick

Silverberg, Robert 1935- .... **CLC 7, 140**
See also AAYA 24; BPFB 3; BYA 7, 9; CA 1-4R, 186; CAAE 186; CAAS 3; CANR 1, 20, 36, 85, 140, 175; CLR 59; CN 6, 7; CPW; DAM POP; DLB 8; INT CANR-20; MAICYA 1, 2; MTCW 1, 2; MTFW 2005; SATA 13, 91; SATA-Essay 104; SCFW 1, 2; SFW 4; SUFW 2

Silverstein, Alvin 1933- .... **CLC 17**
See also CA 49-52; CANR 2; CLR 25; JRDA; MAICYA 1, 2; SATA 8, 69, 124

Silverstein, Shel 1932-1999 .... **PC 49**
See also AAYA 40; BW 3; CA 107; 179; CANR 47, 74, 81; CLR 5, 96; CWRI 5; JRDA; MAICYA 1, 2; MTCW 2; MTFW 2005; SATA 33, 92; SATA-Brief 27; SATA-Obit 116

Silverstein, Sheldon Allan
See Silverstein, Shel

Silverstein, Virginia B. 1937- .... **CLC 17**
See also CA 49-52; CANR 2; CLR 25; JRDA; MAICYA 1, 2; SATA 8, 69, 124

Silverstein, Virginia Barbara Opshelor
See Silverstein, Virginia B.

Sim, Georges
See Simenon, Georges

Simak, Clifford D(onald) 1904-1988 . **CLC 1, 55**
See also CA 1-4R; 125; CANR 1, 35; DLB 8; MTCW 1; SATA-Obit 56; SCFW 1, 2; SFW 4

Simenon, Georges 1903-1989 .... **CLC 1, 2, 3, 8, 18, 47**
See also BPFB 3; CA 85-88; 129; CANR 35; CMW 4; DA3; DAM POP; DLB 72; DLBY 1989; EW 12; EWL 3; GFL 1789 to the Present; MSW; MTCW 1, 2; MTFW 2005; RGWL 2, 3

Simenon, Georges Jacques Christian
See Simenon, Georges

Simic, Charles 1938- .... **CLC 6, 9, 22, 49, 68, 130, 256; PC 69**
See also AAYA 78; AMWS 8; CA 29 32R; CAAS 4; CANR 12, 33, 52, 61, 96, 140, 210; CP 2, 3, 4, 5, 6, 7; DA3; DAM POET; DLB 105; MAL 5; MTCW 2; MTFW 2005; PFS 7, 33, 36; RGAL 4; WP

Simmel, Georg 1858-1918 .... **TCLC 64**
See also CA 157; DLB 296

Simmons, Charles (Paul) 1924- .... **CLC 57**
See also CA 89-92; INT CA-89-92

Simmons, Dan 1948- .... **CLC 44**
See also AAYA 16, 54; CA 138; CANR 53, 81, 126, 174, 204; CPW; DAM POP; HGG; SUFW 2

Simmons, James (Stewart Alexander) 1933- .... **CLC 43**
See also CA 105; CAAS 21; CP 1, 2, 3, 4, 5, 6, 7; DLB 40

Simmons, Richard
See Simmons, Dan

Simms, William Gilmore 1806-1870 .... **NCLC 3, 241**
See also DLB 3, 30, 59, 73, 248, 254; RGAL 4

Simon, Carly 1945- .... **CLC 26**
See also CA 105

Simon, Claude 1913-2005 ... **CLC 4, 9, 15, 39**
See also CA 89-92; 241; CANR 33, 117; CWW 2; DAM NOV; DLB 83, 332; EW 13; EWL 3; GFL 1789 to the Present; MTCW 1

Simon, Claude Eugene Henri
See Simon, Claude

Simon, Claude Henri Eugene
See Simon, Claude

Simon, Marvin Neil
See Simon, Neil

Simon, Myles
See Follett, Ken

Simon, Neil 1927- .... **CLC 6, 11, 31, 39, 70, 233; DC 14**
See also AAYA 32; AITN 1; AMWS 4; CA 21-24R; CAD; CANR 26, 54, 87, 126; CD 5, 6; DA3; DAM DRAM; DFS 2, 6, 12, 18, 24, 27; DLB 7, 266; LAIT 4; MAL 5; MTCW 1, 2; MTFW 2005; RGAL 4; TUS

Simon, Paul 1941(?)- .... **CLC 17**
See also CA 116; 153; CANR 152

Simon, Paul Frederick
See Simon, Paul

Simonon, Paul 1956(?)- .... **CLC 30**

Simonson, Helen 1963- .... **CLC 318**
See also CA 307

Simonson, Rick .... **CLC 70**

Simpson, Harriette
See Arnow, Harriette (Louisa) Simpson

Simpson, Louis 1923- ... **CLC 4, 7, 9, 32, 149**
See also AMWS 9; CA 1-4R; CAAS 4; CANR 1, 61, 140; CP 1, 2, 3, 4, 5, 6, 7; DAM POET; DLB 5; MAL 5; MTCW 1, 2; MTFW 2005; PFS 7, 11, 14; RGAL 4

Simpson, Mona 1957- .... **CLC 44, 146**
See also CA 122; 135; CANR 68, 103, 227; CN 6, 7; EWL 3

Simpson, Mona Elizabeth
See Simpson, Mona

Simpson, N.F. 1919-2011 .... **CLC 29**
See also CA 13-16R; CBD; DLB 13; RGEL 2

Simpson, Norman Frederick
See Simpson, N.F.

Sinclair, Andrew (Annandale) 1935- . **CLC 2, 14**
See also CA 9-12R; CAAS 5; CANR 14, 38, 91; CN 1, 2, 3, 4, 5, 6, 7; DLB 14; FANT; MTCW 1

Sinclair, Emil
See Hesse, Hermann

Sinclair, Iain 1943- .... **CLC 76**
See also BRWS 14; CA 132; CANR 81, 157; CP 5, 6, 7; HGG

Sinclair, Iain MacGregor
See Sinclair, Iain

Sinclair, Irene
See Griffith, D.W.

Sinclair, Julian
See Sinclair, May

Sinclair, Mary Amelia St. Clair (?)-
See Sinclair, May

Sinclair, May 1865-1946 .... **TCLC 3, 11**
See also CA 104; 166; DLB 36, 135; EWL 3; HGG; RGEL 2; RHW; SUFW

Sinclair, Roy
See Griffith, D.W.

Sinclair, Upton 1878-1968 ...... **CLC 1, 11, 15, 63; TCLC 160; WLC 5**
See also AAYA 63; AMWS 5; BPFB 3; BYA 2; CA 5-8R; 25-28R; CANR 7; CDALB 1929-1941; DA; DA3; DAB; DAC; DAM MST, NOV; DLB 9; EWL 3; INT CANR-7; LAIT 3; MAL 5; MTCW 1, 2; MTFW 2005; NFS 6; RGAL 4; SATA 9; TUS; YAW

Sinclair, Upton Beall
See Sinclair, Upton

Singe, (Edmund) J(ohn) M(illington) 1871-1909 .... **WLC**

Singer, Isaac
See Singer, Isaac Bashevis

Singer, Isaac Bashevis 1904-1991 .. **CLC 1, 3, 6, 9, 11, 15, 23, 38, 69, 111; SSC 3, 53, 80, 154; WLC 5**
See also AAYA 32; AITN 1, 2; AMW; AMWR 2; BPFB 3; BYA 1, 4; CA 1-4R; 134; CANR 1, 39, 106; CDALB 1941-1968; CLR 1; CN 1, 2, 3, 4; CWRI 5; DA; DA3; DAB; DAC; DAM MST, NOV; DLB 6, 28, 52, 278, 332, 333; DLBY 1991; EWL 3; EXPS; HGG; JRDA; LAIT 3; MAICYA 1, 2; MAL 5; MTCW 1, 2; MTFW 2005; RGAL 4; RGHL; RGSF 2; SATA 3, 27; SATA-Obit 68; SSFS 2, 12, 16, 27, 30; TUS; TWA

Singer, Israel Joshua 1893-1944 .... **TCLC 33**
See also CA 169; DLB 333; EWL 3

Singh, Khushwant 1915- .... **CLC 11**
See also CA 9-12R; CAAS 9; CANR 6, 84; CN 1, 2, 3, 4, 5, 6, 7; DLB 323; EWL 3; RGEL 2

Singleton, Ann
See Benedict, Ruth

Singleton, John 1968(?)- .... **CLC 156**
See also AAYA 50; BW 2, 3; CA 138; CANR 67, 82; DAM MULT

Siniavskii, Andrei
See Sinyavsky, Andrei (Donatevich)

Sinibaldi, Fosco
See Kacew, Romain

Sinjohn, John
See Galsworthy, John

Sinyavsky, Andrei (Donatevich) 1925-1997 .... **CLC 8**
See also CA 85-88; 159; CWW 2; EWL 3; RGSF 2

Sinyavsky, Andrey Donatovich
See Sinyavsky, Andrei (Donatevich)

Sirin, V.
See Nabokov, Vladimir

Sissman, L(ouis) E(dward) 1928-1976 .... **CLC 9, 18**
See also CA 21-24R; 65-68; CANR 13; CP 2; DLB 5

Sisson, C(harles) H(ubert) 1914-2003 .... **CLC 8**
See also BRWS 11; CA 1-4R; 220; CAAS 3; CANR 3, 48, 84; CP 1, 2, 3, 4, 5, 6, 7; DLB 27

Sitting Bull 1831(?)-1890 .... **NNAL**
See also DA3; DAM MULT

Sitwell, Dame Edith 1887-1964 ..... **CLC 2, 9, 67; PC 3**
See also BRW 7; CA 9-12R; CANR 35; CDBLB 1945-1960; DAM POET; DLB 20; EWL 3; MTCW 1, 2; MTFW 2005; RGEL 2; TEA

Siwaarmill, H. P.
See Sharp, William

Sjoewall, Maj 1935- .... **CLC 7**
See also BPFB 3; CA 65-68; CANR 73; CMW 4; MSW

Sjowall, Maj
See Sjoewall, Maj

Skelton, John 1460(?)-1529 ..... **LC 71; PC 25**
See also BRW 1; DLB 136; RGEL 2

Skelton, Robin 1925-1997 .... **CLC 13**
See also AITN 2; CA 5-8R; 160; CAAS 5; CANR 28, 89; CCA 1; CP 1, 2, 3, 4, 5, 6; DLB 27, 53

Skolimowski, Jerzy 1938- .... **CLC 20**
See also CA 128

Skram, Amalie (Bertha) 1846-1905 .... **TCLC 25**
See also CA 165; DLB 354

Skvorecky, Josef 1924- . **CLC 15, 39, 69, 152**
See also CA 61-64; CAAS 1; CANR 10, 34, 63, 108; CDWLB 4; CWW 2; DA3; DAC; DAM NOV; DLB 232; EWL 3; MTCW 1, 2; MTFW 2005

Skvorecky, Josef Vaclav
See Skvorecky, Josef

Slade, Bernard 1930-
See Newbound, Bernard Slade

Slaughter, Carolyn 1946- .... **CLC 56**
See also CA 85-88; CANR 85, 169; CN 5, 6, 7

Slaughter, Frank G(ill) 1908-2001 ... **CLC 29**
See also AITN 2; CA 5-8R; 197; CANR 5, 85; INT CANR-5; RHW

Slavitt, David R. 1935- .... **CLC 5, 14**
See also CA 21-24R; CAAS 3; CANR 41, 83, 166, 219; CN 1, 2; CP 1, 2, 3, 4, 5, 6, 7; DLB 5, 6

Slavitt, David Rytman
See Slavitt, David R.

Slesinger, Tess 1905-1945 .... **TCLC 10**
See also CA 107; 199; DLB 102

Slessor, Kenneth 1901-1971 .... **CLC 14**
See also CA 102; 89-92; DLB 260; RGEL 2

Slowacki, Juliusz 1809-1849 .... **NCLC 15**
See also RGWL 3

Small, David 1945- .... **CLC 299**
See also CLR 53; MAICYA 2; SATA 50, 95, 126, 183, 216; SATA-Brief 46

Smart, Christopher 1722-1771 .... **LC 3, 134; PC 13**
See also DAM POET; DLB 109; RGEL 2

Smart, Elizabeth 1913-1986 .... **CLC 54; TCLC 231**
See also CA 81-84; 118; CN 4; DLB 88

Smiley, Jane 1949- ...... **CLC 53, 76, 144, 236**
See also AAYA 66; AMWS 6; BPFB 3; CA 104; CANR 30, 50, 74, 96, 158, 196; CN 6, 7; CPW 1; DA3; DAM POP; DLB 227, 234; EWL 3; INT CANR-30; MAL 5; MTFW 2005; NFS 32; SSFS 19

Smiley, Jane Graves
See Smiley, Jane

Smith, A(rthur) J(ames) M(arshall) 1902-1980 .... **CLC 15**
See also CA 1-4R; 102; CANR 4; CP 1, 2, 3; DAC; DLB 88; RGEL 2

Smith, Adam 1723(?)-1790 .... **LC 36**
See also DLB 104, 252, 336; RGEL 2

Smith, Alexander 1829-1867 .... **NCLC 59**
See also DLB 32, 55

Smith, Alexander McCall 1948- ..... **CLC 268**
See also CA 215; CANR 154, 196; SATA 73, 179

Smith, Anna Deavere 1950- ...... **CLC 86, 241**
See also CA 133; CANR 103; CD 5, 6; DFS 2, 22; DLB 341

Smith, Betty (Wehner) 1904-1972 .... **CLC 19**
See also AAYA 72; BPFB 3; BYA 3; CA 5-8R; 33-36R; DLBY 1982; LAIT 3; NFS 31; RGAL 4; SATA 6

Smith, Charlotte (Turner) 1749-1806 .... **NCLC 23, 115; PC 104**
See also DLB 39, 109; RGEL 2; TEA

Smith, Clark Ashton 1893-1961 .... **CLC 43**
See also AAYA 76; CA 143; CANR 81; FANT; HGG; MTCW 2; SCFW 1, 2; SFW 4; SUFW

Smith, Dave
See Smith, David (Jeddie)

Smith, David (Jeddie) 1942- .... **CLC 22, 42**
See also CA 49-52; CAAS 7; CANR 1, 59, 120; CP 3, 4, 5, 6, 7; CSW; DAM POET; DLB 5

Smith, Iain Crichton 1928-1998 .... **CLC 64**
See also BRWS 9; CA 21-24R; 171; CN 1, 2, 3, 4, 5, 6; CP 1, 2, 3, 4, 5, 6; DLB 40, 139, 319, 352; RGSF 2

Smith, John 1580(?)-1631 .... **LC 9**
See also DLB 24, 30; TUS

Smith, Johnston
See Crane, Stephen

Smith, Joseph, Jr. 1805-1844 .... **NCLC 53**

Smith, Kevin 1970- .... **CLC 223**
See also AAYA 37; CA 166; CANR 131,
201

Smith, Lee 1944- .... **CLC 25, 73, 258; SSC 142**
See also CA 114; 119; CANR 46, 118, 173,
225; CN 7; CSW; DLB 143; DLBY 1983;
EWL 3; INT CA-119; RGAL 4

Smith, Martin
See Smith, Martin Cruz

Smith, Martin Cruz 1942- .. **CLC 25; NNAL**
See also Smith, Martin Cruz
See also BEST 89:4; BPFB 3; CA 85-88;
CANR 6, 23, 43, 65, 119, 184; CMW 4;
CPW; DAM MULT, POP; HGG; INT
CANR-23; MTCW 2; MTFW 2005;
RGAL 4

Smith, Patti 1946- .... **CLC 12, 318**
See also CA 93-96; CANR 63, 168

Smith, Pauline (Urmson)
1882-1959 .... **TCLC 25**
See also DLB 225; EWL 3

Smith, R. Alexander McCall
See Smith, Alexander McCall

Smith, Rosamond
See Oates, Joyce Carol

Smith, Seba 1792-1868 .... **NCLC 187**
See also DLB 1, 11, 243

Smith, Sheila Kaye
See Kaye-Smith, Sheila

Smith, Stevie 1902-1971 .... **CLC 3, 8, 25, 44; PC 12**
See also BRWR 3; BRWS 2; CA 17-18; 29-
32R; CANR 35; CAP 2; CP 1; DAM
POET; DLB 20; EWL 3; MTCW 1, 2;
PAB; PFS 3; RGEL 2; TEA

Smith, Wilbur 1933- .... **CLC 33**
See also CA 13-16R; CANR 7, 46, 66, 134,
180; CPW; MTCW 1, 2; MTFW 2005

Smith, Wilbur Addison
See Smith, Wilbur

Smith, William Jay 1918- .... **CLC 6**
See also AMWS 13; CA 5-8R; CANR 44,
106, 211; CP 1, 2, 3, 4, 5, 6, 7; CSW;
CWRI 5; DLB 5; MAICYA 1, 2; SAAS
22; SATA 2, 68, 154; SATA-Essay 154;
TCLE 1:2

Smith, Woodrow Wilson
See Kuttner, Henry

Smith, Zadie 1975- .... **CLC 158, 306**
See also AAYA 50; CA 193; CANR 204;
DLB 347; MTFW 2005; NFS 40

Smolenskin, Peretz 1842-1885 .... **NCLC 30**

Smollett, Tobias (George) 1721-1771 ... **LC 2, 46, 188**
See also BRW 3; CDBLB 1660-1789; DLB
39, 104; RGEL 2; TEA

Snodgrass, Quentin Curtius
See Twain, Mark

Snodgrass, Thomas Jefferson
See Twain, Mark

Snodgrass, W. D. 1926-2009 .... **CLC 2, 6, 10, 18, 68; PC 74**
See also AMWS 6; CA 1-4R; 282; CANR
6, 36, 65, 85, 185; CP 1, 2, 3, 4, 5, 6, 7;
DAM POET; DLB 5; MAL 5; MTCW 1,
2; MTFW 2005; PFS 29; RGAL 4; TCLE
1:2

Snodgrass, W. de Witt
See Snodgrass, W. D.

Snodgrass, William de Witt
See Snodgrass, W. D.

Snodgrass, William De Witt
See Snodgrass, W. D.

Snorri Sturluson 1179-1241 .. **CMLC 56, 134**
See also RGWL 2, 3

Snow, C(harles) P(ercy) 1905-1980 ... **CLC 1, 4, 6, 9, 13, 19**
See also BRW 7; CA 5-8R; 101; CANR 28;
CDBLB 1945-1960; CN 1, 2; DAM NOV;
DLB 15, 77; DLBD 17; EWL 3; MTCW
1, 2; MTFW 2005; RGEL 2; TEA

Snow, Frances Compton
See Adams, Henry

Snyder, Gary 1930- . **CLC 1, 2, 5, 9, 32, 120; PC 21**
See also AAYA 72; AMWS 8; ANW; BG
1:3; CA 17-20R; CANR 30, 60, 125; CP
1, 2, 3, 4, 5, 6, 7; DA3; DAM POET; DLB
5, 16, 165, 212, 237, 275, 342; EWL 3;
MAL 5; MTCW 2; MTFW 2005; PFS 9,
19; RGAL 4; WP

Snyder, Gary Sherman
See Snyder, Gary

Snyder, Zilpha Keatley 1927- .... **CLC 17**
See also AAYA 15; BYA 1; CA 9-12R, 252;
CAAE 252; CANR 38, 202; CLR 31, 121;
JRDA; MAICYA 1, 2; SAAS 2; SATA 1,
28, 75, 110, 163, 226; SATA-Essay 112,
163; YAW

Soares, Bernardo
See Pessoa, Fernando

Sobh, A.
See Shamlu, Ahmad

Sobh, Alef
See Shamlu, Ahmad

Sobol, Joshua 1939- .... **CLC 60**
See also CA 200; CWW 2; RGHL

Sobol, Yehoshua 1939-
See Sobol, Joshua

Socrates 470B.C.-399B.C. .... **CMLC 27**

Soderberg, Hjalmar 1869-1941 ...... **TCLC 39**
See also DLB 259; EWL 3; RGSF 2

Soderbergh, Steven 1963- .... **CLC 154**
See also AAYA 43; CA 243

Soderbergh, Steven Andrew
See Soderbergh, Steven

Sodergran, Edith 1892-1923 .... **TCLC 31**
See also CA 202; DLB 259; EW 11; EWL
3; RGWL 2, 3

Soedergran, Edith Irene
See Sodergran, Edith

Softly, Edgar
See Lovecraft, H. P.

Softly, Edward
See Lovecraft, H. P.

Sokolov, Alexander V. 1943- .... **CLC 59**
See also CA 73-76; CWW 2; DLB 285;
EWL 3; RGWL 2, 3

Sokolov, Alexander Vsevolodovich
See Sokolov, Alexander V.

Sokolov, Raymond 1941- .... **CLC 7**
See also CA 85-88

Sokolov, Sasha
See Sokolov, Alexander V.

Soli, Tatjana .... **CLC 318**
See also CA 307

Solo, Jay
See Ellison, Harlan

Sologub, Fedor
See Teternikov, Fyodor Kuzmich

Sologub, Feodor
See Teternikov, Fyodor Kuzmich

Sologub, Fyodor
See Teternikov, Fyodor Kuzmich

Solomons, Ikey Esquir
See Thackeray, William Makepeace

Solomos, Dionysios 1798-1857 .... **NCLC 15**

Solwoska, Mara
See French, Marilyn

Solzhenitsyn, Aleksandr 1918-2008 ... **CLC 1, 2, 4, 7, 9, 10, 18, 26, 34, 78, 134, 235; SSC 32, 105; WLC 5**
See also AAYA 49; AITN 1; BPFB 3; CA
69-72; CANR 40, 65, 116; CWW 2; DA;
DA3; DAB; DAC; DAM MST, NOV;
DLB 302, 332; EW 13; EWL 3; EXPS;
LAIT 4; MTCW 1, 2; MTFW 2005; NFS
6; PFS 38; RGSF 2; RGWL 2, 3; SSFS 9;
TWA

Solzhenitsyn, Aleksandr I.
See Solzhenitsyn, Aleksandr

Solzhenitsyn, Aleksandr Isayevich
See Solzhenitsyn, Aleksandr

Somers, Jane
See Lessing, Doris

Somerville, Edith Oenone
1858-1949 .... **SSC 56; TCLC 51**
See also CA 196; DLB 135; RGEL 2; RGSF
2

Somerville & Ross
See Martin, Violet Florence; Somerville,
Edith Oenone

Sommer, Scott 1951- .... **CLC 25**
See also CA 106

Sommers, Christina Hoff 1950- ...... **CLC 197**
See also CA 153; CANR 95

Sondheim, Stephen 1930- .. **CLC 30, 39, 147; DC 22**
See also AAYA 11, 66; CA 103; CANR 47,
67, 125; DAM DRAM; DFS 25, 27, 28;
LAIT 4

Sondheim, Stephen Joshua
See Sondheim, Stephen

Sone, Monica 1919- .... **AAL**
See also DLB 312

Song, Cathy 1955- .... **AAL; PC 21**
See also CA 154; CANR 118; CWP; DLB
169, 312; EXPP; FW; PFS 5

Sontag, Susan 1933-2004 ... **CLC 1, 2, 10, 13, 31, 105, 195, 277**
See also AMWS 3; CA 17-20R; 234; CANR
25, 51, 74, 97, 184; CN 1, 2, 3, 4, 5, 6, 7;
CPW; DA3; DAM POP; DLB 2, 67; EWL
3; MAL 5; MBL; MTCW 1, 2; MTFW
2005; RGAL 4; RHW; SSFS 10

Sophocles 496(?)B.C.-406(?)B.C. .... **CMLC 2, 47, 51, 86; DC 1; WLCS**
See also AW 1; CDWLB 1; DA; DA3;
DAB; DAC; DAM DRAM, MST; DFS 1,
4, 8, 24; DLB 176; LAIT 1; LATS 1:1;
LMFS 1; RGWL 2, 3; TWA; WLIT 8

Sordello 1189-1269 .... **CMLC 15**

Sorel, Georges 1847-1922 .... **TCLC 91**
See also CA 118; 188

Sorel, Julia
See Drexler, Rosalyn

Sorokin, Vladimir .... **CLC 59**
See also CA 258; DLB 285

Sorokin, Vladimir Georgievich
See Sorokin, Vladimir

Sorrentino, Gilbert 1929-2006 .... **CLC 3, 7, 14, 22, 40, 247**
See also AMWS 21; CA 77-80; 250; CANR
14, 33, 115, 157; CN 3, 4, 5, 6, 7; CP 1,
2, 3, 4, 5, 6, 7; DLB 5, 173; DLBY 1980;
INT CANR-14

Soseki
See Natsume, Soseki

Soto, Gary 1952- ... **CLC 32, 80; HLC 2; PC 28**
See also AAYA 10, 37; BYA 11; CA 119;
125; CANR 50, 74, 107, 157, 219; CLR
38; CP 4, 5, 6, 7; DAM MULT; DFS 26;
DLB 82; EWL 3; EXPP; HW 1, 2; INT
CA-125; JRDA; LLW; MAICYA 2; MAI-
CYAS 1; MAL 5; MTCW 2; MTFW
2005; PFS 7, 30; RGAL 4; SATA 80, 120,
174; SSFS 33; WYA; YAW

Tannen, Deborah Frances
See Tannen, Deborah

Tanner, William
See Amis, Kingsley

Tante, Dilly
See Kunitz, Stanley

Tao Lao
See Storni, Alfonsina

Tapahonso, Luci 1953- .... **NNAL; PC 65**
See also CA 145; CANR 72, 127, 214; DLB 175

Tarantino, Quentin 1963- .... **CLC 125, 230**
See also AAYA 58; CA 171; CANR 125

Tarantino, Quentin Jerome
See Tarantino, Quentin

Tarassoff, Lev
See Troyat, Henri

Tarbell, Ida 1857-1944 .... **TCLC 40**
See also CA 122; 181; DLB 47

Tarbell, Ida Minerva
See Tarbell, Ida

Tarchetti, Ugo 1839(?)-1869 .... **SSC 119**

Tardieu d'Esclavelles,
Louise-Florence-Petronille
See Epinay, Louise d'

Tarkington, (Newton) Booth
1869-1946 .... **TCLC 9**
See also BPFB 3; BYA 3; CA 110; 143; CWRI 5; DLB 9, 102; MAL 5; MTCW 2; NFS 34; RGAL 4; SATA 17

Tarkovskii, Andrei Arsen'evich
See Tarkovsky, Andrei (Arsenyevich)

Tarkovsky, Andrei (Arsenyevich)
1932-1986 .... **CLC 75**
See also CA 127

Tartt, Donna 1964(?)- .... **CLC 76**
See also AAYA 56; CA 142; CANR 135; LNFS 2; MTFW 2005

Tasso, Torquato 1544-1595 .... **LC 5, 94**
See also EFS 1:2, 2:1; EW 2; RGWL 2, 3; WLIT 7

Tate, (John Orley) Allen 1899-1979 .. **CLC 2, 4, 6, 9, 11, 14, 24; PC 50**
See also AMW; CA 5-8R; 85-88; CANR 32, 108; CN 1, 2; CP 1, 2; DLB 4, 45, 63; DLBD 17; EWL 3; MAL 5; MTCW 1, 2; MTFW 2005; RGAL 4; RHW

Tate, Ellalice
See Hibbert, Eleanor Alice Burford

Tate, James 1943- .... **CLC 2, 6, 25**
See also CA 21-24R; CANR 29, 57, 114, 224; CP 1, 2, 3, 4, 5, 6, 7; DLB 5, 169; EWL 3; PFS 10, 15; RGAL 4; WP

Tate, James Vincent
See Tate, James

Tate, Nahum 1652(?)-1715 .... **LC 109**
See also DLB 80; RGEL 2

Tauler, Johannes c. 1300-1361 ...... **CMLC 37**
See also DLB 179; LMFS 1

Tavel, Ronald 1936-2009 .... **CLC 6**
See also CA 21-24R; 284; CAD; CANR 33; CD 5, 6

Taviani, Paolo 1931- .... **CLC 70**
See also CA 153

Tawada, Yoko 1960- .... **CLC 310**
See also CA 296

Taylor, Bayard 1825-1878 .... **NCLC 89**
See also DLB 3, 189, 250, 254; RGAL 4

Taylor, C(ecil) P(hilip) 1929-1981 .... **CLC 27**
See also CA 25-28R; 105; CANR 47; CBD

Taylor, Charles 1931- .... **CLC 317**
See also CA 13-16R; CANR 11, 27, 164, 200

Taylor, Charles Margrave
See Taylor, Charles

Taylor, Edward 1642(?)-1729 ..... **LC 11, 163; PC 63**
See also AMW; DA; DAB; DAC; DAM MST, POET; DLB 24; EXPP; PFS 31; RGAL 4; TUS

Taylor, Eleanor Ross 1920- .... **CLC 5**
See also CA 81-84; CANR 70

Taylor, Elizabeth 1912-1975 .... **CLC 2, 4, 29; SSC 100**
See also CA 13-16R; CANR 9, 70; CN 1, 2; DLB 139; MTCW 1; RGEL 2; SATA 13

Taylor, Frederick Winslow
1856-1915 .... **TCLC 76**
See also CA 188

Taylor, Henry 1942- .... **CLC 44**
See also CA 33-36R; CAAS 7; CANR 31, 178; CP 6, 7; DLB 5; PFS 10

Taylor, Henry Splawn
See Taylor, Henry

Taylor, Kamala
See Markandaya, Kamala

Taylor, Mildred D. 1943- .... **CLC 21**
See also AAYA 10, 47; BW 1; BYA 3, 8; CA 85-88; CANR 25, 115, 136; CLR 9, 59, 90, 144; CSW; DLB 52; JRDA; LAIT 3; MAICYA 1, 2; MTFW 2005; SAAS 5; SATA 135; WYA; YAW

Taylor, Peter (Hillsman) 1917-1994 .. **CLC 1, 4, 18, 37, 44, 50, 71; SSC 10, 84**
See also AMWS 5; BPFB 3; CA 13-16R; 147; CANR 9, 50; CN 1, 2, 3, 4, 5; CSW; DLB 218, 278; DLBY 1981, 1994; EWL 3; EXPS; INT CANR-9; MAL 5; MTCW 1, 2; MTFW 2005; RGSF 2; SSFS 9; TUS

Taylor, Robert Lewis 1912-1998 .... **CLC 14**
See also CA 1-4R; 170; CANR 3, 64; CN 1, 2; SATA 10; TCWW 1, 2

Tchekhov, Anton
See Chekhov, Anton

Tchicaya, Gerald Felix 1931-1988 .. **CLC 101**
See also CA 129; 125; CANR 81; EWL 3

Tchicaya U Tam'si
See Tchicaya, Gerald Felix

Teasdale, Sara 1884-1933 .... **PC 31; TCLC 4**
See also CA 104; 163; DLB 45; GLL 1; PFS 14; RGAL 4; SATA 32; TUS

Tecumseh 1768-1813 .... **NNAL**
See also DAM MULT

Tegner, Esaias 1782-1846 .... **NCLC 2**

Teilhard de Chardin, (Marie Joseph) Pierre
1881-1955 .... **TCLC 9**
See also CA 105; 210; GFL 1789 to the Present

Temple, Ann
See Mortimer, Penelope (Ruth)

Tennant, Emma 1937- .... **CLC 13, 52**
See also BRWS 9; CA 65-68; CAAS 9; CANR 10, 38, 59, 88, 177; CN 3, 4, 5, 6, 7; DLB 14; EWL 3; SFW 4

Tenneshaw, S.M.
See Silverberg, Robert

Tenney, Tabitha Gilman
1762-1837 .... **NCLC 122, 248**
See also DLB 37, 200

Tennyson, Alfred 1809-1892 ... **NCLC 30, 65, 115, 202; PC 6, 101; WLC 6**
See also AAYA 50; BRW 4; BRWR 3; CD-BLB 1832-1890; DA; DA3; DAB; DAC; DAM MST, POET; DLB 32; EXPP; PAB; PFS 1, 2, 4, 11, 15, 19; RGEL 2; TEA; WLIT 4; WP

Teran, Lisa St. Aubin de
See St. Aubin de Teran, Lisa

Terence c. 184B.C.-c. 159B.C. ...... **CMLC 14, 132; DC 7**
See also AW 1; CDWLB 1; DLB 211; RGWL 2, 3; TWA; WLIT 8

Teresa de Jesus, St. 1515-1582 .... **LC 18, 149**

Teresa of Avila, St.
See Teresa de Jesus, St.

Terkel, Louis
See Terkel, Studs

Terkel, Studs 1912-2008 .... **CLC 38**
See also AAYA 32; AITN 1; CA 57-60; 278; CANR 18, 45, 67, 132, 195; DA3; MTCW 1, 2; MTFW 2005; TUS

Terkel, Studs Louis
See Terkel, Studs

Terry, C. V.
See Slaughter, Frank G(ill)

Terry, Megan 1932- .... **CLC 19; DC 13**
See also CA 77-80; CABS 3; CAD; CANR 43; CD 5, 6; CWD; DFS 18; DLB 7, 249; GLL 2

Tertullian c. 155-c. 245 .... **CMLC 29**

Tertz, Abram
See Sinyavsky, Andrei (Donatevich)

Tesich, Steve 1943(?)-1996 .... **CLC 40, 69**
See also CA 105; 152; CAD; DLBY 1983

Tesla, Nikola 1856-1943 .... **TCLC 88**
See also CA 157

Teternikov, Fyodor Kuzmich
1863-1927 .... **TCLC 9, 259**
See also CA 104; DLB 295; EWL 3

Tevis, Walter 1928-1984 .... **CLC 42**
See also CA 113; SFW 4

Tey, Josephine
See Mackintosh, Elizabeth

Thackeray, William Makepeace
1811-1863 ...... **NCLC 5, 14, 22, 43, 169, 213; WLC 6**
See also BRW 5; BRWC 2; CDBLB 1832-1890; DA; DA3; DAB; DAC; DAM MST, NOV; DLB 21, 55, 159, 163; NFS 13; RGEL 2; SATA 23; TEA; WLIT 3

Thakura, Ravindranatha
See Tagore, Rabindranath

Thames, C. H.
See Marlowe, Stephen

Tharoor, Shashi 1956- .... **CLC 70**
See also CA 141; CANR 91, 201; CN 6, 7

Thelwall, John 1764-1834 .... **NCLC 162**
See also DLB 93, 158

Thelwell, Michael Miles 1939- .... **CLC 22**
See also BW 2; CA 101

Theo, Ion
See Theodorescu, Ion N.

Theobald, Lewis, Jr.
See Lovecraft, H. P.

Theocritus c. 310B.C.- .... **CMLC 45**
See also AW 1; DLB 176; RGWL 2, 3

Theodorescu, Ion N. 1880-1967 .... **CLC 80**
See also CA 167; 116; CDWLB 4; DLB 220; EWL 3

Theriault, Yves 1915-1983 .... **CLC 79**
See also CA 102; CANR 150; CCA 1; DAC; DAM MST; DLB 88; EWL 3

Therion, Master
See Crowley, Edward Alexander

Theroux, Alexander 1939- .... **CLC 2, 25**
See also CA 85-88; CANR 20, 63, 190; CN 4, 5, 6, 7

Theroux, Alexander Louis
See Theroux, Alexander

Theroux, Paul 1941- .... **CLC 5, 8, 11, 15, 28, 46, 159, 303**
See also AAYA 28; AMWS 8; BEST 89:4; BPFB 3; CA 33-36R; CANR 20, 45, 74, 133, 179; CDALBS; CN 1, 2, 3, 4, 5, 6, 7; CP 1; CPW 1; DA3; DAM POP; DLB 2, 218; EWL 3; HGG; MAL 5; MTCW 1, 2; MTFW 2005; RGAL 4; SATA 44, 109; TUS

Theroux, Paul Edward
See Theroux, Paul

Tolson, Melvin B(eaunorus)
   1898(?)-1966 .... **BLC 1:3; CLC 36, 105;
   PC 88**
      See also AFAW 1, 2; BW 1, 3; CA 124; 89-
      92; CANR 80; DAM MULT, POET; DLB
      48, 76; MAL 5; RGAL 4
Tolstoi, Aleksei Nikolaevich
   See Tolstoy, Alexey Nikolaevich
Tolstoi, Lev
   See Tolstoy, Leo
Tolstoy, Aleksei Nikolaevich
   See Tolstoy, Alexey Nikolaevich
Tolstoy, Alexey Nikolaevich
   1882-1945 .... **TCLC 18**
      See also CA 107; 158; DLB 272; EWL 3;
      SFW 4
Tolstoy, Leo 1828-1910 ..... **SSC 9, 30, 45, 54,
   131; TCLC 4, 11, 17, 28, 44, 79, 173,
   260; WLC 6**
      See also AAYA 56; CA 104; 123; DA; DA3;
      DAB; DAC; DAM MST, NOV; DLB 238;
      EFS 1:2, 2:2; EW 7; EXPS; IDTP; LAIT
      2; LATS 1:1; LMFS 1; NFS 10, 28; RGSF
      2; RGWL 2, 3; SATA 26; SSFS 5, 28;
      TWA
Tolstoy, Count Leo
   See Tolstoy, Leo
Tolstoy, Leo Nikolaevich
   See Tolstoy, Leo
Tomalin, Claire 1933- .... **CLC 166**
      See also CA 89-92; CANR 52, 88, 165;
      DLB 155
Tomasi di Lampedusa, Giuseppe
   See Lampedusa, Giuseppe di
Tomlin, Lily 1939(?)- .... **CLC 17**
      See also CA 117
Tomlin, Mary Jane
   See Tomlin, Lily
Tomlin, Mary Jean
   See Tomlin, Lily
Tomline, F. Latour
   See Gilbert, W(illiam) S(chwenck)
Tomlinson, (Alfred) Charles 1927- .... **CLC 2,
   4, 6, 13, 45; PC 17**
      See also CA 5-8R; CANR 33; CP 1, 2, 3, 4,
      5, 6, 7; DAM POET; DLB 40; TCLE 1:2
Tomlinson, H(enry) M(ajor)
   1873-1958 .... **TCLC 71**
      See also CA 118; 161; DLB 36, 100, 195
Tomlinson, Mary Jane
   See Tomlin, Lily
Tomson, Graham R.
   See Watson, Rosamund Marriott
Tonna, Charlotte Elizabeth
   1790-1846 .... **NCLC 135**
      See also DLB 163
Tonson, Jacob fl. 1655(?)-1736 .... **LC 86**
      See also DLB 170
Toole, John Kennedy 1937-1969 ..... **CLC 19,
   64**
      See also BPFB 3; CA 104; DLBY 1981;
      MTCW 2; MTFW 2005
Toomer, Eugene
   See Toomer, Jean
Toomer, Eugene Pinchback
   See Toomer, Jean
Toomer, Jean 1894-1967 ... **BLC 1:3; CLC 1,
   4, 13, 22; HR 1:3; PC 7; SSC 1, 45,
   138; TCLC 172; WLCS**
      See also AFAW 1, 2; AMWS 3, 9; BW 1;
      CA 85-88; CDALB 1917-1929; DA3;
      DAM MULT; DLB 45, 51; EWL 3; EXPP;
      EXPS; LMFS 2; MAL 5; MTCW 1, 2;
      MTFW 2005; NFS 11; PFS 31; RGAL 4;
      RGSF 2; SSFS 5
Toomer, Nathan Jean
   See Toomer, Jean
Toomer, Nathan Pinchback
   See Toomer, Jean

Torley, Luke
   See Blish, James
Tornimparte, Alessandra
   See Ginzburg, Natalia
Torre, Raoul della
   See Mencken, H. L.
Torrence, Ridgely 1874-1950 .... **TCLC 97**
      See also DLB 54, 249; MAL 5
Torrey, E. Fuller 1937- .... **CLC 34**
      See also CA 119; CANR 71, 158
Torrey, Edwin Fuller
   See Torrey, E. Fuller
Torsvan, Ben Traven
   See Traven, B.
Torsvan, Benno Traven
   See Traven, B.
Torsvan, Berick Traven
   See Traven, B.
Torsvan, Berwick Traven
   See Traven, B.
Torsvan, Bruno Traven
   See Traven, B.
Torsvan, Traven
   See Traven, B.
Toson
   See Shimazaki, Haruki
Tourneur, Cyril 1575(?)-1626 ...... **LC 66, 181**
      See also BRW 2; DAM DRAM; DLB 58;
      RGEL 2
Tournier, Michel 1924- .... **CLC 6, 23, 36, 95,
   249; SSC 88**
      See also CA 49-52; CANR 3, 36, 74, 149;
      CWW 2; DLB 83; EWL 3; GFL 1789 to
      the Present; MTCW 1, 2; SATA 23
Tournier, Michel Edouard
   See Tournier, Michel
Tournimparte, Alessandra
   See Ginzburg, Natalia
Towers, Ivar
   See Kornbluth, C(yril) M.
Towne, Robert (Burton) 1936(?)- ..... **CLC 87**
      See also CA 108; DLB 44; IDFW 3, 4
Townsend, Sue 1946- .... **CLC 61**
      See also AAYA 28; CA 119; 127; CANR
      65, 107, 202; CBD; CD 5, 6; CPW; CWD;
      DAB; DAC; DAM MST; DLB 271, 352;
      INT CA-127; SATA 55, 93; SATA-Brief
      48; YAW
Townsend, Susan Lilian
   See Townsend, Sue
Townshend, Pete
   See Townshend, Peter
Townshend, Peter 1945- .... **CLC 17, 42**
      See also CA 107
Townshend, Peter Dennis Blandford
   See Townshend, Peter
Tozzi, Federigo 1883-1920 .... **TCLC 31**
      See also CA 160; CANR 110; DLB 264;
      EWL 3; WLIT 7
Trafford, F. G.
   See Riddell, Charlotte
Traherne, Thomas 1637(?)-1674 .. **LC 99; PC
   70**
      See also BRW 2; BRWS 11; DLB 131;
      PAB; RGEL 2
Traill, Catharine Parr 1802-1899 .. **NCLC 31**
      See also DLB 99
Trakl, Georg 1887-1914 ...... **PC 20; TCLC 5,
   239**
      See also CA 104; 165; EW 10; EWL 3;
      LMFS 2; MTCW 2; RGWL 2, 3
Trambley, Estela Portillo
   See Portillo Trambley, Estela
Tranquilli, Secondino
   See Silone, Ignazio
Transtroemer, Tomas Gosta
   See Transtromer, Tomas

Transtromer, Tomas 1931- .... **CLC 52, 65**
      See also CA 117; 129; CAAS 17; CANR
      115, 172; CWW 2; DAM POET; DLB
      257; EWL 3; PFS 21
Transtromer, Tomas Goesta
   See Transtromer, Tomas
Transtromer, Tomas Gosta
   See Transtromer, Tomas
Transtromer, Tomas Gosta
   See Transtromer, Tomas
Traven, B. 1882(?)-1969 .... **CLC 8, 11**
      See also CA 19-20; 25-28R; CAP 2; DLB
      9, 56; EWL 3; MTCW 1; RGAL 4
Trediakovsky, Vasilii Kirillovich
   1703-1769 .... **LC 68**
      See also DLB 150
Treitel, Jonathan 1959- .... **CLC 70**
      See also CA 210; DLB 267
Trelawny, Edward John
   1792-1881 .... **NCLC 85**
      See also DLB 110, 116, 144
Tremain, Rose 1943- .... **CLC 42**
      See also CA 97-100; CANR 44, 95, 186;
      CN 4, 5, 6, 7; DLB 14, 271; RGSF 2;
      RHW
Tremblay, Michel 1942- .... **CLC 29, 102, 225**
      See also CA 116; 128; CCA 1; CWW 2;
      DAC; DAM MST; DLB 60; EWL 3; GLL
      1; MTCW 1, 2; MTFW 2005
Trevanian
   See Whitaker, Rod
Trevisa, John c. 1342-c. 1402 .... **LC 139**
      See also BRWS 9; DLB 146
Trevor, Frances
   See Teasdale, Sara
Trevor, Glen
   See Hilton, James
Trevor, William 1928- ... **CLC 1, 2, 3, 4, 5, 6,
   7; SSC 21, 58**
      See also BRWS 4; CA 9-12R; CANR 4, 37,
      55, 76, 102, 139, 195; CBD; CD 5, 6;
      DAM NOV; DLB 14, 139; EWL 3; INT
      CANR-37; LATS 1:2; MTCW 1, 2;
      MTFW 2005; RGEL 2; RGSF 2; SSFS
      10, 33; TCLE 1:2; TEA
Triana, Jose 1931(?)- .... **DC 39**
      See also CA 131; DLB 305; EWL 3; HW 1;
      LAW
Trifonov, Iurii (Valentinovich)
   See Trifonov, Yuri (Valentinovich)
Trifonov, Yuri (Valentinovich)
   1925-1981 .... **CLC 45**
      See also CA 126; 103; DLB 302; EWL 3;
      MTCW 1; RGWL 2, 3
Trifonov, Yury Valentinovich
   See Trifonov, Yuri (Valentinovich)
Trilling, Diana (Rubin) 1905-1996 . **CLC 129**
      See also CA 5-8R; 154; CANR 10, 46; INT
      CANR-10; MTCW 1, 2
Trilling, Lionel 1905-1975 ..... **CLC 9, 11, 24;
   SSC 75**
      See also AMWS 3; CA 9-12R; 61-64;
      CANR 10, 105; CN 1, 2; DLB 28, 63;
      EWL 3; INT CANR-10; MAL 5; MTCW
      1, 2; RGAL 4; TUS
Trimball, W. H.
   See Mencken, H. L.
Tristan
   See Gomez de la Serna, Ramon
Tristram
   See Housman, A. E.
Trogdon, William
   See Heat-Moon, William Least
Trogdon, William Lewis
   See Heat-Moon, William Least

Trollope, Anthony 1815-1882 .... **NCLC 6, 33, 101, 215; SSC 28, 133; WLC 6**
See also BRW 5; CDBLB 1832-1890; DA; DA3; DAB; DAC; DAM MST, NOV; DLB 21, 57, 159; RGEL 2; RGSF 2; SATA 22

Trollope, Frances 1779-1863 .... **NCLC 30**
See also DLB 21, 166

Trollope, Joanna 1943- .... **CLC 186**
See also CA 101; CANR 58, 95, 149, 191; CN 7; CPW; DLB 207; RHW

Trotsky, Leon 1879-1940 .... **TCLC 22**
See also CA 118; 167

Trotter, Catharine 1679-1749 .... **LC 8, 165**
See also BRWS 16; DLB 84, 252

Trotter, Wilfred 1872-1939 .... **TCLC 97**

Troupe, Quincy 1943- .... **BLC 2:3**
See also BW 2; CA 113; 124; CANR 43, 90, 126, 213; DLB 41

Trout, Kilgore
See Farmer, Philip Jose

Trow, George William Swift
See Trow, George W.S.

Trow, George W.S. 1943-2006 .... **CLC 52**
See also CA 126; 255; CANR 91

Troyat, Henri 1911-2007 .... **CLC 23**
See also CA 45-48; 258; CANR 2, 33, 67, 117; GFL 1789 to the Present; MTCW 1

Trudeau, Garretson Beekman
See Trudeau, G.B.

Trudeau, Garry
See Trudeau, G.B.

Trudeau, Garry B.
See Trudeau, G.B.

Trudeau, G.B. 1948- .... **CLC 12**
See also AAYA 10, 60; AITN 2; CA 81-84; CANR 31; SATA 35, 168

Truffaut, Francois 1932-1984 ... **CLC 20, 101**
See also AAYA 84; CA 81-84; 113; CANR 34

Trumbo, Dalton 1905-1976 .... **CLC 19**
See also CA 21-24R; 69-72; CANR 10; CN 1, 2; DLB 26; IDFW 3, 4; YAW

Trumbull, John 1750-1831 .... **NCLC 30**
See also DLB 31; RGAL 4

Trundlett, Helen B.
See Eliot, T. S.

Truth, Sojourner 1797(?)-1883 ...... **NCLC 94**
See also DLB 239; FW; LAIT 2

Tryon, Thomas 1926-1991 .... **CLC 3, 11**
See also AITN 1; BPFB 3; CA 29-32R; 135; CANR 32, 77; CPW; DA3; DAM POP; HGG; MTCW 1

Tryon, Tom
See Tryon, Thomas

Ts'ao Hsueh-ch'in 1715(?)-1763 .... **LC 1**

Tsurayuki Ed. fl. 10th cent. - .... **PC 73**

Tsvetaeva, Marina 1892-1941 . **PC 14; TCLC 7, 35**
See also CA 104; 128; CANR 73; DLB 295; EW 11; MTCW 1, 2; PFS 29; RGWL 2, 3

Tsvetaeva Efron, Marina Ivanovna
See Tsvetaeva, Marina

Tuck, Lily 1938- .... **CLC 70**
See also AAYA 74; CA 139; CANR 90, 192

Tuckerman, Frederick Goddard 1821-1873 .... **PC 85**
See also DLB 243; RGAL 4

Tu Fu 712-770 .... **PC 9**
See also DAM MULT; PFS 32; RGWL 2, 3; TWA; WP

Tulsidas, Gosvami 1532(?)-1623 .... **LC 158**
See also RGWL 2, 3

Tunis, John R(oberts) 1889-1975 ..... **CLC 12**
See also BYA 1; CA 61-64; CANR 62; DLB 22, 171; JRDA; MAICYA 1, 2; SATA 37; SATA-Brief 30; YAW

Tuohy, Frank
See Tuohy, John Francis

Tuohy, John Francis 1925- .... **CLC 37**
See also CA 5-8R; 178; CANR 3, 47; CN 1, 2, 3, 4, 5, 6, 7; DLB 14, 139

Turco, Lewis 1934- .... **CLC 11, 63**
See also CA 13-16R; CAAS 22; CANR 24, 51, 185; CP 1, 2, 3, 4, 5, 6, 7; DLBY 1984; TCLE 1:2

Turco, Lewis Putnam
See Turco, Lewis

Turgenev, Ivan 1818-1883 . **DC 7; NCLC 21, 37, 122; SSC 7, 57; WLC 6**
See also AAYA 58; DA; DAB; DAC; DAM MST, NOV; DFS 6; DLB 238, 284; EW 6; LATS 1:1; NFS 16; RGSF 2; RGWL 2, 3; TWA

Turgenev, Ivan Sergeevich
See Turgenev, Ivan

Turgot, Anne-Robert-Jacques 1727-1781 .... **LC 26**
See also DLB 314

Turlin, Heinrich von dem
See Heinrich von dem Tuerlin

Turner, Frederick 1943- .... **CLC 48**
See also CA 73-76, 227; CAAE 227; CAAS 10; CANR 12, 30, 56; DLB 40, 282

Turton, James
See Crace, Jim

Tutu, Desmond M(pilo) 1931- .... **BLC 1:3; CLC 80**
See also BW 1, 3; CA 125; CANR 67, 81; DAM MULT

Tutuola, Amos 1920-1997 .... **BLC 1:3, 2:3; CLC 5, 14, 29; TCLC 188**
See also AAYA 76; AFW; BW 2, 3; CA 9-12R; 159; CANR 27, 66; CDWLB 3; CN 1, 2, 3, 4, 5, 6; DA3; DAM MULT; DLB 125; DNFS 2; EWL 3; MTCW 1, 2; MTFW 2005; RGEL 2; WLIT 2

Twain, Mark 1835-1910 ... **SSC 6, 26, 34, 87, 119; TCLC 6, 12, 19, 36, 48, 59, 161, 185, 260; WLC 6**
See also AAYA 20; AMW; AMWC 1; BPFB 3; BYA 2, 3, 11, 14; CA 104; 135; CDALB 1865-1917; CLR 58, 60, 66, 156; DA; DA3; DAB; DAC; DAM MST, NOV; DLB 11, 12, 23, 64, 74, 186, 189, 343; EXPN; EXPS; JRDA; LAIT 2; LMFS 1; MAICYA 1, 2; MAL 5; NCFS 4; NFS 1, 6; RGAL 4; RGSF 2; SATA 100; SFW 4; SSFS 1, 7, 16, 21, 27, 33; SUFW; TUS; WCH; WYA; YABC 2; YAW

Twohill, Maggie
See Angell, Judie

Tyler, Anne 1941- . **CLC 7, 11, 18, 28, 44, 59, 103, 205, 265**
See also AAYA 18, 60; AMWS 4; BEST 89:1; BPFB 3; BYA 12; CA 9-12R; CANR 11, 33, 53, 109, 132, 168; CDALBS; CN 1, 2, 3, 4, 5, 6, 7; CPW; CSW; DAM NOV, POP; DLB 6, 143; DLBY 1982; EWL 3; EXPN; LATS 1:2; MAL 5; MBL; MTCW 1, 2; MTFW 2005; NFS 2, 7, 10, 38; RGAL 4; SATA 7, 90, 173; SSFS 1, 31; TCLE 1:2; TUS; YAW

Tyler, Royall 1757-1826 .... **NCLC 3, 244**
See also DLB 37; RGAL 4

Tynan, Katharine 1861-1931 .... **PC 120; TCLC 3, 217**
See also CA 104; 167; DLB 153, 240; FW

Tyndale, William c. 1484-1536 .... **LC 103**
See also DLB 132

Tyutchev, Fyodor 1803-1873 .... **NCLC 34**

Tzara, Tristan 1896-1963 .... **CLC 47; PC 27; TCLC 168**
See also CA 153; 89-92; DAM POET; EWL 3; MTCW 2

Uc de Saint Circ c. 1190B.C.-13th cent. B.C. .... **CMLC 102**

Uchida, Yoshiko 1921-1992 .... **AAL**
See also AAYA 16; BYA 2, 3; CA 13-16R; 139; CANR 6, 22, 47, 61; CDALBS; CLR 6, 56; CWRI 5; DLB 312; JRDA; MAICYA 1, 2; MTCW 1, 2; MTFW 2005; NFS 26; SAAS 1; SATA 1, 53; SATA-Obit 72; SSFS 31

Udall, Nicholas 1504-1556 .... **LC 84**
See also DLB 62; RGEL 2

Ueda Akinari 1734-1809 .... **NCLC 131**

Uhry, Alfred 1936- .... **CLC 55; DC 28**
See also CA 127; 133; CAD; CANR 112; CD 5, 6; CSW; DA3; DAM DRAM, POP; DFS 11, 15; INT CA-133; MTFW 2005

Ulf, Haerved
See Strindberg, August

Ulf, Harved
See Strindberg, August

Ulibarri, Sabine R(eyes) 1919-2003 .... **CLC 83; HLCS 2**
See also CA 131; 214; CANR 81; DAM MULT; DLB 82; HW 1, 2; RGSF 2

Ulyanov, V. I.
See Lenin

Ulyanov, Vladimir Ilyich
See Lenin

Ulyanov-Lenin
See Lenin

Unamuno, Miguel de 1864-1936 .... **HLC 2; SSC 11, 69; TCLC 2, 9, 148, 237**
See also CA 104; 131; CANR 81; DAM MULT, NOV; DLB 108, 322; EW 8; EWL 3; HW 1, 2; MTCW 1, 2; MTFW 2005; RGSF 2; RGWL 2, 3; SSFS 20; TWA

Unamuno y Jugo, Miguel de
See Unamuno, Miguel de

Uncle Shelby
See Silverstein, Shel

Undercliffe, Errol
See Campbell, Ramsey

Underwood, Miles
See Glassco, John

Undset, Sigrid 1882-1949 .... **TCLC 3, 197; WLC 6**
See also AAYA 77; CA 104; 129; DA; DA3; DAB; DAC; DAM MST, NOV; DLB 293, 332; EW 9; EWL 3; FW; MTCW 1, 2; MTFW 2005; RGWL 2, 3

Ungaretti, Giuseppe 1888-1970 ... **CLC 7, 11, 15; PC 57; TCLC 200**
See also CA 19-20; 25-28R; CAP 2; DLB 114; EW 10; EWL 3; PFS 20; RGWL 2, 3; WLIT 7

Unger, Douglas 1952- .... **CLC 34**
See also CA 130; CANR 94, 155

Unsworth, Barry 1930- .... **CLC 76, 127**
See also BRWS 7; CA 25-28R; CANR 30, 54, 125, 171, 202; CN 6, 7; DLB 194, 326

Unsworth, Barry Forster
See Unsworth, Barry

Updike, John 1932-2009 .... **CLC 1, 2, 3, 5, 7, 9, 13, 15, 23, 34, 43, 70, 139, 214, 278; PC 90; SSC 13, 27, 103; WLC 6**
See also AAYA 36; AMW; AMWC 1; AMWR 1; BPFB 3; BYA 12; CA 1-4R; 282; CABS 1; CANR 4, 33, 51, 94, 133, 197; CDALB 1968-1988; CN 1, 2, 3, 4, 5, 6, 7; CP 1, 2, 3, 4, 5, 6, 7; CPW 1; DA; DA3; DAB; DAC; DAM MST, NOV, POET, POP; DLB 2, 5, 143, 218, 227; DLBD 3; DLBY 1980, 1982, 1997; EWL 3; EXPP; HGG; MAL 5; MTCW 1, 2; MTFW 2005; NFS 12, 24; RGAL 4; RGSF 2; SSFS 3, 19; TUS

Updike, John Hoyer
See Updike, John

Vega, Lope de 1562-1635 ... **DC 44; HLCS 2; LC 23, 119**
See also EW 2; RGWL 2, 3

Veldeke, Heinrich von c. 1145-c. 1190 .... **CMLC 85**

Vendler, Helen 1933- .... **CLC 138**
See also CA 41-44R; CANR 25, 72, 136, 190; MTCW 1, 2; MTFW 2005

Vendler, Helen Hennessy
See Vendler, Helen

Venison, Alfred
See Pound, Ezra

Ventsel, Elena Sergeevna 1907-2002 .... **CLC 59**
See also CA 154; CWW 2; DLB 302

Venttsel', Elena Sergeevna
See Ventsel, Elena Sergeevna

Verdi, Marie de
See Mencken, H. L.

Verdu, Matilde
See Cela, Camilo Jose

Verga, Giovanni (Carmelo) 1840-1922 ..... **SSC 21, 87; TCLC 3, 227**
See also CA 104; 123; CANR 101; EW 7; EWL 3; RGSF 2; RGWL 2, 3; WLIT 7

Vergil 70B.C.-19B.C. .. **CMLC 9, 40, 101; PC 12; WLCS**
See also AW 2; CDWLB 1; DA; DA3; DAB; DAC; DAM MST, POET; DLB 211; EFS 1:1, 2:1; LAIT 1; LMFS 1; RGWL 2, 3; WLIT 8; WP

Vergil, Polydore c. 1470-1555 .... **LC 108**
See also DLB 132

Verhaeren, Emile (Adolphe Gustave) 1855-1916 .... **TCLC 12**
See also CA 109; EWL 3; GFL 1789 to the Present

Verlaine, Paul 1844-1896 .. **NCLC 2, 51, 230; PC 2, 32**
See also DAM POET; DLB 217; EW 7; GFL 1789 to the Present; LMFS 2; RGWL 2, 3; TWA

Verlaine, Paul Marie
See Verlaine, Paul

Verne, Jules 1828-1905 .... **TCLC 6, 52, 245**
See also AAYA 16; BYA 4; CA 110; 131; CLR 88; DA3; DLB 123; GFL 1789 to the Present; JRDA; LAIT 2; LMFS 2; MAICYA 1, 2; MTFW 2005; NFS 30, 34; RGWL 2, 3; SATA 21; SCFW 1, 2; SFW 4; TWA; WCH

Verne, Jules Gabriel
See Verne, Jules

Verus, Marcus Annius
See Aurelius, Marcus

Very, Jones 1813-1880 .... **NCLC 9; PC 86**
See also DLB 1, 243; RGAL 4

Very, Rev. C.
See Crowley, Edward Alexander

Vesaas, Tarjei 1897-1970 .... **CLC 48**
See also CA 190; 29-32R; DLB 297; EW 11; EWL 3; RGWL 3

Vialis, Gaston
See Simenon, Georges

Vian, Boris 1920-1959(?) .... **TCLC 9**
See also CA 106; 164; CANR 111; DLB 72; 321; EWL 3; GFL 1789 to the Present; MTCW 2; RGWL 2, 3

Viator, Vacuus
See Hughes, Thomas

Viaud, Julien 1850-1923 .... **TCLC 11, 239**
See also CA 107; DLB 123; GFL 1789 to the Present

Viaud, Louis Marie Julien
See Viaud, Julien

Vicar, Henry
See Felsen, Henry Gregor

Vicente, Gil 1465-c. 1536 .... **LC 99**
See also DLB 318; IDTP; RGWL 2, 3

Vicker, Angus
See Felsen, Henry Gregor

Vico, Giambattista
See Vico, Giovanni Battista

Vico, Giovanni Battista 1668-1744 .... **LC 138**
See also EW 3; WLIT 7

Vidal, Eugene Luther Gore
See Vidal, Gore

Vidal, Gore 1925- ...... **CLC 2, 4, 6, 8, 10, 22, 33, 72, 142, 289**
See also AAYA 64; AITN 1; AMWS 4; BEST 90:2; BPFB 3; CA 5-8R; CAD; CANR 13, 45, 65, 100, 132, 167; CD 5, 6; CDALBS; CN 1, 2, 3, 4, 5, 6, 7; CPW; DA3; DAM NOV, POP; DFS 2; DLB 6, 152; EWL 3; GLL 1; INT CANR-13; MAL 5; MTCW 1, 2; MTFW 2005; RGAL 4; RHW; TUS

Viereck, Peter 1916-2006 .... **CLC 4; PC 27**
See also CA 1-4R; 250; CANR 1, 47; CP 1, 2, 3, 4, 5, 6, 7; DLB 5; MAL 5; PFS 9, 14

Viereck, Peter Robert Edwin
See Viereck, Peter

Vigny, Alfred de 1797-1863 .... **NCLC 7, 102; PC 26**
See also DAM POET; DLB 119, 192, 217; EW 5; GFL 1789 to the Present; RGWL 2, 3

Vigny, Alfred Victor de
See Vigny, Alfred de

Vilakazi, Benedict Wallet 1906-1947 .... **TCLC 37**
See also CA 168

Vile, Curt
See Moore, Alan

Villa, Jose Garcia 1914-1997 ... **AAL; PC 22; TCLC 176**
See also CA 25-28R; CANR 12, 118; CP 1, 2, 3, 4; DLB 312; EWL 3; EXPP

Villard, Oswald Garrison 1872-1949 .... **TCLC 160**
See also CA 113; 162; DLB 25, 91

Villarreal, Jose Antonio 1924- .... **HLC 2**
See also CA 133; CANR 93; DAM MULT; DLB 82; HW 1; LAIT 4; RGAL 4

Villaurrutia, Xavier 1903-1950 ...... **TCLC 80**
See also CA 192; EWL 3; HW 1; LAW

Villaverde, Cirilo 1812-1894 .... **NCLC 121**
See also LAW

Villehardouin, Geoffroi de 1150(?)-1218(?) .... **CMLC 38**

Villiers, George 1628-1687 .... **LC 107**
See also DLB 80; RGEL 2

Villiers de l'Isle Adam, Jean Marie Mathias Philippe Auguste 1838-1889 ... **NCLC 3, 237; SSC 14**
See also DLB 123, 192; GFL 1789 to the Present; RGSF 2

Villon, Francois 1431-1463(?) .... **LC 62, 166; PC 13**
See also DLB 208; EW 2; RGWL 2, 3; TWA

Vine, Barbara
See Rendell, Ruth

Vinge, Joan (Carol) D(ennison) 1948- .... **CLC 30; SSC 24**
See also AAYA 32; BPFB 3; CA 93-96; CANR 72; SATA 36, 113; SFW 4; YAW

Viola, Herman J(oseph) 1938- .... **CLC 70**
See also CA 61-64; CANR 8, 23, 48, 91; SATA 126

Violis, G.
See Simenon, Georges

Viramontes, Helena Maria 1954- ... **HLCS 2; SSC 149**
See also CA 159; CANR 182; CLR 285; DLB 122, 350; HW 2; LLW

Virgil
See Vergil

Visconti, Luchino 1906-1976 .... **CLC 16**
See also CA 81-84; 65-68; CANR 39

Vitry, Jacques de
See Jacques de Vitry

Vittorini, Elio 1908-1966 .... **CLC 6, 9, 14**
See also CA 133; 25-28R; DLB 264; EW 12; EWL 3; RGWL 2, 3

Vivekananda, Swami 1863-1902 .... **TCLC 88**

Vives, Juan Luis 1493-1540 .... **LC 170**
See also DLB 318

Vizenor, Gerald Robert 1934- .... **CLC 103, 263; NNAL**
See also CA 13-16R, 205; CAAE 205; CAAS 22; CANR 5, 21, 44, 67; DAM MULT; DLB 175, 227; MTCW 2; MTFW 2005; TCWW 2

Vizinczey, Stephen 1933- .... **CLC 40**
See also CA 128; CCA 1; INT CA-128

Vliet, R(ussell) G(ordon) 1929-1984 .... **CLC 22**
See also CA 37-40R; 112; CANR 18; CP 2, 3

Vogau, Boris Andreevich
See Vogau, Boris Andreyevich

Vogau, Boris Andreyevich 1894-1938 .... **SSC 48; TCLC 23**
See also CA 123; 218; DLB 272; EWL 3; RGSF 2; RGWL 2, 3

Vogel, Paula A. 1951- .. **CLC 76, 290; DC 19**
See also CA 108; CAD; CANR 119, 140; CD 5, 6; CWD; DFS 14; DLB 341; MTFW 2005; RGAL 4

Vogel, Paula Anne
See Vogel, Paula A.

Voigt, Cynthia 1942- .... **CLC 30**
See also AAYA 3, 30; BYA 1, 3, 6, 7, 8; CA 106; CANR 18, 37, 40, 94, 145; CLR 13, 48, 141; INT CANR-18; JRDA; LAIT 5; MAICYA 1, 2; MAICYAS 1; MTFW 2005; SATA 48, 79, 116, 160; SATA-Brief 33; WYA; YAW

Voigt, Ellen Bryant 1943- .... **CLC 54**
See also CA 69-72; CANR 11, 29, 55, 115, 171; CP 5, 6, 7; CSW; CWP; DLB 120; PFS 23, 33

Voinovich, Vladimir 1932- .. **CLC 10, 49, 147**
See also CA 81-84; CAAS 12; CANR 33, 67, 150; CWW 2; DLB 302; MTCW 1

Voinovich, Vladimir Nikolaevich
See Voinovich, Vladimir

Vollmann, William T. 1959- ...... **CLC 89, 227**
See also AMWS 17; CA 134; CANR 67, 116, 185; CN 7; CPW; DA3; DAM NOV, POP; DLB 350; MTCW 2; MTFW 2005

Voloshinov, V. N.
See Bakhtin, Mikhail Mikhailovich

Voltaire 1694-1778 .. **LC 14, 79, 110; SSC 12, 112; WLC 6**
See also BYA 13; DA; DA3; DAB; DAC; DAM DRAM, MST; DLB 314; EW 4; GFL Beginnings to 1789; LATS 1:1; LMFS 1; NFS 7; RGWL 2, 3; TWA

von Aschendrof, Baron Ignatz
See Ford, Ford Madox

von Chamisso, Adelbert
See Chamisso, Adelbert von

von Daeniken, Erich 1935- .... **CLC 30**
See also AITN 1; CA 37-40R; CANR 17, 44

von Daniken, Erich
See von Daeniken, Erich

von dem Turlin, Heinrich
See Heinrich von dem Tuerlin

von Eschenbach, Wolfram c. 1170-c. 1220 .... **CMLC 5**
See also CDWLB 2; DLB 138; EW 1; RGWL 2, 3

Wambaugh, Joseph, Jr. 1937- ...... **CLC 3, 18**
See also AITN 1; BEST 89:3; BPFB 3; CA
33-36R; CANR 42, 65, 115, 167, 217;
CMW 4; CPW 1; DA3; DAM NOV, POP;
DLB 6; DLBY 1983; MSW; MTCW 1, 2

Wambaugh, Joseph Aloysius
See Wambaugh, Joseph, Jr.

Wang Wei 699(?)-761(?) . **CMLC 100; PC 18**
See also TWA

Warburton, William 1698-1779 .... **LC 97**
See also DLB 104

Ward, Arthur Henry Sarsfield
1883-1959 .... **TCLC 28**
See also AAYA 80; CA 108; 173; CMW 4;
DLB 70; HGG; MSW; SUFW

Ward, Douglas Turner 1930- .... **CLC 19**
See also BW 1; CA 81-84; CAD; CANR
27; CD 5, 6; DLB 7, 38

Ward, E. D.
See Lucas, E(dward) V(errall)

Ward, Mrs. Humphry 1851-1920
See Ward, Mary Augusta
See also RGEL 2

Ward, Mary Augusta 1851-1920 ... **TCLC 55**
See Ward, Mrs. Humphry
See also DLB 18

Ward, Nathaniel 1578(?)-1652 .... **LC 114**
See also DLB 24

Ward, Peter
See Faust, Frederick

Warhol, Andy 1928(?)-1987 .... **CLC 20**
See also AAYA 12; BEST 89:4; CA 89-92;
121; CANR 34

Warner, Francis (Robert Le Plastrier)
1937- .... **CLC 14**
See also CA 53-56; CANR 11; CP 1, 2, 3, 4

Warner, Marina 1946- .... **CLC 59, 231**
See also CA 65-68; CANR 21, 55, 118; CN
5, 6, 7; DLB 194; MTFW 2005

Warner, Rex (Ernest) 1905-1986 ...... **CLC 45**
See also CA 89-92; 119; CN 1, 2, 3, 4; CP
1, 2, 3, 4; DLB 15; RGEL 2; RHW

Warner, Susan (Bogert)
1819-1885 .... **NCLC 31, 146**
See also AMWS 18; DLB 3, 42, 239, 250,
254

Warner, Sylvia (Constance) Ashton
See Ashton-Warner, Sylvia (Constance)

Warner, Sylvia Townsend
1893-1978 .. **CLC 7, 19; SSC 23; TCLC
131**
See also BRWS 7; CA 61-64; 77-80; CANR
16, 60, 104; CN 1, 2; DLB 34, 139; EWL
3; FANT; FW; MTCW 1, 2; RGEL 2;
RGSF 2; RHW

Warren, Mercy Otis 1728-1814 .... **NCLC 13,
226**
See also DLB 31, 200; RGAL 4; TUS

Warren, Robert Penn 1905-1989 .. **CLC 1, 4,
6, 8, 10, 13, 18, 39, 53, 59; PC 37; SSC
4, 58, 126; WLC 6**
See also AITN 1; AMW; AMWC 2; BPFB
3; BYA 1; CA 13-16R; 129; CANR 10,
47; CDALB 1968-1988; CN 1, 2, 3, 4;
CP 1, 2, 3, 4; DA; DA3; DAB; DAC;
DAM MST, NOV, POET; DLB 2, 48, 152,
320; DLBY 1980, 1989; EWL 3; INT
CANR-10; MAL 5; MTCW 1, 2; MTFW
2005; NFS 13; RGAL 4; RGSF 2; RHW;
SATA 46; SATA-Obit 63; SSFS 8; TUS

Warrigal, Jack
See Furphy, Joseph

Warshofsky, Isaac
See Singer, Isaac Bashevis

Warton, Joseph 1722-1800 ... **LC 128; NCLC
118**
See also DLB 104, 109; RGEL 2

Warton, Thomas 1728-1790 .... **LC 15, 82**
See also DAM POET; DLB 104, 109, 336;
RGEL 2

Waruk, Kona
See Harris, (Theodore) Wilson

Warung, Price
See Astley, William

Warwick, Jarvis
See Garner, Hugh

Washington, Alex
See Harris, Mark

Washington, Booker T. 1856-1915 . **BLC 1:3;
TCLC 10**
See also BW 1; CA 114; 125; DA3; DAM
MULT; DLB 345; LAIT 2; RGAL 4;
SATA 28

Washington, Booker Taliaferro
See Washington, Booker T.

Washington, George 1732-1799 .... **LC 25**
See also DLB 31

Wassermann, (Karl) Jakob
1873-1934 .... **TCLC 6**
See also CA 104; 163; DLB 66; EWL 3

Wasserstein, Wendy 1950-2006 . **CLC 32, 59,
90, 183; DC 4**
See also AAYA 73; AMWS 15; CA 121;
129; 247; CABS 3; CAD; CANR 53, 75,
128; CD 5, 6; CWD; DA3; DAM DRAM;
DFS 5, 17, 29; DLB 228; EWL 3; FW;
INT CA-129; MAL 5; MTCW 2; MTFW
2005; SATA 94; SATA-Obit 174

Waterhouse, Keith 1929-2009 .... **CLC 47**
See also BRWS 13; CA 5-8R; 290; CANR
38, 67, 109; CBD; CD 6; CN 1, 2, 3, 4, 5,
6, 7; DLB 13, 15; MTCW 1, 2; MTFW
2005

Waterhouse, Keith Spencer
See Waterhouse, Keith

Waters, Frank (Joseph) 1902-1995 .. **CLC 88**
See also CA 5-8R; 149; CAAS 13; CANR
3, 18, 63, 121; DLB 212; DLBY 1986;
RGAL 4; TCWW 1, 2

Waters, Mary C. .... **CLC 70**

Waters, Roger 1944- .... **CLC 35**

Watkins, Frances Ellen
See Harper, Frances Ellen Watkins

Watkins, Gerrold
See Malzberg, Barry N(athaniel)

Watkins, Gloria Jean
See hooks, bell

Watkins, Paul 1964- .... **CLC 55**
See also CA 132; CANR 62, 98

Watkins, Vernon Phillips
1906-1967 .... **CLC 43**
See also CA 9-10; 25-28R; CAP 1; DLB
20; EWL 3; RGEL 2

Watson, Irving S.
See Mencken, H. L.

Watson, John H.
See Farmer, Philip Jose

Watson, Richard F.
See Silverberg, Robert

Watson, Rosamund Marriott
1860-1911 .... **PC 117**
See also CA 207; DLB 240

Watson, Sheila 1909-1998 .... **SSC 128**
See also AITN 2; CA 155; CCA 1; DAC;
DLB 60

Watts, Ephraim
See Horne, Richard Henry Hengist

Watts, Isaac 1674-1748 .... **LC 98**
See also DLB 95; RGEL 2; SATA 52

Waugh, Auberon (Alexander)
1939-2001 .... **CLC 7**
See also CA 45-48; 192; CANR 6, 22, 92;
CN 1, 2, 3; DLB 14, 194

Waugh, Evelyn 1903-1966 ... **CLC 1, 3, 8, 13,
19, 27, 44, 107; SSC 41; TCLC 229;
WLC 6**
See also AAYA 78; BPFB 3; BRW 7; CA
85-88; 25-28R; CANR 22; CDBLB 1914-
1945; DA; DA3; DAB; DAC; DAM MST,
NOV, POP; DLB 15, 162, 195, 352; EWL
3; MTCW 1, 2; MTFW 2005; NFS 13,
17, 34; RGEL 2; RGSF 2; TEA; WLIT 4

Waugh, Evelyn Arthur St. John
See Waugh, Evelyn

Waugh, Harriet 1944- .... **CLC 6**
See also CA 85-88; CANR 22

Ways, C.R.
See Blount, Roy, Jr.

Waystaff, Simon
See Swift, Jonathan

Webb, Beatrice 1858-1943 .... **TCLC 22**
See also CA 117; 162; DLB 190; FW

Webb, Beatrice Martha Potter
See Webb, Beatrice

Webb, Charles 1939- .... **CLC 7**
See also CA 25-28R; CANR 114, 188

Webb, Charles Richard
See Webb, Charles

Webb, Frank J. .... **NCLC 143**
See also DLB 50

Webb, James, Jr.
See Webb, James

Webb, James 1946- .... **CLC 22**
See also CA 81-84; CANR 156

Webb, James H.
See Webb, James

Webb, James Henry
See Webb, James

Webb, Mary Gladys (Meredith)
1881-1927 .... **TCLC 24**
See also CA 182; 123, DLB 34; FW; RGEL
2

Webb, Mrs. Sidney
See Webb, Beatrice

Webb, Phyllis 1927- .... **CLC 18; PC 124**
See also CA 104; CANR 23; CCA 1; CP 1,
2, 3, 4, 5, 6, 7; CWP; DLB 53

Webb, Sidney 1859-1947 .... **TCLC 22**
See also CA 117; 163; DLB 190

Webb, Sidney James
See Webb, Sidney

Webber, Andrew Lloyd
See Lloyd Webber, Andrew

Weber, Lenora Mattingly
1895-1971 .... **CLC 12**
See also CA 19-20; 29-32R; CAP 1; SATA
2; SATA-Obit 26

Weber, Max 1864-1920 .... **TCLC 69**
See also CA 109; 189; DLB 296

Webster, Augusta 1837-1894 .... **NCLC 230**
See also DLB 35, 240

Webster, John 1580(?)-1634(?) ...... **DC 2; LC
33, 84, 124; WLC 6**
See also BRW 2; CDBLB Before 1660; DA;
DAB; DAC; DAM DRAM, MST; DFS
17, 19; DLB 58; IDTP; RGEL 2; WLIT 3

Webster, Noah 1758-1843 .... **NCLC 30, 253**
See also DLB 1, 37, 42, 43, 73, 243

Wedekind, Benjamin Franklin
See Wedekind, Frank

Wedekind, Frank 1864-1918 .... **TCLC 7, 241**
See also CA 104; 153; CANR 121, 122;
CDWLB 2; DAM DRAM; DLB 118; EW
8; EWL 3; LMFS 2; RGWL 2, 3

Weems, Mason Locke
1759-1825 .... **NCLC 245**
See also DLB 30, 37, 42

Wehr, Demaris .... **CLC 65**

Weidman, Jerome 1913-1998 .... **CLC 7**
See also AITN 2; CA 1-4R; 171; CAD;
CANR 1; CD 1, 2, 3, 4, 5; DLB 28

Whalen, Philip (Glenn) 1923-2002 .... **CLC 6, 29**
See also BG 1:3; CA 9-12R; 209; CANR 5, 39; CP 1, 2, 3, 4, 5, 6, 7; DLB 16; WP

Wharton, Edith 1862-1937 ... **SSC 6, 84, 120; TCLC 3, 9, 27, 53, 129, 149; WLC 6**
See also AAYA 25; AMW; AMWC 2; AMWR 1; BPFB 3; CA 104; 132; CDALB 1865-1917; CLR 136; DA; DA3; DAB; DAC; DAM MST, NOV; DLB 4, 9, 12, 78, 189; DLBD 13; EWL 3; EXPS; FL 1:6; GL 3; HGG; LAIT 2, 3; LATS 1:1; MAL 5; MBL; MTCW 1, 2; MTFW 2005; NFS 5, 11, 15, 20, 37; RGAL 4; RGSF 2; RHW; SSFS 6, 7; SUFW; TUS

Wharton, Edith Newbold Jones
See Wharton, Edith

Wharton, James
See Mencken, H. L.

Wharton, William 1925-2008 ..... **CLC 18, 37**
See also CA 93-96; 278; CN 4, 5, 6, 7; DLBY 1980; INT CA-93-96

Wheatley, Phillis 1753(?)-1784 .... **BLC 1:3; LC 3, 50, 183; PC 3; WLC 6**
See also AFAW 1, 2; AMWS 20; CDALB 1640-1865; DA; DA3; DAC; DAM MST, MULT, POET; DLB 31, 50; EXPP; FL 1:1; PFS 13, 29, 36; RGAL 4

Wheatley Peters, Phillis
See Wheatley, Phillis

Wheelock, John Hall 1886-1978 .... **CLC 14**
See also CA 13-16R; 77-80; CANR 14; CP 1, 2; DLB 45; MAL 5

Whim-Wham
See Curnow, (Thomas) Allen (Monro)

Whisp, Kennilworthy
See Rowling, J.K.

Whitaker, Rod 1931-2005 .... **CLC 29**
See also CA 29-32R; 246; CANR 45, 153; CMW 4

Whitaker, Rodney
See Whitaker, Rod

Whitaker, Rodney William
See Whitaker, Rod

White, Babington
See Braddon, Mary Elizabeth

White, E. B. 1899-1985 .... **CLC 10, 34, 39**
See also AAYA 62; AITN 2; AMWS 1; CA 13-16R; 116; CANR 16, 37; CDALBS; CLR 1, 21, 107; CPW; DA3; DAM POP; DLB 11, 22; EWL 3; FANT; MAICYA 1, 2; MAL 5; MTCW 1, 2; MTFW 2005; NCFS 5; RGAL 4; SATA 2, 29, 100; SATA-Obit 44; TUS

White, Edmund 1940- .... **CLC 27, 110**
See also AAYA 7; CA 45-48; CANR 3, 19, 36, 62, 107, 133, 172, 212; CN 5, 6, 7; DA3; DAM POP; DLB 227; MTCW 1, 2; MTFW 2005

White, Edmund Valentine III
See White, Edmund

White, Elwyn Brooks
See White, E. B.

White, Hayden V. 1928- .... **CLC 148**
See also CA 128; CANR 135; DLB 246

White, Patrick 1912-1990 . **CLC 3, 4, 5, 7, 9, 18, 65, 69; SSC 39; TCLC 176**
See also BRWS 1; CA 81-84; 132; CANR 43; CN 1, 2, 3, 4; DLB 260, 332; EWL 3; MTCW 1; RGEL 2; RGSF 2; RHW; TWA; WWE 1

White, Patrick Victor Martindale
See White, Patrick

White, Phyllis Dorothy James
See James, P. D.

White, T(erence) H(anbury) 1906-1964 .... **CLC 30**
See also AAYA 22; BPFB 3; BYA 4, 5; CA 73-76; CANR 37; CLR 139; DLB 160; FANT; JRDA; LAIT 1; MAICYA 1, 2; NFS 30; RGEL 2; SATA 12; SUFW 1; YAW

White, Terence de Vere 1912-1994 ... **CLC 49**
See also CA 49-52; 145; CANR 3

White, Walter
See White, Walter F(rancis)

White, Walter F(rancis) 1893-1955 ..... **BLC 1:3; HR 1:3; TCLC 15**
See also BW 1; CA 115; 124; DAM MULT; DLB 51

White, William Hale 1831-1913 ..... **TCLC 25**
See also CA 121; 189; DLB 18; RGEL 2

Whitehead, Alfred North 1861-1947 .... **TCLC 97**
See also CA 117; 165; DLB 100, 262

Whitehead, Colson 1969- ...... **BLC 2:3; CLC 232**
See also CA 202; CANR 162, 211

Whitehead, E(dward) A(nthony) 1933- .... **CLC 5**
See also CA 65-68; CANR 58, 118; CBD; CD 5, 6; DLB 310

Whitehead, Ted
See Whitehead, E(dward) A(nthony)

Whiteman, Roberta J. Hill 1947- ...... **NNAL**
See also CA 146

Whitemore, Hugh (John) 1936- .... **CLC 37**
See also CA 132; CANR 77; CBD; CD 5, 6; INT CA-132

Whitman, Sarah Helen (Power) 1803-1878 .... **NCLC 19**
See also DLB 1, 243

Whitman, Walt 1819-1892 .. **NCLC 4, 31, 81, 205; PC 3, 91; WLC 6**
See also AAYA 42; AMW; AMWR 1; CDALB 1640-1865; DA; DA3; DAB; DAC; DAM MST, POET; DLB 3, 64, 224, 250; EXPP; LAIT 2; LMFS 1; PAB; PFS 2, 3, 13, 22, 31, 39; RGAL 4; SATA 20; TUS; WP; WYAS 1

Whitman, Walter
See Whitman, Walt

Whitney, Isabella fl. 1565-fl. 1575 ... **LC 130; PC 116**
See also DLB 136

Whitney, Phyllis A. 1903-2008 .... **CLC 42**
See also AAYA 36; AITN 2; BEST 90:3; CA 1-4R; 269; CANR 3, 25, 38, 60; CLR 59; CMW 4; CPW; DA3; DAM POP; JRDA; MAICYA 1, 2; MTCW 2; RHW; SATA 1, 30; SATA-Obit 189; YAW

Whitney, Phyllis Ayame
See Whitney, Phyllis A.

Whittemore, (Edward) Reed, Jr. 1919- .... **CLC 4**
See also CA 9-12R; 219; CAAE 219; CAAS 8; CANR 4, 119; CP 1, 2, 3, 4, 5, 6, 7; DLB 5; MAL 5

Whittier, John Greenleaf 1807-1892 .... **NCLC 8, 59; PC 93**
See also AMWS 1; DLB 1, 243; PFS 36; RGAL 4

Whittlebot, Hernia
See Coward, Noel

Wicker, Thomas Grey
See Wicker, Tom

Wicker, Tom 1926- .... **CLC 7**
See also CA 65-68; CANR 21, 46, 141, 179

Wickham, Anna 1883-1947 .... **PC 110**
See also DLB 240

Wicomb, Zoe 1948- .... **BLC 2:3**
See also CA 127; CANR 106, 167; DLB 225

Wideman, John Edgar 1941- .. **BLC 1:3, 2:3; CLC 5, 34, 36, 67, 122, 316; SSC 62**
See also AFAW 1, 2; AMWS 10; BPFB 4; BW 2, 3; CA 85-88; CANR 14, 42, 67, 109, 140, 187; CN 4, 5, 6, 7; DAM MULT; DLB 33, 143; MAL 5; MTCW 2; MTFW 2005; RGAL 4; RGSF 2; SSFS 6, 12, 24; TCLE 1:2

Wiebe, Rudy 1934- . **CLC 6, 11, 14, 138, 263**
See also CA 37-40R; CANR 42, 67, 123, 202; CN 1, 2, 3, 4, 5, 6, 7; DAC; DAM MST; DLB 60; RHW; SATA 156

Wiebe, Rudy Henry
See Wiebe, Rudy

Wieland, Christoph Martin 1733-1813 .... **NCLC 17, 177**
See also DLB 97; EW 4; LMFS 1; RGWL 2, 3

Wiene, Robert 1881-1938 .... **TCLC 56**

Wieners, John 1934- .... **CLC 7**
See also BG 1:3; CA 13-16R; CP 1, 2, 3, 4, 5, 6, 7; DLB 16; WP

Wiesel, Elie 1928- ...... **CLC 3, 5, 11, 37, 165; WLCS**
See also AAYA 7, 54; AITN 1; CA 5-8R; CAAS 4; CANR 8, 40, 65, 125, 207; CDALBS; CWW 2; DA; DA3; DAB; DAC; DAM MST, NOV; DLB 83, 299; DLBY 1987; EWL 3; INT CANR-8; LAIT 4; MTCW 1, 2; MTFW 2005; NCFS 4; NFS 4; RGHL; RGWL 3; SATA 56; YAW

Wiesel, Eliezer
See Wiesel, Elie

Wiggins, Marianne 1947- .... **CLC 57**
See also AAYA 70; BEST 89:3; CA 130; CANR 60, 139, 180; CN 7; DLB 335

Wigglesworth, Michael 1631-1705 .... **LC 106**
See also DLB 24; RGAL 4

Wiggs, Susan .... **CLC 70**
See also CA 201; CANR 173, 217

Wight, James Alfred
See Herriot, James

Wilbur, Richard 1921- .. **CLC 3, 6, 9, 14, 53, 110; PC 51**
See also AAYA 72; AMWS 3; CA 1-4R; CABS 2; CANR 2, 29, 76, 93, 139; CDALBS; CP 1, 2, 3, 4, 5, 6, 7; DA; DAB; DAC; DAM MST, POET; DLB 5, 169; EWL 3; EXPP; INT CANR-29; MAL 5; MTCW 1, 2; MTFW 2005; PAB; PFS 11, 12, 16, 29; RGAL 4; SATA 9, 108; WP

Wilbur, Richard Purdy
See Wilbur, Richard

Wild, Peter 1940- .... **CLC 14**
See also CA 37-40R; CP 1, 2, 3, 4, 5, 6, 7; DLB 5

Wilde, Oscar 1854(?)-1900 .. **DC 17; PC 111; SSC 11, 77; TCLC 1, 8, 23, 41, 175; WLC 6**
See also AAYA 49; BRW 5; BRWC 1, 2; BRWR 2; BYA 15; CA 104; 119; CANR 112; CDBLB 1890-1914; CLR 114; DA; DA3; DAB; DAC; DAM DRAM, MST, NOV; DFS 4, 8, 9, 21; DLB 10, 19, 34, 57, 141, 156, 190, 344; EXPS; FANT; GL 3; LATS 1:1; NFS 20; RGEL 2; RGSF 2; SATA 24; SSFS 7; SUFW; TEA; WCH; WLIT 4

Wilde, Oscar Fingal O'Flahertie Willis
See Wilde, Oscar

Wilder, Billy
See Wilder, Samuel

Wilder, Samuel 1906-2002 .... **CLC 20**
See also AAYA 66; CA 89-92; 205; DLB 26

Wilder, Stephen
See Marlowe, Stephen

Wilder, Thornton 1897-1975 ..... **CLC 1, 5, 6, 10, 15, 35, 82; DC 1, 24; WLC 6**
See also AAYA 29; AITN 2; AMW; CA 13-16R; 61-64; CAD; CANR 40, 132; CDALBS; CN 1, 2; DA; DA3; DAB; DAC; DAM DRAM, MST, NOV; DFS 1, 4, 16; DLB 4, 7, 9, 228; DLBY 1997; EWL 3; LAIT 3; MAL 5; MTCW 1, 2; MTFW 2005; NFS 24; RGAL 4; RHW; WYAS 1

Wilder, Thornton Niven
See Wilder, Thornton

Wilding, Michael 1942- ...... **CLC 73; SSC 50**
See also CA 104; CANR 24, 49, 106; CN 4, 5, 6, 7; DLB 325; RGSF 2

Wiley, Richard 1944- .... **CLC 44**
See also CA 121; 129; CANR 71

Wilhelm, Kate
See Wilhelm, Katie

Wilhelm, Katie 1928- .... **CLC 7**
See also AAYA 83; BYA 16; CA 37-40R; CAAS 5; CANR 17, 36, 60, 94; DLB 8; INT CANR-17; MTCW 1; SCFW 2; SFW 4

Wilhelm, Katie Gertrude
See Wilhelm, Katie

Wilkins, Mary
See Freeman, Mary E(leanor) Wilkins

Willard, Nancy 1936- .... **CLC 7, 37**
See also BYA 5; CA 89-92; CANR 10, 39, 68, 107, 152, 186; CLR 5; CP 2, 3, 4, 5; CWP; CWRI 5; DLB 5, 52; FANT; MAI-CYA 1, 2; MTCW 1; SATA 37, 71, 127, 191; SATA-Brief 30; SUFW 2; TCLE 1:2

William of Malmesbury c. 1090B.C.-c.
1140B.C. .... **CMLC 57**

William of Moerbeke c. 1215-c.
1286 .... **CMLC 91**

William of Ockham 1290-1349 .... **CMLC 32, 129**

Williams, Ben Ames 1889-1953 ..... **TCLC 89**
See also CA 183; DLB 102

Williams, Charles
See Collier, James Lincoln

Williams, Charles 1886-1945 ..... **TCLC 1, 11**
See also BRWS 9; CA 104; 163; DLB 100, 153, 255; FANT; RGEL 2; SUFW 1

Williams, Charles Walter Stansby
See Williams, Charles

Williams, C.K. 1936- .. **CLC 33, 56, 148, 306**
See also CA 37-40R; CAAS 26; CANR 57, 106, 225; CP 1, 2, 3, 4, 5, 6, 7; DAM POET; DLB 5; MAL 5

Williams, Ella Gwendolen Rees
See Rhys, Jean

Williams, Emlyn 1905-1987 .... **CLC 15**
See also CA 104; 123; CANR 36; DAM DRAM; DLB 10, 77; IDTP; MTCW 1

Williams, George Emlyn
See Williams, Emlyn

Williams, Hank 1923-1953 .... **TCLC 81**
See Williams, Hiram King
See also CA 188

Williams, Helen Maria
1761-1827 .... **NCLC 135**
See also DLB 158

Williams, Hiram King 1923-1953
See Williams, Hank

Williams, Hugo (Mordaunt) 1942- ... **CLC 42**
See also CA 17-20R; CANR 45, 119; CP 1, 2, 3, 4, 5, 6, 7; DLB 40

Williams, J. Walker
See Wodehouse, P. G.

Williams, John A(lfred) 1925- .... **BLC 1:3; CLC 5, 13**
See also AFAW 2; BW 2, 3; CA 53-56, 195; CAAE 195; CAAS 3; CANR 6, 26, 51, 118; CN 1, 2, 3, 4, 5, 6, 7; CSW; DAM MULT; DLB 2, 33; EWL 3; INT CANR-6; MAL 5; RGAL 4; SFW 4

Williams, Jonathan 1929-2008 .... **CLC 13**
See also CA 9-12R; 270; CAAS 12; CANR 8, 108; CP 1, 2, 3, 4, 5, 6, 7; DLB 5

Williams, Jonathan Chamberlain
See Williams, Jonathan

Williams, Joy 1944- .... **CLC 31**
See also CA 41-44R; CANR 22, 48, 97, 168; DLB 335; SSFS 25

Williams, Norman 1952- .... **CLC 39**
See also CA 118

Williams, Paulette Linda
See Shange, Ntozake

Williams, Roger 1603(?)-1683 .... **LC 129**
See also DLB 24

Williams, Sherley Anne
1944-1999 .... **BLC 1:3; CLC 89**
See also AFAW 2; BW 2, 3; CA 73-76; 185; CANR 25, 82; DAM MULT, POET; DLB 41; INT CANR-25; SATA 78; SATA-Obit 116

Williams, Shirley
See Williams, Sherley Anne

Williams, Tennessee 1911-1983 . **CLC 1, 2, 5, 7, 8, 11, 15, 19, 30, 39, 45, 71, 111; DC 4; SSC 81; WLC 6**
See also AAYA 31; AITN 1, 2; AMW; AMWC 1; CA 5-8R; 108; CABS 3; CAD; CANR 31, 132, 174; CDALB 1941-1968; CN 1, 2, 3; DA; DA3; DAB; DAC; DAM DRAM, MST; DFS 17; DLB 7, 341; DLBD 4; DLBY 1983; EWL 3; GLL 1; LAIT 4; LATS 1:2; MAL 5; MTCW 1, 2; MTFW 2005; RGAL 4; TUS

Williams, Thomas (Alonzo)
1926-1990 .... **CLC 14**
See also CA 1-4R; 132; CANR 2

Williams, Thomas Lanier
See Williams, Tennessee

Williams, William C.
See Williams, William Carlos

Williams, William Carlos
1883-1963 .... **CLC 1, 2, 5, 9, 13, 22, 42, 67; PC 7, 109; SSC 31; WLC 6**
See also AAYA 46; AMW; AMWR 1; CA 89-92; CANR 34; CDALB 1917-1929; DA; DA3; DAB; DAC; DAM MST, POET; DLB 4, 16, 54, 86; EWL 3; EXPP; MAL 5; MTCW 1, 2; MTFW 2005; NCFS 4; PAB; PFS 1, 6, 11, 34; RGAL 4; RGSF 2; SSFS 27; TUS; WP

Williamson, David (Keith) 1942- ..... **CLC 56**
See also CA 103; CANR 41; CD 5, 6; DLB 289

Williamson, Jack
See Williamson, John Stewart

Williamson, John Stewart
1908-2006 .... **CLC 29**
See also AAYA 76; CA 17-20R; 255; CAAS 8; CANR 23, 70, 153; DLB 8; SCFW 1, 2; SFW 4

Willie, Frederick
See Lovecraft, H. P.

Willingham, Calder (Baynard, Jr.)
1922-1995 .... **CLC 5, 51**
See also CA 5-8R; 147; CANR 3; CN 1, 2, 3, 4, 5; CSW; DLB 2, 44; IDFW 3, 4; MTCW 1

Willis, Charles
See Clarke, Arthur C.

Willis, Nathaniel Parker
1806-1867 .... **NCLC 194**
See also DLB 3, 59, 73, 74, 183, 250; DLBD 13; RGAL 4

Willy
See Colette

Willy, Colette
See Colette

Wilmot, John 1647-1680 .... **LC 75; PC 66**
See also BRW 2; DLB 131; PAB; RGEL 2

Wilson, A. N. 1950- .... **CLC 33**
See also BRWS 6; CA 112; 122; CANR 156, 199; CN 4, 5, 6, 7; DLB 14, 155, 194; MTCW 2

Wilson, Andrew Norman
See Wilson, A. N.

Wilson, Angus 1913-1991 .... **CLC 2, 3, 5, 25, 34; SSC 21**
See also BRWS 1; CA 5-8R; 134; CANR 21; CN 1, 2, 3, 4; DLB 15, 139, 155; EWL 3; MTCW 1, 2; MTFW 2005; RGEL 2; RGSF 2

Wilson, Angus Frank Johnstone
See Wilson, Angus

Wilson, August 1945-2005 .... **BLC 1:3, 2:3; CLC 39, 50, 63, 118, 222; DC 2, 31; WLCS**
See also AAYA 16; AFAW 2; AMWS 8; BW 2, 3; CA 115; 122; 244; CAD; CANR 42, 54, 76, 128; CD 5, 6; DA; DA3; DAB; DAC; DAM DRAM, MST, MULT; DFS 3, 7, 15, 17, 24; DLB 228; EWL 3; LAIT 4; LATS 1:2; MAL 5; MTCW 1, 2; MTFW 2005; RGAL 4

Wilson, Brian 1942- .... **CLC 12**

Wilson, Colin 1931- .... **CLC 3, 14**
See also CA 1-4R; 315; CAAE 315; CAAS 5; CANR 1, 22, 33, 77; CMW 4; CN 1, 2, 3, 4, 5, 6; DLB 14, 194; HGG; MTCW 1; SFW 4

Wilson, Colin Henry
See Wilson, Colin

Wilson, Dirk
See Pohl, Frederik

Wilson, Edmund 1895-1972 .. **CLC 1, 2, 3, 8, 24**
See also AMW; CA 1-4R; 37-40R; CANR 1, 46, 110; CN 1; DLB 63; EWL 3; MAL 5; MTCW 1, 2; MTFW 2005; RGAL 4; TUS

Wilson, Ethel Davis (Bryant)
1888(?)-1980 .... **CLC 13**
See also CA 102; CN 1, 2; DAC; DAM POET; DLB 68; MTCW 1; RGEL 2

Wilson, Harriet
See Wilson, Harriet E. Adams

Wilson, Harriet E.
See Wilson, Harriet E. Adams

Wilson, Harriet E. Adams
1827(?)-1863(?) ..... **BLC 1:3; NCLC 78, 219**
See also DAM MULT; DLB 50, 239, 243

Wilson, John 1785-1854 .... **NCLC 5**
See also DLB 110

Wilson, John Anthony Burgess
See Burgess, Anthony

Wilson, John Burgess
See Burgess, Anthony

Wilson, Katharina .... **CLC 65**

Wilson, Lanford 1937-2011 ... **CLC 7, 14, 36, 197; DC 19**
See also CA 17-20R; CABS 3; CAD; CANR 45, 96; CD 5, 6; DAM DRAM; DFS 4, 9, 12, 16, 20; DLB 7, 341; EWL 3; MAL 5; TUS

Wilson, Robert M. 1941- .... **CLC 7, 9**
See also CA 49-52; CAD; CANR 2, 41; CD 5, 6; MTCW 1

Wilson, Robert McLiam 1964- .... **CLC 59**
See also CA 132; DLB 267

Wilson, Sloan 1920-2003 .... **CLC 32**
See also CA 1-4R; 216; CANR 1, 44; CN 1, 2, 3, 4, 5, 6

Wilson, Snoo 1948- .... **CLC 33**
See also CA 69-72; CBD; CD 5, 6

Wilson, Thomas 1523(?)-1581 .... **LC 184**
See also DLB 132, 236

Wilson, William S(mith) 1932- .... **CLC 49**
See also CA 81-84

Wilson, (Thomas) Woodrow
  1856-1924 .... **TCLC 79**
    See also CA 166; DLB 47
Winchelsea
    See Finch, Anne
Winchester, Simon 1944- .... **CLC 257**
    See also AAYA 66; CA 107; CANR 90, 130,
    194, 228
Winchilsea, Anne (Kingsmill) Finch
  1661-1720
    See Finch, Anne
    See also RGEL 2
Winckelmann, Johann Joachim
  1717-1768 .... **LC 129**
    See also DLB 97
Windham, Basil
    See Wodehouse, P. G.
Wingrove, David 1954- .... **CLC 68**
    See also CA 133; SFW 4
Winnemucca, Sarah 1844-1891 .... **NCLC 79;**
    NNAL
    See also DAM MULT; DLB 175; RGAL 4
Winstanley, Gerrard 1609-1676 .... **LC 52**
Wintergreen, Jane
    See Duncan, Sara Jeannette
Winters, Arthur Yvor
    See Winters, Yvor
Winters, Janet Lewis
    See Lewis, Janet
Winters, Yvor 1900-1968 .. **CLC 4, 8, 32; PC**
    82
    See also AMWS 2; CA 11-12; 25-28R; CAP
    1; DLB 48; EWL 3; MAL 5; MTCW 1;
    RGAL 4
Winterson, Jeanette 1959- .... **CLC 64, 158,**
    307; SSC 144
    See also BRWS 4; CA 136; CANR 58, 116,
    181; CN 5, 6, 7; CPW; DA3; DAM POP;
    DLB 207, 261; FANT; FW; GLL 1;
    MTCW 2; MTFW 2005; RHW; SATA 190
Winthrop, John 1588-1649 .... **LC 31, 107**
    See also DLB 24, 30
Winthrop, Theodore 1828-1861 ... **NCLC 210**
    See also DLB 202
Winton, Tim 1960- .... **CLC 251; SSC 119**
    See also AAYA 34; CA 152; CANR 118,
    194; CN 6, 7; DLB 325; SATA 98
Wirth, Louis 1897-1952 .... **TCLC 92**
    See also CA 210
Wiseman, Frederick 1930- .... **CLC 20**
    See also CA 159
Wister, Owen 1860-1938 ..... **SSC 100; TCLC**
    21
    See also BPFB 3; CA 108; 162; DLB 9, 78,
    186; RGAL 4; SATA 62; TCWW 1, 2
Wither, George 1588-1667 .... **LC 96**
    See also DLB 121; RGEL 2
Witkacy
    See Witkiewicz, Stanisław Ignacy
Witkiewicz, Stanisław Ignacy
  1885-1939 .... **TCLC 8, 237**
    See also CA 105; 162; CDWLB 4; DLB
    215; EW 10; EWL 3; RGWL 2, 3; SFW 4
Wittgenstein, Ludwig (Josef Johann)
  1889-1951 .... **TCLC 59**
    See also CA 113; 164; DLB 262; MTCW 2
Wittig, Monique 1935-2003 .... **CLC 22**
    See also CA 116; 135; 212; CANR 143;
    CWW 2; DLB 83; EWL 3; FW; GLL 1
Wittlin, Jozef 1896-1976 .... **CLC 25**
    See also CA 49-52; 65-68; CANR 3; EWL
    3
Wodehouse, P. G. 1881-1975 ..... **CLC 1, 2, 5,**
    10, 22; SSC 2, 115; TCLC 108
    See also AAYA 65; AITN 2; BRWS 3; CA
    45-48; 57-60; CANR 3, 33; CDBLB
    1914-1945; CN 1, 2; CPW 1; DA3; DAB;

DAC; DAM NOV; DLB 34, 162, 352;
EWL 3; MTCW 1, 2; MTFW 2005; RGEL
2; RGSF 2; SATA 22; SSFS 10
Wodehouse, Pelham Grenville
    See Wodehouse, P. G.
Woiwode, L.
    See Woiwode, Larry
Woiwode, Larry 1941- .... **CLC 6, 10**
    See also CA 73-76; CANR 16, 94, 192; CN
    3, 4, 5, 6, 7; DLB 6; INT CANR-16
Woiwode, Larry Alfred
    See Woiwode, Larry
Wojciechowska, Maia (Teresa)
  1927-2002 .... **CLC 26**
    See also AAYA 8, 46; BYA 3; CA 9-12R,
    183; 209; CAAE 183; CANR 4, 41; CLR
    1; JRDA; MAICYA 1, 2; SAAS 1; SATA
    1, 28, 83; SATA-Essay 104; SATA-Obit
    134; YAW
Wojtyla, Karol (Jozef)
    See John Paul II, Pope
Wojtyla, Karol (Josef)
    See John Paul II, Pope
Wolf, Christa 1929- ...... **CLC 14, 29, 58, 150,**
    261
    See also CA 85-88; CANR 45, 123; CD-
    WLB 2; CWW 2; DLB 75; EWL 3; FW;
    MTCW 1; RGWL 2, 3; SSFS 14
Wolf, Naomi 1962- .... **CLC 157**
    See also CA 141; CANR 110; FW; MTFW
    2005
Wolfe, Gene 1931- .... **CLC 25**
    See also AAYA 35; CA 57-60; CAAS 9;
    CANR 6, 32, 60, 152, 197; CPW; DAM
    POP; DLB 8; FANT; MTCW 2; MTFW
    2005; SATA 118, 165; SCFW 2; SFW 4;
    SUFW 2
Wolfe, Gene Rodman
    See Wolfe, Gene
Wolfe, George C. 1954- .... **BLCS; CLC 49**
    See also CA 149; CAD; CD 5, 6
Wolfe, Thomas 1900-1938 .... **SSC 33, 113;**
    TCLC 4, 13, 29, 61; WLC 6
    See also AMW; BPFB 3; CA 104; 132;
    CANR 102; CDALB 1929-1941; DA;
    DA3; DAB; DAC; DAM MST, NOV;
    DLB 9, 102, 229; DLBD 2, 16; DLBY
    1985, 1997; EWL 3; MAL 5; MTCW 1,
    2; NFS 18, RGAL 4; SSFS 18; TUS
Wolfe, Thomas Clayton
    See Wolfe, Thomas
Wolfe, Thomas Kennerly
    See Wolfe, Tom, Jr.
Wolfe, Tom, Jr. 1931- .... **CLC 1, 2, 9, 15, 35,**
    51, 147
    See also AAYA 8, 67; AITN 2; AMWS 3;
    BEST 89:1; BPFB 3; CA 13-16R; CANR
    9, 33, 70, 104; CN 5, 6, 7; CPW; CSW;
    DA3; DAM POP; DLB 152, 185 185;
    EWL 3; INT CANR-9; LAIT 5; MTCW
    1, 2; MTFW 2005; RGAL 4; TUS
Wolff, Geoffrey 1937- .... **CLC 41**
    See also CA 29-32R; CANR 29, 43, 78, 154
Wolff, Geoffrey Ansell
    See Wolff, Geoffrey
Wolff, Sonia
    See Levitin, Sonia
Wolff, Tobias 1945- .... **CLC 39, 64, 172; SSC**
    63, 136
    See also AAYA 16; AMWS 7; BEST 90:2;
    BYA 12; CA 114; 117; CAAS 22; CANR
    54, 76, 96, 192; CN 5, 6, 7; CSW; DA3;
    DLB 130; EWL 3; INT CA-117; MTCW
    2; MTFW 2005; RGAL 4; RGSF 2; SSFS
    4, 11, 35
Wolff, Tobias Jonathan Ansell
    See Wolff, Tobias

Wolitzer, Hilma 1930- .... **CLC 17**
    See also CA 65-68; CANR 18, 40, 172; INT
    CANR-18; SATA 31; YAW
Wollstonecraft, Mary 1759-1797 .... **LC 5, 50,**
    90, 147
    See also BRWS 3; CDBLB 1789-1832;
    DLB 39, 104, 158, 252; FL 1:1; FW;
    LAIT 1; RGEL 2; TEA; WLIT 3
Wonder, Stevie 1950- .... **CLC 12**
    See also CA 111
Wong, Jade Snow 1922-2006 .... **CLC 17**
    See also CA 109; 249; CANR 91; SATA
    112; SATA-Obit 175
Wood, Ellen Price
    See Wood, Mrs. Henry
Wood, Mrs. Henry 1814-1887 ...... **NCLC 178**
    See also CMW 4; DLB 18; SUFW
Wood, James 1965- .... **CLC 238**
    See also CA 235; CANR 214
Woodberry, George Edward
  1855-1930 .... **TCLC 73**
    See also CA 165; DLB 71, 103
Woodcott, Keith
    See Brunner, John (Kilian Houston)
Woodruff, Robert W.
    See Mencken, H. L.
Woodward, Bob 1943- .... **CLC 240**
    See also CA 69-72; CANR 31, 67, 107, 176;
    MTCW 1
Woodward, Robert Upshur
    See Woodward, Bob
Woolf, Adeline Virginia
    See Woolf, Virginia
Woolf, Virginia 1882-1941 .... **SSC 7, 79, 161;**
    TCLC 1, 5, 20, 43, 56, 101, 123, 128;
    WLC 6
    See also AAYA 44; BPFB 3; BRW 7;
    BRWC 2; BRWR 1; CA 104; 130; CANR
    64, 132; CDBLB 1914-1945; DA; DA3;
    DAB; DAC; DAM MST, NOV; DLB 36,
    100, 162; DLBD 10; EWL 3; EXPS; FL
    1:6; FW; LAIT 3; LATS 1:1; LMFS 2;
    MTCW 1, 2; MTFW 2005; NCFS 2; NFS
    8, 12, 28; RGEL 2; RGSF 2; SSFS 4, 12,
    34; TEA; WLIT 4
Woollcott, Alexander (Humphreys)
  1887-1943 .... **TCLC 5**
    See also CA 105; 161; DLB 29
Woolman, John 1720-1772 .... **LC 155**
    See also DLB 31
Woolrich, Cornell
    See Hopley-Woolrich, Cornell George
Woolson, Constance Fenimore
  1840-1894 .... **NCLC 82; SSC 90**
    See also DLB 12, 74, 189, 221; RGAL 4
Wordsworth, Dorothy 1771-1855 . **NCLC 25,**
    138
    See also DLB 107
Wordsworth, William 1770-1850 .. **NCLC 12,**
    38, 111, 166, 206; PC 4, 67; WLC 6
    See also AAYA 70; BRW 4; BRWC 1; CD-
    BLB 1789-1832; DA; DA3; DAB; DAC;
    DAM MST, POET; DLB 93, 107; EXPP;
    LATS 1:1; LMFS 1; PAB; PFS 2, 33, 38;
    RGEL 2; TEA; WLIT 3; WP
Wotton, Sir Henry 1568-1639 .... **LC 68**
    See also DLB 121; RGEL 2
Wouk, Herman 1915- .... **CLC 1, 9, 38**
    See also BPFB 2, 3; CA 5-8R; CANR 6,
    33, 67, 146, 225; CDALBS; CN 1, 2, 3,
    4, 5, 6; CPW; DA3; DAM NOV, POP;
    DLBY 1982; INT CANR-6; LAIT 4;
    MAL 5; MTCW 1, 2; MTFW 2005; NFS
    7; TUS
Wright, Charles 1932-2008 ... **BLC 1:3; CLC**
    49
    See also BW 1; CA 9-12R; 278; CANR 26;
    CN 1, 2, 3, 4, 5, 6, 7; DAM MULT,
    POET; DLB 33

PC Cumulative Nationality Index

Nationality Index

PC-127 Title Index